THE OXFORD HANDBOO

THE BRONZE AGE AEGEAN

THE OXFORD HANDBOOK OF

THE BRONZE AGE AEGEAN
(ca. 3000–1000 BC)

Edited by
ERIC H. CLINE

OXFORD
UNIVERSITY PRESS

OXFORD
UNIVERSITY PRESS

Oxford University Press, Inc., publishes works that further
Oxford University's objective of excellence
in research, scholarship, and education.

Oxford New York
Auckland Cape Town Dar es Salaam Hong Kong Karachi
Kuala Lumpur Madrid Melbourne Mexico City Nairobi
New Delhi Shanghai Taipei Toronto

With offices in
Argentina Austria Brazil Chile Czech Republic France Greece
Guatemala Hungary Italy Japan Poland Portugal Singapore
South Korea Switzerland Thailand Turkey Ukraine Vietnam

Copyright © 2010 by Oxford University Press, Inc.

Published by Oxford University Press, Inc.
198 Madison Avenue, New York, New York 10016
www.oup.com

First issued as an Oxford University Press paperback, 2012

Oxford is a registered trademark of Oxford University Press

Library of Congress Cataloging-in-Publication Data
The Oxford handbook of the Bronze age Aegean / edited by Eric H. Cline.
p. cm.
Includes bibliographical references.
ISBN 978-0-19-536550-4 (hardcover); 978-0-19-987360-9 (paperback)
1. Civilization, Aegean.   2. Bronze age—Aegean Sea Region.
3. Aegean Sea Region—Antiquities.
4. Excavations (Archaeology)—Aegean Sea Region.
I. Cline, Eric H.
II. Title: Handbook of the Bronze Age Aegean.
DF220.O946 2010
939.'101—dc22   2009014131

Undertaken with the assistance of the Institute for Aegean Prehistory

Printed in the United States of America
on acid-free paper

Acknowledgments

I would like to thank Stefan Vranka at Oxford University Press for approaching me and suggesting this volume, as well as Brian Hurley and Deirdre Brady at OUP and Rachel Navarro at George Washington University for their assistance throughout, and particularly Keith Faivre at OUP for his heroic efforts during the editing and typesetting phases. Kim Shelton and other scholars provided helpful suggestions concerning the initial proposal. I would also like to thank all of the contributors to this volume for their prompt submissions and relative adherence to the word and illustration limits so that this could appear on schedule and in a timely manner. We are all very grateful to Philip Betancourt, Karen Vellucci, and the Institute of Aegean Prehistory (INSTAP) for a publication subvention that allowed us to include all of the contributions that appear here. Many of the individual contributors wish to thank various colleagues and associates for reading and commenting upon their contributions, sharing unpublished materials, and providing other types of assistance; since space limitations preclude including such acknowledgements after each contribution, a general round of thanks to all involved is issued here.

Contents

List of Contributors and Academic Affiliations (Alphabetical)

Andreadaki-Vlazaki, Maria (25th Ephorate of Prehistoric and Classical Antiquities, Khania, Crete)

Andreou, Stelios (Aristotle University of Thessaloniki)

Barber, Robin (University of Edinburgh)

Bass, George F. (Institute of Nautical Archaeology)

Bryce, Trevor (University of Queensland, Australia)

Burke, Brendan (University of Victoria)

Burns, Bryan E. (Wellesley College)

Cavanagh, William (University of Nottingham)

Chapin, Anne (Brevard College)

Cline, Eric H. (George Washington University)

Dakouri-Hild, Anastasia (University of Virginia)

Davis, Jack L. (American School of Classical Studies, Athens)

Dickinson, Oliver (University of Durham, Emeritus)

Doumas, Christos (University of Athens)

Driessen, Jan (Université Catholique de Louvain)

Evely, Doniert (Curator at Knossos)

Forsén, Jeannette (Göteborg University)

French, Elizabeth (British School at Athens)

GALATY, MICHAEL L. (Millsaps College)

GAUSS, WALTER (Austrian Archaeological Institute at Athens)

GEORGANAS, IOANNIS (Foundation of the Hellenic World)

GREAVES, ALAN M. (University of Liverpool)

HALLAGER, BIRGITTA (University of Aarhus)

HALLAGER, ERIK (University of Aarhus)

HIRSCHFELD, NICOLLE (Trinity University)

HITCHCOCK, LOUISE A. (University of Melbourne)

JABLONKA, PETER (Universität Tübingen)

JUNG, REINHARD (Universität Salzburg)

LA ROSA, VINCENZO (Università di Catania)

LAFFINEUR, ROBERT (Université de Liège)

LUPACK, SUSAN (University College London)

MACDONALD, COLIN (Emeritus Curator at Knossos)

MACGILLIVRAY, J. ALEXANDER (British School at Athens)

MANNING, STURT W. (Cornell University)

MARAN, JOSEPH (Heidelberg University, Germany)

MARKETOU, TOULA (22nd Ephorate of Prehistoric and Classical Antiquities, Dodecanese, Rhodes)

MEE, CHRISTOPHER (University of Liverpool)

MUHLY, JAMES (University of Pennsylvania, Emeritus)

NAKASSIS, DIMITRI (University of Toronto)

PALAIMA, THOMAS G. (University of Texas, Austin)

PARKINSON, WILLIAM (Field Museum of Natural History, Chicago)

PHILLIPS, JACKE (School of Oriental and African Studies, University of London)

PLATON, LEFTERIS (University of Athens)

PULAK, CEMAL (Texas A&M University)

RENFREW, COLIN (Cambridge University, Emeritus)

RUTTER, JEREMY (Dartmouth College)

SACKETT, L. HUGH (British School at Athens)

SCHOEP, ILSE (Katholieke Universiteit Leuven)

SHAW, JOSEPH (University of Toronto, Emeritus)

SHAW, MARIA (University of Toronto, Emerita)

SHELTON, KIM (University of California, Berkeley)

STEEL, LOUISE (University of Wales, Lampeter)

TOMAS, HELENA (University of Zagreb, Croatia)

TOMKINS, PETER (Université Catholique de Louvain)

TZONOU-HERBST, IOULIA (American School of Classical Studies, Athens)

VAGNETTI, LUCIA (CNR–Istituto di studi sulle civiltà dell'Egeo e del Vicino Oriente, Rome)

VOUTSAKI, SOFIA (University of Groningen)

WEINGARTEN, JUDITH (Netherlands)

WIENCKE, MARTHA (American School of Classical Studies, Athens)

YASUR-LANDAU, ASSAF (University of Haifa)

YOUNGER, JOHN (University of Kansas)

ABBREVIATIONS

Journal Titles

AA	*Archäologischer Anzeiger*
AAA	*Archaiologika analekta ex Athenon (Athens Annals of Archaeology)*
AfO	*Archiv für Orientforschung*
AJA	*American Journal of Archaeology*
AM	*Mitteilungen des Deutschen Archäologischen Instituts, Athenische Abteilung*
AnatSt	*Anatolian Studies*
ArchDelt	*Arkaiologikon Deltion*
ASAtene	*Annuario della Scuola archeologica di Atene e delle Missioni italiane in Oriente*
BABesch	*Bulletin antieke beschaving. Annual Papers on Classical Archaeology*
BAR-IS	*British Archaeological Reports–International Series*
BCH	*Bulletin de correspondance hellénique*
BdA	*Bollettino d'arte*
BICS	*Bulletin of the Institute of Classical Studies*
BIFAO	*Bulletin de l'Institut français d'archéologie orientale du Caire*
BSA	*Annual of the British School at Athens*
IEJ	*Israel Exploration Journal*
IJNA	*International Journal of Nautical Archaeology*
IstMitt	*Istanbuler Mitteilungen*
JAS	*Journal of Archaeological Science*
JEA	*Journal of Egyptian Archaeology*
JDAI	*Jahrbuch des Deutschen Archäologischen Instituts*
JHS	*Journal of Hellenic Studies*
JIES	*Journal of Indo-European Studies*
JMA	*Journal of Mediterranean Archaeology*
JRGZM	*Jahrbuch des Römisch-germanischen Zentralmuseums, Mainz*
OJA	*Oxford Journal of Archaeology*
ÖJh	*Jahreshefte des Österreichischen archäologischen Instituts in Wien*
ÖJhBeibl	*Jahreshefte der Österreichischen archäologischen Instituts in Wien, Beiblatt*
OpArch	*Opuscula archaeologica*
OpAth	*Opuscula Atheniensia*

PCPS   *Proceedings of the Cambridge Philosophical Society*
PPS   *Proceedings of the Prehistoric Society*
PZ   *Prähistorische Zeitschrift*
SIMA   *Studies in Mediterranean Archaeology*
SIMA-PB   *Studies in Mediterranean Archaeology Pocket-Book*
SMEA   *Studi Micenei ed Egeo-Anatolici*
TUAS   *Temple University Aegean Symposium*

Book Titles

Aegean and the Orient: Cline, Eric H., and Diane Harris-Cline, eds. 1998. *The Aegean and the Orient in the Second Millennium. Proceedings of the 50th Anniversary Symposium, Cincinnati, April 18–20, 1997.* Aegaeum 18. Liège: Université de Liège.

Aegean Prehistory: Cullen, Tracey, ed. 2001. *Aegean Prehistory: A Review.* AJA Suppl. 1. Boston: Archaeological Institute of America.

Aegean Seals: Palaima, Thomas G., ed. 1990. *Aegean Seals, Sealings, and Administration. Proceedings of the NEH-Dickson Conference of the Program in Aegean Scripts and Prehistory of the Department of Classics, University of Texas at Austin, January 11–13, 1989.* Aegaeum 5. Liège: Université de Liège.

ANCEBA: Erkanal, Hayat, Harald Hauptmann, Vasıf Şahoğlu, and Rıza Tuncel, eds. 2008. *Proceedings of the International Symposium: The Aegean in the Neolithic, Chalcolithic, and the Early Bronze Age: Urla-İzmir (Turkey) October 13–19, 1997.* Research Center for Maritime Archaeology (Anküsam). Publication no. 1. Ankara: Ankara Üniversitesi.

Ariadne's Threads: D'Agata, Anna Lucia, and Jennifer Moody, eds. 2005. *Ariadne's Threads: Connections between Crete and the Greek Mainland in Late Minoan III (LM IIIA2 to LM IIIC). Proceedings of the International Workshop Held at Athens, Scuola Archeologica*

	Italiana, April 5–6, 2003. Tripodes 3. Athens: Dot Repro S.A.
Autochthon:	Dakouri-Hild, Anastasia, and Susan Sherratt, eds. 2005. *Autochthon: Papers Presented to O.T.P.K. Dickinson on the Occasion of His Retirement.* BAR-IS 1432. Oxford: Archaeopress.
BABS:	Galanaki, Ioanna, Helena Thomas, Yannis Galanakis, and Robert Laffineur, eds. 2007. *Between the Aegean and Baltic Seas: Prehistory across Borders. Proceedings of the International Conference, Bronze and Early Iron Age Interconnections and Contemporary Developments between the Aegean and the Regions of the Balkan Peninsula, Central and Northern Europe, University of Zagreb, April 11–14, 2005.* Aegaeum 27. Liège: Université de Liège.
Back to the Beginning:	Schoep, Ilse, Peter Tomkins, and Jan Driessen, eds. Forthcoming. *Back to the Beginning. Proceedings of the Leuven Workshop, 1–2 February 2008.* Oxford: Oxbow.
Bronze Age Trade:	Gale, Noel H., ed. 1991. *Bronze Age Trade in the Mediterranean.* SIMA 90. Jonsered: Åström.
Celebrations of Death:	Hägg, Robin, and Gullög C. Nordquist, eds. 1990. *Celebrations of Death and Divinity in the Bronze Age Argolid. Proceedings of the Sixth International Symposium at the Swedish Institute at Athens, June 11–13, 1988.* Stockholm: Åström.
ΧΑΡΙΣ:	Chapin, Anne P., ed. 2004. *ΧΑΡΙΣ: Essays in Honor of Sara A. Immerwahr.* Hesperia Suppl. 33. Princeton: American School of Classical Studies.
CHIC:	Olivier, Jean-Pierre, and Louis Godart. 1996. *Corpus Hieroglyphicarum Inscriptionum Cretae.* Études Crétoises 31. Paris: L'École française d'Athènes, L'École française de Rome.
CMS:	*Corpus der minoischen und mykenischen Siegel.* Mainz: Akademie der Wissenschaften und der Literatur.

La Crète mycénienne:	Jan Driessen and Alexandre Farnoux, eds. 1997. *La Crète Mycénienne: Actes de la Table Ronde internationale organisée par l'École française d'Athènes (Athènes, 25–28 mars 1991). BCH* Suppl. 30. Paris: De Boccard.
Cyprus-Dodecanese-Crete:	Karageorghis, Vassos, and Nicholas Chr. Stampolidis, eds. *1998. Proceedings of the Symposium: Eastern Mediterranean: Cyprus-Dodecanese-Crete 16th–6th Cent. B.C. Organized by the University of Crete, Rethymnon, and the Anastasios G. Leventis Foundation, Nicosia. Rethymnon, May 13–16, 1997.* Athens: University of Crete and the A. G. Leventis Foundation.
Dodecanese:	Søren, Dietz, and Ioannes Papachristodoulou, eds. 1988. *Archaeology in the Dodecanese.* Copenhagen: Department of the Near Eastern and Classical Antiquities, National Museum of Denmark.
Early Helladic Architecture:	Hägg, Robin, and Dora Konsola, eds. 1986. *Early Helladic Architecture and Urbanization. Proceedings of a Seminar Held at the Swedish Institute in Athens, June 8, 1985. SIMA* 76. Göteborg: Åström.
EIKON:	Crowley, Janice C., and Robert Laffineur, eds. 1992. *EIKON: Aegean Bronze Age Iconography: Shaping a Methodology. Proceedings of the Fourth International Aegean Conference, University of Tasmania, Hobart, Australia, April 6–9, 1992.* Aegaeum 8. Liège: Université de Liège.
Emergence of Civilisation Revisited:	Barrett, John C., and Paul Halstead, eds. 2004. *The Emergence of Civilisation Revisited.* Sheffield Studies in Aegean Archaeology 6. Oxford: Oxbow Books.
Emporia:	Laffineur, Robert, and Emanuele Greco, eds. 2005. *Emporia: Aegeans in the Central and Eastern Mediterranean. Proceedings of the 10th International Aegean Conference/10e Rencontre égéenne internationale, Athens, Italian School of*

Archaeology, April 14–18, 2004. Aegaeum 25. Liège: Université de Liège.

EPOS: Morris, Sarah P., and Robert Laffineur, eds. 2007. *EPOS. Reconsidering Greek Epic and Aegean Bronze Age Archaeology. Proceedings of the 11th International Aegean Conference, Los Angeles, UCLA–J. Paul Getty Villa, April 20–23, 2006.* Aegaeum 28. Liège: Université de Liège.

Escaping the Labyrinth: Isaakidou, Valasia, and Peter Tomkins, eds. 2008. *Escaping the Labyrinth: The Cretan Neolithic in Context. Proceedings of the Workshop Held at the University of Sheffield, January 21–23, 2006.* Sheffield Studies in Aegean Archaeology 8. Oxford: Oxbow.

FGrH: Jacoby, F., ed. 1923–. *Fragmente der Griechischen Historiker.* Berlin: Weidmann.

Function of the Minoan Palaces: Hägg, Robin, and Nanno Marinatos, eds. 1987. *The Function of the Minoan Palaces. Proceedings of the Fourth International Symposium at the Swedish Institute in Athens, June 10–16, 1984.* Skrifter utgivna av Svenska Institutet i Athen 4/35. Stockholm: Åström.

GORILA: Godart, Louis, and Jean-Pierre Olivier. 1976–1985. *Recueil des inscriptions en linéaire A.* Études Crétoises 21. Paris: L'École française d'Athènes.

Horizon: Brodie, Neil J., Jenny Doole, Giorgos Gavalas, and Colin Renfrew, eds. 2008. *Horizon / Ὁρίζων: A Colloquium on the Prehistory of the Cyclades.* Cambridge: McDonald Institute for Archaeological Research.

Knossos: Cadogan, Gerald, Elena Hatzaki, and Adonis Vasilakis, eds. 2004. *Knossos: Palace, City, State. Proceedings of the Conference in Herakleion Organized by the British School at Athens and the 23rd Ephoreia of Prehistoric and Classical Antiquities of Herakleion, in November 2000, for the Centenary of Sir Arthur*

	Evans's Excavations at Knossos. British School at Athens Studies 12. London: British School at Athens.
Knossos Pottery Handbook:	Momigliano, Nicoletta, ed. 2007. *Knossos Pottery Handbook: Neolithic and Bronze Age (Minoan)*. BSA Special Studies 14. London: British School at Athens.
Kommos I:1:	Shaw, Joseph W., and Maria C. Shaw, eds. 1995. *Kommos I: The Kommos Region and Houses of the Minoan Town. Part 1, The Kommos Region, Ecology, and the Minoan Industries.* Princeton: Princeton University Press.
Kommos I:2:	Shaw, Joseph W., and Maria C. Shaw, eds. 1996. *Kommos I: The Kommos Region and Houses of the Minoan Town. Part 2, The Houses of the Minoan Town.* Princeton: Princeton University Press.
Kommos IV:	Shaw, Joseph W., and Maria C. Shaw, eds. 2000. *Kommos IV: The Greek Sanctuary.* Princeton: Princeton University Press.
Kommos V:	Shaw, Joseph W., and Maria C. Shaw, eds. 2006. *Kommos V: The Monumental Minoan Buildings.* Princeton: Princeton University Press.
KRHS TEXNITHS:	Bradfer-Burdet, Isabelle, Béatrice Detournay, and Robert Laffineur, eds. 2005. *KRHS TEXNITHS. L'artisan crétois: Recueil d'articles en l'honneur de Jean-Claude Poursat, publié à l'occasion des 40 ans de la découverte du Quartier Mu.* Aegaeum 26. Liège: Université de Liège.
Krinoi Kai Limenai:	Betancourt, Philip P., Michael C. Nelson, and E. Hector Williams, eds. 2007. *Krinoi Kai Limenai: Studies in Honor of Joseph and Maria Shaw.* Philadelphia: INSTAP Academic Press.
Labyrinth of History:	Evely, Doniert, Helen Hughes-Brock, and Nicoletta Momigliano, eds. 1994. *Knossos: A Labyrinth of History: Papers Presented in Honour of Sinclair Hood.* Oxford: British School at Athens.

LH IIIC:	Deger-Jalkotzy, Sigrid, and Michaela Zavadil, eds. 2003. *LH IIIC Chronology and Synchronisms. Proceedings of the International Workshop Held at the Austrian Academy of Sciences at Vienna, May 7th and 8th, 2001.* Veröffentlichungen der Mykenischen Kommission 20. Vienna: Verlag der Österreichischen Akademie der Wissenschaften.
LH IIIC Middle:	Deger-Jalkotzy, Sigrid, and Michaela Zavadil, eds. 2007. *LH IIIC Chronology and Synchronisms II: LH IIIC Middle. Proceedings of the International Workshop Held at the Austrian Academy of Sciences at Vienna, October 29th and 30th, 2004.* Vienna: Verlag der Österreischishen Akademie der Wissenschaften.
LH IIIC Late:	Deger-Jalkotzy, Sigrid, and Anna Baechle, eds. 2009. *LH IIIC Chronology and Synchronisms III: LH IIIC Late and the Transition to the Early Iron Age. Proceedings of the International Workshop Held at the Austrian Academy of Sciences at Vienna, February 23rd and 24th, 2007.* Veröffentlichungen der Mykenischen Kommission. Vienna: Verlag der Österreichischen Akademie der Wissenschaften.
L'habitat Égéen préhistorique:	Darcque, Pascal, and René Treuil, eds. 1989. *L'habitat Égéen préhistorique.* BCH Suppl. 19. Athens: L'École française d'Athènes.
Mediterranean Peoples:	Gitin, Seymour, Amihai Mazar, and Ephraim Stern, eds. 1998. *Mediterranean Peoples in Transition: Thirteenth to Early Tenth Centuries BCE: In Honor of Professor Trude Dothan.* Jerusalem: Israel Exploration Society.
Meletemata:	Betancourt, Philip P., Vassos Karageorghis, Robert Laffineur, and Wolf-Dietrich Niemeier, eds. 1999. *Meletemata: Studies in Aegean*

	Archaeology Presented to Malcolm H. Wiener as He Enters His 65th Year. Aegaeum 20. Liège: Université de Liège.
Mesohelladika:	Philippa-Touchais, Anna, Gilles Touchais, Sofia Voutsaki, and James Wright, eds. In press. *Mesohelladika: The Greek Mainland in the Middle Bronze Age. Proceedings of the International Conference Held in Athens, March 8–12, 2006.* BCH Suppl. Athens: L'École française d'Athènes.
METRON:	Foster, Karen P., and Robert Laffineur, eds. 2003. *METRON: Measuring the Aegean Bronze Age. Proceedings of the 9th International Aegean Conference, New Haven, Yale University, April 18–21, 2002.* Aegaeum 24. Liège: Université de Liège.
MH Pottery:	Felten, Florens, Walter Gauss, and Rudolfine Smetana, eds. 2007. *Middle Helladic Pottery and Synchronisms. Proceedings of the International Workshop Held at Salzburg, October 31st–November 2nd, 2004.* Vienna: Österreichische Akademie der Wissenschaften.
Minoan Society:	Krzyszkowska, Olga, and Lucia Nixon, eds. 1983. *Minoan Society. Proceedings of the Cambridge Colloquium 1981.* Bristol: Bristol Classical Press.
Minoan Thalassocracy:	Hägg, Robin, and Nanno Marinatos, eds. 1983. *The Minoan Thalassocracy: Myth and Reality. Proceedings of the Third International Symposium at the Swedish Institute in Athens, May 31–June 5, 1982.* Skrifter utgivna av Svenska Institutet i Athen 4/32. Stockholm: Åström.
Minoisch-mykenische Glyptik:	Müller, Walter, ed. 2000. *Minoisch-mykenische Glyptik: Stil, Ikonographie, Function, V. internationales Siegel-Symposium, Marburg 23.–25. September 1999.* Corpus der minoischen und mykenischen Siegel Beiheft 6. Berlin: Mann.
Monuments of Minos:	Driessen, Jan, Ilse Schoep, and Robert Laffineur, eds. 2002. *Monuments of Minos:*

	Rethinking the Minoan Palaces. Proceedings of the International Workshop "Crete of the Hundred Palaces?" Université Catholique de Louvain-la-Neuve, 14–15 December 2001. Aegaeum 23. Liège: Université de Liège.
Periphery of the Mycenaean World:	Kyparissi-Apostolika, Nina, and Mani Papakonstantinou, eds. 2003. *Proceedings of the 2nd International Interdisciplinary Colloquium: The Periphery of the Mycenaean World. September 26–30, Lamia 1999.* Athens: Ministry of Culture, 14th Ephorate of Prehistoric and Classical Antiquities.
PLOES:	Stampolides, Nikolaos C., and Vassos Karageorghis, eds. 2003. *PLOES... Sea Routes... Interconnections in the Mediterranean 16th–6th c. BC. Proceedings of the International Symposium Held at Rethymnon, Crete, September 29th–October 2nd, 2002.* Athens: University of Crete and the A. G. Leventis Foundation.
PM:	Evans, Arthur J. 1921–1935. *The Palace of Minos,* vols. 1–4. London: Macmillan.
Point Iria Wreck:	Phelps, William, Yannos Lolos, and Yannis Vichos, eds. 1999. *The Point Iria Wreck: Interconnections in the Mediterranean ca. 1200 B.C. Proceedings of the International Conference, Island of Spetses, September 19, 1998.* Athens: Hellenic Institute of Maritime Archaeology.
Polemos:	Laffineur, Robert, ed. 1999. *Polemos: Le contexte guerrier en Égée à l'âge du bronze. Actes de la 7e Rencontre égéenne internationale. Université de Liège, 14–17 avril 1998.* Aegaeum 19. Liège: Université de Liège.
Poliochni:	Doumas, Christos G., and Vincenzo La Rosa, eds. 1997. *Η Πολιόχνη και η Πρώιμη Εποχή του Χαλκού στο Βόρειο Αιγαίο, Diethnes Sunedrio Athina, 22–25 Apriliou 1996–Poliochni e l'Antica Età del*

	Bronzo nell'Egeio Settentrionale, Convegno Internazionale, Atene, 22–25 Aprile 1996. Atene: Scuola Archeologica Italiana di Atene.
Politeia:	Laffineur, Robert, and Wolf-Dietrich Niemeier, eds. 2005. *Politeia: Society and State in the Aegean Bronze Age. Proceedings of the 5th International Aegean Conference, University of Heidelberg, Archäologisches Institut, 10–13 April 1994.* Aegaeum 12. Liège: Université de Liège.
Potnia:	Laffineur, Robert, and Robin Hägg, eds. 2001. *Potnia: Deities and Religion in the Aegean Bronze Age. Proceedings of the 8th International Aegean Conference, Göteborg, Göteborg University, April 12–15, 2000.* Aegaeum 22. Liège: Université de Liège.
Prehistoric Cyclades:	MacGillivray, J. Alexander, and Robin N. L. Barber, eds. 1984. *The Prehistoric Cyclades: Contributions to a Workshop on Cycladic Chronology.* Edinburgh: Department of Classical Archaeology, University of Edinburgh.
Problems in Greek Prehistory:	French, Elizabeth B., and Ken A. Wardle, eds. 1988. *Problems in Greek Prehistory: Papers Presented at the Centenary Conference of the British School of Archaeology at Athens, Manchester, April 1986.* Bristol: Bristol Classical Press.
RMP:	Galaty, Michael L., and William A. Parkinson, eds. 1999. *Rethinking Mycenaean Palaces: New Interpretations of an Old Idea.* Los Angeles: Cotsen Institute of Archaeology.
RMP II:	Galaty, Michael L., and William A. Parkinson, eds. 2007. *Rethinking Mycenaean Palaces II.* Rev. and expanded 2d ed. Los Angeles: Cotsen Institute of Archaeology at UCLA.
Role of the Ruler:	Rehak, Paul, ed. 1995. *The Role of the Ruler in the Prehistoric Aegean. Proceedings of a Panel Discussion Presented at the Annual Meeting of the*

Archaeological Institute of America, New Orleans, Louisiana, December 28, 1992, with Additions. Aegaeum 11. Liège: Université de Liège.

Sanctuaries and Cults: Hägg, Robin, and Nanno Marinatos, eds. 1981. Sanctuaries and Cults in the Aegean Bronze Age. Proceedings of the First International Symposium at the Swedish Institute in Athens, May 12–13, 1980. Stockholm: Åström.

Sandy Pylos 1998: Davis, Jack L., ed. 1998. Sandy Pylos: An Archaeological History from Nestor to Navarino. Austin: University of Texas Press.

Sandy Pylos 2008: Davis, Jack L., ed. 2008. Sandy Pylos: An Archaeological History from Nestor to Navarino, 2d ed. Princeton: American School of Classical Studies.

SCIEM II: Bietak, Manfred, ed. 2003. The Synchronisation of Civilisations in the Eastern Mediterranean in the Second Millennium B.C. II, Proceedings of the SCIEM 2000–EuroConference, Haindorf, 2nd of May–7th of May 2001. Wien: Verlag der Österreichischen Akademie der Wissenschaften.

SCIEM III: Bietak, Manfred, and Ernst Czerny, eds. 2007. The Synchronisation of Civilisations in the Eastern Mediterranean in the Second Millennium B.C. III, Proceedings of the SCIEM 2000–2nd EuroConference, Vienna, 28th of May–1st of June 2003. Wien: Verlag der Österreichischen Akademie der Wissenschaften.

Sources for the History of Cyprus: Knapp, A. Bernard, ed. 1996. Sources for the History of Cyprus: Near Eastern and Aegean Texts from the Third to the First Millennia BC. Altamont: Greece and Cyprus Research Center.

SWDS: Cline, Eric H. 1994. Sailing the Wine-Dark Sea: International Trade and the Late Bronze Age Aegean. BAR-IS 591. Oxford: Tempus Reparatum.

TAW I: Doumas, Christos, ed. 1978. *Thera and the Aegean World* I. London: Thera and the Aegean World.

TAW III: Hardy, David, Christos Doumas, Ioannis Sakellarakis, and Peter Warren, eds. 1990. *Thera and the Aegean World* III. London: Thera Foundation.

Tenth ICE: Kousoulis, Panagiotis, ed. 2008. *Tenth International Congress of Egyptologists Abstracts of Papers Rhodes 22–29 May 2008*, 269. Rhodes: Department of Mediterranean Studies, University of the Aegean (detailed publication in preparation).

TEXNH: Laffineur, Robert, and Philip P. Betancourt, eds. 1997. *TEXNH. Craftsmen, Craftswomen, and Craftsmanship in the Aegean Bronze Age. Proceedings of the 6th International Aegean Conference, Philadelphia, Temple University, April 18–21, 1996*. Aegaeum 16. Liège: Université de Liège.

Thalassa: Laffineur, Robert, and Lucien Basch, eds. 1991. *Thalassa: L'Egée préhistorique et la mer. Actes de la 3e Rencontre égéenne internationale de l'Université de Liège, Calvi, Corse, 23–25 avril 1990*. Aegaeum 7. Liège: Université de Liège.

Thanatos: Laffineur, Robert, ed. 1987. *Thanatos : Les coutumes funéraires en Egée à l'âge du Bronze. Actes du colloque de Liège, 21–23 avril 1986*. Aegaeum 1. Liège: Université de Liège.

Timelines: Czerny, Ernst, Irmgard Hein, Hermann Hunger, Dagmar Melman, and Angela Schwab, eds. 2006. *Timelines: Studies in Honour of Manfred Bietak*. Orientalia Lovaniensia Analecta 149. Leuven: Peeters.

TRANSITION: Laffineur, Robert, ed. 1989. *TRANSITION. Le monde égéen du Bronze moyen au Bronze récent. Actes de la 2e Rencontre égéenne internationale de*

	l'Université de Liège, 18–20 avril 1988. Aegaeum 3. Liège: Université de Liège.
Urbanism:	Branigan, Keith, ed. 2001. *Urbanism in the Aegean Bronze Age.* Sheffield Studies in Aegean Archaeology 4. Sheffield: Continuum.
Wace and Blegen:	Zerner, Carol, Peter Zerner, and John Winder, eds. 1993. *Wace and Blegen: Pottery as Evidence for Trade in the Aegean Bronze Age 1939–1989. Proceedings of the International Conference Held at the American School of Classical Studies at Athens, Athens, December 2–3, 1989.* Amsterdam: Gieben.
Wall Paintings of Thera:	Sherratt, Susan, ed. 2000. *The Wall Paintings of Thera. Proceedings of the First International Symposium, Petros M. Nomikos Conference Centre, Thera, Hellas, August 30–September 4, 1997.* Athens: Thera Foundation.
White Slip Ware:	Karageorghis, Vassos, ed. 2001. *The White Slip Ware of Late Bronze Age Cyprus. Proceedings of an International Conference Organized by the Anastasios G. Leventis Foundation, Nicosia in Honour of Malcolm Wiener, Nicosia 29th–October 30th, 1998.* Vienna: Verlag der Österreichischen Akademie der Wissenschaften.

Additional Abbreviations

EBA: Early Bronze Age
EC: Early Cycladic (and/or Early Cypriot in some cases)
EH: Early Helladic
EM: Early Minoan
EN: Early Neolithic
FN: Final Neolithic
IN: Initial Neolithic
LBA: Late Bronze Age
LC: Late Cycladic (and/or Late Cypriot in certain cases)
LH: Late Helladic

LM: Late Minoan
LN: Late Neolithic
MBA: Middle Bronze Age
MC: Middle Cycladic (and/or Middle Cypriot in certain cases)
MH: Middle Helladic
MM: Middle Minoan
MN: Middle Neolithic

Table 1. Aegean Bronze Age Approximate Chronology, Mainland Greece

Early Bronze Age or Early Helladic period	EH I	3000–2650 BC
	EH II	2650–2200 BC
	EH III	2200–2000 BC
Middle Bronze Age or Middle Helladic period	MH I	2000–1900 BC
	MH II	1900–1800 BC
	MH III	1800–1700 BC
Late Bronze Age or Late Helladic period	LH I	1700–1600 BC
	LH II	1600–1400 BC
	LH IIIA	1400–1300 BC
	LH IIIB	1300–1200 BC
	LH IIIC	1200–1100 BC

Source: Courtesy of Eric H. Cline and Sofia Voutsaki.

PREFACE

. . . .

It is my hope that the *Oxford Handbook of the Bronze Age Aegean* will provide a comprehensive overview of our current understanding of the Bronze Age Aegean (ca. 3000–1000 BC) and capture the most important debates and discussions currently ongoing within the discipline. Presented in four separate sections within the handbook, the sixty-six commissioned articles by more than sixty different scholars address a series of useful—and occasionally overlapping—topics ranging from chronological and geographical to thematic and site-specific subjects. Each was written by one or more experts who were asked to present an authoritative précis while adhering to strict word and illustration limits.

GEOGRAPHICAL AND HISTORICAL SCOPE

. . . .

The geographical area of the Aegean, as considered within the handbook, comprises primarily mainland Greece, Crete, and the Cycladic Islands but extends also to Rhodes, the Dodecanese Islands, the western coast of Anatolia (modern Turkey), the eastern Mediterranean (Cyprus, Egypt, and the Levant), and the western Mediterranean (Sicily, Sardinia, and Italy). Individual articles make additional references to the Balkans and Europe. The chronological period under consideration is the Bronze Age, which runs from approximately 3000–1000 BC in the Aegean region and is roughly subdivided into the Early Bronze Age (ca. 3000–2000 BC), the Middle Bronze Age (ca. 2000–1700 BC), and the Late Bronze Age (ca. 1700–1000 BC). For more precise dates, the reader may consult table 1.1 and the entry on chronology, as well as a multitude of individual entries.

CONTENT AND STRUCTURE

. . . .

The first part, Background and Definitions, contains chapters on general topics that are essential to establish the discipline in its historical, geographical, and chronological settings and its relation to other disciplines.

The second part, Chronology and Geography, contains chapters examining the Bronze Age Aegean by chronological period (Early Bronze Age, Middle Bronze Age,

Late Bronze Age). In order to discuss these periods comprehensively, each one has been further subdivided geographically, so that the individual chapters are concerned with mainland Greece during the Early Bronze Age, Crete during the Early Bronze Age, the Cycladic Islands during the Early Bronze Age, and the same for the Middle Bronze Age, followed by the Late Bronze Age.

The third part, Thematic Topics, contains chapters that examine a number of thematic issues that cannot be done justice in a strictly chronological or geographical treatment, including religion, state and society, trade, warfare, pottery, writing, and burial customs, as well as specific topics such as the eruption of Santorini and the Trojan War. Some of these will have been touched upon in the previous major section (Chronology and Geography) but deserve their own extended treatment. Every attempt has been made to ensure that there are no extensive duplications, discrepancies, and/or contradictions within the materials in these different sections.

The fourth part, Specific Sites and Regions, contains chapters that examine some of the most important sites and regions in the Bronze Age Aegean and related areas, including Mycenae, Tiryns, Pylos, Knossos, Kommos, Ialysos, Troy, the Uluburun and Cape Gelidonya shipwrecks, western Anatolia, the Levant, Cyprus, Egypt, and the western Mediterranean. Each of the contributions on a specific site presents the history of the excavations, the discoveries that have been made, and the importance of each to the study of the region and time period under consideration. In almost all of the cases, the entry has been written by the excavator of the site or, if the excavator is deceased, by someone who is considered to be an expert on that site. Similarly, the entries for individual regions have been written by selected scholars who focus on their particular area of expertise.

Contributors

A varied group of scholars has contributed articles to this handbook. A number are established researchers whose names are known even outside their chosen fields; others are younger but highly regarded specialists whose contributions to scholarship are already changing our understanding of Bronze Age Aegean archaeology. All of the contributors have written on their particular area of specialization, whether it is a history of the discipline, an overview of a chronological period, a thematic topic, or a specific site.

Goals and Aims

This handbook is meant to serve as an essential research tool and resource for the Bronze Age Aegean, with reasonably brief entries on the most important periods, places, events, and topics. Based in part on course syllabi used by several Bronze Age

Aegean scholars for advanced undergraduate and graduate classes, the goal was to cover subjects that lend themselves well to individual classroom lectures and discussions and to create a volume that would allow the reader to pick it up, immediately turn to the desired subject, and learn about it in a manageable fashion. It is aimed at professionals who teach undergraduate and graduate courses on the Bronze Age Aegean, as well as advanced undergraduate and graduate students taking such courses and a select portion of the interested general public. It is hoped that the volume will also prove useful to professional scholars and advanced students in related disciplines such as Classics, ancient history, and the ancient Near East and that it will be considered an essential reference work for academic libraries worldwide.

Eric Cline

THE OXFORD HANDBOOK OF

THE BRONZE AGE AEGEAN

PART I

BACKGROUND AND DEFINITIONS

CHAPTER 1

HISTORY OF RESEARCH

JAMES D. MUHLY

OUR modern reconstructions of Greek prehistory have always been influenced by the ways in which the ancient Greeks attempted to create a usable account of their own history. Out of a rich, inherited body of saga, folklore, and myth, the Greeks of the Archaic and Classical periods struggled to assemble a meaningful framework, a sequence of events that satisfied the needs of a contemporary audience. Obviously all of this centered round the Homeric epics, but the establishment of the structural framework seems to have been the work of Hesiod, in his sequence of the "five ages" and in his ordering of genealogical traditions in the work now known as the *Catalogue of Women*.

The *Iliad* and the *Odyssey* established the Trojan War as the culminating event in the prehistory of the Greek people. For Thucydides, writing in the mid-fifth century BC, the separate Hellenic states were weak and disorganized prior to the Trojan War. They lacked even a common name and could not bring themselves to do anything together (Thucydides, I.3). What they did have was a common language that was always the decisive factor in distinguishing between Greeks and barbarians. No one who did not speak Greek could possibly be considered a Greek.

It was the sequence of events associated with the Trojan War and its aftermath that gave Greeks of the historic period their Heroic past. It was this same Heroic past that inspired modern scholars to re-create an archaeological past for a preliterate age. Heinrich Schliemann went to Hisarlık in 1870 to find the capital city of Priam, the king of Troy. He then went to Mycenae in 1876 to find the graves of Agamemnon and all of those involved in the downfall of the House of Atreus. Arthur Evans went to Knossos in 1900 to find the palace of Minos, the king who ruled the seas and for whom the craftsman Daidalos built the Labyrinth. Carl Blegen went back to Troy in 1932 in order to determine what city, out of the nine that made up the prehistoric mound, could best be identified as Homeric Troy. He then went to Ano Englianos, in the southwestern Peloponnese, in 1939 to find the palace of Nestor, the king of Pylos. In other words, our modern reconstruction of Greek prehistory has been motivated and guided by the Heroic past that the ancient Greeks had created for themselves.

The problem is that modern scholars have tried to create a serious history out of fantasy and folklore. In retrospect it is hard to imagine how it could otherwise have happened. What else could possibly have motivated early researchers than the desire to establish the reliability and accuracy of ancient literary traditions? In 1878 Charles Newton, then Keeper of Greek and Roman Antiquities in the British Museum, writing about Schliemann's discoveries at Mycenae in 1876, came to the following conclusion:

> How much the story of Agamemnon is really to be accepted as fact, and by what test we may discriminate between that which is merely plausible fiction and that residuum of true history which can be detected under a mythic disguise in this and other Greek legends, are problems as yet unsolved, notwithstanding the immense amount of erudition and subtle criticism which has been expended on them. (Fitton 1995, 76)

One hundred and thirty years later these problems are, of course, still unresolved, and, in recent years, most Aegean prehistorians have concluded that they can never be resolved because they represent what for George Grote, the great 19th-century historian of ancient Greece, constituted "a past that never was present."

Best to move on to other things, it was argued, and to look upon sites such as Troy, Mycenae, and Pylos not as being inhabited by the likes of Priam, Agamemnon, and Nestor but as important centers of Bronze Age civilization. Yet, our very concepts of Bronze Age and Iron Age go back to Hesiod, and we will never be able to visit Mycenae without thinking of Agamemnon and Clytemnestra. Nor would we necessarily ever want to do so. What Schliemann and Evans did, in its most basic sense, was to take Greek historical and literary scholarship out of the library and into the field. They demonstrated, once and for all, that sites such as Mycenae, Tiryns, Pylos, Thebes, and Orchomenos had a reality that could be uncovered by careful archaeological investigation. The exact nature of the relationship between that reality and the heroic past of ancient Greece will probably never be understood, but most scholars today feel that much more can be accomplished by trying to understand such sites within a framework now identified by terms such as *Late Minoan IA* and *IB* than by worrying about the historicity of Minos and his Labyrinth.

Just as ancient Greece moved from a heroic mythical past in the Bronze Age, to a glorious historical present in the Archaic and Classical periods, so Bronze Age scholarship has moved from a heroic past dominated by larger-than-life figures such as Schliemann, Evans, Tsountas, Wace, and Blegen, to an international, multidisciplinary present that is increasingly dominated by science and technology. Behind all of this, past and present, looms the figure of Homer. Whatever one's own interests and areas of specialization, it is probably true that no Bronze Age scholar has ever worked independently of Homer. Hesiod has always taken a more secondary, subsidiary role, yet his work was critical for the formulation of the Heroic Age, as seen by the ancient Greeks. There are probably good reasons for this. Didactic poetry will never be able to compete with the grand sweep of epic, and, in any case, Homer was simply a much better poet. One need look only at the outpouring of recent scholarship on all aspects of the study of Homer and Hesiod to appreciate the enduring importance of both poets in the 21st century AD.

There is considerable interest today in what can be described as the history of scholarship. Works such as William McDonald and Carol Thomas's *Progress into the Past* and J. Lesley Fitton's *The Discovery of the Greek Bronze Age* give excellent accounts of the historical development of Bronze Age scholarship and of Aegean archaeology from before Schliemann to the decipherment of Linear B by Michael Ventris. Although they both cover the same basic material, they are very different in scope and in approach and complement each other quite nicely. Mention should also be made of the excellent short handbook by Carol Thomas, *Myth Becomes History: Pre-Classical Greece,* written for students of ancient history and containing extensive bibliography.

McDonald's approach is more episodic, analyzing a number of key works of synthesis at different stages of the story, such as Tsountas and Manatt's *The Mycenaean Age,* Gustav Glotz on *The Aegean Civilization,* and H. L. Lorimer's *Homer and the Monuments.* Fitton's work is more analytical. She does a wonderful job of evaluating the work of many important scholars while at the same time putting things together into a grand historical narrative. McDonald, who worked with Blegen at Pylos in 1939 and, as a graduate student, actually excavated the first archive of Linear B tablets found on the Greek mainland, tends to emphasize contributions made by American scholars, whereas Fitton places considerable emphasis upon the role of the British Museum and the writings of early British travelers to Greece. Both McDonald and Fitton have a keen interest in trying to understand the present focus and the future course of Aegean Bronze Age archaeology.

It was the study of seal stones from Crete and their possible evidence for early pictographic writing that first involved Arthur Evans in the antiquities of the island and led to one of his earliest publications, *Cretan Pictographs and Prae-Phoenician Scripts.* The study of Minoan and Mycenaean seal stones and clay sealings soon developed into one of the major research areas in Bronze Age archaeology. The *Corpus der minoischen und mykenischen Siegel,* soon to become known as the *CMS,* published its first volume in 1964. Some twenty-five volumes were to follow, along with six Beiheft or supplementary volumes, making the *CMS* one of the most comprehensive, most significant research enterprises in Aegean archaeology. Originally established by Friedrich Matz, the series has long been edited by Igno Pini at Marburg. An excellent introduction to research in this field has now been published by Olga Krzyszkowska.

Probably the most significant development in the study of Bronze Age archaeology in the 20th century was the recognition of the importance of pottery, resulting in the development of ceramic studies almost as a separate discipline. Carl Blegen began his career as a field archaeologist not at Troy or at Pylos but at the tiny prehistoric site of Korakou, near Cornith, where he uncovered a deep stratigraphic sequence of Early, Middle, and Late Helladic pottery styles (as they came to be called thanks to this excavation). This he published in 1921, and scholarship over the past ninety years has refined and elaborated Blegen's basic sequence. As Blegen himself put it, "Korakou explains Tiryns and Mycenae" (Fitton 1996, 147). The importance of pottery had, to some extent, been recognized right from the start with the pioneering study of *Mykenische Vasen* by Furtwängler and Loeschcke. For the modern study of Mycenaean pottery the basic publication has long been *Mycenaean Pottery: Analysis and Classification* by Furumark, the work that established the chronological sequence for both shapes and motifs. What is most remarkable about this fundamental work is that Furumark worked almost entirely from photographs, with no access to the vases themselves. An excellent synthesis of scholarship since Furumark is *Mycenaean Pottery: An Introduction* by Mountjoy. For Minoan pottery, the basic handbook has long been Betancourt's *The History of Minoan Pottery*.

Pottery study is a field that abounds in specialized studies and monographs. It is important to understand that the establishment of a ceramic sequence establishes a relative chronology. What scholars now realize is that this sequence is usually valid only for a particular region, and the study of variations in regional styles of pottery is one of the major aspects of current research in the field. An excellent account of present-day complexities in the discipline is the two-volume work by Mountjoy titled *Regional Mycenaean Decorated Pottery*. In recent years the trend has been to study the pottery of individual chronological periods. The pottery associated with the collapse of the Bronze Age world in the early 12th century BC, a style known as Late Helladic IIIC, has been the subject of several international conferences sponsored by the Austrian Academy of Sciences in Vienna. Specialization has reached the point where an entire conference can be devoted to LH IIIC Middle (held in Vienna in 2004; published in 2007; see also Thomatos 2006). There are also specialized monographs devoted to individual types of pottery. Outstanding in this regard is *Aegean Bronze Age Rhyta* by Robert Koehl.

What about absolute chronology? When did it all take place? Chronology has always been seen as crucial to any understanding of past events. For Herodotus, Homer lived some four hundred years before his time, or ca. 850 BC, and the Trojan War took place another four hundred years earlier, or ca. 1250 BC. No one in antiquity ever seriously believed that Homer was a contemporary of the world he described in such a haunting fashion. Was there any reason, nevertheless, to take seriously a Hellenistic chronographic tradition, based upon very dubious evidence, that dated the Trojan War at 1193–1184 BC?

When Schliemann presented his discoveries at Mycenae to a very receptive general public, he was greeted with great skepticism by the leading Classical scholars of the day, especially R. C. Jebb, the great editor of the plays of Sophocles. The art of Greece was the art of Phidias and the Parthenon. The gold jewelry from the Shaft Graves at Mycenae was seen as crude and barbarous, probably the work of Scythian nomads. But Charles Newton saw that the pottery from Mycenae was very similar to that found by Biliotti in his excavations at Ialysos on Rhodes in 1868 and 1870. That pottery, sent to the British Museum, had been found in association with a scarab of the Egyptian pharaoh Amenhotep III, now dated to 1391–1353 BC.

The first sherds of what came to be recognized as Kamares ware, the hallmark of the Middle Minoan II period, were discovered by Flinders Petrie at Lahun in Egypt in 1889–1890, ten years before Evans began work at Knossos and five years before John Linton Myers found the pottery at the Kamares Cave itself. Petrie soon recognized that Egypt, with its rich tradition of contemporary historical records, was destined to serve as the basis for the reconstruction of an absolute chronology for the Aegean Bronze Age.

To a great extent this is true still today. Minoan and Mycenaean pottery found in datable Egyptian contexts and inscribed Egyptian objects found in secure Aegean contexts enabled Evans to reconstruct a tripartite framework for Minoan chronology, and Carl Blegen was soon to extend this system to the world of Mycenaean Greece. It might seem surprising, in this high-tech world of Greenland ice cores, Santorini tephra, radiocarbon dating, and dendrochronology, that Egyptian historical records still play such a central role in our understanding of the chronology of the Aegean Bronze Age. The reasons for this are quite simple: The Egyptian records are, for the most part, contemporary with the events they describe (and date). Modern scientific dating techniques, however sophisticated, still represent modern attempts to reconstruct a chronology for events that happened three or four thousand years ago. The more we work with the range of scientific dating techniques available to the modern scholar the more we come to realize the complexity of each technique and the number of variables that have to be understood and accounted for.

The role of Egypt in the establishment of the absolute chronology of the eastern Mediterranean during the second millennium BC has been enhanced in recent years as the result of two spectacular excavations: (1) The excavations by Spyridon Marinatos at the site of Akrotiri on the southern coast of the island of Thera, starting in 1967, uncovered an LM IA settlement buried under pumice and ash from the fallout of a huge volcanic eruption that is to be dated in the mid-second millennium BC; and (2) the excavations by Manfred Bietak at the site of Tell el-Dabᶜa, ancient Avaris, in the eastern delta of the Nile Valley, with spectacular wall paintings in a Minoan style, formerly placed in the period of the Hyksos rulers of Egypt (1638–1540 BC) but now dated to the reign of Thutmose III (1479–1425 BC). The arguments over dating the eruption of Thera and the wall paintings of Tell el-Dabᶜa have split asunder the world of Bronze Age Aegean archaeology. Those who favor the 'scientific' chronology, based upon radiocarbon dates and dendrochronology, place the eruption of Thera at ca. 1620 BC. Those who favor the 'historical' chronology, based upon synchronisms with New Kingdom Egypt, date the eruption to ca. 1520 BC.

These issues were first discussed in a series of three international Thera congresses, organized by Marinatos and starting in 1968. Following the death of Marinatos in 1978, the venue for the discussion of these problems eventually shifted from Athens to Vienna in recognition of the importance of the work of Bietak on behalf of the

Austrian Academy of Sciences. The first volume of studies on the excavations at Tell el-Dab°a appeared in 1975. For absolute chronology, the most important development was the establishment in 2000, by Bietak, of an international conference series to be known as SCIEM 2000 (SCIEM = The Synchronisation of Civilisations in the Eastern Mediterranean in the Second Millennium BC). Volume XX in this series, dealing with *The Bronze Age in the Lebanon*, has just appeared (Bietak and Czerny 2008). In 1990 Bietak established a new journal, *Ägypten und Levante*, soon to also acquire an English version of the title: *Egypt and the Levant* (with vol. VI for 1996). This journal now publishes, among other things, the proceedings of conferences and workshops held under the auspices of SCIEM 2000. The most recent of these, in vol. XVI for 2006, was a workshop on "Egypt and Time: Proceedings of a Workshop on Precision and Accuracy of the Egyptian Historical Chronology." Those who believe that the 'high' or 'scientific' chronology must be correct but who also find it difficult to ignore well-established synchronisms with New Kingdom Egypt, have concluded that Egyptian historical chronology must be off by about one hundred years. This is exceedingly unlikely.

The arguments on both sides of this debate constitute an excellent reflection of the state of Bronze Age archaeology in the early 21st century AD. Many of the technical arguments seem to be a long way from the world of Homer, but relations between Greece and Egypt, and especially Crete and Egypt, have long been part of the archaeology of the world of Homer. In 1930, Pendlebury, who, in the course of his brief career as a field archaeologist, had excavated both in Crete (at Knossos) and in Egypt (at Tell el-Amarna) published his monograph titled *Aegyptiaca: A Catalogue of Egyptian Objects in the Aegean Area*. In that same year, he published an article in the *Journal of Egyptian Archaeology* on "Egypt and the Aegean in the Late Bronze Age." For Pendlebury, the end of Minoan civilization was brought about by a revolt of oppressed Aegean people against hated Minoan domination. These 'historical' events provided the background for the myth of Theseus, who liberated his fellow Athenians from the tyranny of Minos and his Labyrinth. This was Bronze Age archaeology in the grand old tradition of using mythology in an attempt to write history. Today no reputable Bronze Age archaeologist would ever hazard such a reconstruction. The new monograph by Jacqueline Phillips titled *Aegyptiaca on the Island of Crete in Their Chronological Context: A Critical Review,* published as a volume in the SCIEM 2000 series, will be very different from what Pendlebury published in 1930.

These differences reflect the tremendous growth of the discipline of Bronze Age archaeology over the past eighty years. Thanks to the impact and influence of a whole range of disciplines, the Bronze Age archaeologist in now capable of presenting excavated material in ways unthinkable even a few decades ago. Consider, just to give one example, the ways in which a scholar such as Marian Feldman is capable of evaluating the international style of art that developed in the 14th and 13th centuries BC (in her book *Diplomacy by Design* and her earlier article in the *Art Bulletin*).

In the late 19th and early 20th century AD, the Egyptologist Flinders Petrie had a much better understanding of the antiquity of Mycenaean civilization than did his colleagues in Classical Archaeology. It was Petrie who demonstrated to William Ramsay, in his article on "Notes on the Antiquities of Mykenae," that the lions on the Lion Gate at Mycenae had nothing to do with those shown on the façade of the Phrygian tomb at Arslan Taş. Petrie argued that the Lion Gate was to be dated in the 15th century BC, not the 8th.

Ramsay was not alone in believing that Mycenaean civilization was no older than the 8th century BC. For instance, A. S. Murray of the British Museum, in his *Handbook of Greek Archaeology,* published in 1892, argued that the antiquity of the remains of Mycenaean Greece had been greatly exaggerated. He firmly believed that Mycenae and Tiryns were the work of Greek tyrants in the 7th century BC. This is the same Murray who went on to excavate at Enkomi (Cyprus) at the end of the century on behalf of the British Museum.

We tend to forget just how revolutionary the work of Heinrich Schliemann really was. For all his faults as an excavator, Schliemann set the field of Bronze Age archaeology on a path from which it has never deviated. He made it possible for the fantasies of the past to be turned into the solid scholarship of today. Schliemann was more than capable of defending himself against his critics. When Sir Richard Jebb (1882) argued that Hisarlık was not Troy and that Mycenae and Tiryns were Byzantine fortresses, Schliemann replied, in his *Troia* publication (1884, 237): "No courtesy on my part can save Professor Jebb from the fate on which an eminent classical scholar rushes when he mingles in an archaeological debate in ignorance of the first principles of archaeology" (for this debate see Morris 1997, 119). What is remarkable here is that Schliemann is already arguing as an archaeologist in defense of a new discipline that he did so much to bring into existence.

BIBLIOGRAPHY

Betancourt, Philip. 1985. *The History of Minoan Pottery*. Princeton: Princeton University Press.

Bietak, Manfred and Ernst Czerny. 2008. *The Bronze Age in the Lebanon. Studies on the Archaeology and Chronology of Lebanon, Syria and Egypt*. Vienna: SCIEM, Vol. XV, Vienna, Verlag der Österreischen Akademie der Wissenschaften.

Evans, Arthur. 1895. *Cretan Pictographs and Prae-Phoenician Scripts*. London: B. Quaritch.

Feldman, Marian. 2002. "Luxurious Forms: Redefining a Mediterranean 'International Style,' ca. 1400–1200 B.C.E." *Art Bulletin* 84: 6–29.

———. 2006. *Diplomacy by Design*. Chicago: University of Chicago Press.

Fitton, J. Lesley. 1995. "Charles Newton and the Discovery of the Greek Bronze Age." In *Klados: Essays in honour of J. N. Coldstream*, ed. Christine Morris, 73–78. London: British Institute of Classical Studies, Suppl. Vol. 63.

Fitton, J. Lesley. 1996. *The Discovery of the Greek Bronze Age*. Cambridge, Mass.: Harvard University Press.

Furtwängler, Adolf, and Georg Loeschcke. 1886. *Mykenische Vasen*. 3 vols. Berlin: A. Asher.

Furumark, Arne. 1941. *Mycenaean Pottery: Analysis and Classification*. Stockholm: Swedish Institute in Athens.

Glotz, Gustav. 1925. *The Aegean Civilization*. New York: Knopf.

Jebb, SirRichard. 1882. "I. The Ruins of Hissarlik. II. Their Relation to the Iliad." *JHS* 3: 185–217.

Koehl, Robert B. 2006. *Aegean Bronze Age Rhyta*. Philadelphia: INSTAP Academic Press.

Krzyszkowska, Olga. 2005. *Aegean Seals: An Introduction*. BICS Suppl. 85. London: Institute of Classical Studies.

Lorimer, Hilda L. 1950. *Homer and the Monuments*. London: Macmillan.

McDonald, William. 1967. *Progress into the Past*. New York: Macmillan.

McDonald, William, and Carol Thomas. 1990. *Progress into the Past*, 2d ed. Bloomington: Indiana University Press.

Morris, Ian. 1997. "Periodization and the Heroes: Inventing a Dark Age." In *Inventing Ancient Culture: Historicism, Periodization, and the Ancient World*, ed. Mark Golden and Peter Toohey, 96–131. London: Routledge.

Mountjoy, Penelope. 1993. *Mycenaean Pottery: An Introduction*. Oxford: Oxford University Committee for Archaeology.

———. 1999. *Regional Mycenaean Decorated Pottery*. Rahden, Germany: M. Leidorf.

Murray, Alexander S. 1892. *Handbook of Greek Archaeology*. London: J. Murray.

Pendlebury, John D. S. 1930a. *Aegyptiaca: A Catalogue of Egyptian Objects in the Aegean Area*. Cambridge: Cambridge University Press.

———. 1930b. "Egypt and the Aegean in the Late Bronze Age." *JEA* 16: 75–92.

Petrie, Willam M. F. 1891. "Notes on the Antiquities of Mykenae." *JHS* 12: 199–205.

Phillips, Jacqueline. 2008. *Aegyptiaca on the Island of Crete in Their Chronological Context: A Critical Review*. SCIEM 2000, Vienna, Verlag der Österreichen Akademie der Wissenschaften.

Schliemann, Heinrich. 1875. *Troja*. New York: Harper and Brothers.

Thomas, Carol. 1993. *Myth Becomes History: Pre-Classical Greece*. Claremont, Calif.: Regina.

Thomatos, Marina. 2006. *The Final Revival of the Aegean Bronze Age: A Case Study of the Argolid, Corinthia, Attica, Euboea, the Cyclades, and the Dodecanese during LH IIIC Middle*. Oxford: Archaeopress.

Tsountas, Christos, and J. Irving Manatt. 1897. *The Mycenaean Age*. London: MacMillan.

CHAPTER 2

CHRONOLOGY AND TERMINOLOGY

STURT W. MANNING

A Very Brief Historical Introduction

Scholarship that is concerned with the discovery, creation, and interpretation of Aegean prehistory has, throughout its history (mid-19th century AD to present; e.g., McDonald and Thomas 1990; Papadopoulos 2005; Darcque, Fotiadis, and Polychronopoulou 2006; Manning 2008a), been intimately associated with the allocation and categorization of time. Dialectically, the field has been strongly shaped by these time frames as developed by modern scholars. Chronology has become both framework and constraint, friend and problem. If we know nothing else (concretely), we at least hope to put things in order, but how we create this order and how we choose to see the framework entirely creates our 'prehistory.'

The early 19th-century AD concept of the Three Age system developed from Thomsen's reorganization of the National Museum of Denmark (originally Stone Age, Bronze Age, Iron Age; cf. Daniel 1943; Gräslund 1987) and its ideas of evolutionary progression became the standard in most European (region and scholarship) prehistory. In turn, it was transferred to the Near East and the Mediterranean. In the Aegean, via especially the Three Age division of Egyptian history into the Old, Middle, and New Kingdoms for the third-second millennia BC, this framework of classification led to the creation of an Early, Middle, and Late Bronze Age in the Aegean (and before the Bronze Age the Neolithic and afterward the Iron Age) and then to further subdivisions (also typically tripartite, at least to start) of I, II, and III within these periods (Evans 1906 represents a succinct statement and delineation of such a method for Crete). And often further subdivisions, typically of A, B, and C (with a typically tripartite maximum and sometimes even additional subdivisions) were added later; thus, we have 'Late Minoan IIIA2 early' or 'Late Helladic IIIB2' (and even further Early and Late groups; see Vitale 2006) at the extreme. Some additional transitional phases have also been suggested at various times, for example a Middle Minoan III–Late Minoan IA transition (Warren 1991) (see caption to table 2.2).

Each main region, moreover, has its own system: thus Early, Middle, and Late Cycladic and subdivisions; Early, Middle, and Late Helladic and subdivisions; and Early, Middle, and Late Minoan and subdivisions. Western Anatolia has avoided regionalization and either has only key site sequences or Early, Middle, and Late Bronze Ages with various subdivisions. These classifications and their own evolutionary processes have led to an undeniably cumbersome and artificial structure with which scholars actively contend today. Much of our evidence and interpretation does not neatly fit such a unilinear evolutionary framework in terms of both time progression and space (different sites and regions had slightly to more substantially varying histories).

A quest to create some sort of structure and to bring order to a couple of millennia of calendar time has, over the course of the later 19th through the early 21st centuries AD thus come to create an incredibly rich, dense, ad hoc, and arcane system for describing and demarcating the time frame of the Aegean Bronze Age. For some, chronology became an end in itself (and it is almost a subfield of study of its own), forever to be elaborated and pursued to some elusive goal of a totality of knowledge. For others, chronology has, however, become almost a pejorative term—and its central role in Aegean prehistory is argued to distract attention from the more important topics of wider culture change, process, and history, as well as the role of this preclassical world in the creation of later classical civilization. Proponents of such views would argue that we need an agreed approximate framework, yes, but not endless detail and caveats.

An analogous situation exists for the chronology of prehistoric Cyprus, and, in response, Knapp and colleagues (e.g., Given and Knapp 2003, 30) have for some years proposed a much simplified/generalized chronological framework; thus, 'Early Prehistoric,' 'Prehistoric Bronze Age,' and 'Protohistoric Bronze Age' cover the entire previous Epipalaeolithic/Akrotiri phase, Aceramic Neolithic (early, late), Ceramic Neolithic, Early Chalcolithic, Middle Chalcolithic, Late Chalcolithic, Early Bronze/Cypriot I, II, III, Middle Bronze/Cypriot I, II, III, and Late Bronze/Cypriot I, II, III (and various subdivisions) phases. Knapp finds this useful, but many in the field have ignored or criticized this 'brave' attempt to cut through the minutiae (e.g., Frankel 2008).

There are two basic types of chronology in Aegean Bronze Age studies: relative chronology and absolute chronology.

RELATIVE CHRONOLOGY

Relative chronology refers to the temporal ordering of objects and events relative to each other, such that assemblage (or context or object, etc.) 'A' is older or younger than or equivalent to assemblage 'B,' and so on. At a particular site this can be a clear stratigraphic ordering, such that level 10 is followed by level 9, and so on to the most recent level 1. However, on a wider basis, connecting different contexts or sites, comparisons are made between artifact types (and assemblages thereof). Sets of stylistic traits are thus defined to represent one context or phase or period or culture and so on, and assemblages found in different contexts or at different sites with similar stylistic traits are then linked—as seemingly very similar (and more or less) contemporary or as seemingly a bit earlier or later, and so forth. At Knossos on Crete, Evans found a (complicated) stratigraphic sequence at the beginning of the 20th century AD (Evans 1921–1935), which ran from the Neolithic through the post-Minoan, thus almost immediately creating the basis for a long diachronic synthesis (though many details were clarified only many years later, if at all; see Pendlebury 1939, xxxi–xxxii; Evely, Hughes-Brock, and Momigliano 1994; Cadogan, Hatzaki, and Vasilakis 2004).

Ideally, stratigraphic sequences set the order of the typological sequences, but, as Petrie (1899) showed, assemblages that lack stratigraphic order (grave assemblages in his case) can still be plausibly best ordered through what he termed *sequence analysis*. Petrie minimized the relative duration of sets of typological elements on the basis that this was the most efficient general solution (for general archaeological applications of seriation since then, see, e.g., O'Brien and Lee 1999). Turning to the Aegean, we may note that an attempt to better delineate Early Bronze groups (also known largely from cemeteries at the time) in the Cyclades along statistical lines was attempted (with only partial success) by Renfrew (1972, 142–47 and appendix 3). Luckily, subsequent work has found and investigated stratigraphic sequences, which now provide key evidence to better define the Early Cycladic period (e.g., Marangou, Renfrew, Doumas, and Gavalas 2006; Renfrew 2007; Renfrew, Doumas, Marangou, and Gavalas 2007; Brodie, Doole, Gavalas, and Renfrew 2008; Kouka 2009).

By 1903, Montelius had created a typologically derived chronology for Europe, and such work formed the general basis to wider European prehistory for the next two to three generations of scholarship, seen in seminal works such as Childe 1925. A contrast was available in the Aegean, however, as stratigraphic sequences, even if imperfect, informed the efforts to create chronology on Crete and the mainland. Thus, Evans (1906) proposed a Three Age stratigraphic-typological sequence for Crete, taking the term 'Minoan' from its legendary king Minos, and Wace and Blegen (1916–1918) did the same for the mainland, using the term 'Helladic' (thus, Early Helladic, Middle Helladic, Late Helladic—sometimes 'Mycenaean' is used in place of Late Helladic). Purported criticisms of these approximate stratigraphic systems in favor of architecturally or culturally based assessments (notably Åberg 1933) were rejected by most (but see below) and gave the Aegean a key place in the development of European prehistory (see, e.g., Childe 1935; for specific responses regarding Crete, see, e.g., Pendlebury 1939). Åberg's (1933) observations regarding instances of cultural (architectural) sequence and regionalism (and generally in favor of a more compressed European prehistoric chronology) were useful correctives, nonetheless. The Three Age–based, stratigraphy-typology derived structures became largely standard for the chronology of the Aegean Bronze Age, and, as Åberg's (1933) synthesis among others demonstrated (despite criticisms), the mainland, Cretan, and Cycladic sequences could be approximately related, and an overall Aegean chronology was thus available.

Two partial exceptions to this standard, tripartite ordering process also developed. In the Cycladic Islands Renfrew (1972) and then Doumas (1977) proposed to break with the use of Early Cycladic I, II, III, and so forth and instead to employ cultural groupings, principally the Grotta-Pelos culture, the Keros-Syros culture, and the Phylakopi I culture, along with some intermediary groups (especially the Kampos group between Early Cycladic I and Early Cycladic II, and the Kastri group between Early Cycladic II and Early Cycladic III, as well as other subregional or intermediary variants like the now abandoned 'Amorgos Group'). They based their proposal partly on the longstanding lack of stratigraphic sequences in the Cycladic Islands and partly on theoretical or appropriateness grounds. The logic was sensible, but the reality of these groupings as real 'cultural groupings' was questionable, and, to be pragmatic, the groups largely equated with the conventional Early Cycladic I, Early Cycladic II, and Early Cycladic III labels (adding Early Cycladic IIIA and IIIB; see Barber and MacGillivray 1980) and perhaps made less difference than hoped. The complex but fragmented world of the Cycladic Islands offers two other challenges to uniformitarian scholarship. First, the lack of replicated, long stratigraphic sequences leaves some possible gaps in the overall sequence, most notably between the Kastri and Phylakopi I groups in the Early Bronze 3 period (Rutter 1984; Broodbank 2000, 331–35), but see the later discussion. Second, our evidence remains incomplete even today. Just in the last few years new, hitherto unknown, material cultural groupings have been recognized, in particular the 'Rivari Group' found on Melos (Renfrew 2008, 4–5). Differences between islands, moreover, highlight the issues of regionalism and variability in the temporal and spatial dimensions and thus the problem of rigid, overarching chronological frameworks. In the subsequent Middle and Late Bronze Age periods, Cycladic phasing is understood mainly in terms of the sequences at Phylakopi on Melos and Ayia Irini on Kea and increasingly at Akrotiri on Thera (see Barber 1987; MacGillivray and Barber 1984; Renfrew 2007; Nikolakopoulou, Georma, Moschou, and Sofianou 2008), but nonetheless the labels Middle Cycladic I, II, II, and Late Cycladic I, II, and III are standard. (Although it is now dated in light of important subsequent work, MacGillivray and Barber [1984, 301] provide a useful chart of the Cycladic phases and their approximate placement against the mainland and Cretan phases.)

The other main alternative paradigm developed on Crete, where an archaeological framework based on the main architectural/historical phases has appealed to many (beginning with Åberg 1933 and given modern form by Platon 1961; 1968). Thus, we have a Prepalatial period (Early Minoan I–Middle Minoan IA ceramic phases), a Protopalatial period (the first or Old Palace period, comprising the Middle Minoan IB–II ceramic phases), a Neopalatial period (the second or New Palace period, comprising Middle Minoan III to Late Minoan IB), a Monopalatial period (only at Knossos in Late Minoan II to IIIA2 early, when Knossos appears to have been the only functioning palace on the island and to have exerted control over much of central and west Crete at least), and a Postpalatial period (Late Minoan

III, except Knossos, where the palace appears to have functioned until Late Minoan IIIB).

Over the course of the last century, relative chronologies for each Aegean region have thus been constructed, linking assemblages and sites together, with the various typological groups placed into an approximate order (for example, Early Minoan IA, IB, IIA, IIB, III; Middle Minoan IA, IB, II, IIIA, IIIB; sometimes with various individual ceramic wares or classes noted either within or across these periods, like EM Ayios Onouphrios ware or MM Kamares ware on Crete; see Betancourt 1985). Endless elaboration and further subdivision is both possible and inevitable, as new sites and assemblages are found and studied; for example, after many years of debate and some nonclarity, very recent scholarship now offers a much better definition for the beginning of the Middle Bronze Age in the Cycladic islands (Nikolakopoulou, Georma, Moschou, and Sofianou 2008) and largely closes the Early Cycladic III gap (much as suggested by Broodbank 2000, 331–35).

The various regions can then be coordinated with each other to build an overall, relative chronological map of the Aegean by comparing instances of exchanges of material culture or apparent stylistic traits. For example, the sauceboat form and several other indicators are found widely in the earlier to mid-Early Bronze Age 2 period of the Aegean (Early Helladic II, Early Cycladic II, Early Minoan IIA) and serve to link a variety of contexts and cultures from Troy and the northern Aegean to as far south as Knossos on Crete (Broodbank 2000, 305–309). Or, the finds of Phylakopi I duck vases (especially) in the Cyclades and southeast Aegean and then Cretan Middle Minoan IA ceramics in parts of the Cyclades and the mainland tie a series of contexts together in successive time slices and in trade, cultural, and perhaps political ways at the beginning of the Middle Bronze Age (Broodbank 2000, 351–61).

A fundamental problem, though, when one considers the apparent neat framework of the Aegean relative chronology, is the relationship between the typology of material cultural classes—be they ceramic forms and decoration or forms of metal objects and so on—and time, history, and human culture. Some types of material culture tend to be more conservative and stay similar over long periods (for example, storage vessels and cooking utensils are often suggested as belonging in this category), whereas others change rapidly (i.e., as soon as any improvement is available) (weapons and other critical technologies are usually placed in this category), and most lie in some rather ill-understood middle region. Major stratigraphic breaks and building changes at important sites (or across a group of sites) are often seen as demarcating key historical or cultural changes, yet there is no reason that material culture in the form of, let us say, ceramics will reflect these changes (or not immediately). However, in reverse, such major stratigraphic changes at sites (for example, the ubiquitous 'destruction' horizon) usually provide the large bodies of ceramic material that archaeologists then study and use to define the typologies and stylistic phasings and thence chronology. We thus have detailed views through open windows for these destruction events only, from which we can learn a lot, and then closed blinds/curtains for much of the rest of the overall timescale. Thus, some end of phase assemblages (e.g., the Late Minoan IB destruction horizon on Crete) largely define the past we have, leaving out much of the rest of the life of a site and wider regional groupings (in this case early through mid- to mature Late Minoan IB; perhaps also tending to seem to minimize real chronological spans for overall periods in some such cases, as perhaps for Late Minoan IB: see Manning 2009).

The relative chronologies that scholars construct end up with boxes of time labeled as Late Helladic I, then IIA, then IIB, and so on. These are correlated (through exchanges and stylistic similarities) with Late Minoan IA, IB, II, and so on to yield an overall (or macro) Late Bronze 1, 2, and so on regional chronology. This is a useful heuristic device, and the standard framework constructed from years of scholarship is invaluable. However, it is also deeply misleading. Style in material culture is dynamic, and different aspects change or do not change at varying rates within any society and among different groups and places and at different times for many reasons, thereby affecting scales from individual actors to the wider regional settings (including processes linked with biography, status, gender, and ethnicity as much as wider group values, technology, trade, and so on). Fundamentally, one style (and certainly any grouping of styles) neither starts nor ends on any wider basis on a given day, month, year, or maybe even decade, and plural styles and interplays are possible, if not likely. Regionalism can also act to create confusion, with one area apparently conservative with certain 'old' styles continuing in use, whereas another area adopts new styles or influences—yet these different assemblages can be contemporary.

Two examples illustrate the issues. One dynamic form of regionalism/variation occurs on the eastern-central mainland in late Early Helladic II marked by the appearance of new ceramic forms and technology—linked to the Kastri Group in the Cyclades and progenitors in the east Aegean and western Anatolia (in Anatolian terms it is EBIIIA)—conspicuous at some sites and a minor presence at others. Taking its name from the site where it was first recognized as a major element, this grouping or phase is referred to as the Lefkandi I culture/phase (Rutter 1979). It appears largely contemporary with later Early Helladic II (though some see it as representing initial Early Bronze 3 = Early Helladic IIIA (see Manning 1995, 51–63; Rutter 1983; Warren and Hankey 1989, 36–42; Broodbank 2000, 309–19; Kouka 2009). This Lefkandi I phase is not just a regional variant; it also represents new ways of doing things: new technology (wheel-made), new shapes/styles, new external influences, and new or refocused social practices embodied in these new artifact types. These new ways seem to play a central role in restructuring the whole Early Helladic world as seen by the subsequent period.

Another form of regionalism is the more typical occurrence of significant temporal/spatial variation, where one region seems to precede or lag another. An example in general terms can be seen when east Crete continues with its Early Minoan III styles into the temporal period, when central Crete, and especially the sequence as defined at Knossos, has adopted the distinctive new Middle Minoan IA styles— and thus into the chronological period called Middle Minoan IA as a general label (Warren and Hankey 1989, 20; Momigliano 2000).

Table 2.1. Schematic and summary relative chronology for the Aegean Bronze Age showing the main phases and sequences.

	Crete		Cycladic Islands	Greece
Early Bronze 1	Early Minoan IA Early Minoan IB	Early Pre-palatial period	Early Cycladic I—Lakkoudes, Pelos and Plastiras Phases/Groups Kampos Group	Early Helladic I
Early Bronze 2	Early Minoan IIA Early Minoan IIB		Early Cycladic II—Keros-Syros Phase/Group Kastri Phase	Early Helladic II Lefkandi I Phase
Early Bronze 3	Early Minoan III	Late	Early Cycladic III—Phylakopi I Group/Phase	Early Helladic III
Middle Bronze 1	Middle Minoan IA Middle Minoan IB		Middle Cycladic I Middle Cycladic II	Middle Helladic
Middle Bronze 2	Middle Minoan II (A–B at main palaces)	Protopalatial (Old Palace Period)		
Middle Bronze 3	Middle Minoan IIIA Middle Minoan IIIB	Neopalatial (New Palace Period)	Middle Cycladic III	
Late Bronze 1	Late Minoan IA Late Minoan IB		Late Cycladic I	Late Helladic I Late Helladic IIA
Late Bronze 2	Late Minoan II	Monopalatial Period (Knossos only)	Late Cycladic II	Late Helladic IIB
Late Bronze 3	Late Minoan IIIA1 Late Minoan IIIA2 Late Minoan IIIB Late Minoan IIIC	Final Palatial Period	Late Cycladic III	Late Helladic IIIA1 Late Helladic IIIA2 Late Helladic IIIB (phases 1–2 in Argolid) Late Helladic IIIC (with 3 to 5 phases)

Source: Courtesy of the author.

It is important to appreciate these variations and dynamic processes. Yet, for all intensive purposes, Aegean prehistory rather pretends that style-based periods do typically start and end fairly neatly and that time frames can be mapped out in clear boxes of time, one after the other. This might seem practical and harmless enough if everyone understands the true, inherently fuzzy nature, but the problem with abbreviations and labels is that they come to have their own reality as they enter textbooks and common currency, sometimes independently of the information they summarize. They become factoids that are then transferred into other categories of thinking. This can particularly impact Aegean prehistory because of the logical or practical problem that the ceramic and stratigraphic labels are often the same—yet there is no reason they should relate. A system in which the material culture is comprehensively and consistently defined in its own terms (by, e.g., wares), which are then linked to whichever stratigraphic phase *or phases* in which they occur, as on Bronze Age Cyprus, would have merits.

More practically for the student and general reader, relative chronology has become a gate-keeping technology for the academic field: Only the initiated understand the otherwise impenetrable terms such as LH IIIA2 early or EM IB or Transitional LH IIIB2–LH IIIC Early or late Prepalatial, or the Grotta-Pelos culture and so on. Much of this tradition stems from the largely Classical roots of the discipline and its key practitioners; classics has long employed a system of abbreviations, codes, and technical terms known only to those in the field, and Aegean prehistory unfortunately extended this tradition (see table 2.1).

ABSOLUTE CHRONOLOGY

Absolute chronology is simple in concept but fiendish in practice; it means the ability to allocate the Western calendar timescale (thus dates AD/CE or BC/BCE) to archaeological contexts, objects, or discussions. Thus, we hope to be able to make statements that such and such an artifact, type of artifact, building, series of changes in the archaeological record, or burial dates to such and such a century, set of years, or, in a perfect world, even a specific year. The problem is how to establish the calendar years.

Archaeological-Historical Dating

One approach to dating the Aegean Bronze Age tries to link exports or imports of objects or apparent stylistic features or technologies between the Aegean world and the approximately historically dated cultures of Egypt and the Near East. Subject to possible time lags in import/export processes and to how long an imported object remains in use before becoming incorporated in the archaeological context, where it is subsequently found by modern excavations and scholarship, the assumption is that the Egyptian/Near Eastern date associated with either the import or the context of the Aegean export can be roughly applied to the associated Aegean cultural phase. Thus, for example, when Sir Flinders Petrie found Middle Minoan Kamares ware ceramics in Middle Kingdom Egyptian contexts and Late Helladic IIIA2 ceramics at Tell el-Amarna in Egypt, along with finds of other Aegean exports, he provided a solid chronological basis to Mycenaean and Minoan chronology (Petrie 1890; 1891a, 9–10; 1891b; Petrie 1894; Phillips 1997). In this way the Aegean Bronze Age was first established as a genuine pre-Classical period.

The date for the Egyptian or Near Eastern context or object is possible because various written/inscribed records from Egypt, Assyria, Babylonia, and so on provide lists of kings and other officials and sometimes the period of time they reigned or held office (in years and sometimes even the months and days), and in several cases we have long more or less continuous 'king lists.' Calendar dates are then calculated, in some cases on the basis of an ancient record of an astronomical event (like an eclipse, the first reappearance of a conspicuous star, or records of the moon) and in others on the basis of dead reckoning—that is, starting at a known point, like 525BC, when the Greek historian Herodotos tells us Cambyses conquered Egypt and ended the 26th Dynasty (last king Psamtik III), and working backward, adding attested and best interpreted reign lengths to the point of interest.

Occasionally we also have extant written communications between two or more of these various Near Eastern and Egyptian kings, and we can test and refine the chronologies (especially Assyrian/Babylonian dates versus Egyptian). In particular, the Amarna letters from Egypt in the mid-14th century BC (Moran 1992) contain correspondence between the Babylonian kings Kadasman-Enlil I, Burna-Burias II, and Pharaoh Amenhotep III of Egypt and between Burna-Burias II and both Akhenaten and Tutankhamun. Thus, these associated kings were more or less contemporary and have to be fitted together (given the known order of reigns in each country). In this way, the various ancient Near Eastern chronologies can be closely synchronized (see Brinkman 1972, 1976; Kitchen 1996a, 1996b; Beckerath 1997; Hornung, Krauss, and Warburton 2006). Various archaeological contexts in Egypt and the Near East can then be associated with these dated kings or their families or officials—and imported objects from these are approximately historically dated (see, for example, Aston 2003 on New Kingdom examples). In reverse, Egyptian/Near Eastern exports can be related to styles known from dated contexts in Egypt/the Near East—and sometimes the object even carries the name of a specific king (such as the group of items in the Aegean with the name of Amenhotep III; cf. Cline 1987).

Where the linkage comprises a single object or a nonspecific stylistic association, this type of archaeological dating is entirely uncontrolled and could be substantially misleading. When several (and, even better, numerous) linkages exist for a specific period, however, then we may have much more confidence in the dating. In the third millennium BC, for example, we have just a few loose or indirect linkages between the Aegean and the ancient Near East, and the archaeological-historic chronology is approximate and flexible at best. From the First Intermediate Period and the start of the second millennium BC, we begin to see more linkages. The protopalatial period on Crete then has several direct ties with 12th–13th-Dynasty Egypt and is relatively secure in the 19th–18th centuries BC.

We then have very few useful or secure linkages until some Late Minoan I (and mainly IB and mature/late Late Minoan IB, where diagnostic) objects appear in early 18th-Dynasty contexts in Egypt, before mainland Late Helladic IIA and then IIB products replace these during the reign of Thutmose III in the mid-15th century BC (and a vessel with the cartouche—royal name—of Thutmose is found in Crete). Some wall paintings from Egypt also provide likely images of Aegeans ('Keftiu' = Cretans) in Late Minoan I and then Late Minoan II(–IIIA)-style clothing through the reign of Thutmose III. Late Minoan/Helladic IIIA1 is then linked with Amenhotep II and Amenhotep III, and Late Helladic IIIA2 is securely tied to the reign of Amenhotep IV (Akhenaten) and continues subsequently into the late 14th century BC. Late Helladic IIIB and Minoan IIIB subsequently occupy the 13th century BC.

The period c. 1400–1200 BC in broad terms represents the developed palatial era of the east Mediterranean, with major interlinked economies and trading worlds incorporating the Myceneans/Aegeans, the Hittites and other Anatolian powers, Cyprus, the Levant, and Egypt. This all starts to change from around c. 1200 BC and through the 12th century BC, and, as export patterns become less clear, our dates become less certain in the period from the close of the Late Bronze Age through the early Iron Age (for data and discussions, see, e.g., Höflmayer 2007; MacGillivray 1998, 106–108; Merrillees 2003; Kemp and Merrillees 1980; Warren and Hankey 1989, 121–69; Manning 1995, 104–120, 217–29; 1999; 2009; Aston 2003; Wiener 2003; Deger-Jalkotzy and Zavadil 2003; Mountjoy 1999, 2005).

Science-Based Dating

The main science-based dating technique relevant to the Aegean Bronze Age is radiocarbon dating. This enables estimates of the date when organic materials stopped exchanging carbon dioxide with the atmosphere (e.g., when a plant or part thereof—like a tree ring—stops growing or an animal dies; see Taylor 1987, 1997). In archaeology, the critical issue is the use of organic material that relates closely and as directly as possible to the context for which a date is sought (Waterbolk 1971); usually this means that samples of short-lived nature, such as annual growth material, are the ideal candidates because they should yield ages more or less contemporary with the time of human use. In contrast, random wood charcoal (with no evidence of bark or sapwood), when from long-lived tree species, can easily yield correct ages that are many decades to even centuries older than the archaeological context from which they come (and are thus very unhelpful *terminus post quem*—point after which—ranges). Over the last few decades, increased dating precision has become available, and on very much smaller samples (using Accelerator Mass Spectrometry radiocarbon dating; Gove 1992, 1999), making the dating of short-lived samples and other focused materials and contexts practical.

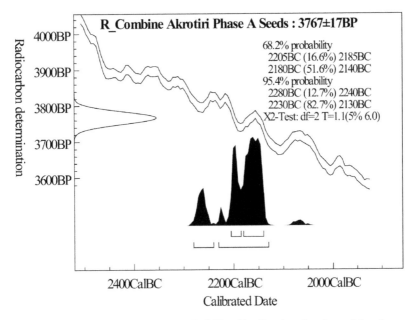

Figure 2.1. Calibrated calendar age probability distribution for the weighted average radiocarbon age from three measurements on charred seeds from a single lump from Locus M31/67 N069 at Akrotiri on Thera/Santorini belonging to the initial Middle Cycladic Phase A (and not the end of the phase). Data from OxCal and IntCal04 (Bronk Ramsey 1995, 2001, 2008; Reimer et al. 2004).

For the Early Bronze Age Aegean, radiocarbon is our main source of absolute dating evidence and provides the available chronology and temporal framework c. 3000–2000 BC (see Manning 1995, 1997, 2008b; Korfmann and Kromer 1993; Kromer, Korfmann, and Jablonka 2003). Additional modern, high-quality dating programs are needed, however, especially to focus on short-lived sample material. A promising example of the progress possible toward the resolution of longstanding problems comes from Akrotiri on Thera/Santorini. Here Phase A is now defined at the very beginning of the Middle Cycladic sequence linking to the Phylakopi I (–ii and –iii) phase (Nikolakopoulou, Georma, Moschou, and Sofianou 2008, 313–17). The weighted average of three very similar radiocarbon measurements on a compressed lump of charred seeds (Manning 2008b, 56) from this phase offers a calibrated calendar age range at 2 standard deviation (95.4%) confidence of 2280–2240 BC (12.7% of probability) or 2230–2130 BC (82.7% of probability); see figure 2.1. Thus, we may start the Middle Cycladic period no later than about the same time; this relatively early date closes the gap somewhat to the late Early Bronze 2 Kastri Group, which seems to cover the early 25th through the later 23rd centuries BC (Manning 2008b). (Some Middle Minoan IA ceramics have also been found in Phase A at Akrotiri; whether this early date applies also to them is an interesting issue for further clarification; the archaeological linkages suggest a date more in the 21st century BC for the start of Middle Minoan IA.)

For the Middle and Late Bronze Ages, there are data and interpretations from both archaeology and radiocarbon evidence. At first, the long-studied and relatively refined archaeological chronologies were much more accurate and precise than anything radiocarbon could offer (Kohler and Ralph 1961). Thus, radiocarbon dating was of interest but at most offered support to an already accepted framework; if there was a conflict, it was obvious that the archaeological chronology was to be preferred (Betancourt and Weinstein 1976; Warren and Hankey 1989, 127).

However, over the last three decades, increasingly precise radiocarbon dates have been obtained, and more sophisticated analytical frameworks developed to refine interpretation (especially Bayesian model-based approaches as employed in the Manning et al. 2006 study). Work on short-lived samples from the Late Minoan IA and IB periods, in particular, have highlighted some apparent discrepancies between the archaeological chronology and the radiocarbon chronology (Manning et al. 2006; Manning 2009). This issue centers on the date of the important eruption of the volcano of Santorini/Thera and the associated archaeological horizon (see chapter 34). A major controversy now exists in the field, and rival (High v. Low) chronologies are in parallel use, depending on whether the radiocarbon evidence (High chronology) or the conventional archaeological evidence (Low chronology) is preferred for the mid-second millennium BC.

An appropriate perspective on this debate is critical, however, as the published literature has become a clash of scholarly cultures, with many arguments made on the basis of assumed truths. The fundamental observation is that the Late Minoan IA period and the earlier part of the Late Minoan IB period (and the preceding Middle Minoan IIIA and IIIB periods) form a time for which very little chronological evidence exists in the form of clearly defined and plural exchanges of material with Egypt and the Near East. Instead, conventional dates were largely estimated for this era between the good Middle Minoan links with the Middle Kingdom and the mature–late Late Minoan IB, as well as Late Helladic IIA and IIB links with the earlier 18th Dynasty and into the reign of Thutmose III. Thus, things were always potentially suspect (or flexible), and phases might be longer or shorter than guessed. Radiocarbon finds age ranges consistent with the archaeological chronology where the latter is well based on numerous exchanges (e.g., Late Minoan II/Late Helladic IIB to Late Helladic IIIB; see, e.g., Manning and Weninger 1992; Manning, Weninger, South, Kling, Kuniholm, Muhly, Hadjisavvas, Sewell, and Cadogan 2001; Betancourt and Lawn 1984), but it suggests a much longer Late Minoan IB period than previously thought (though archaeology now also suggests this; see Rutter n.d.; Betancourt 1998) and a date for Late Minoan IA about one hundred years earlier than the conventional date (Manning et al. 2006; Manning 1998, 1999, 2009). The necessary implication is that Middle Minoan III as a whole was relatively short (something already considered likely; cf. Warren and Hankey 1989, 54–60). The Middle Minoan II linkages with the Middle Kingdom remain untouched and unquestioned, however. Thus radiocarbon redefines some best guesses in the past (where solid evidence was lacking) for Late Minoan IA and IB but does not contradict any good, sound, replicated body of archaeological evidence.

Table 2.2. Approximate Absolute Chronology for the Aegean Bronze Age

Crete	Dates BC	Cyclades	Dates BC	Mainland	Dates BC
Early Minoan I	3100–3000	ECI	3100–3000	Early Helladic I	3100+ to 3000
(EMIB)	(2900–2650)	Kampos Phase	2900–2650		
EMIIA	2650–2450/00	ECII (Keros-Syros phase)	2650–2500	EHII	2650–2500
EMIIB	2450/00–2200	Kastri Phase	2500–2250	Later EHII/Lefkandi I	2500–2200
EMIII	2200–2100/2050	Kastri Phase and into Phylakopi I Phase	2400–2200	EHIII	2250–2100/2050
Middle Minoan IA	2100/50–1925/00	Middle Cycladic–Phylakopi I Phase	2200–	Middle Helladic	2100/2050–
MMIB	1925/00–1875/50				
MMII	1875/50–1750/00				
MMIII(A–B)	1750/00–1700/1675				
Late Minoan IA	1700/1675–1625/00	Late Cycladic I	1700/1675–1625/00	Late Helladic I	1700/1675–1635/00
LMIB	1625/00–1470/60	LCII	1625/00–	LHIIA	1635/00–1480/70
LMII	1470/60–1420/10			LHIIB	1480/70–1420/10
LMIIIA1	1420/10–1390/70	LCIII	1420/1400–	LHIIIA1	1420/10–1390/70
LMIIIA2	1390/70–1330/15			LHIIIA2	1390/70–1330/15
LMIIIB	1330/15–1200/1190			LHIIIB	1330/15–1200/1190
LMIIIC	1200/1190–1075/50			LHIIIC	1200/1190–1075/50

Note: Minoan, Cycladic, and Mainland phases are of course not in exact synchronicity in reality, even when closely aligned; for example, Late Helladic (LH) IIA appears to begin a little before Late Minoan (LM) IB. However, this serves as a general system, so these minor, specialist, issues can often be overlooked (or could fit into the dating ranges indicated for the start/end dates). Similarly, although the table lists specific numbers, these are all approximate. For the EM/EC/EH phases ±50 years should be allowed as a reasonable guide range. For the MM/MH/MC and LM/LC/LH phases, ±25 years may be a reasonable allowance. There is of course one major possible exception. The dates in the table reflect the high or radiocarbon-based dates for LMIA–II and so on (from the study of Manning et al. 2006 in particular). If the conventional archaeological dates are employed instead, then the LMIA period begins closer to ca. 1600 BC, and LMIB begins in the late 16th century BC to ca. 1500 BC. The time period on Crete at the close of the MMIII period and start of the LMIA period has been variously called MMII to LMIA transition, or LMIA Early, or most recently (as again) MMIIB—each label referring to more or less the same interval. On the high chronology shown in table 2.2, this time period lies around the late 18th century BC into the first decades of the 17th century BC (courtesy of the author).

The other dating technique of general relevance to the Aegean Bronze Age is dendrochronology, also called tree-ring dating (Kuniholm 2001; Schweingruber 1987). Where bark or sapwood is present, it is possible to define closely the cutting date and hence human use of timbers. A long near-absolute dendrochronology from Anatolia covers the earlier first and most of the second millennia BC and has major implications for the dating of key sites and even ancient persons in Anatolia and the Near East (Manning, Kromer, Kuniholm, and Newton 2001). Some chronologies, though with a questionable linkage as yet to the second–first millennia dendrochronology, exist also for a good part of the third millennium BC (Newton and Kuniholm 2004).

There has been less success to date in finding good wood or charcoal samples from the Aegean region (but the potential remains, and one reads sadly of apparently large timber remains (now lost) found earlier in the 20th century AD at some of the main palace sites). Nevertheless, some key shorter tree-ring series have been radiocarbon wiggle-matched to yield high-precision information. Examples include a pine timber from Troy I (Korfmann and Kromer 1993; Manning 1997), an oak sample from Miletus that offers a high-resolution *terminus post quem* for the eruption of Santorini/Thera (Manning et al. 2006), and a speculative effort at best-dating some short sequences at Assiros from toward the end of the Late Bronze Age (Newton and Wardle 2005). An approximate absolute chronology for the Aegean Bronze Age is shown in table 2.2.

BIBLIOGRAPHY

Åberg, Nils. 1933. *Bronzezeitliche und früheisenzeitliche Chronologie IV Griechenland.* Stockholm: Kungl. Vitterhets Historie och Antikvitets Akademien.

Aston, David A. 2003. "New Kingdom Pottery Phases as Revealed through Well-dated Tomb Contexts." In *SCIEM* II, 135–62.

Barber, Robin L. N. 1987. *The Cyclades in the Bronze Age.* London: Gerald Duckworth.

———, and J. Alexander MacGillivray. 1980. "The Early Cycladic Period: Matters of Definition and Terminology." *AJA* 84(2): 141–57.

Beckerath, Jürgen von. 1997. "Die Zeitbestimmung der Ägyptischen Geschichte von der Vorzeit bis 332 v. Chr." *Chronologie des pharaonischen Ägypten.* Mainz: Philipp von Zabern.

Betancourt, Philip P. 1985. *The History of Minoan Pottery.* Princeton: Princeton University Press.

———. 1998. "The Chronology of the Aegean Late Bronze Age: Unanswered Questions." In *Sardinian and Aegean Chronology: Towards the Resolution of Relative and Absolute Dating in the Mediterranean.* Studies in Sardinian Archaeology, ed. Miriam S. Balmuth and Robert H. Tykot, 291–96. Oxford: Oxbow.

———, and Barbara Lawn. 1984. "The Cyclades and Radiocarbon Chronology." In *Prehistoric Cyclades,* 277–95.

Betancourt, Philip P., and Gail A. Weinstein. 1976. "Carbon-14 and the Beginning of the Late Bronze Age in the Aegean." *AJA* 80(4): 329–48.

Brinkman, John A. 1972. "Foreign Relations of Babylonia from 1600 to 625 B.C.: The Documentary Evidence." *AJA* 76(3): 271–81.

————. 1976. *Materials and Studies for Kassite History*. Chicago: Oriental Institute of the University of Chicago.

Brodie, Neil. J., Jenny Doole, Giorgos Gavalas, and Colin Renfrew, eds. 2008. *Horizon*.

Bronk Ramsey, Christopher. 1995. "Radiocarbon Calibration and Analysis of Stratigraphy: The OxCal Program." *Radiocarbon* 37: 425–30.

————. 2001. "Development of the Radiocarbon Calibration Program OxCal." *Radiocarbon* 43: 355–63.

————. 2008. "Deposition Models for Chronological Records." *Quaternary Science Reviews* 27: 42–60.

Broodbank, Cyprian. 2000. *An Island Archaeology of the Early Cyclades*. Cambridge: Cambridge University Press.

Cadogan, Gerald, Eleni Hatzaki, and Adonis Vasilakis, eds. 2004. *Knossos*.

Childe, V. Gordon. 1925. *The Dawn of European Civilization*. London: Kegan Paul.

————. 1935. "Review of Nils Åberg, *Bronzezeitliche und fruheisenzeitliche Chronologie: I–IV*." *Man* 35: 75–76.

Cline, Eric. 1987. "Amenhotep III and the Aegean: A Reassessment of Egypto-Aegean Relations in the 14th Century B.C." *Orientalia* 56:1–36.

Daniel, Glyn E. 1943. *The Three Ages: An Essay on Archaeological Method*. Cambridge: Cambridge University Press.

Darcque, Pascal, Michael Fotiadis, and Olga Polychronopoulou, eds. 2006. *Mythos: La prehistoire egeenne de XIXe au XXIe siecle apres J.-C. Actes de la Table Ronde Internationale d'Athènes (21–23 novembre 2002)*. BCH Supplément 46. Athens: École française d'Athènes.

Deger-Jalkotzy, Sigrid, and Michaela Zavadil, eds. 2003. *LH IIIC*.

Doumas, Christos. 1977. *Early Bronze Age Burial Habits in the Cyclades*. SIMA 48. Gothenburg: Åström.

Evans, Arthur J. 1906. *Essai de classification des epoques de la civilisation minoenne. Résumé d'un discours fait au congres d'archeologie à Athènes*. London: B. Quaritch.

————. 1921–1935. *PM*, vols. I–IV.

Evely, Doniert, Helen Hughes-Brock, and Nicoletta Momigliano, eds. 1994. *Labyrinth of History*.

Frankel, David. 2008. "Review of B. Knapp and M. Given, *Sydney Cyprus Survey Project*." *AJA* 112(3): 182–83.

Given, Michael, and A. Bernard Knapp. 2003. *The Sydney Cyprus Survey Project: Social Approaches to Regional Archaeological Survey*. Monumenta Archaeologica 21. Los Angeles: Cotsen Institute of Archeology, University of California, Los Angeles.

Gove, Harry E. 1992. "The History of AMS, Its Advantages over Decay Counting: Applications and Prospects." In *Radiocarbon after Four Decades: An Interdisciplinary Perspective*, ed. Royal E. Taylor, Austin Long, and Renee S. Kra, 214–29. New York: Springer.

————. 1999. *From Hiroshima to the Iceman: The Development and Applications of Accelerator Mass Spectrometry*. Bristol: Institute of Physics Publishing.

Gräslund, Bo. 1987. *The Birth of Prehistory Chronology: Dating Methods and Dating Systems in Nineteenth-century Scandinavian Archaeology*. New York: Cambridge University Press.

Höflmayer, Felix. 2007. "Ägyptische Skarabäen auf Kreta und ihre Bedeutung für die absolute Chronologie der minoischen Altpalastzeit (MM IB–MM IIB)." *Ägypten und Levante* 17: 107–26.

Hornung, Erik, Rolf Krauss, and David A. Warburton, eds. 2006. *Ancient Egyptian Chronology*. Leiden: Brill.

Kemp, Barry J., and Robert S. Merrillees. 1980. *Minoan Pottery in Second Millennium Egypt*. Mainz am Rhein: Philipp von Zabern.

Kitchen, Kenneth A. 1996a. "The Historical Chronology of Ancient Egypt: A Current Assessment." *Acta Archaeologica* 67: 1–13.

———. 1996b. *The Third Intermediate Period in Egypt (1100–650 BC)*, 2d rev. ed. with suppl. Warminster: Aris and Phillips.

Kohler, Ellen L., and Elizabeth K. Ralph. 1961. "C-14 Dates for Sites in the Mediterranean Area." *American Journal of Archaeology* 65: 357–67.

Korfmann, Manfred, and Bernd Kromer. 1993. "Demircihüyük, Besik-Tepe, Troia—Eine Zwischenbilanz zur Chronologie dreier Orte in Westanatolien." *Studia Troica* 3: 135–71.

Kouka, Ourania. 2009. "Third-millennium-BC Aegean Chronology: Old and New Data under the Perspectives of the Third Millennium AD." In *Tree-Rings, Kings, and Old World Archaeology and Environment: Papers Written in Honor of Peter Ian Kuniholm*, ed. Sturt W. Manning and Mary Jaye Bruce, 133–149. Oxford: Oxbow.

Kromer, Bernd, Manfred Korfmann, and Peter Jablonka. 2003. "Heidelberg Radiocarbon Dates for Troia I to VIII and Kumtepe." In *Troia and the Troad: Scientific Approaches*, ed. Günther A. Wagner, Ernst Pernicka, and Hans-Peter Uerpmann, 43–54. Berlin: Springer.

Kuniholm, Peter I. 2001. Dendrochronology and Other Applications of Tree-ring Studies in Archaeology. In *The Handbook of Archaeological Sciences*, ed. Don R. Brothwell and Angela M. Pollard, 35–46. London: John Wiley and Sons.

MacGillivray, J. Alexander. 1998. *Knossos: Pottery Groups of the Old Palace Period*. BSA Studies 5. London: British School at Athens.

———, and Robin L. N. Barber, eds. 1984. *Prehistoric Cyclades*.

Manning, Sturt W. 1995. *The Absolute Chronology of the Aegean Early Bronze Age: Archaeology, History, and Radiocarbon*. Monographs in Mediterranean Archaeology 1. Sheffield: Sheffield Academic Press.

———. 1997. Troy, Radiocarbon, and the Chronology of the Northeast Aegean in the Early Bronze Age. In *Poliochni*, 498–520.

———. 1998. "Aegean and Sardinian Chronology: Radiocarbon, Calibration, and Thera." In *Sardinian and Aegean Chronology: Towards the Resolution of Relative and Absolute Dating in the Mediterranean*. Studies in Sardinian Archaeology, ed. Miriam S. Balmuth and Robert H. Tykot, 297–307. Oxford: Oxbow.

———. 1999. *A Test of Time: The Volcano of Thera and the Chronology and History of the Aegean and East Mediterranean in the Mid-second Millennium BC*. Oxford: Oxbow.

———. 2008a. "An Edited Past: Aegean Prehistory and Its Texts." In *Editing the Image: Strategies in the Production and Reception of the Visual*. Mark A. Cheetham, Elizabeth Legge and Catherine M. Soussloff (eds.), 33–65. Toronto: University of Toronto Press.

———. 2008b. "Some Initial Wobbly Steps towards a Late Neolithic to Early Bronze III Radiocarbon Chronology for the Cyclades." In *Horizon*, 55–69. Cambridge: McDonald Institute for Archaeological Research.

———. 2009. "Beyond the Santorini Eruption: Some Notes on Dating the Late Minoan IB Period on Crete, and Implications for Cretan-Egyptian Relations in the 15th Century BC (and especially LM II)." In *Time's Up! Dating the Minoan Eruption of Santorini*, ed. David Warburton, 207–226. Monographs of the Danish Institute at Athens 10. Athens: Danish Institute at Athens.

Manning, Sturt W., Bernd Kromer, Peter I. Kuniholm, and Maryanne Newton. 2001. "Anatolian Tree-rings and a New Chronology for the East Mediterranean Bronze-Iron Ages." *Science* 294: 2532–35.

Manning, Sturt W., Charles Bronk Ramsey, Walter Kutschera, Thomas Higham, Bernd Kromer, Peter Steier, and Eva M. Wild. 2006. "Chronology for the Aegean Late Bronze Age." *Science* 312: 565–69.

Manning, Sturt W., and Bernhard Weninger. 1992. "A Light in the Dark: Archaeological
    Wiggle Matching and the Absolute Chronology of the Close of the Aegean Late Bronze
    Age." *Antiquity* 66: 636–63.
———, Bernhard Weninger, Alison K. South, Barbara B. Kling, Peter I. Kuniholm,
    James D. Muhly, Sophocles Hadjisavvas, David A. Sewell, and Gerald Cadogan. 2001.
    "Absolute Age Range of the Late Cypriot IIC Period on Cyprus." *Antiquity* 75: 328–40.
Marangou, Lila, Colin Renfrew, Christos Doumas, and Giorgos Gavalas. 2006. *Markiani,
    Amorgos: An Early Bronze Age Fortified Settlement: Overview of the 1985–1991
    Investigations.* BSA supplementary vol. 40. London: British School at Athens.
Merrillees, Robert S. 2003. "The First Appearances of Kamares Ware in the Levant." *Ägypten
    und Levante* 13: 127–42.
McDonald, William A., and Carol G. Thomas. 1990. *Progress into the Past: The Rediscovery
    of Mycenaean Civilization,* 2d ed. Bloomington: Indiana University Press.
Momigliano, Nicoletta. 2000. "On the Early Minoan III and Middle Minoan IA Sequence
    at Knossos." In *Pepragmena H' Diethnous Kritologikou Synedriou, Irakleio, 9–14
    Septemvriou 1996.* Vol. A2, *Proïstoriki kai Archaia Elliniki Periodos,* ed. Alexandra
    Karetsou, Detorakis Theocharis, and Alexis Kalokairinos, 335–48. Irakleio: Etairia
    Kritikon Istorikon Meleton.
Montelius, Oscar. 1903. *Die älteren Kulturperioden im Orient und in Europa.* Stockholm:
    Selbstverlag des Verfassers.
Moran, William. 1992. *The Amarna Letters.* Baltimore: Johns Hopkins University Press.
Mountjoy, Penelope A. 1999. "Late Minoan IIIC/Late Helladic IIIC: Chronology and
    Terminology." In *Meletemata,* 511–16.
———. 2005. "Mycenaean Connections with the Near East in LH IIIC: Ships and Sea
    Peoples." In *Emporia,* 423–27.
Newton, Maryanne W., and Peter I. Kuniholm. 2004. "A Dendrochronological Framework
    for the Assyrian Colony Period in Asia Minor." *Türkiye Bilimler Akademisi Arkeoloji
    Dergisi* 7: 165–76.
———, and Ken A. Wardle. 2005. "A Dendrochronological [14]C Wiggle-match for the Early
    Iron Age of North Greece: A Contribution to the Debate about This Period in the
    Southern Levant." In *The Bible and Radiocarbon Dating Archaeology, Text, and Science*
    ed. Thomas E. Levy and Thomas Higham, 104–13. London: Equinox.
Nikolakopoulou, Irene, Fragoula Georma, Angeliki Moschou, and Photini Sofianou. 2008.
    "Trapped in the Middle: New Stratigraphic and Ceramic Evidence from Middle
    Cycladic Akrotiri, Thera." In *Horizon,* 311–24.
O'Brien, Michael J., and R. Lee Lyman. 1999. *Seriation, Stratigraphy, and Index Fossils: The
    Backbone of Archaeological Dating.* New York: Plenum.
Papadopoulos, John K. 2005. "Inventing the Minoans: Archaeology, Modernity, and the
    Quest for European Identity." *JMA* 18: 87–149.
Pendlebury, John D. S. 1939. *The Archaeology of Crete.* London: Methuen.
Petrie, William M. Flinders. 1890. "The Egyptian Bases of Greek History." *JHS* 11: 271–77.
———. 1891a. *Illahun, Kahun, and Gurob: 1889–90.* London: David Nutt.
———. 1891b. "Notes on the Antiquities of Mykenae." *JHS* 12: 199–205.
———. 1899. "Sequences in Prehistoric Remains." *Journal of the Anthropological Institute*
    29: 295–301.
——— 1894. *Tell el Amarna.* London: Methuen.
Phillips, Jacke. 1997. "Petrie in Egypt." In *Ancient Egypt, the Aegean, and the Near East:
    Studies in Honour of Martha Rhoads Bell,* ed. Jacke Phillip, 407–19. San Antonio:
    Van Siclen.

Platon, Nikolaos. 1961. "Chronologie de la Crète et des Cyclades à l'Age du Bronze." In *Bericht über den V Internationalen Kongress für Vor- und Frühgeschichte, Hamburg 1958*, ed. Gerhard Bersu and Wolfgang Dehn, 671–76. Berlin: Mann.

Platon, Nikolaos. 1968. "Τα προβλήματα χρονολογήσεως των Μινωικών ανακτόρων." Αρχαιολογική Εφημερίς: 1–58.

Reimer, Paula J., Mike G. L. Baillie, Edouard Bard, Alex Bayliss, J. Warren Beck, Chanda J. H. Bertrand, Paul G. Blackwell, Caitlin E. Buck, George S. Burr, Kirsten B. Cutler, Paul E. Damon, R. Lawrence Edwards, Richard G. Fairbanks, Michael Friedrich, Thomas P. Guilderson, Alan G. Hogg, Konrad A. Hughen, Bernd Kromer, Gerry McCormac, Sturt Manning, Christopher Bronk Ramsey, Ron W. Reimer, Sabine Remmele, John R. Southon, Minze Stuiver, Sahra Talamo, F. W. Taylor, Johannes van der Plicht, and Constanze E. Weyhenmeyer. 2004. "IntCa104 Terrestrial Radiocarbon Age Calibration, 0–26 Cal Kyr BP." *Radiocarbon* 46: 1029–58.

Renfrew, Colin. 1972. *The Emergence of Civilization: The Cyclades and the Aegean in the Third Millennium B.C.* London: Methuen.

———, ed. 2007. *Excavations at Phylakopi in Melos, 1974–77*. Suppl. Vol. 42. London: British School at Athens.

Renfrew, Colin, Christos Doumas, Lila Marangou and Giorgos Gavalas. 2007. *Keros, Dhaskalio Kavos: the investigations of 1987–88*. Cambridge: McDonald Institute for Archaeological Research.

———. 2008. "Cycladic Studies Today." In *Horizon*, 1–8.

Rutter, Jeremy B. 1979. *Ceramic Change in the Aegean Early Bronze Age*. Occasional Paper 5. Los Angeles: Institute of Archaeology, University of California.

———. 1983. "Some Observations on the Cyclades in the Later Third and Early Second Millennia B.C." *AJA* 87: 69–76.

———. 1984. "The Early Cycladic III Gap: What It Is and How to Go About Filling It without Making It Go Away." In *Prehistoric Cyclades*, 95–107.

———. n.d. "Late Minoan IB at Kommos: A Sequence of at Least Three Distinct Stages." In *LM IB Pottery: Relative Chronology and Regional Differences*, ed. Thomas M. Brogan and Erik Hallager. Athens: Danish Institute at Athens.

Schweingruber, Fritz H. 1987. *Tree Rings: Basics and Applications of Dendrochronology*. Dordrecht: D. Reidel.

Taylor, Royal E. 1987. *Radiocarbon Dating: An Archaeological Perspective*. Orlando: Academic Press.

———. 1997. "Radiocarbon Dating." In *Chronometric Dating in Archaeology*, ed. Royal E. Taylor and Michael J. Aitken, 65–96. New York: Plenum.

Vitale, Salvatore. 2006. "The LH IIIB-LH IIIC Transition on the Mycenaean Mainland: Ceramic Phases and Terminology." *Hesperia* 75: 177–204.

Wace, Alan J. B., and Carl W. Blegen. 1916–1918. "The Pre-Mycenaean Pottery of the Mainland." *BSA* 22: 175–89.

Warren, Peter M. 1991. "A New Minoan Deposit from Knossos c. 1600 B.C. and Its Wider Relations." *BSA* 86: 319–340.

———, and Vronwy Hankey. 1989. *Aegean Bronze Age Chronology*. Bristol: Bristol Classical Press.

Waterbolk, Harm T. 1971. "Working with Radiocarbon Dates." *Proceedings of the Prehistoric Society* 37: 15–33.

Wiener, Malcolm H. 2003. "The Absolute Chronology of Late Helladic III A2 Revisited." *BSA* 98: 239–50.

PART II

CHRONOLOGY AND GEOGRAPHY

CHAPTER 3

NEOLITHIC ANTECEDENTS

PETER TOMKINS

AT the turn of the twentieth century, excavations beneath Bronze Age strata at Dimini and Sesklo in Thessaly and Knossos on Crete revealed an earlier epoch of human occupation, characterized by stone tools, handmade pottery, and the bones of domesticated animals (Evans 1901; Tsountas 1908). Termed Neolithic by analogy with other European regions, it was immediately clear that this was a phase of village-dwelling farmers, the Aegean's first agricultural society.

AN IMAGINED NEOLITHIC

In these early years and under the influence of nationalist and colonialist agendas, a line was drawn in the sand of prehistory separating the more familiar, village-dwelling, sedentary, pottery-using farmers of the Neolithic and Bronze Age from the more alien, cave-dwelling, mobile foragers of the Palaeolithic and Mesolithic (Zvelebil 1995). In what has become a modern origin myth for Western society, the development of agriculture and sedentism was viewed as 'an escape from the impasse of savagery' (Childe 1942, 55)—a revolutionary beginning in the development of modernity, albeit one eclipsed in modern significance by the 'urban revolution' and the 'emergence of civilization' in the Bronze Age (Childe 1942, 79–163; 1950; Renfrew 1972). To modern eyes accustomed to almost constant change, the nearly constant continuity of the Neolithic seemed backward or uninteresting.

Archaeological engagement with continuity was generally not as profound as its fascination for change, and, as a consequence, Neolithic communities were dismissed as static, small, isolated, and immobile, lacking social stratification, competition, and craft specialization, and preoccupied with subsistence self-sufficiency (e.g., Childe 1936, 1942; Weinberg 1970, 587; Renfrew 1972, 52; Cherry 1983, 33). Understood thus in opposition to the Bronze Age, the Neolithic served a useful purpose as a contrastive device in definitions of civilization (e.g., Renfrew 1972, 3–26; Tomkins 2004, 39–40) and as a means of focusing the narrative of emergence within the Bronze Age. This rhetorical use of the Neolithic is typical of a more general approach to human prehistory (Gamble 2007, 10–83, for a critique). By choosing to divide up the past into major periods such as the Neolithic or Bronze Age, we reduce its complexity to a limited number of categories, about which we develop generalized and largely contrasting characterizations. Inquiry is reduced to a search for origins, change is marshaled into revolutions, usually located at the transitions between major periods, and the role of people in effecting continuity and change is suppressed (Barrett 1994, 2–5, 157–64; Gamble 2007, 10–83).

A New Stone Age

Inevitably this caricature began to unravel when archaeologists started taking a more specific interest in the collection and interpretation of Neolithic data. Early syntheses were able to glimpse hints of complexity and change (e.g., Renfrew 1972, 50–53, 63–80), and in time it has become clear that the Neolithic and the Bronze Age have many features in common, such as craft specialization (Renfrew 1973; Kotsakis 1983; Vitelli 1989; Perlès 1992; Tomkins 2004, 52–53), a diversified agricultural subsistence base, and broadly analogous systems of intensive horticulture (Halstead 2000, 2004). Agricultural surplus, once seen as the preserve of Bronze Age, elite-driven economies (e.g., Childe 1942, 22–23, 54, 61–62), is now viewed as central to the Neolithic economy and a key resource in social competition (Halstead 1989, 1999). Studies of the production and circulation of material culture have made it clear that Neolithic farmers, far from being immobile, were able to sustain contacts at local, regional, and interregional levels (Renfrew 1973; van Andel and Runnels 1988, 236–38; Perlès 1992; Tomkins 2004, 48; Tomkins, Day, and Kilikoglou 2004). Moreover, thanks to the insight that the long-term viability of Neolithic communities was predicated on their ability to maintain external relationships (Sahlins 1974, 41–99; Halstead 1989, 70–71; 1996a, 301–303), exchange is now seen as central to Neolithic society, indeed as one of the principal means by which value in objects (and thus people) was negotiated (van Andel and Runnels 1988, 234–38; Perlès 1992, 149; Andreou, Fotiadis, and Kotsakis 1996, 559; Tomkins 2004, 48; 2007a, 192–93). Regarding consumption, it is widely recognized, not least in the production of fine ceramic tableware (Vitelli 1989; Sherratt 1991; Tomkins

2007a; Urem-Kotsou and Kotsakis 2007), that special, ritualized occasions of com-mensality were central to the reproduction of core values, identities, and relations throughout the Neolithic and Bronze Age. Finally, several studies have concluded that the competitive pursuit of status, once viewed as an emergent property of the emergence of civilization in the Early Bronze Age (e.g., Renfrew 1972, 42), was also a key component of Neolithic social life, albeit one mediated and curtailed by social controls (Kotsakis 1983, 213–14, 264–300; 1999; Halstead 1993, 1999, 90; Tomkins 2004, 48–50; 2007a, 192–95).

It is also the Neolithic that sees the first appearance of commodities such as the vine, the olive, and metal, whose availability has been linked to the emergence of Bronze Age societies (Renfrew 1972; van Andel and Runnels 1988, 240; but see Hamilakis 1996; Halstead 2004, 190–94). During LN and FN, the rarity of metal objects, their special material qualities, and the frequency with which they form part of ritualized depositional practices suggests that they were highly valued (Nakou 1995; Tomkins 2009). Evidence for Neolithic usage of the olive and the vine is sketchy (Hamilakis 1996) but present in regions such as west Crete (olive: Moody, Rackham, and Rapp 1996, 282–89) and Macedonia from the late fifth millennium BC (vine: Valamoti, Mangafa, Koukouli-Chrysanthaki, and Malamidou 2007; Urem-Kotsou and Kotsakis in press).

Recognition of these commonalities between the Neolithic and Bronze Age is important in allowing us to dismantle the artificiality of our inherited periodiciza-tion of the past and to trace development along common axes of variation. Within this more inclusive framework, longstanding Bronze Age research questions regard-ing origins and emergence may be reformulated and readdressed by exploring how these separate axes of variation develop and change in articulation, context, and meaning over a longer timescale stretching back into the Neolithic.

False Dawns

At the same time, a number of superficially attractive but empirically dissatisfying attempts have been made to project certain key elements of Bronze Age 'emergence' back into the Neolithic.

A Neolithic Secondary Products Revolution?

Under the influence of recent traditions of land use in Greece, it has been argued that pastoralism lies behind a domestic usage of caves and the settlement of agricul-turally more marginal upland regions in the later Neolithic (e.g., Jacobsen 1984; van Andel and Runnels 1988, 242; Sampson 1992). Frequently this has been connected with the notion of an Early Bronze Age 'secondary products revolution' (SPR), in which the westward dispersal of a series of Near Eastern innovations in animal management (e.g., traction/transportation, wool/textiles, pastoralism) triggered the emergence of Bronze Age civilization (Sherratt 1981).

More recently, however, the empirical and theoretical foundations of Neolithic pastoralism have been thoroughly questioned, and other models for cave use and marginal colonization have been proposed (Halstead 1996a, 301–302; 1996b; 2000, 111–15; 2008; Tomkins 2008, 38–40; 2009). While aspects of the SPR model such as wool/textile production or the use of animals for dry-shod bulk transportation were clearly intrinsic to Bronze Age economic development, there is nothing in an increasingly cogent body of bioarchaeological data to suggest a sudden, revolutionary shift toward the use of animal secondary products before the Bronze Age (Halstead 2008). Moreover, the first appearance of key components of the SPR model, such as animal traction and dairying, may now be placed much earlier within the Neolithic (Isaakidou 2006, 2008, 101–110; Evershed et al. 2008). Evidence for the use of cows for traction first appears in EN levels at Knossos, where it appears to be embedded within an existing economy of small-scale, intensive horticulture rather than driving a new, extensive form of farming.

Neolithic Urbanism?

A capacity to sustain large aggregations of population is generally seen as a defining feature of Bronze Age Aegean society (e.g., Childe 1950; Renfrew 1972, 5, 7). However, size estimates for several later Neolithic tells (e.g., Knossos: 5 ha; Kouphovouno: 4 ha; Sesklo: 13 ha) and 'extended settlements' (e.g., Vasilika: ca. 25 ha.; Thermi: >12 ha.) would appear to place these sites far beyond the normal Neolithic village size threshold (ca. 0.5–2.0 ha, ca. 300–500 people) (Evans 1971; Halstead 1994, 200; Kotsakis 1999, 67–69; 2006; Mee 2001, 3). This has been interpreted as a precociously early form of asymmetric social restructuring or even urbanism, driven by exceptional, local demographic and ecological conditions (Broodbank 1992; Grammenos 1997, 283–90; Manning 1999; Mee 2001; Cavanagh 2004). However, the empirical basis for these claims is open to question. Excavations at extended settlements suggest habitation by a relatively small group favoring a dispersed and shifting pattern of habitation (Kotsakis 1999, 67–68; 2006). The size of the inhabited area at Knossos has recently been revised down to an unexceptional 2.0–2.5 ha (Tomkins 2008, 35–36), and Kouphovouno, too, may turn out to be more typical once its spatial extent is documented by phased excavated deposits rather than mixed surface scatters.

Neolithic Core-Periphery Relationships?

It has long been recognized that the divergent regional trajectories of socioeconomic development that emerged during the Bronze Age may, at least in part, be understood in terms of human responses to the varying ecological configuration of the Aegean (Renfrew 1972, 265–307; Halstead 1994; Manning 1994). Some have sought to identify similarly divergent, ecologically driven trends of development from the beginning of the Neolithic, viewing the densely settled region of Thessaly as the exceptional core and the southern Aegean as its underpopulated and unimportant periphery (e.g., van Andel and Runnels 1988, 234–40; Perlès 2001, 5, 143–51, 297–98). However, aside from site density, the evidence strongly suggests that regional Neolithic development was broadly isomorphic in character, with communities in different regions sharing fundamental similarities in size, subsistence economy, preferred location, and social organization (Sherratt 1981, 315; Halstead 1981b, 194–95; 1994, 200; Kotsakis 1999, 67; Perlès 2001; Tomkins 2004, 42–50).

Moreover, as has long been recognized (e.g., Sherratt 1972), regional variation in the density of Neolithic settlement is primarily a function of constraints imposed by ecological variation (soils, hydrology) and subsistence technology. The influence of taphonomic and research biases may also be suspected. Meaningful spatial differences in development can be sustained only at a continental level, notable being the disparity between a later Neolithic landscape of villages in the Aegean and the contemporary emergence of urbanism in the Near East (Akkermans and Schwartz 2003, 154–210). While 'escaped technologies' and individuals may occasionally have found their way across this developmental divide (Sherratt and Sherratt 2008), the Neolithic Aegean and its neighbors constituted essentially separate worlds of existence.

SOCIAL LIFE AND SOCIAL TRANSFORMATION DURING THE NEOLITHIC

Over the last decade or so, socioeconomic development during the Neolithic has come to be framed in terms of a developing relationship between two spatial scales of social organization: the household, generally viewed as commensurate with individual residential units (Renfrew 1972, 365; Halstead 1999, 79–81), and the community, broadly equated with the totality of an individual settlement (Halstead 1995, 1999; Kostakis 1999; Tomkins 2004). Although this relationship is often represented as a tension between household self-interest and the necessity of communal cooperation (Halstead 1995), the archaeological record bespeaks continuity and stability suggestive of a comfortable symbiosis. Shifts in the balance of this relationship nevertheless occurred and, at least on present evidence, appear to have taken the form of rapid transformations, the impact of which can be traced in many aspects of existence, from spatial organization and production to storage, consumption, and exchange (e.g. Halstead 1995; Tomkins 2004).

In this way, the Neolithic may be broken down into two relatively stable phases (IN–MN, LN–early FN), punctuated by two shorter periods of socioeconomic transformation, one occurring around the MN–LN transition (ca. 5500/5300 BC) and one beginning late in FN (ca. 3500–3100/3000 BC) and running into the Early Bronze Age. Across this great span of time we can trace the progressive isolation of the household as an independent social, economic, and political unit and its progressive appropriation of communal rights, controls, and obligations until, by the end of FN, a society once subjugated to the interests of the many had been transformed into one driven by the interests of specific groups, who would in time become the 'elite' households of the Bronze Age. From this perspective, the Neolithic emerges as not just the background to the emergence of greater complexity in the Bronze Age but also its beginning, the crucial socioeconomic transformation occurring not, as often assumed, at the transition between our modern periodicizations of the past but a little earlier—in the late FN.

The Submerged Household (ca. 7000–5500 BC)

Within earlier Neolithic (IN–MN) communities, residential units tend to crowd together with cooking facilities located both within and between different structures (Halstead 1995, 16–19; Andreou, Fotiadis, and Kotsakis 1996, 559; Tomkins 2004, 43–45; Nanoglou 2008). This has been interpreted as marking an overarching obligation for households to share food, probably at regular, ritualized occasions of commensality that took place within and on the periphery of residential areas (Halstead 1995, 16–17; Tomkins 2007a, 187–88). Studies of earlier Neolithic craft production have emphasized the role played by communal participation in a production process that was small-scale, inefficient, labor intensive, and characterized by tremendous continuities in practice (Vitelli 1993, 210; Miller 1996; Perlès and Vitelli 1999, 104–105; Tomkins 2004, 45–47).

This raises the question of whether agricultural production, which similarly requires group cooperation at certain stages in the production process, could have been organized at the communal rather than household level (Tomkins 2004, 2007; Nanoglou 2008; Halstead in press for an opposing view). Under such a model, earlier Neolithic households would not have enjoyed a natural right to the products of their labors, produce would have been pooled, and land would have been held in common (Tomkins 2004, 42–43; 2007a, 187–89, 192–93).

At present, the bioarchaeological data for this period are partial, incomplete, and largely equivocal on the question of organization. A possible hint in favor of a more communal model is suggested by the absence of evidence for long-term, bulk agricultural storage at the household level (i.e., over and above normal short-term household provisioning). The existence of such facilities (e.g., granaries, grain pits) at a communal level has not yet been adequately investigated, but one obvious candidate from IN Knossos would be a burnt mud-brick structure, probably raised on posts and of unknown extent, which had clearly contained grain (burnt grain present and grain impressions on the interior surface of mud brick) (Tomkins 2007a, 187–88).

Households during this period may be described as 'submerged' in the sense that they were embedded within a broader system of rights and obligations that continued to assert the primacy of the community (see Düring and Marciniak

2004 for a similar view of the Central Anatolian Neolithic). People lived as separate households but constituted themselves communally, the most significant moments being those seasonal activities of production (craft, food) and consumption (e.g., commensality), which brought households together as a community. Through these collective activities, people constructed a particularly strong and stable vision of their shared origins, values, and identity, which effectively restricted the extent to which individual households could pursue their own self-interest.

If land was held in common and production (craft, food), storage, and the ritualized deployment of agricultural surplus were communally organized and regulated, status competition between households is likely to have been directed into other areas (Halstead 1999, 89–91; Tomkins 2007a, 192–93). If so, this would explain why considerable effort, measured in the circulation of objects (pottery, lithics), appears to have been expended in cultivating external social relationships, often over distances far greater than necessary to ensure demographic viability or offset the risk of productive failure (Perlès 1992; Halstead 1999, 90; Tomkins 2001, 374–75; 2004).

In the case of EN–MN Knossos, for example, stylistic and petrographic studies suggest that up to half of the pottery consumed was not produced directly at the site but in locations ranging from the near vicinity to different regions within and beyond Crete (Tomkins and Day 2001; Tomkins and Kilikoglou 2004). Distance here may be understood to constitute a form of symbolic capital that could be expended through the consumption of exchanged gift items such as ceramic vessels, which symbolized these distant relationships and provided a cue for displays of prowess through the narrating of object biographies and tales of travel and acquisition (Tomkins 2004, 48; 2007a, 192–93). In this way, while communal activities such as commensality reinforced the primacy of the community, they also provided restricted opportunities for households to compete for status.

The Emergent Household (ca. 5500–3500 BC)

Beginning at the end of MN, a series of changes signals a shift in the constitution of Neolithic society (see Halstead 1995, 1999; Kotsakis 1999, 2006; Tomkins 2004). Some communities, such as Dimini in Thessaly and Knossos on Crete, expand to become large villages (ca. 1.5–2.5 ha) and become more clearly partitioned into separate (household) units and enclosed external spaces (Hourmouziadis 1979; Halstead 1995, 14–15; Kotsakis 2006; Tomkins 2008, 33).

This architectural isolation of the household coincides with the appearance of ceramic house models, which reify the household as a separable socioeconomic unit (Gallis 1985; Tomkins 2004, 51–52). The enclosing of external spaces suggests an encroachment on what had previously been a communal space of production and consumption. The size of residential units (ca. 70–100 m^2) suggests an extended household unit larger than a single nuclear family (Halstead 1992, 54). The appearance of a more discrete household unit may have enabled the development of the hamlet (< 0.5 ha), a more compact scale of communal living that first appears late in MN (e.g., MN–LN I Katsamba, Crete; Galanidou in press). Such developments

facilitated a process of settlement infill and expansion into unsettled or agricul-
turally less productive lowland areas of the Aegean (e.g., southern Larisa plain;
Herakleion basin; central Cyclades) (Halstead 1989, 76; 1994, 200; 1995, 14–15, 17;
Broodbank 2000, 144–56; Tomkins 2008, 33–34).

The LN period has been identified as a time of change in the technology, organization, and ownership of production. From the beginning of LN, craft production (e.g., shell beads at Franchthi; pottery at Knossos) sees changes in technology
and dramatic increases in efficiency, intensity, and output, suggestive of the involvement of a smaller, possibly more specialized producing group (Miller 1996; Perlès
and Vitelli 1999, 104–105; Tomkins 2001, 334–48; 2004, 52–53).

Significant change is less clearly identifiable in agricultural production.
Although early syntheses isolated the LN period as a phase of increasing diversification in the subsistence economy (Renfrew 1972, 49, 52, 274–80; Halstead 1981a,
320–27; 1994, 200–202), the incomplete nature of the dataset, especially for the
earlier Neolithic, cautions against confident recognition of temporally specific
patterning (Halstead pers. comm.). In some cases, however, seemingly new agricultural practices find corroboration in associated changes in material culture. Thus,
for example, the appearance of flax in an LN level at Knossos (Sarpaki in press)
broadly coincides with the appearance of ceramic 'shuttles,' which appear to skeuo-
morph weaving equipment (Evans 1964, 233). Similarly, the evidence for Aegean
usage of the olive and the vine from the late fifth and fourth millennia BC broadly
coincides with a horizon of pouring shapes and drinking sets in the pottery typologies of Crete (Tomkins 2007b, 32–44, for a new FN I–IV chronology), northern
Greece (Urem-Kotsou and Kotsakis in press), and elsewhere in Europe (Sherratt
1987). In both examples, the focus seems to be on 'special' crops amenable to being
transformed by a small producing group (household) into low-volume, high-value
products (oil, wine, cloth) that are particularly suitable for deployment in social
networking.

The LN period also sees evidence at some sites for changes in agricultural storage. For example, at LN Dimini an increase in built, indoor storage facilities suggests increased storage capacity at the household level, while the appearance of
large, deep pits in external spaces attests to a greater interest in the long-term storage of agricultural surplus (Renfrew 1972, 288; Halstead 1989, 75–76; 1995, 17; 1996a,
305–306). The increased visibility of agricultural storage at the household level may
suggest that households now enjoyed a greater degree of control over the organization and destination of their productive output.

A shift in the context of production from a communal to a household level
would not only have lessened the influence of social resistance to change—most
powerful when activities take place in a public arena—but also, in giving households
greater control over their productive output, would have created new opportunities for status competition and new incentives for technological change. Changes
in craft production, agricultural production (i.e., introduction of 'special' crops),
and storage may all be read as deliberate attempts to control and increase the quality, quantity, and diversity of household output, which might then be deployed

competitively in the negotiation of status at varying scales and in a variety of contexts (Halstead 1993, 606–608; 1995, 18; 1999, 90; Tomkins 2004, 54–55).

The household during this period may be described as 'emergent' in the sense that it had become a more discrete social, economic, and political unit, but one whose independence continued to be curtailed by a powerful set of communal obligations, manifest perhaps in restrictions on ownership and accumulation. Households continued to live in aggregations, apparently preferring communal living to individual spatial isolation. Moreover, the failure of Neolithic communities to grow beyond the threshold above which egalitarian communities tend to fission or evolve more complex forms of organization (ca. 2–3 ha or 300–500 people; Whitelaw 1983, 340) speaks eloquently of an absence of permanent institutionalized inequalities that would otherwise have developed if household isolation and competition had been allowed to develop unchecked.

Although the centrally located megara at Dimini and other villages in Thessaly have been interpreted as marking the emergence of a 'megaron elite' (Halstead 1989, 78; 1995, 14–15), it is telling that consumption patterns (animals, spondylus) at Dimini reveal no differences in access—and thus no signs of socioeconomic advantage—between the central megaron and other domestic units (Halstead 1992, 1993). Moreover, the central megaron at Dimini is no larger than other domestic units and is marginalized in location and dwarfed in size by a large, centrally located open space. Perhaps the entire central area, megaron included, was given over to communal ritual, constituting perhaps the earliest known instance of a deep tradition of communal ritual in association with central megara on the Greek mainland, which continued into the Bronze Age and perhaps beyond. Indeed, it is in ritual that affirmation of the communal continues to be most clearly represented. The evidence from burial and other forms of corporal manipulation continues to emphasize the primacy of the communal over the individual (Triantaphyllou 1999, 2008) and ritualized occasions of group commensality, sometimes on a truly massive scale (e.g., Pit 212, LN Makriyialos; Halstead 2004, 196; Pappa, Halstead, Kotsakis, and Urem-Kotsou 2004) remained the primary arena for competitive display.

The Modular Household (ca. 3600/3500 BC–Early Bronze Age)

At late FN lowland villages (e.g., Pevkakia, Knossos), residential structures continue to be of a size to suggest an extended household unit larger in size than a single nuclear family. From late FN, cooking facilities in Thessaly either move indoors or are set outdoors in an enclosed yard (Halstead 1989, 77). This hardening of the distinction between the household and the community finds its clearest expression in the emergence during the late FN of two strategies of livelihood, marginality and trading, both of which would be crucial to Bronze Age development.

Marginality might be defined as the settlement of agriculturally less extensive or productive areas of the landscape and is a recognized feature of the FN settlement record of the southern Aegean and other regions of Europe (Sherratt 1981,

292–93; Halstead 1994, 200; 2000, 117–22; 2008; Broodbank 2000, 149–56). For Crete it has recently become clear that this process first began at the end of FN (FN IV; ca. 3300–3100/3000 BC), with some regions not settled until EM I (Tomkins 2008, 38–40). Although less precisely dated in the Peloponnese and the Cyclades, there, too, it was a late FN or EBA phenomenon (Broodbank 1989, 320–21; 2000, 150; Vitelli 1999, 98–99).

Late FN marginal settlement systems generally take the form of networks of small sites (from hamlets to single dwellings) located on more discrete and dispersed pockets of arable land (e.g., Broodbank 1989, 320–27; 2000, 149–51; Branigan 1998). Current evidence suggests that marginal communities continued to rely on mixed farming, supplemented perhaps by forms of economic specialization such as herding, which were appropriate to the specific environment in question (Halstead 2000, 117–22; 2008). The ability to settle these environments depended on two related developments: first, a new possibility for social and spatial disaggregation, perhaps scaling down as far as the nuclear family when stress or the configuration of resources demanded (Halstead 2008); and, second, the construction of a new, dispersed form of community, where intervisibility and mobility served to link scattered sites into larger, more viable entities.

Such changes imply a greater possibility for household isolation and independence and a looser, more flexible understanding of community, developments that are tantamount to a breakdown in the checks and balances that hitherto sustained the stability of the later Neolithic system of village life. Transposed to the lowland village, this suggests a scenario where failing households could have been less certain of communal protection and their land, labor, and livelihood were more open to interference and appropriation by successful households seeking to transform short-term gain into longer-term competitive advantage. Some failing households may have opted to stay, perhaps indebting their land or labor; others may have chosen to take their chances with migration and economic diversification.

An alternative option, at least for some, was trading, defined as the establishment of long-distance exchange relationships in order to secure privileged access to high-value raw materials, objects, and practices (technologies, consumption) and the exploitation of their distribution as a means of negotiating power. While networks of relationships can be traced within and between the regions of the Aegean throughout the Neolithic, it is evident that the late FN saw an intensification in maritime movement and a change in the nature and role of exchange (van Andel and Runnels 1988; Perlès 1992; Broodbank 2000, 166–70).

One obvious aspect of this is a proliferation of late FN–EBA settlements along the coasts of the southern Aegean, many of which continued to be occupied into the Bronze Age (Broodbank 2000, 125, 149–74). While the majority of late FN coastal sites were too small to have mustered the resources necessary for trading (see Broodbank 1989, 330–32), some were comparable in size to the largest EB II trading sites (i.e., ca. 1–2 ha; e.g., Paoura, Kea; Petras Kephala, Crete; cf. Broodbank 1989, 330–32; 2000, 149).

It is becoming increasingly likely that these large, late FN coastal communities, like their later successors (Broodbank 1989), were involved in trading and perhaps already exploiting the longboat, especially those communities located in more marginal locations (e.g., Paoura, Kea; Broodbank 2000, 149). Although the volumes were low and trading still probably looked a lot like gift exchange, for the first time trade relationships seem to have been determined by a desire to secure privileged access to specific commodities and technologies. Thus, late FN Cretan coastal sites such as Nerokourou and Petras Kephala exhibit a particularly close connection (imported pottery, obsidian) with the Attic-Kephala region but appear to lack corresponding links with more proximate regions (Vagnetti 1996; D'Annibale 2008; Papadatos, Tomkins, Nodarou, and Iliopoulos in press). The specificity and scale of these distant connections suggest the involvement of a seacraft with capabilities similar to those of the longboat (cf. Broodbank 1989, 327–35), a conclusion given more credence by the recent discovery of iconographic representations of longboats from the large late FN site of Strophilas on Andros (Televantou 2008).

Although distant raw materials and objects had long been esteemed as status markers (e.g., Perlès 1992; Tomkins 2004, 48), it is only late in FN that people seek overtly to control their acquisition, production, and distribution. In the case of metal, although finished objects, mainly of non-Aegean type, had been circulating for millennia, it is surely significant that our earliest direct evidence for Aegean metallurgy, in the form of ores, crucibles, or slags, comes only late in FN and appears at large coastal sites (e.g., Kea Kephala, Nisiros, Petras Kephala; Broodbank 2000, 158–59; Papadatos 2007) and apparently as deliberate depositions at ritual cave sites (e.g., Kitsos, Alepotrypa; Tomkins 2009). At FN IV Petras-Kephala, obsidian and metal appear to have arrived in raw form and were then processed and transformed into finished products at the site (Papadatos 2007, 164; D'Annibale 2008, 192).

The near absence of obsidian and metal at contemporary inland sites in Crete (Carter 1998) suggests that trading communities like Petras Kephala would have been able to construct advantageous social relationships with other prosperous groups, a scenario that finds support in occasional finds of obsidian blades and metal objects at FN IV inland villages such as Knossos and Phaistos (A. J. Evans 1928, figure 3f; Todaro and Di Tonto 2008, 183, 185). In this way, trading served and stimulated a wider demand for nonlocal products and practices that would have been possible only if communal controls on accumulation and consumption had been loosened and households were now free to pursue more overt and ambitious strategies of accumulation. The development of trading, of restricted control over the production of prestige objects, and of hierarchies of access in the late FN should thus be understood in terms of the first emergence of an economy in prestige goods, smaller in scale but broadly analogous to that of the Bronze Age.

From the late FN, households may thus be described as 'modular' in the sense that they could now operate in isolation as fully separate and separable socioeconomic units that might combine in different ways and at different scales to meet different circumstances. Such flexibility opened the door to the development of new, alternative strategies such as trading and marginality, which were tailored to exploit a wider range of the resources configured across the land and seascapes of the Aegean (Whitelaw 2004; Tomkins and Schoep, this volume). In this way, the late FN emergence of the 'modular' household may be understood to set in train the process of local and regional socioeconomic diversification in the Aegean, which was central to the functioning of Bronze Age and later economies in the Aegean (Sherratt and Sherratt 1998, 334).

From late FN onwards, households appear to become more able to accumulate, appropriate, and compete in ways that brought them into direct conflict with each other and with domains of communal practice and belief that had previously been sacrosanct. This may be seen, for example, in encroachment upon communal ritual space and its appropriation as an arena for more overt expressions of identity and status. For example, the late FN sees an upsurge in the visibility and intensity of burial, manifest in the Cyclades, Euboea, and Attica (e.g., Kephala, Tharrounia) in the appearance of extramural community cemeteries (Broodbank 2000, 150, 154, 170–73). In Crete, caves with older histories of usage as communal ritual sites see a marked intensification in the deposition of human skeletal material in FN IV, a practice that, in EM I, spreads to a host of new caves and rock shelters (Tomkins in press a). At FN IV Knossos and perhaps also Phaistos, certain houses are juxtaposed with large, formal communal areas that hosted large-scale, ritualized occasions of commensality and went on to become the Central and West Courts of the Bronze Age palace buildings (Todaro and Di Tonto 2008; Tomkins in press b).

Ultimate Causes?

At a basic level, all explanations of emergence remain dissatisfying unless they can adequately account for the specific timing of socioeconomic transformation. For much of the twentieth century, technology was viewed as the driving force behind social change, and explanations tended to focus on the timing of the appearance of so-called transformative commodities and technologies (e.g., olive, vine, metals/ metallurgy) whose advantages were taken to be self-evident and to have ensured their rapid acceptance (e.g., Childe 1942, 74; Renfrew 1972, 34, 265–338, 476–504; Sherratt 1981, 285; van Andel and Runnels 1988, 242–45). Allied to this was the notion that population growth, modeled as an ever-present inflationary pressure, left societies especially open to the adoption of technologies that might allow resource expansion (e.g., Sherratt 1981, 286).

In time, however, as the causal relationships in the archaeological data become better understood, it has become clearer that both change and continuity arise from the actions of knowledgeable actors operating within specific, contingent social and material conditions of existence. Technologies spread only because people choose to adopt them (van der Leeuw and Torrence 1989), populations grow only as a consequence of changes in socioeconomic organization, and continuity may be recast as a dynamic and deliberate evocation of established structures, values, and relations and as a socially embedded, cultural resistance to change. In this chapter, it has been argued that technology, production, exchange, consumption, storage, space, and ritual are dimensions along which we may measure Neolithic development and that changes in these areas are causally related to more fundamental shifts in the social conditions of existence, more specifically in social rights, obligations, and identities, represented here in terms of a developing relationship between the community and the household (see also Gamble 2007, 161–204).

In the end, however, archaeology can take us only so far. To go further and understand what ultimately prompted societies structured around continuity to transform themselves, we need to look more closely at the material conditions of existence within which social agency operates and specifically at factors that influence human decision-making but lie beyond human control. It cannot be simply coincidental that the punctuated equilibria of continuity and change in the Neolithic archaeological record broadly parallel major phases and shifts in climate as revealed by modern palaeoclimatic studies (Roberts 1998; Grove and Rackham 2001; Rosen 2007; Broodbank 2008, 284–85).

For most of the Neolithic, the climatic regime was notably different from that which prevails today. Thus, the long and seemingly stable earlier Neolithic period (ca. 7000–5500 BC) broadly coincides with the early Holocene optimum, a relatively stable phase of wetter, milder, and less seasonal weather. Interannual variability increases from the mid-sixth millennium BC (or the late MN/LN transition), broadly corresponding with the series of changes associated here with the emergent household. Finally, from the mid-fourth millennium BC (late FN) and coinciding with the emergence of the modular household, there begins a phase of more extreme aridity, seasonality, and unpredictability that marks the emergence of the modern Mediterranean climatic regime (Grove and Rackham 2001, 144–50). While more work is certainly required to improve the correlation between the archaeological and climatic data, these apparent parallels suggest that we should seriously consider whether the timing and nature of the MN/LN and late FN social transformations across the Aegean reflects a series of broadly analogous, but contextually specific and contingent human responses to ecological change.

Climatic change could not determine the nature and direction of social change, but it did have the potential to disrupt social structures by influencing and altering the conditions of existence within which human actors make choices, thereby opening up new possibilities of behavior. In the case of the emergent household, greater climatic unpredictability may have led to shortages of agricultural surplus and uncertainty about productive capability, thus undermining the role of the community as provider and exposing some of the weaknesses (e.g., inefficiency, underproduction) of the earlier Neolithic communal mode of production. In this way, once sacrosanct rights and obligations may have been called into doubt and become open to negotiation.

The emergence of the household as a more independent productive unit and a greater interest in storage at the household level could be seen as logical outcomes of such a process. Similarly, the emergence of the modern Mediterranean climate, late in FN, could be seen as favoring the development of a more flexible, modular productive unit that was better able to exploit a wider range of resources as a response to greater subsistence insecurity. Unlike the MN/LN transformation, where the process of household isolation was held back by social restrictions and thus stabilized, the late FN shift created the conditions for further change, initiating a continuous process of asymmetric socioeconomic development in the Aegean, characterized by essentially repetitive and analogous cycles of development and decline that run through prehistory and history up to the present day.

BIBLIOGRAPHY

Akkermans, Peter M. M. G., and Glenn M. Schwartz. 2003. *The Archaeology of Syria: From Complex Hunter-gatherers to Early Urban Societies (ca. 16,000–300 BC)*. New York: Cambridge University Press.

Andreou, Stelios, Michael Fotiadis, and Kostas Kotsakis. 1996. "Review of Aegean Prehistory V: The Neolithic and Bronze Age of Northern Greece." *AJA* 100: 537–97.

Barrett, John C. 1994. *Fragments from Antiquity: An Archaeology of Social Life in Britain, 2900–1200 BC*. Oxford: Blackwell.

Branigan, Keith. 1998. "Prehistoric and Early Historic Settlement in the Ziros Region, Eastern Crete." *BSA* 93: 23–90.

Broodbank, Cyprian. 1992. "The Neolithic Labyrinth: Social Change at Knossos before the Bronze Age." *JMA* 5: 39–75.

———. 1989. "The Longboat and Society in the Cyclades in the Keros-Syros Culture." *AJA* 85: 318–37.

———. 2000. *An Island Archaeology of the Early Cyclades*. New York: Cambridge University Press.

———. 2008. "Long after Hippos, Well before Palaces: A Commentary on the Cultures and Contexts of Neolithic Crete." In *Escaping the Labyrinth*, 271–90.

Carter, Tristan. 1998. "The Chipped Stone." *BSA* 93: 47–50.

Cavanagh, William. 2004. "WYSIWYG: Settlement and Territoriality in Southern Greece during the Early and Middle Neolithic Periods." *JMA* 17: 165–89.

Cherry, John F. 1983. "Evolution, Revolution, and the Origins of Complex Society in Minoan Crete." In *Minoan Society*, 33–45.

Childe, V. Gordon. 1936. *Man Makes Himself*. London: Watts.

———. 1942. *What Happened in History*. Harmondsworth, Middlesex, Eng.: Penguin.

———. 1950. "The Urban Revolution." *Town Planning Review* 21(1): 3–19.

D'Annibale, Cesare. 2008. "Obsidian in Transition: The Technological Reorganization of the Obsidian Industry from Petras Kephala (Siteia) between Final Neolithic IV and Early Minoan I." In *Escaping the Labyrinth*, 191–200.

Düring, Bleda, and Arkadiusz Marciniak. 2004. "Households and Communities in the Central Anatolian Neolithic." *Archaeological Dialogues* 12: 165–87.

Evans, Arthur J. 1901. "The Neolithic Settlement at Knossos and Its Place in the History of Early Aegean Culture." *Man* 1: 184–86.

————. 1928. "Chapter 33: Discovery of Late Neolithic Houses beneath Central Court: Traditional Affinities with Mainland East." In *PM* II vol. 1, ed. Arthur J. Evans, 1–21. London: Macmillan.

Evans, John D. 1964. "Excavations in the Neolithic settlement at Knossos, 1957–60." *BSA* 59: 132–240.

————. 1971. "Neolithic Knossos: The Growth of a Settlement." *Proceedings of the Prehistoric Society* 37: 95–117.

Evershed, Richard P., Sebastian Payne, Andrew G. Sherratt, Mark S. Copley, Jennifer Coolidge, Duska Urem-Kotsou, Kostas Kotsakis, et al. 2008. "Earliest Date for Milk Use in the Near East and Southeastern Europe Linked to Cattle Herding." *Nature* 455: 528–31.

Galanidou, Nena. In press. *Katsambas: A Neolithic Settlement by the Kairatos*. Philadelphia: INSTAP Press.

Gallis, Konstantinos I. 1985. "A Late Neolithic Foundation Offering from Thessaly." *Antiquity* 59: 20–24.

Gamble, Clive. 2007. *Origins and Revolutions: Human Identity in Earliest Prehistory*. New York: Cambridge University Press.

Grammenos, Demetrios. 1997. *Neolithiki Makedonia*. Athens: Tameio Arkhaiologikon Poron.

Grove, A. T. and Oliver Rackham. 2001. *The Nature of Mediterranean Europe: An Ecological History*. New Haven, Conn.: Yale University Press.

Halstead, Paul L. J. 1981a. "Counting Sheep in Neolithic and Bronze Age Greece." In *Pattern of the Past: Studies in Honour of David Clarke*, ed. Ian Hodder, Glynn Isaac, and Normand Hammond, 307–39. New York: Cambridge University Press.

————. 1981b. "From Determinism to Uncertainty: Social Storage and the Rise of the Minoan Palace." In *Economic Archaeology*, ed. Andrew Sheridan and Geoff Bailey, 187–213. *BAR-IS* 96. Oxford: British Archaeological Reports.

————. 1989. "The Economy Has a Normal Surplus: Economic Stability and Social Change among Early Farming Communities of Thessaly Greece." In *Bad Year Economics: Cultural Responses to Risk and Uncertainty*, ed. Paul Halstead and John O'Shea, 68–80. New York: Cambridge University Press.

————. 1992. "Dhimini and the 'DMP': Faunal Remains and Animal Exploitation in Late Neolithic Thessaly." *BSA* 87: 29–59.

————. 1993. "*Spondylus* Shell Ornaments from Late Neolithic Thessaly, Greece: Specialized Manufacture or Unequal Accumulation." *Antiquity* 67: 603–609.

————. 1994. "The North-south Divide: Regional Paths to Complexity in Prehistoric Greece." In *Development and Decline in the Mediterranean Bronze Age*, ed. Clay Mathers and Simon Stoddart, 195–219. Sheffield: Sheffield University Press.

————. 1995. "From Sharing to Hoarding: The Neolithic Foundations of Aegean Bronze Age Society." In *Politeia*, 11–21.

————. 1996a. "The Development of Agriculture and Pastoralism in Greece: When, How, Who, What?" In *The Origins and Spread of Agriculture and Pastoralism in Eurasia: Crops, Fields, Flocks, and Herds*, ed. David R. Harris, 296–309. London: UCL Press.

————. 1996b. "Skoteini, Tharrounia: The Cave, the Settlement, and the Cemetery, by Adamantios Sampson." *AJA* 100: 179–80.

————. 1999. "Neighbors from Hell? The Household in Neolithic Greece." In *Neolithic Society in Greece*, ed. Paul Halstead, 77–95. Sheffield Studies of Aegean Archaeology 2. Sheffield: Sheffield Academic Press.

———. 2000. "Land Use in Postglacial Greece: Cultural Causes and Environmental Effects." In *Landscape and Land Use in Postglacial Greece,* ed. Paul Halstead and Charles Frederick, 110–28. Sheffield Studies in Aegean Archaeology 3. Sheffield: Sheffield Academic Press.

———. 2004. "Life after Mediterranean Polyculture: The Subsistence Subsystem and the Emergence of Civilization Revisited." In *Emergence of Civilization Revisited,* ed. Renfrew, 189–206.

———. 2008. "Between a Rock and a Hard Place: Coping with Marginal Colonization in the Later Neolithic and Early Bronze Age of Crete and the Aegean." In *Escaping the Labyrinth,* 232–60.

———. In press. "Farming, Material Culture, and Ideology: Repackaging the Neolithic of Greece (and Europe)." In *Trajectories of Neolithisation,* ed. Angelos Hadjikoumis, Erick Robinson, and Sarah Viner. Oxford: Oxbow.

Hamilakis, Yannis. 1996. "Wine, Oil, and the Dialectics of Power in Bronze Age Crete: A Review of the Evidence." *OJA* 15: 1–32.

Hourmouziadis, Giorgios. 1979. *To Neolithiko Dimini.* Volos, Greece: Society of Thessalian Studies.

Isaakidou, Valasia. 2006. "Ploughing with Cows: Knossos and the 'Secondary Products Revolution.'" In *Animals in the Neolithic of Britain and Europe,* ed. Dale Serjeantson and David Field, 95–112. Oxford: Oxbow.

———. 2008. "'The Fauna and Economy of Neolithic Knossos' Revisited." In *Escaping the Labyrinth,* 90–114.

Jacobsen, Thomas W. 1984. "Seasonal Pastoralism in Southern Greece: A Consideration of the Ecology of Neolithic Urfirnis Pottery." In *Pots and Potters: Current Approaches in Ceramic Archaeology,* ed. Prudence M. Rice, 27–43. Los Angeles: Institute of Archaeology, University of California.

Kotsakis, Kostas. 1983. Keramiki Tekhnologia kai Keramiki Diaforopoiisi: Provlimata tis Graptis Keramikis tis Mesis Neolithikis Epokis tou Sesklou. PhD diss., University of Thessaloniki.

———. 1999. "What Tells Can Tell: Social Space and Settlement in the Greek Neolithic." In *Neolithic Society in Greece,* ed. Paul Halstead, 66–67. Sheffield Studies of Aegean Archaeology 2. Sheffield: Sheffield Academic Press.

———. 2006. "Settlement of Discord: Sesklo and the Emerging Household." In *Homage to Milutin Garašanin,* ed. Nikola Tasic and Cvetan Grozdanov, 207–20. Belgrade: Serbian Academy of Sciences and Arts/Macedonian Academy of Sciences and Arts.

Manning, Sturt W. 1994. "The Emergence of Divergence: Development and Decline on Bronze Age Crete and the Cyclades." In *Development and Decline in the Mediterranean Bronze Age,* ed. Clay Mathers and Simon Stoddart, 221–70. Sheffield: Sheffield University Press.

———. 1999. "Knossos and the Limits of Settlement Growth." In *Meletemata,* 469–82.

Mee, Christopher. 2001. "Nucleation and Dispersal in Neolithic and Early Helladic Laconia." In *Urbanism,* 1–14.

Miller, Michele A. 1996. "The Manufacture of Cockle Shell Beads at Early Neolithic Franchthi Cave, Greece: A Case of Craft Specialization?" *JMA* 9: 7–37.

Moody, Jennifer, Oliver Rackham, and George Rapp. 1996. "Environmental Archaeology of Prehistoric NW Crete." *JFA* 23: 273–97.

Nakou, Georgia. 1995. "The Cutting Edge: A New Look at Early Aegean Metallurgy." *JMA* 8: 1–32.

Nanoglou, Stratos. 2008. "Building Biographies and Households." *Journal of Social Archaeology* 8: 139–60.

Papadatos, Yannis. 2007. "The Beginning of Metallurgy in Crete: New Evidence from the FN–EM I Settlement at Kephala Petras, Siteia." In *Metallurgy in the Early Bronze Age Aegean*, ed. Peter M. Day and Roger C. P. Doonan, 154–67. Sheffield Studies in Aegean Archaeology 7. Oxford: Oxbow.

———, Peter Tomkins, Eleni Nodarou, and Yiannis Iliopoulos. In press. "The Beginning of Early Bronze Age in Crete: Continuities and Discontinuities in the Ceramic Assemblage at Kephala Petras, Siteia." In *The Aegean Early Bronze Age: New Evidence*, ed. Christos Doumas, Colin Renfrew, and Ourania Koukou. Athens, April 11–14, 2008.

Pappa, Maria, Paul Halstead, Kostas Kotsakis, and Dushka Urem-Kotsou. 2004. "Evidence for Large-scale Feasting at Late Neolithic Makriyialos, Northern Greece." In *Food, Cuisine, and Society in Prehistoric Greece*, ed. Paul Halstead and John C. Barrett, 16–44. Sheffield Studies in Aegean Archaeology 5. Oxford: Oxbow.

Perlès, Catherine. 1992. "Systems of Exchange and Organization in Neolithic Greece." *JMS* 5(2): 115–64.

———. 2001. *The Early Neolithic in Greece: The First Farming Communities in Europe.* New York: Cambridge University Press.

———, and Karen D. Vitelli. 1999. "Craft Specialization in the Greek Neolithic." In *Neolithic Society in Greece*, ed. Paul Halstead, 96–107. Sheffield Studies of Aegean Archaeology 2. Sheffield: Sheffield Academic Press.

Renfrew, Colin. 1972. *The Emergence of Civilization: The Cyclades and the Aegean in the Third Millennium B.C.* London: Methuen.

———. 1973. "Trade and Craft Specialization." In *Neolithic Greece*, ed. Detorakis R. Theocharis, 179–91. Athens: National Bank of Greece.

Roberts, Neil. 1998. *The Holocene: An Environmental History.* Oxford: Blackwell.

Rosen, Arlene M. 2007. *Civilizing Climate: Social Responses to Climate Change in the Ancient Near East.* Lanham, Md.: Altamira.

Sahlins, Marshall. 1974. *Stone Age Economics.* London: Tavistock.

Sampson, Adamantios. 1992. "Late Neolithic Remains at Tharrounia, Euboea: A Model for the Seasonal Use of Settlements and Caves." *BSA* 87: 61–101.

Sarpaki, Anaya. In press. "Aspects of the Economy of Neolithic Knossos: A View from the Archaeobotanical (Seed Macrofossil) Data." In *The Neolithic Settlement of Knossos in Crete. New Evidence for the Early Occupation of Crete and the Aegean Islands*, eds. Nikos Efstratiou, Alexandra Karetsou, Maria Ntinou and Eleni Banou. Philadelphia: INSTAP Press.

Sherratt, Andrew. 1972. "Socio-economic and Demographic Models for the Neolithic and Bronze Age of Europe." In *Models in Archaeology*, ed. David L. Clarke, 477–542. London: Methuen.

———. 1981. "Plough and Pastoralism: Aspects of the Secondary Products Revolution." In *Pattern of the Past: Studies in Honour of David Clarke*, ed. Ian Hodder, Glynn Isaac, and Normand Hammond, 261–306. New York: Cambridge University Press.

———. 1987. "Cups That Cheered." In *Bell Beakers of the Western Mediterranean*, ed. William H. Waldern and Rex Claire Kennard, 81–114. BAR 331. Oxford: British Archaeological Reports.

———. 1991. "Palaeoethnobotany: From Crops to Cuisine." In *Paleoecologia e Arqueologia*, vol. 2, ed. Francisco Queiroga and António P. Dinis, 221–36. Vila Nova de Famalicao, Portugal: Centro de Estudios Arquelogicos Famalicenses.

———, and Susan Sherratt. 1998. "Small Worlds: Interaction and Identity in the Ancient Mediterranean." In *Aegean and the Orient*, 329–42.

———. 2008. "The Neolithic of Crete, as Seen from Outside." In *Escaping the Labyrinth*, 291–302.

Televantou, C. A. 2008. "Strofilas: A Neolithic Settlement on Andros." In *Horizon*, 43–54.

Todaro, Simona, and Serena Di Tonto. 2008. "The Neolithic Settlement of Phaistos Revisited: Evidence for Ceremonial Activity on the Eve of the Bronze Age." In *Escaping the Labyrinth*, 177–90.

Tomkins, Peter D. 2001. The Production, Circulation, and Consumption of Ceramic Vessels at Early Neolithic Knossos, Crete. PhD diss., University of Sheffield.

———. 2004. "Filling in the 'Neolithic Background': Social Life and Social Transformation in the Aegean before the Bronze Age." In *Emergence of Civilization Revisited*, 38–63.

———. 2007a. "Communality and Competition: The Social Life of Food and Containers at Aceramic and Early Neolithic Knossos, Crete." In *Cooking Up the Past: Food and Culinary Practices in the Neolithic and Bronze Age Aegean*, ed. Christopher Mee and Josette Renard, 174–99. Oxford: Oxbow.

———. 2007b. "Neolithic: Strata IX–VIII, VII–VIB, VIA–V, IV, IIIB, IIIA, IIB, IIA, and IC Groups." In *Knossos Pottery Handbook*, 9–48.

———. 2008. "Time, Space, and the Reinvention of the Cretan Neolithic." In *Escaping the Labyrinth*, 21–48.

———. 2009. "Domesticity by Default: Ritual, Ritualisation, and Cave Use in the Neolithic Aegean." *OJA* 28(2): 125–53.

———. In press a. "Landscapes of Ritual, Identity, and Memory: Reconsidering Neolithic and Early Bronze Age Cave Use in Crete, Greece." In *Journeys into the Dark Zone*, ed. Holley Moyes. Colorado: University Press of Colorado.

———. In press b. "Behind the Horizon: The Genesis of the 'First Palace' at Knossos (Final Neolithic IV-Middle Minoan IB)." In *Back to the Beginning*.

———, and Peter M. Day. 2001. "Production and Exchange of the Earliest Ceramic Vessels in the Aegean: A View from Early Neolithic Knossos, Crete." *Antiquity* 75: 259–50.

———, and Vasilis Kilikoglou. 2004. "Knossos and the Early Neolithic Landscape of the Herakleion Basin." In *Knossos*, 51–59.

Triantaphyllou, Sevi. 1999. "Prehistoric Makriyialos: A Story from the Fragments." In *Neolithic Society in Greece*, ed. Paul Halstead, 128–35. Sheffield Studies of Aegean Archaeology 2. Sheffield: Sheffield Academic Press.

———. 2008. "Living with the Dead: a Re-consideration of Mortuary Practices in the Greek Neolithic." In *Escaping the Labyrinth*, 137–54.

Tsountas, Christos. 1908. *Ai proïstorikai akropoleis Dhiminiou ke Sesklou*. Athens: I en Athenais Archaiologiki Etaireia.

Urem-Kotsou, Dushka, and Kostas Kotsakis. 2007. "Pottery, Cuisine, and Community in the Neolithic of North Greece." In *Cooking Up the Past: Food and Culinary Practices in the Neolithic and Bronze Age Aegean*, ed. Christopher Mee and Josette Renard, 225–46. Oxford: Oxbow.

———. In press. "Cups of Conversion: Drinking Sets in Social Context in Late Neolithic Northern Greece." In *Wine Confessions: Production, Trade, and Social Significance of Wine in Ancient Greece and Cyprus*, ed. Evi Margaritis, Jane Renfrew, and Martin Jones. Hesperia, Occasional Wiener Laboratory Series. Princeton: American School of Classical Studies at Athens.

Vagnetti, Lucia. 1996. "The Final Neolithic: Crete Enters the Wider World." *Cretan Studies* 5: 29–39.

Valamoti, Soultana M., Maria Mangafa, Chaido Koukouli-Chrysanthaki, and Dimitra Malamidou. 2007. "Grape-pressings from Northern Greece: The Earliest Wine in the Aegean?" *Antiquity* 81: 54–61.

van Andel, Tjeerd H., and Curtis N. Runnels. 1988. "An Essay on the Emergence of Civilisation in the Aegean." *Antiquity* 62: 234–47.

van der Leeuw, Sander E., and Robin Torrence, eds. 1989. *What's New? A Closer Look at the Process of Innovation.* London: Unwin Hyman.

Vitelli, Karen D. 1989. "Were Pots First Invented for Foods? Doubts from Franchthi." *World Archaeology* 21: 17–29.

———. 1993. *Franchthi Neolithic Pottery: Classification and Ceramic Phases 1 and 2.* Excavations at Franchthi Cave, Greece. Fascicle 8. Indianapolis: Indiana University Press.

———. 1999. *Franchthi Neolithic Pottery.* Vol. 2, *The Later Neolithic Ceramic Phases 3 to 5.* Excavations at Franchthi Cave, Greece. Fascicle 10. Indianapolis: Indiana University Press.

Weinberg, Saul S. 1970. "The Stone Age in the Aegean." In *Cambridge Ancient History.* Vol. 1, part 1, *Prolegomena and Prehistory,* 3d ed., ed. I. E. S. Edwards, C. J. Gadd, and N. G. L. Hammond, 557–618. New York: Cambridge University Press.

Whitelaw, Todd M. 1983. "The Settlement at Fournou Korifi, Myrtos, and Aspects of Early Minoan Social Organization." In *Minoan Society,* 323–40.

———. 2004. "Alternative Pathways to Complexity in the Southern Aegean." In *Emergence of Civilisation Revisited,* 232–56.

Zachos, Konstantinos. 2007. "The Neolithic Background: A Reassessment." In *Metallurgy in the Early Bronze Age Aegean,* ed. Peter M. Day and Roger C. P. Doonan, 168–206. Sheffield Studies in Aegean Archaeology 7. Oxford: Oxbow.

Zvelebil, Marek. 1995. "Farmers, Our Ancestors, and the Identity of Europe." In *Cultural Identity and Archaeology: The Construction of European Communities,* ed. Paul Graves-Brown, Sian Jones, and Clive Gamble, 145–66. London: Routledge.

Early Bronze Age

CHAPTER 4

MAINLAND GREECE

JEANNETTE FORSÉN

THE geographical scope of this overview is mainland Greece bordered by Albania, the Former Yugoslav Republic of Macedonia (FYROM), and Bulgaria to the north and the Cyclades and Crete to the south. The period is the Early Bronze Age (EBA), or Early Helladic (EH) denoting the mainland, during the time span between the preceding Final Neolithic period and the ensuing Middle Bronze Age. The absolute dates for the EH period remain unsettled, but if we follow a traditional school, it begins ca. 3100 and ends ca. 2000 BC (Manning 1995).

A tripartite division of the EH period, denoted by Roman numerals EH I–III, was conceived by Blegen, drawing upon his excavation data from Korakou near Corinth (1921, 2–3, 14). This scheme was further elaborated through excavations at Zygouries (Blegen 1928) and Eutresis (Goldman 1931). Goldman was able to apply the term *EH I–III* to three main phases at Eutresis, defined by her through changes in pottery fabric, pottery shapes, and architecture. Thus, a chronological framework based on changes in archaeological material *and* stratigraphical sequencing was created (1931, 227–231).

EH I was then characterized by polished ware, either slipped or unslipped, the earliest most often red slipped, and by incised decorations. EH II was characterized by good-quality glazed ware ("Urfirnis," now Dark-painted ware) and Yellow Mottled ware (now Light-painted, fine-polished ware). Finally, EH III was described as having a degenerated glazed ware, Dark-on-Light ware, a diminishing amount of Yellow Mottled ware, and increasing amounts of Plain ware (Blegen 1928, 76–125, 216–18).

In close to ninety years of archaeological enterprises on mainland Greece, little has altered Blegen's main outline of the EH period, and the stylistic classification of artifactual assemblages for this period has merely been fleshed out. Admittedly, the historical conclusions were modified since Blegen believed that a dramatic and complete cultural break could be seen at the end of the EH III period (Blegen 1928, 221), whereas Caskey—through his excavations at Lerna in Argolis and Eutresis in Boeotia—reached the conclusion that a notable break in southern Greece occurred between EH II and EH III, while a second break took place in central Greece at the end of EH III (Caskey 1960, 299–302; 1973, 136; 1986, 25).

The "cultural break" at the end of EH II and/or EH III has been used to bring one group of foreigners or another to Greece, either through an invasionistic/migrational model or a diffusionistic model (e.g., Blegen 1928; Caskey 1960; Wiencke 1989; Rutter 1995; Maran 1998). However, the historical outline sketched by Caskey, with a pattern of destructions throughout the Peloponnese at the end of EH II, has been shown to be untenable. The traits that he associated with a "foreign invasion" (e.g., apsidal houses, tumuli, and "terracotta anchors") appeared on the mainland at different times during the EH II–MH periods and originated in many different areas (Forsén 1992). Other explanations for the "cultural break" proposed now and then include, for example, climatic changes (Manning 1997) and land degradation (Whitelaw 2000).

However, that the changes seen in the cultural assemblages of EH III date (also called the "Tiryns culture") were due to a local evolution was suggested by Renfrew (1972), French (1973), and Walter and Felten (1981), although they all lacked the means to prove it. A thorough reappraisal of the ceramic changes at the EH II/III boundary at Lerna and Kolonna on Aigina now explain these as a "long-term process within a well-established local population" (Shriner, Murray, Christidis and Brophy in prep.). Behind this process are several decisive elements that ultimately lead to a demand for more robust coarse ware. Such a production began in southern Greece in later EH II and was created by fusing different technological pottery traditions from "central places" (e.g., Lerna, Kolonna) with those from their respective "hinterland" (Shriner, Murray, Christidis and Brophy in prep.). Could these regional sites with more traditional technologies explain the reintroduction of controlled reduction firing during late EH II–III? It should not be doubted that sophisticated technological manufacturing techniques existed at this time, thereby denoting anything *but* a decreased complexity (Spencer in press).

Thrace, Macedonia, and Thessaly

A survey of the principal EBA sites in mainland Greece begins in the northeast with Thrace, Macedonia, and Thessaly, which is an area dominated by large broad plains with conspicuous mounds (magoules) spread out in the landscape.

From the onset of the EBA, the pottery in these regions changed. Whereas it had been diverse, implying many local schools, now coarse ware, principally storage vessels, became the focus of production. This could indicate that a larger degree of self-sufficiency within the agricultural sphere had taken place, but it might also imply the existence of a surplus of agricultural products that could be exchanged for exotica such as gold and tin (cf. Maran 1998, 2007).

Surprisingly little archaeological work has been undertaken in Thrace, considering its setting at the crossroads between northwestern Asia Minor, the Aegean, and the Balkans. The picture of the EBA in Macedonia is clearer, thanks to the seminal work by Heurtley (1939), who laid out a basis for a ceramic cultural sequence. The stratigraphical sequence in combination with radiocarbon dates from several Macedonian sites has recently (Andreou, Fotiadis, and Kotsakis 1996, 586) enabled the identification of an early EBA phase (Dikili Tash IIIA and Sitagroi IV–Va = EH I and early EH II in the southern mainland) and a later EBA phase (Dikili Tash IIIB and Sitagroi Vb = late EH II and EH III in the south).

Dikili Tash, near Philippi, has been excavated intermittently since 1961 (Séfériadès 1983). Circuit walls of EBA date were probably built in order to protect the site from the surrounding marshes (Péristéri and Treuil 1988; Darcque, Touchais, and Treuil 1992). Pottery from the early EBA phase reflects connections to both Troy I and Eutresis in Boeotia (e.g., black polished bowls with tubular lug handles) (Caskey and Caskey 1960, 134–35), while small cups with high, vertical loop handles show influences from the north. Pottery from the later EBA phase retains influences from the north (e.g., bowls with incised lip), while so-called Corded ware has a wider distribution and connects this area with northwestern and central Greece (cf. Christmann 1996, 159–61). The square-spouted jug (Malamidou 1997, 339, figure 12) is more at home in southern Greece than in the north but is an important chronological link between the two regions.

In the Drama plain, Sitagroi magoula was excavated in 1968–1969 (Renfrew, Gimbutas, and Elster 1986; Elster and Renfrew 2003). The main trench on top of the magoula revealed two successive apsidal houses, the "Burnt House" and the "Long House" of early EBA date. These remains were accompanied not only by hearths and storage bins but also by vessels, shaft-hole axes, querns, and spindle-whorls, all artifacts reflecting a farming community. The material culture from Sitagroi can be correlated with both Troy and the important Thessalian site of Argissa. This ties Sitagroi into the Anatolian, as well as the Aegean, sphere, although it remains in the marginal zone. Results of the botanical study indicate a groundwater rise during a phase equivalent to late EH I in the south, recently corroborated by similar results at Chalkis in the Corinthian Gulf (see later discussion).

In Chalkidiki on the eastern side of the Sithonia peninsula, excavations during the late 1990s revealed a large necropolis in a tumulus at Kriaritsi (Asouchidou 2001). The pottery can be correlated with Troy and Thessaly, as well as with southern Greece (e.g., the type 6 jar at Lerna) (cf. Wiencke 2000, 561). The remarkable resemblance in both layout and content between this necropolis and the R-tombs at Steno on Lefkas on the other side of the Greek mainland is noteworthy.

In mountainous western Macedonia, substantial EBA remains, including houses, have been found at Servia (Ridley and Wardle 1979; Ridley, Wardle, and Mould 2000). The pottery reflects the important setting of Servia—at the crossroads and well-trodden passage—to Thessaly in the south and Epirus in the west. Moreover, EH II–III pottery (Light-painted, fine-polished sauceboats and degenerated, Dark-painted ware) correlates Servia with the southern mainland.

Thessaly belongs to a more arid climate zone than that of Macedonia and Thrace. The EBA sites exhibit a different "outlook" in that they are less influenced by northern cultures and more by the southern mainland. Excavations at Argissa magoula in the 1950s revealed—apart from several architectural phases—three main pottery phases, which can be correlated with late EH I–III in the south through similarities in the repertoire of shapes and surface finish and through actual imports (e.g., of Dark-painted pottery [Hanschmann and Milojĉić 1976, 78–80, 185–93, Taf. XI, Beilage 12, 32]).

Pevkakia magoula, on a rocky promontory on the Thessalian coast, shows clear influences from west Anatolia in the appearance at the end of EH II of the "Lefkandi I pottery assemblage" (first identified at Lefkandi on Euboea; see French 1972), accompanied by a change in architecture from an apsidal building to a rectangular megaron. A defensive circuit wall of early EH II date was also exposed (Christmann 1996, 321–25). In the region of Phthiotis in southeastern Thessaly, the evidence for EBA remains is scarce, although a rescue excavation at Rachi Panagias in 1994 exposed two phases of EH I, including bowls with incised lips, one-handled cups, and "Bratislava lids" (Zachou 2004a, 738).

EPIRUS AND LEFKAS

The EBA pottery of Epirus in northwestern Greece reflects northern rather than southern influences, although contacts with the south exist. At Doliana, a site near the source of the river Kalamas, a most interesting pottery assemblage has been found (Dousougli and Zachos 2002). Its importance lies in the fact that the pottery shapes and surface finish (e.g., large storage jars with taenia bands, slipped and polished bowls with incised lips) recall pottery found at most EH I–II sites in the south. The Bratislava lid (figure 4.1) makes Doliana part of a very wide distribution network that includes not only Moravia, Albania, Bulgaria, Macedonia, and Thessaly to the north and east (Maran 1998, 509–17) but also Attica in the south (see later discussion).

The R-necropolis at Steno on Lefkas was excavated by Dörpfeld from 1903 to 1913. The extraordinary finds from the twenty-four tumuli have recently been republished (Kilian-Dirlmeier 2005). The tomb architecture and small finds correspond to burial customs and artifacts found stretching from Lefkas to Kriaritsi in Chalkidiki, Aphidna in Attica, and Olympia in Elis. Lefkas was probably an emporio similar to Aigina, through which goods from Dalmatia and farther north on the Balkan were transmitted to the Peloponnese and Attica in the south (Kilian-Dirlmeier 2005, 155–64).

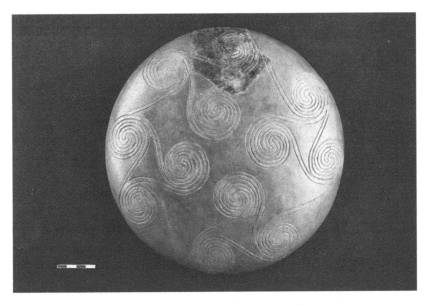

Figure 4.1. A Bratislava lid (restored) from Doliana in Epirus
(courtesy of Angelika Dousougli and Kostas Zachos).

Locris, Phocis, Boeotia,
and Aitolia-Akarnania

Central Greece is characterized by small valleys usually well watered and fertile but
compartmentalized by many mountains. Along the Locrian coast, EH sites abound,
while less than three kilometers from the coast a complex pottery production area
of EH I and early EH II date was recently found at Proskynas. The layout of this
"workshop," including kilns of different size (Zachou 2004b, 1267–76), implies
ceramic craft specialization at a surprisingly early date.

Few EH sites have been excavated in Phocis, although one notable exception is the
large mound of Kirrha next to the Corinthian Gulf (Dor, Jannoray, van Effenterre, and
van Effenterre 1960). However, Boeotia has several important EH sites, such as Lithares, a
vast EH I and early EH II village that includes streets and blocks of houses (Tzavella-Evjen
1985). Lefkandi I pottery is documented at Orchomenos, Eutresis, and Thebes (Forsén
1992). Recently another tumulus of late EH II date was found at Thebes (Aravantinos
2004, 1255–59), which can be correlated both in date and possibly function to tumuli with
similar features previously known at Olympia in Elis and Lerna in Argolis.

In Aitolia on the northern shore of the Corinthian Gulf, excavations at Chalkis
have documented pottery from two subphases of EH I, which can be correlated
with assemblages both in central Greece (Eutresis) and southern Greece (Talioti).
The late EH I phase is accompanied by an environmental change in the form of a
rising sea level (Dietz and Moschos 2006).

ATTICA AND AIGINA

All along the Attic coast, EH sites are to be found either on the coast (e.g., Agios Kosmas) or a little inland, typically on low hills (e.g., Pani and Kontopigado in Alimos) (Kaza-Papageorgiou 2006). The proximity to the Cyclades is felt at most Attic sites usually in the form of pottery (e.g., the Kampos group of EC I/EH I date and the Kastri/Lefkandi I repertoire of late EH II date) or through large quantities of obsidian brought from Melos.

At Tsepi, near Marathon, Kampos group pottery in the cemetery dates the site to EH I, whereas the appearance of Bratislava lids among the grave goods, which include frying-pans (Pantelidou-Gofa 2005), adds Tsepi to the very extensive network of sites mentioned in connection to Doliana in Epirus (thereby stretching from the Carpathian basin to the south Aegean). Moreover, the relationship between the frying-pans and the Bratislava lids needs a careful study (Coleman, forthcoming, suggests that the lids may indicate the beginning of EH I on the mainland).

The cemetery at Agios Kosmas may include a few graves of Cycladic individuals, although the material culture mostly reflects mainland influences, including northern Greece, besides some Kastri/Lefkandi I pottery of west Anatolian inspiration (Mylonas 1959; French 1968, 64–65). A similar case can be made for the burial tumulus near Aphidna, where an amalgam of Anatolian, Cycladic, and mainland influences is evident among the grave goods and in the construction of the tumulus itself, which resembles the ones at Olympia and Lerna in particular. Especially intriguing is the possible link between Aphidna and tomb R-24 at Steno on Lefkas through their identical arrangement of gold rings (Forsén in press).

A large, prehistoric settlement at Kolonna on Aigina has come to light through excavations in the 1970s (Walter and Felten 1981) and from 1993 to 2002 (Felten and Hiller 2004). The importance of the site should not be underestimated as it must have functioned as a hub through which products and influences circulated at a steady pace during the EH II–III periods (EH I is less known). This fortified settlement exhibits similarities in architecture and layout with various areas (e.g., Poliochni on Lemnos, Lithares in Boeotia, and Lerna in Argolis). While the pottery exhibits the usual EH II koiné, it also includes Lefkandi I elements (Berger 2004) and hybrids spanning the crucial EH II–III boundary, allowing for an essentially local development of the pottery (Walter and Felten 1981, 108–16).

CORINTHIA AND ARGOLIS

Corinthia and Argolis are united in the west by a common range of mountains that is divided into two main plains, the Corinthian and the Argive, with smaller upland valleys hidden behind isolated mountains. In Corinthia, the small EH site, Tsoungiza, has supplied data concerning the transition from EH I to early EH II in particular (Pullen, forthcoming), thereby supplementing those already known from the Kephalari Magoula near Argos (Dousougli 1987).

Still, both of these sites are said to represent late EH I, and the question as to whether there is a different material culture assemblage during an early EH I period remains open (see Coleman 2000). However, judging by the EH I pottery found at Asine in Argolis (Frödin and Persson 1938, 200–205), Eutresis in Boeotia (Caskey and Caskey 1960), and Perachora in Corinthia (Fossey 1969), early EH I is denoted by strata containing red-slipped (or unslipped) and polished or dark-burnished ware without traces of Dark-painted ware or other salient features of late EH I (the Talioti repertoire; see Weisshaar 1990) or EH II date.

One of the most famous sites in the region is Lerna, a low artificial mound on the western shore of the Bay of Argos, which was excavated in the 1950s. The site has become one of the key sites in southern Greece due to its well-published artifactual assemblages of EH II–EH III date. During EH II, Lerna was a fortified site dominated by large rectangular "corridor houses" (e.g., the House of the Tiles, which, once destroyed, was turned into a low tumulus). Ceramics were often thin-walled, high-fired, and light colored (Wiencke 2000 and this volume). The subsequent settlement of EH III date consisted of smaller apsidal houses without fortification, while the pottery was often thick-walled, porous, and low-fired (Rutter 1995). The contrast between the two settlement layers could not have been greater, and it is no wonder that Caskey (1971) concluded that an "invasion" or "influx" of new and different people had taken place.

On the eastern side of the Bay of Argos opposite Lerna, important EH II architecture is documented at Tiryns, for example, the Rundbau and apsidal houses of early EH II date (Kilian 1986, 65–71), the latter feature recently corroborated by similar finds at Epidauros (Theodorou-Mavrommatidi 2004, 1167–82). Much controversy over a slightly divergent pottery chronology as documented at Tiryns and Lerna has been solved by Maran (1998, 460), who inserted a "Wendezeit," thus allowing different sites to follow slightly different historical trajectories during this period of change.

ACHAEA AND ARCADIA

On a narrow strip of land along the southern coast of the Corinthian Gulf, remarkable EH remains are found at Helike in Achaea. This was a coastal site, a "central place" with a "corridor house" of EH II date, late EH II pottery of Lefkandi I type, and rectangular houses of EH III date (Katsonopoulou, forthcoming). A *depas amphikypellon* of Anatolian origin (figure 4.2) indicates that Helike was most likely part of an extensive exchange network during EH II–EH III between the Peloponnese and west Anatolia, which, according to Rahmstorf (2006), also encompassed the Near East.

In the upland valleys of Arcadia, data from Asea Paleokastro indicates that this seemingly remote site also took part in far-reaching exchange networks during the EH period, as evidenced by exotica such as non-local pottery, obsidian, and honey flint (Forsén 1996; 2003, 195). The existence of a land route across the Peloponnese,

Figure 4.2. The depas amphikypellon found at Helike in Achaea (courtesy of Dora Katsonopoulou).

along which goods originating, for instance, in Dalmatia reached the Bay of Argos (Rambach 2004, 1233–42), has been postulated in order to explain Asea's status as a "central place" during the later EH period.

ELIS AND MESSENIA

In the Altis at Olympia in Elis, important EH remains were excavated by Dörpfeld (1935) and Kyrieleis (1990) e.g., the Pelopeion, a large tumulus of late EH II date, and several apsidal houses of late EH III date. The fact that much non-local pottery of EH III date was found is seen as the result of Olympia's serving as a trading post, like Asea, along a land corridor across the Peloponnese (Rambach 2004, 2007).

Excavations at Akovitika in Messenia have revealed "corridor houses" similar to the ones at Lerna (Themelis 1984, 344–47). The pottery includes Attic and Lefkandi I type ceramics (Koumouzelis-Bouchard 1981), implying that Akovitika was part of the far-reaching exchange network postulated for the late EH II period.

LACONIA

Renewed research centered on Kouphovouno, a low hill just southwest of Sparta, including both survey and excavations, has revealed a high level of interconnectivity between sites of EH II date ranging in size from "central places" to single farmsteads.

Specialist potters supplied a network of smaller sites with their products, indicating some sort of commercial activity and/or shared cultural values (Mee 2009). At the fortified acropolis site at Geraki, southeast of Sparta, a thriving community existed during EH II (Crouwel, Prent, Thorne, and van der Vin 2000), whereas the EH III period until recently (Banou 1999) has been lacking in the archaeological record of Laconia.

Summary

It seems that extensive exchange networks existed from the onset of EH I, when the Bratislava lid spread over large areas of mainland Greece. Social hierarchies might be inferred from early EH II, when the earliest fortifications were built (e.g., at Pevkakia in Thessaly). A wider distribution occurs during the late EH II period, when, for example, Askitario and Plasi in Attica, Kolonna on Aigina, Lerna in Argolis, and Geraki in Laconia were fortified. This propensity to fortify in late EH II can possibly be connected to a rise in internal competition between different communities. It is not impossible that environmental changes (cf. Sitagroi and Chalkis) triggered this development.

The dramatic cultural break seen especially at Lerna between EH II and EH III was in the past interpreted as evidence of invaders at the site, who supposedly built the apsidal houses of Lerna IV. However, the appearance at several Argive sites of apsidal houses during early EH II could imply that people from these nearby sites (i.e., Tiryns or Epidauros) moved to Lerna after the most famous of "corridor houses", the House of the Tiles, burned down. That it was the local people who turned the debris of the house into a low tumulus (to commemorate it?) should not be doubted. The notion to build a tumulus might initially have emanated from actual visits to Thebes or Olympia.

In this chapter I have suggested that complex exchange networks and sophisticated technological manufacturing techniques, especially within pottery production, existed during late EH II–III. Thus, envisioning a decreased social complexity at the end of EH is not necessarily accurate. On the contrary, the demand for coarse ware, which increased during late EH II–III, implies a new form of complexity that we cannot yet decipher. It is bedeviling that functions that must have been self-evident to EH humans—for instance, sealings or potter's marks—are lost to us since they could feasibly be part of deciphering this complexity.

In any event, the spectacular jewelry hoard of late EH III date found at Kolonna on Aigina (Reinholdt 2004) indicates the existence of social elites with far-reaching trading contacts at this time. One hopes that more research and archaeological finds will bring solutions that will help to explain the cultural shift at the end of the EH period.

BIBLIOGRAPHY

Andreou, Stelios, Michael Fotiadis, and Kostas Kotsakis. 1996. "Review of Aegean Prehistory V: The Neolithic and Bronze Age of Northern Greece." *AJA* 100: 537–97.

Aravantinos, Vassilis. 2004. "New Evidence about the EH II Period in Thebes: A New Architectural Complex and a Group Burial within the Kadmeia." In *Die ägäische Frühzeit: Die Frühbronzezeit in Griechenland*, ed. Eva Alram-Stern, 1255–59. Vienna: Verlag der Österreichischen Akademie der Wissenschaften.

Asouchidou, Sofia. 2001. "Καύσεις της εποχής του χαλκού στη Μακεδονία." In Καύσεις στην Εποχή του Χαλκού και την Πρώιμη Εποχή του Σιδήρου, ed. Nicholas Chr. Stampolidis, 31–46. Athens: Πανεπιστήμιο Κρήτης.

Banou, Emilia. 1999. "New Evidence on Early Helladic Laconia." *BSA* 94: 63–79.

Berger, Lydia. 2004. "Neue Ergebnisse zur FH II-Keramik aus der prähistorischen Innenstadt." In *Die ägäische Frühzeit: Die Frühbronzezeit in Griechenland*, ed. Eva Alram-Stern, 1093–1103. Vienna: Verlag der Österreichischen Akademie der Wissenschaften.

Blegen, Carl W. 1921. *Korakou: A Prehistoric Settlement near Corinth*. Boston: American School of Classical Studies.

———. 1928. *Zygouries: A Prehistoric Settlement in the Valley of Cleonae*. Cambridge, Mass.: Harvard University Press.

Caskey, John L. 1960. "The Early Helladic Period in the Argolid." *Hesperia* 29: 285–303.

———. 1971. "Greece, Crete, and the Aegean Islands in the Early Bronze Age." In *The Cambridge Ancient History*, vol. 1, part 2, 3d ed., ed. I. E. S. Edwards, C. J. Gadd, and N. G. L. Hammond, 771–807. New York: Cambridge University Press.

———. 1973. "Greece and the Aegean Islands in the Middle Bronze Age." In *The Cambridge Ancient History*, vol. 2, part 1, 3d ed., ed. I. E. S. Edwards, C. J. Gadd, and N. G. L. Hammond, 117–40. New York: Cambridge University Press.

———. 1986. "Did the Early Bronze Age End?" In *The End of the Early Bronze Age in the Aegean*, ed. Gerald Cadogan, 9–30. Leiden: Brill.

———, and Elizabeth G. Caskey. 1960. "The Earliest Settlements at Eutresis: Supplementary Excavations, 1958." *Hesperia* 29: 126–67.

Christmann, Elmar. 1996. *Die deutschen Ausgrabungen auf der Pevkakia-Magula in Thessalien II: Die Frühe Bronzezeit*. Bonn: Dr. Rudolf Habelt.

Coleman, John E. 2000. "An Archaeological Scenario for the 'Coming of the Greeks' ca. 3200 B.C." *JIES* 28: 101–53.

———. Forthcoming. "The Petromagoula-Doliana Group and the Beginning of the Aegean Early Bronze Age." In *Helike IV: The Early Helladic Peloponnesos: Proceedings of the Fourth International Conference*, ed. Dora Katsonopoulou. Athens: Helike Society.

Crouwel, Joost H., Mieke Prent, Stuart MacVeigh Thorne, and Jos van der Vin. 2000. "Geraki: An Acropolis Site in Laconia: Preliminary Report on the Sixth Season (2000)." *Pharos* 8: 41–76.

Darcque, Pascal, Giles Touchais, and René Treuil. 1992. "Dikili Tash." *BCH* 116: 715–19.

Dietz, Søren, and Ioannis Moschos, eds. 2006. *Chalkis Aitolias I: The Prehistoric Periods*. Monographs of the Danish Institute at Athens, vol. 7. Århus, Denmark: Århus University Press.

Dor, Léopold, Jean Jannoray, Henri van Effenterre, and Micheline van Effenterre. 1960. *Kirrha: Étude de préhistoire phocidienne*. Paris: E. de Boccard.

Dörpfeld, Wilhelm. 1935. *Alt-Olympia: Untersuchungen und Ausgrabungen zur Geschichte des ältesten Heiligtums von Olympia und der älteren griechischen Kunst*. Berlin: E. S. Mittler und Sohn.

Dousougli, Angelika. 1987. "Makrovouni-Kefalari Magoula-Talioti: Bemerkungen zu den Stufen EH I und II in der Argolis." *PZ* 62: 164–220.

———, and Konstantinos Zachos. 2002. "L'archéologie des zones montagneuses: Modèles et interconnexions dans le Néolithique de l'Épire et de l'Albanie méridionale." In *L'Albanie dans l'Europe préhistorique*, ed. Gilles Touchais and Josette Renard, 111–43. BCH Supplementaire 42. Athens: École française d'Athènes.

Elster, Ernestine S., and Colin Renfrew. 2003. *Prehistoric Sitagroi: Excavations in Northeast Greece, 1968–1970*. Vol. 2, *The Final Report*. Monumenta Archaeologica 20. Los Angeles: Cotsen Institute of Archaeology, University of California.

Felten, Florens, and Stefan Hiller. 2004. "Forschungen zur Frühbronzezeit auf Ägina-Kolonna 1993–2002." In *Die ägäische Frühzeit: Die Frühbronzezeit in Griechenland*, ed. Eva Alram-Stern, 1089–92. Vienna: Verlag der Österreichischen Akademie der Wissenschaften.

Forsén, Jeannette. 1992. *The Twilight of the Early Helladics: A Study of the Disturbances in East-central and Southern Greece towards the End of the Early Bronze Age*. SIMA-PB 116. Partille, Sweden: Åström.

———. 1996. "Prehistoric Asea Revisited." *OpAth* 21: 41–72.

———. 2003. "The Early and Middle Bronze Age." In *The Asea Valley Survey: An Arcadian Mountain Valley from the Palaeolithic Period until Modern Times*, Jeannette Forsén and Björn Forsén, 192–96. Acta Instituti Atheniensis Regni Sueciae 4°, 51. Sävedalen, Sweden: Åström.

———. In press. "Aphidna in Attika Revisited." In *Mesohelladika*.

Fossey, John M. 1969. "The Prehistoric Settlement by Lake Vouliagmeni, Perachora." *BSA* 64: 53–69.

French, David H. 1968. "Anatolia and the Aegean in the Third Millennium B.C." Ph.D. diss., Cambridge University.

———. 1972. "The Pottery." In *Excavations at Lefkandi, Euboea 1964–66*, ed. Mervyn R. Popham and L. Hugh Sackett, 7–8. London: British School of Archaeology at Athens.

———. 1973. "Migrations and 'Minyan' Pottery in Western Anatolia and the Aegean." In *Bronze Age Migrations in the Aegean*, ed. R. A. Crossland and Ann Birchall, 51–57. London: Duckworth.

Frödin, Otto, and Axel W. Persson. 1938. *Asine: Results of the Swedish Excavations 1922–1930*. Stockholm: Generalstabens litografiska anstalts förlag.

Goldman, Hetty. 1931. *Excavations at Eutresis in Boeotia*. Cambridge, Mass.: Harvard University Press.

Hanschmann, Eva, and Vladimir Milojčić. 1976. *Die deutschen Ausgrabungen auf der Argissa-Magula in Thessalien III: Die frühe und beginnende mittlere Bronzezeit I–II*. Bonn: Rudolf Habelt.

Heurtley, Walter A. 1939. *Prehistoric Macedonia*. Cambridge: Cambridge University Press.

Katsonopoulou, Dora. Forthcoming. "The Early Helladic Settlement at Helike: An Early Bronze Age Center in Achaea." In *Helike IV: The Early Helladic Peloponnesos: Proceedings of the Fourth International Conference*, ed. Dora Katsonopoulou. Athens: Helike Society.

Kaza-Papageorgiou, Konstantina. 2006. "Euonimon and Alimos" In *Alimos: A Greek-English Edition of the City's History*, ed. Dimitris Lucas, 16–151. Athens: Alexandros Publications.

Kilian, Klaus. 1986. "The Circular Building at Tiryns." In *Early Helladic Architecture*, 65–71.

Kilian-Dirlmeier, Imma. 2005. *Die bronzezeitlichen Gräber bei Nidri auf Leukas: Ausgrabungen von W. Dörpfeld 1903–1913*. Römisch-Germanisches Zentralmuseum Monographien Bd. 62. Mainz: Verlag des Römisch-Germanisches Zentralmuseum.

Komouzelis-Bouchard, Margarita. 1981. "The EH II Site of Akovitika in Messenia (Abstract)." *AJA* 85: 202–203.

Kyrieleis, Helmut. 1990. "Neue Ausgrabungen in Olympia." *Antike Welt* 21: 177–88.

Malamidou, Dimitra. 1997. "Eastern Macedonia during the Early Bronze Age." In *Poliochni*, 329–43.

Manning, Sturt W. 1995. *The Absolute Chronology of the Aegean Early Bronze Age: Archaeology, Radiocarbon, and History.* Monographs in Mediterranean Archaeology 1. Sheffield: Sheffield Academic Press.

———. 1997. "Cultural Change in the Aegean c. 2200 BC." In *Third Millennium BC Climate Change and Old World Collapse*, ed. H. Nüzhet Dalfes, George Kukla, and Harvey Weiss, 149–71. Berlin: Springer.

Maran, Joseph. 1998. *Kulturwandel auf dem griechischen Festland und den Kykladen im späten 3. Jahrtausend v. Chr.: Studien zu den kulturellen Verhältnissen in Südosteuropa und dem zentralen sowie östlichen Mittelmeerraum in der späten Kupfer- und frühen Bronzezeit.* Universitätsforschungen zur prähistorischen Archäologie 53. Bonn: Dr. Rudolf Habelt.

———. 2007. "Seaborne Contacts between the Aegean, the Balkans, and the Central Mediterranean in the 3rd Millennium BC: The Unfolding of the Mediterranean World." In *BABS*, 3–23.

Mee, Christopher. 2009. "Interconnectivity in Early Helladic Laconia." In *Sparta and Laconia from Prehistory to Pre-modern*, ed. William G. Cavanagh, Chrysanthi Gallou, and Mercourios Georgiadis, 43–53. London: British School at Athens.

Mylonas, George E. 1959. *Aghios Kosmas: An Early Bronze Age Settlement and Cemetery in Attica.* Princeton: Princeton University Press.

Pantelidou-Gofa, Maria. 2005. Τσέπι Μαραθώνος. Το προτοελλαδικό νεκροταφείο. (Βιβλιοθήκη της εν Αθήναις Αρχαιολογικής Εταιρείας, 235). Athens: Η έν Αθήναις Αρχαιολογική Εταιρεία.

Péristéri, Katérina, and René Treuil. 1988. "Dikili Tash." *BCH* 112: 727–31.

Pullen, Daniel J. Forthcoming. *The Early Bronze Age Village on Tsoungiza Hill.* Nemea Valley Archaeological Project. Vol. 1. Princeton: American School of Classical Studies at Athens.

Rahmstorf, Lorenz. 2006. "Zur Ausbreitung vorderasiatischer Innovationen in die früh-bronzezeitliche Ägäis." *PZ* 81: 49–96.

Rambach, Jörg. 2004. "Olympia im ausgehenden 3. Jahrtausend v. Chr.: Bindeglied zwischen zentralem und östlichem Mittelmeerraum." In *Die ägäische Frühzeit: Die Frühbronzezeit in Griechenland*, ed. Eva Alram-Stern, 1199–1254. Vienna: Verlag der Österreichischen Akademie der Wissenschaften.

———. 2007. "Olympia and Andravida-Lechaina: Two Bronze Age Sites in the Northwest Peloponnese with Far-reaching Overseas Cultural Connections." In *BABS*, 81–90.

Reinholdt, Claus. 2004. "Der frühbronzezeitliche Schmuck-Hortfund von Kap Kolonna/Ägina." In *Die ägäische Frühzeit: Die Frühbronzezeit in Griechenland*, ed. Eva Alram-Stern, 1113–19. Vienna: Verlag der Österreichischen Akademie der Wissenschaften.

Renfrew, Colin. 1972. *The Emergence of Civilisation: The Cyclades and the Aegean in the Third Millennium B.C.* London: Methuen.

———, Maria Gimbutas, and Ernestine Elster, eds. 1986. *Excavations at Sitagroi: A Prehistoric Village in Northeast Greece*, vol. 1. Monumenta Archaeologica 13. Los Angeles: Institute of Archaeology, University of California.

Ridley, Cressida, and Kenneth A. Wardle. 1979. "Rescue Excavations at Servia 1971–1973: A Preliminary Report." *BSA* 74: 185–230.

————, and Catharine A. Mould. 2000. *Servia I: Anglo-Hellenic Rescue Excavations 1971–1973 Directed by Katerina Rhomiopoulou and Cressida Ridley.* BSA Supplementary volume 32. London: British School at Athens.

Rutter, Jeremy B. 1995. *Lerna: A Preclassical Site in the Argolid.* Vol. 3, *The Pottery of Lerna IV.* Princeton: American School of Classical Studies at Athens.

Séfériadès, Michel. 1983. "Dikili Tash: Introduction à la préhistoire de la Macédoine orientale." *BCH* 107: 635–77.

Shriner, Christine, Haydn H. Murray, George E. Christidis, and James G. Brophy. In prep. "A Method of Explanation for the Nature of Cultural Change. Archaeological and Theoretical Implications."

Spencer, Lydia. In press. "The Regional Specialisation of Ceramic Production in the EH III through MH II Period." In *Mesohelladika.*

Themelis, Petros, G. 1984. "Early Helladic Monumental Architecture." *AM* 99: 335–51.

Theodorou-Mavrommatidi, Anthi. 2004. "An Early Helladic Settlement in the Apollon Maleatas Site at Epidauros." In *Die ägäische Frühzeit: Die Frühbronzezeit in Griechenland*, ed. Eva Alram-Stern, 1167–88. Vienna: Verlag der Österreichischen Akademie der Wissenschaften.

Tzavella-Evjen, Hara. 1985. *Lithares: An Early Bronze Age Settlement in Boeotia.* Institute of Archaeology, University of California. Occasional Paper 15. Los Angeles: UCLA Institute of Archaeology Publications.

Walter, Hans, and Florens Felten. 1981. *Alt-Ägina* III, 1. *Die vorgeschichtliche Stadt: Befestigungen, Häuser, Funde.* Mainz am Rhein: Philipp von Zabern.

Weisshaar, Hans-Joachim. 1990. "Die Keramik von Talioti." In *Tiryns, Forschungen und Berichte*, Band XI, 1–34. Mainz am Rhein: Philipp von Zabern.

Wiencke, Martha H. 1989. "Change in Early Helladic II." *AJA* 93: 495–509.

————. 2000. *Lerna: A Preclassical Site in the Argolid.* Vol. 4, *The Architecture, Stratification, and Pottery of Lerna III.* Princeton: American School of Classical Studies at Athens.

Whitelaw, Todd. 2000. "Settlement Instability and Landscape Degradation in the Southern Aegean in the Third Millennium BC." In *Landscape and Land Use in Postglacial Greece*, ed. Paul Halstead and Charles Frederick, 135–61. Sheffield Studies in Aegean Archaeology 3. Sheffield: Academic Press.

Zachou, Eleni. 2004a. "Rachi Panagias." In *Die ägäische Frühzeit: Die Frühbronzezeit in Griechenland*, ed. Eva Alram-Stern, 738. Vienna: Verlag der Österreichischen Akademie der Wissenschaften.

————. 2004b. "Die frühbronzezeitliche Siedlung in Proskynas/Lokris." In *Die ägäische Frühzeit: Die Frühbronzezeit in Griechenland*, ed. Eva Alram-Stern, 1267–83. Vienna: Verlag der Österreichischen Akademie der Wissenschaften.

CHAPTER 5

CRETE

PETER TOMKINS
ILSE SCHOEP

TRADITIONALLY, the story of the Cretan Early Bronze Age (hereafter Early Minoan) has been one constructed between two pivotal points of change. The first, at the Neolithic–EM I transition, is viewed as the birth of a culture considered to be definably Minoan (Betancourt 1999), fostered by a major impulse from the east, conventionally modeled as a migration (Evans 1928, 1–24; Warren 1973, 42–43; Hood 1990, 371–75; Nowicki 2002, 66–69). The second, at the transition to the Middle Bronze Age (MM IB), is seen as the emergence of Europe's first civilization—a redistributive theocracy of kings or princes, cities and palaces, art and writing—which in subsequent millennia spread to the rest of Europe, famously 'irradiating European "barbarism"' (Evans 1921, 26; Childe 1958, 70; Renfrew 1972, 51).

In the later language of neoevolutionism, the emergence of the palaces in MM IB marked the transition from an egalitarian to a more complex, statelike society with a clear hierarchical structure crowned by a central, administrative elite authority that resided in the palaces (Cherry 1986, 27). The long 'prepalatial' period that lay between these two traditional pivotal points tended to be defined in terms similar to those of the Neolithic and in opposition to the succeeding 'protopalatial' period (e.g., Cherry 1983, 33; 1986; Tomkins 2004, 39–40, table 3.1). Debate was at its sharpest over the pace of EM development, with many favoring a gradualist model of slow, incremental change with a notable increase in complexity from EM II (Renfrew 1972; Whitelaw 1983; Warren 1987; Branigan 1988; Soles 1988) and others a long, relatively static period followed by a rapid explosion of complexity around MM IB (Cherry 1983; 1984; Watrous 1987; 2001, 174–79).

RECENT PERSPECTIVES

The last two decades have seen dramatic advances in our understanding of the Early Minoan period. There has been not only a significant increase in the quantity and quality of data but also a broadening of the theoretical and analytical range and a more critical evaluation of Minoan archaeology's intellectual inheritance (for overviews see Manning 1994; Haggis 1999; Watrous 2001; Wilson 2008). The chronological framework first established by Arthur Evans has been given important new rigor and resolution thanks to a series of detailed stratigraphic and ceramic studies at Knossos, Phaistos, and other sites mainly in the center and east of the island (Wilson and Day 1994; 2000; Wilson 2007; Todaro 2005; Tomkins 2007b; Momigliano 2007; Papadatos, Tomkins, Nodarou, and Iliopoulos in press). Not only have there been new refinements such as early and late phases of EM I and EM IIA and a revised FN chronology, but much of the previous confusion about the phasing, labeling, and relationship of regional sequences, especially at the transition to and from the Early Bronze Age, has also been laid to rest.

As EM has come into clearer focus, the two traditional horizons of change have been pulled apart. The notion that EM I marks a sudden, new cultural beginning, in which Crete emerges from millennia of isolation under the stimulus of a wave of external migration, is gradually giving way to a more nuanced understanding of cultural development and change. Studies of ceramic and lithic material from Knossos now suggest that Neolithic Crete was always connected in some way to the rest of the Aegean but in ways that changed over time (Tomkins 2007b, 21–44; Conolly 2008). Moreover by the end of FN (FN IV; c.3300–3100/3000 BC; Tomkins 2007b), certain coastal sites already appear to have enjoyed preferential access to high-value materials and technologies (e.g., obsidian, metal) over inland sites in their vicinity in a manner reminiscent of later EM 'gateway communities' (Papadatos 2007, 2008; Tomkins 2008, 40; this volume; Papadatos, Tomkins, Nodarou, and Iliopoulos in press).

Likewise, marginal colonization of less productive or extensive areas of arable land, such as upland basins or islands, a process once considered to originate in EM I (e.g., Watrous 2001, 163, 168), actually begins as early as FN IV in some areas (e.g., Siteia uplands) (Tomkins 2008, 38–40). The beginning of EM I is thus emerging as a prominent point within a longer period of socioeconomic reconfiguration, a point privileged in traditional cultural histories mainly because of the appearance of painted ceramic wares. Explanations of change during this period now also need to take account of clear signs of residential, cultural, and technological continuity across the FN IV–EM I transition not just at large inland sites such as Knossos and Phaistos but also at those coastal sites, such as Petras Kephala, that appear to have been the main mediators of cultural interaction with the rest of the Aegean (Todaro 2005; Tomkins 2007b, 44; in press b; Todaro and Di Tonto 2008; Papadatos, Tomkins, Nodarou, and Iliopoulos in press).

In much the same way, many of the cultural features traditionally associated with an MM IB horizon have been realigned, stretching the timetable of 'emergence' to more than a millennium. Certain aspects of the traditional palatial model, such as permanent forms of social inequality, long-distance trade, specialized craft production, urbanism, settlement hierarchy, and central places, can now be identified in the Early Minoan period, well before MM IB (Wilson and Day 1994; Whitelaw et al. 1997; Day, Wilson, and Kiriatzi 1997; Knappett 1999; Schoep and Knappett 2004; Schoep 2006). In addition, our understanding of Minoan social complexity, which for so long was focused on a contentious search for steep social hierarchies and single elite authorities (Watrous 2001, 174–75), has been usefully broadened to include situations of weak hierarchy, where multiple groups compete for power (Haggis 1999; Schoep 2002; in press a).

The more we learn about the prehistoric past, the more arbitrary become the divisions between the blocks of time into which it is conventionally divided. In both of the preceding cases, an overestimation of later complexity, combined with difficulties in understanding what came before, led change to be simplified into origin points and dramatized into revolutions, a tendency by no means peculiar to Minoan archaeology (see Gamble 2007 for a recent critique). Clearly the burgeoning EM dataset demands a more inclusive and subtle interpretative framework, one that allows change to be assessed along a continuum stretching from the Neolithic to the Middle Bronze Age and recognizes that continuity and change are best understood, from the bottom up, as flowing from the actions of people operating under specific conditions of existence (Day, Wilson, and Kiriatzi 1997; Barrett and Damilati 2004; Tomkins 2004, 39–41).

One way of doing this is to focus on lower-level analytical categories of practice, context, and agency, such as production, burial, and the household, and to see how these change in articulation, context, scale, and meaning over time. From 'art' and writing to urbanism and monumental ceremonial centers, all that has been traditionally understood to characterize 'civilization' (Childe 1950; Renfrew 1972, 7, 13) may be understood to derive from the emergence and subsequent development of elite households, elite material culture, and the political cultures of production and consumption that sustained them (Baines and Yoffee 2000; Van Buren and Richards 2000; Wright 2004).

Production

During the Cretan later Neolithic, production appears to have been one area where households could compete for status by manipulating the quantity and quality of their productive output, albeit one regulated and restricted at a communal level (Tomkins 2004, 50–57; this volume; Isaakidou 2008, 108–13). During LN and FN, the technology and organization of local ceramic production at Knossos shows no sign of change and would be consistent with some form of low-level household specialization oriented towards the needs of the local community. This picture of communally regulated productive stability first seems to be challenged from FN IV with the colonization of agriculturally more marginal areas of the Cretan landscape by a wave of farmers, perhaps forced out of older, more productive locations by the newly unfettered, acquisitive strategies of successful households (Halstead 2008, 244–47; Tomkins 2008, 38–42; this volume).

From the beginning of EM I, there are signs of a shift in ceramic production, characterized by the development of a new and distinctive range of burnished, slipped, and painted ware types, by marked regionality in material expression, by increasingly elaborate *chaînes opératoires,* and by rising productive intensity and output. This may mark the emergence of independent, regionally located, full-time specialists who were producing a range of distinctive products for a large, mainly local, external market (Wilson and Day 1994, 2000; Day, Wilson, and Kiriatzi 1997; Whitelaw et al. 1997). As in the Neolithic, access to the products of more distant Cretan producers provided opportunities for the marking of social differences through consumption (Whitelaw et al. 1997, 269; Wilson and Day 1994, 85; Tomkins 2004, 2007a).

In contrast to the spatial ubiquity of agricultural and ceramic production, the distribution of other, newer technologies producing high-value or 'prestige' products in stone or metal appears to be restricted to specific, prominent sites. Although earlier stone vessels are known, the first substantial indigenous stone vase industry on Crete dates from EM IIA (e.g., Mochlos; Bevan 2004, 112). Recent excavations at Petras Kephala have produced evidence for copper smelting and the use of copper punches in obsidian blade production from FN IV (Papadatos 2007, 2008; D'Annibale 2008), while from the beginning of EM I the biconical form, fenestrated pedestals, and decorative 'rivets' of ceramic chalices attest indirectly to the existence of sheet-metal containers. Two crucibles from the late EM I cemetery at Ayia Photia were probably used for the production of copper objects (Betancourt and Muhly 2007). Metallurgical debris in EM I–II levels at Poros indicates the deliberate production of arsenical copper alloys and the casting of mid-rib and long daggers (Doonan, Day, and Dimopoulou-Rethemniotaki 2007).

Although the evidence for copper production activity in the EBA Aegean is characterized by notable temporal and spatial variation (Catapotis 2007), the establishment by EM III of a specialized smelting site at Chrysokamino may mark an intensification in Cretan metallurgical production and perhaps a desire to regulate and control specific stages of the production process through spatial segregation (Betancourt 2006; Muhly 2002; cf. Nakou 1995; Broodbank 2000, 294–96). Such discoveries continue to affirm the connection between metallurgy, the production of prestige goods, and the marking of social difference (Renfrew 1972; Nakou 1995) but push its origins back into the last few centuries of FN. Intensification of metal production, the so-called *metallschok* of the EB II period, may now be pushed back into the late EM I (Doonan, Day, and Dimopoulou-Rethemniotaki 2007), while periods where metal objects are rarer, such as EM III, may more plausibly reflect differences in depositional practice than fluctuations in the supply of metal or metal objects (Nakou 1995 2007).

Exchange

For the later Neolithic stylistic and petrographic analyses suggest a low-volume circulation of ceramic vessels, compatible with gift exchange, over short and long distances between different communities within and occasionally beyond the island (Tomkins and Day 2001; Tomkins, Day, and Kilikoglou 2004; Tomkins 2004, 48; 2007b; 2008, 41). By FN IV, it would appear that certain coastal sites such as Nerokourou and Petras Kephala enjoyed a more intimate and intense relationship with the Aegean, specifically the Attic-Kephala region, in which the low-volume procurement and technological transformation of rare materials such as obsidian and metal, as well as control over their subsequent distribution within Crete, played a defining role (Vagnetti 1996; Carter 1998; Papadatos 2007; 2008; Tomkins 2008, 40; this volume; Papadatos, Tomkins, Nodarou, and Iliopoulos in press).

During EM, trading sites that focused on the procurement and working of greater volumes of obsidian, metal, and stone have been identified at Poros, Mochlos, and other locations along the north coast of Crete (Warren 1965, 28–36; Branigan 1991; Dimopoulou-Rethemiotaki, Wilson, and Day 2007). Late in EM I and into EM IIA, off-island relationships further intensify, as indicated by an increase in Cycladic imports (Kampos and Keros-Syros Groups) and raw materials (e.g., obsidian, copper, lead, silver), the local production of material culture in Cycladic styles or technologies, and a possible relocation of Cycladic groups to sites such as Ayia Photia or Poros, along the north coast of Crete (Renfrew 1964; Warren 1984; Karantzali 1996; Day, Wilson and Kiriatzi 1998; Papadatos 2005; Dimopoulou-Rethemiotaki Wilson, and Peter M. Day 2007).

From EM IIB, there are signs of a shift in the nature and directionality of external relations. At EM IIB Poros and Knossos, imports from the Cyclades entirely disappear while those from the east of the island increase (Wilson 1994, 41–44; Dimopoulou-Rethemiotaki, Wilson, and Day 2007, 87, 93). Cycladic imports are rare in EM III and increase only in MM I (Momigliano and Wilson 1996, 55). Nevertheless, the continued presence of Cycladic raw materials (e.g., obsidian, copper) in EM IIB Cretan contexts and Cretan exports in EC IIB (Kastri Group; e.g., Akrotiri; Day pers. comm.) suggests that this was not an absence of contact but a shift in the nature of Cretan-Cycladic trading activity.

During EM II–III, the presence of Egyptian and Syrian imports and local Cretan imitations indicate contact with East Mediterranean sites, probably to be connected with the adoption of the masted sailing ship, representations of which appear on Cretan seals from EM III (Evans 1925; Broodbank 2000, 341–49; Bevan 2004, 111–21). Although low in volume, such contacts were critical in ensuring the supply of exotic prestige goods and technologies that were so essential to emergent elites (Sherratt and Sherratt 1991; Schoep 2006), as suggested by the consistent presence of imports or imitations of off-island material culture in funerary contexts throughout the Early Bronze Age. In this way, Cretan elite culture appears to exhibit a shift from favoring Aegean to Eastern Mediterranean models and forms during the course of the Early Bronze Age (Schoep 2006).

Sealing, Writing, and Administration

Seals and sealings are present on Crete from EM II and appear at broadly the same time as on the Greek mainland (e.g., Lerna, Geraki). Whereas Early Minoan seals are attested primarily in grave contexts, sealings are usually found in nonfunerary contexts. Although, two sealings from an EM IIA fill below the West Court at Knossos have recently been redated on stylistic grounds to EM III/MM I (see references in Krzyszowkska 2005, 78), restudy of context and associated pottery argues in favor of the original EM IIA date. Sealings dating to EM IIB have been found at both small (Myrtos, Trypeti) and larger, proto-urban settlements (e.g. Malia, within court building; for references see Schoep 2004). Although the quantity of sealings is very small, especially compared to the Greek mainland, their social importance should not be underestimated.

The varied findspots of EM sealings suggest that this was not an isolated, local practice (contra Weingarten 1994). Rather, the practice of sealing needs to be situated within the wider context of the emergence and development of elite identities and elite culture. The attestation of sealings on Crete is important because the practice of sealing lumps of clay with seal stones is not an Aegean invention but, like script, is adopted from outside and adapted to suit local needs. Although typologically similar to sealings from regions further east, Cretan sealings were used differently and in a way that clearly did not involve a hierarchically organized bureaucratic administration (Weingarten 2000, 147).

On present evidence, script appeared slightly later, the oldest examples being the 'Archanes script,' attested on several seal stones from the Phourni cemetery in MM IA or at the latest MM IB contexts. There can be no doubt that these represent a real script (i.e., signs conveying phonetic values) since some sign groups are later attested in Linear A and Cretan Hieroglyphic documents (for different views, see Godart 1999 and Olivier 1996). The possibility of still earlier attestations of writing is hinted at by the incised signs found on nonjoining fragments of a vase of EM III type from Malia (Schoep and Allegrette 1999).

The significance of the EM evidence for the origins of administration has been hotly debated (Vlasaki and Hallager 1995; Weingarten 1990; Pini 1990). It was long assumed that the appearance of script implied the existence of a complex bureaucracy and was thus associated with an MM IB horizon of palace-building and, in particular, the economic needs of a managerial elite resident in the palaces (Weingarten 1990, 1994; Olivier 1989). The handful of known EM sealings tended to be judged unfavorably from the perspective of later and larger MM II collections (e.g., Phaistos) and dismissed as evidence for administration (Weingarten 1990; see Pini 1990 and Schoep 1999 for an alternative view).

More recently, it has been recognized that there is no need to make a direct equation between the presence of administrative documents and centralized economic control (Weingarten 2000; Schoep 2004). Sealing and writing also have important social and symbolic connotations, especially as markers of privilege and difference (Postgate, Wang, and Wilkinson 1995), and the logic behind their deployment at

EM sites may have been social and symbolic rather than strictly economic (Schoep 2004). Certainly the deposition of seal stones with early script in funerary contexts, as at Phourni, suggests that they played a role in the marking of identity and social difference (Schoep 2006).

Settlement and Urbanism

From FN IV, it is possible to identify three distinct dwelling strategies tied to different parts of the Cretan landscape, each of which exhibits differing long-term growth potentials (Whitelaw 2004; Tomkins this volume): agricultural sites, located in extensive and productive agricultural hinterlands (e.g., Knossos, Malia); trading sites, located on the coast (e.g., Petras Kephala, Mochlos, Poros); and marginal sites, located in less productive, predictable or extensive agricultural environments (e.g., Ziros region in east Crete; Branigan 1998; Halstead 2008; Tomkins 2008, 38–40). By EM II, many of the more extreme marginal areas see a contraction in settlement or abandonment (e.g., Branigan 1998). Marginal sites that thrived in EM II, such as the hamlets of Myrtos Fournou Korifi or Trypeti (Whitelaw 1983, 2004; Whitelaw et al. 1997), did so in part because of their position within wider exchange networks, often facilitated by a coastal location. This combination of marginal and trading strategies sustained a string of EM village communities around the Cretan coast, whose prospects for further expansion were, nevertheless, curtailed by the limited size or productivity of their agricultural hinterlands (Haggis 1999, 67; Whitelaw 2004).

During EM II, many agricultural sites (e.g., Knossos, Malia) undergo a phase of growth, which, though dwarfed by the scale of later expansions (e.g., Whitelaw 2004, 243, figure 13.8), represents a doubling or more of their Neolithic or EM I extent (Whitelaw 1983; Watrous 2001, 167; Tomkins 2008, 37–38). A similar pattern of growth, associated with an early stage of urbanism, may be identified in other regions of the EB II Aegean (Halstead 1981, 196–200; Hägg and Konsola 1986). Significantly, this expansion took these sites for the first time beyond the organizational threshold of the village, indirectly implying that social restructuring had taken place (cf. Whitelaw 1983).

Further growth at these proto-urban centers took place during EM III–MM IA, and in some areas this may be linked to a wave of small rural sites, which have been associated with agricultural intensification and extensification (Haggis 1999, 61–65). Although the generation of ever-greater agricultural surpluses was essential to growth (Manning 1994; Haggis 1999), the newly emerging EM II–III social hierarchies also needed to secure privileged access to the prestige goods and knowledge that flowed through trading sites. Agricultural sites located on coastal plains, such as Malia and Palaikastro, were well placed to combine agricultural and trading strategies in this way; inland sites such as Knossos and Phaistos, rooted in deeper Neolithic histories of place, were not. In the case of Knossos, this was perhaps resolved by the foundation in EM I of the nearby trading site of Poros, with which it enjoyed a close, symbiotic relationship for the rest of the Bronze Age (Dimopoulou-Rethemniotaki, Wilson, and Day 2007).

Claims of site hierarchies of three or more tiers from as early as EM I, on the basis of site size alone (e.g., Hayden, Moody, and Rackham 1992; Watrous et al. 1993; Driessen 2001), are thus probably premature in projecting stratified or hierarchical relationships onto what appears to have been a diversified but not an obviously politically integrated landscape (cf. Haggis 2002). Evidence for integration becomes less ambiguous only when demographic expansion at a center is of an order that exceeds the carrying capacity of its immediate hinterland and thus implies an extension of control over neighboring polities. In the case of Knossos, one of the most developed of the EM proto-urban centers, this is unlikely to have taken place before MM IA (Whitelaw 2004, 245).

Central Places and Arenas of Consumption

Recent work at Knossos, Malia, and Phaistos shows that the Middle Minoan court buildings are built on top of or incorporate elements of Early Bronze Age buildings also constructed around a large court. At Knossos, the origins of the open spaces of the central and west courts may be traced back to the end of FN (Tomkins 2007b, 41–42; in press b), while the construction of the first court buildings may be plausibly associated with a series of large-scale terracing and leveling episodes during EM II that transformed the summit of the Kephala Hill into a large, platform with specific, restricted ramped access points (Wilson 1994; Tomkins in press b for a discussion). Further such episodes of construction and modification during EM III, MM IA and MM IB created the monumental structure which convention terms the 'First Palace' (MacGillivray 1994; Tomkins in press b).

At Malia, remains of a large EM IIB building, beneath and on an orientation similar to that of the First Palace and laid out to the north and west of a large open space, have been brought to light in a series of tests (Pelon 1992; contra Watrous 2001, 171, 175). The 'First Palace' at Malia seems to have been constructed in EM III/MM IA, but, perhaps significantly, this building seems in one area (Magazine I1) to have deliberately incorporated part of its predecessor, namely a sort of vault with EM IIB vases in situ.

At Phaistos, the monumental structure known as the First Palace was constructed in MM IB and MM IIA. However, it has recently been shown that the open areas of the Lower West Court and the Central Court, as at Knossos, have a history of use going back to late FN (FN III–IV), when there is evidence to suggest that they were frequented for ritualized gatherings involving large-scale group consumption of liquids and foodstuffs (Todaro and Di Tonto 2008). Moreover, a sequence of monumental ramped entrances connecting these two areas can be traced back to EM II (Todaro in press). Such work provides a new context within which to situate enigmatic stretches of monumental EM IIB architecture at Palaikastro, Tylissos, and Mochlos (Branigan 1988, 43–44; Schoep 1999; Haggis 1999, 61–62).

What unites these monumental central places is the presence of formalized open spaces or courts, the origins of which may be traced at least as far back as the end of FN, if not deeper into the Neolithic (Tomkins 2004, 43–45; 2007a, 187–90; in press b; Todaro and Di Tonto 2008). During FN IV–EM III, other arenas used for communal ritual include built tombs and natural places such as caves, hilltops, and mountain peaks (Haggis 1999, 73–79; Tomkins in press a). In this way, the appearance in EM II of large public buildings in association with courts at large settlements such as Knossos, Malia, and Phaistos should be understood, on the one hand, as being rooted within deeper histories and traditions of communal ritual practice, but, on the other, as bound up with strategies of social restructuring and reproduction at the newly emergent and expanding proto-urban centers (Schoep in press a; Tomkins in press b). In this way the first court buildings mark the birth of a new type of communal space, out of which the later palaces would eventually develop. Much detail remains to be learned about the biographies of construction and renewal of the EM court buildings, the nature of the practices that went on within them, and the social relations and values that such practices reproduced (Schoep this volume). There are, however, good reasons for thinking that communal arenas at all scales served as formal places where groups of people could come together to construct and experience a sense of their place in the world through ritual practice.

A key component of communal ritual is commensality, and consideration of its changing articulation during the Neolithic and Bronze Age can reveal additional insights into social relations. At present, commensality during EM is perhaps best appreciated from the perspective of the containers used. During EM I–IIA, consumption of food and drink took place using individual sets of vessels whose form and size are suggestive of consumption by household groups (Wilson and Day 2000, 59–60), albeit relatively small in scale and similar to that which characterized the Neolithic (Tomkins 2007a).

The introduction of the footed goblet late in EM IIA (Wilson 2007, 64) thus marks a significant shift in the structure of commensality toward a larger group of people consuming smaller, equal, and more measured quantities (Wilson and Day 2000). The possibility remains strong that the ubiquitous ceramic goblet functioned alongside rarer and now largely absent containers in metal or stone (Nakou 2007) in a hierarchy of container value, which via commensality could have reproduced similarly asymmetrical relationships in people (cf. Macdonald and Knappett 2007). In this we might perhaps be glimpsing the beginning of a process of growth and extension to the later Neolithic household unit (see Tomkins this volume for a discussion), whereby larger and more complex corporate groups were formed, perhaps composed of a privileged (elite) social group and their affiliates and dependents.

Burial

Easily overlooked and often glossed as egalitarian, when approached from the perspective of later burial, the nature and significance of Early Minoan funerary practice is perhaps best appreciated when set against what went before.

During the Cretan Neolithic, grave goods are as good as absent, and human skeletal material is extremely rare, confined mainly to isolated fragments and occasional interments in settlement contexts or caves (Triantaphyllou 2008; Tomkins in press a). A high degree of selection must have been involved, with the vast majority of people receiving no archaeologically visible form of disposal.

Thus, one of the more striking changes to occur at the beginning of EM I, if not slightly earlier in FN IV, is the marked increase in visible forms of burial, typically in locations beyond the space of habitation. Initially these appear in caves or rock shelters (Branigan 1993, 152–54; Tomkins in press a), but from EM I these are joined by purpose-built round tombs or 'tholoi' (south-central Crete; e.g., Branigan 1970, 1993; Warren 2004; Tomkins 2007b, 20, table 1.6, 46–48) and cemeteries (Davaras and Betancourt 2004), and from EM II by house tombs (Soles 1992). This explosion in visible forms of burial may be understood as reflecting increased social competition, in particular a new interest in death as a means of marking status differences among the living, and a greater desire to use ritual as a means of appropriating or contesting the ownership of particular, strategic places in the landscape.

The development of conspicuous burial foci forms part of a broader EM expansion in the materiality and theatricality of death. From the carrying of the dead to their final resting place to funerary commensality (Hamilakis 1998, 124–26), the construction and use of permanent burial monuments offered new possibilities for the dramatization of social difference through funerary practice. From EM I, these practices included the interment of grave goods such as bronze daggers, gold jewelry, gold diadems, seal stones, amulets, pendants, and beads—high-value items in rare materials, which could be worn upon the person as markers of identity and status (Nakou 1995; Colburn 2008; Schoep in press a) and whose removal from circulation may have marked a form of conspicuous consumption. The presence from EM II of artifacts associated with personal body maintenance, such as obsidian blades or metal tweezers, suggests an interest in marking social differences by techniques of corporal inscription (Carter 1994; 1996; Doonan, Day, and Dimopoulou-Rethemniotaki 2007, 117).

Taken together, the EM burial data broadly indicate a situation of social competition and diversification, but not one that was necessarily always strongly hierarchical. While we cannot entirely exclude the possibility that a section of the population could be excluded from formal burial, estimates suggest that most people did have access (Whitelaw 1983). This burying population appears to have been eager to advertise identity and status through the display and disposal of valued material and symbolic resources. Sustained and systematic differences in wealth and status may on occasion be identified within this burying group, principally in the cemeteries attached to larger, wealthier communities such as Mochlos, Malia, Platanos, and Koumasa (Whitelaw 1983, 2004, 235–38; Soles 1988; 1992; Branigan 1993, 111).

THE EMERGENCE OF ELITE HOUSEHOLDS AND ELITE CULTURE

During the Neolithic and Early Bronze Age, at least two related units of social organization may be identified: the household, represented by discrete architectural units or houses, and the community, composed of agglomerations of coexisting households (see Halstead 1999; Tomkins 2004; this volume).In general, social change during this period can be read as a progression away from a communal model of society, where households are subordinate to and regulated by higher-level or communal forms of organization, to one where the communal becomes subordinate to the interests of specific households, who take responsibility for the ongoing wellbeing of the community and become the main (elite) agents of socioeconomic development. The appropriation of the communal thus formed a central role in the emergence of elite households on Crete between FN IV and EM III and may be glimpsed in the development not only of specific arenas (e.g., courts, tombs), where hierarchies of space could increasingly be exploited to incorporate, exclude, and thus define differential identity and status within and between communities, but also of an elite culture of objects, practices and knowledge, which from the end of the Neolithic drew increasingly on off-island sources in order to reproduce and legitimate social affiliation and difference.

From FN IV and through EM, Cretan communities appear to have been quick to diversify and differentiate themselves socially and economically but slow to integrate politically (Haggis 2002; Whitelaw 2004). The most successful, measured in terms of demographic growth, were those like Malia and Knossos-Poros, which were located in environments where trading, specifically access to and control over the resource of distance, might be combined with an ability to generate large agricultural surpluses. While there was a clear shifting of gears during the EM II period, sustained and extended during EM III (Haggis 1999, 61–65), it is only during MM I that there are signs of a major acceleration in growth significant enough to imply the development of larger-scale organizational forms and only then in the vicinity of the larger urban polities such as Knossos, Malia, and Phaistos. Outside the still-limited orbit of these urban centers, Crete remained a mosaic of independent and often tiny polities, operating at different scales and controlled by small-time, local elites who would, during the Middle Bronze Age, increasingly look to affiliate themselves with wealthier and better-connected elites in one or more of the larger, urban centers.

BIBLIOGRAPHY

Baines, John, and Norman Yoffee. 2000. "Order, Legitimacy, and Wealth: Setting the Terms." In *Order, Legitimacy, and Wealth in Ancient States,* ed. Janet Richards and Mary Van Buren, 13–17. New York: Cambridge University Press.

Barrett, John C., and Kristalli Damilati. 2004. "Some Light on the Early Origins of Them All: Generalization and the Explanation of Civilization Revisited." In *Emergence of Civilization Revisited,* 145–69.

Betancourt, Philip P. 1999. "What Is Minoan? FN/EM I in the Gulf of Mirabello Region." In *Meletemata,* 33–39.

Betancourt, Philip P. 2006. *The Chrysokamino Metallurgy Workshop and its Territory.* Hesperia Supplement 36. American School of Classical Studies/Oxbow Press.

———, and James Muhly. 2007. "The Crucibles from the Aghia Photia Cemetery." In *Metallurgy in the Early Bronze Age Aegean,* ed. Peter M. Day and Roger C. P. Doonan, 146–53. Sheffield Studies in Aegean Archaeology 7. Oxford: Oxbow.

Bevan, Andrew. 2004. "Emerging Civilized Values? The Consumption and Imitation of Egyptian Stone Vessels in EM II–MM I Crete and Its Wider Eastern Mediterranean Context." In *Emergence of Civilization Revisited,* 107–26.

Branigan, Keith. 1970. *The Tombs of Mesara.* London: Duckworth.

———. 1974. *Aegean Metalwork of the Early and Middle Bronze Age.* Oxford University Press.

———. 1988. *Pre-palatial: The Foundations of Palatial Crete: A Survey of Crete in the Early Bronze Age.* Amsterdam: Hakkert.

———. 1991. "Funerary Ritual and Social Cohesion in EBA Crete." *JMS* 1(2): 9–13.

———. 1993. *Dancing with Death: Life and Death in Southern Crete c. 3000–2000 B.C.* Amsterdam: Hakkert.

———. 1998. "Prehistoric and Early Settlement in the Ziros Region, Eastern Crete." *BSA* 93: 23–90.

Broodbank, Cyprian. 2000. *An Island Archaeology of the Early Cyclades.* New York: Cambridge University Press.

Carter, Tristan. 1994. "Southern Aegean Fashion Victims: An Overlooked Aspect of Early Bronze Age Burial Practices." In *Stories in Stone,* ed. Nick Ashton and Andrew David, 127–44. Lithics Study Society Occasional Paper 4. London: Lithics Study Society.

———. 1996. "Blood from Stones: Obsidian, Death, and Ethnicity in the Early Bronze Age." *BICS* 41: 142–43.

———. 1998. "The Chipped Stone." *BSA* 93: 47–50.

Catapotis, Michalis. 2007. "On the Spatial Organization of Copper Smelting Activities in the Southern Aegean during the Early Bronze Age." In *Metallurgy in the Early Bronze Age Aegean,* ed. Peter M. Day and Roger C. P. Doonan, 207–23. Sheffield Studies in Aegean Archaeology 7. Oxford: Oxbow.

Cherry, John. 1983. "Evolution, Revolution, and the Origins of Complex Society in Minoan Crete." In *Minoan Society,* 33–46.

———. 1984. "The Emergence of the State in the Prehistoric Aegean." *PCPS* 210, n.s., 30: 18–48.

———. 1986. "Polities and Palaces: Some Problems in Minoan State Formation." In *Peer Polity Interaction and Socio-Political Change,* ed. Colin Renfrew and John Cherry, 19–45. New York: Cambridge University Press.

Childe, V. Gordon. 1950. "The Urban Revolution." *Town Planning Review* 21(1): 3–19.

———. 1958. "Retrospect." *Antiquity* 32: 69–74.

Colburn, Cynthia. 2008. "Exotica and the Early Minoan Elite: Eastern Imports in Prepalatial Crete." *AJA* 112(2): 203–24.

Conolly, James. 2008. "The Knapped Stone Technology of the First Occupants at Knossos." In *Escaping the Labyrinth,* 73–89.

D'Annibale, Cesare. 2008. "Obsidian in Transition: The Technological Reorganization of the Obsidian Industry from Petras Kephala (Siteia) between Final Neolithic IV and Early Minoan I." In *Escaping the Labyrinth,* 191–200.

Davaras, Costis, and Philip P. Betancourt. 2004. *The Hagia Photia Cemetery,* vol. 1. Philadelphia: INSTAP Academic Press.

Day, Peter M., and Roger C. P. Doonan. 2007. *Metallurgy in the Early Bronze Age Aegean.* Sheffield Studies in Aegean Archaeology 7. Oxford: Oxbow.

Day, Peter M., David E. Wilson, and Evangelia Kiriatzi. 1997. "Reassessing Specialization in Prepalatial Cretan Ceramic Production." In *TEXNH,* 275–89.

Day, Peter M., David E. Wilson, and Evangelia Kiriatzi. 1998. "Pots, Labels, and People: Burying Ethnicity in the Cemetery at Aghia Photia, Siteias." In *Cemetery and Society,* 133–49.

Dimopoulou-Rethemniotaki, Nota, David E. Wilson, and Peter M. Day. 2007. "The Earlier Prepalatial Settlement of Poros-Katsambas: Craft Production and Exchange at the Harbour Town of Knossos." In *Metallurgy in the Early Bronze Age Aegean,* ed. Peter M. Day and Roger C. P. Doonan, 84–97. Sheffield Studies in Aegean Archaeology 7. Oxford: Oxbow.

Doonan, Roger, Peter M. Day, and Nota Dimopoulou-Rethemniotaki. 2007. "Lame Excuses for Emerging Complexity in Early Bronze Age Crete: The Metallurgical Finds from Poros-Katsambas and Their Context." In *Metallurgy in the Early Bronze Age Aegean,* ed. Peter M. Day and Roger C. P. Doonan, 98–122. Sheffield Studies in Aegean Archaeology 7. Oxford: Oxbow.

Driessen, Jan. 2001. "History and Hierarchy: Preliminary Observations on the Settlement Pattern of Minoan Crete." In *Urbanism,* 51–71.

Evans, Arthur. 1921. *PM,* vol. 1.

———. 1925. "The Early Nilotic, Libyan and Egyptian Relations with Minoan Crete." *Journal of the Royal Anthropological Institute of Great Britain and Ireland* 55: 199–228.

———. 1928. *PM,* vol. 2.

Gamble, Clive. 2007. *Origins and Revolutions: Human Identity in Earliest Prehistory.* New York: Cambridge University Press.

Godart, Louis. 1999. "L'écriture d'Arkhanès: Hiéroglyphique ou Linéaire A?" In *Meletemata,* 299–302.

Hägg, Robin, and Dora Konsola. 1986. *Early Helladic Architecture.*

Haggis, Donald C. 1999. "Staple Finance, Peak Sanctuaries, and Economic Complexity in Late Prepalatial Crete." In *From Minoan Farmers to Roman Traders: Sidelights on the Economy of Ancient Crete,* ed. Angelos Chaniotis, 53–86. Stuttgart: Franz Steiner.

———. 2002. "Integration and Complexity in the Late Prepalatial Period: A View from the Countryside in Eastern Crete." In *Labyrinth Revisited: Rethinking 'Minoan' Archaeology,* ed. Yiannis Hamilakis, 120–42. Oxford: Oxbow.

Halstead, Paul. 1981. "From Determinism to Uncertainty: Social Storage and the Rise of the Minoan Palace." In *Economic Archaeology,* ed. Andrew Sheridan and Geoff Bailey, 187–213. *BAR-IS* 96. Oxford: British Archaeological Reports.

———. 1999. "Neighbours from Hell? The Household in Neolithic Greece." In *Neolithic Society in Greece,* ed. Paul Halstead, 77–95. Sheffield Studies of Aegean Archaeology 2. Sheffield: Sheffield Academic Press.

———. 2008. "Between a Rock and a Hard Place: Coping with Marginal Colonization in the Later Neolithic and Early Bronze Age of Crete and the Aegean." In *Escaping the Labyrinth,* 232–60.

Hamilakis, Yannis. 1998. "Eating the Dead: Mortuary Feasting and the Politics of Memory in Aegean Bronze Age Societies," In *Cemetery and Society,* 115–32.

Hayden, Barbara, Jenny Moody, and Oliver Rackham. 1992. "The Vrokastro Survey Project, 1986–1989: Research Design and Preliminary Results." *Hesperia* 61: 293–353.

Hood, Sinclair. 1990. "Autochthons or Settlers? Evidence for Immigration at the Beginning of the Early Bronze Age in Crete." In *Pepragmena tou ST' Diethnous Kritologikou Synedriou* A1, 367–75. Heraklion: Etairia Kritikon Istorikon Meleton.

Isaakidou, Valasia. 2008. "'The Fauna and Economy of Neolithic Knossos' Revisited." In *Escaping the Labyrinth*, 90–114.

Karantzali, Efi. 1996. *Le Bronze Ancien dans les Cyclades et en Crète: Les Relations Entre les Deux Regions—Influence de la Grèce Continentale.* BAR-IS 631. Oxford: Archaeopress.

Knappett, Carl J. 1999. "Tradition and Innovation in Pottery-forming Technology: Wheel-throwing at Middle Minoan Knossos." *BSA* 94: 101–29.

Krzyszowkska, Olga. 2005. *Aegean Seals: An Introduction.* Bulletin of the Institute of Classical Studies Suppl. 85. London: Institute of Classical Studies, School of Advanced Study, University of London.

Macdonald, Colin. F., and Carl J. Knappett. 2007. *Knossos: Protopalatial Deposits in Early Magazine A and the South-West Houses.* BSA Supplementary Volume 41. London: British School at Athens.

MacGillivray, J. Alexander. 1994. "The Early History of the Palace at Knossos (MM I–II)." In *Labyrinth of History*, 45–55.

Manning, Sturt. 1994. "The Emergence of Divergence: Development and Decline on Bronze Age Crete and the Cyclades." In *Development and Decline in the Mediterranean Bronze Age*, ed. Clay Mathers and Simon Stoddart, 221–70. Sheffield: Sheffield University Press.

Momigliano, Nicoletta. 2007. "Late Prepalatial (EM III–MM IA): South Front House Foundation Trench, Upper East Well and House C/Royal Road South Fill Groups." In *Knossos Pottery Handbook*, 79–103.

———, and David E. Wilson. 1996. "Knossos 1993: Excavations outside the South Front of the Palace." *BSA* 91: 1–57.

Muhly, James. 2002 "Early metallurgy in Greece and Cyprus." In *Der Anschnitt. Zeitschrift fur Kunst und Kultur im Bergbau* 15: 77–82.

Nakou, Georgia. 1995. "The Cutting Edge: A New Look at Early Aegean Metallurgy." *JMA* 8(2): 1–32.

———. 2007. "Absent Presences: Metal Vessels in the Aegean at the End of the Third Millennium BC." In *Metallurgy in the Early Bronze Age Aegean*, ed. Peter M. Day and Roger C. P. Doonan, 224–44. Sheffield Studies in Aegean Archaeology 7. Oxford: Oxbow.

Nowicki, Krzysztof. 2002. "The End of the Neolithic in Crete." *Aegean Archaeology* 6: 7–72.

Olivier, Jean-Pierre. 1989. "Les écritures crétoises." In *Les civilisations egeennes du néo-lithique et de l'âge du bronze*, ed. Réné Treuil, Pascal Darcque, Jean-Claude Poursat, and Gilles Touchais, 237–52. Paris: Presses Universitaires de France.

———. 1996. "Les écritures crétoises: Sept points à considérer. In *Atti e memorie del secondo Congresso internazionale di micenologia, Roma-Napoli, 14–20 ottobre 1991. Incunabula Graeca 98:I*, ed. Ernesto De Miro, Louis Godart, and Anna Sacconi, 101–13. Rome: Gruppo editoriale internazionale.

Papadatos, Yannis. 2005. *Tholos Tomb Gamma: A Prepalatial Tholos Tomb at Phourni, Archanes.* Philadelphia: INSTAP Press.

———. 2007. "The Beginning of Metallurgy in Crete: New Evidence from the FN–EM I Settlement at Kephala Petras, Siteia." In *Metallurgy in the Early Bronze Age Aegean*, ed. Peter M. Day and Roger C. P. Doonan, 154–67. Sheffield Studies in Aegean Archaeology 7. Oxford: Oxbow.

———. 2008. "The Neolithic–Early Bronze Age Transition in Crete: New Evidence from the Settlement at Petras Kephala, Siteia." In *Escaping the Labyrinth*, 258–72.

————, Peter Tomkins, Eleni Nodarou, and Yiannis Iliopoulos. In press. "The Beginning of Early Bronze Age in Crete: Continuities and Discontinuities in the Ceramic Assemblage at Kephala Petras, Siteia." In *The Aegean Early Bronze Age: New Evidence,* ed. Christos Doumas, Colin Renfrew, and Ourania Koukou. Athens, April 11–14, 2008.

Pelon, Olivier. 1992. *Guide de Malia: Le palais et la nécropole de Chrysolakkos.* Paris: Ecole française d'Athènes.

Pini, Ingo. 1990. "The Hieroglyphic Deposit and the Temple Repositories Deposit at Knossos." In *Aegean Seals,* 33–60.

Postgate, Nicolas, Tao Wang, and Toby Wilkinson. 1995. "The Evidence for Early Writing: Utilitarian or Ceremonial?" *Antiquity* 69: 459–80.

Renfrew, Colin. 1964. "Crete and the Cyclades before Rhadamanthus." In *Kritika Chronika* 18: 107–41.

————. 1972. *The Emergence of Civilization.* London: Methuen.

Schoep, Ilse. 1999. "The Origins of Writing and Administration on Crete." *OJA* 18: 265–75.

————. 2002. "Social and Political Organisation on Crete in the Proto-palatial Period: The Case of Middle Minoan II Malia." *JMA* 15: 101–32.

————. 2004. "The Socio-economic Context of Seal Use and Administration at Knossos." In *Knossos,* 283–329.

————. 2006. "Looking beyond the First Palaces: Elites and the Agency of Power in EM III–MM II Crete." *AJA* 110: 37–64.

————. In press a. "Bridging the Gap between Early and Middle Minoan." In *Back to the Beginning.*

————. In press b. "Making Elites: Political Economy and Elite Culture(s) in Middle Minoan Crete." In *Political Economies of the Aegean Bronze Age,* ed. Daniel Pullen.

————, and Alvaro Allegrette. 1999. "Quatre tessons incisés provenant des sondages au sud-est de la crypte hypostyle à Malia." *Kadmos* 38: 109–13.

Schoep, Ilse, and Carl J. Knappett. 2003. "Le Quartier Nu (Malia, Crète): L'occupation du Minoen moyen II." *BCH* 117(1): 49–86.

————. 2004. "Dual Emergence: Evolving Heterarchy, Exploding Hierarchy." In *Emergence of Civilization Revisited,* 21–37.

Sherratt, Andrew, and Susan E. Sherratt. 1991. "From Luxuries to Commodities: The Nature of Mediterranean Bronze Age Trading Systems." In *Bronze Age Trade,* 351–86.

Soles, Jeffrey S. 1988. "Social Ranking in Prepalatial Cemeteries." In *Problems in Greek Prehistory,* 49–61.

————. 1992. *The Prepalatial Cemeteries at Mochlos and Gournia and the House Tombs of Bronze Age Crete.* Hesperia Suppl. 24. Princeton: Princeton University Press.

Todaro, Simona. 2005. "EM I–MMIA Ceramic Groups at Phaistos: Towards the Definition of a Prepalatial Ceramic Sequence in South Central Crete." *Creta Antica* 6: 11–46.

————. In press. "Craft Production and Social Practices at Prepalatial Phaistos: The Background to the First 'Palace.'" In *Back to the Beginning.*

————, and Serena Di Tonto. 2008. "The Neolithic Settlement at Phaistos Revisited: Evidence for Ceremonial Activity on the Eve of the Bronze Age." In *Escaping the Labyrinth,* 177–90.

Tomkins, Peter. 2004. "Filling in the 'Neolithic Background': Social Life and Social Transformation in the Aegean before the Bronze Age." In *Emergence of Civilization Revisited,* 38–63.

————. 2007a. "Communality and Competition: The Social Life of Food and Containers at Aceramic and Early Neolithic Knossos, Crete." In *Cooking Up the Past: Food and*

Culinary Practices in the Neolithic and Bronze Age Aegean, ed. Christopher Mee and Josette Renard, 174–99. Oxford: Oxbow.

———. 2007b. "Neolithic: Strata IX–VIII, VII–VIB, VIA–V, IV, IIIB, IIIA, IIB, IIA, and IC Groups." In *Knossos Pottery Handbook,* 9–48.

———. 2008. "Time, Space, and the Reinvention of the Cretan Neolithic." In *Escaping the Labyrinth,* 21–48.

———. In press a. "Landscapes of Identity, Ritual, and Memory: Reconsidering the Use of Caves on Crete during the Neolithic and Early Bronze Age." In *Journeys into the Dark Zone,* ed. Holley Moyes. Colorado: University Press of Colorado.

———. In press b. "Behind the Horizon: The Genesis of the 'First Palace' at Knossos (Final Neolithic IV–Middle Minoan IB)." In *Back to the Beginning.*

———, and Peter M. Day. 2001. "Production and Exchange of the Earliest Ceramic Vessels in the Aegean: A View from Knossos." *Antiquity* 75: 259–60.

———, Peter M. Day and Vasilis Kilikoglou. 2004. "Knossos and the Early Neolithic Landscape of the Herakleion Basin." In *Knossos,* 51–59.

Triantaphyllou, Sevi. 2008. "Living with the Dead: A Re-Consideration of Mortuary Practices in the Greek Neolithic." In *Escaping the Labyrinth,* 136–54.

Vlasaki, Maria, and Erik Hallager. 1995. "Evidence for Seal Use in Pre-palatial Western Crete." In *Sceaux minoens et mycéniens,* ed. Walter Müller, 251–70. *CMS* Beiheft 5. Berlin: Mann.

Vagnetti, Lucia. 1996. "The Final Neolithic: Crete Enters the Wider World." *Cretan Studies* 5: 29–39.

———, and Paolo Belli. 1978. "Characters and Problems of the Final Neolithic in Crete." *SMEA* 19: 125–63.

Van Buren, Mary, and Janet Richards. 2000. "Introduction: Ideology, Wealth, and the Comparative Study of Civilizations." In *Order, Legitimacy, and Wealth in Ancient States,* ed. Janet Richards and Mary Van Buren, 3–12. New York: Cambridge University Press.

Warren, Peter. 1965. "The First Minoan Stone Vases and Early Minoan Chronology." *Kritika Chronika* 19: 7–43.

———. 1973. "Crete, 3000–1400 B.C.: Immigration and the Archaeological Evidence." In *Bronze Age Migrations in the Aegean: Archaeological and Linguistic Problems in Greek Prehistory,* ed. R. A. Crossland and Ann Birchall, 41–47. Park Ridge, N.J.: Noyes.

———. 1984. "Early Minoan–Early Cycladic Chronological Correlations." In *Prehistoric Cyclades,* 55–62.

———. 1987. "The Genesis of the Minoan Palace." In *Function of the Minoan Palaces,* 39–42.

———. 2004. "Part II: The Contents of the Tombs." In *The Early Minoan Tombs of Lebena, Southern Crete,* ed. Stelios Alexiou and Peter Warren, 23–218. *SIMA* XXX. Sävedalen, Sweden: Åström.

Watrous, L. Vance. 1987. "The Role of the Near East in the Rise of the Cretan Palaces." In *Function of the Minoan Palaces,* 65–70.

———. 2001. "Crete from the Earliest Prehistory through the Protopalatial Period." In *Aegean Prehistory,* 157–223.

———, Despoina Xatzi-Vallianou, Kevin Pope, Nikos Mourtzas, Jennifer Shay, C. Thomas Shay, John Bennet, et al. 1993. "A Survey of the Western Mesara Plain in Crete: Preliminary Report on the 1984, 1986, and 1987 Field Seasons." *Hesperia* 62: 191–248.

Weingarten, Judith. 1990. "Three Upheavals in Minoan Sealing Administration: Evidence for Radical Change." In *Aegean Seals,* 105–14.

————. 1994. "Sealings and Sealed Documents at Bronze Age Knossos." In *Labyrinth of History,* 171–88.

————. 2000. "Lerna: Sealings in a Landscape." In *Administrative Documents in the Aegean and Their Near Eastern Counterparts,* ed. Massimo Perna, 103–24. Turin: Paravia Scriptorium.

Whitelaw, Todd. 1983. "The Settlement at Fournou-Korifi, Myrtos and Aspects of Early Minoan Social Organisation." In *Minoan Society,* 323–45.

Whitelaw, Todd. 2004. "Alternative Pathways to Complexity in the Southern Aegean." In *The Emergence of Civilization Revisited,* 232–56.

————, Peter M. Day, Evangelia Kiriatzi, Vasilis Kilikoglou, and David E. Wilson. 1997. "Ceramic Traditions at EMIIB Myrtos, Fournou Korifi." In TEXNH, 265–74.

Wilson, David E. 1994. "Knossos before the Palaces: an Overview of the Early Bronze Age (EM I-EM III)." In *Knossos: A Labyrinth of History.* Papers Presented in Honour of Sinclair Hood, ed. Don Evely, Helen Hughes-Brock and Nicoletta Momigliano, 23–44. London: British School at Athens.

————. 2007. "Early Prepalatial (EM I–EM II): EM I Well, West Court House, North-East Magazines, and South Front Groups." In *Knossos Pottery Handbook,* 49–77.

————. 2008. "Early Prepalatial Crete." In *The Cambridge Companion to the Aegean Bronze Age,* ed. Cynthia W. Shelmerdine, 77–104. New York: Cambridge University Press.

————, and Peter M. Day. 1994. "Ceramic Regionalism in Prepalatial Central Crete: The Mesara Imports from EM IB to EM IIA Knossos." *BSA* 89: 1–87.

————. 2000. "EM I Chronology and Social Practice: Pottery from the Early Palace Tests at Knossos." *BSA* 95: 21–63.

————. 2004. "The Pottery from Early Minoan I-IIB Knossos." In *Knossos,* 67–74.

Wright, James C. 2004. "The Emergence of Leadership and the Rise of Civilization in the Aegean." In *Emergence of Civilization Revisited,* 64–89.

CHAPTER 6

....

CYCLADES

....

COLIN RENFREW

THE Cycladic Islands, lying in the southern Aegean in a group almost equidistant from the Greek and Anatolian coasts and from Crete, have played a central role in the prehistory of the Aegean. Even in the late Upper Palaeolithic period, before there is evidence of permanent settlement in the islands, the volcanic glass known as obsidian—and very suitable as a raw material for chipped stone tools—was being brought from its principal Aegean source on the island of Melos to Franchthi Cave in the Argolid (Renfrew and Aspinall 1990). From the Neolithic period onward, interactions between the Cycladic Islands and neighboring lands were frequent. And, of course, the Cyclades were significant in the Archaic period of Greek civilization, when islands such as Naxos, Paros, Siphnos, and Melos played a prominent role until the period of Athenian domination.

In the Early Bronze Age, the inhabitants of the Cyclades took an active part in the trade and commerce of the time. Cycladic sources of lead and copper were economically significant. The influence of the Early Cycladic cultures was felt in settlements, and notably in cemeteries, in northern Crete and in Attica and Euboea. The characteristic marble sculptures or figurines, usually no more than thirty centimeters high but sometimes reaching almost life-sized, are among the most characteristic Cycladic products and much prized by collectors today. Their influence upon the burial customs in neighboring areas is evident.

The Early Bronze Age cultures of the Cyclades first came to scholarly attention during the nineteenth century, when the Early Cycladic cemeteries became known to travelers and collectors (e.g., Bent 1884). They were first systematically investigated in the pioneering excavations of Christos Tsountas (1898, 1899), whose careful account has become the basis for later studies (Papathanassopoulos 1962; Doumas 1977; Rambach 2000a, 2000b). At about the same time, the first Cycladic settlement was excavated at Phylakopi in Melos, under the day-to-day supervision of Duncan Mackenzie, who went on to play a key role in the excavations conducted by Sir Arthur Evans at Knossos in

Figure 6.1. Photograph of the Early Cycladic site of Skarkos on the island of Ios (courtesy of Dr. Marisa Marthari).

Crete. Good stratigraphic control at Phylakopi allowed the division of the sequence into what were termed the First, Second, and Third Cities (Atkinson et al. 1904), interpreted as belonging broadly to the Early, Middle, and Late Bronze Age. Later work (Dawkins and Droop 1911; Barber 1974; Renfrew 2007) has allowed more detailed analysis. However, the recovered building remains of the Early Bronze Age were not extensive, and the site has proved more illuminating for the later periods (e.g., Renfrew 1985).

The second major Bronze Age settlement to be investigated in the Cyclades was Ayia Irini on Kea, again a multiperiod site, studied by J. L. Caskey: Periods I to III constitute the Early Bronze Age levels (Wilson 1999). The third such town site, again better known for the Middle and Late Bronze Age levels, is Akrotiri on Thera, excavated first by Spyridon Marinatos and then by Christos Doumas. In recent years at Akrotiri, the cutting of shafts into earlier levels in order to allow the insertion of steel pylons to support the protective roofing has yielded important Early Bronze Age materials (Doumas 2008; Sotirakopoulou 2008), but little is known of the structure of the Early Bronze Age settlement.

Few Early Bronze Age settlements lacking an overburden of later materials have yet been investigated in the Cyclades, although Tsountas himself excavated at the important site of Kastri in Syros (Bossert 1967), and the small rural site of Markiani on Amorgos has recently been published (Marangou et al. 2006). Mention should also be made of the settlement on the island of Dhaskalio, opposite the ritual center of Kavos on the island of Keros (Renfrew et al. 2007; Renfrew et al. 2008), and of the extensive excavations at Skarkos on Ios (Marthari 2008). The work at Skarkos will, when fully published, give the most complete picture yet available of an Early Cycladic village or small town (figure 6.1).

It is fair to say that our current knowledge of the Early Cycladic period remains somewhat reliant on material from the cemeteries. There is good agreement over the broad cultural sequence (Renfrew 1972; Doumas 1977), and the development of the Cycladic Early Bronze Age has been well surveyed by Broodbank (2000). There are, however, still divergences of view about the concluding phases of the period, including the so-called Kastri Group' (see later discussion). Excavations on the west coast of Turkey, notably at the important site of Liman Tepe, are now revealing relationships that had not previously been well understood (see Sahoglu 2005). After many years of relative neglect, the past decade has shown a marked resurgence of interest in Cycladic studies (see Davis 1992; Barrett and Halstead 2004; Brodie et al. 2008).

THE NEOLITHIC BACKGROUND

Almost nothing was known of the Neolithic period in the Cyclades until the discovery of the settlement of Saliagos near Antiparos (Evans and Renfrew 1968). This was a small village of farmers and fishermen. Stone foundations for buildings were found: The superstructures may have been of pisé (unbaked clay). Barley was the most frequent cereal—as it has been ever since in the Cyclades—followed by wheat (both emmer wheat and einkorn). Among the animal remains, sheep and goat were the most frequent—as they have since remained in the islands— with some cattle, pigs, and deer. Abundant fish bones were recovered, with sea perch exceeding a meter in length. The most abundant were tuna fish, reaching a length of more than two meters and caught seasonally, perhaps using the carefully pressure-flaked obsidian points that are a particular feature of the Saliagos culture. Spinning, and by inference weaving, is attested by numerous spindle whorls. The characteristic dark-faced, well-burnished pottery frequently has decoration in white paint. There were numerous tools of stone, bone, obsidian, and shell, including a series of small axes made of emery from the nearby island of Naxos. Trace-element analysis has confirmed that the obsidian was from Melos. The marble figurines so frequent in the Early Bronze Age were anticipated here by a schematic (violin-shaped) figurine and by a small, headless representation of a seated female—the 'fat lady of Saliagos.' These features are relevant to the early (and later) Bronze Age occupation of the Cyclades since they document the agrarian life that persisted in the islands until the twentieth century AD. Radiocarbon dates set the Saliagos culture, after calibration, in the Late Neolithic period of the Aegean, between 5000 and 4500 BC. Other sites of the Saliagos culture have since been investigated (Sampson 2008a).

More recent work in the Cyclades has not documented an earlier Neolithic phase of occupation, although it is clear that Melos was the source of nearly all of the obsidian used in the Aegean throughout the Neolithic and Early Bronze Age periods (Renfrew, Cann, and Dixon 1965; Torrence 1986). Perhaps earlier Neolithic finds are still to be expected since traces of both a Mesolithic settlement and cemetery are found at the site of Maroulas on Kythnos (Sampson 2008b).

The type site for the Final Neolithic (or Chalcolithic) period in the Cyclades is Kephala on Kea (Coleman 1977), represented by rather scanty traces of a settlement, with clear indications of copper metallurgy, accompanied by a well-preserved cemetery with built graves of stone containing multiple burials. This is one of the earliest cemeteries in the Aegean, initiating the tradition of well-constructed graves of stone, which continues through the Early Bronze Age. The pottery is characteristically red and burnished, often with pattern burnish decoration, comparable to material found in Attica (hence the term 'Attic-Kephala culture'). The links extend more widely, with pottery resemblances (or 'parallels') extending to Thessaly and even to Albania to the northwest. The marble beaker with pointed base found in one of the graves may be compared with Chalcolithic finds in western Anatolia and even with Copper Age Varna in Bulgaria. Thus, it is clear that the maritime links indicated by the obsidian trade also extended in other directions. Related finds have been made in the Cave of Zas in Naxos (Zachos 1990), where the cultural sequence from the Saliagos culture through to the Early Bronze Age Grotta-Pelos culture may be followed.

Our understanding of the Final Neolithic in the Cyclades and indeed of the Early Bronze Age which follows has been transformed by the discovery of the settlement at Strophilas on Andros (Televantou 2008). It is a fortified site—the earliest fortifications known in the Cyclades—and features clear incisions on the rock depicting longships of a kind previously thought to be an innovation during the Keros-Syros culture dating perhaps a millennium later.

THE EARLY CYCLADIC CULTURE SEQUENCE

The Early Bronze Age of the Cyclades is traditionally divided into a series of periods (EC I, EC II, EC III) or cultures and groups. These do not, however, succeed one another smoothly across the Cyclades, so that the Kampos Group has not yet been identified on Syros in the north, while the Kastri Group is not well documented at Phylakopi on Melos in the south. For that reason, the 'culture' nomenclature is to be preferred and is followed here. The cultural succession, as seen in the pottery sequence on three published sites, is reasonably clear. At Phylakopi on Melos, the sequence from Grotta-Pelos to Keros Syros to Phylakopi I culture is evident (Renfrew and Evans 2007). At Ayia Irini on Kea, the transition from Keros-Syros culture to Kastri Group is firmly documented (Wilson 1999), and at Markiani on Amorgos there is a clear sequence from Kampos Group to Keros-Syros culture to Kastri Group (Marangou et al. 2006). The absolute chronology emerges clearly from the radiocarbon dates at Markiani (Renfrew, Housley, and Manning 2006; Manning 2008). The basic sequence as set out forty years ago (Renfrew and Sterud 1969; Renfrew 1972; Doumas 1977; Broodbank 2000) has thus been supported by later work. It also harmonizes in general with the cemetery seriation achieved by Rambach (2000b, Beilage 15), although his seriation analysis has the defect that it places most of the graves at the important site of Chalandriani on Syros later than all of those at the cemetery of Aplomata on Naxos. Clearly we are not speaking of a mass migration from Naxos to Syros, and some aspects of his chronology must be an artifact of the seriation process used (see Renfrew and Sterud 1969; Hage, Harary, and James 1999).

The Grotta-Pelos Culture

The Grotta-Pelos culture (Early Cycladic I; ca. 3400–3000 BC) is best known from cemeteries of cist graves, notably on Melos (at Pelos), Paros (Pyrgos, Plastiras), Antiparos (Krassades), Dhespotikon (Zoumbaria), Naxos (Krassades, Lakkoudes, Louros), and Siphnos (Aktoriraki). The graves are simple boxes consisting of marble slabs and were in effect family graves, often with several inhumations. The pottery in the graves is dark faced, often with incised (herringbone) decoration. It is accompanied by obsidian blades and marble vessels: open bowls, flat-based beakers, and footed jars ('kandiles'). The marble figurines are in general schematic, but a simple form delineating legs and head (the Louros type), and another, more detailed, with arms meeting at the waist (the Plastiras type) are known. There are no well-published settlements, although Grotta-Pelos pottery is found at Phylakopi in Melos, Grotta in Naxos, and Markiani in Amorgos but without clear building remains.

The Kampos Group

The Kampos Group (transitional EC I–EC II; ca. 3000–2800 BC), first recognized from the Kampos cemetery on Paros, is now more fully documented from the cemetery of Agrilia on Ano Kouphonisi (Zapheiropoulou 1984, 2008) and is also represented at the settlement of Markiani on Amorgos (Marangou et al. 2006). The most characteristic forms include a specific form of frying pan, a characteristic ceramic bottle, and a footed bowl or 'fruit stand.' These materials have been well considered by Karantzali (1996; cf. Marangou et al. 2006). They have strong resemblances to finds from the Haghia Photia cemetery in northeast Crete (Davaras and Betancourt 2004; Betancourt 2008), the port of Pros-Kastambas in north-central Crete (Wilson, Day, and Dimopoulou-Rethemiotaki 2008), and other north Cretan coastal sites. It is possible that groups of settlers from the southern Cyclades may have come to Crete at this time.

The Keros-Syros Culture

The Keros-Syros culture (EC II; ca. 2800–2300 BC) takes its name from the cemetery and settlement at Chalandriani on Syros and from the site of ritual deposition at Kavos on Keros (Renfrew et al. 2007), with the accompanying settlement on the

Figure 6.2. Two early Cycladic figurines made of marble; found in a grave at the Dokathismata cemetery on Amorgos (by John Bigelow Taylor).

small island of Dhaskalio nearby (Renfrew et al. 2008). It is well represented by numerous cemeteries on Amorgos (notably Dokathismata) and Naxos (Aplomata, Spedos).

The rather scanty settlement remains documented for Phylakopi on Melos and Grotta-Aplomata on Naxos are supplemented by those at Markiani on Amorgos and by phases II and III at Ayia Irini on Kea. The most extensively investigated settlement is Skarkos on Ios (Marthari 2008).

It is at this time that the Cyclades developed an outstanding dynamism. The material culture includes not only notably fine ceramic wares, many of them with painted decoration, but also a range of sophisticated marble forms, both marble vessels (Getz-Gentle 1996) and the celebrated sculptures in folded-arm position (figure 6.2; Renfrew 1969; Getz-Preziosi 1987). Metallurgy developed conspicuously, with copper or daggers now a frequent form, and there is a range of personal ornaments in copper or silver now as well. One ceramic form seen mainly in the graves at Chalandriani on Syros is the frying pan (of Syros type), notable for the decorative incision depicting Cycladic longboats. There are numerous resemblances between

Cycladic finds and those in the Peloponnese at this time, most characteristically seen in the sauceboat form in the pottery, which itself imitates prototypes in precious metal. There are links, too, with Troy and Liman Tepe on the Anatolian coast, and it is possible to speak of an 'international spirit' that pervades southern Greece and the Aegean at this time.

The Kastri Group

The Kastri Group (EC II–III; ca. 2500–2200 BC) (Renfrew 1972, 533–34; Sotirakopoulou 1983) takes its name from the fortified settlement of Kastri near Chalandriani on Syros (Bossert 1967) first excavated by Tsountas. It is well represented in the earliest levels at the site of Lefkandi in Euboea (as well as the cemetery at Manika) and is seen stratified at the site of Markiani on Amorgos (Markiani IV), as well as at Ayia Irini on Kea (Ayia Irini III: Wilson 1999). Its Anatolian affinities have been obvious from the outset, but with the excavation of Liman Tepe near Izmir the focus of attention has shifted south from Troy (Sahoglu 2005). It is important to stress, however, that at most of the Cycladic sites where the Kastri Group has been recognized, it represents not a break but a continuation of the Keros-Syros culture. Indeed, it was initially defined as a subgroup within the Keros-Syros culture, and this may well be an appropriate way of looking at the new forms, mostly of Anatolian origin (the one-handled cup, the two-handled 'depas' cup, the wheel-made plates), which now make their appearance in the Cyclades. It seems that tin bronze now becomes more common, replacing the arsenical bronze that was previously a feature of Cycladic metallurgy (see Charles in Renfrew 1967; Nakou 1995; Gale and Stos-Gale 2008). Many of the sites of the Kastri Group are fortified, including Panormos on Naxos and the type site of Kastri itself.

The Phylakopi I Culture

The Phylakopi I culture (Early Cycladic III; ca. 2200–1900 BC) is best attested at the type site of Phylakopi and also well documented at the site of Paroikia on Paros. On Melos this is a period of settlement nucleation: The number of settlements declines drastically, but the importance of Phylakopi increases (see Cherry in Renfrew and Wagstaff 1982, 10–23), although the size of the settlement at this time has been questioned (Whitelaw 2004).

The dark-faced pottery, often decorated with incisions and including the well-known askos ('duck-vase' form), was well documented in the early excavations at Phylakopi (Atkinson 1904) and may constitute a phase not so evident in the more recent excavations (Renfrew 2007), where the dark-on-light painted decoration of the succeeding subphase was quite well represented (Renfrew and Evans 2007). This is characteristic of the material recovered in the nineteenth century from rock-cut tombs at Phylakopi.

The stratigraphic and chronological relationship between the Kastri Group and the Phylakopi I culture is not yet well established, which has led some authors (e.g., Rutter 1984) to speak of a 'gap' between the two.

SOCIAL DEVELOPMENTS

The richness and variety of the material of the Keros-Syros culture documents an increasing prosperity and some increase of population beyond that of the Grotta-Pelos culture (Cherry 2004). The subsistence base remained one of mixed farming already established since the time of the Saliagos culture. However, these cereal crops were supplemented by olives and vines (Renfrew 1972, 265–307; Halstead 2004), and the frequency of drinking vessels in the Keros-Syros culture is suggestive of wine drinking and perhaps of feasting. As noted earlier, metallurgical production increases notably at this time (see Wagner and Weissgerber 1985).

Some of the more prosperous settlements of the Keros-Syros culture show an abundance of fine wares, and Broodbank (2000, 237–41) has suggested that there were up to four nodes of intense communication in the Cyclades at this time (Chalandriani-Kastri, Ayia Irini, Grotta-Aplomata, and Dhaskalio-Kavos), all centers with "unusually large population, skilled craft production in several media, marked involvement in maritime trade and high levels of consumption of prestige material culture." Certainly the range of choice products documented contrasts with the simpler repertoire found at Markiani on Amorgos or even at the large settlement at Skarkos on Ios. It is also possible to argue that we may speak of a ranked society at this time (Renfrew 1974; Wright 2004), and some degree of administrative organization is perhaps implied by the clay sealings (see Pullen 1994) found at Markiani on Amorgos (Marangou et al. 2006, 219–22) and at the Cave of Zas on Naxos (Zachos and Dousougli 2008). The recognition by Rahmstorf (2003) that the 'spools' or 'pestles' of fine stone or of *Spondylus* shell, seen for instance at Markiani (Marangou et al. 2006, 176 and pl. 40) and at Kavos (Renfrew et al. 2008, 25, figure 15), may represent balance weights is a further indication of commercial organization at this time. Arguments for the transformative role at this period of the Cycladic longship, seen on the Syros frying pans, are undermined, however, by the recognition of depictions of what appear to be very similar vessels at Strophilas on Andros (Televatou 2008) a millennium earlier.

The pottery forms of the Kastri Group, in the later stages of the Keros-Syros culture, undoubtedly indicate more intense contacts with the Anatolian coast and are seen by Sahoglu (2005) as indicating the incorporation of the Cyclades within the 'Anatolian Trade Network.' The precise nature of these interactions requires further investigation. Certainly, however, they heralded the decline of the Keros-Syros culture, of the period of consolidation, and of the settlement nucleation that followed.

CYCLADIC SYMBOLIC CULTURE

One of the most striking features of the Cycladic cultures has always been the rich repertoire of finds of pottery, marble, and metal (as well as some beautifully carved vessels in chlorite schist) found in the Cycladic cemeteries and documented also at the major settlements. The marble figures or figurines have been much admired over the past century by collectors and connoisseurs (Zervos 1957; discussed later). They represent, particularly in the folded-arm figurine, a very well-defined form that is carved according to well-understood rules (to produce the so-called canonical varieties) that must have had a clear-cut and well-established meaning. The evolution of the forms and varieties is now reasonably well understood (Renfrew 1969; Getz-Preziosi 1987), but their function is not entirely clear. Why were some figures made so large—almost life-sized—that they could not be fitted, entire and unbroken, in a standard cist grave?

Until recently it has been widely assumed that these figures were made with a specifically funerary purpose: to be buried with the deceased in the Cycladic cemeteries. However, the realization that the site of Dhaskalio Kavos on Keros constitutes a location of ritual deposition of such materials (fine pottery, marble vessels, marble figurines, etc.) all deliberately broken, calls into question their uniquely funerary function. Consideration of the painted decoration on some of the figures, notably by Hendrix (2003), suggests that they were used, sometimes repeatedly, during the life of their owners. It has been suggested that Dhaskalio Kavos acted as a ritual center or 'symbolic attractor' (Renfrew et al. 2007, 435–42) for the Cyclades and perhaps beyond, and functions beyond the purely funerary now seem likely. Goodison (1989) has already used the rich symbolism of the Early Cycladic cultures as a starting point for the discussion of Early Cycladic religion. It is possible that the abundance of evidence for these cultures yielded by the Cycladic cemeteries has led scholars to lay too much emphasis upon a funerary interpretation.

THE RECEPTION OF CYCLADIC CULTURE IN THE TWENTIETH CENTURY AD

The simplicity and purity of form of many of the Early Cycladic sculptures and other artifacts has been appreciated aesthetically for more than a century. Picasso, Brancusi, and Giacometti were among the artists of the early Modern school who greatly admired Cycladic sculpture, followed in more recent times by Henry Moore and others. Such 'esteem' (Gill and Chippindale 1993) has contributed to an ever-increasing price for such antiquities on the art market. Unfortunately, collectors and major museums have not hesitated to pay substantial sums for unprovenanced antiquities, thus fueling this ready market in looted objects, which almost invariably lack any archaeological provenance or context. The extent of looting in the Cycladic cemeteries, especially since the Second World War, has been devastating. Most of the Early Cycladic finds in the world's museums outside of Greece lack any archaeological context. The loss to knowledge has been considerable. For instance, of the several near-life-sized Cycladic figures known, not one comes from a secure and published context. We simply do not know how they were used.

Disquiet about the purchase and acquisition of such looted materials increased notably in the years following the exhibition 'Art and Culture of the Cyclades,' held in 1977 at the Badisches Landesmuseum in Karlsruhe (Thimme and Getz-Preziosi 1997; see Renfrew 2006), where as much as half the material on display was without any stated provenance and therefore, by inference, looted. It was there that figurines, illicitly removed from the ritual site of Dhaskalio Kavos on Keros, the so-called Keros Hoard, first made their public appearance (see Sotirakopoulou 2005). Scholars in general have now come to realize that to publish or give prominence to unprovenanced antiquities (as for instance in Renfrew 1991) risks offering legitimacy to their purchase and thus to the whole cycle of destructive looting and sale. Many museums now follow the logic of the 1970 UNESCO Convention on the Illicit Traffic of Cultural Property and decline to acquire antiquities that lack a documented provenance going back before 1970. The loss to scholarship has, however, been immense. And that is the main reason that we still know and understand relatively little about the Cyclades in the Early Bronze Age despite the apparent richness of the material.

BIBLIOGRAPHY

Atkinson, Thomas D., Robert C. Bosanquet, Campbell C. Edgar, Arthur J. Evans, David G. Hogarth, Duncan Mackenzie, Cecil Smith, and Francis B. Welch. 1904. *Excavations at Phylakopi in Melos.* Society for the Promotion of Hellenic Studies Supplementary Paper 4. London: Macmillan.

Barber, Robin L. N. 1974. "Phylakopi 1911 and the History of the Later Cycladic Bronze Age." *BSA* 69: 1–53.

Barrett, John C., and Paul Halstead, eds. 2004. *The Emergence of Civilization Revisited.*

Bent, James T. 1884. "Researches among the Cyclades." *JHS* 5: 42–58.

Betancourt, Philip P. 2008. "The Cemetery at Haghia Photia, Crete." In *Horizon*, 237–40.

Bossert, Eva-Maria. 1967. "Kastri auf Syros." *Archaiologikon Deltion* 22(A): 53–76.

Broodbank, Cyprian. 2000. *An Island Archaeology of the Early Cyclades.* New York: Cambridge University Press.

Cherry, John. 2004. "Chapter 14 Revisited: Sites, Settlements, and Populations in the Prehistoric Aegean since *The Emergence of Civilization*." In *Emergence of Civilization Revisited*, 1–20.

Coleman, John E. 1977. *Keos 1: Kephala: A Late Neolithic Settlement and Cemetery.* Princeton: Princeton University Press.

Davaras, Costis, and Philip P. Betancourt. 2004. *Hagia Photia Cemetery I: The Tomb Groups and Architecture*. Prehistory Monographs 14. Philadelphia: INSTAP Academic Press.

Davis, Jack L. 1992. "Review of Aegean Prehistory: The Islands of the Aegean." *AJA* 96: 699–756.

Dawkins, Richard M., and John L. Droop. 1911. The Excavations at Phylakopi in Melos. *BSA* 17: 1–22.

Doumas, Christos. 1977. *Early Bronze Age Burial Habits in the Cyclades*. Studies in Mediterranean Archaeology 48. Gothenburg: Åström.

———. 2008. "Chambers of Mystery." In *Horizon*, 165–76.

Evans, John D., and Colin Renfrew. 1968. *Excavations at Saliagos near Antiparos*. British School at Athens Suppl. 5. London: British School at Athens.

Gale, Noel H., and Zofia A. Stos-Gale. 2008. "Changing Patterns in Prehistoric Cycladic Metallurgy." In *Horizon*, 387–408.

Getz-Gentle, Patricia. 1987. *Sculptors of the Cyclades: Individual and Tradition in the Third Millennium BC*. Ann Arbor: University of Michigan Press.

———. 1996. *Stone Vessels of the Cyclades in the Early Bronze Age*. Philadelphia: Pennsylvania State University Press.

Gill, David, and Christopher Chippindale. 1993. "Material and Intellectual Consequences of Esteem for Cycladic Figures." *AJA* 97: 602–73.

Goodison, Lucy. 1989. *Death, Women, and the Sun: Symbolism of Regeneration in Early Aegean Religion*. Institute of Classical Studies Bulletin Suppl. 53. London: University College London.

Hage, Per, Frank Harary, and Brent James. 1999. "The Minimum Spanning Tree Problem in Archaeology." *American Antiquity* 61: 149–55.

Halstead, Paul. 2004. "Life after Mediterranean Polyculture: The Subsistence Subsystem and the Emergence of Civilization Revisited." In *Emergence of Civilization Revisited*, 189–206.

Hendrix, Elizabeth A. 2003. "Painted Early Cycladic Figures: An Exploration of Context and Meaning." *Hesperia* 72: 405–46.

Hoffman, Gail L. 2002. "Painted Ladies: Early Cycladic II Mourning Figures?" *AJA* 106: 525–50.

Karantzali, Efi. 1996. *Le Bronze ancien dans les Cyclades et en Crète: Les relations entre les deux régions; influence de la Grèce continentale*. BAR-IS 631. Oxford: Tempus Reparatum.

Manning, Sturt W. 2008. "Some Initial Wobbly Steps towards a Late Neolithic to Early Bronze III Radiocarbon Chronology for the Cyclades." In *Horizon*, 55–60.

Marangou, Lila, Colin Renfrew, Christos Doumas, and Giorgios Gavalas, eds. 2006. *Markiani, Amorgos: An Early Bronze Age Fortified Settlement. Overview of the 1985–1991 Investigations*. British School at Athens Supplementary vol. 40. London: British School at Athens.

Marthari, Marisa. 2008. "Aspects of Pottery Circulation in the Cyclades during the EB II Period: Fine and Semi-fine Imported Ceramic Wares at Skarkos, Ios." In *Horizon*, 71–84.

Nakou, Georgia. 1995. The Cutting Edge: A New Look at Early Aegean Metallurgy. *JMA* 8: 1–32.

Papathanassopoulos, George A. 1962. "Kykladika Naxov." *Archaeologikon Deltion* 17(A): 104–51.

Pullen, Daniel J. 1994. "A Lead Seal from Tsoungiza, Ancient Nemea, and Early Bronze Age Aegean Sealing Systems." *AJA* 98: 35–52.

Rahmstorf, Lorenz. 2003. "The Identification of Early Helladic Weights." In *METRON*, 293–302.

Rambach, Jorg. 2000a. *Kykladen I: Die frühe Bronzezeit. Grab- und Siedlungsbefunde.* Beiträge zur ur-und frühgeschichtlichen Archäologie des Mittelmeer-Kulturraumes 33. Bonn: Habelt.

———. 2000b. *Kykladen II: Die frühe Bronzezeit. Frühbronzezeitliche Beigabensittenkreise auf den Kykladen, Relative Chronologie, und Verbreitung.* Beiträge zur ur-und frühgeschichtlichen Archäologie des Mittelmeer-Kulturraumes 34. Bonn: Habelt.

Renfrew, Colin. 1967. Cycladic Metallurgy and the Aegean Early Bronze Age. *AJA* 71: 1–20.

———. 1969. The Development and Chronology of the Early Cycladic Figurines. *AJA* 73: 1–32.

———. 1972. *The Emergence of Civilisation: The Cyclades and the Aegean in the Third Millennium BC.* London: Methuen.

———. 1974. "Beyond a Subsistence Economy: The Evolution of Social Organisation in Prehistoric Europe." In *Reconstructing Complex Societies,* ed. Charlotte B. Moore, 69–85. Cambridge, Mass.: American Schools of Oriental Research.

———, ed. 1985. *The Archaeology of Cult: The Sanctuary at Phylakopi.* British School at Athens Supplementary vol. 18. London: Thames and Hudson.

———. 1991. *The Cycladic Spirit: Masterpieces from the Nicholas P. Goulandris Collection.* London: Thames and Hudson.

———. 2006. "Museums Acquisitions: Responsibilities for the Illicit Trade in Antiquities." In *Archaeology, Cultural Heritage, and the Antiquities Trade*, ed. Neil J. Brodie, Morag M. Kersel, Christina Luke, and Kathryn Walker Tubb, 245–57. Gainesville: University Press of Florida.

———, ed. 2007. *Excavations at Phylakopi in Melos 1974–77.* British School at Athens Supplementary vol. 42. London: British School at Athens.

———, and Arnold Aspinall. 1990. "Aegean Obsidian and the Franchthi Cave." In *Les industries lithiques taillées de Franchthi (Argolide, Grèce).* Tome I, *Présentation générale et industries paléolithiques,* ed. Catherine Perlès, 257–70. Excavations at Franchthi Cave, Greece, Fascicle 3. Indianapolis: Indiana University Press.

Renfrew, Colin, Johnston R. Cann, and John E. Dixon. 1965. "Obsidian in the Aegean." *BSA* 60: 225–47.

Renfrew, Colin, Christos Doumas, Lila Marangou, and Giorgios Gavalas, eds. 2007. *Keros, Dhaskalio Kavos: The Investigations of 1987–88.* McDonald Institute Monographs. Cambridge: McDonald Institute for Archaeological Research.

Renfrew, Colin, and Robert K. Evans. 2007. "The Early Bronze Age Pottery." In *Excavations at Phylakopi in Melos 1974–77,* ed. Colin Renfrew, 129–80. British School at Athens Supplementary vol. 42. London: British School at Athens.

Renfrew, Colin, Rupert Housley, and Sturt Manning. 2006. "The Absolute Dating." In *Markiani, Amorgos: An Early Bronze Age Fortified Settlement. Overview of the 1985–1991 Investigations,* ed. Lila Marangou, Colin Renfrew, Christos Doumas, and Giorgios Gavalas, 71–80. British School at Athens Supplementary vol. 40. London: British School at Athens.

Renfrew, Colin, Olga Philaniotou, Neil J. Brodie, and Giorgios Gavalas. 2008. "Keros: Dhaskalio and Kavos, Early Cycladic Stronghold and Ritual Centre. Preliminary Report of the 2006 and 2007 Excavation Seasons." *BSA* 102: 1–33.

Renfrew, Colin, and Gene Sterud. 1969. "Close Proximity Analysis: A Rapid Method for the Ordering of Archaeological Materials." *American Antiquity* 34: 265–77.

Renfrew Colin, and J. Michael Wagstaff, ed. 1982. *An Island Polity: The Archaeology of Exploitation in Melos.* New York: Cambridge University Press.

Rutter, Jeremy B. 1984. "The Early Cycladic Gap: What It Is and How to Go About Filling It without Making It Go Away." In *Prehistoric Cyclades*, 95–107.

Sahoglu, Vasif. 2005. "The Anatolian Trade Network and the Izmir Region during the Early Bronze Age." *OJA* 24: 339–60.

Sampson, Adamantios. 2008a. "The Architectural Phases of the Neolithic Settlement of Ftelia on Mykonos." In *Horizon*, 29–36.

———. 2008b. "The Mesolithic Settlement and Cemetery of Maroulas on Kythnos." In *Horizon*, 13–18.

Sotirakopoulou, Panayiota I. 1993. "The Chronology of the 'Kastri Group' Reconsidered." *BSA* 88: 5–20.

———. 2005. *The "Keros Hoard": Myth or Reality?* Athens: Goulandris Foundation.

———. 2008. "Akrotiri, Thera: The Late Neolithic and Early Bronze Age Phases in the Light of Recent Excavations at the Site." In *Horizon*, 121–34.

Televantou, Christina A. 2008. "Strofilas: A Neolithic Settlement on Andros." In *Horizon*, 43–54.

Thimme, Jurgen, and Patricia Getz-Preziosi, eds. 1977. *Art and Culture of the Cyclades in the Third Millennium BC*. Chicago: University of Chicago Press.

Torrence, Robin. 1986. *Production and Exchange of Stone Tools: Prehistoric Obsidian in the Aegean*. New York: Cambridge University Press.

Tsountas, Christos. 1898. "Kykladika." *Archaiologike Ephemeris* 1898: 137–212.

———. 1899. "Kykladika II." *Archaiologike Ephemeris* 1899: 74–134.

Wagner, Gunther A., and Gerd Weissgerber, eds. 1985. *Silber, Blei, und Gold auf Sifnos: Prähistorische und antike Metallproduktion*. Der Anschnitt 3. Bochum: Deutsches Bergbau-Museum.

Whitelaw, Todd M. 2004. "The Development of an Island Centre: Urbanization at Phylakopi on Melos." In *Explaining Social Change: Studies in Honour of Colin Renfrew*, ed. John Cherry, Christopher Scarre, and Stephen Shennan, 149–66. McDonald Institute Monographs. Cambridge: McDonald Institute for Archaeological Research.

Wilson, David E. 1999. *Keos 9: Ayia Irini Periods I–III, The Neolithic and Early Bronze Age Settlements*. Part 1, *The Pottery and Small Finds*. Mainz: Philipp von Zabern.

———, Peter M. Day, and Nota Dimopoulou-Rethemiotaki. 2008. "The Gateway Port of Poros-Katsambas: Trade and Exchange between North-central Crete and the Cyclades in EB I–II." In *Horizon*, 261–70.

Wright, James C. 2004. "The Emergence of Leadership and the Rise of Civilization in the Aegean." In *Emergence of Civilisation Revisited*, 64–89.

Zachos, Konstantinos. 1990. "The Neolithic Period in Naxos." In *Cycladic Culture: Naxos in the Third Millennium B.C.*, ed. Lila Marangou, 29–38. Athens: Goulandris Foundation.

———, and Angelika Dousougli. 2008. "Observations on the Early Bronze Age Sealings from the Cave of Zas at Naxos." In *Horizon*, 85–96.

Zapheiropoulou, Photeini. 1984. "The Chronology of the Kampos Group." In *Prehistoric Cyclades*, 31–40.

———. 2008. "Early Bronze Age Cemeteries of the Kampos Group on Ano Kouphonisi." In *Horizon*, 183–94.

Zervos, Christian. 1957. *L'art des Cyclades du début à la fin de l'Âge du Bronze, 2500–1100 avant notre ère*. Paris: Cahiers d'Art.

Middle Bronze Age

CHAPTER 7

MAINLAND GREECE

SOFIA VOUTSAKI

THE Middle Helladic (MH) period is caught between two peaks of economic growth and cultural achievement, the Early and Late Bronze Ages. In addition, the MH mainland has suffered from comparison with Minoan palatial societies and the maritime polities of the Aegean (Rutter 2001, 32). As a result, the MH period has until recently received little attention.

For most of the 20th century, research concentrated on the origins of the MH civilization or on typological sequences, although studies by Dickinson (1977), Zerner (1979), Nordquist (1987), and papers in the journal *Hydra* have laid the foundations for subsequent research. The last fifteen years have seen a renewed interest in the period, spurred by seminal new publications (Maran 1992), Rutter's excellent synthesis (Rutter 2001), renewed investigations at important sites (e.g., Kolonna: Gauss and Smetana 2007; Aspis: Touchais 1998; Philippa-Touchais in press b), and the reexamination of old data (e.g., pre-Mycenaean finds from Ano Englianos: Davis and Stocker in press; MH Argolid: Voutsaki 2005). These investigations and discussions, many of which have been assembled in two recent conferences on the MH period (Felten et al. 2007; Philippa-Touchais et al. in press), have cast doubt on the traditional perception of MH societies as static, backward, isolated, and largely homogeneous (as pointed out already by Rutter 2001, 132). The MH period is now seen as witnessing important social, political, and cultural changes that lead to the formation of the early Mycenaean polities and the later palatial states. The following discussion presents some of the new evidence, as well as new approaches to old data, which have brought about the modification (or at least the qualification) of these earlier views.

DEMARCATION IN SPACE

The core area of the MH mainland includes the Peloponnese, Attica, Boeotia, Euboea, and coastal Thessaly, while the areas to the west and the north (Ionian islands, Aetolia-Acarnania, inland Thessaly, Epirus, Macedonia) can be said to belong to the periphery of the Helladic world. The discussion here covers primarily the core areas of the southern mainland, although relations and exchanges with neighboring areas are also discussed.

DURATION

The MH period begins around 2100 BC or somewhat earlier. While there is agreement about the earlier part of the period, the transition to the LH period is caught in the wider debate between the 'High Chronology,' which supports a date around 1700 BC (Manning et al. 2006), and the 'Low Chronology,' which prefers the traditional date at 1600 BC (Warren and Hankey 1989). The issue can be resolved only if more extensive programs of radiocarbon analyses from mainland sites are undertaken.

Defining the internal subdivisions of the period is difficult for several reasons. Regional differences hinder comparison between local sequences (see Maran 1992, 370, figure 25), while establishing synchronisms with Minoan Crete and the Aegean is not without difficulties (Hatzaki 2007; Girella 2007). Moreover, there are only a few reliable radiocarbon dates from the mainland. It is worth noting that recent ^{14}C analyses from Lerna (Voutsaki, Nijboer, and Zerner in press) render support to the High Chronology. Table 7.1 shows some recent suggestions for the chronology of the period. The discussion here concentrates on the MH period and thereby follows the accepted periodization of Aegean prehistory, based on the ceramic sequence. However, if one considers historical and social developments, as well as changes in material culture, it makes more sense to discuss the earlier part of the period (MH I–MH II phases) together with the EH III phase and to consider MH III together with LH I. For this reason, an effort is made to discuss earlier and later developments for each aspect presented.

SUMMARY OF MAIN DEVELOPMENTS

The southern mainland suffers a severe crisis at the end of the EH period, the nature of which is now better understood, though its causes are still debated (Forsén 1992; Maran 1998). The EH II/EH III transition and the EH III period witness depopulation and destruction in various sites, changes in the settlement pattern and the settlement

Table 7.1. The MH Period: Relative and Absolute Chronologies

| | Suggested Calendar Years BC | | | |
	Dietz 1991	Dickinson 1994	Rutter 2001 (based on Manning 1995)	Voutsaki, Nijboer and Zerner (in press)
EH III			2200/2150–2050/2000	–2100
MH I		2100–1900	2050/2000–1950/1900	2100–1900
MH II	–1775	1900–1700	1950/1900–1750/1720	1900–1800
MH III	1775–1700	1700–1580	1750/1720–1680	1800–1700
LH I	1700–1625/1600	1580–1500	1680–1600/1580	1700–

Source: Courtesy of the author.

hierarchy, the use of settlement space, mortuary practices, and the material culture. Traditionally these changes were attributed to invasions and migrations (Howell 1973; Hood 1986). Recently, more emphasis has been placed on environmental causes such as land degradation and erosion (see Zangger 1992; Whitelaw 2000; Rutter 2001, 136) or climate change (Manning 1997), as well as their impact on the social system. However, migrations (or at least infiltration of ethnic groups) are still part of the explanatory framework (papers in Galanaki et al. 2007)—though whether these were the cause or the consequence of the crisis in the south needs to be discussed more explicitly. As Rutter (2001, 145) concludes, an old explanatory model has been rejected, but alternative interpretations have not been formulated as yet. He stresses, nevertheless, that the realization that we are dealing with a complex and protracted process affecting different regions and sites in an uneven manner is a significant and positive development.

The situation in MH I–MH II is not very well understood since these periods have received very little attention. While prevailing opinion holds that there is little development during the early part of the MH period, closer analyses of well-documented bodies of data indicate that changes *are* taking place in this period. For instance, the MH I period in Lerna sees the appearance (and subsequent disappearance) of larger or more complex domestic structures and perhaps some accumulation of wealth (Voutsaki forthcoming), while in MH II a subtle increase in the complexity of mortuary practices is evident (Milka n.d.). However, *irreversible* changes seem to take place only in MH III–LH I (Dickinson 1989, 133).

In the last phase of the MBA, the mainland societies indeed undergo a deep transformation. The changes are manifested primarily in the mortuary practices and are accompanied by an intensification of exchanges with areas within and beyond the Aegean. The influx of prestige items found (primarily though not exclusively) in the Shaft Graves of Mycenae represent the most spectacular aspect of this change in external relations—but more mundane items such as pottery circulate more widely as well. Exchanges not only with Minoan Crete and the Aegean but also with areas farther afield become denser, while the local material culture becomes much more receptive to Aegean and Minoan influences.

The reasons underlying this transformation are complex. The evolution of the debate gives us interesting insights into the history of the discipline. Under the diffusionist paradigm, the transformation of the mainland was attributed first to invasion and later to heavy cultural influence by the more advanced Minoan palatial societies. In the last decades of the 20th century, under the influence of Renfrew's evolutionist model (Renfrew 1972), the explanation for social change was sought in internal social developments. Most recently, an attempt has been made to bring together external stimuli and internal developments (Voutsaki 1999, 2005; Wright 2004b; Dickinson in press).

SETTLEMENT PATTERN

The transition from the EH to the MH period is marked by a severe discontinuity in the settlement pattern: Many sites are destroyed and/or abandoned between the end of the EH II period and the beginning of MH I. The number of sites in use decreases dramatically (Rutter 2001, 122–23; Wright 2004a, 119; Zavadil in press); most notably, the small rural sites are abandoned (Bintliff in press). There is also evidence for the decrease in the size of settlements and for an ensuing disappearance of the site hierarchy (Rutter 2001, 113). However, some poorly documented sites, such as Argos (Touchais 1998), Thebes (Demakopoulou and Konsola 1975; Dakouri-Hild 2001), and Mycenae (Shelton in press), were perhaps fairly large throughout the period. In certain regions, the evidence for EH III is limited or nonexistent, while MH I sites are quite rare across the entire southern mainland. This process of abandonment and regression, as well as the recovery from MH II or MH III onward, proceeds in an uneven fashion in the different regions (Wright 2004a; Zavadil in press).

In the MH III period, we observe population growth, as attested by an increase in the number of sites (Zavadil in press), the resettlement of areas that lay abandoned during the MH I–II periods, and a possible increase in the size of some settlements, for instance in Thebes, Argos, and Mycenae. In addition, survey data suggest a more intensive land use (Wright 2004a, 122). A three-tiered site hierarchy can once more be reconstructed (Rutter 2001, 130–31)—although, in the absence of information on settlement size, the criterion is often the presence of rich tombs.

SETTLEMENT ORGANIZATION AND DOMESTIC ARCHITECTURE

Few MH settlements have been extensively excavated (Malthi constitutes an exception, but its dating remains debated—see Darcque 2005, 343–344). In addition, neither settlement organization nor the development of domestic architecture during the MH period has ever been studied systematically (but see now Philippa-Touchais in press; Voutsaki in press). Few settlements are fortified: Kolonna has already been mentioned; the circuit wall in Malthi most likely dates to the Mycenaean period (Darcque 1980, 32–33); and the function or date of the enclosures in Thebes, Aspis, and Megali Magoula, Galatas (for the latter see Konsolaki-Yannopoulou in press) are uncertain.

Houses are self-standing and usually positioned in an irregular fashion—at least in MH I–II. They are fairly homogeneous: Most consist of two rooms, are rarely larger than 50–60 m², and have stone foundations with a mud-brick superstructure. There are differences in size and contents even in the earlier period. For example, MH I House 98A in Lerna consists of a main house and a smaller structure serving as a storage/kitchen area—where several large, imported Minoan jars have been found—within a rectangular enclosure. Similarly, house 311B in Pefkakia had large storage pithoi and a concentration of Aeginetan imports (Maran 2007a, 172ff.). In the later phases, differences between houses become more marked: Some MH III houses in Asine are up to four times larger than ordinary MH houses, have a more complex layout, and are built on either side of a path, sharing a similar orientation (Nordquist 1987, 76ff.; Voutsaki in press). Other large houses are reported from other settlements (e.g., in Plasi, Marathon) (Marinatos 1970). Finally, in MH III–LH I, a few sites acquire a more organized layout: For instance, in the southeastern sector in the Aspis, the haphazardly positioned MH IIIA houses are replaced in MH IIIB–LH I by a row of complexes that adjoin each other and encircle the top of the hill, that is, following the (possible) outer enclosure (Philippa-Touchais in press).

Throughout the period, Kolonna stands out because of its heavy fortification wall, the more organized arrangement of the houses (Felten 2007, 13, 15), and the presence of a monumental structure from MH I onward (Felten 2007; Gauss and Smetana in press). It should be emphasized that Kolonna differs from the mainland centers in terms of social and economic organization and has many similarities with the large, cosmopolitan harbor towns of the Aegean.

Mortuary Practices

Mortuary practices are quite homogeneous in the earlier phases (EH III–MH I–MH II), although subtle variations can be observed. Burials are in general intramural, though few burials (mostly of infants) are interred under the floor of houses still in use; many graves are cut into or among ruined houses (Nordquist 1987, 95; Milka in press; Aravantinos and Psaraki in press). Extramural cemeteries are in use probably from MH II onward. Tumuli are also found, but their distribution is uneven (Müller 1989). Different grave types are used: simple pits, cists of various types, as well as large pithoi or smaller jars (the latter exclusively for infants and children). The mode of disposal is fairly uniform: As a rule, the graves contain single, contracted inhumations, although a few double or even multiple burials exist. Offerings are rare and unimpressive: a vase, a few beads, a bone pin. Once more, there are notable exceptions, such as the tumuli in Aphidna (Wide 1896; Hielte-Stauropoulou and Wedde 2002) and Kastroulia (Rambach 2007) or the built grave in Kolonna (Kilian-Dirlmeier 1997).

The situation changes in a fairly dramatic fashion in MH III–LH I, though the transformation is actually gradual and uneven across space. Extramural cemeteries are used more widely, and reuse of the grave and the secondary treatment of the body become more common. New tomb types, especially designed for reuse—the shaft grave, the tholos tomb, and the chamber tomb—are adopted. Finally, there is a general increase in the quantity and diversity of funerary offerings, although no tombs equal in any way the splendor of the Shaft Graves of Mycenae. Conspicuous consumption in the mortuary sphere clearly becomes the main strategy for the creation of power and prestige in this period (Voutsaki 1997).

Cult

Interestingly, evidence for cult or ritual practices is absent from the MH mainland: There are virtually no cult places (Rutter 2001, 144) or artifacts that have an unambiguous ritual function, with the exception of a few late figurines or zoomorphic vases, such as the two bull *rhyta* found in Eleusis (Mylonas 1975, 203). Needless to say, the archaeological invisibility of religion in MH times need not imply the absence of religious beliefs. It has been suggested that the ritual focus in MH times was in the mortuary sphere, as can be attested, for instance, by the evidence of rites taking place on or in the vicinity of some tumuli (Whittaker in press).

One shrine dates from the very end of the MH period at Apollo Maleatas in Epidauros. While votives (pottery, weapons, and ornaments found in ashy layers intermingled with animal bones—Lambrinudakis 1981) were deposited from LH I onward, at a short distance away, on the very top of the Kynortion hill, an MH pit was cut and subsequently filled with feasting debris in the middle of a settlement abandoned since EH times. As the area was never built over, Theodorou-Mavrommatidi (in press) suggests that we may observe here the process of the 'sanctification' of a precinct.

Material Culture

The discussions regarding early MH material culture have largely concentrated on the issue of the origins of MH culture. However, Forsén's (1992) study has by now demonstrated that changes in material culture (the appearance of apsidal buildings, terracotta 'anchors,' stone shaft-hole hammer axes, tumuli) attributed by scholars of the previous generation to invaders from the north or migrants from the east do not all appear at the same time, nor are they consistently associated with destruction (or postdestruction) layers.

While MH pottery is considered fairly simple and conservative (Rutter 2007, 35), there are marked differences between regions and even between neighboring sites, as each site contains different proportions of local wares, local imitations, and imports from different regions. Nonceramic finds (tools, ornaments) are equally simple and basic, and show little development through time. However, recent studies emphasize that technological advances *did* take place even very early on in the period—for example, the replacement of arsenic copper with bronze metallurgy (Kayafa in press) and the adoption of the potter's wheel (Spencer in press). On the other hand, the range and quantities of metal objects remained limited throughout the period, while technological advances in pottery remained largely restricted to Boeotia. One may conclude that a certain introvertedness and conformity to tradition characterized some, though not all, of the mainlanders: For instance, Aeginetan pottery was imitated in Thessaly (Maran 2007a, 174) but not in Boeotia (Sarri 2007, 163).

Needless to say, the situation changed dramatically toward the end of the period, when the mainland became open to external cultural influences. It is only by reference to changing social conditions and cultural orientation that we can explain the transformation of material culture in MH III–LH I: the diversification of pottery styles and technologies; the appearance of a uniform ceramic style (the LH I style: Rutter 2001, 137); the adoption of figurative elements in the hitherto uniconic MH culture (Rutter 2001, 141–42); the increased receptivity to external influences and stimuli; and, of course, the influx of valuable items.

External Contacts

This last point brings us to the issue of external contacts. The EH II–EH III–MH I discontinuity affected trade relations as well, as one can deduce from the circulation of both ceramics and chipped stone (Rutter 2001, 122). However, even in early MH I there is an increase in contacts between the Greek mainland (especially the eastern coast) and Aegina, the Aegean islands, and Crete (Rutter and Zerner 1984; Rutter 2001, 124). The distribution of (primarily) ceramic imports (Rutter and Zerner 1984; Nordquist 1987, 61ff.; Zerner 1993) allows us to reconstruct small-scale, overlapping networks whose extent and intensity fluctuate. The presence of Minoan imports mostly along the eastern coast is well documented, though there are now interesting new additions to the corpus, for instance at Kastroulia (Rambach 2007) and Pylos (Davis and Stocker in press). Aeginetan pottery (Zerner 1993; Lindblom 2001) reached primarily the Argolid and Corinthia and to a lesser extent Arcadia, Laconia, Boeotia, Euboea, Thessaly, and the Cyclades, while a few pieces are found along the coasts of Italy and Asia Minor (Lindblom 2001, 43–44; Maran 2007a, 171). Lustrous Decorated and other Minoanizing wares (whose provenance remains uncertain—Kiriatzi in press) have a more southerly distribution. Central Greek pottery, produced in Boeotia, was exported to the south (Zerner 1993, 47 and notes 44–48; Sarri 2007, passim). A Thessalian network reaching the northeastern Aegean has recently been reconstructed (Maran 2007a). There are substantial differences in the distribution of imports throughout the period: While coastal sites had obvious advantages, certain communities (or social groups) were clearly more successful than others in establishing and maintaining trade contacts. For instance, imports concentrate in Lerna (Zerner 1993) and Argos (Kilikoglou et al. 2003), while more modest quantities are imported to Asine (Nordquist 1987, 61ff.), and none are found in Tsoungiza (Rutter 1990). As already stated, the MH III–LH I period sees an intensification of pottery exchanges, as well as clearer Cycladic and Minoan influences on mainland pottery (Graziadio 1998; Rutter 2001, 142).

Turning now to metal trade, most of the copper and all of the lead used in the MH period came from the Aegean, though some of the copper may have come from sources in the Aegean islands, Rodopi in Thrace and perhaps Cyprus (see references on provenance analyses in Kayafa in press). Less is known about the provenance of the few gold and silver objects found in the MH mainland.

Contacts were not restricted to the Aegean: The interaction between the southern mainland and the areas to the west and north, primarily Epirus and Macedonia, is now better understood, thanks to recent discoveries and investigations (see Andreou, Fotiadis, and Kotsakis 2001). Minyan imports and local imitations are found in a few coastal sites (Horejs 2007). In recent years, contacts with the Adriatic and the Balkans (Maran 2007b) have received more attention, and their significance has been discussed in a much more nuanced manner (though overtly diffusionist approaches persist as well). The significance of contacts with the central Mediterranean—as evidenced by the presence of mainland pottery in the Aeolian Islands and in Vivara (Vianello 2005; Merkouri in press)—cannot be overemphasized. It becomes evident that the traditional notions of an isolated and introverted mainland need to be abandoned, although a certain resistance to external influences in the early part of the period is apparent as well.

Social Organization and Social Change

In the MH period communities were organized in villages whose economic life was based on agriculture and animal husbandry (Nordquist 1987; for recent studies see Forstenpointner et al. in press; Gardeisen in press). Basic craft activities (e.g., the preparation of stone tools—Hartenberger and Runnels 2001) may have taken place within the household. A certain degree of craft specialization existed, although we are dealing mostly with what Nordquist has called 'household industries' (Nordquist

1995). Needless to say, pottery production in Aegina must have been highly organized, but in economic and social organization, Kolonna clearly differed from MH villages.

Society in the MH period was traditionally considered to be fairly simple, undifferentiated, and static. However, Imma Kilian-Dirlmeier, in her publication of the MH II built grave at Kolonna (Kilian-Dirlmeier 1997), has argued for the existence of elites as early as MH I–II on the basis of some rich burials. Although the early date of some of her examples has been questioned (Voutsaki 2005, 136; Dickinson in press), there undoubtedly *are* some rich tombs in MH I–II (see earlier discussion). However, we should be careful when equating wealth with status—whether achieved, claimed, or aspired to (Dickinson in press). In addition, we should not interpret these burials in isolation (and see them as antecedents of the Shaft Grave elites) but examine them alongside all of the contemporary graves in the region. We certainly need to acknowledge the possibility that different regions of the MH world had different forms of social organization.

James Wright (2001, 2004b) has offered a slightly different reading of these rich burials, which he attributes not to established elites but to aggrandizing leaders of unstable and fluid factions stretching across different communities. However, the emphasis in the mortuary sphere in the mainland (with the exception of the Kolonna grave) is not really on the individual but on the burial group (presumably representing a kinship group). Indeed, the clustering of graves and their close association to houses (Milka in press) suggest that kinship was an important element of social organization (Voutsaki 2005, 137). Recent analyses of mortuary and osteological data have stressed the significance of age and gender—both dimensions underlying kinship positions—in the MH period (Ingvarsson-Sundström 2003; Voutsaki 2004; Milka in Voutsaki, Triantaphyllou, and Milka 2005, 37; Triantaphyllou in press; Pomadère in press; Ruppenstein in press). It has therefore been suggested that the main organizational principle in the MH I–II period was kinship rather than status and that authority was embedded in kinship relations and therefore did not require ostentatious practices or elaborate material culture for its legitimation (Voutsaki 2001, 183–84).

However, the question remains, why did the situation change in MH III–LH I? To attribute social changes solely to growing prosperity (following Renfrew's [1972] systemic model) is not convincing: Economic growth on the mainland takes place primarily *after* or at best *parallel to* the so-called Shaft Grave phenomenon (Voutsaki 2005, 139–140; see earlier discussion of the intensification of land use and trade in MH III–LH II). In addition, attempts to attribute the rise of the mainland centers to control of specific economic resources, usually (precious) metal, remain inconclusive (Dickinson 1989, 136; Rutter 2001, 145). Of course, the integration of the mainland in ever-expanding networks of exchange played a very important role (Sherratt and Sherratt 1991; Voutsaki 1997)—and here Wright's arguments about the manipulation of external contacts by competing leaders are directly relevant (Wright 2004b; see also Voutsaki 1997). However, we need to reflect more about the *political* ramifications, the impact of the expansionist policies of the Minoan palaces, and the shifting significance of (and possible competition between) the

Aegean maritime centers (Broodbank 2000, 350ff.). These expanding horizons and fluid 'international' conditions created new arenas of social action and provided unique opportunities for diplomatic alliances. The sudden wealth acquired by a couple of families in Mycenae cannot be seen as the result of gradual enrichment and growth but should be attributed to cunning political maneuvers by opportunistic leaders. However, only close empirical analyses of both funerary and settlement data in the mainland will allow us to reconstruct the changing position of individuals, social groups, and communities in this expanding new world.

BIBLIOGRAPHY

Andreou, Stelios, Michael Fotiadis, and Kostas Kotsakis. 2001. "The Neolithic and Bronze Age of Northern Greece." In *Aegean Prehistory*, 259–328.

Aravantinos, Vassilis, and Kyriaki Psaraki. In press. "The Middle Helladic Cemeteries of Thebes: General Review and Remarks in the Light of New Investigations and Finds." In *Mesohelladika*.

Bintliff, John. In press. "The Middle Bronze Age through the Surface Survey Record of the Greek Mainland: Demographic and Sociopolitical Insights." In *Mesohelladika*.

Broodbank, Cyprian. 2000. *An Island Archaeology of the Early Cyclades*. New York: Cambridge University Press.

Dakouri-Hild, Anastasia. 2001. "Plotting Fragments: A Preliminary Assessment of the Middle Helladic Settlement in Boeotian Thebes." In *Urbanism*, 103–18.

Darcque, Pascal. 2005. *L'habitat mycénien: Formes et fonctions de l'espace bâti en Grèce continentale à la fin du IIe millénaire avant J.-C.* Athens: École française d'Athènes.

Davis, Jack, and Shari Stocker. In press. "Early Helladic and Middle Helladic Pylos: The Petropoulos Trenches and Pre-Mycenaean Remains on the Englianos Ridge." In *Mesohelladika*.

Demakopoulou, Katie, and Dora Konsola. 1975. "Leipsana protoelladikou, mesoelladikou kai ysteroelladikou oikismou sti Thiva." *Archaiologiko Deltio* 30 A: 44–89.

Dickinson, Oliver T. P. K. 1977. *The Origins of the Mycenaean Civilisation*. SIMA 49. Gothenburg: Åström.

———. 1989. "'The Origins of Mycenaean Civilisation' Revisited." In *TRANSITION*, 131–36.

———. 1994. *The Aegean Bronze Age*. Cambridge: Cambridge University Press.

———. In press. "The 'Third World' of the Aegean? Middle Helladic Greece Revisited." In *Mesohelladika*.

Dietz, Soren. 1991. *The Argolid at the Transition to the Mycenaean Age*. Copenhagen: National Museum of Denmark.

Felten, Florens, Walter Gauss and Rudolfine Smetana, eds. 2007. *MH Pottery*.

Felten, Florens. 2007. "Aegina-Kolonna: The History of a Greek Acropolis." In *MH Pottery*, 11–34.

Forsén, Jeannette. 1992. *The Twilight of the Early Helladics: A Study of the Disturbances in East-central and Southern Greece towards the End of the Early Bronze Age*. Jonsered, Sweden: Åström.

Forstenpointner, Gerhard, Alfred Galik, Gerald E. Weissengruber, Stefan Zohmann, Ursula Thanheiser, and Walter Gauss. In press. "Subsistence and More in Middle Bronze Age Aegina Kolonna: Patterns of Husbandry, Hunting, and Agriculture." In *Mesohelladika*.

Galanaki, Ioanna, Helena Tomas, Yannis Galanakis, and Robert Laffineur, eds. 2007. *BABS*.

Gardeisen, Armelle. In press. "Approche comparative de contextes du Bronze Moyen égéen à travers les données de l'archéozoologie." In *Mesohelladika*.

Gauss, Walter, and Rudolfine Smetana. 2007. "Aegina Kolonna: The Stratigraphic Sequence of the Middle Bronze Age." In *MH Pottery*, 57–80.

———. In press. "Aegina Kolonna in the Middle Bronze Age." In *Mesohelladika*.

Girella, Luca. 2007. "Toward a Definition of Middle Minoan III Ceramic Sequence in South-central Crete: Returning to MM IIIA and IIIB Traditional Division?" In *MH Pottery*, 233–56.

Graziadio, Giampaolo. 1998. "Trade Circuits and Trade-routes in the Shaft Grave Period." *SMEA* 40(1): 29–76.

Hartenberger, Britt, and Curtis Runnels. 2001. "The Organization of Flaked Stone Production at Bronze Age Lerna." *Hesperia* 70(3): 255–83.

Hatzaki, Eleni. 2007. "Ceramic Groups of Early Neopalatial Knossos in the Context of Crete and the South Aegean." In *MH Pottery*, 273–94.

Hielte-Stauropoulou, Maria, and Michael Wedde. 2002. "Sam Wide's Excavation at Aphidna—Stratigraphy and Finds." In *Peloponnesian Sanctuaries and Cults*, ed. Robin Hägg, 21–24. Skrifter utgivna av Svenska Institutet i Athen. 4°, 48. Stockholm: Åström.

Hood, Sinclair. 1986. "Evidence for Invasions at the End of the Early Bronze Age." In *The End of the Early Bronze Age in the Aegean*, ed. Gerald Cadogan, 31–68. Leiden: Brill.

Horejs, Barbara. 2007. "Transition from Middle to Late Bronze Age in Central Macedonia and Its Synchronisms with the 'Helladic' World." In *MH Pottery*, 183–200.

Howell, Roger J. 1973. "The Origins of the Middle Helladic Culture." In *Bronze Age Migrations in the Aegean*, ed. R. A. Crossland and Ann Birchall, 73–106. Park Ridge, N.J.: Noyes.

Ingvarsson-Sundström, Anne. 2003. "Children Lost and Found: A Bioarchaeological Study of Middle Helladic Children in Asine with a Comparison to Lerna." PhD diss., University of Uppsala.

Kayafa, Maria. In press. "Middle Helladic Metallurgy and Metalworking: Review of the Archaeological and Archaeometric Evidence from the Peloponnese." In *Mesohelladika*.

Kilian-Dirlmeier, Imma. 1997. *Das mittelbronzezeitliche Schachtgrab von Ägina*. Mainz: Philip von Zabern.

Kilikoglou, Vassilis, Evangelia Kiriatzi, Anna Philippa-Touchais, Gilles Touchais, and Ian Whitbread. 2003. "Pottery Production and Supply at MH Aspis, Argos: The Evidence of Chemical and Petrographic Analyses." In *METRON*, 131–36.

Kiriatzi, Evangelia. In press. "'Minoanising' Pottery Traditions in the Southwest Aegean during the Middle Bronze Age: Understanding the Social Context of Technological and Consumption Practice." In *Mesohelladika*.

Konsolaki-Yannopoulou, Eleni. In press. "The Middle Helladic Establishment at Megali Magoula, Galatas (Troizinia)." In *Mesohelladika*.

Lambrinudakis, Vasileios. 1981. "Remains of the Mycenaean Period in the Sanctuary of Apollon Maleatas." In *Sanctuaries and Cults*, 59–65.

Lambropoulou, Anastasia. 1998. "The Middle Helladic Period in the Corinthia and the Argolid: An Archaeological Survey." PhD diss., Bryn Mawr College.

Lindblom, Michael. 2001. *Marks and Maker: Appearance, Distribution, and Function of Middle and Late Helladic Manufacturers' Marks on Aeginetan Pottery*. SIMA 128. Jonsered, Sweden: Åström.

Manning, Sturt W. 1995. *The Absolute Chronology of the Aegean Early Bronze Age.* Monographs in Mediterranean Archaeology 1. Sheffield: Sheffield Academic Press.

———. 1997. "Cultural Change in the Aegean c. 2200 BC." In *Third Millennium BC Climate Change and Old-world Collapse,* ed. Hasan N. Dalfes, George Kukla, and Harvey Weiss, 149–71. NATO ASI Series I, vol. 49. Berlin: Springer.

———, Christopher Bronk Ramsey, Walter Kutschera, Thomas Higham, Bernd Kromer, Peter Steier, and Eva M. Wild. 2006. "Chronology for the Aegean Late Bronze Age 1700–1400 BC." *Science* 312 (5573): 565–69.

Maran, Joseph. 1992. *Die deutschen Ausgrabungen auf der Peukakia–Magula in Thessalien III: Die mittlere Bronzezeit.* Bonn: Habelt.

———. 1998. *Kulturwandel auf dem griechischen Festland und den Kykladen in späten 3. Jahrtausend v. Chr.* Bonn: Habelt.

———. 2007a. "Emulation of Aeginetan Pottery in the Middle Bronze Age of Coastal Thessaly: Regional Context and Social Meaning." In *MH Pottery,* 167–82.

———. 2007b. "Seaborne Contacts between the Aegean, the Balkans, and the Central Mediterranean in the 3rd Millennium BC: The Unfolding of the Mediterranean World." In *BABS,* 3–23.

Marinatos, Spyridon. 1970. "Further News from Marathon." *AAA* 3: 153–66.

Merkouri, Christina. In press. "MH III/LH I Pottery from Vivara (Gulf of Naples, Italy): A Contribution to the Understanding of an Enigmatic Period." In *Mesohelladika.*

Milka, Eleni. In press. "Burials upon the Ruins of Abandoned Houses in the MH Argolid." In *Mesohelladika.*

———. n.d. "An Analysis of Mortuary Practices in MH Lerna." Unpublished paper.

Müller, Sylvie. 1989. "Les tumuli helladiques: où? quand? comment?" *BCH* 113: 1–41.

Mylonas, G. 1975. *To dytikon nekrotafeion tis Elevsinos.* 3 Vols. *Vivliothiki tis en Athinais Archailogikis Etaireias 81.* Athens: Archailogiki Etaireia.

Nordquist, Gullög C. 1987. *A Middle Helladic Village: Asine in the Argolid.* Studies in Ancient Mediterranean and Near Eastern Civilization 16. Uppsala: Boreas.

———. 1995. "Who Made the Pots? Production in the Middle Helladic Society." In *Politeia,* 201–207.

Philippa-Touchais, Anna. In press a. "Settlement Planning and Social Organisation in Middle Helladic Greece." In *Mesohelladika.*

Philippa-Touchais, Anna. In press b. "Les tombes intra muros de l'Helladique Moyen à la lumière des fouilles de l'Aspis d'Argos," in A. Banaka and S. Huber (eds.) *Sur les pas de Wilhelm Vollgraff. Cent ans d'activités archéologiques à Argos,* Recherches Franco-Helléniques 4.

Philippa-Touchais, Anna, Gilles Touchais, Sofia Voutsaki and James Wright, eds. In print. *Mesohelladika.*

Pomadère, Maia. In press. "De l'indifférenciation à la discrimination spatiale des sépultures? Variété des comportements à l'égard des enfants morts pendant l'HM–HR I." In *Mesohelladika.*

Rambach, Jörg. 2007. "Investigations of Two MH I Burial Mounds at Messenian Kastroulia." In *MH Pottery,* 137–50.

Renfrew, A. Colin. 1972. *The Emergence of Civilisation: The Cyclades and the Aegean in the Third Millennium B.C.* London: Methuen.

Ruppenstein, Florian. In press. "Gender and Regional Differences in Middle Helladic Burial Customs." In *Mesohelladika.*

Rutter, Jeremy B. 1990. "Pottery Groups from Tsoungiza of the End of the Middle Bronze Age." *Hesperia* 59: 375–458.

———. 2001. "The Pre-palatial Bronze Age of the Southern and Central Greek Mainland." In *Aegean Prehistory*, 95–156.

———. 2007. "Reconceptualizing the Middle Helladic 'Type Site' from a Ceramic Perspective: Is 'Bigger' Really 'Better'?" In *MH Pottery*, 35–44.

———, and Carol W. Zerner. 1984. "Early Hellado-Minoan Contacts." In *Minoan Thalassocracy*, 75–83.

Sarri, Kalliope. 2007. "Aeginetan Matt-painted Pottery in Boeotia." In *MH Pottery*, 151–66.

Shelton, Kim. In press. "Living and Dying in and around Middle Helladic Mycenae." In *Mesohelladika*.

Sherratt, Andrew, and Sue Sherratt. 1991. "From Luxuries to Commodities: The Nature of Mediterranean Bronze Age Trading Systems." In *Bronze Age Trade*, 351–86.

Spencer, Lindsay. In press. "The Regional Specialisation of Ceramic Production in the EH III through MH II Period." In *Mesohelladika*.

Theodorou-Maurommatidi, Anthi. In press. "Defining Ritual Action: A Middle Helladic Pit at the Site of Apollo Maleatas in Epidauros." In *Mesohelladika*.

Touchais, Gilles. 1998. "Argos à l'époque Mesohelladique: Un habitat ou des habitats?" In *Argos et l'Argolide: Topographie et urbanisme*, ed. Anne Pariente and Gilles Touchais, 71–84. Paris: de Boccard.

Triantaphyllou, Sevasti. In press. "Prospects for Reconstructing the Lives of Middle Helladic Populations in the Argolid: Past and Present of Human Bone Studies." In *Mesohelladika*.

Vianello, Andrea. 2005. *Late Bronze Age Mycenaean and Italic Products in the West Mediterranean: A Social and Economic Analysis*. BAR-IS 1439. Oxford: Archaeopress.

Voutsaki, Sofia. 1997. "The Creation of Value and Prestige in the Late Bronze Age Aegean." *Journal of European Archaeology* 10: 34–52.

———. 1999. "The Shaft Grave Offerings as Symbols of Power and Prestige." In *Eliten in der Bronzezeit: Ergebnisse zweier Colloquien in Mainz und Athen*, ed. Imma Kilian-Dirlmeier and Markus Egg, 103–17. Monographien des Römisch-Germanischen Zentralmuseums 43. Mainz: Römisch-Germanisches Zentralmuseum.

———. 2001. "The Rise of Mycenae: Political Interrelations and Archaeological Evidence." *BICS* 45: 183–84.

———. 2004. "Age and Gender in the Southern Greek Mainland, 2000–1500 BC." *Ethnographisch-archäologische Zeitschrift* 46(2–3): 339–63.

———. 2005. "Social and Cultural Change in the Middle Helladic Period: Presentation of a New Project." In *Autochthon*, 134–43.

———. In press. "The Domestic Economy in MH Asine." In *Mesohelladika*.

———. Forthcoming. "Houses and households in MH Lerna." *Hesperia*.

———, Albert J. Nijboer, and Carol Zerner. In press. "Radiocarbon Analysis and Middle Helladic Lerna." In *Mesohelladika*.

———, Sevasti Triantaphyllou, and Eleni Milka. 2005. "Project on the Middle Helladic Argolid: A Report on the 2004 Season." *Pharos* 12: 31–40.

Warren, Peter, and Vronwy Hankey. 1989. *The Absolute Chronology of the Aegean Bronze Age*. Bristol: Bristol Classical Press.

Whittaker, Helène. In press. "Some Thoughts on Middle Helladic Religious Beliefs and Ritual and Their Significance in Relation to Social Structure." In *Mesohelladika*.

Whitelaw, Todd. 2000. "Settlement Instability and Landscape Degradation in the Southern Aegean in the Third Millennium BC." In *Landscape and Land Use in Postglacial Greece*, ed. Paul Halstead and Charles Frederick, 135–61. Sheffield Studies in Aegean Archaeology 3. Sheffield: Sheffield Academic Press.

Wide, Sam. 1896. "Aphidna in Nordattika." *Athenische Mitteilungen* 21: 385–409.

Wright, James C. 2001. "Factions and the Origins of Leadership and Identity in Mycenaean Society." *BICS* 45: 182.

———. 2004a. "Comparative Settlement Patterns during the Bronze Age in the Northeastern Peloponnesos, Greece." In *Side-by-Side Survey: Comparative Regional Studies in the Mediterranean World*, ed. Susan E. Alcock and John F. Cherry, 114–31. Oxford: Oxbow.

———. 2004b. "The Emergence of Leadership and the Rise of Civilization in the Aegean." In *Emergence of Civilisation Revisited*, 64–89.

Zangger, Eberhard. 1992. "NL to Present Soil Erosion in Greece." In *Past and Present Soil Erosion: Archaeological and Geographical Perspectives*, ed. John Boardman and Martin Bell, 133–47. Oxbow Monograph 22. Oxford: Oxbow.

Zavadil, Michaela. In press. "The Peloponnese in the Middle Bronze Age: An Overview." In *Mesohelladika*.

Zerner, Carol W. 1979. "The Beginning of the Middle Helladic Period at Lerna." PhD diss., University of Cincinnati.

———. 1993. "New Perspectives on Trade in the Middle and Early Late Helladic Periods on the Mainland." In *Wace and Blegen*, 39–56.

CHAPTER 8

··

CRETE

··

ILSE SCHOEP

THE emergence of the 'First' or 'Old' Palaces is generally considered to be the main event of the Middle Bronze Age on Crete. These 'palaces' are widely believed to have emerged in MM IB or around 1925/1900 BC (Cherry 1986) in several places on Crete (Knossos, Malia, Phaistos, Petras). In the last couple of years it has become clear, however, that some of these structures have a much older biography and in fact go back to the Early Minoan period (see Tomkins and Schoep this volume; Schoep, Tomkins, and Driessen forthcoming) since some of their key features (e.g., orientation, presence of major courts and of architectural wings) are attested as early as EM IIB.

The designation 'palace' and its interpretation as the residence of a king, as with many of our ideas about Minoan society, go back to Arthur Evans (Evans 1921). Struck by the absence of the sort of temples that were already known from Egypt and the Near East and influenced by perceived resemblances to Anatolian theocracies, Evans interpreted the large court building he excavated at Knossos as the residence of a dynasty of priest-kings who stood at the head of a hierarchical power structure (Evans 1921, 26). It has been convincingly demonstrated that the discovery of a 'palace' at Knossos corresponded to Evans's expectations, which were determined by his sociopolitical and cultural background (MacGillivray 2000). From our perspective, it is surprising that the *presence* of such large structures did not evoke more surprise, given that there is no such development anywhere else in the Aegean and even the wider Mediterranean at that time.

After the decipherment of Linear B in 1952, the economic role of the Minoan palace became more emphasized, and the 'palace' became the center of a redistributive economy analogous to the redistributive temple economy in the Near East. The Linear B tablets were assumed to "reveal a massive redistributive operation, in which all personnel and all activities, all movements of both persons and goods, so to speak, were administratively fixed" (Finley 1957, 135). Heavily influenced by neo-evolution-ism (Hamilakis 2002), Renfrew further developed the Minoan 'palace' as a regional redistributive center that was linked to an agricultural hinterland, also for the Middle Bronze Age (Renfrew 1972, 51, 307): "The palace [from its emergence] is both the redistributive centre for the economic activities of a region, and the residence of a prince, the leading personage of a society now stratified" (Renfrew 1972, 51).

However, although the economic transactions recorded in the Knossian Linear B tablets illustrate that in its latest phase (LM II–III) the palace at Knossos was an important economic hub, it is premature to project this model onto earlier phases (MM I–II, as well as MM III–LM I) of the palace and to other 'palaces' on Crete. In addition, the redistributive model as suggested by Renfrew (1972) has been exten-sively critiqued (Halstead 1988, 2004; Hamilakis 1996).

An important contribution was made by Cherry, who argued that the 'palaces' as residences of a political, religious, and economic authority are indicative of a state-level society (Cherry 1984, 1986). At the same time, the emergence of these buildings signals an important change in the organizational base of society, which is now hierarchically organized: "The twentieth century BC saw the appearance, in several regions of Crete, of complex monumental building (i.e., palaces) of closely similar form, the material embodiment of radically new institutional features and major changes in the organizational basis of Minoan society" (Cherry 1986, 27). However, considering the long biography of the 'palaces' of Malia, Knossos, and Phaistos, the question of whether the MM IB phase indeed constitutes a drastic change in the organizational basis of society needs to be carefully reconsidered (Schoep and Tomkins this volume; Schoep forthcoming).

The idea that 'palaces' were the residence of a political, religious, and economic authority has found wide acceptance (Renfrew 1972; Cherry 1986; Halstead 1988; Branigan 1988; Watrous 1987; Dickinson 1994; Hood 1995). Recently, however, as more emphasis is being placed on the historiography of the palace model, this inter-pretation has increasingly been questioned (Bintliff 1984; Farnoux 1995; Hamilakis 2002; Driessen 2002; Schoep 2002a, 2002b). One of the first areas to have come under fire is the presumed economic function of these structures. The function of the kouloures as large-scale receptacles for grain has been criticized (Strasser 1997). In addition, the notion that palaces were the main producers of high-quality items or elite culture in Minoan society has been called into question. There is no evidence that the production of Kamares ware, traditionally attributed to palatial workshops (cf. Cherry 1986, 37–38), was taking place under palatial control. Petrographic analy-sis of Kamares ware from Knossos has shown that a significant proportion of this high-quality pottery was produced not locally but somewhere in south-central Crete (Day and Wilson 1998, 352, 358). The First 'Palace' at Knossos emerges as less of an active producer of fine pottery than as a consumer. It may be doubted that the entire Minoan economy functioned through redistribution or that the Minoan pal-aces controlled all agricultural production and commercial activity since this is not even true of the temple economy in the Near East, on which this model was based (Postgate 1995; Cherry 1999). As Postgate (1992, 109) notes: "We cannot any longer maintain that because the temple collected commodities and distributed them to its dependants the entire economy operated through 'redistribution,' or that the priests controlled all agricultural production and commercial activity." However, one must be careful not to completely discard the idea that the 'palaces' had an economic aspect, as some production was clearly taking place in these buildings (Branigan 1987, 1988, and see later discussion). There is, however, no reason to assume that the latter in any way controlled the production of high-quality (or other) items in Middle Bronze Age society or that the presence or absence of production activities can be used as an argument for the interpretation of these buildings as 'palaces.'

DEFINING THE 'PALACE'

Although the large central buildings that have been excavated at Knossos, Malia, Phaistos, and Petras are identified as 'palaces,' the monumental buildings at Kommos (Shaw 2002), Monastiraki (Kanta and Tzigounaki 2000), and perhaps also Archanes (Sakellarakis and Sapouna-Sakellaraki 1997) are not. The definition of the Minoan palace is mainly based on the physical appearances of the Late Bronze Age buildings and often combines both objective (architectural) and subjective (interpretative) criteria: "Each palace included a central court; generally there were other courts as well. Around the central court were grouped storage facilities, production areas, archives of inscribed tablets, rooms for ritual activity and rooms for state functions" (Warren 1985, 94). Watrous's (1987, 204) definition of a palace as the residence of a powerful authority that controls a system of redistribution assisted by a literate bureaucracy is even more subjective. The discovery in recent years of high-profile buildings with courts at Petras (Tsipopoloulou 2002), Kommos (Shaw 2002), Archanes (Sakellarakis and Sapouna-Sakellaraki 1997), and Monastiraki that do not resemble the canonical palace form has posed additional challenges to the traditional definition. Such confusion arises in part from both a desire to establish islandwide homogeneities, patterns, and typologies and a reluctance to acknowledge the apparent variation and regionalism that existed within the island throughout the Bronze Age. The traditional definitions of 'palace' were created on the basis of a single palace (i.e., Knossos) and a single phase (i.e., the latest and best-preserved phase), and any variation in time, form, and scale were not taken into account, thereby generating confusion as to whether some buildings should be identified as palaces or not. Considering that each palace plays a very specific role in a community, it seems logical that their size, embellishment, and specific layout should be determined in relation to the changing size, affluence, and organization of the community it served. Indeed, a comparison of the actual remains of the Middle Bronze Age court palaces reveals a number of differences in size, arrangement, number of courts, and architectural elaboration and layout of the architecture bordering the courts (Schoep 2004). In addition, too little attention is paid to the social practices taking place in these buildings, although it is exactly these that are likely to inform us about the role of these buildings (Day and Relaki 2002).

A key part of the critical reassessment of the Minoan palace in the last couple of years is the acknowledgement that the term 'palace' carries with it a host of perhaps unhelpful baggage, which consciously or unconsciously encourages interpretation of the palace as the residence of a royal elite who occupies a supreme position within a hierarchical social and political structure (Schoep 2002a). Therefore, scholars have suggested alternative designations such as court-centered buildings, court buildings, and court compounds (Driessen 2002; Schoep 2002a, 2002b). The obvious advantage of the use of these terms is that they describe the buildings without imposing ideas about the ways in which they functioned; an alternative term such as 'court building' more accurately reflects our lack of knowledge of the identity and nature of these buildings and is therefore here preferred.

The Organization of Society in the Middle Bronze Age: From a Palace-Centered to an Elite-Centered Model?

In the traditional palatial model, the court building is considered to be the physical embodiment of a complex state structure or a state and the residence of a political, religious, and economic authority (Cherry 1984, 1986). This interpretation has encouraged a top-down view, with all of the activities taking place outside the palaces viewed from a palatial perspective. As such, workshops outside the palaces or palatial centers producing high-quality and labor-intensive prestige goods, monumental structures, and the presence of administration are generally considered to be 'palatial,' implying a certain dependency upon the court building that cannot in fact be empirically justified.

This bias toward the Minoan palace in theorizing about Minoan society is reminiscent of the way that, in the Near East until the 1950s, the temple was thought to be the state (Postgate 1995, 109). This extreme view has now been revised, and it is clear that in the Near East the temple was counterpoised by the palace, and these respective authorities exercised their power from two geographically different locations. Despite being associated with different sources of power in society, both the palace and the temple were run along similar lines, and they might have had property in more than one place and engaged in a variety of productive and commercial activities (Postgate 1995, 109). At the same time, although part of the economy was based on redistribution (i.e., to feed dependent personnel), this does not imply that the whole economy functioned in this manner.

This brief comparison leads to two important observations. First, it is not because some of the activities that took place in the court buildings involved storage, production, and perhaps the collection and distribution of commodities that they can be identified as the residences of a king, who also controlled the religious and the economic sectors. Second, the attestation of these activities in the court buildings does not imply that, in the Middle Bronze Age, these buildings controlled the whole economy to the exclusion of other parties. Third, the traditional Minoan palatial model of society is unusual because in none of the contemporary societies in the East Mediterranean were the political and the religious authorities housed under a single roof, not even in theocratic societies such as Egypt and the Hittites (Macqueen 1986). This raises the question of whether we should continue to view the court buildings as housing these different aspects under a single roof.

THE COURT BUILDINGS IN CONTEXT

One of the best ways to shed light on the function of the court buildings in Minoan society and on their relationship to other parties and agents in society is to explore the practices that took place in these structures (Day and Relaki 2002). It will become clear in the following section that some of the practices attested in them, such as administration and production and consumption of high-value goods, are not exclusive to them but are also confirmed in other high-profile buildings belonging to affluent households (e.g., Quartier Mu at Malia) (Schoep 2002a). From this it follows that the court buildings in themselves cannot be used as "the basis for a reconstruction of the entire Minoan society" as is sometimes thought (Warren 1985, 94).

PRODUCTION

The Minoan palaces have attracted so much attention and been invested with so much power because "in them were concentrated the kind of high-quality artifacts that delight the discoverer and encapsulate the culture," as was the case for the temples in the Near East (Postgate 1995, 109). However, the presence of such objects need not imply that the palaces were the only producers of high culture since such artifacts occur in a range of ritual contexts such as tombs and rural shrines, as well as large residential/ceremonial complexes outside the court buildings, for example, Quartier Mu at Malia. Similarly, in the Near East, such activities evidently took place in the palace, in the temple, and in wealthy households (Postgate 1995).

The evidence for actual on-the-spot production in the court buildings is limited (see also Branigan 1988, 64). At Phaistos, polishers, spatulas, and debris were found in rooms LI–LV and LXII, in association with some twenty stone vases and a number of administrative documents (Branigan 1988, 64). The main evidence for production consists of loomweights, pointing toward the production of textiles (Militello 2006, 176). Concentrations of loomweights are not exclusive to court buildings, and considerable numbers of loomweights have been found in Quartier Mu in Malia. The palatial production may have been intended for consumption within the confines of this building or for activities taking place on these premises.

The Loomweight Basement at Knossos yielded more than four hundred loomweights, but the date of this deposit is contested, whether MM IIB (MacGillivray 1998, 41; Macdonald 2005, 66–69) or MM IIIA (Warren and Hankey 1989, 52–53). Interestingly, there are possible indications of the procurement of the raw material needed for the production of textiles: a number of Cretan Hieroglyphic bars containing large even numbers but no logogram. Since these large numbers are unlikely to record people, they may be indicating flocks of sheep (Olivier 1994–1995; Schoep 2001a). It suggests that at the time of the Cretan Hieroglyphic documents (whether MM IIB or MM IIIA; see Schoep 2001b) the court building at Knossos was managing an estate that produced wool (Schoep 2004, 287–88). The attestation of logograms denoting cereals, figs, olives, and other unidentified commodities on further tablets suggests that these commodities also formed part of the transactions recorded on other bars.

Besides the possible production of textiles, there is no evidence that the high-value objects such as found stored or deposited in the Vat Room deposit and the Loomweight Basement at Knossos (mentioned earlier) were produced on the premises, with the exception of the obsidian, but the knapping of these has been connected with transformative processes as ritual action (Carter 2004, 273). One of the sealings sealed the string binding of a document or some other item (Macdonald 2005, 52), which could have accompanied any of these objects or the raw material out of which they were made.

Storage and Consumption

Another aspect that has been closely connected with the identification of the court buildings as palaces is the presence of elaborate storerooms (cf. Renfrew 1972). Besides the storage of agricultural commodities, the large-scale storage of tableware is evidenced. At Knossos, the MM IIA Royal Pottery Stores contain piled-up stacks of very plain drinking wares (saucers, conical cups, and teacups) (MacGillivray 1998, 155–58, Group G) and some of the finest pottery found at Knossos (especially in southwest room; MacGillivray 1998, 36, Group F). The quantity of MM IIA cups and goblets exceeds the number of vases used for the storage of liquids, suggesting an assemblage primarily for the serving of food and drink on a large scale.

Quantities of tableware were found elsewhere in the court building at Knossos. Recent work in Early Magazine A has revealed a deposit that reflects an interesting hierarchy of drinking vessels; the majority of shapes are crudely made, footed goblets and straight-sided cups, and at the top of the hierarchy is an astonishing eggshell cup (Macdonald and Knappett 2007). The MM IB Vat Room deposit from a plaster-lined pit contained mainly drinking and pouring vessels, obsidian cores, blades and flakes, fragments of objects in ivory, ostrich shell, rock crystal, and two sealings (Panagiotaki 1999; MacGillivray 1998; Macdonald 2005, 50–51).

It is remarkable that a proportion of the Kamares pottery consumed at Knossos was derived from a workshop in the Mesara, which also supplied the court building at Phaistos (Day and Wilson 1998). In MM I, a considerable part of the fine pottery was imported from Pediada (Rethemniotakis and Christakis 2004). The pottery from the MM I–II court building in Malia has not been published in detail, but if the pottery from Quartier Mu (Poursat and Knappett 2005) is anything to go by, the court building was probably consuming pottery from different local and nonlocal workshops. It would thus seem that the court buildings were consumers of tableware that was produced elsewhere.

At Phaistos, high-quality Kamares tableware was stored in large quantities in the south part of the west wing, said to contain more than 25% of all pottery (Branigan 1988). There is a clear connection between these stores of tableware and the presence of large open spaces, where the consumption presumably took place. In addition, room LVIII contains pithoi from which foodstuffs and/or liquids could have been dispensed. This large-scale storage of tableware, destined to be used for communal consumption, contrasts with the pattern attested in the north sector of the west wing, where the rooms contained small deposits of vases, again mainly drinking and pouring shapes (see Pernier 1935). Since these were concerned with small-scale dispensation of liquids (due to the restricted number of drinking vessels), it is clear that consumption in these contexts was neither communal nor aimed at a large public. In the north wing, the storage of agricultural goods is attested in magazine XXXIV, which was equipped with thirty-one pithoi and located near an open space (i.e., a later central court).

Besides the large-scale storage of tableware, there is also evidence in the court building for the storage of high-status and labor-intensive objects such as several bronze swords, a schist leopard ax, and a dagger have been found (Pelon 1992). There is no evidence, however, that these were produced in the court building. The acrobat's sword forms part of a group of Egyptianizing metal objects, including a dagger from Quartier Mu and the gold bees from Chrysolakkos, which were presumably produced locally (Poursat 2000, 29–30). At Phaistos, some of the rooms were equipped with stone vases and occasionally bronze objects and on one occasion an ivory knife heft and gold sheet fragments (Pernier 1935), but in general the absence of metals and high-status goods is striking (Carinci 2000, 33). Similarly, high-value items were found in the Vat Room Deposit at Knossos and the same could be argued for the objects from the Loomweight Basement (terracotta models, Town Mosaic, etc.) (Macdonald 2005, 67–68).

WRITING AND SEALING

Writing and sealing practices are traditionally closely connected with the interpretation of the court buildings as palaces, and the presence of Linear A and Cretan hieroglyphic documents is usually interpreted as evidence not only for the economic role of the palace (cf. Renfrew 1972; Weingarten 1990) but also for the existence of an administrative authority (Weingarten 1990). The origins of sealing and writing are traditionally associated with the assumed MM IB emergence of the palaces and their economic needs (Weingarten 1990, 1994; Treuil et al. 2007; Krzyszkowska 2005, 79). However, both writing as well as seal use are already attested in the late Early Minoan period (Schoep 2006), although it seems that a significant increase and an increased sophistication in their deployment occurred in the Middle Bronze Age. A more complex typology of sealed documents appears besides the already existing, direct object sealings and *noduli* involving crescents, roundels, and hanging nodules (Schoep 1999; Krzyszkowska 2005, 99–104).

Written documents usually occur together with sealed documents, although the ratio of one to the other varies considerably among deposits. Major MM II collections of written and sealed documents have been found in the court buildings of Phaistos (Militello 2000) and Petras (Tsipopolou and Hallager 1996, 1997). The 'archives' from Knossos and Malia probably postdate MM II and are more likely to be MM III in date (Schoep 2001b, 2004; Krzyszkowska 2005, 111, 114). However, the use of sealings and script is also attested in high-profile buildings outside the settlement. The most extensive archive to date comes from Quartier Mu at Malia, where Cretan hieroglyphic bars were used in conjunction with an array of sealed documents (Olivier and Godart 1996). Cretan hieroglyphic bars were also used in a building complex discovered to the southwest of Quartier Mu during the Malia survey, and inscriptions on pottery suggest that some of the pottery workshops were also deploying writing; at Malia, besides the court building there is evidence of administration in at least two locations (Schoep 2002a; Müller and Olivier 1991). At Knossos, a nodulus and a fragment of an inscribed tablet were found in conjunction with production debris (Macdonald and Knappett 2007, 131–37).

PLACING THE PRACTICES IN THE COURT BUILDINGS IN A WIDER FRAMEWORK

It is important to view the Minoan court buildings within a wider spatial context—hence the emphasis in the 1980s and 1990s on surveys (Driessen 2001)—but also with regard to the practices attested in these buildings and the way they relate to similar practices outside them. As noted earlier, it is not because they were engaging in activities of production, collection and storage, consumption, and even distribution that they controlled all of the production, collection, and distribution in Minoan society. A comparison of the production, exchange, and consumption strategies of affluent households and the court buildings allows us to chart similarities and differences in production, exchange, and consumption strategies and to assess the role of the latter in the community. The best example of a context of an affluent household in the Middle Bronze Age is Quartier Mu at Malia, which consists of two main buildings (A and B) and a number of workshops around them (see Poursat 1996; Schoep 2002a, forthcoming b). That the elite of Quartier Mu was overseeing production is suggested by the location of the workshops around them (Poursat 1996). Some (but not all) of the goods produced in the workshops were also consumed and/or stored in the main buildings (A, B, and D). However, not all of the goods that were stored and consumed in buildings A, B, and D were produced in the workshops, and almost all of the pottery was obtained from other local and nonlocal workshops. Other houses in Malia seem to have been consuming the same pottery (Schoep and Knappett 2003). However, the terracotta Egyptianizing appliqué elements and presumably the exotic knowledge they imply are as yet exclusive to Quartier Mu (Poursat 1996).

Although the court building was considerably larger than the total area covered by Quartier Mu, the former did on present evidence not contain significantly more storage vases (liquids in East Wing, two pithoi in West Wing). There is less evidence for production in the court building than in Quartier Mu, as in fact few loom-weights have been found, and the evidence for craft activities is almost nonexistent (Schoep 2002a, 113). At least some of the polychrome pottery (from Quartier III) is local polychrome of the type that was also attested in Quartier Mu ('marguerites') (Pelon 1992, plate III:2) and was produced in a local workshop. Seal stones of the type that was produced in the Sealstone workshop of Quartier Mu were consumed in the court building (Pelon 1984, 885, figure 7) were also found in the court building (Pelon 1984, 885 fig. 7; Pelon 1992, 47, figure 24; 60, figure 37). Other unpublished finds from the MM I–II building include stone and faience objects, an ivory pendant in the shape of a lioness, and gold leaf fragments (Daux 1969, 1056). The two swords and the dagger are stunning objects, but there is no evidence for metalworking in the MM I–II building. Although a metal workshop was identified in Mu, the latter seems in the first place to have produced metal tools (Poursat 1996). There is no evidence that the high-quality metal dagger with inlays from Mu was produced in the Mu workshop. The swords from the Malia palace, the bees from Chrysolakkos, and the Mu dagger all share Egyptianizing features (Poursat 2000) and may perhaps be ascribed to a single (as yet unidentified) workshop. However, we cannot rule out the possibility that objects that were used in ritual practice inside the palace were also produced in these buildings, as is suggested by the obsidian cores from the Vat Room Deposit (Macdonald 2005, 50).

CONCLUSIONS

In this chapter I suggest that the palatial model in which complete power is concentrated in the 'palaces' should be revised because such a model is unrealistic on several levels. There is no empirical evidence to support the traditional interpretation of the 'palaces' as the residence of a single, centralized authority whose domain was the political, religious, and economic affairs of the community. Even though evidence that points toward production, storage, consumption, and recordkeeping is found in the court buildings, we cannot simply conclude that the latter controlled these activities in society. In fact, the excavation of Quartier Mu at Malia has shown conclusively that an affluent household such as that was engaged in activities similar to those carried out in the contemporary court building at Malia. From the evidence at hand, it seems that production in the court buildings pertains in the first place to textiles and not to the production of high-quality prestige goods, as is assumed all too often. Going on the evidence from the Quartier Mu workshops, a case can be made that affluent households in the settlement were actively involved in the production of high-profile elite objects, perhaps through attached specialists. Consumption of not only foodstuffs but also high-status objects is attested in both the court buildings and affluent households. A clear difference in scale is suggested by the large amounts of tableware in the court buildings and the size of the communal spaces. In contrast to the venues and the consumption in the affluent households, the court buildings were aimed at a much wider public than any happenings staged by the latter.

BIBLIOGRAPHY

Bintliff, John. 1984. "Structuralism and Myth in Minoan Studies." *Antiquity* 58: 33–38.

Branigan, Keith. 1987. "The Economic Roles of the First Palaces." In *Function of the Minoan Palaces*, 245–49.

———. 1988. "Some Observations on State Formation in Crete." In *Problems in Greek Prehistory*, 63–71.

Carinci, Filippo M. 2000. "Western Messara and Egypt during the Protopalatial Period: A Minimalist View." In *Krete-Aigyptos: Politismikoi desmoi trion chilieton. Meletes*, ed. Alexandra Karetsou, 31–37. Athens: Hypourgeio Politismou.

Carter, Tristan. 2004. "Transformative Processes in Liminal Space: Craft as Ritual Action in the Throne Room Area." In *Knossos*, 273–82.

Cherry, John. 1984. "The Emergence of the State in the Prehistoric Aegean." *PCPS* 210, n.s., 30: 18–48.

———. 1986. "Polities and Palaces: Some Problems in Minoan State Formation." In *Peer Polity Interaction and Socio-political Change*, ed. Colin Renfrew and John Cherry, 19–45. New York: Cambridge University Press.

————. 1999. "Introductory Reflections on Economies and Scale in Prehistoric Crete." In *From Minoan Farmers to Roman Traders: Sidelights on the Economy of Ancient Crete*, ed. Angelos Chaniotis, 17–23. Stuttgart: Steiner.

Daux, Georges. 1969. "Chronique des fouilles en Grèce." *BCH* 93: 1056.

Day, Peter M., and David E. Wilson. 1998. "Consuming Power: Kamares Ware of Protopalatial Knossos." *Antiquity* 72: 350–58.

Day, Peter M., and Maria Relaki, "Past Factions and Present Fictions: Palaces in the Study of Minoan Crete." In *Monuments of Minos*, 217–34.

Dickinson, Oliver T. P. K. 1994. *The Aegean Bronze Age*. New York: Cambridge University Press.

Driessen, Jan. 2001. "History and Hierarchy: Preliminary Observations on the Settlement Pattern of Minoan Crete." In *Urbanism*, 51–71.

————. 2002. "The King Must Die: Some Observations on the Use of Minoan Court Compounds." In *Monuments of Minos*, 1–13.

Evans, Arthur. 1921. *PM*, vol. 1.

Farnoux, Alexandre. 1995. "La fondation de la royauté minoenne: XXème siècle avant ou après Jésus-Christ?" In *Politeia*, 323–34.

Finley, Moses I. 1957. "The Mycenaean Tablets and Economic History." *Economic History Review* 10: 128–41.

Halstead, Paul. 1988. "On Redistribution and the Origins of Minoan-Mycenaean Palatial Economies." In *Problems in Greek Prehistory*, 519–30.

————. 2004. "Life after Mediterranean Polyculture: The Subsistence Subsystem and the Emergence of Civilisation Revisited." In *The Emergence of Civilisation Revisited*, 189–206.

Hamilakis, Yannis. 1996. "Wine, Oil, and the Dialectics of Power in Bronze Age Crete: A Review of the Evidence." *OJA* 15: 1–32.

————. 2002. "What Future for the 'Minoan' Past? Rethinking Minoan Archaeology." In *Labyrinth Revisited: Rethinking 'Minoan' Archaeology*, ed. Yannis Hamilakis, 2–28. Oxford: Oxbow.

Hitchcock, Louise A. 2000. *Minoan Architecture: A Contextual Analysis*. Jonsered, Sweden: Aström.

Hood, Sinclair. 1995. "The Minoan Palaces as Residences of Gods and Men." In *Pepragmena tou Z' Diethnous Kretologikou Synedrio*, 393–407. Rethymnon, Crete: Historical Society of Crete.

Kanta, Athanasia, and Anastasia Tzigounaki. 2000. "The Protopalatial Multiple Sealing System: New Evidence from Monastiraki." In *Proceedings of the International Conference of Sphragistic Studies (1996)*, ed. Massimo Perna, 193–210. Turin: Paravina Scriptorium.

Knappett, Carl J. 1999. "Assessing a Polity in Proto-palatial Crete: The Malia-Lasithi State." *AJA* 103: 615–39.

Krzyszkowska, Olga. 2005. *Aegean Seals: An Introduction*. BICS Suppl. 85. London: Institute of Classical Studies.

Macdonald, Colin F. 2005. *Knossos*. London: Folio Society.

————, and Carl J. Knappett. 2007. *Knossos: Protopalatial Deposits in Early Magazine A and the South-west Houses*. BSA Supplementary vol. 41. London: British School at Athens.

MacGillivray, J. Alexander. 1994. "The Early History of the Palace at Knossos." In *Labyrinth of History*, 45–55.

————. 1998. *Pottery Groups of the Old Palace Period*. BSA Studies 5. Athens: British School at Athens.

————. 2000. *Minotaur: Sir Arthur Evans and the Archaeology of the Minoan Myth*. New York: Farrar, Straus, and Giroux.

Macqueen, J. G. 1986. *The Hittites and Their Contemporaries in Asia Minor*. London: Thames and Hudson.

Militello, Pietro. 2000. "L'archivio di cretule" del Vano 25 e un nuovo sigillo da Festòs." In *Administrative Documents in the Aegean and Their Near Eastern Counterparts*, ed. Massimo Perna, 221–43. Turin: Paravina Scriptorium.

————. 2006. "Attività tessile a Festòs ed Haghia Triada del Neolitico al Bronzo Tardo." *Proceedings of the 8th Cretological Conference*, 175–88. Heraklion: Historical Society of Crete.

Müller, Sylvie, and Jean-Pierre Olivier. 1991. "Prospection à Malia: Deux documents hiéroglyphiques." *BCH* 115: 65–70.

Olivier, Jean-Pierre. 1994–1995. "Un simili-raccord dans les barres en hiéroglyphique de Knossos (CHIC #057, #058)." *Minos* 29–30: 257–69.

Panagiotaki, Marina. 1999. *The Central Palace Sanctuary at Knossos*. BSA Suppl. 31. London: British School at Athens.

Pelon, Olivier. 1982. *Guide de Malia: Le palais et la nécropole de Chrysolakkos*. Sites et Monuments IX. Paris: Diffusion de Boccard.

————. 1984. "Travaux de l'école française d'Athènes en Grèce en 1988: Malia. Le palais." *BCH* 108: 881–87.

Pernier, Luigi. 1935. *Il palazzo minoico di Festòs*, vol. 1. Rome.

Platon, Nikolaos. 1983. "The Minoan Palaces: Centres of organisation of a Theocratic, Social, and Political System." In *Minoan Society*, 273–80.

Postgate, John N. 1995. *Early Mesopotamia: Society and Economy at the Dawn of History*. London: Routledge.

Poursat, Jean-Claude. 1996. *Fouilles exécutées à Malia: Le quartier Mu III: Artisans minoens: Les maisons-ateliers du quartier Mu*. Études crétoises 32. Athens: Geuthner.

————. 2000. "Malia et l'Egypte." In *Krete-Aigyptos: Politismikoi desmoi trion chilietion. Meletes*, ed. Alexandra Karetsou, 29–30. Athens: Hypourgeio Politismou.

————, and Carl J. Knappett. 2005. *Fouilles exécutées à Malia: Le quartier Mu IV. La poterie du Minoen Moyen II: Production et utilisation*. Etudes crétoises 33. Athens: Geuthner.

Renfrew, Colin. 1972. *The Emergence of Civilization*. London: Methuen.

Rethemniotakis, Georgios, and Konstantinos Christakis. 2004. "Cultural Interaction between Knossos and Pediada: The Evidence from the Middle Minoan IB Pottery." In *Knossos*, 169–76.

Sakellarakis, Ioannis, and Effie Sapouna-Sakellaraki. 1997. *Minoan Crete in a New Light*. Athens: Ammos.

Schoep, Ilse. 1999. "The Origins of Writing and Administration on Crete." *OJA* 18: 265–76.

————. 2001a. "Managing the Hinterland: The Rural Concerns of Urban Administration." In *Urbanism*, 87–102.

————. 2001b. "Some Notes on the "Hieroglyphic" Deposit from Knossos." *SMEA* 43(1): 143–58.

————. 2002a. "Social and Political Organisation on Crete in the Proto-palatial Period: The Case of Middle Minoan II Malia." *JMA* 15(1): 101–32.

————. 2002b. "The State of the Minoan Palaces or the Minoan Palace-state?" In *Monuments of Minos*, 15–33.

————. 2004. "Assessing the Role of Architecture in Conspicuous Consumption in the Middle Minoan I–II Periods." *OJA* 23: 243–69.

————. 2006. "Looking beyond the First Palaces: Elites and the Agency of Power in EM III–MM II Crete." *AJA* 110(1): 37–64.

————. Forthcoming a. "Bridging the Divide between the Prepalatial and the Protopalatial Period." In Schoep, Tomkins and Driessen.

————. Forthcoming b. "Making Elites: Political Economy and Elite Cultures in Middle Minoan Crete." In D. Pullen (ed.), *Political Economies of the Aegean Bronze Age*. Oxford: Oxbow.

————, and Carl J. Knappett. 2003. "Le Quartier Nu (Malia, Crète): L'occupation du Minoen moyen II." *BCH* 117(1): 49–86.

Schoep, Ilse, Peter Tomkins, and Jan Driessen, eds. Forthcoming. *Back to the Beginning. Proceedings of the Leuven workshop*, February 1–2, 2008. Oxford: Oxbow.

Shaw, Joseph. 2002. "The Minoan Palatial Establishment at Kommos: An Anatomy of Its History, Function, and Interconnections." In *Monuments of Minos*, 99–110.

Strasser, Tom. 1997. "Storage and States on Prehistoric Crete: The Function of the Koulouras in the First Minoan Palaces." *JMA* 10: 73–100.

Treuil, Réné, Pascal Darcque, Gilles Touchais, and Jean-Claude Poursat. 2007. *Les civilisations égéennes du Néolithique et de l'Age du Bronze*. Paris: Presses Universitaires de France.

Tsipopoulou, Metaxia. 2002. "Petras, Siteia: The Palace, the Town, the Hinterland, and the Protopalatial Background." In *Monuments of Minos*, 133–44.

————, and Erik Hallager. 1996. "Hieroglyphic and Linear A Inscriptions from Petras, Siteia." *SMEA* 37: 7–46.

————. 1997. "A New Hieroglyphic Archive at Petras, Siteia." *Kadmos*: 165–67.

Warren, Peter. 1985. "Minoan Palaces." *Scientific American* 253: 94–103.

————, and Vronwy Hankey. 1989. *Aegean Bronze Age Chronology*. Bristol: Bristol Classical Press.

Watrous, L. Vance. 1987. "The Role of the Near East in the Rise of the Cretan Palaces." In *Function of the Minoan Palaces*, 65–70.

————. 2001. "Crete from the Earliest Prehistory through the Protopalatial Period." In *Aegean Prehistory*, 157–223.

Weingarten, Judith. 1990. "Three Upheavals in Minoan Sealing Administration: Evidence for Radical Change." In *Aegean Seals, Sealings, and Administration*, ed. Thomas G. Palaima, 105–14. *Aegeaum* 5. Liège: Université de Liège.

————. 1994. "Sealings and Sealed Documents at Bronze Age Knossos." In *Labyrinth of History*, 171–88.

CHAPTER 9

....

CYCLADES

....

ROBIN L. N. BARBER

GEOGRAPHY

....

While there is no reason to believe that the physical geography of the Cyclades underwent any significant change from the Early to the Middle Cycladic (MC) period, it is possible that there were gradual alterations in the patterns of currents, wind, and so on, which themselves help to define the group by moulding routes of communication (Morton 2001; Papageorgiou 2008).

There may have been adjustments too in what may be termed 'cultural geography.' The name Cyclades, derived in the Classical period from the islands that formed a loose circle (*kyklos*) around the sacred centre of Delos, nowadays signifies a modern administrative region—from Andros and Tenos in the north to Melos and Thera in the south. In the Byzantine and Mediaeval periods, the boundaries of the region were different at different times. In the Bronze Age, when we can judge its extent only by the kinship of sites in material culture, they may have been different again since, in the Early Cycladic period, places on the coasts of Attica (Ayios Kosmas, Tsepi [Marathon]), Crete (Ayia Photia), and even Asia Minor (Iasos) display, in varying degrees, features characteristic of the material culture of the core Cycladic islands (Barber 1987, 134–37). Some of these have, on occasion, been dubbed 'colonies,' but it can be suggested, with perhaps greater plausibility, that they belonged to a Cycladic cultural area, dissimilar to that with which we are now familiar and about whose extent there is undoubtedly more to be learnt.

If defined in this way, Middle Cycladic geography seems to show yet another grouping since no sites with similarly strong island characteristics have so far been located outside the area known today as the Cyclades.

MIDDLE CYCLADIC MATERIAL CULTURE

The particular character of Middle Cycladic culture (Barber 1987, 142–58; Sotirakopoulou in press) is defined mainly by the pottery classes that are reviewed below. Pictorial designs offer glimpses—often enigmatic—of various aspects of life and attitudes and deserve further study since they range quite widely in date and location and are sometimes found, for instance, also on Cycladic Geometric pottery and earlier Melian Cycladic White (for Theran material, cf. Papagiannopoulou 2008).

The pottery also provides the only detailed framework for the relative dating of historical events, external relations, and other developments. Of the other minor artefacts recovered, little has so far been identified as especially characteristic of the period, although some of the terracotta figurines from Naxos (Mikre Vigla) should be of this date.

Typical of MC times, however, are relatively large, carefully laid out and organised townships in which island populations seem to have become concentrated, to the virtual exclusion of smaller settlements. Although some modification of this view may be necessary in the light of the recent identification of greater numbers of minor MC sites on one or two islands (Sotirakopoulou in press), it still seems true that centralisation of settlement was a feature of the period and that this was reflected at the major sites by growth in size and greater sophistication of architecture and planning. Fortification systems also appear to be a characteristic of MC sites.

Graves are poorly known (except on Kea) but seem to represent a continuation of Early Cycladic types, though with more variation and less emphasis on the cist.

As regards external contacts, relationships with the Mainland—which stylistic rather than import-export evidence suggests were strong in EC IIIB—continue in the earlier MC stage, when more imports are found. These are accompanied by increasing numbers of Minoan pottery fragments of MM IA and MM II date. The later stage of MC is associated with MM III and later MH pottery.

IDENTIFICATION OF THE MC PERIOD AND HISTORY OF INVESTIGATION

The terms used today for discussion of the cultures of the Aegean Bronze Age and their relative chronology are the result of a long process of development. The Cretan sequence was the first to be codified (Momigliano 2007, 3–4), on the basis of excavations at Knossos, and involved coincident architectural and ceramic phases (e.g., First and Second Palaces—Middle and Late Minoan pottery). Increasingly detailed subdivision of the pottery sequence, which became possible with the progress of research, has inevitably resulted in the separation of the two types of phasing—

architectural and ceramic—since it is no longer possible, for example, to equate exactly the chronological duration of the Middle Minoan pottery phase with that of the First Palace. Thus the construction of the First Palace is now set after, rather than at the beginning of, the ceramic period Middle Minoan IA (MacGillivray 2007, 106).

A similar process has also applied in the other main regional subdivisions—Helladic (Mainland) Greece and the Cyclades.

A system based on the Cretan was first applied to the Helladic area by Wace and Blegen (1918, 186–87). Blegen (1921, 121), whose scheme was later modified by Furumark (1941, 217), also incorporated the Cyclades into an overall framework in which the Bronze Age in each area (Helladic, Cycladic, Minoan) was divided into Early, Middle, and Late (further subdivided into I, II, III) and the probable relationships between the phases shown.

Although the logic of the process was not made fully explicit, it was ultimately geared to the already-established Cretan system, so that ceramic stages on the Mainland and in the Cyclades that could be related via imports/exports or stylistic similarities to those in Crete were regarded as representing corresponding 'Early,' 'Middle,' or 'Late' stages in the Helladic or Cycladic areas.

It is instructive, however, that, although Blegen equated exactly the Cycladic and Minoan periods, presumably because of the generally rather broad subdivisions that then existed, he did not regard the ceramic phases in the different areas as necessarily corresponding in detail. Although this point seems self-evident, the use of expressions such as 'the Middle Bronze Age in the Aegean,' which are regrettably now in common use, suggest that it is often forgotten. Cultural areas must first be defined, and the sequences for each established separately and then related to each other as appropriate, without any assumption that what belongs to the 'Middle' phase, for example, in one must be directly related to the 'Middle' phase in another.

Such a 'traditional' scheme has been followed here for discussion of the Middle Cycladic period. Some scholars reject the overall framework and prefer to concentrate on sequences at individual sites and their interrelationships. Nevertheless, so long as the existence of a unified and reasonably distinct culture in the Cycladic area is accepted, it is important to have a broad framework for discussion of developments of all kinds and so that older literature, where such a system is taken for granted, can be readily assimilated by students and researchers.

THE CYCLADIC SEQUENCE

A *Cycladic* pottery sequence was worked out initially on the basis of finds from the first (1896–99) well-stratified site to be excavated in the Cyclades—Phylakopi on Melos (see especially Atkinson et al. 1904, 238–72). Although this was, to be precise, rather a *Melian* sequence, its primary role in the history of research and the fact that subsequent finds from other islands can be related to it in a reasonably satisfactory way make its use as the foundation of a wider system entirely acceptable.

At Phylakopi, a widespread destruction ended the primarily Early Cycladic 'First City' and separated it from the primarily Middle Cycladic 'Second City.' Both destruction and reconstruction probably fell within a transitional pottery phase, which is discussed later. The fact that the Second was the 'Middle' of the three 'Cities' identified may have encouraged its designation as the 'Middle' Cycladic phase at the site but was not decisive (or indeed universally accepted—witness Furumark 1941, 217n1, who sets the beginning of Middle Cycladic before the end of the First City) since that attribution was based rather on ceramic parallels with Middle Minoan Crete and Middle Helladic Greece.

It should be noted here that the original excavators identified three phases of the Second City at Phylakopi (subsequently abbreviated II–i, II–ii, II–iii). Recent analyses (Barber 1987, 30, and references; see further below) have tended to discount the II–i phase, resulting in use of the terms 'early' and 'late' Middle Cycladic, equivalent to Phylakopi II–ii (Kea IV) and Phylakopi II–iii (Kea V), respectively.

OTHER IMPORTANT SITES

At Ayia Irini on Kea (Caskey 1972), there was a gap in occupation of the site between Period III (C) (Wilson 1999), dated to Early Cycladic IIIA (a stage sometimes referred to as 'EC IIB' or the 'Kastri phase') and Periods IV (D) (Overbeck 1989b) and V (F) (Davis 1986), which are the earlier and later phases of the reestablished Middle Cycladic settlement.

At Akrotiri on Thera, the MC structures mostly lie concealed beneath the later town, but a good deal of pottery was found in later deposits, and recent work, not yet reported in detail, has revealed deposits of the period (Nikolakopoulou et al. 2008; cf. Sotirakopoulou in press, n. 5). Assessment of the sequence proposed in this and other brief notices must await detailed publication. Other sites on Thera (Ftellos, Ayios Ioannis Eleemon) have also produced late EC III/early MC material (Marthari 1983, 2001).

At Paroikia on Paros, undoubtedly an important settlement with both EC III and MC pottery (Overbeck 1989a; Sherratt 2000, 224n14), it is difficult to make distinctions between or within the two periods on the basis of the stratigraphic information available.

In addition, work on Naxos (Philaniotou 2001, 30, 33) suggests that the Kastro was the acropolis of a substantial MC site that also covered part of the lower-lying area of Grotta; a surface survey of Mikre Vigla (Barber and Hadjianastasiou 1989) recovered a significant amount of MC pottery, as well as terracotta figurines (also Sakellarakis 1996, 94–96), some of which should belong to the same period.

Excavations at Plaka on Andros, so far only briefly reported (Televantou 2005, 214–15; 2008, 53, with further references) indicate the existence of an important MC centre.

ABSOLUTE CHRONOLOGY

Recent commentators (Warren and Hankey 1989, 169; Manning 1995, figure 2) appear to be in rough agreement as to the beginning of the MC period at ca. 2000 BC (+/– fifty years). The end date (equivalent to the beginning of LM IA in Crete) is partly dependent on estimates of that of the volcanic catastrophe on Thera and can be set between 1675+/– (Manning 1999, 340) and 1600 +/– BC (Warren and Hankey 1989, 169; Warren 1999, 902).

RELATIVE CHRONOLOGY: THE POTTERY SEQUENCE

The Early–Middle Cycladic transitional phase is discussed in the next section, following a description of the characteristic features of the mature MC period.

Middle Cycladic—Early

The second stage of the Second City (Phylakopi II–ii), as defined by the first excavators (Atkinson et al. 1904, 259–61), and Period IV at Ayia Irini give a consistent picture of the pottery of this phase. There is related material from Akrotiri (Nikolakopoulou et al. 2008, where pl. 32. 5 is distinctive) and from other islands.

The two main fabric groups are Dark Burnished and Cycladic White (CW). The former (Barber 1987, 146–48; 2007, 186–96) was not recognised as a significant category until the second excavation campaign at Phylakopi in 1911 (Dawkins and Droop 1911, 19–21) but has been found widely on island sites. At Phylakopi, pottery of this class is slipped and burnished to a glossy finish—sometimes a brilliant red but also in various shades of brown and black. It is found in a range of shapes, including barrel jars and inturned-rim bowls, also the ring-stemmed goblet and other forms borrowed from the mature phase of MH Minyan pottery of the Mainland (Dickinson 2007, 242–44). Vases are not infrequently decorated with white painted patterns (Barber 2007, 194–95) that are often now visible only in shadow; others have grooved or ribbed decoration.

Dark Burnished was evidently more important in the earlier part of the MC period. Later, at Phylakopi, there was apparently a tendency for burnish to be replaced by a matt wash. A similar decline in high burnish was noted on Kea, although the class remained prominent in Period V (later MC) (Davis 1986, 4–5).

The other main fabric, Cycladic White (Barber 1987, 148–50; 2007, 196–207), is found in EC III at both Phylakopi and Akrotiri. At the former site it is rare and always undecorated; at the latter it is more common and decorated in the contemporary Geometric style. The fabric shows some variation in colour and quality but can be thin, white, and finely levigated—features that seem more common in this earlier MC stage. Sometimes there is a buff or greenish tinge. The paint is dull matt and powdery brown-black.

In the early MC period, CW pottery is almost always decorated in a style that Furumark called 'early Curvilinear' (in contrast to the 'Geometric' of EC IIIB) and is related to Cretan MM II (Furumark 1941, 220f.). Distinctive shapes include the beaked jug and shallow bowl (with decoration on the interior), the former clearly distinguishable in shape and spout form from its EC predecessors. The panelled cup (decoration in a panel on the side away from the drinker) made its appearance in early MC but is more common later. Abstract motifs and zonal decoration are prominent, the former sometimes used to form fantastical creatures. On many island sites, including Ayia Irini (Overbeck 1989b, 11), pottery of the CW class has been thought all to have been imported from Melos, though this is probably not true of Akrotiri.

The continued significance of Geometric pottery in the MC period remains unclear (Barber 2008, 60), although some was probably still being made (Atkinson et al. 1904, 259). A group of vases with decoration over a chalky white slip and in paint somewhat resembling that of CW was identified in the original report (Atkinson et al. 1904, 102–106) but may rather belong mainly to the transitional stage (discussed later).

Although the notebooks of the 1911 excavation (Brodie, Boyd, and Sweetman 2008, 413) and comments of Dawkins and Droop (1911, 10) show that Geometric pottery was found in later levels, a good deal of this may have consisted of survivals from earlier times (Renfrew and Evans 2007, 131), and it seems unlikely to have continued as a major class after the transitional phase. Certainly, it was virtually nonexistent in the MC levels of the recent excavations (Barber 2007, 213—there called Soft Matt-painted [SMP]).

Middle Cycladic—Late

A later phase of MC pottery can be distinguished on the basis of finds in Phylakopi II–iii and Ayia Irini Period V, when the DB category changes character (see above) while Cycladic White remains prominent, though with a perceptible difference in the decoration and often some coarsening of the fabric. The new style has been called 'later Curvilinear' or 'Naturalistic' (Scholes 1956, 19–20) and involves particularly the use of minor floral and other motifs (spirals) often related to the pottery of Crete in MM III. Similar material has been illustrated from Akrotiri (e.g., Nikolakopoulou et al. 2008, pl. 32.4b, bottom left).

A series of carinated cups, closely related to the later MH matt-painted pottery of the Mainland, may be rather earlier than most of the later CW pottery.

An aesthetically distinctive style of decoration ('Black and Red'), mostly related by Furumark (1941, 222) to MM III, uses burnished red circles or bands, with matt black outlines and appendages, sometimes forming pictorial motifs, combining features of DB and CW. This makes its appearance on CW fabric in earlier MC but is much more common in the later phase and lasts into the Late Cycladic period (often on LL fabric). It is found on all major Cycladic sites and appears too on the Mainland and in Crete in late MH/LH I and LM IA (Barber 1974, 35).

The Transition from Early to Middle Cycladic

Although Middle Cycladic pottery (chiefly Dark Burnished and Cycladic White) can, in general terms, be clearly distinguished from that of later Early Cycladic III (where Geometric is the most distinctive of several classes; see Renfrew and Evans 2007), the process of transition from the one to the other is harder to pin down.

For the present, attempts to do this must be based on the Phylakopi material since, at Ayia Irini, there was a gap in occupation at this time while, at Akrotiri, preliminary notices of finds from Phase A of recent investigations suggest that it covers a long period of time (equivalent at least to Phylakopi I–ii to II–ii) and cannot be used accurately to define this transition.

At Phylakopi, there are indications that the pottery from the latest floors of City I show its beginnings, particularly in the presence of what has been called (Sherratt 2000, 237) 'Combination Ware.' This, mainly found in the classic form of the 'Melian bowl' (Atkinson et al. 1904, pl. xxxiii 3–5; Barber 1974, 44 Type 3), combines a version of MC-type slip and burnish with (on the inturned rim) Geometric decoration on a band of white slip, a style and technique otherwise exclusive to Geometric pottery. The technique is occasionally employed also on other shapes.

The pottery from Phase B (= Phylakopi I–iii) of recent work at the site (Renfrew and Evans 2007, 157–76), which has produced no MC-type burnish, Combination Ware, or Melian bowls, may therefore represent the stage preceding the transition, while it must be later than the primary stage of EC IIIB since Dark-faced Incised (DFI), one of the two main ceramic components of that phase, is lacking.

For the present, this suggestion must remain provisional since clarification is still needed both of the distinction between EC and MC burnished ware and of the extent to which Geometric pottery survived into the Second City at Phylakopi. Nonetheless, it helps to accommodate several observations that have not always been easy to reconcile: Mackenzie's view (Atkinson et al. 1904, 258) of ceramic continuity from City I to II; the identification of an early stage of City II (II–i), which we have hitherto been tempted to discard but would be represented by such a transitional ceramic phase; and the observation made by Dawkins and Droop (1911, 19) that burnished ware (if MC-type burnish is meant, which is not certain) was common in Geometric levels. Further, the occupation of 'south Phylakopi,' recently proposed by Brodie, Boyd, and Sweetman (2008, 412–15) to postdate the EC III period, would probably also belong here.

While this proposal is based only on study of the Phylakopi deposits, the incontrovertibly transitional character of the Combination Ware, of which examples are found on other sites, encourages the supposition that it has a wider relevance.

MC Coarse Pottery has begun seriously to be studied only in recent years and is dated mainly by shape relationships with the classes already described.

The End of Middle Cycladic

In ceramic terms, the MC period is readily distinguished from the LC since the latter, despite many points of ceramic continuity, is marked by imports and imitations of LM IA pottery in quantity. At Phylakopi, the change coincides closely with the destruction of the Second City and the building of the Third, although the chronology of this process may be more complex than has usually been thought (Brodie forthcoming).

CONCORDANCE OF DESCRIPTIVE TERMS

Vases with Geometric Designs in Lustrous Paint (Atkinson et al. 1904, chapter IV, section 6) = Early Matt painted (EMP) (Renfrew and Evans 2007)

Geometric Pottery with Designs in Matt Black (Atkinson et al. 1904, chapter IV, section 7) = Soft Matt painted (SMP) (Renfrew and Evans 2007)

Both of the preceding were subsumed under the general heading of 'Geometric Pottery' in Barber (2008, 59–76) but separately identified, where possible, by the abbreviations used by Renfrew and Evans

Pottery of the Early Mycenaean Style with Designs in Matt Black (Atkinson et al. 1904, chapter IV, section 9) = Cycladic White (Barber 1987, etc).

Pottery of the Early Mycenaean Period with Designs in Black and Red (Atkinson et al. 1904, chapter IV, section 10) = Black and Red (BandR) (Barber 1987, etc).

Note also that, at Phylakopi, the Second City (II) (Atkinson et al. 1904, 254) is Phase C of the recent excavations (Renfrew et al. 2007, 10 table 2. 2).

SAMPLE ILLUSTRATIONS OF CERAMICS

Dark Burnished: Barber (1987, 147–49, figs. 103, 105, 107)

Cycladic White: Barber (1987, 151, 152, figs. 109, 100 [early Curvilinear style]); Sherratt (2000, pl. 385 [later Curvilinear or Naturalistic style])

Black and Red style: Atkinson et al. (1904, pls. xx, xxi); Barber (1987, 150, fig. 108)
Transitional:

Combination Ware: Atkinson et al. (1904, pl. xxxiii, nos. 3–4); Barber (1987, 147, fig. 104)

Soft Matt painted: Atkinson et al. (1904, pls. xi–xiii)

General: Zervos (1957) contains good photographs of Cycladic pottery of various periods.

BIBLIOGRAPHY

Atkinson, Thomas D., Robert C. Bosanquet, Campbell C. Edgar, Arthur J. Evans, David G. Hogarth, Duncan Mackenzie, Cecil Smith, and Francis B. Welch. 1904. *Excavations at Phylakopi in Melos*. Society for the Promotion of Hellenic Studies. Supplementary Paper 4. London: Macmillan.

Barber, Robin L. N. 1974. "Phylakopi 1911 and the History of the Later Cycladic Bronze Age." *BSA* 69: 1–53.

———. 1987. *The Cyclades in the Bronze Age*. London and Iowa City: Duckworth and University of Iowa Press.

———. 2007. "The Middle Cycladic Pottery." In *Excavations at Phylakopi in Melos 1974–77*, eds. Colin Renfrew et al., 181–238. British School at Athens Supplementary vol. 42. London: British School at Athens.

———. 2008. "Unpublished Pottery from Phylakopi." *BSA* 103: 43–222.

———, and Olga Hadjianastasiou. 1989. "Mikre Vigla: A Bronze Age Settlement on Naxos." *BSA* 84: 63–162.

Betancourt, Philip P., Vassos Karageorghis, Robert Laffineur, and Wolf-Dietrich Niemeier, eds. 1999. *Meletemata*.

Blegen, Carl W. 1921. *Korakou: A Prehistoric Settlement near Corinth*. New York: American School of Classical Studies at Athens.

Brodie, Neil J. Forthcoming. "A Reassessment of Mackenzie's Second and Third Cities at Phylakopi." *BSA* 104 (2009).

———, Michael Boyd, and Rebecca Sweetman. 2008. "The Settlement of South Phylakopi: A Reassessment of Dawkins and Droop's Excavations." In *Horizon*, 409–15.

Brodie, Neil J., Jenny Doole, Giorgos Gavalas, and Colin Renfrew, eds. 2008. *Horizon*.

Caskey, John L. 1972. "Investigations in Keos. Part II: A Conspectus of the Pottery." *Hesperia* 41: 357–401.

Δανέζης, Ιωάννης, ed. 2001. *Σαντορίνη: Θήρα, Θηρασία, Ασπρονήσι, Ηφαιστεία*. Athens: Adam/Pergamos.

Davis, Jack L. 1986. *Keos V: Ayia Irini Period V*. Mainz: von Zabern.

Dawkins, Richard M., and John P. Droop. 1911. "The Excavations at Phylakopi in Melos." *BSA* 17: 1–22.

Dickinson, Oliver T. P. K. 2007. "The Middle Helladic Pottery." In *Excavations at Phylakopi in Melos 1974–77*, ed. Colin Renfrew et al., 238–48. British School at Athens Supplementary vol. 42. London: British School at Athens.

Furumark, Arne. 1941. *The Mycenaean Pottery: Analysis and Classification*. Stockholm: Victor Petterson.

Lentini, Maria Costanza, ed. 2001. *The Two Naxos Cities: A Fine Link between the Aegean Sea and Sicily*. Palermo: Gruppo Editoriale Kalos.

MacGillivray, J. Alexander. 2007. "Protopalatial (MM IB–MM IIIA): Early Chamber beneath the West Court, Royal Pottery Stores, the Trial KV, and the West and South Polychrome Deposits Groups." In *Knossos Pottery Handbook*, 105–49.

Manning, Sturt. 1995. *The Absolute Chronology of the Aegean Early Bronze Age: Archaeology, History, and Radiocarbon*. Monographs in Mediterranean Archaeology 1. Sheffield: Sheffield Academic Press.

———. 1999. *A Test of Time: The Volcano of Thera and the Chronology and History of the Aegean and East Mediterranean in the Mid-second Millennium BC*. Oxford: Oxbow.

Μαρθάρη, Μαρίζα. 1983. "Ανασκαφή στο Φτέλλο Θήρας (Περίοδος 1980)." *AAA* 15 (1982): 86–101.

———. 2001. "Η Θήρα από την Πρώιμη στη Μέση Εποχή του Χαλκού. Τα αποτελέσματα των ανασκαφών στον Φτέλλο και τον Άγιο Ιωάννη τον Ελεήμονα." In *Σαντορίνη: Θήρα, Θηρασία, Ασπρονήσι, Ηφαιστεία*, ed. Ιωάννης Δανέζης, 105–20. Athens: Adam/Pergamos.

Momigliano, Nicoletta, ed. 2007. *Knossos Pottery Handbook*.

Morton, Jamie. 2001. *The Role of the Physical Environment in Ancient Greek Seafaring*. Mnemosyne Suppl. 213. Leiden: Brill.

Nikolakopoulou, Irene, Fragoula Georma, Angeliki Moschou, and Photini Sofianou. 2008. "Trapped in the Middle: New Stratigraphical and Ceramic Evidence from Middle Cycladic Akrotiri, Thera." In *Horizon*, 311–25.

Overbeck, John C. 1989a. *The Bronze Age Pottery from the Kastro at Paros*. SIMA Pocket Book 78. Jonsered, Sweden: Åström.

———. 1989b. *Keos VII: Ayia Irini Period IV*. Part I: *The Stratigraphy and the Find Deposits*. Mainz: von Zabern.

Papageorgiou, Despoina. 2007. "Sea Routes in the Prehistoric Cyclades." In *Horizon*, 9–11.

Papagiannopoulou, Angelia. 2008. "From Pots to Pictures: Middle Cycladic Figurative Art from Akrotiri, Thera." In *Horizon*, 433–49.

Philaniotou, Olga. 2001. "New Evidence for the Topography of Naxos in the Geometric Period." In *The Two Naxos Cities: A Fine Link between the Aegean Sea and Sicily*, ed. Maria Costanza Lentini, 29–34. Palermo: Gruppo Editoriale Kalos.

Renfrew, Colin, Neil Brodie, Christine Morris, and Chris Scarre, eds. 2007. *Excavations at Phylakopi in Melos 1974–77*. British School at Athens Supplementary vol. 42. London: British School at Athens.

———, and Robert K. Evans. 2007. "The Early Bronze Age Pottery." In *Excavations at Phylakopi in Melos 1974–77*, eds. Colin Renfrew et al., 129–80. British School at Athens Supplementary vol. 42. London: British School at Athens.

Sakellarakis, Ioannis. 1996. "Minoan Religious Influence in the Aegean." *BSA* 91: 81–99.

Scholes, Kathleen. 1956. "The Cyclades in the Later Bronze Age: A Synopsis." *BSA* 51: 7–40.

Sherratt, Susan. 2000. *Catalogue of Cycladic Antiquities in the Ashmolean Museum: The Captive Spirit*. 2 vols. Oxford: Oxford University Press.

Sotirakopoulou, Panayiota. In press. "The Cycladic Middle Bronze Age: A 'Dark Age' in Aegean Prehistory or a Dark Spot in Archaeological Research?" In *Mesohelladika*.

Τελεβάντου, Χριστίνα. 2005. "Άνδρος." In *Αρχαιολογία. Νησιά του Αιγαίου*, ed. Ανδρέας Γ. Βλαχόπουλος, 214–19. Athens: Melissa.

Televantou, Christina A. 2008. "Strofilas: A Neolithic Settlement on Andros." In *Horizon*, 43–53.

Βλαχόπουλος, Ανδρέας Γ., ed. 2005. *Αρχαιολογία. Νησιά του Αιγαίου*. Athens: Melissa.

Wace, Alan J. B., and Carl W. Blegen. 1918. "The Pre-Mycenaean Pottery of the Mainland." *BSA* 22: 175–89.

Warren, Peter. 1999. "LM IA: Knossos, Thera, Gournia." In *Meletemata*, 893–903.

———, and Vronwy Hankey. 1989. *Aegean Bronze Age Chronology*. Bristol: Bristol Classical Press.

Wilson, David E. 1999. *Keos IX: Ayia Irini Periods I–III, the Neolithic and Early Bronze Age Settlements*. Part 1: *The Pottery and Small Finds*. Mainz: von Zabern.

Zervos, Christian. 1957. *L'art des Cyclades du début a la fin de l'Age du Bronze, 2500–1100 avant notre ère*. Paris: Cahiers d'Art.

Late Bronze Age

CHAPTER 10

....

MAINLAND GREECE

....

KIM SHELTON

MYCENAEAN civilization developed, grew to great heights, and collapsed, all during the Late Bronze Age. Rooted on the Greek mainland, where the period is called Late Helladic (LH), the beginning, internal divisions (I, II, IIIA, IIIB, and IIIC), and end of this historical framework are based almost entirely on pottery styles.

These ceramic phases do not necessarily correspond to historical periods, however, so there is occasionally a preference for chronological divisions centered on the life cycle of the palace—a defining cultural and architectural feature—following more closely the economic and political character of the society (e.g., prepalatial, palatial, and postpalatial). The pottery sequence, though, allows for more narrowly refined periods that also take advantage of the most prevalent material artifact and one that is subject to relatively rapid style change and wide distribution.

An absolute chronology, or numerical calendar dates, can also be reckoned by linking these ceramic sequences to Egyptian sites and finds, especially where Mycenaean pottery occurs in Egypt or Egyptian objects are found in the Aegean (Dickinson 1994, 9–22). The absolute dates are necessarily approximate but are now becoming much more refined, with scientific dating methods such as ^{14}C and dendrochronology effectively used to check the relatively derived absolute or historical dates. As a result, recent studies suggest that the upper end of the LH period should begin earlier (ca. 1700 BC) and extend longer than originally assumed; the absolute dates for the Late Helladic III period (14th–12th centuries BC), on the other hand, seem to correspond very closely with the traditional relative dating sequence (Manning et al. 2001).

The best entrée into the Mycenaean culture of the Late Bronze Age is through the archaeological record that has produced the remains of settlements and cemeteries, artifacts of life and death, from their emergence as a power at the end of the Middle Helladic (MH) period to the destruction of their palaces at the end of LH IIIB. Research has been ongoing for more than 130 years, yet there is still much that we do not know about the Mycenaeans and the mainland in this period. The scene is also continuously changing, with new sites and new evidence carrying the potential to completely alter what we now know. Additional work in settlements and chamber tomb cemeteries, for example, will certainly fill many gaps in our knowledge, while expanding and exciting subfields such as bioarchaeology will add greatly to both the vast artifactual and the limited textual evidence (Tzedakis, Martlew, and Jones 2008).

EARLIEST BEGINNINGS

The culture that we refer to as Mycenaean, named after the palatial site of Mycenae, began developing in the previous MH period. The diverse seeds of the recognized Mycenaean cultural forms were planted in this earlier period; through internal indigenous growth together with closer and more consistent contacts with Minoan Crete and the Cyclades, the early Late Helladic period marks a rise in more uniform developmental stages and material culture out of complex and heterogeneous processes, as yet not completely understood. Excavated material culture from the entire period, especially the earlier phases, often originates from cemeteries rather than settlements, while the search for palaces and the elite has dominated research goals for many decades, with smaller sites and settlements receiving less attention. The situation is changing, however, with survey strategy and methodology creating great advances in the location of sites across the landscape and providing invaluable information on settlement patterns, density, and habitation phases (Wright 2004a, 114–31).

It is now becoming clear that the formative processes of Mycenaean states were influenced by a variety of factors, including competitive interaction of mainland elites based on hunting and military prowess, exposure and access to outside cultures and materials, and a likely role in brokering Cycladic and Cretan access to resources and opportunities on the mainland. It is also now fairly clear that Mycenaean sites, large and small, all share similar characteristics, including a focus on an architectural center, usually in a commanding position and sometimes fortified, located close to water and good agricultural land, and sitting along lines of communication from the sea to farther inland.

LH I–II PERIOD (16TH–15TH CENTURIES BC)

During the Early Mycenaean or LH I–II period (16th–15th centuries BC), also known as the Prepalatial/Early Palatial period, the geographical center of the Mycenaean world was located in the heart of the mainland, specifically within southern and central Greece: important regions for the development of administrative and cultural polities as a whole included the Argolid, Messenia, and probably Laconia, much of Attica, Boeotia, eastern Phocis, and coastal Thessaly.

The first recognizable Mycenaean tombs, pottery, and other material culture belong to the 16th century BC, essentially the LH I period, and are confined to the Peloponnese, Attica, and central Greece. Our knowledge of the culture in this period is derived in large part from cemetery/burial evidence, with grave goods providing the assemblages of material culture that indicate levels of prosperity, social complexity, and artistic influences. The cemeteries are well defined, organized, and divided, some formally for exclusion or inclusion—either conceptual or physical. Habitation is in small settlements, perhaps organized into functional and/or social divisions. Throughout this period, the settlements become increasingly consolidated while the cemeteries become highly differentiated.

Overall, individual regions on the mainland seem to develop independently, with local rulers who may have been either individual chiefs or an allied group (i.e., an oligarchy of successful elites who consolidated power over communities and regions, through persuasion, whether peaceful or violent) (Wright 1995, 63–80). Pronounced regional variations can be seen developing within larger uniform trends; while individual characteristics are more diverse early on, features then combine or cross-pollinate into a more common cultural style over time.

Wealthy societal groups also emerged. The new prosperity was manifested in valuable funerary gifts, usually symbolic. Weapons and objects of foreign manufacture suggest power, wealth, and possibly warfare; the best known are those from the Shaft Graves at Mycenae (Graziadio 1991). Because of the strong cultural continuity with the MH period in areas such as burial customs, weapons, and shapes and decoration of pottery, it is very likely that these groups developed from within the culture rather than being newcomers.

Multiple burials and cemeteries, including all ages and genders, stress the importance of family and lineage. Marked diversity of tomb types (shaft grave, tumulus, tholos) and conspicuous consumption in burials indicate competition and status marking, as well as fluctuation within and among regional ranking systems. A combination of local, traditional, and imported ideas and artifacts is evident particularly in the rich burials of the Shaft Graves at Mycenae and in tumuli and early tholoi, especially in Messenia.

Acquisition of the considerable wealth that had become available—as seen both preserved in and perhaps exclusively intended for burials—occurs as a result of stimuli derived from growing contacts with and influences from Minoan Crete and the Eastern Mediterranean. Mycenae and Pylos are two early success stories inasmuch as both show important contact with Crete, while other areas with rich and/or imported finds from this period include Laconia, Corinth, Athens, Marathon, Thebes, and Orchomenos, Kirrha, and Krisa near Delphi, as well as coastal Thessaly. From the evidence of pottery and weapons, the Mycenaeans were already in contact as well with Macedonia, Albania, and Italy.

The ceramic assemblage on the mainland during this time includes a number of different fine wares from indigenous traditions combined with Minoan, Cycladic, and Aeginitan influences (Dietz 1991). The distinctive and defining LH I lustrous dark-on-light pottery may have developed in Laconia as a result of Cretan influence by way of the island of Kythera and then spread quickly to the Argolid. Throughout the period, though, it remains a significant minority alongside the traditional MH wares. Mycenaean pottery also arrives in the Cyclades as early as the 16th century BC, very soon after its occurrence on the mainland, highlighting the extent and efficiency of the early trade network in the Aegean.

The stratification of society was complete by LH II, but again, regional variation continues. Some districts start out with numerous independent settlements that are gradually consolidated into competing polities, probably by strong families or chiefs at a smaller number of larger sites (those marked with tholoi); for instance, those in Messenia cede complete autonomy to Pylos when it becomes the single palatial center (Voutsaki 1998, 41–58; Bennet 1999, 29–39). A similar arrangement of small settlements that then consolidate into larger polities is also evident in the Argolid and Laconia through LH II, but there they develop quite differently as several—rather than simply one—palatial centers appear in the Argolid, including Mycenae, Tiryns, and Midea. In contrast, none develop in Laconia; instead, here several successful nonpalatial polities, including Ayios Stephanos, Vapheio, Menelaion, and Pellana, continue into the following period (Cavanagh 1995, 81–88).

Cultural contact with the Minoan palaces and the central Aegean is of basic importance to the successful acquisition of wealth by the Mycenaeans and to the adaptation of technology and practices that enables the formation of their palatial system. The effect of stimuli from Minoan Crete can be seen most clearly in crafts, which include both imported finished objects and raw materials, together with specialized local production, that mark status both socially and politically (Voutsaki 1995, 55–66). At the same time, one can see the adoption, imitation, or adaptation of Minoan styles, which accompanies a veritable explosion of pictorial arts, in stark contrast to the earlier and practically aniconic MH tradition. It can be difficult to distinguish Mycenaean arts from the Minoan originals or inspirations, although there are always some underlying, continuous Helladic elements present as well. Iconography and its inherent meaning to the Mycenaeans are also blurred; often it is impossible to isolate distinctly Mycenaean beliefs.

Also to be emphasized is the importance of the island of Aegina—possibly as a conduit from Crete and the islands into the southern and central mainland and as a witness to continuous cultural development from the Middle into the Late Bronze Age (Rutter 2001, 126–30). The very successful polity on Aegina exhibits close contact with the mainland, evident in its ceramics—fine ware storage vessels and kitchenware especially—until at least early LH III, even at production centers such as Mycenae. The island hubs of Aegina, Kythera, and probably Keos played an influential role in the development of the Mycenaean centers on the mainland.

As large regions and their significant resources became increasingly centralized during LH II, organization and administration became necessary. The emergent elite with access to wealth and control of specialized labor was in a position to consolidate power further, creating a sociopolitical center stratified horizontally, according to specialist capabilities, as well as vertically. The formal state structure was thus created.

During the Pre–/Early Palatial period on the Greek mainland, a number of destructions occur on Crete. Afterward, Mycenaean control clearly expands in the southern Aegean, and, as Mycenaean goods appear more frequently and systematically in the east, a takeover of Minoan trade routes and depots occurs. At this time in LH II, Mycenaean pottery becomes the dominant fine ware beyond the mainland, influencing pottery made on Crete—a reversal of the earlier pattern. Mainland influence continues into the next period, at which time Greek—in the form of Linear B—becomes the administrative language at Knossos.

The Early Mycenaean period comes to an end on the Greek mainland with the emergence of the palaces.

Late Helladic IIIA–B (14th–13th Centuries BC)

The Palatial period of Late Helladic IIIA–B (14th–13th centuries BC) sees the successful development and evolution of several competing polities from the previous period into centrally focused and administered states. Following the second destruction of Knossos in the 14th century BC, administrative features of the Minoan palaces are transferred to the Greek mainland, probably during the first major phase of palace construction. These centuries also witnessed a great expansion of culture when Mycenaean Greece extended northward to Mount Olympus, westward to Epirus, eastward to the Dodecanese, and south to Crete.

Particularly during the LH IIIA2 phase of the later 14th century BC, the Mycenaean civilization rapidly became dominant in the Aegean. It was a period of political security, giving rise to a flourishing economy and to great expansion: to the east, especially the coast of Asia Minor; to the west, with Sardinian metal sources serving as a likely carrot; and well to the north into Macedonia, the northern Aegean, and beyond, possibly up into the Black Sea. The extensive contact, trade, and reciprocal influences afforded by cultural interfaces outside the polities and even beyond the mainland (Cline 1994, 2007) became important for the further development of Mycenaean cultural and political features and for the success of the states and their hierarchical population.

The Palatial period sees a stabilization of social organization and an institutionalization of power structures. This is most clearly visible in the archaeological record in the centers with palaces, such as Mycenae, Tiryns, Pylos, and Thebes. They functioned like Minoan palaces—as administrative, ceremonial, production, and storage centers—but with a different internal structure centered around an architectural unit called the megaron and with settlements of various sizes and forms. The latter are still very little understood, whether in palatial or rural context. Research bias toward the lives of the Mycenaean elite has left much to be learned about the wider spectrum of the population, although important exceptions include Nichoria, Ayios Stephanos, Tsoungiza, Korakou, Berbati, and Asine. The growth of regional studies has made the greatest contribution to our knowledge of settlement patterns and density; current excavation work (e.g., at Iklaina, Korfos, and Mitrou) also indicates a very welcome trend toward settlements and the investigation of Mycenaeans from other social strata.

Most of the information about Mycenaean citadels, palaces, and settlements, gathered through archaeological excavation, comes from the 13th century BC and reveals extensive building programs, engineering, and infrastructure to support a large but exclusive elite class and a substantial population located at varying distances from the center. By this time, citadels built in Cyclopean masonry are seen at Mycenae, Tiryns, Midea, Athens, and Gla, along with probably Thebes and possibly Orchomenos in Boeotia, as well as Pylos in Messenia. Major improvements to the infrastructure (fortification, roads, drainage, and water supply) are also part of the systematic public building program, created especially for a more widespread transportation and communication network both intra- and interregionally. With the expansion of settlements and a growing population comes also a growing exploitation of land for the support of the population, for trade resources, and for specialized labor forces.

From this period, too, comes most of the evidence contained on the unbaked clay tablets written in Linear B script, an early form of the Greek language used primarily, if not exclusively, at palatial centers as notations or temporary annual/seasonal records of commodities or economic administration. The archive of Linear B tablets from Pylos illuminates many aspects of Mycenaean palatial administration, as well as a complex economy and social structure in those areas where palace centers had become established (Duhoux and Morpurgo-Davies 2008). The volume of recovered knowledge of intangible aspects is immense and helps to create the impression that Pylos was a typical Mycenaean palatial state, which it probably was not.

Additional tablets, usually found in small numbers within scattered 13th-century contexts, have been recovered at Mycenae, Tiryns, and Thebes. Most recently, tablets from late 14th century BC context were uncovered in the settlement of Mycenae at Petsas House, showing that written administrative accounting was already in use on the mainland at that time, nicely filling a gap leading back to the Linear B archives from Knossos of the early 14th century BC.

These two primary sources of information (the archaeological record and texts) enable us to visualize the basic elements of the Mycenaean economy and social organization (Shelmerdine 2001a, 113–28; Wright 2004b, 13–48). Over many decades, excavation and survey that have focused on increasingly larger sites and the palatial citadels have revealed widespread settlement patterns throughout the mainland. Through LH IIIA and into LH IIIB, the number and scale of settlements gradually increase. At the centers, organized workforces concentrate on massive building programs directed toward habitation and industry, while decidedly less effort and fewer resources are put into tomb construction. The number of new tholoi are much less widespread, with the last/largest built early in the period (Cavanagh and Mee 1998, 61–79). Sumptuary controls on elite mortuary practice must also have been implemented since the elaboration of burial features and the inclusion of prestige items are entirely lacking in chamber tombs during LH IIIB (French 2002, 75).

Evidence for the Mycenaean economy, as well as the administrative system that supported it, as viewed through the tablets, shows a power hierarchy with the wanax at the top. Material and human resources are mobilized from the center for the needs of the political economy. Below the wanax are many administrators who are individual landowners, but land is also owned and leased by the palace. The successful exploitation of the landscape for agricultural production allowed the labor force to be mustered for major public works or for military purposes. At the palatial level, specialized, large-scale cultivation of limited crops enabled the production of perfumed oil, textiles, and other crafts. Agricultural products and other commodities could be provided from elsewhere in taxes (Shelmerdine 2001b, 358–62). The economic success of the Mycenaean palaces both depended on and fostered trade over a wide area of the Mediterranean; fully involved in trade, the palaces import raw materials (metals, ivory, glass) and export processed commodities and objects made from these materials, together with local products: oil, perfume, wine, and wool (Cline 1994, 2007). Pottery is also essential in this system.

Mycenaean pottery now spread over the entire Greek mainland and the Aegean islands. Extremely homogeneous and thus often called 'the Mycenaean koine,' pottery of LH IIIA and IIIB is of very high technical quality, while at the same time also mass produced (Mountjoy 1993). This is also true of other craft items; seals, jewelry, weapons, and ivories were produced in large numbers with an increasingly stylized and narrow repertoire of designs. Mycenaean pottery is exported over much of the Mediterranean—necessary for the trade of its contents, especially oil and wine, but also popular in and of itself; such vessels were kept in circulation for long stretches of time as heirlooms and frequently imitated in local clays (Leonard 1994; van Wijngaarden 2002).

Everywhere on the mainland, palaces were built and rebuilt during the long and prosperous Palatial phase, with ever-increasing signs of centralized control. Several widespread but localized destructions were usually followed by rebuilding on a massive scale. However, even in the late 13th century, indications of trouble began to appear: a tightening up of control and of the economy, with isolated instances of destruction and decline, all of which indicate likely strains within society. The period ends with yet another destruction from which recovery was much more difficult (Mycenae, Tiryns) or impossible (Pylos, Thebes). Although there is some indication of continuing central organization, there is no longer evidence for the remarkable administration recorded in Linear B script.

LATE HELLADIC IIIC (12TH–11TH CENTURIES BC)

The Late Mycenaean phases of the 12th–11th centuries BC (LH IIIC) are, in almost all regions of the mainland, Postpalatial. Sometime around 1200 BC, all of the palaces suffer from a major destructive event and are not rebuilt. Many nonpalatial sites in most regions also show signs of either destruction or abandonment. Along with the loss of the large-scale construction and monumental buildings, we also see the disappearance of the administrative system, the writing system employed in it, and other palatial features such as imported luxury crafts and frescoes.

These instances of destruction, which take place over several decades, coincide with much upheaval in the eastern Mediterranean. Some are certainly the result of natural disasters such as earthquakes, but clearly there are different causes in different regions. Most significant is the total lack or—at best—a reduced level of recovery in virtually every instance (Shelmerdine 2001b, 372–76, 381).

Following the palatial destructions, a marked instability appears. Although some sites recovered and prospered for a brief time, they did so with a different orientation and organization, perhaps more intraregionally focused. Tiryns, and probably Mycenae as well, has a central structure built on the ruins of the palaces but on a different scale (a reflection, surely, of the reduced level of organization and control).

The homogenous nature of the Palatial period is interrupted or lost during the Postpalatial period of LH IIIC. Regional and local preferences and styles become intensified in most cultural features, including architecture, burial customs, communication networks, and pottery production. Tomb evidence suggests a great decrease in population in many regions such as the Argolid, which worsens during the period; in other areas such as Attica, however, burials increase. The period of temporary recovery is followed by an ever more rapid economic decline, and by the 11th century BC there is little still recognizable as "Mycenaean" in the archaeological record (Deger-Jalkotzy 2003, 455–70; Deger-Jalkotzy and Zavadil 2007).

BIBLIOGRAPHY

Bennet, John. 1999. "The Expansion of a Mycenaean Palatial Center." In *RMP*, 9–18.

Cavanagh, William. 1995. "Development of the Mycenaean State in Laconia: Evidence from the Laconia Survey." In *Politeia*, 81–88.

———, and Christopher Mee. 1998. *A Private Place: Death in Prehistoric Greece. SIMA* 125. Jonsered, Sweden: Åström.

Cline, Eric H. 1994. *SWDS*.

———. 2007. "Rethinking Mycenaean International Trade." In *RMP II*, 190–200.

Deger-Jalkotzy, Sigrid. 2003. "Work in Progress: Report on the 'End of the Mycenaean Civilization' Project for the Years of 1999–2001." In *SCIEM* II, 455–70.

———, and Michaela Zavadil, eds. 2007. *LH IIIC Middle*.

Dickinson, Oliver T. P. K. 1994. *The Aegean Bronze Age*. Cambridge World Archaeology. New York: Cambridge University Press.

Dietz, Søren. 1991. *The Argolid at the Transition to the Mycenaean Age: Studies in the Chronology and Cultural Development in the Shaft Grave Period*. Copenhagen: National Museum, Denmark, Department of Near Eastern and Classical Antiquities.

Duhoux, Yves, and Anna Morpurgo Davies, eds. 2008. *A Companion to Linear B: Mycenaean Greek Texts and Their World*. Louvain-la-Neuve, Belgium: Peeters.

French, Elizabeth B. 2002. *Mycenae, Agamemnon's Capital: The Site and Its Setting*. Charleston, S.C.: Tempus.

Graziadio, Giampaolo. 1991. "The Process of Social Stratification at Mycenae in the Shaft Grave Period: A Comparative Examination of the Evidence." *AJA* 95: 403–40.

Leonard, Albert 1994. *An Index to the Late Bronze Age Aegean Pottery from Syria-Palestine. SIMA* 114. Jonsered, Sweden: Åström.

Manning, Sturt W., Bernd Kromer, Peter I. Kuniholm, and Maryanne W. Newton. 2001. "Anatolian Tree Rings and a New Chronology for the East Mediterranean Bronze-Iron Ages." *Science* 294.5551: 2532–35.

Mountjoy, Penelope. 1993. *Mycenaean Pottery: An Introduction*. OUCA Monograph. Oxford: Oxbow.

Rutter, Jeremy B. 2001. "Review of Aegean Prehistory II: The Prepalatial Bronze Age of the Southern and Central Greek Mainland." In *Aegean Prehistory*, 95–155.

Shelmerdine, Cynthia W. 2001a. "The Evolution of Administration at Pylos." In *Economy and Politics in the Mycenaean Palace States: Proceedings of a Conference Held on 1–3 July 1999 in the Faculty of Classics, Cambridge*, ed. Sofia Voutsaki and John Killen, 113–28. Cambridge: Cambridge Philological Society.

———. 2001b. "Review of Aegean Prehistory VI: The Palatial Bronze Age of the Southern and Central Greek Mainland." In *Aegean Prehistory*, 329–81.

———. 2006. "Mycenaean Palatial Administration." In *Ancient Greece from the Mycenaean Palaces to the Age of Homer*, ed. Sigrid Deger-Jalkotzy and Irene S. Lemos, 73–86. Edinburgh Leventis Studies 3. Edinburgh: Edinburgh University Press.

Tzedakis, Yannis, Holley Martlew, and Martin K. Jones, eds. 2008. *Archaeology Meets Science: Biomolecular Investigations in Bronze Age Greece*. Oxford: Oxbow.

van Wijngaarden, Gert J. 2002. *Use and Appreciation of Mycenaean Pottery in the Levant, Cyprus, and Italy (ca. 1600–1200 BC)*. Amsterdam: Amsterdam University Press.

Voutsaki, Sofia. 1995. "Social and Political Processes in the Mycenaean Argolid: The Evidence from Mortuary Practices." In *Politeia*, 55–66.

————. 1998. "Mortuary Evidence, Symbolic Meanings, and Social Change: A Comparison between Messenia and the Argolid in the Mycenaean Period." In *Cemetery and Society in the Aegean Bronze Age,* ed. Keith Branigan, 41–58. Sheffield Studies in Aegean Archaeology 1. Sheffield: Sheffield Academic Press.

Wright, James C. 1995. "From Chief to King in Mycenaean Society." In *Role of the Ruler,* 63–80.

————. 2004a. "Comparative Settlement Patterns during the Bronze Age in the Northeastern Peloponnesos, Greece." In *Side-by-Side Survey: Comparative Regional Studies in the Mediterranean World,* ed. Susan E. Alcock and John F. Cherry, 114–31. Oxford: Oxbow.

————. 2004b. "A Survey of Evidence for Feasting in Mycenaean Society." In *The Mycenaean Feast,* ed. James C. Wright, 13–58. *Hesperia* 73(2). Princeton: American School of Classical Studies at Athens.

CHAPTER 11

CRETE

ERIK HALLAGER

Two of the most outstanding single finds from the Late Minoan period discovered during the last twenty-five years are the Palaikastro Kouros and the clay sealing known as the Master Impression from Khania. Both finds have been published via an individual monograph (MacGillivray, Driessen, and Sackett 2000; Hallager 1985), and both have demonstrated how little we actually know about important aspects of the period. To the inhabitants of Late Minoan I Crete, the meaning of both objects would have been obvious, but we can only guess what they actually represent, at least on present evidence. And this is characteristic of the period: A great deal of good evidence enables us to agree on most of the facts, but uncertainties start emerging as soon as we begin to interpret the facts.

Very succinctly, the history of Late Minoan Crete can be described as a period of many changes. In the beginning, we find the flourishing time of the Minoan palaces with the first real urban society on European soil. This palatial society was destroyed by conflagrations all over the island. Of the palaces, it seems that only Knossos survived. In connection with, or some time after, these destructions we know that Mycenaean mainlanders settled in Crete, after which many aspects of the Cretan society changed. Toward the end of the Bronze Age, almost all coastal towns and settlements were abandoned, and people either moved to the mountains or emigrated.

CHRONOLOGY

Three different systems describe the relative chronology of the Late Minoan period: (1) the traditional chronology, based on stratigraphy and typology of pottery; (2) a chronology based on palatial periods; and (3) a chronology based on administrative issues. The only one of the three where there is a reasonable agreement among scholars today is the first the traditional, relative chronology based on pottery, which can be divided into ten periods, of which LM IIIC and Subminoan are still under discussion (table 11.1).

Regarding the second system, there is little agreement on the palatial periods, with the single exception that the LM I period belongs to the Neopalatial period. In the original system introduced by Platon, the Neopalatial period lasted until the destruction of Knossos, which was thought to date to the end of LM II (Platon 1949), and was followed by the Postpalatial period. However, most scholars writing after Platon ended the Neopalatial period not at the close of LM II but rather with the numerous destructions all over Crete by the end of LM IB.

Then, as it became clear that the *wanax* (the Mycenaean word for king) and with him one or more palaces must also have existed in Crete after a destruction of the palace at Knossos at the beginning of LM IIIA2, I suggested in 1988 that the Neopalatial period was followed by a Monopalatial period during LM II–early LM IIIA2, followed by a Final Palatial period during LM IIIA2 and IIIB1. Since the palatial administration seems to cease in Crete after LM IIIB1, LM IIIB2 was considered

Table 11.1. Chronological Table Indicating Some of the Different Relative and Absolute Chronologies of the Late Minoan Period.

Natural science	Historical	Pottery	Palaces			Administration	
1613	1540	LM IA	Neo-palatial	Neo-palatial	Neo-palatial	Minoan	Minoan
1525	1450	LM IB					
1425	1400	LM II		Mono-palatial	Final palatial	Mycenaean	Intermediate
		LM IIIA:1					
1300	1300	LM IIIA:2	Post-palatial	Final palatial			Mycenaean
		LM IIIB:1					
1200	1200	LM IIIB:2		Post-palatial	Post-palatial		
		LM IIIC early					
1050	1050	LM IIIC late					
		Subminoan					

Source: Courtesy of the author.

the start of the Postpalatial period (Hallager 1988). In their *AJA* article on the Late Minoan Period, Rehak and Younger kept the phrase 'Final Palatial period,' but they extended it to include the Monopalatial period as well (Rehak and Younger 2001).

If we turn to the third system—a chronology based on administrative issues—there is also no agreement except for the LM I period, which is surely Minoan, with its characteristic Linear A system. To those scholars who argue for the LM II arrival and political dominance of the mainlanders, who used the Linear B administrative system, the Mycenaean period started immediately after LM I. However, other scholars are uncertain what happened in Crete during the LM II–early LM IIIA2 period and maintain that the Mycenaean period started after the LM IIIA2 destruction of the palace at Knossos and that the period in between could be designated as the Intermediate period (Hallager 1988; Niemeier 1982, 219–87).

As mentioned, the relative chronology based on pottery is reasonably secure, while other relative chronologies are exposed to individual interpretations of the archaeological data and are rather confusing concerning the LM II–LM III periods. If we turn to the absolute chronology, there is a reasonable agreement concerning the LM III period, while the LM I–II periods are under serious discussion. The absolute chronology has traditionally been based on synchronisms with Egypt. According to this approach, the Late Minoan IB period could not very well have started before c. 1540 BC (Warren 2006), while, according to recent results in the natural sciences, the eruption at Thera/Santorini, which probably happened in the later part of the LM IA period, must have taken place between 1623 BC and 1600 BC (Warburton 2009).

THE NEOPALATIAL PERIOD

Both the architecture and the administration clearly indicate a prosperous and well-organized society in the LM I period. Palaces have been excavated at Knossos, Phaistos, Malia, Zakro, and Galatas, and a palatial building has been uncovered in Petras in eastern Crete. In all probability, additional undiscovered palaces also exist in western Crete at Khania and Stavromenos, a little east of Rethymnon. Undoubtedly, in the LM I period, Knossos was the largest and at the same time the major palace in Crete.

The architecture of the palaces is rather uniform, containing more or less the same elements, although differently situated within each complex. Multistory buildings are constructed around a central court. With the possible exception of the newly discovered palace at Galatas, the west wing of the palaces is the most consistently laid out and has an impressive façade. On the ground floor are cult rooms and large storage areas, while archives and reception areas are usually found on the upper floor.

Another characteristic element in the architecture is the so-called Minoan Hall, which consists of a light well with column and a front hall with a pier-and-door partition leading into the main hall. There is no general agreement on the function of the Minoan Hall, which may have served as representative, private, or religious rooms. Likewise, there is no general agreement as to the function of another characteristic architectural element, the lustral basin.

Large pillar halls—possibly with banquet halls above—have been identified in the north wing of the palaces, while workrooms and storerooms are spread over the entire area. Many of the characteristic architectural elements of the palaces are repeated in the large, two-storied villas and town houses all over the island (Graham 1969). The settlements around the palaces were quite extensive and well planned, as were other towns with major (palatial?) buildings, such as Palaikastro and Gournia.

The administration of the period was quite extensive. The tools of the administration were the Linear A script and the seals, the use of which has been discovered at all of the major settlements in LM I Crete. The physical remains consist of Linear A tablets and five main types of sealings. The Linear A script is as yet not deciphered, but the tablets were probably a kind of preliminary economic document. They are found scattered throughout the settlements, while the sealings, with the exception of the *nodulus,* seem to have been kept in archives. One of the documents, the roundel, in all probability functioned as a receipt—a document that disappeared in the later Linear B administration. Among the most interesting are the flat-based (or parcel) nodules, which were apparently used to seal inscribed parchment documents. This evidence, taken together with the fact that the Linear A script was used on many noneconomic items and was also written in ink, seems to indicate that the script was much more extensively used during the LM I period than the preserved inscriptions might otherwise lead us to think.

Another interesting observation in this regard is the fact that flat-based nodules stamped with the same golden signet rings have been discovered at several different sites in LM I Crete, indicating that written documents were sent from one place to another. The signet rings used for these documents were undoubtedly official seals, which were in use for generations. This is shown by the fact that nodules impressed with one of those rings (*CMS* V S.3 391) have been found both in the LM IA destruction at Thera and in the LM IB destructions at Sklavokambos and Hagia Triada.

We do not know for sure the function of the one-hole hanging nodules, but there are indications that they were applied to documents written on papyrus. Furthermore, it seems certain that these nodules were impressed by both official and unofficial seals, which indicates that transactions between officials and individuals were kept in the archives. It has been suggested that these nodules were specifically attached to legal documents (Hallager 1996).

The Thera eruption had an undeniable impact on LM I Crete (Driessen and Macdonald 1997). Layers of airborne volcanic ash and seaborne pumice have been found at several sites on the northeastern coast of Crete, at Mochlos, Pseira, and Palaikastro, for example. Below a threshold in Nirou Khani was found a foundation deposit of conical cups containing pumice. The final destruction of the palace at Malia (LM IA or LM IB) is still under discussion but may also be related. In the town of Gournia, several quarters of the town were apparently not rebuilt after a destruction in LM IA, while profound changes took place in the architecture of settlements such as Khania (Splanzia). Intriguingly, for instance, the lustral basin seems to have gone out of use in the LM IB period (Driessen 1982).

However severe the impact, the Minoans managed to overcome these immediate problems, and at several sites we see impressive new buildings constructed in the LM IB period. By the time the Neopalatial period came to an end, the island was again wealthy and prosperous, as attested by the rich finds from all of the destroyed buildings. The many instances of copper ingots (Hagia Triada and Zakro), tin ingots (Mochlos), and elephant tusks (Zakro) clearly show that raw materials for tools, weapons, and luxury items were imported to the island, while finds of LM IB pottery in Cyprus, Egypt, and the Levant, as well as several paintings of Minoan delegations in Egyptian tombs, likewise point to the cultural interconnections at this time. Even the impact of Minoan art is visible in Egypt during this period.

The end of the LM IB period also marks the end of the flourishing Neopalatial civilization. In the archaeological record, we note instances of severe destruction by fire in palaces, towns, and villas all over the island—events that changed the Minoan civilization profoundly. Three explanations have been advanced as to the cause of these events. One advanced by Evans and later supported by Furumark was internal unrest—uproars against the dominant power of Knossos. After the decipherment of Linear B, the prevailing theory was that the destructions were caused by an invasion of the Mycenaean mainlanders. Still others have suggested natural catastrophes. Combinations of the three explanations have also been suggested.

As with so many other topics, we cannot be certain about the exact source of this devastation at the end of the LM IB period, but some important points for reflection should be raised. One is that not all of the settlements were destroyed, and it was not always the entire settlement that was ruined. Thus, for example, at Knossos, extensive parts of the settlement were destroyed by fire, but not the palace proper. In Khania, rescue excavations in 1990 indicated that parts of the settlement were not damaged, but, more important, the major harbour town in southern Crete, Kommos, was not afflicted. These points seem to indicate decision makers behind the acts.

Another question we should ask in connection with the theory of the Mycenaean takeover is quite simple: Was the Mycenaean society by the end of LM IB/LH IIA sufficiently developed and politically organized to be able to conquer and maintain control over the prosperous island of Crete?

THE MONOPALATIAL OR 'INTERMEDIATE' PERIOD

The following period, LM II, does not really provide us with answers to the preceding questions since it is relatively poorly known in the archaeological record. For years it was even suggested that the period was confined to Knossos, but it has since been documented all over the island in the more important settlements. An intensi-

fied contact with the Mycenaean mainland is visible, as is demonstrated by the warrior tombs, weaponry, Ephyraean goblets, and squat alabastra, to mention just some
of the most traditional arguments. Many of these points are presently the subject of
debate, however, and we cannot argue the presence of a Mycenaean administrative
elite in Crete at this time. Linear A is still the only certain script in use during this and
the following LM IIIA1 period, but it is very limited (Popham 1976; Demopoulou,
Olivier, and Rethemiotakis 1993). Driessen's attempt to date the Linear B tablets from
the Room of the Chariot Tablets and the Room of the Fallen Column Bases to the
LM II or LM IIIA1 period is well argued but remains unproven, and it has been questioned by one of the Knossos excavators (Popham 1993), among others.

Leaving aside the uncertain evidence of the Linear B deposits from Knossos, the
evidence for administration in this period is extremely limited: There are no tablets
and only a few sealings, all from Khania. Two of these are odd, flat-based nodules
(*CMS* V s.3 103 and V S.1A 141), with a sealing system similar to that seen on some
from the Room of the Chariot Tablets but also found in LM IB Hagia Triada. They
have been dated to LM IB, while a third sealing from an LM IIIA1 context that does
not belong to the Neopalatial types might be considered the earliest Mycenaean sealing in Crete. Many points could be—and have been—put forward that the Minoan
administration continued in this period, and the answer to this problem must—on
present evidence—remain open.

The architecture of the period is also not well known. The best-preserved example is the Unexplored Mansion at Knossos—a Minoan building founded during LM
IA but finished only in LM II. At Kommos, it seems that the habitation continued
undisturbed in the LM I buildings with some alternations, while in Khania, for example, many of the rooms in the destroyed LM I buildings were cleared of destruction
debris and reinhabited with temporary repairs.

During the LM IIIA1 period, many more sites are recognized in Crete compared
to the previous period. It seems, to judge from the pottery, that most of those sites
were influenced by Knossos, which by then (according to our present knowledge)
was the only existing palace in Crete and—one may assume—in some kind of political control.

This "Intermediate" period ended with one major event: a (but not *the*) destruction of the palace at Knossos. As to what happened, it is tempting—with parallels to many historical events—to suggest a foreign invasion. Conquer the capital,
with its central administration, and you have conquered the whole—in this case—
island. Moreover, by the LM/LH IIIA2 period, the Mycenaeans had likely developed
a strong and well-organized society capable of continuing the administrative maintenance of Crete. However, this unproven hypothesis focuses on the still-debated
question of the final destruction of the palace at Knossos and the date of the Linear
B tablets.

As Popham (1970) has clearly shown, the palace at Knossos suffered a destruction at the beginning of the LM IIIA2 period. Some of the key evidence originated
from the deep cists in the West Magazines and their Long Corridor. The cists contained LM IIIA2 pottery (also burnt); furthermore, many contained lots of charcoal

and building material swept into them, which relate the fill of the cists to a destruction by fire. The point here, however, is that all of this material was sealed below the latest floors in use, meaning that the palace—or at least the West Wing—was rebuilt and still functioning after an early LM IIIA2 destruction. In addition, many of the Linear B tablets and sealings were discovered in the undisturbed destruction debris excavated above the sealed deep cists (Hallager 1977).

So, the question is, when did this second LM III destruction take place: immediately after the previous one in IIIA2 or a century later—probably at the end of LM IIIB1? The preserved evidence from Knossos is not enough to prove which choice is more likely, although many more complete vases of the LM IIIB period than of the LM IIIA2 period have been found scattered in the palace and surrounding buildings. In this connection, it may also be worthwhile to recall that the Linear B tablets found in 1990 in a secure late LM IIIB1 context in Khania clearly belonged to the Knossian and not the mainland scribal tradition (Hallager, Vlasaki, and Hallager 1992).

THE FINAL PALATIAL PERIOD

The importance and the meaning of the Linear B tablets are treated elsewhere in this volume, but here it should be stressed that since this is the script of the Mycenaean mainlanders and was used for the administration of Crete's wealth, it shows that at the time of the Linear B tablets we must envisage a Mycenaean elite in economic and perhaps political control of Crete. The script is now different, and so is the use of the other administrative tool, the seals. While sealings in the Minoan period were found mainly in archives and were attached to written documents, they are found in the Mycenaean administration scattered primarily in storerooms and workshops, with extremely few in archives and none—at least on present evidence—attached to written documents (figure 11.1).

While the use of script and seals in the Minoan period seemed to cover a large range of people in the society, it appears in the Mycenaean period to be confined to the administration of economic matters. Apart from tablets and sealings, the Linear B script is found inscribed only on stirrup jars, in a system that recalls the tablets and may perhaps also be part of the administrative system. Probably all of these inscribed stirrup jars, regardless of findspot, were produced in Crete; none can be dated earlier than LM IIIB. The same stirrup jars are also undeniable evidence for the presence of a *wanax* in Crete in this period. Simply put, the change in administrative practices indicates the presence of Mycenaeans in Crete from LM IIIA2 onward. Other archaeological evidence—at least in west Crete (Hallager and Hallager 2003, 287)—indicates the same, but there is nothing to suggest a mass invasion from the Greek mainland.

During the Minoan period, the settlements and architecture are well known and the tombs rare and poorly known, but the situation is the opposite during the

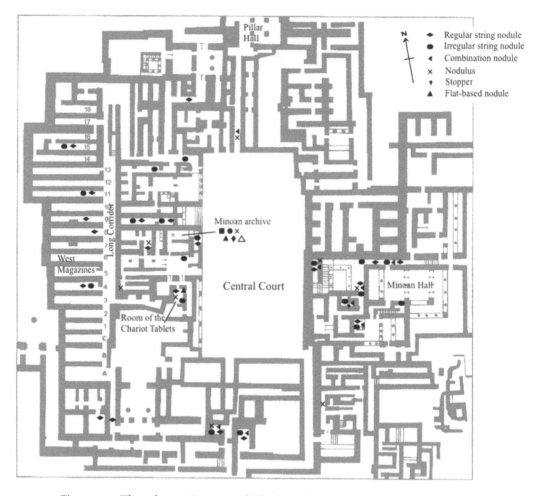

Figure 11.1. The palace at Knossos, which shows the distribution of administrative documents. With two exceptions the Minoan administrative documents were all found in the Temple Repositories (courtesy of the author).

LM III period, when the Mycenaeans are apparently in control. In this period, tombs and cemeteries are plentiful, while more substantial evidence from settlements has been brought to light only during the later years. The architecture changed from multistoried buildings, often based on wooden structures, to one-story buildings mainly constructed in stone, but the basic Minoan idea of a building where one can communicate between the different rooms was maintained.

At first glance, it seems that the material culture became much more uniform in the LB III period, but the three main areas—the mainland, the Aegean islands, and Crete—kept their strong local traditions. In Crete, the Kydonian Workshop of western Crete became dominant (perhaps together with the Knossian workshop), and its products have been found all over the island, as well as in the Cyclades, on the Greek mainland, and in Sardinia and Cyprus. It is probably only a matter of time before it is also recognized in the Levant and Egypt (figure 11.2). Imports from

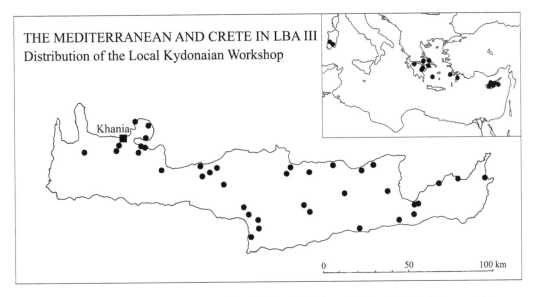

THE MEDITERRANEAN AND CRETE IN LBA III
Distribution of the Local Kydonaian Workshop

Khania

0   50   100 km

Figure 11.2. Distribution of the Local Kydonian Workshop during LM IIIA/B (copyright B. P. Hallager).

these places have also been found all over Crete, which prospered during the Final Palatial period (Cline 1994, 1999). The Handmade Burnished Ware is both interesting and significant not only because it shows the connection to southern Italy and Sardinia but also because it was locally produced in Crete, which seems to indicate the presence of south Italians as residents on the island.

THE POSTPALATIAL PERIOD

Toward the end of the Bronze Age, in LM IIIB2, the settlement pattern starts to slowly change. Large coastal sites such as Kommos, Malia, and Palaikastro have produced only very little evidence for habitation in this period, whereas many of the so-called refuge settlements of the LM IIIC period, such as Kastrokefala, Karphi, and Kastri, are actually founded in the LM IIIB2 period. We can see a clear prelude for what is going to happen in LM IIIC.

Communication within the island continued during LM IIIC early, but only a few of the old coastal settlements continued to exist—and only for a short period of time. The question is again, what happened? There is no doubt that this question must be seen in relation to what was going on in Europe and especially the eastern Mediterranean around 1200 BC, with the fall of the great powers—the Hittites, the Assyrians, the weakening of Egypt, the Sea Peoples, possible migrations from central Europe, and so on. These events, which have been discussed in the scholarly world for more than a century, clearly affected Crete in that the coast was no longer a safe place to live. The Cretan Bronze Age civilization, however, continued to exist for a century or more, although all evidence of administration disappears, as does most of the evidence for close contacts with the surrounding world—indeed a period of a troubled island.

BIBLIOGRAPHY

Cline, Eric H. 1994. *SWDS*.
————. 1999. "The Nature of the Economic Relations of Crete with Egypt and the Near East during the Bronze Age." In *From Minoan Farmers to Roman Traders: Sidelights on the Economy of Ancient Crete*, ed. Angelos Chaniotis, 115–43. Munich: Steiner.
Demopoulou, Nota, Jean-Pierre Olivier, and George Rethemiotakis. 1993. "Une statuette en argile MR IIIA de Poros/Irakliou avec inscription en linéaire A." *BCH* 117: 501–21.
Driessen, Jan. 1982. "The Minoan Hall in Domestic Architecture on Crete: To Be in Vogue in Late Minoan IA?" *Acta Archaeologica Lovanensia* 21: 27–92.
————, and Colin Macdonald. 1997. *The Troubled Island: Minoan Crete before and after the Santorini Eruption*. Aegaeum 17. Liège: Université de Liège.
Graham, James Walter. 1969. *The Palaces of Crete*, 2nd ed. Princeton: Princeton University Press.
Hallager, Erik. 1977. *The Mycenaean Palace at Knossos*. Medelhavsmuseet, Memoir 1. Stockholm: Medelhavsmuseet.
————. 1985. *The Master Impression*. SIMA LXIX. Gothenburg: Åström.
————. 1988. "Final Palatial Crete: An Essay in Minoan Chronology." In *Studies in Ancient History and Numismatics Presented to Rudi Thomsen*, ed. Erik Christiansen, Aksel Damsgaard-Madsen, and Erik Hallager, 11–21. Aarhus, Denmark: Aarhus University Press.
————. 1996. *The Minoan Roundel and Other Sealed Documents in the Neopalatial Linear A Administration*. Aegaeum 14. Liège: Université de Liège.
————, and Birgitta P. Hallager, eds. 2003. *The Greek-Swedish Excavations at the Agia Aikaterini Square Kastelli, Khania 1970–1987 and 2001*. Vol. 3, *The Late Minoan IIIB:2 Settlement*. ActaAth-40, XLVII:III. Stockholm: Svenska Institutet i Athen.
Hallager, Erik, Maria Vlasaki, and Birgitta P. Hallager. 1992. "New Linear B Tablets from Khania." *Kadmos* 31: 61–87.
MacGillivray, J. Alexander, Jan M. Driessen, and L. Hugh Sackett. 2000. *The Palaikastro Kouros: A Minoan Chryselephantine Statuette and Its Aegean Bronze Age Context*. BSA Studies 6. London: British School of Archaeology.
Niemeier, Wolf-Dietrich. 1982. "Mycenaean Knossos and the Age of Linear B." *SMEA* 23: 219–87.
Platon, Nicholas. 1949. "Η χρονολόγια τον μινοικών ανάκτορων της Φαιστού." *KrChron* 1949: 150–66.
Popham, Mervyn. 1970. *The Destruction of the Palace at Knossos: Pottery of the Late Minoan IIIA Period*. SIMA XII. Gothenburg: Åström.
————. 1976. "An Inscribed Pithoid Jar from Knossos," with an appendix by Maurice Pope and Jacques Raison. *Kadmos* 15: 102–107.

————. 1993. "Review of Jan Driessen, *An Early Destruction in the Mycenaean Palace at Knossos* (Acta Archaeologica Lovenensia Monographiae 2)." *JHS* 113: 174–78.

Rehak, Paul, and John Younger. 2001. "Neopalatial, Final Palatial, and Postpalatial Crete." In *Aegean Prehistory,* 91–173.

Warburton, David A., ed. 2009. *Time's Up! Dating the Minoan eruption of Santorini. Acts of the Minoan chronology workshop, Sandbjerg November 2007.* Monographs of the Danish Institute at Athens, vol. 10. Athens: Danish Institute at Athens.

Warren, Peter. 2006. "The Date of the Thera Eruption in Relation to Aegean-Egyptian Interconnections and the Egyptian Historical Chronology." In *Timelines,* vol. 2, 305–21.

CHAPTER 12

....

CYCLADES

....

ROBIN L. N. BARBER

THE archaeological evidence is now more varied than that for Middle Cycladic and requires different treatment. From the beginning of the period, Cycladic material culture ceases to have a distinctively local character, falling first under the strong influence of Minoan Crete and later of Mycenaean Greece. Therefore, the subdivisions Late Cycladic (LC) I, II, and III are mostly defined by the Minoan and Mycenaean pottery (imported or imitated) associated with them (LC I = LM IA; LC II = LM IB/LH IIA; LC III = LH IIIA–C, with further subdivisions). Thus, in the literature, relative dates for Cycladic material or events are found expressed in either form.

An earlier review (Barber 1981; cf. also Barber 1987, 32–34, with a minor modification to LC III) discussed the Late Cycladic period in terms of a series of historical phases to which dates were applied mainly on the basis of imported pottery. The excellent recent survey of Mountjoy (2008) employs a slightly different approach, taking the phases of the Mycenaean pottery sequence as the framework and setting cultural and historical developments within this. The latter study incorporates new evidence and provides some corrections to the former, and the two can profitably be used in combination. Divergences between their methods are most evident from middle LC III onward.

Evidence cited here is chiefly from the major sites—Akrotiri on Thera (until the site's volcanic destruction in late LC I), Ayia Irini on Kea, Phylakopi on Melos, and (from LC III) Grotta on Naxos. The two studies mentioned above (also Vlachopoulos 2008) make reference to other sites and surface finds.

The sequence at Phylakopi still provides a useful key for much of the period—not least because of its primary role in the history of research. To this, developments at other sites can be generally, if not always precisely, related. There, the change from MC to LC coincides closely with a general destruction of the Second City (though see chapter 9 in this volume) and the building of the Third.

Throughout the Cyclades, LC I sees ever-increasing Minoanisation. In LC II, Mainland ceramic influence in the Cyclades expands at the expense of Minoan, presaging the situation in early LC III, when there is widespread Mycenaean cultural dominance. In later LC III, complex changes in settlement and patterns of material culture probably reflect the state of flux in the Aegean following the decline and destruction of the Mycenaean palace system on the Mainland (cf. Lemos 2002, 192–93).

The end of the period comes not with a bang but a whimper, for, at the end of LH IIIC, the population of the islands seems to have declined at an accelerating rate, with most sites abandoned and hardly any material remains of the following sub-Mycenaean and earlier Protogeometric periods (Lemos 2002, 207).

Main Sites

Ayia Irini

The Late Cycladic town (Periods VI–VIII), rebuilt after an earthquake at the end of the Middle Cycladic period, is most fully reported by Cummer and Schofield (1984, House A; cf. also Caskey 1972). The later phases are represented only by pottery because of erosion of the site.

Akrotiri

The volcanic destruction of Akrotiri, late in LC I, has left amazingly well-preserved structures and finds of that phase (Doumas 1983). The town took its final form as the result of rebuilding near the beginning of the period.

Phylakopi

The Third City (III–i/III–iii; Atkinson et al. 1904, 263–72), rebuilt after the destruction of the Second, represents the Late Cycladic phase at the site. Both III–i (LC I) and III–ii (LC II) fall within Phase D of the report of recent excavations (Renfrew et al. 2007, 10, table 2.2). City III–iii is the 'Mycenaean' stage, which can now be subdivided as the result of recent work (Phases E and F).

Geography

In the Late Cycladic period, the concept of a cultural area with a distinct Cycladic identity, as defined earlier in relation to the EC and MC periods, becomes impossible to apply. The level of Minoan and Mycenaean influence suggests that the islands should more properly be incorporated first in a Cretan, then in a Mycenaean, cultural zone that must also take into account the evidence for Minoan and Mycenaean influence, similar to that on Cycladic sites, noted at centres in the Dodecanese and the coast of Asia Minor (Mountjoy 1998). Thus, in LC times, the term 'Cycladic' normally signifies the region as recognised today.

Further alterations in cultural alignment become apparent in later LC III, when they are expressed in the idea of the *koine*—an area or group of sites that share common, mostly ceramic, features (cf. Desborough 1964, 228; Vlachopoulos 2008, 491; Mountjoy 2008, 476).

Historical Summary

For easier reference between this survey (Barber 1987, 32–34) and that of Mountjoy (2008), a list of her dates (in Mycenaean [LH] pottery terms) for sites and events mentioned is set out later in this chapter. The relative chronology of the Middle, Late, and Final stages of LC III is dependent on the detailed sequences worked out for the Argolid and Lefkandi (cf., for a brief summary, Barber 1981, 12n117 and, fuller and more recent, Mountjoy 1999, 75–79). It should be carefully noted that the adjective 'early' has different meanings when applied, on the one hand, in the historical summary ('Late Cycladic III Early') and, on the other, as a stage in the Mycenaean pottery sequence ('LH IIIC early').

Approximate dates are given for the subdivisions of the later LC III period to aid appreciation of the length of time over which the developments described took place. They represent rough averages of dates given by Warren and Hankey (1989; cf. Mountjoy 1999). Since dating by pottery is not sufficiently precise as to allow the sequence of events at different sites to be exactly correlated, the details of the picture presented here are likely to require modification in the light of future research.

Late Cycladic I

Phylakopi III–i, Akrotiri Main Period, Ayia Irini Period VI (with further stratigraphic subdivisions at Kea and Akrotiri). Extensive LM IA and (later) sporadic LH I imports.

With regard to pottery, the onset of the Late Cycladic period (LC I) is defined by the widespread appearance in the islands of Cretan LM IA imports and their pervasive influence on the forms and decoration of the still extensive local production (Furumark 1950). The process by which this took place is now thought to have been gradual rather than sudden (Davis and Gorogianni 2008, 341). Recent analysis (Mountjoy 2008, 461) indicates that Mainland imports appeared only later in the period and in small quantities. Although the volcanic destruction of Thera can be seen historically as bringing LC I to a close, this may not be strictly true in ceramic terms since, at Phylakopi, the phase seems to continue for some time after that event (Davis and Cherry 2007, 301).

It is not only in the pottery that the Cyclades succumb to Minoan influence (Doumas 1983 passim; Barber 1987, chapter 7). There seems little doubt that the frescoes found at all major LC sites are derived from those of Minoan Crete, which they strongly recall, even if there is likely to have been local innovation in certain features (E. Davis 1990; Morgan 1990). Minoan architectural style, techniques, and forms such as the lustral basin and pillar room, are also found in the islands, most prominently at Akrotiri. Other finds of Minoan type, some imported, include bronze vessels, stone vases, and terracotta figurines. Weights on the Minoan standard appear, and there are instances of the use of the Minoan Linear A script. Many of these objects and images imply the adoption of Minoan practices, systems, and sometimes perhaps beliefs, although, in the latter case, it is always possible that the use of foreign forms is merely superficial and they were simply grafted on to the local Cycladic tradition.

It has been argued (Schofield 1982) that Minoan influence is mainly to be found on the islands (Thera, Melos, and Kea) situated on a trade route between Crete and the Greek Mainland, although subsequent finds on Naxos and elsewhere in the central Cyclades (Hadjianastasiou 1989) cast doubt on this conclusion. Akrotiri seems to show much stronger Minoan characteristics than the other sites. While this situation may be partly explained by technical factors (the better preservation of the buildings and finds; the availability of stone more suited to the adoption of Minoan architectural styles; the proximity of the site to Crete and its potentially greater role in Minoan trade), it still seems not unlikely that Thera was Minoanised more extensively and in a different way from other island centres.

This overwhelming of Cycladic culture by Cretan (Barber 1987, 194–200, with further references) has often been seen as symptomatic of the existence of a Minoan *thalassocracy* (sea empire) in the islands, as recounted by Thucydides (I. 4) and the thalassocracy itself as consisting not only of military control of the seas but also of a colonial presence and political and economic government of the area. It has been suggested, too (MacGillivray 1984, 157), that the destructions of Phylakopi II and Ayia Irini (end of Period V) and the subsequent cultural phenomena may be the result of a forcible imposition of Minoan authority by one or more of the Cretan palaces. Others see the islands' towns as still essentially independent but having adopted Minoan forms for efficiency of production and saleability of their goods or for more complex reasons of emulation for social status (Davis and Gorogianni 2008).

These are not strictly alternative interpretations, and there may well be some truth in all of them. Nor is there any reason why changes on all of the islands should have been identical in form or brought about in the same way.

Direct Minoan military intervention on one or more islands certainly cannot be excluded.

Late Cycladic II

> Phylakopi III–ii; (Akrotiri no longer existent); Ayia Irini Period VII. On Kea, the period can again be subdivided. At Phylakopi, part of the site suffered fire damage with pottery of this period on floors. LM IB and LH IIA imports.

In terms of pottery finds, the chief difference from the preceding phase is the much higher proportion of Mainland products among the imports. These amount to ca. 50% at Ayia Irini, and a similar trend is evident at Phylakopi. A likely, if very general, historical explanation of this phenomenon lies in the appearance and development of the Mycenaean palaces and the early expansion of their spheres of influence, of which the destruction at Phylakopi (III–ii, discussed later) may be a symptom. At the same time, Minoan power regressed after the volcanic catastrophe on Thera, with its severe side effects, effectively brought about the collapse of the Cretan palace system.

Imported pottery of the succeeding Minoan and Mycenaean phases (LM II/ LH IIB) is rare in the islands. Only Kea has stratified deposits of the periods, and Mountjoy (2008, 471) has suggested that those may belong to a period of squatter occupation preceding rebuilding after earthquake destruction.

Late Cycladic III Early (ca. 1390–1260 BC)

> Phylakopi III–iii (early) (= Phases E and F [part] of recent excavations); Ayia Irini Period VIII; Grotta (Naxos); tombs at Angelika (Mykonos), Ayia Thekla (Tenos), Khosti (Naxos; no firm dating evidence). LH IIIA1–early B imports.

At Phylakopi, this phase saw the building of a palace (III–iii/Phase E) of recognisably Mycenaean form in the area of the site destroyed by fire at the end of III–ii and, soon after, the construction of a shrine, later extended, whose contents are Mycenaean in character (Renfrew 1985). To the present author (Barber 1999), there seems persuasive circumstantial evidence that these developments at Phylakopi represent a Mycenaean takeover of the site, but this conclusion has not appealed to others (e.g., Mountjoy 2008).

Pottery found in the islands is now all of Mycenaean, rather than Minoan, type, almost all imported, and further evidence of Mycenaeanisation comes in the form of the tholos tombs on Mykonos, Tenos, and Naxos. Superficially, at least, the situation resembles the 'Minoan thalassocracy' of Late Cycladic I. As was suggested there, the process of Mycenaeanisation did not necessarily take the same form on all of the islands. If some were forcibly subdued, others may well have succumbed to less direct pressures or simply become drawn into the expanding Mycenaean economic zone. Certainly there is no evidence (except possibly on Paros, and there only later) of palatial installations similar to that at Phylakopi. The physical presence of Mainlanders is also open to question.

Although the archaeological picture, as it is at present, may be deceptive, Phylakopi now seems to occupy a position—relative to the other Cycladic sites—similar to that of Akrotiri in LC I; that is to say, it appears more thoroughly Mycenaean in character. Thus, it can be surmised (Barber 1984) that, after a gradually changing balance of influence and then the grand turmoil that accompanied Akrotiri's volcanic demise, the change from Minoan to Mycenaean dominance also involved the replacement of the former main seat of authority in the islands on Thera by Phylakopi on Melos.

The end of this historical phase is tentatively set in the middle of the 13th century BC (end of LH IIIB1), when direct mainland contacts weaken.

Late Cycladic III Middle (ca. 1260–1150 BC)

> Phylakopi new fortifications (Phase F); Grotta new fortifications (Lambrinoudakis and Philaniotou-Hadjianastasiou 2001); defensive sites: Ayios Andreas (Siphnos), Koukounaries (Paros); also perhaps Xombourgo (Tenos) and Monolithos (Thera). Decline of imports from LH IIIB1–LH IIIB2.

This phase is marked by a perceptible reduction (Mountjoy 2008, 473) in the quantities of Mycenaean imports (between LH IIIB1 and LH IIIB2) and a corresponding increase in local production. A sense of unease, if not something stronger, is further induced by the massive new fortification wall at Phylakopi and the (rather later) foundation of a series of remote, fortified, and obviously defensive settlements (Karageorghis and Morris 2001).

While the material culture of the islands continued to be Mycenaean in character, it is clear that connections with the Mainland centres of Mycenaean civilisation were much reduced. It is logical to connect the instability suggested by this evidence with the troubles that had begun to beset the Mainland palatial system and eventually saw the destructions of the palace sites at the end of LH IIIB2.

If the ultimate cause of the Mycenaean collapse was climatic, or partly so, as has sometimes been suggested, the Cyclades may not have been immune to its likely consequences, including the breakdown of the preceding network of mutually beneficial trade and commerce, a situation that could have engendered local rivalries and disputes and perhaps piracy (Mountjoy 2008; Schallin 1993, 175f.).

Late Cycladic III Late (ca. 1150–1090 BC)

Phylakopi III, Sanctuary phases 2b–3a, then destroyed; Koukounaries Main Period, then destroyed; Grotta (Naxos), with Aplomata and Kamini cemeteries; To Froudhi tis Baronas (Siphnos). Mainland parallels LH IIIC middle (developed and advanced).

This stage has recently been the subject of particular study by Vlachopoulos (2008, which contains a summary with further bibliography), with special reference to Grotta (Naxos). Grotta seems to have been an exceptionally rich place at this time, and many finds from the two cemeteries indicate wide contacts.

The overall picture may be distorted by the wealth of finds from Naxos. In any case, the situation on the other Cycladic islands is less clear since, apart from an uneven spread of finds, there is considerable local variation in the character of the material culture, and clear chronological relationships are hard to establish.

Particularly characteristic of the pottery is the widely distributed stirrup jar with stylised octopus decoration. This feature, together with other shapes and motifs and the introduction of the cremation burial rite, led Desborough (1964, 228) to propound the idea of a Mycenaean *koine*, or cultural area, in the central and southern Aegean, including Miletus on the coast of Asia Minor, untouched by the problems that had affected the Mainland. His proposal, however, is now less favoured (Vlachopoulos 2008, 491), though the concept has been used to define other areas of apparent common culture later in LC III (e.g., Mountjoy 2008, 476), when such new groupings can also be identified.

If Grotta is representative, this seems to have been a period of stability, possibly inaugurated by the arrival of refugees from the Mainland palaces (discussed later).

Late Cycladic III Final (ca. 1090–1065/1015 BC)

Grotta abandoned; Ayia Irini (Temple); Koukounaries (minor reoccupation); Ayios Andreas (reoccupied or never deserted?). Mainland parallels: LH IIIC late.

The final phase of the Bronze Age in the Cyclades is marked once again by disruption—most strikingly the destruction of the flourishing settlement at Grotta but also the reoccupation or continuation of earlier refuge sites. Evidence for habitation over the area is restricted, and many sites previously used seem to have been deserted. The pottery is limited in quantity and simple in character.

At Ayia Irini, finds have been made only in part of the temple, suggesting that, reduced in scale, it was the focus for a community either scattered or living nearby in flimsy dwellings that have not been traced. The restricted quantity and quality of finds indicates poverty and decline in population. On Naxos, the settlement was abandoned now, to be rebuilt not long after, in the Protogeometric period, on a different alignment— a feature that suggests radical change, perhaps involving a new population element.

Refugees in the Cyclades in LC III

It has been suggested that some of the finds made and disturbances recognised in the LC III period may be due to the arrival in the Cyclades of Mainlanders who were fleeing in the face of the problems that beset the Mycenaean area from the middle of the 13th century BC (e.g., Barber 1987, 227 [Naxos]; contra Mountjoy 2008, 475; Vlachopoulos 2008, 490).

A scatter of settlements away from the old Mycenaean centres after the destruction of the palaces is well documented, and the Cyclades seem to provide a series of prime destinations, but, while the probability of some refugees arriving in the islands is high, the likelihood of the reestablishment of palatial communities seems low, and the question of what form their presence took is hard to answer. Perhaps most likely is the exploitation of preexisting contacts that had been established through trade. In some cases, these would have resulted in the peaceful integration of outsiders into local Cycladic communities; in others there may have been violence. In this light may be seen the appearance of new wealth on some Cycladic sites (especially the Naxos tombs), the variety of material culture, and new local groupings.

A further movement of Mainlanders into the area—this time in LC III Final and perhaps to be related to the later tradition of the Ionian migrations—is suggested to Mountjoy (2008, 476) by the appearance of an extensive new pottery koine of Mainland origin, which includes several of the Cyclades.

Dating of Late Cycladic III Sites and Events by Mycenaean (LH) Pottery Phases

The pottery dating information in the following section is from Mountjoy (2008), except where other references are given.

Late Cycladic III Early

Phylakopi III–iii (early), Phases E and F (part of recent excavations)
palace (III–iii, Phase E): LH IIIA1
construction of shrine (later extended): LH IIIA2

Grotta (Naxos): LH IIIA1
Angelika (Mykonos): LH IIIA2, used until LH IIIB
Ayia Thekla (Tenos): LH IIIB, used until LH IIIC early
Khosti (Naxos): no dating evidence

Late Cycladic III Middle

Phylakopi III, new fortifications (Phase F): LH IIIB
Grotta, new fortifications: LH IIIC early (Lambrinoudakis and Philaniotou-
    Hadjianastasiou 2001)
Ayios Andreas (Siphnos): LH IIIB or LH IIIC early
Koukounaries (Paros): LH IIIC early
Perhaps Xombourgo (Tenos): date uncertain
Monolithos (Thera): LH IIIC early? (Vlachopoulos 2008, 479–80)

Late Cycladic III Late

Phylakopi III, Sanctuary phases 2b–3a, then destroyed early in LH IIIC middle
    (advanced)
Koukounaries Main Period, then destroyed early in LH IIIC middle
    (advanced)
Grotta (Naxos), with Aplomata and Kamini cemeteries: LH IIIC middle
    (advanced) (main period)/late
To froudhi tis Baronas (Siphnos): LH IIIC middle (advanced)/late
    (Vlachopoulos 2008, 490)

Late Cycladic III Final

Grotta abandoned: LH IIIC late
Ayia Irini (Temple): use in LH IIIC late
Koukounaries (minor reoccupation): LH IIIC late
Ayios Andreas (reoccupied or never deserted?): LH IIIC late

ABSOLUTE CHRONOLOGY

The absolute chronology of this period in the Aegean has been the subject of extensive discussion (Bietak and Höflmayer 2007; see also Mountjoy 1999, 16–18, with
table 1). The traditional lower chronology is adopted here: ca. 1600 BC (LC I)–ca.
1065/1015 BC (end of LC III Final) (Warren and Hankey 1989, 169, table 3.1); Warren
1999, 900–902).

SAMPLE ILLUSTRATIONS OF CERAMICS

Imported Minoan and Mycenaean pottery (all periods): Mountjoy (1999, 861–965)

Local pottery: (LC I) (Barber 1987, figures 118–24); (LC II) (Dawkins and Droop 1911, pl. x, nos. 77, 138, 188); (LC III) (Mountjoy 1999, 861–965)

Other LC material culture: (LC I) (Doumas 1983); (LC I–II) (Barber 1987, chapter 7); (LC III) Barber (1987, chapter 9)

BIBLIOGRAPHY

Atkinson, Thomas D., Robert C. Bosanquet, Campbell C. Edgar, Arthur J. Evans, David G. Hogarth, Duncan Mackenzie, Cecil Smith, and Francis B. Welch. 1904. *Excavations at Phylakopi in Melos*. Society for the Promotion of Hellenic Studies Supplementary Paper 4. London: Macmillan.

Barber, Robin L. N. 1981. "The Late Cycladic Period: A Review." *BSA* 76: 1–21.

———. 1984. "The Status of Phylakopi in Creto-Cycladic Relations." In *Minoan Thalassocracy*, 179–82.

———. 1987. *The Cyclades in the Bronze Age*. London and Iowa City: Duckworth and Iowa University Press.

———. 1999. "Hostile Mycenaeans in the Cyclades?" In *Polemos*, 133–40.

Betancourt, Philip P., Vassos Karageorghis, Robert Laffineur, and Wolf-Dietrich Niemeier, eds. 1999. *Meletemata*.

Bietak, Manfred, and Felix Höflmayer. 2007. "Introduction: High and Low Chronology." In *SCIEM III*, 13–23.

Brodie, Neil J., Jenny Doole, Giorgos Gavalas, and Colin Renfrew, eds. 2008. *Horizon*.

Caskey, John L. 1972. "Investigations in Keos. Part II: A Conspectus of the Pottery." *Hesperia* 41: 357–401.

Cummer, W. Willson, and Elizabeth Schofield. 1984. *Keos III: Ayia Irini. House A*. Mainz: von Zabern.

Davis, Ellen N. 1990. "The Cycladic Style of the Thera Frescoes." In *TAW III*, 214–38.

Davis, Jack L., and John F. Cherry. 2007. "The Cycladic Pottery from the Late Bronze I Levels." In *Excavations at Phylakopi in Melos 1974–77*, ed. Colin Renfrew et al., 265–306. BSA Supplementary vol. 42. London: British School at Athens.

Davis, Jack L., and Evi Gorogianni. 2008. "Potsherds from the Edge: The Construction of Identities and the Limits of Minoanised Areas of the Aegean." In *Horizon*, 339–48.

Desborough, Vincent R. d'A. 1964. *The Last Mycenaeans and Their Successors*. Oxford: Clarendon Press.

Doumas, Christos. 1983. *Thera: Pompeii of the Ancient Aegean*. London: Thames and Hudson.

Furumark, Arne. 1950. "The Settlement at Ialyssos and Aegean History c. 1550–1400 B.C." *Op Arch* 6: 150–271.

Hadjianastasiou, Olga. 1989. "Some Hints of Naxian External Connections in the Earlier Late Bronze Age." *BSA* 84: 205–15.

Hägg, Robin, and Nanno Marinatos, eds. 1984. *Minoan Thalassocracy*.

Hardy, David A., Christos G. Doumas, Ioannis Sakellarakis, and Peter M. Warren, eds. 1990. *Thera and the Aegean World III* (3 vols.). London: Thera Foundation.

Karageorghis, Vassos, and Christine E. Morris. 2001. *Defensive Settlements of the Aegean and the Eastern Mediterranean after c. 1200 BC*. Nicosia: Leventis Foundation.

Lambrinoudakis, Vassilios, and Olga Philaniotou-Hadjianastasiou. 2001. "The Town of Naxos at the End of the Late Bronze Age and the Mycenaean Fortification Wall." In *Defensive Settlements of the Aegean and the Eastern Mediterranean after c. 1200 BC*, ed. Vassos Karageorghis and Christine E. Morris, 157–69. Nicosia: Leventis Foundation.

Lemos, Irene. S. 2002. *The Protogeometric Aegean: The Archaeology of the Late Eleventh and Tenth Centuries B.C.* Oxford: Oxford University Press.

MacGillivray, J. Alexander. 1984. "Cycladic Jars from Middle Minoan III Contexts at Knossos." In *Minoan Thalassocracy*, 153–58.

Morgan, Lyvia. 1990. "Island Iconography: Thera, Kea, Milos." In *TAW III*, 252–66.

Mountjoy, Penelope A. 1998. "The East Aegean–West Anatolian Interface in the Late Bronze Age: Mycenaeans and the Kingdom of Ahhiyawa." *AnatSt* 48: 33–67.

———. 1999. *Regional Mycenaean Decorated Pottery*. Rahden, Germany: Leidorf.

———. 2008. "The Cyclades during the Mycenaean Period." In *Horizon*, 467–77.

Renfrew, Colin, ed. 1985. *The Archaeology of Cult: The Sanctuary at Phylakopi*. BSA Supplementary vol. 18. London: Thames and Hudson.

———, et al., eds. 2007. *Excavations at Phylakopi in Melos 1974–77*. British School at Athens Supplementary vol. 42. London: British School at Athens.

Schallin, Anne-Louise. 1993. *Islands under the Influence: The Cyclades in the Late Bronze Age and the Nature of Mycenaean Presence*. SIMA vol. 111. Jonsered, Sweden: Åström.

Schofield, Elizabeth. 1982. "The Western Cyclades and Crete: A Special Relationship?" *OJA* 1: 9–25.

Warren, Peter M. 1999. "LM IA: Knossos, Thera, Gournia." In *Meletemata*, 893–903.

———, and Vronwy Hankey. 1989. *Aegean Bronze Age Chronology*. Bristol: Bristol Classical Press.

Vlachopoulos, Andreas. 2008. "A Late Mycenaean Journey from Thera to Naxos: The Cyclades in the Twelfth Century BC." In *Horizon*, 479–91.

CHAPTER 13

END OF THE BRONZE AGE

REINHARD JUNG

RELATIVE CHRONOLOGY

Today our knowledge of the last phases of the Aegean Bronze Age (Late Helladic/ Late Minoan IIIC) can be based on a few but very important vertical settlement stratigraphies spanning most of the 12th and 11th centuries BC (for a general overview see Deger-Jalkotzy 2008); additional evidence comes from cemetery sites. Apart from the tell sequences of central Macedonia, from the outset of the Early Iron Age (Submycenaean/Subminoan and Protogeometric [PG]), the relative chronology rests mainly on tomb seriations, as there are still very few settlement stratigraphies available, although the situation is currently improving.

The longest settlement stratigraphy for the Postpalatial period is provided by the Lower Citadel ("Unterburg") at Tiryns in the Argolid. A large area of roughly 20 x 80 m was uncovered in its western half during the 1970s and 1980s (Kilian 1988, 132, figure 9, 134–35) and was followed by new excavations close to the north gate (*AA* 2002, 147–48; *AA* 2003, 184–85). The Tiryns Lower Citadel shows very short intervals of destruction events, rebuilding phases, and floor remakes (for an overview, see Mühlenbruch 2007), which allow a fine-phased pottery sequence to be reconstructed from the early Palace Period (LH IIIA1) to the Submycenaean phase (Papadimitriou 1988; Podzuweit 2007; Stockhammer 2009). This sequence (table 13.1) provides us with the largest quantity of stratified settlement pottery known in the Postpalatial Aegean and therefore is of considerable statistical significance for establishing the production periods of chronologically important types, motifs, and linear decorations. Further

Table 13.1. Relative and Absolute Chronology of the End of the Aegean Late Bronze and the Beginning of the Early Iron Age

Phases and Architectural Horizons at Tiryns, Lower Citadel (Podzuweit 2007)	Tell Kazel, Ugarit (Historic-Archaeological; Jung 2008)	Italy and Switzerland (Dendro and ^{14}C)	Kastanás (^{14}C)	Calendar Age (BCE)
1 Hor. LH IIIB Final (palace destruction)			Level 15 (LH IIIB Developed and Final)	−1210/00
1st Hor. LH IIIC Early	ca. 1197/75 destruction at the beginning of IIIC Early		Levels 14b and 14a	1210/00− **LH IIIC Early**
2nd Hor. LH IIIC Early			1180/70 start Level 13 (still in LH IIIC Early?)	−1170/60
1st Hor. IIIC Developed				1170/60− **LH IIIC Developed**
2nd Hor. LH IIIC Developed				−1150/40
1st Hor. LH IIIC Advanced				1150/40− **LH IIIC Advanced**
2nd Hor. LH IIIC Advanced			1130/20 start Level 12 (in LH IIIC Advanced)	−1100
3rd Hor. LH IIIC Advanced				
1 Hor.LH IIIC Late				1100−1085/80 **LH III C Late**
1 Hor. Submycenaean		−1070/40FBA 2/ Submycenaean		1085/80−1070/40 **Submycenaean**
				1070/40−1000 **EPG**
			c. 1000 start Level 11 (MPG)	
			middle of 10th cent. during Level 10 (LPG)	

Source: After Weninger and Jung (2009, p. 416).

Postpalatial settlement levels were uncovered in the northwestern (ca. 115 m²) and northeastern parts (ca. 208 m²) of the Lower Town surrounding the citadel (Kilian 1978, 449–57; Maran and Papadimitriou 2006).

At Mycenae, also located in the Argolid, deposits providing a continuous Late Palatial through Postpalatial stratigraphy were excavated in parts of the settled area inside the citadel. Most of these excavations took place during the 1960s. For a limited extension of roughly 500 m², in the so-called Citadel House Area, settlement deposits from the first two Postpalatial phases of LH IIIC Early are available. The middle phases of LH IIIC Developed and Advanced are represented mainly by wash layers in the same area (see, e.g., French and Taylour 2007, 4 tab. 1), which still makes the long-known LH IIIC Advanced floor deposit of the so-called Granary an exceptional context at Mycenae (French 2007). Important stratified settlement levels with floor deposits ranging from LH IIIC Early to Advanced were excavated close to the so-called Hellenistic Tower but are not published yet (Iakovidis 2003, 121). The Submycenaean phase is basically represented by tombs in the area of the former settlement (Eder 1998, 56–58). The Argolid also provides important closed-tomb contexts for the Middle and Late phases of LH IIIC (e.g., the cremation and single inhumation burials under tumuli inside the modern town of Argos) (Piteros 2001).

In Attica, our knowledge of the later Bronze Age and Early Iron Age phases is based chiefly on the cemeteries of Perati in eastern Attica and the Kerameikos in Athens. At Perati, a tripartite phase division was achieved based on single graves and closed find-groups inside the chamber tombs with multiple burials (Iakovidis 1969/1970). The excavations in the Kerameikos cemetery established the backbone of Submycenaean and PG pottery chronology for Greece (Ruppenstein 2007 with bibliography). It is still the type site for the Early Iron Age on the southern Greek mainland because the pottery production of Athens seems to have been especially innovative at the very end of the second and the outset of the first millennium BC.

At Thebes in Boeotia, recent excavations at Pelopidou Street (a trench of ca. 6 x 25 m) have shown that the destruction of the palace in LH IIIB Final was followed by a resettlement of the site in LH IIIC Early. Habitation in that area continued until LH IIIC Advanced (Andrikou 2006).

In central Greece, the settlements of Lefkandi on the Euboean coast and Pyrgos Livanaton on the coast of Phtiotis, as well as the sanctuary of Kalapodi in its hinterland, are important points of reference for the relative chronological phases of the Postpalatial period and the start of the Early Iron Age. At the tell site of Xeropolis at Lefkandi, in a main area of roughly 20 x 20 m and several smaller trenches, three architectural levels were brought to light. According to floor levels and destruction deposits, they could be further divided into subphases (Evely 2006; Schofield 2007). The published Lefkandi sequence covers the phases from LH IIIC Early to IIIC Late (cf. Mountjoy 1999, 38–39, table II), but the ongoing new excavations add Submycenaean and PG settlement strata (Lemos 2007). The older excavations brought to light only tombs for the initial phases of the Iron Age (Popham, Sackett, and Themelis 1979/1980).

At Kalapodi, a trench of 37.5 m² in the Greek sanctuary area has revealed a rare, unbroken vertical stratigraphy reaching from LH IIIC Early all the way through the Early Iron Age (Jacob-Felsch 1996). The many floor and ash levels allow for a fine-phased pottery chronology, but the pottery is very fragmentary. Recent excavations extend the investigated LH IIIC and PG levels (Niemeier 2007, 42–43).

Another central Greek site with a continuous occupation bridging the Late Bronze–Early Iron Age border is the coastal tell site of Pyrgos Livanaton (Kynos), where settlement levels from LH IIIC Advanced to a later phase of PG were excavated and are currently being studied for final publication (Dakoronia 2003; Dakoronia and Kounouklas 2009).

In the northwestern Peloponnese (Achaea, Elis), the relative chronology of the Postpalatial period still has to rely mainly on cemetery data. Thanks to modern excavations with separate documentation of closed burial contexts inside the chamber tombs of Kallithea, Achaea Clauss, Portes, and Voudeni among others, a six-phased relative chronology with additional subphases was constructed. It covers the time from LH IIIB Final until Submycenaean/Early Protogeometric (EPG), when the use of chamber tombs stopped (Moschos in press; Paschalidis and MacGeorge in press; for single Submycenaean and PG burials in Elis, see Eder 2001). The settlement of Aigeira in eastern Achaea with a three-phased vertical stratigraphy in an excavated area of ca. 15 x 22.5 m is still an exceptional case in the northwest Peloponnese, but the style of its pottery differs slightly from those in western Achaea and Elis (Deger-Jalkotzy 2003). Other multiphased Achaean settlements have only recently been excavated and are not yet published.

On the islands of the Cyclades, several excavations brought to light important stratigraphic sequences of Postpalatial date. First, one has to name the different LH IIIC building phases of the cult complex of Phylakopi on Melos (excavated area ca. 10 x 30 m), ranging from LH IIIC Early to IIIC Advanced (Renfrew 1985). An important closed context of the LH IIIC Developed phase is the destruction level of the fortified coastal settlement of Koukounaries on Paros, where an area of 24 x 30 m was excavated (Schilardi 1984; Koehl 1984). Finally, the two-phased LH IIIC settlement of Grotta and its cemeteries at Aplomata and Kamini in western Naxos provide stratigraphic contexts for the phases LH IIIC Developed–Late (Vlachopoulos 2003, 2006).

Based on the stratigraphic evidence of the major sites of the Argolid, Attica, and Euboea, a robust relative chronological sequence has been established in the last few decades. This could also be verified at other find places of the southern and central Greek mainland and on the Aegean islands, although one has to emphasize that the Postpalatial period is characterized by a marked regionalism, which poses problems for comparative chronology.

Traditionally, LH IIIC Early is defined as the first phase of the Postpalatial period, starting after the palace destructions, which happened at the end of LH IIIB in the Argolid (during the phase called LH IIIB Final at Tiryns). Some years ago, a LH IIIB2/IIIC Early Transitional phase was defined (Mountjoy 1999, 36–38), which would mark the beginning of the Postpalatial period. However, most and probably all of the types used in its definition are already present (in small quantities) in the Argive palace destructions of the end of LH IIIB. This reflects the difficulty of recognizing the fundamental political change marked by the breakdown of the palace system in archaeological find assemblages and underlines the need for quantitative analysis of closed-find assemblages. The change in percentages of different types in relation to each other may be the only way to separate a Final Palatial from an Early Postpalatial pottery assemblage, provided that the sample is large enough to allow a chronological rather than a functional interpretation of such differences. While some researchers have adopted the term "LH IIIB2/IIIC Early Transitional" and begin LH IIIC Early only after that phase, others prefer to use the label "LH IIIC Early" from as early as the outset of the Postpalatial period.

At Tiryns and Mycenae, there is evidence for a further subdivision of LH IIIC Early into LH IIIC Early 1 and 2. The middle of the period also includes two phases, LH IIIC Developed and Advanced. These are frequently subsumed under the heading "LH IIIC Middle." However, most of the characteristic mid-IIIC pottery types were invented only by LH IIIC Advanced. Therefore, in many cases it should be possible to recognize that subphase, while in some it might be feasible to talk only of LH IIIC Middle instead.

The LH IIIC Late phase is characterized principally by an impoverishment of the pottery type repertory with the introduction of few new types, while a further impoverishment is noted for the following Submycenaean phase. This phase, resting mainly on tomb assemblages, is for various reasons difficult to identify in settlement levels even if continuous vertical stratigraphies exist (such as in central Greece; see Lis 2009). However, at least Tiryns has a settlement layer stratified above LH IIIC Late, containing pottery of Submycenaean style while at the same time lacking PG elements.

Although Greek relative chronology is based principally on pottery, from the later LH/LM IIIC phases onward, metal types become increasingly important as dating criteria. For instance, while bow fibulae with two knots and asymmetric bow are found in LH IIIC (Advanced–)Late contexts, twisted-bow fibulae with symmetric semicircular bow are a new feature of Submycenaean (Jung 2006, 190, 192–94).

On Crete, recent excavations provide us with several stratigraphies that are relevant for the periodization of the final Bronze and earliest Iron Age phases. In western Crete, inside the old town of Khania, at the Agia Aikaterini Square, a settlement area of roughly 660 m² was excavated and yielded basically one LM IIIC Early building level on top of a LM IIIB2 destruction level. Three stratigraphical units are later than the LM IIIC Early buildings and were tentatively dated to a middle phase of LM IIIC (Hallager and Pålsson Hallager 2000). East of Rethymno, at the settlement site of Khamalevri, several field plots have been excavated. Three LM IIIC building phases can be stratigraphically differentiated (Andreadaki-Vlazaki and Papadopoulou 2005, 2007). At the inland site of Thronos Kephala, most of the LM IIIC stratigraphic evidence covering the phases from LM IIIC Early until PG comes from a series of pit contexts, but some also comes from nearby buildings (D'Agata 2003).

At Knossos, at the Stratigraphical Museum site, three settlement levels of LM IIIC were examined in an area of ca. 12 x 17 m, of which the lowermost (stratigraphical "stage I") represents the earliest LM IIIC, while the uppermost ("stage III") was dated by the excavator to a later stage of LM IIIC Early (Warren 2007). For the definition of Subminoan and the subsequent phases of the Early Iron Age, the rich necropolises of Knossos are of fundamental importance (Hood, Huxley, and Sandars 1958–1959, 205–208; Coldstream and Catling 1996). Apart from Knossos, in central Crete the settlement excavation of Kastelli Pediada provides a two-phased vertical stratigraphy that ends before the late phase of LM IIIC (Rethemiotakis 1997). At Prinias, a number of closed Subminoan tomb contexts with bronze and iron weapons was found (Rizza 1996).

In eastern Crete, at the Gulf of Ierapetra, several Postpalatial settlement sites were investigated. The Kastro of Kavousi, with its main area of ca. 60 x 35 m, is important for its continuous stratigraphy of LM IIIC throughout PG and even later Early Iron Age phases (local Phases I–V, see Mook 2004; also Mook and Coulson 1997). By contrast, the settlement of Khalasmenos is basically one phase (with a few secondary architectonic alterations and new floors in some buildings) and dated by its excavator to a middle phase of LM IIIC. A total of more than three thousand square meters has been uncovered (Tsipopoulou 2005, 317–26).

At the end of this enumeration of stratigraphical contexts on the island of Crete, it is appropriate to point out that no general agreement has so far been reached for the periodization of LM IIIC and its synchronization with the well-established mainland sequence (for the relevant discussions, see chapters in Hallager and Pålsson Hallager 1997; Deger-Jalkotzy and Zavadil 2003, 2007). While some scholars subdivide LM IIIC into Early and Late (e.g., Pålsson Hallager 2007; D'Agata 2007), others single out an additional LM IIIC Middle phase (e.g., Borgna 2007; Warren 2007, 333). Similar problems occur when it comes to defining Subminoan, its possible subdivision, and its correlation with Submycenaean and EPG.

Turning to the northern areas of modern Greece, the situation changes considerably. In the northwestern part of the country, in Epirus (Papadopoulos and Kontorli-Papadopoulou 2003, 1–37), the lack of excavated stratigraphies and the scarcity of wheel-made and painted pottery reflecting southern and central Greek pottery styles inhibit any precise chronological classification of LBA and EIA finds. Thus, it is often not possible to tell LH IIIC from Submycenaean and PG contexts.

In Macedonia, and more precisely in its central part, a number of excavated tell sites provide long-lived vertical stratigraphies. The tells (locally called "toumba") of Ayios Mamas/Prehistoric Olynthus, Assiros, Kastanas, and Thessaloniki allow for a fine-phased assessment of architecture, pottery, and small finds (for an overview with bibliography, see Andreou, Fotiadis, and Kotsakis 2001, 298–308, 323–26). During the Late Bronze and partly during the Early Iron Age, central Macedonia belonged to the inner-Balkanic cultural sphere but at the same time was the northernmost region of the Balkans, in which many Aegean cultural traits were adopted by the local population. As a result, only a minor fraction of the different find categories can be compared to southern/central Greek typologies (e.g., the majority of the pottery is handmade and not wheel made throughout the Late Bronze and Early Iron Ages). However, especially for the last decades of the 11th century and all of the 10th century, the Macedonian toumbas provide the most complete settlement plans available to date in Greece.

ABSOLUTE CHRONOLOGY

Establishing an absolute chronology for the last centuries of the Aegean Bronze Age is a difficult task for two reasons. First, the last secure historical dates from the Near East that can be linked both to the Pharaonic chronology and to Aegean pottery sequences are the destructions of Syrian city-states by the "Sea Peoples" in the early 12th century BC. Second, the radiocarbon calibration curve has a rather flat shape throughout the 12th and 11th centuries, which implies that no precise calendric age can be assigned to a sample from those centuries.

For the absolute chronology of the Postpalatial Aegean, key sources are the inscription of Rameses' III regnal year 8 at Medinet Habu and an Egyptian letter written in Akkadian and found at Ugarit. That letter was sent by Bay (Freu 1988), Pharaoh Siptah's chancellor, who seems to have been executed as a traitor in Siptah's regnal year 5 (Grandet 2000). According to different current calculations of pharaonic regnal periods (von Beckerath 1997; Kitchen 2000; Krauss 2007), Siptah reigned from 1197 or 1194/1193, which means that Bay's execution would have happened in 1193 or 1190/1189. This date sets a *terminus post quem non* for the sending of the letter.

According to the aforementioned Medinet Habu inscription of Rameses' III year 8 (1180, 1177, or 1176/1175 BC), a coalition of enemies that came from some Mediterranean islands—which means they were most probably coming from the Aegean—attacked Egypt. These peoples, referred to in the scholarly literature as "Sea Peoples," are further reported in the inscription to have destroyed various countries, including Carchemish (i.e., the region of northern Syria, where Ugarit is situated). The same inscription mentions that the aggressors set up a camp in Amurru before moving on toward Egypt. In those years the kingdom of Amurru included regions of modern southern Syria along the coast and northern Lebanon. The largest Late Bronze Age tell in Amurru (and probably its capital) is Tell Kazel in Syria. The year 8 inscription states that Amurru was destroyed by that foreign peoples' coalition, and a total destruction is also reported in another inscription from Medinet Habu dated to year 5 of Rameses III (1183, 1180, 1179/1178 BC). However, the historicity of this last inscription is debated (for different positions, cf. Cifola 1988, 291; Bietak 1993, 299; Cline and O'Connor 2003, 136–37). Thus, the Medinet Habu inscriptions set *termini ante quem* for the destructions of Ugarit and Amurru.

Both Ugarit and Tell Kazel show clear signs of violent destructions that can be best explained as the result of the Sea Peoples' attacks. Moreover, both destruction levels contain Mycenaean-type pottery imported from various regions of the Aegean but at Tell Kazel also locally made (yet adhering closely to the Hellado-Mycenaean style). The typologically latest Mycenaean-type pottery is not earlier than LH IIIB Final, and most probably it dates to the beginning of LH IIIC Early—also called LH IIIB2/IIIC Early Transitional (Monchambert 2004, 269–300, 321–22; Mountjoy 2004; Jung 2008). However, although a reoccupation of Ugarit has recently been identified in certain places (around the royal palace and to the south), based on an architectural phase built over the ruins of the great destruction (Callot 2008), that reoccupation cannot be connected to any pottery deposits. One may therefore conclude that LH IIIC Early started before the 1190s/70s BC. This is the last secure synchronism between the pottery-based Aegean relative chronology and the historical chronologies of the ancient Near East and Egypt. For the middle and the second half of the 12th century BC, synchronisms are less stable due to insecure links of Near Eastern contexts to pharaonic regnal dates on the one hand and to still unresolved problems of the chronological phasing of Aegean-type and Aegeanizing pottery classes in Cyprus and Palestine on the other (see articles in Bietak and Czerny [2007, 501–620, with bibliography]).

Radiocarbon dating can be useful for the period from 1200 to 1000 BC but only under very specific circumstances. The tree-ring calibration curve is rather flat for these two centuries, and it exhibits a number of quite strong wiggles. These properties of the calibration curve imply that ^{14}C dates from a one-phased context (e.g., a destruction layer) of Postpalatial date are more or less useless (i.e., they cannot contribute toward refining the existing historical-archaeological chronology no matter how many samples are taken from such a context or how well chosen the samples are, that is, even if they are short-lived plants, seeds, or bones). Dates from annual events in the 12th and 11th centuries fit nearly everywhere on the calibration curve.

If, however, during sampling certain conditions are fulfilled, the wiggly nature of the curve may be very useful. First, a long and continuous settlement sequence spanning a larger part of the time span between the 13th and 11th centuries should be available. Second, this sequence should be characterized by destructions and/or rebuildings in short intervals. Third, short-lived samples should be taken from every building phase (or subphases, if these can be defined, for example with the help of superimposed floors). In such cases, it may be possible to establish an exact match of the date sequence with the calibration curve by using advanced statistical procedures (e.g., Bayesian calibration, "archaeological wiggle matching"). Alternatively, an independently established archaeological age model may be tested.

In the first case (i.e., the statistical procedures), for example, it may be possible to identify a statistically significant "best calendric age fit" of the series by making use of stratigraphical information and estimates of possible phase durations to refine the dating. In the second case (i.e., the archaeological age model), the individual measurements in a given sequence are artificially placed on the ^{14}C scale (y-direction) according to the measured ^{14}C values and on the calendric time scale (x-direction) according to historical age expectations, as derived from the stratigraphy and the pottery chronology. The deviations between the measured ^{14}C ages and the calibration curve then supply information that may either help to validate the established absolute dating or imply that corrections are necessary.

Recently the first dendrochronological dates for the end of the second millennium BC were published. They derive from the central Macedonian tell site of Assiros Toumba. Here a series of construction timbers and posts from mud-brick houses of building Phases 3 and 2 was dated by both dendrochronology and dendrochronological ^{14}C wiggle-matching (Newton, Wardle, and Kuniholm 2005; Wardle, Newton, and Kuniholm 2007). For the post and the fallen timber of Phase 2, a cutting date of ca. 1070 BC is reconstructed, while ca. 1080 BC is proposed for the two fallen timbers of the earlier Phase 3. The finds of Phase 3 would thus fall into an interval between ca. 1080 BC and 1070 BC. A PG amphora of central/northern Greek style found scattered through Phases 3 and 2 is ascribed to Phase 3 and then used to arrive at a *terminus ante quem* for the invention of the Protogeometric style. Thus, the scholars who are working with the Assiros material propose to date the beginning of the PG period to 1120 BC rather than to the years around 1050, 1025, or even 1020/1000, as in different conventional chronologies (cf. Desborough 1952, 294–95; 1964, 241; 1972, 79, 134–35; Mountjoy 1988, 27; Hankey in Mountjoy 1988, 33–37; Lemos 2002, 26).

While the dendro- and the ^{14}C dates of the Assiros wood samples are robust, the stratigraphical position of the only wheel-made PG vessel from the phases in question might leave some room for doubt. More serious, however, is the possibility that all of the dated timbers were in fact reused from houses of the preceding building Phase 4, which did not burn down in a fiery destruction and must therefore have provided reusable wooden construction elements in quantity. (In contrast to Phase 4, Phase 3 did burn down, but with the wooden posts built into the mud-brick walls, there is a good possibility that such posts would have survived that destruction and be usable even for the following Phase 2.) If this hypothesis is true, the cutting date of 1070 BC supplies only a *terminus post quem* with an unknown number of years following for the introduction of the PG style into northern Aegean pottery production.

The tell site of Kastanas, also situated in central Macedonia, provides a long series of ^{14}C dates from the Mycenaean palace period down to the LPG phase and a rich sequence of wheel-made Mycenaean and PG pottery (Jung 2002). For the ^{14}C dates on charcoal, a pattern of wood reuse versus the fresh cutting of trees can be reconstructed, which depended on the availability of timbers as determined by construction technique (mud-brick vs. wattle-and-daub houses), density of houses standing on the tell, and fiery destruction events. While the charcoal samples, which do not stem from reused posts, date the beginning of their relative building phases, dates on animal bone samples are related to the use phases of the houses in or in front of which they were discarded. The Kastanas ^{14}C sequence is in good agreement with the historical date of around 1200 calBC for the start of LH IIIC Early. It supplies a *terminus ad quem* for a developed stage of LH IIIC Early of ca. 1180 calBC, another terminus ad quem for LH IIIC Advanced of ca. 1130 calBC, and a less secure terminus ante quem for the end of EPG around 1000 calBC

(Weninger and Jung 2009). The absolute dates for LH IIIC Early can also be supported by a parallel ^{14}C sequence from the tell site of Thessaloniki Toumba (Jung, Andreou, and Weninger 2009).

For the very end of the Aegean Late Bronze Age, good Aegean synchronisms with the Italian Final Bronze Age (FBA) can be used to link the Aegean relative chronology across the Alps to the dendrochronologically dated lake settlements of Switzerland. Submycenaean pottery and fibulae with Aegean Submycenaean parallels are found in the burnt destruction of Rocavecchia in Apulia, which dates to the later part of FBA 2. The earliest building phases of the Swiss settlements with cutting dates between 1055 and 1035 denBC have a bronze inventory (tools, implements, and dress accessories) that has close parallels in that same later stage of FBA 2 in northern but also central and southern Italy. In combination with the settlement of Livorno-Stagno in Tuscany, which provides slightly higher dates for the end of FBA 2 (by dendrochronological ^{14}C wiggle matching), one arrives at a dating range for the end of the Submycenaean phase between 1070 and 1040 BC (Weninger and Jung 2009).

Bibliography

Andreadaki-Vlazaki, Maria, and Eleni Papadopoulou. 2005. "The Habitation at Khamalevri, Rethymnon, during the 12th Century BC." In *Ariadne's Threads*, 353–97.
———. 2007. "Recent Evidence for the Destruction of the LM IIIC Habitation at Khamalevri, Rethymnon." In *LH IIIC Middle*, 27–53.
Andreou, Stelios, Michael Fotiadis, and Kostas Kotsakis. 2001. "Review of Aegean Prehistory V: The Neolithic and Bronze Age of Northern Greece." In *Aegean Prehistory*, 259–327.
Andrikou, Eleni. 2006. "The Late Helladic III Pottery." In *Thèbes: Fouilles de la Cadmée II.2. Les tablettes en linéaire B de la Odos Pelopidou. Le contexte archéologique. La céramique de la Odos Pelopidou et la chronologie du linéaire B*, ed. Eleni Andrikou, Vassilis L. Aravantinos, Louis Godart, Anna Sacconi, and Joanita Vroom, 11–179. Rome: Istituti Editoriali e Poligrafici Internazionali.
von Beckerath, Jürgen. 1997. *Chronologie des pharaonischen Ägypten : Die Zeitbestimmung der ägyptischen Geschichte von der Vorzeit bis 332 v. Chr.* Münchner Ägyptologische Studien 46. Mainz: von Zabern.
Bietak, Manfred. 1993. "The Sea Peoples and the End of the Egyptian Administration in Canaan." In *Biblical Archaeology Today, 1990: Proceedings of the Second International Congress on Biblical Archaeology, Jerusalem, June–July 1990*, ed. Avraham Biran and Joseph Aviram, 292–306. Jerusalem: Israel Exploration Society.
———, and Ernst Czerny, eds. 2007. *The Synchronisation of Civilisations in the Eastern Mediterranean in the Second Millennium B.C. III: Proceedings of the SCIEM 2000, 2nd EuroConference, Vienna, May 28–June 1, 2003*. Vienna: Verlag der Österreichischen Akademie der Wissenschaften.
Borgna, Elisabetta. 2007. "LM IIIC Pottery at Phaistos: An Attempt to Integrate Typological Analysis with Stratigraphic Investigations." In *LH IIIC Middle*, 55–72.

Callot, Olivier. 2008. "Réflexions sur Ougarit après ca 1180 av. J.-C." In *Ras Shamra-Ougarit au Bronze Moyen et au Bronze Récent : Actes du colloque international tenu à Lyon en novembre 2001,* ed. Yves Calvet and Marguerite Yon, 119–25. Travaux de la Maison de l'Orient et de la Méditerranée 47. Lyon: Maison de l'Orient et de la Méditerranée.

Cifola, Barbara. 1988. "Ramses III and the Sea Peoples: A Structural Analysis of the Medinet Habu Inscriptions." *Orientalia (Rome)* 57: 275–306.

Cline, Eric H., and David O'Connor. 2003. "The Mystery of the 'Sea Peoples.'" In *Mysterious Lands,* ed. David O'Connor and Stephen Quirke, 107–38. London: UCL Press.

Coldstream, J. Nicolas, and Hector W. Catling, eds. 1996. *Knossos North Cemetery: Early Greek Tombs.* BSA Supplementary vol. 28. Stroud: Sutton.

D'Agata, Anna Lucia. 2003. "Late Minoan IIIC–Subminoan Pottery Sequence at Thronos/Kephala and Its Connections with the Greek Mainland." In *LH IIIC,* 23–35.

———, and Jennifer Moody, eds. 2005. *Ariadne's Threads: Connections between Crete and the Greek Mainland in Late Minoan III (LM IIIA2 to LM IIIC): Proceedings of the International Workshop Held at Athens, Scuola Archeologica Italiana, 5–6 April 2003.* Tripodes 3. Athens: Dot Repro S.A.

Dakoronia, Fanouria. 2003. "The Transition from Late Helladic IIIC to the Early Iron Age at Kynos." In *LH IIIC,* 37–51.

———. 2007. "LH IIIC Middle Pottery Repertoire of Kynos." In *LH IIIC Middle,* 119–27.

Dakoronia, Fanouria, and P. Kounouklas. 2009. "Kynos' Pace to the Early Iron Age." In *LH IIIC Late,* 61–76.

Deger-Jalkotzy, Sigrid. 2003. "Stratified Pottery Deposits from the Late Helladic IIIC Settlement at Aigeira/Achaia." In *LH IIIC,* 53–75.

———. 2008. "Decline, Destruction, Aftermath." In *The Cambridge Companion to the Bronze Age,* ed. Cynthia W. Shelmerdine, 387–415. New York: Cambridge University Press.

———, and Michaela Zavadil, eds. 2003. *LH IIIC.*

———, eds. 2007. *LH IIIC Middle.*

Desborough, Vincent Robin d'Arba. 1952. *Protogeometric Pottery.* Oxford: Clarendon.

———. 1964. *The Last Mycenaeans and Their Successors: An Archaeological Survey c. 1200–c. 1000 B.C.* Oxford: Clarendon.

———. 1972. *The Greek Dark Ages.* London: Ernest Benn.

Eder, Birgitta. 1998. *Argolis, Lakonien, Messenien: Vom Ende der mykenischen Palastzeit bis zur Einwanderung der Dorier.* Vienna: Verlag der Österreichischen Akademie der Wissenschaften.

———. 2001. *Die submykenischen und protogeometrischen Gräber von Elis.* Vivliothiki tis en Athinais Archaiologikis Etaireias 209. Athens: I en Athinais Archaiologiki Etaireia.

Evely, Don, ed. 2006. *Lefkandi IV: The Bronze Age: The Late Helladic IIIC Settlement at Xeropolis.* BSA Supplementary vol. 39. Oxford, Northampton: Alden.

French, Elizabeth B. 2007. "Late Helladic IIIC Middle at Mycenae." In *LH IIIC Middle,* 243–51.

French, Elisabeth B., and William D. Taylour. 2007. *The Service Areas of the Cult Centre.* Oxford: Oxbow Books.

Freu, Jacques. 1988. "La tablette RS 86.2230 et la phase finale du royaume d'Ugarit." *Syria* 65: 395–98.

Grandet, Pierre. 2000. "L'exécution du chancelier Bay. O.IFAO 1864." *BIFAO* 100: 339–45.

Hallager, Erik, and Birgitta Pålsson Hallager, eds. 1997. *Late Minoan III Pottery Chronology and Terminology: Acts of a Meeting Held at the Danish Institute at Athens, August 12–14, 1994.* Monographs of the Danish Institute at Athens 1. Athens: Clemenstrykkeriet, Århus.

————, eds. 2000. *The Late Minoan IIIC Settlement: The Greek-Swedish Excavations at the Agia Aikaterini Square, Kastelli, Khania 1970–1987 II*. Stockholm: Åström.

Hood, Sinclair, George Huxley, and Nancy Sandars. 1958–1959. "A Minoan Cemetery on Upper Gypsades (Knossos Survey 156)." *BSA* 53–54: 194–262.

Iakovidis, Spyridon E. 1969/1970. *Περατή. Το νεκροταφείον Α´-Γ´*. Vivliothiki tis en Athinais Archaiologikis Etaireias 67. Athens: I en Athinais Archaiologiki Etaireia.

————. 2003. "Late Helladic IIIC at Mycenae." In *LH IIIC*, 117–23.

Jacob-Felsch, Margrit. 1996. "Die spätmykenische bis frühprotogeometrische Keramik." In *Kalapodi: Ergebnisse der Ausgrabungen im Heiligtum der Artemis und des Apollon von Hyampoli in der antiken Phokis I*, ed. Rainer C. S. Felsch, 1–213. Mainz: von Zabern.

Jung, Reinhard. 2002. *Kastanas. Ausgrabungen in cinem Siedlungshügel des Bronze- und Eisenzeit Make doniens 1975–1979. Die Drehseheibenkeramik der Schichten 19–11*. Prähistorische Archäologie in Südo steuropa 18 (Keil 2002).

————. 2006. *Χρονολογία comparata. Vergleichende Chronologie von Südgriechenland und Süditalien von ca. 1700/1600 bis 1000 v. Chr.* Veröffentlichungen der Mykenischen Kommission 26. Vienna: Verlag der Österreichischen Akademie der Wissenschaften.

————. 2008. Die mykenische Keramik von Tell Kazel (Syrien)." *Damaszener Mitteilungen* 15, 2006 [2008]: 147–218.

————, Stelios Andreou, and Bernhard Weninger. 2009. "Synchronisation of Kastanás and Thessaloníki Toumba at the End of the Bronze and the Beginning of the Iron Age." In *LH IIIC Late*, 183–202.

Kilian, Klaus. 1978. "Ausgrabungen in Tiryns 1976: Bericht zu den Grabungen." *AA* 1978: 449–70.

————. 1988. "Mycenaeans Up to Date: Trends and Changes in Recent Research." In *Problems in Greek Prehistory*, 115–52.

Kitchen, Kenneth A. 2000. "Regnal and Genealogical Data of Ancient Egypt (Absolute Chronology I): The Historical Chronology of Ancient Egypt: A Current Assessment." In *The Synchronisation of Civilisations in the Eastern Mediterranean in the Second Millennium B.C.: Proceedings of an International Symposium at Schloß Haindorf, 15th–17st of November 1996 and at the Austrian Academy, Vienna, 11th–12th of May 1998*, ed. Manfred Bietak, 39–52. Vienna: Verlag der Österreichischen Akademie der Wissenschaften.

Koehl, Robert. 1984. "Observations on a Deposit of LC IIIC Pottery from the Koukounaries Acropolis on Paros." In *Prehistoric Cyclades*, 207–24.

Krauss, Rolf. 2007. "An Egyptian Chronology for Dynasties XIII to XXV." In *SCIEM III*, 173–89.

Lemos, Irene S. 2002. *The Protogeometric Aegean: The Archaeology of the Late Eleventh and Tenth Centuries BC*. Oxford Monographs on Classical Archaeology. New York: Oxford University Press.

————. 2007. "Lefkandi." *Archaeological Reports for 2006–2007*: 38–40.

Lis, Bartłomiej. 2009. "The Sequence of Late Bronze/Early Iron Age Pottery from Central Greek Settlements: A Fresh Look at Old and New Evidence." In *LH IIIC Late*, 203–33.

MacGillivray, J. Alexander, and Robin L. N. Barber, eds. 1984. *Prehistoric Cyclades*.

Maran, Joseph, and Alkestis Papadimitriou. 2006. "Forschungen im Stadtgebiet von Tiryns 1999–2002." *AA* 2006: 97–169.

Monchambert, Jean-Yves. 2004. *La céramique d'Ougarit : Campagnes de fouilles 1975 et 1976*. Ras Shamra-Ougarit XV. Paris: Éditions Recherche sur les Civilisations.

Mook, Margaret S. 2004. "From Foundation to Abandonment: New Ceramic Phasing for the Late Bronze Age and Early Iron Age on the Kastro at Kavousi." In *Crete beyond the*

Palaces: Proceedings of the Crete 2000 Conference, ed. Leslie Preston Day, Margaret S. Mook, and James D. Muhly, 163–79. Prehistory Monographs 10. Philadelphia: INSTAP Academic Press.

————, and William D. E. Coulson. 1997. "Late Minoan IIIC Pottery from the Kastro at Kavousi." In *Late Minoan III Pottery Chronology and Terminology: Acts of a Meeting Held at the Danish Institute at Athens, August 12–14, 1994,* ed. Erik Hallager and Birgitta Pålsson Hallager, 337–70. Monographs of the Danish Institute at Athens 1. Athens: Clemenstrykkeriet, Århus.

Moschos, Ioannis. In press. "Evidence of Social Re-organisation and Reconstruction in Late Helladic IIIC Achaea and Modes of Contacts and Exchange via the Ionian Sea and Adriatic." In *Dall'Egeo all'Adriatico: Organizzazioni sociali, modi di scambio, e interazione in età post-palaziale (XII–XI sec. a. C.). From the Aegean to the Adriatic: Social Organizations, Modes of Exchange, and Interaction in the Post-palatial Times (12th–11th c. BC). Seminario internazionale, 1–2 Dicembre 2006/International Workshop, December 1st–2nd, CISM, Piazza Garibaldi 18, Udine,* ed. Elisabetta Borgna and Paola Cassola Guida.

Mountjoy, Penelope A. 1988. "LH IIIC Late versus Submycenaean." *JdI* 103: 1–37.

————. 1999. *Regional Mycenaean Decorated Pottery.* Rahden, Westfalen: Leidorf.

————. 2004. "Miletos: A Note." *BSA* 99: 189–200.

Mühlenbruch, Tobias. 2007. "The Post-palatial Settlement in the Lower Citadel of Tiryns." In *LH IIIC Middle,* 243–51.

Newton, Maryanne, Ken A. Wardle, and Peter Ian Kuniholm. 2005. "Dendrochronology and Radiocarbon Determinations from Assiros and the Beginning of the Greek Iron Age." *To Archaiologiko Ergo sti Makedonia kai sti Thraki* 17, 2003 [2005]: 173–90.

Niemeier, Wolf-Dietrich. 2007. "Kalapodi." *Archaeological Reports for 2006–2007:* 41–43.

Pålsson Hallager, Birgitta. 2007. "Problems with LM/LH III B/C Synchronisms." In *LH IIIC Middle,* 189–202.

Papadimitriou, Alkestis. 1988. "Bericht zur früheisenzeitlichen Keramik aus der Unterburg von Tiryns. Ausgrabungen in Tiryns 1982/83." *AA* 1988: 227–43.

Papadopoulos, Thanasis, and Litsa Kontorli-Papadopoulou. 2003. Προϊστορική Αρχαιολογία Δυτικής Ελλάδας, Ιόνιων Νησιών. Ioannina: University of Ioannina.

Paschalidis, Costas, and Patrick J. P. McGeorge. In press. "Life and Death in the Periphery of the Mycenaean World at the End of the Late Bronze Age: The Case of the Achaea Klauss Cemetery." In *Dall'Egeo all'Adriatico: Organizzazioni sociali, modi di scambio, e interazione in età post-palaziale (XII–XI sec. a. C.). From the Aegean to the Adriatic: Social Organizations, Modes of Exchange, and Interaction in the Post-palatial Times (12th–11th c. BC). Seminario internazionale, 1–2 Dicembre 2006/International Workshop, December 1st–2nd, CISM, Piazza Garibaldi 18, Udine,* ed. Elisabetta Borgna and Paola Cassola Guida.

Piteros, Christos. 2001. "Ταφές και τεφροδόχα αγγεία τύμβου της ΥΕ ΙΙΙΓ στο Άργος." In *Πρακτικά του συμποσίου «Καύσεις στην εποχή του Χαλκού και την πρώιμη εποχή του Σιδήρου», Ρόδος, 29 Απριλίου-2 Μαΐου 1999,* ed. Nicholas Chr. Stampolidis, 99–120. Athens: Pergamos Ektypotiki Ekdhotiki.

Podzuweit, Christian. 2007. *Studien zur spätmykenischen Keramik.* Tiryns. Forschungen und Berichte XIV. Wiesbaden: Reichert.

Popham, Mervyn R., L. Hugh Sackett, and Petros G. Themelis, eds. 1979/1980. *Lefkandi I: The Iron Age: The Settlement, the Cemeteries.* Oxford: Alden.

Renfrew, Colin. 1985. *The Archaeology of Cult: The Sanctuary at Phylakopi.* British School of Archaeology at Athens Supplementary vol. 18. Oxford: Alden.

Rethemiotakis, Georgos. 1997. "Late Minoan III Pottery from Kastelli Pediada." In *Late Minoan III Pottery: Chronology and Terminology: Acts of a Meeting Held at the Danish Institute at Athens, August 12–14, 1994*, ed. Erik Hallager and Birgitta Pålsson Hallager, 305–336. Monographs of the Danish Institute at Athens 1. Athens: Clemenstrykkeriet, Århus.

Rizza, Giovanni. 1996. "Prinias in età micenea." In *Atti e memorie del secondo congresso internazionale di miceneologia, Roma-Napoli, 14–20 Ottobre 1991*, ed. Ernesto Di Miro, Louis Godart, and Anna Sacconi, 1101–1110. Incunabula Graeca XCVIII. Rome: Gruppo Editoriale Internazionale.

Ruppenstein, Florian. 2007. *Die submykenische Nekropole: Neufunde und Neubewertung.* Kerameikos. Ergebnisse der Ausgrabungen XVIII. Munich: Hirmer.

Schilardi, Demetrius U. 1984. "The LH IIIC Period at the Koukounaries Acropolis, Paros." In *Prehistoric Cyclades*, 184–206.

Schofield, Elizabeth, V. 2007. "Lefkandi in Late Helladic IIIC Middle." In *LH IIIC Middle*, 301–13.

Stockhammer, Philipp. 2009. "New Evidence for LH IIIC Late Pottery from Tiryns." In *LH IIIC Late*, 345–358.

Tsipopoulou, Metaxia. 2005. " 'Mycenoans' at the Isthmus of Ierapetra: Some (Preliminary) Thoughts on the Foundation of the (Eteo)Cretan Cultural Identity." In *Ariadne's Threads*, 303–33.

Vlachopoulos, Andreas. 2003. "The Late Helladic IIIC 'Grotta Phase' of Naxos: Its Synchronisms in the Aegean and Its Non-synchronisms in the Cyclades." In *LH IIIC*, 217–34.

———. 2006. Η Υστεροελλαδική ΙΙΙΓ περίοδος στη Νάξο. Τα ταφικά σύνολα και οι συσχετισμοί τους με το Αιγαίο. Vol. A. Τα Υστεροελλαδικά ΙΙΙΓ ταφικά σύνολα της Νάξου. Sira Dimosievmaton Periodikou "Archaiognosia" no. 4. Athens: Kardamitsa.

Wardle, Kenneth, Maryanne Newton, and Peter Ian Kuniholm. 2007. "Troy VIIb2 Revisited: The Date of the Transition from Bronze to Iron Age in the Northern Aegean." In *The Struma/Strymon River Valley in Prehistory: Proceedings of the International Symposium Strymon Praehistoricus, Kjustendil-Blagoevgrad (Bulgaria), Serres-Amphipolis (Greece), 27.09–01.10.2004*, ed. Henrieta Todorova, Mark Stefanovich, and Georgi Ivanov, 481–97. Sofia: Gerda Henkel Stiftung.

Warren, Peter. 2007. "Characteristics of Late Minoan IIIC from the Stratigraphical Museum Site at Knossos." In *LH IIIC Middle*, 329–43.

Weninger, Bernhard, and Reinhard Jung. 2009. "Absolute Chronology of the End of the Aegean Bronze Age." In *LH IIIC Late*, 373–416.

PART III

THEMATIC TOPICS

Art and Architecture

CHAPTER 14

MINOAN ARCHITECTURE

LOUISE A. HITCHCOCK

Minoan architecture is characterized by both tradition and innovation. Although regionalism (suggesting lack of cultural integration) was more typical of tomb architecture of the Early Bronze Age (EBA), there are also some regional distinctions among Minoan palatial buildings. These distinctions are frequently overshadowed by the emphasis placed on the organization of the palaces around a central court, resulting in the use of the essentialist term "court-centered building" to describe them in recent literature (Driessen, Schoep, and Laffineur 2002). Houses were characterized by a radial plan with rooms organized around a squarish hall. A preference for corner doorways and a liberal use of corridors and staircases in the palaces and villas enhanced their complexity. Greater cultural uniformity with mainland Greece at the end of the Bronze Age is indicated by the predominance of rectilinear halls with entry on the short side throughout the Aegean.

While fortifications typify the mainland, they have also turned up on Crete, most notably at Petras. Construction techniques varied regionally and chronologically but include a variety of techniques such as timber and rubble construction in the Palatial period, mud-brick superstructures on a stone socle, drywall masonry, and ashlar masonry on a stone socle (cf. Shaw 1971). Ashlar blocks in the Aegean had a finished face but were typically cut back in a "V" or trapezoidal shape for easy fitting so that the joints between the blocks could be filled with clay and small stones. Dovetail mortises were sometimes used to anchor blocks in place. A handful of blocks on Crete preserve drafted margins with a raised and rusticated central panel that typifies later Cypriot architecture (see Hood 2000), but these are unusual. Mud bricks were used to construct the upper-story walls and were also used for repairs. Terraced platforms and especially terracing into the slope of a hill also characterized Minoan building, and these techniques persist into the present. Use of local stone predominates in building. Stone was also used decoratively, as seen in the lavish use of gypsum orthostates at Knossos and for revetment at Phaistos and Ayia Triada. Other types of decoration include carved stone elements such as horns of consecration, sparing use of carved relief, and wall paintings.

EARLY BRONZE AGE

Early Bronze Age domestic architecture on Crete is characterized by a radial arrangement of rooms around a roughly square, central hall that served as the circulation hub of the building, which stands in contrast to the use of corridors to promote circulation and privacy in later periods. This multifunctional central room also served as the main gathering area of the structure. A central pillar or column served as a support for a roof, although this was sometimes omitted, and the space could be turned into an open courtyard. This form typified houses at the EBA settlement of Myrtos–Fournou Korifi on the south coast of eastern Crete, as well as at multihousehold complexes as at Gournia and Trypeti. It also characterized vernacular architecture of the Middle–Late Bronze Age and occurs as a module in some of the palaces and palatial villas (Hitchcock forthcoming b).

A more complex example of EBA architecture is the "House on the Hill" at Vasiliki, which is, in reality, a compound made up of multiple and conjoined structures added to over time. Although no longer regarded as a protopalace, it contains features that anticipate the later palaces: (1) a paved western court with a cupule stone (*kernos*) set into the pavement; (2) carefully planned rooms with square corners and the use of corridors and stairways; (3) timber and rubble construction; and (4) red-colored stucco walls, a precursor to fresco painting.

BURIAL MONUMENTS

While house tombs of the "but-and-ben" style harking back to the Neolithic tradition represent east Crete, round (*tholos*) tombs of the Mesara Valley in southern Crete represent a regional distinction. The but-and-ben structure is characterized by a roughly square plan divided into two parts by a spur wall running down the middle with an opening at one end. This plan was also used as a module (*en chicane*) in the later Minoan palaces (Hitchcock 2000, 34–35). The lower walls were constructed of available fieldstones and larger boulders held together by mortar consisting of mud, pebbles, and broken pottery, with the upper part of the walls of mud brick. The roof was constructed of wooden beams, mud, and reeds and was coated with plaster.

The vaulted walls of the free-standing Mesara *tholoi* were constructed of roughly worked blocks preserved as high as 2 m. at Kamilari. The rough workmanship of the stone and the lack of fallen blocks from collapsed roofs of the *tholoi* argue against their having been corbelled like later mainland Greek tombs, to which they appear unrelated. Flat roofs of wood and stone or conical roofs constructed of mud brick (common in traditional round houses in contemporary Syrian and Anatolian villages) remain possibilities, although no evidence of mud brick is preserved. Entrance to the tombs is typically on the east, and Goodison (1989) argues that beliefs about the afterlife were linked to the rising of the sun. Hearths may have been used for fumigation or funerary feasting.

The MM I funerary complex of Chrysolakkos (Malia) is a rectangular, multi-chambered, ossuary structure with a court that was renewed and reused in subsequent periods, obscuring the internal arrangement of the original building. The building also had a paved court and is notable for the introduction of limestone orthostates, the use of saw-cut blocks, and dowel holes (cf. Shaw 1983).

EMERGENCE OF THE MINOAN PALACES

The first "palaces" on Crete were built in the Middle Bronze Age, around 1900 BC. Although they seem to have appeared out of nowhere, recent research indicates that the earliest versions were more modest than the second palaces, which reached their final form in the Middle to Late Bronze Age transition (Schoep 2004, 2006). Although palatial Minoan buildings quickly assumed a unique style, they may have been inspired by trade with the Near East, through a process of emulation. Monumentality implies planning, full-time craftsmen, organization of materials and labor, a high level of social complexity based on agricultural surplus, and social ranking. Monumental structures communicate permanence, power, and status (cf. Trigger 1990). Technical expertise likely developed out of the construction of impressive monumental tombs of the preceding period (Hitchcock forthcoming a). The stratified social structure that would have led to their construction likely emerged out of the activities required to oversee large-scale building projects and out of the prestige-goods economy based on acquisition of foreign and exotic luxury goods known from the earlier tombs.

Repair and rebuilding restricts our knowledge of the first Minoan palaces. What is known about them includes their paved, public west courts with stone-lined pits (*kouloures*) and raised, triangular causeways (presumably for processions); indented west façades fronting storage magazines; rectangular central courts with 2:1 proportions and oriented north-south; and remnants of pillared halls in the east wing at Knossos (MacGillivray 1994).

The indented façades, which create a play of light and shade, may indicate Egyptian and Near Eastern influences. Commonly accepted views that the west courts of the palaces served as public gathering places is influenced by the depiction of ritual dancing among sacred trees on the "Sacred Grove" fresco from Knossos. The function of these features changed by the Second Palace period, when the *kouloures* were filled in at Knossos and Phaistos. At Phaistos, the causeway was also paved over.

New evidence for understanding the first palaces comes from the monumental building at Monastiraki (Amari Valley, western Crete) and from Quartier Mu at Malia, where features we associate with the largest and most famous Minoan palaces occurred earlier. Two gamma-shaped doorjambs carved out of limestone from Monastiraki represent what may be the earliest example of a feature typically associated with later pier-and-door-partition (*polythyron*) halls (Kanta, comment in Perna 2000, 208). A Middle Minoan IB–II architectural parallel for the "throne room" at Knossos consisting of anteroom, hall with "lustral basin," rear service room, and four side chambers was uncovered in Quartier Mu at Malia (Niemeier 1987). The appearance of multiple buildings with palatial features at Malia has led to proposals of competing factions or heterarchy in Crete (Schoep 2004, 2006). The first palaces suffered damage and/or destruction, probably from earthquakes, just before the beginning of the Late Bronze Age, ca. 1700 BC. At this time some of the buildings were remodeled, and new palaces and smaller, palatial "villas" were constructed all over Crete.

Late Bronze Age: The Second Palace Period on Crete

The plans and organization of the second palaces at Knossos, Phaistos, Malia, and Kato Zakro are similar enough to suggest that they were initially designed and executed for each community by the same team of professional planners (Preziosi 1983). However, their construction was executed with varying degrees of skill, and the unit of measurement used is contested (see Hitchcock 1997). The most striking characteristic of the Minoan palaces is their monumentality, which combines ashlar masonry, multiple stories, and architectural decoration such as horns of consecration. Some of the ashlar blocks were engraved with symbols of uncertain significance, termed "mason's marks." The use of timber and rubble in building the walls may have provided flexibility in times of earthquake (cf. Driessen 1987).

Spacious, paved, and public west courts continued, as did the north-south orientation of the central court. Frequently this orientation also referenced a sacred mountain housing peak and/or cave sanctuaries. Goodison (2001) has shown that the east-west orientation was also important, whereby the rising sun might illuminate particular features in the west wings. The coastal locations of the second palaces also communicated prestige to visiting traders.

Whether navigating a Minoan building or looking at a ground plan, one is impressed by their labyrinthine layout. Upon careful study, the visitor becomes aware of a specific architectural vocabulary, recurring types of rooms, and a complex organizational structure (cf. Preziosi 1983). This vocabulary includes elaborate halls that are located in the northwest and/or east wing, small sunken rooms (lustral basins), small dark rooms ("pillar crypts") located near storage areas, other areas devoted to ritual activity in the west wing, storage and industrial quarters frequently located in the west or northwest wing, a main entrance, additional minor entrances, and a hypostyle (pillared) hall in the north wing (Hitchcock 2003). The palaces were also decorated with wall paintings, painted stucco, and/or veneering. In addition, each building has certain features that make it unique—for example, the famous "Throne Room" that occurs only at Knossos, round and rectangular pools built of cut stone that occur only at Kato Zakro, the *baetyls,* which are found in the west court at Gournia and in the central court at Malia, and the presence of four lustral basins at Phaistos (more than at any other palace). Variation in the distribution of corridors, stairways, and doorways gives each building a complex uniqueness that underlies superficial similarities in the location of rooms. For example, two rooms might share a common wall yet may be separated by a long, winding route. These kinds of distinctions make the palaces and villas one-of-a-kind architectural masterpieces.

The "Minoan hall" is one of the most notable features of Minoan architecture and enhances its mazelike qualities (Palyvou 1987; Driessen 1982). It is composed of several rectangular rooms separated by a row of columns and a set of square piers. The piers support double doors that fold back into shallow recesses, allowing for the manipulation of light, ventilation, and movement. These pier-and-door partitions separate a hall into two parts, a hall and a forehall. A lightwell is separated from the other two rooms by a row of columns and allows light and ventilation into the building. The pier-and-door partitions can be used to either collapse or open up a room. If they form two or more walls of a room, the complexity of circulation within a building is further increased. The Minoan hall constitutes a feature that is uniquely Minoan.

Minoan halls were lavishly appointed, sometimes with gypsum dadoes, sometimes with fresco paintings. They tended to be located in the northwest and/or east wings of the Minoan palaces. A second, smaller hall was frequently built adjacent to a larger pier-and-door partition hall. It was sometimes appointed with pier-and-door partitions or was more exposed to the elements with multiple windows or columns replacing a wall, sometimes with benches and/or a lightwell. A lack of objects found in Minoan halls makes it difficult to know how to interpret them. They have been viewed as ritual spaces and as sleeping areas, with the smaller hall designated as a "Queen's" or "women's" quarters (e.g., Graham 1987). A consideration of context affords additional possibilities. Minoan halls could be put to multiple purposes depending on the time of day, the season, and specific needs. Possible functions include, but are not limited to, a circulation hub within a building, a ceremonial gathering and/or meeting area, as well as a general living space (cf. Hitchcock 2000, 157–76).

In at least two instances (especially Ayia Triada, Kato Zakro), Minoan halls were located near tablet archives. This raises the possibility that they served as a meeting place for palace administrators. Ritual, administrative, and social activity does not exclude other, more practical uses for the Minoan hall, such as sleeping at the end of the day. In short, we can view them as all-purpose gathering spaces, although changing their relationship to neighboring rooms could radically alter their purpose. For example, they have been utilized as entrances when placed at the front of a building (Nirou Khani, Phaistos), circulatory areas when placed in the center of a cluster of rooms (Tylissos A), and private gathering spaces when segregated at the rear (Tylissos C).

Another architectural feature that is uniquely Minoan is a small room referred to as a "lustral basin" (Hitchcock 2000, 163–79). This is a small, rectangular room sunken below the floor level and reached by a short flight of stairs, making a turn and running along a parapet and always open off of a rectangular anteroom. They are interpreted as sites of ritual initiation, purification, symbolic descent into the earth, and bathing. Sir Arthur Evans (1921, 405–22) named them "lustral basins," believing that the oil jars found in a Knossian basin were used for ritual cleansing. Horns of consecration are another frequent association. They are sometimes decorated, often with gypsum veneering; one example is frescoed (Chania). Contextual differences suggest that they were multifunctional. However, bathing is unlikely based on the water-soluble nature of the gypsum revetment, the public nature of some of the basins near entrances and opposite the "throne" at Knossos, and the absence of drainage. This is most clearly indicated in house Xeste 3 (Akrotiri), where, in addition to a lustral basin, there are two tubs set into clay benches with drains attached. In the Minoan villas, most (if not all) of the lustral basins were filled in when pier-and-door partition halls with lightwells were added (Driessen 1982), indicating that the palaces took over control of their function.

The palaces had multiple entrances, which segregated the activities taking place in the various wings. Certain entrances were more ceremonial in character: appointed with special pavements, procession frescoes, or pier-and-door partitions. The main entrance at Kato Zakro at the northeast end of the building connects the palace with the road to the harbor. At other palaces the main entrance is frequently on the west or southwest end of the building. A variety of drains carried water and runoff away from the palaces. They were constructed using slab-lined channels of various sizes, U-shaped clay segments, clay drain pipes, and a unique series of settling basins at Knossos that were joined by drains with parabolic runnels, believed to slow down the speed of the water (see Shaw 1971).

The palaces also featured rows of long, narrow storage magazines, which were frequently located in the west and north wings and sometimes held large storage jars (*pithoi*) that were rarely (if ever) moved. As much as one-third of the ground space of the Minoan palaces was devoted to storage (Begg 1987), and this area was even greater at Malia, where the east, west, and a substantial part of the north wing was utilized.

Workrooms in Minoan buildings tended to be slightly wider than storerooms. These well-lit spaces were undecorated and were sometimes distinguished by special features connected with a particular activity; they might also contain raw or partially worked materials. Open areas and rooftops were also used for industrial activity. Additional storage areas were distributed among other wings of the palaces—in the crawl space beneath stairways and on upper floors, as indicated by fallen objects.

Sockets and bases for columns and fresco representations indicate that wooden columns were frequently used as architectural supports. They are depicted as red with a black, bulbous capital and tapering downward, sometimes with double axes embedded in them, but there is no clear evidence that the Minoans employed a canon of proportions with regard to a base-to-height ratio. Impressions from the lustral basin in a villa known as the Little Palace at Knossos preserve the only evidence of fluted columns. Columns were used in staircases, lustral basins, colonnades, and peristyle courts and as supports in square and impluvium (so-called Palaikastro-style) halls (Driessen 1989–1990, 14n85). Another preferred form of support was the stone pillar. Although monolithic pillars are attested, they were more frequently segmented. Pillars were used in hypostyle halls, colonnades, and storage rooms but have attracted the most attention when found in pillar crypts.

The term "pillar crypt" was coined by Evans to refer to small, dark rooms located near the storage magazines at Knossos that contained a central pillar with incised double-ax markings. They are regarded as architectural and aniconic representations of the stalactites and stalagmites worshiped by the populace in sacred caves (cf. Evans 1901). They occur in palaces and villas in close association with or connected to storage areas. At some sites they also served as storerooms. Possible ritual symbols associated with them include mason's marks, pyramidal stone stands for holding cult emblems, and cists cut into the floor, possibly for pouring libations into the earth (see Gesell 1985, 148).

CYCLADIC ARCHITECTURE

Cycladic buildings on Kea, Thera, and Melos show both Minoan and, later, Mycenaean influences. Ayia Irini on Kea is notable for the numerous Minoan architectural features and fresco motifs found at House A. These can be contrasted with a local building technique and design differences in the neighboring houses. Most notable in its contrast to House A is House F, which consists of a series of axially aligned rooms arranged in a linear fashion, one behind the other.

House A was a multiroomed structure divided into a service wing and a wing containing residential rooms. This type of arrangement is comparable to Tylissos House A (Crete) and Xeste 3 (Akrotiri), although it was constructed using drywall masonry, a local technique, in contrast to ashlar masonry used in these other houses. House A incorporates numerous Minoan features, including a lightwell, pillar room, dual halls, a courtyard, a labyrinthine circulation pattern, a nonaxial layout of rooms, some attempt at cut or ashlar masonry in wall façades, traces of indented façades, cut-slab pavement with red plaster in its interstices, a U-shaped stone drain, slots for a wooden door frame, terraced construction techniques, a staircase-and-entry combination, an auxiliary staircase, the bipartite division of the building into storage/work and living areas with a west orientation for the storage/workrooms, and the presence of figural frescoes (Hitchcock 1998).

Most of the houses at Akrotiri on Thera incorporated Minoan architectural features, and some were clearly altered to give them a more Minoan-looking, radial style of plan. Minoan features known from Akrotiri include ashlar masonry, mason's marks, horns of consecration, the wrap-around lightwell in the House of the Ladies, which parallels Knossos in miniature, a lustral basin in house Xeste 3, pier-and-door partitions in a number of houses, liberal use of figural frescoes and auxiliary staircases, an association of stairways and entrances, and division of Xeste 3 into service and living/ceremonial areas. Although a couple of features (pillar crypt and canonical pier-and-door partition hall with lightwell) are conspicuously absent, this is a broader range of features than occurred at either Ayia Irini or Phylakopi on Melos, where just a pillar crypt and figural frescoes have been detected. This may have been a result of Akrotiri's proximity to Crete.

Religious Architecture

Peak Sanctuaries

As the Minoan palaces gained prominence, these sites became more formalized, suggesting elite control. This was indicated by the introduction of simple structures at some sanctuaries including a built altar, terraces to level out the approach, some storage rooms, sometimes a *temenos*, and sometimes horns of consecration. Linear A–inscribed offering tables and other luxury offerings also indicate palatial influence.

Bench Shrines

Cult activity at Postpalatial sites in Crete such as Gazi, Gournia, and Kavousi tends to take place in small rectangular rooms with benches running along one wall for placing offerings. These are commonly referred to as bench shrines or sanctuaries. Sometimes such shrines were established in the ruins of existing structures (ruin cult) as at Knossos (Prent 2004).

Postpalatial Architecture

Postpalatial architecture on Crete is characterized by the appearance of the mainland style *megaron,* a hall and porch structure with side corridor that provides access to a series of side chambers. Monumental versions of such a building are found at Gournia and at Ayia Triada. Also, at Ayia Triada is a stoa that replicates the main features found much later in the classical stoa: a row of rooms with a porch supported by a colonnade composed of alternating pillars and columns with a stairway on the side. The occasional use of saw-cut blocks and the Minoan practice of setting column bases into a stylobate persisted in LM III Crete. At LM IIIC Kavousi-Vronda, the "chieftain's" house, preserved Minoan design features in the form of rectangular magazines combined with a mainland-style megaroid hall and a paved west court with cupule stone (*kernos*). More typically, Postpalatial architecture featured a rectilinear hall, a hearth, and sometimes a linear arrangement of columns as in the "chieftain's" house at Kavousi-Kastro. Doorways might be placed axially in these structures, as preferred on the mainland, or located to one side, as preferred in Crete.

Conclusion

Administrative devices, the setting aside of numerous spaces for storage, and the presence of large, public courts have led archaeologists to view Minoan palaces as centers for organizing redistribution and trade in a prestige-goods economy and for holding rituals at special times of the year such as the planting and harvest seasons, as well as to mark transitional periods. The purpose of such celebrations would be to promote community solidarity and legitimize the role of the palaces in these processes. Toward the end of their histories, the Minoan palaces developed restricted access (see Driessen and MacDonald 1997) but not before their technical sophistication was passed on to their Mycenaean successors.

Bibliography

Begg, Donald J. I. 1987. "Continuity in the West Wing at Knossos." In *Function of the Minoan Palaces,* 179–84.

Driessen, Jan. 1982. "The Minoan Hall in Domestic Architecture on Crete: To Be in Vogue in Late Minoan IA?" *Acta archaeologica Lovanensia* 21: 27–92.

———. 1987. "Earthquake-resistant Construction and the Wrath of the 'Earth-Shaker.'" *Journal of the Society of Architectural Historians* (June): 171–78.

————. 1989–1990. "The Proliferation of Minoan Palatial Architectural Style: (I) Crete." *Acta archaeologica Lovanensia* 28–29: 3–23.

————, and Colin MacDonald. 1997. *The Troubled Island: Minoan Crete before and after the Santorini Eruption.* Aegaeum 17. Liège: Université de Liège.

Driessen, Jan, Ilse Schoep, and Robert Laffineur, eds. 2002. *Monuments of Minos.*

Evans, Arthur J. 1901. "Mycenaean Tree and Pillar Cult." *JHS* 21: 99–204.

————. 1921. *PM,* vol. 1.

Gesell, Geraldine C. 1985. *Town, Palace, and House Cult in Minoan Crete. SIMA* 67. Gothenburg: Åström.

Goodison, Lucy. 1989. *Death, Women, and the Sun: Symbolism of Regeneration in Early Aegean Religion.* Bulletin of the Institute of Classical Studies Supplement 53. London: University of London, Institute of Classical Studies.

————. 2001. "From Tholos Tomb to Throne Room: Perceptions of the Sun in Minoan Ritual." In *Potnia,* 77–88.

Graham, James W. 1987. *Palaces of Crete.* Reprint of 1962 edition. Princeton: Princeton University Press.

Hitchcock, Louise A. 1997. "The Best Laid Plans Go Astray: Modular (Ir)regularities in the 'Residential Quarters' at Phaistos." In *TEXNH,* 243–50.

————. 1998. "Blending the Local with the Foreign: Minoan Features at Ayia Irini, House A." In *Kea-Kythnos: History and Archaeology: Proceedings of an International Symposium, Kea-Kythnos, 22–25 June 1994,* ed. Lina G. Mendoni and Alexander J. Mazarakis-Ainian, 169–74. Athens: Research Centre for Greek and Roman Antiquity National Hellenic Research Foundation.

————. 2000. *Minoan Architecture: A Contextual Analysis. SIMA* Pocket Book 155. Jonsered, Sweden: Åström.

————. 2003. "Understanding the Minoan Palaces." *Athena Review* 3.3: 27–35.

————. Forthcoming a. "Monumentalizing Hierarchy: The Significance of Architecture in the Emergence of Complexity on Minoan Crete." *Proceedings of the 10th International Congress of Cretan Studies, October 2006,* vol. A. Chania, Crete.

————. Forthcoming b. "Never Momentary, but Always Fluid and Flexible: Revisiting the Vernacular Tradition in Bronze Age Crete and Cyprus." In *STEGA: The Archaeology of Houses and Households in Ancient Crete,* ed. Kevin Glowacki and Natalia Vogeikoff-Brogan. Hesperia Suppl. Princeton: American School of Classical Studies at Athens Press.

Hood, Sinclair. 2000. "Masonry with Drafted Margins in Bronze Age Crete." *Eirene* 36: 20–26.

MacGillivray, J. Alexander. 1994. "The Early History of the Palace at Knossos (MM I–II)." In *Labyrinth of History,* 45–55.

Niemeier, Wolf-Dietrich. 1987. "On the Function of the 'Throne Room' in the Palace at Knossos." In *Function of the Minoan Palaces,* 163–68.

Palyvou, Clary. 1987. "Circulatory Patterns in Minoan Architecture." In *Function of the Minoan Palaces,* 195–203.

Perna, Massimo, ed. 2000. *Administrative Documents in the Aegean and Their Near-Eastern Counterparts: Proceedings of the International Colloquium, Naples, February 29–March 2, 1996.* Torino: Centro internazionale di ricerche archeologiche antropologiche e storiche.

Prent, Mieke. 2004. "Cult Activities at the Palace of Knossos from the End of the Bronze Age: Continuity and Change." In *Knossos,* 411–19.

Preziosi, Donald. 1983. *Minoan Architectural Design.* Berlin: Mouton.

————, and Louise A. Hitchcock. 1999. *Aegean Art and Architecture.* New York: Oxford University Press.

Schoep, Ilse. 2004. "Assessing the Role of Architecture in Conspicuous Consumption." *OJA* 23(3): 243–69.

————. 2006. "Looking beyond the First Palaces: Elites and the Agency of Power in EM III–MM II Crete." *AJA* 110(1): 37–64.

Shaw, Joseph W. 1971. *Minoan Architecture: Materials and Techniques.* Annuario della Scuola archeologica di Atene e delle Missioni in Oriente 49. Roma: L'Erma.

————. 1983. "The Development of Minoan Orthostates." *AJA* 87(2): 213–16.

Trigger, Bruce. 1990. "Monumental Architecture: A Thermodynamic Explanation of Symbolic Behaviour." *World Archaeology* 22(2): 119–32.

CHAPTER 15

....

MYCENAEAN ARCHITECTURE

....

LOUISE A. HITCHCOCK

FROM the final Neolithic/Early Bronze to the end of the Bronze Age, Aegean and Mycenaean architecture is characterized by both continuity and innovation, as well as by the adoption and adaptation of neighboring practices. The most obvious feature of mainland architecture is that it is hall centered, dominated by a central rectangular hall or *megaron,* thereby combining both axiality and simplicity. It forms the core element of the Mycenaean palaces, with additional rooms and courtyards organized around it.

Construction techniques varied regionally and chronologically but include a variety of techniques including mud-brick superstructures on a stone socle, drywall masonry, rubble masonry, Cyclopean (massive unworked and partially worked boulders) masonry, and ashlar masonry on a stone socle. Mud bricks were used to construct upper-story walls and to make repairs. Terraces consisting of retaining walls with fills were used to extend the habitable area on hillsides and serve as platforms for buildings, typifying Mycenaean palatial architecture (Wright 1978, 54–107). The use of local stone predominates in building. Ashlar was typically sand or limestone, although saw-cut, dressed conglomerate blocks were used in special places such as thresholds and the entrances of fortifications and *tholos* tombs. Conglomerate is composed of naturally cemented-together pebbles, cobblestones, and other sediments, giving the worked blocks a colorful, variegated appearance. This type of rock made up the Panagia Ridge in Mycenae and also occurs in Laconia at Vapheio. There was also a sparing use of decorative stone such as gypsum, which might reference Crete, in the palaces and other monumental structures such as tombs. Other types of decoration include carved stone elements such as "horns of consecration," sparing use of carved relief, wall paintings, and painted plaster floors. Mycenaean architecture is also characterized by a liberal use of the corbel arch, which was used to relieve the downward pressure on the lintel blocks of monumental doorways and to create niches. Corbel vaults were used to build culverts in bridges, construct galleries and passageways, and create the domed beehive or *tholos* tombs.

NEOLITHIC ARCHITECTURE

Late Neolithic–Early Bronze Age architecture on the mainland is characterized by variations on a theme, namely the rectilinear hall. For example, the site of Dimini in the plain of Thessaly in central Greece is dominated by a large central, *megaroid-style* building (Preziosi and Hitchcock 1999). It is comprised of a large hall with a horseshoe-shaped hearth that is roughly centered, with four columns supporting the roof as indicated by postholes. A forehall and smaller porch connected to the hall by axially placed doorways were later additions. Rectangular Neolithic houses might also be apsidal at one end and include a rectangular porch. Apsidal houses are also well attested in the Middle Bronze Age (discussed later).

Neolithic houses were more frequently composed of just a small, single rectangular room that contained a variety of internal features including bins, hearths, and platforms. Hearths might be constructed out of stones that may or may not have been coated with clay. Bins were constructed from stone slabs; pits coated with clay served as storage areas. Rainy weather in many parts of Greece suggests that roofs were slanted or gabled with a covering of clay and reeds. Neolithic houses typically employed stone foundations that would have supported a mud-brick superstructure and postholes for wooden supports. House models give some indication as to what houses may have looked like and reflect an interest in symbolically representing them. While the practice of making house models does not seem to continue in later Bronze Age Greece (with the exception of the Menelaion), it did occur in Crete. Other types of installations—such as pottery kilns—also characterize Neolithic settlements.

THE MAINLAND IN THE EARLY BRONZE AGE

Larger, hall-centered rectangular or *megaroid* buildings appear in significant numbers during the Early Bronze I from Troy and Poliochni in the northeastern Aegean and throughout mainland Greece. They were commonly entered on their short side, with axially connected rooms. A variant of this form, the *corridor house,* is distinguished by a more complex internal arrangement. It is composed of large, square, axially aligned halls that are encircled by long narrow corridors and/or stairways.

The more elaborate and monumental corridor houses begin to appear on the mainland later, in Early Helladic II (ca. 2900–2400 BC). Although once believed to be limited to the "House of the Tiles" at Lerna in the southwestern Argolid, more examples of this form have been detected, most notably at Kolonna on the island of Aegina.

The House of the Tiles was named for the enormous quantity of fired clay roof tiles associated with the building. It was built of mud brick over a substantial stone foundation course (ca. 12 x 25 m), with traces of wood-sheathed doorjambs and stucco-plastered walls in some rooms. It was two stories high, as indicated by traces of stairways, and may have had several verandas upstairs, partially covered by a pitched roof, as suggested by Shaw (1990). The House of the Tiles was preceded by an earlier structure of similar type, House BG. These buildings sometimes also incorporated elaborate clay hearths that are decorated with stamped-seal impressions.

In addition, while monumental fortifications typify the mainland, they are well known in the Cyclades during the EBA as well. These fortifications were characterized by thick, stone-built walls; round (Lerna, Kastri) or square (Troy, Poliochni) towers; heavily protected and/or hidden entranceways (Preziosi and Hitchcock 1999). Dwellings were characterized by groupings of rooms into what may have been compounds for extended families, separated by alleys, streets, or courtyards. Burial architecture was simple, consisting of rectangular cists lined with stone slabs.

MIDDLE HELLADIC ARCHITECTURE

On the mainland, cities were located on citadels from at least the Middle Helladic period. Early examples of the prototypes for Mycenaean palaces may be proposed for the MH through LH II periods. Among them, House D at Asine is the most convincing. It is composed of a rectangular hall and porch but lacks the column bases and hearth of a canonical *megaron* (see the following section). Other early structures that are worthy of mention include a Middle Helladic building with hall and porch at Eutresis; Building F at Krisa in Phocis, which was composed of a hall with ancillary chambers and side corridor as early as LH I; a large LH II hall with two preserved column bases at Kakavatos in Elis (Barber 1992); the MH settlement at Kolonna on Aegina, where a reused ashlar block with double-ax "mason's mark" hints at a Cretan connection (Niemeier 1995); and a substantial MH building at Plasi (Marinatos 1970), which features a rectangular hall rather than the apsidal hall more common to this period.

The LH II building known as Mansion I at the Menelaion in Laconia is the earliest building of some importance on the mainland. It was a hall-centered building with a porch and a forehall, as well as rear and side chambers accessed by circulatory corridors. Its carefully rendered foundation beddings anticipate the Mycenaean palaces of the 13th century BC. Mansion I and its successor,

Mansion II, contain some of the earliest ashlar blocks on the mainland in the form of reused poros blocks, which imply the presence of an earlier, hypothetical building dubbed the "Old Menelaion" (also Catling 1976–1977).

CHARACTERISTICS OF MYCENAEAN PALACES

Mycenaean palaces of the Late Helladic III period are best known from Pylos, Mycenae, and Tiryns, while less typical variants are known from Midea and Gla. Thebes and Orchomenos are only partially preserved, and the presumed Mycenaean palace at Athens was obliterated by later structures. In terms of design, the main Mycenaean palaces included a core set of recognizable architectural features and modules arranged in a set pattern, additional recurring features that were deployed in a varied syntax, and unusual elements that were site specific and formed the central part of a larger compound that included buildings unique to each site. This is most clearly illustrated at Tiryns and Pylos and to a lesser extent at Mycenae, where much of the palace was lost over a precipice.

The core element of the Mycenaean palace is the *megaron,* or hall. This is generally not very large and would have fit easily within the central court at Knossos. It consists of a hall, a forehall, and a porch of rectangular outline with two columns in *antis* to support the roof. Both the forehall and the porch are approximately one-half the depth of the inner hall. The internal arrangement of the megaron was dominated by a monumental circular hearth decorated with painted plaster and surrounded by four columns. The best-preserved hearth is at Pylos and is ca. 4 m. in diameter with an inner ring of 3 m. It is decorated with a painted stucco design depicting a running spiral motif around the top and a flame pattern around the side. There, the columns probably supported a clerestory with a balcony to admit light and draw off smoke through a two-part clay chimney found in the excavations. The megaron frequently had rear chambers, with side corridors giving access to smaller, square service rooms. All megarons incorporate variations of this basic arrangement.

Most dominant among the additional recurring features alluded to earlier is a smaller, subsidiary megaron that is frequently referred to as a "Queen's" megaron by analogy with Evans's suggestions for Knossos. At Tiryns, this feature is located to the northeast of the palace across a court, though still within the confines of the palace. In contrast, at Pylos this feature is tightly incorporated into the fabric of the palace and is located to the south of the east row of side chambers and on the east end of the courtyard leading into the palace. An H-shaped *propylon* with a central doorway and one or two columns between projecting *antae* is another characteristic feature. Layers of plaster around the column bases at Pylos preserved impressions of fluted wooden columns. The propylon gives access to a colonnaded courtyard that leads to the palace at both Pylos and Tiryns. Tiryns had an additional outer courtyard and propylon, which initially formed the entrance to the citadel in LH IIIA1 and became the inner part of a more complex entry system by LH IIIB. At Mycenae, the palace and its associated structures was spread over multiple levels situated on three artificially constructed Cyclopean terraces. A lengthy passage separates the propylon at Mycenae from the courtyard that fronts on the palace. A grand staircase also leads to the courtyard. Soles (1995) regards this staircase, throne emplacements, and heraldic decoration in Mycenaean palaces as a Knossian inspiration.

Beyond the commonalities in the megaron hall, propylon, court, and similar construction techniques (discussed later), there is an extraordinary amount of variation in the appointments in the palaces, as well as in the rest of the compound. Some examples include the storage jars for oil set into benches behind the megaron and a decorated clay bathtub set into a clay bench behind the "Queen's megaron," both at Pylos. In contrast, Tiryns boasts a colossal, sloping, monolithic black slab with channel and mortises, which may be for washing or libation. The megaron at Mycenae was decorated with a gypsum slab pavement, which may reference earlier Minoan prestige architecture.

Many of the rooms deployed around the megaron at Tiryns are included within the fabric of the building, while Pylos and Mycenae had a number of nearby but discrete buildings that were functionally associated with them. At Pylos, these include the Southwest Building, an earlier megaron-style building with a different orientation and many interconnected rooms that give the compound an indented west façade, and the Wine Magazine, a rectilinear hall to the northeast of the palace, where wine was stored. To the east of the palace at Mycenae and at another level lie several buildings, including the Artisan's Quarter, a square building that may have served as an annex to the House of the Columns (also Maggidis 2008). The House of the Columns was a colonnaded, court-centered building with a north-south orientation and a west wing composed of what may be storage or workrooms. The many differences in Mycenaean palatial compounds warrant a closer functional analysis.

Many of the building techniques employed in Mycenaean palatial architecture are quite similar to those used earlier by the Minoans. These include the use of timber framing and a rubble core in the interior walls, which were usually covered with plaster. The exterior walls of the palaces were constructed of ashlar blocks, many containing dovetail mortises or clamp cuttings to secure them to the rubble core and square dowels to hold horizontal timbers along the outer face of blocks, with the occasional use of mortar. A few Minoan-style mason's marks have turned up on the mainland, notably on an ashlar block with a double ax found beneath the palace at Pylos and two others on the *dromos* of the tholos tomb at Peristeria. Although "horns of consecration" have also turned up at Pylos and at Gla, they are actually more common in Cypriot architecture. Doors are indicated by cut-stone doorjambs similar to those found in Crete, while the absence of these in some doorways suggested to Blegen that hangings were also used (Blegen and Rawson 1966).

The floors of the Mycenaean palaces were coated with plaster that was decorated by means of an incised grid of small squares painted with nonfigural patterns. The absence of symmetry in the arrangement of the grid has been contrasted to earlier Minoan floor patterns that were executed with more precision and logically related to the architecture (Hirsch 1977). The variegated stone of Minoan paved slab floors has been suggested as possible inspiration for these floors. A similar painted floor, but incorporating floral motifs, is known from the MBA Canaanite palace at Tel Kabri, where there are also Aegean-style frescoes, suggesting that the Mycenaean painted plaster floor had its origins in Crete or the Cyclades (Niemeier and Niemeier 1998). Another painted plaster floor of Minoan inspiration has been found at Tell el Dabᶜa. Pedestals or platforms located opposite the hearths of the palaces indicate that a throne (Linear B as *to-no*) stood there, while other pedestals near doorways at Pylos may indicate guard stands. A narrow channel with depressions at either end, perhaps for pouring libations, was cut in the floor at Pylos near the pedestal for a throne. The Mycenaean palaces were also decorated with elaborate fresco programs, which included processions, heraldic animals, and agonistic scenes.

TOMBS

Although the round or tholos tomb seems to evolve independently from humble beginnings in the western Peloponnese, the Late Helladic II period marks the appearance of monumental beehive or tholos tombs of ashlar construction. Stone architecture frequently symbolizes permanence, and Mycenaean *tholoi* may have been modeled on MH tumuli based on the superimposition of one of the earliest Mycenaean tholoi at Voïdokoilia (Messenia) on an MH tumulus. The earliest tholoi, built as free-standing monuments, were subject to roof collapse. Building them into the hillside in order to support the vaulted dome solved this problem. They dominated the landscape as unprecedented territorial and genealogical markers of wealth and power (cf. Wright 1987). The most famous and elaborately constructed tholos tomb is the so-called Treasury of Atreus at Mycenae.

The Treasury of Atreus consists of a great chamber (14.5 m. in diameter) built into a cutting in the hillside and entered by a long corridor (*dromos*). The corbeled dome of ashlar blocks is built of circular courses progressively extending inward and upward to a central, round capstone. Traces of nails in the interior are regarded as the remnants of bronze ornament (rosettes?). Although robbed in antiquity, burials would have been placed in a side chamber. The building originally had a sculpted façade that included two engaged columns of greenish marble, finely carved with chevrons and spirals, and above the door a façade of alternating red and white bands of running spirals and lozenges between two smaller engaged columns. Behind the carved façade is the relieving triangle over the massive lintel, its great size symbolizing the power to harness resources (Frizell 1997–1998).

More characteristic in the Mycenaean world is the use of chamber tombs carved into rock.

FORTIFICATIONS

The drive to fortify places such as Mycenae, Tiryns, Midea, Athens, Thebes, and Gla occurred in stages rather than suddenly (Iakovidis 1983; Loader 1998; Scoufopoulos 1971). The beginnings of Mycenaean fortifications can be traced to earlier MH and LH defensive structures in Messenia and Laconia (Wright 1978, 162). The earliest LH III fortifications were modest, lacking the elaborate features of the Tiryns gate or the unique monumental sculpture of the rampant antithetic lions of the famous Lion Gate and Great Ramp leading up the citadel at Mycenae. The fortification walls tended to follow the contour of the acropolis and were built in sections, as is especially evident in the west at Tiryns, where there are distinct offsets reminiscent of the west façades of the Minoan palaces. Sections ranged to 8 m. in thickness and reach a maximum preserved height of 13 m. Saw-cut and hammer-dressed conglomerate blocks were used for highly visible sections of the entrance systems, while the bulk of the wall was constructed of unworked limestone boulders. Although recent interpretations (Maran 2006) argue that Mycenaean fortification walls were more about display, they certainly were also intended to help the city function as a place of refuge during times of stress.

The initial fortifications begun in the 14th century in LH IIIA1 at Tiryns—and twenty-five years later at Mycenae—surrounded only a limited portion of each site, primarily encircling the megaron with simple entry systems: an H-shaped propylon at Tiryns and an overlapping break reconstructed at Mycenae. By their third phase, some eighty years later, around 1250 BC, both citadels had doubled in size, encompassing a much larger area. At Tiryns, the famous corbel vaulted galleries were added on the south and the east, and a complex series of ascending ramps and gateways was also added on the east. It was at this time at Mycenae that the famous Lion Gate with projecting bastion was constructed, and the west wall was extended to enclose Grave Circle A and the nearby Cult Center.

At both sites, the entry systems would have served to spread out and diminish the effectiveness of an attacking force. In the west wall at Tiryns, a sally port that progressively narrowed inward would have served a similar purpose. At this time, the monumental Great Ramp leading up the Acropolis at Mycenae was constructed over the broken slabs of Grave Circle A and an earlier ramp of hard-packed earth and pebbles. A new Postern Gate was added on the north, and a tower was built on the southeast a short time later. Although undecorated, the design of the Postern Gate incorporates the same features of the Lion Gate on a smaller scale, a slab of stone placed in the relieving triangle of the corbeled arch over the lintel of the doorway.

Final changes enacted around 1200 BC saw the addition of sally ports, while a further extension of the fortifications at Mycenae on the northeast enclosed an underground cistern, reached by a zigzag underground staircase leading to a rectangular shaft fed by an aqueduct from a nearby spring. It was coated with plaster, allowing the water to rise into the lower passage. At Tiryns, tunnels leading out of the citadel also gave access to the water supply.

Other Large Building Projects

Other large-scale building projects undertaken by the Mycenaeans included roads, dams combining earthen embankments with Cyclopean walls, and drainage projects achieved by using the natural terrain combined with dykes utilizing Cyclopean masonry to create canals that channeled the seasonal lake at Kopais in Boeotia into sinkholes (*katabothroi*).

Religious Architecture

The LC I Temple at Kea represents a regional development as indicated by its unusual plan, spectacular hoard of wheel-made, terra-cotta statuettes of females, and long history of importance to Aegean and later Greek religion. Its use continued into the Iron Age, and by at least the sixth century BC it had become a shrine of Dionysos. Preserved remains form a long, narrow, trapezoidal structure built of drywall masonry in which the northwestern wall angles inward toward the south. The entrance was probably located at the eroded southeastern end. A rectangular hall with several stone installations takes up the full southeastern end and opens onto a rectangular hall at the northwestern end, which is divided into two small, rectangular rooms on the northeast side. A small court at the west end is connected to processional walkways along the north and south sides of the temple.

Other Aegean shrines, as typified at Phylakopi and at the Cult Center at Mycenae, were usually double shrines, possibly influenced by and influencing Near Eastern cult buildings (contrast Gilmour 1993; Negbi 1988). A possible Canaanite prototype can be found at Tell Mevorakh, and there may have been Philistine successors as at Tell Qasile and Tell Miqne-Ekron (cf. Mazar 2000). Mycenaean shrines are characterized by rectangular halls with rear chambers, small benches and/or platforms for the display of cult offerings, and a small rear chamber serving as a holy of holies or storage area for ritual paraphernalia. They also had column supports. A spherical stone *baetyl* was located in the court between the two shrines at Phylakopi, while the Cult Center at Mycenae included a bathtub and fresco paintings.

Postpalatial Domestic Architecture

Following the destruction of the Mycenaean citadels in the LH IIIC or Early Iron Age, rectilinear halls and various types of hearths characterized houses. At Tiryns, a new east wall was built in the palace, which may have been reused, although its status as a palace is uncertain. The construction of chamber tombs was replaced by the use of cist graves and cremation burials in jars, while the construction of small tholos tombs persisted in Crete.

CONCLUSION

The houses and palaces of mainland Greece were characterized by their organization around the rectilinear megaron hall. The palaces served as redistributive centers and regulated access to prestige goods and imported commodities such as bronze, ivory, and gold. These activities would have made it possible for craftsmen to obtain needed staples in exchange for their wares. Although the Mycenaeans augmented their traditional megaron and tholos plans with other types of buildings that may have been adapted from abroad, it is possible to speculate that some of their construction techniques were developed through the presence of Minoan builders who found their way to the mainland as part of elite gift exchanges and/or as refugees seeking new patronage after the fall of the Minoan palaces (Hitchcock 2008). The sheer monumentality of Mycenaean fortifications, tombs, and public works symbolized the power of the ruling elite. As in Crete, access became more restricted in the Mycenaean palaces toward the end of their histories.

BIBLIOGRAPHY

Barber, Robin L. N. 1992. "The Origins of the Mycenaean Palace." In *ΦΙΛΟΛΑΚΩΝ: Lakonian Studies in Honour of Hector Catling*, ed. Jan M. Sanders, 11–23. London: British School at Athens.

Blegen, Carl W., and Marion Rawson. 1966. *The Palace of Nestor at Pylos I: The Buildings and Their Contents*. Part 1, *Text*; Part 2, *Illustrations*. Princeton: Princeton University Press.

Catling, Hector W. 1976–1977. "Excavations at the Menelaion, Sparta, 1973–1976." *Archaeological Reports* 23: 24–42.

Frizell, B. Santillo. 1997–1998. "Monumental Building at Mycenae: Its Function and Significance." *OpAth* 22–23: 103–16.

Gilmour, Garth H. 1993. "Aegean Sanctuaries and the Levant in the Late Bronze Age." *BSA* 88: 125–34.

Hirsch, Ethel S. 1977. *Painted Decoration on the Floors of Bronze Age Structures on Crete and the Greek Mainland. SIMA* 53. Gothenburg: Åström.

Hitchcock, Louise A. 2008. " 'Do You See a Man Skillful in His Work? He Will Stand before Kings': Interpreting Architectural Influences in the Bronze Age Mediterranean." *Ancient West and East* 7: 17–48.

Iakovidis, Spyros E. 1983. *Late Helladic Citadels on Mainland Greece*. Monumenta Graeca et Romana IV. Leiden: Brill.

Loader, N. Claire. 1998. *Building in Cyclopean Masonry with Special Reference to the Mycenaean Fortifications on Mainland Greece. SIMA-PB* 148. Gothenburg: Åström.

Maggidis, Christofilis. 2008. *The Royal Workshops of Mycenae: The Artisans' Workshop and the House of Columns.* Athens: Athens Archaeological Society.

Maran, Joseph. 2006. "Mycenaean Citadels as Performative Space." In *Constructing Power: Architecture, Ideology, and Social Practice,* ed. Joseph C. Maran, Carsten Juwig, Hermann Schwengel, and Ulrich Thaler, 75–91. Hamburg: LIT.

Marinatos, Spyridon. 1970. "Further News from Marathon." *Athens Annals of Archaeology* 3: 153–55.

Mazar, Amihai. 2000. "The Temples and Cult of the Philistines." In *The Sea Peoples and Their World: A Reassessment,* ed. Eliezer D. Oren, 213–29. University Museum Monograph 108. University Museum Symposium Series 11. Philadelphia: University Museum, University of Pennsylvania.

Negbi, Ora. 1988. "Levantine Elements in Sacred Architecture of the Aegean at the Close of the Bronze Age." *BSA* 83: 330–57.

Niemeier, Wolf-Dietrich. 1995. "Aegina: First Aegean 'state' Outside of Crete?" In *Politeia,* 73–78.

———, and Barbara Niemeier. 1998. "Minoan Frescoes in the Eastern Mediterranean." In *Aegean and the Orient,* 69–98.

Preziosi, Donald, and Louise A. Hitchcock. 1999. *Aegean Art and Architecture.* New York: Oxford University Press.

Scoufopoulos, Niki C. 1971. *Mycenaean Citadels. SIMA* 22. Gothenburg: Åström.

Shaw, Joseph W. 1990. "The Early Helladic II Corridor House: Problems and Possibilities." In *L'habitat egeen prehistorique,* ed. René Treuill and Pascal Darque, 183–94. BCH Suppl. 19. Athens: L'École française d'Athènes.

Soles, Jeffrey S. 1995. "The Functions of a Cosmological Center: Knossos in Palatial Crete." In *Politeia,* 405–14.

Wright, James C. 1978. Mycenaean Masonry Practices and Elements of Construction. PhD diss., Bryn Mawr College.

———. 1987. "Death and Power at Mycenae: Changing Symbols of Mortuary Practice." In *Thanatos,* 171–84.

CHAPTER 16

FIGURINES

IOULIA TZONOU-HERBST

A recent thought concerning Aegean prehistoric figurines was penned by Colin Renfrew in one of his latest books:

> We do not know, and we shall probably never know, quite why they were made. They may not have been created simply and solely to be "good to look at." They may also have had ritual functions, or served as toys, or as educational aids. But it is difficult not to imagine that at least one of the intentions of the maker of each was that the work should be well made and indeed be "good to look at." (Renfrew 2003, 77)

The trajectory of Renfrew's scholarship parallels the trends in the study of Aegean Bronze Age figurines. In 1969 he produced the typological sequence of Early Cycladic (EC) figurines; at Phylakopi in 1985 he established the criteria for the identification of Bronze Age Aegean sanctuaries in the archaeological record, in which figurines play a central role; and in 2003 he doubted whether we will ever know their meanings. After the establishment of typologies and chronologies, scholars have searched for interpretations based on certain criteria, and then they questioned whether the archaeological record preserves any clues to help uncover the meaning figurines had for their makers and owners. Before discussing the intricate problem of meaning, I describe the archaeological evidence, the various types of figurines—Helladic, Minoan, and Cycladic—and their excavated contexts. I also consider methodologies of interpretation from different points of view: religion, identity, and archaeological context.

PRELIMINARY OBSERVATIONS

Figurines are small-scale representations of humans, animals, and objects that were regularly produced throughout the Bronze Age in the Aegean, continuing an extant tradition from the Neolithic period (figure 16.1). While Cycladic and Minoan products develop continuously, the mainland tradition of female figurines with exaggerated body features dies out in the Early Bronze Age (figures 16.1.1, 16.1.6, 16.2.1).

Materials differ from period to period and between regions. While clay seems to have been the most common material used, stone (particularly marble) is also prevalent; moreover, metal, bone, ivory, faience, sea pebble, and shell examples also exist.

Size distinguishes figurines from figures, which approach the size of small statues (figure 16.2). Thus, Mycenaean figurines range between 0.05 and 0.20 m. in height, while figures reach 0.35 m. (type A) to 0.69 m. (type B) (figure 20.1). Minoan figurines are small, 0.10–0.15 m. at Petsophas, while the faience snake figures are up to 0.35 m. tall; the figures with upraised hands range from 0.22 to 0.85 m., and the figures from the temple at Ayia Irini in Kea measure between 0.70 and 1.35 m. EC examples measure from 0.05 to 1.5 m. Apart from size, the technique of manufacture of the terracottas also differs. Figurines are handmade; figures wheel made.

The quantity of figurines present in the archaeological record is indicative of their use. Fewer than 2,000 EC figurines are known, produced over some 600–700 years in the third millennium BC. In contrast, at least 4,500 have been uncovered at a single site, Mycenae, dating between 1400–1100 BC. Figures are much rarer. Seventeen Mycenaean figures exist to date, along with 43 Minoan from the Postpalatial period.

The archaeological contexts in which figurines have been excavated encompass architectural settings and object assemblages that relate them to various spheres of human activity. Throughout the Bronze Age, people buried figurines with their dead. They also used them in other ritual activities that are more difficult for us to reconstruct, but they had them in their houses as well. They recycled them and eventually threw them away when they no longer had any use for them. On the other hand, figures appear only in settings related to ritual.

EARLY BRONZE AGE

In the EBA, anthropomorphic marble figurines were produced in the Cyclades. Traces of paint indicate that bright colors originally highlighted the details of face and body (Hendrix 2003). Schematic representations early in the EC period are replaced later in the period by more anatomically detailed examples, the canonical or Folded-Arm Figurines (FAF). The schematics include the violin, notch-waisted, and pebble types, among others, which are self-explanatory of the shape. The FAF stand on tiptoe with the head tilted back and the arms folded over the stomach. Seated and double

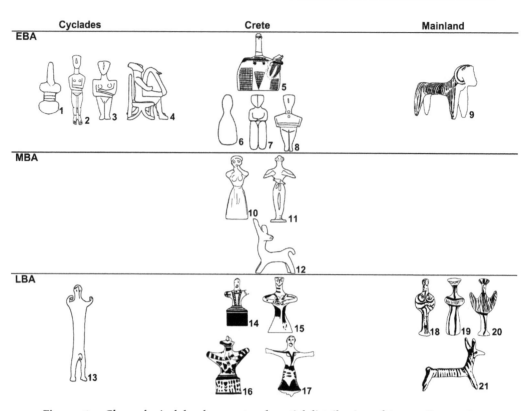

| Cyclades | Crete | Mainland |

Figure 16.1. Chronological development and spatial distribution of Aegean Bronze Age figurines (not to scale): (1) EC I white marble figurine, Violin type; (2) EC II white marble figurine, Late Spedos variety; (3) EC II white marble figurine, Chalandriani variety; (4) EC II white marble harpist, from Keros? (National Archaeological Museum); (5) "Goddess of Myrtos," EM terracotta female figurine from Myrtos, Fournou Korifi; (6) EM schematic figurine, Troy I type from Lebena; (7) EM female figurine, Trapeza type from Trapeza; (8) EM female figurine, Koumasa variety; (9) EH terracotta animal figurine from Corinth; (10) MM I–II terracotta female figurine from the peak sanctuary of Petsophas, near Palaikastro; (11) MM I–II terracotta male figurine from the peak sanctuary of Petsophas, near Palaikastro; (12) MM I–II terracotta deer figurine from a communal tomb at Porti, Mesara Plain; (13) LC terracotta male figurine from the sanctuary at Phylakopi, Melos; (14) LM IIIA terracotta female figurine from Mavrospilio; (15) LM III A–B terracotta female figurine from a grave at Khania; (16) LM II–IIIA1 terracotta female figurine with smaller male figurine in her arms, from Mavrospilio; (17) LM IIIA terracotta female dancer figurine from Palaikastro; (18) Mycenaean (LH IIIB) terracotta female figurine, Phi type, from Zeli, Lamia; (19) Mycenaean (LH IIIB) terracotta female figurine, Tau type, from chamber tomb XXXVI, Prosymna, Argolid; (20) Mycenaean (LH IIIB) terracotta female figurine, Psi type, from chamber tomb XXXIII, Zygouries, Corinthia; (21) Mycenaean (LH IIIA–B) terracotta animal figurine from chamber tomb XXII, Prosymna, Argolid (all drawings by J. A. Herbst).

Figure 16.2. Figurines and figures. (1) Late Neolithic white marble schematic figurine
from Paros; (2) EC II white marble female figurine, Late Spedos variety, Fine Arts
Museums of San Francisco, from "Keros Hoard"; (3) EM white marble female figurine,
Koumasa variety, from Teke, Crete; (4) EH terracotta animal figurine from Corinth;
(5) bronze male figurine, "Minoan salute" type, British Museum; (6) Neopalatial male
statuette made out of serpentine, rock crystal, wood, gold, and ivory, from Palaikastro;
(7) neopalatial faience "snake goddess" from Temple Repositories, Knossos; (8) LM IIIA
terracotta female figurine from Myrsini, Ayios Nikolaos; (9) LM II–IIIA1 terracotta female
figurine with smaller male figurine in her arms, from Mavrospilio; (10) LM IIIA terracotta
female figurine from Mavrospilio; (11) Mycenaean (LH IIIB) terracotta female figurine,

continued

Tau type, from chamber tomb XXXVI, Prosymna, Argolid; (12) Mycenaean (LH IIIA1) terracotta female figurine of kourotrophos from cist tomb 12, Deiras, Argos; (13) Mycenaean (LH IIIB) terracotta female figurine, Phi type, from Zeli, Lamia; (14) Mycenaean (LH IIIB) terracotta female figurine, Psi type, from chamber tomb XXXIII, Zygouries, Corinthia; (15) Mycenaean (LH IIIA–B) terracotta animal figurine from chamber tomb XXII, Prosymna, Argolid; (16) Mycenaean (LH IIIA–B) terracotta chariot figurine from chamber tomb XXII, Prosymna, Argolid; (17) Mycenaean (LH IIIA2) terracotta female figure, type A, from Room 19, Temple, Cult Center, Mycenae; (18) Mycenaean (LH IIIC) terracotta female figure, type A, Lower Citadel, Tiryns; (19) LM IIIB–C terracotta female figure, "Goddess with Upraised Arms," from shrine at Gazi (arranged by J. A. Herbst).

figurines, musicians, and warriors also exist (Renfrew 1969, 28, figure 4; 1991, 90–91; Peggy Sotirakopoulou 2005, 50–51) (figures 6.2, 16.1.1–4, 16.2.2).

Scholars are divided as to whether EC figurines were made exclusively as funerary goods or intended for consumption in other settings as well (Davis 1984; Renfrew 1984; Panayiota Sotirakopoulou 1998, 153–158). They have been excavated mainly in cemeteries and occasionally in settlements such as Phylakopi on Melos, Ayia Irini on Kea, and Akrotiri in Thera. Excavations are under way at the enigmatic site at Kavos Daskaleio on Keros and will provide answers regarding the site from which numerous figurines were recovered in the 1950s and 1960s, the "Keros Hoard." Was it a sanctuary, settlement and cemetery, or a ritual deposit (Renfrew 2006; Peggy Sotirakopoulou 2008)? In tombs, one or many figurines (up to fourteen) accompany a single burial. Both male and female figurines are interred with many valuable grave goods or none at all. They are not equally common in all islands (Gill and Chippindale 1993, 609). For example, Tsountas (1899, 78–79, 100) excavated six figurines in 540 graves at Chalandriani in Syros.

Archaeological contexts of figurines indicate different customs on the mainland. Early Helladic (EH) terracotta representations of cattle and goats were predominantly excavated not in cemeteries or shrines but in settlements, as at Lithares in Boeotia, and at Tsoungiza and Corinth in the Peloponnese (figures 16.1.9, 16.2.4). The representations paint a picture of everyday life. The people at Lithares made figurines of bulls, an animal they loved to eat (Tzavella-Evjen 1985, 20). In Corinth, the figurines with slits in their bellies may represent slaughtered and gutted animals, if the slits were not simply part of the manufacturing processes (Phelps 1987; Pullen 1992, 50). The yoked oxen from Tsoungiza show that people used animal traction and the plow in cultivating their fields in EH times (Pullen 1992).

Early Minoan or Prepalatial anthropomorphic and zoomorphic clay figurines were used in Crete in domestic contexts, as at Myrtos and Vasiliki; in cemeteries, as at Koumasa; and in caves, as at Trapeza. The so-called Goddess of Myrtos, a figurine holding a jug, was used in a room with a bench and storage, along with pouring and cooking pots (Warren 1972) (figure 16.1.5). Another figurine from the same settlement was reused in road packing. In addition to terracotta figurines, ones made in stone and ivory were placed as grave goods in tholos and, more rarely, in house tombs. In contrast to the Minoan taste for ivory, bone and ivory figurines are rare on the mainland (Andrikou 1998). Figurines of Troadic and Cycladic inspiration produced in Crete show that people and ideas traveled between these areas of the Aegean in the EBA (Branigan 1971) (figures 16.1.6, 16.1.8, 16.2.3).

MIDDLE BRONZE AGE

Figurine production diminishes in the Cyclades and the mainland in the Middle Bronze Age, whereas it flourishes in Crete. In the Protopalatial (MM I–II) period, thousands of terracottas were dedicated at peak sanctuaries located on mountaintops. Finds include human and animal figurines and votive limbs. Mount Jouktas, for example, produced far more male than female figurines. Among other votives were human heads, hands, and torsos; sheep/goats, pigs, birds, snakes, and bucrania; clay balls, floral branches, women in childbirth, and phalloi.

Similar finds were made at Petsophas above Palaikastro within the enclosure wall of the sanctuary and in the rocks and crevices outside the confines of it. Male and female are differentiated by their gestures: The males fold their hands on the chest, the females extend their arms upward or outward (figures 16.1.10, 16.1.11).

At the small rural sanctuary at Atsipades, hundreds of clay phalloi were found. Rethemiotakis (1998, 51) believes the votives were dedicated by farmers and shepherds asking the god to intervene and protect plants and animals. Watrous (1995, 402) interprets them as part of a cult concerned with male and female maturation. While figurines were repeatedly deposited in the peak sanctuaries, few have been excavated in domestic contexts—at Malia, Tylissos, Vasiliki, at the farm house at Khamaizi—and they are rare among tomb offerings (figure 16.1.12).

LATE BRONZE AGE

At the end of the Protopalatial and beginning of the Neopalatial (MM III–LM IB) period, the production of terracottas diminishes markedly. Bronze and ivory are favored, while clay figurines imitate examples in those materials. Well more than one hundred bronze Neopalatial human figurines have been excavated in peak sanctuaries, caves, palaces, and villas. They are distinguished by at least eight different gestures: 'the Minoan salute,' or one hand on the forehead; both arms bent toward the face, placed on the hips, or folded or crossed on the chest; one on the chest and the other at the side (Hitchcock 1997) (figure 16.2.5).

The production and distribution of bronze was controlled by the palace. The high quality of workmanship, evident in the detailed and possibly individuating features of the figurine from Kato Symi, strengthens the argument that the owners of these bronzes belonged to an elite stratum of Minoan society that had access to the palace. Similarly, the Palaikastro chryselephantine statuette certainly belonged to a higher-status member of society because of the exquisite workmanship of the luxury material (figures 16.2.6, 43.2).

In contrast to the bronze figurines, schematic and naturalistic, male and female terracottas have no canonical poses in the Neopalatial and Postpalatial (LM II to LM IIIC) periods (figures 16.1.14–17, 16.2.8–10). There are fantastic and domestic animals: oxen, bulls, cats, dogs, sheep, agrimia, birds, and beetles. Kourotrophoi and dancers are represented, while a clay model from Kamilari with individuals bringing offerings to larger persons may depict a scene of honoring the dead.

Gesell's studies (1985, 2004) of the architecture and find combinations have identified as shrines structures containing figurines associated with other cult equipment. Neopalatial shrines in the palaces at Phaistos and Malia, peak sanctuaries at Traostalos and Kophinas, open-air shrines, villa shrines, and Postpalatial town and house shrines all contained these items. Other ritual settings with figurines include graves, such as those at Mavrospilio and Kalou Temenous.

Figurines do not appear solely in ritual settings in Crete. Less well known are domestic contexts such as those at Siva in Mesara and Malia in Neopalatial times, as well as an LM IIIB2–IIIC trash deposit at Khania. Within Rubbish Area North, many pits contained pottery, animal bones, stone tools, bronzes, and a large concentration of females and animal figurines. There is no evidence that this was a religious waste deposit (Hallager 2001). The presence of figurines in ritual, domestic, and trash deposits indicates that they had multiple meanings for the Minoans.

Mycenaean terracottas recovered in comparable assemblages support their multivocality as well. Contrary to the Minoan examples, which are individual in their gestures, Mycenaean or Late Helladic (LH) III figurines were mass produced. Phi, Tau, and Psi female types derive their names from the similarity of their form to the respective Greek letters (figures 16.1.18–20; 16.2.11, 16.2.13–14). Wavy, Linear, Spine, and Ladder animals are named based on designs in red paint (figures 16.1.21, 16.2.15). Other types represent enthroned figures, riders, charioteers, and kourotrophoi (figures 16.2.12, 16.2.16).

At Mycenae, Prosymna, and other sites on the mainland, archaeological assemblages with figurines show how their owners used them (Tzonou-Herbst 2002, 2003, 2009). Funerary settings indicate that they were appropriate grave offerings for the dead and at the same time used by the living in funerary or memorial ceremonies. The patterns of association of figurine types with burial types are complex. Men, women, and children were buried with them and presumably owned them in life. Poor and wealthy tombs contain them, sometimes in abundance, but interment with figurines was not obligatory for all. The regional inconsistency in burial practices suggests that figurines had different meanings for different people. Additionally, the practice of burial with figurines was introduced at different times. In LH IIIA1, the inhabitants of Mycenae used their figurines at home and threw them in the trash more readily than they put them in their tombs. Later, in LH IIIA2, they offered them to the dead. One can thus discern a change in the significance of figurines or in the ideas about death.

Apart from their use as grave goods, figurines were used in ceremonies honoring the dead. Libations and ritual feasting, along with the offering of figurines, may have been performed in front of the stomion of tombs and in front of monumental walls around ancestral tombs such as the Great Poros Wall at Mycenae and the Kyklos at Peristeria. Figurines, kylikes, and stirrup jars are most frequently associated in those settings.

Incorporation of figurines in burials, in ceremonies to the dead outside the tomb, and in sanctuaries at Mycenae (Moore and Taylour 1999), Tiryns (Kilian 1981), and Phylakopi (Renfrew 1985) leads us to conclude that they were used ritually. They are also found, however, in storage and cooking areas in houses and in household trash. Some reused them as stoppers for vessels or as temper in mud bricks. If some considered their terracottas sacred, others reused them as functional objects, and still others discarded them.

The disposal of figurines shows that a functional transformation occurred during their use lives. Their significance was altered, and after a period of use, Mycenaeans threw them out. Alternatively, occurrence in trash may indicate that some Mycenaeans believed in them, whereas others did not. Mycenaeans may not have shared the same religion or beliefs, and a number of scholars support the idea of different religions for different social groups (Hägg 1981; Wright 1994).

Thus, people of all walks of life used figurines in both sacred and profane settings. Find contexts of the figures, on the other hand, indicate that they were not individual possessions but rather belonged to the community as a whole. Specialists must have manufactured them since they were elaborately made on the wheel.

In contrast to the mass of figurines, few figures have been excavated in ritual architectural settings that share the same features as those at Mycenae, Tiryns, and Phylakopi (figure 16.2.17–18). Additionally, only one was in a grave, and none have been uncovered in houses to date. When their initial purpose was fulfilled, figures were respectfully buried.

Similarly, the Neopalatial faience snake figures were buried beneath the Temple Repositories in the palace at Knossos (figure 16.2.7). Their Postpalatial (LM IIIB–LM IIIC) counterparts are likewise discovered in contexts with repetitive architectural and artifactual features. Large terracotta snake and bird figures with upraised hands are usually found on a bench or in a room with a bench, and other ritual equipment such as kalathoi, with or without snake tubes, and plaques in public town shrines at Gournia, Karphi, Kavousi, Gazi, and Prinias (figure 16.2.19). The variety of settings with figurines shows that their meaningfulness was fluid and flexible, while the figures had a constant significance.

Interpretation and Discussion

The preceding description of contexts and representations of Bronze Age Aegean figurines generates questions about the function of these objects. Their meaning was discussed as soon as they were discovered at the end of the 19th century.

Typologies and chronologies were attempted early on as well. However, in the 1960s, work by scholars such as French (1961, 1971) and Renfrew (1969) established types and dates used widely today and continues to provide the foundation on which further research is undertaken.

Theories regarding the function and meaning of the figurines to their makers and users cover a wide range of possibilities from the sacred to the mundane. Religious interpretations dominate much of the scholarship. Figurines do not have an obvious function. Because they are not immediately explicable, they are identified with the divine. According to another line of argument, figurines are religious because they have been found in sanctuaries. Consequently, all should be interpreted as religious even when they are not found in religious contexts. However, the argument turns full circle on itself if sanctuaries are characterized or identified because of the figurines in them.

Schliemann and Evans were the instigators of relating Mycenaean and Minoan figurines to religious beliefs and cult practices. Schliemann (1880, 13) regarded them as symbols of the goddess Hera. Evans believed Minoan figurines were images of the 'Mother Goddess.' After a century of research, scholarship still centers on the explanation of the images as goddesses. Dickinson (1994, 169) wrote that "It seems reasonable to suppose that most had some symbolic function in the related spheres of religion, magic and ceremony." Gesell (2004, 143–144) asked, regarding the figures with upraised arms, "The major unanswered question regarding these images is always: are they in fact images of the goddess, and if so, is she one or many? There is of course no answer to this question that will satisfy all. The figures could represent the same goddess, several different goddesses, priestesses representing goddesses, priestesses representing themselves, or worshipers. How can one tell?"

Because figurines are often considered religious, and because religion is viewed by some as a criterion of ethnic and/or cultural identity, scholars cite figurines as evidence for the presence of specific groups of people when found in areas away from their producing centers. Thus, it is debated whether EC figurines found in Crete show that immigrants from the Cyclades used them (Doumas 1976; Sakellarakis 1977). The presumed relationship of figurines to Mycenaean religion and cult practices makes them an appropriate symbol of Mycenaean identity. They "constitute expression of a religious ideology, which contributes to the reconnaissance of ethnic identity" (Pilali-Papasteriou 1998, 29). Niemeier (1997, 347) and Barber (1999, 315) substantiated the Mycenaean presence at Miletus and Phylakopi, respectively, based on figurines. Boulotis (1997, 267) believed that figurines reveal the identity of their owners, as "carriers of deeply rooted religious beliefs."

Interpretations deriving from ideas such as religion or identity focus on a priori assumptions. It is taken for granted that the figurines were religious, and thus the question becomes which deity was represented or whether the figurines depicted the deities or the worshippers. The religious meaning becomes universally accepted, and meanings associated with other intangible spheres, such as identity, are proposed.

In addition to interpretations that relate figurines to abstract concepts, more mundane readings have been put forth. One of them is that figurines were toys or educational aids. Blegen (1937) suggested that Mycenaean figurines were toys because they were associated with tomb burials of children at Prosymna. Another theory is that EC figurines may have been educational aids used to instruct about the female body and the customs of the society. Horizontal parallel incised lines at the abdomen are seen as postpartum lines (Renfrew 1969, 18; Getz-Gentle 2001, 10). The red striations painted on the cheeks of a number of them may represent the bloody lines scratched by women as part of mourning (Hoffman 2002).

Meanings derive not only from analysis of the figurines' inherent features but also from contextual associations of artifact assemblages and architectural settings. Without contexts, interpretation is difficult. The praise of EC figurines as art pieces led to illicit digging and dealings with museums and collectors throughout the world. Lacking archaeological information, research concentrated on features of the figurines themselves to get to information about their producers. Getz-Gentle defined sculptural hands (1987, 2001), but a number of scholars question the usefulness of such attributions since they do not relate to real people and places (Renfrew 1991, 137–41; Cherry 1992; Gill and Chippindale 1993; Davis 2001, 24).

To reconstruct the activities in which owners used their figurines in the past, scholarship in the 1990s focused on the facts of recovery (Conkey and Tringham 1995). Scholars proposed hypotheses based on patterns of deposition, the archaeological contexts of the objects. An example of the application of information from archaeological context in interpretation is given earlier in the chapter in the reading of Mycenaean figures and figurines. The find contexts show that figurines had a varied existence. They were not religious objects for all people at all times. Some considered them religious especially if or when they had been made efficacious through ritual. Others recycled, reused, and threw them in the trash. Figures, on the other hand, were used in specific activities in certain spaces. When their use was deemed to have ended, they were ritually buried and sealed. Mycenaeans would not have considered throwing them away in their trash, as they did with the figurines.

Conclusions

The variety of types of figurines and contexts in which they have been found in the Aegean throughout the Bronze Age cannot all be explained by religion. Alternative interpretations and functions must be sought. To be able to produce these, we need to record the location and number of found figurines, the other objects they are found with, their depositional histories, how they were made and later broken, the history of their existence, and their use life from the moment they were formed, through the many uses and reuses, to their recycling and eventual discard. We can then infer the lifestyle of figurine owners.

Multiple interpretations of the figurines exist both because their meaning or meaningfulness is fluid and variable and because archaeologists construct those interpretations, which reflect their readings of the sociocultural environment that created the figurines. Archaeologists produce meanings according to their own perceptions and interests. In answer to Renfrew's worry that we will probably never know why figurines were produced, Hourmouziadis (2007, 58) replies that he is not interested in knowing why figurines were meaningful to their owners; rather, he is excited about hypothesizing the reasons he, the archaeologist, believes they were produced.

Inevitably, archaeological interpretation consists of facts, but it also depends on the imagination and speculation of the archaeologist. The multiple interpretations produced for figurines demonstrate that. Figurines are enigmatic and will continue to puzzle us. They have their own idiosyncratic characteristics since they are creations of landscapes, times, and people that no longer exist. We attempt to revive their worldview, thoughts, and perceptions as they portrayed them in these objects.

BIBLIOGRAPHY

Andrikou, Eleni. 1998. "An Early Helladic Figurine from Thebes, Boeotia." *BSA* 93: 103–106.

Barber, Robin L. N. 1999. "Μυκηναίοι στη Φυλακωπή;" In *Η Περιφέρεια του Μυκηναϊκού Κόσμου. Α´ Διεθνές Διεπιστημονικό Συμπόσιο, Λαμία, 25–29 Σεπτεμβρίου 1994*, ed. Fanouria Dakoronia, 315–20. Lamia: Ministry of Culture, 14th Ephoreia of Prehistoric and Classical Antiquities.

Blegen, Carl W. 1937. *Prosymna: The Helladic Settlement Preceding the Argive Heraeum.* London: Cambridge University Press.

Boulotis, Christos. 1997. "Κουκονήσι Λήμνου, Τέσσερα Χρόνια Ανασκαφικής Έρευνας: Θέσεις και Υποθέσεις. " In *Poliochni*, 230–72.

Branigan, Keith. 1971. "Cycladic Figurines and Their Derivatives in Crete." *BSA* 66: 57–78.

Cherry, John F. 1992. "Beazley in the Bronze Age? Reflections on Attribution Studies in Aegean Prehistory." In *EIKON*, 123–44.

Conkey, Margaret W., and Ruth E. Tringham. 1995. "Archaeology and the Goddess: Exploring the Contours of Feminist Archaeology." In *Feminisms in the Academy*, eds. Domna C. Stanton and Abigail J. Stewart, 199–247. Ann Arbor: University of Michigan Press.

Davis, Jack L. 1984. "A Cycladic Figure in Chicago and the Non-funereal Use of Cycladic Marble Figures." In *Cycladica: Studies in Memory of N. P. Goulandris*, ed. J. Lesley Fitton, 15–23. London: British Museum Press.

———. 2001. "Review of Aegean Prehistory I: The Islands of the Aegean." In *Aegean Prehistory*, 19–76.

Dickinson, Oliver. 1994. *The Aegean Bronze Age.* New York: Cambridge University Press.

Doumas, Christos G. 1976. "Προϊστορικοί Κυκλαδίτες στην Κρήτη." *Athens Annals of Archaeology* 12: 104–109.

French, Elizabeth B. 1961. The Development of Mycenaean Terracotta Figurines with Special Reference to Unpublished Material from Mycenae. PhD diss., University of London.

———. 1971. "The Development of Mycenaean Terracotta Figurines." *BSA* 66: 102–87.

Gesell, Geraldine C. 1985. *Town, Palace, and House Cult in Minoan Crete.* SIMA 67. Gothenburg: Åström.

———. 2004. "From Knossos to Kavousi: The Popularizing of the Minoan Palace Goddess." In *ΧΑΡΙΣ*, 131–50.

Getz-Gentle, Pat. 1987. *Sculptors of the Cyclades: Individual and Tradition in the Third Millennium B.C.* Ann Arbor: University of Michigan Press–J. Paul Getty Trust.

———. 2001. *Personal Styles in Early Cycladic Sculpture.* Madison: University of Wisconsin Press.

Gill, David W. J., and Christopher Chippindale. 1993. "Material and Intellectual Consequences of Esteem for Cycladic Figures." *AJA* 97(4): 601–59.

Hägg, Robin. 1981. "Official and Popular Cults in Mycenaean Greece." In *Sanctuaries and Cults*, 35–40.

Hallager, Erik. 2001. "A Waste Deposit from an LBA Shrine in Khania (?)" In *Potnia*, 175–80.

Hendrix, Elizabeth A. 2003. "Painted Early Cycladic Figures: An Exploration of Context and Meaning." *Hesperia* 72(4): 405–46.

Hitchcock, Louise A. 1997. "Engendering Domination: A Structural and Contextual Analysis of Minoan Neopalatial Bronze Figurines." In *Invisible People and Processes: Writing Gender and Childhood into European Archaeology*, eds. Jenny Moore and Eleanor Scott, 113–30. New York: Leicester University Press.

Hoffman, Gail L. 2002. "Painted Ladies: Early Cycladic II Mourning Figures?" *AJA* 106(4): 525–50.

Hourmouziadis, Giorgios H. 2007. "Η Μικρογραφία του Δισπηλιού ή με Αφορμή τα Ειδώλια Ενός Λιμναίου Οικισμού." *Εγνατία* 11: 51–71.

Kilian, Klaus. 1981. "Zeugnisse mykenischer Kultausubung in Tiryns." In *Sanctuaries and Cults*, 49–58.

Moore, Andrew D., and William D. Taylour. 1999. *The Temple Complex: Well-built Mycenae.* Fascicule 10 of *The Helleno-British Excavations within the Citadel at Mycenae, 1959–1969*, eds. William D. Taylour, Elizabeth B. French, and Ken A. Wardle. Oxford: Oxbow.

Niemeier, Wolf-Dietrich. 1997. "The Mycenaean Potters' Quarter at Miletus." In *TEXNH*, 347–52.

Phelps, William W. 1987. "Prehistoric Figurines from Corinth." *Hesperia* 56: 233–53.

Pilali-Papasteriou, A. 1998. "Idéologie et commerce: Le cas des figurines mycéniennes." *BCH* 122(1), Études: 27–52.

Pullen, Daniel J. 1992. "Ox and Plow in the Early Bronze Age Aegean." *AJA* 96(1): 45–54.

Renfrew, Colin. 1969. "The Development and Chronology of the Early Cycladic Figurines." *AJA* 73(1): 1–32.

———. 1984. "Speculations in the Use of Early Cycladic Sculpture." In *Cycladica: Studies in Memory of N. P. Goulandris*, ed. J. Leslie Fitton, 24–30. London: British Museum Press.

———. 1985. *The Archaeology of Cult: The Sanctuary at Phylakopi.* BSA Suppl. 18. London: British School at Athens.

———. 1991. *The Cycladic Spirit: Masterpieces from the Nicholas P. Goulandris Collection.* New York: Harry N. Abrams.

———. 2003. *Figuring It Out: What Are We? Where Do We Come From? The Parallel Visions of Artists and Archaeologists.* London: Thames and Hudson.

———. 2006. "Dhaskalio Kavos (Keros): Reflections and a Question." In *Γενέθλιον. Αναμνηστικός Τόμος για τη Συμπλήρωση Είκοσι Χρόνων Λειτουργίας του Μουσείου*

Κυκλαδικής Τέχνης, ed. Nikolaos Chr. Stampolides, 25–34. Athens: Goulandris Foundation–Museum of Cycladic Art.

Rethemiotakis, Giorgos. 1998. *Ανθρωπόμορφη Πηλοπλαστική στην Κρήτη από τη Νεοανακτορική έως την Υπομινωϊκή Περίοδο*. Athens: Archaeological Society.

Sakellarakis, Ioannis. 1977. "Τα Κυκλαδικά Στοιχεία των Αρχανών." *Athens Annals of Archaeology* 10: 93–115.

Schliemann, Heinrich. 1880. *Mycenae: A Narrative of Researches and Discoveries at Mycenae and Tiryns*. New York: Scribner's.

Sotirakopoulou, Panayiota. 1998. "The Early Bronze Age Stone Figurines from Akrotiri on Thera and Their Significance for the Early Cycladic Settlement." *BSA* 93: 107–65.

Sotirakopoulou, Peggy. 2005. *The "Keros Hoard": Myth or Reality? Searching for the Lost Pieces of a Puzzle*. Athens: Goulandris Foundation–Museum of Cycladic Art.

———. 2008. "The Keros Hoard: Some Further Discussion." *AJA* 112(2): 279–94.

Tsountas, Christos. 1899. "Κυκλαδικά II." *ArchEph*: 73–134.

Tzavella-Evjen, Hara. 1985. *Lithares, an Early Bronze Age Settlement in Boeotia*. Los Angeles: Institute of Archaeology, University of California.

Tzonou-Herbst, Ioulia N. 2002. A Contextual Analysis of Mycenaean Terracotta Figurines. PhD diss., University of Cincinnati.

———. 2003. "Η Πολυσημία των Μυκηναϊκών Ειδωλίων." In *ΑΡΓΟΝΑΥΤΗΣ: Τιμητικός Τόμος για τον Καθηγητή Χρίστο Γ. Ντούμα από τους Μαθητές του στο Πανεπιστήμιο Αθηνών (1980–2000)*, eds. Andreas Vlachopoulos and Kiki Birtacha, 645–64. Athens: Η Kathimerini.

———. 2009. "Trashing the Sacred: The Use-life of Mycenaean Figurines." In *Encounters with Mycenaean Figurines*, eds. Anne-Louise Schallin and Petra Pakkanen. Athens: Swedish Institute.

Warren, Peter. 1972. *Myrtos: An Early Bronze Age Settlement in Crete*. London: British School of Archaeology at Athens.

Watrous, L. Vance. 1995. "Some Observations on Minoan Peak Sanctuaries." In *Politeia*, 393–403.

Wright, James C. 1994. "The Spatial Configuration of Belief: The Archaeology of Mycenaean Religion." In *Placing the Gods: Sanctuaries and Sacred Space in Ancient Greece*, eds. Susan E. Alcock and Robin Osborne, 37–78. Oxford: Clarendon.

CHAPTER 17

....

FRESCOES

....

ANNE P. CHAPIN

PICTORIAL painting in fresco is a defining characteristic of Aegean material culture, yet the art form presents numerous challenges to modern study. Prehistoric frescoes are durable but fragile, and as little as 5–10% of any given composition may survive to the present day. Attempts to restore the original appearance of such fragmentary paintings often result in errors or overly imaginative reconstructions.

Dating frescoes to specific phases of prehistory is also difficult. Prehistoric buildings typically have complex architectural histories marked by frequent remodeling and repair. Fresco fragments are often found in secondary contexts (e.g., dumps, or reused as fill material), and mixed stratigraphy and/or scant documentation of excavations often obscure the dating of surviving frescoes.

In addition, the anonymity of the art form and an incomplete understanding of its stylistic development complicate both individual and collective study. In the absence of written history, however, the pictorial imagery preserved on frescoes provides crucial information about the social practices and beliefs of the prehistoric Minoan, Cycladic, and Mycenaean populations of the Aegean. This brief summary of Aegean wall painting focuses on recent scholarship; detailed discussion of individual frescoes, together with earlier relevant bibliography, can be found in Immerwahr (1990).

THE RISE OF PICTORIAL PAINTING

....

Painted in true (*buon*) fresco on wet lime plaster (though there is also evidence for painting on dry surfaces [*fresco secco*]), Aegean frescoes are technically distinct from Egyptian paintings made directly on limestone or dry gypsum plaster

(Jones 2005, 217–22). The origins of Aegean fresco painting can be found on FN and EM Crete, where the floors and walls of important buildings were coated in plaster made of lime mixed with clay and colored monochrome red (sometimes black).

With the construction of the first Minoan palaces on Crete came technical advances in fresco, including the introduction of a high-purity lime plaster and improved pigments. Early frescoes from Phaistos, Knossos, and Kommos demonstrate that MM II artists created abstract designs and imitations of stonework (Blakolmer 1997; Militello 2001, 45–46; Hood 2005, 48–49; Shaw and Shaw 2006, 182, 224–25).

Pictorial painting first appears in MM IIIA at Knossos. Preferred subjects were drawn from nature and include bulls and (reportedly) a human figure in relief, as well as spirals (Knossos palace: Hood 2005, 49, 76–78), various plants and a foliate lily band (Royal Road, Knossos: Cameron 1974, 725–26), and abstract plants (Galatas palace: Rethemiotakis 2002, 57, pl. XVIa). Stylistic comparanda also suggest an MM IIIA date for the Saffron Gatherer Fresco from Knossos (Walberg 1986, 58–62; Hood 2005, 49–50, 62). The motivations for adopting figural painting remain unknown, but Minoan rulers, patrons, and artists were probably influenced by the monumental artistic traditions of Egypt and the Near East. Small-scale pictorial imagery already present in Minoan seal decoration and ceramics, together with foreign models, could have provided the basis for the development of Minoan monumental painting (Immerwahr 1990, 21–37). Middle Cycladic bichrome pictorial vase painting may also have played a role.

Neopalatial Painting on Minoan Crete

Knossos remained a center of artistic production throughout the Neopalatial era (MM III–LM I). The palace was heavily frescoed after a late MM IIIB earthquake (Evans's "Great Restoration"), as were many houses situated near the palace. Structures built across Crete, including those at Amnisos, Archanes, Ayia Triada, Chania, Epano Zakros, Kommos, Palaikastro, Pseira, and Tylissos, received fresco decoration. Interestingly, the other palatial centers of Phaistos, Malia, Kato Zakros, and Galatas received comparatively little pictorial painting.

Minoan frescoes were distributed across wall surfaces in three decorative zones: an upper level above windows and doorways for border designs (bands, spirals, etc.) and pictorial friezes, the main wall surface for large compositions, and a dado at floor level, often painted with imitations of stonework (Evely 1999, 68–69, 133–35). Pictorial subjects range in scale from miniature (figure height: 6–10 cms.) to life sized. Ceiling and floor frescoes are also known, but the suggestion that the Dolphin Fresco from Knossos was a floor fresco cannot be confirmed (Hirsch 1977; Hood 1978, 71, 76–77; Koehl 1986b).

Most frescoes were painted on flat surfaces, but relief frescoes were sculptural in conception. Figures modeled in plaster relief receive careful attention to anatomical detail. The Aegean palette featured blues from Egyptian blue (synthesized from copper compounds), glaucophane, and riebeckite; reds, browns, oranges, and yellows from haematite, iron oxides, and ochres; white from lime; and black from charcoal/carbon (Jones 2005). Greens, pinks, and grays were achieved by mixing pigments, but chiaroscuro (shading in light and dark) was virtually unknown.

Frescoes from Knossos

Ongoing efforts to clarify the architectural history of Knossos offer hope for achieving a better understanding of the palace's pictorial program in its Neopalatial phase (excluding compositions from its final phase of Mycenaean occupation). A principal assumption is that the program served the prevailing ideology of the ruling elite, even though the rulers' identities remain unknown. Additionally, certain frescoes appear to have served as "signposts" marking important spaces and indicating how they were used (e.g., painting corridors and stairways with procession frescoes).

At Knossos, north and west palace entrances displayed bull/taureador frescoes. Stucco reliefs of athletes (perhaps boxers or taureadors) from the restored East Hall underscore a palatial interest in athletes and athletic competition. Large-scale relief fragments of female breasts and leashed griffins allude to imagery better preserved at Xeste 3 in Akrotiri, Thera (discussed later). Women are prominent in an early Procession Fresco, in the "Ladies in Blue" and the "Lady in Red" Frescoes, and in two miniature frescoes, the Grandstand Fresco and the Sacred Grove and Dance Fresco. These miniature compositions depict elite women, large crowds, and palatial settings. Together they emphasize Minoan social relations and the likely priorities of the Neopalatial rulers (i.e., elite display, public performance, and communal identity).

These Knossos frescoes illustrate the Aegean color convention borrowed from Egyptian art in which male figures have red skin tones and women are painted white. The famous Priest-King Fresco from Knossos, however, preserves ambiguous "rosy" skin surfaces that are neither red nor white (figure 17.1). This has prompted the suggestion that the figure represents a female athlete, perhaps a bull leaper (Cameron 1974, 122), even though the figure's powerful upper body and lack of breast development appear male. Suggestions that the fragments that constitute the Priest-King Fresco actually represent a boxer (Coulomb 1979) or a deity (Niemeier 1987) facing right are now disproved (M. Shaw 2004).

Landscapes

Minoan landscapes rank among the first in the world to portray plants and animals in their natural environments without human presence. Vibrant rocky terrain, lively flora and fauna, and unusual spatial conventions characterize the best-preserved landscapes, including the Monkeys and Birds Fresco from the House of the Frescoes,

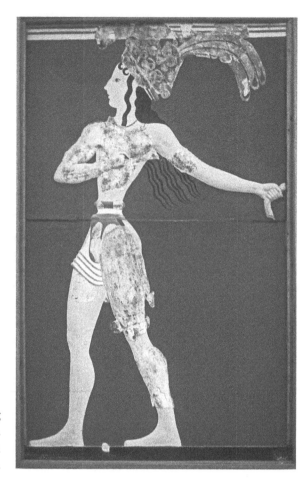

Figure 17.1. The Priest-King Fresco from Knossos, Crete. Neopalatial, LM I (photograph courtesy of the author).

the Partridge and Hoopoe Fresco from the Caravanserai, and the Floral Fresco from the Unexplored Mansion, all at Knossos (Chapin 1997; M. Shaw 2005). Landscape frescoes often extend across the walls of a room, ignoring corners and surrounding the viewer with idealized depictions of plants and animals. Some species can be identified, but artistic hybrids create new motifs, and flowers of all seasons bloom profusely and simultaneously, contrary to nature. The popularity of landscape as room decoration in elite estates suggests their importance in social display, while their latent religious symbolism implies that landscape painting visualized essential Minoan religious beliefs (Chapin 2004).

Female Figures

Large-scale frescoes of female figures (many in relief) decorated numerous, well-appointed buildings in Minoan towns across Crete (e.g., Archanes, Chania, Katsamba, Palaikastro, Pseira). The best preserved come from the villa at Ayia Triada, where two women are painted in a lush landscape. One kneels over sacred baetyls, and the other stands beside a stepped structure similar to platforms used as seats for presumably divine female figures in other media. The Ayia Triada fresco may therefore depict a goddess (or a goddess imperson-ator) and her votary (Militello 1998, 250–82). Without inscriptions, distinctive costumes, or identifying attributes, however, it remains difficult to differentiate divine personages from those with priestly status in Minoan art. This ambigu-ous iconography permeates other frescoes with large-scale female figures and may intentionally blur the boundaries between mortal and divine.

Cycladic Painting in the Neopalatial Period: Akrotiri, Thera

Minoan culture influenced prehistoric sites throughout the Aegean, and the Cycladic town of Akrotiri on Thera, the island closest to Crete, preserves the strength of this influence. The LC I eruption of the Santorini volcano buried the town and pro-tected its many frescoes to a degree not found elsewhere in the Aegean.

Xeste 3

Images of women dominate the extensive fresco program of Xeste 3, a large villalike structure built with *polythyra* and a lustral basin (Doumas 1992, 127–31, pls. 93–137; Vlachopoulos 2008). The programmatic focus is a fresco of a seated goddess attended by a leashed griffin. Associated frescoes depict pubertal girls collecting an offering of saffron (an initiation rite?) and young women of marriageable age together with a painted shrine (Marinatos 1984, 61–84; Davis 1986; Rehak 1999; Chapin 2002). Associated nature frescoes identify the goddess as a *potnia theron*, a mistress of animals. A procession of mature women imparts a multigenerational aspect to com-munal participation. A secondary programmatic focus on boys and men emerges in space 3b, painted with three youths and an adult male, and in newly restored scenes of bull catching and goat leaping painted at the building's entrance. Large, complex spiral compositions decorated the uppermost level of Xeste 3. Crocuses were painted with organic purple pigment from murex mollusks (Chrysikopoulou 2005).

The West House

A fresco program linked by maritime themes and the predominance of men deco-rated Rooms 4 and 5 of the West House (Doumas 1992, 45–49, pls. 14–64). A minia-ture frieze depicted coastal towns, a ship procession, a sea raid, a Nilotic landscape, and other scenes (Televantou 1990, 1994). The fresco's imagery compares closely to the themes, formulae, and episodes of Homeric epic and may be inspired by a lost poetic source (Morris 1989; Hiller 1990; Watrous 2007). Alternatively, the ship procession could celebrate a seasonal nautical festival (Morgan 1988). The West House also preserves frescoes of adolescent boys holding lines of fish, a youthful "Priestess," *ikria* (sea captain's cabins), and cut lilies.

Other Frescoes

Every house thus far excavated at Akrotiri has produced pictorial frescoes, demonstrating that the art form was not restricted to elite structures. The Spring Fresco from Building Delta is famous for its brightly colored landscape with swaying lilies and darting swallows painted calligraphically in foreshortened views (Doumas 1992, pls. 66–76). The House of the Ladies preserves frescoes of sea daffodils and women engaged in a costuming ceremony (Marinatos 1984, 97–105; Peterson Murray 2004). Xeste 4 has a male procession fresco in a staircase (Doumas 1992, pls. 138–41) and a frieze of boar's tusk helmets, an emblem of prestige often associated with Mycenaean culture (Akrivaki 2003). Athletic training figures prominently in the Boxing Boys and Antelopes Fresco from Building Beta (Doumas 1992, pls. 79–84). From the Porter's Lodge, a female figure with a yellow face (Vlachopoulos 2007, 135, pl. 15.16) preserves a clear departure from the usual red-and-white color convention used by Aegean artists but recalls numerous depictions of Egyptian women in New Kingdom painting. Studies of painting technique reveal that the flowing lines of some figural and spiral frescoes were painted with the aid of mechanical devices (Birtacha and Zacharioudakis 2000; Papaodysseus et al. 2006a, 2006b).

Images of Children

More images of children and adolescents have been found at Akrotiri than any other Aegean site. Many seem engaged in ritual activities, perhaps of initiation. Attempts to sort them into age grades, primarily by analyzing hairstyles, have failed to produce consensus (e.g., E. Davis 1986; Koehl 1986a), but recent studies of figural proportion show that Theran artists followed a grid system based on the Egyptian canon and adjusted it for individual figures (Guralnik 2000). This flexibility allowed artists to portray the changing figural proportions of youthful growth and development, so that the Akrotiri frescoes figure among the world's earliest naturalistic images of children (Chapin 2007).

Neopalatial Frescoes from Other Islands

Contemporary frescoes from Melos, Keos, and Rhodes are also closely related to Neopalatial Minoan painting. From Phylakopi on Melos come frescoes of female figures, a monkey, lilies, and flying fish (Morgan 1990). House A from Ayia Irini on Keos yielded griffin fragments and a frieze of blue doves (E. Davis 2007); Area M produced a miniature frieze similar to that of the West House of Akrotiri

(Morgan 1998). Evidence for a Cycladic school of painting includes shared thematic interests, a stylistic preference for thin washes of paint, and figures painted on white plaster grounds (Davis 1990; Morgan 1990). Yet recent identification of distinctive splash-pattern frescoes at Knossos and Petras (Crete), Ayia Irini (Keos), and Trianda (Rhodes) offer intriguing evidence for traveling artists (Davis 2007; see also Boulotis 2000). It may be premature to identify regional schools of painting in an anonymous art form with mobile workshops.

AEGEAN ARTISTS ABROAD

Aegean-style frescoes (painted on wet plaster) have been identified at a growing number of Near Eastern and Egyptian sites. The palace of Yarim-Lim at Alalakh (Level VII) has produced fragments of painted dados, reeds, a bull's horn, and a griffin fresco of Aegean type (Niemeier and Niemeier 2000). A painted plaster floor and a miniature fresco resembling that of the West House at Akrotiri, Thera, was found at the Canaanite palace at Tell Kabri (Niemeier and Niemeier 2002), and fresco fragments preserving Aegean-style motifs, including spirals, rockwork, palm trees, and watery scenes with crabs and turtles, were discovered at the Royal Palace at Qatna in Syria (Pfälzner 2008).

From Tell el-Dabᶜa (ancient Avaris), Egypt, come frescoes dating to the early 18th Dynasty that were painted with Aegean motifs, including acrobats, Aegean-style griffins, and rocky landscapes (Bietak and Marinatos 1995). An intriguing Bull and Maze Fresco depicts Minoan-style bull leaping in a setting of undulating bands, a maze pattern, and a half-rosette frieze (Bietak, Marinatos, and Palyvou 2007). The partially shaved scalp of one leaper recalls Theran hairstyles, and his yellowish skin color is notable. Technical and stylistic features demonstrate the Aegean character of the Tell el-Dabᶜa paintings, but whether they were painted by artists of Minoan nationality, as has been suggested, remains difficult to prove.

FRESCOES FROM MYCENAEAN CRETE, LM II–IIIA

Mycenaean Greeks ruled Crete after the LM IB collapse of Neopalatial Minoan society, but the Knossos palace remained an important center of power with a significant fresco program. The Procession Fresco, the Taureador Fresco, the griffins (wingless, as at Pylos) of the Throne Room, and several bull frescoes all reproduce earlier Minoan themes. Martial subjects associated with Mycenaean culture appear in the Shield and Palanquin-Charioteer Frescoes. The Camp Stool

Fresco features pairs of men raising Mycenaean kylikes and Minoan chalices in a possible drinking ceremony. The appearance of registers, monochromatic grounds, and repeated pictorial motifs may reflect renewed artistic influence from Egypt, while human figures become simpler and more schematic, often outlined in black. These stylistic features are also found in the LM IIIA frescoes and painted sarcophagus of Ayia Triada (Militello 1998, 132–48, 154–67, 283–320) and develop further in later Mycenaean painting. The growing figural abstraction also undermines the legibility of the Aegean color convention. The Taureador Fresco, subject of much recent investigation (e.g., Damiani-Indelicato 1988; Marinatos 1993, 219–20; Morgan 2000, 939–40), preserves such schematic figural proportions that sex, gender, and age-grade distinctions become difficult to read (Alberti 2002, 109–15; Chapin 2007, 231–32).

MYCENAEAN FRESCOES FROM THE
GREEK MAINLAND

Evidence for early Mycenaean fresco painting remains scarce. Tiryns yielded MH monochrome plasters painted in various colors and fresco fragments (unpublished) from LH II contexts (Müller 1930, 178; Kilian 1987, 213). Fragments painted with plant motifs were found at Mycenae under the East Lobby floor in LH IIA contexts and demonstrate that at least one Mycenaean building contemporary with Neopalatial Crete was decorated with pictorial frescoes (Wace 1923, 155–59, pl. 25b.1–2). Fragments from Mycenae or Tiryns (now lost) also demonstrate knowledge of the relief technique (Immerwahr 1990, 194; see also Blakolmer 2000, 401).

Fresco painting became more widespread in LH IIIA, though frescoes of this period are seldom found in sealed, stratified deposits and are often difficult to date. Based on stratigraphical and stylistic criteria, the Theban female Procession Fresco is likely the earliest rendition of this favorite Mycenaean theme, with other processions known from Mycenae, Tiryns, and Pylos. These compositions seem to represent a continuation of Neopalatial subject, costuming, and ritual action, though figures are rendered more schematically. Bull leaping is represented by a fragment from Pylos and a fresco from the Ramp House Deposit at Mycenae (M. Shaw 1996). Whether Mycenaeans engaged in bull leaping remains uncertain (many scholars are doubtful), but taureador imagery virtually disappears from Mycenaean iconography after the final destruction of Knossos in LM IIIA or early IIIB.

Most of the surviving Mycenaean frescoes date from LH IIIB, when wall paintings decorated palaces, houses, and many other types of buildings. Technical evidence suggests that artists of the Mycenaean era continued earlier painting practices. As before, walls were organized into decorative zones for dados, pictorial scenes, and decorative friezes. At Pylos, decorative and figurative friezes are sometimes stacked in registers, one atop the next, in Egyptian fashion (e.g., the frescoes of Hall 64). Some compositions are so repetitive that they resemble modern wallpaper. Rare pigments include lapis lazuli (Gla, the Ayia Triada sarcophagus), the organic dye indigo (Thebes), and malachite (Shield Fresco, Tiryns) (Brysbaert and Vandenabeele 2004; Jones 2005, 216; Brysbaert 2006). Relief fresco disappears, but the Mycenaeans adopted their own "miniature" painting style with figures larger than those of Neopalatial miniature frescoes and even painted some frescoes in sepia, without color. Floor frescoes painted with grid patterns are known from the megarons of Mycenae, Tiryns, and Pylos (Hirsch 1977).

The pictorial programs of Mycenaean palaces are best preserved at Pylos, where the ritual focus of the main megaron frescoes is balanced by battle scenes in Hall 64. From Linear B evidence, it has been suggested that these chambers functioned as seats of authority for the *wanax* (king) and the *lawagetas* ("leader of the people," perhaps a military leader) (Killen 1994; Davis and Bennet 1999, 116). Recent investigations confirm a lack of evidence for the antithetical arrangement of lions and griffins about the Pylos throne, as suggested by Piet de Jong's widely reproduced drawing (McCallum 1987; Shank 2007), though lions and griffins are abundant in Hall 46.

Frescoes from the palace at Mycenae preserve martial themes with horses, chariots, and warriors. A fragmentary scene depicting a Mycenaean warrior falling before an Aegean city found in the megaron suggests epic inspiration, while the Boar Hunt Fresco from Tiryns depicts a favorite sport of the Mycenaean elite (figure 17.2). Women driving chariots, huntsmen leading hounds, and spearmen closing in for the kill all seem to proclaim the ability of the Mycenaean ruling class to protect the land and its people from the forces of chaos represented by the highly destructive and dangerous wild boar. Stylistically this fresco represents a Mycenaean interest in stylized abstraction at the expense of naturalism. The celebration of nature that characterized Neopalatial Minoan painting is gone. The discovery of a nearly identical boar hunt fresco from Orchomenos further suggests traveling workshops or the use of pattern books.

Religious imagery is preserved most frequently at Mycenae. In addition to the lovely "Mykenaia," for whom a divine identity has been suggested but not confirmed, there is the important and unique fresco composition from Room 31 (the Room of the Frescoes) that depicts three female figures and an altar painted with horns of consecration. Position and scale identify the two larger female figures as divinities, and each one is distinguished by costume and attribute (sword and staff). However, they lack identifying inscriptions and thus remain anonymous. Between them, two small and crudely painted figures with outstretched arms may represent souls or votaries. The third female figure raises sheaths of grain before the altar in an offertory gesture. Her mantled costume, plumed hat, and seal stone are distinctive, and she is smaller in scale than the presumed divinities. Beside her a guardian animal is preserved only by its yellow paws and

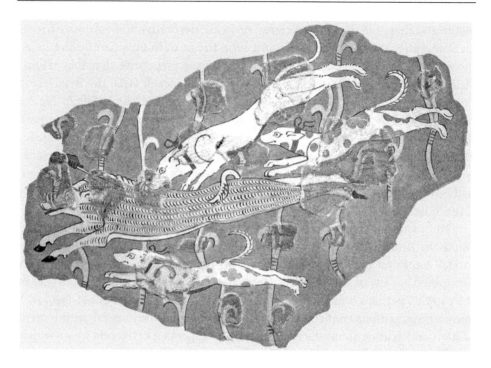

Figure 17.2. Boar Hunt Fresco from Tiryns. Mycenaean, LH IIIB (drawing by author after Rodenwaldt 1912, figure 55, pl. XIII).

tail—perhaps a griffin but more likely a lion. Both divine and priestly identities have been proposed for this female figure, but a consensus has yet to emerge (Marinatos 1988; Rehak 1992; Morgan 2005b). Another puzzling fresco fragment from Mycenae depicts a helmeted woman carrying a small griffin, perhaps a goddess or a priestess carrying a model.

Frescoes decorated many other Mycenaean buildings, including local seats of authority at Argos, Nichoria, and Sparta (the Menelaion), houses/workshops located outside the citadel at Mycenae, a potter's workshop at Zygouries, and storerooms, kitchens, and workshops at Gla (references in Blakolmer 2000, 401, 403). The Dolphin Fresco from Gla recalls the earlier Dolphin Fresco from Knossos and demonstrates an unexpected persistence of themes drawn from nature (Iakovidis 2001, 138–41). Frescoes also decorated tombs at Mycenae, Tiryns, Prosymna, Kokla (near Argos), and Thebes (references in Blakolmer 2000, 401).

However, fresco painting disappeared with the collapse of palatial society at the end of LH IIIB. A fragment of a woman with a lily found at Mycenae in LH IIIC contexts is likely LH IIIB in date, while a limestone stele stuccoed and painted with registers of warriors and deer in mid-LH IIIC marks the end of the fresco technique in the Bronze Age Aegean.

BIBLIOGRAPHY

Akrivaki, Natasa. 2003. "Τοιχογραφια μεΠαρασταση Οδοντοφρακτου Κρανους απο την Ξεστη 4 του Ακρωτηριου Θηρας," with English summary. In *ΑΡΓΟΝΑΥΤΗΣ: Τιμητικός Τόμος για τον Καθηγητή Χρίστο Γ. Ντούμα απο τους μαθητές του στο Πανεπιστήμιο Αθηνών (1980–2000)*, ed. Andreas Vlachopoulos and Kiki Birtacha, 527–41. Athens: H. Kathimerini.

Alberti, Benjamin. 2002. "Gender and the Figurative Art of Late Bronze Age Knossos." In *Labyrinth Revisited: Rethinking "Minoan" Archaeology*, ed. Yannis Hamilakis, 98–117. Oxford: Oxbow.

Betancourt, Philip P., Michael C. Nelson, and E. Hector Williams, eds. 2007. *Krinoi Kai Limenai.*

Bietak, Manfred, and Nannó Marinatos. 1995. "The Minoan Wall Paintings from Avaris." *Ägypten und Levante* 5: 49–62.

———, and Clairy Palyvou. 2007. *Taureador Scenes in Tell el-Dabʿa (Avaris) and Knossos.* Denkschriften der Gesamtakademie 43. Vienna: Verlag der Österreichischen Akademie der Wissenschaften.

Birtacha, Kiki, and Manolis Zacharioudakis. 2000. "Stereotypes in Theran Wall Paintings: Modules and Patterns in the Procedure of Painting." In *Wall Paintings of Thera*, 159–72.

Blakolmer, Fritz. 1997. "Minoan Wall-painting: The Transformation of a Craft into an Art Form." In *TEXNH*, 95–105.

———. 2000. "The Function of Wall Painting and Other Forms of Architectural Decoration in the Aegean Bronze Age." In *Wall Paintings of Thera*, 393–412.

Boulotis, Christos. 2000. "Travelling Fresco Painters in the Aegean Late Bronze Age: The Diffusion Patterns of a Prestigious Art." In *Wall Paintings of Thera*, 844–58.

Brysbaert, Ann. 2006. "Lapis Lazuli in an Enigmatic 'Purple' Pigment from a Thirteenth-century BC Greek Wall Painting." *Studies in Conservation* 51: 252–66.

———, and Peter Vandenabeele. 2004. "Bronze Age Painted Plaster in Mycenaean Greece: A Pilot Study on the Testing and Application of Micro-Raman Spectroscopy." *Journal of Raman Spectroscopy* 35: 686–93.

Cameron, Mark A. S. 1974. A General Study of Minoan Frescoes with Particular Reference to Unpublished Wall Paintings from Knossos. 4 vols. PhD diss., University of Newcastle upon Tyne.

Chapin, Anne P. 1997. "A Re-examination of the Floral Fresco from the Unexplored Mansion at Knossos." *BSA* 92: 1–24.

———. 2002. "Maidenhood and Marriage: The Reproductive Lives of the Girls and Women from Xeste 3, Thera." *Aegean Archaeology* 4 (1997–2000): 7–25.

———. 2004. "Power, Privilege, and Landscape in Minoan Art." In *ΧΑΡΙΣ*, 47–64.

———. 2007. "Boys Will Be Boys: Youth and Gender Identity in the Theran Frescoes." In *Constructions of Childhood in Ancient Greece and Italy*, ed. Ada Cohen and Jeremy Rutter, 229–55. *Hesperia* Suppl. 41. Princeton, N.J.: American School of Classical Studies.

Chrysikopoulou, Elisabeth. 2005. "Use of Murex Purple in the Wall-paintings at Akrotiri, Thera." *ΑΛΣ*3: 77–80.

Coulomb, Jean. 1979. "Le 'Prince aux Lis' de Knossos reconsidéré." *BCH* 103: 29–50.

Damiani-Indelicato, Silvia. 1988. "Were Cretan Girls Playing at Bull Leaping?" *Cretan Studies* 1: 39–47.

Davis, Ellen. 1986. "Youth and Age in the Thera Frescoes." *AJA* 90: 399–406.

————. 1990. "The Cycladic Style of the Thera Frescoes." In *TAW III*, 214–38.

————. 2007. "Brush Work." In *Krinoi Kai Limenai*, 145–50.

Davis, Jack L., and John Bennet. 1999. "Making Mycenaeans: Warfare, Territorial Expansion, and Representations of the Other in the Pylian Kingdom." In *Polemos*, 105–20.

Doumas, Christos. 1980. "Ανασκαφή Θήρας." *Praktika tes en Athenais Arkhaiologikes Hetaireias*: 289–96.

————. 1992. *The Wall-paintings of Thera*. Athens: Thera Foundation.

Evely, Doniert. 1999. *Fresco: A Passport into the Past: Minoan Crete through the Eyes of Mark Cameron*. Athens: British School at Athens, Goulandris Foundation, Museum of Cycladic Art.

Guralnick, Eleanor. 2000. "Proportions of Painted Figures from Thera." In *Wall Paintings of Thera*, 173–90.

Hardy, David A., Christos G. Doumas, Ioannis A. Sakellarakis, and Peter M. Warren, eds. 1990. *TAW III*.

Hiller, Stefan. 1990. "The Miniature Frieze in the West House: Evidence for Minoan Poetry?" In *TAW III*, 437–52.

Hirsch, Ethel. 1977. *Painted Decoration on the Floors of Bronze Age Structures in Crete and the Greek Mainland*. SIMA 53. Gothenburg: Åström.

Hood, Sinclair. 1978. *The Arts in Prehistoric Greece*. New York: Penguin.

————. 2005. "Dating the Knossos Frescoes." In *Aegean Wall Painting: A Tribute to Mark Cameron*, ed. Lyvia Morgan, 45–81. BSA Studies 13. London: British School at Athens.

Iakovidis, Spyros. 2001. *Gla and the Kopais in the 13th Century B.C.* Athens: Archaeological Society at Athens.

Immerwahr, Sara A. 1990. *Aegean Painting in the Bronze Age*. University Park: Pennsylvania State University Press.

Jones, R. E. 2005. "Technical Studies of Aegean Bronze Age Wall Painting: Methods, Results, and Future Prospects." In *Aegean Wall Painting: A Tribute to Mark Cameron*, ed. Lyvia Morgan, 199–228. BSA Studies 13. London: British School at Athens.

Kilian, Klaus. 1987. "L'architecture des résidences mycéniennes: Origine et extension d'une structure du pouvoir politique pendant l'âge du bronze récent." In *Le système palatial en Orient, en Grèce, et à Rome*, ed. Edmond Lévy, 203–17. Strasbourg: Université des Sciences Humaines de Strasbourg.

Killen, John T. 1994. "Thebes Sealings, Knossos Tablets, and Mycenaean State Banquets." *BICS* 39: 67–84.

Koehl, Robert. B. 1986a. "The Chieftain Cup and a Minoan Rite of Passage." *JHS* 106: 99–110.

————. 1986b. "A Marinescape Floor from the Palace at Knossos." *AJA* 90:4: 407–17.

Marinatos, Nannó. 1984. *Art and Religion in Thera: Reconstructing a Bronze Age Society*. Athens: Mathioulakis.

————. 1988. "The Fresco from Room 31 at Mycenae: Problems of Method and Interpretation." In *Problems in Greek Prehistory*, 245–51.

————. 1993. *Minoan Religion: Ritual, Image, and Symbol*. Columbia: University of South Carolina Press.

McCallum, Lucinda R. 1987. Decorative Program in the Mycenaean Palace of Pylos: The Megaron Frescoes. PhD diss., University of Pennsylvania.

Militello, Pietro. 1998. *Haghia Triada I: Gli affreschi*. Monografie della Scuola Archeologica di Atene e delle Missioni Italiane in Oriente 9. Padua: Bottega d'Erasmo.

————. 2001. *Gli Affreschi Minoici di Festòs*. Studi di Archeologia Cretese 2. Padua: Bottega d'Erasmo.

Morgan, Lyvia. 1988. *The Miniature Wall Paintings of Thera: A Study in Aegean Culture and Iconography*. New York: Cambridge University Press.

———. 1990. "Island Iconography: Thera, Kea, Milos." In *TAW III*, 252–66.

———. 1998. "The Wall Paintings of the North-east Bastion at Ayia Irini, Kea." In *Kea-Kynthos: History and Archaeology. Proceedings of an International Symposium, Kea-Kynthos, 22–25 June 1994*, ed. Lina G. Mendoni and Alexander J. Mazarakis AinianAinian J. Mazarakis, 201–10. Paris: Diffusion de Boccard.

———. 2000. "Form and Meaning in Figurative Painting." In *Wall Paintings of Thera*, 925–44.

———, ed. 2005a. *Aegean Wall Painting: A Tribute to Mark Cameron*. BSA Studies 13. London: British School at Athens.

———. 2005b. "The Cult Centre at Mycenae and the Duality of Life and Death." In *Aegean Wall Painting: A Tribute to Mark Cameron*, ed. Lyvia Morgan, 159–71. BSA Studies 13. London: British School at Athens.

Morris, Sarah. 1989. "A Tale of Two Cities: The Miniature Frescoes from Thera and the Origins of Greek Poetry." *AJA* 93: 511–35.

Müller, Kurt F. 1930. *Tiryns III: Die Architektur der Burg und des Palastes*. Augsburg: Filser.

Niemeier, Barbara, and Wolf-Dietrich Niemeier. 2000. "Aegean Frescoes in Syria-Palestine: Alalakh and Tel Kabri." In *Wall Paintings of Thera*, 763–802.

———. 2002. "The Frescoes in the Middle Bronze Age Palace." In *Tel Kabri: The 1986–1993 Excavation Seasons*, ed. Aharon Kempinski, Na'ama Scheftelowitz, and Ronit Oren, 254–98. Tel Aviv: Tel Aviv University.

Niemeier, Wolf-Dietrich. 1987. "Das Stuckrelief des 'Prinzen mit der Federkron' aus Knossos und minoische Götterdarstellungen." *AM* 102: 65–98.

Papaodysseus, Constantin, Dimitrios Fragoulis, Mihalis Panagopoulos, Thanasis Panagopoulos, Panayiotis Rousopoulos, Mihalis Exarhos, and Angelos Skembris. 2006a. "Determination of the Method of Construction of 1650 B.C. Wall Paintings." *IEEE Transactions on Pattern Analysis and Machine Intelligence* 28(9): 1361–71.

Papaodysseus, Constantin, Thanasis Panagopoulos, Mihalis Exarhos, Dimitrios Fragoulis, George Roussopoulos, Panayiotis Rousopoulos, Angelos G. Galanopoulos, Constantin Triantafillou, Andreas Vlachopoulos, and Christos Doumas. 2006b. "Distinct, Late Bronze Age (ca. 1650 BC) Wall-paintings from Akrotiri, Thera, Comprising Advanced Geometrical Patterns." *Archaeometry* 48(1): 97–114.

Peterson Murray, Suzanne. 2004. "Reconsidering the Room of the Ladies at Akrotiri." In ΧΑΡΙΣ, 101–30.

Pfälzner, Peter. 2008. "Between the Aegean and Syria: The Wall Paintings from the Royal Palace of Qatna." In *Fundstellen: Gesammelte Schriften zur Archäologie und Geschichte Altvorderasiens ad honorem Hartmut Kühne*, ed. Dominik Bonatz, Rainer M. Czichon, and F. Janoscha Kreppner, 95–118. Wiesbaden: Harrassowitz.

Rehak, Paul. 1992. "Tradition and Innovation in the Fresco from Room 31 in the 'Cult Center' at Mycenae." In *EIKON*, 39–62.

———. 1999. "The Aegean Landscape and the Body: A New Interpretation of the Thera Frescoes." In *From the Ground Up: Beyond Gender Theory in Archaeology. Proceedings of the Fifth Gender and Archaeology Conference, University of Wisconsin–Milwaukee, October 1998*, ed. Nancy L. Wicker and Bettina Arnold, 11–22. BAR-IS 812. Oxford: Archaeopress.

Rethemiotakis, Giorgos. 2002. "Evidence on Social and Economic Changes at Galatas and Pediada in the New-palace Period." In *Monuments of Minos*, 55–69.

Rodenwaldt, Gerhart. 1912. *Tiryns II: Die Fresken des Palastes*. 1976 reprint. Mainz: von Zabern.

Shank, Elizabeth. 2007. "Throne Room Griffins from Pylos and Knossos." In *Krinoi Kai Limenai*, 159–65.

Shaw, Joseph, and Maria C. Shaw. 2006. *Kommos V*.

Shaw, Maria C. 1996. "The Bull-leaping Fresco from below the Ramp House at Mycenae: A Study in Iconography and Artistic Transmission." *BSA* 91: 167–90.

———. 2004. "The "Priest-king" Fresco from Knossos: Man, Woman, Priest, King, or Someone Else?" In ΧΑΡΙΣ, 65–84.

———. 2005. "The Painted Pavilion of the 'Caravanserai' at Knossos." In *Aegean Wall Painting: A Tribute to Mark Cameron*, ed. Lyvia Morgan, 91–111. BSA Studies 13. London: British School at Athens.

Sherratt, Susan, ed. 2000. *Wall Paintings of Thera*.

Televantou, Christina. 1990. "New Light on the West House Wall-paintings." In *TAW III*, 309–23.

———. 1994. *Ακρωτήρι Θήρας: Οι Τοιχογραφίες της Δυτικής Οικίας*. Βιβλιοθήκη της εν Αθήναις Αρχαιολογικής Εταιρείας 143. Athens: Archaeological Society.

Vlachopoulos, Andreas. 2007. "*Disiecta Membra:* The Wall Paintings from the 'Porter's Lodge' at Akrotiri." In *Krinoi Kai Limenai*, 131–38.

———. 2008. "The Wall Paintings from the Xeste 3 Building at Akrotiri: Towards an Interpretation of the Iconographic Programme." In *Horizon*, 451–65.

Wace, Alan J. B. 1923. "Mycenae: Report on the Excavations of the British School at Athens 1921–1923." *BSA* 25. Athens: British School at Athens.

Walberg, Gisela. 1986. *Tradition and Innovation: Essays in Minoan Art*. Mainz: von Zabern.

Watrous, L. Vance. 2007. "The Fleet Fresco, the Odyssey and Greek Epic Narrative." In *EPOS*, 97–105.

Society and Culture

....

CHAPTER 18

STATE AND SOCIETY

....

DIMITRI NAKASSIS
MICHAEL L. GALATY
WILLIAM A. PARKINSON

STATES are notoriously difficult to define. Archaeologists usually describe them as complex, centralized institutions with administrative and social hierarchies that regulate access to resources and monopolize legitimate force within substantial territories. Some features typically associated with ancient states are settlement hierarchies of four tiers (with three levels of administrative decision-making), social stratification that divides the ruling elite from the nonelite, and a recognizable structure, or "palace," which serves as a base of operations for the ruling households (Marcus and Feinman 1998, 6–8).

AEGEAN STATE FORMATION
AND DEVELOPMENT

....

In the Aegean, states did not form until the beginning of the Middle Bronze Age at the earliest. We can define three general periods of state formation:

(1) the Protopalatial ("Old Palace") states of Minoan Crete, which date to ca. 1900–1725 BC (MM IB–MM II)

(2) the Neopalatial ("New Palace") states of Minoan Crete, which date to ca. 1725–1500 BC (MM III–LM IB)

(3) the Mycenaean states of the Greek mainland and Crete (at Knossos and Khania only), which date to ca. 1500–1200 BC (LM II–LM IIIB on Crete, LH IIIA1–LH IIIB2 on the Greek mainland).

The states of these three periods have a number of features in common. All of them are "secondary," meaning that they formed while in contact with well-developed, "primary" and secondary states elsewhere. Crete, for example, was certainly in contact with the older states of Egypt and the Near East before and after the emergence of the first palaces, although the relative importance of external contacts is still debated (Cherry in press). It is widely acknowledged, however, that contact with Neopalatial Crete (both directly and through interaction with the island societies of the Aegean) was crucial to the development of Mycenaean states on the Greek mainland. Both Minoan and Mycenaean states were relatively small, with territories of about 1500 km^2 and central settlements of 20–100 ha (figure 18.1). They coalesced and developed through processes of "peer polity" interaction (i.e., the exchange of goods and ideas, accompanied by competitive display and emulation) between similarly structured emergent state systems (Renfrew and Cherry 1986). Despite these similarities, however, processes of state formation followed radically different trajectories in Crete and on the Greek mainland, and the resulting states were quite different from each other.

One major axis of difference between Minoan (Protopalatial and Neopalatial) and Mycenaean states is that Minoan states pursued group-oriented, "corporate" strategies of political rule, whereas Mycenaean states pursued individualizing "network" strategies (Parkinson and Galaty 2007). Corporate political strategies typically emphasize and encourage group cohesion, deploy ideologies that value knowledge and ritual, and are financed through the production and redistribution of staple goods (Blanton et al. 1996). Network political strategies typically allow and promote individual rule and depend on systems of wealth finance (Feinman, Lightfoot, and Upham 2000). That Minoan and Mycenaean states pursued different strategies of political rule is reflected in different architectural plans found at Minoan and Mycenaean palaces.

Minoan palaces are designed around a large central court flanked by residential quarters, storage facilities, and ritual suites (for plans of Knossos, Malia, and Phaistos, see below, figures 40.1, 42.1, and 44.1). The central court is the main space around which palace traffic circulated, and various wings of the building were most easily (or only) accessible via the central court (Driessen 2002, 2004). Many Aegean prehistorians have accordingly advocated replacing the term "palace" with "court compound." while the palace at Knossos has a "throne room," its function appears to have been related more to ritual practices rather than political ones, and the throne itself is probably a later feature added during the Mycenaean period (Driessen 2002, 3). Other Minoan palaces do not have throne rooms, and an iconography of the ruler is missing from Minoan representational art until the very end of the Neopalatial period (Davis 1995), which is very typical of corporate states (Blanton et al. 1996).

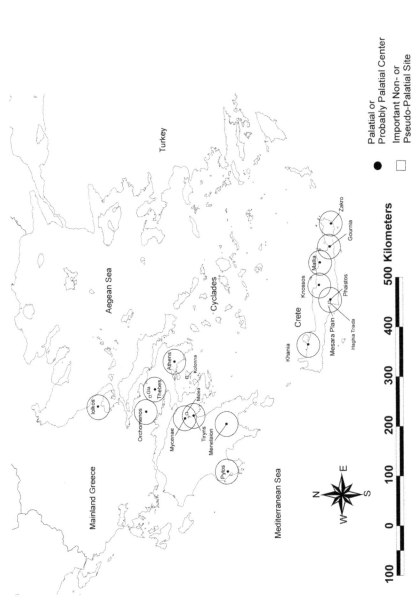

Figure 18.1. Map of state centers in the Aegean with hypothetical polity boundaries indicated as circles with diameters of fifty km. Palatial centers are marked by circles, and important non- or pseudopalatial centers by squares. The map of Crete is for the Neopalatial period, whereas the map of the mainland pertains to the late Mycenaean period (figure drawn by the authors).

Moreover, there is an absence of very wealthy burials in Protopalatial and Neopalatial Crete that we might call "royal," although there are major depositions of wealth within the palaces themselves. Recent work on Minoan palaces has, in fact, suggested that they were "communal, ceremonial centers that were used both by non-elite (outside) and by elite groups (inside) as meeting places for ritual, integrative actions" (Driessen 2002, 8). That the courts of the Minoan palaces were used for major communal rituals is indicated by two miniature frescoes found at Knossos, the Grandstand Fresco and the Sacred Grove Fresco.

The ritual role of Minoan palaces should not, however, diminish their administrative and economic roles, which were crucially important. Storage of agricultural staples was extensive in both Protopalatial and Neopalatial palaces (Christakis 2004, 2008), and the administrative texts of the Minoan palaces, while undeciphered, clearly monitor large amounts of foodstuffs alongside other valuable commodities and human labor (Palmer 1995). Even if these foodstuffs were ultimately destined for communal banqueting ceremonies, the economic impact of the Minoan palace cannot be ignored. It appears that Minoan economy and ritual were tightly integrated, not mutually exclusive, components of the larger, corporate state system (Day and Relaki 2002, 219–20).

Mycenaean palaces on the Greek mainland, on the other hand, are organized around a central "megaron" complex, which consists of a porch, an anteroom, and a large rectangular room with a central hearth bracketed by four columns and a throne regularly located to the right of the entrance (see figure 18.2). Flanking this megaron complex are small courts, storerooms, administrative quarters, and residential suites. Mycenaean architecture thereby emphasizes the importance of the enthroned king, whose title, as we know from the clay administrative tablets written in Linear B, was *wanax* (*wa-na-ka*).

Wealthy burials are an endemic feature of Mycenaean palatial societies and the communities that preceded them. At the palatial sites of Mycenae and Pylos, large corbeled "tholos" tombs are closely associated with the palace itself. These tombs have architectural precursors on the mainland in the form of Middle Bronze Age tumuli and on Crete in the form of large, circular tomb chambers (Rutter 1993, 789; Parkinson and Galaty 2007, 122). Mycenaean art, like Minoan art, lacks a clear iconography of the king himself; rather, the wall paintings of the palace act as a frame or focalizing device for the *wanax*, providing a 'first-person' (rather than 'third-person') iconography of power (Bennet 2007). As with the tholos tombs, the iconographic vocabulary of these artistic frames at Mycenaean palaces (e.g., heraldic lions/griffins, in-curved altars) is largely borrowed from the Minoan world.

In terms of political economy, Mycenaean palaces were interested in controlling the acquisition of exotic raw materials such as ivory, as well as their distribution as finished products (Burns 1999). Many of these goods are found deposited in rock-cut chamber tombs and corbeled tholos tombs, some of which are truly monumental (Cavanagh and Mee 1998). Palace-sponsored feasting (see articles in

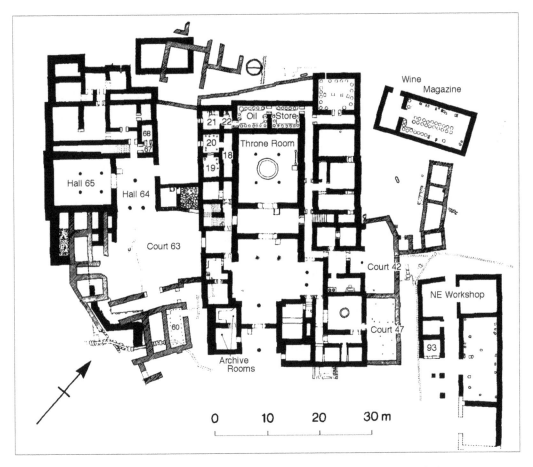

Figure 18.2. Plan of the palace at Pylos (courtesy of the Department of Classics,
University of Cincinnati).

Wright 2004) is a feature common to all Mycenaean centers and arguably was one
way for the palace to promote the centrality of the state, along with the individuals and corporate groups who contributed staples and material, in ritual practice.
These features can be associated with network (as opposed to corporate) strategies
that center on the individual and the control of prestige goods.

Despite the variation present within each type of Aegean state, the basic distinction between more corporate Minoan states and more networked Mycenaean states
can still be made, and these characterizations can be attributed to the processes of
their formation. The earliest Minoan states did not dominate the landscape to the
same degree as their Neopalatial and Mycenaean successors. As such, the first palaces were relatively simple, one-story structures that lacked the elaborate architectural features, such as ashlar masonry, associated with the palaces of the Neopalatial
period (Schoep 2004). On the contrary, these architectural elaborations are attested

in early houses and building complexes surrounding the palace at Malia. All of this suggests that the first Minoan palaces emerged as centers of communal ritual within a context of elite competition and emulation (Schoep 2006).

Mycenaean states, on the other hand, were preceded in the Middle Bronze Age by small communities organized around kin groups (Voutsaki in press). Elites in these small-scale societies were buried in sometimes grand fashion, with an emphasis on wealth, goods imported from the islands and elsewhere, the hunt, and warfare. These burials often contain one individual or a small number of individuals within a larger burial ground (a grave circle or tumulus) that may represent a kinship group larger than the nuclear family (Dickinson 1977, 41; Cavanagh and Mee 1998, 34).

With the growth of settlements at the start of the Late Bronze Age, however, the dominant burial form became the rock-cut chamber tomb in cemeteries that were carefully separated from settlement space. Although chamber tombs were typically reused over generations in contrast to the individualizing pit and cist graves of the early Mycenaean period, the burial group had shifted to the nuclear family. Thus, Wright (2008) argues that the chamber tomb represents promotion of the nuclear family as a political unit in Mycenaean society.

This emphasis on the nuclear family and most probably the individual head of this household was a stable feature of Mycenaean palatial society and found its most grandiose expression in the transformation of the standard Middle Bronze Age longhouse into the monumental throne room of Mycenaean palaces, the megaron with its central circular hearth (Kilian 1985, 1988; Wright 1994, 2006). As Kilian has put it, "the Mycenaean palace can be seen as a vast embodiment of personal propaganda" (Kilian 1988, 299).

AEGEAN STATE ECONOMY AND SOCIETY

The economic function of the Aegean states is now understood in more nuanced ways than was the case previously. Earlier work on Minoan and Mycenaean states envisioned the palaces as classic, Near Eastern–style redistributive centers that dominated the production, storage, and regional distribution of agricultural staples and wealth items (Renfrew 1972; Branigan 1987). However, this picture was largely the product of work on economy based on the Mycenaean Linear B texts (e.g., Killen 1985), which then was projected backward onto earlier, developing states and outward onto states that lacked such evidence on both Crete and the mainland. However, recent work on the Mycenaean states themselves argues that palatial control was far more selective than has been hitherto appreciated and emphasizes the need to examine areas outside of palatial control (Halstead 1992; Galaty and Parkinson 2007a, 2007b).

It now appears that the redistributive model does not apply to Mycenaean states, whose economies depended on mobilization (not, strictly speaking, redistribution)—by which we mean that surpluses were collected primarily in order to finance the operations of the state (Halstead 2007). Moreover, their control over resources may have been highly selective in spatial terms and in terms of how different industries were managed. For example, perfumed oil and bronze production were directly monitored by the palace (Shelmerdine 1984), but the production of ceramics was only indirectly monitored (Galaty 1999, 2007, in press), and most aspects of chipped stone production were not controlled at all (Parkinson 2007). We have argued elsewhere on the basis of the textual and archaeological evidence that the Mycenaean palace at Pylos supported a "prestige economy" that operated through the distribution of both staples and wealth (Galaty and Parkinson 2007a, 2007b; Nakassis in press).

The Minoan palatial economy is also seen in a different light, especially since its redistributive role was previously inferred on the basis of the interpretation of the later Mycenaean evidence. Research has suggested that the Minoan palaces were, like their Mycenaean counterparts, largely consumers rather than producers of some palatial goods. The finely made ceramics of Protopalatial Crete, Kamares ware, whose production was previously believed to have taken place in palatial workshops, has been shown to be the product of specialized pottery workshops that were in operation prior to the emergence of the palaces (Day and Wilson 1998). Kamares ware was imported to Knossos, the largest of the Minoan centers, from the central Mesara Plain rather than being produced exclusively by palace-controlled workshops. So, although this high-quality, display-oriented good was largely consumed at palatial centers, its production was probably not managed by them.

This decentralized picture of the economic role of Minoan and Mycenaean states has led to new models of their formation and reproduction. Minoan states have been increasingly studied not as a concrete objects with static systems of hierarchy but through the lens of heterarchy (*Monuments of Minos*; Schoep and Knappett 2004), which in the context of political complexity means that given social units (such as corporate groups) are unranked with respect to each other or can be ranked in different ways depending on context (Crumley 1995).

Some have argued that it may be fruitful to think of the Minoan state (especially in the Protopalatial period) not as a unified territorial entity largely controlled by the palace but as composed of several corporate groups or "houses" (Driessen in press) in competition with each other. Thus, the state appears as an emergent property that results from and is reproduced by elite competition and emulation (not unlike recent studies of the Greek polis [Osborne 1996, 187–97] or state formation in the New World [Brumfiel and Fox 1994]).

Schoep (2004), for example, has shown that the features typically associated with Minoan palaces (architectural and otherwise) appear for the first time not in the palaces themselves but rather in houses and other architectural complexes located in the towns surrounding them. She therefore argues that the main social forces of Protopalatial Crete were not the palaces but elites at large. These individuals and households were consumers of exotic goods imported from Egypt and the Near East (Schoep 2006). Consequently, the emergence of the palace as an institution needs to be seen in its larger systemic context as a product of social forces outside of its purview and control. A further result of this is that each palace needs to be examined separately since each was enmeshed in different social and historical environments (Day and Relaki 2002, 221).

Schoep's model applies primarily to the Protopalatial period. In the later Neopalatial period of Minoan Crete, palaces are much larger, ornate buildings with extensive storage capacities (Christakis 2004, 2008), the hinterlands of which reflect political expansion and settlement hierarchies (Haggis 2002). It therefore seems likely that authority was more concentrated in this period (Dabney and Wright 1990). Palmer's careful study (1995) has shown that the quantities of agricultural goods from the Neopalatial Linear A texts found at Haghia Triada are comparable to entries from Mycenaean Knossos, suggesting that the scale of administration was similar to that of later Mycenaean states.

On the other hand, Neopalatial Crete is far from a static period or homogenous entity (Driessen and Macdonald 1997; Macdonald 2002). The administrative center at Haghia Triada just mentioned, for example, is physically separate from the court-centered palace at Phaistos, which does not seem to have a significant administrative role in LM I. This situation seems incompatible with a model in which the elite resident in the palace exerted strict control over the hinterland and suggests instead that groups outside the palace were important to the maintenance and reproduction of the Neopalatial state.

Similar research trends have affected the study of Mycenaean states. As noted earlier, recent work has challenged the traditional picture of the palace as the center of a classic redistributive system that dominated the economic and public affairs of the polity as a whole. In terms of its internal structure, Mycenaean states are usually modeled as static bureaucracies occupied by impersonal offices and controlled by the wanax (on these offices, see Shelmerdine 2008).

Based on a prosopographical study of the Linear B texts at Pylos, however, Nakassis (2006) has argued that a large number of individuals identified primarily by personal name in the administrative texts of the palace were agents to whom important economic activities were assigned by the palatial administration. Previous work had distinguished quite sharply between elite office holders and nonelite peasants and dependent labor (Chadwick 1976, 77), but named individuals appear to constitute a class of administrators ranging from relatively low-level laborers to high-status "collectors" who were intimately involved in the highest levels of palatial administration.

Thus, the state at Pylos can be understood as the product of interaction among a network of elites with substantial nonpalatial interests in addition to their roles as administrators. The activities of these elites actively reproduced the palatial system and at the same time were simultaneously constrained by preexisting institutional systems of production, remuneration, taxation, and so on. Thus, the Mycenaean state can be seen, in general, as the direct result of elite participation in the palatial system and was likely the central arena for elite competition (cf. Blanton 1998).

CONCLUSION

Recent models of Minoan and Mycenaean states emphasize three major points. First, there is no such thing as *the* Minoan or Mycenaean state; rather, there is evidence for similarity and difference between individual polities. Consequently, each polity needs to be studied individually in order to observe this variability and to explain it. Second, the state cannot be studied as a freestanding entity in splendid isolation from society at large, particularly since state boundaries are not easily drawn even in modern societies (Mitchell 1999). The third point, closely related to the second, is that the internal operation of the state is not simple but is the product of dynamic interaction between individuals, social groups, and institutional structures.

The dual-processual approach, which points out that early states used different methods of political unification distributed along a continuum between corporate and network strategies, allows us to draw basic distinctions between Minoan and Mycenaean states. Minoan states, with their strategies of inclusion, present us with larger corporate groups that participated in a palatial system focused on unification through large-scale rituals. Mycenaean states, on the other hand, were focused on individual aggrandizement, the acquisition of material wealth through participation in the palatial system, and its display through sponsorship of feasts and wealth deposited with the dead in sometimes monumental graves. The differences between these different states are the result of their local historical trajectories and the processes by which they developed in interaction with other, closely and distantly related, societies.

BIBLIOGRAPHY

Bennet, John. 2007. "Representations of Power in Mycenaean Pylos: Script, Orality, Iconography." In *ΣΤΕΦΑΝΟΣ ΑΡΙΣΤΕΙΟΣ: Archäologische Forschungen zwischen Nil und Istros. Festschrift für Stefan Hiller zum 65. Geburtstag*, ed. Felix Lang, Claus Reinholdt, and Jörg Weilhartner, 11–22. Vienna: Phoibos.

Blanton, Richard E. 1998. "Beyond Centralization: Steps toward a Theory of Egalitarian Behavior in Archaic States." In *Archaic States*, ed. Gary M. Feinman and Joyce Marcus, 135–72. Santa Fe: School for American Research Press.

———, Gary M. Feinman, Stephen A. Kowalewski, and Peter N. Peregrine. 1996. "A Dual-processual Theory for the Evolution of Mesoamerican Civilization." *Current Anthropology* 37: 1–14.

Branigan, Keith. 1987. "The Economic Role of the First Palaces." In *Function of the Minoan Palaces*, 245–49.

Brumfiel, Elizabeth M., and John W. Fox, eds. 1994. *Factional Competition and Political Development in the New World*. New York: Cambridge University Press.

Burns, Bryan E. 1999. Import Consumption in the Bronze Age Argolid (Greece): Effects of Mediterranean Trade on Mycenaean Society. PhD diss., University of Michigan.

Cavanagh, William, and Christopher Mee. 1998. *A Private Place: Death in Prehistoric Greece.* SIMA 125. Jonsered, Sweden: Åström.

Chadwick, John. 1976. *The Mycenaean World.* New York: Cambridge University Press.

Cherry, John F. In press. "Sorting Out Crete's Prepalatial Interactions." In *Archaic State Interaction: The Eastern Mediterranean in the Bronze Age,* ed. William Parkinson and Michael Galaty. Santa Fe: School for Advanced Research.

Christakis, Kostandinos S. 2004. "Palatial Economy and Storage in Late Bronze Age Knossos." In *Knossos,* 299–309.

———. 2008. *The Politics of Storage: Storage and Sociopolitical Complexity in Neopalatial Crete.* Philadelphia: INSTAP Academic Press.

Crumley, Carole L. 1995. "Heterarchy and the Analysis of Complex Societies." In *Heterarchy and the Analysis of Complex Societies,* ed. Robert M. Ehrenreich, Carole L. Crumley, and Janet E. Levy, 2–5. Archeological Papers of the American Anthropological Association 6. Arlington: American Anthropological Association.

Dabney, Mary K., and James C. Wright. 1990. "Mortuary Customs, Palatial Society, and State Formation in the Aegean Area: A Comparative Study." In *Celebrations of Death,* 45–53.

Davis, Ellen N. 1995. "Art and Politics in the Aegean: The Missing Ruler." In *Role of the Ruler,* 11–12.

Day, Peter M., and Maria Relaki. 2002. "Past Factions and Present Fictions: Palaces in the Study of Minoan Crete." In *Monuments of Minos,* 217–34.

Day, Peter M., and David E. Wilson. 1998. "Consuming Power: Kamares Ware in Protopalatial Knossos." *Antiquity* 72: 350–58.

Dickinson, Oliver T. P. K. 1977. *Origins of Mycenaean Civilisation.* Studies in Mycenaean Archaeology 49. Gothenburg: Åström.

Driessen, Jan. 2002. " 'The King Must Die.' Some Observations on the Use of Minoan Court Compounds." In *Monuments of Minos,* 1–13.

———. 2004. "The Central Court of the Palace at Knossos." In *Knossos,* 75–82.

———. In press. "Spirit of Place: Minoan Houses as Major Actors." In *Political Economies of the Aegean Bronze Age,* ed. Daniel J. Pullen. Oxford: Oxbow.

———, and Colin Macdonald. 1997. *The Troubled Island: Minoan Crete before and after the Santorini Eruption.* Aegaeum 17. Liège: Université de Liège.

Feinman, Gary, Kent Lightfoot, and Steadman Upham. 2000. "Political Hierarchies and Organizational Strategies in the Puebloan Southwest." *American Antiquity* 65(3): 449–70.

Galaty, Michael L. 1999. *Nestor's Wine Cups: Investigating Ceramic Manufacture and Exchange in a Late Bronze Age 'Mycenaean' State.* BAR-IS 766. Oxford: British Archaeological Reports.

———. 2007. "Wealth Ceramics, Staple Ceramics: Pots and the Mycenaean Palaces." In *RMP II,* 74–86.

———. In press. "Wedging Clay: Combining Competing Models of Mycenaean Pottery Industries." In *Political Economies of the Aegean Bronze Age,* ed. Daniel J. Pullen. Oxford: Oxbow.

———, and William A. Parkinson. 2007a. "Introduction: Mycenaean Palaces Rethought." In *RMP II,* 1–17.

———. 2007b. "Introduction: Putting Mycenaean Palaces in Their Place." In *RMP II,* 21–28.

Haggis, Donald. 2002. "Integration and Complexity in the Late Pre-palatial Period: A View from the Countryside in Eastern Crete." In *Labyrinth Revisited: Rethinking 'Minoan' Archaeology,* ed. Yiannis Hamilakis, 120–42. Oxford: Oxbow.

Halstead, Paul. 1992. "The Mycenaean Palatial Economy: Making the Most of the Gaps in the Evidence." *Proceedings of the Cambridge Philological Society* 38: 57–86.

———. 2007. "Toward a Model of Mycenaean Palatial Mobilization." In *RMP II*, 66–73.

Kilian, Klaus. 1985. "L'Architecture des residences mycénienne: Origine et extension d'une structure du pouvoir politique pendant l'âge du Bronze recent." In *Le système palatial en Orient, en Grèce et à Rome*, ed. Edmond Lévy, 203–17. Leiden: Brill.

———. 1988. "The Emergence of *Wanax* Ideology in the Mycenaean Palaces." *OJA* 7(3): 291–302.

Killen, John T. 1985. "The Linear B Tablets and the Mycenaean Economy." In *Linear B: A 1984 Survey. Mycenaean Colloquium of the VIII Congress of the International Federation of the Societies of Classical Studies*, ed. Anna Morpurgo Davies and Yves Duhoux, 241–305. Bibliothèque des Cahiers de l'Institut de Linguistique de Louvain 26. Louvain-la-Neuve, Belgium: Cabay.

Macdonald, Colin F. 2002. "The Neopalatial Palaces of Knossos." In *Monuments of Minos*, 35–54.

Marcus, Joyce, and Gary M. Feinman. 1998. "Introduction." In *Archaic States*, ed. Gary M. Feinman and Joyce Marcus, 3–13. Santa Fe: School for American Research Press.

Mitchell, Timothy. 1999. "Society, Economy, and the State Effect." In *State/Culture: State Formation after the Cultural Turn*, ed. George Steinmetz, 76–97. Ithaca: Cornell University Press.

Nakassis, Dimitri. 2006. The Individual and the Mycenaean State: Agency and Prosopography in the Linear B Texts from Pylos. PhD diss., University of Texas at Austin.

———. In press. "Reevaluating Staple and Wealth Finance at Mycenaean Pylos." In *Political Economies of the Aegean Bronze Age*, ed. Daniel J. Pullen. Oxford: Oxbow.

Osborne, Robin. 1996. *Greece in the Making: 1200–479 BC*. New York: Routledge.

Palmer, Ruth. 1995. "Linear A Commodities: A Comparison of Resources." In *Politeia*, 133–55.

Parkinson, William A. 2007. "Chipping Away at a Mycenaean Economy: Obsidian Exchange, Linear B, and 'Palatial Control' in Late Bronze Age Messenia." In *RMP II*, 87–101.

———, and Michael L. Galaty. 2007. "Secondary States in Perspective: An Integrated Approach to State Formation in the Prehistoric Aegean." *American Anthropologist* 109(1): 113–29.

Renfrew, Colin. 1972. *The Emergence of Civilisation: The Cyclades and the Aegean in the Third Millennium B.C.* London: Methuen.

———, and John F. Cherry, eds. 1986. *Peer Polity Interaction and Socio-political Change*. New York: Cambridge University Press.

Rutter, Jeremy B. 1993. "Review of Aegean Prehistory II: The Prepalatial Bronze Age of the Southern and Central Greek Mainland." *AJA* 97: 745–97.

Schoep, Ilse. 2004. "Assessing the Role of Architecture in Conspicuous Consumption in the Middle Minoan I–II Period." *OJA* 23(3): 243–69.

———. 2006. "Looking beyond the First Palaces: Elites and the Agency of Power in EM II–MM II Crete." *AJA* 110: 37–64.

———, and Carl Knappett. 2004. "Dual Emergence: Evolving Heterarchy, Exploding Hierarchy." In *Emergence of Civilisation Revisited*, 21–37.

Shelmerdine, Cynthia W. 1984. *The Perfume Industry of Mycenaean Pylos*. SIMA-PB 34. Gothenburg: Åström.

———. 2008. "Mycenaean Society." In *A Companion to Linear B: Mycenaean Greek Texts and their World. Volume 1*, ed. Yves Duhoux and Anna Morpurgo Davies, 115–58. Dudley, Mass.: Peeters.

Voutsaki, Sophia. In press. "From Kinship Economy to Prestige Economy." In *Political Economies of the Aegean Bronze Age*, ed. Daniel J. Pullen. Oxford: Oxbow.

Wright, James C. 1994. "The Spatial Configuration of Belief: The Archaeology of Mycenaean Religion." In *Placing the Gods: Sanctuaries and Sacred Space in Ancient Greece*, ed. Susan Alcock and Robin Osborne, 37–78. Oxford: Clarendon.

———, ed. 2004. *The Mycenaean Feast. Hesperia* 73(2). Princeton: American School of Classical Studies at Athens.

———. 2006. "The Formation of the Mycenaean Palace." In *Ancient Greece: From the Mycenaean Palaces to the Age of Homer*, ed. Sigrid Deger-Jalkotzy and Irene S. Lemos, 7–52. Edinburgh Leventis Studies 3. Edinburgh: Edinburgh University Press.

———. 2008. "Chamber Tombs, Family, and State in Mycenaean Greece." In *DIOSKOUROI: Studies Presented to W. G. Cavanagh and C. B. Mee on the Anniversary of their 30-year Join Contribution to Aegean Archaeology*, BAR-IS 1889, ed. Chrysanthi Gallou, Mercouris Georgiadis, and Gina M. Muskett, 144–153. Oxford: Archaeopress.

CHAPTER 19

MINOAN RELIGION

SUSAN LUPACK

THE FOUNDATIONS OF MINOAN RELIGION

Minoan religion appears to have had its foundations in rituals associated with funerary rites. Starting in the EM I period, the Minoans of south central Crete built tholos tombs, and in the EM II period, rectangular house tombs appeared in north central and east Crete (Branigan 1970, 1988; Soles 1992). In the EM II period, rooms located either within the tombs or before their entrances were used for ritual activities that were not associated with rites performed for the dead. Several sites had niches, altars, bench shrines, and paved courtyards.

The fact that the rituals performed at the tombs were being taken beyond simple funerary rites is indicated by some of their finds (Branigan 1998, 22; Soles 1992, 226–36), which included offering tables, triton shells, clay phalli, cups with molded breasts, anthropomorphic and zoomorphic figurines and rhyta, some in the form of bulls, and bronze double axes. Branigan (1993, 133) suggests that bulls and perhaps bull sacrifices were part of the ceremonies. Certainly the cult was concerned with human fertility and the seasonal cycle. A series of female figurines who either carried a vessel or whose breasts were pierced so that they could function as rhyta supports the idea that fertility was a major concern of early Minoan cult. One figurine from Koumasa, ca. 2000 BC, has a snake wound around her shoulders and may be an early Snake Goddess (Gesell 1983). These figurines were found not only in the tombs but also in caves and at the settlement shrine of Myrtos (Warren 1972).

Peak Sanctuaries

The shrines situated on mountains, called peak sanctuaries, are a distinctive feature of Minoan religion. Peak sanctuaries were not always located on the highest point of a mountain. Rather, as Peatfield (1983, 275) points out, it was more important "that the sanctuary should be seen from the region it served, and also that it should 'see' that region." Thus, peak sanctuaries were "topographic and religious focal points for groups of settlements" (Peatfield 1987, 90).

The peak sanctuary of Knossos on Mount Jouktas dates to the EM II period (Karetsou 1981, 1987), but generally they appear in the EM III/MM I periods and flourish throughout the Protopalatial period, at which time there were approximately twenty-five sites (Peatfield 1994a). In the Neopalatial period that number is reduced to a mere eight.

The most common finds are clay figurines, which appear in the form of animals, human votaries (who "seem to memorialise the action of peak sanctuary ritual itself" Peatfield [1994b]), and parts of the human body, such as feet, eyes, and genitalia. These votives reflect the concerns of the worshippers—their own fertility and well-being and that of their animals. Richer peak sanctuaries have stone vessels, Linear A inscriptions, jewelry, seals, bronze blades, figurines, and double axes. The more costly finds were found at a limited number of sites and generally date to the Neopalatial period. The ritual focus of the shrine may consist of a flat rock, a cairn of stones, and/or (Nowicki 1994) concentrations of white pebbles. Actual architectural remains appear at only nine sites, eight of which were those that continued into the Neopalatial period (Peatfield 1994a). Jouktas is exceptional in that it had a built altar, three terraces, and a multiroomed cult building.

The inspiration for the foundation of the peak sanctuaries has been debated. Rutkowski (1972, 185) says that the "peak sanctuaries came into existence mainly to relieve the fears and cares of the shepherds and cattle breeders." Peatfield (1983) agrees, pointing to the vast numbers of domestic farm animal figurines. Cherry (1978, 1986) has proposed that the peak sanctuaries were established by the emerging elite of the palaces to support their newly founded control over Minoan society, while Watrous (1987, 1995) has proposed that the establishment of the peak sanctuaries was part of a larger cultural change that was influenced by the Near Eastern and Egyptian cultures.

Peatfield, who sees peak sanctuaries as having developed naturally from tomb cult, believes that Watrous has overplayed the Eastern influence and discounts Cherry's specific proposal because it is now recognized that no chronological link exists between the emergence of the elite and the first appearance of the peak sanctuaries. Nonetheless, Peatfield (1990, 130) and Kyriakidis (2005, 124–27) believe that the palatial elite of the Neopalatial period appropriated the already established cult of the peak sanctuaries to "maintain its hierarchical position" by taking on the "social prestige" associated with the Mountain Goddess. Evidence for this can be seen in the fact that iconographic references to peak sanctuaries, such as the

Figure 19.1. The "Mother of the Mountains" seal impression from Knossos. The goddess, flanked by two lions, stands atop a mountain and holds a staff in a commanding gesture. A shrine with horns of consecration appears at the left, and a male adorant is on the right (courtesy of Ingo Pini, *CMS*).

Knossos 'Mother of the Mountains' impression (figure 19.1) and the Zakros Peak Sanctuary stone rhyton, are found only in the Neopalatial palaces.

In addition, the peak sanctuaries that were in use during the Neopalatial period not only had built structures and palatially manufactured goods but were also associated with palatial and urban centers, while those that served smaller settlements fell out of use. A reflection of the palatial appropriation of the cult may be seen in the Procession fresco at the West entrance of Knossos, which Cameron (1987, 324) argues represents a ritual in which a "goddess-impersonator would have arrived and been welcomed into the Palace," presumably from the peak sanctuary of Jouktas.

Cave Sanctuaries

Cave sanctuaries were also a prominent type of cult site in Minoan religion. The appearance of the first sacred cave (on Mount Ida) is contemporaneous with that of the first peak sanctuaries, and, like the peak sanctuaries, the caves were generally visible from a nearby settlement (Tyree 1994, 2006).

The main ritual areas in Proto- and Neopalatial times were deep within the cave; hence, getting to them could be "an intense sensory experience" (Tyree 1994, 41). Stalagmites were often used to mark the most important area of the cave, and in some cases, the stalagmites themselves were marked, as at Psychro, where double axes were inserted into them. The pouring of libations (e.g., at Kamares) and drinking rituals (e.g., at Psychro, Amnisos, and Skotino) were part of the rites performed in the caves. Evidence of feasting is also attested at a few caves. Marinatos (1993, 124) proposes that an agricultural festival was celebrated in Kamares cave because of the heap of grain that was found within it. Male and female bronze figurines constitute one of the most common finds from the caves, which may indicate that the elite played a key role in the rituals performed there.

Tyree (1994) proposes that ecstatic trances may have been one of the religious experiences associated with the caves. She points out that the caves, with their "potential for repetitive sound and light effects," would have been conducive to such altered states of consciousness. The goal of such a trance may have been to achieve a visionary experience involving the epiphany of the deity, an important element of Minoan religion (Hägg 1983).

Town and Palace Cult:
The Pre- and Protopalatial Periods

Cult areas in settlements did not become common until the Protopalatial period. The only sanctuary found in association with a settlement in the EM period (specifically, EM II) is the one found at Myrtos (Warren 1972). This sanctuary shared walls with the settlement's single building complex of ninety-three rooms, but access to the shrine rooms was from the courtyard. The westernmost room of the complex, room 92, was designated as the shrine proper because within it was found a terracotta goddess figurine holding a vessel, which must have fallen from the room's stone bench altar. Room 91, with its sixty-six predominantly fineware vessels, seems to have been the shrine's storeroom. Against the east wall of Room 89 was what Warren describes as "a tripartite structure consisting of two little, low benches or tables with a hearth between them" (Warren 1972, 81). The fragments of a skull from a young adult male were uncovered in this room, causing Warren to comment that "ancestor worship, or even human sacrifice cannot be ruled out" (Warren 1972, 83). In room 90, evidence was found for the preparation of wine.

The "Bench Shrine" type of cult site first seen at Myrtos, with its main shrine room accompanied by various storerooms and preparation rooms, becomes a common pattern for cult sites in the following Protopalatial and Neopalatial periods. There is limited evidence for the Protopalatial period, but the examples that are extant fit this pattern. Gesell (1985, 9; 1987, 124) cites the MM II Bench Sanctuary of Malia as an early example with its shrine room, anteroom, and storeroom. Also, it was common for bench shrines of the time to be accessible both from within the building and from their exterior courtyards, showing that they were meant to serve both the elite and the public (Gesell 1987, 125). This pattern continues into the Neopalatial period.

Among the finds uncovered in these shrines were early examples of the symbols and cult equipment that are characteristic of Minoan religion: double axes, horns of consecration, bulls, birds, triton shells, animal figurines, fixed and moveable offering tables (some covered with red glaze), and libation tables. The goddess herself is attested only in the decoration found on a bowl and a fruit stand found in the Lower West Court Sanctuary Complex of Phaistos, both of which depict a female figure surrounded by dancers (Gesell 1985, 17). The first has loops running down her robe and is therefore interpreted as a "Snake Goddess," while the figure on the fruit stand holds flowers in her upraised arms and has been dubbed the 'Goddess of the Lilies' (Gesell 1983).

TOWN AND PALACE CULT: THE NEOPALATIAL PERIOD

The Palace

Scholars have long debated the religious nature of the monumental Minoan buildings traditionally called "palaces." Rutkowski (1986, 229), on one end of the spectrum, sees the palace as a purely secular building and therefore claims that urban shrines were not important in Minoan Crete. Marinatos (1993, 39–40), on the other hand, states that "what have been termed 'palaces' are, in reality…primarily cult centers, although they had important administrative and economic functions as well." It seems that Gesell (1987, 126) hits the right note when she says, "it is clear that the Minoan palace was the center of cult in the Minoan town." Religion definitely played a significant part in determining the layout of the palaces' West Wings, which held a variety of cult rooms and storerooms.

The Throne Room

The pithos and several alabastra that were found within the throne room at Knossos show that it was used for religious ceremonies: A ceremony involving anointment with unguents must have been about to take place there just before the palace was destroyed (Hägg 1988). Also, the frescoes flanking the throne depicting griffins and palm trees connect the occupant of the throne with the divine realm. However, the question that has troubled scholars is this: Precisely who sat on the throne?

Traditionally, the occupant of the throne was assumed to be the male ruler of Knossos. However, recently several scholars have taken the view that the more likely occupant was the high priestess playing the part of the Goddess in an epiphany ritual. Niemeier (1987) and Cameron (1987) maintain that the shape of the throne resembles the rock upon which the goddess stands in the "Mother of the Mountains" impression. This may then be another indication that the cult of the peak sanctuaries was transferred to the palaces.

Tripartite Shrine

Tripartite shrines are known mostly from their artistic representations (Gesell 1985, 29; Shaw 1978). Their façades have three sections, the middle of which is built higher than the two wings. Each had at least one column, and horns of consecration were placed on their roofs.

Tripartite shrines have been restored at Vathypetro and most famously in the center of the façade of the West Wing at Knossos. This latter restoration was modeled after the Grandstand Fresco, which shows a tripartite shrine in its center. It is thought that the high priestess as the goddess would appear to the crowds in the space between the columns during epiphany rituals.

The Central and Western Courts

The Central Courts of Knossos, Phaistos, and Malia are remarkably similar in size (ca. 24 x 52 m), while that of Zakros is smaller (ca. 12 x 29 m). All are laid out north to south and had cult rooms on their western sides. Several scholars have proposed that the bull-leaping festivals that are so often depicted at Knossos were actually held in the Central Courts. It seems unlikely, however, that this was the case because the paving stones would have proved hazardous to both the running bulls and the leapers (Younger 1995). Marinatos (1993) also maintains that holding the festival in the Central Court, where the number of spectators would have been restricted since the courtyard would have been given over to the bull leaping, makes no sense for an event that the whole community would want or need to see. An area with a soft, earthen floor would be more suitable for bull-leaping ceremonies. Nonetheless, the altars found in the Central Courts at Phaistos, Malia, and Gournia, in addition to the "Grandstand Fresco," which may represent the Central Court (Davis 1987), demonstrate that rituals were held there; perhaps it was the actual sacrifice of the bull, as the finale of the bull-leaping ceremony, that was performed within them.

The more public nature of the rituals held in the West Courts, which were open to the towns surrounding the palaces (while access to the Central Court could be restricted), has been emphasized by Gesell (1987), Marinatos (1987), and Hägg (1987). Hägg (1987) reconstructs the west façade of the Neopalatial palace at Knossos as a monumental tripartite structure, reminiscent of the one in the "Grandstand Fresco," and proposes that it had a "window of appearance" in which an epiphany ritual could be viewed by people gathered below. The existence of a sanctuary on the upper floor is indicated by fresco fragments that depict architectural façades with columns, double axes, and horns of consecration.

The Sacred Grove Fresco, with its raised walkways that are reminiscent of those found in the West Court, most likely depicts a festival held in that court. Marinatos (1987), citing the underground granaries found in the West Courts of Knossos, Phaistos, and Malia, has proposed that it was a harvest festival that was being celebrated. She also believes that the Minoans would have continued to celebrate the harvest in the West Court despite the eventual filling in of the granaries at Knossos and Phaistos and that an offering or tribute of grain to a palatial official (the high priestess/goddess?) was a key element of the Neopalatial festival.

Lustral Basins and Pillar Crypts

Minoan religious practice gave rise to two very distinctive types of cult rooms, the lustral basin and the pillar crypt, both of which appear in the Protopalatial period but take on their canonical form in the Neopalatial period. The lustral basin (so named by Evans because of the unguent flasks found in one) consisted of a room with a sunken floor that was lined with gypsum, plaster, or cement and was reached via an L-shaped or dogleg staircase. The walls above the lining were plastered and sometimes decorated with frescoes. Lustral basins were clearly very popular since they have been found in all of the palaces (Knossos had at least three, while Phaistos had five) and most of the villas.

The ritual use of many lustral basins is clear from the material remains found within them. For instance, one of the Phaistos lustral basins (room 63d) contained a bull's head rhyton, a piriform rhyton, two horns of consecration, and bronze double axes. Moreover, frescoes with religious themes have been found in and around lustral basins, including horns of consecration on top of altars at Zakros (Platon 1971, 182). In Xeste 3 at Akrotiri, a horns of consecration with blood dripping down it was painted within the lustral basin, while the fresco program in the surrounding room reflects an initiation ritual (Marinatos 1984, 73–84).

Despite the various indications of the religious nature of the lustral basin, several (particularly those found in residential areas) lack any sure signs of cult usage, which has caused some scholars, such as Graham (1987, 99–108) and Platon (1971, 183), to propose that they were sometimes used for cult practice, but primarily as bathrooms. One problem with this suggestion is that the lustral basins lack drains; another is that the finds do not suggest an extensive use of water. It seems more reasonable to give the religious evidence pride of place and presume that all lustral basins had a ritual use (Gesell 1985, 25; Nordfeldt 1987). Marinatos has proposed that they were a kind of adyton that offered a physical separation from the normal environment and that they were used in association with pier and door rooms that could be shut so as to plunge individuals into darkness or opened to bathe them in light (1993, 77–87).

The pillar crypt was basically a rectangular room with one, two, or three square pillars in the center. Very often a cult room with a column was situated directly above the pillar crypt. Several pillars have basins or channels for liquids set in the floor at their bases. Double axes were very often incised on the pillars, and stands for actual double axes were sometimes found. Bull's head rhyta also appear in the pillar crypts.

Hallager (1987) saw the pillar crypts in the West Wing of Knossos, which were situated on the path from the West Wing entrance to the storage magazines, as the location of a harvest or purification festival celebrated when the crops were brought in. Pillar crypts also occur in tombs, which may suggest a connection between funerary and palace cult (Gesell 1985, 26; Marinatos 1993). This connection, however, is not in conflict with the agricultural ceremony proposed by Hallager since stored grain, with its potential for rebirth, could have been linked to funerary cult's concern with the cycle of life and death.

The Practice of Minoan Religion

It is clear from the numerous representations of female goddesses in various media that a female deity was the major religious focus of Minoan religion. She appears as the Mother Goddess, the Mistress of the Animals, and the Guardian of Cities. However, the question that has been debated is whether the Minoans worshipped many different female deities or if one Great Goddess appeared in a multitude of aspects. Traditionally, the one Great Goddess theory has prevailed and has often been taken as a given among scholars. Nonetheless, Dickinson (1994) has made the case that it would be strange for Minoan religion to be so different from the contemporaneous religions of the Mediterranean and the Near East. He therefore favors the idea of a multiplicity of female deities. Moss (2005) argues that there was indeed a full Minoan pantheon and bases her hypothesis on the different representations of both male and female deities.

The act of summoning the goddess and her resulting epiphany appears to have been a major part of Minoan religion. In many rituals, the presence of the goddess was probably represented by a high priestess, but her presence could also have been experienced in a nonmaterial way (Warren 1988). Minoan iconography shows men and women in positions of ecstatic worship, the focus of which could be a baetyl (La Rosa 2001; Warren 1990), a tree, the goddess's dress (which was probably presented to the deity as part of the ritual), or even a figure-of-eight shield (figure 19.2). Hägg (1983) has termed these two types of worship "enacted" and "ecstatic."

Male deities, while not nearly as prominent in the iconography as female ones, are suggested by scenes of small figures floating in the air, which seem to be descending or arriving (figure 19.2). The "Master Impression," a sealing that shows a male holding a staff atop a town, may also represent a male deity. Also, various cult paraphernalia such as horns of consecration, bull's head rhyta, double axes, and images of bull leaping and sacrifice (Rehak 1995; Younger 1995) show the importance of the bull in Minoan (particularly Knossian) religion.

It has also been suggested that the Minoans practiced human sacrifice. Within a Protopalatial (MM II) sanctuary near Archanes at Anemospelia on the lower slopes of Mount Jouktas, four human skeletons were found (Sakellarakis and Sapouna-Sakellaraki 1991). Three of these people were killed when the building collapsed in an earthquake, but one eighteen-year-old male was found lying on his side on

Figure 19.2. A Cretan gold ring showing a woman worshipping a double baetyl on the right, the high priestess (goddess?) on the left, and an armed male deity who floats in between (courtesy of Ingo Pini, *CMS*).

a platform in the middle of the room in a contracted position, as if he had been trussed. A bronze dagger was found among his bones.

A second example comes from an LM IB building, part of which was used for cult practice, in the town of Knossos. Within a small chamber were found the remains of four children whose bones had cut marks, which indicate that their flesh had been removed, implying that the children had been killed and eaten as part of a ritual (Warren 1981). Some doubt exists that these examples actually provide evidence that the Minoans performed human sacrifice, but if human sacrifice was part of Minoan religious practice, it must have been rare.

POSTPALATIAL CRETE

At the end of LM IB, a disaster struck Minoan society that destroyed all of the palaces and villas except for Knossos. After this disaster, we see evidence that the Mycenaeans established themselves at Knossos and ruled over what was in many respects a flourishing economy.

Changes in the expression of Minoan religion at this time are fairly dramatic. Most of the peak sanctuaries fall out of use (Peatfield 1990), while open rock shelters are preferred to the previous period's deep stalagmitic sacred caves (Tyree 1994). Lustral basins were filled in, and pillar crypts were used for different purposes. Any newly built shrines were of the bench-shrine type, such as those found at Gournia and the Shrine of the Double Axes at Knossos (Gesell 1985, 47).

A new type of cult image is also found in these shrines: the Goddess with Upraised Arms. These terracotta figures are sometimes quite large, up to 0.85 m, and it is likely that their bell-shaped lower halves wore flounced skirts. The crowns of the idols usually held the deity's attributes, such as poppies, birds, snakes, horns of consecration, and disks. These attributes could be combined on individual figures, and two figures with the same attributes could appear in one shrine. Thus, it may be that the statues do not depict particular goddesses but rather represent a general goddess of nature (Marinatos 1993, 227; cf. Peatfield 1994a).

One of the most common pieces of cult equipment in this period is also new: tubular stands that have loops of snakes running along the sides of the vessel, which were therefore called "snake tubes." The snake tubes may have come in sets with particular Goddesses with Upraised Arms (Gesell 1985, 44).

It has been proposed that at this point the Mycenaeans influenced the practice of Minoan cult (Renfrew 1981), and some change is evident in the predominance of the bench shrine, the use of terracotta cult figures (although there is no exact parallel for the Goddess with Upraised Arms on the mainland), and the disuse of lustral basins and pillar crypts. Nonetheless, although the form of the goddess is new, the attributes that accompany the cult figures are familiar from Proto- and Neopalatial iconography. This implies that the deities of the different periods were the same. Furthermore, horns of consecration and double axes were commonly used in the Postpalatial shrines, thereby contributing to the idea that the belief system founded in the Protopalatial period was still in use despite the presence of the mainlanders (Gesell 1983; Hägg 1997). The LM III Ayia Triadha sarcophagus, a stone example of the terracotta larnakes used for burials, with its scenes of animal sacrifice and double axes associated with a man's burial, seem to connect Minoan religion in its latest stages with its origins—as intertwined with funerary cult and the cycle of life and death.

BIBLIOGRAPHY

Branigan, Keith. 1970. *The Tombs of Mesara: A Study of Funerary Architecture and Ritual in Southern Crete, 2800–1700 B.C.* London: Duckworth.

———. 1988. *Pre-palatial: The Foundations of Palatial Crete: A Survey in the Early Bronze Age*, 2d ed. Amsterdam: Hakkert.

———. 1993. *Dancing with Death: Life and Death in Southern Crete c. 3000–2000 B.C.* Amsterdam: Hakkert.

———. 1998. "The Nearness of You: Proximity and Distance in Early Minoan Funerary Behaviour." In *Cemetery and Society in the Aegean Bronze Age*, ed. Keith Branigan, 13–26. Sheffield Studies in Aegean Archaeology 1. Sheffield: Sheffield Academic Press.

Cameron, Mark. 1987. "The 'Palatial' Thematic System in the Knossos Murals." In *Function of the Minoan Palaces*, 321–28.

Cherry, John F. 1978. "Generalisation and the Archaeology of the State." In *Social Organisation and Settlement*, ed. David Green, Colin Haselgrove, and Matthew Spriggs, 411–37. *BAR-IS* 47. Oxford: British Archaeological Reports.

———. 1986. "Polities and Palaces: Some Problems in Minoan State Formation." In *Peer Polity Interaction and Socio-political Change*, ed. Colin Renfrew and John F. Cherry, 19–45. New York: Cambridge University Press.

Davis, Ellen. 1987. "The Knossos Miniature Frescoes and the Function of the Central Courts." In *Function of the Minoan Palaces*, 157–61.

Dickinson, Oliver T. P. K. 1994. "Comments on a Popular Model of Minoan Religion." *OJA* 13: 173–84.

Gesell, Geraldine. 1983. "The Place of the Goddess in Minoan Society." In *Minoan Society*, 93–99.

———. 1985. *Town, Palace, and House Cult in Minoan Crete*. SIMA 67. Gothenburg: Åström.

———. 1987. "The Minoan Palace and Public Cult." In *Function of the Minoan Palaces*, 123–28.

Graham, James W. 1987. *The Palaces of Crete*. Princeton: Princeton University Press.

Hägg, Robin. 1983. "Epiphany in Minoan Ritual." *BICS* 30: 184–85.

———. 1987. "On the Reconstruction of the West Façade of the Palace at Knossos." In *Function of the Minoan Palaces*, 129–34.

———. 1988. "The Last Ceremony in the Throne Room at Knossos." *OpAth* 17: 99–105.

———. 1997. "Religious Syncretism at Knossos in Post-palatial Crete?" In *La Crète mycénienne*, 163–68.

Hallager, Erik. 1987. "A 'Harvest Festival Room' in the Minoan Palaces? An Architectural Study of the Pillar Crypt Area at Knossos." In *Function of the Minoan Palaces*, 169–77.

Karetsou, Alexandra. 1981. "The Peak Sanctuary of Mount Juktas." In *Sanctuaries and Cults*, 137–53.

Kyriakidis, Evangelos. 2005. *Ritual in the Bronze Age Aegean: The Minoan Peak Sanctuaries*. London: Duckworth.

La Rosa, Vincenzo. 2001. "Minoan Baetyls: Between Funerary Rituals and Epiphanies." In *Potnia*, 221–27.

Marinatos, Nanno. 1984. *Art and Religion in Thera: Reconstructing a Bronze Age Society*. Athens: Mathioulakis.

———. 1987. "Public Festivals in the West Courts of the Palace." In *Function of the Minoan Palaces*, 135–43.

———. 1993. *Minoan Religion: Ritual, Image, and Symbol*. Columbia: University of South Carolina Press.

Moss, Marina. 2005. *The Minoan Pantheon: Towards an Understanding of Its Nature and Extent*. BAR-IS 1343. Oxford: British Archaeological Reports.

Niemeier, Wolf-Dietrich. 1987. "On the Function of the 'Throne Room' in the Palace at Knossos." In *Function of the Minoan Palaces*, 163–68.

Nordfeldt, Ann Charlotte. 1987. "Residential Quarters and Lustral Basins." In *Function of the Minoan Palaces*, 188–94.

Nowicki, Krzysztof. 1994. "Some Remarks on the Pre- and Protopalatial Peak Sanctuaries in Crete." *Aegean Archaeology* 1: 31–48.

Peatfield, Alan. 1983. "The Topography of Minoan Peak Sanctuaries." *BSA* 78: 273–80.

———. 1987. "Palace and Peak: The Political and Religious Relationship between Palaces and Peak Sanctuaries." In *Function of the Minoan Palaces*, 89–93.

———. 1990. "Minoan Peak Sanctuaries: History and Society." *OpAth* 18: 117–31.

———. 1994a. "After the 'Big Bang'—What? Or Minoan Symbols and Shrines beyond Palatial Collapse." In *Placing the Gods: Sanctuaries and Sacred Space in Ancient Greece*, ed. Susan E. Alcock and Robin Osborne, 19–36. Oxford: Clarendon.

———. 1994b. "Divinity and Performance on Minoan Peak Sanctuaries." In *Potnia*, 51–55.

Platon, Nicholas. 1971. *Zakros: The Discovery of a Lost Palace of Ancient Crete*. New York: Charles Scribner's Sons.

Rehak, Paul. 1995. "The Use and Destruction of Minoan Stone Bull's Head Rhyta." In *Politeia*, 435–60.

Renfrew, Colin. 1981. "Questions of Minoan and Mycenaean Cult." In *Sanctuaries and Cults*, 27–31.

Rutkowski, Bogdan. 1972. *Cult Places in the Aegean World*. Wroclaw: Polish Academy of Sciences, Institute of the History of Material Culture.

———. 1986. *Cult Places of the Aegean*. New Haven: Yale University Press.

Sakellarakis, John A., and Efi Sapouna-Sakellaraki. 1991. *Archanes*. Athens: Ekdotike Athenon S.A.

Shaw, Joseph W. 1978. "Evidence for the Minoan Tripartite Shrine." *AJA* 82: 429–48.

Soles, Jeffrey S. 1992. *The Prepalatial Cemeteries at Mochlos and Gournia and the House Tombs of Bronze Age Crete*. Hesperia Suppl. 24. Princeton: American School of Classical Studies at Athens Press.

Tyree, Loeta. 1994. "Diachronic Changes in Minoan Cave Cult." In *Potnia*, 39–50.

———. 2006. "Minoan Sacred Caves: The Natural and Political Landscape." In *Proceedings of the 9th International Congress of Cretan Studies, 1–7 October 2001*, 329–42. Heraklion: Society of Cretan Historical Studies.

Warren, Peter. 1972. *Myrtos: An Early Bronze Age Settlement in Crete*. London: Thames and Hudson.

———. 1981. "Minoan Crete and Ecstatic Religion: Preliminary Observations on the 1979 Excavations at Knossos." In *Sanctuaries and Cults*, 155–67.

———. 1988. *Minoan Religion as Ritual Action*. Gothenburg: Gothenburg University.

———. 1990. "Of Baetyls." *OpAth* 18: 192–206.

Watrous, L. Vance. 1987. "The Role of the Near East in the Rise of the Cretan Palaces." In *Function of the Minoan Palaces*, 65–70.

———. 1995. "Some Observations on Minoan Peak Sanctuaries." In *Politeia*, 393–403.

Younger, John. 1995. "Bronze Age Representations of Aegean Bull-Games, III." In *Politeia*, 507–545.

CHAPTER 20

MYCENAEAN RELIGION

SUSAN LUPACK

THE FOUNDATIONS OF MYCENAEAN RELIGION

The evidence for the Mycenaean period is different from that for the Minoan in two important respects. First, in general the Mycenaean evidence is not as abundant as it is for the Minoan culture. Because of this, scholars can be dismissive of the evidence we do have, thereby giving the impression that not much can be said about Mycenaean religion. However, the body of archaeological material is now not as scanty as is often portrayed, and positive information can be gleaned from the sites that have been discovered. Furthermore, when the archaeological evidence is combined with the information provided by the Linear B tablets, a fairly informative picture of Mycenaean religion results.

The second difference between Minoan and Mycenaean religion is that the archaeological evidence for religious structures does not extend over as long a period as the Minoan, which means that it is not possible to trace the origins and development of Mycenaean religion with much precision or fullness. Many authors have remarked on the relative dearth of evidence for religious practice on the mainland in the early periods (see, e.g., Dickinson 1994; Mylonas 1966, 137).

Nevertheless, Caskey (1990, 20) has found evidence for EH ritual in the large, decorated hearths that are found in geographically diverse mainland sites and proposed that they at least parallel and may even constitute the "remote but direct ancestors of the Megaron hearth of Mycenaean times." Unfortunately, nothing similar has been found in the MH period, but evidence for communal sacrificial rites has been found on the Kynortion hilltop above Epidauros (Lambrinudakis 1981) and on the island of Nisakouli near Methoni (Choremis 1969). At both sites, MH sherds were found in layers of ash that contained burnt animal bones, and those on Nisakouli were associated with an altar/hearth structure. The types of bones and the associated pottery indicate that the sacrifices were probably followed by communal feasting (Hägg 1997a; see Wright 1994, 39, and Kilian 1992 for other MH–LH II religious sites).

Another feature of ritual practice that Hägg thinks must have originated in the MH period is the pouring of libations (Hägg 1990, 184; 1997a). He proposes that we have not detected this cult practice archaeologically because specialized vessels, like rhyta, had not yet been adopted. Whittaker (2001), in line with this proposal, sees the practice of funerary libations in the jugs and cups found at gravesites in the MH period. Thus, religion in the MH period may have been rather simple, but the traces of Helladic cult that are extant foreshadow the cult practices of the later Mycenaeans. Whittaker (2001, 357) argues that the increasing complexity of Helladic religion can be seen in the elaboration of early LH burial rituals, as the rising "Mycenaean elite was starting to utilize ritual activity in order to reinforce its claims to socio-political power." It was at this point, she argues, that Helladic religion took on a social function that it had not had in the MH period, one that fueled the development of its iconography and architecture.

When shrine buildings do appear on a significant scale, it is at the same time as the earliest palace structures: in the LH IIIA period. Hence, Wright (1994, 38) has stated that the "formalization of religious activity in Mycenaean society was largely a phenomenon of the period of the palaces." And indeed, religion is specifically associated with the rulers of the citadels through its practice in the physical and symbolic heart of the Mycenaean palaces—the megaron.

MEGARON (THRONE ROOM)

There are several indications that the megara of the Mycenaean palaces were used for religious rituals. At Tiryns, an altar was located in the porticoed courtyard in front of the megaron complex (Kilian 1990; Maran 2000, 2001). At Mycenae, the remains of an altar, an offering table, and an alabaster basin set into the floor were found in the porch of the megaron (Papadimitriou 1955). At Pylos, the miniature kylikes found on an offering table next to the hearth and the circular depressions linked by a channel in the floor next to the throne indicate that libations were an important part of the rituals conducted in the megaron (Blegen and Rawson 1966, 88–89). Also, the hearth of the megaron, which was larger than necessary, was probably seen as the heart of the Mycenaean state (Wright 1994). The religious nature of the megaron is also demonstrated by the frescoes found at Pylos (Lang 1969; McCallum 1987a, b). On the walls of the megaron's vestibule was a procession in which a bull was being led to a shrine, and in the megaron the succeeding ceremonial banquet was depicted.

Most scholars believe that the *wanax*, the Mycenaean ruler, derived much of his power from his position within the religious realm (Kilian 1988; Palaima 1995;

Whittaker 2001; Wright 1995b) and that he presided over sacrificial feasts conducted in the palace (cf. Rehak 1995, who proposed that it was actually a priestess who sat on the throne). The *wanax*'s strong ties to religion seem to be demonstrated by the Lion Gate at Mycenae: The lions rest their paws on incurved altars, showing that the power of the ruler is founded upon religion (Mylonas 1966, 175). In addition, at Pylos, painted lions and griffins guard the throne, symbolizing the divine protection bestowed upon the *wanax*. The tablet PY Un 2 seems to support this, in that it refers to the celebration of the *wanax*'s initiation, which was to be held at *Pa-ki-ja-ne*, the prime sanctuary for the Pylians. Thus, the religious officials of *Pa-ki-ja-ne* may have had a role to play in legitimizing the power of the *wanax* (Lupack 2008b, 47–48).

It must be true, though, that while cult activities took place in the megaron, it did not constitute an actual sanctuary (Albers 2001, 133). Sanctuaries that were devoted to the worship of deities are found in close proximity to the citadels of Mycenae, Tiryns, Phylakopi, Midea, and possibly Pylos, but also at smaller settlements such as Asine, Methana, and Berbati, while there was a hilltop sanctuary near Epidauros on the heights of Kynortion. (This list is meant to be representative but is not exhaustive.)

RELIGIOUS SITES IN MYCENAEAN CITADELS

Cult Center of Mycenae

The Cult Center of Mycenae is the most impressive Mycenaean sanctuary. As such it has been described elsewhere in great detail (see most recently French 2002; French and Taylour 2007; Moore and Taylour 1999). Therefore, we need here only touch briefly on its most important attributes.

The Cult Center was connected to the palace by a Processional Way (French 2002, 85; Mylonas 1972, 1983), one portion of which was roofed and decorated with a chariot procession fresco (French 2002, 85). Its five main buildings, the Megaron, the Temple, the Room with the Fresco Complex, Tsountas's House Shrine (now Shrine Gamma), and Tsountas's House produced a wealth of religious artifacts and various types of cult installations. Tsountas's House Shrine had an unusual horseshoe-shaped altar with an installation attached for libations, and a large unworked stone was sunk into the floor.

In its main room (18), the Temple had three columns that ran along a staircase, which led to room 19. In the middle of room 18 was a plaster-coated platform, and at its northern end was a series of benches on which were found an offering table and a "Type B" figure. Type B figures, which have been found only at Mycenae, are generally large (0.35 to 0.69 m) and painted black all over the body and face except for some reserved areas around the face. They are thought to represent cult celebrants,

Figure 20.1. Two Type-A figures, both from the Cult Center of Mycenae. The one on the left was found in room 19 of the Temple, while the one on the right was found in shrine room 32 of the Room with the Fresco Complex (copyright Mycenae Archive).

while the more finely decorated Type A figures (figure 20.1) are thought to represent deities (Moore and Taylour 1999, 93–101). The handmade anthropomorphic "psi" and "phi" figurines, along with the zoomorphic figurines, are smaller than both of these and have a much wider distribution (French 1981).

Twenty-seven Type B figures were found along with fifteen coiled clay snakes and three Type A figures in room 19 and in a small alcove behind room 18. In several instances fragments of the same figures were found separately in the two rooms. Room 19 was sealed up, and the cult objects effectively decommissioned, presumably after the early LH IIIB disaster (probably an earthquake). The Temple opened onto the Cult Center's central court, within which stood a round altar, near which was a pit of burnt offerings (French 2002, 87; French and Taylour 2007, 10; Mylonas 1972).

The Room with the Fresco Complex is so named for the fresco painted over an altar in the main room (31). An ivory head lay in front of the altar, which may have represented a deity. Another cult image, a Type A female figure, was found on a bench shrine in room 32 to the east of room 31 (Taylour 1970). The fresco (figure 20.2), with its two female figures and two small, floating male figures, is also thought to depict the deities of the sanctuary (Marinatos 1988; Rehak 1992). The woman on the left holds a sword and may be a War Goddess (Rehak 1984), while the woman facing her, dressed in a Minoan-style flounced skirt and holding a staff, may be her daughter (Moore and Taylour forthcoming). On the lower register a priestess or goddess, who is holding a sheaf of wheat in each of her hands, appears with a griffin. The wheat here may indicate that one of the female figures in the fresco is the "Mistress of the Grains," who is recorded on a Linear B tablet found nearby.

Figure 20.2. Reconstruction of the fresco from Room 31 of the Room with the Fresco Complex. The altar with the horns of consecration is positioned underneath the main part of the fresco (copyright Diana Wardle).

Pylos

The Northeast Building of Pylos was predominantly a storage facility and an administrative clearinghouse, but one of its rooms, 93, was identified as a shrine (Blegen and Rawson 1966, 301–305). No objects of a definite cultic nature were found within the room, but standing outside it was a frescoed altar. The façade of the room also indicates its special nature with its decorative antae. Textual evidence found within the building also indicates that the occupants had a religious association. Thus, the "seat of Potnia Hippeia" referred to on Linear B tablet An 1281 may be the Northeast Building itself (Lupack 2008a, 2008b). It is also possible that a sanctuary will be found once the Lower Town is excavated.

Tiryns

The shrine, Room 117, found in the Lower Town of Tiryns dates to the LH IIIC period, but there is evidence that the area was used for cult practice in the LH IIIB period (Kilian 1981). Inside Room 117 were a bench-altar and typical Mycenaean anthropomorphic and zoomorphic figurines, two large female figures, and a bull-shaped rhyton. To the north of Room 117 was an oval altar with traces of ash (Kilian 1979). Various bones show that animal sacrifice was practiced.

Phylakopi

In the LH IIIA1 period, a megaron-centered structure replaced the earlier Minoan "mansion." At this time, the West Shrine of Phylakopi was built (Renfrew 1981b, 1985). This Shrine was in use for approximately 260 years. In the LH IIIB period, the East Shrine was built, which, with the West shrine, created a courtyard within which a rounded baetyl was found. The figurines found associated with the two altars in the West Shrine were separated by gender. The Lady of Phylakopi, a Type A figure and probably the main cult image of the sanctuary, was found in one of the two adyta/storage rooms behind the main room. Wheel-made bovid figures and ten seal stones were found around the altar in the East Shrine. Other cult equipment included a male gold facemask, conch shells, and a tortoise-shell lyre, which shows that music was part of the shrine's cult.

Midea

The LH IIIB sanctuary found on the lower terraces of Midea (Walberg 1998, 177; 2007, 196) consisted of several rooms. Room XXXII had an elliptical hearth and a tripod offering table, while parts of two wheel-made figures, a female and a bull, were found in room VIII with a stirrup jar decorated with double axes and horns of consecration. Further evidence for cult practice at Midea is provided by the more than two hundred figurines found near the West Gate (Demakopoulou and Divari-Valakou 2001). The most outstanding of these is a complete LH IIIB Type A female figure, whose polos hat has a hole that runs through her body. She may have been used for libations or carried in processions.

TOWN AND OPEN-AIR RELIGIOUS SITES

Asine

House G of Asine, which dates to the LH IIIC period, was located at the northern edge of a Mycenaean town (Hägg 1981a). Its main cult room (XXXII) had two columns along its central axis and a cult bench in the northeast corner, around which were found a kernos, an inverted jug whose bottom had been deliberately broken, female figurines, and a large terracotta, probably female, head.

Methana

The LH IIIA–B site of Ayios Konstantinos, Methana, has produced a five-room shrine complex located within a Mycenaean settlement (Konsolaki 2002; Konsolaki-Yannopulou 1999, 2001). The main shrine, room A, contained a stepped bench shrine, around which approximately 150 figurines were found. Most of the figurines are individual bovids, but many are composite constructions of animals with riders and chariot groups. Remarkably, there was only one female figurine. A separate deposit included an animal-head rhyton and a fragmentary jar neck, which were probably used for a libation ceremony. The hearth in the southeast corner contained a number of burnt animal bones, providing secure evidence for animal sacrifice.

The Potter's Workshop at Berbati

A bench shrine was found in a building near to the LH II–IIIA kiln that had Psi figurines, a decorated spoon, and an amphora whose bottom was missing (Akerström 1968, 1987; Schallin 1997). In the LH IIIB period, another building was built over the first, and a new cult installation that consisted of a stone channel with the base of a kylix fixed in one end replaced the bench shrine. A second LH III installation, found in a nearby building, consisted of a large krater whose bottom had been deliberately pierced and half-buried in the earth. It seems the potters poured libations for the gods to ensure the successful outcome of their work.

Kynortion Hill above Epidauros

This site is remarkable for the length of time that it was active: from the MH through the LH periods (Lambrinudakis 1981). As mentioned earlier, burnt bones, including skulls and horns from bulls and goats, were found mixed in a deep layer of ash. A wide array of Mycenaean figurines was also found, along with a sheet-bronze animal face, bronze double axes, votive and real swords, seals, and a steatite vessel decorated with a relief of warriors in a boat. This site has been called a "peak sanctuary" by its excavator because of the Minoan influence seen in the double axes, but Peatfield (1990, 120–22) and Hägg (1988, 207) argue convincingly that it is not in the Minoan tradition.

Other sites of LH III cult activity located outside the palaces are found at Amyklai, Tsoungiza, Aigina, and Delphi, all of which produced Mycenaean figurines and fragments of larger cult figures (Wright 1994). Open-air sites have been found at Ayia Triada near Klenies and in a cave on Profitis Elias near Ayios Hadrianos (Kilian 1990), and French (1971) notes many sites that have produced religious deposits consisting primarily of figurines.

MYCENAEAN CULT

These summaries of sites and their finds establish a basic picture of Mycenaean cult practice. The cult buildings are usually of the bench-shrine type, but a variety of altars existed alongside them. Some show signs of burnt sacrifices, while others must have been used for cereal and liquid offerings. Cult equipment, such as rhyta, kylikes, offering tables, and vessels with deliberately pierced bottoms, indicate the importance of libations in Mycenaean cult (Hägg 1990). The handmade figurines, both anthropomorphic and zoomorphic, are nearly ubiquitous in Mycenaean cult, while the less numerous Type A figures, such as the Lady of Phylakopi, probably represented deities.

Processions were also a central feature of Mycenaean cult practice (Hägg 2001), as evidenced by the fresco in the megaron complex at Pylos. This fresco, coupled with the evidence for burnt sacrifices, also indicates the importance of communal feasting and drinking, which probably followed sacrificial rituals (see Wright 1995a).

The importance of religion to the elite is suggested by the number of cult sites found in citadels. Nonetheless, it is clear from the numerous deposits of figurines that religion was widely practiced. Hägg (1981b, 1995) has attempted to classify Mycenaean religious sites as either 'official/state' or 'popular,' but this oversimplifies the situation (as he himself has recognized) and ignores the fact that the religion practiced by the elite must have derived from Helladic religious traditions.

The iconography of Mycenaean religion as practiced by the elite was, however, heavily influenced by Minoan culture. For example, double axes are found both in archaeological assemblages (as on Kynortion and at Lerna) and in religious imagery, while horns of consecration are found at Pylos, Gla, Tiryns, and Mycenae. Scholars have questioned whether and to what extent the Mycenaeans had adopted the religious beliefs of the Minoans when they took on their iconography (Hägg 1981b, 1988; Renfrew 1981a). However, it seems most likely, given the close contact between the Minoans and the Mycenaeans in the 15th century BC, when the use of Minoan iconography was at its height, that the Mycenaeans were not ignorant (or careless) of Minoan religious meaning (Niemeier 1990), and the way that the Mycenaeans used many of the symbols demonstrates this (Walberg 1988). For instance, the Mycenaeans used the horns of consecration as markers of religious buildings on gold rings and frescoes.

Rather, it seems that the Mycenaeans selectively adopted certain types of symbols and scenes that had meaning to them within their own religious construct. Thus, Whittaker (2001) proposes that the double axe "was taken over from Crete precisely because it was a symbol of power that could be easily assimilated into Helladic military symbolism," which was "becoming visibly associated with religious activity." The fact that the double axe was associated with animal sacrifice, which was part of Mycenaean cult practice, probably also contributed to its adoption (Hägg 1988).

In contrast, images of ecstatic and enacted epiphany, which are an essential element of Minoan iconography, are all but absent in Mycenaean religious scenes. Also absent from Mycenaean cult are lustral basins, pillar crypts, and clay snake tubes. Rhyta and offering tables, however, were adopted early in the Mycenaean period, but Hägg (1988, 1997a, 18) proposes that this was "to embellish, as it were, an already existing cult practice."

The Minoan religious iconography, therefore, seems to have provided the Mycenaeans with an already established—and esteemed—repertoire of symbols. Since they were lacking such an elaborate system themselves, the Mycenaeans were happy to adopt and adapt these symbols wherever and whenever appropriate for the illustration and aggrandizement of their own religion. This is not to say that the Minoan influence was entirely superficial. It is, of course, possible that in this process certain elements of the original religion were emphasized over others or were modified to become more like the Minoan concepts. Nonetheless, it does seem that the Mycenaeans did not simply accept concepts into their religious system that were entirely foreign to their own.

Linear B Evidence

The Helladic nature of Mycenaean religion is also made clear by the Linear B tablets. Our information regarding cult practice is derived predominantly from the tablets that record offerings (which include perfumed oil, grain, honey, spices, cloth, and, in one case, golden vessels) made by the palace to various deities and religious sanctuaries. Sometimes the offering tablets record a month name that was based on a religious festival (Hiller 1981), which means that the Mycenaeans had a religious calendar similar in nature to that of the historical Greeks (Burkert 1985, 225–26).

The Mycenaeans referred to their shrines as *nawoi*, and they could be named after the deity that presided over each of them (e.g., the Posidaion). Of the deities mentioned on the tablets, many are immediately recognizable as gods that were also worshipped in Classical times, such as Zeus, Hera, Poseidon, Athena, Artemis, Ares, Hermes, Dionysos, Eileuthia, and Erinys (Chadwick 1985). Others are Greek names, but ones that were not used in Classical times, such as Diwia and Posidaia, female versions of Zeus and Poseidon.

The most prominent female deity in the Mycenaean corpus is Potnia. The word on its own denotes a female who wields power and can be translated as "Mistress" (Trümpy 2001). However, the word is associated with several epithets and locations (Chadwick 1957, 1985) such as the Horses, the Grains, the Labyrinth, Athens (Gulizio, Pluta, and Palaima 2001), and Asia (Morris 2001). The question here, as it was with the Goddess of Minoan religion, is whether Potnia was one goddess who could be worshipped under several different aspects or whether each epithet represented a distinct goddess. Boëlle (2001) leans toward the latter explanation but acknowledges that this question is not easily resolved.

The Mycenaean rulers at Knossos also sent offerings to several non-Greek divinities such as *mba-ti* and *pi-pi-tu-na* (Gulizio and Nakassis 2002) and to a generic "all the gods," which they may have done so as not to incur the wrath of the local gods (Gulizio 2008). Hägg (1997b) sees a possible syncretism of Minoan and Mycenaean religions in the appearance of Greek deities who have taken on local epithets, such as Diktaian Zeus. However, he points out that the common attributes of cult in Postpalatial Crete, such as the Goddess with Upraised Arms, the snake tube, and hut urns, do not have a Mycenaean origin. Hägg (1997b, 168) therefore concludes that the syncretism demonstrated by the textual evidence "was probably a phenomenon of limited scope, with little if any impact on the Cretan population at large."

The archaeological evidence for sacrificial communal feasts is fleshed out by the textual evidence. Several tablets record the gathering of animals, wine, cheese, and other foodstuffs, while others provide festival names. One such is the "Festival of the New Wine," which may have been similar to the Anthesteria (Bennett 1958). A second is the "Lechestroterion," which has been taken as a festival celebrating the "Spreading of the Couches"— the couches were being spread either for a banquet of the gods (Ventris and Chadwick 1973) or for a sacred wedding (Bennet 1958). A third festival name may be taken as the "Festival of the Throne" (Bennet 1958; Hiller 1970; cf. Petrakis 2002–2003). It is possible that this festival was celebrated in honor of an ancestral, founding *wanax* (Lupack 2001). In a fourth example, the "Theophoria" or "Carrying of the God(s)," we may see a festival that involved the carrying of Type A cult images in processions (Hägg 2001; Hiller 1984).

Many religious officials are named on the tablets, which demonstrates that the Mycenaeans had a well-developed religious hierarchy. Among them, we find the Priestess of *Pakijane*, a Keybearer, who in historical times had custody of a shrine; the *hieroworgos* or sacrificial priest; a *sphageus* or 'sacrificer'; several generic priests; many "servants of the god"; a "skin bearer," whom Olivier (1960) believes wore a garment made of animal skin as the insignia of his position; and the "guardians of the fire." Female religious officials, such as the priestess of *Pa-ki-ja-ne*, who is actually recorded as challenging the *demos* over the classification of a piece of land, constitute the only examples in the tablets of women taking on roles of authority. Many religious officials hold their own land or have other economic resources (Bendall 2007; Lupack 2006, 2008a), and some are active within the palatial administration. Thus, the highest religious officials may have been on a par with, and in some cases may have been members of, the Mycenaean palatial elite.

Conclusions

From this brief survey of the tablets, it seems that the Linear B tablets affirm the Helladic nature of Mycenaean religion rather than providing a sense that Minoan religion had a heavy influence on Mycenaean religious practice or belief. It could also be said that much that is found on the Linear B tablets regarding Mycenaean religion fits well with a religion that is in some senses the precursor to Classical Greek religion. Despite the vast influence of the Minoans on the Mycenaeans in many aspects of their culture, it is the Helladic characteristics of Mycenaean religion that seem to be the ones that are retained and that resurface in historical Greek times.

BIBLIOGRAPHY

Akerström, A. 1968. "A Mycenaean Potter's Factory at Berbati near Mycenae." In *Atti e memorie del I Congresso Internazionale di Micenologia, Roma 1967*. Vol. 1, *Incunabula Graeca* 25, 3–6. Rome: Edizione dell'Ateno.

———. 1987. *Berbati*.Vol. 2, *The Pictorial Pottery*. Stockholm: Svenska Institut i Athen.

———. 1988. "Cultic Installations in Mycenaean Rooms and Tombs." In *Problems in Greek Prehistory*, 201–209.

Albers, Gabriele. 2001. "Rethinking Mycenaean Sanctuaries." In *Potnia*, 131–41.

Bendall, Lisa M. 2007. *Economics of Religion in the Mycenaean World: Resources Dedicated to Religion in the Mycenaean Palace Economy*. Oxford: Oxford University School of Archaeology.

Bennett, Emmett L. 1958. *The Mycenae Tablets II. TAPS* 48.

Blegen, Carl W., and Marion Rawson. 1966. *The Palace of Nestor at Pylos in Western Messenia*.Vol. 1, *The Buildings and Their Contents*. Princeton: Princeton University Press.

Boëlle, Cecille. 2001. "*Po-ti-ni-ja*: Unité ou pluralité?" In *Potnia*, 403–409.

Burkert, Walter. 1985. *Greek Religion*. Trans. J. Raffan. Cambridge, Mass.: Harvard University Press.

Caskey, Miriam E. 1990. "Thoughts on Early Bronze Age Hearths." In *Celebrations of Death*, 13–21.

Chadwick, John. 1957. "Potnia." *Minos* 5: 117–29.

———. 1985. "What Do We Know about Mycenaean Religion?" *Linear B: A 1984 Survey* (*BCILL* 26), ed. Anna Morpurgo Davies and Yves Duhoux, 191–202. Louvain-la-Neuve, Belgium: Peeters.

Choremis, Angelos. 1969. "ΜΕ βώμος εἰς Νησακούλι Μεθώνη" (with English summary). *AAA* 2: 10–14.

Demakopoulou, Katie, and Nicoletta Divari-Valakou. 2001. "Evidence for Cult Practice at Midea: Figures, Figurines, and Ritual Objects." In *Potnia*, 181–91.

Dickinson, Oliver T. P. K. 1994. *The Aegean Bronze Age*. New York: Cambridge University Press.

French, Elizabeth B. 1971. "The Development of Mycenaean Terracotta Figurines." *BSA* 66: 101–87.

———. 1981. "Mycenaean Figures and Figurines: Their Typology and Function." In *Sanctuaries and Cults*, 173–77.

———. 2002. *Mycenae: Agamemnon's Capital—The Site in Its Setting*. Gloucestershire: Stroud, Tempus.

French, Elizabeth B., and William D. Taylour. 2007. *The Service Areas of the Cult Centre, Well Built Mycenae: The Helleno-British Excavations within the Citadel of Mycenae*

1959–1969, fascicule 13, series ed. William D. Taylour, Elizabeth B. French, and Ken A. Wardle. Oxford: Oxbow.

Gulizio, Joanne. 2008. "Mycenaean Religion at Knossos." In *The Proceedings of the 12th International Mycenological Colloquium*, ed. Anna Sacconi, Louis Godart, and Maurizio Del Freo, 351–58. Rome: Biblioteca di Pasiphae.

————, and Dimitri Nakassis. 2002. "The Minoan Goddess(es): Textual Evidence for Minoan Religion." Talk presented at the Classical Association of the Middle West and South (CAMWS), April 4–6, 2002.

Gulizio, Joanne, Kevin Pluta, and Thomas G. Palaima. 2001. "Religion in the Room of the Chariot Tablets." In *Potnia*, 453–61.

Hägg, Robin. 1981a. "The House Sanctuary at Asine Revisited." In *Sanctuaries and Cults*, 91–94.

————. 1981b. "Official and Popular Cults in Mycenaean Greece." In *Sanctuaries and Cults*, 35–40.

————. 1988. "Mycenaean Religion: The Helladic and the Minoan Components." In *Linear B: A 1984 Survey (BCILL 26)*, ed. A. Morpurgo Davies and Yves Duhoux, 203–25. Louvain-la-Neuve, Belgium: Peeters.

————. 1990. "The Role of Libations in Mycenaean Ceremony and Cult." In *Celebrations of Death*, 177–84.

————. 1995. "State and Religion in Mycenaean Greece." In *Politeia*, 387–91.

————. 1997a. "Did the Middle Helladic People Have Any Religion? *Kernos* 10: 13–18.

————. 1997b. "Religious Syncretism at Knossos in Post-palatial Crete?" In *La Crète mycénienne*, 163–68.

————. 2001. "Religious Processions in Mycenaean Greece." In *Contributions to the Archaeology and History of the Bronze and Iron Ages in the Eastern Mediterranean*, ed. Peter M. Fischer, 143–48. Vienna: Österreichisches Archäologisches Institut.

Hiller, Stefan. 1970. "Wanasoi Tonoeketerijo." *Minos* 10: 78–92.

————. 1981. "Mykenische Heiligtümer: Das Zeugnis der Linear B-Texte." In *Sanctuaries and Cults*, 95–126.

————. 1984. "*Te-o-po-ri-ja.*" In *Aux origins de l'helénisme: La Crète et la Grèce*, ed. Le Centre G. Glotz, 139–50. Paris: Université de Sorbonne.

Kilian, Klaus. 1979. "Ausgrabungen in Tiryns 1977." *AA*: 379–411.

————. 1981. "Zeugnisse mykenisher Kultausubung in Tiryns." In *Sanctuaries and Cults*, 49–58.

————. 1988. "The Emergence of Wanax Ideology in the Mycenaean Palaces." *OJA* 7: 291–302.

————. 1990. "Patterns in the Cult Activity in the Mycenaean Argolid: Haghia Triada (Klenies), the Profitias Elias Cave (Haghios Hadrianos) and the Citadel of Tiryns." In *Celebrations of Death*, 185–97.

————. 1992. "Mykenischer Heiligtümer der Peloponnese." *Kotinos: Festschrift für Erika Simon*, ed. Heide Froning, Tonio Hölscher, and Harald Mielsch, 10–25. Mainz on Rhine: von Zabern.

Konsolaki, Eleni. 2002. "A Mycenaean Sanctuary on Methana." In *Peloponnesian Sanctuaries and Cults*, ed. Robin Hägg, 25–36. Stockholm: Svenska Institutet i Athen.

Konsolaki-Yannopoulou, Eleni. 1999. "A Group of New Mycenaean Horseman from Methana." In *Meletemata*, 427–33.

————. 2001. "New Evidence for the Practice of Libations in the Aegean Bronze Age." In *Potnia*, 213–20.

Lambrinudakis, Vasileios. 1981. "Remains of the Mycenaean Period in the Sanctuary of Apollon Maleatas." In *Sanctuaries and Cults*, 59–65.

Lang, Mabel. 1969. *The Palace of Nestor at Pylos in Western Messenia.*Vol. 2, *The Frescoes.* Series ed. Carl W. Blegen and Marion Rawson. Princeton: Princeton University Press.

Lupack, Susan. 2001. "The Mycenaean *Wanax* in the Fr Series: An Ancestral Deity?" Paper presented at the 102nd Annual Meeting of the Archaeological Institute of America.

———. 2006. "Deities and Religious Personnel as Collectors." In *Fiscality in Mycenaean and Near Eastern Archives*, ed. Massimo Perna, 89–108. Naples: Studi Egei e Vicinorientali.

———. 2008a. "The Northeast Building of Pylos and An 1281." In *The Proceedings of the 12th International Mycenological Colloquium*, ed. Anna Sacconi, Louis Godart, and Maurizio Del Freo, 467–84. Rome: Biblioteca di Pasiphae.

———. 2008b. *The Role of the Religious Sector in the Economy of Late Bronze Age Mycenaean Greece.* Oxford: British Archaeological Reports.

Maran, J. 2000. "Das Megaron im Megaron." *AA* 2000: 1–16.

———. 2001. "Political and Religious Aspects of Architectural Change on the Upper Citadel of Tiryns: The Case of Building T." In *Potnia*, 113–22.

Marinatos, Nanno. 1988. "The Fresco from Room 31 at Mycenae: Problems of Method and Interpretation." In *Problems in Greek Prehistory*, 245–51.

———. 2001. "Minoan and Mycenaean Larnakes: A Comparison." In *La Crète mycénienne*, 281–92.

McCallum, Lucinda R. 1987a. Decorative Program in the Mycenaean Palace of Pylos: The Megaron Frescoes. PhD diss., University of Pennsylvania.

———. 1987b. "Frescoes from the Throne Room at Pylos: A New Interpretation." *AJA* 91: 296.

Mee, Christopher B., and William G. Cavanagh. 1984. "Mycenaean Tombs as Evidence for Social and Political Organisation." *OJA* 3: 45–64.

Moore, Andrew D., and William D. Taylour. 1999. *The Temple Complex, Well Built Mycenae: The Helleno-British Excavations within the Citadel of Mycenae 1959–1969,*fascicule 10, series ed. William D. Taylour, Elizabeth B. French, and Ken A. Wardle. Oxford: Oxbow.

———. Forthcoming. *The Room with the Fresco Complex, Well Built Mycenae: The Helleno-British Excavations within the Citadel of Mycenae,* 1959–1969fascicule 11, series ed. William D. Taylour, Elizabeth B. French, and Ken A. Wardle. Oxford: Oxbow.

Morris, Sarah. 2001. "Potnia Aswija: Anatolian Contributions to Greek Religion." In *Potnia*, 423–34.

Mylonas, George. 1966. *Mycenae and the Mycenaean Age.* Princeton: Princeton University Press.

———. 1972. Τὸ Θρησκευτικὸν Κέντρον τῶν Μυκηνῶν, or *The Cult Center of Mycenae* (with English summary). Athens: Archaiologiki Etaireia.

———. 1983. *Mycenae Rich in Gold.* Athens: Ekdotike Athenon S.A.

Niemeier, Wolf-Dietrich. 1990. "Cult Scenes on Gold Rings from the Argolid." In *Celebrations of Death*, 165–70.

Olivier, Jean-Pierre. 1960. *A propos d'une 'liste' de desservants de sanctuaire dans les documents en linéaire B de Pylos.* Brussels: Presses Universitaires.

Palaima, Thomas G. 1995. "The Nature of the Mycenaean *Wanax*: Non-Indo-European Origins and Priestly Functions." In *Role of the Ruler*, 119–39.

Papadimitriou, I. 1955. "Anaskaphai eis Mykenon." *Praktika* 1955: 230–32.

Peatfield, Alan. 1990. "Minoan Peak Sanctuaries: History and Society." *OpAth* 18: 117–31.

Petrakis, Vassilis P. 2002–2003. "*To-no-e-ke-te-ri-jo* Reconsidered." *Minos* 37–38: 293–316.

Rehak, Paul. 1984. "New Observations on the Mycenaean 'War Goddess.'" *AA* 1984: 535–45.

———. 1992. "Tradition and Innovation in the Fresco from Room 31 in the 'Cult Center' at Mycenae." In *EIKON*, 39–62.

———. 1995. "Enthroned Figures and the Function of the Mycenaean Megaron." In *Role of the Ruler*, 95–118.

Renfrew, Colin. 1981a. "Questions of Minoan and Mycenaean Cult." In *Sanctuaries and Cults*, 27–31.

———. 1981b. "The Sanctuary at Phylakopi." In *Sanctuaries and Cults*, 67–80.

———. 1985. *The Archaeology of Cult: The Sanctuary at Phylakopi*. BSA Supplementary vol. 18. London: Thames and Hudson.

Schallin, Anne-Louise. 1997. "The Late Bronze Age Potter's Workshop at Mastos in the Berbati Valley." In *Trade and Production in Premonetary Greece: Acquisition and Distribution of Raw Materials and Finished Products. Proceedings of the 6th International Workshop, Athens 1996*, ed. Carole Gillis, Christina Risberg, and Birgitta Sjöberg, 73–88. *SIMA-PB* 154. Jonsered, Sweden: Åström.

Taylour, William D. 1970. "New Light on Mycenaean Religion." *Antiquity* 44: 270–80.

———. 1981. *Well Built Mycenae: The Helleno-British Excavations within the Citadel of Mycenae 1959–1969*, fascicule 1, series ed. William D. Taylour, Elizabeth B. French and Ken A. Wardle. Warminster: Aris and Phillips.

Trümpy, C. 2001. "Potnia dans les tablettes mycéniennes: Quelques problèmes d'interprétation." In *Potnia*, 411–21.

Ventris, Michael, and John Chadwick. 1973. *Documents in Mycenaean Greek*. Cambridge: Cambridge University Press.

Walberg, Gisela. 1988. "Problems in the Interpretation of Some Minoan and Mycenaean Cult Symbols." In *Problems in Greek Prehistory*, 211–18.

———. 1998. *Excavations on the Acropolis of Midea*.Vol. 1, 1–27, *The Excavations on the Lower Terraces 1985–1991*. Stockholm: Svenska Institutet I Athen.

———. 2007. *Midea: The Megaron Complex and Shrine Area. Excavations on the Lower Terraces 1994–1997*. Philadelphia: INSTAP Academic Press.

Whittaker, Helène. 2001. "Reflections on the Socio-political Function of Mycenaean Religion." In *Potnia*, 355–60.

Wright, James C. 1987. "Death and Power at Mycenae: Changing Symbols in Mortuary Practice." In *Thanatos*, 171–84.

———. 1994. "The Spatial Configuration of Belief: The Archaeology of Mycenaean Religion." In *Placing the Gods: Sanctuaries and Sacred Space in Ancient Greece*, ed. Susan E. Alcock and Robin Osborne, 37–78. Oxford: Clarendon.

———. 1995a. "Empty Cups and Empty Jugs: The Social Role of Wine in Minoan and Mycenaean Societies." In *The Origins and Ancient History of Wine*, ed. P. E. McGovern, S. J. Fleming, and S. H. Katz, 287–309. Luxembourg: Gordon and Breach.

———. 1995b. "From Chief to King in Mycenaean Society." In *Role of the Ruler*, 63–80.

CHAPTER 21

....

DEATH AND BURIAL

....

CHRISTOPHER MEE

NEOLITHIC GREECE
....

In the Mesolithic period, several adults and infants were buried near the entrance
of the Franchthi cave in the Argolid (Jacobsen and Cullen 1981). Two of the adults,
a male and a female, had apparently been cremated (Cullen 1995). Clearly, funeral
practices were already well developed before the start of the Neolithic period. As
the population increased with the growth of settlements, we would expect more
graves. However, the number of excavated Neolithic burials can be counted in the
hundreds, whereas tens of thousands of people lived and died in Greece between
7000 and 3000 BC. Obviously we will never find everyone, but the Neolithic dead
do seem unusually elusive.

Intramural burial within settlements was not common for adults. Most of the
cases that have been recorded were infants or young children (Cavanagh and Mee
1998, 7; Perlès 2001, 276–79). The situation is different in caves that were occupied at
this time, such as Franchthi and Alepotrypa in Laconia (Papathanassopoulos 1996,
175–77). The remains of adults and children have been found at both of these sites,
but few of the skeletons were articulated. Although some may have been disturbed,
it is clear that secondary burial was a regular practice. At Alepotrypa, two ossuaries have been excavated; each contained a mass of bones. Particular attention had
been paid to the skulls, which were sometimes surrounded by a circle of stones. The
darkness of the cave would undoubtedly have heightened the psychological impact
of these rituals.

Secondary burials have occasionally been reported in settlements (Cavanagh
and Mee 1998, 9; Perlès 2001, 279–80). Under one of the houses at Prodromos in
Thessaly were eleven skulls. However, most of the dead must have been buried
elsewhere. An Early Neolithic cemetery was discovered a short distance from

Souphli, another Thessalian site (Gallis 1982; Perlès 2001, 274–76). The dead had been cremated on pyres and included adults and juveniles. Once the body had burned, the remains were removed from the pyre while still hot and buried in a pit. Some of the pottery with the burials was scorched and had obviously been placed on the pyre. Cremation is a more elaborate rite that requires a considerable amount of fuel, so it is significant that no distinction seems to have been made regarding the age or gender of the deceased.

Although Neolithic cremations have been found at a number of other sites, inhumation was probably the most common practice (Cavanagh and Mee 1998, 7–9). So where were most of the dead buried? Excavators would almost certainly miss a cemetery that was some distance from a settlement, yet it is remarkable that more accidental discoveries have not been made, particularly in Thessaly, which has hundreds of Neolithic sites. The explanation may be that most graves were quite shallow and have consequently been destroyed or disturbed by later activities.

This makes it sound as though death was treated rather casually, perhaps because it was such a common occurrence at a time when life expectancy was so short. Children were especially susceptible, and most would have died before they reached adulthood. Neolithic society has also been perceived as relatively egalitarian, which meant that families did not use the funeral as an opportunity to stress status distinctions, and in any case they could not afford a lavish ceremony. Yet some communities did have complex ritual practices that they observed in the case of both children and adults, which may well reflect a more widely held set of beliefs. Moreover, there is evidence of inequality in the Late Neolithic period, if not earlier. Neolithic funerals were probably not as simple as they seem (Cavanagh and Mee 1998, 10–11).

Early Bronze Age

In the Final Neolithic cemetery at Kephala on Keos, the graves were built of stone (Coleman 1977). As a result, the dead had a much more visible presence, and this new trend was soon taken up elsewhere in the Cyclades. Early Bronze Age cemeteries have been excavated on most of the islands (Doumas 1977; Barber 1987, 74–85). Generally they consist of 15–20 graves, though some were much larger, in particular Chalandriani on Syros, with more than 600. The typical grave is a cist, a rectangular or trapezoidal stone-lined pit covered by slabs. Because the graves were usually less than a meter in length, the dead were buried in a contracted position with their legs bent up. It is possible that this was symbolic and not just a practical necessity. Quite often graves were used again, presumably for another family member. The remains of previous burials would then be moved aside to make room, though the skull was usually left undisturbed. In some cists, an extra floor was added so that the upper chamber could be used for burials and the lower chamber as an ossuary.

Many graves produced no finds, though we must bear in mind that perishable items may have been left with the dead. No doubt they wore clothes or a shroud and could have been given items of food that have not survived. Pottery is the most common type of grave good that is present, particularly bowls, cups, and jugs, which suggests the belief that the dead needed provisions for the afterlife. If the obsidian blades were razors, they were probably also expected to look well groomed. Wealth is sometimes emphasized with metal or marble vessels, weapons, jewelry, and figurines.

Once buried, these items had been taken out of circulation in what was clearly intended as a reminder of the status that the deceased had enjoyed in life and which was expected to continue even after death. This display of wealth no doubt promoted the position of the family as well. The marble figurines are particularly impressive, and their artistic appeal is unfortunately the reason so many Early Cycladic graves have been looted. They underline the religious dimension of the rituals that were performed at the funeral, and the discovery of stone platforms in some cemeteries is an indication that ceremonies may also have been held at other times.

In Greece, most of the Early Bronze Age cemeteries are concentrated in the eastern mainland, in the Argolid, Corinthia, Attica, Boeotia, and on Euboea (Cavanagh and Mee 1998, 15–21). At Tsepi in Attica is a cemetery of rectangular built graves that were laid out in rows (Pantelidou-Gofa 2005). Each grave was carefully outlined with a border of stones. The sides of the grave were lined with rubble or slabs, a row of slabs formed the roof, and one end had a narrow entrance. The graves were used repeatedly. The latest burial had generally been left just inside the entrance. At the back of the chamber was a mass of stacked bones, though more care was taken with the skulls, which were sometimes lined up on one side. This is reminiscent of the way that earlier burials were treated in the islands, and much of the pottery, though locally made, is Cycladic in style.

A number of cemeteries contained chamber tombs (Cavanagh and Mee 1998, 17). At Manika on Euboea, the entrance to such tombs was a vertical shaft, off of which opened the chamber, which could be rectangular, trapezoidal, or circular (Sampson 1985, 1988). The chamber was carefully blocked off by slabs or stones. The dead had usually been buried in a contracted position despite the fact that the chambers were often more than two meters in diameter. Thus, the size of the tomb did not necessarily dictate how the body would be laid out. Earlier burials were pushed to one side, and in some cases the bones had apparently been removed and put in an ossuary. The quantity and quality of the finds varies, presumably because of differences in status. A connection with the Cyclades is evident, and the presence of marble figurines suggests that these shared tastes reflect similar beliefs.

On Lefkas in western Greece, the dead were cremated, and the grave goods were also placed on the pyre (Dörpfeld 1927). Once this had burned down, the remains and some of the grave goods were collected and put into a pithos, which was sealed with a slab. A circular stone platform was then built around the pithos, and this also covered the pyre. The platform was in turn covered by a mound of earth and stones, which formed a tumulus. In many of the tumuli, additional graves were later inserted in the stone platform. This marks the start of a vogue for circular tombs in western Greece that continues in the Middle Bronze Age, though elsewhere on the mainland there is more of a break (Cavanagh and Mee 1998, 17).

Different regional traditions also developed on Crete. The tombs in the south of the island were circular stone tholoi (Branigan 1993). The first tholoi were constructed in EM I, and this was still the most common tomb type in the Protopalatial period. Around seventy have been discovered in cemeteries of one, two, or three tombs. At sites with more than one tomb, their use overlaps. They were built a short distance from the settlement, often within 100 meters or so (Branigan 1998). The dead were nearby, but the tombs were oriented so that the entrance faced away from the settlement. Consequently, they could not see their homes and would be less inclined to return. The fact that the tomb entrances were carefully blocked highlights this desire to keep the dead in their place. Nevertheless, because of the size and solid construction of the tombs, they were a very visible and permanent presence. Many of them remained in use for centuries and would have been a powerful symbol of the entitlement that a community could claim to land and other key resources (Murphy 1998).

A tholos has a circular wall made up of a rubble core faced with larger blocks of stone, which can be more than two meters thick in the case of the largest tombs, which have a diameter of ten meters or more (Branigan 1998). There has been considerable speculation about the type of roof. Because the walls lean in and masses of fallen stone have sometimes been found in the chamber, the obvious solution is a stone vault. However, the walls were not buttressed in any way, so they could not have supported the weight of a stone roof. Mud brick is an alternative, though this would be identifiable and has not been reported from any of the excavated tombs. Thatch is another possibility, but no consensus exists as yet. The entrance was almost always on the east side of the tomb, so sunrise may have had a special significance. A number of tholoi also had annexes in front of the entrance, which had been added later.

Because of the length of time the tholoi remained in use and the fact that most have been looted, it is not easy to reconstruct the funeral rites (Branigan 1993). The dead were apparently laid out on the floor of the tomb with personal possessions, which could include weapons, tools, jewelry, seal stones, and pottery. Food and drink were provided, some of which may have been consumed by the mourners at the funeral. The number of cups suggests that a toast was drunk or libations poured before the entrance of the tomb was sealed. Few skeletons have been found in situ, and it is evident that, once the body had decomposed, the bones were swept aside. It seems that the tombs were periodically cleaned out and purified. The bones would then be transferred to one of the annexes, which were used as ossuaries. When the remains of earlier burials were moved, no doubt a ceremony marked this final stage of the journey. The presence of stone platforms suggests that the tombs may have been a focus for cult and ritual activity at other times as well, which implies that the dead were venerated if not worshipped. As far as we can tell, the entire community was buried in these tombs. There was certainly no discrimination on the basis of age or gender. Some tombs were probably reserved for particular groups of families, which would explain why settlements had two or three tholoi, but differences in status were not emphasized.

At Ayia Photia in eastern Crete is a cemetery with more than 250 EM I/II tombs. Most have a vertical shaft and a rectangular or oval chamber sealed by a stone slab (Davaras and Betancourt 2004). Similar tombs appear in the Cyclades, and much of the pottery and metalwork is Cycladic in style. The possibility that this was a case of colonization rather than acculturation or close contact has therefore been raised. There were also rectangular stone-built tombs in the northern and eastern parts of the island (Soles 1992; Vavouranakis 2007). In some respects they resemble houses, but it is questionable whether they were conceived as a home away from home for the dead. The cemetery on the island of Mochlos was located so that the tombs would be visible from the sea as ships approached, but they cannot be seen from the settlement. Approximately thirty tombs have been excavated, built up against the rock face in such a way that they seem like part of the landscape. A processional path winds up through the cemetery to the most elaborate tombs I/II/III and IV/V/VI. In front of IV/V/VI were a paved court and a platform, possibly an altar. Although the tombs have been disturbed, they were evidently used for primary burials. In due course, the bones were moved to another compartment, where the skulls were carefully stacked together. Much of the jewelry that was buried in the tombs is of gold or silver. Many superb stone vessels have also been found. The finest objects were not found exclusively in the largest tombs, though they were concentrated in I/II/III and IV/V/VI. Status must have been a more contentious issue at Mochlos and was certainly the case at Malia, where one of the tombs is enormous. Known as the Chrysolakkos, or gold pit (from the spectacular finds, most of which were looted), the tomb measures approximately forty by thirty meters, and the interior was divided into rows of burial compartments. Built at the start of the Protopalatial period, at around the same time as the palace at Malia, it was surely reserved for the elite (Soles 1992, 163–71).

The burial record is not always an accurate barometer of social change, but the political upheavals on Crete clearly had an impact. The cemetery at Archanes in the north of the island is unusual in that it contains tholoi and rectangular built tombs (Sakellarakis and Sapouna-Sakellaraki 1997). This fusion of two distinct architectural styles integrated different traditions and continued in the Middle Minoan period, when the cemetery was expanded. Tomb B, a two-story structure with a tholos enclosed on three sides by annexes, is particularly impressive. Many of the dead were buried in clay jars or terracotta larnakes. It is unclear whether this was an indication of higher status or reflects a greater emphasis on individuality, which is evident from the choice of personal items in these tombs. The seal stones especially were a mark of identity. It is significant that the level of activity at Archanes increased in MM IA, just before the old palaces were constructed, a time when the competition for power must have intensified.

MIDDLE BRONZE AGE

In Greece, the situation was very different. Many of the Early Helladic cemeteries went out of use, and burial in simple pit or cist graves became the rule (Cavanagh and Mee 1998, 23–35). The most impressive Middle Helladic tombs were tumuli, which can be as much as 25 meters in diameter. However, even though a central grave sometimes occurs, which suggests a recognition of higher status, the finds are generally rather modest, especially in comparison with the Early Helladic tumuli on Lefkas (Boyd 2002). In the pit and cist graves, this impression of austerity is even more apparent. Less than 30% of the two hundred Middle Helladic burials at Lerna had any recognizable grave goods, and this figure is fairly typical. Some settlements did have cemeteries with clusters of graves in which members of the same family had presumably been buried. Intramural burial was also very common, though the graves were often in a part of the settlement that had been abandoned or was not occupied at the time. It was usually children who were buried under the houses.

As an example of a Middle Helladic cemetery, one may look at Kouphovouno in Laconia, where sixteen graves have been excavated, as well as the remains of skeletons that had been disturbed (Cavanagh and Lagia in press). Some of the graves were pits that were often edged with stones that had supported a roof made of perishable material. There were also cists constructed of upright slabs (figure 21.1). The dead had usually been buried on their sides in a contracted position. Only a few had grave goods. The remains of twenty-seven individuals have been identified, adults and children, males and females (table 21.1).

The greatest likelihood of death was in infancy/early childhood and late adolescence/young adulthood. The mortality rate between birth and five years was very high in these communities. At Lerna, the figure is almost 50%, so parents could expect that half of their children would die before they were five. The reason for this was nutritional deficiency combined with childhood diseases. The second phase of increased mortality in late adolescence/young adulthood is usually due to the risks of childbirth, but women of this age are underrepresented at Kouphovouno, and they may have been buried in another part of the cemetery. A number of the males in this group had suffered serious injuries; one had somehow been cut in two. Some graves contained the remains of adults and infants. The natural assumption is that a mother and infant were buried together, but in one case the adult was male, and DNA analysis has shown that the two individuals were related.

The people of Kouphovouno were not very healthy (Cavanagh and Lagia in press). Study of the skeletons has shown that, as children, they were malnourished and suffered from diseases, in particular rickets, scurvy, measles, and smallpox. Hard work had caused degenerative changes in the adult skeletons of both sexes. Arthritis and osteoporosis were also common. Stable isotope analysis of the carbon and nitrogen in bone samples from Kouphovouno indicates a diet that mainly consisted of plant foods, such as wheat, barley, and fruits. Some animal protein was consumed, either as meat or dairy products, but not in significant quantities.

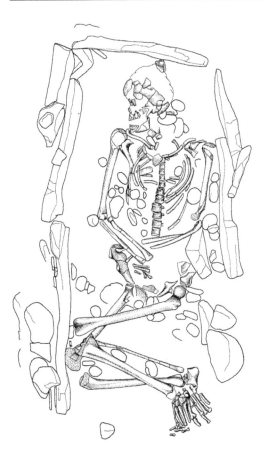

Figure 21.1. Cist grave at Kouphovouno (courtesy of the author).

Table 21.1. Middle Helladic cemetery at Kouphovouno in Laconia

Age Group	Number of Individuals	Male	Female	Indeterminate Sex
Infants (0–1 yrs.)	5			5
Young children (2–5 yrs.)	3			3
Older children (6–12 yrs.)	1			1
Adolescents (13–19 yrs.)	5	3	1	1
Young adults (20–34 yrs.)	3	3		
Middle-aged adults (35–49 yrs.)	4	3	1	
Old adults (50+ yrs.)	2		2	
Adults (20+ yrs.)	4	1		3
Total	27	10	4	13

Source: Courtesy of the author.

For many Middle Helladic communities, life must have been fairly grim, and it is difficult to escape the conclusion that this was a period when most people were desperately poor. However, there were exceptions. Kolonna on Aigina was a fortified settlement that had built up a network of trade contacts and was consequently quite prosperous. Just in front of the main gate in the fortifications, a man was buried with a sword, a dagger, a spear, a helmet, and a gold diadem (Kilian-Dirlmeier 1997). He was clearly an exceptional individual who was commemorated as a warrior, perhaps because of his military prowess. He also set a precedent for the spectacularly rich burials in the shaft graves at Mycenae.

LATE BRONZE AGE

Although the two shaft grave circles at Mycenae were in use before the end of the Middle Helladic period, they nonetheless mark the start of a new era. Circle A is prominently positioned just inside the Lion Gate, but this arrangement dates from LH IIIB, when the fortifications were extended. At the same time, the grave circle was carefully restored, and the original enclosure wall was replaced. This was done three centuries or so after the final burial had taken place and indicates a reverence for the dead that suggests that they were worshipped as the founders of the royal dynasty, whatever their relationship with the later rulers of Mycenae may in fact have been.

There were six shaft graves in Circle A, the largest of which measured 4.50 by 6.40 meters and was 4.00 meters deep (Karo 1930–1933; Dickinson 1977, 46–50). The graves consisted of a rectangular shaft cut through the earth and rock, with a ledge at the lower end to support the roof. Nineteen people had been buried in the graves: eight men, nine women, and two children. The men had an extraordinary array of weapons, an arsenal of finely crafted swords, daggers, spears, and knives. They are depicted as heroic warriors and hunters on some of the gold rings from the graves. Men and women were covered in jewelry, in particular gold discs that were sewn on their clothes or shrouds. Some of the men wore gold funeral masks. The dead were also provided with gold and silver cups and goblets, presumably so that they could dine in style in the underworld.

Grave Circle B was only a short distance from the citadel but had evidently been forgotten by the LH IIIB period (Mylonas 1973; Dickinson 1977, 40–46). The fourteen shaft graves were generally not as large as those in Circle A, and there were also eleven cist and pit graves. A built grave, tomb Rho, was added later. It was not possible to determine the age and sex of all of the burials, but adults outnumber children 24:8, and there are also three times as many men as women. The maximum number of burials was four in grave Gamma: three men and a woman. One of the men had been buried first, followed by the woman. Their skeletons were subsequently moved aside for the burial of the man in the center. Finally, another man was laid across one end of the grave. After each burial, the roof was replaced and sealed with clay. The shaft was then filled with earth, and the grave was marked by a low mound and sometimes a carved gravestone.

Men, women, and children were buried in Grave Circle B with an impressive range of grave goods, but many of the dead had only pottery. The Circle A burials were generally much richer (Laffineur 1989; Graziadio 1991). However, it is important to note that, although the two circles coexisted for a time, Circle B was in use first. Thus, it could be argued that what we see is an escalation in conspicuous consumption because the wealth that was taken out of circulation when it was deposited in these graves had effectively been destroyed. The reason for this extravagance was a desire for prestige and consequently status (Voutsaki 1995). This was evidently a period of political instability, and funerals were an occasion for legitimizing the transfer of power and rights of succession. Those buried in the grave circles were clearly an élite who had set themselves apart. Yet there must also have been divisions within this group, which would explain why Circle A was established.

The shaft graves were essentially enlarged pit graves and could be viewed as an example of the ostentation that is such a feature of this period. However, their size also facilitated a move to collective burial, which is equally true of tholos and chamber tombs (Cavanagh and Mee 1998, 41–49). Tholos tombs originated in Messenia at the end of the Middle Helladic period (Voutsaki 1998). These new types of tomb were designed to be reopened periodically for the burial of individuals who were no doubt related in some way, so this practice places a much greater emphasis on hereditary status. The narrow *dromos* leads to the entrance of the tomb. The circular burial chamber has a corbeled stone vault (Pelon 1976). Unlike Minoan tholoi, the Mycenaean tombs were cut into the bedrock, so that the vault was buttressed, and they were covered by an earth mound.

Soon there were tholos tombs in the Argolid and Laconia, as well as Messenia. In LH II, seven were constructed at Mycenae, where they replaced shaft graves as the high-status option. It seems quite likely that some were royal tombs, though tholoi were probably not reserved just for rulers. Most had been robbed, but a few were still intact or had pits in the chamber floor that had not been opened. This was the case at Dendra in the Argolid and Vapheio in Laconia, for example. The character and quality of the finds emphasizes how important the funeral had become for these image-conscious individuals.

Chamber tombs have a similar layout but were rock cut rather than stone built (Cavanagh and Mee 1998, 54–55). Some have circular chambers like tholos tombs or are rectangular. At Prosymna in the Argolid, the size of the chamber ranges from 5–30 square meters (Blegen 1937), though one of the tombs at Pellana in Laconia has a chamber more than 10 meters in diameter, as large as a tholos. It is questionable whether there were any rigid rules about who could be buried in a tholos or chamber tomb in LH I–II (Voutsaki 1995). The Minoans also had rock-cut chamber tombs (Pini 1968), which the Mycenaeans may well have seen and adapted. The distinctive mainland style of tomb is then found at Knossos in LM II–IIIA, when it is believed that the palace was under Mycenaean control. The warriors who were buried in these tombs have quite naturally been identified as Mycenaeans, but this assumption has been questioned (Preston 1999, 2004). It is equally possible that they were Minoans whose way of life had been influenced by the warrior ethos, which was prevalent in Greece at this time. There may be a more subtle explanation for changes in the burial record than an alteration in the ethnic makeup of a community.

Although LH III is often regarded as a period of greater uniformity (and it is true that there is less experimentation during this time), regional differences are apparent (Cavanagh and Mee 1998, 77–79). For example, Messenia had few chamber tomb cemeteries, unlike in Boeotia, where tholos tombs were a rarity. Variation is also evident at a more local level, possibly because communities wished to maintain their traditions and consequently an independent identity as the Mycenaean palaces grew more powerful and influential. Some rulers may well have imposed restrictions.

Mycenae and Tiryns were the only sites in the Argolid where tholos tombs were constructed in LH IIIA–B. Moreover, the tombs at Mycenae were the magnificent Treasury of Atreus and the Tomb of Clytemnaestra. It would have taken around twenty thousand man days to build the Treasury of Atreus (Cavanagh and Mee 1999). The tomb is approached down a *dromos* 36 meters in length, which is lined with ashlar masonry. The façade was decorated with green and red marble columns. Above the entrance, which was sealed by double doors sheathed in bronze, is a lintel block that weighs approximately 120 tons. The chamber is 14.5 meters in diameter and 13.6 meters high, with thirty-three smoothly finished courses of masonry (Pelon 1976). The ruler who built this tomb was no doubt buried in the side chamber.

Chamber tombs were much more common in LH III and must have been used by a wider cross-section of society (Cavanagh and Mee 1998, 65–79). They were likely family tombs, but at those sites where the skeletal remains have been properly studied, children were clearly underrepresented. Moreover, they had often been buried in a niche in front of the entrance rather than in the chamber or were given separate tombs. The fact that children were treated differently does not imply a lack of concern or respect. Parents would have grieved when a child died, but with the mortality rate hovering around 50% for those under the age of ten, the death of a child was a frequent occurrence. To cope psychologically with their loss, parents may not have viewed children as full-fledged members of society who needed to be ritually reunited with their ancestors. Of course, some children were buried alongside adults, and it is evident that the conventions that governed behavior were very flexible. Curiously, men also outnumber women in Mycenaean tombs. Although it is true that female skeletons are not as robust and would therefore be more likely to have disintegrated, this does not fully account for the discrepancy. There seems to have been a gender bias, which may be linked with the dependent status of most of the women as wives and daughters in Mycenaean society (Mee 1998).

We can reconstruct the ceremonies at the graveside from the hundreds of excavated chamber tombs, but the first part of the funeral took place away from the cemetery, probably in or outside the home of the person who had died. Terracotta

Figure 21.2. Tanagra larnax (after Cavanagh and Mee 1995, 48, figure 1).

larnakes from Tanagra in Boeotia depict processions of women who raise their hands to their heads in a gesture that clearly expresses their grief (Cavanagh and Mee 1995; Immerwahr 1995) (figure 21.2). Their dress suggests that they led the mourners when the corpse was laid out and the community members came to pay their respects. Other women with shaved heads and lacerated faces were presumably close relatives. In one highly emotional scene, they lower the body of a child into a larnax. Men occasionally appear on the larnakes but do not seem to have been as closely involved, perhaps because there were taboos that restricted how they could act.

The journey to the cemetery began a process of separation that took the dead physically and symbolically away from family and friends (Cavanagh and Mee 1998, 71–76, 103–20; Gallou 2005, 82–132). Once the body had been brought into the tomb, it was laid out, normally in an extended position, on the floor or a bench (Wace 1932). Terracotta larnakes and wooden coffins were occasionally used. The pottery provided often includes jars of perfumed oil, a tradition that would continue for centuries. The oil was a luxury and also signified purity. Vessels with food and drink may be the residue of a funeral feast, though it was evidently expected that the dead would need supplies for the afterlife. They were given jewelry and no doubt wore their finest clothes as well. There is less of an emphasis on weaponry, perhaps because it was now believed that bronze should be kept in circulation. Terracotta female figurines, found with children, probably offered protection. The entrance was then carefully blocked with stone, a toast was drunk, and the cups were shattered against the wall. Finally, the *dromos* was backfilled with earth. When the next funeral took place, the *dromos* and the entrance would be unblocked and the process repeated. However, the time would come when the chamber offered no more room. At this point, earlier burials were moved to one side, or the bones were collected and placed in a pit.

This practice has often been seen as rather cavalier, and a contrast has been drawn between the care taken when the dead were first buried and their later treatment. However, tombs have been excavated in which none of the skeletons was undisturbed. It seems likely that the chamber had been reopened for a ceremony that involved the rearrangement of the last burial. Ceremonies of this type were probably a regular occurrence and marked the final stage in the journey that the dead had undertaken. Like many societies, the Mycenaeans evidently believed in a liminal phase between life and death. This ended when the body had decomposed and the spirit was freed. Ceremonies ensured that the dead were placated and would not cause trouble. They also gave the bereaved time to adjust to their loss.

After the destruction of the palaces at the end of the LH IIIB period, no more major tholos tombs and fewer chamber tombs were built (Cavanagh and Mee 1998, 89–97; Dickinson 2006, 178–83). Sometimes tombs that had gone out of use were cleared and reused, presumably by a different group. Some new chamber tombs appeared, notably at Perati in Attica, but they were small and not as well constructed (Iakovidis 1969). This is not a sign of poverty, however, because some of the Perati tombs were quite rich. Nevertheless, many of the tombs held only one or two skeletons, which suggests a change of beliefs. It was no longer the custom that generations of the same family would be buried together, which anticipates the move to individual burial in the Early Iron Age. The funeral ceremony may also have been curtailed, which could explain the introduction of cremation. The first Mycenaean cremations were at Müskebi in western Anatolia, and the rite may have spread from there. The puzzle is that, at Perati, for example, we find cremations and inhumations in the same tomb. Thus, it seems unlikely that those who were cremated came from a different ethnic group. Changes such as the move to individual burial (Lewartowski 2000) and the adoption of cremation were once used as evidence of population movements in the twelfth and eleventh centuries. What they actually reflect is the sense of insecurity that had undermined confidence in the social order and the traditions that underpinned this.

BIBLIOGRAPHY

Barber, Robin L. N. 1987. *The Cyclades in the Bronze Age*. London: Duckworth.
Blegen, Carl W. 1937. *Prosymna: The Helladic Settlement Preceding the Argive Heraeum*. Cambridge: Cambridge University Press.
Boyd, Michael. 2002. *Middle Helladic and Early Mycenaean Mortuary Practices in the Southern and Western Peloponnese*. Oxford: Archaeopress.

Branigan, Keith. 1993. *Dancing with Death: Life and Death in Southern Crete c. 3000–2000 BC*. Amsterdam: Hakkert.

———. 1998. "The Nearness of You: Proximity and Distance in Early Minoan Funerary Behavior." In *Cemetery and Society in the Aegean Bronze Age*, ed. Keith Branigan, 13–26. Sheffield Studies in Aegean Archaeology 1. Sheffield: Sheffield Academic Press.

Cavanagh, William, and Anna Lagia. In press. "Burials from Kouphovouno, Sparta, Lakonia." In *Mesohelladika*.

Cavanagh, William G., and Christopher Mee. 1995. "Mourning before and after the Dark Age." In *Klados: Festschrift for Nicolas Coldstream*, ed. Christine Morris, 45–61. London: Institute of Classical Studies.

———. 1998. *A Private Place: Death in Prehistoric Greece*. Jonsered, Sweden: Åström.

———. 1999. "Building the Treasury of Atreus." In *Meletemata*, 93–102.

Coleman, John E. 1977. *Keos I: Kephala*. Princeton: American School of Classical Studies.

Cullen, Tracey. 1995. "Mesolithic Mortuary Ritual at Franchthi Cave, Greece." *Antiquity* 69: 270–89.

Davaras, Costis, and Philip P. Betancourt. 2004. *The Hagia Photia Cemetery I: The Tomb Groups and Architecture*. Philadelphia: INSTAP Academic Press.

Dickinson, Oliver T. P. K. 1977. *The Origins of Mycenaean Civilisation*. Gothenburg: Åström.

Dickinson, Oliver T. P. K. 2006. *The Aegean from Bronze Age to Iron Age*. London: Routledge.

Dörpfeld, Wilhelm. 1927. *Alt-Ithaka: Ein Beitrag zur Homer-Frage*. Munich: Uhde.

Doumas, Christos. 1977. *Early Bronze Age Burial Habits in the Cyclades*. Gothenburg: Åström.

Gallis, Konstantinos I. 1982. *Kafseis Nekron apo ti Neolithiki Epochi sti Thessalia*. Athens: Archaiologiki Etaireia.

Gallou, Chrysanthi. 2005. *The Mycenaean Cult of the Dead*. Oxford: Archaeopress.

Graziadio, Giampaolo. 1991. "The Process of Social Stratification at Mycenae in the Shaft Grave Period: A Comparative Examination of the Evidence." *AJA* 95: 403–40.

Iakovidis, Spiros. 1969. *Perati: To Nekrotapheion*. Athens: Archaiologiki Etaireia.

Immerwahr, Sara A. 1995. "Death and the Tanagra Larnakes." In *The Ages of Homer: A Tribute to Emily Vermeule*, ed. Jane B. Carter and Sarah P. Morris, 109–21. Austin: University of Texas Press.

Jacobsen, Thomas W., and Tracey Cullen. 1981. "A Consideration of Mortuary Practices in Neolithic Greece: Burials from Franchthi Cave." In *Mortality and Immortality: The Anthropology of Death*, ed. Sally C. Humphreys and Helen King, 79–101. London: Academic Press.

Karo, Georg. 1930–1933. *Die Schachtgräber von Mykenai*. Munich: Bruckmann.

Kilian-Dirlmeier, Imma. 1997. *Das mittelbronzezeitliche Schachtgräb von Ägina*. Mainz: Von Zabern.

Laffineur, Robert. 1989. "Mobilier funéraire et hiérarchie sociale aux cercles des tombes de Mycènes." In *Transition: Le monde égéen du Bronze moyen au Bronze récent*, ed. Robert Laffineur, 227–38. Liège: Université de Liège.

Lewartowski, Kazimierz. 2000. *Late Helladic Simple Graves: A Study of Mycenaean Burial Customs*. Oxford: Archaeopress.

Mee, Christopher. 1998. "Gender Bias in Mycenaean Mortuary Practices." In *Cemetery and Society in the Aegean Bronze Age*, ed. Keith Branigan, 165–70. Sheffield Studies in Aegean Archaeology 1. Sheffield: Sheffield Academic Press.

Murphy, Joanne M. 1998. "Ideologies, Rites, and Rituals: A View of Prepalatial Minoan Tholoi." In *Cemetery and Society in the Aegean Bronze Age*, ed. Keith Branigan, 27–40. Sheffield Studies in Aegean Archaeology 1. Sheffield: Sheffield Academic Press.

Mylonas, George E. 1973. *O Taphikos Kyklos B ton Mykinon.* Athens: Archaiologiki Etaireia.

Pantelidou-Gofa, Maria. 2005. *Tsepi Marathonas: To Protoelladiko Nekrotapheio.* Athens: Archaiologiki Etaireia.

Papathanassopoulos, George A. 1996. *Neolithic Culture in Greece.* Athens: Goulandris Foundation.

Pelon, Oliver. 1976. *Tholoi, tumuli, et cercles funéraires: Recherches sur les monuments funéraires de plan circulaire dans l'Egée de l'âge du Bronze (IIIe et IIe millénaires av. J-C.).* Paris: de Boccard.

Perlès, Catherine. 2001. *The Early Neolithic in Greece: The First Farming Communities in Europe.* New York: Cambridge University Press.

Pini, Ingo. 1968. *Beiträge zur minoischen Gräberkunde.* Wiesbaden: Franz Steiner.

Preston, Laura. 1999. "Mortuary Practices and the Negotiation of Social Identities at LM II Knossos." *BSA* 94: 131–43.

———. 2004. "A Mortuary Perspective on Political Changes in Late Minoan II–IIIB Crete." *AJA* 108: 321–48.

Sakellarakis, Ioannis, and Effie Sapouna-Sakellaraki. 1997. *Archanes: Minoan Crete in a New Light.* Athens: Ammos.

Sampson, Adamantios. 1985. *Manika I: Mia Protoelladiki Poli sti Khalkida.* Athens: Etaireia Euboikon Spoudon.

———. 1988. *Manika II: O Protoelladikos Oikismos kai to Nekrotapheio.* Athens: Demos Khalkideon.

Soles, Jeffrey S. 1992. *The Prepalatial Cemeteries at Mochlos and Gournia and the House Tombs of Bronze Age Crete.* Princeton: American School of Classical Studies.

Vavouranakis, Giorgos. 2007. *Funerary Landscapes East of Lasithi, Crete, in the Bronze Age.* Oxford: Archaeopress.

Voutsaki, Sofia. 1995. "Social and Political Processes in the Mycenaean Argolid: The Evidence from the Mortuary Practices." In *Politeia,* 55–66.

———. 1998. "Mortuary Evidence, Symbolic Meanings, and Social Change: A Comparison between Messenia and the Argolid in the Mycenaean Period." In *Cemetery and Society in the Aegean Bronze Age,* ed. K. Branigan, 41–58. Sheffield Studies in Aegean Archaeology 1. Sheffield: Sheffield Academic Press.

Wace, Alan J. B. 1932. *Chamber Tombs at Mycenae.* Oxford: Society of Antiquaries.

Watrous, L. Vance. 2001. "Crete from Earliest Prehistory through the Protopalatial Period." In *Aegean Prehistory,* 157–223.

CHAPTER 22

TRADE

BRYAN E. BURNS

TRADE is typically defined as the exchange of good and services within a mercantile or economic framework that may or may not involve currency. Political and ideological dynamics, however, may structure commercial exchange as much as economic rules. The transfer of goods, furthermore, is necessarily accompanied by the movement of people, which enables additional interaction such as the sharing of technology or the communication of ideas and beliefs. Thus, the archaeological study of trade necessarily includes a spectrum of activities that are often difficult to distinguish from one another, based on surviving artifacts and corollary evidence. It is clear that these various processes by which communities interacted greatly influenced the development of polities and the lives of people—providing foodstuffs and luxuries, enabling new crafts and new artistic statements, and potentially reshaping the means of power and persuasion.

The individual societies of the Aegean developed while in frequent contact with each other throughout the Bronze Age and with varying intensities they maintained ties with more distant regions of Europe, Africa, and Asia. From these different directions came a diverse range of useful materials, such as lapis lazuli from Afghanistan, amber from the Baltic, ivory from Egypt and the Levant, and copper from Cyprus. The source of some materials remains elusive, but it is clear that desirable commodities such as tin and gold do not naturally occur within the Aegean. While there is little doubt that the need for bronze-making metals spurred interregional trade in the Mediterranean (Knapp 1990; Muhly 2003), the exchange of luxury, or less utilitarian, items enabled powerful statements. In this regard, eastern regions made the strongest contribution, as the sophisticated states of Egypt, the Levant, Mesopotamia, and Anatolia provided a wealth of precious items that functioned as technological and artistic models for the development of Aegean arts and society.

The nature and extent of eastern influence on the Aegean has been the subject of vigorous scholarly debate, beginning with the initial presentations of Mycenaean and Minoan culture. Sir Arthur Evans attributed the creation of Minoan civilization to the movement of people and ideas from north Africa and western Asia, which he deduced from shared styles of dress, crafts, and architecture. He further proposed the possibility of "more intangible influences that may have been brought to bear in the domain of ideas—in Cretan religion for instance, in law and government, or even in literary tradition" (Evans 1921, 19), thus providing an extended example for V. Gordon Childe's theory of cultural diffusion (1925, 22–40).

A divergent thread of scholarship has turned inward in the search for the causes of growing social complexity. Again for Crete, Colin Renfrew (1972) put forward a comprehensive theory that tied the rise of a social and political elite to perceived needs for the redistribution of agricultural commodities. Nonetheless, the arrival of goods and technologies from the Near East was contemporary with the increased social stratification on Crete, demonstrating the availability of a model for the nascent palatial administration. Similarly, the introduction of foreign goods from sophisticated neighbors in the Shaft Graves at Mycenae appears to be intertwined with the rise of an indigenous elite on mainland Greece.

A balanced approach to the role of foreign exchange in the rise of Aegean states and the continued development of social structures stresses the opportunities and pressures created by external contacts. Rather than expecting to find the wholesale importation of an administrative system or asserting "some vaguely defined 'civilis-ing influence' from the East as the direct cause of state origins" (Cherry 1984, 38), comparative studies suggest that exchange with a more highly structured neighbor may provoke changes in settlement distributions, resource management, or admin-istrative hierarchy through internal processes that follow the primary interaction (Renfrew 1975, esp. 32–35; cf. Parkinson and Galaty 2007).

The impact of exchange need not be measured on a societal scale alone. Mary Helms (1988) has demonstrated the ways in which travel and the acquisition of foreign items operate as pathways to power, by which individuals lay claim to the special status accorded to geographically distant peoples and places. In some cul-tures, the emphasis is found "primarily in the very activity and practice of maritime movement itself" (Broodbank 2000, 290), yet power can also be accrued through the acquisitions of foreign items themselves (Helms 1993). The sustained exploita-tion of resources from an outside realm can demonstrate ongoing international relationships, and leaders' oversight of the process that converts exotic materials into locally significant items creates an opportunity to create new instruments of influence in the form of prestige objects (cf. D'Altroy and Earle 1985).

I have chosen specific cases of Aegean trade and exchange for this chapter with these possibilities in mind, aiming not only to describe general trends and eco-nomic implications of exchange but also to emphasize the importance of trade for the functioning of social and political structures. Andrew Sherratt and Susan Sherratt (1991) have taken a similar tack by calling attention to the importance of demand and "conspicuous consumption" within the societies taking part in

Mediterranean exchange. Their general model for interregional trade posits a phase of initial exchange of high-value, low-bulk preciosities that eventually leads to "full linkage," wherein each side provides bulk materials and products. In reaching this final step, though, local production is not only stimulated by external trade but also often restructured, as new social institutions become necessary to control increased production and circulation.

As indicated earlier, the rise of complex civilizations in the Aegean is at least chronologically related to new instances of foreign interaction, and social changes were arguably intermeshed with transferred technology, shifts in style, and the new availability of key materials. Political leaders, whether claiming or legitimizing power, often take advantage of the social and economic benefits of long-distance exchange (cf. Liverani 1990; Brumfiel 1994, 6), and the connection between local authority and foreign trade grew more complex over the course of the Bronze Age. The elite ruling from palatial sites like Knossos, Mycenae, and Thebes enjoyed rare luxuries and also manipulated exchange networks to maintain centralized power.

Yet to fully appreciate the impact of international trade on Aegean society, one needs to also point to a broad range of contexts with activities that were stimulated, enabled, and empowered by external impulses. As the scale of exchange increased during the Bronze Age, so too must the diversity of interactions have grown. That is to say, no single description of trade can explain the complicated scenarios of the Late Bronze Age Mediterranean, and we should bear in mind the likely coexistence of a number of means of exchange (Knapp and Cherry 1994, 127–28). Among these is the possibility that the transfer of goods was not necessarily a voluntary exchange but rather accompanied by physical force or political aggression.

EARLY BRONZE AGE

Exchange during the Early Bronze Age was largely contained within the Aegean, with distinct cultural zones arising through interaction of limited distances. For example, northern Aegean sites such as Poliochni on Lemnos shared cultural traits with Macedonia and Thrace and participated in exchange networks with the Troad. Through this route imports from western Anatolia may have penetrated as far south as Euboea and into the Cyclades (Lambrou-Phillipson 1990, 100). Travel and trade were particularly important to development in the Cyclades (Broodbank 2000), where inhabitants depended on interisland travel to acquire limited resources, such as copper from Kythnos and silver and lead from Siphnos (Stos-Gale and Macdonald 1991), as well as the Melian obsidian, which had been exploited for millennia.

The possibility of contact farther beyond the Aegean during the EBA has been raised by the discovery of early Egyptian stone vessels at Mycenae and Knossos, including a predynastic jar that Peter Warren pronounced one of the oldest imported items in the Aegean (1969, 114). This vessel, however, was found in a well-provisioned chamber tomb of the Late Helladic III period (Tomb 55), indicating a final deposition a thousand years after its manufacture. Rather than consider this to be an heirloom, recirculated in its new cultural context, it was more plausibly imported long after it was first manufactured. As such, it finds good company in the small group of predynastic stone vessels found at Knossos but in problematic, likely later, contexts (Bevan 2004, 110–11).

Egyptian contact with Crete during the third millennium is better evidenced by the style and material of Early Minoan seals, such as those in ivory or carved in distinctly Egyptian shapes like scarabs (Aruz 2008, 53–76). This introduction of non-Aegean imagery and objects in the Prepalatial period has been suggested as the beginning of significant interaction between Egypt and Minoan Crete, though the number of relevant artifacts is strictly limited (Warren 1995). The relative rarity of these imported objects arguably intensifies the value that each one carried and suggests that they functioned as powerful objects with which emergent elites were able to distinguish themselves (Manning 1994, 243–44; Manning and Huhlin 2005, 282).

The Prepalatial cemetery at Mochlos, where social stratification is visible in a community's treatment of the dead, provides a good example of the exploitation of foreign contacts by a limited few. Twenty-eight tombs of the "house type" were used during the EM II and EM III periods, only a few of which also contained MM I material (Seager 1912; Soles 1992, 41–42). Cynthia Colburn's analysis of the tombs' contents shows the stark concentration of imported stone, metal, and ivory objects in only three of the tombs (2008, 210–12, table 2). Two of these are also the largest, most architecturally complex tombs of the Mochlos cemetery (Tombs I/II/III and IV/V/VI), each combining three separate chambers that held a number of separate interments. As locations of repeated activity, where previously entombed bodies were rearranged and earlier burial goods reencountered, each tomb contained an accumulation of valued symbols. For example, the items of gold, faience, and chalcedony found in compartment IV (Seager 1912, 48–49, figure 20) were not so much taken out of circulation as given further meaning through their deposition in a funerary context. Colburn (2008, 217–20) further emphasizes the personal, corporeal nature of the surviving imports as items of adornment and argues that these were markers of status used by living individuals, primarily women, as well as for depositions with the dead. This makes material such as the Mochlos jewelry even more compelling, as items of individual identity consolidated to mark an elite group monument.

Palatial Crete

The appearance of the palatial centers during the Middle Minoan period signals a new level of economic centralization that fostered increased local exchange and strengthened regional styles of production (Knappet 1999). The first palaces were, arguably, well positioned to take control over long-distance trade routes. Yet the nature and distribution of the surviving imports from Protopalatial Crete—with those from MM Knossos, for example, fairly well balanced by a number of seals and weapons from the Mesara tombs—do not themselves indicate palatial control (Lambrou-Phillipson 1990; Wiener 1991). A remarkable absence of imported objects has been noted, for example, from the well-preserved portions of the first palace at Phaistos (Carinci 2000), and Ilse Schoep (2006) has emphasized the interests of nonpalatial elite in participating in foreign ventures. Even if the agents of trade are difficult to define, a steady pulse of high-value, low-bulk imports flowed into Middle Minoan Crete, and evidence for the export of Minoan products beyond Crete points to a growing importance of trade.

Increased contact with Eastern Mediterranean polities clearly provided opportunities for early palatial rulers to exploit. Although numerous components of the Minoan administration—from the architectural form of the palace to the seal- and tablet-using bureaucracy—have eastern predecessors, no single point of influence is easily identified (Warren 1987, Watrous 1987). Similarly, it is challenging to link many of the imported objects found in early palatial contexts with specific points of origin. A terracotta plaque from Quartier Mu at Malia, for example, was manufactured locally but has been described as an Egyptianizing sphinx that combines the body of a lion with the face of a bearded pharaoh (Poursat 1980, 116–18), though some scholars identify it with the Anatolian type of hybrid creatures also seen in MM seals (Rehak and Younger 1998, 234; Aruz 2008, 86). The distinction of stylistic provenance, while important to mapping the network of exchange, is not necessary to recognize the adoption of a powerful symbol, and in this way foreign exchange contributed to the prestige of palatial environments and elite people through strategies that become more visible over the course of the Middle Minoan period.

The adoption of imported iconography and techniques evident in the palatial arts of Crete is balanced by the introduction of Aegean objects and styles into Eastern Mediterranean contexts, beginning with exports of Kamares ware vessels and signs of Minoan influence in objects of the Tôd treasure (Warren 1995, 2–4). The expansion of Minoan material culture beyond Crete brings the dynamics of exchange into a larger set of questions about cultural influence, colonialism, and control. Archaeological counterparts for the tradition of the Minoan thalassocracy have been advanced in relation to a number of sites in the Aegean where Cretan styles of living were adopted by Cycladic communities (e.g., Akrotiri) or where trade emporia were hosted (e.g., Kastri on Kythera) (Hägg and Marinatos 1984). A process that increased cultural influence, or Minoanization, seems to have proceeded steadily throughout the Middle Bronze Age by means of repeated interaction and the adoption of select technologies and styles by local communities (Broodbank 2004; Knappett and Nikolakopoulou 2008). This would seem to be separate from the distant outposts such as at Miletus, where a settlement with Minoan material spanning Old and New Palace periods remained distinct from an indigenous population, followed by a similarly contained Mycenaean presence in LH III (Niemeier 2005).

The reach of Minoan products and influence across the Aegean and throughout the Eastern Mediterranean strengthened in the Neopalatial era, and the benefits of a thriving exchange network are evident in the rebuilt palaces. Palatial workshops depended upon the import of raw materials from the east, such as the uncarved elephant tusks and copper ingots preserved at Zakros (Platon 1971, 210–21; cf. Stos-Gale 2001), but also excelled in their own adaptations of eastern technologies such as faience working (Foster 1979). The high point of Minoan international exchange, however, is best represented by the evidence for Minoans traveling and working abroad, which I discuss later.

Mycenaean Mainland

While contact between Crete and the East Mediterranean became more regular over the course of the Middle Bronze Age, this was not an era of prosperous exchange for the communities of mainland Greece. The period of the Shaft Graves at Mycenae spans the transition from Middle to Late Bronze Age and also marks the beginning of a cultural dynamic that bound the use of exotic arts, both of foreign-made goods and new materials, with strategies for building and maintaining social power.

Like the elite who defined themselves through funerary activity at Mochlos, a small segment of society at Mycenae marked their emerging status through the deposition of exotic items in burial places that were already distinguished by their elaborate construction and spatial position (Voutsaki 1999). The high number of Cretan works in these graves indicates that the Egyptian, Mesopotamian, and Levantine objects also deposited therein came to Mycenae through the well-established Minoan networks, yet new interactions with Anatolia and Europe suggest independent Mycenaean contacts to the north (Hughes-Brock 2005).

In the Late Helladic III period, Mycenae became a major center of exchange, drawing in raw materials for palatial workshops, as well as elite objects that may represent high-level exchange with eastern polities (Cline 1994; Phillips and Cline 2005). The concentrated use of imports at Mycenae during the palatial period was rivaled by the inhabitants of neighboring Tiryns. Specific patterns in the types of imported objects found at different sites, such as a high concentration of Cypriot goods at Tiryns and Egyptian objects at Mycenae (Cline 1994), suggest that rival centers developed particular trade partnerships. Furthermore, the distribution of foreign objects across the Argolid indicates that participation in long-distance exchange was not the exclusive domain of the palatial administrations and that elite individuals at Asine, Midea, and Nauplion had a share among imported objects (Burns 2010).

A sharp contrast is found in Boeotia, where nearly all of the imports of the LH IIIA–IIIB period are found in palatial contexts at Thebes, mostly from a single deposit of three dozen cylinder seals in the "Treasure Room" of the New Kadmeion

(Porada 1981; Cline 1994). Not only was the vast majority of the region's imported items found in the administrative center, but exotic raw materials were tightly concentrated here as well. The Treasure Room contained onyx jewelry and fragments of ivories, and a contemporary jewelry workshop also yielded sizable quantities of imported stone, glass, and ivory (Symeonoglou 1973, 44–62, 66–70).

The range of imported materials in tombs and workshops at Mycenae and Thebes accords well with the descriptions found in the Linear B tablets from Pylos and Knossos. Items catalogued for palatial use, for example, include vessels made of gold *(ku-ru-so, chrysos)* and tables inlaid with ivory *(e-re-pa, elephas)*. The network of craftspeople engaged by the palatial centers include workers of bronze *(ka-ko, chalkos)* and blue glass *(ku-wa-no, kyanos)*, which was another material imported from the East Mediterranean. Clearly, sophisticated living was enhanced by imported luxuries, and key industries depended upon exotic materials even if the use of foreign commodities is not explicitly catalogued (Palaima 1991).

THE MEDITERRANEAN CONTEXT

As the preceding survey has shown, the most widespread evidence for ancient trade is the corpus of artifacts identified as imports (i.e., those recovered in contexts outside their region of manufacture and those made of exogenous materials) (Lambrou-Phillipson 1990; Cline 1994). The contexts in which these items are found were determined by factors of their use within their new cultural sphere, but the general distribution indicates both the geographical scope of exchange and the social landscape of import consumption. The various categories of finds combine to describe a network of Mediterranean exchange through which the Aegean was linked to the eastern empires of the Hittites in Anatolia and pharaonic Egypt; smaller kingdoms such as Alalakh and Ugarit; key production centers, including the island of Cyprus; and also places where Aegean products were consumed, such as the settlement on Vivara off the western coast of Italy (see figure 22.1).

The presence of Mycenaean ceramics across the Mediterranean indicates the fullest extension of Aegean participation in an international market (Smith 1987; Leonard 1994, 2003; Dabney 2007). The distribution of stirrup jars, kraters, and kylikes, however, does not indicate an expanding series of simple transactions but rather the compilation of repeated interactions and shifts in local craft economies. The adoption of Aegean styles in the ceramic production of both East and West Mediterranean settlements has been cited as evidence of merchant colonies, or emporia (Marazzi, Tusa, and Vagnetti 1986; Laffineur and Greco 2005), though scientific analyses show that many larger deposits are in all likelihood produced from mainland Greek clay (Jones, Levi, and Bettelli 2005). Contextual studies suggest that Mycenaean ceramics were highly valued outside the Aegean (van Wijngaarden 2003; Vianello 2005), but these may simply be the most durable (i.e., archaeologically

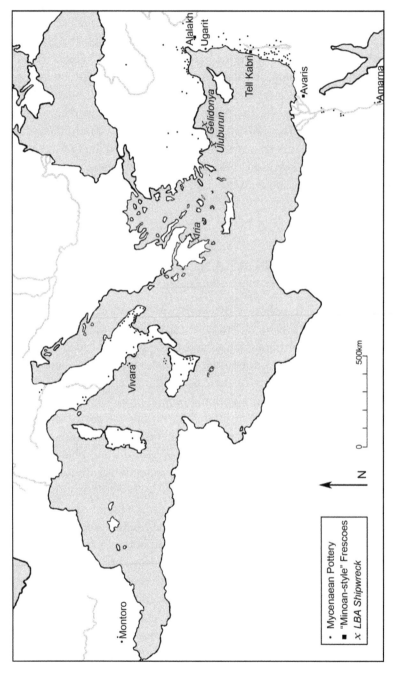

Figure 22.1. Evidence for the trade network of the Late Bronze Age Mediterranean, including shipwrecks sites, extra-Aegean finds of Mycenaean pottery, and Minoan-style frescoes (courtesy of the author).

visible) of a range of Aegean products that included textiles, scented oils, and other organic products (Barber 1991; Knapp 1991).

Ceramics, textiles, and more precious objects are among the commodities that Aegean merchants may have offered, based on the paintings of traders labeled as the "Keftiu" in Egyptian tomb paintings. These men were depicted wearing kilts and breechcloths similar to those seen in Cretan art, especially the frescoes from Knossos, suggesting that Minoans were shown bringing "tribute" to the pharaoh (Wachsmann 1987; Rehak 1996). A more specific account of Aegean peoples as subject to Egyptian power was found on an inscribed statue base from Amenhotep III's mortuary temple at Kom el-Hetan (Wachsmann 1987, 95–99; Cline 1987). The "Aegean list" names nine places that potentially include Knossos, Mycenae, and Thebes, claiming the major centers of the Mycenaean world came under the political dominance of the Egyptian pharaoh. These same sites preserve a number of artifacts inscribed with the name of Amenhotep, suggesting that the Kom el-Hetan base corresponds to a route of exchange, perhaps even the journey of an embassy from Egypt to the Aegean (Hankey 1981; Cline 1998). The more grandiose claims of these monuments, however, would seem to misrepresent foreign interaction of a commercial or even diplomatic nature for the sake of propaganda aimed at an internal audience (Liverani 1990).

The possibility that some Aegeans served foreign kings may be suggested on a more limited scale by the finds of "Minoan" fresco fragments at Avaris (Tell el-Dabᶜa) in the Nile Delta (Bietak 2005) and at Alalakh and Tel Kabri in the Levant (Niemeier and Niemeier 1998). The subject matter is best preserved at Avaris, including bull-leaping figures and large-scale griffins, which offer an especially close connection with the palace at Knossos. In addition to the iconographic links with Cretan frescoes, detailed scientific study reveals that the techniques employed at Avaris are remarkably consistent with those of Aegean painting (Brysbaert 2002). It is clear, therefore, that artists traveled between Crete and Egypt, and it may suggest that the Aegean was included in a broader system of Eastern Mediterranean exchange that functioned as part of international relations of the highest level.

A series of texts known as the Amarna Letters document the material-conscious correspondence that passed between the pharaohs Amenhotep III and Akhenaten and kings of states such as Assyria, Babylonia, and the Hittite Empire (Bryce 2003). The letters contain detailed inventories of their gifts to each other, including basic commodities, such as Cypriot copper, but highlighting rare objects of sophisticated crafting that often transcended regional styles (Feldman 2006). Despite the valuable shipments reported and requested by leaders of states of varied scale, invocations of kinship and expressions of respect and affection between the kings artfully mask differences of power and economic strength (Cline 1995). Whether Minoan or Mycenaean leaders were accepted as trading partners and peers in name remains an unresolved question, but evidence from the seabed seems to indicate that state-sponsored trade networks of the East Mediterranean expanded to include the Aegean periphery.

The shipwreck at Uluburun is the largest of three underwater sites that represent the diverse types of maritime exchange in the LBA (see again figure 22.1). Two smaller shipwrecks that date to the thirteenth century BC have more uniform cargo: the Iria wreck in the Gulf of Argos with its vessels from Cyprus and Crete (Phelps, Lolos, and Vichos 1999) and the ship at Cape Gelidonya, off the southern coast of Anatolia, which specialized in metal exchange (Bass 1967). By comparison, the ship at Uluburun, which sank off the southeast coast of Turkey in the late fourteenth century BC, was richly stocked with goods gathered from various East Mediterranean regions (Bass 1998; Pulak 2001). The quantity and range of items on board, including ten tons of copper ingots, indicate the investment of resources that the excavators have associated with a Levantine polity, perhaps assembled as a royal gift of the sort described in the Amarna Letters. The ship was apparently sailing west toward the Aegean; there is no doubt that its cargo would have greatly enhanced the industries and strategies of a Cretan or mainland Greek palace (Cline and Yasur-Landau 2007; cf. Bachhuber 2006).

Although the intended Aegean destination for the Uluburun cannot be determined, the shipwreck preserves some further evidence for the complicated nature of Bronze Age trade. On board the ship were a small number of items that were manufactured in the Aegean, including Mycenaean pottery, glass beads, two seal stones, and two swords (Pulak 2005). The small quantity and personal nature of these objects—in particular the weapons and seals—suggest that these items belonged to two individuals from the Aegean. These might have been independent travelers catching a ride home, wealthy merchants returning with their wares, or state envoys of a ruler who awaited the arrival of the Uluburun ship. The fact that possessions of these two individuals can be identified among the thousands of artifacts the ship was transporting and that their identities and activities can be debated is amazing. It serves as a compelling example of the far-reaching effects of trade and the ability of archaeological inquiry to focus on individuals, social groups, and the networks that bound them together.

BIBLIOGRAPHY

Aruz, Joan. 2008. *Marks of Distinction: Seals and Cultural Exchange between the Aegean and the Orient (ca. 2600–1360 B.C.).* CMS Beiheft 7. Mainz: von Zabern.

Bachhuber, Christopher. 2006. "Aegean Interest on the Uluburun Ship." *AJA* 110: 345–63.

Barber, Elizabeth J. W. 1991. *Prehistoric Textiles: The Development of Cloth in the Neolithic and Bronze Ages with Special Reference to the Aegean.* Princeton: Princeton University Press.

Bass, George F., ed. 1967. *Cape Gelidonya: A Bronze Age Shipwreck.* TAPS 57, part 8. Philadelphia: American Philosophical Society.

———. 1998. "Sailing between the Aegean and the Orient in the Second Millennium BC." In *Aegean and the Orient,* 183–91.

Bevan, Andrew. 2004. "Emerging Civilized Values? The Consumption and Imitation of Egyptian Stone Vessels in EM II–MM I Crete and Its Wider Eastern Mediterranean Context." In *Emergence of Civilisation Revisited*, 107–26.

Bietak, Manfred. 2005. "The Setting of the Minoan Wall Paintings at Avaris." In *Aegean Wall Painting: A Tribute to Mark Cameron*, ed. Livia Morgan, 83–90. BSA Studies 13. London: British School at Athens.

Broodbank, C. 2000. *An Island Archaeology of the Early Cyclades*. New York: Cambridge University Press.

———. 2004. "Minoanisation." *PCPS* 50: 46–91.

Brumfiel, Elizabeth M. 1994. "Factional Competition and Political Development in the New World: An Introduction." In *Factional Competition and Political Development in the New World*, ed. Elizabeth M. Brumfiel and John W. Fox, 1–13. New York: Cambridge University Press.

Bryce, Trevor. 2003. *Letters of the Great Kings of the Ancient Near East: The Royal Correspondence of the Late Bronze Age*. London: Routledge.

Brysbaert, Ann. 2002. "Common Craftsmanship in the Aegean and East Mediterranean Bronze Age. Preliminary Technological Evidence with Emphasis on the Painted Plaster from Tell el-Dabᶜa, Egypt." *Ägypten und Levante* 12: 95–107.

Burns, Bryan E. 2010. *Mycenaean Greece, Mediterranean Commerce, and the Formation of Identity*. New York: Cambridge University Press.

Carinci, Filippo M. 2000. "Western Messara and Egypt during the Protopalatial Period: A Minimalist View." In *Krete-Aigyptos: Politismikoi desmoi trion chilietion. Meletes*, ed. Alexandra Karetsou, 31–37. Athens: Hypourgeio Politismou.

Cherry, John F. 1984. "The Emergence of the State in the Prehistoric Aegean." *PCPS* 30: 18–48.

Childe, V. Gordon. 1925. *The Dawn of European Civilisation*. New York: Knopf.

Cline, Eric H. 1987. "Amenhotep III and the Aegean: A Reassessment of Egypto-Aegean Relations in the 14th Century B.C." *Orientalia* 56: 1–36.

———. 1994. *SWDS*.

———. 1995. " 'My Brother, My Son': Rulership and Trade between the LBA Aegean, Egypt, and the Near East." In *Role of the Ruler*, 143–50.

———. 1998. "Amenhotep III, the Aegean, and Anatolia." In *Amenhotep III: Perspectives on His Reign*, ed. David O'Connor and Eric H. Cline, 236–50. Ann Arbor: University of Michigan Press.

———, and Assaf Yasur-Landau. 2007. "Musings from a Distant Shore: The Nature and Destination of the Uluburun Ship and its Cargo." *Tel Aviv* 34: 125–41.

Colburn, Cynthia S. 2008. "Exotica and the Early Minoan Elite: Eastern Imports in Prepalatial Crete." *AJA* 112: 203–24.

Dabney, Mary. 2007. "Marketing Mycenaean Pottery in the Levant." In *Krinoi kai Limenes: Studies in Honor of Joseph and Maria Shaw*, ed. Philip P. Betancourt, Michael C. Nelson, and E. Hector Williams, 191–97. Philadelphia: INSTAP.

D'Altroy, Terrence N., and Timothy K. Earle. 1985. "State Finance, Wealth Finance, and Storage in the Inka Political Economy." *Current Anthropology* 26: 187–206.

Evans, Arthur. 1921. *PM*, vol. 1.

Feldman, Marion H. 2006. *Diplomacy by Design: Luxury Arts and an "International Style" in the Ancient Near East, 1400–1200 BCE*. Chicago: University of Chicago Press.

Foster, Karen P. 1979. *Aegean Faience of the Bronze Age*. New Haven: Yale University Press.

Hägg, Robin, and Nanno Marinatos, eds. 1984. *Minoan Thalassocracy*.

Hankey, Vrowney. 1981. "The Aegean Interest in el Amarna." *Journal of Mediterranean Anthropology and Archaeology* 1: 38–49.

Helms, Mary W. 1988. *Ulysses' Sail: An Ethnographic Odyssey of Power, Knowledge, and Geographical Distance*. Princeton: Princeton University Press.

———. 1993. *Craft and the Kingly Ideal: Art, Trade, and Power*. Austin: University of Texas Press.

Hughes-Brock, Helen. 2005. "Amber and Some Other Travellers in the Bronze Age Aegean and Europe." In *Autochthon*, 301–16.

Jones, Richard E., Sara T. Levi, and Marco Bettelli. 2005. "Mycenaean Pottery in the Central Mediterranean: Imports, Imitations, and Derivatives." In *Emporia*, 539–45.

Knapp, A. Bernard. 1990. "Ethnicity, Entrepreneurship, and Exchange: Mediterranean Inter-Island Relations in the Late Bronze Age." *BSA* 85: 115–53.

———. 1991. "Spice, Drugs, Grain, and Grog: Organic Goods in Bronze Age Eastern Mediterranean Trade." In *Bronze Age Trade*, 19–66.

———, and John F. Cherry. 1994. *Provenience Studies and Bronze Age Cyprus: Production, Exchange, and Politico-economic Change*. Monographs in World Archaeology 21. Madison: Prehistory Press.

Knappett, Carl. 1999. "Assessing a Polity in Protopalatial Crete: The Malia-Lasithi State." *AJA* 103: 615–39.

———, and Irene Nikolakopoulou. 2008. "Colonialism without Colonies? A Bronze Age Case Study form Akrotiri, Thera." *Hesperia* 77: 1–42.

Laffineur, Robert, and Emanuele Greco, eds. 2005. *Emporia*.

Lambrou-Phillipson, Connie. 1990. *Hellenorientalia: The Near Eastern Presence in the Bronze Age Aegean, ca. 3000–1100 B.C. SIMA-PB 95*. Gothenburg: Åström.

Leonard, Albert. 1994. *An Index to the Late Bronze Age Aegean Pottery from Syria-Palestine. SIMA* 114. Jonsered, Sweden: Åström.

———. 2003. "Mycindex 3.1." In *SCIEM* II, 539–44.

Liverani, Mario. 1990. *Prestige and Interest: International Relations in the Near East ca. 1600–1100 BC*. Padua: Sargon.

Manning, Sturt W. 1994. "The Emergence of Divergence: Development and Decline on Bronze Age Crete and the Cyclades." In *Development and Decline in the Mediterranean Bronze Age*, ed. Clay Mathers and Simon Stoddart, 221–70. Sheffield Archaeological Monographs 8. Sheffield: Sheffield University Press.

———, and Linda Huhlin. 2005. "Maritime Commerce and Geographies of Mobility in the Late Bronze Age of the Eastern Mediterranean: Problemizations." In *The Archaeology of Mediterranean Prehistory*, ed. Emma Blake and A. Bernard Knapp, 270–91. Oxford: Blackwell.

Marazzi, Massimiliano, Sebastiano Tusa, and Lucia Vagnetti, eds. 1986. *Traffici micenei nel Mediterraneo: Problemi storici e documentazione archeologica*. Taranto: Instituto per la storia e l'archeologia della Magna Grecia.

Muhly, James D. 2003. "Trade in Metals in the Late Bronze and Iron Ages." In *PLOES*, 141–50.

Niemeier, Wolf-Dietrich. 2005. "Minoans, Mycenaeans, Hittites, and Ionians in Western Asia Minor: New Excavations in Bronze Age Miletus-Millawanda." In *The Greeks in the East*, ed. Alexandra Villing, 1–36. British Museum Research Publication 157. London: British Museum.

———, and Barbara Niemeier. 1998. "Minoan Frescoes in the Eastern Mediterranean." In *Aegean and the Orient*, 69–98.

Palaima, Thomas G. 1991. "Maritime Matters in the Linear B Tablets." In *Thalassa*, 273–310.

Parkinson, William A., and Michael Galaty. 2007. "Secondary States in Perspective: An Integrated Approach to State Formation in the Prehistoric Aegean." *American Anthropologist* 109: 113–29.

Phelps, William, Yannos Lolos, and Yannis Vichos, eds. 1999. *The Point Iria Wreck.*

Phillips, Jacke, and Eric H. Cline. 2005. "Amenhotep III and Mycenae. Further Evidence." In *Autochthon*, 317–28.

Platon, Nicholas. 1971. *Zakros: The Discovery of a Lost Palace of Ancient Crete.* New York: Scribner.

Porada, Edith. 1981. "The Cylinder Seals Found at Thebes in Boeotia." *AfO* 28: 1–70.

Poursat, Jean-Claude. 1980. "Reliefs d'applique moulés." In *Fouilles exécutées à Mallia: Le Quartie Mu* II, ed. Béatrice Detournay and Jean-Claude Poursat, 116–32. Études crétoises 26. Athens: L'École française d'Athènes.

Pulak, Cemal. 2001. "The Cargo of the Uluburun Ship and Evidence for Trade with the Aegean and Beyond." In *Italy and Cyprus in Antiquity, 1500–450 BC: Proceedings of an International Symposium Held at the Italian Academy for Advanced Studies in America at Columbia University, November 16–18 2000*, ed. Larissa Bonfante and Vassos Karageorghis, 13–60. Nicosia: Severis Foundation.

———. 2005. "Who Were the Mycenaeans aboard the Uluburun Ship?" In *Emporia*, 295–310.

Rehak, Paul. 1996. "Aegean Breechcloths, Kilts, and the Keftiu Paintings." *AJA* 100: 35–51.

———, and John G. Younger. 1998. "International Styles in Ivory Carving in the Bronze Age." In *Aegean and the Orient*, 229–54.

Renfrew, A. Colin. 1972. *The Emergence of Civilisation: The Cyclades and the Aegean in the Third Millennium B.C.* London: Methuen.

———. 1975. "Trade as Action at a Distance: Questions of Integration and Communication." In *Ancient Civilization and Trade*, ed. Jeremy A. Sabloff and Clifford C. Lamberg-Karlovsky, 3–59. Albuquerque: University of New Mexico Press.

Schoep, Ilse. 2006. "Looking beyond the First Palaces: Elites and the Agency of Power in EM III–MM II Crete." *AJA* 110: 37–64.

Seager, Richard B. 1912. *Excavations in the Island of Mochlos.* New York: American School of Classical Studies at Athens.

Sherratt, Andrew, and Susan Sherratt. 1991. "From Luxuries to Commodities: The Nature of Mediterranean Bronze Age Trading Systems." In *Bronze Age Trade*, 351–86.

Smith, Thyrza R. 1987. *Mycenaean Trade and Interaction in the West Central Mediterranean, 1600–1000 B.C.* BAR-IS 371. Oxford: British Archaeological Reports.

Soles, Jeffrey S. 1992. *The Prepalatial Cemeteries at Mochlos and Gournia and the House Tombs of Bronze Age Crete.* Hesperia Suppl. XXIV. Princeton: American School of Classical Studies at Athens.

Stos-Gale, Zofia A. 2001. "Minoan Foreign Relations and Copper Metallurgy in MM III–LM III Crete." In *The Social Context of Technological Change*, ed. Andrew J. Shortland, 195–210. Oxford: Oxbow.

———, and Colin Macdonald. 1991. "Sources of Metals and Trade in the Bronze Age Aegean." In *Bronze Age Trade*, 249–88.

Symeonoglou, Sarantis. 1973. *Kadmeia.* Vol. 1, *Mycenaean Finds from Thebes, Greece. SIMA* 35. Gothenburg: Åström.

van Wijngaarden, Gert-Jan. 2003. *Use and Appreciation of Mycenaean Pottery in the Levant, Cyprus, and Italy ca. 1600–1200 BC.* Amsterdam Archaeological Studies 8. Amsterdam: Amsterdam University Press.

Vianello, Andrea. 2005. *Late Bronze Age Mycenaean and Italic Products in the West Mediterranean: A Social and Economic Analysis.* BAR-IS 1439. Oxford: British Archaeological Reports.

Voutsaki, Sophia. 1999. "Mortuary Display, Prestige, and Identity in the Shaft Grave Era." In *Eliten in der Bronzezeit: Ergebnisse zweier Colloquien in Mainz und Athen*, ed. Imma

Kilian-Dirlmeier and Markus Egg, 103–17. Monographien des Römisch-Germanischen Zentralmuseums 43. Mainz: Verlag des Römisch-Germanischen Zentralmuseum.

Wachsman, Shelley. 1987. *Aegeans in the Theban Tombs.* Leuven: Peeters.

Warren, Peter M. 1969. *Minoan Stone Vases.* London: Cambridge University Press.

———. 1987. "The Genesis of the Minoan Palace." In *Function of the Minoan Palaces*, 47–56.

———. 1995. "Minoan Crete and Pharaonic Egypt." In *Egypt, the Aegean, and the Levant: Interconnections in the Second Millennium BC*, ed. W. Vivian Davies and Louise Schofield, 1–18. London: British Museum.

Watrous, L. Vance. 1987. "The Role of the Near East in the Rise of the Cretan Palaces." In *Function of the Minoan Palaces*, 65–70.

Wiener, Malcolm H. 1991. "The Nature and Control of Minoan Foreign Trade." In *Bronze Age Trade*, 325–50.

CHAPTER 23

....

WEAPONS AND WARFARE

....

IOANNIS GEORGANAS

Since the dawn of human history, conflict and warfare have been an integral part of life. The earliest concrete evidence for warfare in the Aegean comes from the Early Bronze Age, as the large number of daggers on Crete indicates. However, it is with the rise of the Mycenaeans on mainland Greece that a warlike ethos becomes more prominent, as is evident by the numerous and spectacular weapons retrieved from the Shaft Graves at Mycenae, as well as the numerous representations of warriors and combat scenes. Thanks to Homer's *Iliad* and *Odyssey*, the Aegean Bronze Age has always been perceived as a time when warrior-heroes roamed the land and engaged in military campaigns in Greece, the Aegean, and beyond.

This chapter provides a concise history of weapons and warfare in the Aegean during the Bronze Age. Aspects to be covered are offensive equipment, defensive equipment, and chariotry.

OFFENSIVE EQUIPMENT

Included under this heading are daggers and swords, spears, bows, and slings. Each class of weapons is examined separately in rough chronological order from the Early Bronze to the Late Bronze Age.

Daggers and Swords

The most characteristic weapon of the Early Bronze Age was the dagger. The earliest types had short, double-edged blades, which were thin and had thick midribs. Their wooden hilts were attached by rivets to the shoulder of the blade. A great number of such daggers is known from early Minoan Crete, where Branigan has estimated that about 80% of metal production on the island went into weapons (Branigan 1999, 88). Although the majority of scholars have interpreted most of those weapons as status symbols, Peatfield (1999) has pointed out that some of the Cretan daggers had actually been damaged, and subsequent changes in their design indicate attempts to make them stronger and more efficient in combat.

As time passed, these daggers became longer and were furnished with even more prominent midribs. It is almost certain that the first Aegean swords evolved directly from these daggers, as is evident by the many similarities in shape and construction features. The earliest swords are long and thin and have rounded shoulders, very short tangs, and prominent midribs. These early swords, known as Type A, have been found in great numbers on both Crete and the mainland. The earliest specimens, dated to ca. 1850–1750 BC, come from Malia and have a length of about 90 cm. Even longer examples are known from the Shaft Graves at Mycenae, which yielded numerous swords of this type, some of which had elaborately decorated hilt attachments and/or blades. This, however, reduced their practical value, as a heavy blow on the edge of the sword could snap the tang or even break the blade itself. The Mycenaeans soon identified this problem and came up with a new type of sword (Type B), which remained in use from ca. 1600 to 1375 BC. This was of medium length, mostly resembling daggers, and was equipped with a longer tang and a slightly wider blade. These modifications increased the weapon's strength and durability.

The next stage in the development of swords was the modification of the hilts and the shoulders of the blade in order to provide protection for the hand. We can identify two main types: Type C was furnished with a pair of horns projecting from the hilt, while Type D had two cruciform projections. Experimental archaeology has shown that these two types were designed for different fighting styles (Molloy 2008; Peatfield 2008, 89–90). The handle of the Type C sword favors a 'saber' grip, which allows for style of fighting that somewhat resembles fencing. In contrast, the handle of the Type D sword favors a 'hammer' grip, which allows more cutting actions. Both types were in use throughout the mainland, Crete, and the islands from ca. 1450 to 1300 BC. The next two types (F and G) were much shorter and more robust, ideal for a range of thrusting and limiting cutting attacks.

The last and probably most important development was the introduction of the so-called Naue II sword (figure 23.1). This type most probably has a Central European origin and appeared in Greece ca. 1230 BC. It has a flanged hilt that is secured with rivets, and the blade has parallel edges for the greater part of its length before tapering to a sharp point. Most of the Naue II swords known are between

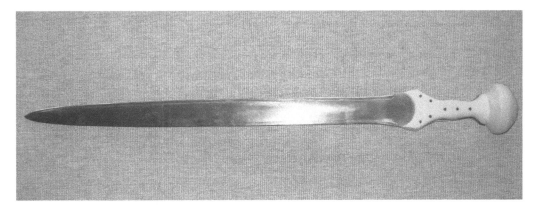

Figure 23.1. Replica of a Naue II sword (photograph by the author).

60 and 80 cm long. This type has been considered as the cut-and-thrust sword par excellence; its design was so effective that the iron version became virtually the only sword used in the Aegean during the subsequent Early Iron Age.

Spears and Javelins

The most common type of spearhead was a narrow, leaf-shaped blade (some of the earlier ones were as much as 50 cm long) with a strongly marked midrib and a socketed base. The spearhead was secured to the shaft by a metal collar at the base of the socket, as well as by pins. Many of such spearheads have been recovered from the Shaft Graves at Mycenae and the 'Warrior Graves' at Knossos. Representational evidence in the form of seals and the 'Lion Hunt' dagger from Shaft Grave IV shows that these large spears were wielded with two hands at shoulder level, although the warriors depicted on the Thera frescoes seem to wield them single-handed. However, as Grguric (2005, 12) points out, the method of holding the spear with both hands, horizontal at shoulder level, is seen only when the shield is placed to the warrior's back. When the spearman is wielding the spear in any other way, his shield is in front of his body. This type of spear would have been used by both infantry (as shown on the Thera frescoes) and by chariot warriors. At the same time, spears were also used for hunting, as the scene from the 'Lion Hunt' dagger indicates.

By 1300 BC, the spear had become a much smaller and lighter weapon, with a length of about 2 m and a blade of 20–30 cm. A wall painting from Pylos, dated to the 13th century BC, shows Mycenaean soldiers fighting barbarians dressed in goat-skins. One of the Mycenaean men carries a spear that he uses underarm, killing his opponent. Moreover, on the one side of the famous 'Warrior Vase' from Mycenae, dated to the 12th century BC, the warriors are portrayed using their small spears overarm, again as thrusting weapons.

Let us now move to the discussion of javelins. Evidence for javelins (or throwing spears) for the earlier periods is meager. There are some examples of small spearheads, which may have been for such weapons, but we cannot be certain whether they were implements of war or merely hunting equipment (Everson 2004, 31–32). More concrete evidence for their use comes from two frescoes from Knossos. The first, known as the 'Captain of the Blacks' fresco, shows a male figure carrying two light javelins; no other weapons or armor are present. The second, known as the 'Warriors Hurling Javelins' fresco, shows what are probably javelin-armed light infantry, hurling their javelins upward (Grguric 2005, 30).

Bows and Slings

Although no physical remains of bows survive, representational evidence, as well as the large number of arrowheads found all over the Aegean, suggest that the bow was an indispensable part of the Minoan and Mycenaean arsenal. The earliest arrowheads were made of flint and obsidian, while bronze ones started appearing during the 15th century BC. The Shaft Graves yielded several flint and obsidian arrowheads of fine craftsmanship. These could have been used for both hunting and warfare, but as Everson (2004, 32) notes, the barbed heads of some of the arrows clearly suggest warfare, as they inflicted more damage and were difficult to retrieve. On the contrary, in hunting, it was better for arrows to create less damage and be easier to withdraw from the prey.

Under the palaces, the production and distribution of arrowheads clearly became a state affair. At Knossos, 110 bronze specimens were found, while at Pylos some 500 turned up. Moreover, Linear B tablets record large numbers of arrowheads; at Knossos, for instance, a single tablet records 8,640 arrowheads (Snodgrass 1999, 23).

The only depictions of bows used in warfare come from the so-called Siege Rhyton from Shaft Grave IV at Mycenae, which shows three archers in battle in front of the besieged towns walls, and the silver krater, again from Shaft Grave IV, on which archers fight side by side with spearmen (Hiller 1999, 323, pls. LXIX.1b and LXX.9a).

Another missile weapon, the sling, was also in use in Bronze Age warfare. Originally used for hunting, by the 15th century BC the sling had acquired a military role. Sling bullets were initially rounded stones, pebbles, and baked clay pieces, while toward the end of the Mycenaean period lead bullets also appeared. The only representation of slings being used in battle comes from the 'Siege Rhyton' found in Shaft Grave IV, which shows three slingers fighting alongside archers.

DEFENSIVE EQUIPMENT

Minoan and Mycenaean warriors were provided with an array of defensive equipment such as helmets, body armor, greaves, and shields. Our information about these comes from actual finds, Linear B tablets, and representations on wall paintings, pottery, and jewelry.

Helmets

The most common type of helmet used throughout the Bronze Age Aegean was covered with boar's tusk plates (figure 23.2). So far, more than fifty graves have been found containing plates of boar's tusks that date from ca. 1650 to 1150 BC (Everson 2004, 5). This type of helmet, which is certainly of Aegean origin, was made by a series of small, almost crescent-shaped boar's tusk plates, pierced in the corners with holes and sewn onto a cup-shaped piece of leather or felt in alternating rows. Some of these helmets were furnished with either a plume or a crest or simply terminated in a knob, while most of the latest examples were also equipped with cheek and/or neck guards.

Boar's tusk helmets are frequently depicted on frescoes, seals, and metal vessels. They also appear in ivory inlay work. The Thera frescoes, which date to the 16th century BC, provide one of the earliest depictions, while the wall paintings from the palace of Pylos, which date to the late 13th century BC, provide one of the latest.

Figure 23.2. Boar's tusk helmet from Crete (photograph by the author).

This type of helmet was not the only one used in the Aegean. Metal specimens were also known, as evidence from sites like Knossos indicates. The Knossian example was found in one of the 'Warrior Graves' and is dated to the 15th century BC. It has a conical bowl that terminates in a knob and is furnished with two cheek guards that were sewn onto the bowl.

Around 1200 BC, new types of helmets appear. The warriors on the 'Warrior Vase' are shown wearing horned, black helmets with white dots, which have been interpreted as bronze studs on a leather helmet or an embossed bronze helmet (Everson 2004, 37, with references). Others wear helmets with low 'hedgehog' crests, most probably made of horsehair.

Body Armor

When one thinks of Aegean Bronze Age armors, the first thing that comes to mind is the impressive bronze cuirass found in an early Mycenaean tomb at Dendra in the Argolid. The armor comprises a simple corselet, a breastplate, and a backplate. The neck was covered by a large cylindrical guard, and the shoulders were covered by curved plates. A 'skirt' of six overlapping plates—three at the front and three at the back—hung from the waist, which facilitated movement of the lower body and legs. The plates of the cuirass are about 1 mm thick, and holes with a diameter of 2 mm were punched around the edge for the attachment of a lining. Larger holes about 4 mm in diameter are also present near the edge of all of the plates; these were used to attach the various plates to each other by means of leather straps.

Most scholars have argued that the heavy weight (about 15 kg) and cumbersome appearance of this armor would have made fighting on foot extremely difficult and therefore that it was suitable only for warriors fighting from a chariot. Experimental archaeology, however, has shown that the armor was quite flexible and not especially uncomfortable during hand-to-hand combat (Molloy, personal communication). Peatfield (2008, 93), however, has stressed the fact that "the Dendra armour was not battlefield gear, but rather was designed for dueling." This seems to fit well with the aristocratic nature of the Mycenaean society, where rulers and other members of the elite measured their status and prestige by personal skill at arms.

Another misconception connected with this armor is its supposed uniqueness. Careful examination of finds from Thebes and of representations on pottery has shown that metal armors were quite common in the Bronze Age Aegean. Various metal artifacts found in the 'Arsenal' of the palace at Thebes and dated to ca. 1300 BC have been identified as parts of metal armors. Among them was a pair of shoulder guards, which are smaller than those of the Dendra armor and lack the wide 'wings' that cover the Dendra cuirass at the chest and back (Andrikou 2007, 402). Such differences are clearly due to the development of this type of armor over time, indicating an evolution toward simpler forms that improved the warriors' flexibility (Andrikou 2007, 403).

Metal armors are also mentioned in Linear B tablets from Pylos and Knossos, either in the form of ideograms or with the word *to-ra-ke* (Greek *thorax)*. It is worth noting that the ideogram for 'armor' on the Knossos tablets looks astonishingly like the Dendra cuirass.

Later armors seem to be of completely different types. The 'Warrior Vase' from Mycenae shows warriors wearing short, most probably leather, corselets reinforced with metal studs. Scholars have also argued for the use of scale armors, a type typical of the Near East. The evidence for that, however, is extremely scanty as only two scale plates are known from the Aegean—one from Mycenae and another from the site of Kanakia on the island of Salamis.

Greaves

The earliest known greave dates to the 14th century BC and comes from the same grave where the Dendra cuirass was found. It was made from a thin bronze sheet and worn over a legging of linen, leather, or felt. At 32.5 cm long and 8 cm wide, it covered the leg from knee to ankle (Everson 2004, 22). It seems, however, that metal greaves fell out of use, and the majority of warriors wore linen or leather leggings. Frescoes from Mycenae and Pylos show several soldiers wearing white leggings. Their white color most probably denotes the material used (i.e., linen), while three or more bands of red, dark brown, or black under the knees and around the ankles probably designate the leather straps used to hold them in place.

Metal greaves again made their appearance in the late 12th century BC. Two graves in Achaea (Kallithea and Portes-Kephalovryso) and one in Athens yielded a pair each. The Kallithea examples are oval shaped, 25.5 cm long, and 12.6 cm wide. They are embossed with repouseé borders and studs. They are also equipped with lacing wires. For the pair from Kephalovryso we do not have sufficient information, but according to Papadopoulos (1999, 271–72), they are "simpler and undecorated" as compared to the Kallithea ones. The pair from Athens was found in a grave on the slopes of the Acropolis (Everson 2004, 58, figure 23). The greaves are very fragmentary and have no surviving lacing wires. They are oval shaped and are decorated with punch-marked decoration that consists of a border and a central vertical line and six circles on each greave.

Shields

The lack of any physical remains of shields means that our knowledge of their types and function relies almost totally on representations. The several depictions of shields available to us show that during the early phases of the Bronze Age two main types of shield were in use: the 'figure-of-eight' shield and the 'tower' shield. Both types were very large, covering the warrior from neck to toe and were most likely made of several layers of oxhide on a wicker frame, while metal or wooden reinforcements could have also been placed on their faces.

The figure-of-eight shield, as its name suggests, looks like a figure of eight if seen from the front or back, while its profile is highly concave. Slightly smaller is the tower shield, which has straight rims at the sides but an upward curve at the top edge and a slightly concave profile. Both shields were held and maneuvered by means of a leather strap that passed diagonally over the left shoulder. The highly concave profile and the addition of wooden reinforcements on the surface of the figure-of-eight shield would have rendered it especially efficient for breaking into packed formations and also ideal for deflecting missile weapons and blows from swords and spears.

Tower shields went out of use after the early Mycenaean period, unlike the figure-of-eight ones, which seem to have been used until the end of the palatial period, as wall paintings from Knossos, Mycenae, and Tiryns indicate. It was in ca. 1300 BC that smaller shields, either round or with a part cut out from the lower edge, were introduced. The latter are featured on the 'Warrior Vase' from Mycenae.

CHARIOTS

Two-horse war chariots appeared on the Greek mainland during the 16th century BC, as pictorial evidence from Mycenae demonstrates. Their origin must be sought in the Near East, where chariots had been used in battle from as early as the Middle Bronze Age. Although no actual remains have survived, we can get a clear picture of the different Aegean types from numerous depictions on frescos, jewelry, and pottery, as well as mentions in Linear B tablets.

The earliest type, known as the 'box chariot,' was in use between ca. 1550 and 1450 BC. Its name derives from the boxlike shape of the cab, whose sidings rose to thigh or hip height and were covered with some sort of screening material (e.g., leather or basketry) (Crouwel 1981, 59–62). The most common type of chariot, however, was the 'dual chariot,' which was in use between ca. 1450 and 1200 BC. It is so named because its cab was furnished with curved side extensions or 'wings' at the rear. The main sidings and wings were usually covered with oxhide or leather (Crouwel 1981, 63–70). Every type of chariot had two four-spoked wheels and a single pole.

Various theories have been put forward regarding the way these chariots were used in the Aegean. Greenhalgh (1973) has argued that heavily armed spearmen, like the Dendra warrior, charged headlong at each other in mass formation, while Drews (1993) has suggested that chariots were used as archery platforms, much like in Egypt. However, the only Aegean representations of archers operating from chariots concern hunting and not warfare. On the contrary, the majority of scholars believe that chariots were simply used as 'taxis' to take warriors to and from battle. The lack of evidence for protection of the chariots or their horses clearly indicates that chariots "were not designed to appear in the thick of battle, or even to come within range of enemy missiles" (Crouwel 1981, 145). It is not a coincidence that such a role is echoed in Homer's descriptions in the *Iliad*.

CONCLUSION

Scholars and students of the Aegean Bronze Age still have to deal with the great misconception that the Minoans were peaceful while the Mycenaean Greeks were warlike. Such notions are too simplified and naïve, and as we have seen, it was on Early Minoan Crete that the first proper weapons appeared. In addition, evidence for conflict *does* exist, as the destruction and abandonment of several Protopalatial sites demonstrate.

It is true, however, that the Mycenaean Greeks took things a step further and invested more in the development of their military infrastructure. The great number and the quality of the weaponry retrieved from the Shaft Graves at Mycenae, as well as the representations of war scenes on the offerings and funerary stelae, clearly illustrate this point.

The early Mycenaeans were efficient warriors who knew and appreciated the skills of both siege warfare and group warfare with units of heavy spearmen, swordsmen, archers, slingers, and chariots. Because all of these soldiers were equipped with the best possible arms of the time, they were eventually enabled to conquer Knossos in ca. 1400 BC and take over the precious maritime trade routes from the Minoans.

During the 13th century BC, however, the Mycenaean military infrastructure underwent a major change both in equipment and tactics. Weapons became smaller and lighter and focused on uniformity and mobility. We are not certain why these changes occurred, but possibly the Mycenaeans had to face new, unknown enemies who fought differently. History has a name for such invaders: the 'Sea People.' Despite all of the changes in equipment and tactics, the Mycenaean civilization collapsed shortly after 1200 BC, and the Aegean sank into a darker age.

BIBLIOGRAPHY

Andrikou, Eleni. 2007. "New Evidence on Mycenaean Bronze Corselets from Thebes in Boeotia and the Bronze Age Sequence of Corselets in Greece and Europe." In *BABS*, 401–409.

Branigan, Keith. 1999. "The Nature of Warfare in the Southern Aegean during the Third Millennium B.C." In *Polemos*, 87–94.

Crouwel, Joost H. 1981. *Chariots and Other Means of Land Transport in Bronze Age Greece.* Allard Pierson Series 3. Amsterdam: Allard Pierson Museum.

Drews, Robert. 1993. *The End of the Bronze Age: Changes in Warfare and the Catastrophe ca. 1200 B.C.* Princeton: Princeton University Press.

Everson, Tim. 2004. *Warfare in Ancient Greece: Arms and Armour from the Heroes of Homer to Alexander the Great.* Stroud, Gloucestershire: Sutton.

Greenhalgh, Peter, A. L. 1973. *Early Greek Warfare: Horsemen and Chariots in the Homeric and Archaic Ages.* Cambridge: Cambridge University Press.

Grguric, Nicolas. 2005. *The Mycenaeans c. 1650–1100 BC.* Elite Series 130. Oxford: Osprey.

Hiller, Stefan. 1999. "Scenes of Warfare and Combat in the Arts of Aegean Late Bronze Age: Reflections on Typology and Development." In *Polemos*, 319–30.

Molloy, Barry. 2008. "Martial Arts and Materiality: A Combat Archaeology Perspective on Aegean Swords of the Fifteenth and Fourteenth Centuries BC." *World Archaeology* 40(1): 116–34.

Papadopoulos, Thanasis J. 1999. "Warrior-graves in Achaean Mycenaean Cemeteries." In *Polemos*, 267–74.

Peatfield, Alan. 1999. "The Paradox of Violence: Weaponry and Martial Art in Minoan Crete." In *Polemos*, 67–74.

———. 2008. "Minoan and Mycenaean Warfare." In *The Ancient World at War*, ed. Philip de Souza, 87–99. London: Thames and Hudson.

Snodgrass, Anthony M. 1999. *Arms and Armor of the Greeks.* Rev. ed. Baltimore: John Hopkins University Press.

Seals and Writing/Administrative Systems

CHAPTER 24

MINOAN SEALS
AND SEALINGS

JUDITH WEINGARTEN

SEALS are small semi-precious or common stones cut into standard shapes, polished, pierced, and then engraved with ornamental patterns, figures or, occasionally, inscriptions. When pressed into clay or wax, the seal leaves a legible impression in relief. A relatively small group of seals are metal rings with broad engraved bezels that can be viewed both on the ring and in relief.

More than any other ancient work of art, seals are intimate objects which are literally bound to their owners, whether worn on a bracelet or necklace or as pendant or pin. Given the diversity of materials, colors, images, and purposes, seals resonate on multiple levels. Their basic function is to identify the seal owner, but they can be worn, too, as conspicuous jewelry. Sometimes they indicate the seal-owner's rank or set apart a specific social group, or they may serve amuletic or magical purposes. In ancient societies, their primary purpose was to secure property—whether in the home or the public arena—and to assign responsibility by means of clay sealings impressed by a specific individual who is identified by the seal's impression.

The study of Minoan seals began even before the discovery of Minoan civilization. Long before archaeologists arrived on the scene, Cretan women were wearing 'milk-stones'—brightly colored Minoan engraved gems—on their breasts or around the neck. These were believed to contain magical powers to ensure the milk of a nursing mother. Shepherds and farmers had been finding such "milk-stones" for generations on the Kephala hill at Knossos. When Arthur Evans first traveled to Crete in 1894, he visited Knossos and soon began collecting gemstones. He was excited by the miniature scenes on the gems, including some with peculiar, inscribed pictographic characters. His trips to Crete led to the excavations at Knossos and the revelation of the Minoan world (MacGillivray 2000).

Prepalatial Minoan Seals and Sealings

The story of Minoan glyptic begins in EM II, when the first seals and one sealing were found at the southern coastal settlement of Myrtos–Fournou Korifi (*CMS* V.1, 14–20; Warren 1972, 226–70), in tombs at Lebena on the south coast (*CMS* II.1, 195–200, 202, 203; Alexiou and Warren 2004, 134), and at Arkhanes in the north-center of the island (Sakellarakis 1976, 515–18, 1–8, figure 2; 1980, figure 4, 1–8). Based on these, a fair number of other seals, primarily from the Mesara tombs but also some from as far away as Mochlos in the north and Palaikastro in the far east, can also be ascribed with some confidence to EM II (Sbonias 1995, 74–83).

Like their northern neighbors in the Cyclades and on the Greek mainland, the early Minoans chose to use stamp seals. Seal shapes were predominantly irregular pyramids and cones and made of soft stone and bone. Seal designs mostly range from simple scratches to cross- or diagonal-hatching, with the few more elaborate patterns, such as the chip-cut seals from Lebena and the trilobes and opposed C-spirals from Arkhanes suggesting northern connections (Sbonias 1995, 79; Aruz 2008, 29–30). One striking link across the Aegean is the angle-filled cross that appears on the sealing from Myrtos. This was one of the most popular ways of decorating seals in Anatolia: From there, the motif appears to have migrated to the Greek mainland, the Cyclades, and Crete (Aruz 2008, 29).

The new craft, needing only simple tools, was probably carried out at the village level (Sbonias 2000, 280–82). In truth, there seem to be few EM II settlements larger than villages on Crete at this time, and even the striking tholos tombs need not have served anything grander than large villages. There is nothing comparable on the island to the monumental buildings or fortifications that appear in EB II on the mainland and some islands—which may be why there is nothing comparable to the quality and variety of mainland seals as known from their impressions. The single sealing from Myrtos does show, however, that seals could be understood as sphragistic instruments even if the connection was not always made: There are also EM II sealings without any seal impressions at all (Weingarten forthcoming).

While there may have been a gap in settlement and craft development after the end of EM II (Watrous, Hadzi-Vallianou, and Blitzer 2004, 251–52), a glyptic gap remains problematic. Nevertheless, at some time during EM III–MM I, a common glyptic tradition evolves that seems to run in tandem with the growth of settlements like Knossos, Malia, and Phaistos. Smaller communities, too, such as Gournia and Palaikastro, show signs of growth and town planning, while substantial free-standing houses appear on several sites. No site, however, appears to have had a chief building dominating the rest of the settlement.

As in many early seal traditions, glyptic 'take off' is reflected in a rich variety of seal shapes. Many seals now display quite sophisticated and complex motifs and there is a general advance in the quality of carving. Designs often follow clear compositional schemes, some of which become characteristic of Minoan art ever after, especially Rotation, Radiation, and Rapport (Yule 1980, 185–91).

Figure 24.1. Modern impression of Parading Lions Seal (hippopotamus ivory) from Platanos Tholos A (*CMS* II 1 248a; photo courtesy *CMS*).

The first definable style-groups now emerge, notably the Parading Lions-Spiral group and the large Border/Leaf Group, both undoubtedly manned by specialist craftsmen (Yule 1980, 208–210; Sbonias 1995, 89–106). Bone and soft stone remain in common use, but there is also much imported hippopotamus ivory.

Many seals of the Border/Leaf group display Egyptianizing patterns. This workshop is also responsible for the so-called white pieces, a material that mimics Egyptian burnt steatite (Weingarten 2005, 760 and note 8). Seals of the Parading Lions-Spiral group show an intriguing borrowing: The lion iconography (which appears on 66% of their seals) comes from the south, and it may not be coincidence that most of these seals, often large stamp cylinders, are made of hippopotamus ivory (figure 24.1). The earliest seal from Knossos was stamped with a Parading Lions seal (Hood and Kenna 1973, 103–106; *CMS* II.8 6). Parading Lions seals seem altogether special, and the seals may have served as badges for an emerging elite in this period, leading up to the foundation of the palaces. The choice of the lion as the premier emblem of this group was not an artistic choice but a social and political one—imagery intentionally adopted from Egypt in order to convey the idea of power (Weingarten 2005, 763–65).

In MM IA, a burst of tomb building took place in the great cemetery of Arkhanes, 8 km to the north of Knossos. Building bigger and better tombs may in itself have been part of the process by which hierarchy became established in north-central Crete (Hitchcock forthcoming). The abundant seal evidence from Arkhanes supports the idea of an elite who were busy acquiring power—and the symbols of power—in the MM IA–IB periods. Hierarchy and emblematic power come together with the appearance here of the first inscribed seals, often elaborately carved bone seals engraved with simple Hieroglyphic signs. These 'Arkhanes script' seals are repeatedly described as Prepalatial in date: This is by no means certain as the relevant tombs were also in use in MM IB (Macdonald and Knappett 2007, 137 and note 51), so the seals could be contemporary with the foundation of the palace at Knossos. Be that as it may, the development of script is undoubtedly a key step in the centralization of economic power, and inscribed seals become a major bureaucratic tool at Knossos and elsewhere in the Protopalatial period.

There is still no evidence that Prepalatial seals were used for any purpose greater than that of household management (*pace* Pini 1990, 34–37; Vlasaki and Hallager 1995, 251–70; Hallager 2000, 97–99). That is, sealings are found scattered in houses and workshops, follow no patterns, and are rarely, if ever, repetitive. Administrative sealings, on the other hand, which are part of a structured process dealing with the centralized management of goods, should be evidenced by clusters of sealings in central buildings (or linked to central buildings), following set patterns and often repetitive; there may also be associated evidence of bureaucratic administration, such as door sealings and/or scribal records.

This is the kind of evidence that we do find, limited at first but steadily growing after the foundation of the First Palaces in MM IB.

FIRST PALACE SEALS AND SEALINGS

The earliest closely dated Minoan seal depicting a long-horned goat (*CMS* II.8, 374; see figure 24.2)—an enduring glyptic theme on Crete—stamped three clay noduli found in an MM IB storeroom at Knossos (Weingarten and Macdonald 2005). Noduli have no string holes or other means of attachment to objects and could not have sealed or labeled anything. They may have served as *laisser passer* or receipts given for occasional work; they are simple documents, practical in a society already too populous for entirely face-to-face contacts but where literate instruments are limited or lacking.

Of the nine sealings found in the Room of the Olive Press (MM IA = Panagiotaki 1993; MM IB = Weingarten and Macdonald 2005, 397 and nn. 9, 10), one was impressed by two *different* seals (*CMS* II.8, 17+18), the first in a long line of *multiple* sealings—a sphragistic habit that continues through LM I at Knossos and also at LM IB Zakro. Inscribed seals are now being used: A fragmentary sealing in the MM IB (or MM IIA?) Vat Room Deposit is stamped by a seal engraved with the Hieroglyphic 'arrow' sign, CHIC 050 (Panagiotaki 1999, 39); and a nodulus from a Knossos MM IIA workshop was impressed by an ivory/bone seal displaying two signs: a human hand (CHIC 008) and a heart-shaped sign (*CMS* II.8, 15; Weingarten 2003).

At Knossos, sealing evidence shows the use of sealings and noduli both within and immediately outside the palace structure. This does not support the view that the First Palaces are purely ceremonial centers (Schoep 2005). In any case, what matters is not the intra- or extra-mural location of the administrative power, but the existence of that power.

Figure 24.2. MM IB nodulus, Knossos southwest palace angle ("Early Magazine A") (*CMS* II.8 374; photo courtesy *CMS*).

In Middle Minoan II, Cretan craftspersons adopted the horizontal bow lathe from the Near East, a tool that allowed them to carve hard stones for the first time. This led to a colorful range of semiprecious seal stones, a richly visual, perhaps symbolic choice, characteristic of Minoan glyptic and without parallel in the Near East or elsewhere. While soft stone seals continued to be made throughout the Minoan period, seals of bone and ivory soon vanish. New seal shapes appear—especially the handled signet (*petschaft*) and three- and four-sided prisms, which were put to use by palace bureaucracies.

The end of MM IIB is marked by major destructions, leaving abundant evidence of sealing and scribal administration.

In the palace of Knossos, Quartier Mu at Malia, and Petras in the east, scribes were writing in the Hieroglyphic script on three- and four-sided clay bars and medallion-shaped 'labels.' Inscribed Hieroglyphic seals, often of hard stone, were used for unquestionably bureaucratic purposes, most often appearing on crescent-shaped sealings. At Knossos, a group of seal users—striking in that most of their seals bore figurative designs—stamped a new, flat-based sealing type that had sealed leather documents—so I simply call them 'document sealings' (Pini 1990; Weingarten 1995).

In southern Crete, scribes wrote in the Linear A script on bars, tablets, and roundels. Bureaucrats at Phaistos and Monastiraki stamped thousands of sealings in a day-to-day accounting system almost identical to that known from the Near East—as indicated by the diagnostic knob and peg traces on the sealing reverses (Fiandra 1968; Heath-Wiencke 1976). In all, more than 327 different seals were used to stamp sealings at Phaistos—so storeroom management was comparable in scale to that of a Near Eastern bureaucracy. The majority of seals at Phaistos had geometric or interlace designs and were made of soft materials, but almost 22% bore more 'advanced' figurative images of plants, animals, and even human figures. Some were from hard seal stones, and at least five were from metal rings: Such rings may have led to the 'flowering of glyptic naturalism' since any mistakes in the rendering of details could be corrected by reheating the metal.

The administrative systems expressed in the Hieroglyphic and Linear A scribal spheres are almost entirely different and geographically distinct. After the great destructions, Hieroglyphic administration and its script disappear. Henceforth, all Crete uses Linear A. The production of inscribed seals, too, came to an end: Whatever the meaning of the texts on the seals, they were not translated into Linear A. Such an abrupt loss of script and inscribed seals could hardly have occurred without a major shift in social or political power, probably violent. To my mind, therefore, the New Palace period really begins not with architectural modifications but with the appearance of the Linear A script over the whole island.

Second Palace Seals and Sealings

Late Minoan I is a time of growing prosperity throughout Crete. New buildings are erected above the older palatial structures, and palaces are founded at Zakro and Galatas. From the administrative viewpoint, the most striking feature is the construction or expansion of the villas and rich farmhouses throughout the north, south, and, east of the island. Located in fertile valleys, the villas presumably functioned as provincial centers of authority in a complex series of geographically related units (Rehak and Younger 2000, 278–85). When this system collapsed, with widespread burnt destructions at the end of LM IB, some villas left evidence of sealing activities but little or no indications of scribal administration.

Neopalatial glyptic shows steadily improved engraving of animated and lifelike images of animals and humans, sometimes placed in elaborate landscapes reminiscent of fresco paintings. Perhaps at the behest of the new bureaucracy, sealing shapes are pared down to just three: cushion and lentoid seals, which developed out of earlier shapes, and the new amygdaloid, first confined to the large and distinctive class of talismanic seals before spreading to more conventional subjects.

Neopalatial naturalistic glyptic is sharply skewed to depictions of animals: 85% compared to 15% with humans (Younger 1988, x–xii). There is, however, a bias toward human subjects on metal rings. Although only about two hundred rings and ring impressions survive, rings occupy a prominent place in Minoan iconography, with scenes of hunting, fighting, chariot driving, and bull leaping especially, although not exclusively, associated with metal rings.

Despite the often lifelike effect, it is wrong to describe these seals as naturalistic. It is doubtful that any Minoan artist ever tried to make a literal representation or to reproduce anything as an exact portrayal of a given scene or object. Nor are they in any meaningful sense "inspired by nature" (*pace* Krzyszkowska 2005, 146). Whether portraying human figures or bulls in flying gallop or butterflies and flowers, naturalism was not the Minoan artists' aesthetic goal. One need only look at the Minoan male figure to see that they do not accurately represent the human body: wasp-waisted and wiry, the physical body is distorted in order to create an impression of youth and agility (Boardman 1970, 38).

The image projects the focal points of the Minoan worldview—not the world as it is. Seal carvers emphasized some aspects of the subject while minimizing or omitting others. For example, it has been argued that the aniconic or featureless heads of female figures on some LM I gold rings result from the techniques of punching and engraving (Krzyszkowska 2005, 138n63). While glyptic style and technique are undoubtedly entwined, technical restraints should apply equally to all parts of the ring, which is simply not the case: The women's flounced skirts on the same rings are almost always so finely detailed that they explicitly "encourage attention" (Boardman 1970, 38). Put another way, whether the women are goddesses, priestesses, or worshippers is not the issue: They are wearing the skirt of the goddess, and *that*, not human features, is the focus of the scene. These images are statements of what the seal engravers wanted to show, not an objective account of a religious scene (*pace* Krzyszkowska 2005, 142)—in this case that the women's skirts are more important than their heads or limbs.

Despite the high technical and artistic quality of rings and many hard stone seals, the Minoan elite did not always choose to use such pieces as they went about palatial or villa business. Surprisingly, at LM IB Ayia Triada, only three of the top sealing leaders (i.e., those who used their seals most often [= *CMS* II.6 11, 101, 70]) had excellent seals, while many of the most active seal owners used mediocre or even poor-quality seals: a quasi-talismanic bird, a wretched Bird-Lady, a sausage-shaped female griffin, talismanic fish, and a lion so poorly engraved that it might be a scratching dog about to fall over (*CMS* II.6 110, 28, 99, 134, 85). It seems that seals were not chosen primarily for their aesthetic excellence but for reasons that mattered more to the seal owner, perhaps because of family connections or amuletic efficacy (Weingarten 1988).

At LM IB Zakro, the local sealing leader used a ring that depicts a cult procession. But this ring breaks down into *two* rings (*CMS* II.7 16, 17): two almost identical cult scenes of the same size but in two very slightly different versions. The Zakro sealing leader (or leaders) is using what we call "replica" rings: rings made intentionally similar in order to exercise some similar political or social authority. Impressions from such replica rings are found in all of the main LM IB sealing deposits (Betts 1967) and now on LC I Thera, too (Doumas 2000).

Some scholars argue that the replica rings—many of which were large metal rings, often with cult scenes or of bulls and bull leaping—are no more than reflections of fashion or of craftspersons simply repeating themselves (Pini 2006; Krzyszkowska 2005, 141–42, 188–92). However, this is to miss our most important evidence for the activities of social and political elites at this time. For the issue is not the mere existence of slightly different large metal rings but how they are *used*. Because of the Zakro habit of stamping nodules with two or even three different seal impressions, we can see replica rings in action (Figure 24.3): a cult ring used by the sealing leader at Zakro

Figure 24.3. Cult Scene + bull leaping, Document sealings stamped
by two gold rings, Zakro House A (*CMS* II.7 16 + 37;
photo courtesy *CMS*).

is paired with another replica ring, in this case a bull-leaping ring; both the cult ring
and the bull-leaping ring, in fact, break down into two almost identical rings always
paired together (= CMS II.7, 16 + 37CMS II.7, 17 + 38). Since they can hardly have been
distinguished in sealing practice, it follows that it cannot have mattered which of the
two (or four) had written, sent, or sealed these documents (Weingarten 1993). The
simplest explanation is that the cult rings are nearly identical because they are used by
people having the same rank or duties—and so, too, are the two bull-leaping rings.

The quality and imposing imagery of the best of these rings indicate a central
palatial workshop, probably at Knossos. This need not mean Knossian political
control of large parts of the island, still less of Thera: Current evidence suggests

no more than documents and messengers moving back and forth between LM I sites under the authority of a select group of ring owners (Weingarten 1991; *pace* Betts 1967).

FINAL PALACE SEALS AND SEALINGS

If we had only seals to go by, we would never have guessed that the Mycenaeans took control of Crete in LM II/IIIA. Undoubtedly many artisans survived the great destructions and ensured glyptic continuity. One striking example (*CMS* VII, 113, 162, II.3, 212) shows three rock crystal gems of the same size (± 2 cm) treated by three different stylistic groups: The composition is virtually identical—a standing bull, regardant, palm tree in front, figure-8 shield below—but, if the stylistic dating is correct, they were engraved sequentially, probably from late LM I to LM IIIA (Younger 2000, 353 and figures 8–10). It may well be that the seals were made intentionally similar for persons of the same bureaucratic level, even as administration switched from Minoan to Mycenaean hands.

Nonetheless, craftspersons inevitably responded to the new political situation. Among the large group of Spectacle-Eye seals (LM II(?)–LM IIIA1), some show continuity with the Minoan past, but many seem to take explicitly new directions: (1) using otherwise unusual lapis lacedaemonius and Near Eastern black haematite; (2) developing distinctive, conventional compositions, such as animal pairs in symmetrically reversed and mirror-image poses; and (3) creating emblematic themes, most strikingly, the Minotaur—perhaps the origin of the best-known Cretan myth (Younger 2000, 349–51). These innovations might be meant to personify early Mycenaean rule at Knossos—a difficult proposal to prove but a stimulating one to think about.

The Knossos sealings, on the other hand, are good indicators of regime change—most obviously those inscribed in Linear B, signaling the arrival of another new script. Document sealings disappear: The Mycenaeans apparently had no need for those documents so necessary to Minoan administration. Changes in the sealing pattern, too, indicate that the sealings no longer represent internal storeroom management (as did most Minoan deposits) but probably a tax-based or tributary system with sealed goods arriving at the palace from elsewhere (Weingarten 1994, 184–87).

Shortly before the fall of the palace, a new glyptic style began to emerge. A very large metal ring impression depicting two winged griffins attacking a stag (*CMS* II.8, 192) belongs within the Rhodian Hunt Group (RHG), characterized by elongated, 'scooped out' animal bodies in mannered, elegant poses (Younger 1987, 63–64; Aruz 2008, 204–205; Pini 1986). The RHG seals are better known from the islands and Greek mainland in LM IIIA2–IIIB, the last workshop to have carved hard-stone seals in the prehistoric Aegean (Younger 1979, 97). The style reappears in Cypro-Aegean glyptic: On a haematite cylinder now in the Metropolitan Museum of Art, the small Master of Animal scene in the upper field is clearly extracted from a Minoan lentoid, and the stag below is remarkably similar to that on the Knossos ring impression (Weingarten 1996; Aruz 2008, 218–19, figure 434). The RHG scooped-out animal style thus began at Knossos. It may have been the fall of the palace that sent gem engravers fleeing eastward toward Cyprus, where they or their immediate descendants went on to influence the iconography and style of Cypro-Aegean glyptic.

With the fall of the palace of Knossos, a thousand years of Minoan seals comes to an abrupt end.

BIBLIOGRAPHY

Alexiou, Stylianos, and Peter M. Warren. 2004. *The Early Minoan Tombs of Lebena, Southern Crete. SIMA* 30. Sävedalen, Sweden: Åström.

Aruz, Joan. 2008. *Marks of Distinction: Seals and Cultural Exchange between the Aegean and the Orient (ca. 2600–1360 B.C.). CMS* Beiheft 7. Mainz: von Zabern.

Betts, John. 1967. "New Light on Minoan Bureaucracy: A Re-examination of Some Cretan Sealings." *Kadmos* 6: 15–40.

Boardman, John. 1970. *Greek Gems and Finger Rings.* London: Thames and Hudson.

Doumas, Christos. 2000. "Seal Impressions from Akrotiri, Thera: A Preliminary Report." In *Minoisch-mykenische Glyptik*, 57–65.

Fiandra, Enrica. 1968. "A che cosa servivano le cretule di Festòs." In *Proceedings of the 2nd International Cretological Congress*, 383–95. Athens: University of Crete.

Hallager, Erik. 2000. "New Evidence for Seal Use in the Pre-palatial and Protopalatial Periods." In *Minoisch-mykenische Glyptik*, 97–105.

Heath-Wiencke, Martha. 1976. "Clay Sealings from Shechem, the Sudan, and the Aegean," *JNES* 35: 127–30.

Hitchcock, Louise. Forthcoming. "Monumentalizing Hierarchy: The Significance of Architecture in the Emergence of Complexity on Minoan Crete." In *Proceedings of the 10th International Cretological Congress, Khania.*

Hood, Sinclair, and Victor E. G. Kenna. 1973. "An Early Minoan III Sealing from Knossos." *Antichità Cretesi: Studi in onore di Doro Levi 1, Cronache di Archeologia* 12: 103–106.

Krzyszkowska, Olga. 2005. *Aegean Seals: An Introduction.* BICS Suppl. 85. London: Institute of Classical Studies.

Macdonald, Colin F., and Carl Knappett. 2007. *Knossos Protopalatial Deposits in Early Magazine A and the South-west Houses,* BSA Suppl. 41. London: Institute of Classical Studies.

MacGillivray, J. Alexander. 2000. *Minotaur: Sir Arthur Evans and the Archaeology of the Minoan Myth.* London: Jonathan Cape.

Panagiotaki, Marina. 1993. "Sealings from the Olive Press Room, Knossos: New Information from the Unpublished Notes of Sir Arthur Evans." *BSA* 88: 29–47.

———. 1999. The Central Palace Sanctuary at Knossos, BSA Supplementary Volume 31, London.

Pini, Ingo. 1986. "Nochmals zu einem tönernen Siegelabdruck des Museums Iraklion." In *Philia epi Georgion E. Mylonan*, 300–303. Athens: Library of the Archaeological Society of Athens.

———. 1990. "The Hieroglyphic Deposit and the Temple Repositories at Knossos." In *Aegean Seals*, 33–54.

———. 2006. "Look-alikes, Copies, and Replicas." In *Pepragmena Th' Diethnous Kritologikou Synedriou (Proceedings of the 9th International Cretological Congress), Elounta, 1–6 October 2001. A3: Proïstoriki Periodos, Techni kai Latreia, Elounda*, ed. Eugenia Tampakaki and Agisilaos Kaloutsakis, 51–64. Irakleio: Etairia Kritikon Istorikon Meleton.

Rehak, Paul, and John G. Younger. 2000. "Minoan and Mycenaean Administration in the Early Late Bronze Age." In *Administration Documents in the Aegean and Their Near Eastern Counterparts*, ed. Massimo Perna, 277–301. Turin: Centro internazionale di ricerche archeologiche antropologiche e storiche.

Sakellarakis, Ioannis A. 1976. "Χρονολογημένα σύνολα μινωικών σφραγίδων τις Αρχάνες." *Proceedings of the 4th Cretological Congress* (Heraklion), 510–32. Irakleio: Etairia Kritikon Istorikon Meleton.

———. 1980. Gruppen minoischer Siegel der Vorpalatzeit aus datierten geschlossenen Funden. JRGZM 27, 1–12.

Sbonias, Konstantinos. 1995. *Frühkretische Siegel. BAR-IS* 620. Oxford: Tempus Reparatum.

———. 2000. "Specialization in the Early Minoan Seal Manufacture: Craftsmen, Settlements, and the Organization of Production." In *Minoisch-mykenische Glyptik*, 277–93.

Schoep, Ilse. 2005. "The Socio-economic Context of Seal Use and Administration at Knossos." In *Knossos*, 283–93.

Vlasaki, Maria, and Erik Hallager. 1995. "Evidence for Seal Use in Pre-palatial Western Crete." In *Sceaux minoens et mycéniens*, ed. Ingo Pini and Jean-Claude Poursat, 251–70. *CMS* Beiheft 5. Mainz: von Zabern.

Warren, Peter. 1972. *Myrtos, an Early Bronze Age Settlement in Crete*. Athens: British School of Archaeology at Athens.

Watrous, L. Vance, Despoina Hadzi-Vallianou, and Harriet Blitzer. 2004. *The Plain of Phaistos: Cycles of Social Complexity in the Mesara Region of Crete*. Los Angeles: University of California at Los Angeles, Institute of Archaeology.

Weingarten, Judith. 1988. "Seal-use at LM IB Ayia Triada: A Minoan Elite in Action, II: Aesthetic Considerations." *Kadmos* 27: 81–114.

———. 1991. "Late Bronze Age Trade within Crete: The Evidence of Seals and Sealings." In *Bronze Age Trade*, 303–24.

———. 1993. "The Multiple Sealing System of Minoan Crete and Its Possible Antecedents in Anatolia." *Oxford Journal of Archaeology* 11: 25–37.

———. 1994. "Sealings and Sealed Documents at Bronze Age Knossos." In *Labyrinth of History*, 171–88.

———. 1995. "Sealing Studies in the Middle Bronze Age. III; The Minoan Hieroglyphic Deposits at Malia and Knossos." In *Sceaux minoens et mycéniens, IVe Symposium International 10–12 septembre 1992, Clermont-Ferrand*, ed. Walter Müller, 285–311. *CMS* Beiheft 5. Mainz: Akademie der Wissenschaften und der Literatur.

———. 1996. "The Impact of Some Aegean Gem Engravers on Cypriot Glyptic Art: Thoughts on a Chicken or Egg Problem." In *Minotaur and Centaur: Studies in the Archaeology of Crete and Euboea Presented to Mervyn Popham*, ed. Don Evely, Irene Stavros Lemos, and Susan Sherratt, 79–86. *BAR-IS* 638. Oxford: Tempus Reparatum.

———. 2003. "A Tale of Two Interlaces." In Yves Duhoux, ed., *Briciaka: A Tribute to W. C. Brice. Cretan Studies* 9: 285–99.

———. Forthcoming. "Some Early Unstamped Sealings from EM IIB Palaikastro." In *Proceedings of the 10th International Cretological Congress, Khania*.

———. 2005. "How Many Seals Make a Heap: Seals and Interconnections on Prepalatial Crete." In *Emporia*, 759–66.

———, and Colin F. Macdonald. 2005. "The Earliest Administrative Sealed Documents from Knossos (MM IB): Three Noduli in the so-called Early Magazine A. In *Studi in Onore di Enrica Fiandra*, ed. Massimo Perna, 393–404. Paris: De Boccard.

Younger, John G. 1979. "The Rhodian Hunt Group." In *Papers in Cycladic Prehistory*, ed. Jack L. Davis and John F. Cherry, 97–73. Institute of Archaeology, Monograph 14. Los Angeles: University of California at Los Angeles, Institute of Archaeology.

———. 1987. "Aegean Seals of the Late Bronze Age VI." *Kadmos* 26: 44–73.

———. 1988. *The Iconography of Late Minoan and Mycenaean Sealstones and Finger Rings.* Bristol: University of Bristol Press.

———. 2000. "The Spectacle-eyes Group: Continuity and Innovation." In *Minoisch-mykenische Glyptik*, 348–60.

Yule, Paul. 1980. *Early Cretan Seals: A Study of Chronology.* Marburger Studien zur Vor- und Frühgeschichte 4. Mainz: von Zabern.

CHAPTER 25

MYCENAEAN SEALS
AND SEALINGS

JOHN G. YOUNGER

AFTER the introduction of a sealing system from the Near East into southern Greece in the Early Helladic period (see Wiencke, this volume) and the destruction of that culture ca. 2200 BCE, there is no demonstrable sign of seal use on the Greek mainland until the sudden appearance of seals in the Mycenae Shaft Graves at the end of the Middle Helladic period.

After the Shaft Grave period, seals are known on the Greek mainland, but there is almost no evidence that seals are being carved there, with the possible exception of the Mycenae-Vapheio group (mentioned later). A stone mold for a gold ring found in a tomb at Eleusis (*CMS* V, 422) constitutes the slim evidence for the making of seals on the Greek mainland (cf. Evely 1993, 146–71).

Perhaps almost all seals used on the Greek mainland in the Late Bronze were made in Crete. Certainly the seals in most stylistic groups cluster predominantly in Crete, and after the fall of Knossos brought an end to hard stone seal engraving (ca. 1300 BCE; Weingarten this volume), the administrators at Mycenae and Pylos used heirloom seals to impress sealings (Younger 1981a). Furthermore, after the fall of Knossos, Mycenaeans produced the Mainland Popular group, a series of beads in soft stones and glass that look like seals but were (almost) never used administratively (Younger 1987a; Pini 1995; Dickers 2001). One might say, then, that the Mycenaeans used seals in imitation of Minoan seal use but that tradition sat thinly on Mycenaean culture.

Before the Late Bronze Age

In the Late Neolithic period, clay and stone stamps are found from central Europe and Italy to the eastern Mediterranean (Makkay 1984, 2005; Younger 1987b). Because their intaglio designs are simple and a few preserve traces of color (yellow and red), it is believed that they were used to imprint designs on cloth—whence the term *pintaderas*.

The Early Helladic stamp seals (Wiencke this volume) may have arisen from pintaderas—their shapes are similar and their designs look like textile patterns. These stamps were used in a sealing administration, apparently derived from the Near East (see Weingarten, this volume).

One seal impression from Kea points in the direction that the EH/EC II culture would have taken if left to flourish. A stamped hearth rim (*CMS* V, 478) parodies Egyptian hieroglyphs, including a *djed* pillar, *Ra* sun sign, and a vase sign. The last is especially clever, for in Egyptian it would be the typical amphora, but here, in the EC II Aegean, it is the typical sauceboat. Obviously someone in the central Aegean knew enough about Egyptian writing to poke intelligent fun at it.

After the EH II destructions, the mainlanders abandoned seals. Yet a few clay stamps are found in Middle Helladic contexts (Younger 1992); perhaps these represent a resuscitation of pintaderas, as if lurking beneath the sophisticated surface of EH II administrative sealing there had been a local tradition of stamping waiting to reemerge.

The Shaft Grave Period

Until the end of the Middle Helladic period, only the islands (e.g., Kea and Samothrace) are acquainted with Minoan seals. But in MH III–LH I, the shaft graves at Mycenae begin attracting seals in number. In Grave Circle B come two Talismanics (*CMS* I, 6, 7) and a tiny amethyst disk (*CMS* I, 5) engraved with a portrait head of a bearded man; both are Minoan imports.

From Circle A come three gold cushions (*CMS* I, 9–11) and three stone seals (*CMS* I, 12–14), all from Shaft Grave III and two gold rings (*CMS* I, 15, 16) from Shaft Grave IV; a third gold ring (*CMS* I, 17) comes from the nearby "Mycenae Treasure." These trios from Grave Circle A (and vicinity) provoke a thought: Might they refer to another triadic series? Grave Circle B encloses approximately twelve major tombs, and Grave Circle A contains six shaft graves. After the Shaft Grave period, the Mycenae elite are buried in tholoi, which cluster in three geographical areas (near the citadel, and on both sides of the Panagia Ridge) and in three distinct periods (LH I–II, II late, and IIIA–B early). Is it possible that Mycenae had three major kinship groups that shared power (French 1989)? The

Lion Gate relief may present the venue for their power: Two lions (military) stand on two altars with concave sides (religion) and flank a column (palatial administration).

THE MAJOR MYCENAEAN, OR MYCENAEAN-INSPIRED, STYLISTIC GROUPS

The Mycenae-Vapheio Lion Group

The three gold cushions from Shaft Grave III present a distinct kind of lion: powerful body, fishgill-like separation between head and mane, heavy forelegs rounded at the top and outlined by a separate line topped by a dot, a sinuous saphenous vein over the legs, fur on belly and haunch, and heavily dotted paws (figure 25.1; MH III–LH I [–LH II]; Younger 1978, 1984, 1987a). The same lion appears on many seals from the Vapheio cist (LH IIA; e.g., *CMS* I, 243, 250). Another seal from the Vapheio cist (*CMS* I, 223) presents an equally powerful griffin, also with saphenous veins, led on a leash by a robed man wearing a seal stone on his left wrist (Rehak 1994). Other objects also present the same lion (e.g., the lion-hunt niello dagger and the gold lioness-head rhyton, both from Shaft Grave IV; Marinatos and Hirmer 1960, color pls. XXXV, XXXVII, XXXIX).

These seals and other objects constitute a major style called the Mycenae-Vapheio style because many of the pieces come from these two sites. To this core

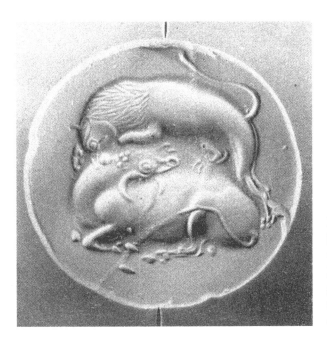

Figure 25.1. Modern impression of a lentoid (*CMS* V 435) in the Mycenae-Vapheio Lion group, from the Nichoria tholos (photo courtesy *CMS*).

group other seals are related (Younger 1981b), for instance the badly cut lion on *CMS* I, 228, from the Vapheio chamber, which has the fishgill but nothing else. The Lion Gate relief has powerful lions with the saphenous vein and outlined forelegs, but it adds "bracelets" across the ankles paralleled on a seal (*CMS* I, 46) from Mycenae Chamber Tomb 8 (LH II context?) that carries almost the same scene: two lions on an altar with concave sides sharing a frontal face.

Only a few examples of the Mycenae-Vapheio group come from Crete. From Knossos comes one sealing (*CMS* II.8, 297), while a few others may be peripherally related (from Kato Zakro, *CMS* II.7, 75, cf. 74, and from Ayia Triada, *CMS* II.6, 104).

If the Mycenae-Vapheio group was created on the Mainland, it is the only seal stone workshop that can, with any plausibility, be located there.

The Spectacle Eye Group (LH IIIA)

When the Mycenaeans took over Knossos, they commissioned a new style for seals, the Spectacle Eye group (Weingarten this volume; Younger 2000; Müller 2000); its animals look like they are wearing eyeglasses. Since the group also employs lapis lacedaemonius (a stone found only south of Sparta on the Greek mainland) and creates a new iconography (animals in bilateral symmetry and the Minotaur), it is likely that this group is an invention to mark the new Mycenaean administration at Knossos.

The Island Sanctuaries Group (End of LH IIIA)

Known for its animals with svelte bodies, linear legs with dotted hooves and joints, and contorted poses, the Island Sanctuaries seals, and its subset, Rhodian Hunt, are the last seals to be made in hard stone; no more developed stylistic group of seals exists (Younger 1979, 1981a). Since only one, possibly three, Rhodian Hunt seals impressed Knossos sealings (*CMS* II.8, 192, possibly 186, 187) and since most seals in this group have been found in the Cyclades and Dodecanese, including many in Mycenaean sanctuaries, it is tempting to hypothesize that the group had just begun to develop at Knossos when the palace fell and the artists dispersed.

Mainland Popular Seals and Related Groups (End of LH IIIA–IIIB)

With the demise of hard stone seal engraving (perhaps always more a Minoan art), there arose a group of soft stone seals with schematic, linear depictions of animals, occasionally people, known as the Mainland Popular group (Younger 1987a; Pini 1995; Dickers 2001). The name derives from the fact that the seals are restricted to the Greek mainland (a subset, the Armenoi group, in Mycenaean Crete) and to humble tombs scattered broadly across the Aegean; two Mainland Popular seals even come from the Uluburun wreck (dated after 1306 BC by dendrochronology; *CMS* VS.1B, 473; VS.3, 454). This widespread dispersal of Mainland Popular seals, their appearance at nonpalatial sites, and the fact that they impressed virtually no sealings (one exception from Thebes: *CMS* VS 3.373), all make it likely that these seals served as the identity markers of commoners, much as did the Mesara dentine seals of EM II–III, soft stone prisms from the Malia Workshop in MM II (Poursat 1996), and the Cretan Popular group in LM I (Younger 1983).

With the Mainland Popular group, the manufacture of seals in the Bronze Age Aegean comes to an end.

The Prepalatial Use of Seals on the Greek Mainland

There is no direct evidence for seal use in the Prepalatial Mycenaean period (LH I–II), but if the trios of seals and rings from Grave Circle A relate to the concept of cooperative power, then we can identify groups of two and three seals from the early tholoi that may have functioned similarly (Rehak and Younger 2000). I give two examples. From the Kazarma tholos (LH I; *CMS* V, 577–85) come two Talismanic amygdaloids, two red lentoids (sard and cornelian), two quasi-Talismanic amygdaloids, and three cylinder seals, two of which are amethyst and two of which carry griffins. And from the Rutsi tholos (LH II), shaft 2 (*CMS* I, 269–74, VS.1A, 345), come two cushions with female griffins, two three-sided amethyst prisms, and three amygdaloids (one of which is glass and the other of gold with a netted bull); from the floor of the tholos (*CMS* I, 275–86) come two sardonyx lentoids, two agate lentoids, four cornelian lentoids, two cylinder seals of red stone (cornelian and sardonyx), a glass lentoid (cf. the glass amygdaloid from the shaft), and a second gold amygdaloid (this one with a wounded bull).

These pairs and trios of seals imply that two or three administrators shared authority and expressed that cooperation by owning seals with similar motifs and in similar shapes and materials (compare "replica" rings in Neopalatial Crete: Weingarten this volume). Evidence for a similar sharing of authority by lieutenants can be seen in sealings from Pylos (mentioned later).

The Use of Seals in the Mycenaean Palaces

A seal represents the individual who owns it; impressing the seal into clay is an act that stipulates that individual's responsibility in the transaction represented by the sealing. For example, while the clay stopper of a wine jar prevents contamination (e.g., *CMS* VS.1B, 348, from the Menelaion, LH II–IIIA), impressing the stopper certifies and guarantees its contents. For the Mycenaeans, seals are used only when it is necessary to document the participation of the particular individual who was responsible (immediately or ultimately) for the transaction that is being authenticated. Minoan seal use was more casual, authenticating most transactions regardless of the necessity to identify the responsible individual.

Except for a few other impressed jar stoppers (e.g., *CMS* I, 160–62; V, 669; and VS.3, 164, 218), one document sealing (*CMS* VS.3, 217), and one impressed *nodulus* (*CMS* I, 19), almost all other mainland seal impressions are found only on nodules (clay sealing around a knotted string)—and only one seal per nodule. Moreover, while many hundreds of seals impressed sealings from Minoan Crete, there are only some 250 seals that impressed some 500 sealings from the Mycenaean mainland (Palaima 1987). This restricted use parallels the restriction of Linear B writing to just tablets, labels, and nodules (Linear A was used more widely; Godart and Olivier, 1976–1985).

Most Mycenaean nodules document transactions between outlying production centers and the palace (for instance, a seal from Elis [*CMS* XI, 27] impressed a sealing from Pylos [*CMS* IS, 180] inscribed (Wr 1416) "nanny" [CAP^f], apparently recording the shipment of female goats). Most of the Pylos sealings written by persons outside the palace are inscribed in an "archaic" hand, reminiscent of the handwriting styles at Knossos almost two centuries earlier (Palaima 2000)—within the palace the official style was more modern.

Also within the palace, seal impressions were usually not necessary (the parties were well known), and few sealings (impressed or inscribed or both) are actually found in the Mycenaean palaces. We should imagine, therefore, that most sealings traveled out from the palaces to the outlying production centers accompanying raw goods to be finished. The excavation of the lower towns of Pylos and Mycenae will probably produce the kinds of documents that have been found in the houses on the Chania acropolis (Hallager and Vlasaki 1997, with earlier bibliography).

Another type of sealing no doubt to be found in the outlying production centers are those that were attached to tablets. Some leaf-shaped tablets (e.g., the Pylos Eb [landholding] and Sa [chariot wheels] series, and Thebes Ug 5 and 17) reveal traces of a horizontal string running through them, to which a sealing could have been fastened "with the impression of the seal of the scribal administrator" to be taken away by the person who had delivered commodities to the palace (e.g., Ameja in Pylos Sa 834 and Sh 736 and Akosota in Va 842) as a receipt that he had finished his task and furnished the commodities and "that the scribal administrator had indeed approved his work through inspection" (Palaima 1996). Such proof of delivery might be necessary if the furnisher were ever suspected of fraud, as in the trial of two Hittite supervisors during the reign of Hattusilis III (ca. 1286–1265 BC; Justus 1997; Palaima 1996).

Inscribed sealings record short, individual bits of information that are then entered on summary tablets (Palaima 2000). For instance, Pylos sealing Wr 1326 records the delivery of a bed (tablet Vn 851 presents the summary) and is impressed by a lentoid depicting a central octopus surrounded by dolphins (*CMS* I, 312); the seal may have belonged to an important individual: An octopus is painted on the floor directly in front of the throne, and dolphins are painted on floors in the "Queen's Megaron" suite (Hirsch 1977, 32–36, pls. 7.16, 7.17a, 9).

Inscribed and impressed sealings sometimes also give additional details, like those from Thebes that record individual animals, their sex, and their condition. Occasionally there is a pattern in seal use, too. For instance, Thebes seal type J (bull leaping) authorizes the delivery of pigs from Sameus (the swineherd?), while seal type L (two goats) authorizes fodder (logogram PYC), and R (two goats), male sheep (Aravantinos, Godart, and Sacconi 2002, 20, 51–75). Similar information for a feast at Pylos "when the wanax was initiated" must have arrived via similar sealed deliveries, summarized on tablets Un 2 and 138 (Palaima 2000).

At Pylos we can see delivery sealings. From the oil magazine (room 24) comes a sealing (Wr 1437) inscribed with "unguent" (logogram AREPA) and impressed with a lentoid that depicts crossed goats (*CMS* I, 382), presumably belonging to the supplier. Four sealings (Wr 1358–1361) from the Wine Magazine (room 105) each carry the inscription "wine" (logogram VIN); the impressing seals may have belonged to the vintners. Sealing Wr 1361 was impressed by a gold ring (*CMS* I, 361), while the other three sealings (1358–1360) were all impressed by a single lentoid (*CMS* I, 363, a stag hunt). Two of these sealings also record a man's name, both different and both in a different hand—presumably these are the vintner's lieutenants, who may have had access to the same seal. The seal would then signify that the person possessing it has ultimate authority, while the inscribed names would be those immediately responsible for the deliveries.

Mycenae also preserves delivery sealings. From the House of Sphinxes (LH IIIB middle; Bennett 1958) come eight sealings, seven impressed by the same seal (*CMS* I 163, in the Rhodian Hunt group) and an eighth (*CMS* VS.217, in the Island Sanctuaries group), whose reverse preserves the impressions of thick leather straps. These were found clustered for discard in the doorway of room 1; the inscribed sealings (Wt 501–507; figure 25.2) record pots (possibly those found in that room) that are summarized on the obverse of tablet Ue 611 found down the hall in the archives room 6. The seals were presumably owned by the potter and/or the transporter.

Similarly, many sealings from the Arsenal at Knossos (Ws 1704, etc.) were found among the remains of two wooden boxes and hundreds of bronze points. Most of the sealings were inscribed by the same scribe with the appropriate logogram (Linear B *254 JAC), apparently to identify the contents for delivery; three sealings had been impressed by a single lentoid (*CMS* II.8, 305), probably belonging to the armorer (or his scribe), who then wrote the logogram across the impressions.

Unimpressed sealings are predictably inscribed with the kind of written information that the seal impression would have given visually. For instance, unimpressed Pylos labels (the Wa and Wo series) record personnel (e.g., the name of the supplier) and other details; Knossos label Wm 8499 records the name of a man furnishing cloth being supplied by another, while Wm 8493 records a collective at the place Setoija (Arkhanes?) furnishing a special *te* cloth to another place, Kirita.

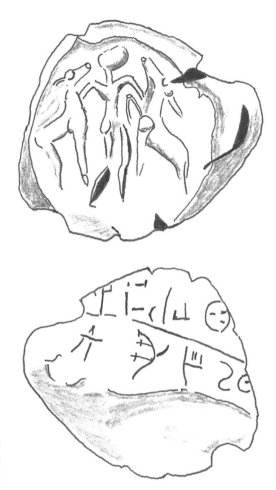

Figure 25.2. Mycenae sealing Wt 501
impressed by a lentoid (*CMS* I 163;
drawing by the author).

After inspectors within the palace received and unsealed the delivered goods, they would gather the sealings for discard, and the responsible administrator would have the deliveries summarized on tablets to be sent to the central archives. At Knossos, one sealing is impressed by a lentoid depicting a female dog (*CMS* II.8, 287); it is inscribed (Ws 8754) with the name of the purveyor, Kuwata, in the bureau of *(opi)* Anuwiko. We do not know the commodity that was sealed, nor do we know anything more about Kuwata (unless he is the immediately responsible scribe, Hand 101).

Anuwiko, however, may have been the "lawaketa" recorded on personnel tablets As 40+5093 and 1516 written by the same Hand 101; he would then be one of the most important officials at Knossos, second to the wanax (king) and more important than the qasirewe (classical "basileus") (Olivier 1968; Weingarten 1997). If the seal with the female dog is Anuwiko's (or his bureau's), it impressed sealings found in the west, south, and east wings of the palace. These sealings belong to the class known as "combination" sealings: A stringhole runs through them, and they were pressed up against a wicker basket, presumably the basket that held the recording tablets (see *CMS* II.8, fig. 29a, for the wicker impression on the reverse of Anuwiko's sealing).

At Pylos, combination sealings were found only in the Central Archives, room 8 (Weingarten 1991). There are six of these, impressed by three seals: *CMS* I, 302, a ring (?) depicting a man battling a lion; *CMS* I, 305, a ring with a bull-leaping scene; and *CMS* IS, 173, a ring with two men battling two lions—two certainly, maybe three, gold rings for our high-placed administrators within the palace. A regular sealing (*CMS* I, 307) was found next door in room 7 of the central archives. It was impressed either by the same ring as that with men battling lions or by a slightly different "replica." In any case, a "replica" ring does exist, the slightly larger, gold "Danicourt" ring (*CMS* XI, 272, said to come from Thessaloniki). Thus, we have, for the ultimately responsible administrator with access to the Central Archives, one, if not two, replica rings for his lieutenants.

Summary

From this discussion it is apparent that Mycenaeans valued Minoan seals but produced few, if any, of their own for administrative use, though they did produce soft stone identity markers (the Mainland Popular group) when hard stone seals were no longer being supplied by Knossian artists (ca. 1300 BC).

In the Prepalatial period (LH I–II) pairs or trios of Mycenaean administrators, working cooperatively, may have used similar seals to conduct their shared duties.

In the Palatial period (LH III), Mycenaean administrators preferred to write their transactions out in full. When doing so was inconvenient (the sealing was too small, the transaction too complicated, or the participants were illiterate), then the personal seals of those responsible for conducting the transactions would be used in place of naming them. It is therefore probable that most Mycenaean sealings are delivery sealings to the palace (or palatial workshops outside the palace) accompanying commodities being furnished by persons in the outlying regions.

While some sealings accompanied goods that were circulating within the palace, others, the combination sealings, accompanied baskets of preliminary tablets to the central archives and recorded the receipt of commodities at the delivery points on the periphery. These were impressed by the seals that belonged to high officials (the lawaketa or the qasirewe) or by the replicas that belonged to their lieutenants, following an old tradition of shared cooperation on the mainland.

Mycenaeans may have commissioned a new seal stone style to mark their takeover of Knossos, but after that palace fell they no longer commissioned seals and were content to use heirlooms.

BIBLIOGRAPHY

Aravantinos, Vassilis L., Louis Godart, and Anna Sacconi. 2002. *Thèbes: Fouilles de la Cadmée*. Vol. 3, *Corpus des documents d'archives en Linéaire B de Thèbes*. Rome: Istituti editoriali e poligrafici internazionali.

Bennett, Emmett L., Jr., ed. 1958. "The Mycenae Tablets II." *TAPS* 48.1.

Dickers, Aurelia. 2001. *Die spätmykenischen Siegel aus weichem Stein: Untersuchungen zur spätbronzezeitlichen Glyptik auf dem griechischen Festland und in der Ägäis*. Rahden, Westfalia: Leidorf.

Evely, Don. 1993, 2000. *Minoan Crafts: Tools and Techniques. An Introduction. SIMA* 92: 1 and 2. 2 vols. Gothenburg: Åström.

French, Elizabeth B. 1989. " 'Dynamis' in the Archaeological Record at Mycenae." In *Images of Authority: Papers Presented to Joyce Reynolds on the Occasion of her 70th Birthday*, ed. Mary M. Mackenzie and Charlotte Roueché, 122–30. Cambridge Philosophical Society Suppl. 16. Cambridge: Cambridge University Press.

Godart, Louis, and Jean-Pierre Olivier. 1976–1985. *Recueil des inscriptions en Linéaire A: ÉtCrét* 21, 1–5. 5 vols. Paris: Librairie Orientaliste Paul Geuthner.

Hallager, Erik, and Maria Vlasaki. 1997. "New Linear B Tablets from Khania." In *La Crète mycénienne*, 169–74.

Hirsch, Ethel. 1977. *Painted Decoration on the Floors of Bronze Age Structures in Crete and the Greek Mainland. SIMA* 53. Gothenburg: Åström.

Justus, Carol F. 1997. "The Case of the Missing *dusdumi* and *lalami*." *Minos* 29–30 (1994–1995): 213–38.

Makkay, János. 1984. *Early Stamp Seals in South-east Europe*. Budapest: Akadémia Press.
———. 2005. *Supplement to the Early Stamp Seals of South-east Europe*. Budapest: Akadémia Press.

Marinatos, Spyridon, and Max Hirmer. 1960. *Crete and Mycenae*. New York: Abrams.

Müller, Walter. 2000. "Zu Stil und Zeitstellung des Bildthemas 'Herr der Löwen.' " In *Minoisch-mykenische Glyptik*, 181–94.

Mylonas, George E. 1966. *Mycenae and the Mycenaean Age*. Princeton: Princeton University Press.

Olivier, Jean-Pierre. 1968. "La serie Ws de Cnossos." *Minos* 9: 173–83.

Palaima, Thomas G. 1987. "Mycenaean Seals and Sealings in Their Economic and Administrative Contexts." In *Tractata Mycenaea*, ed. Petar Ilievski and Ljiljana Crepajac, 249–66. Skopje: Macedonian Academy of Sciences.
———. 1996. "Sealings as Links in an Administrative Chain." In *Administration in Ancient Societies: Proceedings of Session 218 of the 13th International Congress of Anthropological and Ethnological Sciences, Mexico City, July 29–August 5, 1993*, ed. Piera Ferioli, Enrica Fiandra, and Gian Giacomo Fissore, 37–66. Turin: Ministero per i Beni Culturali e Ambientali Ufficio Centrale per i Beni Archivistici.
———. 2000. "The Palaeography of Mycenaean Inscribed Sealings from Thebes and Pylos and Their Place within the Mycenaean Administrative System." In *Minoisch-mykenische Glyptik*, 219–38.

Pini, Ingo. 1995. "Die spätminoische Weichsteinglyptik." In *Sceaux minoens et mycéniens*, ed. Walter Müller, 193–207. *CMS* Beiheft 4. Berlin: Mann.

Poursat, Jean-Claude. 1996. *Fouilles exécutées à Malia: Le quartier Mu III. Artisans minoens: Les maisons-ateliers du quartier Mu. ÉtCrét* 32. Athens: L'École française d'Athènes.

Rehak, Paul. 1994. "The Aegean 'Priest' on *CMS* I.223." *Kadmos* 33(1): 76–84.

————, and John G. Younger. 2000. "Minoan and Mycenaean Administration in the Early Late Bronze Age." In *Administration Documents in the Aegean and Their Near Eastern Counterparts*, ed. Massimo Perna, 277–301. Turin: Centro internazionale di ricerche archeologiche antropologiche e storiche.

Vermeule, Emily T. 1967. "A Mycenaean Jeweler's Mold." *BMFA* 64(339): 19–31.

Weingarten, Judith. 1997. "The Sealing Bureaucracy of Mycenaean Knossos: The Identification of Some Officials and Their Seals." In *La Crète mycénienne*, 517–35.

————. 1991. 'Late Bronze Age Trade Within Crete: the evidence of seals and sealings,' in *Bronze Age Trade in the Mediterranean*. *SIMA* 90, ed. Nicholas H. Gale, 303–324. Jonsered; Åström.

Younger, John G. 1978. "The Mycenae-Vapheio Lion Group." *AJA* 82: 285–99.

————. 1979. "The Rhodian Hunt Group." In *Papers in Cycladic Prehistory*, ed. Jack L. Davis and John F. Cherry, 97–105. Institute of Archaeology, University of California at Los Angeles, Monograph XIV. Los Angeles: University of California at Los Angeles, Institute of Archaeology.

————. 1981a. "The Island Sanctuaries Group: Date and Significance." In *Studien zur minoischen und helladischen Glyptik. Beiträge zum 2. Marburger Siegel-Symposium 26.–30. September 1978*, ed. Wolf-Dietrich Niemeier, 263–72. *CMS* Beiheft 1. Berlin: Mann: http://kuscholarworks.ku.edu/dspace/handle/1808/4497.

————. 1981b. "The Mycenae-Vapheio Lion Workshop, III." *Temple University Aegean Symposium* 6: 67–71.

————. 1983. "Aegean Seals of the Late Bronze Age: Masters and Workshops, II. The First Generation Minoan Masters." *Kadmos* 22: 109–36.

————. 1984. "Aegean Seals of the Late Bronze Age: Masters and Workshops, III. The First Generation Mycenaean Masters." *Kadmos* 23: 38–64.

————. 1987a. "Aegean Seals of the Late Bronze Age: Stylistic Groups VI. Fourteenth-century Mainland and Later Fourteenth-century Cretan Workshops." *Kadmos* 26: 44–73.

————. 1987b. "A Balkan-Aegean-Anatolian Glyptic Koine in the Neolithic and EBA Periods." A paper given at the VIth International Aegean Symposium, Athens, Greece, 31 August–5 September 1987; http://kuscholarworks.ku.edu/dspace/handle/1808/4303.

————. 1988. *The Iconography of Late Minoan and Mycenaean Sealstones and Finger Rings*. Bristol: Bristol Classical Press.

————. 1992. "Seals? from Middle Helladic Greece." *Hydra* 8: 35–54; http://kuscholarworks.ku.edu/dspace/handle/1808/4302.

————. 2000. "The Spectacle-eyes Group: An Assessment of Its Iconography, Techniques, and Style." In *Minoisch-mykenische Glyptik*, 347–60.

CHAPTER 26

....

CRETAN HIEROGLYPHIC AND LINEAR A

....

HELENA TOMAS

THE existence of Bronze Age literacy in the Aegean was first recognized thanks to Arthur Evans's insightful study of seals and other inscribed objects that he saw or purchased while traveling through Crete. The seals bore signs of a script thereafter called Hieroglyphic or Pictographic—the name was based on Evans's interpretation of the appearance of the signs but was also influenced by his awareness of other Bronze Age hieroglyphic scripts known at the time (Evans 1894, 1897). With his further research on Crete, he established the existence of two other linear-looking scripts, and he envisaged an evolutionary progression from Hieroglyphic → Linear A → Linear B (Evans 1909, 18, 38; 1921, 612–13; 1952, 1–2).

As Evans suspected, Linear B is indeed the youngest of the three scripts; as for the other two, it is still unclear which one is older (mentioned later). Since all three scripts are now shown to be syllabic in their nature, the 'hieroglyphic' one bears a misleading name. The prefix 'Cretan' has therefore been suggested in order to differentiate it from other Bronze Age hieroglyphic scripts (Olivier 1989, 40–41).

Although the very first inscriptions are of Prepalatial date and may have had symbolic value which enhanced power of élites (as suggested by Schoep 2006, 44–47, 2007b, 56), wider use of Cretan Hieroglyphic and Linear A is best explained as a result of expanding economic activities that accompanied the growth of Cretan palatial centers and a consequent need for a well-structured administrative system (Schoep 1999, 267–68). It is precisely this administrative usage that allows us a partial understanding of texts in these two scripts, even though they both remain undeciphered.

The lack of decipherment is due partly to a relative paucity of documents and therefore a limited vocabulary specimen (ca. 300 different words are preserved in Cretan Hieroglyphic; ca. 800 in Linear A) and partly to the unknown language (or possibly two different languages) behind the scripts (Olivier 1986, 1989; Duhoux 1989, 1998). Thus, although correspondences with deciphered Linear B syllabograms give us an idea of the pronunciation of some Cretan Hieroglyphic and Linear A sign groups (words), we cannot understand their meaning.

CHRONOLOGY AND DISTRIBUTION

According to the archaeological evidence, the earliest examples of both scripts come from the MM IIB period. In the Southwest House at Knossos, an even earlier—MM IIA—document has been discovered (KN 49), but it has a poorly preserved inscription, probably in Linear A (Del Freo 2007, 204–205), although Cretan Hieroglyphic has also been proposed (Schoep 2007a).

During the MM III period, Cretan Hieroglyphic was abandoned, and Linear A remained the single script on the island until the end of LM IB, when it was succeeded by Linear B. The geographical distribution of the two scripts during the MM II–III periods may reflect a political fragmentation on the island: Linear A was used mostly in its southern part, whereas Cretan Hieroglyphic was used mostly in north-central and northeastern Crete (Schoep 1999). A clear division, however, is not possible since intrusions of one script into the area typically covered by the other have been observed on a number of sites, and, in the MM III palace at Malia, documents in both scripts appear even in the same deposit (succinct overviews in Schoep 1995). This coexistence of the two scripts has resulted in a range of common types of documents, as well as in numerous exchanges of scribal features.

Cretan Hieroglyphic Inscriptions

The earliest securely dated Cretan Hieroglyphic inscriptions on clay date from MM IIB, while the latest secure deposit comes from the MM III palace at Malia (see the concise overview in Younger 1996–1997). Production of seals with Cretan Hieroglyphic signs may have started even before MM IIB (*CHIC*, 27–32). Whereas these seals have been found often as isolated finds at a large number of sites, mostly in north-central and northeastern Crete, clay documents have been discovered in significant numbers only at Knossos, Malia, and Petras (cf. map in *CHIC*, 20).

Malia has yielded some fifty documents, the majority coming from either a MM IIB context of the Quartier Mu (Godart and Olivier 1978; Olivier 1996a) or a MM IIIB context of the palace (Chapouthier 1930). Forty or so documents come from the MM IIB deposit at Petras but were discovered only in 1996–1997 (Tsipopoulou 1998), which is why they are not included in *CHIC*.

With some one hundred specimens, however, the Hieroglyphic Deposit at Knossos constitutes the largest assemblage of documents. It was discovered in 1900 in the West Wing, in a fill beneath a staircase at the end of the Long Corridor (Evans 1899–1900). The circumstances of the discovery and the lack of pottery make the precise dating of this deposit difficult (Schoep 2001, 147–48): after much ambivalence, a late MM II date was suggested by Evans (1921, 272) and later supported by Yule (1978, 9). However, on the basis of their advanced seal motifs, Pini suggests an MM III date for some sealings and concludes that not all of the documents belonged to the same period but were accumulated over a longer time (1990, 41–43; *CMS* II.8, 2002, 6–7).

Linear A Inscriptions

During Evans's lifetime, no MM II Linear A inscriptions were yet known, which was one of the reasons he believed that Cretan Hieroglyphic was older than Linear A. However, discoveries at Phaistos in 1955 (Pugliese Carratelli 1958) showed that Linear A was already in use in MM IIB, while the 1992 discovery of a Knossian document pushes its beginnings into MM IIA (see earlier). The regular use of Linear A came to a halt at the end of the LM IB period, although rare inscriptions, mostly on nonadministrative objects (e.g., on a clay figurine; Dimopoulou, Olivier, and Rethemiotakis 1993), occurred even later (see the succinct overview in Bennet 2008, 12–13).

Whereas in the MM II and MM III periods, Linear A appears to have been used at a limited number of sites, during LM IB it was employed all over Crete, as well as on a few sites outside the island (Schoep 1995; Karnava 2008). With some 150 tablets and more than one thousand sealings discovered in the early years of the 20th century, Haghia Triada has provided the largest assemblage so far (Halbherr, Stefani, and Banti 1977). Here the documents were divided between two areas—the Villa and the Villaggio; the exact findspots of most of the former have been difficult to reconstruct (Militello 2002). All of the documents are from the LM IB period, a time when Haghia Triada, although not a palace, appears to have acted as an administrative center of the Mesara plain, while the nearby palace at Phaistos is administratively 'silent' (La Rosa 2002). Other assemblages of numerous Linear A documents come from Khania, Phaistos, and Zakro (see the relevant volumes of *GORILA*).

The Question of the Archanes Script

It is well known that writing does not necessarily indicate the beginning of administration and that sealing practice typically predates the use of writing (Palaima 1990; Ferioli et al. 1994, 1996; Perna 2000). This was the case in Crete, where certain Prepalatial sealings, although uninscribed, may have had an administrative purpose (Pini 1990, 34–35; Schoep 1999, 267–69; 2004, 283–86; Hallager 2000, 99).

Prepalatial administration is also reflected by the so-called Archanes script (as christened by Yule 1980, 170), attested on a small number of seals from Archanes Phourni, Pangalochori near Rethymnon, and Moni Odigitria in the vicinity of the Mesara Plain (Grumach and Sakellarakis 1966; Godart and Tzedakis 1992, 108, 121–22; for Prepalatial seals in general see Krzyszkowska 2005, 57–78). These seals are dated to EM III–MM IA and display signs similar to those in later Cretan Hieroglyphic and Linear A, even a sign group resembling the later 'Minoan libation formula' (Olivier 1996b, 107).

If the Archanes script is a separate script (doubts expressed by Olivier 1986, 377), then it is the oldest in the Aegean. However, *CHIC* includes it among Cretan Hieroglyphic texts, whereas Godart wonders whether we should instead consider it as Linear A, which would make Linear A the oldest script in the Aegean (Godart 1999). The main reason it is now included in *CHIC* is that seals with engraved signs of a script are abundant in Cretan Hieroglyphic but absent in Linear A (for three Linear A exceptions to this rule, see Olivier 1999, 422–26). The status of the Archanes script and its association with either Cretan Hieroglyphic or Linear A thus remain debatable.

SIGNARY

Both scripts are of syllabic nature. Clustered syllabograms form sign groups, most likely words. On inscribed clay documents, sign groups can be followed by logograms representing commodities and associated quantities. In both scripts, individual syllabograms are sometimes also used as logograms and can be ligatured.

Cretan Hieroglyphic Signary

Some ninety syllabograms have been distinguished in Cretan Hieroglyphic, as well as thirty or so logograms, probably denoting agricultural commodities. In addition, there are signs for numbers and fractions (Karnava 2001; Jasink 2005), as well as punctuation marks. The latter include a cross sign, interpreted as an indication of the beginning of a sign group and therefore an indication of the direction of reading, as already suggested by Evans (1921, 280; the classification of all Cretan Hieroglyphic signs can be found in *CHIC*, 17).

Since Cretan Hieroglyphic is still undeciphered, little can be said about the exact meaning of its inscriptions. Instead, only some very general interpretations can be made. Due to the few tablets available, we cannot even achieve much from comparing them to the well-understood system of Linear B tablets. Cretan Hieroglyphic therefore remains the least understood Aegean script (for the latest attempt at interpretation, see Younger 2003, 2005).

Linear A Signary

Linear B has been of crucial help in understanding the Linear A signary. About ninety syllabograms have been preserved in Linear A, nearly 70% of which have parallels in Linear B (*GORILA* V, XXII). As for the logograms, the percentage of correspondence is much lower. Linear A logograms are frequently ligatured with syllabic signs, probably in order to designate varieties or subtypes of commodities, as is the case in Linear B (Palaima 1994, 321, 327,n62). For the purpose of designating commodities, Linear A also employed monograms (i.e., signs composed of two or three syllabograms). Apart from several exceptions, this feature is largely abandoned in Linear B.

Signs for numbers do not differ in Linear A and B. They follow the so-called step-tally system; the only distinction between the two systems is that Linear A has no attested sign for ten thousand (Bennett 1999, 162). The way of expressing measures, however, is completely different. Linear A uses a complex system of signs for aliquot fractions (klasmatograms), whereas Linear B employs metrical signs to express units (with a scale of subunits) for weight, dry goods, and liquid goods. The values of Linear A fractions have not been established with certainty, although several keys have been proposed (the pioneering study was by Bennett 1950).

TYPES OF DOCUMENTS

With a fair amount of certainty, we can say that the majority of objects with Cretan Hieroglyphic script and a large number of those with Linear A had an administrative purpose, which is why we refer to them as documents (see overviews in Hallager 1996, 31–38; Krzyszkowska 2005, 98–118). Linear A has also been attested on a large number of nonadministrative objects, most of which are related to cult. These include votive stone tables from peak sanctuaries and sacred caves, votive cups and ladles, golden and silver pins, a figurine, and so on (Schoep 1994; Whittaker 2005). Unlike the administrative texts that contain lists of people and goods, these latter objects have more continuous texts, possibly even sentences, and may thus give us an insight into the syntax of the unknown language (Duhoux 1978, 1992).

Cretan Hieroglyphic Documents

Cretan Hieroglyphic documents can be divided into two groups: nonsealed and sealed. The former have an inscription incised on their clay surface, whereas the latter are stamped by seals with engraved Cretan Hieroglyphic signs and may have an incised inscription in addition (figure 26.1).

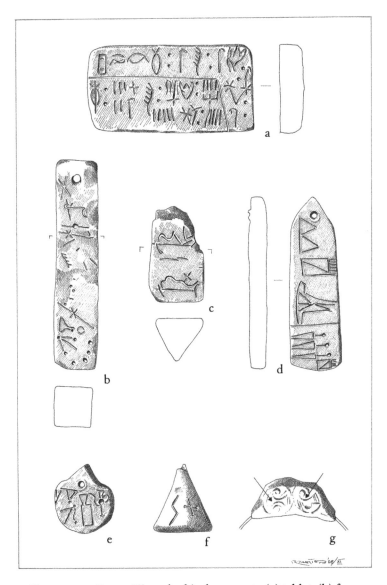

Figure 26.1. Cretan Hieroglyphic documents: (a) tablet; (b) four-sided bar; (c) three-sided bar; (d) two-sided bar; (e) medallion; (f) cone; (g) crescent. Arrows indicate the position of seal impressions (drawings by K. Rončević, based on images from *CHIC*). Combination nodules and irregular string nodules are not included into this plate since the Petras documents are still unpublished. For noduli, flat-based nodules, roundels, one-hole hanging nodules and direct object sealings, see the Linear A plate (figure 26.2).

Nonsealed Documents

Compared to other Aegean Bronze Age administrative systems, nonsealed types of documents are much more diverse in Cretan Hieroglyphic. Altogether, these nonsealed items amount to a total of ca. ninety-five documents.

Basically, the only nonsealed Linear A type of document is a clay *tablet*. While this type of document is employed in Cretan Hieroglyphic as well, it is rare: one tablet has been discovered in Phaistos, two have been found in the palace of Malia, and two in the Hieroglyphic Deposit at Knossos.

Clay *bars* are more numerous. One is three-sided, and the rest are four-sided (all of these sides are inscribed); some bars are pierced. The type of information on the bars resembles that inscribed on the tablets, with sign groups, sometimes also logograms and numerals recorded (Karnava 2006), but their function appears to be different. Olivier at first suggested that pierced bars with high numbers and no logograms were population census records, strung together and filed as a homogeneous document. Later on, he agreed with Godart's suggestion that these high numbers probably refer to livestock (Olivier 1994–1995, 266–67).

Two-sided bars (*lames à deux faces*) are smaller than three- and four-sided bars. They are oblong, pointed and pierced on one end, and inscribed on one or both sides. Piercing suggests that they were designed to be attached to another object.

Medallions are small clay disks, pierced and often inscribed on both sides with sign groups, logograms, and numerals. Again, their piercing suggests that they may have been fastened to something.

Finally, two nonpierced but hollow inscribed *cones* have been discovered. Several inscribed clay pots have also been found, but it is less certain whether the inscriptions on the pots were of an administrative nature as well.

Sealed Documents

In addition to the documents that were only inscribed, Cretan Hieroglyphic employed a wide range of those that could be both inscribed and sealed or only sealed. Altogether, this group consists of ca. eighty documents.

The most numerous type of document in this category is the *crescent*. Due to its shape and traces of a string, this type was at first seen as a predecessor to a Linear A two-hole hanging nodule (Weingarten 1986a, 295,n8; Hallager 1996, 38). However, recently discovered Cretan Hieroglyphic documents at Petras make this hypothesis less plausible. As to its function, the crescent may not be related to day-to-day administrative business but to a single, specialized activity, perhaps tax or tribute payments (Weingarten 1995, 308).

Other types of Cretan Hieroglyphic documents that belong to this group, although represented in smaller numbers, are *combination nodules, irregular string nodules, noduli, flat-based nodules, roundels,* and *direct object sealings.* Whereas the crescent is typical only of Cretan Hieroglyphic, the combination nodule (i.e., a document that is both pressed against an object and secured with a string inside the lump, resulting in a combination of a direct object sealing and a string nodule) and the irregular string nodule (see later), attested in the Petras deposit, are shared with the Linear B system (Tsipopoulou 1998, 437; Hallager 2005, 253). The other document types are also characteristic of the Linear A system and are addressed in more detail later. Several clay pots and a loomweight with hieroglyphic seal impressions have been found as well.

Most of the seals used for stamping these documents contain engraved Cretan Hieroglyphic signs. So far, some 140 such seals have been discovered. In addition to more elaborate forms of signs on them, they differ from Cretan Hieroglyphic incised inscriptions primarily in their lack of numerals. Although the meaning of engraved sign groups is not yet well understood and some scholars actually believe that these seals do not represent writing *stricto sensu* but are perhaps ornamental writing, they played a vital role in administration, having been used for stamping clay documents (Olivier 1981, 2000; Poursat 2000). Apart from a few rare exceptions, seals and seal impressions with signs of the script are absent from Linear A and B systems and are therefore principally characteristic of the Cretan Hieroglyphic system. Some take this as an indication of a more widespread Cretan Hieroglyphic literacy (Weingarten 1995, 302).

Linear A Documents

Although fewer types are identified, the total number of extant documents with Linear A, as well as the amount of information recorded thereon, significantly exceeds those with Cretan Hieroglyphic. They can be again classified into nonsealed and sealed groups (figure 26.2).

Nonsealed Documents

The only nonsealed type of Linear A document is a clay *tablet*. A total of some four hundred such tablets have been discovered, although many are in a fragmentary state. Unlike Linear B, which used two shapes of tablets (page shaped and elongated), page-shaped tablets were primarily used in Linear A, whereas elongated tablets were discovered only in small numbers among the MM IIB documents in Phaistos. As is the case with Linear B as well, tablets with Linear A contain more substantial textual information than do any other types of documents with Linear A.

Sealed Documents

In addition to tablets, a wide variety of sealed documents was used, some inscribed in addition to being sealed (for the nomenclature and classification of Linear A documents see Hallager 1999; for an overview of sealing types and their find-spots, see Krzyszkowska 2005, 154–92).

With nearly a thousand examples, the *single-hole hanging nodule* is the most numerous type of Linear A document and can have both an inscription and a seal impression. Most of the inscriptions consist of a single sign (only occasionally is more than one sign present), usually syllabic, whose meaning is still unresolved (some possibilities are suggested in Weingarten 1986a, 288–89; Palaima 1994, 315). The document obviously hung from something, possibly papyrus rolls. According to its shape, it is divided into five subtypes: pendant, pyramid, cone, dome, and pear (Hallager 1996, 162–63, 198–99). The document is unique to the Linear A administration.

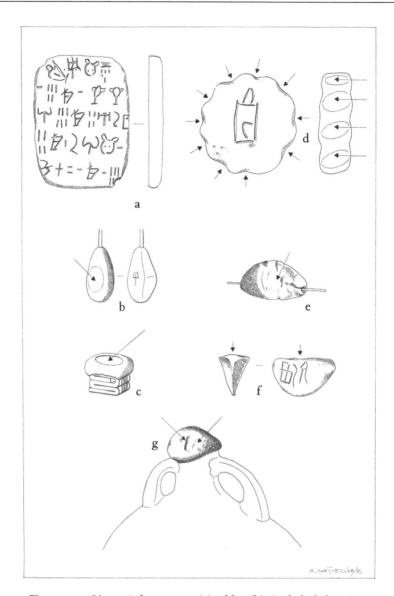

Figure 26.2. Linear A documents: (a) tablet; (b) single-hole hanging nodule (subtype: pendant); (c) flat-based nodule (subtype: recumbent); (d) roundel; (e) two-hole hanging nodule; (f) nodulus (subtype: dome); (g) direct object sealings on a stirrup jar (clay stopper). Arrows indicate the position of seal impressions (drawings by K. Rončević, based on images from *GORILA*; Fiandra 1968, 1975; Hallager 1996, 2001).

Flat-based nodules are rarely inscribed but are regularly sealed. They appear in two different shapes: standing and recumbent. This type of document serves as the best evidence that material other than clay was used for certain Minoan administrative records, for flat-based nodules often have, on their flat undersides, impressions of folded parchment held by a string. Once attached, it was impossible to unfold the parchment without breaking the seal, which prevented unauthorized viewing of the document (Hallager 1996, 135–45). Some flat-based nodules have been found in the Hieroglyphic Deposits at Knossos and Malia (Pini 1990, 39–40; Weingarten 1995, 296). With several examples, this type of sealing appears among the earliest of the Linear B documents as well, namely those from the Room of the Chariot Tablets at Knossos (Driessen 1990, 64; Hallager 2005, 252).

The *roundel* is a round clay disc with seal impressions along the edge and, in most cases, an inscription on one or both sides. These inscriptions sometimes consist of sign groups but are usually logograms; in a very few cases, numerals are also inscribed. It has been convincingly argued that an inscribed logogram stands for a commodity, while seal impressions represent units of a commodity: each impression equals one item or unit. Hallager argues that the roundel probably functioned as a receipt that was issued and kept by palace officials upon dispatching commodities from the storerooms (1996, 116–18). Until recently, the roundel was considered a document unique to Linear A, but the discovery of a roundel at Petras has now changed this picture (Hallager 2000, 101–103).

Two-hole hanging nodules were probably attached to commodities as labels (Hallager 1996, 36). They are regularly sealed but rarely inscribed. Their name was initially applied to the most common Linear B type of sealing. Hallager, however, rightly points out that in their nature the two are quite different (the latter is, for example, regularly inscribed). This is why he has introduced a new name for the Linear B documents—string nodules—and divided them into two subtypes: regular and irregular (Hallager 2005, 253–58). Similar-looking Cretan Hieroglyphic documents in Petras were also initially described as two-hole hanging nodules (Hallager 2000, 100), but with further studies they were renamed irregular nodules (Hallager forthcoming). Thus the document called a two-hole hanging nodule now remains unique to Linear A.

The *nodulus* is the most widespread Aegean Bronze Age document, both geographically and chronologically. It is one of the rare types of document that is present in all three Cretan administrative systems. The document appears in two shapes: dome and disk. Many noduli were not inscribed but only sealed. They functioned either as dockets (i.e., receipts for work accomplished, which may have been exchanged for goods as wages) (Weingarten 1986b, 17–21) or as receipts given to individuals for goods delivered to storerooms (which is why we often find them in private houses) (Hallager 1996, 132). It has also been suggested that some noduli functioned as tokens and were exchanged for goods or services (e.g., food, accommodation), while their initial possessor was traveling (Weingarten 1990, 19–20).

The last document type that belongs to this group is the *direct object sealing*, probably the simplest type of an administrative document. This is a lump of clay placed directly onto objects, such as pithoi covered with cloth or reed mats, jars and other vases (clay stoppers), chests and containers, leather sacks, or door pegs; imprints of all of these materials are preserved on the reverse of the sealing. Direct sealings are never inscribed but only sealed. Such seal impressions were meant to prevent unauthorized access to the sealed container or room; thus, they had a twofold function: control of movable goods and control of centralized storage

(Fiandra 1968). Direct sealings were generally an MM II feature, and nearly disappeared thereafter, only to reappear in Linear B administration (Weingarten 1988, 6–7). Direct sealings were abundantly present in MM IIB contexts, with some sixty-five hundred examples at Phaistos alone (Levi 1958; here they were found together with Linear A tablets and inscribed sealings, which is why they are included in this overview of Linear A documents although they are uninscribed). Further MM IIB examples come from Monastiraki (Kanta and Tzigounaki 2000).

As we have seen, apart from tablets, six other types of administrative document were widespread in the Linear A system. Understanding the correlation between Linear A sealings and tablets is problematic. In Linear B we have clear evidence that sealings served as primary documents whose data were thereafter summarized on page-shaped tablets (see discussion in Driessen 1999, 207–208). In Linear A, on the other hand, there is no evidence that tablets summarized records from sealings (Schoep 1996–1997, 412–15; for a single possible exception, see Palaima 1994, 317; Hallager 2002), which is why it has been suggested that information from Linear A sealings was summarized directly onto perishable material (Hallager 1996, 225). This means that Linear A sealings did not necessarily precede tablets in the information cycle, as is the case in Linear B.

Conclusion

Although Linear A is, like Cretan Hieroglyphic Script, still undeciphered, a larger number of documents offers better grounds for contextual comparisons, the result of which is a basic understanding of Linear A administrative texts (most thoroughly achieved by Schoep 2002). The meaning of two Linear A sign groups has been established: KU-RO 'total' and PO-TO-KU-RO 'grand total,' while the sign group KI-RO may stand for 'deficit' (see individual discussions in Schoep 2002, 160–64). Comparisons with similarly organized Linear B texts on tablets suggest that most other sign groups are probably toponyms and anthroponyms, followed by logograms (a significant number of which have been understood) and numerals. All of this clearly shows—at least from our current stage of knowledge—that the Linear A script was mostly used to record transactions of administrative centers.

As already pointed out, the coexistence of Cretan Hieroglyphic and Linear A resulted in exchanges of scribal features and common types of documents. As a result, it is sometimes difficult to distinguish Cretan Hieroglyphic from Linear A inscriptions; in some cases an inscription has initially been interpreted as one script, only to be reinterpreted later as the other (*CHIC*, 18). It is therefore impossible to regard Cretan Hieroglyphic and Linear A as two entirely separate systems; although they are usually separately dealt with, the links described must always be kept in mind.

In addition to mutual influences, similarities between Cretan Hieroglyphic and Linear A have been explained as a consequence of having a common ancestor. If this is the case, then it is possible that political fragmentation on the island resulted in the use of the two systems (Schoep 1999, 267). Political reasons may have also caused the disappearance of Cretan Hieroglyphic in MM III and brought about its replacement by Linear A, just as sometime later Linear A was for cultural and/or political reasons replaced by Linear B (Palaima 1988; Driessen and Langohr 2007, 187–88; Schoep 2007b, 59–60; Bennet 2008, 19–22).

BIBLIOGRAPHY

Bennet, John. 2008. "Now You See It; Now You Don't! The Disappearance of the Linear A Script on Crete." In *The Disappearance of Writing Systems: Perspectives on Literacy and Communication*, ed. John Baines, John Bennet, and Stephen Houston, 1–29. London: Equinox.

Bennett, Emmett L. 1950. "Fractional Quantities in Minoan Bookkeeping. *AJA* 54: 204–22.

———. 1999. "Minos and Minyas: Writing Aegean Measures." In *Floreant Studia Mycenaea: Akten des X. Internationalen Mykenologischen Colloquiums in Salzburg vom 1.–5. Mai 1995*, ed. Sigrid Deger-Jalkotzy, Stefan Hiller, and Oswald Panagl, 159–75. Vienna: Verlag der Österreichischen Akademie der Wissenschaften.

Chapouthier, Fernand. 1930. *Les écritures minoennes au palais de Mallia*. Études Crétoises 2. Paris: Geuthner.

Del Freo, Maurizio. 2007. "Rapport 2001–2005 sur les textes en écriture hiéroglyphique crétoise, en linéaire A et en linéaire B." In *Colloquium Romanum: Atti del XII Colloquio Internazionale di Micenologia. Roma, 20–25 febbraio 2006*, vol. 1, ed. Anna Sacconi, Maurizio del Freo, Louis Godart, and Mario Negri, 199–222. Rome: Pasiphae.

Dimopoulou, Nota, Jean-Pierre Olivier, and Georges Rethemiotakis. 1993. "Une statuette en argile avec inscription en linéaire A de Poros/Irakliou." *BCH* 117: 501–21.

Driessen, Jan. 1990. *An Early Destruction in the Mycenaean Palace at Knossos: A New Interpretation of the Excavation Field-notes of the South-east Area of the West Wing*. Acta Archaeologica Lovaniensia, Monographiae 2. Leuven: Katholieke Universiteit Leuven.

———. 1999. "The Northern Entrance Passage at Knossos: Some Preliminary Observations on Its Potential Role as 'Central Archives.'" In *Floreant Studia Mycenaea: Akten des X. Internationalen Mykenologischen Colloquiums in Salzburg vom 1.–5. Mai 1995*, ed. Sigrid Deger-Jalkotzy, Stefan Hiller, and Oswald Panagl, 205–26. Vienna: Verlag der Österreichischen Akademie der Wissenschaften.

———, and Charlotte Langohr. 2007. "Rallying 'round a 'Minoan' Past: The Legitimation of Power at Knossos during the Late Bronze Age." In *Rethinking Mycenaean Palaces II*, ed. Michael Galaty and William Parkinson, 178–89. Rev. and exp. 2d ed. Los Angeles: Cotsen Institute of Archaeology at UCLA.

Duhoux, Yves. 1978. "Une analyse linguistique du linéaire A." In *Études minoennes, I. Le linéaire A*, ed. Yves Duhoux, 65–129. Louvain: Institut de Linguistique de Louvain.

———. 1989. "Le linéaire A: Problèmes de déchiffrement." In *Problems in Decipherment*, ed. Yves Duhoux, Thomas G. Palaima, and John Bennet, 59–119. Louvain-la-Neuve, Belgium: Peeters.

———. 1992. "Variations morphosyntaxiques dans les textes votifs linéaires A." *Cretan Studies* 3: 65–88.

———. 1998. "Pre-Hellenic language(s) of Crete." *Journal of Indoeuropean Studies* 26(1–2): 1–39.

Evans, Arthur J. 1894. "Primitive Pictographs and a Prae-Phoenician Script from Crete and the Peloponnese." *JHS* 14: 270–372.

———. 1897. "Further Discoveries of Cretan and Aegean Script: With Libyan and Proto-Egyptian Comparisons." *JHS* 17: 327–95.

———. 1899–1900. "Knossos: Summary Report of the Excavations in 1900. I. The Palace." *BSA* 6: 3–70.

———. 1909. *Scripta Minoa I*. Oxford: Oxford University Press.

———. 1921. *PM I*.

———. 1952. *Scripta Minoa II*, ed. John Myres. Oxford: Clarendon.

Ferioli, Piera, Enrica Fiandra, and Gian Giacomo Fissore. 1996. *Administration in Ancient Societies: Proceedings of the Session 218 of the 13th International Congress of Anthropological and Ethnological Sciences, Mexico City, July 29–August 5, 1993*. Rome: Ministero per i Beni Culturali e Ambientali.

———, and Marcella Frangipane, eds. 1994. *Archives before Writing: Proceedings of the International Colloquium Oriolo Romano, October 23–25, 1991*. Rome: Centro Internazionale di Richerche Archeologiche, Antropologiche e Storiche.

Fiandra, Enrica. 1968. "A che cosa servivano le cretule di Festòs." *Pepragmena tou B' Diethnous Kritologikou Synedriou*. Vol. 1, 383–97. Athens: Filologikos Syllogos "O Hrysostomos."

———. 1975. "Ancora a proposito delle cretule di Festòs: connessioni tra i sistemi amministrativi centralizzati e l'uso delle cretule nell'età del bronzo, *Bolletino d'arte* 60: 1–25.

Godart, Louis. 1999. "L'écriture d'Arkhanès: hiéroglyphique ou linéaire A?" In *Meletemata*, 299–302.

———, and Jean-Pierre Olivier. 1978. *Fouilles exécutées à Mallia: Le Quartier Mu*. Vol. 1, *Introduction générale: Écriture hiéroglyphique crétoise*. Études Crétoises 23. Paris: L'École Française d'Athènes.

———, and Yannis Tzedakis. 1992. *Témoignages archéologiques et épigraphiques en Crète occidentale du Néolithique au Minoen récent III B*. Incunabula Graeca 93. Rome: Istituto per gli Studi Micenei ed Egeo-Anatolici.

Grumach, Ernst, and Ioannis Sakellarakis. 1966. "Die neuen Hieroglyphensiegel vom Phourni (Archanes) I". *Kadmos* 5: 109–14.

Halbherr, Federico, Enrico Stefani, and Luisa Banti. 1977. "Haghia Triada nel periodo tardo palaziale." *Annuario della Scuola Archeologica di Atene* 55: 9–296.

Hallager, Erik. 1996. *The Minoan Roundel and Other Sealed Documents in the Neopalatial Linear A Administration*. Aegaeum 14. Liège: Université de Liège.

———. 1999. "Nomenclature of Administrative Linear A Documents." In *Floreant Studia Mycenaea: Akten des X. Internationalen Mykenologischen Colloquiums in Salzburg vom 1.–5. Mai 1995*, ed. Sigrid Deger-Jalkotzy, Stefan Hiller, and Oswald Panagl, 277–88. Vienna: Verlag der Österreichischen Akademie der Wissenschaften.

———. 2000. "New Evidence for Seal Use in the Pre- and Protopalatial Periods." In *Minoisch-mykenische Glyptik*, 97–105.

———. 2001. "Sealing without Seals: An Explanation." *Arbejdspapirer/Work in Progress* 99, 2–16.

———. 2002. "One Linear A Tablet and 45 Noduli." *Creta Antica* 3: 105–109.

———. 2005. "The Uniformity in Seal Use and Sealing Practice during the LH/LM III Period." In *Ariadne's Threads*, 243–65.

———. Forthcoming. "On the Origin of Linear B Administration." In *Proceedings of the 10th Cretological Conference.*

Jasink, Anna Margherita. 2005. "The so-called Klasmatograms on Cretan Hieroglyphic Seals." *Kadmos* 44: 23–39.

Kanta, Athanasia, and Anastasia Tzigounaki. 2000. "The Protopalatial Multiple Sealing System: New Evidence from Monastiraki." In *Administrative Documents in the Aegean and Their Near Eastern Counterparts: Proceedings of the International Colloquium, Naples, February 29–March 2, 1996*, ed. Massimo Perna, 193–210. Rome: Centro Internazionale di Richerche Archeologiche, Antropologiche e Storiche.

Karnava, Artemis. 2001. "Fractions and Measurement Units in the Cretan Hieroglyphic Script." In *Manufacture and Measurement: Counting, Measuring and Recording Craft Items in Early Aegean Societies*, ed. Anna Michailidou, 45–51. Athens: Research Centre for Greek and Roman Antiquity, National Hellenic Research Foundation.

———. 2006. "Indications of Minoan Fiscal Registrations." In *Fiscality in Mycenaean and Near Eastern Archives: Proceedings of the Conference Held at Sopraintendenza Archivistica per la Campania, Naples, 21–23 October 2004*, ed. Massimo Perna, 59–68. Studi Egei e Vicinorientali 3. Paris: De Boccard.

———. 2008. "Written and Stamped Records in the Late Bronze Age Cyclades: The Sea Journeys of an Administration." In *Horizon*, 377–86.

Krzyszkowska, Olga. 2005. *Aegean Seals: An Introduction.* BICS Supplement 85. London: Institute of Classical Studies.

La Rosa, Vincenzo. 2002. "Pour une révision préliminaire du second palais de Phaistos." In *Monuments of Minos*, 71–98.

Levi, Doro. 1958. "L'archivio di cretule a Festòs." *Annuario della Scuola Archeologica di Atene* 35–36: 7–122.

Militello, Pietro. 2002. "A Notebook by Halbherr and the Findspots of the Ayia Triada Tablets." *Creta Antica* 3: 111–20.

Olivier, Jean-Pierre. 1981. "Les sceaux avec des signes hiéroglyphiques. Que lire? Une question de définition." In *Studien zur minoischen und helladischen Glyptik. Beiträge zum 2. Marburger Siegel-Symposium 26.–30. September 1978*, ed. Wolf-Dietrich Niemeier, 105–15. *CMS* Beiheft 1. Mainz: Akademie der Wissenschaften und der Literatur.

———. 1986. "Cretan Writing in the Second Millennium B.C." *World Archaeology* 17(3): 377–89.

———. 1989. "The Possible Methods in Deciphering the Pictographic Cretan Script." In *Problems in Decipherment*, ed. Yves Duhoux, Thomas G. Palaima, and John Bennet, 39–58. Louvain-la-Neuve, Belgium: Peeters.

———. 1994–1995. "Un simili-raccord dans les barres en hiéroglyphique de Knossos (*CHIC* #057 ⊕ #058)." *Minos* 29–30: 257–69.

———. 1996a. "Addenda: Écriture hiérogliphique crétoise." In *Fouilles exécutées à Mallia: Le Quartier Mu. III. Artisans minoens: Les maisons-ateliers du Quartier Mu*, ed. Jean-Claude Poursat, 155–99. Études Crétoises 32. Paris: L'École Française d'Athènes.

———. 1996b. "Les écritures crétoises: Sept points à considérer." In *Atti e memorie del secondo congresso internazionale di micenologia. Roma-Napoli, 14–20 ottobre 1991* (Incunabula Graeca 98), ed. Ernesto de Miro, Louis Godart, and Anna Sacconi, 101–13. Rome: Istituto per gli Studi Micenei ed Egeo-Anatolici.

———. 1999. "Rapport 1991–1995 sur les textes en écriture hiéroglyphique crétoise, en linéaire A en en linéaire B." In *Floreant Studia Mycenaea: Akten des X. Internationalen Mykenologischen Colloquiums in Salzburg vom 1.–5. Mai 1995*, ed. Sigrid Deger-Jalkotzy,

Stefan Hiller, and Oswald Panagl, 419–35. Vienna: Verlag der Österreichiscen Akademie der Wissenschaften.

———. 2000. "Les sceaux avec des inscriptions hiéroglyphiques. Comment comprendre?" In *Administrative Documents in the Aegean and Their Near Eastern Counterparts: Proceedings of the International Colloquium, Naples, February 29–March 2, 1996*, ed. Massimo Perna, 141–69. Rome: Centro Internazionale di Richerche Archeologiche, Antropologiche e Storiche.

Palaima, Thomas G. 1988. "The Development of the Mycenaean Writing System." In *Texts, Tablets and Scribes: Studies in Mycenaean Epigraphy Offered to Emmett L. Bennett Jr.*, ed. Jean-Pierre Olivier and Thomas G. Palaima, 269–342. Suppl. to Minos 10. Salamanca: Universidad de Salamanca.

———, ed. 1990. *Aegean Seals*.

———. 1994. "Seal-users and Script-users: Nodules and Tablets at LM IB Hagia Triada." In *Archives before Writing: Proceedings of the International Colloquium Oriolo Romano, October 23–25, 1991*, ed. Piera Ferioli, Enrica Fiandra, Gian Giacomo Fissore, and Marcella Frangipane, 307–37. Rome: Centro Internazionale di Richerche Archeologiche, Antropologiche e Storiche.

Perna, Massimo. 2000. *Administrative Documents in the Aegean and Their Near Eastern Counterparts: Proceedings of the International Colloquium, Naples, February 29–March, 2, 1996*. Rome: Centro Internazionale di Richerche Archeologiche, Antropologiche e Storiche.

Pini, Ingo. 1990. "The Hieroglyphic Deposit and the Temple Repositories at Knossos." In *Aegean Seals*, 33–60.

Poursat, Jean-Claude. 2000. "Les sceaux hiéroglyphiques dans l'administration minoenne: Usage et fonction." In *Administrative Documents in the Aegean and Their Near Eastern Counterparts: Proceedings of the International Colloquium, Naples, February 29–March 2, 1996*, ed. Massimo Perna, 187–91. Rome: Centro Internazionale di Richerche Archeologiche, Antropologiche e Storiche.

Pugliese Carratelli, Giovanni. 1958. "Nuove epigrafi minoiche di Festo." *Annuario della Scuola Archeologica di Atene* 35–36: 363–88.

Schoep, Ilse. 1994. "Ritual, Politics, and Script on Minoan Crete." *Aegean Archaeology* 1: 7–25.

———. 1995. "Context and Chronology of Linear A Administrative Documents." *Aegean Archaeology* 2: 29–65.

———. 1996–1997. "Sealed Documents and Data Processing in Minoan Administration: A Review Article." *Minos* 31–32: 401–15.

———. 1999. "The Origin of Writing and Administration on Crete." *OJA* 18(3): 265–76.

———. 2001. "Some Notes on the 'Hieroglyphic' Deposit from Knossos." *SMEA* 43(1): 143–58.

———. 2002. *The Administration of Neopalatial Crete: A Critical Assessment of the Linear A Tablets and Their Role in the Administrative Process*. Suppl. to Minos 17. Salamanca: Universidad de Salamanca.

———. 2004. "The Socio-economic Context of Seal Use and Administration at Knossos." In *Knossos*, 283–93.

———. 2006. "Looking beyond the First Palaces: Elites and the Agency of Power in EM III–MM II Crete." *AJA* 110: 37–64.

———. 2007a. "The Inscribed Document." In *Knossos: Protopalatial Deposits in Early Magazine A and the South-west Houses*, Colin F. Macdonald and Carl Knappett, 131–34. BSA Supplementary vol. 41. London: British School at Athens.

————. 2007b. "The Social and Political Context of Linear A Writing on Crete." In *Literacy and the State in the Ancient Mediterranean*, ed. Kathryn Lomas, Ruth D. Whitehouse and John B. Wilkins, 53–62. Accordia Specialist Studies on the Mediterranean vol. 7. London: University of London.

Tsipopoulou, Metaxia. 1998. "The Hieroglyphic Archive at Petras, Siteia." In *Recherches récentes en épigraphie créto-mycénienne*, ed. Françoise Rougemont and Jean-Pierre Olivier. *BCH* 122: 436–40.

Weingarten, Judith. 1986a. "The Sealing Structures of Minoan Crete: MM II Phaistos to the Destruction of the Palace of Knossos. Part I, The Evidence until the LM IB Destructions." *OJA* 5(3): 279–98.

————. 1986b. "Some Unusual Minoan Clay Nodules." *Kadmos* 25: 1–21.

————. 1988. "The Sealing Structures of Minoan Crete: MM II Phaistos to the Destruction of the Palace of Knossos. Part II, The Evidence from Knossos until the Destruction of the Palace." *OJA* 7(1): 1–25.

————. 1990. "More Unusual Minoan Clay Nodules: Addendum II." *Kadmos* 29: 16–23.

————. 1995. "Sealing Studies in the Middle Bronze Age. III: The Minoan Hieroglyphic Deposit at Mallia and Knossos." In *Sceaux minoens et mycéniens: IVe Symposium International 10–12 septembre 1992, Clermont-Ferrand*, ed. Walter Müller, 285–311. *CMS* Beiheft 5. Mainz: Akademie der Wissenschaften und der Literatur.

Whittaker, Hélène. 2005. "Social and Symbolic Aspects of Minoan Writing." *European Journal of Archaeology* 8: 29–41.

Younger, John. 1996–1997 [1998]. "The Cretan Hieroglyphic Script: A Review Article." *Minos* 31–32: 379–400.

————. 2003. "Cretan Hieroglyphic Transaction Terms: 'Total Paid' and 'Total Owed.'" In *Briciaca: A Tribute to W. C. Brice*, ed. Y. Duhoux, 301–16. Cretan Studies 9. Amsterdam: Hakkert.

————. 2005. "Cretan Hieroglyphic Wool Units (LANA, Double Mina)." In *Studi in onore di Enrica Fiandra: Contributi di archeologia egea e vicinorientale*, ed. Massimo Perna, 405–409. Studi egei e vicinorientali 1. Paris: De Boccard.

Yule, Paul. 1978. "On the Date of the 'Hieroglyphic Deposit' at Knossos." *Kadmos* 17: 1–9.

————. 1980. *Early Cretan Seals: A Study of Chronology.* Marburger Studien zur Vor- und Frühgeschichte 4. Mainz: von Zabern.

CHAPTER 27

LINEAR B

THOMAS G. PALAIMA

LINEAR B is a Late Bronze Age (ca. 1500–1200 BCE) writing system within the distinctive tradition of Cretan and Cretan-inspired scripts (Cretan Hieroglyphic and Linear A, Cypro-Minoan, and Cypriote Syllabic) that spanned nearly two millennia (ca. 2100 to ca. 225 BCE) (Bartoněk 2003, 16–49; Chadwick 1987; Duhoux 1989; Palaima 1989, figures 4 and 9; Olivier 2008). It is an adaptation of the earlier (ca. 1900–1450 BCE) Linear A, with which it shares peculiarities in the use of both the signs that represent sounds (phonograms) and the signs that represent objects (ideograms) or the words for those objects (logograms) (Duhoux 1985; 1989, 63, 72–76).

Unlike the other Bronze Age scripts in this tradition (Cretan Hieroglyphic, Linear A, and Cypro-Minoan), Linear B has been deciphered—by British architect Michael Ventris. Ventris announced his achievement for the first time in personal handwritten letters of June 18, 1952, to two close collaborators, Emmett L. Bennett Jr. and Sir John L. Myres (Robinson 2002, 102–106; Palaima, Pope, and Reilly 2000). The primary language in the preserved Linear B texts is Greek (Ventris and Chadwick 1953), as it was developing in the 14th and 13th centuries BCE. Like the historical Greek lexicon, the lexicon of the Linear B texts (Ventris and Chadwick 1973, 527–94; Aura Jorro 1985, 1993) contains loan words that come from the languages of the many cultures with which first the Minoans during their two palatial periods (MM II–LM IB) and then the Mycenaeans during their palatial period (LH II–LH IIIB) were in contact. This includes the languages of the so-called substrate cultures with which the Greek speakers interacted when they entered the Balkan peninsula and as they then spread out over the Aegean area (Brown 1985, 1–19; Hester 1968; Renfrew 1998).

The Linear B texts, therefore, give us information about an important formative stage of the Greek language and how it was affected by language contact with surrounding cultures. They also provide our earliest primary written evidence about all facets of Mycenaean palatial civilization. Finally, because what we call the *Mycenaean* Linear B script is an adaptation of *Minoan* Linear A, Linear B texts give us insights into how speakers of the still undeciphered Minoan language(s) and of early Greek analyzed spoken language and how they represented it in writing as 'visible speech' (Sharypkin 2008; Woodard 1997; Palaima and Sikkenga 1999).

THE DISCOVERY AND PUBLICATION OF TEXTS

The first scientifically excavated Linear B tablets were uncovered by Sir Arthur Evans at the site of Knossos on Crete on March 30, 1900 (Evans 1900, 18, 55–58; MacGillivray 2000, 177–78, 181–85). Many more texts were uncovered in the succeeding years of excavation. There are now about forty-two hundred texts from Knossos, many of which are small fragments (Shelmerdine 2008b, 18n33; Bartoněk 2003, 30).

Evans was the first great scholar of Aegean writing systems (Palaima 2000a). The adjective 'great' is no exaggeration. In fact, Evans's interests in early writing systems are what led him to become an excavator (Myres 1941). Evans devised the first typology of Bronze Age Aegean scripts in *Scripta Minoa* I (Evans 1903–1904, 1909) and then turned his attention to other matters (e.g., reconstruction of the Knossos site and full, synthetic publication of its excavation [Evans 1921–1935] and even Balkan diplomacy in the aftermath of World War I).

Consequently, Evans's planned companion volume on Linear B, *Scripta Minoa* II, was published only in 1952. It was a major reworking of the manuscript he left at his death in 1941 to the care of Sir John L. Myres. Myres, who was not a specialist in scripts, first enlisted in 1947 major help from Alice E. Kober, arguably the foremost scholar working on Aegean writing in the 1940s. After Kober's death in 1950, Myres received help from Emmett L. Bennett Jr., whose work on the Pylos tablets had been interrupted by his service analyzing Japanese encoded texts during World War II. The only other scholar who did sustained and consistently sober analytical work on the linear scripts before 1941 was Johannes Sundwall of Finland (Sundwall 1920, 1932, 1936).

Scripta Minoa II (Evans 1952), however, was prevented from becoming the fully scientific publication that Alice Kober wanted it to be for two reasons. First, dire postwar economic conditions made it necessary for the Clarendon Press to use plates and fonts (for charts of signs and drawings and transcriptions of texts) that had been produced for Evans when *Scripta Minoa* I and *Palace of Minos* were published. Second, Myres viewed it as his obligation to publish a faithful edited version of the book that Evans had partially written, not the up-to-date scientific study that Kober and Bennett were capable of producing. *Scripta Minoa* II, when it appeared, was already a fossil.

In the decades after Evans's initial finds at Knossos, there were two major impediments to further progress on Linear B: Few of the nearly eighteen hundred tablets that Evans had uncovered from Knossos were carefully published and available to scholars, and there were no further discoveries to add to the variety and quantity of the Linear B data. The problem with nonpublication of the Knossos material was partly remedied when *Palace of Minos*, volume IV, appeared in 1935 (Evans 1921–1935). It presented a selection of tablets with learned commentary. Significant help with the second problem came when Professor A. D. Keramopoullos at Thebes in 1921 began his discovery of a large deposit of transport stirrup jars, twenty-eight of which bore painted Linear B inscriptions (Wace 1921, 272–73).

The other important predecipherment discovery of tablets was made by Carl W. Blegen in 1939, when excavating at the site of Pylos in Messenia in the southwest Greek mainland (Blegen and Kourouniotis 1939). The advent of World War II delayed the publication of these 636 tablets, but in 1951 they were given to the scholarly world in a careful, regularized transcription by Emmett L. Bennett Jr. (Bennett 1951), based upon his equally painstaking work on the forms of signs of the syllabary in his earlier dissertation (Bennett 1947).

Numbers and General Time Period of Texts

In the fifty-six years since the decipherment of Linear B, the corpus of Linear B inscriptions has greatly expanded. We now have more than five thousand inscribed clay records from Khania and Knossos on Crete and from Pylos, Mycenae, Tiryns, Midea, and Thebes on the mainland (Bartoněk 2003, 30; Del Freo 2008, 213–22). The limited numbers of clay records are explained by the fact that they are preserved only when accidentally fired in the destruction of the buildings in which they were located. The rule is: no fire, no tablets.

This also severely limits the coverage that these economic documents provide of human economic, political, religious, and social activities. The Linear B texts were never intended to be long lasting. They were written, stored, and consulted in connection with the administrative year in progress. They look back at the year past and ahead at the year coming. There is no system in the tablets equivalent to the historical Greek practice of dating decrees or other inscriptions by reference to eponymous magistrates (archons), priests, or priestesses. We have evidence for only one or at most two or three randomly selected and undated years at any given Mycenaean site. Thus, we have little way of reconstructing trends, beyond a single year, over time. There has been, however, some attention paid to the chronology of texts within a given administrative phase (Palaima 1995).

In addition, painted inscriptions on ca. 160 transport stirrup jars are known from five sites on Crete (Malia, Knossos, Armenoi, Khania, and Monastiraki) and seven sites on the Greek mainland (Tiryns, Midea, Mycenae, Eleusis, Kreusis, Thebes, and Orchomenos) (Van Alfen 2008). There is also a single stone 'parallelepiped' from the important northern site of Iolkos, which was identified long ago by Nilsson (1932) as a potential major palatial site. It has three signs inscribed into it (Del Freo 2008, 215–16 and note 82).

All of the inscribed material comes from the 14th and 13th centuries BCE (at Pylos the transition into the 12th), and all of it comes from the environs of significant settlements (Driessen 2008). We have no good evidence yet that Linear B was used at the smaller settlements within the structure of regional organization in Mycenaean palatial territories that are called second- or third-order centers (Bennet 1990, 1998).

An Unlikely Inscribed Pebble

It has been proposed that our earliest Linear B text is an inscribed pebble from an insignificant Middle Helladic settlement in the district of Elis, found supposedly in a mid-MH III (i.e., ca. 1650 BCE) context (Del Freo 2008, 216–17). Here follow the many reasons to reject this proposal (as argued fully by Palaima 2006b).

The very status of the site where it was found makes it highly dubious, as does the fact that the *galet*, as it is known in Mycenological circles, was discovered on April Fool's Day (April 1, 1994). Also humorously suspicious is the inscribed image of a double ax surrounded by cartoonlike rays (completely unparalleled in Minoan or Mycenaean art). As regards writing style, the Linear B signs are not early prototypical forms that we would expect in 1650 BCE, but they are in the style of the main scribe at Pylos ca. 1200 BCE (450 years after the date of the pebble). When the sign groups are read, they give the names and nicknames of the son of the excavator and possibly his father. It is surprising that this object has been published as a genuine inscription and almost unconscionable that it is now being cited, whether uncritically or with reservations, in handbooks and discussions of the history of Linear B (e.g., Bartoněk 2003, 73–74; Driessen 2008, 76).

Typology of Clay Document Inscriptions

Even before the decipherment, Kober and Bennett exploited the typology of the clay inscriptions in Linear B as a means of studying their texts. All Linear B tablets are devised so that they can be held in one hand, while writing with the other. We even find the finger impressions of scribes along the edges of the texts where they gripped the tablets (Palaima 1988).

The two main shapes are (1) long, narrow tablets that Evans called leaf shaped because they reminded him of palm-leaf documents from south Asia; and (2) rectangular, page-shaped texts (Palmer, 2008a, 61, figure 2.1). The leaf-shaped tablets are used mainly for documents focused on discrete records within larger bookkeeping assignments. Good examples are the inspection inventories of individual sets of armor (and helmets) in the Pylos Sh series (Palaima 1996a); ration allotments to dependent women work groups in the Pylos Aa, Ab, and Ad series (Chadwick 1988; Palmer 1989); the receipts of six taxed commodities in the Pylos Ma series, which the principal districts making up the territory of the palatial state of Pylos each have to give (Ventris and Chadwick 1973, 289–95, 464–66); honey being shipped to the sanctuary of Zeus specifically for Zeus and Dionysos in Khania Gq 5 (Palaima 2004a, 448); and the assignment of armor, a chariot, and a pair of horses to individual warriors in the Room of the Chariot Tablets at Knossos (Driessen 1996).

Page-shaped tablets are used to compile and summarize the information that might originally have gone on a number of leaf-shaped documents or to record the responsible parties involved in transactions and activities involving large numbers of individuals, localities, or institutions. These tablets generally are records of distribution, delivery, collection, mobilization, inventory, or census. Good examples are a simple record of rowers of a single ship coming from five communities in Messenia (Pylos An 1: Killen 1983); bronze allocation to groups of smiths (Pylos Jn series: Smith 1993); the mundane daily allotment of grain to individuals and workers who perform different services within the palatial system (Thebes Fq series: Palaima 2006a); and the list of human beings connected with organizations involving the *lawagetas* and the *basileus* (KN As 1516: Driessen 1985).

Clay is used in Mycenaean administration also for nodules. These are small lumps of clay molded around knotted string and impressed with a seal (Hallager 1996, 31–38; [Palmer, 2008a, 61, figure 2.1]). Linear B–inscribed nodules usually serve as records of single transactions (Palaima 1996b, 2000b). The best example here is the set of sixty-one such devices (fifty-six inscribed) discovered at Thebes and dealing with animals being provided for a sacrificial feast (Piteros, Olivier, and Melena 1990). The inscriptions and seal impressions in the Theban nodules identify responsible parties, place names (including Thebes itself and Amarunthos and Karustos in Euboea), the kinds of animals, and the conditions under which these contributions are made (whether 'paid' as a kind of religious obligation or 'finished off,' i.e., brought into a state fit for sacrifice) (translation and discussion in Palaima 2004b, 220–21, 225–28, 237–39).

Finally, clay was pressed flat against the outer surface of transport baskets made of woven, pliant plant fiber (generically 'wicker'). These 'labels' were then inscribed with brief descriptions of the tablets that were placed inside the baskets. The baskets were carried from one location to another. The labels from Pylos all come from the centrally located Archives Complex.

General Techniques of Analysis

A key resource in interpreting the Linear B documents is palaeography (Palaima forthcoming), literally the study of 'old writing.' Many of the common signs of the Linear B script are complex in form, with lines crossing or running into one another. Moist clay generally preserves a clear record of the habitual order in which individual tablet writers made particular signs and the peculiar ways they drew component elements. This and other idiosyncratic features, such as tablet layout, vocabulary, subject matter, and spelling variants, have made it possible to identify 'scribal hands.' By studying their work, we can reconstruct, at least partially, the administrative systems (including central archives) in which the tablet writers functioned (Palaima 2003a).

Three specialized studies (Olivier 1967, Palaima 1988, Driessen 2000) of scribes and their work have been crucial in determining how to interpret sets and other groups of tablets from Knossos and Pylos and even how to establish the relative chronology of the tablets from a particular site. The study of traces of palmprints on tablet surfaces, made, it seems, by young apprentices and older retirees who assisted the tablet writers in their work (Sjöquist and Åström 1985, 1991) has also added to our understanding of how tablet writers interacted with each other.

A major recent advance is the application of phylogenetic systematics to the palaeographical data (Skelton 2008). Skelton has used this biological research method to determine the most probable line of chronological development of the styles of the identifiable scribal hands and to trace possible affinities among tablet writers. Significantly, Skelton's study independently isolated the same groups of texts that scholars of palaeography had considered somehow problematical or anomalous. The phylogenetically determined chronology is right in line, too, with the relative chronology devised by palaeographers. It also puts the forgery (see earlier) known as the Kafkania *galet* where it would belong stylistically, 1200 BCE, if it were genuine.

CHRONOLOGY OF THE TABLETS

The Linear B tablets have a chronological range. Most problematical, as might be expected because scientific methods for the control and recording of data were not very advanced at the time, are the earliest excavated tablets from the site of Knossos, specifically those that come from the Room of the Chariot Tablets (RCT). Driessen (2000, 2008, 70–72) has argued convincingly on the basis of text typology, small linguistic peculiarities, the discovery among these tablets of 'transitional' types of clay sealings, palaeographical singularity, and the decided lack of any prosopographical connection between the RCT texts and the rest of the Knossos tablets, that the RCT tablets are earlier than other Knossos tablets. The RCT tablets may be dated to LH IIIA1 (ca. 1390–1340 BCE).

In spring 1990, three tablets were discovered at the Khania site in a secure end of LH IIIB1 context (early to mid-13th century BCE). The handwriting and formatting style of these tablets was very similar but not identical to that found on the tablets of Scribe 115 at Knossos (Olivier 1993, 1996; Palaima 1993). This suggests that at least some of the remaining Knossos tablets should be dated to this phase.

On the mainland, tablets from the so-called houses at Mycenae and various locations on the citadel of Thebes, as well as from Midea, Tiryns, and the major destruction phase at Pylos, date from mid- to very late LH IIIB, even transitional into LH IIIC (ca. 1250–1190 BCE). Exceptions are a few contextually isolated tablets from Pylos that also show palaeographical and lexical peculiarities. These may come from LH IIIA (Driessen 2008, 73). A tablet from Petsas House at Mycenae (Shelton 2003) comes from an LH IIIA2 context.

THE STRUCTURE OF THE LINEAR B SCRIPT

Even before the decipherment of Linear B, scholars like Bennett, Evans, Kober, Sundwall, and Ventris could distinguish within the Linear B texts signs that represented words through their phonetic parts (phonograms) and signs that stood for objects (ideograms) or the whole words (logograms) for those objects. For these components and how they work separately and together, see Duhoux (1985, 11–19) and Palmer (2008a, 31–35).

As mentioned earlier, Linear B has a set of phonograms (see figure 27.1) that represent discrete elements of sound (pure vowels [V] or open-syllabic combinations of consonant plus vowel [CV]). There are about eighty-seven such signs now identified. About seventy-five of these have been given secure or very probable values. The 'spelling rules,' we have lately come to think, reflect the natural ways in which native speakers of Minoan and Greek, or bilingual Minoan/Greek speakers, conceived of words. For example, writers of Linear B spell the later Greek word for 'human being' *anthrōpos a-to-ro-kwo*, where both the *n* that precedes the later Greek theta /th/ and the final *s* are not written; the aspiration of the /t/ is not written; the length of the first /o/ vowel is not represented; and the sequence *thr* is written *to-ro* with what is called a 'dummy vowel' taken from the syllable that this sequence of consonants begins. Finally, the last syllable in this example begins with a consonant called a labiovelar (a combination of a palatal stop and the glide /w/ treated as a basic sound, or *phoneme*, in the language). Labiovelars in specific environments develop into various simple consonants in historical Greek (i.e., they disappear from Greek speech).

In order to represent the peculiar features of the Minoan language, Linear A script used a set of syllabic signs that stand for combinations of stop consonants (e.g., /t/ and /d/) and palatal and labial glides (/y/ and /w/) plus, of course, vowels. Linear B preserves some of these signs as holdovers (Duhoux 1985, 41–48). So, for example, the word in the sphere of chariot wheel construction that means 'provided with a *termis*' (referring to a kind of insertion technique used at the points on wheels where the spokes met the rims) is spelled alternatively *te-mi-de-we-te* and *te-mi-dwe-te*. In

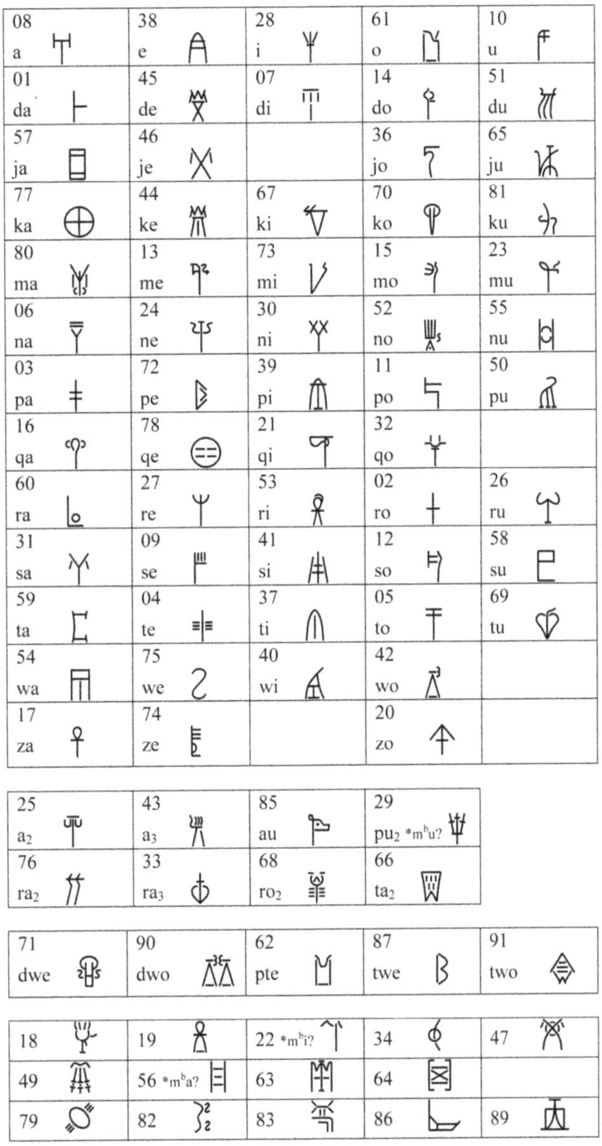

08 a	38 e	28 i	61 o	10 u
01 da	45 de	07 di	14 do	51 du
57 ja	46 je		36 jo	65 ju
77 ka	44 ke	67 ki	70 ko	81 ku
80 ma	13 me	73 mi	15 mo	23 mu
06 na	24 ne	30 ni	52 no	55 nu
03 pa	72 pe	39 pi	11 po	50 pu
16 qa	78 qe	21 qi	32 qo	
60 ra	27 re	53 ri	02 ro	26 ru
31 sa	09 se	41 si	12 so	58 su
59 ta	04 te	37 ti	05 to	69 tu
54 wa	75 we	40 wi	42 wo	
17 za	74 ze		20 zo	

25 a$_2$	43 a$_3$	85 au	29 pu$_2$ *m^{b}u?	
76 ra$_2$	33 ra$_3$	68 ro$_2$	66 ta$_2$	

71 dwe	90 dwo	62 pte	87 twe	91 two

18	19	22 *m^{b}i?	34	47
49	56 *m^{b}a?	63	64	
79	82	83	86	89

Figure 27.1. Linear B phonograms classified by their phonetic values (based on images from Duhoux and Morpurgo Davies 2008; courtesy of Ruth Palmer).

both of these spellings, the /r/ that precedes /m/ is not represented. However, in one spelling the consonant sequence arising in word formation from suffixation (*termid-went-*) is treated as a sequence of two consonant sounds (*de-we*), while in the other spelling, this consonant cluster is heard and represented in a Minoan way—almost as a single phoneme (*dwe*). 'Extra' signs, like *dwe*, which are useful but not necessary, and the 'partial spellings' we just looked at give the Linear B syllabary a look of inefficiency, especially in contrast with the later Cypriote syllabary (Olivier 2008). However, they are rightly explained as good evidence for the continuing influence

Humans	100 MAN	102 WOMAN		
Animals	104 DEER	105 HORSE	105[f] HORSE[f]	105[m] HORSE[m]
	106[f] SHEEP[f]	106[m] SHEEP[m]	107[f] GOAT[f]	107[m] GOAT[m]
	108[f] PIG[f]	108[m] PIG[m]	109[f] BOVID[f]	109[m] BOVID[m]
Vegetable products	120 BARLEY?	121 WHEAT?	122 OLIVE	123 SPICE
	125 CYPERUS	129 FLOUR	130 OIL	131 WINE
	144 SAFFRON	174	176 TREE	30 FIGS
Metal	140 BRONZE	141 GOLD	167 INGOT	
Fiber and cloth	31 FLAX	145 WOOL	146 CLOTH	159 CLOTH
Animal products	151 HORN	152 OX HIDE	153 SHEEPSKIN	154
Vases	155[VASE]	200[VASE]	201[VASE] TRIPOD	202[VASE]
	203[VASE]	204[VASE]	205[VASE]	206[VASE]
	207[VASE]	208[VASE]	209[VASE] AMPHORA	210[VASE] STIRRUP JAR
	211[VASE]	212[VASE]	213[VASE]	215[VASE] KYLIX
	226[VASE]	227[VASE] RHYTON	229[VASE]	250[VASE]
Armor and weapons	162 BREASTPLATE	163 ARMOR SET	191 HELMET	230 SPEAR
	231 ARROW	232 SACRIFICIAL AX	233 SWORD	254 JAVELIN
Chariots	240 CHARIOT	241 CHASSIS	242 CHARIOT BOX	243 WHEEL

Figure 27.2. Selected Linear B ideograms according to category (based on images from Duhoux and Morpurgo Davies 2008; courtesy of Ruth Palmer).

of Minoan culture within Mycenaean culture. Several hundred tablet writers had no difficulty using the script effectively and routinely on a daily basis.

One final way that we can trace Minoan elements in the Linear B script is among the ideograms (see figure 27.2). The ideogram for 'figs' in Linear B is also used as the phonogram for the phonetic value /ni/. Greek used the loan word *sukon* for 'figs,' with initial syllable /su/, so we assume that /ni/ in Linear A was the initial syllable of the Minoan word for 'figs.' This is confirmed by a lexicographical entry that tells us that the word *nikuleon* is the Cretan word for 'figs' (Duhoux 1989, 71). There are several other such examples.

In the repertory of Linear B signs for objects, many of the signs for military equipment, vessels, and cloth are representational. We can immediately see that a sign represents a tripod, a chariot chassis, or fringed cloth. The sign for 'horse' is clearly a horse. Other signs have been made more abstract by their long history in Cretan writing, which goes back to the earliest period of Linear A economic records. Thus, whether signs *120 and *121 represent 'wheat' and 'barley' or vice versa (Palmer 2008b) is a controversial issue that has to be decided on the basis of their occurrence within specific Linear B texts and sets of texts and not on the basis of their appearance.

EDITIONS AND OTHER TOOLS OF RESEARCH

An extensive, up-to-date list of research tools is provided by Palmer (2008a, 51–55), so it need not be duplicated here. Nonetheless, some commentary and slight supplementing are in order.

All but the most recently discovered Linear B tablets are now published in official corpus editions or carefully edited volumes of transcriptions. However, these editions are designed for the handful of specialists who have learned how the script works, mastered the technicalities of language, and learned enough about the archaeological and historical background of the texts to be able to work firsthand with the tablets and their transcriptions and propose interpretations of their texts that fit what we know about Greek in the late Bronze Age and the protohistorical contexts of the records.

Special collections of tablets, like the inscribed sealings from Thebes, perfumed oil tablets, or the tablets from the RCT at Knossos, have had comprehensive studies published. Arguably the greatest aid to interpretation is the publication by a single scholar, Francisco Aura Jorro, of a bibliographically comprehensive, two-volume lexicon of Mycenaean Greek (Aura Jorro 1985, 1993). There has been no new full grammar of Linear B since Vilborg (1960).

The main general handbooks (Ventris and Chadwick 1973; Hiller and Panagl 1976; Hooker 1980; Morpurgo Davies and Duhoux 1985) that offer translations and interpretations of selected documents are now supplemented (Ruipérez and Melena 1990; Bartoněk 2003; Bernabé and Luján 2006; Duhoux and Morpurgo Davies 2008). A multiauthored update of Ventris and Chadwick (1973) is well under way, as is another systematic survey of textual evidence for themes in Aegean prehistory that Italian scholar Massimo Perna is editing. Descriptive analytical bibliographies of specialized work connected with the Linear B texts also appear regularly in *Studies in Mycenaean Inscriptions and Dialect* (SMID), now published by the Program in Aegean Scripts and Prehistory at the University of Texas at Austin and available online at http://paspserver.class.utexas.edu/index.html.

Finally, Mycenological specialists hold a major international conference about once every five years. These provide a fairly comprehensive look at advances and trends in the field over time.

There are two final points to make about scholarship surrounding the Linear B texts, one positive and one a warning. First, the focus of the field has shifted away from the originally inevitable (in the twenty-five or so years after the decipherment) concentration on publication of the documents and interpreting the language of the texts and the specialized semantics of their vocabulary. All of the general studies of aspects of the Mycenaean palatial period now include specialist articles and chapters that give state-of-the art looks at what the tablets tell us and, even more important, what they do not tell us (i.e., the limitations that we have to impose on speculation).

Second, because interpretation of these texts requires such an array of scholarly skills, the interpretation of newly discovered tablets has until recently involved extensive informal collaboration during a period of intensive preliminary study. It is necessary to say that the interpretation of the most recently discovered Thebes tablets did not follow this practice. Many radical and outright wrong ideas were put forward in the first official publication of the texts. Unfortunately, specialists in other areas, without any way of judging, may use these ideas as definitive explanations of the texts and what they mean. Reviews (Palaima 2003b) and special seminars have tried to correct this anomaly (Deger-Jalkotzy and Panagl 2006). *Caveant lectores.*

WHAT THE TEXTS TELL US

A survey of the ideograms and the numbers associated with them gives us a general sense of the main focuses of the economies of Mycenaean palatial territories.

Basic agricultural ideograms (grains, figs, olives, olive oil, wine) are standard in Linear A and Linear B. Linear B tablets from Knossos give us records of major harvests. One Knossos tablet records about a million liters of grain as a harvest (*amā*) at the site of *da-wo* in the Mesara. Other texts give us terminology for agricultural specialists (e.g., 'overseers of figs' *opisūkoi*; 'overseers of digging' *opiskaphēwes*; 'winnowers' **akhnēwes*). Food and land parcels on which food crops could be grown are the major ways palatial centers and village communities compensated individuals for labor and other services. In each locality, the apportioning and use of communal land was overseen by a *dāmos*, a collective group, presumably of elders, which is etymologically connected with the idea of 'apportioning.' The 'holding' of land parcels brought with it obligations, and it was often a reward for services rendered to local communities or the palatial centers.

There are extensive land tenure series at Pylos (Ventris and Chadwick 1973, 252–74, 443–56) involving individuals termed 'servants'—in what sense is hard to know—of the deity, specialist craftspersons of the *wanax* ('king'), and individuals (again including work specialists) who are associated with the *lāwāgetās* (a military leader and official in charge of overseeing the role of 'aliens' in a palatial territory; see Nikoloudis 2006, 2008). Nonfood products like flax, terebinth, and wood are also carefully monitored because they were essential for vital palatial industries:

flax in the manufacture of articles made out of cloth (in this case, linen), including sails; terebinth in perfumed oil production; and wood in the construction of ships, buildings, furniture, chariots, and weaponry.

Animals are also carefully monitored in texts that reveal how the palatial centers controlled economic activities and organized economic operations. The texts also give evidence of the degree to which the palatial system relied on (1) influential individuals (elites known conventionally as 'collectors' and also 'followers' of the king; and local 'big men' known as *gwasilēwes*); (2) institutions (especially councils of elders, *geronsiai*; collectives under the influence of *gwasilēwes*; and sanctuaries); and (3) locales that had status and power before the palatial centers came into existence and that continue to play a major role in controlling economic affairs.

Sheep were the focus of administration in the wool production industry (Nosch 2008). The Knossos tablets famously monitor a hundred thousand sheep in flocks controlled by collectors, sheep owners, and the deity known at *potnia*. However, sheep are also singled out as sacrificial offerings (*sphaktēria*) and listed as such on records of the resources assembled for commensal ceremonies. Likewise, bulls, goats, and pigs are listed as sacrificial offerings, but they are also recorded as economic items, used for their hides and other body parts. Male bovids are allocated in teams as draught animals, and we also have groups of cowherds listed together with wall builders on a major construction project. For all of these animals, words for specialized attendants (i.e., herdsmen, although the social implications of the modern equivalents are doubtless misleading) are attested.

Here we have already given the correct impression that the palatial centers constructed remarkably successful economic engines within their regions. The palatial system maximized productivity and made it possible for the Mycenaeans to compete in the international economy of the period (Palaima 2007). The picture the tablets give us of the successful mobilization of resources within regions is reflected in the archaeologically attested development (Bennet 2007).

Of primary concern, as Thucydides stresses in his survey of Greek prehistory and history, is military preparedness, which provided protection against attacks, whether from rival palatial territories or foreign cultures. These had the potential to disrupt and reduce the effectiveness of the exploitation of natural resources (foodstuffs and raw materials like timber) that were the basis of the palatial economies.

The Mycenaean military industrial complex, therefore, had a dominant position within the economy and society of the palatial territories (Palaima 1999). Nearly half of the definitive monograph on archaeological ideograms (Vandenabeele and Olivier 1979) is devoted to armor, weaponry, horses, chariots, and wheels. A single tablet from Pylos (Jn 829) records a prospective collection of recycled bronze (from sanctuaries and from officials overseeing agricultural labor) sufficient for 33,000 arrowheads or 142 spearheads. All of the sites except Midea (with very few tablets) attest to the production, refurbishing, and distribution of military equipment.

One tablet alone at Pylos lists 151 chariot wheels. The chariot force at Knossos in the period of the RCT texts numbers between 173 and 250 chariots with horses and accompanying sets of armor. Other Knossos records deal with the manufacture of swords. Of the four tablets from Khania, one fragmentary text records 10 pairs of chariot wheels. At Pylos, one recently interpreted record (An 1282) lists assignments of groups of men (broken down into groups of 18 and 36) assigned to work on chariots, chariot wheels, flint (for spear- or arrowheads), horse feeding sacks, and spear and javelin shafts. Pylos also has page-shaped tablets that track the assignment of large numbers of men to 'coastal watcher' contingents and to rowing groups. In the latter case there are explicit references to their obligation to row, to groups of men designated by foreign ethnics, and to the involvement of the *lāwāgetās* and possibly even the *wanaks* in the mobilization of these men.

There are some 5,000 persons listed in collective groups as dependent labor on the Pylos texts (Hiller 1988) and roughly another 800 or so of more elevated status, listed by personal name (Nakassis 2008, 560). Set against the estimated population of 50,000 (Whitelaw 2001, 64) for the entire region and keeping in mind the haphazardly incomplete nature of the texts that we have, the Linear B tablets from Pylos give us a good impression of successful state formation and relative prosperity in a region that in later historical times never reached such a level of general well-being. The texts help us to see that the palatial centers in the various regions of the Mycenaean world relied on their status, powers of coercion, control of religious ceremonies, manipulation of networks of social institutions, and continually renegotiated relationships with high-status individuals. All of these techniques are visible in the Linear B tablets. They give us good evidence of the general human instinct for what Thucydides and Aristotle call *autarkeia*, the self-sufficiency and self-determination that comes to Mycenaean palatial centers or historical Greek *poleis* only when they acquire, exploit, and protect the resources of their regions.

I dedicate this chapter to my friend and mentor Emmett L. Bennett, Jr., who turned ninety-one years of age on July 12, 2009, the birthday he is very pleased to share with Michael Ventris.

BIBLIOGRAPHY

Aura Jorro, Francisco. 1985. *Diccionario micénico*, vol. 1. Madrid: Consejo Superior de Investigaciones Científicas.

———. 1993. *Diccionario micénico*, vol. 2. Madrid: Consejo Superior de Investigaciones Científicas.

Bartoněk, Antonin. 2003. *Handbuch des mykenischen Griechisch*. Heidelberg: Winter.

Bennet, John. 1990. "Knossos in Context: Comparative Perspectives on the Linear B Administration of LM II–III Crete." *AJA* 94: 193–211.

———. 1998. The Linear B Archives and the Kingdom of Nestor. In *Sandy Pylos* 1998, 111–33.

———. 2007. "PYLOS: The Expansion of a Mycenaean Palatial Center." In *RMP II*, 29–39.

Bennett, Emmett L., Jr. 1947. The Minoan Linear Script from Pylos. PhD diss., University of Cincinnati.

———. 1951. *The Pylos Tablets: A Preliminary Transcription*. Princeton: Princeton University Press.

Bernabé, Alberto, and Eugenio R. Luján. 2006. *Introducción al griego micénico*. Monografías de Filología Griega 18. Zaragoza: Universidad de Zaragoza.

Blegen, Carl W., and Konstantinos Kourouniotis. 1939. "Excavations at Pylos, 1939." *AJA* 43: 537–76.

Brown, Raymond A. 1985. *Evidence for Pre-Greek Speech on Crete from Greek Alphabetic Sources*. Amsterdam: Hakkert.

Chadwick, John. 1987. *Linear B and Related Scripts*. Los Angeles: University of California Press/British Museum.

———. 1988. "The Women of Pylos." In *Texts, Tablets, and Scribes: Studies in Mycenaean Epigraphy and Economy in Honor of Emmett L. Bennett Jr.*, ed. Thomas G. Palaima and Jean-Pierre Olivier, 43–95. *Minos* Supl. 10. Salamanca: Ediciones Universidad de Salamanca.

Deger-Jalkotzy, Sigrid, and Oswald Panagl. 2006. *Die neuen Linear B-Texte aus Theben*. Vienna: Verlag der Österreichischen Akademie der Wissenschaften.

Del Freo, Maurizio. 2008. "Rapport 2001–2005 sur les textes en écriture hiéroglyphique crétoise, en linéaire A et en linéaire B." In *Colloquium Romanum: Atti del XII Colloquio Internazionale di Micenologia. Roma, 20–25 febbraio 2006*, vol. 1, ed. Anna Sacconi, Maurizio Del Freo, Louis Godart, and Mario Negri, 199–222. Rome: Fabrizio Serra.

Driessen, Jan. 1985. "Quelques remarques sur la 'Grande Tablette' (As 1516) de Cnossos." *Minos* 19: 169–94.

———. 1996. "The Arsenal of Knossos (Crete) and Mycenaean Chariot Forces." *Acta Archaeologica Lovaniensia* 8, 481–98.

———. 1997. "Le palais de Cnossos au MR II–III: Combien de destructions?" In *La Crète mycénienne*, 113–34.

———. 2000. *The Scribes of the Room of the Chariot Tablets: Interdisciplinary Approach to the Study of a Linear B Deposit*. Suplementos a *Minos* 16. Salamanca: Ediciones Universidad de Salamanca.

———. 2008. "Chronology of the Linear B Texts." In *A Companion to Linear B*, vol. 1, ed. Yves Duhoux and Anna Morpurgo Davies, 69–79. Bibliothèque des Cahiers de l'Institut de Linguistique de Louvain 120. Louvain-la-Neuve, Belgium: Peeters.

Duhoux, Yves. 1985. "Mycénien et écriture grecque." In *Linear B: A 1984 Survey*, ed. Anna Morpurgo Davies and Yves Duhoux, 7–74. Bibliothèque des Cahiers de l'Institut de Linguistique de Louvain 26. Louvain-la-Neuve, Belgium: Cabay.

———. 1989. "Le linéaire A: Problèmes de déchiffrement." In *Problems in Decipherment*, ed. Yves Duhoux, Thomas G. Palaima, and John Bennet, 59–119. Bibliothèque des Cahiers de l'Institut de Linguistique de Louvain 49. Louvain-la-Neuve, Belgium: Peeters.

———, and Anna Morpurgo Davies. 2008. *A Companion to Linear B*, vol. 1. Bibliothèque des Cahiers de l'Institut de Linguistique de Louvain 120. Louvain-la-Neuve, Belgium: Peeters.

Evans, Arthur E. 1900. "Knossos, I. The Palace." *BSA* 6: 3–70.

———. 1903–1904. "The Pictographic and Linear Scripts of Minoan Crete and Their Relations." *Proceedings of the British Academy* 1: 137–39.

———. 1909. *Scripta Minoa*, vol. 1. Oxford: Clarendon.

———. 1952. *Scripta Minoa*, vol. 2, ed. John L. Myres. Oxford: Clarendon.

Hallager, Erik. 1996. *The Minoan Roundel and Other Sealed Documents in the Neopalatial Linear A Administration*. Aegaeum 14. Liège: Université de Liège.

Hester, D. A. 1968. "Recent Developments in Mediterranean 'Substrate' Studies." *Minos* 9: 219–35.

Hiller, Stefan. 1988. "Dependent Personnel in Mycenaean Texts." In *Society and Economy in the Eastern Mediterranean (c. 1500–1000 B.C.)*, ed. Michael Heltzer and Edward Lipiński, 53–68. Leuven, Belgium: Peeters.

———, and Oswald Panagl. 1976. *Die frühgriechischen Texte aus mykenischer Zeit*. Erträge der Forschung 49. Darmstadt: Wissenschaftliche Buchgesellschaft.

Hooker, James T. 1980. *Linear B: An Introduction*. Bristol: Bristol Classical Press.

Killen, John T. 1983. "PY An 1." *Minos* 18: 71–79.

MacGillivray, J. Alexander. 2000. *Minotaur: Sir Arthur Evans and the Archaeology of the Minoan Myth*. London: Cape.

Morpurgo Davies, Anna, and Yves Duhoux. 1985. *Linear B: A 1984 Survey*. Bibliothèque des Cahiers de l'Institut de Linguistique de Louvain 26. Louvain-la-Neuve, Belgium: Cabay.

Myres, John L. 1941. "Sir Arthur Evans." *Proceedings of the British Academy* 27: 323–57.

Nakassis, Dimitri. 2008. "Named Individuals and the Mycenaean State at Pylos." In *Colloquium Romanum: Atti del XII Colloquio Internazionale de Micenologia. Roma, 20–25 febbraio 2006*, vol. 2, ed. Anna Sacconi, Maurizio del Freo, Louis Godart, and Mario Negri, 549–61. Rome: Fabrizio Serra.

Nikoloudis, Stavroula. 2006. The *ra-wa-ke-ta*, Ministerial Authority and Mycenaean Cultural Identity. PhD diss., University of Texas at Austin.

———. 2008. "The Role of the *ra-wa-ke-ta*: Insights from PY Un 718." In *Colloquium Romanum: Atti del XII Colloquio Internazionale de Micenologia. Roma, 20–25 febbraio 2006*, vol. 2, ed. Anna Sacconi, Maurizio del Freo, Louis Godart, and Mario Negri, 587–94. Rome: Fabrizio Serra.

Nilsson, Martin P. 1932. *The Mycenaean Origin of Greek Mythology*. Berkeley: University of California Press.

Nosch, Marie-Louise. 2008. "Administrative Practices in Mycenaean Palace Administration and Economy." In *Colloquium Romanum: Atti del XII Colloquio Internazionale de Micenologia. Roma, 20–25 febbraio 2006*, vol. 2, ed. Anna Sacconi, Maurizio del Freo, Louis Godart, and Mario Negri, 595–604. Rome: Fabrizio Serra.

Olivier, Jean-Pierre. 1967. *Les scribes de Cnossos*. Incunabula Graeca 17. Rome: Edizioni dell' Ateneo.

———. 1993. "KN 115 = KH 115. Un meme scribe à Knossos et à la Canée au MRIIIB: Du soupçon à la certitude." *BCH* 117: 19–33.

———. 1996. "KN 115 et KH 115: Rectification." *BCH* 120: 823.

———. 2008. "Les syllabaires chypriotes des deuxième et premier millénaires avant notre ère: État des questions." In *Colloquium Romanum: Atti del XII Colloquio Internazionale de Micenologia. Roma, 20–25 febbraio 2006*, vol. 2, ed. Anna Sacconi, Maurizio del Freo, Louis Godart, and Mario Negri, 605–620. Rome: Fabrizio Serra.

Palaima, Thomas G. 1988. *The Scribes of Pylos*. Incunabula Graeca 87. Rome: Edizioni dell' Ateneo.

———. 1989. "Cypro-Minoan Scripts: Problems of Historical Context." In *Problems in Decipherment*. Bibliothèque des Cahiers de l'Institut de Linguistique de Louvain 49, ed. Yves Duhoux, Thomas G. Palaima and John Bennett, 121–87. Louvain-la-Neuve, Belgium: Peeters.

———. 1993. "Ten Reasons Why KH 115 ≠ KN 115." *Minos* 27–28: 261–81.

———. 1995. "The Last Days of the Pylos Polity." In *Politeia*, 623–33.

———. 1996a. " 'Contiguities' in the Linear B Tablets from Pylos." In *Atti e Memorie del Secondo Congresso Internazionale di Micenologia*, ed. Ernesto de Miro, Louis Godart, Anna Sacconi, 379–396. Rome: Gruppo editoriale internazionale.

————. 1996b. "Sealings as Links in an Administrative Chain." In *Administration in Ancient Societies*, ed. Piera Ferioli, Enrica Fiandra, and Gian Giacomo Fissore, 37–66. Turin: Centro Internazionale di Ricerche Archeologiche Antropologiche e Storiche.

————. 1999. "Mycenaean Militarism from a Textual Perspective. Onomastics in Context: *lawos, damos, klewos*." In *Polemos*, 367–78.

————. 2000a. Review of J. Alexander MacGillivray, *Minotaur: Sir Arthur Evans and the Archaeology of the Minoan Myth*. London: Cape, 2000. *Times Higher Education Suppl.* August 18, 2000, 19.

————. 2000b. "Transactional Vocabulary in Linear B Tablet and Sealing Administration." In *Administrative Documents in the Aegean and Their Near Eastern Counterparts*, ed. Massimo Perna, 261–76. Turin: Centro Internazionale di Ricerche Archeologiche Antropologiche e Storiche.

————. 2003a. " 'Archives' and 'Scribes' and Information Hierarchy in Mycenaean Greek Linear B Records. " In *Ancient Archives and Archival Traditions*, ed. Maria Brosius, 153–94, figures 8.1–8.9. New York: Oxford University Press.

————. 2003b. "Reviewing the New Linear B Tablets from Thebes." *Kadmos* 42: 31–38.

————. 2004a. "Linear B Sources." In *Anthology of Classical Myth*, ed. Stephen M. Trzaskoma, R. Scott Smith, and Stephen Brunet, 439–54. Indianapolis: Hackett.

————. 2004b. "Sacrificial Feasting in the Linear B Tablets." In *The Mycenaean Feast*, ed. James C. Wright, 217–46. *Hesperia* 73(2). Princeton: American School of Classical Studies.

————. 2006a. "FAR? or *ju?* and Other Interpretative Conundra in the New Thebes Tablets." In *Die neuen Linear B-Texte aus Theben*, ed. Sigrid Deger-Jalkotzy and Oswald Panagl, 139–48. Vienna: Verlag der Österreichischen Akademie der Wissenschaften.

————. 2006b. "OL Zh 1: *Quousque tandem?*" *Minos* 37–38: 373–85.

————. 2007. "Mycenaean Society and Kingship: *Cui bono?* A Counter-speculative View." In *EPOS*, 129–40.

————. Forthcoming. "Scribes, Scribal Hands and Palaeography." In *A Companion to Linear B*, vol. 2, ed. Yves Duhoux and Anna Morpurgo Davies. Bibliothèque des Cahiers de l'Institut de Linguistique de Louvain. Louvain-la-Neuve, Belgium: Peeters.

————, Elizabeth Pope, and F. Kent Reilly. 2000. *Unlocking the Secrets of Ancient Writing: The Parallel Lives of Michael Ventris and Linda Schele and the Decipherment of Mycenaean and Mayan Writing*. Catalogue of an Exhibition Held at the Nettie Lee Benson Latin American Collection, March 9–August 1, 2000. Austin: Program in Aegean Scripts and Prehistory.

Palaima, Thomas G., and Elizabeth Sikkenga. 1999. "Linear A > Linear B. How?" In *Meletemata*, 599–608.

Palmer, Ruth. 1989. "Subsistence Rations at Pylos and Knossos." *Minos* 24: 89–124.

————. 2008a. "How to Begin?" In *A Companion to Linear B*, vol. 1, ed. Yves Duhoux and Anna Morpurgo Davies, 25–68. Bibliothèque des Cahiers de l'Institut de Linguistique de Louvain 120. Louvain-la-Neuve, Belgium: Peeters.

————. 2008b. "Wheat and Barley 15 Years Later." In *Colloquium Romanum: Atti del XII Colloquio Internazionale di Micenologia. Roma, 20–25 febbraio 2006*, vol. 2, ed. Anna Sacconi, Maurizio del Freo, Louis Godart, and Mario Negri, 621–39. Rome: Fabrizio Serra.

Piteros, Christos, Jean-Pierre Olivier, and José L. Melena. 1990. "Les inscriptions en linéaire B des nodules de Thèbes (1982): La fouille, les documents, les possibilités d'interprétation." *BCH* 104: 103–84.

Renfrew, Colin. 1998. "Word of Minos: The Minoan Contribution to Mycenaean Greek and the Linguistic Geography of the Bronze Age Aegean." *Cambridge Archaeological Journal* 8: 239–64.

Robinson, Andrew. 2002. *The Man Who Deciphered Linear B*. London: Thames and Hudson.

Ruipérez, Martin S., and José L. Melena. 1990. *Los griegos micénicos*. Historia 16. Madrid: MELSA.

Sharypkin, Serguey. 2008. "Irrelevant Phonetic Features and the Rules of the Linear B Script." In *Colloquium Romanum: Atti del XII Colloquio Internazionale de Micenologia. Roma, 20–25 febbraio 2006*, vol. 2, ed. Anna Sacconi, Maurizio del Freo, Louis Godart, and Mario Negri, 735–52. Rome: Pasiphae.

Shelmerdine, Cynthia W. 2008a. "Background, Sources, and Methods." In *The Cambridge Companion to the Aegean Bronze Age*, ed. Cynthia W. Shelmerdine, 1–18. New York: Cambridge University Press.

———, ed. 2008b. *The Cambridge Companion to the Aegean Bronze Age*. New York: Cambridge University Press.

Shelton, Kim. 2003. "A New Linear B Tablet from Petsas House, Mycenae." *Minos* 37–38: 387–96.

Sjöquist, Karl-Erik, and Paul Åström. 1985. *Pylos: Palmprints and Palmleaves*. SIMA-PB 31. Gothenburg: Åström.

———. 1991. *Knossos: Keepers and Kneaders*. SIMA-PB 82. Gothenburg: Åström.

Skelton, Christina. 2008. "Methods of Using Phylogenetic Systematics to Reconstruct the History of the Linear B Script." *Archaeometry* 50: 158–76.

Smith, Joanna S. 1993. "The Pylos Jn Series." *Minos* 27–28: 167–259.

Sundwall, Johannes. 1920. "Zur Deutung kretischer Tontäfelchen." *Acta Academiae Aboensis Humaniora* 2: 1–12.

———. 1932. "Zu dem minoischen Währungssystem." In *Mélanges Gustave Glotz*, vol. 2, 827–29. Paris: Les Presses Universitaires de France.

———. 1936. "Altkretische Urkundenstudien." *Acta Academiae Aboensis Humaniora* 10, 2: 1–45.

Van Alfen, Peter. 2008. "The Linear B Inscribed Vases." In *A Companion to Linear B*, vol. 1, ed. Yves Duhoux and Anna Morpurgo Davies, 235–42. Bibliothèque des Cahiers de l'Institut de Linguistique de Louvain 120. Louvain-la-Neuve, Belgium: Peeters.

Vandenabeele, Frieda, and Jean-Pierre Olivier. 1979. *Les idéogrammes archéologiques du Linéaire B*. Études Crétoises 24. Paris: Geuthner.

Ventris, Michael, and John Chadwick. 1973. *Documents in Mycenaean Greek*, 2d ed. Cambridge: Cambridge University Press.

———, and John Chadwick. 1953. "Evidence for Greek Dialect in the Mycenaean Archives." *JHS* 73: 84–103.

Vilborg, Ebbe. 1960. *A Tentative Grammar of Mycenaean Greek*. Studia Graeca et Latina Gothoburgensia 9. Gothenburg: Almqvist and Wiksell.

Wace, Alan J. B. 1921. "Archaeology in Greece, 1919–1921." *JHS* 41: 260–76.

Whitelaw, Todd. 2001. "Reading between the Tablets: Assessing Mycenaean Involvement in Ceramic Production and Consumption." In *Economy and Politics in the Mycenaean Palace States*, ed. Sophia Voutsaki and John T. Killen, 51–79. Transactions of the Philological Society Suppl. 27. Cambridge: Cambridge Philological Society.

Woodard, Roger D. 1997. *Greek Writing from Knossos to Homer*. New York: Oxford University Press.

CHAPTER 28

....

CYPRO-MINOAN

....

NICOLLE HIRSCHFELD

THERE are approximately two hundred identified Cypro-Minoan inscriptions (excluding potmarks). Most are very short (one or two sequences totaling fewer than ten signs). They are impressed, incised, or painted on a variety of objects and materials in an assortment of lengths and formats and are found in a diversity of contexts widely dispersed across the island of Cyprus and at Ras Shamra-Ugarit on the mainland. They span the entire Late Bronze Age (16th–11th centuries BC) and perhaps continue into the very early Iron Age.

The earliest discoveries were made at the end of the 19th century; most recently, Cypro-Minoan has been recognized at Ras Shamra-Ugarit and perhaps at Ashkelon. The script has not been deciphered, and any claims to have done so are premature, for the extant corpus is too limited, and there is no bilingual.

A BRIEF HISTORY OF CYPRO-MINOAN STUDIES
....

A bronze plaque with a bilingual inscription discovered at Idalion in 1869 confirmed the existence of a distinctive Cypriote Iron Age script. The inscription was long enough to provide sufficient material in itself for a decipherment, and further discoveries of Cypriote inscriptions confirmed the hypothesis that Greek-speaking Cypriotes of the Iron Age often used an indigenous script (in several regional variations) to express Greek. The identification of an indigenous script raised the question of the date and circumstances of its origins.

Thirty years later, a British Museum expedition discovered Bronze Age writing in the form of short inscriptions cut into five small clay balls found at Enkomi and

Hala Sultan Tekke, as well as similar marks cut singly into the handles of Mycenaean vases. However, it was Arthur Evans who, in his search to establish the broader context of his discoveries of the linear scripts of Crete, recognized the importance of the early Cypriote evidence and coined the term "Cypro-Minoan" to refer to the Bronze Age script of Cyprus (Evans 1909, 70–73).

For the first half-century of discovery, Cypro-Minoan inscriptions were recognized in short sequences, indeed even isolated marks, on a variety of media. This is reflected in the first systematic compilation of a Cypro-Minoan corpus, published by Stanley Casson in 1937. Although Casson listed separately the occurrences and media for each of the sixty-one signs of his corpus, he and his peers indiscriminately lumped together all of the available material—in part because it was so meager—in their studies of Cypriote Bronze Age writing.

It was John Franklin Daniel who, in his appropriately titled "Prolegomena to the Cypro-Minoan Script" (1941), established a sober methodology for progress in analysis and decipherment. Daniel advocated the consideration of an inscription within the context of its medium. He separated Casson's agglomerative corpus and set specific criteria for reintegrating the signs of any particular object group into the Cypro-Minoan corpus. Unfortunately, Daniel died before the apogee of Cypro-Minoan discoveries, most significantly at Enkomi (where the first tablet and the first lengthy inscription were discovered in 1952) and Ras Shamra-Ugarit in the 1950s and 1960s, at Kition and Hala Sultan Tekke in the 1970s, and at Kalavassos–*Ayios Dhimitrios* in the 1980s.

Through her diligent inventory of much material from many sites, Emilia Masson is the scholar most responsible for advancing the study of Cypro-Minoan. Her 1974 synthesis, and in particular the table of signs published therein (Masson 1974, 13–15), still remains the standard reference (Olivier 2007, 21, 24). However, for several reasons this now needs to be changed.

The first reason is not Masson's fault: Namely, the discoveries since 1974 need to be incorporated into the corpus. However, even as it stands, there are serious shortcomings. Masson's tables of signs ignore Daniel's precepts; they include without remark signs impressed, incised, or painted on a variety of object types. The lack of annotation makes it impossible to evaluate individually her reasons for identifying variants as alternate or as distinctive sign forms. Moreover, Masson's initial readings have several times been fundamentally corrected or enhanced by a second set of eyes. Thus, for example, Smith saw that the texts on two of the cylinders from Kalavassos–*Ayios Dhimitrios* are palimpsests, a feature Masson did not notice or consider in her rendering of the signs from those inscriptions (Smith 2002, 23–25; 2003, 283–84), and Ferrara has further noted a three-sign inscription (not mentioned by Masson or Smith) on one of the flat surfaces of a third cylinder (Ferrara 2005, 199–200).

Cypro-Minoan studies have until very recently been piecemeal; the scattered and sometimes obscure publications have made access even to the primary material difficult except to the most determined researcher, and this, as much as the vicissitudes of archaeological discovery, has hindered progress in the analysis of the scripts. Two new publications now change this state of affairs. A recent PhD dissertation (Ferrara 2005) proffers an updated and comprehensive edition of the Cypro-Minoan corpus based on and accompanied by extensive contextual, epigraphic, and palaeographical analyses. The dissertation awaits publication and evaluation. Meanwhile, Olivier (2007) offers a welcome compilation of photographs, drawings, essential bibliography, and current provenance of 217 Cypro-Minoan inscriptions.

THE EVIDENCE

The corpus of Cypro-Minoan signs has yet to be securely identified. Masson (1974, 13–15) lists 125, whereas Ferrara (2005, 264–67) recognizes 84. The reduction in the sign list is due in part to the expanded corpus of inscriptions now available and in part to different readings by the different individuals. Both factors alter the identification of repetitive sequences that are crucial, in an undeciphered script, to recognizing variant sign forms. In addition to scribal idiosyncrasies, the variety of writing tools, media, and modes of inscribing attested for Late Bronze Age Cyprus produced a diversity of forms for each Cypro-Minoan sign.

The great majority of Cypro-Minoan inscriptions are drawn or impressed into moist clay. The most commonly inscribed objects are eighty-three small (avg. 20–22 mm) clay balls on which only a few (2–8) signs were written, frequently separated into two shorter sequences. The purpose of these balls and/or their inscriptions is not known. The variety of suggested functions—weights, taxation records, votive pebbles, gaming marbles, divination pieces, and identity cards—reflects the diverse archaeological contexts in which these balls were found (almost all were found at Enkomi).

A second type of inscribed object is clay cylinders, one larger (4 cm. dia., 13 cm. H.) found at Enkomi and five smaller and mostly fragmentary from Kalavassos–*Ayios Dhimitrios*. These six cylinders, plus eight tablets (figure 28.1), preserve the only long Cypro-Minoan texts, the longest consisting of fewer than five hundred signs. Like the cylinders, most of the tablets are heavily damaged. The tablets are all page shaped and thick, with one or both sides convex. Four were discovered in residential archives in Ras Shamra-Ugarit; the rest were found in various secondary contexts at Enkomi.

Many short inscriptions are cut or stamped (and there is at least one painted example) into hard materials (ivory, metals, stone, fired clay) fashioned into an assortment of forms: bowls, tools, perhaps *obeloi,* rings, ring stands, (miniature) ingots, pithos lids, spindle whorls, weights, labels, a wall plaque, basin, votive kidney, pipe, rod, Bes plaque, bull figurine, and more than two dozen stamp and cylinder seals. Almost half of these inscriptions consist of a single sequence; the great majority of Cypro-Minoan inscriptions consist of only one or two sequences.

Figure 28.1. Enkomi tablet 1687 (obverse) (photograph courtesy of Joanna Smith).

There are many objects with single marks, and Cypro-Minoan studies (with the notable exception of Daniel 1941) have conventionally included most of these, especially potmarks. This is partly because it was certainly Cypriote practice occasionally to incise inscriptions on the shoulders and handles of plain jugs and pithos rims. More often, single marks were incised into the same features of those same kinds of vases, and those single marks are sometimes identical to or reminiscent of the signs found in "true" inscriptions. Thus, it is reasonable to consider such marks as possible signs of writing.

Second, marks incised into the handles of Mycenaean containers were among the discoveries noted by the earliest archaeological expeditions to the island, in an era when decipherments of hieroglyphs and cuneiform and the discovery of Cretan linear scripts encouraged identification of writing systems. The mindset of seeing potmarks as evidence of writing was bolstered by subsequent discoveries of definite inscriptions on vases, and thus today potmarks are still regularly cited as evidence for Cypro-Minoan writing.

To what extent this is true is crucial to Cypro-Minoan studies because the number of marked vases found on Cyprus and marked Cypriote vases found abroad has the potential to contribute significantly to defining the corpus of Cypro-Minoan signs and to establishing the geographical and chronological boundaries of its use.

DISTRIBUTION (CYPRUS)

The greatest concentration of Cypro-Minoan writing has been found at Enkomi. This site has produced the earliest extant examples of Cypro-Minoan, referred to as "Archaic CM," and is the only place on the island where Cypro-Minoan tablets have been discovered. Clearly this was an important site in the history of Bronze Age writing on Cyprus, but whether its centrality is in whole or in part magnified by the relatively extensive excavations of the site remains to be ascertained. It is particularly frustrating that many of the inscriptions found at this site either have no recorded context or are from secondary deposits.

Cypro-Minoan inscriptions have been found at the other important coastal urban centers, though in much smaller quantities (figure 28.2). For example, in contrast to the more than one hundred inscriptions discovered at Enkomi, the wealthy and cosmopolitan settlements ringing Larnaca Bay (Kition and Hala Sultan Tekke) yielded altogether perhaps thirty inscriptions. The Cypriote hinterland is less well explored, but here, too, sites excavated to any significant extent have produced Cypro-Minoan inscriptions (usually only one or two), and these are often on objects that may well have been imported to the site. *If* "Cypro-Minoan" potmarks are accepted as signs of writing, then the argument for some level of participation in a literate administrative system by inhabitants of rural manufacturing or agricultural sites is greatly increased, for "Cypro-Minoan" potmarks are almost always found even at these sites (albeit usually in very small numbers).

No adequate study of the distribution patterns of Cypro-Minoan has yet been published (though see the excellent initiation in Ferrara 2005, 48–136, and supporting appendices and plans). Although writing is cited as a defining feature in currently proposed models of site hierarchies in Late Bronze Age Cyprus, a study that considered all aspects of the inscriptions—the inscribed objects and their archaeological contexts, as well as the paleographic and epigraphic features of the inscriptions themselves—would contribute significantly to the discussion of political, economic, or other interrelationships among the coastal centers or between a coastal center and its hinterland.

The corpus of Cypro-Minoan inscriptions is too small and varied to enable us to define regional differences. This is further complicated by the comparative lack of published material from the northern third of the island.

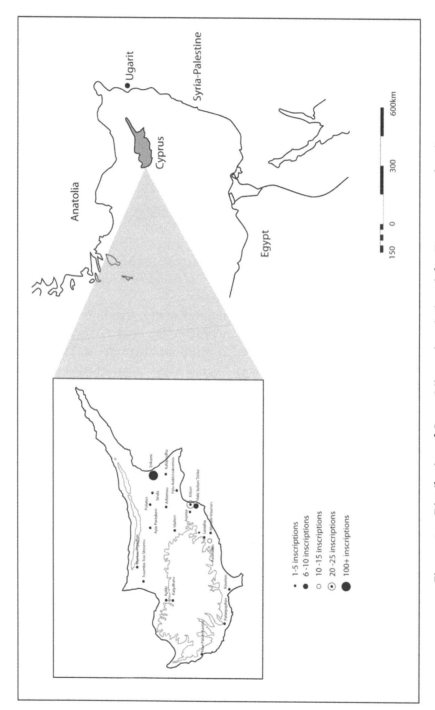

Figure 28.2. Distribution of Cypro–Minoan inscriptions (after Ferrara 2005, plan 2).

DISTRIBUTION (BEYOND CYPRUS)

Outside the island, Cypro-Minoan was certainly in use only at Ras Shamra–Ugarit. The corpus is at first glance small (eight objects), but this is comparable to the quantity found at Kition and Kalavassos–*Ayios Dhimitrios*, and Ugarit is the only site other than Enkomi to have yielded tablets (one complete and fragments of three others). In other words, Ugarit is one of the primary sources of Cypro-Minoan texts. The circumstances of Cypriote writing at Ugarit are a topic of both acute interest and profound enigma. Were they written at Ugarit or sent from Cyprus? Who in Ugarit could read (write?) these texts? For whom and what purpose were they intended? Masson, in her primary publication of the tablets and a silver bowl (Masson 1974, 18–46), focused especially on their lexical features for the purpose of defining the content or even reading (sections of) the inscriptions. Current scholarship is reconsidering in greater depth aspects Masson discussed only briefly: palaeography, formatting features, the tablets' physical characteristics, archaeological context, and archival context (Smith 2003, 284; Ferrara 2005, 123–33).

Potmarks *may* indicate a wider foreign familiarity and perhaps use of Cypriote Bronze Age writing. I have argued that a Cypriote marking system, partially based on Cypro-Minoan signs, is evident in most of the marks incised into the handles and painted under the bases of exported Mycenaean fine wares and Minoan coarse-ware stirrup jars (Hirschfeld 1993). Thus, these characteristic marks found on Aegean vases deposited at sites along the shores of the eastern Mediterranean, as far west as Sicily, north to Troy, and south to Egypt and Libya, are evidence of handling by individuals who used Cypriote bureaucratic methods to keep track of their wares.

The most recent discoveries of Cypro-Minoan, if the identification is accepted, would significantly extend the geographical and temporal range of this script in foreign contexts. Cross and Stager (2006) claim that one ostracon with a painted inscription and twelve inscribed jar handles found in levels from the 12th–11th century BC are evidence that the Philistines of Ashkelon had appropriated and modified the Cypro-Minoan script for local use. I do not consider those claims to be adequately substantiated by the evidence presented (Hirschfeld 2007; Olivier 2007, 21n5, is neutral), although I do not discount the possibility of a Cypro-Minoan afterlife on the Levantine coast.

CHRONOLOGICAL DISTRIBUTION

Cypro-Minoan is first attested at Enkomi in Late Cypriote IA levels (ca. 1600 BC). It was in its floruit throughout the LC IIC–IIIA periods (LH IIIB–early LH IIIC1 in Aegean terms). Its continuity into LC IIIB is attested only at Enkomi and Kition.

How long Cypro-Minoan lasts on Cyprus is unclear. Partly by coincidence and partly by agenda, archaeological investigations have straddled either side of the Cypro-Minoan/Cypriote Syllabic transition, sometime in the Cypro-Geometric period (11th century BC). That lacuna is now beginning to be addressed, and those studies hold great interest for students of Cypriote script. Meanwhile, it is a matter of debate where in the Cypro-Minoan/Cypriote Syllabic spectrum the two *obeloi* and two stone blocks found in association with a Cypriote Syllabic *obelos* in an 11th-century tomb at Palaepaphos-*Skales* should be situated.

Cypro-Minoan and Other Scripts

Cypro-Minoan characters are morphologically closest to Linear A (Palaima 1989, 136–38), but it has also been observed that the earliest Cypro-Minoan text, a tablet found at Enkomi, was written in a cuneiform style, the characters punched and bent rather than drawn (Godart and Sacconi 1979; Smith 2003, 281). The cuneiform influence makes sense, given the island's geographical situation and archaeological indications of close connections with a literate mainland. The Cretan element is surprising in light of the otherwise limited evidence for Minoan presence on Cyprus (or vice versa) at the time when transmission must have occurred. Here is a clear instance of text trumping archaeology. Why Minoan? Palaima suggests that the Aegean linear script was much easier to learn than Akkadian/Sumerian cuneiform (Palaima 1989, 161–62, but see Ferrara 2005, 64–66).

The hybridization of Cypro-Minoan continued throughout its history, certainly in terms of sign form and ductus (the manner of its writing), perhaps also in its vocabulary and dialects (mentioned later). Characterizations of the script have in the past not taken full account of the scale, materials, and writing implements of an inscription, but that is now being remedied (Smith 2003; Ferrara 2005, 25–29).

Sometime in the 11th century BC, the Greek language began to be written on Cyprus. However, rather than adapt the alphabetic script employed by the Phoenicians, as the Greeks would later do, in the 8th century, the Cypriotes continued to use a syllabic writing system reminiscent of Cypro-Minoan but now with morphological and phonological affinities to Linear B (Palaima 2005, 36–38). The complicated transition from native Bronze Age script to native Iron Age script has yet to be understood.

Cypro-Minoan Script Systems

There is general agreement that the earliest Cypro-Minoan texts—a tablet and a weight (?) from Enkomi—exhibit a somewhat different, perhaps experimental, form of Cypro-Minoan.

In her seminal publication, Masson (1974, 11–17) divided developed Cypro-Minoan into three subcategories on the basis of epigraphic and paleographical observations, geographical distribution, and (postulated) language differences:

- CM 1, the "standard," is the most common; it appears islandwide on a variety of objects;
- CM 2 comprises only the tablets from Enkomi, written by an ethnic group newly settled on the east coast of Cyprus who adapted CM 1 to their language;
- CM 3 is the form of the script extant only on two tablets and a cylinder seal found in Syria.

Although Masson subsequently refined details of these classifications, she has consistently maintained their essence (most recently Masson 2007); they have been generally quoted and are accepted with minor qualifications in the recent corpus (Olivier 2007, 21).

Nonetheless, there is increasing unease with Masson's tripartite division. Palaima (1989, 152–62) has presented the most detailed argument to date for dismissing Masson's divisions as artificial; Ferrara (2005, 209–281 and supporting appendices) has taken up his challenge and presented a wholesale reappraisal.

Decipherment

Fewer than three thousand signs in total constitute the entire corpus of Cypro-Minoan inscriptions (excluding potmarks). In other words, the corpus is too small to support decipherment methodologies. Decipherment is not possible unless substantial archives are uncovered or a bilingual is discovered.

Of course, those facts do not hinder attempts at decipherment, which generally are based on some combination of assuming Cypriote Syllabic or Linear B values, proposing a language based on historical probability, observation of character frequencies, sequence repetition, text layout, and archaeological context. Hiller (1985) presents a thorough treatment of the various efforts; only Faucounau (2007) actively continues.

It is possible in some cases to make reasonable inferences about the content of an inscription based on observation of the sign patterns, formatting, and context (object, archaeological) of the inscription. For example, there are the five inscribed cylinders, all found in the same context at Kalavassos–*Ayios Dhimitrios*. Masson suggests that they were foundation deposits, based on a comparison of their form to cylindrical Mesopotamian building deposits and the observation that the first line of each inscription begins with the same word, which Masson has interpreted as indicative of formulaic dedications (Masson 1983, 139). Smith proposes instead that the cylinders had an administrative function and bases her argument on reevaluations of the comparanda and the archaeological context and exact observation of the traces of writing (Smith 2002, 21–25). She demonstrates that Masson had missed the fact that some of the texts were palimpsests and that her "formulas" were based on reconstructions and normalizations of signs. Both arguments demonstrate how much can be extracted by a holistic approach to interpreting the texts; Smith's counterargument illustrates the necessity of firsthand examination or, at the very least, accurate representations of the texts.

The (Foreseeable) Future of Cypro-Minoan Studies

Even lacking new discoveries, Cypro-Minoan research is making positive and significant headway in two directions: refining the signary and vocabulary and contextualizing Cypro-Minoan writing.

As discussed earlier, the signary published by Emilia Masson needs to be updated and annotated, and its tripartite division should be scrutinized and probably eliminated. Ferrara has taken on the challenge of establishing a revised corpus; the forthcoming book based on her 2005 dissertation will likely replace Masson's 1974 signary as the standard reference. The detailed observations that form the basis of Ferrara's corpus will, in turn, need to be evaluated. In addition, close reexaminations of the inscriptions are leading to revised vocabulary lists and observations about sign patterns and syntax.

More eyes looking at the original texts are resulting in increasingly nuanced observations about the different writing styles and perhaps even the identification of individual hands. Smith has demonstrated that the identification of multiple writing traditions has important implications for our understanding of the adoption and transmission of Cypro-Minoan (2003). Ferrara's identification of hands in the corpus of Enkomi clay balls has great significance for discussions of scribal organization, literacy, and especially the Late Cypriote IIC/IIIA transition (Ferrara 2005, 173–78). The groundbreaking paths of these two studies need to be extended.

The contexts of writing on Cyprus need and can be investigated more thoroughly. Smith's restudy of the cylinders from Kalavassos–*Ayios Dhimitrios* and Hirschfeld's continuing studies of potmarks have already been mentioned. A third example is Ferrara's reexamination of the inscribed Kition ivories, in which equal attention is paid to inscription, object, and archaeological context, leading to a preliminary understanding of the group's functions and the role of its inscriptions (Ferrara 2005, 156–60).

On a broader scale, the role of Cypro-Minoan within the increasingly broad spectrum of the excavated Cypriote Late Bronze Age landscape requires evaluation. It is gradually becoming possible to evaluate the use of Cypro-Minoan in terms of models of hierarchical systems within a valley system, within a region, and between regions.

Finally, the forms and contexts of Cypro-Minoan writing can already and should be more thoroughly placed within the greater context of contemporary writing and administrative systems in the Aegean, the Levant, and Egypt.

In summary, the groundwork is currently being laid for a methodologically sound presentation of the evidence for Cypriote Bronze Age writing. The discovery of an archive is a desideratum, but in the meantime it is still possible to make substantive progress.

BIBLIOGRAPHY

Casson, Stanley. 1937. "The Cypriot Script." In *Ancient Cyprus: Its Art and Archaeology,* 72–109. London: Methuen.

Cross, Frank M., and Lawrence E. Stager. 2006. "Cypro-Minoan Inscriptions Found in Ashkelon." *IEJ* 56(2): 129–59.

Daniel, John Franklin. 1941. "Prolegomena to the Cypro-Minoan Script." *AJA* 45: 249–82.

Evans, Arthur J. 1909. *Scripta Minoa: The Written Documents of Minoan Crete, with Special Reference to the Archives of Knossos,* vol. 1. Oxford: Clarendon.

Faucounau, Jean. 2007. *Les inscriptions chypro-minoénnes.* Paris: L'Harmattan.

Ferrara, Sylvia. 2005. An Interdisciplinary Approach to the Cypro-Minoan Script. PhD diss., University College London.

Godart, Louis, and Anna Sacconi. 1979. "La plus ancienne tablette d'Enkomi et le Linéaire A." In *Acts of the International Archaeological Symposium: The Relations between Cyprus and Crete, ca. 2000–500 B.C.,* ed. Vassos Karageorghis, 128–33. Nicosia: Department of Antiquities, Cyprus.

Hiller, Stefan. 1985. "Die kyprominoische Schriftsysteme." *AfO* 20: 61–93.

Hirschfeld, Nicolle. 1993. "Incised Marks (Post-firing) on Aegean Wares." In *Wace and Blegen,* 311–18.

———. 2007. "'Cypro-Minoan' beyond the Island." Annual Meetings of the American Schools of Oriental Research (ASOR), San Diego, November 16, 2007 (2007 Annual Meeting Abstract Book, 56–57).

Masson, Emilia. 1974. *Cyprominoica. Répertoires: Documents de Ras Shamra. Essais d'Interpretation.* SIMA 31(2). Gothenburg: Åström.

———. 1983. "Premiers documents chypro-minoens du site Kalavasos–Ayios Dhimitrios." *RDAC:* 131–41.

———. 2007. "Cypro-Minoan Scripts." In *A History of Ancient Greek from the Beginnings to Late Antiquity,* ed. Anastassios-Fivos Christidis, 235–38. New York: Cambridge University Press.

Olivier, Jean-Pierre. 2007. *Edition holistique des textes chypro-minoens.* Biblioteca di "Pasiphae" VI. Rome: Fabrizio Serra.

Palaima, Thomas G. 1989. "Cypro-Minoan Scripts: Problems of Historical Context." In *Problems in Decipherment,* ed. Y. Duhoux, T. G. Palaima, and J. Bennett, 121–87. Bibliothèque des Cahiers de l'Institut de Linguistique de Louvain 49. Louvain-la-Neuve, Belgium: Peeters.

————. 2005. *The Triple Invention of Writing in Cyprus and Written Sources for Cypriote History.* Fourteenth Annual Lecture in memory of Constantine Leventis, November 6, 2004. Nicosia: Leventis Foundation.

Smith, Joanna. 2002. "Problems and Prospects in the Study of Script and Seal Use on Cyprus in the Bronze and Iron Ages." In *Script and Seal Use on Cyprus in the Bronze and Iron Ages,* ed. Joanna Smith, 1–47. AIA Colloquia and Conference Papers 4. Boston: Archaeological Institute of America.

————. 2003. "Writing Styles in Clay of the Eastern Mediterranean Late Bronze Age." In *PLOES,* 277–89.

Material Crafts

CHAPTER 29

MATERIALS AND INDUSTRIES

DONIERT EVELY

GREECE is adequately endowed with stones (nonprecious), clays, timber, and plant products; metals are somewhat more localized, indeed effectively lacking in Crete (Dickinson 1994, 23–29; Higgins and Higgins 1996; Rackham and Moody 1996). Overseas contacts, thus, were always crucial; 'trade networks' catered to the material needs in the more complex societies and developed periods but arguably existed in less centralized forms long before (Laffineur and Greco 2005). The roots of such procurement and the fundamentals of all crafts utilizing local products reach down into the Neolithic period; the utilization of obsidian is a clear case, but, as is becoming ever more apparent, so is metalworking. The factors behind increased use and acquisition/dissemination of materials, skills, and knowledge have varied; the establishment in EB I/II of settlements with Cycladic links on the north coast of Crete and the east seaboard of the mainland is quite possibly how the early exploitation of copper/bronze and silver/lead was carried forward; the later Minoan 'colonies' on the Asia Minor coastline could have tapped into the resources of the hinterland or existing trade routes—the lack of a translator knowing 'Minoan' is referred to in the tin trade. The same root cause is true for Mycenaean contacts with Italy.

'Tribute scenes' involving Aegean peoples and copies of their textiles, both depicted in New Kingdom Egyptian tombs (Barber 1991, 338–51; Dziobeck 1994; Evely 1999, 137), demonstrate how raw materials and finished goods circulated in more complicated times. Craftsmen, too, may have traveled, as the Minoanizing frescoes at the Hyksos city of Avaris or at Alalakh both arguably reveal (Niemeier and Niemeier 1998). The Uluburun shipwreck (of ca. 1300 BC) illustrates actual transportation of a wide range of exotics and valuables of a decidedly international flavor (Bass 1986, 1991; Pulak 1988); the contemporary Gelidonya wreck carried a less extensive but still expensive cargo of metals (Bass 1967). Alongside physical items went ideas and words: A Minoan (Keftiu) incantation against sickness is referred to in Egypt (Kyriakidis 2002, 213–16).

Emporia, in the Aegaeum series, has plenty of discussion on matters mercantile, overseas contacts, and the movement of materials (Laffineur and Greco 2005). Localized trading exists in all periods (e.g., in LBA, andesite from Aegina [Runnels and Evely 1992]; lapis lacedaemonius from near Sparta [Warren 1969, 132–33]).

Investigation into the workings of crafts is extensive; far less research is done on the individual tools, assembled toolkits, and their particular usage. Evely has attempted an overview for Minoan Crete (Evely 1993 and 2000); Tournavitou writes on the Mainland (Tournavitou 1988, 1997); and numerous other accounts exist for this or that tool type (note Catling 1964, for Cyprus as a good example). An exception to this empirical approach is made for obsidian and ground stone tools in Carter's work: Based on a thorough study of the data, the deductions are constantly given a social perspective (Carter 1994, 1998, 2004).

Few archaeologists are, or know, skilled craftsmen. Mental efforts and library reading certainly help comprehension, but ultimately ideas need to be tested practically. Experimental archaeology is time consuming and often expensive: Skilled specialists may work with societies outside the Aegean BA time frame. Recent work that applies to Bronze Age Greece includes Minoan potters' wheels and kilns, Mycenaean ceramics, Minoan crucibles, Aegean plaster production and painting, Minoan faience and glasswork, Minoan obsidian blades, and Mycenaean ship construction.

Insofar as one can generalize, recent academic tendencies (e.g., Day and Doonan 2007), while still producing and building on fundamental typologies and categories, are increasingly concerned with the human 'why' rather than the material 'how' or 'what.'

Several crafts made extensive and fundamental use of fire and/or heat in the transformation of their raw materials into finished products: metalworking, pottery making, and the production of faience and glass items.

The working of *metals* is rooted in the later Neolithic into EB I (e.g., Petras, Crete, and Attica [Kakavoianni 2005; Papadatos 2007; Zachos 2007]). Exploitation of these practically useful and socially desirable materials continued most spectacularly where and when the elites could organize matters. Literature detailing the range, typology, and fortunes of object types is extensive (e.g., Branigan 1974; the *Praehistorische Bronzefunde* series); more insights are continually being gained through excavation (e.g., Palaikastro, Crete: Hemingway 1996, 213–52).

For *metals of utilitarian usage* (copper/bronze), the evolutionary model of their discovery and usage is as follows: native copper/simple ores > arsenical copper > tin bronze, with the superior qualities given by each subsequent alloying process leading to its preferment. This still has some essential truth in it, as copper items that contain arsenic exist before the widespread adoption of tin bronzes. Recent work has suggested that at least some arsenical coppers were produced deliberately (Doonan, Day, and Dimopoulou-Rethemiotaki 2007, 111–13) by adding an arsenic-rich mineral in the smelting process (as opposed to using ores that contained arsenic minerals naturally) in full cognizance, sooner or later, that a more useful product resulted. The deliberateness of later alloying techniques with tin (and at times lead) is clear. Such 'advances' are not necessarily uniformly adopted everywhere and at the same time: Neopalatial products from Palaikastro (east Crete) have a larger presence of arsenic (perhaps from a greater recycling of earlier metal pieces) than do those at Knossos, where tin was more readily available (Evely and Stos 2004, 269–71). One cannot be sure that practical concerns were always uppermost in determining choices or habits.

In the EBA (3500–2000 BC), copper and its arsenical version were used mostly for a range of relatively small and simple objects: Some are tools, while others have to do with demonstrations of power and personal appearance (see Evely 2000, 323–97 generally for Crete). The importance of the Cyclades in the spread of these metals and their working has been emerging for a while. In the islands themselves, sites employing varying metal-extracting techniques are known from Kythnos, Syros, and Seriphos among others, and where specific surveys have been carried out (e.g., Kythnos: Bassiakos and Philaniotou 2007), their numbers grow. Along the eastern seaboard of Greece (at Manika and Aghios Kosmas) and the north coast of Crete (Aghia Photia and Chrysokamino to the east; Gournes and Poros from the Herakleion area at the center), sites that look to have deliberate connections with the Cyclades, as early as EB I and II, have been found (Sampson 1988; Mylonas 1959; Davaras and Betancourt 2004; Betancourt 2007; Catapotis and Bassiakos 2007; Galanaki forthcoming; Dimopoulou-Rethemiotaki, Wilson, and Day 2007): metalworking approaches that were part of the cultural assemblage of these newcomers are observable.

Smelting could be undertaken in tapering cylinders of clay, aerated by natural breezes and drafts from bellows (figure 29.1; Bassiakos and Philaniotou 2007, 46; Betancourt 2007, 63; Catapotis and Bassiakos 2007, 76). Fluxes are likely to have been a regular addition to the ore and fuel charge: calc-ferrous at Chrysokamino, Crete. The metals produced sank to the base, where they could have been tapped or allowed to collect in a scoop. Some, trapped as prills in the slags produced, were released by pounding with stone hammers or were even ground out. The subsequent melting and casting processes are better represented: Crucibles are essentially clay bowls on low stems, pierced through to permit a stick, say, to be inserted to aid manipulation (e.g., Betancourt and Muhly 2007); tongs or paired withies as depicted in Egyptian scenes were needed, too. The ceramic technology to make such—and indeed the furnaces, bellow's nozzles, and tuyères—was developed in tandem with the alloying and so on. Here is an early example of one craft's awareness of and indebtedness to another: namely the production of ceramic cooking utensils that also had to withstand thermal shocks.

Casting processes are simple: The existence of an open or single-piece mold of stone or clay is witnessed in the sorts of objects produced, as well as by actual surviving items. The recovery of a two-piece mold of copper in an apparently EM context at Vasiliki suggests that this comprehension may be skewed and oversimplistic (Evely 2000, 358). Such molds, as well as the lost-wax and sand-casting procedures (Fri 2007, 70–72), were made more use of in subsequent phases (MB and LB).

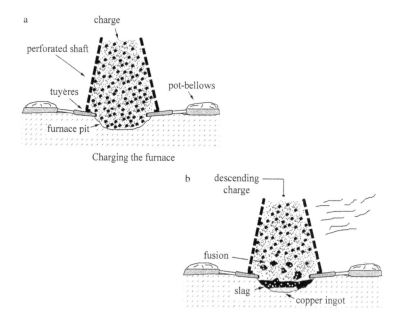

Charging the furnace

The smelting operation in progress

Figure 29.1. Smelting copper at Chrysokamino, Pre-palatial Crete: (a) and (b) the smelt; (c) preparing the furnace (all courtesy of the copyright of Oxbow; Day and Doonan, eds., 2007; [a] and [b] by M. Catapotis, [c] drawing by L. Brock, courtesy of P. Betancourt).

Following the millennium-long development of the EBA, a crucial stage was reached with the rise of the First or Old Palaces on Crete (ca. 2000–1700 BC). This watershed applies to most crafts—on Crete and through it the rest of the Aegean—but can seldom be properly understood. The social changes and stimuli operating seem to have allowed the mastering, within the three centuries involved, of most of the techniques that any craft required; of course, both fashions and the products alter thereafter. The more significant developments were the wider exploitation of metal sources within (e.g., Lavrion) and without (e.g., Cyprus for copper; tin via the Near East) the Balkans and an increased movement of prepared metals as ingots as opposed to raw ores. Changes in foundry furnishings also occur, if gradually: hemispherical crucibles, at first with a groove on the underside to facilitate handling, improved bellows, tuyères, and so on (Crete: Blitzer 1995, 500–508; Evely forthcoming); a full range of mold types; and the beginning of wider adoption of tin bronze. Now, too, the Minoans first established a network of overseas settlements to secure access to all sorts of materials (Dickinson 1994, 243).

The role of Lead Isotope analysis in establishing the provenance of copper (and silver/lead) has proven vital (Gale and Stos-Gale 2002); chemical analysis of the individual elements within the makeup of an item provides other insights. As with all such scientific advances, initial hopes will always be tempered as the complexities of realities become appreciated (e.g., tin isotopes: Gillis et al. 2003).

As in other crafts, all such fundamental matters become greatly intensified within the time of the so-called Second or New Palaces on Crete (1700–1425 BC). Increasingly, the mainland sphere (the Peloponnese and central Greece at least) borrows the trappings of Minoan finery and knowhow, either directly or through the Cyclades. Around 1450 BC the mainlanders emerge as the dominant force within the Aegean: Crete remains an integral part of this until the loss of the final palaces there by 1300 BC, after which the island's role declines. Now and in the ultimate Postpalatial phase (down to 1050 BC), a still wider search for metal sources deserves attention: Copper from Sardinia is part of the new Mycenaean interest in the West, while Cypriot mines are tapped more than ever before (Gale and Stos-Gale 2002). Aegean groups begin to settle and roam the east Mediterranean, some in the guise of the Sea Peoples.

The replacement of copper and bronze by *iron* is a complex issue and still not well understood. Present thinking can be summarized thus: The standard model (Snodgrass 1980) sees 12th-century BC shortages of tin leading to a growing appreciation of iron, whose ores were in any event more widely available. This postulated lack of bronze is questioned. Sherratt (1994) argues that Cypriot entrepreneurs began to market iron, which can be regularly produced in small quantities as a byproduct in copper smelting. Haarer (2001) sees a deliberate development from a still broader, Near Eastern use of iron in the Bronze Age.

For *precious metals* (gold and silver), the cupellation of silver and lead late in the Neolithic and the start of the EB (see earlier) marks a significant discovery beyond what scholarship had earlier deemed likely. Lead Isotope work has assisted with the provenancing of silver, but little yet can be done with gold—and may never be possible, given its ready reuse and mixing. Otherwise, advances are mostly in the realm of technical appreciation, for instance, the manufacture and use of granulation (Politis 2001).

The increasing sophistication and levels of skills within the EBA have long been appreciated (e.g., an early reliance on inserting, folding, and twisting as the means of assemblage starts to give way by EB III to fusing and soldering inasmuch as the development of colloid hard solder allows great subtlety of handling). By MB in Crete, all of the required processes were in place; thereafter, advances were again more in the nature of design and complexity in assembling component parts. The creation of the gold bezel rings (requiring both three-piece and lost-wax molds;

chasing and engraving; at times inlaying) demonstrates the mastery attained. Comprehension of their manufacture has been aided by the recent use of X-ray photographic techniques and ultrasound (Müller 2003a, 147–50; 2003b, 475–81). In contrast, the gold foil beads of the LB are made in molds in numbers that speak almost of mass production (Boulotis 2000). The exploitation of niello (Boss and Laffineur 1997) recalls the interest in developing manufactured compounds, elsewhere most readily seen in faience/Egyptian blue.

The handling of fine sheet, foils, granules, and wires was developed particularly by this side of metalworking (Evely 2000, 401–44 generally for Crete), but developments ran broadly in parallel with the utilitarian, which is not surprising as the skills of each are frequently found combined on the one object (swords in particular).

In *ceramics,* interest has focused mostly upon provenance/trade and the technology of manufacture (Evely 2000, 259–322); deductions made from these have permitted speculation on social dimensions. Crucial to all has been the expansion of fabric analyses, departing somewhat from the strictly chemical-based approaches in favor of categorizing the physical makeup and components of the paste (see much of the work by Day, e.g., Wilson and Day 2000). Typical conclusions so reached have indicated Early Neolithic sites outside Knossos in the Mirabello area (Tomkins and Day 2001) and allowed the appreciation of the extensive degree of local production in EM Crete and accompanying movement of vessels within the island (Whitelaw et al. 1997). Quite subtle conclusions are possible now as the reference collections expand.

Information is also obtainable on and through manufacturing techniques. The recognition of an unusual combination of different clays for different parts of the body in some Mesara EM wares not only demonstrates the existence of a local tradition well removed from, say, that of contemporary Knossos but also shows the strength or conservatism that may operate regionally (Todaro, pers. comm.). In turn, the identification of such regional patterns (a combination of clay, manufacture, shapes, and decorative finishing) has been offered as a potential indicator of the growth of social identities, groupings, and even 'states' (Cadogan 1994; Knappett 1997). Xeroradiography and kindred techniques help reveal how a vase was formed (Müller 2003a, 150–51; the research project of Berg at Manchester University): The focus here is often on questions of hand- versus wheel-made pieces. As well as illuminating local traditions again, potential insights are offered into matters such as the adoption of the wheel. Were such, for example, taken up first and most fully under the stimulus of elite groups? Experiments assist greatly: The physical form and capabilities of the Minoan wheel are now better appreciated (figure 29.2; Evely et al. 2008), and kiln firings, too, help comprehension of the controlling of temperature and atmosphere critical to such as the mottled Vasiliki and Urfinis wares of the EB and the Kamares pottery of MM times (unpublished experiments by both Moody and Politis on Crete).

In the EB period, pots were handmade: Leaves, basketry mats, and clay discs provided the moveable bases for the smaller and medium vessels, as imprints on their bases show. Coil production is the approach most commonly recognized, though slab and paddle-and-anvil techniques sometimes occur. An interest in

Figure 29.2. Experiments with a Minoan potter's wheel (courtesy of the author).

decoration—in paint (contrasting with the fabric's color) and burnishing—is manifest from the start; in this both regionalism and an overarching awareness on a broader scale are noted (Betancourt 1985; Wilson and Day 1994; Momigliano 2007). Firing techniques were controlled and sophisticated enough to produce the Vasiliki and Urfinis wares, as were others when a reducing atmosphere and gray finish were desired. These achievements all argue for the existence of kilns proper, which is no surprise, given what metallurgists did regularly in smelting furnaces. In early MM times this promising start was taken further on Crete, where the best of the Kamares wares combine exquisite control of the fabric to produce eggshell thin wares, of a wide range of pigments and their application in complex patterns, and of the controlled kiln firing, which produced the semiglaze effects in the black iron-rich background coloration (Evely 2000, 291; Faber et al. 2002). The wheel, too, now gains ground, but coils were now and later always used for larger vessels. The LB period sees the decorative aspect reach its zenith first on Crete and then in the hands of the mainland Greeks, whose technical skills produced harder-fired fabrics. The kiln types evolve: The short-lived, channeled kiln of Neopalatial Crete is replaced by the updraft version of probable mainland development (Evely 2000, 300–11). Unlike many crafts, ceramics was not especially depressed by the demise of the palace-centered lifestyles at the end of the BA (less time was spent in decoration), a fact that demonstrates both its central role and widely dispersed distribution.

For the last of this pyrotechnical trio, namely *faience* and *glassmaking,* research has built on the like of Foster's account (1979), largely of late concentrating on faience. As well as seeking to analyze and define more accurately the composition of cores (and thus distinguish between different approaches and times), effort has gone into elucidating possible manufacturing techniques by using analytical and macroscopic avenues (Panagiotaki 2005). Insights so obtained have guided choices of raw materials and preparation procedures in experimental work (Sklavenitis 2007).

A 'high-tech' pair of crafts (Evely 2000, 445–69), that of faience, was introduced first into the Aegean from the Near East in the EBA: only small pieces, often simple jewelry, were first manufactured. The Minoans made the most of this in the MM and early LM periods by extending the polychrome potentials. Blue frit (Egyptian blue), a material intermediate between faience and glass, is an example of a purely synthetic substance. (The short-lived trial in EM Crete with the 'white pieces' appears to be a comparable venture into synthetic substances: Krzyszkowska 2005, 72–74.) Glasses (and related enamels) were more to mainland tastes and a later development. At present it is not clear whether glass was itself manufactured in the Aegean as opposed to being imported in ingot form for remelting.

Both substances rely first on a proportional preparation of the ingredients, frequently on molding techniques and then the application of heat. The items produced in faience in MB and LB times were often still small in size but intended for inlay on a grand scale (e.g., the Town Mosaic of Knossos); such may closely recall the products of ivory/bone working. Larger composite pieces in the round, such as the Snake Goddesses from Knossos, can also share features of concept and preparation with that same craft. The mold-made glass beads of the LBA are the equivalent of the gold-foil ones mentioned earlier: every bit as much production on the grand scale. Whether glass vessels were made in the Aegean is uncertain.

As a postscript come *plasters* and *frescoes.* The role of fires and furnaces is here limited to the initial production of the raw material, which when slaked makes the basic plaster. Earlier art-historical approaches always considered the workings of the societies depicted in them, but they have now been linked to scientific analyses of the pigments and the actual makeup of the plaster (Cameron 1975; Evely 1999, 2000; Morgan 2005; Brysbaert 2009). The recovery of Minoan-style/executed frescoes in the Near East and Egypt have opened up the possibilities of traveling/loaned craftsmen, a phenomenon that certainly occurred in the Near East (Bloedow 1997; Niemeier and Niemeier 1998, 2000; Boulotis 2000).

Plasters (of mud) were well exploited in the Neolithic period, and this basic use was never lost in the Aegean. Within the EBA, the earliest lime plaster is adulterated with clays and coarser aggregates; decoration is simple in range and manner. The next step is associated with the palatial structures on Crete; gradually improving in the lime percentage, by the Neopalatial era, plaster regularly attains at least a 90% level in lime (Brysbaert 2004; Jones 2005). Similar plasters may be used from floor to ceiling (with especially durable admixtures containing small pebbles developed for floors): All may be painted, and some can incorporate low relief work. Methods of application (pegs, trowels, floats, and burnishing tools) and of the layout of the decorative techniques (strings, rulers, sketches in ink or with a point) are often detectable (Evely 2000, 471–84).

At its zenith between 1700–1500 BC, fresco painting was undertaken all over the Aegean and attained exquisite levels within the elite buildings. Akrotiri, on Thera, is proving the best source for understanding all aspects of this craft, as well as being a constant source of visual pleasure (Morgan 1988; Sherratt 2000). Though the 'buon fresco' technique is well attested from the malleable state of the plaster, 'secco fresco' was also likely known; indeed, the two can be found on the same wall. The pigments were prepared from naturally occurring soils (many involving iron compounds), with blues alone being a synthetic compound; mixing gave a wide range of hues. The overall effects are to encompass the viewer in a total visual effect; stories are being referred to (social events; scenes set in the natural world)—it is never just wallpaper. With the loss of such patronage, matters reverted fairly swiftly to fundamental and practical standards of lime and mud plasters.

Working in stone followed two main and distinct paths. The first, not discussed here, is concerned with architecture and engineering, some of which works were on a monumental scale—tombs, fortifications, and aspects of land reclamation and water control (Knauss 2005; Palyvou 2005). Occasional pieces of associated ornament are also on the large size. Otherwise, the two main focuses are smaller items: stone vases and again seal stones and jewelry elements. In both cases, scholarship has concentrated mostly on questions of technology and categorization, though work by Bevan and Krzyszkowska introduces the social, too (2007 and 2005, respectively).

Stone vases have a link to the Neolithic past (Devetzi 2005). The traditions of the EBA emerged most strongly on both the Cyclades and Crete, with an initial emphasis on a relatively small size. On Crete, the toolkit first included chisels, blades, saws, hammers, and abrasives, and only later did drilling become a standard and important practice (Evely 1993, 172–94 generally). Once conversant, the Minoans produced works of a startling quality and in quantity; making use of imported materials alongside native ones, they practiced their craft at many sites, combining appreciations of form, color, and patterning every bit as complex as those seen in ceramics (Warren 1969). The relief vases contain valuable renditions of events of daily and ritual nature/occurrence (Warren 1969, 174–81). With the emergence of the mainlanders in the LBA, this craft largely went into recession. Vases continued to be made—some indeed elegant and ornate (Sakellarakis 1976). However, the range of products collapsed; softer stones were again employed for a while. This pattern indisputably reveals how much an 'elite' craft this had become and in this case especially connected with Minoan Crete.

Seal stones are valuable evidence today for understanding spheres such as administration and economy, whose role in the past was more personal but also connected with status. Neolithic stamps (pintaderas) belong to the peripheries of the Aegean and do not obviously connect with what arises in the EBA. At that time the mainland and Crete pursue different trajectories, but both produce complex pieces of aesthetic merit (Krzyszkowska 2005). Cretan evidence is far fuller and seems to cover a wider range of materials. Common to both are soft stones (wood, too, may be assumed); the mainland has clay in addition, while Crete utilizes bone, hippo ivory, and the 'white pieces' (see earlier). Knives, burins, and handheld drills are the basic toolkit (Evely 1993, 146–71 generally). By MM II, hard semiprecious stones are worked alongside the softer; new tools (bow-driven drills and cutting wheels; emery abrasives) were the secret of these often bravura treatments in miniature. Numerous styles are recognized, and attempts to divide the corpus up, à la Beazley, abound (e.g., Boardman 1970; Yule 1980; Betts 1981; Younger 1983). The mainland adopted all of this early in the LBA, though eschewing the softer stones at first. After LB IIIA, a shift occurs in both regions, perhaps again indicating the prime position of Crete in this craft. New Cretan production is limited, while the mainland adopts softer materials to satisfy its still considerable need for seals. The eventual demise of the palaces left only older pieces in circulation, sometimes for centuries.

Ivory/bone and *shell* working is a long-lived craft whose Neolithic antecedents are largely domestic in nature but also involved the decorative (figurines). Monographs by Poursat, Sakellarakis, and Krzyszkowska cover many aspects of BA typology, manufacture, and development, both utilitarian and ornamental (1977, 1979, 1990, respectively). Experiments on the toolkit have been made by Evely (1992, 1993). Since ivory was always imported, it serves as another indicator of trade and contacts. The craft as a whole acts as a mirror for comparable work in wood and has ties, too, with stone working on a smaller scale.

In addition, EBA production involves small-size pieces. The Cyclades continued in particular to exploit a source of Spondylus shell; the Minoans worked in all classes (note that of the ivories, only hippo is known at first: Krzyszkowska 1988) and produced mainly seals outside the domestic range of items (Evely 1993, 219–56; 2005). As metal tools became more common, the potential for small-scale inlay, as well as pieces in the round (figurines), was advanced in MM Crete (local preferences/availabilities are evident: Malia makes more use of shell than Knossos). Saws, chisels, blades, drills, and abrasives have all left their traces. With the Neopalatial era and the regular availability of the larger elephant ivory tusks, the quantity and physical size both increased. The Minoan composite figurines are justly praiseworthy: The Palaikastro 'kouros,' with its combination of hippo ivory with serpentine, rock crystal, gold, a blue pigment, and probably wood, is a prime example (MacGillivray, Driessen, and Sackett 2005). Indeed, this admixture with other substances (faience, silver, and other stones and pigments are also represented) is a hallmark of the craft now. A craftsman's house at Knossos yields a rounded picture of the production sequences (Evely 1992).

The mainlanders continue much of this in the LB (e.g., Tournavitou 1995, 123–206); figurines drop from the repertoire, but other items were developed (e.g., mirror handles). Inlaid furniture is a favorite. Their aesthetic style alters (as is evident in pottery and frescoes, too), with a stiffer, more grandiose, and even overly ornate feel prevailing. Certain materials and object types of local origin circulate in the Aegean now—often utilitarian in character: The possible spatula made of red-deer antler can be placed alongside the tripod mortars of volcanic stone and the clay 'spool.'

The remaining crafts can be categorized as perishables. Inevitably, only rather indirect lines of inquiry now exist. For *woodworking,* any evidence of major concerns such as shipbuilding will come only from shipwrecks (Uluburun, for example), though the recent discovery of shipsheds in Herakleion may add ancillary details. Here, too, experimental work is adding a further dimension (Kamarinou and Baika 2005). Though the Linear B tablets record wide and subtle appreciation of different timbers and their uses, only Thera regularly provides examples (in negative, by means of plaster casts) of actual furniture (beds, stools, and such: Speciale 2000; Polychronakou-Sgouritsa 2001). Work on a smaller scale can be more directly surmised from such as ivory inlay work; the toolkit is well represented with some impressive pieces in recovered bronze, such as the two-man saws (Evely 2000, 528–37).

Perfumes are served slightly better. A considerable body of receptacles for burning aromatics, of largely later MBA and LBA date, has been collected (Georgiou 1980). Two other avenues exist; the first concerns references in Linear B tablets from Crete and the mainland (Knossos and Pylos), which detail aspects of land usage and the harvest size expected, and also lists of ingredients that could be so utilized (Enegren 2000, 33–34; Shelmerdine 1985). The second approach is through analytical archaeology (organic residue, still a much-debated process): From the cemetery of LM Armenoi, traces of an oil allegedly derived from iris was recovered from fireboxes, themselves decorated with iris flowers (Tzedakis and Martlew 1999).

Finally come *textiles.* Well enough served as this topic is, if indirectly, by the evidence of frescoes, by innumerable loomweights of clay, and occasionally by other weaving apparatus (also by experimental work: Andersson and Nosch 2003), yet nothing much else remains (Evely 2000, 485–510; Tzachili 2005). Rather it is the unraveling of the tablets' cryptic listings by Linear B specialists that represents a triumph, thereby revealing the organization of the breeding of sheep, the collection of their wool, and its subsequent transformation at the hands of labor forces and specialists, usually supported on rations (Killen 1964). The evidence is most extensive for the period of mainland control at Knossos (1425–1350 BC): The social aspects of the labor force, the systems of exploitation, and the degree of control exerted by the elite are remarkably apparent.

As has been touched upon throughout, the drawing out of social insights has been a major concern of recent research. The evidence presented by Linear B assists greatly in this endeavor (*Documents in Mycenaean Greek,* new edition forthcoming); it encompasses, most obviously, simple names of craftsmen (e.g., kowirowoko: seal engravers; kuwanowokoi: glassworkers), products (erepatejo: of ivory; eteja: a type of oil; topeza: a table), and the system that ran it all (tarasija: the standard work cycle). The teasing out from the tablets of such sets of information as the textile production at Knossos or the bronze working and perfume making at Pylos represent major achievements (also Shelmerdine 1987). Outside this window of literacy, the view of necessity remains stubbornly obscured. The degree to which one now ventures into the realms of supposition, analogy, and metaphor to seek explanations will depend on the individual scholar's proclivities and character.

BIBLIOGRAPHY

Andersson, Eva, and Marie-Louise B. Nosch. 2003. "With a Little Help from My Friends: Investigating Mycenaean Textiles with Help from Scandinavian Experimental Archaeology." In *METRON*, 197–205.

Barber, Elizabeth J. W. 1991. *Prehistoric Textiles: The Development of Cloth in the Neolithic and Bronze Ages, with Special Reference to the Aegean*. Princeton: Princeton University Press.

Bass, George F. 1967. *Cape Gelidonya: A Bronze Age Shipwreck*. Transactions of the American Philosophical Society, n.s., 57, part 8. Philadelphia: American Philosophical Society.

———. 1986. "A Bronze Age Shipwreck at Ulu Burun (Kas): 1984 Campaign." *AJA* 90(3): 269–96.

———. 1991. "Evidence of Trade from Bronze Age Shipwrecks." In *Bronze Age Trade*, 69–82.

Bassiakos, Yannis, and Olda Philaniotou. 2007. "Early Copper Production on Kythnos: Archaeological Evidence and Analytical Approaches to the Reconstruction of Metallurgical Process." In *Metallurgy in the Early Bronze Age Aegean*, ed. Peter M. Day and Roger C. P. Doonan, 19–56. Sheffield Studies in Aegean Archaeology 7. Oxford: Oxbow.

Betancourt, Philip P. 1985. *The History of Minoan Pottery*. Princeton: Princeton University Press.

———. 2007. "The Final Neolithic to Early Minoan III Metallurgy Site at Chrysokamino, Crete." In *Metallurgy in the Early Bronze Age Aegean*, ed. Peter M. Day and Roger C. P. Doonan, 57–67. Sheffield Studies in Aegean Archaeology 7. Oxford: Oxbow.

———, and James D. Muhly. 2007. "The Crucibles from the Aghia Photia Cemetery." In *Metallurgy in the Early Bronze Age Aegean*, ed. Peter M. Day and Roger C. P. Doonan, 146–53. Sheffield Studies in Aegean Archaeology 7. Oxford: Oxbow.

Betts, John H. 1981. "The 'Jasper Lion Master': Some Principles of Establishing LM/LH Workshops and Artists." In *Studien zur minoischen und helladischen Glyptik*, ed. Wolf-Dietrich Niemeier, 1–16. *CMS* Beiheft 1. Berlin: Mann.

Bevan, Andrew. 2007. *Stone Vessels and Values in the Bronze Age Mediterranean*. New York: Cambridge University Press.

Blitzer, Harriet. 1995. "Minoan Implements and Industries." In *Kommos I, The Kommos Region and Houses of the Minoan Town*. Part 1, *The Kommos Region, Ecology, and Minoan Industries*, ed. Joseph W. Shaw and Maria C. Shaw, 403–535. Princeton: Princeton University Press.

Bloedow, Edmund F. 1997. "Itinerant Craftsmen and Trade in the Aegean Bronze Age." In *TEXNH*, 439–47.

Boardman, John. 1970. *Greek Gems and Finger Rings: Early Bronze Age to Late Classical*. London: Thames and Hudson.

Boss, Martin, and Robert Laffineur. 1997. "Mycenaean Metal Inlay: A Technique in Context." In *TEXNH*, 191–98.

Boulotis, Christos. 2000. "Travelling Fresco Painters in the Aegean Bronze Age: The Diffusion Patterns of a Prestigious Art." In *Wall Paintings of Thera*, 844–58.

Branigan, Keith. 1974. *Aegean Metalwork of the Early and Middle Bronze Age*. Oxford: Clarendon.

Brysbaert, Ann. 2004. Technology and Social Agency in Bronze Age Aegean and Eastern Mediterranean Painted Plaster. PhD diss., University of Glasgow.

———. 2009. *The Power of Technology in the Bronze Age Eastern Mediterranean: The Case of the Painted Plaster*. Monographs in Mediterranean Archaeology 12. London: Equinox.

Cadogan, Gerald. 1994. "An Old Palace Period Knossos State?" In *Labyrinth of History*, 57–68.

Cameron, Mark A. S. 1975. A General Study of Minoan Frescoes, with Particular Reference to Unpublished Wall Paintings from Knossos. PhD diss., University of Newcastle-upon-Tyne.

Carter, Tristan. 1994. "Southern Aegean Fashion Victims: An Overlooked Aspect of Early Bronze Age Burial Practices." In *Stories in Stone*, ed. Nick Ashton and Andrew David, 127–44, Occasional Paper 4. London: Lithics Study Society.

———. 1998. "Reverberations of the International Spirit: Thoughts upon 'Cycladica' in the Mesara." In *Cemetery and Society in the Aegean Bronze Age*, ed. Keith Branigan, 59–77. Sheffield Studies in Aegean Archaeology 1. Sheffield: Sheffield Academic Press.

———. 2004. "Transformative Processes in Liminal Spaces: Crafts as Ritual Action in the Throne Room Area." In *Knossos: Palace, City, State: Proceedings of the Conference in Herakleion organised by the British School at Athens and the 23rd Ephoreia of Prehistoric and Classical Antiquities of Herakleion, in November 2000, for the Centenary of Sir Arthur Evans's Excavations at Knossos*, eds. Gerald Cadogan, Eleni Hatzaki, and Adonis Vasilakis, 273–82. British School at Athens Studies 12, London: The British School at Athens.

Catapotis, Mihalis, and Yannis Bassiakos. 2007. "Copper Smelting at the Early Minoan Site of Chrysokamino on Crete." In *Metallurgy in the Early Bronze Age Aegean*, ed. Peter M. Day and Roger C. P. Doonan, 68–83. Sheffield Studies in Aegean Archaeology 7. Oxford: Oxbow.

Catling, Hector W. 1964. *Cypriot Bronzework in the Mycenaean World*. Oxford: Clarendon.

Cullen, Tracey, ed. 2001. *Aegean Prehistory: A Review*. AJA Suppl. 1. Boston: Archaeological Institute of America.

Davaras, Costis, and Philip P. Betancourt. 2004. *The Hagia Photia Cemetery I: The Tomb Groups and Architecture*. Prehistory Monographs 14. Philadelphia: INSTAP Academic Press.

Day, Peter M., and Roger C. P. Doonan. 2007. *Metallurgy in the Early Bronze Age Aegean*. Sheffield Studies in Aegean Archaeology 7. Oxford: Oxbow.

Devetzi, Tania. 2005. "I petra stin upiresia tis technis kai tis zois: Lithina angeia." *Archaiologia and Technes* 94 (Martios): 58–66.

Dickinson, Oliver. 1994. *The Aegean Bronze Age*. New York: Cambridge University Press.

Dimopoulou-Rethemiotaki, Nota, David E. Wilson, and Peter M. Day. 2007. "The Earlier Prepalatial Settlement of Poros-Katsambas: Craft Production and Exchange at the Harbour Town of Knossos." In *Metallurgy in the Early Bronze Age Aegean*, ed. Peter M. Day and Roger C. P. Doonan, 84–97. Sheffield Studies in Aegean Archaeology 7. Oxford: Oxbow.

Documents in Mycenaean Greek. New edition, forthcoming.

Doonan, Roger C. P., Peter M. Day, and Nota Dimopoulou-Rethemiotaki. 2007. "Lame Excuses for Emerging Complexity in Early Bronze Age Crete: The Metallurgical Finds from Poros Katsambas and Their Context." In *Metallurgy in the Early Bronze Age Aegea* n, ed. Peter M. Day and Roger C. P. Doonan, 98–122. Sheffield Studies in Aegean Archaeology 7. Oxford: Oxbow.

Dziobek, Eberhard. 1994. *Die Gräber des Vezirs User-Amun. Theben Nr. 61 und 131*. Archäologische Veröffentlichungen des Deutschen Archäologischen Instituts, Abteilung Kairo 84. Mainz: von Zabern.

Enegren, Hedvig L. 2000. "Craft Production at Knossos—Raw Materials and Finished Goods—the Linear B Evidence." In *Trade and Production in Premonetary Greece: Acquisition and Distribution of Raw Materials and Finished Products. Proceedings of the 6th International Workshop, Athens 1996*, ed. Carole Gillis, Christina Risberg, and Birgitta Sjöberg, 29–42. SIMA-PB 154. Jonsered, Sweden: Åström.

Evely, R. Doniert G. 1992. "Towards an Elucidation of the Ivory-worker's Tool-kit in Neo-palatial Crete." In *Ivory in Greece and the Eastern Mediterranean from the Bronze Age to the Hellenistic Period*, ed. J. Lesley Fitton, 7–16. British Museum Occasional Papers 85. London: British Museum.

———. 1993 and 2000. *Minoan Tools and Techniques: An Introduction*. SIMA 92: 1–2. Gothenburg and Jonsered, Sweden: Åström.

———. 1999. *Fresco: A Passport into the Past. Minoan Crete through the Eyes of Mark Cameron*. Athens: British School at Athens/Goulandris Foundation–Museum of Cycladic Art.

———. 2005. "I epexergasia tou elephantodontou sto Aigaio tis Chalkokratias." *Archaiologia and Technes* 94 (Martios): 71–75.

———. Forthcoming. *Small Finds of Building 1, Palaikastro*.

Evely, R. Doniert G., Vasilis Politakis, Jerolyn Morrison, and Doug Park. 2008. "The Minoan Potter's Wheel: Experimental Reproduction and Usage." A contribution to the ICAANE workshop 'Modes of Development of Wheel-fashioning Techniques,' Rome, May 8, 2008.

Evely, R. Doniert G., and Zofia Stos. 2004. "Aspects of Late Minoan Metallurgy at Knossos." In *Knossos*, 267–71.

Faber, Edward W., Vassilis Kilikoglou, Peter M. Day, and David E. Wilson. 2002. "Technologies of Middle Minoan Polychrome Pottery: Traditions of Paste, Decoration, and Firing." In *Modern Trends in Scientific Studies on Ancient Ceramics:*

Papers Presented at the 5th European Meeting on Ancient Ceramics, Athens 1999, ed. Vassilis Kilikoglou, Anno Hein, and Yannis Maniatis, 129–41. *BAR-IS* 1011. Oxford: Archaeopress.

Foster, Karen P. 1979. *Aegean Faience of the Bronze Age*. New Haven: Yale University Press.

Fri, Maria L. 2007. The Double Axe in Minoan Crete: A Functional Analysis of Production and Use. PhD diss., Stockholm University, Sweden.

Galanaki, Calliope. Forthcoming. *The Site of Gournes on Crete*.

Gale, Noel H., and Zofia A. Stos-Gale. 2002. "The Characterisation by Lead Isotopes of the Ore Deposits of Cyprus and Sardinia and Its Bearing on the Possibility of the Lead Isotope Provenancing of Copper Alloys." In *Archaeometry 98: Proceedings of the 31st Symposium, Budapest, April 26–May 3, 1998, II*, ed. Erzsébet Jerem and Katalin T. Biró, 351–62. Archaeolingua Central European Series 1. *BAR-IS* 1043. Oxford: Archaeopress.

Georgiou, Hara. 1980. "Minoan Fireboxes: A Study of Form and Function." *SMEA* 21. *Incunabula Graeca* 72: 123–92.

Gillis, Carole, Robin Clayton, Ernst Pernicka, and Noel Gale. 2003. "Tin in the Aegean Bronze Age." In *METRON*, 103–10.

Gillis, Carole, Christina Risberg, and Birgitta Sjöberg, eds. 1995–2000. *Trade and Production in Premonetary Greece: Aspects of Trade. Proceedings of the International Workshops, Athens. SIMA-PB*. Jonsered, Sweden: Åström.

Haarer, Peter. 2001. "Problematising the Transition from Bronze to Iron." In *The Social Context of Change: Egypt and the Near East, 1650–1550 BC*, ed. Andrew J. Shortland, 255–73. Oxford: Oxbow.

Hemingway, Seán A. 1996. "Minoan Metalworking in the Postpalatial Period: A Deposit of Metallurgical Debris from Palaikastro." *BSA* 91: 213–52.

Higgins, Michael D., and Reynold Higgins. 1996. *A Geological Companion to Greece and the Aegean*. London: Duckworth.

Jones, Richard E. 2005. "Technical Studies of Aegean Bronze Age Wall Painting: Methods, Results, and Future Prospects.' In *Aegean Wall Painting. A Tribute to Mark Cameron*, ed. Lyvia Morgan, 199–228. BSA Studies 13. London: British School at Athens.

Kakavoigianni, Olga. 2005. "Ergasterio metallourgias argyrou tis Protoelladikis I Epochis sta Lambrika Koropiou." *Archaiologia and Technes* 94 (Martios): 45–48.

Kamarinou, Dimitra, and Kalliopi Baika. 2005. "Omerika kai mikinaika ploia." *Archaiologia and Technes* 94 (Martios): 12–18.

Killen, John T. 1964. "The Wool Industry of Crete in the Late Bronze Age." *BSA* 59: 1–15.

Knappett, Carl. 1997. "Ceramic Production in the Protopalatial Mallia 'State': Evidence from Quartier Mu and Myrtos Pyrgos." In *TEXNH*, 305–11.

Knauss, Jost. 2005. "Proistorika engeioveltiotika erga." *Archaiologia and Technes* 94 (Martios): 19–22.

Krzyszkowska, Olga H. 1988. "Ivory in the Aegean Bronze Age: Elephant Tusk or Hippopotamus Ivory?" *BSA* 83: 209–34.

———. 1990. *Ivory and Related Materials: An Illustrated Guide*. Classical Handbook 3, Bulletin Suppl. 59. London: Institute of Classical Studies.

———. 1990. *Ivory and Related Materials: An Illustrated Guide*. Classical Handbook 3, Bulletin Suppl. 59. London: Institute of Classical Studies.

Kyriakidis, Evangelos. 2002. "Indications on the Nature of the Language of the Keftiw from Egyptian Sources." *Egypt and the Levant* XII: 211–19.

Laffineur, Robert, and Emanuele Greco, eds. 2005. *Emporia*.

MacGillivray, J. Alexander, Jan M. Driessen, and L. Hugh Sackett, eds. 2005. *The Palaikastro Kouros: A Minoan Chryselaphantine Statuette and Its Aegean Bronze Age Context*. BSA Studies 6. London: British School at Athens.

Momigliano, Nicoletta, ed. 2007. *Knossos Pottery Handbook*.

Morgan, Lyvia. 1988. *The Miniature Wall Paintings of Thera: A Study in Aegean Culture and Iconography*. New York: Cambridge University Press.

———, ed. 2005. *Aegean Wall Painting: A Tribute to Mark Cameron*. British School at Athens Studies 13. London: British School at Athens.

Müller, Walter. 2003a. "Minoan Works of Art—Seen with Penetrating Eyes: X-ray Testing of Gold, Pottery, and Faience." In *METRON*, 147–55.

———. 2003b. "Precision Measurements of Minoan and Mycenaean Gold Rings with Ultrasound." In *METRON*, 475–82.

Mylonas, Georgios E. 1959. *An Early Bronze Age Settlement and Cemetery in Attica*. Princeton: Princeton University Press.

Niemeier, Barbara, and Wolf-Dietrich Niemeier. 2000. "Aegean Frescoes in Syria-Palestine: Alalakh and Tel Kabri." In *Wall Paintings of Thera*, 763–802.

Niemeier, Wolf-Dietrich, and Barbara Niemeier. 1998. "Minoan Frescoes in the Eastern Mediterranean." In *Aegean and the Orient*, 69–98.

Palyvou, Clairy. 2005. "Oikodomiki technologia ton proistorikon chronon." *Archaiologia and Technes* 94 (Martios): 8–11.

Panagiotaki, Marina. 2005. "Technologies aichmis sto Proistoriko Aigaio tin Epochi tou Chalcou: ualodeis ules." *Archaiologia and Technes* 94 (Martios): 76–82.

Papadotos, Yiannis. 2007. "The Beginning of Metallurgy in Crete: New Evidence from the FN–EM I Settlement at Kephala Petras, Siteia." In *Metallurgy in the Early Bronze Age Aegean*, ed. Peter M. Day and Roger C. P. Doonan, 154–67. Sheffield Studies in Aegean Archaeology 7. Oxford: Oxbow.

Politis, Thea. 2001. "Gold and Granulation: Exploring the Social Implications of a Prestige Technology in the Bronze Age Mediterranean." In *The Social Context of Technological Change: Egypt and the Near East, 1650–1550 BC. Proceedings of A Conference Held at St. Edmund Hall, Oxford, 12–14 September 2000*, ed. Andrew J. Shortland, 161–94. Oxford: Oxbow.

Polychronakou-Sgouritsa, Naya. 2001. "Epipla kai epiplourgia ston proistoriko oikismo tou Akrotiriou." In *Santorini: Thira, Thirasia, Aspronisi, Ifaisteia*, ed. Ioannis M. Danezis, 133–39. Athens: Adam Ekdoseis and Pergamos Ekdotiki.

Poursat, Jean-Claude. 1977. *Les ivoires mycénien: Essai sur la formation d'un art mycénien*. Bibliothèque des écoles françaises, Fascicule 230. Paris: L'École française d'Athènes. *Praehistorische Bronzefunde* series.

Pulak, Cemal. 1988. "The Bronze Age Shipwreck at Ulu Burun, Turkey: 1985 Campaign." *AJA* 92: 1–38.

Rackham, Oliver, and Jennifer Moody. 1996. *The Making of the Cretan Landscape*. New York: Manchester University Press.

Runnels, Curtis, and Doniert Evely. 1992. "Ground Stone." In *Well-built Mycenae: The Helleno-British Excavations within the Citadel at Mycenae, 1959–1969*, ed. William D. Taylour, Elizabeth B. French, and Kenneth A. Wardle. Fascicle 27. Oxford: Oxbow.

Sakellarakis, Ioannis. A. 1976. "Mycenaean Stone Vases." *SMEA* 62: 173–87.

———. 1979. *To elephantodonto kai i katergasia tou sta mikinaika chronia*. Library of the Athens Archaeological Etaireia 93. Athens: Athens Archaeological Etaireia.

Sampson, Adamantios. 1988. *Manika II: An Early Helladic Settlement and Cemetery*. Athens: Demos Khalkideon.

Shelmerdine, Cynthia W. 1985. *The Perfume Industry in Mycenaean Pylos*. SIMA-PB 34. othenburg: Åström.

———. 1987. "Industrial Activity at Pylos." In *Tractata Mycenaea: Proceedings of the Eighth International Colloquium on Mycenaean Studies, Held in Ohrid (15–20 September 1985)*, ed. Petar Ilievski and Ljiljana Crepajac, 333–42. Skopje: Macedonian Academy of Sciences and Arts.

Sherratt, E. Susan. 1994. "Commerce, Iron, and Ideology: Metallurgical Innovation in 12th–11th Century Cyprus." In *Cyprus in the 11th Century BC: Proceedings of the International Symposium Organized by the Archaeological Research Unit of the University of Cyprus and the A. G. Leventis Foundation, Nicosia, 30–31 October 1993*, ed. Vassos Karageorghis, 59–106. Nicosia: Leventis Foundation.

———, ed. 2000. *Wall Paintings of Thera. Proceedings of the First International Symposium, Petros M. Nomikos Conference Centre, Thera, Hellas, 30 August–4 September 1997*, Athens Thera Foundation—Petros M. Nomikos and The Thera Foundation.

Sklavenitis, Christophoros. 2007. "Minoiki Maza." *Kritiko Panorama* 23 (Septembrios-Oktobrios): 46–69.

Snodgrass, Anthony M. 1980. "Iron and Early Metallurgy in the Mediterranean." In *The Coming of the Age of Iron*, ed. Theodore A. Wertime and James D. Muhly, 335–74. New Haven: Yale University Press.

Speciale, Maria Stella. 2000. "Furniture in Linear B: The Evidence from Tables." In *Pepragmena H' Diethnous Kritologikou Synedriou, Irakleio, 9–14 Septemvriou 1996.* Vol. A3, *Proïstoriki kai Archaia Elliniki Periodos*, ed. Alexandra Karetsou, Theocharis Detorakis, and Alexis Kalokairinos, 227–39. Irakleio: Etairia Kritikon Istorikon Meleton.

Stos-Gale, Zofia A., and Noel H. Gale. 2003. "Lead Isotopic and Other Isotopic Research in the Aegean." In *METRON*, 83–102.

Tomkins, Peter, and Peter M. Day. 2001. "Production and Exchange of the Earliest Ceramic Vessels in the Aegean: View from Early Neolithic Knossos, Crete." *Antiquity* 75(288): 259–60.

Tournavitou, Iphigenia. 1988. "Towards an Identification of a Workshop Space." In *Problems in Greek Prehistory*, 447–67.

———. 1995. *The "Ivory Houses" at Mycenae*. BSA Supplementary vol. 24. London: British School at Athens.

———. 1997. "Jewellers' Moulds and Jewellers' Workshops in Mycenaean Greece: An Archaeological Utopia." In *Trade and Production in Premonetary Greece: Production and the Craftsman. Proceedings of the 4th and 5th International Workshops, Athens 1994 and 1995*, ed. Carole Gillis, Christina Risberg, and Birgitta Sjöberg, 209–56. SIMA-PB 143. Jonsered, Sweden: Åström.

Tzachili, Iris. 2005. "I uphantiki Techni tin epochi tou chalkou." *Archaiologia and Technes* 94 (Martios): 67–70.

Tzedakis, Yannis, and Holley Martlew, eds. 1999. *Minoans and Mycenaeans: Flavours of Their Time. National Archaeological Museum, 12 July–27 November 1999*. Athens: Greek Ministry of Culture, General Directorate of Antiquities.

Warren, Peter M. 1969. *Minoan Stone Vases*. London: Cambridge University Press.

Whitelaw, Todd, Peter M. Day, Evangelia Kiriatzi, Vassilis Kilikoglou, and David E. Wilson. 1997. "Ceramic Traditions at EM IIB Myrtos, Fournou Korifi." In *TEXNH*, 265–74.

Wilson, David E., and Peter M. Day. 1994. "Ceramic Regionalism in Prepalatial Central Crete: The Mesara Imports at EM I to EM II A Knossos." *BSA* 89: 1–87.

———. 2000. "EM I Chronology and Social Practice: Pottery from the Early Palace Tests at Knossos." *BSA* 95: 21–63.

Younger, John G. 1983. "Aegean Seals of the Late Bronze Age: Masters and Workshops: II. The First-generation Minoan Masters." *Kadmos* 22(2): 109–36.

Yule, Peter. 1980. *Early Cretan Seals: A Study of Chronology*. Marburger Studien zur Vor- und Frühgeschichte 4. Mainz am Rhein: von Zabern.

Zachos, Konstantinos. 2007. "The Neolithic Background: A Reassessment." In *Metallurgy in the Early Bronze Age Aegean*, ed. Peter M. Day and Roger C. P. Doonan, 168–206. Sheffield Studies in Aegean Archaeology 7. Oxford: Oxbow.

CHAPTER 30

MINOAN POTTERY

BIRGITTA HALLAGER

ALTHOUGH major subsequent modifications and revisions have been made to Arthur Evans's pottery sequence, his suggested tripartite division of the Neolithic and the Minoan period is still by and large in use. Most scholars are also using a parallel, broader, and more simplified division of the Minoan era: the Prepalatial (EM I–MM IA), Protopalatial (MM IB–MM IIIA), Neopalatial (MM IIIB–LM IB), Final palatial (LM II–LM IIIB1) and Postpalatial (LM IIIB2–LM IIIC/Subminoan) periods.

Only the most important novelties and characteristic traits in each period are highlighted in this chapter, and it must be emphasized that "a specific period is defined not only by the exclusive presence of certain features but by the fact that some wares are common while others are just beginning or ending their periods of greatest popularity" (Betancourt 1985, 21). References to sites with pottery characteristic of the different periods can be found in Betancourt (1985) with additional new sites in Momigliano (2007b).

NEOLITHIC

Evans divided the Neolithic period into Early, Middle, and Late periods. Subsequently, the Early Neolithic has been subdivided into two phases (Furness 1953; J. D. Evans 1964) and the Late Neolithic period into three phases: Late Neolithic I, II, and Final Neolithic (Manteli 1993). Recently Tomkins (2007) has presented a complete revision of Neolithic Knossos that he has subdivided into nine phases. The beginning of the Early Neolithic I period has been dated to ca. 6500 BC. All Neolithic vessels are handmade and fired to a relatively low temperature. Their surfaces are dark burnished or polished. So far only Knossos has produced the whole pottery sequence for the Neolithic period.

In Early Neolithic I, large and small bowls are the most common shapes, but other shapes include hole-mouthed jars, low-collared jars, flat-based mugs, and flared cups. Various types of handles are present, such as strap handles on bowls and jars, pairs of 'ears' on bowls, and wishbone handles. Some vessels have plastic decoration in the form of pellets and cordons, while others have an incised decoration in the form of short horizontal lines, stripes, and triangles. Typical for this period is the so-called pointillé decoration, which usually consists of incised zigzag or straight lines filled with small pricked dots. Early Neolithic I pottery is confined mainly to Knossos.

Different shapes of bowls and jars are also made in Early Neolithic II, but flat-based mugs are rare and disappear thereafter. House models (legged receptacles) and 'shuttles' decorated with incised lines and/or pointillé decoration occasionally occur. Plastic cordons are rare, and pellets are no longer in vogue, while incised decoration continues with many new motifs like 'barbed wire,' herringbone, tree, rows of chevrons, zigzag lines, and hatched lozenges. Although a few vases burnished with rippled lines were present in the former period, they are somewhat more common in Early Neolithic II. Scribble Burnished Ware is common.

Several Early Neolithic shapes continue in the Middle Neolithic period, including house models and 'shuttles.' Among new introductions, we find flared cups with a flat base, shallow lids, ladles with pronged wishbone handles, pedestal bowls, bridge-spouted bowls, and cylindrical vessels with an opening in the side. Pointillé decoration, Rippled, and Scribble Burnished Ware decline toward the end of the period, while pottery with incised decoration increases. The variety of motifs, including hatched triangles, branches, lozenge chains, horizontal ladders, rope patterns, and 'sewn' motifs, is much greater than in the previous period and continue to be linear, usually in continuous horizontal friezes.

Most of the shapes in the Late Neolithic period are known from the previous period, but they become more varied than before. We find a variety of carinated bowls and jars, hole-mouthed and collared jars, as well as specialized vessels like pyxides and tall, one-handled, small-diameter vessels that may have a pointed, flat, or pedestal base. Flared bowls with a small, triangular wishbone handle projecting above the rim are also typical for the period. All main incised motifs from the previous period continue but decrease toward the end of Late Neolithic, when several new types of impressed decoration appear (e.g., pattern jabbed, triangular jabbed, borderless punched ladder).

Features from the Late Neolithic as defined from Knossos continue in Final Neolithic, along with several new features. Closed shapes like jug and jars become much more frequent. New shapes include two-handled globular vessels with narrow tall neck (bottles), pyxides with tall horned lids, footed cups, cups and bowls with horns flanking the handle, and bowls or basins with a row of holes (so-called cheese pots). Incised decoration continues, but it is not very common, and almost all types of jabbed decoration disappear. Few are scribble burnished or have burnished patterns. Final Neolithic is the best represented of all of the Neolithic phases.

EARLY MINOAN

Evans (1904, figure 7) published an idealized section of the tripartite division of the Early Minoan period at Knossos, but he did not find a single stratigraphic sequence for this division. It was not until the early 1960s, due to stratigraphic tests, that the Early Minoan I, II, and III periods could be clearly defined (Hood 1962, 1966). Further tests made in the early 1970s made it possible to separate EM II at Knossos into two subphases, EM IIA and EM IIB (J. D. Evans 1972; Warren 1972a). In addition, EM III has been a controversial ceramic period, but most scholars today agree that it is a proper ceramic phase, although it presently is recorded at only a few sites (Momigliano 2007a, 79–80).

The Scored (or Wiped) Ware is characteristic of the Early Minoan I deposits across the island. The surface of the vessels is decorated with rough vertical, diagonal, or horizontal lines wiped in the moist clay. The most common pattern-wiped shape is the large globular jug with wide-mouthed neck and rounded or flat bottom, but other shapes like bowls, collared jars, and cooking pots are also present. The so-called Pyrgos Ware is also typical of the period. It has a dark gray burnished surface, often with pattern-burnished decorations. The two most distinctive shapes in this ware are the chalice and the pedestal bowl; less common are jars, pyxides, cups, and jugs.

Another fine ware is the so-called Agios Onouphrios Ware. Groups of vertical, diagonal, or horizontal lines are painted in red, sometimes shading to brown, on a buff ground. The jug with a globular body and a high cut-away spout seem to be the favorite shape in this Dark-on-Light Ware. Other shapes include cups, bowls, teapots, two-handled globular vessels with a low to tall neck (tankards), askoi, pyxides, and animal-shaped vessels. Presently this Dark-on-Light Ware occurs mainly in central Cretan sites, while vessels with a white on red decoration, the so-called Lebena Ware, seems restricted mainly to southern Crete.

Pottery inspired by Cycladic incised vessels are mainly found on the north coast of Crete. Finally, two important shapes that continue throughout the remainder of the Minoan period appear in the Early Minoan I settlements: the cooking dish (baking plate) and the pithos.

Early Minoan IIA is divided into two subphases at Knossos (Wilson 2007, 56–69), but this division is presently not discernable at other sites. Unpivoted turntables, probably used in pottery production, have been found in the settlement at Myrtos (Warren 1972b), but the vessels are still handmade. Vessels made in a Fine Gray Ware, often incised with diagonal lines, herringbone, punctuations, and semicircles in horizontal bands, are confined mainly to this period. The pyxis with short neck, vertically pierced lugs, and sometimes footed or with tripod legs is a favorite shape, but other shapes include bowls, stemmed goblets, and strainers; in tombs we often find miniature vessels.

Dark-on-Light Wares are also appreciated in several parts of the island. One of these, the so-called Koumasa Ware, is recognized by its linear decorations, which usually include hatched or crosshatched motifs, but several other motifs, like the butterfly motif, solid triangles, and groups of diagonal lines, are used on shapes like cups, bowls, jugs, teapots, jars, goblets, and askoi. Foreign shapes, like the sauceboat (known on the contemporary mainland and the Cyclades), are introduced in this period.

Dark-on-Light Wares continue in Early Minoan IIB, and Red/Brown/Black Burnished Wares are quite common, especially in east Crete. Light-on-Dark Wares—usually white paint on a red or black slip—are also produced. While there are good ceramic links across the island in Early Minoan I–IIA, they are somewhat more difficult to trace in Early Minoan IIB. Perhaps the best candidate for a pan-Cretan style in this period is the so-called Vasiliki Ware, which is largely a feature of this period. The surface of the vessels is slipped, burnished, and fired so that it varies from red to brown to black. This mottled decoration is found on a large variety of shapes foremost on jugs with a high cut-away spout, goblets, and teapots, but other shapes include shallow bowls, spouted, conical bowls, bridge-spouted jars, and several types of cups. Mottled pottery occurs in western and central Crete but is most common in the eastern part of the island. Its enigmatic techniques of manufacture have been much debated (Betancourt et al. 1979).

Early Minoan III seems presently to be a time of isolation and strong regionalism. Dark-on-Light Ware, with vessels decorated with linear designs, is produced alongside what is perhaps the most characteristic ware in this period: Light-on Dark Ware. Vessels from western and central Crete are sparsely adorned with simple lines, often with only horizontal bands. In the eastern part of the island, however, the light-on-dark decorations are more varied, with motifs like spirals, quirks, semicircles, dot bands, hatched lozenges, paneled patterns, and circles, which are often combined in bold, ornamental ways. Shapes like goblets, tumblers, rounded and conical cups, bowls, and jugs with cut-away spouts are common, but others like teapots, jars, and undecorated, coarse storage and cooking vessels are also produced. The one-handled cup, which becomes the most common drinking vessel in the Middle and Late Minoan periods, is introduced in this period.

MIDDLE MINOAN

At Knossos, the Middle Minoan period has been divided into six pottery phases. The subdivision of MM II can presently best be distinguished at sites associated with the palace workshops, whereas it is more difficult in provincial contexts. The subdivision of Middle Minoan III outside Knossos is presently also somewhat problematic, as very few sites have provided a clear stratigraphy for this division. Another 'problem' appeared when the Middle Bronze Age material from the old palace at Phaistos was divided into four phases (Levi 1960, 1976) that could not immediately be synchronized with Evans's division. These phases have subsequently been resorted (Fiandra 1962, 1980; Levi and Carinci 1988), but there is still some confusion in the literature (MacGillivray 2007, 105–106). There are many regional styles in this period, and only some are mentioned here.

The Middle Minoan IA period is usually defined by the presence of polychrome decoration—separating it from the Early Minoan III period—and the absence of wheel-made pottery, which was introduced in the following Middle Minoan IB period. Dark-on-Light Wares are still produced, alongside the Light-on-Dark Ware of Early Minoan III, which was particularly long lived in the eastern part of the island. The introduction of red paint (together with white) on the dark surface (Polychrome Ware) is a salient feature of the period. Many shapes known from EM III continue; straight-sided and carinated cups, however, are new additions. The enigmatic, so-called sheep bells are also new, but in spite of many suggestions, their function remains a mystery. Vessels with incised decorations like diagonal bands, zigzags, or crosshatched areas enjoyed a late revival.

The potter's wheel was introduced in Middle Minoan IB, but handmade and wheel-made vessels are often found side by side in the beginning. Dark-on-Light Ware continues to be popular, and several regional variations are discernable. The decorations are usually simple; for example, dipping, blot and trickle, and banding are common in the Mesara, while additional and somewhat more varied motifs like dots, groups of bands, sprays, chevrons, and occasionally zoomorphic and anthropomorphic designs appear in eastern Crete. Orange and yellow paint is added to the Polychrome Ware (Kamares Ware), which is usually adorned with linear motifs, but in the Knossos region we find patterns that may have been inspired by textiles.

Although the so-called Barbotine Ware is sparsely present before this period, the height of its popularity comes in the period MM IB–MM IIA. It is characterized by rough plastic reliefs on the surfaces of the vessels. Several types of decoration coexist, including large and small pellets, thin relief bands, and dabs of slurry (barnacle work). Barbotine decoration occurs especially on jugs, often in combination with white or polychrome painting. Incised decoration dies out at the end of the period.

Monochrome and Light-on-Dark Wares (adorned with white bands) continue in Middle Minoan IIA, but most attention has been drawn to the Polychrome (Kamares) Ware found at the two main palatial centers of its production, Knossos and Phaistos. Drinking and pouring vessels are the most common items, but other shapes like bowls and pyxides are also present. The sophisticated so-called Eggshell Ware is a hallmark of MM IIA: cups with walls less than 1 mm thick. Vessels with painted patterns and additional horizontally stamped or impressed designs, as well as those on which a device was used to print sponge, crescent, or seed patterns, are also made in this period. Another characteristic ware introduced in MM

IIA is the so-called Crude Ware. The small, rough vessels are mass produced on wheels in a fine buff ware. The shapes include shallow bowls, cups, juglets, pyxides, and conical cups. As the provincial pottery is usually a very simple version of the palatial styles, the synchronisms with other sites are presently somewhat tenuous.

The Polychrome (Kamares) Ware reaches its last flourishing period in Middle Minoan IIB. Drinking and pouring vessels are still the most common, but large storage jars, amphorae, rhyta, and many other specialized forms are in use. The repertoire and, not least of all, the combination of motifs seem almost endless. Spirals, petals, tendrils, rosettes, foliate bands, and chevrons are only a few of the many motifs often arranged in creative whirling and twisting compositions. It is not impossible that some of these motifs were borrowed from woven textiles; others come from the flora and fauna (e.g., trees, plants, octopi, fish). The repoussé technique is now used for the Stamped Ware: The thin wall of the vase is pushed from within over die stamps like circles, star or sun motifs, spirals, concentric circles, and shells, all of which leave the potter's fingerprint on the inside. Printed Ware and Crude Ware continue, as well as a variety of utilitarian coarse ware vessels, including pithoi.

Contrary to the polychrome and complex motifs of the preceding period, the Middle Minoan III pottery in general is adorned with simple and sober motifs, including flowers like lilies and crocuses. The subdivisions of the Middle Minoan III period are presently better defined in central Crete than in other parts of the island. Light-on-Dark Ware continues in Middle Minoan IIIA; at Knossos, cups with evenly spaced ridges are typical, and small, white-painted spots and spirals appear on shapes like cups, tumblers, and jugs. The bridge-spouted jar on an elongated foot may also belong to this period.

Dark-on-Light Ware decorated with ripple pattern seems to appear in this period, but it becomes more common in Middle Minoan IIIB on shapes like cups, bowls, and jars. Two new shapes are introduced: the so-called Vapheio cup and the in-and-out bowl. Light-on-Dark Ware decorated with white-painted motifs like spirals, irises, quirks, dots, and semicircles is also common. The very first stirrup jars appear in south central Crete. Middle Minoan III vessels in coarse fabrics include basins and specialized shapes like lamps, braziers, vats, cooking vessels, shallow dishes, and pithoi, which are more numerous than before.

LATE MINOAN

The Late Minoan period is subdivided into more pottery phases than any of the previous periods. Efforts to subdivide both LM IA and LM IB into an early and a late phase have turned out to be more confusing than helpful, as the arguments are based mainly on stylistic features rather than on stratigraphic evidence (Hatzaki

2007, 154–60). After some controversy, LM II has been established as a separate pottery phase, but so far it is found stratified in only a few sites. The differences between LM IIIA1 and LM IIIA2 pottery were defined in the 1970s, and the subdivision of LM IIIB into B1 and B2 was made in this millennium (Popham 1970; Hallager 2003a, 2003b). Problems remain concerning the subdivisions of LM IIIC. While LM IIIC early has been identified at several sites on Crete, the later part of the period is presently more diffuse, and the question is whether the so-called Subminoan period will eventually be regarded as the very last period of the Bronze Age or the first in the Iron Age.

Late Minoan IA is characterized by a strong ceramic regionalism. The long-lived Light-on-Dark Ware has almost disappeared in central Crete, although it is still quite common in the eastern part of the island. Dark-on-Light Ware is, however, the most prevalent, and in spite of several regional shapes and decorative motifs, reed patterns become a hallmark of the period; other appreciated motifs include ripple patterns, foliate bands, and floral decorations. Monochrome cups are often present, and the number of plain conical cups increases. Several shapes of cups, jugs, and jars continue from the previous period, and the conservative cooking equipment cannot be more closely dated within LM I. The decorated cylindrical jar seems to be a new shape, and among the coarse-fabric vessels we now also find so-called fire-boxes, which may have been used in perfume making.

Several shapes and motifs continue in Late Minoan IB. Foliate bands, spirals, and floral decorations are still favorite motifs, together with wavy bands and semi-circles; in eastern Crete, red and white accessory ornaments are not unusual. The hallmark of the period is a group of vessels made in a style called the Special Palatial Tradition. They were probably produced in a Knossian workshop, and although there are rather few within the total LM IB material, they are crucial in separating the two LM I periods. Based on the vessels' iconography, the tradition has been separated into four subdivisions: the Marine Style, the Floral Style, the Geometric and Abstract Style, and the Alternating Style. As a new feature we find motifs arranged freely on the entire body of the vessel, and occasionally motifs from more than one style are combined. New LM IB shapes include the S-shaped bowl, the one-handled squat alabastron, and the baggy alabastron; among the several shapes of rhyta, the cup/rhyton seems to be the most common.

The repertoire of Late Minoan II shapes and motifs is so far best illustrated in the publication of the Unexplored Mansion at Knossos (Popham et al. 1984). Many shapes and motifs survive from the LM IB period, and in spite of several shapes that have been claimed to be newcomers in LM II, presently only the goblet can be pointed out. We find both plain and decorated goblets, the latter usually with a single motif (e.g., octopus, iris cross, triple Cs, rosette) on each side of the vessel and often with droplets on the rim. Tin-coated vessels like goblets, cups, jugs, and squat alabastra also appear as a new feature. Imports of Knossian LM II are occasionally found in the eastern part of the island, but presently the synchronisms with this area are somewhat problematic as the pottery here bears no resemblance to central or west Cretan products.

Central and west Cretan Late Minoan IIIA1 pottery is more or less influenced by the Knossian workshops, while the east Cretan workshops continued their own ceramic traditions. Important synchronisms are found at sites on the border between the two areas, where vessels from both worlds are found together. Repeated motifs framed by bands become standard; the most common are foliate bands, festoon patterns, alternating arcs, net patterns, foliate scrolls, and zigzags, which are often combined with additional rows of dots or framed by wavy bands. Pictorial decoration in the form of flowers, birds, and fish are found mainly on cups, pyxides, and baggy alabastra. A single motif on each side of the decorated goblet has gone out of fashion and is replaced by repeated motifs. New shapes include ledge-rimmed cups, incense burners with lids, amphoroid kraters, funnel-necked jugs, juglets, and the shallow bowl, the latter always undecorated.

In Late Minoan IIIA2, west and central Cretan workshops are in close contact, and although the eastern part of the island continued its local styles, the limit of west and central Cretan influence has moved somewhat farther east. Many repeated motifs continue from LM IIIA1 and are thus unreliable for dating purposes. Among the new shapes found in most of the island are the kylix, which has a long stem—in contrast to the short stem of the goblet—and often loop handles and the footed cup (also called champagne cup). Several shapes in fine ware, now including kylikes, footed cups, deep cups, jugs, jars, and kalathoi, are produced both in a plain and a decorated version. Decorated larnakes and bathtubs appear in the tombs, but they also have a domestic function, as witnessed by the many examples found in the settlements. Vessels in coarse fabric like cooking dishes and trays continue unchanged, but the old, straight-sided tripod cooking pot has finally been replaced by one with a globular body and a high everted rim; handles may be horizontal or vertical.

In the Late Minoan IIIB1 period, a close contact between all areas of Crete is finally established. Export of vessels from the Kydonian workshop reaches a peak now and also includes several sites in the east Cretan area. The quantity of large (transport) stirrup jars, a shape known from MM III, increases. By now they are produced in three areas—north-central, south-central, and western Crete—and are usually adorned with horizontal bands or high wavy bands; some have Linear B inscriptions. The repeated motifs, including alternating arcs, hatched lozenges and loops, festoons, chevrons, stylized shells, multiple arcs, whorl shells, spirals, and stylized flowers, are usually less densely packed. New shapes are added (e.g., the shallow kylix, the bowl with an upright profile, and small squat and conical stirrup jars); although a few small globular stirrup jars have occasionally appeared since LM I, they are now among the most commonly produced vessels.

Most shapes from LM IIIB1 continue in Late Minoan IIIB2, but type fossils like cups and bowls with flaring rims—in west Crete often with interior double rim bands and in central Crete with monochrome interiors—are found at several sites. The carinated cup is also a new LM III shape, and in west Crete the banded cup with high-slung handle is a new and prominent feature of the period. The motifs are simple and applied in a more spacious manner than in the previous period. They include paneled patterns in which the wavy border is often a component, antithetic spirals, quirks, simple foliate bands, zigzags, wavy bands, isolated lozenges, multiple stemmed spirals, comb patterns, and above all concentric semicircles. Among the coarse-fabric pottery, finger impressions on the upper legs of tripod cooking pots appear for the first time.

The close cross-island contacts continue in Late Minoan IIIC early. Carinated bowls and kraters become popular, and a new (Mycenaean) technique of making small stirrup jars is quickly spreading across the island: The false neck/disc, modeled on a flat disc, is now made in solid clay and placed on a separately made body. Long handle attachments on kraters and pyxides and reserved rim bands on the interiors of bowls and kraters are new features. Vessels decorated in the so-called open style and close style appear simultaneously at the beginning of the period. Among the new motifs, we find the buttonhook and the tricurved streamer, and pictorial motifs including horses, fish, trees, and above all birds are not uncommon. Vertical slashes or finger impressions on the upper part of the tripod legs is now a pan-Cretan trait, and a new coarse-fabric shape appears: the disclike lid with a central, high, solid knob handle decorated with relief patterns, which was perhaps used as a damper.

It may eventually turn out to be crucial that the important settlement at Knossos, which was continuously inhabited in antiquity, so far has no deposits stratified between LM IIIC early and the so-called Subminoan period. Among the features that have been put forward as characteristic of Late Minoan IIIC late, we find stirrup jars with a cone top on the false disc and an airhole close to the neck or handle, bulging stems on kylikes, conical feet on cups, bowls, and stirrup jars, and the absence of large stirrup jars. These features seem to continue in the Subminoan period, and the question is whether we can separate LM IIIC late and Subminoan into two successive phases or whether they eventually are one and the same period.

NB: Several scholars in addition to those mentioned in this chapter have contributed to our present knowledge of Minoan pottery. They are far too many to be listed here, but a good up-to-date bibliography may be found in Momigliani (2007b).

BIBLIOGRAPHY

Betancourt, Philip P. 1985. *The History of Minoan Pottery*. Princeton: Princeton University Press.
———, Thomas K. Gaisser, Eugene Koss, Robert F. Lyon, Frederick R. Matson, Steven Montgomery, George H. Myer, and Charles P. Swann. 1979. *Vasilike Ware: An Early Bronze Age Pottery Style in Crete*. Gothenburg: Åström.
Evans, Arthur J. 1904. "The Palace of Knossos." *BSA* 10: 1–62.
Evans, John D. 1964. "Excavations in the Neolithic Settlement at Knossos, 1957–60." *BSA* 59: 132–240.
———. 1972. "The Early Minoan Occupation of Knossos: A Note on Some New Evidence." *AnatSt* 22: 115–28.

Fiandra, Enrica. 1962. "I periodi struttivi del primo palazzo di Festòs." Πεπραγμένα του
    Α' Διεθνούς Κρητολογικού Συνεδρίου, 112–26. Athens: Εταιρια Κρητικων Ιστορικων
    Μελετων.

———. 1980. "Precisazioni sul MM IIA Festòs." Πεπραγμένα του Δ' Διεθνούς
    Κρητολογικού Συνεδρίου, 169–96. Athens: Πανεπιστημιον Κρητης.

Furness, Audrey. 1953. "The Neolithic Pottery of Knossos." *BSA* 48: 94–134.

Hallager, Birgitta P. 2003a. "Late Minoan IIIB2 and Late Minoan IIIC Pottery in Khania." In
    LH IIIC, 105–16.

———. 2003b. "The Late Minoan IIIB:2 Pottery." In *The Greek Swedish Excavations at the
    Agia Aikaterini Square Kastelli, Khania 1970–1987 and 2001*. Vol. III:1, ed. Birgitta P.
    Hallager and Erik Hallager, 197–265. Skrifter utgivna av Svenska Institutet i Athen, 4°,
    XLVII:III:1. Stockholm: Åström.

Hatzaki, Eleni. 2007. "Neopalatial (MM IIIB–LM IB): KS 178, Gypsades Well (Upper
    Deposit) and SEX North House Groups." In *Knossos Pottery Handbook*, 151–96.

Hood, M. Sinclair F. 1962. "Stratigraphic Excavations at Knossos, 1957–61." Πεπραγμένα του
    Α' Διεθνούς Κρητολογικού Συνεδρίου, 92–98. Athens: Εταιρια Κρητικων Ιστορικων
    Μελετων.

———. 1966. "The Early and Middle Minoan Periods at Knossos." *BICS* 13: 110–11.

Levi, Doro. 1960. "Per una nuova classificazione della civiltà Minoica." *La parola del passato*
    15: 81–121.

———. 1976. *Festòs e la civiltà minoica*. Incunabula Graeca 60. Rome: Edizioni dell'Ateneo.

———, and F. Carinci. 1988. *Festòs e la civiltà minoica IIb*. Incunabula Graeca 77. Rome:
    Edizioni dell'Ateneo.

MacGillivray, J. Alexander. 2007. "Protopalatial (MM IB–MM IIIA): Early Chamber
    beneath the West Court, Royal Pottery Stores, the Trial KV, and the West and South
    Polychrome Deposits Groups." In *Knossos Pottery Handbook*, 105–49.

Manteli, Katya. 1993. The Transition from the Neolithic to the Early Bronze Age in Crete,
    with Special Reference to Pottery. PhD diss., Institute of Archaeology, University of
    London.

Momigliano, Nicoletta. 2007a. "Late Prepalatial (EM III–MM IA): South Front House
    Foundation Trench, Upper East Well, and House C/Royal Road South Fill Groups." In
    Knossos Pottery Handbook, 79–103.

———, ed. 2007b. *Knossos Pottery Handbook*.

Popham, Mervyn, R. 1970. *The Destruction of the Palace at Knossos: Pottery of the Late
    Minoan IIIA Period*. SIMA 12. Gothenburg: Åström.

———, J. H. Betts, M. Cameron, H. W. and E. A. Catling, D. Evely, R. A. Higgins,
    D. Smyth, et al. 1984. *The Minoan Unexplored Mansion at Knossos*. London: British
    School at Athens/Thames and Hudson.

Tomkins, Peter. 2007. "Neolithic: Strata IX–VIII, VII–VIB, VIA–V, IV, IIIB, IIIA, IIB, IIA
    and IC Groups." In *Knossos Pottery Handbook*, 9–48.

Warren, Peter. 1972a. "Knossos and the Greek Mainland in the Third Millennium B.C."
    Athens Annals of Archaeology 5: 392–98.

———. 1972b. *Myrtos: An Early Bronze Age Settlement in Crete*. BSA Suppl. 7. London.

Wilson, David E. 2007. "Early Prepalatial (EM I–EM II): EM I Well, West Court House,
    North-East Magazines, and South Front Groups." In *Knossos Pottery Handbook*, 49–77.

CHAPTER 31

MYCENAEAN POTTERY

JEREMY B. RUTTER

Serious study of Mycenaean pottery, the ceramic assemblage characteristic chiefly of the central and southern Greek mainland during the Aegean Late Bronze Age (ca. 1550, or possibly as early as 1650, until ca. 1050/1000 BC), began within a decade of the first discovery of substantial quantities of this artifactual class in the initial exploration of the chamber tomb cemeteries at Ialysos on Rhodes by Billiotti and Salzmann (1868, 1870) and Schliemann's better-known excavations at Troy (1870–1873, 1878–1879, 1882, 1890), Mycenae (1876), Tiryns (1884–1885), and Orchomenos (1880, 1886) (McDonald 1967; Mountjoy 1993, 1; Fitton 1996). Furtwängler and Löschcke were the first scholars to devote an entire book to the subject (1879), soon followed by a second, which incorporated many of Schliemann's recent findings at Tiryns (1886). But it was Blegen's careful stratigraphic excavations of 1915–1916 at the Corinthian coastal site of Korakou that first permitted virtually the full temporal range of Mycenaean ceramics to be outlined (Blegen 1921) by employing a tripartite chronological system modeled after that devised by Sir Arthur Evans for the Bronze Age pottery of Minoan Crete less than twenty years earlier.

The recovery of thousands of additional Mycenaean terracotta containers, especially intact or fully restorable vessels from tomb contexts, eventually made possible a definitive classification of the full typological range of Mycenaean ceramics during some ten stages of development spanning five centuries, thanks to publications by an international cast of excavators active in Greece during the 1920s and 1930s: Keramopoullos at Thebes, Kourouniotes and Mylonas at Eleusis, Marinatos on Kephallenia (Greece); Jannoray and Van Effenterre at Kirrha and Krisa (France); Karo at Mycenae (Germany); Maiuri and Iacopi at Ialysos (Italy); Frödin and Persson at Asine and Dendra (Sweden); Wace at Mycenae (United Kingdom); Blegen at Zygouries and Prosymna, Goldman at Eutresis, and Broneer at Athens (United States).

This complex system of morphological, as well as decorative, taxonomy, which included a much more finely tuned relative chronology and ultimately also absolute chronology, thanks to exported Mycenaean vases from well-dated contexts in Egypt and the Levant, was the great achievement of the Swedish scholar Arne Furumark (1941a, 1941b). The continuing value of his system of 103 forms, 336 shapes, various syntaxes, 78 motifs, and eight chronologically distinct styles is readily apparent from the simple fact that it is still in use more than six decades after its initial publication, notwithstanding challenges to it by no less an authority than Blegen (Blegen and Rawson 1966, 353–54) and minor modifications to it introduced by two full generations of subsequent scholars.

Developments in the subspecialty of Mycenaean ceramic studies that emerged as a consequence of Furumark's classification are best highlighted through the work of Elizabeth Wace French at Mycenae (especially 1963, 1964, 1965, 1966, 1967, 1969a, 1969b) and that of the students she trained there for nearly fifteen years (ca. 1965–1980) (e.g., Mee 1982; Mountjoy 1976, 1981, 1983, 1985; Rutter 1974, 1977, 1978, 1979; Rutter and Rutter 1976; Sherratt 1980, 1981; Wardle 1969, 1973), especially the extensive contributions of Penelope Mountjoy over the past three decades (most recently and especially 1986, 1988, 1993, 1995, 1997, 1998, 1999). French's most important contribution was the adaptation of Furumark's taxonomy to the analysis of substantial deposits of highly fragmentary material from settlement deposits, but she also pioneered the subdivision of the LH IIIB phase (13th century), as well as a much more refined approach to the definition and subdivision of the subsequent LH IIIC phase (12th–11th centuries).

Of course, even if most of the scholarship on Mycenaean pottery has been published in English, whether by native speakers or not (e.g., Andrikou, Cosmopoulos, Crouwel, Th. Papadopoulos, Vlachopoulos), by no means all of it has. For example, continuing fieldwork at Tiryns and other sites in the Argolid, Achaea, Arcadia, Attica, Phocis, Thessaly, and Macedonia has generated numerous important publications in German (site-based reports by Alram-Stern, Damm, Deger-Jalkotzy, Döhl, Gauss, Güntner, Hiller, Jacob-Felsch, Jung, Kalogeropoulos, Maran, Podzuweit, Schönfeld, Slenczka, Stockhammer, and Voigtländer, as well as major syntheses by Schachermeyr), and the same can be said for French (Deshayes), Italian (Benzi, Morricone), and especially Greek (Dakoronia, Demakopoulou, Iakovidis, Kardara, Mylonas, Pantelidou-Gofa).

The chronological development of Mycenaean pottery may be broken down into four stages of unequal duration, corresponding to major changes in the cultural history of the Aegean basin as a whole. Most, if not all, of these changes can be expected to have had a significant impact on the production and consumption of ceramic containers in styles typical of the Greek mainland and on their spatial distribution.

The first stage, which lasted at least a century and perhaps as long as two (for the vexed problem of the absolute chronology of the earlier part of the Aegean Late Bronze Age, see Mountjoy 1999, 16–18; Manning et al. 2006; Wiener 2007), comprises the phases known as Late Helladic (LH) I–IIA, during which Mycenaean culture took shape in the Peloponnese (Argolid, Messenia, and perhaps Laconia) with a heavy debt for many of its forms to Neopalatial Minoan Crete in the south and with a significant debt to Aigina as well in the northeast (Rutter 2001, 125–30, 135–40).

The earliest pottery termed "Mycenaean" in a stylistic (as opposed to purely chronological) sense is a decorated fine ware characterized by Minoan-derived patterns and syntaxes in a dark-on-light style executed with a lustrous, iron-based clay slip (or "paint"), ranging in color from red to black and usually mottled to some degree (depending on firing conditions and the thickness of the paint's application) on a pale clay ground. Such pattern-painted Mycenaean pottery accounts for only a tiny fraction (less than 1%) of the total pottery recovered in early LH I contexts. It is sometimes described as "Lustrous Decorated" to distinguish it from contemporary painted classes ornamented with one or more manganese-based matte paints that have a long history on the mainland going back to the beginning of the Middle Bronze Age some four to five centuries earlier.

Plain versions of several of the six to eight earliest (LH I) Mycenaean shapes exist (Mountjoy 1986, 9–16; 1993, 33–35), but are generally less common. The shape range of such plain, light-surfaced vessels is, however, at first substantially broader than that of the decorated Mycenaean class, although by LH IIA most of these plain types have been incorporated into the expanded pattern-painted repertoire of more than 25 distinct shapes (Mountjoy 1986, 17–36; 1993, 40–42). Whether plain or painted, these shapes are invariably wheelmade, whereas the contemporary plain and painted wares of the prolific ceramic workshops located at and around the site of Kolonna on Aigina are handmade, in addition to having the banding and patterns on their decorated vessels executed in either dull or matte paints. The dark-surfaced cooking wares of this period are either locally made descendants of handmade Middle Helladic (MH) types or else imports from Aigina, likewise handmade but usually featuring potter's marks (Lindblom 2001).

During the LH I phase, Mycenaean Lustrous Decorated was competing for dominance of the market in tablewares with several other decorated classes, especially Mainland Polychrome Matt-painted (probably Boeotian), Light on Lustrous Dark-burnished (probably Corinthian), and Aiginetan Matt-painted, each of which was produced in its own range of shapes. By the developed LH IIA phase, only Aeginetan Matt-painted pottery was still being produced, in a shape repertoire that had been reduced to large open and closed shapes (kraters, stamnoi, hydrias, and amphoras). Among undecorated wares, Mycenaean light-surfaced plain ware likewise appears to have displaced LH I competitors such as Gray Minyan (probably Boeotian) and Fine Orange (likewise central Greek). Even the popularity of Aeginetan dark-slipped-and-burnished kraters and goblets seems to have been waning in the face of increasing numbers of Mycenaean monochrome painted vessels. The bulk of the progress on this earliest stage of Mycenaean pottery since Furumark has been published in English: Davis (1979), Dickinson (1972, 1974, 1977, 1992), Dietz (1980, 1991), Graziadio (1988, 1991), Kalogeropoulos (1998), Lindblom (2007), Lolos (1987), Maran (1992), Mountjoy (2008), Mylonas (1973, 1975), Rutter (1989, 1993), Rutter and Rutter (1976), and Zerner (1986, 1988, 1993,

2009). Almost all of this work has been helpfully synthesized recently by Mountjoy (1993, 5–10, 33–56, 167–68; 1999, 18–24).

The second major stage of Mycenaean ceramic development encompasses the LH IIB and IIIA1 phases, lasted for a century or less, and corresponds with the period during which Knossos was the only functioning palatial administration surviving on Crete following the destruction of all other known Minoan Neopalatial centers. Although Mycenaean palatial centers may already have come into being in Messenia during the previous stage (at least at Pylos: Nelson 2007), it is during this stage that the earliest such complexes may have appeared in Laconia at the Menelaion and in the Argolid at Tiryns (Darcque 2005).

Mycenaean decorated pottery now ceases to be slavishly dependent on Minoan sources of inspiration for both shapes and decoration and instead begins to exert its own influence abroad, not only on Crete during the corresponding Late Minoan (LM) II–IIIA1 phases but also in the Cyclades and the Dodecanese, as well as in the form of imports from as far afield as Cyprus, the Levant, and Egypt (Hankey 1967; Leonard 1994; Sherratt 1999; Steel 1998, 2004; van Wijngaarden 2002; Yon, Karageorghis, and Hirschfeld 2000). Symptomatic of the decline in dependence on Crete for inspiration are the overall reduction in the number of decorated shapes by as much as a third (due to the elimination of the so-called "Palatial Class" of LH IIA: Mountjoy 1993, 41–42, 52) and the increased abstraction of the once naturalistic plant and marine motifs adopted from the LM I decorative repertoire.

The beginning of this stage witnesses the appearance of the first distinctively Mycenaean style of ceramic decoration in the form of the Ephyraean style, designed to ornament the principal forms of a standardized drinking assemblage (goblets, beaked jugs, dippers, and an occasional krater) perhaps produced previously only in metallic form (Wright 1996, 2004a, 2004b). Also appearing at this time, perhaps as a result of the sustained intense interaction with the Knossos area manifested in the LM II Warrior Graves and contemporary tombs in the Argolid, is the unpainted and lipless conical cup, occasionally used in the Minoan fashion as a lamp (Mountjoy 1993, 58).

To a somewhat later phase (LH IIIA1) belongs the earliest purely Mycenaean production of pictorially decorated pottery, for the most part consisting of amphoroid kraters bearing scenes of chariots in procession (Åkerström 1987; Morris 1989; Crouwel 1991; Sakellarakis 1992; Vermeule and Karageorghis 1982). An expanded range of plain shapes includes some that appear contemporaneously in metallic form in the Warrior Graves at Knossos, as well as in Argive tombs, along with a penchant for coating plain shapes with a thin layer of tin so as to imitate silver or perhaps even gold versions of these forms (Immerwahr 1966; Gillis 1991, 1992, 1994, 1997; Mountjoy 1993, 66; Gillis, Holmberg, and Widelöv 1995). The last of Mycenaean decorated fine ware's competitors, Aeginetan Matt-painted, disappears toward the end of this stage or at the very beginning of the next. The major deposits of these phases are well spread out on the Greek mainland, from Attica (Mountjoy 1981) and the Corinthia (Dickinson 1972) through the Argolid (French 1964, Åström 1977, Frizell 1980) down to Laconia (Catling 1977, 2009; Mountjoy 2008), once again helpfully synthesized by Mountjoy (1993, 11–15, 52–70, 168–70; 1999, 24–28).

The third stage, that of the so-called Mycenaean *koiné,* which flourished contemporaneously with the palatial centers of Athens, Dimini, Gla, Iolkos (?), Mycenae, Orchomenos, Pylos, Thebes, and Tiryns, spans the LH IIIA2–B phases of roughly 175 years' duration between the LM IIIA burning of Knossos and the violent destructions of all known mainland palaces within a comparatively short stretch of time between the end of the 13th and the first couple of decades of the 12th century BC. As the term *koiné* suggests, the ceramic repertoire during this lengthy palatial apogee of Mycenaean culture was more standardized than ever before, while at the same time boasting an expanded shape range (ca. 35 painted and 10–20 unpainted types in common use) and an ever more abstract but still impressively varied range of painted patterns.

During the earlier LH IIIA2 part of this stage, the dominant painted shapes are kylikes, small piriform jars, and small stirrup jars, and the most popular motifs are Flower and Whorl shell; during the later LH IIIB stage, the most common painted open form changes from the kylix to the deep bowl and the stemmed bowl, and Paneled Patterns become increasingly common. Massive quantities of decorated pottery are exported to western Anatolia, Cyprus, the Syro-Palestinian coast, Egypt, Sicily, and southern Italy, and small amounts are found as far west and north as Spain and the head of the Adriatic. In some of these regions, imitations of subsets of these imports have begun to be produced before the end of the 13th century; these appear to be responses to an inability to acquire genuine imports any longer (e.g., the Pastoral or Rude Style on Cyprus; small linear stirrup jars in southern Palestine and the Sinai). In other regions, a broader range of imitations suggests that migrant Aegean potters may have established workshops in what some authorities consider to be colonial settings (e.g., Miletus on the coast of western Anatolia; Broglio di Trebisacce in Calabria).

This entire stage marks the highpoint in the production of Mycenaean pictorial pottery, most of it evidently distributed to Cyprus and from there to the Levant in the form of amphoroid and bell kraters, but some also as other shapes (jugs, chalices, kylikes, conical rhyta) associated with ceremonial drinking (Steel 1999; van Wijngaarden 2002; Jung 2006b). Substantial settlement deposits of the LH IIIA2 subphase have been found in the Corinthia (Tsoungiza), Laconia (Ayios Stephanos), Messenia (Nichoria), the Argolid (Mycenae), and eastern Locris (Mitrou), but so far only those from Nichoria and some from Mycenae have been published, so the subphase's definition continues to rely more on tomb deposits than is normally the case (Mountjoy 1993, 71–79; 1999, 28–32).

LH IIIB, however, is better documented by published settlement deposits from all areas of the Greek mainland than any previous ceramic phase (Mountjoy 1993, 80–90; 1999, 32–36; Voigtländer 2003), with the result that subphases within it are readily recognizable (e.g., LH IIIB1 vs. LH IIIB2, the first probably two or even three times longer than the second, which has itself been recently subdivided: Vitale 2006). A hallmark of the earlier subphase is the Zygouries style, a distinctively spare system of ornament featuring vertical Whorl shell and hybrid Flower patterns applied chiefly to drinking vessels (kylikes, jugs, and kraters) and thus broadly comparable in both functional and aesthetic senses to the earlier Ephyraean style of LH IIB (Thomas 1997, 2004, 2005). Some developments toward the end of LH IIIB herald trends that will become much more pronounced in the succeeding stage, namely the dramatic decline in ceramic exports to Cyprus, the Levant, and Egypt already mentioned, as well as the possible restriction of the diagnostic features of the LH IIIB2 subphase—the decorative variants of the deep bowl known as the Group B and rosette types (Sherratt 1980; Mountjoy 1999, 35–36, figure 39: 295–98)—to the Argolid, central Greece, and the Corinthian Gulf.

A fourth and final stage in the development of Mycenaean pottery corresponds to the Postpalatial era of Mycenaean culture, the LH IIIC phase (Desborough 1964; Deger-Jalkotzy 1998; Dickinson 2006, 58–78; Evely 2006; Stockhammer 2007), which for some includes a brief subphase transitional to the Iron Age that is termed "Submycenaean." Roughly as long as the preceding LH IIIA2–B palatial era in calendar years, this stage witnesses as impressive a movement toward regionally diverse ceramic assemblages as its predecessor did to that of a uniform ceramic *koiné*. Thanks to the highly unsettled conditions that prevailed throughout the eastern Mediterranean world during the 12th and 11th centuries BC, large numbers of settlement destruction contexts have been identified, and thus a more sensitive system of relative chronology has been devised that recognizes up to as many as seven short-lived subphases (Mountjoy 1999, 39, table II; 2007, 229, figure 1; Rutter 2007, 293, figure 4, with Vitale 2006, 201, table 3) that are commonly clustered into three or four broader subdivisions termed LH IIIC Early, Middle, and Late (the last either including or followed by "Submycenaean").

The LH IIIC Early phase (Mountjoy 1993, 90–97; 1999, 36–47; Deger-Jalkotzy and Zavadil 2003; Vitale 2006; Stockhammer 2007) is characterized by a significant impoverishment in the pattern-painted repertoire, which results in a greater percentage of vessels being decorated either with simple banding or a solid coating of paint or else left altogether plain. Virtually the only vessels to attract substantial amounts of patterned ornament are kraters and stirrup jars, along with a few deep bowls. Most closely akin to this stage of LH IIIC ceramic development are the large quantities of Mycenaeanizing pottery that appear as local products at numerous sites on Cyprus and have been considered to represent a wave of Aegean migration to that island.

Also of considerable historical interest is a dramatic rise in the number of sites that at this time have furnished evidence for a technologically and formally alien class of handmade, dark-surfaced, and crudely burnished (HMB) pottery in a variable but sometimes fairly wide range of shapes (Jung 2006a, 21–51; Strack 2007). These HMB containers from mainland Greek contexts, when examined by means of petrographic or trace-element analysis, have been shown to be likely local products at sites where they occur in significant quantities, thus presumably made where they were found by immigrant potters rather than being imported (Jung 2006a, 24n98). The most plausible region of origin of these potters is presently considered to be southern Italy, although a large number of other candidates (e.g., Epirus, the Morava Valley of Yugoslavia, the Black Sea Coast of Romania) have been proposed and for good reason rejected. Regionalism at this time is manifested largely by distinctive preferences drawn from a shared tradition, whether for particular forms of drinking cups and bowls or for special ways of decorating these, rather than by altogether new directions in vessel shapes or decorative motifs. That is, localized styles now tend to be defined more by narrowed groupings of inherited shape and decorative ranges than by creative additions to traditional assemblages.

The LH IIIC Middle phase (Mountjoy 1993, 97–108; 1999, 47–51; Thomatos 2006, 2007; Deger-Jalkotzy and Zavadil 2007) witnesses an artistic resurgence in ceramics exemplified above all by a renewed interest in elaborately decorated pottery that typically differs markedly from that of earlier stages in the complexity of its patterns and sometimes even of the overall syntax, as well as in the choice of pictorial themes (Rutter 1992, 62–67). One result of this shift is the emergence of a series of regionally restricted, decoratively elaborate styles (e.g., Argive Close Style, Lefkandi Pictorial Style, several classes of Octopus Style) that as a group have been described by Schachermeyr with the term "pleonastic" (1979, 1980; Deger-Jalkotzy and Zavadil 2007, 347, 350–51).

When combined with the regional preferences for specific groupings of open shapes (in particular) that characterized the previous phase, this new enthusiasm for ornamental elaboration makes ceramic regionalism at this time appear more pronounced throughout the Mycenaean world than it had been at any other time since the end of LH I four centuries before. The enhanced interest in more ornamental ceramic containers at first appears to be a development at variance with the unsettled conditions of the later 12th century but makes good sense as a broad-based response to the increasing rarity of richly decorated objects in other media such as seals, wall paintings, and containers of stone, metal, and exotic imported materials like ivory, ostrich eggs, or ebony. By the end of the century, the only pictorial media still readily available to Mycenaean consumers were objects made of terracotta, whether containers or figurines.

The LH IIIC Late phase (Mountjoy 1993, 109–17; 1999, 51–58) appears to have been fairly short-lived and is marked by substantial declines in the artistic range and technical accomplishment of Aegean potters. Shapes now number only about two-thirds of those current in the preceding phase, and much the same appears to be true with respect to painted patterns. These figures shrink still further at the end of the phase, so that at the very end of the mainland Greek Bronze Age the ceramic repertoire is at its lowest ebb in terms of range and quality in more than two millennia. Pictorialism disappears entirely, and so, too, may fine plain pottery. Regionalism becomes more difficult to detect due to the extreme simplicity of the ceramic assemblage, whether used for domestic, funerary, or ritual purposes.

Mycenaean pottery was among the earliest Mediterranean pottery of any date to be subjected to trace-element analysis with an eye to determining specific locales of manufacture (i.e., provenience analysis); the first analyses of this kind were applied more than forty years ago in the form of optical emission spectroscopy to transport stirrup jars bearing painted inscriptions in Linear B found in the 1920s by Keramopoullos in the palatial building at Thebes, which he christened the "House of Kadmos" (Catling and Millett 1965; Jones 1986, 477–94). Since then, a variety of other chemical techniques have been explored with varying degrees of success, along with petrological examination that focuses on macroscopic mineralogical components of the fired clay with similar goals in mind.

The preferred chemical techniques are now instrumental neutron activation analysis (INAA) and inductively coupled plasma atomic emission spectrometry (ICP-AES), and the centers of such analytical work as applied to specifically Mycenaean samples have thus far been located at Oxford (UK), Athens, Berkeley, Bonn, and Manchester (UK). Databanks that comprise well over five thousand analyzed samples now exist for Aegean Late Bronze Age pottery of one kind or another (e.g., Jones 1986, 99–299, 439–521; Tomlinson 1997; Mountjoy and Ponting 2000; Mommsen et al. 2001; Mommsen 2003; Badre, Boileau, Jung, and Mommsen 2005). Petrology, typically applied to somewhat coarser fabrics than those characteristic of Mycenaean fine wares, has proved to be an effective technique for investigating the provenience of HMB, as well as transport stirrup jars (Whitbread 1992; Day 1995). The application of organic residue analysis to Mycenaean pottery with the aim of determining the nature of vessel contents is still in its infancy but is expected to produce useful results soon (Martlew 2004; Koh 2006).

The natures and histories of Mycenaeanizing ceramic assemblages that were produced at sites outside of those regions conventionally considered to have been culturally "Mycenaean," whether in Macedonia (e.g., Jung 2002), southern Italy (e.g., Vagnetti 1999), or the Levant (e.g., Steel 2004; Yasur-Landau 2002, 2005), have frequently been the targets of ambitious research projects, as has been the related issue of how the borders of the region considered to be culturally Mycenaean can be mapped at various points in time with the aid of Mycenaean pottery (Kilian 1976; Feuer 1983).

Notwithstanding the very impressive progress that the study of Mycenaean pottery has made during the 140 years since its inception, a number of major questions involving this large body of prehistoric Greek material culture remain either unresolved or underinvestigated. Still unknown, for example, is where the production of the earliest pottery universally recognized as Mycenaean—the Lustrous Decorated class of LH I—actually began. Much also remains to be learned about how its producers established their product as the dominant decorated fine ware of Mycenaean civilization.

At the other end of the chronological spectrum, agreement has yet to be reached on whether a discrete "Submycenaean" phase can be defined in terms of ordinary settlement pottery without taking contemporary funerary practices and burial assemblages into consideration (Rutter 1978; Jacob-Felsch 1988; Mountjoy 1988; Papadimitriou 1988; Lis in press; Van de Moortel in press). Neglected topics that merit far more attention than they have so far received are the history and regional variability of Mycenaean cooking pottery, a similar history of Mycenaean pithoi along the lines of Christakis's recent work (2005) on Minoan bulk storage vessels, and the specific role played by Mycenaean (Haskell 1981), as opposed to Minoan (Haskell 2005) or Aeginetan (Lindblom 2001), transport vessels in intra-Aegean exchanges, as well as more broadly in eastern Mediterranean trade throughout the Late Bronze Age.

BIBLIOGRAPHY

Åkerström, Åke. 1987. *Berbati* II: *The Pictorial Pottery.* Stockholm: Swedish Institute in Athens.

Åström, Paul. 1977. *The Cuirass Tomb and Other Finds at Dendra.* Part 1, *The Chamber Tombs. SIMA* 4. Gothenburg: Åström.

Leila Badre, Marie-Claude Boileau, Reinhard Jung, and Hans Mommsen. 2005. "The Provenance of Aegean and Syrian-Type Pottery Found at Tell Kazel (Syria)." *Ägypten und Levante* 15: 15–47.

Blegen, Carl W., and Marion Rawson. 1966. *The Palace of Nestor at Pylos in Western Messenia,* vol. 1. Princeton: Princeton University Press.

———. 1921. *Korakou. A Prehistoric Settlement near Corinth.* Boston: American School of Classical Studies at Athens.

Catling, Hector W. 1977. "Excavations at the Menelaion, Sparta, 1973–76." *AR* 1976–1977: 23–42.

———. 2009. *Sparta: Menelaion I. The Bronze Age.* London: British School at Athens.

———, and Anne Millett. 1965. "A Study of the Inscribed Stirrup Jars from Thebes." *Archaeometry* 8: 3–85.

Christakis, Kostandinos S. 2005. *Cretan Bronze Age Pithoi: Traditions and Trends in the Production and Consumption of Storage Containers in Bronze Age Crete.* Philadelphia: INSTAP Academic Press.

Crouwel, Joost H. 1991. *The Mycenaean Pictorial Pottery: Well-built Mycenae.* Fascicule 21. Oxford: Oxbow.

Darcque, Pascal. 2005. *L'habitat mycénien: Formes et fonctions de l'espace bâti en Grèce continentale à la fin du IIe millénaire avant J.-C.* Athens: L'École française d'Athènes.

Davis, Jack L. 1979. "Late Helladic I Pottery from Korakou." *Hesperia* 48: 234–63.

Day, Peter M. 1995. "Appendix C: Petrographic Analysis of Transport Stirrup Jars from the House of the Oil Merchant, Mycenae." In *The "Ivory Houses" at Mycenae,* ed. Iphigeneia Tournavitou, 309–16. London: British School at Athens.

Deger-Jalkotzy, Sigrid. 1998. "*The Last Mycenaeans and Their Successors* Updated." In *Mediterranean Peoples,* 114–28.

———, and Michaela Zavadil, eds. 2003. *LH IIIC.*

———. 2007. *LH IIIC Middle.*

Desborough, Vincent R. d'A. 1964. *The Last Mycenaeans and Their Successors.* Oxford: Clarendon.

Dickinson, Oliver T. P. K. 1972. "Late Helladic IIA and IIB: Some Evidence from Korakou." *BSA* 67: 103–12.

———. 1974. "The Definition of Late Helladic I." *BSA* 69: 109–20.

———. 1977. *The Origins of Mycenaean Civilization. SIMA* 49. Gothenburg: Åström.

———. 1992. "Part I: The Late Helladic I and II Pottery." In *Excavations at Nichoria in Southwest Greece II: The Bronze Age Occupation,* ed. William A. McDonald and Nancy C. Wilkie, 469–88. Minneapolis: University of Minnesota Press.

———. 2006. *The Aegean from Bronze Age to Iron Age: Continuity and Change between the Twelfth and Eighth Centuries B.C.* London: Routledge.

Dietz, Søren. 1980. *Asine* II, 2: *The Middle Helladic Cemetery, the Middle Helladic, and Early Mycenaean Deposits.* Stockholm: Åström.

———. 1991. *The Argolid at the Transition to the Mycenaean Age: Studies in the Chronology and Cultural Development in the Shaft Grave Period.* Copenhagen: National Museum, Dept. of Near Eastern and Classical Antiquities.

Evely, Doniert, ed. 2006. *Lefkandi IV: The Bronze Age. The Late Helladic IIIC Settlement at Xeropolis.* London: British School at Athens.

Feuer, Bryan. 1983. *The Northern Mycenaean Border in Thessaly.* Oxford: British Archaeological Reports.

Fitton, J. Lesley. 1996. *The Discovery of the Greek Bronze Age.* Cambridge, Mass.: Harvard University Press.

French, Elizabeth. 1963. "Pottery Groups from Mycenae: A Summary." *BSA* 58: 44–52.

———. 1964. "Late Helladic IIIA1 Pottery from Mycenae." *BSA* 59: 241–61.

———. 1965. "Late Helladic IIIA2 Pottery from Mycenae." *BSA* 60: 159–202.

———. 1966. "A Group of Late Helladic IIIB1 Pottery from Mycenae." *BSA* 61: 216–38.

———. 1967. "Pottery from Late Helladic IIIB1 Destruction Contexts at Mycenae." *BSA* 62: 149–93.

———. 1969a. "The First Phase of LH IIIC." *AA:* 133–36.

———. 1969b. "A Group of Late Helladic IIIB2 Pottery from Mycenae." *BSA* 64: 71–93.

Frizell, Barbro S. 1980. *An Early Mycenaean Settlement at Asine: The Late Helladic IIB–IIIA1 Pottery.* Gothenburg: Dept. of Ancient Culture and Civilization, Classical Institute, University of Gothenburg.

Furtwängler, Adolf, and Georg Loeschcke. 1879. *Mykenische Thongefässe: Festschrift zur Feier des fünfzigjährigen Bestehens des Deutschen Archaeologischen Institutes in Rom im Auftrage des Institutes in Athen herausgegeben.* Berlin: Asher.

———. 1886. *Mykenische Vasen: Vorhellenische Thongefässe aus dem Gebiete des Mittelmeeres.* Berlin: Asher.

Furumark, Arne. 1941a. *The Chronology of Mycenaean Pottery.* Stockholm: Kungl. Vitterhets, Historie och Antikvitets Akademien.

———. 1941b. *Mycenaean Pottery: Analysis and Classification.* Stockholm: Kungl. Vitterhets, Historie och Antikvitets Akademien.

Gillis, Carole. 1991. "Tin-covered Vessels in the Aegean Bronze Age." *Hydra* 8: 1–30.

———. 1992. "How I Discovered Gold and Solved the Alchemists' Dream, or Tin-covered Vessels: Part II." *Hydra* 10: 13–16.

———. 1994. "Binding Evidence. Tin Foil and Organic Binder on Aegean Late Bronze Age Pottery." *OpAth* 20: 57–61.

———. 1997. "Tin-covered Late Bronze Age Vessels: Analyses and Social Implications." In *Trade and Production in Premonetary Greece: Production and the Craftsman,* ed. Carole Gillis, Christina Risberg, and Birgitta Sjöberg, 131–38. *SIMA-PB* 143. Jonsered: Åström.

———, Bertil Holmberg, and Anders Widelöv. 1995. "Aegean Bronze Age Tinned Vessels: Analyses and Social Implications." In *8th CIMTEC: The Cultural Ceramic Heritage,* ed. Pietro Vincenzini, 251–60. Monograph in Materials and Society 2. Faenza: Techna.

Graziadio, Giampaolo. 1988. "The Chronology of the Graves of Circle B at Mycenae: A New Hypothesis." *AJA* 92: 343–72.

———. 1991. "The Process of Social Stratification at Mycenae in the Shaft Grave Period: A Comparative Examination of the Evidence." *AJA* 95: 403–40.

Güntner, Wolfgang. 2000. *Tiryns: Forschungen und Berichte XII: Figürlich bemalte mykenische Keramik aus Tiryns.* Mainz: von Zabern.

Hankey, Vronwy. 1967. "Mycenaean Pottery in the Near East: Notes on Finds since 1951." *BSA* 62: 107–47.

Haskell, Halford W. 1981. "Coarse-ware Stirrup-jars at Mycenae." *BSA* 76: 225–38.

————. 2005. "Region to Region Export of Transport Stirrup Jars from LM IIIA2/B Crete." In *Ariadne's Threads*, 205–21.

Immerwahr, Sara A. 1966. "The Use of Tin on Mycenaean Vases." *Hesperia* 35: 381–96.

Jacob-Felsch, Margrit. 1988. "Compass-drawn Concentric Circles in Vase Painting: A Problem of Relative Chronology at the End of the Bronze Age." In *Problems in Greek Prehistory*, 193–99.

————. 1996. "Die spätmykenische und frühprotogeometrische Keramik." In *Kalapodi: Ergebnisse der Ausgrabungen im Heiligtum der Artemis und des Apollon von Hyampolis in der antiken Phokis* I, ed. Rainer C. S. Felsch, 1–213. Mainz: von Zabern.

Jones, Richard E. 1986. *Greek and Cypriot Pottery: A Review of Scientific Studies*. London: British School at Athens.

Jung, Reinhard. 2002. *Kastanas: Ausgrabungen in einem Siedlungshügel der Bronze- und Eisenzeit Makedoniens 1975–1979: Die Drehscheibenkeramik der Schichten 19 bis 11*. Kiel: Oetker/Voges.

————. 2006a. *Chronologia Comparata: Vergleichende Chronologie von Südgriechenland und Süditalien von ca. 1700/1600 bis 1000 v. u. Z.* Vienna: Verlag der Österreichishen Akademie der Wissenschaften.

————. 2006b. "Ευποτον Ποτεριον: Mykenische Keramik und mykenische Trinksitten in der Ägäis, in Syrien, Makedonien und Italien." In *Studi in Protostoria in Onore di Renato Peroni*, ed. Renato Peroni, 407–23. Florence: Insegna del Giglio.

Kalogeropoulos, Konstantinos. 1998. *Die frühmykenischen Grabfunde von Analipsis (Südostliches Arkadien) mit einem Beitrag zu den Palatialen Amphoren des griechischen Festlandes*. Athens: He en Athenais Archaiologike Hetaireia.

Kilian, Klaus. 1976. "Nordgrenze des ägäischen Kulturbereiches im mykenischer und nackmykenischer Zeit." *Jahresbericht des Instituts für Vorgeschichte, Universität Frankfurt-am-Main 1976*: 112–29.

Koh, Andrew J. 2006. The Organic Residues of Mochlos, Crete: An Interdisciplinary Study of Typological and Spatial Function at an Archaeological Site. PhD diss., University of Pennsylvania.

Leonard, Albert, Jr. 1994. *An Index to the Late Bronze Age Aegean Pottery from Syria-Palestine*. SIMA 114. Jonsered, Sweden: Åström.

Lindblom, Michael. 2001. *Marks and Makers: Appearance, Distribution, and Function of Middle and Late Helladic Manufacturers' Marks on Aeginetan Pottery*. SIMA 128. Jonsered, Sweden: Åström.

————. 2007. "Early Mycenaean Mortuary Meals at Lerna VI with Special Emphasis on Their Aeginetan Components." In *Middle Helladic Pottery*, 115–35.

Lis, Bartolomej. In press. "The Sequence of Late Bronze/Early Iron Age Pottery from East-central Greek Settlements: A Fresh Look at Old and New Evidence." In *LH IIIC Late*.

Lolos, Yannos. 1987. *The Late Helladic I Pottery of the Southwestern Peloponnesos and Its Local Characteristics*. SIMA 50. Gothenburg: Åström.

Manning, Sturt W., Christopher Bronk Ramsey, Walter Kutschera, Thomas Higham, Bernd Kromer, Peter Steier, and Eva M. Wild. 2006. "Chronology for the Aegean Late Bronze Age 1700–1400 B.C." *Science* 312: 565–69.

Maran, Joseph. 1992. *Kiapha Thiti: Ergebnisse der Ausgrabungen II.2: 2. Jt. v. Chr.: Keramik und Kleinfunde. Marburger Winckelmann-Programm 1990*. Marburg/Lahn: Phillips-Universität.

Martlew, Holly. 2004. "Minoan and Mycenaean Technology as Revealed through Organic Residue Analysis." In *Invention and Innovation: The Social Context of Change 2: Egypt, the Aegean, and the Near East 1650–1150 B.C.*, ed. Janine Bourriau and Jacke S. Phillips, 121–48. Oxford: Oxbow.

McDonald, William A. 1967. *Progress into the Past: The Rediscovery of Mycenaean Civilization*. New York: Macmillan.

Mee, Christopher. 1982. *Rhodes in the Bronze Age: An Archaeological Survey*. Warminster: Aris and Phillips.

Mommsen, Hans. 2003. "Attic Pottery Production, Imports, and Exports during the Mycenaean Period by Neutron Activation Analysis." *Mediterranean Archaeology and Archaeometry* 3: 13–30.

———, Anno Hein, Doris Ittameier, Joseph Maran, and Phanouria Dakoronia. 2001. "New Production Centres of Ceramics from Bronze Age Settlements in Central Greece Obtained by Neutron Activation Analysis." In *Archaeometry Issues in Greek Prehistory and Antiquity*, ed. Yiannis Bassiakos, Eleni Aloupi, and Giorgos Facorellis, 343–54. Athens: Elliniki Archaiometriki Etaireia.

Morris, Christine E. 1989. The Mycenaean Amphoroid Krater: A Study in Form, Design, and Function. PhD diss., University College London.

Mountjoy, Penelope A. 1976. "Late Helladic IIIB1 Pottery Dating the Construction of the South House at Mycenae." *BSA* 71: 77–111.

———. 1981. *Four Early Mycenaean Wells from the South Slope of the Acropolis at Athens*. Miscellanea Graeca 4. Gent: Belgian Archaeological Mission in Greece.

———. 1983. *Orchomenos V: Mycenaean Pottery from Orchomenos, Eutresis, and Other Boeotian Sites*. Munich: Verlag der Bayerischen Akademie der Wissenschaften.

———. 1985. "The Pottery." In *The Archaeology of Cult: The Sanctuary at Phylakopi*, ed. Colin Renfrew, 151–208. London: British School at Athens.

———. 1986. *Mycenaean Decorated Pottery: A Guide to Identification*. Gothenburg: Åström.

———. 1988. "LH IIIC Late versus Submycenaean: The Kerameikos Pompeion Cemetery Reviewed." *JdI* 103: 1–33.

———. 1993. *Mycenaean Pottery: An Introduction*. Oxford: Oxford University Committee for Archaeology.

———. 1995. "Thorikos Mine no. 3: The Mycenaean Pottery." *BSA* 90: 195–228.

———. 1997. "The Destruction of the Palace at Pylos Reconsidered." *BSA* 92: 109–35.

———. 1998. "The East Aegean–West Anatolian Interface in the Late Bronze Age: Mycenaeans and the Kingdom of Ahhiyawa." *AnatSt* 48: 33–67.

———. 1999. *Regional Mycenaean Decorated Pottery*. Rahden: Leidorf.

———. 2008. "The Late Helladic Pottery." In *Ayios Stephanos. Excavations at a Bronze Age and Medieval Settlement in Southern Laconia*, ed. William D. Taylour and Richard Janko, 299–387. London: British School at Athens.

———, and Matthew J. Ponting. 2000. "The Minoan Thalassocracy Reconsidered: Provenance Studies of LH IIA/LM IB Pottery from Phylakopi, Ay. Irini, and Athens." *BSA* 95: 141–84.

Mylonas, George E. 1973. *O taphikos kyklos B ton Mykenon*. Athens: He en Athenais Archaiologike Hetaireia.

———. 1975. *To dytikon nekrotapheion tes Eleusinos*. Athens: He en Athenais Archaiologike Hetaireia.

Nelson, Michael C. 2007. "Pylos, Block Masonry, and Monumental Architecture in the Late Bronze Age Peloponnese." In *Power and Architecture: Monumental Public Architecture in the Bronze Age Near East and Aegean*, ed. Joachim Bretschneider, Jan Driessen, and Karel van Lerberghe, 143–59. Leuven: Peeters.

Papadimitriou, Alkestis. 1988. "Bericht zur früheisenzeitlichen Keramik aus der Unterburg von Tiryns: Ausgrabungen in Tiryns 1982–83." *AA*: 227–43.

Podzuweit, Christian. 2007. *Tiryns: Forschungen und Berichte XIV: Studien zur spätmykenischen Keramik.* Wiesbaden: Reicheert.

Rutter, Jeremy B. 1974. The Late Helladic IIIB and IIIC Periods at Korakou and Gonia in the Corinthia. PhD diss., University of Pennsylvania.

———. 1977. "LH IIIC Pottery and Some Historical Implications." In *Symposium on the Dark Ages in Greece,* ed. Ellen N. Davis, 1–20. New York: Archaeological Institute of America.

———. 1978. "A Plea for the Abandonment of the Term 'Submycenaean.'" *TUAS* 3: 58–65.

———. 1979. "The Last Mycenaeans at Corinth." *Hesperia* 48: 348–92.

———. 1989. "A Ceramic Definition of Late Helladic I from Tsoungiza." *Hydra* 6: 1–19.

———. 1992. "Cultural Novelties in the Post-palatial Aegean World: Indices of Vitality or Decline?" In *The 12th Century B.C.: The Crisis Years,* ed. William A. Ward and Martha S. Joukowsky, 61–78. Dubuque: Kendall/Hunt.

———. 1993. "A Group of Late Helladic IIA Pottery from Tsoungiza." *Hesperia* 62: 53–93.

———. 2001. "Review of Aegean Prehistory II: The Prepalatial Bronze Age of the Southern and Central Greek Mainland." In *Aegean Prehistory,* 95–155.

———. 2007. "How Different Is LH IIIC at Mitrou? An Initial Comparison with Kalapodi, Kynos, and Lefkandi." In *LH IIIC Middle,* 287–300.

———, and Sarah H. Rutter. 1976. *The Transition to Mycenaean: A Stratified Middle Helladic II to Late Helladic IIA Pottery Sequence from Ayios Stephanos in Lakonia.* Los Angeles: Institute of Archaeology, University of California at Los Angeles.

Sakellarakis, Giannis A. 1992. *The Mycenaean Pictorial Style in the National Archaeological Museum of Athens.* Athens: Kapon Editions.

Schachermeyr, Fritz. 1979. "The Pleonastic Pottery of Cretan Middle IIIIC and Its Cypriote Relations." In *Acts of the International Archaeological Symposium "The Relations between Cyprus and Crete ca. 2000–500 B.C.": Nicosia, 16th April–22nd April 1978,* 204–14. Nicosia: Department of Antiquities, Cyprus.

———. 1980. *Die ägäische Frühzeit IV: Griechenland im Zeitalter der Wanderungen vom Ende der mykenischen Ära bis auf die Dorier.* Vienna: Verlag der Österreichishen Akademie der Wissenschaften.

Sherratt, E. Susan. 1980. "Regional Variation in the Pottery of Late Helladic IIIB." *BSA* 75: 175–202.

———. 1981. The Pottery of Late Helladic IIIC and Its Significance. PhD diss., Oxford University.

———. 1999. "*E pur si muove*: Pots, Markets, and Values in the Second Millennium Mediterranean." In *The Complex Past of Pottery: Production, Circulation, and Consumption of Mycenaean and Greek Pottery [Sixteenth to Early Fifth Centuries B.C.],* ed. Jan P. Crielaard, Vladimir Stissi, and Gert J. van Wijngaarden, 163–211. Amsterdam: Gieben.

Slenczka, Eberhard. 1974. *Tiryns: Forschungen und Berichte VII: Figürlich bemalte mykenische Keramik aus Tiryns.* Mainz: von Zabern.

Steel, Louise. 1998. "The Social Impact of Mycenaean Imported Pottery in Cyprus." *BSA* 93: 285–96.

———. 1999. "Wine Kraters and Chariots: The Mycenaean Pictorial Style Reconsidered." In *Meletemata,* 803–10.

———. 2004. "A Reappraisal of the Distribution, Context, and Function of Mycenaean Pottery in Cyprus." In *La céramique mycénienne de l'Égée au Levant: Hommage à*

Vronwy Hankey, ed. Jacqueline Balensi, Jean-Yves Monchambert, and Sylvie Müller Celka, 69–85. Lyon: Maison de l'Orient et de la Méditerranée–Jean Pouilloux.

Stockhammer, Philipp W. 2007. *Kontinuität und Wandel: Die Keramik der Nachpalastzeit aus der Unterstadt von Tiryns.* PhD diss., University of Heidelberg; http://www.ub.uni-heidelberg.de/archiv/8612.

Strack, Sara. 2007. *Regional Dynamics and Social Change in the Late Bronze and Early Iron Age: A Study of Handmade Pottery from Southern and Central Greece.* PhD diss., University of Edinburgh.

Thomas, Patrick M. 1997. "Mycenaean Kylix Painters at Zygouries." In *TEXNH,* 377–83.

———. 2004. "Some Observations on the 'Zygouries' Kylix and Late Helladic IIIB Chronology." In *XAPIΣ,* 207–24.

———. 2005. "A Deposit of Late Helladic IIIB:1 Pottery from Tsoungiza." *Hesperia* 74: 451–573.

Thomatos, Marina. 2006. *The Final Revival of the Aegean Bronze Age: A Case Study of the Argolid, Corinthia, Attica, Euboea, the Cyclades, and the Dodecanese during LH IIIC Middle.* Oxford: Archaeopress.

———. 2007. "*Koine* and Subsidiary *Koines:* Coastal and Island Sites of the Central and Southern Aegean during LH IIIC Middle." In *LH IIIC Middle,* 315–27.

Tomlinson, Jonathan E. 1997. "Statistical Evaluation of the Asaro-Perlman Neutron Activation Data on Mycenaean Pottery from the Peloponnese." *BSA* 92: 139–64.

Vagnetti, Lucia. 1999. "Mycenaean Pottery in the Central Mediterranean: Imports and Local Production in Their Context." In *The Complex Past of Pottery: Production and Consumption of Mycenaean and Greek Pottery ca. 1500–500 B.C.,* ed. Jan P. Crielaard, Vladimir Stissi, and Gert J. van Wijngaarden, 137–61. Amsterdam: Gieben.

Van de Moortel, Aleydis. In press. "The Late Helladic IIIC–Protogeometric Transition at Mitrou in East Lokris." In *LH IIIC Late.*

van Wijngaarden, Gert J. 2002. *Use and Appreciation of Mycenaean Pottery in the Levant, Cyprus, and Italy (ca. 1600–1200 BC).* Amsterdam: Amsterdam University Press.

Vermeule, Emily, and Vassos Karageorghis. 1982. *Mycenaean Pictorial Vase Painting.* Cambridge, Mass.: Harvard University Press.

Vitale, Salvatore. 2006. "The LH IIIB–LH IIIC Transition on the Mycenaean Mainland: Ceramic Phases and Terminology." *Hesperia* 75: 177–204.

Voigtländer, Walter. 2003. *Tiryns: Forschungen und Berichte X: Die Palaststilkeramik.* Mainz: von Zabern.

Wardle, Kenneth A. 1969. "A Group of Late Helladic IIIB1 Pottery from within the Citadel at Mycenae." *BSA* 64: 261–97.

———. 1973. "A Group of Late Helladic IIIB2 Pottery from within the Citadel at Mycenae: The Causeway Deposit." *BSA* 68: 297–342.

Whitbread, Ian. 1992. "Petrographic Analysis of Barbarian Ware from the Menelaion, Sparta." In *Philolakon: Lakonian Studies in Honour of Hector Catling,* ed. Jan M. Sanders, 297–306. London: British School of Athens.

Wiener, Malcolm H. 2007. "Times Change: The Current State of the Debate in Old World Chronology." In *SCIEM* III, 25–48.

Wright, James C. 1996. "Empty Cups and Empty Jugs: The Social Role of Wine in Minoan and Mycenaean Societies." In *The Origins and Ancient History of Wine,* ed. Patrick E. McGovern, Stuart J. Fleming, and Solomon H. Katz, 287–309. Amsterdam: Gordon and Breach.

———. 2004a. "Mycenaean Drinking Services and Standards of Etiquette." In *Food, Cuisine, and Society in Prehistoric Greece,* ed. Paul Halstead and John C. Barrett, 90–104. Sheffield Studies in Aegean Archaeology 5. Oxford: Oxbow.

————. 2004b. "A Survey for Evidence of Feasting in Mycenaean Society." In *The Mycenaean Feast,* ed. James C. Wright, 13–58. *Hesperia* 73(2). Princeton: American School of Classical Studies.

Yasur-Landau, Assaf. 2002. Social Aspects of Aegean Settlement in the Southern Levant at the End of the 2nd Millennium BCE. PhD diss., Tel Aviv University.

————. 2005. "Old Wine in New Vessels: Intercultural Contact, Innovation and Aegean, Canaanite, and Philistine Foodways." *Tel Aviv* 32(2): 168–91.

Yon, Marguerite, Vassos Karageorghis, and Nicolle Hirschfeld. 2000. *Céramiques mycéniennes d'Ougarit. Ras Shamra-Ougarit* XIII. Paris: ERC-ADPF.

Zerner, Carol W. 1986. "Middle Helladic and Late Helladic I Pottery from Lerna." *Hydra* 2: 58–74.

————. 1988. "Middle Helladic and Late Helladic I Pottery from Lerna: Part II: Shapes." *Hydra* 4: 1–10.

————. 1993. "New Perspectives on Trade in the Middle and Early Late Helladic Periods on the Mainland." In *Wace and Blegen,* 39–56.

————. 2008. "The Middle Helladic Pottery, with the Middle Helladic Wares from Late Helladic Deposits and the Potters' Marks." In *Ayios Stephanos. Excavations at a Bronze Age and Medieval Settlement in Southern Laconia,* ed. William D. Taylour and Richard Janko, 177–298. London: British School at Athens.

CHAPTER 32

....

TEXTILES

....

BRENDAN BURKE

SPINNING fibers and weaving garments predates by thousands of years nearly every other known craft or technology, including freestanding architecture, metallurgy, and ceramics. Unlike contemporary Egypt (e.g., Kemp and Vogelsang-Eastwood 2001), scant traces of cloth from the Bronze Age Aegean survive, yet by using multidisciplinary approaches, including visual culture, textual sources, and tools of production, it is possible to understand cloth manufacture, distribution, and consumption. In this chapter the tools of cloth production are contextualized within their economic, political, and social realms and thereby show that this was one of the most important economic activities of the Bronze Age Aegean. Within the Minoan and Mycenaean spheres, many craft activities, including the many phases of textile production, were controlled by elites in order to maintain and finance social, religious, and military institutions.

Cloth manufacture is labor intensive and involves many different stages of production, including the mobilization of agricultural resources, the preparation of raw materials, the spinning of thread, weaving, storage, and, finally, distribution, all of which are best administered under the direct control of a regional center or palace. There are three main sources of information for Aegean cloth: excavated craft residues (tools of production), administrative documents (seals, sealings, tablets), and visual culture (representations of garments in Bronze Age art).

In the Aegean, the warp-weighted loom was used for the production of the majority of textiles, beginning as early as the Middle Neolithic period. The basic technology of this type of loom is simple: A shed is created by leaning a simple frame against a flat upright wall. Rows of vertical warp threads fall downward and can be divided into any number of smaller sheds. Weft threads run horizontally through these sheds, and, by using a shuttle, a skilled weaver can create a variety of patterns with the interwoven threads. The woven design generally starts from the top, and the weave is packed upward. This technology is fairly simple, which may explain its great popularity, especially in comparison to the ground looms and two-beam vertical looms of Egypt and the Near East (Hoffmann 1964; Crowfoot 1936; Carington Smith 1975, 97–99; Kemp and Vogelsang-Eastwood 2001).

PREPALATIAL CRETE

Radiocarbon dates suggest that textile equipment at Knossos first appeared in the Middle Neolithic, in approximately the first quarter of the fourth millennium BC (J. Evans 1968, 272; Carington Smith 1975, 182–84). Tools for cloth production first occur in wide distribution throughout the site, illustrating that individual household units were making cloth for their own needs. By the Late Neolithic, however, equipment is concentrated only in certain areas of the site, suggesting a change to a system of specialization, wherein autonomous individuals or household units aggregated to produce cloth for group consumption and exchange.

By the Early Bronze Age, Myrtos Fournou Koriphi on the south coast of Crete provides a great deal of evidence for the role of cloth production in the third millennium BC. Myrtos, dating primarily to the EM II period, was viewed by the excavator, Warren, as a single, integrated community with specialized areas for economic, political, and ritual purposes (Warren 1972, 267). Branigan, however, has interpreted the one-hundred-room site as an integrated whole: a mansion, or protopalace, for a local chief (Branigan 1970, 47–48). Whitelaw's reinvestigation of EM II A–B Myrtos indicates that the social organization shows no signs of complexity beyond that of a large nuclear family comprising perhaps six separate households (1983).

Along with significant numbers of loomweights and spindle whorls of the Early Minoan period, the earliest known spinning bowls are found at Myrtos, and Barber has suggested the possibility that the Egyptians and other spinners in the Near East adopted the idea of fiber-wetting bowls from Minoan spinners across the Libyan Sea (1991, 74–76). She also suggests that since 10th Dynasty wall paintings in Egypt show a Minoan double-heart spiral pattern that was probably inspired by Cretan textiles, some of the textiles produced at Myrtos could have been elaborate, patterned textiles created for export (1994, 109; 1997, 516, and pl. CXCIII a and b; 1998, 14). The large number of tools associated with cloth production, the proximity of Myrtos to Egypt, the growing number of goods originating from Egypt and the Near East on Crete dating to the Early Minoan period, and the long history of international textile trade all suggest that trade in textiles between Crete and Egypt in the third millennium was not unlikely.

At Knossos, Wilson reports that in the West Court Houses, excavated in 1969–1970, spindle whorls and loomweights of Early Minoan II A date were found (1984, 214–19). Both spinning and weaving activities were practiced in tandem at Early Minoan sites like Knossos and Myrtos. The co-occurrence of weaving and spinning is significant since it indicates that there was no degree of specialization in certain parts of the site but rather independent, household production. Presumably individuals participated in all aspects of cloth production, from spinning raw thread to weaving finished textiles. After the Early Minoan period, at about 2000 BC, with the rise of the Minoan palaces, the archaeological distribution of textile equipment changes: No longer are spinning and weaving tools found together as they were at Prepalatial sites. This change and new textile technologies, such as purple dying from murex (Burke 1999), suggest multiple developments that contributed to the emergence of the Minoan palace system.

PALATIAL CRETE

By the early part of the second millennium BC, there are three basic types of Minoan loomweight: the rectangular or cuboid weight (figure 32.1a), the spherical 'melon' weight (figure 32.1b), and the disc weight (figure 32.1c). The cuboid most often has four small suspension holes, one in each corner, placed along the longitudinal axes, and shows thread wear. The earliest examples are from the Neolithic Knossos, and a variant of this cuboid type occurs in the Middle Minoan period concentrated in eastern Crete, for example at Palaikastro and Petras (Burke 2006). Some of these weights are stamped in a manner similar to other known loomweights, and they appear fairly standardized in form and weight, suggesting that they were indeed used as textile tools.

Figure 32.1. (left) Stamped loomweight; *CMS* V Suppl. 1A no. 61 (permission from Prof. Dr. Ingo Pini, *CMS* editor, Marburg); (middle) spherical Minoan loomweight from Knossos (photograph by Brendan Burke); (right) discoid loomweight from Knossos (photographs by Brendan Burke).

Next, spherical, or 'melon,' weights occur primarily on Crete during the MM III to LM III periods (Popham et al. 1984, 249). These weights are fairly large, approximately the size of an orange, and often with grooves running parallel to the suspension hole across the entire surface of the weight. Both the grooves and the interior of the central suspension hole are often painted with the same dark red–brown, iron-based paint used on fine ware ceramics, perhaps in order to prevent snagging when the weights were threaded. Spherical weights have been found on Crete in Neopalatial contexts but not at any of the prominent Minoan-influenced sites off-island (Burke 2003). For example, none have been found at Akrotiri, Kythera, Kea, or Rhodes, sites that otherwise contain a great deal of Minoan material culture, including examples of discoid weights (discussed later). Most of the Cretan examples seem to be concentrated in the northern and eastern parts of the island, at Malia (Pelon 1970, pl. xxvi.3), Vathypetro (Marinatos 1951, 269), Archanes-Phourni Building 4 (Sakellarakis and Sapouna-Sakellaraki 1991, 87, figure 62), and especially around the area of Knossos, including the North Building of the Stratigraphical Museum excavations (Warren 1980–1981, figures 42–43), the Houses by the Acropolis (Catling, Catling, and Smyth 1979, figures 43–44), and the Unexplored Mansion (Popham et al. 1984, 247–49). The contexts of these finds indicate retainer workshops of full-time weavers employed by the ruling elites at Knossos.

The third type of Minoan loomweight is the discoid, which was in use on Crete from EM II through LM III. Carington Smith suggests, in fact, that the Minoan discoid weight is just as culturally distinctive of the Minoans as is the double ax or the horns of consecration (1975, 275). The deposit of more than four hundred highly standardized discoid loomweights in the Loomweight Basement at Knossos, discovered by Evans in 1902, suggests 10–15 working looms, if we assume that each loom used 20–30 weights. The uniformity of the weights with their single suspension holes, similar fabric, and shape, as well as their concentrated numbers, suggests that these weights were part of a regulated textile industry administered by Knossos. Cross marks incised on some of the weights may also have been used to indicate sets of weights. This deposit is good evidence for retainer workshops with full-time weavers working for the Minoan state, centered at the palace of Knossos.

In contrast to the limited distribution of the spherical weights (discussed earlier), large deposits of discoid loomweights occur throughout the Aegean, including such off-island sites as Akrotiri (Tzachili 1990, 407–19; 1997, 183–93), Ialysos, Iasos, and Ayia Irini (Davis 1984). Davis's study of the distribution of these discoid weights and other textile tools throughout the settlement of Ayia Irini on Keos discusses the cultural implications of large quantities of cloth production tools.

Middle Bronze Age loomweights found on Keos have closer parallels to weights found in Anatolia than to those on Crete. Terracotta spools, about five to seven centimeters in height with a pinched waist, are also prevalent on Keos and occur in Anatolia. The function of these objects has long puzzled scholars although they are catalogued with other textile equipment from sites throughout the Aegean, such as Zygouries (Blegen 1928, 190–191, figure 179.4–5) and Eutresis (Goldman 1931, 193; Davis 1984, 162–63). Barber suggests that they may have been used to give tension to threads while being twisted into a belt cord (1997, 515–19). Carington Smith associates them with a warping creel or spool rack that was used to warp a horizontal loom (1975, 400–404). If they are associated with a horizontal loom, Davis remarks that two fundamentally different weaving technologies are present at Ayia Irini in the Middle Bronze Age: the warp-weighted loom and the horizontal loom (Davis 1984, 163).

By the LC I period on Keos, however, it is the Minoan discoid type that dominates the textile equipment assemblage. The type of loom using this weight had an advantage over the others; it provided increased control over warp thread tension and permitted cloths of greater width. More than 185 clay loomweights are found in LC I levels at Ayia Irini, where they are heavily concentrated in the north-central part of the site. Davis (1984) speculates that this concentration of standardized clay weights indicates the production of specialized textiles woven using Minoan technologies for trade within the Aegean sphere.

In marked contrast to the high number of preserved Minoan loomweights is the relative absence of Minoan spindle whorls used for spinning thread. In many parts of Crete, for example, the proportion of excavated spindle whorls to loomweights is very low, suggesting either that the majority of spinning was done using some tool other than the canonical spindle whorl or that it was dispersed throughout the island of Crete. Some have suggested that the Minoans may have used perishable materials such as wood for the whorls at the ends of their spindles. While this is possible, it may also be the case that archaeologists have not been looking in areas where most of the spinning took place: the domestic settlements of working Minoans.

In addition to tools of cloth production, we also can look at administrative documents that provide evidence for the organized production of cloth on Bronze Age Crete (Burke 1997). A certain type of three-sided seal stone, most examples of which come from MM IB–MM II contexts (i.e., the Old Palace period), depict three to five loomweights attached to bars at the bottom of a warp-weighted loom. The round objects suspended from poles shown on some of the seals are very similar to the circular or discoid loomweights found throughout Crete and the Aegean. Wear marks on discoid loomweights indicate that the one- and two-holed weights were attached by straps to some horizontal object to which warp threads were attached. The grooves found on the upper edges of the loomweights are most likely where small poles would be attached to the weights, just as we see depicted on the seals. This placement would give equal tension to all of the warp threads, thereby reducing the need for large numbers. Many of the seal images show tassels or fringes running upward, perpendicular to the bar and the weights, which may be the warp threads of the loom.

Evans initially suggested that the images on these seal stones showed vessels attached to poles for transport (Evans 1909, 131–32, figures 69a, 70b, 71a). Publications of similar seals since have followed Evans's identification: Yule, for example, classifies these seals along with others displaying vessel motifs (1980, 166–67); Younger calls them 'Vertical Supports with Globular Attachments' (1995, 336). There are prism seals that clearly show vessels with lips, handles, and rims delineated by the glyptic artist. To my mind, the seals under discussion here seem to be showing something completely different from suspended globular vessels: I believe that they are the one- or two-holed Minoan disc loomweights attached to the bottom of a warp-weighted loom, indicating weaving under the administration of Minoan authorities from the beginning of the palatial periods.

Mycenaean Cloth Production

By the middle Late Bronze Age, ca. 1400 BC, the Mycenaeans played a dominant role in the economic history of the Aegean both on the mainland and on Crete. Clay tablets inscribed in the Linear B script record a variety of transactions at Mycenaean palaces in the earliest form of written Greek and are the best source for understanding the complex organization of the Mycenaean economy. A large percentage of these tablets refer in some way to a well-organized textile industry.

The Mycenaean tablets are our best source of information for the organization of labor in Bronze Age Greece, and from such records we see that Mycenaean textile production, like its Minoan counterpart, was subject to the central authority of the palace (Bennet 1990). Tablets record large amounts of raw textile material, wool and flax for linen, from surrounding towns and villages under the administration of the palaces. Palace scribes use a variety of ideograms and terms to make distinctions between various types of cloth, usually indicating the heaviness and amounts of wool used. We can see some of the various ideograms in figure 32.2.

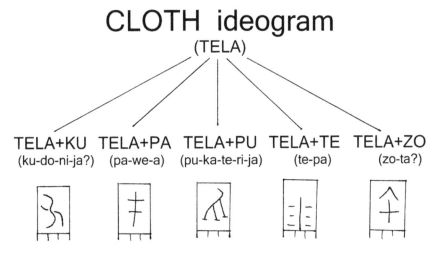

Figure 32.2. Linear B ideogram for cloth (drawing by Brendan Burke).

The documents also provide information about textile personnel, including food rations for dependent workers involved in this industry. All indications are that the craftsmen and craftswomen listed were highly specialized, recording specific occupations such as spinners, weavers, and fullers (Killen 1962, 1964, 1979, 1984, 1988, 2007; Nosch 2000b; Bennet 1992; Chadwick 1988; Palaima 1997).

Textiles were more probably woven in outlying Mycenaean settlements, but production was administered by palatial centers such as Pylos and Knossos. From tablets at these centers we learn that many of the women textile workers listed have ethnic descriptions locating their origin in Anatolia, at places such as Knidos (*ki-ni-di-ja*), Miletus (*mi-ra-ti-ja*), and Halikarnassos (Zephyra, *ze-pu$_2$-ra$_3$*), suggesting a shared continuous tradition of cloth working in the Aegean and Anatolia, which allows us to make some inferences about textile working throughout the eastern Mediterranean and the organization of labor (Chadwick 1988; Killen 1988).

By cross-checking sheep-shearing documents, target accounts, and workers' rations with various place names and ethnic descriptions, analyses of Linear B texts allow us to reconstruct a highly structured and well-organized textile industry. Linear B tablets from Knossos describe flock management (tablet series Da-Dg, Dn), sheep shearing (Dk/Dl), and wool allocations (Od) recorded by the palace scribes for outlying areas of the kingdom (Bennet 1989, 27; Halstead 1981, 1991, 1992, 1999).

Raw wool was distributed to textile workers with the expectation that set production targets would be met with finished textiles delivered back to the palace. The distribution and requisition of raw materials to dependent workers is known as the *ta-ra-si-ja* system (Nosch 2000a, 2000b, 2001). The word occurs in later Greek as *talasia,* where it is solely associated with textile work, especially with wool processing (Barber 1991, 265). In Mycenaean times, the word is attested in several areas of craft production, including bronze smiths' obligations at Pylos and wheel making for chariots at Knossos, and in textile industries at Pylos, Knossos, and Mycenae.

Two major points distinguish textile production at Pylos from Knossos: First, in comparison to Mycenaean Knossos, the palace economy at Pylos shows a greater degree of regionalized specialization among its various provinces and towns. The Linear B records found at the Palace of Nestor reflect centralized control of craft activities at two major centers, Pylos and Leuktron, which monitored activities dispersed throughout the kingdom (Shelmerdine 1987). As Killen (1984) summarizes, Pylos had twenty-eight separate work groups, nearly half of which contained more than twenty women in each group. Leuktron had six or seven work groups, one with thirty-seven women. The other place names in the tablets usually have only one work group of less than a dozen adult workers.

Second, linen production had a much larger role in the palace textile industry at Pylos than at Knossos. The various phases of linen cloth production in centers of differing size are fairly well attested in the Pylian records, although they are far fewer in number than the wool records at Knossos. From the collection records of one hundred different towns and villages under the administration of Mycenaean Pylos, we see that textiles and related crops compose 78% of the records, while food and livestock, for example, are only 16%. On the Na, Ng, and Nn records, the commodity SA has been identified as some form of flax product (Robkin 1979, 473), and in the tablets we find *ri-no*, which is almost certainly related to *linon* 'linen.' From the collection target tablet Ng 319, the Hither province alone yielded nearly fifty thousand kg of this fiber in one year. The region of Messenia today in the southwest Peloponnese covers an area roughly equivalent to the extent of the ancient Pylian kingdom. In the 1950s this region produced more than half of the linen in Greece (McDonald and Rapp 1972, 240).

Archaeological evidence in the form of tools for spinning thread and weaving cloth at Pylos or anywhere in the kingdom is slight, as is the case with other Mycenaean centers. No significant finds of organized cloth production were found at the Palace of Nestor itself. Four loomweights similar in form to those at the settlement of Nichoria were found in the aqueduct in the southeast corner of the palace (Blegen and Rawson, vol. 1, 1966, 301, figure 305.1, pl. lv; vol. 3, Blegen, Rawson, Taylour, and Donovan 1973, 7–16, 336, figure 105.1–3).

The best evidence for Mycenaean cloth production comes from Nichoria, identified as the Pylian town of *Ti-mi-to-a-ke*. This lower-order settlement was assigned one of the largest amounts of flax, according to the Pylos tablets, suggesting a specialization in linen production (Carington Smith 1992; Shelmerdine 1981). Craft residues of cloth production include 153 spindle whorls from houses containing mixed ceramic deposits that date to the Middle and Late Bronze Age. The whorls are generally of two types, medium and large, and the majority are biconical in shape.

Carington Smith (1992) compares the Messenia whorls to those found at Troy and sees a similarity in the new forms appearing in Greece in the Middle Bronze Age to those of Troy VI (Goldman 1931, 198). There is, however, no new type of loomweight in Greece for the Middle Helladic period, and Carington Smith suggests that different weaving technologies (i.e., nonwarp, weighted looms) were used during the MH period. Twelve Mycenaean loomweights have been found at Nichoria, the majority probably from a set of LH II–LH IIIA1 date in Area VI. One loomweight and a possible spinning bowl are of Minoan type. These data provide a unique view of a nonpalatial, subordinate center from the Mycenaean period, comparable perhaps to the nonpalatial Minoan sites of Crete.

AEGEAN ART AND ARTIFACTS

The study of Aegean dress as depicted on wall paintings and figurines is significant for issues related to cultural influence, self-presentation, and modes of production. The flounced skirt of the snake goddesses and other garments in Minoan art are skillfully crafted garments that show a great deal of effort by individual seamstresses and weavers (Barber 1994). This does not seem to be the work of mass-produced textiles, as we infer for Mycenaean cloth from both the Linear B texts and Mycenaean representations. Elite Minoan clothing was probably individually made with great skill, perhaps the work of women of leisure or their servants.

In contrast, representations of Mycenaean garments often show plain, white cloth elaborated only with decorative edgings or bands. Elite Mycenaean women continue to use some styles inherited or borrowed from the Minoans, such as the open bodice and full skirt, but the textiles themselves are simpler and less individualistic. For men, the clothes of both the Minoans and the Mycenaeans remained fairly simple: Minoan men wore a fairly skimpy loincloth or breechcloth that is found in bull-jumping frescoes and on male figurines. The Mycenaean men wore a kilt in religious and military contexts. Some wall paintings from Egypt actually show the underpainting of a Minoan breechcloth replaced by a Mycenaean warrior's kilt (Barber 1993, 350; Rehak 1996).

CONCLUSIONS

Textile production is a highly specialized craft in which attached laborers participated in redistributive economies. This kind of organization could occur only at urban centers that had close ties to rural hinterlands. The evidence presented here demonstrates that differences in social complexity and productive strategies translate into differential distributions of textile equipment.

Having looked at many examples of centralized textile production, both with textual and archaeological sources, what can we say about palace production? We have documentary records of cloth manufacture from Minoan and Mycenaean palaces. Many archaeologists have focused a great deal of attention on these major centers while not investigating smaller settlements, where activities such as pottery, metallurgy, and textile production are more likely to have been located.

The production of cloth probably occurred in smaller villages located in the hinterlands of the palaces, at settlements like Nichoria. It seems that large-scale production of textiles was primarily the work of women who were dependent upon the central authority, possibly against their will, as captives in war, for example, if one makes inferences from the *Iliad*. Palace-made cloth was probably used to appease potentially hostile neighbors, impress valuable trading partners, and legitimize the elite power base. Textiles produced by commoners in household settings were often assessed and collected as tribute by the center and then redistributed as a form of currency to nonfood producers. This circulation of textiles would have continued as long as the centralized economic system was working.

After the Bronze Age, the organization of textile production changes dramatically in the Archaic and Classical periods in Greece. The contribution of women's labor to Classical household economics, as described in Xenophon's *Oeconomicus* 7, or the role of textiles in Greek religion, are subjects for further investigation. This chapter has briefly examined the many different sources of information that help us to understand the role of controlled textile production at large palatial centers of the Bronze Age Aegean. Changes in textile technology and organization reflect developments in both complexity and craft specialization. The rich archaeological record demonstrates that humbler artifactual evidence can inform us about larger issues of emerging complexity.

BIBLIOGRAPHY

Barber, Elizabeth. 1991. *Prehistoric Textiles: The Development of Cloth in the Neolithic and Bronze Ages, with Special Reference to the Aegean.* Princeton: Princeton University Press.

———. 1993. "Late Bronze Age Kilts and the Reconstruction of Aegean Textile Connections," *AJA* 97: 350.

———. 1994. *Women's Work: The First 20,000 Years.* New York: Norton.

———. 1997. "Minoan Women and the Challenges of Weaving for Home, Trade, and Shrine." In *TEXNH*, 515–19.

———. 1998. "Aegean Ornament and Designs in Egypt." In *Aegean and the Orient*, 13–17.

Bennet, John. 1989. "Outside in the Distance: Problems in Understanding the Economic Geography of Mycenaean Palatial Territories." In *Texts, Tablets, and Scribes: Studies in Mycenaean Epigraphy and Economy Offered to Emmett L. Bennett Jr.*, ed. Jean-Pierre Olivier and Thomas Palaima, 19–42. Minos Suppl. 10. Salamanca: Universidad de Salamanca.

———. 1990. "Knossos in Context: Perspectives on the Linear B Administration of LM II–III Crete," *AJA* 94: 193–211.

———. 1992. " 'Collectors' or 'Owners'? An Examination of Their Possible Functions within the Palatial Economy of LM III Crete." In *Mykénaïka: Actes du IXe Colloque international sur les textes mycéniens et égéens organisé par le Centre de l'Antiquité Grecque et Romaine de la Fondation Hellénique des Recherches Scientifiques et l'École française d'Athènes, Athènes, 2–6 octobre 1990*, ed. Jean-Pierre Olivier, 65–101. Supplément au BCH 25. Athens: L'École française d'Athènes.

Blegen, Carl. 1928. *Zygouries: A Prehistoric Settlement in the Valley of Cleonae.* Cambridge, Mass.: Pub. for the American School of Classical Studies at Athens, Harvard University Press.

———, and M. Rawson. 1966. *The Palace of Nestor at Pylos in Western Messenia* I, Princeton.

———, M. Rawson, W. Taylour, and W. Donovan. 1973. *The Palace of Nestor at Pylos in Western Messenia* III, Princeton.

Branigan, Keith. 1970. *The Foundations of Palatial Crete.* New York: Routledge.

Burke, Brendan. 1997. "The Organization of Textile Production in Bronze Age Crete." In *TEXNH*, 413–24.

———. 1999. "Purple and the Aegean Textile Trade of the Early Second Millennium B.C." In *Meletemata*, 75–82.

———. 2003. "The Spherical Loom Weights." In *Knossos: The South House*, ed. Penelope Mountjoy, 195–97. BSA Suppl. 34. London: BSA.

———. 2006. "Textile Production at House II, Petras." In *Proceedings of the 8th Cretological Conference* 279–95. Heraklion: Historical Society of Crete.

Carington Smith, Jill. 1975. Weaving, Spinning, and Textile Production in Greece: The Neolithic to Bronze Age. PhD diss., University of Tasmania.

———. 1992. "Textiles at Nichoria." In *Excavations at Nichoria in Southwestern Greece.* Vol. 2, *The Bronze Age Occupation*, ed. William McDonald and Nancy Wilkie, 674–711. Minneapolis: University of Minnesota Press.

Catling, Hector, E. A. Catling, and D. Smyth. 1979. "Knossos 1975: Middle Minoan III and Late Minoan I Houses by the Acropolis." *BSA* 74: 1–78.

Chadwick, John. 1988. "The Women of Pylos." In *Texts, Tablets, and Scribes: Studies in Mycenaean Epigraphy and Economy Offered to Emmett L. Bennett Jr.*, ed. Jean-Pierre Olivier and Thomas Palaima, 43–96. Minos Suppl. 10. Salamanca: Universidad de Salamanca.

Crowfoot, Grace. 1936. "Of the Warp-weighted Loom." *BSA* 37: 36–47.

Davis, Jack. 1984. "Cultural Innovation and the Minoan Thalassocracy at Ayia Irini." In *Function of the Minoan Palaces*, 159–66.

Evans, Arthur. 1909. *Scripta Minoa: The Written Documents of Minoan Crete with Special Reference to the Archives of Knossos*. Vol. 1, *The Hieroglyphic and Primitive Linear Classes I*, Oxford: Clarendon.

Evans, John. 1968. "Knossos Neolithic, Part II." *BSA* 63: 239–76.

Goldman, Hetty. 1931. *Excavations at Eutresis in Boeotia*. Cambridge, Mass.: Harvard University Press.

Halstead, Paul. 1981. "Counting Sheep in Neolithic and Bronze Age Greece." In *Pattern of the Past: Studies in Honour of David Clarke*, ed. Ian Hodder, Glynn Isaac, and Norman Hammond, 307–39. New York: Cambridge University Press.

———. 1991. "Lost Sheep? On the Linear B Evidence for Breeding Flocks at Knossos and Pylos." *Minos* 22: 343–65.

———. 1992. "The Mycenaean Palatial Economy: Making the Most of the Gaps in the Evidence." *Proceedings of the Cambridge Prehistoric Society* 38: 57–86.

———. 1999. "Missing Sheep: On the Meaning and Wider Significance of the Knossos Sheep Records." *BSA* 94: 145–66.

Hoffman, Marta. 1964. *The Warp-weighted Loom: Studies in the History and Technology of an Ancient Implement. Studia Norvegica* 14. Oslo: Norsk folkemuseum.

Kemp, Barry, and Gillian Vogelsang-Eastwood. 2001. *The Ancient Textile Industry at Amarna*. London: Egypt Exploration Society.

Kenna, Victor. 1960. *Cretan Seals: With a Catalogue of the Minoan Gems in the Ashmolean Museum*. Oxford: Clarendon.

Killen, John. 1962. "The Wool Ideogram in Linear B Texts." *Hermathena* 96: 38–72.

———. 1964. "The Wool Industry of Crete in the Late Bronze Age." *BSA* 59: 1–15.

———. 1979. "The Knossos Ld (1) tablets." In *Colloquium Mycenaeum: Actes du sixième Colloque International sur les textes mycéniens et égéens à Chaumont sur Neuchâtel du 7 au 13 Septembre 1975*, ed. Ernst Risch and Hugo Mühlestein, 151–81. Geneva: Université de Neuchâtel.

———. 1984. "The Textile Industry at Pylos and Knossos." In *Pylos Comes Alive: Industry and Administration in the Mycenaean Palace*, ed. Cynthia Shelmerdine and Thomas Palaima, 49–64. Boston: Archaeological Institute of America.

———. 1985. "The Linear B Tablets and the Mycenaean Economy." In *Linear B: A 1984 Survey*, ed. Anna Morpurgo-Davies and Yves Duhoux, 241–305. Louvain: Peeters.

———. 1988. "Epigraphy and Interpretation of Knossos Woman and Cloth Records." In *Texts, Tablets, and Scribes: Studies in Mycenaean Epigraphy and Economy Offered to Emmett L. Bennett Jr.*, ed. Jean-Pierre Olivier and Thomas Palaima, 167–83. Minos Suppl. 10. Salamanca: Universidad de Salamanca.

———. 2007. "Cloth Production in Late Bronze Age Greece: The Documentary Evidence." In *Ancient Textiles: Production, Craft, Society*, ed. Carole Gillis and Marie-Louise Nosch, 50–58. London: Oxbow.

———, and Jean-Pierre Olivier. 1968. "155 raccords de garments dans les tablettes de Cnossos." *BCH* 92: 115–41.

McDonald, William, and George Rapp Jr., eds. 1972. *Minnesota Messenia Expedition*. Minneapolis: University of Minnesota Press.

Nosch, Marie-Louise. 2000a. "Acquisition and Distribution: *Ta-ra-si-ja* in the Mycenaean Textile Industry." In *Trade and Production in Premonetary Greece: Acquisition and Distribution of Raw Materials and Finished Products. Proceedings of the 6th International Workshop, Athens 1996*, ed. Carole Gillis, Christina Risberg, and Birgitta Sjöberg, 43–61. *SIMA-PB* 154. Jonsered, Sweden: Åström.

———. 2000b. The Organization of the Mycenaean Textile Industry. PhD diss., University of Salzburg.

———. 2001. "The Geography of the *Ta-ra-si-ja*." *Aegean Archaeology* 4: 27–44.

———. 2003. "The Women at Work in the Linear B Tablets." In *Gender, Cult, and Culture in the Ancient World from Mycenae to Byzantium*, ed. Agnete Strömberg and Lena Larsson Lovén, 12–26. *SIMA-PB* 166. Gothenburg: Åström.

———. 2004. "Red Coloured Textiles in the Linear B Inscriptions." In *Colour in the Ancient Mediterranean World*, ed. Liza Cleland, Karen Stears, and Glenys Davies, 32–39. *BAR-IS* 1267. Oxford: Hedges.

———, and Massimo Perna. 2001. "Cloth in Cult." In *Potnia*, 471–77.

———. 2007. *The Knossos Od Series: An Epigraphical Study*. Mykenische Studien Bd. 20. Vienna: Verlag der Österreichischen Akademie der Wissenschaften.

Palaima, Thomas. 1997. "Potter and Fuller: The Royal Craftsmen." In *TEXNH*, 407–12.

Pelon, Olivier. 1970. *Mallia: Exploration des maisons et quartiers d'habitation, 1963–1966*. *Études Crétoises* XVI. Paris: L'École française d'Athènes.

Popham, Mervyn, et al. 1984. *The Minoan Unexplored Mansion*. BSA Suppl. 17. Athens: British School of Archaeology at Athens.

Rehak, Paul. 1996. "Aegean Breechcloths, Kilts, and the Keftiu Paintings." *AJA* 100: 35–51.

Robkin, Ann Lou H. 1979. "The Agricultural Year, the Commodity SA, and the Linen Industry of Mycenaean Pylos." *AJA* 83: 469–74.

Sakellarakis, Ioannis, and Effie Sapouna-Sakellaraki. 1991. *Archanes*. Athens: Ekdotike Athenon.

Shelmerdine, C. 1981. "Nichoria in Context: a Major Town in the Pylos Kingdom," *AJA* 85: 324–88.

———. 1987. "Industrial Activity at Pylos." In *Tractata Mycenaea: Proceedings of the VIIIth International Colloquium on Mycenaean Studies, held in Ohrid, 15–20 September 1985*, ed. P. Ilievski and L. Crepajac, Skopje, pp. 333–42.

Tzachili, Iris. 1990. "All Important yet Elusive: Looking for Evidence of Cloth-making at Akrotiri." In *TAW III*, 380–89.

———. 1997. Υφαντική και Υφάντρες στο Προϊστορικό Αιγαίο 2000–1000 π.Χ. Ηράκλειο: Πανεπιστημιακές Εκδόσεις Κρήτης.

Warren, Peter. 1968. "A Textile Town 4500 Years Ago?" *Illustrated London News* 252, 25–27.

———. 1972. *Myrtos: An Early Bronze Age Settlement in Crete.* BSA Suppl. 7. Athens: British School of Archaeology at Athens.

———. 1980–1981. "Knossos: Stratigraphical Museum Excavations, 1978–1980." *Archaeological Reports* 27: 73–92.

Whitelaw, Todd. 1983. "The Settlement at Fournou Korifi Myrtos and Aspects of Early Minoan Social Organization." In *Minoan Society*, 323–45.

Wilson, David E. 1984. The Early Minoan II A West Court Houses at Knossos. PhD diss., University of Cincinnati.

Younger, John. 1995. "Aegean Seals and Other Minoan-Mycenaean Art Forms." *CMS Beiheft* 5: 336–39.

Yule, Paul. 1980. *Early Cretan Seals: A Study of Chronology. Marburger Studien zur Vor- und Frühgeschichte* 4. Mainz: von Zabern.

CHAPTER 33

....

JEWELRY

....

ROBERT LAFFINEUR

JEWELRY, usually designating both gold and silver work, is undoubtedly one of the most significant classes among the so-called small finds in the prehistoric Aegean. It is attested from the Final Neolithic period, with the gold pendants in the shape of stylized female figures exhibited in 1998–1999 in Athens (Demakopoulou 1998; for other Neolithic finds, see Zachos 2007), until the very end of the Bronze Age, with small objects such as the ornaments found in the Late Helladic IIIC tombs at Perati in Attica. The corpus of finds is especially rich between these two extremes in all periods of development and in the various areas of expansion of Aegean cultures, the Cycladic islands, Crete, western Asia Minor, and the Greek mainland. Some peaks in production, however, can easily be observed.

The Early Bronze Age has produced the first series of jewelry exhibiting a real variety of types. Most of them belong to the category of items made especially for use in the funerary context, with a great majority of objects made of thin gold sheet, mainly diadems and discs, usually without ornament. They are designed both to protect the body of the deceased, thanks to the durable character of gold, and to emphasize the social importance of the buried persons. Finds have been made in the Cyclades and on the Greek mainland, but they are still rather rare in comparison with the rich finds on Crete and in the northern part of western Asia Minor, respectively, in the house tombs on the islet of Mochlos in the Mirabello region in eastern Crete and in the circular tombs of the Mesara plain in the southern part of the island, as well as in Troy and sites in the neighboring islands of Lemnos (Poliochni) and Lesbos (Thermi) (Branigan 1974, 183–96).

The so-called treasures of Troy IIg are certainly the most impressive collection of Early Bronze Age jewelry. They were excavated by H. Schliemann in the 1870s, lost in Berlin at the end of World War II, and recently "rediscovered" in the Pushkin Museum in Moscow, where they have now been exhibited since 1996 (Tolstikow and

Trejster 1996). Highly significant is that the components of those "treasures"—the "treasures of Priam," according to the excavator—belong to types of more solid structure (e.g., earrings, necklaces, elaborated pendants, bracelets, and pins), most probably made for use in everyday life as well, with additional ornamentation implying more difficult techniques such as filigree and granulation. Some specific items are directly related in techniques of manufacture, suggesting the existence of local workshops, and many features in the treasures show clear similarities with productions from sites in the "circum-Pontic" areas and in the Aegean (the objects from Poliochni and Thermi already mentioned, some objects from Prepalatial Crete, and a necklace in the Berlin Museum coming from the Thyreatis in the eastern Peloponnese; cf. Reinholdt 1993 and, for the treasure from Cape Kolonna on Aegina, Reinholdt 2008). Such affinities are clear signs of the existence of a sort of *koine* at such an early date (Laffineur 2002, 2008). Gold and silver vessels are also attested in Troy IIg, among them a two-handled sauceboat of perfect workmanship, a real masterpiece with its incredible weight of 600 gr.

The succeeding period of the Middle Bronze Age appears rather poor in contrast, especially in the Cyclades and on the Greek mainland, where production is limited to rare and very simple examples of funerary jewelry (Branigan 1974). Minoan Palatial Crete is an exception, however. Finds of Protopalatial and Neopalatial date—extending to the beginning of the Late Bronze Age—form a rich corpus indeed, in terms of types, shapes, ornamentation, techniques, and functions (cf. the systematic catalogue in Effinger 1996). Thin gold sheet continues to be used mainly for plating bronze weapons, such as specimens from both the palace and Quartier Mu at Malia—the first with a gold roundel with the repoussé figure of an acrobat decorating the hilt of a sword, the second with the plating of the haft of a dagger worked in openwork technique—and a gold plating of a dagger from the Mitsotakis collection in Athens (Marangou 1992, 258). Engraving is also known at the beginning of the Late Bronze Age, on votive gold double axes from the cave at Archalokori in central Crete, as well as granulation and filigree on a nice series of solid gold earrings in the shape of a stylized bull's head (Laffineur 1980).

Two important finds deserve special attention: the famous "bee pendant" from the necropolis of Chrysolakkos at Malia and the so-called Aegina treasure in the British Museum. The Malia pendant, which is dated to late Prepalatial or Protopalatial times (Effinger 1996, 241), is another masterpiece of craftsmanship, with a highly skilful use of granulation, a sophisticated composition, and a likely symbolic meaning that has inspired many comments—beginning with the identification of the insects—bees, hornets, or wasps.

The "Aegina treasure" is a particularly rich collection of pieces of probably late Protopalatial date that has been looted in Mycenaean times, probably from Crete (Higgins 1979). Its supposed homogeneity and the many affinities with the precious metal finds from Chrysolakkos have led some scholars to suggest an ultimate origin in Malia. There are clear affinities, however, with productions from other parts of the Aegean as well, from the early Mycenaean mainland in particular (Laffineur 2009), that lead one to question the homogeneity of the whole (Laffineur 2003a,

Figure 33.1. Gold pendant with Master of animals in the Aegina treasure
(photograph courtesy of Robert Laffineur).

2006b, 40–42). Whatever the exact provenance—or provenances—may be, some masterpieces have again to be mentioned: a gold pendant in the shape of a "master of the animals" holding two geese (figure 33.1) and related openwork pendants with antithetic images of dogs that are very close to a gold pendant recently excavated at Tell el-Dabʿa in the eastern Nile delta (Walberg 1991).

Silver vessels are also attested during Palatial times in Crete. The richest collection is the so-called Tod treasure, found in the temple of Montu at Tod in upper Egypt in copper chests inscribed with the name of Amenhemhat II and kept in the museum in Cairo and in the Louvre. The objects provide metal equivalents of shapes and decorations of Middle Minoan Ib and II clay vases and represent most probably the first known Cretan tribute to Egypt, an antecedent of later ones depicted on the *Keftiu* scenes in XVIIIth-dynasty tombs of the Theban necropolis. But again, the homogeneity of the whole has to be questioned since some of the silver vessels in the treasure exhibit clear affinities with precious metal vessels of late Middle Helladic and early Late Helladic date from the Greek mainland (Maran 1987; Laffineur 1988).

In the Late Minoan period, an intriguing series of gold objects deserves mention, the so-called Zakro treasure reputedly found at Kato Zakro in east Crete and consisting of a gold diadem with a repoussé image of a mistress of the goats, a three-dimensional bull's head, and a shallow cup with running spirals. The authenticity of the whole has been questioned (Buchholz 1970), but doubts can be expressed for the Bronze Age date of the treasure instead since the layout of ornamentation on the diadem and various details on the three pieces indicate similarities with gold work of the classical period (Laffineur 1986).

The Mycenaean mainland has yielded undoubtedly the richest production of gold and silver items in the Aegean, at the very end of the Middle Bronze Age and at the beginning of the Late Bronze Age, during the so-called Shaft Graves period (Laffineur 1996b, 1990–1991, 2006a). The bulk of these has been excavated in the Argolid, especially in Grave Circles A and B at Mycenae—a city that fully deserves the denomination of *polychrysos* attached to it in the Homeric poems—but important finds are attested in other areas of the Peloponnese and in central Greece as well (Laffineur 2003b). The significant quantity of precious material revealed in those tombs by Heinrich Schliemann and by a Greek team under George Mylonas has caused much discussion since the respective discovery and publication (Karo 1930–1933; Mylonas 1972–1973).

The first problem involved is, of course, the supply of raw material. Silver does not cause a problem in that respect since the Laurion mines in Attica have certainly been exploited as early as the Early Bronze Age and since cupellation—the method for separating lead and silver from the local argentiferous lead ore—has been known and practiced as early as the EH period, during the third millennium BC. The Laurion ore has proved to be the dominant source for the manufacture of Aegean lead and silver objects, but the possibility has to be considered that silver was perhaps in addition a very useful commodity in the trade for other materials, especially tin, as seems to be confirmed by references to silver and gold used as exchange for the purchase of tin in the Mari archives. There is no such evidence, however, that gold sources situated in the Aegean, Siphnos in the Cyclades, or Thasos close to the Thracian shores were exploited before historical times.

This lack of evidence has led most scholars to search for sources of gold supply outside the Aegean, and the question is especially crucial for the prolific production of the beginning of the Mycenaean age. According to the classic view that has long been accepted, the kings buried in the shaft graves at Mycenae would have purchased the precious metal in Egypt as a reward for the help they had given the pharaoh for driving the Hyksos out of the Nile valley. However, the fact that the enrichment had begun at Mycenae before the Late Helladic I phase, in the late Middle Helladic and transitional grave circle B, though on a more limited scale, and that it consequently predates the end of the Hyksos dynasty in Egypt has been considered as a major obstacle to the Egyptian theory (Laffineur 1990–1991, 252–54).

Instead of restricting the possible sources to the Eastern Mediterranean, either Egypt or Anatolia (with reference to the use of gold from the Pactolus River in Lydia in historical times), which are traditionally considered as the most probable ones, it is perhaps worth trying an alternative direction—toward the north. Ellen Davis has emphasized the connections between the Mycenae shaft graves and central Romania and suggested that the basic reason for such a trade and contacts with the north—what she calls the "Transylvanian connection"—was a mutual and complementary need for metal, Romania having much gold but no bronze, whereas early Mycenaean Greece was in quite the opposite situation (Davis 1983). Close relations with the Black Sea shores, investigated by Stefan Hiller (Hiller 1991), could also lead to the possibility of an additional "Pontic connection" since the area is well known to be rich in gold, as echoed in the classical traditions of the expedition of the Argonauts and the Golden Fleece.

As for the techniques of manufacture, several major observations have to be put forward when considering mainland gold work, especially in the early Mycenaean phases. Direct or freehand repoussé is well attested in the shaft graves (e.g., on gold bands with relief designs that consist mostly of groups of bosses and dots), and that style and process of decoration can be traced back to Middle Helladic times. However, the great majority of finds consist of small gold leaf ornaments made of a relatively thin sheet of metal and decorated with figurative motifs that prove in many instances to be identical and that have consequently been produced by beating the sheet over a mold bearing the corresponding intaglio design. Stone molds of that type have been found in the excavations, but other materials like wood or metal may have been used as well and either have not been preserved or were smelted for reuse. Some details can be given by additional chasing, with the sheet of gold usually cut along the outline of the design. The repertoire includes floral elements, animals, and human figures and more exceptional motifs, like the façade of a tripartite shrine.

The implications of such a technical process are certainly not unimportant, and it has been extensively used in later times, especially in jewelry workshops of Geometric and Archaic Greece. Most interesting is that it provides form and decoration simultaneously and further that it allows a repetition of similar objects with identical decoration and hence a certain mass production. This appears quite suitable to meet the complementary needs of early Mycenaeans both for displaying abundant production that is easily manufactured and for simple and nonsolid ornaments made just for funerary use.

Equally worth emphasizing are the close connections that the manufacture of molds implies with gem cutting and that may well account for some iconographical and stylistic similarities between gold ornaments and seals. These might lead to the suggestion that the engraving was made in both cases by the same people and in the same workshops since it requires much the same skill. A still closer relation must have existed between jewelry and the manufacture of colored glass beads. The perfect identity of design and dimensions that may be observed and measured on some ornaments in the two series, in the material excavated in the slightly later chamber tombs at Mycenae especially, gives evidence that cavities on the same molds were sometimes used both for beating sheet gold and for pouring liquid glass paste (Laffineur 1978). That the different items are in each case more or less contemporary is not the least important implication. The chronological difference indeed must have been limited since a single mold does not appear suitable for lengthy use. Faience relief beads were manufactured by the same process as early as the shaft graves period, when the use of hollow molds again allowed the repetition of identical designs on different series of ornaments.

The picture that we get from these observations is that craftspersons working in different media, including gold ornaments, glass paste, and faience beads, as well as seals, were technically dependent on each other—the relation is confirmed by gilded seals and by glass seals (Laffineur 1995).

Slight variation can be reached on similarly produced gold relief beads by the addition of granulation. A further variant of the same process of manufacture consists in repeating an identical relief design several times on a single artifact through successive hammerings of the sheet in the same cavity of a mold. Beating gold foil in a hollow mold has been used most probably also for three-dimensional human and animal figures, the former made of a front half and a rear half soldered together, the latter of a single sheet attached to a flat base. Identical figures are attested in only one instance, in Grave Circle A at Mycenae, but the regularity of modeling and details that other single figures exhibit confirms that they could be achieved only by such a process. Each part was produced by beating a sheet of gold in a hollow mold, and, as in the case of relief beads, glass paste and faience may have been poured into the cavities as well.

Among the techniques attested by Mycenaean precious metal finds, mention has to be made of gold plating, which has been extensively used in the Shaft Graves period for the decoration of prestige weapons, and of metal inlay, a much-elaborated process applied to weapons with pictorial ornamentation and to vases, a technique that was probably imported from the Levant, where it is known in the first half of the second millennium.

Besides the dominating class of gold sheet ornaments and beads with reliefs specifically made for funerary use, Mycenaean gold work has produced a series of gold finger rings with engraved designs, very frequently pictorial motifs, with animal and human figures and even elaborated scenes of a religious nature (Vassilicou 2000) (figure 33.2). Inlaying colored materials in cells outlined by metal strips—a process known as cloisonné—appears as early as the shaft graves period on a dagger haft from Grave Circle A and has been applied in the subsequent phases, especially to the decoration of finger rings. Specimens have been found in Mycenae, Vapheio, Volos, Thebes, Achaea, and, more recently, Corinthia, although their inlays consisting most probably of glass paste have generally been lost. The finger ring from Achaea also gives one rare example of filigree, both of the plain and the twisted varieties, a technique that must have been adopted at a rather late date since the ring comes from a Late Helladic IIIC context.

Characteristic of the early Mycenaean period are also the numerous gold or silver vessels of various shapes with repoussé designs (Davis 1977; Laffineur 1977), among which are many masterpieces (e.g., the shallow cups with octopi and ivies from Dendra in the Argolid, some of the specimens from Grave Circle A at Mycenae with images of animals and human figures, and still others with elaborate curvilinear ornaments from Mycenae and Peristeria in Messenia, not to mention the two famous gold cups from the tholos tomb at Vapheio in Laconia, with their remarkably naturalistic scenes of the capture and domestication of wild bulls).

Figure 33.2. Gold finger ring from chamber tomb 91 at Mycenae
(after Dimakopoulou 1988, figure on p. 195).

This review of the principal techniques practiced by mainland goldsmiths during the Late Bronze Age allows for an identification of some specific and recurring features. The most characteristic appears to be a certain mass production that is made possible by using molds and has been applied to different types of objects, to various ornaments and beads, and also (most probably though less frequently) to precious metal vessels, as well as to different materials (e.g., gold, silver, glass paste, faience). This emphasizes the great homogeneity of the production, and this in turn is an obvious sign of its essentially local character.

A confirmation is provided by the evidence we have of the organization of jewelry workshops, especially at Thebes. Here the excavations have revealed that different materials have been worked into shape at the same place: not only precious metals, fragments of which were discovered in both finished and unfinished forms, but also glass paste, shells, and amber and raw stones like rock crystal, steatite, onyx, amethyst, agate, and lapis lazuli (Symeonoglou 1978).

Especially significant is the presence of small gold sheet ornaments of regular geometric shapes but also cut along the outline of pictorial designs. These were surely intended as inlays for bronze objects, most probably vases rather than daggers since the manufacture of the latter had ceased at the time the Thebes workshop was active, which was immediately before its destruction at the end of Late Helladic IIIB1, whereas inlaid metal vessels were still being made at the end of the Late Helladic IIIB period. This seems to indicate that at least in this particular case ornaments made of precious metal, semiprecious stones, and other colored materials were manufactured in the same workshop as the inlaid precious metal vessels.

No less important for the reconstruction of the successive stages in the manufacture are the six small pieces of rock crystal, identified by the excavator as inlays to be assembled on a panel but that could be interpreted rather as magnifying glasses.

The craftspersons certainly were in need of a magnifying system when working on small items such as gold beads and especially when they had to add granulation to them. The slight convexity of the six items from Thebes gives them some properties to enlarge things that are looked at through them—the same feature as on similar rock crystal items in the Troy "treasures"—and the double cutting at the bottom may be the best means of allowing an easier grip for the lenses.

The information about jewelry workshops appears, in the end, rather scanty. We should not forget, however, that a substantial part of Mycenaean precious metal objects belongs to the category of funerary ornaments made specifically for funerary use. Moreover, it has been suggested that at least in one case the manufacture of gold ornaments took place within the tomb itself, during the process of laying down the deceased and the offerings. This is the way in which Protonotariou-Deïlaki quite convincingly interprets the tiny pieces of gold sheet found near one of the skeletons in the tholos tomb at Kazarma in the Argolid, which are most probably the scraps that fell on the ground while the craftspersons was cutting the pieces of the funerary ornamentation (Protonotariou-Deïlaki 1990). This particular practice, which is attested also in the shaft graves but has probably not been used systematically, seems to give additional insight into the conditions in which the goldsmiths were working.

The preceding observation of the prevailing funerary nature of Mycenaean gold jewelry implies an essentially local use and certainly not a wide distribution of objects. The function and the meaning of the items favor a similar conclusion. Mycenaean jewelry and precious metal plate were certainly intended in some cases for everyday use. Obvious signs of this are the solid construction of most gold finger rings and of some gold relief beads, with additional granulated decoration, as well as the various techniques used for increasing the structure and stability of metal vessels. The majority of gold items, however, exhibit on the contrary a clearly simplified quality of work, as well as an extremely thin and quick fabric that is hardly suitable for repeated use and is compatible only with a strictly limited function within the funerary ritual. Examples of such a simplified technique are numerous, especially in the class of gold sheet ornaments with small holes along the edges intended to be sewn to the shroud.

What about the reasons for the Mycenaeans' evident preference for a class of jewelry that appears particularly and exclusively suited to serve a specific function in burial practices—an exclusivity that is quite clear from the Kazarma evidence mentioned earlier? An inventory of the designs embossed on the gold sheet ornaments enables one to observe that most of them refer to categories of fauna either considered as having a protective value or exhibiting rather unexpected features. The owl and the eagle belong to the former, as well as probably some hybrids, such as the sphinx and the griffin and perhaps also the swan. To the latter belong the butterfly, the bee, the cicada, the frog, the triton shell, the octopus, and probably the stag (i.e., animals that hibernate and thus regularly awaken after a long period of immobility, animals that develop by metamorphosis, or animals that possess some faculty of regeneration such as tentacles or antlers) (Laffineur 1985). The protective value has certainly been understood as quite profitable for the deceased in the after-world. The other features may reasonably be expected to have been considered as symbolical guarantees of the accession of the dead to a new life after death. They may have influenced the choice of motifs represented on the funerary ornaments and resulted in a preference for images of animals that incorporate those highly beneficial qualities.

A related interpretation could be proposed in the funerary context for the gold ornaments with images of plants and flowers, which may be viewed as hints at the annual renewal of vegetation and at the suggestive evidence that vegetal life grows out of earth. Their representations may consequently be considered as equally pre-cious guarantees of the accession to a new life for the deceased. More specific associ-ations may be added, especially the pomegranate, a well-known symbol of fertility, illustrated on gold beads from Shaft Grave III at Mycenae, as well as associations of plants with animals, particularly stags, which have in themselves a symbolic value of regeneration.

Increasing the efficiency of the symbolism of regeneration was certainly intended through the repetition of identical motifs on several gold ornaments and the tech-nique of mass production that makes it possible, as well as through the association of several images of different animals to the same burial or even the association of hints at vegetal renewal and animal regeneration. The frequent emblematical pre-sentation of the designs is likely to have been intended as a further way to duplicate the message. Finally, the predominant use of gold is not insignificant: Its imper-ishable character was no doubt considered as contributing to the conservation of the ornaments and to a sort of eternal functioning of the symbolical action of the images on them. This last feature has to be connected with the value of immortality, which has often been attached to gold in later times and has likely its origin in the solar connotations of the shining metal.

The high value of gold, which is increased by the fact that it likely had to be imported from abroad, would imply that its possession and use were limited to wealthy individuals belonging to a high class, in much the same way as prestige weapons and other luxury items do. Social, political, and economic status can best be expressed in funerary contexts, where the signs of the appurtenance to a specific class are definitely and deliberately attached to individuals when they are buried and are given specific objects as grave goods. Especially indicative of a high status is, in this respect, the more or less high value of the personal belongings of the deceased, both taken separately and considered as a whole, and depending on the material in which they are made, the skill and artistic value that they reflect and their eventual rarity. However, the quantitative aspect of a funerary assemblage seems undoubt-edly another illustration of high status, in particular of its value as an indication of social status and as a means of legitimizing political status and power.

Coming back to typology and the techniques of manufacture, one should finally raise the question of the survival of Mycenaean jewelry in later Greek jewelry (Laffineur 1987, 1998). Signs of survival appear especially numerous in the Dark Ages, for which the excavations have yielded examples of types reminiscent of Late

Bronze Age types, especially and paradoxically of the earliest ones—and in spite of the obvious decline observable in the last Mycenaean phase (Higgins 1983): circular ornaments made of thin sheet gold from Skyros in the Goulandris collection, from Lemnos and Rhodes, "Gamaschenhalter" or closely related pieces from Skyros and from tombs at Lefkandi in Euboea (Laffineur 1996a), tubular beads with four spirals from Skyros (to be compared with specimens from Shaft Grave III and grave Omikron at Mycenae), and earrings with two spirals from Lefkandi.

Most significant for a connection to a Late Bronze Age tradition is also the predominant nonsolid construction and funerary use of geometric jewelry and the probably much similar meaning of symbolic protection attached to it. Survivals are also attested as far as technique is concerned. The process of cloisonné has to be mentioned here (earrings from Eleusis and Athens, a necklace from Spata), as well as granulation, which experiences a significant revival in Geometric and Orientalizing jewelry. The most typical link, however, is emphasized by the techniques of mass production through beating sheet gold over hollow molds that have been extensively used for the Attic Geometric gold bands and the Rhodian Orientalizing gold plaques with raised figures. Iconography, in fact, shows the only noticeable differences and true renewal with the introduction of oriental designs as early as the late Geometric period.

BIBLIOGRAPHY

Branigan, Keith. 1974. *Aegean Metalwork of the Early and Middle Bronze Age.* Oxford: Clarendon.

Buchholz, Hans-Günter. 1970. "Ägäische Kunst gefälscht." *Acta Praehistorica et Archaeologica* 1: 121–22.

Davis, Ellen N. 1977. *The Vapheio Cups and Aegean Gold and Silver Ware.* New York: Garland.

———. 1983. "The Gold of the Shaft Graves: The Transylvanian Connection." *Temple University Aegean Symposium* 8: 32–38.

Demakopoulou, Katie. 1988. *Das mykenische Hellas: Heimat der Helden Homers.* Athens: Ministry of Culture.

———. 1990. *Troja, Mikines, Tirins, Orchomenos: Ekato chronia apo to thanato tou Enrikou Sliman.* Athens: Ministry of Culture.

———. 1998. *Kosmimata tis ellinikis proïstorias: O neolithikos thisavros.* Athens: TAP Press.

Effinger, Maria. 1996. *Minoischer Schmuck.* BAR-IS 646. Oxford: British Archaeological Reports.

Higgins, Reynold. 1979. *The Aegina Treasure: An Archaeological Mystery.* London: British Museum Publications.

———. 1983. "Goldwork of the Extreme End of the Aegean Bronze Age." *Temple University Aegean Symposium* 8: 50–52.

Hiller, Stefan. 1991. "The Mycenaeans and the Black Sea." In *Thalassa,* 207–16.

Karo, Georg. 1930–1933. *Die Schachtgräber von Mykenai.* Munich: Bruckmann.

Laffineur, Robert. 1977. *Les vases en métal précieux à l'époque mycénienne.* Gothenburg: Åström.

———. 1978. "La technique du verre mycénien et ses rapports avec les techniques de l'orfèvrerie." In *Annales du 7e Congrès de l'Association internationale pour l'histoire du verre (Berlin, 1977),* 31–39. Liège: Secrétariat général de l'Association internationale pour l'histoire du verre.

———. 1980. "Les pendants d'oreilles minoens en forme de bucrane." In *Pepragmena tou D diethnous kritologikou sinedriou [Proceedings of the 4th International Cretological Congress (Herakleion, 1976)],* A I, 281–96. Athens: University of Crete.

———. 1985. "Iconographie minoenne et iconographie mycénienne à l'époque des tombes à fosse." In *L'iconographie minoenne: Actes de la Table Ronde d'Athènes (21–22 avril 1983),* ed. Pascal Darcque and Jean-Claude Poursat, 245–66. BCH Suppl. XI. Athens: École française d'Athènes.

———. 1986. "Le trésor de Zakro: Datation et authenticité." In *Pepragmena tou E diethnous kritologikou sinedriou [Proceedings of the 5th International Cretological Congress (A. Nikolaos, 1981)],* A, 181–89. Heraklaion: Society of Cretan Historical Studies.

———. 1987. "Der Zusammenhang von Mykenischem und Frühgriechischem in der Goldschmiedekunst." In *Akten des Internationalen Kolloquiums Forschungen zur ägäischen Vorgeschichte: Das Ende der mykenischen Welt (Köln, 1984),* ed. Eberhard Thomas, 73–92. Berlin: Wasmuth KG.

———. 1988. "Réflexions sur le trésor de Tôd." *Aegaeum* 2: 17–30. Liège: University of Liège.

———. 1990–1991. "Material and Craftsmanship in the Mycenae Shaft Graves: Imports vs. Local Production." *Minos,* n.s., 25–26: 245–95.

———. 1995. "Craftsmen and Craftsmanship in Mycenaean Greece: For a Multimdia Approach." In *Politeia,* 189–99.

———. 1996a. "A propos des 'Gamaschenhalter' des tombes à fosse de Mycènes." In *Atti e Memorie del secondo Congresso Internazionale di Micenologia (Roma-Napoli, 14–20 ottobre 1991)* III, ed. Ernesto De Miro, Louis Godart, and Anna Sacconi, 1229–38. Rome: Gruppo Editoriale Internazionale.

———. 1996b. "Polychrysos Mykene: Toward a Definition of Mycenaean Goldwork." In *Ancient Jewelry and Archaeology,* ed. Adriana Calinescu, 89–116. Bloomington: Indiana University Press.

———. 1998. "Bronze Age Traditions in Dark Age and Orientalising Jewellery." In *The Art of the Greek Goldsmith,* ed. Dyfri Williams, 9–13. London: British Museum Press.

———. 2002. "Reflections on the Troy Treasures." In *Mauerschau: Festschrift für Manfred Korfmann,* vol. 1, ed. Rüstem Aslam, Stephan Blum, Gabriele Kastl, Frank Schweitzer, and Diane Thumm, 237–44. Remshalden-Grunbach: Greiner.

———. 2003a. "The 'Aegina Treasure' Revisited." In *Argosaronikos: Praktika 1ou diethnous sinedriou istorias ke archaiologias tou Argosaronikou. Proceedings of the 1st International Congress of History and Archaeology of the Argosaronikos (Poros 26–29 June 1998),* ed. Eleni Konsolaki-Iannopoulou, A, 41–45. Athens: Municipality of Poros.

———. 2003b. "Mycenaean Jewellery in the Periphery." In *Periphery of the Mycenaean World,* 81–85.

———. 2006a. "Mycènes riche en or: L'orfèvrerie et la bijouterie mycéniennes." In *Les ors des mondes grec et barbare: Actes du Colloque de la Société Française d'Archéologie classique du 18 novembre, Paris 2000,* ed. Gérard Nicolini, 35–62. Paris: Picard.

———. 2006b. "Les trésors en archéologie égéenne: Réalité ou manie ?" In *Mythos: La préhistoire égéenne du XIXe au XXIe s. ap. J.-C. Actes de la Table ronde internationale d'Athènes (21–23 novembre 2002),* ed. Pascal Darcque, Michael Fotiadis, and Olga Polychronopoulou, 37–46. *BCH* Suppl. 46. Paris: École française d'Athènes.

———. 2008. "Aspects of Early Bronze Age Jewellery in the Aegean." In *ANCEBA,* 323–32.

———. 2009. "The Aigina Treasure: The Mycenaean Connection." In *The Aigina Treasure. Aegean Bronze Age Jewellery and Mystery Revisited,* ed. J. Lesley Fitton, 40–42. London: The British Museum Press.

Maran, Joseph. 1987. "Die Silbergefässe von et-Tôd und die Schachtgräberzeit auf dem griechischen Festland." *PZ* 62: 221–27.

Marangou, Lila. 1992. *Minoan and Greek Civilization from the Mitsotakis Collection.* Athens: Goulandris Foundation.

Mylonas, George E. 1972–1973. *O tafikos kiklos B ton Mikinon.* Athens: Archaeological Society at Athens.

Protonotariou-Deïlaki, Evangelia. 1990. "Burial Customs and Funerary Rites in the Prehistoric Argolid." In *Celebrations of Death,* 79–80.

Reinholdt, Claus. 1993. "Der Thyreatis-Hortfund in Berlin: Untersuchungen zum vormyke-nischen Edelmetallschmuck in Griecheland." *JdI* 108: 23–26.

———. 2008. *Der frühbronzezeitliche Schmuckhortfund von Kap Kolonna: Ägina und die Ägäis im Goldzeitalter des 3. Jahrtausends v. Chr.* Vienna: Verlag der Österreichischen Akademie der Wissenschaften.

Symeonoglou, Sarantis. 1978. *Kadmeia I: Mycenaean Finds from Thebes, Greece. Excavation at 14 Oedipus St.,* 63–66. Gothenburg: Åström.

Tolstikow, Wladimir P., and Trejster, Michail J. 1996. *Der Schatz aus Troja: Schliemann und der Mythos des Priamos-Goldes.* Zürich: Belser.

Vassilicou, Dora. 2000. *Mycenaean Signet Rings of Precious Metal with Cult Scenes.* Athens: Archaeaological Society at Athens.

Walberg, Gisela. 1991. "A Gold Pendant from Tel el-Dabᶜa." *Ägypten und Levante* II: 111–12.

Zachos, Konstantinos. 2007. "The Neolithic Background: A Reassessment." In *Metallurgy in the Early Bronze Age Aegean,* ed. Peter M. Day and Roger C.P. Doonan, 168–206. Oxford: Oxbow.

Events

CHAPTER 34

....

ERUPTION OF THERA/ SANTORINI

....

STURT W. MANNING

ALTHOUGH human lives, and history, are full of specific and key moments, finding these in a useful form in the archaeological record is a rare occurrence; too often one is faced with a challenging palimpsest. But one especially dramatic type of archaeological moment, or short-lived horizon, occurs when a large volcanic eruption devastates a region. A world is, tragically, captured (entombed, frozen) forever at a specific time—in toto. The most famous example is the eruption of Vesuvius in AD 79. Although this catastrophe extinguished and entombed Pompeii and Herculaneum, it has provided archaeology with an unparalleled set of evidence (e.g., Berry 2007). The prehistoric 'Pompeii' of the Aegean world is the horizon of time sealed by the great eruption of the Thera/Santorini volcano in the Aegean in the mid-second millennium BC (Friedrich 2000). This eruption entombed a thriving city with international links (referred to as Akrotiri, from the name of the nearby modern village) and other settlements on Thera, and, through the spread of a tephra blanket (airfall volcanic ash/debris), laid down a clear marker horizon across much of the southern and eastern Aegean, western Anatolia, and some of the East Mediterranean (which can be traced by modern scientific means, e.g., Bichler et al. 2003).

The prehistoric archaeology buried by the volcano on Thera was recognized in the late 19th century AD (Tzachili 2005), but modern excavations started under Spyridon Marinatos only in 1967 (Marinatos 1968–1976); work has continued from 1974 to the present under the direction of Christos Doumas (e.g., 1983, chapter 56 this volume). The extraordinary and unique finds at Akrotiri—a large town of buildings preserved to several stories (and with earlier remains underneath), millions of artifacts, and, most famously, room after room of astonishing wall paintings—make the site—and the eruption that both destroyed and created it (for the modern world)—pivotal and compellingly central to Aegean and wider East Mediterranean prehistory (Palyvou 2005; Sherratt 2000; Manning 1999; Forsyth 1997; Doumas 1983, 1991, 1992; Doumas, Marthari, and Televantou 2000; Hardy et al. 1990). The volcanic eruption itself was an epoch-scale event—one of the larger volcanic eruptions of the last several thousand years (with recent work making it only larger: Sigurdsson et al. 2006)—and it had a substantial, shorter-term impact on the region beyond Santorini, ranging from direct airfall tephra damage in the southeast Aegean, associated seismic and especially tsunami impacts, to (debated) effects on the environment and even the climate over the subsequent months to years (Bruins et al. 2008; Frisia et al. 2008, 26; Bottema and Sarpaki 2003; Eastwood et al. 2002; McCoy and Heiken 2000; Manning and Sewell 2002; cf. Pyle 1997). Marinatos (1939) famously suggested that the eruption might even have caused the destruction of Minoan Crete (also Page 1970). Although this simple hypothesis has been negated by the findings of excavation and other research since the late 1960s (e.g., Renfrew 1979; Doumas 1990; Hardy and Renfrew 1990; Soles, Taylor, and Vitaliano 1995), which demonstrate that the eruption occurred late in the Late Minoan IA ceramic period, whereas the destructions of the Cretan palaces and so on are some time subsequent (late in the following Late Minoan IB ceramic period), some scholars nonetheless continue to see the volcanic eruption as a pivotal event that caused the downturn (or beginning of the end) of Minoan civilization (Driessen and Macdonald 1997).

When did this important eruption occur?

This seemingly innocent question has been the source of a major controversy in Aegean prehistory for a generation (e.g., Michael 1976; Warren 1984; Betancourt 1987; Manning 1988, 1999, 2007; Hardy and Renfrew 1990; Bietak 2003a; Wiener 2006, 2007). Let us begin with what is agreed and then move on to what is debated and why.

Relative Date

The placement of the eruption in the archaeological sequence of the southern Aegean is now more or less universally agreed: toward the end of the Late Minoan (LM) IA period in terms of the Cretan sequence (this is based both on comparison of the Minoan ceramics buried by the eruption at Akrotiri with Crete and on the presence of direct airfall Minoan eruption products in late LM IA strata/contexts on Crete). A final posteruption stage of LM IA may have followed, but a mature/late LM IA date is clear. In terms of the mainland sequence, the eruption is very late in Late Helladic (LH) I or perhaps even LH I/IIA border or into the very start of LH IIA (one vase in particular from preeruption Akrotiri looks LH IIA in style) (Warren 2007; Hardy and Renfrew 1990; Manning 1999, 12–19). This relative archaeological placement can be extended outside the Aegean through linkages between the Aegean worlds and those in the East Mediterranean especially. In particular, a direct linkage between preeruption Thera and Cyprus likely exists with apparent imports/exports in both directions, tying Late Cypriot IA to Late Minoan IA (Cadogan 1990, 95; Vermeule and Wolsky 1990, 382 and note 76, 394; Merrillees 2001).

So when did the eruption and late LM IA occur?

Absolute Date

The Problem

The traditional approach to absolute dating in Aegean prehistory has been to find exports to or imports from the approximately historically dated world of Egypt and then best estimating the Aegean ceramic periods around these. For periods during which there were clear and plentiful contacts, this procedure works well. Examples are the linkages of the main Old Palace (Kamares) phase (Middle Minoan II) on Crete with Middle Kingdom Egypt (and so the 19th–18th centuries BC) or the (very specific) correspondence between the LH IIIA2 period and the short-lived Egypt capital of Tell el-Amarna under Amenhotep IV (Akhenaten) in the mid-14th century BC. No one contests these dating 'pegs,' which have long been clear (e.g., Cadogan 1978), and recent science dating, where available, finds compatible outcomes.

However, there is no good evidence from Egypt for the date of the LM IA period. A couple of LM I (B or maybe A) or contemporary LH items and then a few agreed mature/late LM IB objects are found in Egypt in contexts of the earlier 18th Dynasty (with the LM I characterizing the earliest but least well known horizon from Ahmose to Thutmose II, ca.1540–1482 BC and the transition from the late LM IB material to Mycenaean vessels occurring during the reign of Thutmose III, ca.1479–1425 BC, with an example of LH IIB—largely contemporary with LM II on Crete—found also in a 'typical tomb group datable to the reign of Thutmose III' [Aston 2003, 140–45; see also Warren and Hankey 1989, 138–46; Egyptian dates taken from Kitchen 1996; Hornung Kraut, and Washburton 2006]). All of this, however, merely sets a point before which (*terminus ante quem*) for the LM IA period. Depending on variables such as whether these vessels were interred immediately or later after use, some to most of the LM IB period lies before the time they arrived in Egypt. If the LM IB period is considered short—as it was thought to be until recently—this could suggest that late LM IA was perhaps in the later 16th century BC (an end-date of 1500 BC was the initial 'round number' approximation, e.g., Warren 1984; more recently, dates a couple or a few decades earlier have been entertained: e.g., Warren and Hankey 1989, esp. 215; Warren 2006, 2007; Wiener 2006). If the LM IB period is long—as now is seemingly clear from both the archaeological and the science-dating evidence from Crete (Betancourt 1998, 293; Rutter n.d.; Manning

2009)—then this same evidence could indicate that late LM IA was somewhere in the later 17th century BC down to around 1600 BC (or roughly a century earlier).

The 'Short chronology' was the interpretation of the mid-second millennium BC Aegean that became conventional or orthodox in scholarship through the AD 1980s (see, for example, the chronology of Warren and Hankey 1989, 169). However, subsequent archaeological work (see especially Rutter n.d.), as well as reconsideration of how to interpret the archaeological linkages between the Aegean and Egypt (Kemp and Merrillees 1980; Betancourt 1987; Manning 1988, 1999, 2007), and especially the application of science-dating techniques (in particular, radiocarbon dating: discussed later) have raised major questions about this dating in recent decades. This evidence suggests a long LM IB period (early/earlier 16th century to the first half of the 15th century BC) and a date for the eruption of Thera in the late 17th century BC. Dates for the eruption from environmental records (especially ice cores and tree rings) have also been suggested as relevant (see later). Some are possible (although some have been strongly criticized), but as of now (AD 2009), none are clear or established (and generally what seemed more plausible in the late AD 1980s–1990s has became less evident or more complicated as a result of more critical examination and further work).

A clash of scholarly cultures has developed. Some archaeologists simply state that the conventional interpretation of the archaeological evidence is secure and superior and that any suggestion to the contrary by science dating simply means something is wrong with the science dating or its analysis (Bietak 2003a; Wiener 2003, 2007). A variety of supposed or claimed possible problems with radiocarbon dating are listed—but never demonstrated as relevant—to justify ignoring this evidence. Meanwhile, others have accepted the worth of the case built from a large number of radiocarbon determinations and have concluded that the archaeological evidence can be reinterpreted in a consonant fashion. Warburton (2009, 139–144) goes even further: critically questioning the supposed stratigraphic sequence at the key site of Tell el-Dabᶜa in the Nile Delta (noting the conspicuous lack of suitable published evidence to support the many specific stratigraphic and assemblage claims made), and suggests that it is perhaps the claimed interpretation of this site, and not radiocarbon, that is the main problem. There has been little common ground.

Archaeology

No fundamentally key archaeological evidence for this problem has helpfully turned up in the last generation to resolve or advance matters. The situation remains where there is a conventional interpretation or viewpoint (Short or Low chronology), but it abides now simultaneously or in parallel with an alternative analysis (High or Long chronology) or at least a clear ambiguity that allows plural interpretations, as argued by Betancourt (1987, 1990; see also Kemp and Merrillees 1980; Manning 1988, 1999, 2007; and see generally conference volumes such as Hardy and Renfrew 1990; Balmuth and Tykot 1998; Bietak 2003b; Bietak and Czerny 2007).

This lack of progress has not been for want of effort. Some spectacular wall painting fragments of a Minoan-like type have been found at a major site (Tell el-Dabᶜa) in the Nile delta (Bietak, Marinatos, and Palyvou 2007). After first being dated to the Hyksos period, they are now assigned to the Thutmosid period, likely the reign of Thutmose III (see Bietak, Marinatos, and Palyvou 2007, 39–40, with key stratigraphic support summarized on pages 21, 27). A secure linkage to Thutmose III awaits publication of the full ceramic evidence. The limits seem to be as follows: First, from his ceramic seriation, Aston (2003, 143) says the relevant upper stratum 'cannot really be any earlier than the reign of Thutmose III,' and the lower limit seems to be Amenhotep II (see Bietak, Marinatos, and Palyvou 2007, 21, 27, and the description of the phase C/2 = stratum c magazines that cut into deposits with painting fragments on p. 21). The paintings are in the earlier part of this range and are therefore likely Thutmose III in date.

These paintings have been much discussed. The excavator, Manfred Bietak, trenchantly argues that they are very similar to the Akrotiri wall paintings from Thera and thus that they are of earlier LM I date. He sees a very short/low chronology, with this context of the early to mid-15th century BC only some decades at most after the Thera eruption (which he would date ca. 1500 BC *or later*). Nonetheless, the paintings are simply not LM IA in style. At the earliest they are late LM I (i.e., late LM IB) and, in all sense and likelihood, are in fact LM II-IIIA in style and date (Shaw 2009 and Younger 2009), linking especially to a group of LM II wall paintings known from Knossos, which was the new, single-palace supersite of Crete and the southern Aegean at this time and with good evidence for high-level contacts with Egypt, including, from its port area at Katsamba, Thutmose III (Manning 2009 and references). Thus, one could merely state that these paintings offer ambiguous evidence; alternatively, they may well support a rethinking of the Short chronology. However, they do not offer a clear resolution that everyone will accept.

Finds of pumice in the East Mediterranean from the Minoan eruption have been noted, and their presence especially in Tuthmosid contexts in Egypt has been held by some to suggest that the eruption occurred around this time (e.g., Bietak and Höflmayer 2007, 17 and references; Bietak 2003a, 28). However, this argument has failed to gain traction. The pumice was used in craft workshops and was collected (and maybe even traded), and we have no idea how long it had been lying around before use (just as it has been regularly used in many other, later prehistoric contexts down through the Classical period and beyond). We also lack many contexts for the 16th century BC from which to see whether they, too, have Minoan pumice—thus, the presence/absence case is weak.

Other recent attempts to claim that a category of artifact type does or does not resolve the short/long debate have failed to convince those already not committed to one side or the other. Either the evidence is not of sufficient resolution or clarity to preclude one side or the other, or it can reasonably be reinterpreted (or less determinedly interpreted in one way). For example, it is argued that a couple of stone vases (one from Shaft Grave IV at Mycenae, one from Akrotiri) are Egyptian and specifically of 18th-Dynasty date (with linkages especially drawn from the reign of Thutmose III) (Warren 2006). Therefore, the implication is that the LH I/LM IA periods must overlap into the 18th Dynasty (and hence continue after ca. 1540 BC) and, given the specified Thutmose III parallel, perhaps last even into the 15th century BC. As stated, this seems key evidence, but it is not in fact certain that the vessels are Egyptian (there has been debate over several other claimed Egyptian stone vessels: Lilyquist 1996, 1997), and, more critically, the stylistic dating, which places them exclusively in the 18th Dynasty, is not demonstrated. Although there are undoubtedly good 18th-Dynasty parallels from the several known 18th-Dynasty assemblages, the types could also date earlier (a notable feature of earlier 18th-Dynasty material is that much of it is a last stage of development of Second Intermediate Period types, as is also the clear case for the ceramics; see, e.g., Aston 2003, 142). Here we have less convenient assemblages for comparison also, which makes it especially hard either to prove or to rule out a pre-18th-Dynasty (Second Intermediate Period) dating. Thus, the case is neither clear nor resolved.

There are several other examples of a similarly ambiguous or nondecisive nature (unless a particular interpretative slant is applied). For example, Koehl (2000) has suggested that rhyta made in Egypt in the earlier to mid-18th Dynasty are more like LM IA types (and so some see this as evidence that LM IA was contemporary: e.g., Bietak 2003a, 29), but the situation is not so simple. The mechanism, directness, and specificity of the link between the Aegean form and those in Egypt is unclear (which have non-Aegean decorations—the supposed link is just the shape/form); moreover, LM IA–style rhyta continue into LM IB (as Koehl 2000, 95, notes), even if a direct influence is sought (and, of course, they appear, even if modified, also in the later years of Thutmose III, held by figures dressed in kilts of LM II–IIIA style: Koehl 2000, 97–99; for the kilts see Rehak 1996, 36–37; Betancourt 1998, 293; Barber 1991, 348; 1993). Furthermore, other LM IB, LH IIA, and even LM II objects occur in earlier to mid-18th-Dynasty contexts (Kemp and Merrillees 1980; Warren and Hankey 1989; Warren 2006). Moreover, during the reign of Thutmose III there is good evidence for a linkage to LM II (Manning 2009); hence, these rhyta may not offer a suitably sensitive comparison. Similarly, analysis of the metal vessels depicted with the Keftiu (= Cretans, it is assumed) in paintings in some Egyptian tombs (Mätthaus 1995) is capable of being consistent with either the short or the long Aegean chronology.

The net result is something of a stalemate from the point of view of archaeology. The main arguments offered to supposedly prove a Short or Low chronology position are in no case decisive and in several cases have been argued in fact to support an alternative Long or High chronology.

Perhaps the most dramatic example of the last is a Cypriot White Slip I bowl that was found on Thera in the late 19th century under the volcanic pumice (Merrillees 2001). The vessel has been lost since at least AD 1922. Bietak argues that because no White Slip I is found in Egypt in a secure context before the 18th Dynasty (though the corpus is in fact quite small, and some sherds from insecure contexts might in fact have been original Second Intermediate Period imports), then this vessel cannot date before the 18th Dynasty, and so the eruption must also date after the beginning of the 18th Dynasty (e.g., Bietak 2003a, 23–28; Wiener 2001). However, the vessel can be recognized as an early type of White Slip I and is probably of northwestern Cypriot origin (see Manning 1999, 150–92; Manning and Sewell 2002; Manning, Crewe, and Sewell 2006, 482–85; Manning 2007, 118–19). White Slip I appears in west/northwest Cyprus from Late Cypriot IA2 but was not really present in eastern Cyprus (and especially around Enkomi) until (late) Late Cypriot IB; there is a marked regionalism on Cyprus at the start of the Late Bronze Age (Merrillees 1971; Manning 2001; Crewe 2007, esp. p.153), just as in Egypt in the Second Intermediate Period (Bourriau 1997), which lasts into the early 18th Dynasty (Aston 2003, 142). Yet, known Cypriot exports to Egypt in the Late Cypriot I period mainly come from the east. Thus, White Slip I and other new Late Cypriot wares like Base Ring I, largely appear in Egypt only *after* the eastern region adopts them. The Egyptian evidence is therefore at best a partial record of *east* Cypriot fashions at this time and is in no sense a measure of the overall range of Cypriot ceramic history in Late Cypriot IA–IB. In contrast, there is other evidence for LM IA contacts between Thera and northwest Cyprus (Cadogan 1990, 95; Vermeule and Wolsky 1990, 382 and note 76, 394), so we can envisage two very different Cypriot ceramic-regional groupings as represented when we compare the sparse evidence from both the Aegean and Egypt. There is no reason this evidence should be compatible and also no reason to limit early White Slip I to an 18th Dynasty start.

Science Dating

In contrast to the archaeological gridlock, the science-dating situation has become somewhat clearer over the last twenty years.

Radiocarbon

Radiocarbon dates on organic materials of annual growth from contexts buried by the volcanic eruption—like seeds stored in jars when the town of Akrotiri was abandoned—should give ages more or less contemporary with the time humans abandoned the site very shortly before the eruption. These have consistently produced ages indicating a date around one hundred years earlier than the conventional Short chronology date in work by a number of laboratories over several decades (with recent work merely more precise) (see Michael 1976; Michael and Betancourt 1988; Manning 1988, 1990; Manning et al. 2006; Housley et al. 1990; Friedrich, Wagner, and Tauber 1990). The latest study, employing both a large dataset and a coherent sequence of evidence from before, around, and after the time of the Thera eruption to best define the volcanic destruction horizon, offered an age of 1660–1613 BC at 95.4% probability for the volcanic destruction level (with the subrange of 1639–1616 BC the most likely) (Manning et al. 2006).

It is also important to note what is not possible. The original Short chronology date of ca. 1500 BC is simply incompatible with the radiocarbon evidence. Even ignoring the integrated LM IA–LM II sequence and its sophisticated analysis

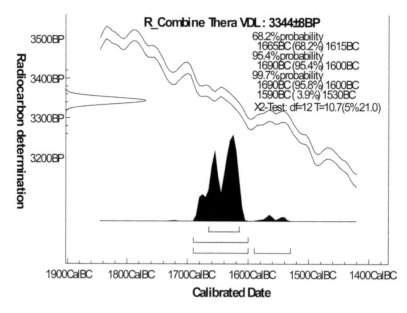

Figure 34.1. Calibrated calendar age probability distribution for the weighted average of the AD2000s analyzed radiocarbon measurements by the Oxford (OxA) and Vienna (VERA) laboratories on short-lived seed samples from the volcanic destruction level at Akrotiri Thera (*n* = 13). Calibration using OxCal and the current IntCal04 data set (calibration curve resolution set at 5: Bronk Ramsey 1995, 2001, 2008; Reimer et al. 2004). For details on the thirteen samples and the individual measurements, see Manning et al. (2006a), supporting online material table S1. As indicated by the χ^2 test (Ward and Wilson 1978), the thirteen samples are all consistent with the hypothesis of representing the same real age at the 95% confidence level. Hence, the weighted average is reasonably the best estimate of the real radiocarbon age (courtesy of the author).

in the Manning et al. (2006a) study, just the high-quality, recently analyzed (measured in the AD 2000s), short-lived data from the volcanic destruction level at Akrotiri by themselves indicate that a date after ca. 1600 BC has less than 5% probability and that a date after ca. 1530 BC has less than a 1% possibility (see figure 34.1).

In response, critics note that plants that grow close (and usually only very close—tens to hundreds of meters) to volcanic vents can take in volcanic (and thus old or depleted) carbon dioxide, which causes them to yield anomalously old (usually very old and highly obvious) apparent radiocarbon ages. Thus, some scholars suggest that or speculate whether this volcanic effect (or something similar) somehow caused an anomaly in the radiocarbon ages for samples from Akrotiri (Wiener 2003, 2007). However, consideration of the very consistent pattern of data from Akrotiri for short-lived samples from the volcanic destruction level (no clear very old ages) and the likely distance from the volcanic vent to the locations where crops were likely growing (several kilometers) both argue against the relevance of the volcanic carbon dioxide effect based on modern case studies of volcanic islands (e.g., Pasquier-Cardin et al. 1999; Manning et al. 2009). Moreover, samples from sites beyond Thera, where no plausible volcanic effect could apply, indicate a similar age. A recent study (Manning et al. 2006), which employed a large set of radiocarbon evidence from before, during, and after the eruption, considered an analysis that excluded all of the data from Thera/Santorini itself (and so excluded any plausible volcanic effect). This study shows that these non-Santorini data nonetheless clearly indicate the same early age range for the late LM IA period (and therefore for the eruption date). Hence, placing the volcanic destruction level and the late LM IA period in the later 17th century BC seems real and fairly solid.

Another recent study examined an olive sample found in the Minoan pumice on Thera and attempted to date (or wiggle-match) a time-order sequence of segments from this sample out to the bark (or the time of death of the sample) (Friedrich et al. 2006). This placed the time of death (and it was argued the eruption) between 1627 and 1600 BC at 95.4% probability or, considering the range of error possible in their analysis, as wide as 1654–1597 BC also at 95.4% probability (Friedrich et al. 2006, supporting online material table S2). This age appears compatible with the findings from the Akrotiri short-lived samples. The use of olive wood in such a study is unusual as it is not regarded as suitable for tree-ring analysis because clear, visible annual growth rings are not produced; hence, the Friedrich et al. study employed X-ray tomography to try to find the growth increments. However, it is certainly possible that some of the 'rings' identified are not annual or that the count is less accurate than thought. Friedrich et al. considered up to a 50% error in the ring count and found that only modest changes occurred, but a degree of uncertainty undoubtedly exists concerning the reality of the 'ring' count, and replication and further investigation would certainly be desirable.

Worst case? If the 'ring' count is entirely abandoned and one looks only at the indisputable order (from oldest to most recent) across the sample, then a Sequence analysis (employing the data in Friedrich et al. 2006 and the OxCal software with the current IntCal04 radiocarbon calibration curve: Bronk Ramsey 1995, 2001, 2008; Reimer et al. 2004) finds that the last dated segment lies between either 1650 and 1600 BC (57.6% probability) or 1590–1530 BC (37.8% probability), with the most likely 51.7% of the total probability indicating the range 1635–1605 BC. This finding, of course, allows Short chronology proponents to claim that the less likely 37.8% range could allow a date down to around 1530 BC or so. Yes, but it also continues to indicate that the most likely age for the death of this sample is shortly after 1635–1605 BC and thus in line with the other evidence from Thera related to the volcanic eruption (regardless of whether one can really count olive growth 'rings'). (Skeptics and those who prefer a later age for the eruption will also speculate on whether it is certain that the sample was actually killed by the eruption or was not an already-dead section of an olive tree; either assertion is possible, of course, but the coincidence of age range with the other evidence from the Akrotiri volcanic destruction level suggest these assertions probably are not correct.)

Overall, the radiocarbon evidence is fairly clear and indicates a likely date for the eruption of Thera in the later 17th century BC.

Other Science Dating Claims?

In the AD 1980s, analysis of ice cores from Greenland identified acidity peaks that correspond to major volcanism (Hammer, Clausen, and Dansgaard 1980), and it was argued that a volcanic signal ca. 1645 BC could indicate the Thera eruption since this date was compatible with the radiocarbon evidence, and the signal indicated a very large eruption (Hammer et al. 1987). The case was one of coincidence. No positive link was possible between the acid spike and Thera. Thera just happened to be the best-known eruption of the mid-second millennium BC.

Meanwhile, it was observed that tree-ring growth in sensitive locations correlated in some cases with the impacts of major volcanic eruptions. A growth anomaly observed between 1628 and 1626 BC was tentatively identified as perhaps the Thera eruption (LaMarche and Hirschboeck 1984; Baillie and Munro 1988). There was no positive evidence for the specific linkage, but at the time it seemed that an unusual 'package' of evidence indicated a major volcanic eruption around the same time, and the radiocarbon said this could be Thera. A date of 1628/1626 BC seemed a possibility for the Thera eruption. However, these simplistic and sweeping would-be teleconnections and hypotheses were undoubtedly naive (Buckland, Dugmore, and Edwards 1997).

In the subsequent two decades, few new methods have really entered the fray. An attempt to apply luminescence techniques to the dating of the older (Cape Riva) eruption of Santorini, even selecting only quartz to avoid known problems with feldspars, was unsuccessful (Bonde, Murray, and Friedrich 2001). However, it is potentially of importance that recent work has begun on identifying past volcanic eruptions and impacts by employing speleothems, and a stalagmite from Sofular Cave in western Turkey is suggested to have a signal caused by the Santorini/Thera eruption (Frisia et al. 2008, 26; photo of the stalagmite on the front cover of issue no. 2). The dating of the Sofular Cave stalagmite is not yet by itself of the high resolution needed to address the Thera debate independently (contrast the recent higher-resolution record from Grotta di Ernesto in Italy: Frisia et al. 2008:25–26, figure 1), but that dating or similar records may prove useful in the future. A short-lived ^{13}C peak and then a slightly delayed and sustained sulphur response (suggesting increased sulphur levels available for mobilization from surface to subsurface for several decades) is noted in the Sofular Cave starting around ca. 1600 BC (which the authors suggest is consistent with an eruption on Santorini in the late 17th or early 16th century BC). This is an area of research to watch for further developments and for full publications (see e.g. Siklósy et al. 2009).

One other potentially promising avenue of research is dendrochemistry. Pilot work has shown some success linking tree-ring chemistry to major volcanic eruptions (Pearson, Manning, Coleman, and Jarvis 2005; Pearson 2006 and references), and ongoing work may suggest a volcanic association for the ca. 1650 BC growth anomaly in the Aegean dendrochronology (Pearson et al. 2009; Pearson and Manning 2009).

Meanwhile, further research in the subsequent two decades has both changed and clarified the simple initial hypotheses drawn from the ice cores and tree rings. Attempts to identify tiny volcanic glass particles in the ice led first to claims of a positive Thera identification (Hammer et al. 2003) but then to strong criticism, including arguments in one case for an Alaskan volcano instead (Aniakchak) (Keenan 2003; Pearce et al. 2004; Denton and Pearce 2008). Most recently, a date of 1642 ±5 BC has been stated for the one clear major volcanic acidity peak (in all three synchronized Greenland ice cores for the period) in the time span indicated for the Thera eruption by the radiocarbon evidence (Vinther et al. 2006, 2008). Could the ice-core event be Thera? Denton and Pearce (2008) claimed that it could not. However, the careful and considered response of Vinther et al. (2008) makes important reading. It is correct that the chemistry of the volcanic glass is indistinguishable from that from the Aniakchak eruption, but Vinther et al. make a good case that the analyses do not rule out Thera as a source, especially if the clear complexities of the Thera case are considered (they also correctly observe the inappropriateness of Keenan's (2003) t-test approach to this type of analytical situation, remarking that it would also rule out Aniakchak). The most persuasive point is that the tephra arrived several months before the sulphate aerosol in the Greenland ice, typical of major lower-latitude eruptions like Thera and *not* high-latitude eruptions (as noted by Hammer et al. 2003; Vinther et al. 2006).

Thus, an ice-core date of ca. 1642 ±5 BC remains in play (while not established). From the tree-ring side, recent work has found additional years during which growth anomalies plausibly indicate volcanic impacts (Salzer and Hughes 2007). Thera candidates include 1652–1648 BC, 1628–1626 BC, and 1619–1617 BC in the later 17th century BC (contemporary with the age range indicated by radiocarbon for the Thera eruption). Considering the total date range suggested by radiocarbon and conventional archaeology, other possibilities could include 1597 BC, 1544 BC, and 1524 BC. Whether the first or second can be synchronized so as to link with the ice-core evidence is not clear at this time. An extraordinary growth anomaly in the Aegean dendrochronology is dated ca. 1650 +4/−7 BC (Manning et al. 2001), and it is tempting to speculate whether this might be linked with the 1652–1648 BC tree-ring package noted by Salzer and Hughes (2007) and, in turn, whether we might be able to associate this with the ca. 1642 ±5 BC ice-core signal. However, if the Thera eruption is regarded as a lesser signal in the ice-core records, then 1619–1617 BC or 1597 BC could come into play. No other environmental proxy indicates a major volcanic event ca. 1544 BC, so this seems an unlikely association. Wiener (2006) has noted the tree-ring growth anomaly attested in 1524 BC, and, as this is almost at the very margin of the latest possible part of the radiocarbon range and, in reverse, at the top end of the conventional short chronology estimates for the date of eruption, he has suggested this might be Thera in an attempt to keep the short chronology in play. At present no other proxy evidence supports this association.

Thus, with regard to Thera, no clear ice-core and tree-ring tie-in exists as of AD 2009 (contra the situation that seemed to perhaps exist in the AD 1980s, e.g., Hughes

1988). In addition, we have no clear positive evidence, although Vinther et al. (2008) make a reasonable case for seriously considering 1642 ± 5 BC despite recent criticism (and the date may be a little more flexible, even to around 20 years, according to one recent analysis; Muscheler 2009). We simply have several possible candidates.

Conclusions

It might seem that archaeologists and scientists ought to be able to date a very large volcanic eruption less than 4000 years ago. However, although archaeologists in the Aegean can place its relative position in the cultural sequence quite precisely (late in the Late Minoan IA cultural phase), there has been much controversy about the absolute date: later 17th century BC *or* late 16th century BC (or even later for some). The weight of the science-based evidence seems to point to a likely age around a century earlier than archaeologists' best estimate through the AD 1980s. This potential direct contradiction of a long tradition of work by archaeologists has been met with stiff resistance over the last three decades. Acceptance of such a change would involve some significant reworking of the conventional culture-historical synthesis. It would undermine years of work and publications by many leading figures. As a result, it has to be wrong.

What is the right answer? It remains too early to say. Notably, a great deal of radiocarbon work by several laboratories, using samples from Thera, as well as samples *not* from Thera (and thus immune from claims that volcanic carbon dioxide somehow affected the samples on Thera), and from periods before, around, and after the eruption, consistently produces more or less the same result: a date most likely in the later 17th century BC. If so, we may be able to associate some events noted in ice-core and tree-ring records—if a positive connection can ever be established. Based on the ice-core and tree-ring evidence, some major volcano seems to have erupted around 1650 BC, give or take a few years. But which volcano is not known—Vinther et al. (2008) merely argue persuasively that Thera remains a possibility. If this turns out not to be Thera, then the other signals noted earlier could be relevant. The stalagmite from Sofular Cave, and other such records (see for example Siklósy et al. 2009) may also prove useful; this evidence already tends to support the Long or High scenario rather than the Short or Low chronology.

Meanwhile, proponents of the Short Aegean chronology continue vigorously to defend a date in the later 16th century BC (or lower in some cases) and to express skepticism regarding science-dating claims. Those who consider dates in the mid-16th century BC down to ca. 1530 BC can claim to be within the less likely range of the radiocarbon evidence. However, those who argue for dates later than this have entirely to ignore or dismiss the large body of high-quality radiocarbon evidence available. There is no sound justification for this position.

The archaeological and radiocarbon evidence from the next archaeological phase on Crete, Late Minoan IB, is also relevant. The archaeology today indicates a long period based on the recognition of several phases within the overall period (Rutter n.d.), while the radiocarbon evidence is consonant, indicating a date for the end of the phase in the first half of the 15th century BC, but also indicating that this long phase began at least in the mid-16th century BC (placing the Thera eruption at least a little earlier again) (Manning 2009). All of this is another challenge for the Short chronology, whereas it can work very happily with the Long or High chronology and with an overall LM IA to LM II radiocarbon-based chronological framework (Manning et al. 2006).

The date of the great eruption of Thera Santorini thus remains for the present an unsolved question. The arguments on both sides reflect a clear clash of academic cultures and generations.

BIBLIOGRAPHY

Aston, David A. 2003. "New Kingdom Pottery Phases as Revealed through Well-dated Tomb Contexts." In *SCIEM* II, 135–62.

Baillie, Michael G. L., and Martin A. R. Munro. 1988. "Irish Tree Rings, Santorini, and Volcanic Dust Veils." *Nature* 332: 344–46.

Balmuth, Miriam S., and Robert H. Tykot, eds. 1998. *Sardinian and Aegean Chronology: Towards the Resolution of Relative and Absolute Dating in the Mediterranean.* Studies in Sardinian Archaeology V. Oxford: Oxbow.

Barber, Elizabeth J. W. 1991. *Prehistoric Textiles: The Development of Cloth in the Neolithic and Bronze Ages with Special Reference to the Aegean.* Princeton: Princeton University Press.

———. 1993. "Late Bronze Age Kilts and the Reconstruction of Aegean Textile Connections." *AJA* 97: 350.

Berry, Joanne. 2007. *The Complete Pompeii.* New York: Thames and Hudson.

Betancourt, Philip P. 1987. "Dating the Aegean Late Bronze Age with Radiocarbon." *Archaeometry* 29: 45–49.

———. 1990. "High Chronology or Low Chronology: The Archaeological Evidence." In *TAW III*, 19–23.

———. 1998. "The Chronology of the Aegean Late Bronze Age: Unanswered Questions." In *Sardinian and Aegean Chronology*, ed. Miriam Balmuth and Robert Tykot, 291–96. Studies in Sardinian Archaeology V. Oxford: Oxbow.

Bichler, Max, Martin Exler, Claudia Peltz, and Susanne Saminger. 2003. "Thera Ashes." In *SCIEM* II, 11–21.

Bietak, Manfred. 2003a. "Science versus Archaeology: Problems and Consequences of High Aegean Chronology." In *SCIEM* II, 23–33.

———, ed. 2003b. *The Synchronisation of Civilisations in the Eastern Mediterranean in the Second Millennium B.C. II. Proceedings of the SCIEM 2000, EuroConference, Haindorf, 2nd of May–7th of May 2001.* Vienna: Verlag der Österreichischen Akademie der Wissenschaften.

————, and Ernst Czerny, eds. 2007. *The Synchronisation of Civilisations in the Eastern Mediterranean in the Second Millennium B.C. III. Proceedings of the SCIEM 2000, 2nd EuroConference, Vienna, 28th of May–1st of June 2003.* Vienna: Verlag der Österreichischen Akademie der Wissenschaften.

Bietak, Manfred, and Felix Höflmayer. 2007. "Introduction: High and Low Chronology." In *SCIEM III,* 11–23.

Bietak, Manfred, Nanno Marinatos, and Claire Palyvou. 2007. *Taureador scenes in Tell el-Dabʿa (Avaris) and Knossos.* Vienna: Verlag der Österreichischen Akademie der Wissenschaften.

Bonde, Anette, Andrew Murray, and Walter L. Friedrich. 2001. "Santorini: Luminescence Dating of a Volcanic Province Using Quartz?" *Quaternary Science Reviews* 20: 789–93.

Bottema, Sytze, and Anayia Sarpaki. 2003. "Environmental Change in Crete: A 9000-year Record of Holocene Vegetation History and the Effect of the Santorini Eruption." *Holocene* 13: 733–49.

Bourriau, Janine. 1997. "Beyond Avaris: The Second Intermediate Period in Egypt outside the Eastern Delta." In *The Hyksos: New Historical and Archaeological Perspectives,* ed. Eliezer D. Oren, 159–82. Philadelphia: University Museum, University of Pennsylvania.

Bronk Ramsey, Christopher. 1995. "Radiocarbon Calibration and Analysis of Stratigraphy: The OxCal Program." *Radiocarbon* 37: 425–30.

————. 2001. "Development of the Radiocarbon Calibration Program OxCal." *Radiocarbon* 43: 355–63.

————. 2008. "Deposition Models for Chronological Records." *Quaternary Science Reviews* 27: 42–60.

Bruins, Hendrik J., J. Alexander MacGillivray, Costas E. Synolakis, Chaim Benjamini, Jörg Keller, Hanan J. Kisch, Andreas Klügel, and Johannes van der Plicht. 2008. "Geoarchaeological Tsunami Deposits at Palaikastro (Crete) and the Late Minoan IA Eruption of Santorini." *JAS* 35(1): 191–212.

Buckland, Paul C., Andrew J. Dugmore, and Kevin J. Edwards. 1997. "Bronze Age Myths? Volcanic Activity and Human Response in the Mediterranean and North Atlantic Regions." *Antiquity* 71: 581–93.

Cadogan, Gerald. 1978. "Dating the Aegean Bronze Age without Radiocarbon." *Archaeometry* 20: 209–14.

————. 1990. "Thera's Eruption into Our Understanding of the Minoans." In *TAW III.1,* 93–97.

Crewe, Lindy. 2007. *Early Enkomi: Regionalism, trade and society at the beginning of the Late Bronze Age on Cyprus.* BAR International Series 1706. Oxford: Archaeopress.

Denton, Joanna S., and Nicholas J. G. Pearce. 2008. "Comment on 'A Synchronized Dating of Three Greenland Ice Cores throughout the Holocene' by Bo M. Vinther *et al.:* No Minoan Tephra in the 1642 B.C. Layer of the GRIP Ice Core." *Journal of Geophysical Research* 113: D04303, doi:10.1029/2007JD008970.

Doumas, Christos G. 1983. *Thera: Pompeii of the Ancient Aegean.* London: Thames and Hudson.

————.1990. "Archaeological Observations at Akrotiri relating to the Volcanic Destruction." In *TAW III,* 48–49.

————. 1991. "High Art from the Time of Abraham." *Biblical Archaeology Review* 17: 40–51.

————. 1992. *The Wall-paintings of Thera.* Athens: Thera Foundation, Petros M. Nomikos.

————, Mariza Marthari, and Christina Televantou. 2000. *Museum of Prehistoric Thera: Brief Guide.* Athens: 21st Ephorate of Prehistoric and Classical Antiquities.

Driessen, Jan, and Colin F. Macdonald. 1997. *The Troubled Island: Minoan Crete before and after the Santorini Eruption.* Aegaeum 17. Liège: Université de Liège.

Eastwood, Warren J., John C. Tibby, Neil Roberts, H. John B. Birks, and Henry F. Lamb. 2002. "The Environmental Impact of the Minoan Eruption of Santorini (Thera): Numerical Analysis of Palaeoecological Data from Gölhisar, Southwest Turkey." *Holocene* 12: 431–44.

Forsyth, Phyllis Y. 1997. *Thera in the Bronze Age.* New York: Lang.

Friedrich, Walter L. 2000. *Fire in the Sea: The Santorini Volcano: Natural History and the Legend of Atlantis.* Trans. A. R. McBirney. New York: Cambridge University Press.

Friedrich, Walter L., Bernd Kromer. Michael Friedrich, Jan Heinemeier, Tom Pfeiffer, and Sahra Talamo, S. 2006. "Santorini Eruption Radiocarbon Dated to 1627–1600 B.C." *Science* 312: 548.

———, Peter Wagner, and Henrik Tauber. 1990. "Radiocarbon-dated Plant Remains from the Akrotiri Excavation on Santorini, Greece." *TAW III.3*, 188–96.

Frisia, Silvia, S. Badertscher, A. Borsato, J. Susini, O.M. Göktürk, H. Cheng, R.L. Edwards, J. Kramers, O. Tüysüz, and D. Fleitmann. 2008. "The Use of Stalagmite Geochemistry to Detect Past Volcanic Eruptions and Their Environmental Impacts." *PAGES News* 16(3): 25–26.

Hammer, Claus U., Henrik B. Clausen, and Willi Dansgaard. 1980. "Greenland Ice Sheet Evidence of Post-glacial Volcanism and Its Climatic Impact." *Nature* 288: 230–35.

Hammer, Claus U., Henrik B. Clausen, Walter L. Friedrich, and Henrik Tauber. 1987. "The Minoan Eruption of Santorini in Greece Dated to 1645 BC?" *Nature* 328: 517–19.

Hammer Claus U., Gero Kurat, Peter Hoppe, Walter Grum, and Henrik B. Clausen. 2003. "Thera eruption date 1645BC confirmed by new ice core data?" In *SCIEM* II, 87–94.

Hardy, David A., Christos G. Doumas, Ioannis Sakellarakis, and Peter M. Warren, eds. 1990. *Thera and the Aegean world III. Vol.1.* London: Thera Foundation.

Hardy, David A. and A. Colin Renfrew, eds. *Thera and the Aegean World III. Vol.3.* London: The Thera Foundation.

Hornung, Erik, Rolf Krauss, and David A. Warburton, eds. 2006. *Ancient Egyptian Chronology.* Leiden: Brill.

Housley, Rupert A., Robert E. M. Hedges, Ian A. Law, and Christopher R. Bronk. 1990. "Radiocarbon Dating by AMS of the Destruction of Akrotiri." In *TAW III.3*, 207–51.

Hughes, Malcolm K. 1988. "Ice Layer Dating of the Eruption of Santorini." *Nature* 335: 211–12.

Keenan, Douglas J. 2003. "Volcanic Ash Retrieved from the GRIP Ice Core Is Not from Thera." *Geochemistry, Geophysics, Geosystems* 4(11): 1097, doi:10.1029/2003GC000608.

Kemp, Barry J., and Robert S. Merrillees. 1980. *Minoan Pottery in Second Millennium Egypt.* Mainz am Rhein: von Zabern.

Kitchen, Kenneth A. 1996. "The Historical Chronology of Ancient Egypt: A Current Assessment." *Acta Archaeologica* 67: 1–13.

Koehl, Robert. 2000. "Minoan Rhyta in Egypt." In *Krete-Aigyptos: Politismikoi desmoi trion chilietion. Meletes,* ed. Alexandra Karetsou, 94–100. Athens: Hypourgeio Politismou.

LaMarche, Valmore C., Jr., and Katherine K. Hirschboeck. 1984. "Frost Rings in Trees as Records of Major Volcanic Eruptions." *Nature* 307: 121–26.

Lilyquist, Christine. 1996. "Stone Vessels at Kamid el-Loz: Egyptian, Egyptianizing, or Non-Egyptian? A Question at Sites from the Sudan to Iraq to the Greek Mainland." In *Kamid el-Loz 16*, ed. Rolf Hachmann, 133–73. Schatzhausstudien. Bonn: Dr. Rudolf Habelt.

———. 1997. "Egyptian Stone Vases? Comments on Peter Warren's Paper." In *TEXNH*, 225–28.

Manning, Sturt W. 1988. "The Bronze Age Eruption of Thera: Absolute Dating, Aegean Chronology and Mediterranean Cultural Interrelations." *JMA* 1(1): 17–82.

———. 1990. "The Eruption of Thera: Date and Implications." In *TAW III.3*, 29–40.

———. 1999. *A Test of Time: The Volcano of Thera and the Chronology and History of the Aegean and East Mediterranean in the Mid-second Millennium BC*. Oxford: Oxbow.

———. 2001. "The chronology and foreign connections of the Late Cypriot I period: times they are a-changin." In *The chronology of Base-Ring ware and Bichrome wheel-made ware*, ed. P. Åström, 69–94. Stockholm: The Royal Academy of Letters, History and Antiquities.

———. 2007. "Clarifying the "High" v. "Low" Aegean/Cypriot Chronology for the Mid-second Millennium BC: Assessing the Evidence, Interpretive Frameworks, and Current State of the Debate." In *SCIEM* III, 101–37.

———. 2009. "Beyond the Santorini Eruption: Some Notes on Dating the Late Minoan IB Period on Crete, and Implications for Cretan-Egyptian Relations in the 15th century BC (and Especially LM II)." In *Time's Up! Dating the Minoan Eruption of Santorini*, ed. David A. Warburton, 207–26. Monographs of the Danish Institute at Athens 10. Athens: Danish Institute at Athens.

Manning Sturt W., Christopher Bronk Ramsey, Walter Kutschera, Thomas Higham, Bernd Kromer, Peter Steier, and Eva M. Wild. 2006. "Chronology for the Aegean Late Bronze Age 1700–1400 BC." *Science* 312(5573): 565–69.

———. 2009. "Dating the Santorini/Thera Eruption by Radiocarbon: Further Discussion (AD 2006–2007)." In *Tree-Rings, Kings, and Old World Archaeology and Environment: Papers Written in Honor of Peter Ian Kuniholm*, ed. Sturt W. Manning and Mary Jaye Bruce, 299–316. Ithaca: Cornell University Press.

Manning, Sturt W., Lindy Crewe, and David A. Sewell. 2006. "Further Light on Early LC I Connections at Maroni." In *Timelines*, vol. 2, 471–88.

———, Bernd Kromer, Peter I. Kuniholm, and Marianne W. Newton. 2001. "Anatolian Tree-rings and a New Chronology for the East Mediterranean Bronze–Iron Ages." *Science* 294: 2532–35.

Manning, Sturt W., and David A. Sewell. 2002. "Volcanoes and History: A Significant Relationship? The Case of Santorini." In *Natural Disasters and Cultural Change*, ed. Robin Torrence and John Grattan, 264–91. London: Routledge.

Marinatos, Spyridon. 1968–1976. *Excavations at Thera I–VII*. Athens: Arkhaiologike Hetaireia.

Matthäus, Hartmut. 1995. "Representations of Keftiu in Egyptian Tombs and the Absolute Chronology of the Aegean Late Bronze Age." *BICS* 40: 177–94.

McCoy, Floyd W., and Grant Heiken. 2000. "The Late-Bronze Age Explosive Eruption of Thera (Santorini), Greece: Regional and Local Effects." In *Volcanic Hazards and Disasters in Human Antiquity*, ed. Floyd W. McCoy and Grant Heiken, 43–70. Geological Society of America Special Paper 345. Boulder: Geological Society of America.

Merrillees, Robert S. 1971. "The Early History of Late Cypriot I." *Levant* 3: 56–79.

———. 2001. "Some Cypriote White Slip Pottery from the Aegean." In *White Slip Ware*, 89–100.

Michael, Henry N. 1976. "Radiocarbon Dates from Akrotiri on Thera." *Temple University Aegean Symposium* 1: 7–9.

————, and Philip P. Betancourt. 1988. "The Thera Eruption: II. Further Arguments for an Early Date." *Archaeometry* 30: 169–75.

Muscheler, Raimund. 2009. "^{14}C and ^{10}Be around 1650 cal B.C." In *Time's Up! Dating the Minoan Eruption of Santorini*, ed. David A. Warburton, 275–284. Monographs of the Danish Institute at Athens 10. Athens: Danish Institute at Athens.

Page, Denys L. 1970. *The Santorini Volcano and the Desolation of Minoan Crete*. London: Society for the Promotion of Hellenic Studies.

Palyvou, Clairy. 2005. *Akrotiri Thera: An Architecture of Affluence 3,500 Years Old*. Philadelphia: INSTAP Academic Press.

Pasquier-Cardin, Aline, Patrick Allard, Teresa Ferreira, Christine Hatte, Rui Coutinho, Michel Fontugne, and Michel Jaudon. 1999. "Magma-derived CO_2 Emissions Recorded in ^{14}C and ^{13}C Content of Plants Growing in Furnas Caldera, Azores." *Journal of Volcanology and Geothermal Research* 92: 195–207.

Pearce, Nicholas J. G., John A. Westgate, Shari J. Preece, Warren J. Eastwood, and William T. Perkins. 2004. "Identification of Aniakchak (Alaska) Tephra in Greenland Ice Core Challenges the 1645 BC Date for Minoan Eruption of Santorini." *Geochemistry, Geophysics, Geosystems* 5(3), Q03005, doi:10.1029/2003GC000672.

Pearson, Charlotte L. 2006. *Volcanic Eruptions, Tree Rings, and Multielemental Chemistry: An Investigation of Dendrochemical Potential for the Absolute Dating of Past Volcanism*. BAR 10191. Oxford: John and Erica Hedges.

Pearson, Charlotte L., Darren S. Dale, Peter W. Brewer, Peter I. Kuniholm, Jeffrey Lipton, and Sturt W. Manning. 2009. "Dendrochemical analysis of a tree-ring growth anomaly associated with the Late Bronze Age eruption of Thera." *JAS* 36: 1206–14.

————, and Sturt W. Manning. 2009. "Could Absolutely Dated Tree-ring Chemistry Provide a Means to Dating the Major Volcanic Eruptions of the Holocene?" In *Tree-rings, Kings, and Old World Archaeology and Environment: Papers Written in Honor of Peter Ian Kuniholm*, ed. Sturt W. Manning and Mary Jaye Bruce, 97–109. Oxford: Oxbow.

————, Sturt W. Manning, Max L. Coleman, and Kym Jarvis. 2005. "Could Tree-ring Chemistry Reveal Absolute Dates for Past Volcanic Eruptions?" *JAS* 32: 1265–74.

Pyle, David M. 1997. "The Global Impact of the Minoan Eruption of Santorini, Greece." *Environmental Geology* 30: 59–61.

Rehak, Paul. 1996. "Aegean Breechcloths, Kilts, and the Keftiu Paintings." *AJA* 100: 35–51.

Reimer Paula J., Mike G. L. Baillie, Edouard Bard, Alex Bayliss, J. Warren Beck, Chanda J. H. Bertrand, Paul G. Blackwell, Caitlin E. Buck, George S. Burr, Kirsten B. Cutler, Paul E. Damon, R. Lawrence Edwards, Richard G. Fairbanks, Michael Friedrich, Thomas P. Guilderson, Alan G. Hogg, Konrad A. Hughen, Bernd Kromer, Gerry McCormac, Sturt Manning, Christopher Bronk Ramsey, Ron W. Reimer, Sabine Remmele, John R. Southon, Minze Stuiver, Sahra Talamo, F. W. Taylor, Johannes van der Plicht, and Constanze E. Weyhenmeyer. 2004. "IntCal04 Terrestrial Radiocarbon Age Calibration, 0–26 Cal Kyr BP." *Radiocarbon* 46: 1029–58.

Renfrew, A. Colin 1979. "The Eruption of Thera and Minoan Crete." In *Volcanic Activity and Human Ecology*, ed. Payson D. Sheets and Donald K. Grayson, 565–85. New York: Academic Press.

Rutter, Jeremy B. n.d. "Late Minoan IB at Kommos: A Sequence of at Least Three Distinct Stages." In *LM IB Pottery: Relative Chronology and Regional Differences*, ed. Thomas M. Brogan and Erik Hallager. Athens: Danish Institute at Athens.

Salzer, Matthew W., and Malcolm K. Hughes. 2007. "Bristlecone Pine Tree Rings and Volcanic Eruptions over the Last 5000 yr." *Quaternary Research* 67: 57–68.

Shaw, Maria C. 2009. "A Bull-Leaping Fresco from the Nile Delta and a Search for Patrons and Artists." *AJA* 113: 471–77.

Sherratt, Susan, ed. 2000. *Wall Paintings of Thera.*

Siklósy, Zoltán, Attila Demény, Torsten W. Vennemann, Sebastien Pilet, Jan Kramers, Szabolcs Leél-Őssy, Mária Bondár, Chuan-Chou Shen, and Ernst Hegner. 2009. Bronze Age volcanic event recorded in stalagmites by combined isotope and trace element studies. *Rapid Communications in Mass Spectometry* 23: 801–808.

Sigurdsson, Haraldur, Steven Carey, Matina Alexandri, Georges Vougioukalakis, Katherine Croff, Chris Roman, Dimitris Sakellariou, Christos Anagnostou, Grigoris Rousakis, Chrysanthi Ioakim, Aleka Gogou, Dionysis Ballas, Thanassis Misaridis, and Paraskevi Nomikou. 2006. "Marine Investigations of Greece's Santorini Volcanic Field." *Eos. Transactions American Geophysical Union* 87(34), doi:10.1029/2006E0340001.

Soles, Jeffrey S., S. R. Taylor, and Charles J. Vitaliano. 1995. "Tephra Samples from Mochlos and Their Chronological Implications for Neopalatial Crete." *Archaeometry* 37: 385–93.

Tzachili, Iris. 2005. "Excavations on Thera and Therasia in the 19th Century: A Chronicle." *JMA* 18: 231–57.

Vermeule, Emily D. T., and Florence Z. Wolsky. 1990. *Toumba tou Skourou: A Bronze Age Potter's Quarter on Morphou Bay in Cyprus. The Harvard University–Museum of Fine Arts, Boston Cyprus Expedition.* Cambridge, Mass.: Harvard University Press.

Vinther, Bo M., H. B. Clausen, S. J. Johnsen, S. O. Rasmussen, K. K. Andersen, S. L. Buchardt, D. Dahl-Jensen, I. K. Seierstad, M.-L. Siggaard-Andersen, J. P. Steffensen, A. Svensson, J. Olsen, and J. Heinemeier. 2006. "A Synchronized Dating of Three Greenland Ice Cores throughout the Holocene." *Journal of Geophysical Research* 111, D13102, doi:10.1029/2005JD006921.

———. 2008. "Reply to Comment by J. S. Denton and N. J. G. Pearce on 'A Synchronized Dating of Three Greenland Ice Cores throughout the Holocene.'" *Journal of Geophysical Research* 113, D12306, doi:10.1029/2007JD009083.

Warburton, David A., ed. 2009. *Time's Up! Dating the Minoan Eruption of Santorini.* Monographs of the Danish Institute at Athens 10. Athens: Danish Institute at Athens.

Ward, Graeme K., and Sue R. Wilson. 1978. "Procedures for Comparing and Combining Radiocarbon Age Determinations: A Critique." *Archaeometry* 20: 19–31.

Warren, Peter M. 1984. "Absolute Dating of the Bronze Age Eruption of Thera (Santorini)." *Nature* 308: 492–93.

Warren, Peter M. 2006. The Date of the Thera Eruption in Relation to Aegean-Egyptian Interconnections and the Egyptian Historical Chronology. In *Timelines, vol. 2,* 305–21.

———. 2007. "A New Pumice Analysis from Knossos and the End of Late Minoan IA." In *SCIEM* III, 495–99.

Warren, Peter, and Vronwy Hankey. 1989. *Aegean Bronze Age Chronology.* Bristol: Bristol Classical Press.

Wiener, Malcolm H. 2001. "The White Slip I of Tell el-Dabᶜa and Thera: Critical Challenge for the Aegean Long Chronology." In *White Slip Ware,* 195–202.

———. 2003. "Time Out: The Current Impasse in Bronze Age Archaeological Dating." In *METRON,* 363–99.

———. 2006. "Chronology Going Forward (with a Query about 1525/4 B.C.)." In *Timelines,* vol. 2, 317–28.

———. 2007. "Times Change: The Current State of the Debate in Old World Chronology." In *SCIEM* III, 25–47.

Younger, John G. 2009. "The Bull-Leaping Scenes from Tell el-Dabᶜa." *AJA* 113: 479–80.

CHAPTER 35

THE TROJAN WAR

TREVOR BRYCE

THE story of Troy's war with the Greeks is one of the best-known narrative episodes from the Greek and Roman literary tradition. Apart from the scholarly analyses to which the tale is constantly subjected, it has enjoyed many reincarnations in more popular forms—novels, plays, and presentations on television and cinema screens. To the ancient Greeks and Romans, it provided the inspiration for a wide range of artistic representations in the fields of painting, sculpture, poetry, drama, and philosophy. The romance of the story, which began with a love affair, the scale of the conflict, which brought together two allegedly great international powers, the heroic exploits of its main participants, and the final Greek triumph all contribute to the popularity the story enjoyed in the Classical period and continues to enjoy in the Western world today.

In the Classical tradition, the *casus belli* was the abduction of Helen, wife of the Spartan king, Menelaus, by the Trojan prince Paris while he was on a 'goodwill' visit to Sparta. Helen's flight with Paris back to Troy prompted the mustering of a Panhellenic naval expedition under the command of Agamemnon, king of Mycenae, whose mission was to sail to Troy, then ruled by Paris's father, Priam, capture the city, and reclaim the stolen queen. The Greeks encamped on the plains outside Troy and placed the city under siege when the Trojans refused to release Helen. For ten years Troy held out before it fell to the Greeks, who secured entry to the city by the stratagem of the so-called Trojan Horse. Troy was sacked and abandoned, one group of fugitives traveling west with Prince Aeneas, member of a collateral branch of Priam's family. In the version favored by Roman tradition, the refugees resettled in southwestern Italy, where Aeneas became the founder of the Roman nation.

Ancient Greek writers proposed widely varying dates for the Trojan War, ranging from as early as 1334 to as late as the tenth century BC. The 1334 date was proposed by the 4th–3rd century BC historian Duris, tyrant of Samos, for whom the war occurred 1,000 years before Alexander's arrival on the site of Troy (*FGrH* 76 F41). The historian Herodotus, writing in the fifth century, dated the war 800 years before his time (i.e., early in the thirteenth century) (2.145). The third-century Greek geographer Eratosthenes believed that it took place 407 years before the first Olympiad (i.e., 1183) (*FGrH* 241 F1, 244 F61). This last date was the one most favored in the Hellenistic period. However, although they differed on the war's actual date, the ancient writers all agreed in assigning it to Greece's prehistoric period, many generations before the appearance of the first written records (after the Linear B script) in the Greek world. In modern terms, the period to which they assigned the war belongs to the last century (or a little earlier in the case of Duris) of the Late Bronze Age.

In the interval between the war and the earliest written records of it, traditions about the conflict were kept alive and orally transmitted by a succession of storytellers, no doubt like the bards and minstrels who, according to Homer, entertained the courts of Mycenaean kings and noblemen (*Odyssey* 9.5–11). By far the most famous version of the tale is that narrated by Homer in the *Iliad*. However, the Trojan War story must already have been told many times by many generations of bards and minstrels before Homer first recited his poem in the late eighth or early seventh century. Indeed, much of our information about events associated with the war, including the abduction of Helen, the stratagem of the Trojan Horse, and the fall of Troy, comes not from Homer but from other sources. The most notable of these are the remains of a group of poems making up the so-called Epic Cycle. These post-date the *Iliad* but are probably no later than the seventh or early sixth century. They include works such as the *Cypria*, which deals with the seduction of Helen, the *Little Iliad*, which tells the story of the Trojan Horse, and the *Iliu Persis* ('Sack of Troy'), which describes the capture and destruction of the city by the Greeks. Though only small fragments of these works survive, they clearly reflect stories of the war that predate Homer's own narrative.

Homer himself refers only in passing to some of the war's best-known episodes and in the *Iliad* makes not one single mention of the Trojan horse. He has no wish to repeat all of the details of an already well-known story. Instead, he confines his attention to the last weeks of the ten-year conflict—fifty-one days to be precise—and most of his account is limited to just six days, four days of fighting divided by two days of truce.

The chief theme of his poem is the wrath of the Greek hero Achilles, which was directed initially against Agamemnon for commandeering his favorite slave girl, Chryseis, and finally against the Trojan prince Hektor, who has killed his beloved friend Patroklos. Achilles' all-consuming desire for revenge is not satisfied until he has met and slaughtered Hektor in hand-to-hand combat and desecrated his body by dragging it back to his tent behind his chariot. The *Iliad* ends with Hektor's funeral rites. It thus stops short of an account of the Greeks' final victory and the sack of Troy, though the city's fall is foreshadowed a number of times throughout the poem. Homer is less concerned with the outcome of the war than with the range of human qualities and emotions the conflict reveals, as well as the personal triumphs and tragedies to which it gives rise. In this respect, no distinction is drawn between those who fought on the Greek side and those who fought on the Trojan. All were united in both a common culture and their adherence to a common set of ideals and values.

We should not lose sight of the fact that Homer was a poet, not a historian. Moreover, it does him an injustice to assess the merits of his composition on the basis of whether it reflects historical fact. Even so, the ancient commentators had no doubt about the fundamental truth of the *Iliad* and of the Trojan War tradition in general. Nonetheless, they were sometimes skeptical about various aspects of the tradition, particularly as Homer presented it. Herodotus, for example, accepted the story the Egyptian priests told him—that Helen had never reached Troy (2.112–18). Rather, she had been detained in Egypt, whither the ship in which she and Paris were traveling had been blown by violent winds. The Egyptian king, Proteus, had held her in custody until her husband, Menelaus, could rescue her. When later challenged by the Greeks to hand Helen over, the Trojans declared that they could not do so because she was not in Troy. Homer well knew the truth, Herodotus declares, but ignored it because it did not suit his epic theme. Herodotus's younger contemporary Thucydides also had no doubts about the basic historicity of the Greek-Trojan conflict and cited Homer as its main source (1.10). However, he believed that Homer, like other reciters of tales, was prone to exaggeration (2.41).

According to Thucydides, Homer set the size of the Greek fleet at 1,200 ships. This is a rounded-off figure, for the precise total obtained by adding together all of the vessels listed in Homer's 'Greek Catalogue of Ships' (*Iliad* 2.484–760) is actually 1,186. A fleet of this size is inconceivable in a Bronze Age context. Late Bronze Age fleets may have contained no more than a dozen ships at most. We know, for example, that around the time the Trojan War allegedly took place, a fleet of seven ships was sufficient to attack and inflict severe damage on the Syrian coastal city of Ugarit (Nougayrol et al. 1968, 87–89n24).

This is consistent with what the *Iliad* tells us about a first Trojan War in the days when Priam's father, Laomedon, ruled Troy. In this war, the Greek leader was Herakles, who captured and sacked Troy with just six ships (*Iliad* 5.640–42) and apparently in a much shorter time than the ten-year siege of the 'second' Trojan War. A naval-based military operation on this scale is much more feasible in a Bronze Age context than one involving an armada of 1,186 ships. Thucydides makes some attempt to rationalize Homer's figures by suggesting that the actual number of combatants on board the fleet may not have been particularly large and that the siege continued for ten years because the majority of the Greek forces had to be deployed on plundering and crop-production activities to ensure adequate provisioning for the actual besiegers (1.11).

What of scholarship today? Making allowances for a conflict conceived on an 'epic' scale and magnified by successive generations of bards for the entertainment of their audiences, have modern scholars been able to find a kernel of historical truth in the Trojan War tradition? There is now little doubt that the site of Hisarlık, which the Classical Greeks called Ilion ('Troy VIII') and the Romans Ilium ('Troy

IX'), was the setting Homer used for his account of the Trojan War. Furthermore, it is commonly assumed that one of Ilion's Late Bronze Age predecessors ('Troy VI' or 'Troy VII') was the *actual* setting of a historical conflict or conflicts that gave rise to the Greek tradition of a Trojan War.

Bronze Age settlement at Troy reached its peak in the Troy VI period, dated on archaeological grounds from ca. 1700 to the early thirteenth century BC (see Mountjoy 1999). The material remains of this level are not inconsistent with Homer's description of Priam's Troy—though the correspondence does not extend beyond a few general features. The final sublevel of Troy VI (VIh) suffered violent destruction. A date of ca. 1280 BC for this destruction would fit well with Herodotus's date of the Trojan War. There is some evidence to support the conclusion that Troy VIh was destroyed by human agency, though it is not sufficient to rule out destruction by earthquake.

Among the most important results produced by Manfred Korfmann's work at Hisarlık is the identification of a Late Bronze Age lower settlement attached to the citadel mound. Korfmann's excavations, conducted between 1988 and 2005, appear to have increased tenfold the known area occupied by Troy, from some 20,000 square meters (the citadel on its own) to approximately 200,000 square meters (see Korfmann et al. 2001; Korfmann 2006). Such a dramatic increase in the city's size has presumably laid to rest the concerns of Homeric literalists (beginning with Heinrich Schliemann), who have found it difficult to reconcile the previously known area of Troy with the Homeric representation of a city that took a force of tens of thousands of Greeks ten years to conquer.

Korfmann's excavations (which have been subject to criticism by some scholars) indicate that Troy was a much more substantial city than had previously been evident. Its population at its peak in the Troy VI period is now estimated to have been somewhere between 4,000 and 10,000. The city was still not large by ancient Near Eastern standards, but if well fortified, as it clearly was, it could have resisted a large besieging force for a considerable period of time—but probably only for a matter of months, not years. Walled cities attacked by the contemporary Hittites might sometimes hold out for six months against their besiegers, and the investment of such cities could in some instances have strained the resources of the besiegers almost as much as those of the besieged.

There is some validity in Thucydides' claim that a much larger force than the one directly employed for the siege of Troy was necessary to ensure that the besiegers were adequately provisioned. However, the notion of a protracted siege lasting ten years is simply out of the question. A more realistic conclusion would be that a city like the Troy that Korfmann has now revealed may have been subject to a siege of up to six months (or not much more) by an attacking force of around ten thousand men. Some of the attackers may have arrived in ships, while others were very likely land-based forces, recruited in some cases from local regions and populations allied with or subject to the attackers.

Do Hittite sources provide any answers to the question of whether there really was a Trojan War? The proposed identification of the Late Bronze Age states Wilusa/

Wilusiya and Taruisa in Hittite texts with Homer's (W)ilios and Troia has led to much inconclusive debate among scholars since the Swiss philologist Emil Forrer first suggested the equivalence in the 1930s. However, recent studies on the political geography of western Anatolia have considerably strengthened the case for locating Wilus(iy)a and Taruisa in northwestern Anatolia, in the region later called the Troad (see Starke 1997; Hawkins 1998). These studies increase the likelihood that Wilus(iy)a/Taruisa was the historical prototype of Homer's (W)ilios/Troy. The significance of the equation is that if it is valid, Hittite texts do provide us with a few scraps of information about Troy's (i.e., Wilusa's) history during the Late Bronze Age (see Güterbock 1986; Bryce 2006, 107–12, 182–86). It was for a time a subject kingdom of the Hittite empire and perhaps for this reason became embroiled in disputes and uprisings, probably involving pro- and anti-Hittite internal factions, as well as external forces.

Directly or indirectly, Mycenaean Greeks may have become involved in these conflicts. Few scholars now doubt that the term 'Ahhiyawa' was used in Hittite texts to refer to the Mycenaeans, sometimes called Achaeans in the Homeric poems. A specific king of Ahhiyawa had established control over Milawata (Classical Miletus) on the southwestern Aegean coast of Anatolia by the end of the thirteenth century, and he may well have used Milawata as a base for the further expansion of his influence and power throughout the western Anatolian coastal regions. In the inappropriately named 'Tawagalawa letter,' one of the best known of the 'Ahhiyawa documents' in the Hittite archives, the Hittite king, probably Hattusili III (ca. 1267–1237 BC), hints at the prospect of war over Wilusa with his Ahhiyawan counterpart (see Güterbock 1986, 37) and complains of the latter's support of insurrectionist activity in the area.

Another well-known letter, the so-called Milawata letter, informs us that Wilusa's king Walmu had been removed from his throne and sought refuge with his Hittite overlord, on this occasion probably Hattusili's son and successor, Tudhaliya IV. The Hittite king, author of the letter, is making arrangements with the addressee, unnamed in the letter's fragmentary remains but probably the king of the large nearby state, Mira, for Walmu's restoration (see Bryce 2005, 306–308). To judge from the fragmentary Hittite records that refer to it, Wilusa may well have suffered periods of political and military turbulence, like all other states in the region. In addition, it is not at all unlikely that a territorially ambitious Ahhiyawan/Mycenaean kingdom, which had already established a base on the Anatolian mainland, turned predatory eyes on the northern Anatolian kingdom—acting in some instances with the support of local insurgents. However, it is a major step from there to assert that we have in the small number of relevant Hittite documents evidence for the historical reality of the Trojan War tradition.

Warfare that resulted in the capture and sacking of cities was a normal state of affairs in the history of the Late Bronze Age, and the likelihood is that there were many 'wars' involving the people of Wilusa and outside attackers, the latter very likely including Greeks. Of course, some such wars may have been little more than small-scale raids designed to plunder merchandise as it was arriving in or departing from the city. Still, this does not rule out the possibility of a substantial and pro-tracted conflict between northwestern Anatolians and Ahhiyawan/Mycenaean Greeks that provided the genesis of the Trojan War tradition, best known from Homer's version of it. Korfmann himself has argued such a case, and one of his staunchest supporters, J. Latacz (2004), has done so at greater length. However, the historical reality of a single, discrete conflict on a scale and of a duration consistent with the epic tale has yet to established. My own view is that the tale told by Homer and by generations of bards before him is based on an accumulation of stories of conflict that span perhaps several centuries and came to be distilled into a single episode supposedly lasting for ten years and involving a cast of many thousands. In *this* respect, there may well be a factual basis, or indeed many factual bases, for the story of the Trojan War.

Hittite documentary sources provide no close parallels for what in Greek tradi-tion was the fundamental cause of the Trojan War—the abduction of a Greek queen by a foreign prince. However, Hittite kings were certainly prepared to go to war with other rulers who abducted their subjects or provided refuge for them when they fled Hittite authority. On one occasion, too, the Hittite king declared war on Egypt when his son was allegedly murdered by Egyptian agents while on his way to Egypt to marry the pharaoh's widow (see Bryce 2005, 180–83). The abduction no less than the murder of a member of a royal family by representatives of a foreign kingdom might well have provided—in the real as in the legendary world—the catalyst for conflict between two kingdoms. There is no need to find a more prosaic explana-tion for the Trojan War, as some scholars have done, by proposing (for example) a squabble over fishing rights in the Hellespont (Dardanelles) or a contest for control over the waterways leading from the Aegean to the Black Sea.

Due largely to the Homeric version of Troy's conflict with Greece, the Trojan War became firmly embedded in legendary tradition and provided a major source of inspiration for many generations of writers and artists in the Classical and later worlds. It served other purposes as well. Herodotus claims that the Persians dated their hostility toward Greece to the time of Troy's fall and reports (7.43) that just before crossing the Hellespont for his invasion of the Greek mainland in 480, the Persian king Xerxes ascended Troy's citadel and was told the whole story of what had happened there; he then sacrificed a thousand oxen to the goddess Athena of Ilion and ordered his priests to offer libations to the heroes of the Trojan War.

Xerxes would have been fully aware of the political value of a visit to Troy at the beginning of his Greek campaign, and this was no doubt reflected in the symbolic acts he performed on the site. Quite possibly he *now* sought to represent himself as the avenger, finally, of Troy's destruction. Nevertheless, there is no suggestion in any of our sources that a desire to take vengeance on the Greeks for what they had done to Troy figured among the reasons for the Persian campaign against Greece, let alone provided a fundamental cause for it.

In 334, Alexander the Great visited Troy immediately after landing on Asian soil. Here he paid homage to the goddess Athena and to the heroes of the Trojan War. This was in effect a response to the similar acts Xerxes had performed on the same site 150 years earlier. The situation was now reversed. Alexander's visit to Troy marked the beginning of his campaign against the Persian empire, as Xerxes' visit had marked the beginning of his campaign against Greece. For both Alexander and Xerxes, the rites they performed on the site of the alleged Trojan War had important symbolic significance and made clear political statements.

The Trojan War tradition gained a new lease on life in the last decades of the first century BC, when Vergil composed an epic poem that used the sack of Troy as its starting point. Vergil's poem, the *Aeneid*, shifts the focus from the main characters of the *Iliad* to the minor Trojan prince Aeneas. The poem has to do with Aeneas's flight from the burning city, his subsequent travels, and his final settlement in Italy, where he founded the Roman nation. In fact, only one of the twelve books of the *Aeneid* is devoted to the Trojan War. This is Book II, which contains a number of well-known episodes of the war preserved in Greek tradition but not found in the *Iliad*. Notable among these are the stories of the Trojan Horse and the sack of Troy, as well as a description of the murder of Priam. However, there is no doubt that Homer's poem provided the basic inspiration for the Vergilian composition. Even so, the *Aeneid*'s main purpose was a political one. It was intended to justify the extraordinary status that Rome's 'first citizen,' Augustus, enjoyed by depicting the emperor as the lineal descendant of Aeneas and the founder of a new golden age, one whose coming had been foretold by destiny back in the time of Aeneas's arrival in his promised land.

We have referred to Xerxes' and Alexander's visits to Troy in 480 and 334, respectively, and the symbolic and political significance of these visits. Ten years after his conquest of Constantinople in 1453, the Ottoman sultan Mehmet II also came to Troy. There he declared that, in capturing the Byzantine Greek capital, he had defeated the descendants of those responsible for the destruction of Troy; they had at last paid the debt they owed to the people of Asia (Vermeule 1995, 447–48).

BIBLIOGRAPHY

Bryce, Trevor R. 2005. *The Kingdom of the Hittites.* New ed. Oxford: Oxford University Press.
———. 2006. *The Trojans and Their Neighbours.* London: Routledge.
Güterbock, Hans G. 1986. "Troy in Hittite Texts? Wilusa, Ahhiyawa, and Hittite History." In *Troy and the Trojan War: Proceedings of a Symposium Held at Bryn Mawr College, October 1984*, ed. Machteld J. Mellink, 33–44. Bryn Mawr, Penn.: Bryn Mawr College.
Hawkins, J. David. 1998. "Tarkasnawa, King of Mira: 'Tarkondemos,' Boğazköy Sealings and Karabel." *AnatSt* 48: 1–31.
Korfmann, Manfred O., ed. 2006. *Troia: Archäologie eines Siedlungshügels und seiner Landschaft.* Trans. Dirk Bennett, Jan Breder, and Petra Lilith Höhne. Mainz am Rhein: von Zabern.
———, et al. 2001. *Troia: Traum und Wirklichkeit.* Stuttgart: Theiss.

Latacz, Joachim. 2004. *Troy and Homer: Towards a Solution of an Old Mystery.* Oxford: Oxford University Press.

Mountjoy, Penelope. 1999. "The Destruction of Troy VIh." *Studia Troica* 9: 253–93.

Nougayrol, Jean, Emmanuel Laroche, Charles Virolleaud, and Claude Schaeffer. 1968. *Ugaritica V.* Paris: Klincksieck.

Starke, Frank. 2007. "Troia im Kontext des historischen-politischen und sprachlichen Umfeldes Kleinasiens in 2 Jahrtausend." *Studia Troica* 7: 447–87.

Vermeule, Cornelius C., III. 1995. "Neon Ilion and Ilium Novum: Kings, Soldiers, Citizens, and Tourists at Classical Troy." In *The Ages of Homer: A Tribute to Emily Townsend Vermeule,* ed. Jane B. Carter and Sarah P. Morris, 467–80. Austin: University of Texas.

CHAPTER 36

THE COLLAPSE AT THE END OF THE BRONZE AGE

OLIVER DICKINSON

THE history of the Aegean Bronze Age has often been presented in terms of long periods of development and apparent stability that are brought to an end by a disaster that afflicts one or more of the major subdivisions of the Aegean region. Such disasters are typically recognized in "destruction horizons," which show evidence for the destruction of major buildings, often by fire, at a series of important sites at roughly the same time, as defined by the presence of types of diagnostic finds, particularly pottery, in the destruction strata. In Crete, such disasters have generally, though not always, been attributed to earthquakes, but destruction horizons identified on the mainland have more commonly been attributed to hostile attack, most often by external "invaders."

This was an interpretation favored for many years in dealing with the last such horizon, which I hereafter refer to simply as the Collapse. This occurred around the end of the Late Helladic IIIB pottery phase, probably a bit after 1200 BC on the currently accepted absolute chronology (Shelmerdine 2001, 332–33). Originally the destructions were identified as the archaeological evidence for the population movements and resulting conquests that are reported in the Greek legends to have occurred after the Trojan War, the most famous of which is generally referred to as the "Dorian invasion," though this is a modern term. Some modern accounts have directly linked the legendary movements of other Greek groups to the east Aegean, referred to generically as the "Ionian migration," to this "Dorian invasion" by interpreting them as representing the flight of refugees before the Dorian advance. However, this is not what the legends say, for they place the "Ionian migration" a generation or more after the supposed Dorian conquests in the Peloponnese and attack on Athens.

General loss of faith in "invasion theories" as explanations of cultural change, doubts about the value of the Greek legends as sources for Bronze Age history, and closer dating of the sequence of archaeological phases have undermined the credibility of this reconstruction, and other explanations for the Collapse have been proposed. In part, these have reflected a heightened appreciation of what was involved in the Collapse. In the first flush of the enthusiasm aroused by the decipherment of the Linear B script as Greek, Wace, wishing to see continuity of development from Mycenaean Greeks to Classical Greeks, attempted to minimize the cultural changes involved in the transition from the period of the Mycenaean palaces to later times (1956, xxxiii–xxxiv). However, it has become abundantly clear from detailed analysis of the Linear B material and the steadily accumulating archaeological evidence that this view cannot be accepted in the form in which he proposed it. There was certainly continuity in many features of material culture, as in the Greek language itself, but the Aegean world of the period following the Collapse was very different from that of the period when Mycenaean civilization was at its height, here termed the Third Palace Period. Further, the differences represent not simply a change but also a significant deterioration in material culture, which was the prelude to the even more limited culture of the early stages of the Iron Age.

Mycenaean civilization of the Third Palace Period is discussed elsewhere (Nakassis, Galaty, and Parkinson, this volume). Here it is sufficient to recall that the general impressions given by the material suggest a relatively prosperous and stable world dominated by a few major centers, the capitals of the "palace societies"; the best known are Mycenae (with which Tiryns and Midea, impressive sites in their own right, were surely closely associated), Thebes, and Pylos. These are the sites, along with Khania in Crete, that have produced almost all of the evidence from the thirteenth century BC for a sophisticated system of administration. This system, comparable in many ways to those used in the Near Eastern states, relied on the use of the seal and the Linear B script (I here follow the view that the Linear B archives from Knossos are fourteenth century). To what extent the rulers of the most important centers were in diplomatic contact with their contemporaries in the Near East remains debatable. It seems virtually certain that the state Ahhiyawā, whose kings had diplomatic contacts with Hittite kings, was Mycenaean, and its center is very likely to have been Mycenae or Thebes, but there are no certain references to this state outside Hittite documents, and, while there is plausible evidence for some Aegean diplomatic contacts with Egypt in the fourteenth century, there is nothing later.

However, there is much evidence to show that the Aegean was closely tied into the international trade networks that encompassed much of the Mediterranean at this time, and the leading Aegean centers could well have acted as emporia for their less important neighbors by distributing the commodities acquired by trade, particularly raw materials like metals. Thus, their activities could have been fundamental to the general standard of living in the Aegean as a whole, even outside their own territories.

To judge from the evidence of Pylos, the palace centers also supplied and supported teams of craftworkers who produced specialized commodities such as perfumed olive oil and decorated textiles, which were probably used in foreign, as well as Aegean, trade. These and other sites, that seem just as large as the leading centers but have not yet produced clear evidence of the administrative use of Linear B, were also able to invest considerable resources in major building projects, especially fortifications. However, by no means all of the really large sites were fortified, and the spread of a multitude of apparently undefended settlements, ranging from substantial to small, over the countryside in many parts of Mycenaean Greece suggests general stability. It also suggests that the land was farmed on a scale not seen again until Classical times, but it remains unclear whether this led to overexploitation, and the data hardly support any theory of overpopulation. Nevertheless, the level of "civilization" attained should not be overemphasized. Even the biggest centers are dwarfed by the great capitals of the Near Eastern civilizations, and no Aegean centers conformed to the Near Eastern pattern of the walled city.

The impression of stability given by the archaeological remains of phases that lasted at least several decades may be deceptive. Arguments have been advanced for supposing that in the final stages of the Third Palace Period difficulties were beginning to beset the palace societies (Dickinson 2006, 41–46; Shelmerdine 2001, 372–73). There are hints that their economic position was deteriorating, as well as rather more tangible indications from the construction or extension of fortifications that precautions were being taken to guard against attack. This development seems to follow a group of destructions that affect important buildings at Mycenae, Tiryns, Zygouries, Thebes, and the massive fortified site at Gla, but these were not all contemporary and cannot be assumed to have had the same cause, let alone one related to warfare (that at Mycenae seems more likely to reflect earthquake damage).

There is also a famous set of Linear B tablets from Pylos recording what are apparently military detachments stationed at various points along the coasts of the Pylos state. However, as Shelmerdine has pointed out (2001, 375), the arguments that these form part of the evidence for an immediate crisis at Pylos are not cogent, and it would be dangerous to assume that this was an extraordinary, rather than normal, arrangement.

The most telling evidence of troubled times is provided by the abandonment of Gla and the building/extending of fortifications at other sites, but, since constructing these massive walls would have taken a considerable time, such projects can hardly be interpreted as evidence of reaction to an immediately perceived threat. (In this connection, no reliance should be placed on the "Isthmus wall" as evidence that a specific threat was perceived from north of the Peloponnese. The nature and even the date of this structure remain in doubt.) Also, several major centers apparently remained unfortified even at this stage, of which two (Orchomenos in Boeotia and Dhimini [= Iolkos?] in Thessaly) would seem particularly vulnerable to any threat that might originate in central or northwestern Greece. If some of the mid–LH IIIB destructions are to be interpreted as evidence of warfare, as seems possible, this could have occurred between Mycenaean states and, like the new fortifications, could bear witness to the development of dangerous tensions in a period of economic decline. However, the new defenses also indicate a capacity to marshal major resources at some leading centers even in the final stages of the Third Palace Period, and overall the Collapse still comes as something of a surprise.

It is far easier to summarize the main features of the Collapse and its most obvious effects than to explain it. A whole series of leading centers, widely spread on the mainland—Mycenae, Tiryns, Midea, the Menelaion site, Pylos, Thebes, Krisa, Dhimini (the Megara A and B complex), and probably Teikhos Dymaion (Achaea)—has produced evidence of severe destruction, frequently including fire. Such evidence has also been identified at some less important sites, and the process of abandoning settlements, both small and substantial, which has been deduced from the results of excavation and survey in many parts of the Greek mainland, began now if not before. Although it is hard to establish a precise chronology for this abandonment, it is noteworthy that a great many of the deserted sites, even the most substantial, show no evidence of reoccupation for many centuries, if ever. A major and surely highly significant shift in the distribution of population was clearly taking place, and the total population seems to have diminished very markedly in some regions (e.g. Messenia). Unfortunately, it cannot be stated with any certainty when this process ended, but it was probably completed by the end of the Postpalatial Period.

The sequel to the destructions at the major excavated sites varied: Some seem to have been totally abandoned (e.g. Krisa), while at others there was continued occupation and rebuilding. But at no site were new buildings erected over the old on a comparable scale, as typically happened in Crete earlier in the Bronze Age. The new rulers of these centers were evidently no longer able to command resources and labor for the large-scale architectural projects that were typical previously. This as much as anything symbolizes the complete disappearance of the palace societies, which is apparent also in the absence of evidence for the use of Linear B and seals in strata following the Collapse. Similarly, the high-quality arts of the Third Palace Period such as fresco painting, ivory working, and the production of precious vessels and inlaid items of furniture barely survived, if at all; the need for them disappeared with the ruling elite whose position they were used to enhance. Although there undoubtedly were rulers in the Postpalatial Period, their distinction from their subjects was not so conspicuously marked.

However, there is no need to present the effects of the Collapse in the apocalyptic terms sometimes used. Many major sites continued to be occupied, and some even seem to have grown in size (e.g. Tiryns, Lefkandi). There is evidence for exchange both within the Aegean and beyond it to east and west, in the course of which various innovations were spread, including the first functional iron items, and some notable indications of prosperity can be identified, especially in the middle stages of the Postpalatial Period (Dickinson 2006, 67–69, 73–74). Still, these features cannot be identified in every part of the Aegean, and the recovery that they represent was not sustained. The Collapse did not cause a total and immediate catastrophe, but it fatally undermined the stability of Aegean society. Indeed, the evidence from the Postpalatial Period suggests chronic instability. A significant section of the population

seems to move about restlessly, gathering at major sites and then after a few generations abandoning them again, and sites that had survived the Collapse and apparently prospered for a considerable while were eventually abandoned (e.g., Korakou)
or dwindled to shadows of their former selves (e.g., Tiryns).

There were wide variations in experience. In some of the provinces and islands
(e.g., Laconia, Achaea, Rhodes), it is impossible to identify a single site that was
certainly occupied in the earliest stages of the Iron Age, although this must partly
reflect the chances of discovery and the much greater difficulty in identifying pottery types diagnostic for this period. However, there is a multitude of sites in Crete,
and their material includes signs of prosperity and overseas contacts that are hard to
parallel elsewhere in the Aegean. Even on and near the mainland, sites like Lefkandi,
Mitrou, and the Elateia-Alonaki cemetery provide evidence that the picture was
less gloomy than that traditionally presented. Nevertheless, centuries were to pass
before levels of stability and prosperity comparable with those of the Third Palace
Period were achieved again throughout the Aegean.

If, then, the Collapse had such a marked effect on social development in the
Aegean, what caused it? The explanations advanced fall into three classes: some
form of warfare, whether invasion or raids from outside the Mycenaean world or
internecine or civil war, which could include revolts by overburdened subjects;
natural disasters of some kind, such as earthquake, drought-induced famine, or
disease; and "systems collapse," an internally generated failure of the palace societies
to function, which might represent the culmination of inherent weaknesses in their
management or an inability to withstand unexpected shocks.

Such explanations, which tend to focus on a single cause for the Collapse, characteristically fail to take account of all facets of the evidence, including the potential
signs of trouble and decline earlier, and they frequently involve the use of questionable premises. Among the reasons for caution in advancing explanations, most
important is that the time period over which the Collapse took place cannot be
closely measured. There are no outstanding diagnostic types that could suggest that
the destructions took place within a very few years of each other (as in the destruction horizon that ended the Second Palace Period in Crete). Although some, as in
the Argolid, are agreed to fall very closely together, there is no reason why the whole
group should not have been spread over twenty or thirty years, and, as already noted,
the process of abandonment of sites may have taken much longer. Such points are
bound to undermine all theories that rely on the idea of a single intolerable shock,
whether natural or human-delivered.

Also, theories that start from a view that the palace societies were overcentralized, even rigid and oppressive, and dependent upon a narrow economic base are
quite open to question. In particular, doubt can be cast on any theory that argues
that the palaces encouraged specialization in just one or two crops throughout the
territories they controlled, or fostered local specialization that required exchange of
commodities through the palace to secure all of the foodstuffs required. Neither of
these quite popular ideas can actually be sustained on the evidence of the Linear B
tablets or archaeology. Rather, it seems likely that the intensive production of a few

commodities was a feature of the palaces' own estates and that the average settlement had a broadly based agricultural economy (Shelmerdine 2001, 359–60; Galaty and Parkinson 2007, 4–5; Halstead 2007). It follows that the removal of the palaces would probably have meant that the communities they controlled found it harder to get supplies of essential metals and of good-quality manufactured goods, but it should not have affected their ability to farm and otherwise exploit the land, and they would no longer have to pay whatever taxes were previously demanded.

Further, it seems highly unlikely that the palace administrations—and the ruling elites in less complex societies—would not have taken the possibility of bad years into account in their planning, in a region where such years are a recurrent feature. So they would have tried to maintain substantial stores to use in an emergency, and would not have been so vulnerable to some short-term natural disaster (such as a drought resulting from a freak weather pattern in one year) that they could not recover. Palynological and dendrochronological evidence does not support the theory of a long-term (but ultimately reversed) shift in weather patterns put forward by Rhys Carpenter (1966), which, like the theory of a freak alteration in one or two years, is not supported by the settlement pattern following the Collapse (Shrimpton 1987; Drews 1993, ch. 6, especially 79–80).

Earthquakes, another recurring hazard in the Aegean, have greater capacity to deliver a really damaging blow because they may destroy stores and administrative records as well as buildings. But the history of the great centers in Crete shows an ability to recover from severe earthquakes, and while there seems to be growing agreement that the Argive centers were quite probably destroyed by earthquake, perhaps simultaneously, it is hard to accept that earthquake should also have badly damaged so many other places, more widely separated than in Crete, in the same period.

This is a reminder that the experience of any one site or region, however important, cannot be taken as typical, a point of particular relevance when the quite exceptional level of site abandonment in Messenia is considered. Here it is tempting to suggest a special explanation, such as the outbreak of serious disease, although the fourteenth century "plague" in the Hittite empire is not reported to show such a marked effect archaeologically. It is perfectly possible that disease was one of the problems affecting Aegean society, but it is not easy to see why the destruction of major centers should be one of its effects; it is no more likely to have caused complete social breakdown than historically recorded plagues did.

Explanations that see warfare as the main cause also have considerable drawbacks. It is hard to believe that any form of warfare should be so destructive, especially if this was no more than raids, however damaging temporarily, while theories that the ruling elites were overthrown by rebelling subjects must raise certain questions: "Where are the victorious subjects? Why is this followed by such evident decline and movements of population?" Theories that a successful invasion was the cause also have to explain, first, why the putative invaders wrecked the centers of power rather than simply taking them over, as is more normally the case with conquerors (e.g., the Hyksos in Egypt), and second, why there is no material trace of such invaders. For the material culture of the Postpalatial Period essentially continues earlier traditions, without major change in any important feature. The much-discussed handmade burnished ware is found at certain centers before the Collapse and occurs far too sporadically to represent a whole new population; rather, it seems to reflect trade links with Italy.

Drews has argued (1993) that the Collapse in the Aegean and serious disruption in the Near East were the result of the introduction of new weapons and tactics, that allowed hordes of "barbarian" infantry to defeat armies centered upon chariotry and to sack most of the centers of wealth in the Aegean and Near East over a period of decades. This raises a host of questions (Dickinson 1999; 2006, 47–50), not least whether traditionally organized Bronze Age armies were so dependent upon chariotry, especially in the Aegean; whether the "barbarians" can be shown to have adopted the new weapons first; and whether the "Sea Peoples," who figure so largely in the theory, were as extraordinarily effective a fighting force as represented in this and other modern reconstructions. Drews's attribution of the destructions in the Aegean partly to warlike "north Greeks," who then take over territories, again provokes the questions posed earlier.

All of these difficulties and objections, taken together with the growing evidence for variations of experience in different parts of the Aegean, point to the conclusion that it is a waste of effort to try to isolate a single cause or prime mover for the Collapse. It seems very likely that the course of events was too complicated to be reconstructed without the help of written documents. Nevertheless, it does seem possible that the system that depended to a great extent on the palace societies was coming under increasing strain in the later thirteenth century BC, one element of which was the tensions developing between some of the major Mycenaean states. One or more localized incidents, which could be of very varied types—interstate wars, civil wars, earthquakes, crop failures—could have set a process in motion that grew beyond the ability of any power to control it. The more difficult conditions became, the more the palace-based elites would lose the trust of their followers and subjects (earthquakes and other natural disasters might especially be taken as evidence of the gods' anger with the ruling elite; cf. the Hittite "plague"). Conditions may have been truly chaotic for a short while. The more or less concurrent sequence of damaging events in the Near East, especially the collapse of the Hittite empire, ensured that, when some degree of order was restored in the Aegean, the old systems could not be resurrected, for the conditions in which they had flourished were gone forever.

BIBLIOGRAPHY

Carpenter, Rhys. 1966. *Discontinuity in Greek Civilization*. Cambridge: Cambridge University Press.

Dickinson, Oliver. 1999. "Robert Drews's Theories about the Nature of Warfare in the Late Bronze Age." In *Polemos*, 21–27.

———. 2006. *The Aegean from Bronze Age to Iron Age*. New York: Routledge.

Drews, Robert. 1993. *The End of the Bronze Age*. Princeton: Princeton University Press.

Galaty, Michael L., and William A. Parkinson, eds. 2007. *RMP II*.

Halstead, Paul. 2007. "Towards a Model of Palatial Mobilization." In *RMP II*, 66–72.

Shelmerdine, Cynthia W. 2001. "The Palatial Bronze Age of the Southern and Central Greek Mainland." In *Aegean Prehistory*, 329–81.

Shrimpton, Gordon. 1987. "Regional Drought and the Economic Decline of Mycenae." *Echos du monde classique/Classical Views* 6: 137–77.

Wace, Alan J. B. 1956. "Foreword." In Ventris, Michael and John Chadwick, *Documents in Mycenaean Greek*. Cambridge: Cambridge University Press.

PART IV

SPECIFIC SITES AND REGIONS

Crete

CHAPTER 37

....

AYIA TRIADA

....

VINCENZO LA ROSA

AYIA Triada was first explored in May 1902 by F. Halbherr and was originally thought to be a necropolis of Phaistos (figure 37.1). Exploration of the site continued, with a few interruptions, until 1914. Halbherr bore in mind the crucial issue of the relationship between the two sites from the start and hypothesized a single political entity divided between an "Ano polis" (Phaistos) and a "Kato polis" (Ayia Triada), with a hierarchy between the two sites.

After three years of consolidating campaigns carried out by L. Pernier from 1934 to 1936, L. Banti, who had been entrusted with the publication of the excavations that Halbherr had left unpublished (Halbherr, Stefani, and Banti 1977), opened a few test pits in the area of the *sacello* in 1939 and 1950. Episodic or occasional excavations took place in the 1970s by C. Laviosa and D. Levi, and a new systematic cycle of excavations was begun by the Italian archaeological school at Athens in 1977, which aimed to clarify a series of chronological, architectural, and planimetrical problems left unsolved by the old excavations (La Rosa 2003). The new excavations have led to explanations of the parallel histories of Ayia Triada and Phaistos in terms of a 'complementarity of roles' (La Rosa 2003).

The settlement of Ayia Triada was located on the western slope of a low hill, the top of which, now leveled for the construction of a parking area, reached a height of 60 m above sea level. The natural terrace where the church of St. George Galatian was built is 41.70 m above sea level; the small hill to the west, above which the *casale veneziano* was built, was slightly higher (43.70 m). The site, very close to the Ieropotamos River, was easily reached from Phaistos and, therefore, from the western Mesara (via the river) and also from the port of Kommos (perhaps via a coastal road). The junction of these two communication routes made it easy to travel toward the northwestern part of the island in the direction of the Amari valley. A north-south axis that led to the plain passed through the settlement from at least the Neopalatial period; another east-west axis led to the sea.

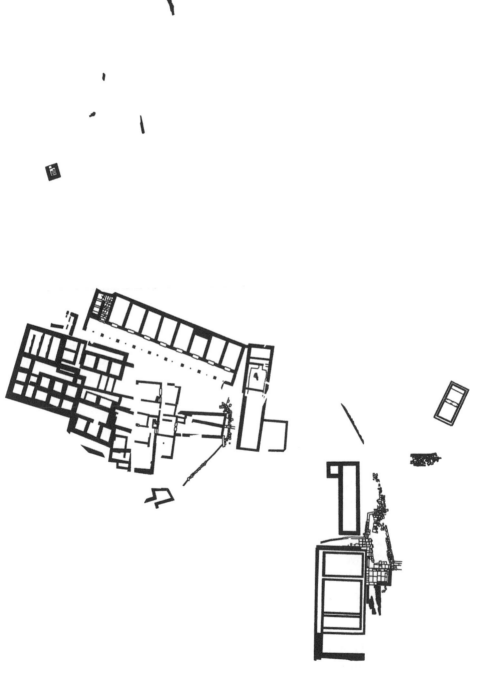

Figure 37.1. General plan of the Ayia Triada archaeological site in the LM IIIA2 period (drawing by E. Stefani, with additions by B. Salmeri; elaboration by M. Tanasi).

The name of the site in prehistoric or historical times is unknown, and the suggestion that it be identified with *da-wo*, mentioned in the Linear B tablets of Knossos in relation to large amounts of grain, is only hypothetical. It is possible that the entire area was indicated with the single name *pa-i-to* in that period, which was more properly related to Phaistos. The modern name Ayia Triada (i.e., Holy Trinity) belonged to the Venetian hamlet and is derived from the small two-aisled church that is still preserved to the southwest of the archaeological area.

The size of the settlement appears to have been relatively limited throughout its various periods (at least from the time in which there was a single inhabited area, the extension of which has been estimated at about 10,000 m²), when potential sacred areas or peripheral sanctuaries are discounted.

No traces of Neolithic occupation or frequentation have so far been located, but a large EM I votive deposit has been identified (and only partially excavated) beneath the Venetian cemetery immediately to the south of *Piazzale dei Sacelli* (Todaro 2003a, 2003b). A recent interpretation of the assemblage has connected it with a foundation rite that involved the communal consumption of food and drink (meat and wine), as well as the ritual burial of all of the ceramics that had been used (generally of high quality), together with animal bones and other food remains. The presence of clay house models is particularly meaningful, as it underlines the foundation project (Todaro 2003a).

The in situ discard and burial of the debris of that ceremony led to the creation of a low tumulus, delineated by a curvilinear wall that is still partly visible today. It remained deprived of architectural construction, as though the memory of that ancestral rite was still vividly remembered by the various inhabitants of the site (Todaro 2003a). The settlement history of Phaistos and the analogy of pottery and ritual have also led to the hypothesis that the 'founder group' had moved from Phaistos, perhaps as a result of episodes of internal competition (Todaro forthcoming).

Another group of EM I vases (also of ritual but not necessarily funerary nature) has been found to the southwest of Tholos A and has been related to a communal liturgy. A small ceramic deposit attributable to an early stage of EM IIA was identified immediately above bedrock, behind the rear wall of the so-called Tomba degli ori.

A habitation quarter attributable to a final stage of EM IIA has been partly excavated to the northeast of the archaeological area, by the edge of the road that descends toward the river (Todaro 2003b). The presence of pithoi that were found smashed onto the floors suggests that the quarter was abandoned as the result of an earthquake.

The materials retrieved from the abandonment level seem to predate the construction of Tholos A, which dates to the beginning of EM IIB (Stefani and Banti 1930–1931). The considerable dimensions of the structure (internal diam. 8.70 m) suggest a rather large settlement (which has not yet been identified); the relatively small number of depositions attributable to the structure's earliest stage of use is surprising, as is the temporary abandonment of the tomb. Copper daggers, seals, and other prestige items suggest, however, the presence of emerging groups (Cultraro 2003).

The graves of the upper burial level (arranged above the abandonment level) date to the end of the EM III–beginning of the MM IA period. The so-called *annessi* (small rooms that originally housed the paraphernalia used during the funerary liturgies) were built at the same time on the east side of the tholos and were later used as ossuaries, thus allowing new depositions to be made within the tomb.

The identification of a wall with two baetyls within the necropolis area in the MM IA period (La Rosa 2001) and of an assemblage of more than two hundred vessels clearly represent liturgies connected to the world of the dead in which a ritual set that comprised a jug, a shallow bowl, and four handleless cups was used (Carinci 2004). The ritual, probably open to a large group (including children), involved the consumption of solid food (such as honey, fruit, and unleavened bread) and drinks (such as milk, beer, wine, or various infusions) in an apparently egalitarian context, with canonical and standardized vases. These vases were kept (either as offerings or for reuse) in the ten rooms identified to the south of Tholos A. In such a context, it seems inevitable to suppose that the religious sphere was under the control of an elite.

At the beginning of MM IB, workers and elites could have been involved in the construction of the nearby palace at Phaistos. In any case, the ceremonial activity near Tholos A at Ayia Triada continued, although the rite seems to have become limited to libations and perhaps to a more restricted number of participants (also due to the interruption of burials with Tholos A).

In addition, MM IB dwellings have been identified in the area of the "Mycenaean" shrine; at the same time Tholos B was built immediately to the south of Tholos A and was used until MM II, with a reuse in LM II–IIIA1 (Carinci 2003). An interconnected paved road and a paved area of about 40 m², which was reused in later periods, was found within the *Complesso della Mazza della Breccia* and has recently been correlated with processions and ceremonies performed in the necropolis.

Here, a very small *hieròn* was in use, which had incorporated the baetyls located to the southeast of Tholos A and had a stone offering table embedded in the center of its paved floor (La Rosa 2001). It is, in other words, possible to hypothesize that these communal ceremonies, although performed within a funerary context, were similar to those that took place in the west court of the palace at Phaistos.

The last deposition within Tholos A was made in MM II and belonged to the elites (Stefani and Banti 1930–1931). Dwellings (in the same area of the shrine), a stucco floor in the area of the villa, and rich pottery assemblages (in various areas of the settlement), together with a thick dump/landslide in the area of the *Complesso della Mazza di Breccia* (probably belonging to structures located along the upper slope), are the new reference points for the MM II period (Carinci 2003).

The site, apparently deprived of monumental buildings and administrative documents, was certainly subjected to Phaistos in this period but had nevertheless reached a high level of social complexity (at least judging from its pottery) and a notable extension, which has recently been hypothesized to be 26–30 ha., as compared to the 60 ha. of contemporary Phaistos (Watrous, Hadzi-Vallianou, and Blitzer 2004). The MM IIB seismic destruction, so evident in the palace at Phaistos, is mainly attested in Ayia Triada by the large dumps and the terracing containing pottery of that period.

The extent of the settlement in MM III is less certain, although a tract of paved road has been identified near the paved road of the previous period, immediately to the east of the *Complesso della Mazza di Breccia* (La Rosa 1992–1993). Deposits that belong to the first part of the period (MM IIIA) are scarce, perhaps due to a partial and temporary depopulation of the site. Habitation remains have been recorded to the south of the shrine; a small pottery deposit has been found in the area of the *Bastione*, and another one beneath the *Complesso della Mazza di Breccia*. A large dump of materials retrieved from trench M/4 (near the same '*Complesso*') dates to the MM IIIB period (Girella 2003, 2007, forthcoming).

The so-called Royal Villa, a structure of palatial type that planimetrically corresponds to half a palace, represents the most notable building of the Neopalatial period and contains a rich and intact destruction level. It is a building with an L-shaped plan and an upper story that was divided into four quarters, with significant spaces reserved for storage and residential and sacred areas. The Villa, although seen by some scholars as the result of the unification of two contiguous complexes (Watrous 1984), can be considered (after some stratigraphic tests conducted along the northern limit) to be a single building, although some reconstruction and reuse are clear, especially in the eastern residential quarter (La Rosa 1997b).

The identification of the foundation deposit (beneath the white stucco floor of *corridoio* 74), which consists of a group of vases purposely situated within a pit with ash and burnt remains (La Rosa appendix in Halbherr, Stefani, and Banti 1977), together with materials from MM IIIA, has recently been questioned and referred to previous structures (Girella forthcoming). It is possible that the foundation of the Villa at Ayia Triada (at the expense of Phaistos) was a political action favored by the Knossian elite at a time in which the Phaistian palace was not in use (between MM IIIB and LM IA).

The new building became the reference point for the administration of the surrounding area. The most consistent archive in Linear A tablets ever found in the Aegean was in fact retrieved from the Villa (and from a house in the village). It consists of 147 tablets, about a thousand cretulae with one or two sealings, more than twenty roundels, and a few inscriptions on vases or other objects (with sealings in some cases identical to those found in other centers of the island: evidence of the existence of a centralized administrative system rather than of simple exchange activity).

The Linear A records focus mainly on agricultural products and personnel and to a much lesser extent on animals or textiles, only a few units of which are mentioned; two tablets that record vases doubtless need to be considered as exceptions. The exact nature of the registrations is uncertain; they might refer to inputs and outputs from the storerooms, to the distribution of goods in exchange for work, to transactions, and perhaps also to taxes.

Groups of people, probably workers, are also recorded: some are almost certainly bronze smiths and are sometimes associated with agricultural products that can be interpreted as food portions (perhaps monthly), which consist of wheat, figs, and wine (Schoep 2002). It is difficult to estimate the extent of some of these records: the groups of men rarely exceed 100 units and only in one case reached 355 (?) individuals. The total has recently been proposed to be 2,788 persons (Schoep 2002).

The value of the agricultural products varies considerably from one tablet to another. In the case of wheat, for example, the value ranges from 3 units to a maximum of 1,060 units (in tablet HT 102), which, applying the same values as in Linear B, should correspond to 101,760 liters. Since a large pithos could contain about 565 liters of wheat, the 1,060 units mentioned would have required 180 pithoi. The 50 pithoi from the Villa alone would give a potential capacity of about 28,000 liters. In the case of the oil in tablet HT 2, an individual or a place (Kiretana) contributes 101 units, equal to 2,828 liters, which can be contained in 4–5 pithoi.

A sum of the units of the various products recorded in the tablets provides a figure for the volume of the Villa's business, which, judging from the overall results, must not have been very high: wheat, oil, and wine mentioned in the tablets could have been produced by a territory of about 15 km². For the wheat alone, an extension of 8.5 km² has been estimated (Palaima 1994). An inscription incised on a pithos (su-ki-ri-ta) probably refers to the toponym of a relatively distant site (identified with the Greek Sybrita, perhaps near the modern village of Thronos in the Amari province) and probably alludes to a type of product rather than to the Villa's range of economic interests and activities.

A certain number of weapons, concentrated especially in the southwestern quarter of the building (sixteen in total, with daggers and the heads of spears and javelins retrieved from the destruction level), attests to the existence of individuals entrusted with the defense of goods stored in the Villa (La Rosa and Militello 1999). The elite group in power in this period has been estimated, on the basis of the sealings and the hands of the scribes, at fewer than twenty individuals.

A recent reading of the architecture and of the finds tends, however, to stress the Villa's cultic aspect rather than its political-economic one (Puglisi 2003a). A cycle of frescos decorated the small *hieron* of the building (Militello 1998). The monumental and contiguous *Casa Est*, similarly two-storied and with elite architectural details, was probably linked to the Villa (in a cultic-ceremonial hub?).

A huge indented wall (clearly not conceived as a defensive structure) cut the village in half in an east-west direction and probably delimited a sector that was linked to the Villa (in the second Neopalatial phase). As mentioned earlier, a good number of Linear A tablets was also retrieved from the *Casa del Lebete* (immediately to the south of the indented wall), some of which were inscribed by the same scribes who had worked for the villa. Rather than thinking of a decentralized administration, one could conceive of a parallel involvement in records linked to the sacred sphere (directly linked to the important owner of the house).

A monumental structure (traditionally known as the *bastione* but which certainly functioned as a storage area: Puglisi 2003b) marked the boundary between the area of the Villa and that of the village, a junction that was probably demarcated by a *propylon* (La Rosa 2006).

A series of indicators allows us to distinguish two principal phases within the LM I settlement, each with subphases (certain in LM IA and probable in LM IB); a fifth phase should perhaps be identified between LM IB and LM II (Puglisi 2006, forthcoming). The available evidence for Ayia Triada in the Neopalatial period therefore allows a closer chronological definition than the one provided by Phaistos, starting from the articulation on the settlement's terraces (Puglisi 2007). However, not a single trace of tephra or pumice from Thera has yet been identified at Ayia Triada or Phaistos, in contrast to the situation recorded in a few northern Cretan sites.

A seismic event (accompanied by a violent fire) ended the life of the Villa (Monaco and Tortorici 2003), destroying the entire settlement toward the end of LM IB. The lack of bodies in the destruction levels seems to indicate a series of earthquakes, only the last of which occurred at a time in which many lamps and braziers were in use.

Recent excavations have brought to light a new building in the area of the necropolis, within which it has been possible to distinguish three architectural phases, all attributable to LM IB (figure 37.2). Labeled *Complesso della Mazza di Breccia* (after the retrieval of a stone mace head probably used in bull sacrifice or as a sacerdotal attribute), it housed sacred paraphernalia (such as a group of mobile clay altars) and was connected via a paved area with the *Tomba degli Ori* building excavated in 1903, which was also possibly involved in special liturgies (La Rosa 1992–1993).

An old interpretation of this building as a House Tomb or Temple Tomb has recently been reproposed, which is of course not incompatible with a simultaneous sacred function (Puglisi 2003b). Future explorations will allow the hypothesis of an exclusive connection of this new architectural hub with the nearby necropolis (where no contemporary burials have so far been identified) to be further examined.

A well-preserved pottery kiln has been identified in close proximity to the elite *Casa Est* (Levi and Laviosa 1979–1980; Tomasello 1996; Belfiore et al. 2007). It is therefore plausible that the artisan quarter was established immediately after the destruction of that house: the kiln was apparently used for only a brief period of time because the potsherds retrieved from within it date to the end of LM IB (Puglisi 2003b).

The altar platform that was built against the ruined *Complesso della Mazza di Breccia* has been dated to LM II (it was previously dated to LM IB or LM IIIA1), together with a few homogenous ceramic assemblages from the area of the *Edificio Ovest*.

The scant remains from this period, if not due to archaeological bias, document not only a notable topographic and demographic contraction of the settlement (perhaps for a couple of decades) but also a close stylistic continuity in ceramic productions (D'Agata 1999a). There is no convincing evidence to directly link this situation with a Mycenaean conquest of the island.

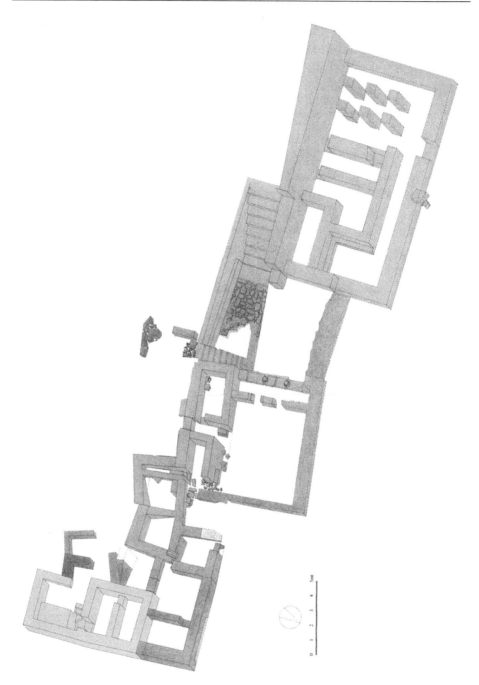

Figure 37.2. Axonometric reconstruction of the Complesso della Mazza di Breccia and the so-called Tomba degli Ori in the LM IB final period (elaboration by R. Vitale).

In LM III, Ayia Triada apparently maintained its role as a center of power over the surrounding territory at the expense of Phaistos. In its period of maximum splendor, the site shows two distinct nuclei with specific functions, exemplified by monumental buildings that are so far unparalleled on the rest of the island. The buildings of the political and religious sphere are constructed on the terrace where the small church of St. George was later constructed, while the storage structures and structures of a general economic purpose are instead built to the north, on the lower plateau (La Rosa 1997a; Cucuzza 2003). This reflects a precise functional model that, through the Mycenaean experiences of mainland Greece (to which Ayia Triada can be only superficially compared), finally developed into the constituent model of the Greek polis, with the two nuclei of acropolis and agora.

It is not possible to precisely establish when the process of monumentalization started at Ayia Triada, in which influences of a clear Mycenaean type are mixed with elements of continuity of Minoan tradition. It seems highly probable, however, that the first public building was the megaron, which was, significantly, built above the Royal Villa and inherited its function (Cucuzza 2003). The builders of the new structure founded their wall very deep—in the destruction level of the Villa—but respected the floor assemblage and even left in situ the 600 kg of copper stored in the basement of the destroyed building. This eloquent detail seems to confirm the lack of war and looting episodes and to favor the institutional and religious continuity of the local elites during the transition from LM I to LM III.

The stoa to the east of the megaron and the shrine was seemingly built immediately afterward, but it is uncertain whether this architectural distinction between political and religious buildings corresponded to an effective managerial division of the two spheres. The fact that the three buildings were organized around an area that was probably used during ceremonial activities, as in previous periods, reveals a stronger influence from Minoan palatial architecture (use of ashlar masonry, *polythyra*, mason's marks) (Cucuzza 2003).

In addition, LM IIIA1 ceramic assemblages and structures (especially in the area of the agora), testify to the richness of the settlement with an autonomous architectural phase.

The rich houses at Chalara and Phaistos, as well as the royal tombs at Kalivia, perhaps show that the LM IIIA1 period, although definitely reflecting a strong resurgence in comparison to the LM II period, was a delicate transitional period for the surrounding area; in the end (at the very beginning of the 14th century BC), the territorial equilibrium appears to have been rebalanced in favor of Ayia Triada.

In LM IIIA2, a double and generalized urban phase is marked by an intentional destruction that was presumably contemporary with an event of strong symbolic and political meaning: the *damnatio memoriae* (the condemnation or deletion of the memory) of the chieftain to whom the famous painted larnax belonged (La Rosa 1999). This tomb is dated by the fact that the gold items and the scarab of Tiyi, wife of the pharaoh Amenhotep III, probably formed part of its grave goods (at the beginning of his thirty-nine years of reign, at some point between 1417 and 1390; the pharaoh ascended to the throne at the age of twelve and seemingly married two years later). The gold items and the scarab were apparently thrown into a nearby building after the tomb was looted (the so-called *Tomba degli Ori*), which was already in ruins (La Rosa 2000).

A series of figurative scenes, together with the painted larnax, demonstrate the quality of the workshops active in LM IIIA2 (Militello 1998). The same is true for ceramic production (D'Agata 1999a).

A further proof of the new political and urban life of the LM IIIA2 site was identified in the so-called pit of the frescoes, an apparent dump of frescoes with figurative scenes retrieved within a room of the village during the old excavations. It had been hypothesized that these frescoes had been purposely detached from the walls and hidden at the time of the urban reorganization (La Rosa 1997; Militello 1998). However, a recent reexamination of the excavation notebooks has instead suggested that the frescoes (which belong to a mature phase of LM IIIA2) decorated the walls of the room in which they were found (room D of the *Casa dei Vani aggiunti progressivamente*): The building, of ceremonial function, was apparently abandoned in a nontraumatic way, so that the frescoes detached progressively from the walls (Privitera 2008).

In the second urban phase, the commercial quarter underwent a series of transformations as part of a single project of reorganization, the major outcome of which is represented by the large public storerooms on the east side (with an interesting portico in the front, which has been compared to the Hellenistic stoai) and by building P on the north side.

On the basis of a Linear B tablet from the archive at Pylos, as well as some information concerning the organization of building sites in Egypt in the 12th century BC, it has recently been surmised that a group of workmen consisting of twenty builders, five stonemasons, a master mason, and two foremen would have to work between 78 and 128 days in order to cut the 600 m3 of hill and preexisting ruins for the construction of the public storerooms (Cucuzza 2003). It has also been suggested, on the basis of the bodies preserved in the necropolis, that the LM IIIA elite was composed of a very restricted group of 5–12 individuals (i.e., one or two families). It might have been the family of the collector *we-we-si-jo*, mentioned more than once in relationship to *pa-i-to* in the Linear B tablets from Knossos and perhaps represented in the painted larnax (Cucuzza 2002, 2003). The overall population of the Mesara in the Mycenaean period has been estimated at around 18,500 inhabitants on the basis of the tablets (Cucuzza 2003).

The level of the *Piazzale* (600 m²) was raised for the second time during this radical reorganization and made with a layer of lime and pebbles and not, as before, with a layer of reddish clay. The so-called *Bastione* (the western half of which was perhaps turned into a panoramic terrace) closed the *Piazzale* along the southern side (Puglisi 2003a).

An important moment in the life of the LM IIIB center is represented by the closing of the *Piazzale* of the so-called agora on the northern side, and by the creation of a new access point on the southern side, through a staircase leading to the panoramic terrace of the so-called *Bastione*. At the same time, a few habitation structures invaded the area of the *Piazzale* on the western side, suggesting that the political-religious structures that controlled that public space had perhaps become weaker (La Rosa 1997a; Cucuzza 2003). A frequentation phase is documented within the Casa *VAP Vani Aggiunti Progressivamente*, i.e., rooms progressively added), the destruction level of which has recently been shown to have contained two large, globular painted pithoi that were found during the old excavations and are now stored at the Iraklion museum (Privitera 2001).

The situation at Ayia Triada seems to strengthen the high chronology for the destruction of the palace at Knossos. The division between the two LM IIIA2 urban phases could have been a consequence of that event. Ayia Triada likely constituted the administrative capital of the surrounding area, still under Knossian control, with the single name *pa-i-to*. Comparing the data provided by Linear A and B sources from our area, it is necessary to underline the relevant differences either in the quantities or in the products mentioned. Rather than thinking of a radical and abrupt change in the economy of the western Mesara region, it is opportune to think of interests and practices that differed in the two administrations, the Minoan and the Mycenaean. The Linear B documents, in fact, refer to a situation in which the area of Phaistos–Ayia Triada is part of a wider system led by Knossos, which controlled the region through the collectors (Cucuzza 2003).

Very little has been identified of the destruction or abandonment levels of the large LM III buildings. A level recognized in the test pit opened behind the large stoa, a deposit immediately to the west of Edificio Nord-Ovest, and a poor floor assemblage in room R, immediately to the north of the *Piazzale* of the agora, allow the moment of abandonment of the site (apparently without violent destruction) to be dated to the end of the 13th century BC (La Rosa 1997a; Cucuzza 2003). Episodes of synoecism with nearby Phaistos have recently been hypothesized for such events. Afterward, however, the settlement at Ayia Triada ceased to exist as such and was resettled only during the Hellenistic period.

A large open-air sanctuary without formal cultic buildings was organized in the LM IIIC period in the area to the south of the megaron and the stoa, an area that had previously remained free of structures. Hundreds of votive offerings, especially bull figurines but also fantasy animals such as sphinxes and centaurs, were perhaps deposited in groups within perishable or temporary enclosures. From a religious point of view, these represent a sharp change from the cult of the goddess with raised hands, which was identified within the 14th–13th century BC shrine. This new sanctuary represented the focus of cult for pilgrims from a larger territory: pilgrims for whom the bull had acquired an economically important role. It cannot be excluded that the new religious practices reflect influences from mainland Greece. The depositions probably continued until the end of the 11th century BC and began to diminish during the 10th century BC, temporarily disappearing between the end of the 10th and the first half of the 9th centuries BC (D'Agata 1999b).

Overall, the settlement, probably founded by a group from Phaistos at the beginning of the EM I period, lived in a substantial autarchy during the Prepalatial period, perhaps with several clusters of habitations spread out in the area of the river, and possibly with other large circular tombs. The fragmentary nature and discontinuity of architectural structures and deposits—topographically and chronologically—could have been a characteristic determined by mobility or a succession of human groups, possibly caused by a more general territorial instability.

A gradual process of stabilization of the elites (also in the nearby sanctuary site of Paterikiès) seems to have been completed, in the funerary sphere, toward the end of the Prepalatial period (MM IA), when the vitality of the settlement at Phaistos is demonstrated by the artisans' quarter, which has recently been identified in an area close to the future palace.

The foundation of the first palace at Phaistos might have represented a change in the organization of the territory, in which Ayia Triada had a subordinate (although strictly correlated) position perhaps until MM IIIA, when the building of power at Phaistos was rearranged after the MM IIB earthquake. The settlement was probably concentrated in the area of the modern archaeological area, where it also remained in later periods.

The foundation of the Royal Villa (which has a unique plan when compared to similar buildings) took place toward the end of the MM IIIB period, after the temporary abandonment of the palace at Phaistos following the MM IIIA earthquake, thanks to a political intervention of the Knossian elites. After this event, Ayia Triada became the territorial capital, a sort of (relatively small) "business city" at the expense of the previous territorial hierarchy in the Mesara. This situation does not seem to have changed with the construction, at the beginning of LM IB, of the new palace at Phaistos, which seems to have had a limited function. An earthquake seemingly ended the life of the Villa, and also destroyed the village.

After a period during which data are limited (between LM II and LM IIIA1), which corresponds to the Mycenaean conquest of Knossos, the 'utopia of the capital city' seemingly proceeded during LM IIIA and for a good part of LM IIIB but always at the expense of Phaistos and under Knossian protection. The monumental and stratigraphic situation at Ayia Triada, with its double urban phase, might reflect changes connected to the destruction of Knossos. Ayia Triada in the second of the two LM IIIA2 phases, like *ku-do-ni-ja*/Chanià (a center that now also has Linear B tablets), would have represented the political reference point of a greater or lesser territory.

The abandonment (rather than the destruction) of the Mycenaean capital seems to mark a further chapter in the "complementarity of roles" between Phaistos and Ayia Triada. The open-air sanctuary of the Piazzale dei Sacelli was probably now controlled by the new and rich Phaistian elites of LM IIIC, as documented by the large deposit from the Acropoli mediana. The trend seemingly continued in the sanctuary's second phase of use until the vigorous resurgence of Phaistos in the last quarter of the 7th century BC, which saw the construction of the large sanctuary. The destruction by Gortyn in the second half of the 2nd century ended the long history of Ayia Triada.

BIBLIOGRAPHY

Belfiore, Cristina M., P. M. Day, A. Hein, V. Kilikoglou, V. La Rosa, P. Mazzoleni, and
A. Pezzino. 2007. "Petrographic and Chemical Characterization of Pottery Production
of the Late Minoan I Kiln at Haghia Triada, Crete." *Archaeometry* 49(4): 621–53.

Carinci, Filippo. 2003. "Haghia Triada nel periodo Medio Minoico." *Creta Antica* 4: 97–141.

———. 2004. "*Priests in Action:* Considerazioni sulla fine dell'età prepalaziale ad Haghia
Triada." *Creta Antica* 5: 25–40.

Cucuzza, Nicola. 2002. "Osservazioni sui costumi funerari dell'area di Festòs ed Haghia
Triada nel TM IIIA1–A2." *Creta Antica* 3: 133–66.

———. 2003. "Il volo del grifo: Osservazioni: Sulla Haghia Triada 'micenea.' " *Creta Antica*
4: 199–271.

Cultraro, Massimo. 2003. "La grande tholos di Haghia Triada: Nuovi dati per un vecchio
complesso." *Creta Antica* 4: 301–27.

D'Agata, Anna Lucia. 1999a. "Hidden Wars: Minoans and Mycenaeans at Haghia Triada in
the LM III Period: The Evidence from Pottery." In *Polemos*, 47–55.

———. 1999b. *Statuine minoiche e post-minoiche dai vecchi scavi di Haghia Triada (Creta).*
Monografie Scuola Archeologica Italiana di Atene, no. XI. Padua: Bottega d'Erasmo-
Ausilio editore.

Girella, Luca. 2003. "Un *pitharaki* MM III dal nuovo 'Settore Nord-Est' di Haghia Triada."
Creta Antica 4: 343–57.

———. 2007. "Towards a Definition of the Middle Minoan III Ceramic Sequence in
South-central Crete: Returning to the Traditional MM IIIA and B Division?" In *Middle
Helladic Pottery*, 233–55.

———. Forthcoming. "Evidence for an MM III Occupation at Ayia Triada." In *Intermezzo:
Intermediacy and Regeneration in Middle Minoan III Crete.* International workshop
held at Knossos (Villa Ariadne, July 3–5, 2008), ed. Carl Knappett, Eleni Banou, and
Colin Macdonald. BSA Studies.

Halbherr, Federico, Enrico Stefani, and Luisa Banti. 1977. "Haghia Triada nel periodo tardo
palaziale." *ASAtene* LV: 13–296. (with an appendix by Vincenzo La Rosa, 297–342).

La Rosa, Vincenzo. 1992–1993. "La c.d. Tomba degli ori e il nuovo settore nord-est
dell'insediamento di Haghia Triada." *ASAtene* LXX–LXXI: 121–72.

———. 1997a. "Haghia Triada à l'époque mycénienne: L'utopie d'une ville capitale." In *La
Crète mycénienne*, 249–66.

———. 1997b. "La 'Villa Royale' de Haghia Triada." In *The Function of the "Minoan Villa"
(Athens, 6–8 June 1992)*, ed. Robin Hägg, 79–89. Acta Instituti Atheniensis Regni
Sueciae, ser. in 4°, no. XLVI. Stockholm: Svenska Institutet i Athen.

———. 1999. "Nuovi dati sulla tomba del sarcofago dipinto di Haghia Triada." In *επι
ποντον πλαζομενοι, Simposio italiano di studi egei in onore di L. Bernabò Brea e G.
Pugliese Carratelli*, ed. Vincenzo La Rosa, Dario Palermo, and Lucia Vagnetti, 177–88.
Rome: Scuola Archeologica Italiana di Atene.

———. 2000. "To Whom Did the Queen Tiyi Scarab Found at Hagia Triada Belong?" In
Krete-Aigyptos: Politismikoi desmoi trion chilietion. Meletes, ed. Alexandra Karetsou,
86–93. Athens: Hypourgeio Politismou.

———. 2001. "Minoan Baetyls: Between Funerary Rituals and Epiphanies." In *Potnia*,
221–26.

———. 2003. " 'Il colle sul quale sorge la chiesa ad ovest è tutto seminato di cocci….'
Vicende e temi di uno scavo di lungo corso." *Creta Antica* 4: 11–65.

———. 2006. "Considerazioni sull'area ad Ovest del c.d. Bastione ad Haghia Triada." *ASAtene* LXXXIV(2): 819–77.

———, and Pietro Militello. 1999. "Caccia, guerra, o rituale? Considerazioni sulle armi minoiche da Festòs e Haghia Triada." In *Polemos*, 241–63.

Levi, Doro, and Clelia Laviosa. 1979–1980. "Il forno minoico da vasaio di Haghia Triada." *ASAtene* LVII–LVIII: 7–47.

Militello, Pietro. 1998. *Gli affreschi: Haghia Triada I*. Monografie Scuola Archeologica Italiana di Atene 9. Padua: Bottega d'Erasmo-Ausilio editore.

Monaco, Carmelo, and Luigi Tortorici. 2003. "Effects of Earthquakes on the Minoan 'Royal Villa' at Haghia Triada (Crete)." *Creta Antica* 4: 409–16.

Palaima, Thomas G. 1994. "Seal-users and Script-users: Nodules and Tablets at LM I B Hagia Triada." In *Archives before Writing* (Proc. Int. Colloq., Oriolo Romano October 23–25, 1991), ed. Piera Ferioli, Enrica Fiandra, Gian Giacomo Fissore, and Marcella Frangipane, 307–30. Turin: Paravia/Scriptorium.

Privitera, Santo. 2001. "I due pithoi globulari di Haghia Triada e la cronologia della 'Casa dei Vani aggiunti progressivamente.'" *Creta Antica* 2: 141–46.

———. 2008. "Gli affreschi TM III del 'Villaggio' di Haghia Triada: Nuove osservazioni sul contesto e sulla cronologia." *Creta Antica* 9: 111–37.

Puglisi, Dario. 2003a. "Il Bastione Tardo Minoico I ad Haghia Triada: Nuove osservazioni su cronologia e funzione." *ASAtene* LXXXI(2): 573–93.

———. 2003b. "Haghia Triada nel periodo Tardo Minoico I." *Creta Antica* 4: 145–97.

———. 2006. Produzioni ceramiche Tardo Minoico I ad Haghia Triada nel contesto della Creta centro-meridionale. PhD diss., Università di Udine.

———. 2007. "L'organizzazione a terrazze nel Villaggio TM I di Haghia Triada." *Creta Antica* 8: 169–98.

———. Forthcoming. "From the End of LM IA to the End of LM IB: The Pottery Evidence from Haghia Triada." In *LM IB Pottery: Examining New Evidence for Relative Chronology and Regional Differences* (Athens, July 27–29, 2007), ed. Erik Hallager and Tom Brogan. Athens: Danish Institute at Athens and INSTAP.

Schoep, Ilse. 2002. *The Administration of Neopalatial Crete*. Minos suppl.17. Salamanca: Ediciones Universidad de Salamanca.

Stefani, Enrico, and Luisa Banti. 1930–1931. "La grande tomba a *tholos* di Haghia Triada." *ASAtene* XIII–XIV: 147–251.

Todaro, Simona. 2003a. "Il deposito AM I del Piazzale dei Sacelli ad Haghia Triada: I modellini architettonici." *ASAtene* LXXXI(2): 547–72.

———. 2003b. "Haghia Triada nel periodo Antico Minoico." *Creta Antica* 4: 69–94.

———. Forthcoming. "Craft Production and Social Practice at Prepalatial Phaistos: The Background to the First Palace." In *Back to the Beginning*.

Tomasello, Francesco. 1996. "Fornaci a Festòs ed Haghia Triada dall'età mediominoica alla geometrica." In *Keramika Ergastiria stin Kriti apo tin archaeotita os simera (Actes du Ier Colloque international 1995 de Margaritès, Crète)*, ed. Irini Gavrilaki, 27–37. Réthymno, Greece: Istoriki Laografiki Etaireia Rethymnis.

Watrous, L. Vance. 1984. "Ayia Triada: A New Perspective on the Minoan Villa." *AJA* 88: 123–34.

———, Despoina Hadzi-Vallianou, and L. Harriet Blitzer. 2004. *The Plain of Phaistos: Cycles of Social Complexity in the Mesara Region of Crete*. Monumenta Archaeologica 23. Los Angeles: Cotsen Institute of Archaeology, University of California at Los Angeles.

CHAPTER 38

KATO ZAKROS

LEFTERIS PLATON

History of Research

Zakros was known as an archaeological site from the reports of nineteenth-century travelers T. Spratt and L. Mariani. Nevertheless, its significance was first understood by Sir Arthur Evans, who visited it during his travels across the island in 1894. Evans pushed David Hogarth, at that time director of the British School at Athens, to investigate the site by excavation.

The site lies at the southeastern end of Crete, south of Palaikastro, where another important Minoan settlement is located. Actually, Zakros Bay is the only safe haven along the steep southeastern shores of Crete. Although the strong northwesterly winds afflict the area, they do not affect the waters inside the gulf, which is protected by its orientation and two rather long promontories.

From the interior, the valley of Zakros is approached with difficulty since it is surrounded by steep, rocky, barren slopes split only by a single reasonably passable gorge. Excavation has shown that this served the prehistoric inhabitants as a passageway from the valley inland, while a fair number of caves and rocky shelters in its walls were used during various periods for burials or as temporary protection by shepherds.

Hogarth excavated Zakros for a single period—in 1901. His search concentrated mainly on two low hills that dominate a small valley. The excavation brought to light the architectural remains of several megalithic buildings that constituted part of a densely built harbor settlement in Minoan times and had preserved a quantity of rich finds. Among them was a good deal of pottery—a large part of which came from two pits excavated in the rock, which Hogarth identified as "shrine repositories"—as well as bronze tools, stone vases and tools, and different types of loomweights. However, the most impressive finds were a total of almost three hundred clay sealings made by seal stones and signet rings—presenting motifs of religious character. Particularly interesting was a series of scenes showing hybrid human forms and fabulous beasts that have no parallels in Minoan iconography. Hogarth published his preliminary excavation report without imagining that his spade had touched the edges of a Minoan palace whose finds would surpass in richness those preserved at Knossos.

Sixty years later, in 1961, Nikolaos Platon, Ephor of Cretan Antiquities at the time, started a trial trench in the gulf of "Kato Zakros," as the site is now known. Zakros, the ancient—probably prehistoric—name today has been transferred inland to the nearest, probably nineteenth-century, village. Platon was led to Zakros by the following evidence:

1. Zakros was the reported provenance of an important Minoan treasure consisting of three gold items kept in the Herakleion Museum: a diadem with embossed decoration, whose central medallion bore a goddess mastering two wild goats, a bull's head pendant, and a bowl decorated inside with a twisted spiral motif

2. evidence for a likely palatial pottery workshop whose products apparently radiated from a center in the wider area of eastern Crete. Before his visit to Zakros, Nikolaos Platon had investigated a number of Minoan sites in the Siteia district. In the most significant of these he had identified and excavated large structures he called "villas."

3. a more careful examination of Hogarth's finds. The finding of such extensive records, including, apart from the sealings, a Linear A tablet, actually constituted evidence for the existence of a bureaucracy, which was well known to be used mainly in Minoan times by the palaces for better financial control of their periphery. The observation that some of the sealings were obviously produced by metal signet rings originating in Knossos strengthened the hypothesis of a palatial correspondence.

4. the accidental discovery of some huge pithoi at Zakros when agricultural machinery was introduced in the area

The trial excavation of 1961 brought to light, in the valley lying between the two hills, a row of spacious storerooms full of pithoi, together with a great number of other finds, in an architectural structure resembling a similar one excavated in the East Wing of the palace at Knossos. Additionally, the quantity and quality of the finds was such that it could not be ascribed to a common settlement. Thus, Nikolaos Platon, after his first contact with the area, spoke of the possible existence of a further palace, the contents of which seemed intact as a result of having been buried in the debris of a huge destruction.

The next season, with the financial support of both the Archaeological Society of Athens and Leon Pomerance, an American amateur archaeologist, excavation was expanded. In Sector Γ, which lies in the narrow valley between the two hills investigated by Hogarth, a great structure comprising several rooms was revealed, the contents of which exceeded all expectations. The strong possibility of the existence of a palace became certainty during the following season (1963), when an unplundered palatial treasury was brought to light—with the total of its contents remaining in situ.

More than fifty stone vases of various types, some of which had until that moment been known only from Minoan iconography and were made of various materials imported from different places around the Mediterranean Sea, such as Egypt, Gyali near Nissyros in the Dodecanese, the Cycladic islands, the district of Sparta in the Peloponnese, and elsewhere, comprised the most impressive part of the total. Together with these were ceremonial emblems and vessels made of bronze, faience, stone, and other materials and jewels or inlays of rock crystal, faience, and ivory.

Several rooms typical of a palace were also confirmed in this sector of the great building. Among these were the archive room, from the contents of which only thirteen Linear A tablets were preserved, magazines for agricultural surplus, cupboards, and storage areas for raw materials imported from abroad such as elephant tusks and bronze ingots shaped in molds. Rooms devoted to the cult were also discovered and included a small shrine and a room of the type known as a "Lustral Basin."

During excavations, which continued until 1967, the rest of the palace was investigated. The West Wing contained two large halls that were likely used in ceremonies and symposia. The northern sector includes a spacious kitchen, identified from the presence of some permanent fireplaces, remnants of animal bones, and equipment related to cooking.

The Central Court is surrounded by three more wings, of which the east one, just as at Knossos, is the largest. The latter has suffered greatly from modern agricultural usage, and almost none of the contents of its rooms have survived. Nevertheless, it has been possible to construct a drawing of the plan of two halls equipped with polythyra and bordered by a long portico facing the Central Court, of a great square hall with a central, rounded cistern, and, finally, of two detached structures used for drawing underground water.

In the north part of the East Wing, a further "Lustral Basin" was discovered, with a badly preserved wall painting depicting ceremonial symbols. The South Wing is not so extensive, but it seems that it housed the palatial workshops, to judge from the discovery of some partly worked or raw materials found alongside a number of finished products. A magnificent stepped, processional entrance gave access to the palace at its northeastern end. The whole picture is rounded out by a full network of drains that dealt with rainwater under the pavement of an inner courtyard, a small portico with a stone bench at the north end of the central court, some antechambers and secondary rooms, and a number of staircases, which prove the existence of at least one upper story.

Platon dated the final destruction of the Zakros palace to the end of the LM IB period, namely the mid-fifteenth century BC, on the evidence of the pottery found in the last "closed stratum." He believed this great destruction to be a result of the Thera volcanic explosion. Nowadays most scholars believe that the explosion of the volcano took place by the end of the previous LM IA phase since certain related geological evidence appears in the archaeological layers of that period both in the Aegean and on Crete.

The excavation of the palace was followed by the extensive recovery of the surrounding Minoan town. Over the course of twenty-one additional excavation seasons, more than thirty buildings came to light. These constitute a densely built settlement that utilized a well-planned grid of roads or passageways.

The buildings at Zakros, although they do not exhibit advanced architectural features, were rich in finds that prove the existence of a prosperous community contemporary with the palace. Their contents show that they constituted primarily private housing, although some of them may have been under the control of the palatial administration. Industrial installations and equipment, as well as storage rooms for agricultural produce and various domestic utensils, imply a relative economic independence for the inhabitants of these buildings, although their social status has not yet been thoroughly studied.

Another subject of interest to Nikolaos Platon was the location of the Minoan cemeteries. This matter constitutes a more general problem for Minoan archaeology since few graves dated to the period of the new palaces have been identified until now, but the enclosed landscape of Zakros has made it possible to carry out such an investigation. In addition to the slopes at the edge of the Minoan town, several caves and rock shelters in the steep walls of the gorge and elsewhere were explored. A search brought to light graves and temporary refuges of different periods, beginning with the Neolithic, as well as the Prepalatial and the Protopalatial periods, and ending with the Postpalatial and Geometric periods but failed to locate the cemeteries of the prosperous settlement period (i.e., the period of the palace).

Aware of the difficulties presented by a final publication of the huge volume of his finds, Nikolaos Platon proceeded to write a concise book in which he presented the main results of his research. He also kept the scholarly community informed of the progress of his work through detailed reports that were published in the two annual journals edited by the Archaeological Society of Athens. He published information related to the dating of archaeological layers at Zakros, the kinds of destruction that ravaged the site, and the function of particular installations and areas in archaeological journals or in the proceedings of international congresses. General reports of his findings were included in his own writings on Aegean or Cretan prehistory and in general works by other scholars. In addition, several of his collaborators presented material from Zakros in papers referring to specific subjects of Aegean prehistory.

Nevertheless, the material from Minoan Zakros remains largely unknown, and some important conclusions that could be drawn from it have been underexposed in the modern bibliography. It became clear that only the full scholarly publication of the results of the site excavations could enable the scientific community to evaluate properly the rich data extracted from this very important site.

This realization led to the suspension of digging at Zakros in early 1990, at which time I undertook the long-term project of cataloguing, evaluating, and additional conservation of the material. This important project is being carried out with the assistance of a team of specialists that includes archaeologists, architects, painters, and photographers. Apart from the Archaeological Society, important financial support is granted annually by the Institute for Aegean Prehistory in the United States.

The following brief survey presents some fresh data on the dating of pottery groups and the archaeological layers related to them. The information has been drawn from the recent study for the Zakros final publication.

THE NEW DATA ON RELATIVE CHRONOLOGY

Nikolaos Platon, in his excavation reports and papers on special subjects, made extensive use of the traditional chronological system devised by Evans and Mackenzie. He often combined this with a system that he himself first proposed and introduced and which is based on the general destruction and reestablishment of the palaces.

Experience has shown that neither system is applicable to every part of Crete. Certain pottery styles, which in the Evans-Mackenzie system actually define chronological phases, have been shown to be rather the products of local workshops. On the other hand, the chronological system that Platon introduced, which is based on the acceptance of a simultaneous establishment and destruction of all of the Minoan palaces, has also been shaken by the realization that Knossos survived the destruction of the other palaces and by the probable identification of a second palace in the so-called Postpalatial period at Chania. Finally, different dates for the establishment and abandonment of the palaces at Galatas, Phaistos, and Zakros have recently been proposed.

Under these conditions, another system of relative chronology for the Zakros material is proposed here, one that is based exclusively on the stratigraphy of the site itself. It should be noticed that in a time span represented by twelve phases in the system devised by Evans and Mackenzie, to date only five stratigraphically confirmed phases have been identified for the district of Kato Zakros and a total of seven for the wider Zakros area.

The first phase, denoted by the capital letter N (Zakros Neolithic), is represented by finds that belong to the final Neolithic period, which were found in the cave at Mavro Avlaki, a small fjord just to the south of Zakros Bay. To the next phase, designated Zakros I, belong finds from caves and rock shelters in the Zakros gorge, corresponding to the EM I and II phases of Evans and Mackenzie. The harbor settlement appears in the Zakros II phase, which is well represented by the stratified group found under the "kitchen" of the Late Minoan palace. On the floor of a room in a structure whose type and extent remain unclear, some vases representative of the White on Dark East Cretan pottery were found alongside vessels that represent the early polychrome style (figure 38.1). Consequently, Zakros II is identified with the EM III and MM IA phases of Evans and Mackenzie.

Figure 38.1. Pottery found under the "Kitchen" of the Late Minoan palace (Zakros II phase) (courtesy of the author).

The next phase, Zakros III, is represented by a destruction layer identified at various spots in the Zakros settlement and especially in the north hill quarter. Most representative are the finds from three successive rooms under Neopalatial Building H. There, the pots are decorated in a more advanced polychrome style, imitating the decoration of Kamares ware. Nevertheless, the discovery in the same context of a bridge-spouted jar with a close parallel from phase IA of Phaistos supports a dating for this layer closer to the MM IB–IIA of Evans and Mackenzie.

Similar pottery comes from many other contexts located in both the Zakros settlement and the wider district. One group comes from the probably closed context of Kalyvomouri, possibly a shrine deposit near the rim of the gorge wall. Here, no secure specimen of the so-called mature Kamares style has yet been found at Zakros, and, consequently, no layer can be assigned with any certainty to the MM IIB period, when the first palaces at Knossos and Phaistos were destroyed. A possible solution to the problem is that the MM IB–IIA style in Zakros remained in vogue until the end of the next ceramic phase of central Crete.

The following period, Zakros IV, represented by a wide destruction horizon, is particularly important for Zakros. Destruction layers that contain homogeneous pottery

ZAKROS IV=MMIIIB/LMIA

Figure 38.2. Clay vessels representative of the Zakros IV phase (courtesy of the author).

from this period have so far been identified in a room underneath the megalithic Building G, in buildings near the edges of the West and South Palace Wings, in the filled basement rooms of two buildings that border the palace on the north ("Building of the NW Sector," "Building to the North of the Palace Kitchen") and, finally, in the filled part of a great building, some rooms of which were filled during the construction of the new palace's East Wing. This last building is very important in defining this phase since, according to Platon, it formed part of the first palace of Zakros.

In all of these contexts, the pottery is decorated in a style that is usually called MM IIIB–LM IA or early LM IA (figure 38.2). The main features of the style are the simultaneous use of both of the painted decoration techniques (dark on light and light on dark), the frequent presence of particular motifs such as the scroll and the feather, the latter usually on the inside of open bowls, the row of crescents, and, principally, the wide use of the ripple motif. However, in the same contexts, the style that would in other Cretan contexts be called the "mature LM IA style" is well represented with motifs such as the reed pattern and spirals with solid discs usually overlaid with white spots, to mention only the most typical. Thus, it appears that the so-called MM IIIB–LM IA style in Zakros continues to the end of the LM IA period. Levels with pure LM IA pottery on the site are missing.

This conclusion revises the history of the site because the so-called Old Palace was obviously filled at the latest during the construction of the New Palace since part of it is underneath the East Wing of the latter. The dating of the Old Palace fill pottery has now been reassigned to the end of the LM IA; therefore, the establishment of the new palace must date at the earliest from that period. In this case, the palace that is visible today at Zakros must be at least a century later (i.e., younger) than that at Knossos.

The clearest chronological phase on the site is that assigned to the following stage, Zakros V, which corresponds to the LM IB period of Evans and Mackenzie. It is perfectly represented by the finds of a destruction horizon spread throughout the settlement. It is evident that this stage was the last of the palace but not of the settlement.

Thousands of pots that, when published, will constitute a kind of corpus for the LM IB pottery come from this horizon. The typological variety and differing quality create subgroups that, in spite of their dissimilarity, we must place within the same chronological bracket. Vessels of high quality, probably imported from Knossos or other sites in central Crete, coexist with significant products of local workshops and with pots of much lower quality in such great numbers that one can talk of mass production.

Another important observation is that vases decorated in styles that had previously been considered representative of earlier chronological steps are found in the same levels with the much more developed artistic creations, usually dated to the lowest limits of the LM I period. This indicates that some contexts outside Zakros previously thought to belong to phases earlier than the LM IB should probably now be redated: They include those of the so-called villas at Epano Zakros, Prophetes Helias Praissos, and Akhladia Siteia.

The next stage, Zakros VI, is represented by the pottery assigned by the excavator to a period of reoccupation, which was confined to only part of the settlement. Nikolaos Platon placed the reoccupation in the LM IIIA2 phase. The data drawn from the study of the pottery confirm that he underestimated the chronological and topographical extent of this period. The finding of even a few imported LM II vases from Knossos proves the existence of such a period at Zakros, which should be traced in subgroups of pottery considered as LM IIIA2. Moreover, even though limited, the presence of LM III pottery in contexts from the north and northeast hills shows that occupation during the Postpalatial period was not confined to a single quarter of the settlement.

In spite of the complete absence of LM IIIB sherds at Zakros, the site appears to have been reoccupied once again, on a truly limited scale this time, during the 11th century, to judge from some pottery found in a room of house E on the southwest hill.

To sum up, the port settlement was established in the MM IA, was flourishing and significantly expanding during the MM IB–IIA, grew even more in importance during the LM IA, and reached its zenith in the LM IB with the construction of a palace. The influence of Knossos on the palace is obvious in the pottery, the use of specific emblems, the type of archives, and the choice of architectural features, all of which suggest the strong possibility that this palace was a Knossian establishment.

Whether an earlier palace existed at Zakros cannot yet be determined. Nonetheless, the great structure underneath the East Palace Wing is obviously something more than a private house. The quantity and quality of its finds, the clear definition of the various functions in different parts arranged on successive terraces (the higher of which consist of workshops and a pottery kiln), its spacious, well-paved rooms interconnected by wide doorways, and, finally, its location on a site later occupied by part of the LM IB palace indicate that perhaps it should be considered an administrative center that functioned at least during the LM IA.

After a general destruction of the site around the end of the LM IB period, the palace was abandoned, but part of the settlement continued to exist until the end of the LM IIIA2, when it was also deserted.

BIBLIOGRAPHY

Hogarth, David G. 1901. "Excavations at Zakro, Crete." *BSA* 7 (1900–1991): 121–49.

Platon, Lefteris. 1993. "Ateliers palatiaux minoens: une nouvelle image." *BCH* 117(1): 103–22.

———. 1999a. "Ανυπόγραφα «έργα τέχνης» στα χέρια ιδιωτών, κατά τη νεοανακτορική περίοδο στην Κρήτη." In *Eliten in der Bronzezeit: Ergebnisse zweier Kolloquien in Mainz und Athen*, ed. Imma Kilian-Dirlmeier and Markus Egg, 37–50. Monographien des Römisch-Germanischen Zentralmuseums 43. Mainz: Römisch-Germanischen Zentralmuseums.

———. 1999b. "New Evidence for the Occupation at Zakros, before the LM I Palace." In *Meletemata*, 671–81.

———. 2002. "The Political and Cultural Influence of the Zakros Palace on Nearby Sites and in a Wider Context." In *Monuments of Minos*, 145–56.

———. 2004. "Το Υστερομινωικό I ανάκτορο της Ζάκρου: μία «Κνωσός» έξω από την Κνωσό." In *Knossos*, 381–92.

Platon, Nikolaos. 1961–1990. "Ανασκαφή Ζάκρου." *Praktika* 1961–1990.

———. 1971. *Zakros: The Discovery of a Lost Palace of Ancient Crete*. New York: Scribner.

———. 1974. *Ζάκρος. Το νέον μινωϊκόν ανάκτορον*. Athens: Athens Archaeological Society.

———. 1992. "Zakro." In *The Aerial Atlas of Ancient Crete*, ed. J. Wilson Myers, Eleanor E. Myers, and Gerold Cadogan, 293–301. Berkeley: University of California Press.

———, and William C. Brice. 1975. *Inscribed Tablets and Pithos of Linear A System from Zakros*. Athens: Athens Archaeological Society.

Shaw, Joseph W. 1971. *Minoan Architecture: Materials and Techniques*. ASAtene 49. Rome: Instituto Poligrafico dello Stato.

CHAPTER 39

KHANIA (KYDONIA)

MARIA ANDREADAKI-VLAZAKI

IT is generally agreed that the modern town of Khania has been established on the ruins of classical Kydonia, one of the first-order city-states of Crete. According to Diodorus, Kydonia was one of the three cities founded by Minos in Crete (V, 78.2). This indicates that it existed even in Minoan times, which is confirmed by the reference to Kydonia in the Knossian Linear B tablets (Chadwick et al. 1986). Taking all of this into account, as well as the wealth and significance of the Minoan settlement of Khania, we are compelled to locate the seat of a very important Minoan and Mycenaean palatial center in the same site occupied by the classical city (Andreadaki-Vlazaki 2002, in press b).

In the beginning of the 20th century, modern Khania was rapidly extending outside the old city walls, and quite a few rich chamber tombs of the LM III period were revealed at that time (Jantzen 1951). Questions about the settlement of these Minoan people arose at once. The low hill of Kastelli, east of the Old Harbor, where traces of ancient buildings and Minoan pottery were visible, was the most probable settlement. This is confirmed by the extensive excavations that began in 1964 and are still continuing today in a few open areas of this densely occupied region.

The hill has been inhabited without interruption from Early Minoan times. Recently, the excavations in a small street of Kastelli revealed very interesting evidence for the early human activity. Below the ruins of various periods, quite a few narrow and mostly deep pits were dug into the rock, perhaps recalling pile dwellings. Later on, large houses with well-built rooms, carefully laid floors with circular hearths, walls coated with plaster, and pottery of exceptionally fine quality indicate that this was an important Prepalatial center. Furthermore, EM imports and local imitations suggest that the settlement had contacts with Knossos, the Peloponnese, the Cyclades, and even lands farther afield, as a unique EM III ivory plate, perhaps part of a game board from the Near East, may indicate (Andreadaki-Vlazaki in press b).

A lasting, close contact between the Khania area and the eastern part of the Peloponnese (especially the Argolid), a connection that existed throughout antiquity, originated in EM times. The geographic position of Khania, opposite the Peloponnese, favored travel. Even by chance, a Peloponnesian sailor could arrive in west Crete just by following the sea currents, as Menelaos did (Odyssey γ, 303 ff.). The island of Kythera was instrumental in this communication. The similarity between the EM III/MM IA pottery (e.g., cups with protobarbotine and incised decoration) of Kastelli at Khania and Kastri on Kythera is indicative in this respect (Coldstream and Huxley 1972, pl. 18, nos. 7–9, 13–15).

In the first half of the second millennium BC, the settlement at Khania developed into a dynamic center. The products of the local pottery workshop followed the styles of central Crete, and a number of vases were also imported. Unfortunately, the MM II constructions on Kastelli have been destroyed by the extensive building activity of the periods immediately following, and very few remains have survived.

The majority of the Minoan finds in Khania date from the Neopalatial period. At that time the built-up area was restricted to the hill and the south and southeast part of its base (Andreadaki-Vlazaki 2002, pl. La). This concentration is probably due to the different structure and organization of the settlement when tied to a palatial center. Up to now, no central court has been revealed. However, the Greek Swedish excavations in Haghia Aikaterini Square, as well as fifteen Greek excavations in private plots and public areas, suggest the idea of a nearby palace. The direct and indirect evidence that prompts such a view includes the Linear A archives, the palatial features in the architecture, the emphasis on ceremonial and cult areas, the scenes on seal impressions, and the mason's marks.

The archives consist of 99 pieces of clay tablets, 124 roundels, and 28 nodules (Papapostolou, Godart, and Olivier 1976; GORILA 5; Andreadaki-Vlazaki and Hallager 2007). Most of these articles were found in the Katre no. 10 plot. Preserved by their accidental hardening during the violent conflagration at the end of LM IB, they contain lists of agricultural products and censuses of people and animals. They attest to the functioning of an advanced administrative system connected with the centralized economy of a powerful society. Regarding the number of Linear A tablets, Khania is in second position among the Minoan centers and in first position with regard to the roundels (Hallager 1996).

Many of the architectural features in the Khania settlement have been identified: a lustral basin, Minoan halls with pier-and-door partitions, lightwells, ashlar façades, fresco paintings, columns, pillars, well-organized storage rooms, well-developed drainage systems, and paved floors with red-painted plaster in the joints of the slabs. The palatial elements found at Khania were at first attributed to private buildings owned by the elite. However, the increase in number of these elements, in combination with the recovery of ceremonial and cult places, has allowed us to formulate the hypothesis that part of the excavated constructions could well be included as further evidence of a palace.

In the Neopalatial settlement, three main architectural phases have been recognized. The first one dates back to the MM III period, the second starts in the beginning of the LM IA, and the third starts at the beginning of the LM IB. The final destruction by conflagration comes at the end of the LM IB. The following transitional years, known as the LM II period, can be characterized as an intermediate period. In these years, the inhabitants of Khania roughly repaired the ruined buildings, thereby setting the scene for the following grand period characterized by the Mycenaean presence in the Minoan culture.

The most important and characteristic Neopalatial areas in the Kastelli hill and the Splantzia quarter are the following (Andreadaki-Vlazaki 2002, 2005):

a. Haghia Aikaterini Square (Greek Swedish Excavations)

Excavation over an area of 550 square m. and to a depth of 2 m. has revealed parts of two streets, an open area, and five buildings (for one of which we have a complete plan). This structure covers 220 square m. and has a second story, the larger part of which was an unroofed area. It consists of fourteen rooms on the ground floor, with a huge threshold at the entrance. It includes a Minoan polythyron hall, a lightwell, a kitchen, a storeroom, and a double staircase for the upper story. In the center of the kitchen, a rectangular clay hearth has been preserved, and the discovery of numerous loomweights indicates the existence of a loom in the vicinity.

The findings from House IV, such as an offering table and a clay foot model, denote a cult activity in the area.

b. Lionakis Plot

Located to the west of the previous area, this plot contains an important Neopalatial building with mud-brick walls, paved floors with red plaster in the joints, and the characteristic doorjamb bases.

c. Katre No. 10 Plot

Most of the Linear A tablets, roundels, and nodules of the archives of Khania come from this excavation. Found in a thick layer of red soil above a floor of beaten earth, they had probably fallen from the upper story.

d. Mathioudakis Plot

Situated in the eastern extremity of the Kastelli hill, this plot contains part of a vast Neopalatial building that has been uncovered here. In one of its rooms, a thick layer of pumice stone was spread all over the floor, which may hint at the presence of a shrine. On top of the pumice stone room, a great pillar may have been erected during the Mycenaean period.

e. Daskaloyannis Street Complex (Figure 39.1)

Daskaloyannis Street is one of the main streets in the town of Khania, located in the Splantzia quarter, east of the Kastelli hill. Due to municipal works projects, part of the street (74 m long by 8 m wide) had to be excavated. A very important Neopalatial building complex emerged, the excavated part of which is more than one thousand square meters in total. The strong outer walls are founded on huge, rough limestone blocks, while the inner ones are usually made of mud brick. The complex is divided in two parts.

In the southeast, an impressive threshold marks the main entrance. Inside the building, two rooms on the west lead to an adyton or lustral basin, which has a square ground plan, each side measuring 4 m. outside and 2 m. inside (Andreadaki-Vlazaki 1993). Its walls were preserved up to a height of 70 cm, and it was full of debris from the superstructure. During the LM IA period, this underground room was converted into a room on the ground-floor level. The pillar of the staircase and the walls of the room were decorated with fresco wall paintings down to the paved floor. The motifs are an imitation of marble revetment at the bottom and a frieze with a running spiral at the top—a decoration similar to that of the adyton in the east wing of the palace at Knossos. The pillar carries the most impressive decoration: a depiction of the core of the marble.

The proportions of a grand hall, located to the right of the lustral basin, permitted many people to gather there. The north end gives access to an immense platform or podium surrounded by drains and constructed of large rectangular limestone blocks 45 cm in thickness. In the middle, a low, thin wall encloses a plain rectangular area, and the drain held quite a few conical cups. The drainage system starts from the extensive courtyard to the west. In this area, in the northwestern corner of the building, a special structure with a luxurious double drain has been revealed. In front of it, another pit was found—again full of conical cups. A huge number of similar cups, many of which have a hole in the bottom, have been collected from the different earthen floors of the courtyard. Most of the cups were found upside down.

In the northeastern niche of the courtyard was a thick, loose layer of ash that contained many conical cups and animal bones, mainly from young pigs, as well as sheep, goats, cows, a wild goat, a deer, and a dog (Tzedakis and Martlew 1999, 106: Mylona). Straight to the north, more ceremonial activities took place in another open area. In the southeastern corner, a ritual *bothros* came to light among different earthen floors full of conical cups like those found in the courtyard. A group of five rooms found farther to the north, all of them with sunken floors, contained an abundance of conical cups and cooking utensils. These rooms also have ground floors.

Strong ritual and cult elements are noted in the Daskaloyannis complex. Its particular architectural structure, in combination with its multiple pottery finds, suggests special ceremonies, some of which were probably successive instances of feasting (Andreadaki-Vlazaki in press a). The lustral basin may represent one

Figure 39.1. Daskaloyannis street. Part of the neopalatial building complex (from the south) (photograph by Maria Andreadaki-Vlazaki).

of the focal points of the complex since it can hold only a limited number of persons. On the contrary, the great hall, which ends at the platform, points to the gathering of many visitors. The platform hints at an open-air rite, and the west courtyard completes the picture. The Splantzia platform reminds us of the raised *loggia* of Malia. Similar structures were also uncovered in the central building in the Neopalatial settlement of Kastelli Pediados (Rethemiotakis 1992–1993, 44–45, plans 2 and 4).

Another elongated structure outside the Archanes complex has been interpreted as a similar exedra (Sakellarakis and Sapouna-Sakellaraki 1997, 79, plans 6, 7, 81, 145). Such platforms seem to be a common feature of open-air ritual scenes depicted on Neopalatial seals. In the rural sanctuary of Kato Syme in Viannos, the Neopalatial podium, surrounded by a drain, provides a ready parallel (Lebessi and Muhly 1990, 324–29, figure 3). During the final Minoan centuries and even the Classical period, the Splantzia area retains a ceremonial and sacred character, according to quite a few findings in huge pits dug there (Andreadaki-Vlazaki in press b).

Figure 39.2. The Master
Impression; Haghia
Aikaterini square (Khania
Archaeological Museum;
photograph by Ilias Iliadis).

Quite a few Neopalatial seal impressions with interesting cult scenes derive from Khania (Papapostolou 1977). Among them, the unique Master Impression was found (figure 39.2) in a pit in the Greek Swedish excavations among LM IB and II material (Hallager 1985; Andreadaki-Vlazaki 2005, 23–26, pl. III). The sealing represents a low hill by the sea, with a steep, rocky shore (i.e., a landscape identical to the topography of the Kastelli hill, where it was found). A fortified complex of multistory buildings crowned with horns of consecration occupies the hill and the surrounding plain. At the top of the central and higher wing, a male figure is holding a spear or staff in the gesture and position of a young Master. The fact that he stands among horns of consecration emphasizes the sacred character of the scene and reminds us of the Young God in the well-known LM III Kydonian seal stone (*PM* IV, 708, figure 532; Andreadaki-Vlazaki 2005, 23, pl. Vd).

Like most of the centers on the island, the settlement was destroyed suddenly in 1450 BC by an enormous fire. Some of the building sections were reused during the following LM II period. In those days, the name Kydonia was incised on one of the ten stelai bases of the funerary monument of Amenhotep III at Kom el-Hetan in Egypt, together with the names of various Cretan and Greek mainland cities. This epigraphic testimonium may reflect the itinerary of an official journey of the pharaonic court to the Aegean. Just by chance, a scarab with Amenhotep's cartouche was found in Kastelli (cf. Banou in Karetsou, Andreadaki-Vlazaki, and Papadakis 2000, 246; also Keel and Kavoulaki in ibid, 320, cat. no. 329).

During the Final Palatial period, Mycenaeans took Aegean commerce under control and incorporated Crete into their "koine." In Kydonia, the Mycenaean element seems to be stronger, and the 14th and 13th centuries represent the apex of the town's urban development. The beginning of the period witnessed a new building program; large constructions, organized in a different way, appeared (Hallager 1997). Khania evolved into a very important center with Mycenaean, Cypriot, Syro-Phoenician, Egyptian, and probably Italian imports. It also enjoyed close relations with the Argolid and Boeotia. The local pottery workshop, known as the "Kydonia workshop," developed into one of the predominant such places on the island. Its products, which are distinguished by the exceptionally high quality of the clay and slip, have been found at Rethymnon, Knossos, eastern Crete, and Patra and even in Cyprus and Sardinia. Representative of this workshop is the famous pyxis with a scene of a kithara player, found in a tomb in the area of Aptara (Tzedakis 1969, 1970; Kanta 1980, 288–89).

Kydonia seems to have been the center of an important overseas trade network in the LM III period, as it emerges from the study of a specific vase type, the inscribed stirrup jar. Outside Khania, such vases have been found at Rethymnon, Knossos, Thebes, Orchomenos, Mycenae, and Tiryns. It is noteworthy that the adjective *wa-na-ka-te-ro* was painted on the shoulder of some of the stirrup jars (Catling *et al.* 1980; Andreadaki-Vlazaki and Hallager 2007). Chemical analysis has revealed that 75% of these vases were made of clay from the Khania area and that they were used to transport aromatic oils or locally produced wine. This trade must partly explain the need for a literate bureaucracy.

The discovery during the Greek Swedish excavations of the first Linear B tablets, dating from LM IIIB early, was an event of major importance for the history of Khania (Hallager, Vlasakis, and Hallager 1992; Godart and Tzedakis 1995; Palaima 1995). These tablets point to a centralized administration and very probably to a palace structure. The first one (KH Sq 1) records ten pairs of wheels and recalls a tablet from Knossos that mentions chariots without wheels from or to Kydonia.

In the offering tablet KH Gq 5, amphorae with honey are being offered to Zeus and Dionysos in the shrine of Zeus (Dion). The occurrence of Dionysos on this tablet of undeniable religious context is conclusive proof that the god existed even in LM III Crete. His connection with Ariadne, Minos's daughter, cannot be just a coincidence. Besides, the Greek tradition presents Dionysos as a chthonic deity, the son of Zeus and Persephone, Dionysos-Zagreus. Furthermore, in classical Greece, honey was connected with chthonic rituals performed on the day of the dead during the Anthesteria, the old wine festival of Dionysos (Andreadaki-Vlazaki 2005, 25).

In the second tablet, KH Ar 4, a palimpsest, we read masculine proper names in connection with the cities in Crete *punaso* and *wato*. The most important thing on this tablet, which deals with the administration of personnel, is that the scribe's handwriting is similar to that of Knossian scribe 115 of an earlier date. This shows that the same scribal tradition existed in both cities.

The population of Kydonia probably included a number of nonnative people, according to the indications of both artifact types and skeletal material. Although the evidence concerning the prehistoric settlement in Khania covers the entire

Bronze Age, the evidence on the necropolis is limited almost exclusively to the LM IIIA and B phases. More than 170 tombs have been recovered to the east of the center, in a region that consists almost exclusively of soft limestone (Andreadaki-Vlazaki 1997). Most of these are chamber tombs, although there are quite a few pit caves, as well as a few pit graves and even shaft graves.

In 2004, part of the eastern cemetery was excavated and yielded unexpected finds. Just east of the Mazali plot, where Nikolaos Platon had found quite a few chamber tombs, fifty-four tombs came to light, dating mostly to LM IIIA (Andreadaki-Vlazaki in press b). These are pit caves and shaft graves mingled with chamber tombs. The most important tomb is the LM III A1 shaft grave of Mycenaean type, which contained an intact burial. Its pit is 3 m. deep. Stone walls have been built along the four sides in order to support the cover, which consisted of very thick, heavy stone slabs. This burial was protected from plunder because of the stones' great weight. The interment of a high-status warrior, a chieftain, was found intact, surrounded by bronze weapons and a bronze bowl. The most valuable find is the 80-cm-long sword of the 'horned' Ci type (Driessen and Macdonald 1984), with an ivory pommel, a gold ring below it, and gold-plated rivets. A precious seal stone with a female figure in a tree cult scene also accompanied the burial.

The pit caves consist of an elongated, rectangular trench up to 3.30 m. in depth, on one long side of which a cavity was dug, corresponding to the dimensions of the dead and blocked up by a rough stonewall. Only a single person was buried in the cave, which was never reused. Among these tombs, there are three double examples with the burial of a warrior and his companion, who always had only a miniature jug and a spindle whorl as grave gifts. The large groups of weapons were associated with only a few clay vases, mainly three-handled, piriform jars and squat alabastra. The pit cave is a tomb type very rare in Crete and without immediate forerunners, and only the Zapher Papoura cemetery near Knossos has yielded it (Evans 1906; Alberti 2004). On the Greek mainland, only a few examples are reported from Argolid and Attica. Since no direct prototype can be traced in Greece, some scholars suggest an eastern origin. The closest parallel seems to be cave tombs in Cyprus and the eastern Mediterranean area.

The earliest pit cave, dated to the beginning of the LM II phase, is a very impressive construction. Its pit is 3.30 m. deep, and the cavity, blocked by a double stone wall, contained the interment of another high-ranking warrior. Two big, three-handled jars and two more beaked jugs of exceptional decoration, a silver hair-dress, a bronze mirror, an ivory comb with relief decoration, a necklace with glass beads, and three precious seal stones accompanied the burial. His bronze armor consisted of an excellent long sword of the Ci type, two knives, and twenty-two arrowheads. Of special interest is a haematite seal with a unique representation of the Master of Animals (Andreadaki-Vlazaki 2005, 23–24, pl. Va).

Despite the time gap, this part of the burial ground has clear links with the mainland, particularly the Argolid, with regard to the shaft grave and pit cave tomb types, as well as the chamber tomb. It also looks very similar to the Zapher Papoura cemetery of Knossos, with its well-known warrior graves. We are able to say that the similarities between mainland, Knossian, and Kydonian cemeteries are undeniably close.

This recent find is crucial for the history of Khania and emphasizes the great importance and role of Kydonia in Mycenaean times as a Cretan center in a period of rapid, large-scale political and cultural changes in Crete. An interpretation that sees the warrior burials as representing officials of different ranks in the palatial military organization, drawn from different levels of society and of different origins (e.g., mercenaries) seems to be the most plausible explanation of the evidence.

By LM IIIA2 and IIIB, a period with obviously more regionalized polities on the island, the chamber tomb became increasingly common as the most convenient rock-cut tomb for multiple burials instead of single ones. The height of the dromos in front of the chamber entrance varies from 1.80 to 6.75m, and the doorway is always blocked by a rough stone wall. The dead were put on the floor of the chamber in a position determined by the available space. Wooden coffins and the removal of relics were common practices. The clay larnax burial, a major distinguishing feature of LM III Crete, is absent in Kydonia. Only a bathtub decorated with octopi has been found.

Most of the burials were accompanied by funerary gifts. There is a clear distinction between the LM IIIA1 and IIIA2/B pottery assemblages. The later burials are characterized by several types of vases, mostly products of the local Kydonian workshop. There are also some Mycenaean imports and part of a Canaanite amphora among them. The most common vase shape is the stirrup jar, which is usually decorated with an octopus with its tentacles suited to any kind of belly. The small stirrup jar is likely designed specifically for perfumed oil. Bronze utensils and weapons compose another interesting group of funerary gifts. Only one intact tomb contained a great accumulation of bronze, reminding us of the tomb of the Tripod Hearth at Zapher Papoura: a big amphora, two bucket-shaped vases, three bowls, two ladles, a tripod cauldron, two mirrors, two pairs of scales, a sword, two cleavers, knives, and a spearhead.

Jewelry is not absent. Nice necklaces of glass and faience have been found. Golden artifacts are rare. Among the representations on the seal stones, the hybrid beings are noteworthy (Andreadaki-Vlazaki 2005, 25, pl. IV f–h).

In an important chamber tomb of a high-ranking individual were revealed finely wrought pieces of ivory, such as heads of warriors with boar's tusk helmets, one of them *en face*, heraldically confronted lions, eight-shaped shields, columns with capitals, female figures carrying flowers, and lions attacking deer (Sakellarakis 1979; Poursat 1977; Andreadaki-Vlazaki in press b). These pieces were probably attached to a wooden box.

Until now, only a few skeletons from Kydonia have been studied (Hallager and McGeorge 1992). It seems that the average life span of women was 25.6 years, while for men it was 34.14 years. The average height of a male was 1.645 m, and for a woman, only 1.488 m. The women looked very fatigued. The rise in the death rate was due to pregnancy and childbirth; the low height was attributed to malnutrition and chronic ailments. The high infant death rate was a fact. As the studied skeletal sample comes from a group of tombs that appear to be inferior in comparison to the rest of the cemetery, another study is essential for more reliable conclusions. Dr. McGeorge has begun studying the skeletal material of the warriors' graves. With regard to pit and shaft graves, her initial results are different: These graves have yielded tall men and women, as well as robust men with traces of wounds on the bones.

The Minoan settlement of Kydonia was suddenly abandoned in the LM IIIC period, as were most of the other settlements in Crete. The causes of this abandonment are unknown. The various hypotheses advanced revolve around the internal weakening and decline of Minoan civilization, in combination with more general upheavals throughout the entire Eastern Mediterranean basin, with the appearance of the Sea Peoples and the destruction of the Hittite kingdom. It is worth stressing that the city of Khania was not destroyed but simply deserted. This is clear from the almost empty rooms and the complete absence of signs of destruction (Hallager and Hallager 2000).

BIBLIOGRAPHY

Alberti, Lucia. 2004. Οι νεκροπόλεις της Κνωσού κατά την υστερομινωική II–IIIA1 περίοδο. PhD diss., University of Athens.

Andreadaki-Vlazaki, Maria. 1993. "Υπόγειο άδυτο ή δεξαμενή καθαρμών στα Χανιά." AAA 1988 (1993): 56–76.

———. 1997. "La nécropole du Minoen Récent III de la ville de La Canée." In *La Crète mycénienne*, 487–509.

———. 2002. "Are We Approaching the Minoan Palace of Khania?" In *Monuments of Minos*, 157–66.

———. 2005. "Cultes et divinités dans la ville minoenne de La Canée." In ΚΡΗΣ ΤΕΧΝΙΤΗΣ, 17–28.

———. In press a. "Τελετουργικές αποθέσεις των νεοανακτορικών χρόνων στη Δυτική Κρήτη." In *Πεπραγμένα του Ι' Διεθνούς Κρητολογικού Συνεδρίου, Khania, October 1–8, 2006*.

———. In press b. "Το 'παλίμψηστον' της αρχαίας πόλης των Χανίων." In *Πεπραγμένα του Ι' Διεθνούς Κρητολογικού Συνεδρίου, Khania, October 1–8, 2006*.

———, and Erik Hallager. 2007. "New and Unpublished Linear A and Linear B Inscriptions from Khania." *Proceedings of the Danish Institute at Athens V*, Athens, 7–22.

Catling, Hector W., John F. Cherry, Richard E. Jones, and John T. Killen. 1980. "The Linear B Inscribed Stirrup Jars and West Crete." *BSA* 75: 49–113.

Chadwick, John, Louis Godart, John T. Killen, Jean-Pierre Olivier, Anna Sacconi, and Ioannis A. Sakellarakis. 1986. *Corpus of Mycenaean Inscriptions from Knossos*. New York: Incunabula Graeca 88.

Coldstream, Nicolas, J., and George L. Huxley, eds. 1972. *Kythera: Excavations and Studies*. London: Faber and Faber.

Driessen, Jan, and Colin Macdonald. 1984. "Some Military Aspects of the Aegean." *BSA* 79: 49–74.

Evans, Sir Arthur, J. 1906. *The Prehistoric Tombs of Knossos. Archaeologia* 49. London.

Godart, Louis, and Jean-Pierre Olivier. 1976–1985. *Recueil des inscriptions en Linéaire A.* 5 vols. Paris: Études crétoises 21.

Godart, Louis, and Yannis Tzedakis. 1992. *Témoignages archéologiques et épigraphiques en Crete occidentale du Néolithique au Minoen récent IIIB.* Rome: Incunabula Graeca 93.

———. 1995. "La chute de Cnossos, le royaume de Kydonia et le scribe 115." *BCH* 119: 27–33.

Hallager, Birgitta P., and Photini J. P. McGeorge. 1992. *Late Minoan III Burials at Khania: The Tombs, Finds, and Deceased in Odos Palama.* SIMA 93. Gothenburg: Åström.

Hallager, Erik. 1985. *The Master Impression: A Clay Sealing from the Greek-Swedish Excavations at Kastelli, Khania.* SIMA 69. Gothenburg: Åström.

———. 1996. *The Minoan Roundel and Other Sealed Documents in the Neopalatial Linear A Administration.* Aegaeum 14. Liège: Université de Liège.

———. 1997. "Architecture of the LM II/III Settlement in Khania." In *La Crète mycénienne,* 175–85.

———, and Birgitta P. Hallager, eds. 2000. *The Greek Swedish Excavations at the Agia Aikaterini Square Kastelli, Khania, 1970–1987: The LM IIIC Settlement.* 2 vols. Acta Instituti Atheniensis Regni Sueciae, Series in 4o, XLVII:II. Stockholm: Åström.

Hallager, Erik, Maria Vlasakis, and Birgitta P. Hallager. 1992. "New Linear B Tablets from Khania." *Kadmos* 31: 61–87.

Jantzen, Ulf. 1951. "Die spätminoische Nekropole von Kydonia." In *Forschungen auf Kreta 1942,* ed. Friedrich Matz, 72–81. Berlin: de Gruyter.

Kanta, Athanasia. 1980. *The Late Minoan III Period in Crete: A Survey of Sites, Pottery, and Their Distribution.* SIMA 58. Gothenburg: Åström.

Karetsou, Alexandra, Maria Andreadaki-Vlazaki, and Nikos Papadakis, eds. 2000. *Krete-Aigyptos: Politismikoi desmoi trion chilietion. Meletes.* Athens: Hypourgeio Politismou.

Lebessi, Angeliki, and Polymnia Muhly. 1990. "Aspects of Minoan Cult: Sacred Enclosures: The Evidence from the Syme Sanctuary (Crete)." *AA* 3: 315–36.

Palaima, Thomas G. 1995. "Ten Reasons Why KH 115 ≠ KN 115." *Minos* 27–28 (1992–1993): 261–81.

Papapostolou, Ioannis A. 1977. Τα σφραγίσματα των Χανίων. Συμβολή στη μελέτη της μινωικής σφραγιδογλυφίας. PhD diss., Aristotle University of Thessaloniki.

———, Louis Godart, and Jean-Pierre Olivier. 1976. *Η Γραμμική Α στο μινωικό αρχείο των Χανίων.* Rome: Incunabula Graeca LXII.

Poursat, Jean-Claude. 1977. *Les ivoires mycéniens: Essai sur la formation d'un art mycénien. Bibliothèques des Écoles françaises d'Athènes et de Rome* 230. Athens: Diffusion de Boccard.

Rethemiotakis, Giorgos. 1992–1993. "Το μινωικό 'κεντρικό κτίριο' στο Καστέλλι Πεδιάδας." ΑΔ 47–48. A: 29–64.

Sakellarakis, Ioannis. 1979. Το ελεφαντόδοντο και η κατεργασία του στα μυκηναϊκά χρόνια. Athens: Βιβλιοθήκη της εν Αθήναις Αρχαιολογικής Εταιρείας 93.

———, and Effie Sapouna-Sakellaraki. 1997. *Archanes: Minoan Crete in a New Light.* 2 vols. Athens: Ammos.

Tzedakis, Yannis. 1969. "L'atelier de céramique postpalatiale à Kydônia." *BCH* 93(I): 346–418.

———. 1970. "Μινωικός κιθαρωδός." *ΑΑΑ* 3: 111–12.

———, and Holley Martlew, eds. 1999. *Minoans and Mycenaeans: Flavours of Their Time. National Archaeological Museum 12 July–27 November 1999.* Athens: Greek Ministry of Culture, General Directorate of Antiquities.

CHAPTER 40

KNOSSOS

COLIN MACDONALD

KNOSSOS was the main prehistoric settlement of the island of Crete and is best known for its monumental palace, the so-called Palace of Minos (figure 40.1a–b). It lies in the north of the center part of the island, about 5 kilometers south of its ancient harbor town at Poros-Katsabas. The palace is 100 meters above sea level on one of the few *tells* of the prehistoric Aegean, the Kephala hill, first inhabited around 7000 BC, some four thousand years before the inception of the Bronze Age.

The earliest settlement of Knossos in the prepottery or Aceramic Neolithic may have been the earliest formal settlement in the whole of Crete. While new discoveries and a wide range of archaeological methods are helping to clarify and challenge our views of early human habitation on Crete, it is important to note that the earliest signs of human activity on the island are found precisely where the ceremonial center of Knossos, the palace, was later built. The Bronze Age palace itself was, among other things, both a monument to the ancient religious ceremonies that had taken place on this spot and an expression of the new authority that was in place, initially at the Knossian level and later at a regional and perhaps even an island-wide level.

The fact that five thousand years of tradition and history lay behind the foundation of the Bronze Age palace at Knossos may help to explain why this was the only site in Crete where occupation was never seriously interrupted by the destructions that periodically visited this and other sites. Only during the 14th century BC was the face of Bronze Age civilization changed, with the destruction of the palace at a time when mainland influence on Crete was strong.

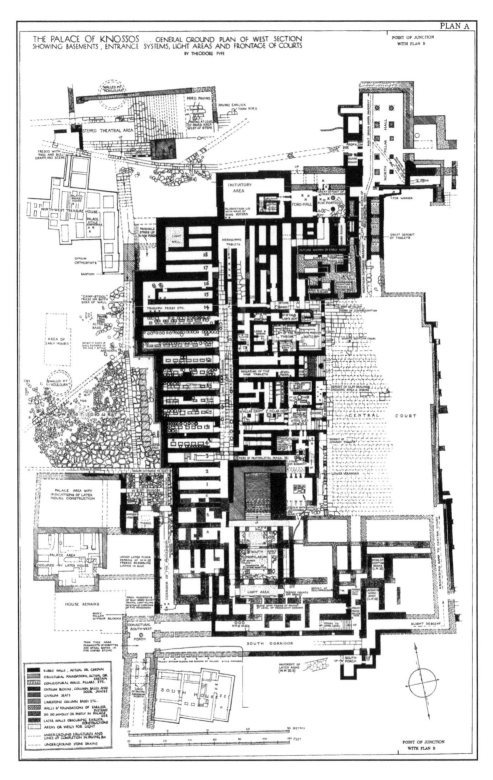

Figure 40.1a. General ground plan of the West Section of Knossos (from *The Palace of Minos* by Sir Arthur Evans, used by permission of Paterson Marsh Ltd. on behalf of the Sir Arthur Evans Trust).

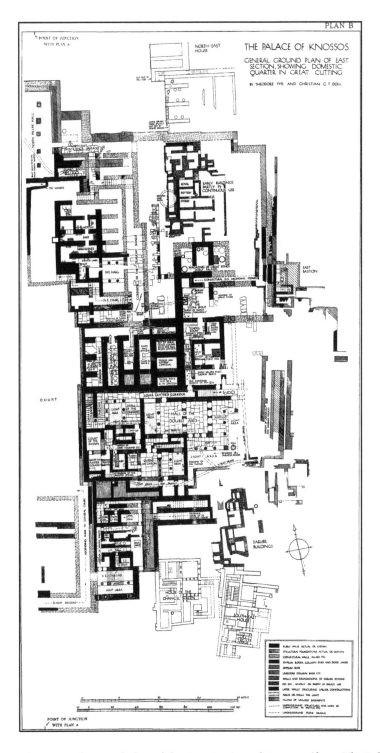

Figure 40.1b. General ground plan of the East Section of Knossos (from *The Palace of Minos* by Sir Arthur Evans, used by permission of Paterson Marsh Ltd. on behalf of the Sir Arthur Evans Trust).

The Neolithic and Early Bronze Age

There is no reason to imagine that the Neolithic population of Knossos was displaced by new, metal-using groups even if the arrival of some new people in Crete toward the end of the 4th millennium BC seems likely. Both the north-south orientation of houses in the area (mid- to late 4th millennium BC) later occupied by the Central Court of the Palace and the continuity of the burnishing ceramic tradition support a more gradual change from Neolithic to the Bronze Age than has usually been suggested. The large chalices of Early Minoan I, dark burnished to a finish approaching the finest Neolithic ceramics, have their origin both in the Final Neolithic of the 4th millennium BC and in contemporary EB I developments in the Cyclades and the north Aegean. Their use at Knossos, demonstrated particularly by their occurrence in an Early Minoan I well deposit, implies communal feasting activities on a large scale in the area where later the palace and its central court would be built.

Ceremonial activities for the community of Knossos certainly took place regularly on the Kephala hill during the 3rd millennium BC. The small, individual drinking cup, the footed goblet or eggcup, was introduced in the middle of the third millennium and continued to be the main drinking vessel at Knossos until the 19th century BC. Toward the end of the 3rd millennium BC or Early Minoan III, the first large-scale structure appears to have been built, although its character is unclear. It took the form of an impressive wall made of small, roughly worked blocks balanced by small stones in the interstices, which ran at least from the northwest corner of the later palace south, west, and south again to the level of the later Magazines XI/X, where it is lost east under the later walling. It may have been a platform of some kind for a building that dominated the hill. It is also possible that the so-called Early Keep or 'Prisons' date to this period, perhaps all together forming some form of complex with deep, underground storage facilities. Whatever the precise nature of this complex, it seems as though there was an attempt to build an impressive public building that overlooked one or more ceremonial areas and perhaps the northern approach from the sea. The building was not a palace in any sense of the word, and only its orientation and preservation by later builders implies any formal connection with later monumentality.

The Middle Bronze Age and the Construction of the Palace

The construction of the monumental Palace of Minos at Knossos in the later 20th and early 19th centuries BC and its subsequent development for almost five hundred years (some expansion; frequent repair and remodeling after destructive episodes) can be considered a crucial point of departure from the gradual processes of development until then evident on the island. Although there is currently a trend to diminish the importance of the construction of 'palaces' in Crete and to bolster the Early Bronze Age evidence for large-scale ceremonial activity in open areas that later became the palatial courts, with the construction of the palace, the modest, clan-based community completed its transformation to a hierarchical, urban society controlled by one or more elite groups.

There was clearly greater central organization of a range of activities, not least religious and ceremonial, facilitated by writing and sealing. To what extent the palace became deeply involved in broad economic control of the region cannot be ascertained from the few, and undeciphered, documents of Cretan Hieroglyphic. It may be that in the first couple of centuries, the palace relied on largely local contributions as the main, regional ceremonial center (labor to build it and produce to maintain its personnel and the ceremonial and ritual events it organized) rather than formal revenues through taxes and tribute. The latter was a role more appropriate for its final century when, due to mainland Mycenaean influence if not control, the Linear B script was used on clay tablets and sealings for detailed accounting of the arrival of goods from a wide geographical area.

Although there is by no means agreement on how much of the palace that is visible today was built in the first hundred years of what we call the Old Palace or Protopalatial Period, it seems that the area covered by the Old Palace was almost the same as that covered by the 'New.' It is for this reason that, although the bipartite division into Old and New Palace periods may work for sites on the rest of the island, not the least of which is Phaistos, at Knossos it is misleading because it gives the mistaken impression that one palace building gave way to or was replaced by another.

In fact, after the first palace was built during Middle Minoan IB–IIA or 1950–1800 BC, despite numerous destructive episodes, it was not replaced at any time by a 'new' structure, although important architectural innovations of the late 18th to the mid-17th centuries (Middle Minoan III) were adopted in reconstructed or newly built areas of the palace (e.g., the NW Portico and Initiatory Area, as well as the Domestic or Residential Quarter of the East Slope). By the 16th century, or Late Minoan IA, these Neopalatial architectural leitmotifs (e.g., the finest ashlar masonry, pier-and-door partitions) and arrangements (e.g., the Minoan hall and the lustral basin) had been adopted throughout much of the island and beyond (Akrotiri, Thera and Trianda, Rhodes).

Apart from the great Central Court, which may have been a largely open space even before the palace was built, one of the most impressive elements of the architecture of the early palace is the long west façade, with its orthostatic, gypsum blocks and indentations. Another striking feature will have been an upper story with windows overlooking the West Court and looking toward the Minoan town as it stretched west up the Acropolis Hill, where occupation is attested from around 2000 BC at a distance of some 370 m from the palace (Warren 1987, 53). Some would place this façade in Middle Minoan III or the 17th century BC, but my opinion is that it is a construction of MM IIA at the latest, with traces of an earlier façade beneath its north end (Macdonald and Knappett 2007, 170). Even if a later date is correct, what we see today would then be a rebuilding of the original façade in order to maintain continuity and a link with the past.

The entrance system of raised walkways was certainly in place by the 19th century, as were three large, circular, stone-lined pits called the *kouloures* in the area of the west court; a fourth was found in the Theatral Area where people from the town of Knossos would have approached the palace region along the so-called Royal Road, a public way that was first paved by the early 19th century BC or Middle Minoan IIA, if not a little earlier (Warren 1994, 201–202). The road and the other paved thoroughfares of Knossos leading to and around the palace area were major public works carried out under the aegis of the palatial administration and marked a great leap forward in urban organization compared with the Prepalatial era of the 3rd millennium BC. Similarly, the great stone-lined *kouloures* were public constructions that may have been for storage, perhaps for produce like grain, which was poured into them during a harvest festival of some kind. Those in the west court went out of use at the end of the 18th century BC or a little later (i.e., Middle Minoan IIB or IIIA) (MacGillivray 1998, 33), when storage space both within and outside the palace may have decreased.

Rather less is known of Protopalatial houses (MM IB–II) than those of the Neopalatial period (MM III–LM I) and later. However, excavation southwest of the palace has shown that major terracing of the hill in MM IB and MM IIA allowed modest rectangular dwellings and workshops to be built. Drainage systems were installed to serve houses northwest of the palace by the Royal Road as early as MM IB (Evans 1928, 368, figure 204), so it is no surprise that very well-built drainage systems are installed inside the palace (Domestic Quarter and North Entrance) by Middle Minoan III, if not earlier (Macdonald and Driessen 1988, 235–58). The terracing of the Kephala hill, on which the palace stood, combined with the creation of a road network serviced by drains, transformed the Early Bronze Age settlement into a well-organized urban center run by a palatial administration that bore more than a passing resemblance to towns and cities in the Near East.

As in the palaces of the Near East, interior storage was of great importance from the beginning. The serried ranks of oblong Magazines of the West Wing were in place during the Protopalatial period, even if the walls dividing them today are much later; other magazines nearby, perhaps of Middle Minoan IB date, have tall gypsum doorjambs carved with large, deeply cut mason's marks (*croix pommée*) but were cut off by later developments in the area of the East and West Pillar Rooms, whose gypsum pillars were adorned with carved 'double axes' belonging to the 17th century BC or Middle Minoan III, if not earlier.

Still more magazines and storage areas were located on the lower terraces of the East Slope, beneath spaces that later became the Court of the Stone Spout, the School Room, Room of the Stone Pier, and so on. How early storage in this area is attested is uncertain although it probably goes back to Middle Minoan II (19th/18th centuries BC); the latest storage jars or *pithoi*, including the aptly named 'Giant Pithoi,' are probably Middle Minoan IIIA in date or early 17th century BC (*pace*

Evans 1921, 231–34), but the *kalderim* or cobbled paving on which they were found probably dates back at least to Middle Minoan IIB.

Apart from storing food and drink for consumption by palace officials and workers on a daily basis, as well as at ceremonies, and keeping the ritual paraphernalia and feasting vessels used in these events (e.g., 'Early Magazine A,' Macdonald and Knappett 2007, 161–65, figure 164; 'Royal Pottery Stores,' Evans 1921, 240–47), the first palace had several other functions, including production (Cadogan 1987). In addition, some palatial workshops lay outside but close to the palace (e.g., soft-stone seal carving and a horn workshop in the Southwest Houses: Macdonald and Knappett 2007).

Weaving may have been an important industry, producing fine cloths and, no doubt, ships' sails; the Cretan melon-shaped loomweight for manufacturing special fabrics is first found inside the palace in the Loomweight Basement of the east slope (Evans 1921, 248–55) toward the end of the 18th century BC. It is of great interest that much later, when cloth became even more important within the Linear B palace economy of the late 15th and 14th centuries BC, this same, uniquely Cretan, shape of loomweight was still in use (unpublished Late Minoan II set of loomweights from the Southwest Houses excavated under the supervision of C. F. Macdonald in 1992–1993 and in 1996 with E. Hatzaki). Many of those who were involved in these industries could have lived within the palace itself or in its immediate environs and been supported by it.

We do not know whether those involved in more polluting industries, such as potting and metallurgy, were directly subject to and supported by the early palace, as they were under the later Linear B administration. However, there is no sign as yet of a large, possibly independent administrative and crafts quarter, like Quartier Mu at Malia. Indeed, it is possible to argue that the use of clay sealings in Middle Minoan IB and IIA contexts outside the palace indicates that the palace's physical boundaries did not mark the limits of its power and control.

From the very earliest days of the palace, when a monumental façade stood at the southwest corner of the highest terrace (Macdonald and Knappett 2007, plates 1–4), a store of cups, jugs, jars, and bowls was kept for use during a feast nearby, in the West or Central Courts or in a hall of the west wing. The composition of the Middle Minoan IB deposit indicates that whatever feast the pots were used in, there was a strong hierarchical element to the composition of the groups attending, where the small number of fine vessels corresponds to small numbers of elite members, and the finest eggshell goblet represents the head of the ceremony, if not the leader of Knossos itself. The deposit appears to have been stored for use in a patron-role feast, and we may be witnessing the institutionalization of a feast in which the palace authority or ruler is the patron and host of an event during which the relative levels of subordination within society of those attending are cemented by their roles and position at the feast. The three clay *noduli*, a counter, and twenty-three miniature vase tokens from the same store indicate that the form of the feast was very much under palatial control (Weingarten and Macdonald 2005; Macdonald and Knappett 2007, 161–64).

If some form of line or dynasty was instituted in Middle Minoan I, perhaps to build, certainly to run the palace, we should not assume that it continued uninterrupted until the end of the Neopalatial period (Late Minoan IB or mid-15th century BC). The end of the Protopalatial period might be considered an appropriate moment for a change in the ruling body at Knossos on the basis of numerous changes that take place about this time. One of the most obvious is the abandonment of the Hieroglyphic script in favor of Linear A, the script that had been in use in the south of the island at Phaistos in Middle Minoan II. However, the more we learn about the 17th century, or Middle Minoan III, this crucial period of change, the more we see a gradual transformation into the Neopalatial palace and city that is largely visible today.

The great Hieroglyphic Deposit (Evans 1921, 271–85), probably from a disturbed deposit beneath stairs that lead to the upper floor of the west wing from the north end of the Long Corridor, cannot be closely dated. However, because it appears fairly advanced compared with the scattered sealings and single tablet of earlier periods (MM IB–IIA), with new types of sealings—the document sealing or flat-based nodules and crescent-shaped sealings—it is usually placed in Middle Minoan IIIA. By Middle Minoan IIIB, Linear A is the script of choice and very widespread, implying that it had some time at Knossos to develop into a well-known and widely used script. Two large goblets with pinched bases, a Middle Minoan IIIA shape that harks back to the classic shape of drinking cup from Early Minoan II to Middle Minoan IIA, were painted with Linear A inscriptions (Evans 1921, 588, 613). Thus, two scripts were being used in the same broad period, although not precisely side by side. It may have taken some time to wean the traditional palace scribes and administrators away from Cretan Hieroglyphic. However, I am not sure that we can view the replacement of Cretan Hieroglyphic by Linear A as sudden, although it was decisive.

THE MIDDLE MINOAN III–LATE MINOAN I PALACE (C. 1700–1450 BC)

Whereas many other sites in Crete had suffered greatly from destructive events at the end of Middle Minoan IIB, Knossos may have suffered less and perhaps not in the same way. In Middle Minoan IIIA, Knossos does not show signs of large-scale architectural transformation, but it does enter a new era in other ways, some of which have already been mentioned.

For example, foreign trade takes off, marked by significant contact with Thera and the Dodecanese, as well as with the coast of Asia Minor. We do not yet understand why this occurred, but Middle Minoan IIIA can be considered the beginning of Knossian involvement in established and new networks of the south Aegean at a time when the other sites of Crete appear to have been recovering from the disasters of Middle Minoan IIB. This might also be the period when Knossos begins to dictate aspects of Cretan material culture and even dominate the island on some political level (Wiener 2007), highlighted at a regional level by the construction of a palace at Galatas in the Pediada during Middle Minoan III.

At Knossos, during Middle Minoan III, the most characteristic elements of the palace were laid out, even if some did not achieve their final form until Late Minoan I. Without going into the precise dating of each, some of the main features were the following:

The West Court, now larger due to the filling of the *kouloures*, divided the town to the west from the palace on the east. The palace's West Wing cast an early morning shadow over the court with its two stories, the upper walls of which were of plastered and painted mud brick with large windows. The entrance around the southwest, by the Corridor of the Procession Fresco, existed at this time, although the wall painting itself is probably a work of the later 15th century BC or Late Minoan II.

The entrance route could take the visitor through a large columned entrance porch called the South Propylaeum, a hubristic structure that was narrowed in Late Minoan I after an earthquake. The figures preserved in reproduction wall paintings, like the Cup-Bearer, belonged to the later Procession Fresco. Stairs led to the first floor and possibly top story of the West Wing. The main feature of the west side of the wing is the row of West Magazines, although their present dividing walls belong to a phase of repairs in Late Minoan II–IIIA since there is so much reused, broken ashlar masonry. The Long Corridor divides the West Wing and links its two sides.

On the east side, which borders the west of the Central Court, there are two important complexes, one dubbed the Central Palace Sanctuary (Panagiotaki 1999) and the other known as the Throne Room complex. The former includes the well-known East and West Pillar Rooms or Crypts, the Vat Room (with its deposit of Prepalatial and early Protopalatial objects), and the Temple Repositories, where the faience figures of the Snake Goddess and votaries were found. The arrangement of the spaces here—essentially a series of six squares—changed over time as the function also evolved. However, it appears that it at least remained an area for storing shrine paraphernalia over a long period since, once the Temple Repositories had gone out of use, a collection of stone vases, many of them religious rhyta of the finest quality, was stored in a room above and to one side of the East Pillar Crypt.

The Room of the Throne and the Lustral Basin, with its complex of preparatory ancillary rooms behind, is one of the most important areas of the palace and is directly linked with the Central Court by an antechamber. The present state of the room with the gypsum seat/throne and benches may date to the early 15th century or Late Minoan IB, as may the accompanying wall paintings of heraldic griffins and palms. However, the arrangement, which focuses on a Lustral Basin, goes back to Middle Minoan III, when there may also have been access via the area of three cists south of the antechamber through to the Central Palace Sanctuary. Ceremonies in the Central Court are likely to have been controlled from the west side of the palace, where so much emphasis has been laid on ritual.

The east side of the Central Court, like the west in Late Minoan I, may have been lined with a stoa of pillars or columns (Shaw 2002). One story would have been visible behind, although in the case of the Domestic Quarter, there were at least two more floors to reach ground level via the Grand Staircase. A great cutting was made into the side of the hill to accommodate the new quarter as early as Middle Minoan II. The Domestic Quarter of the 17th–15th centuries BC is a showcase of Minoan palatial architecture, from colonnaded staircases and lightwells to columned halls divided by pier-and-door partitions, and all were adorned with wall and sometimes floor paintings (Fish or Dolphin Fresco). This was Cretan Bronze Age living at its most elegant. There was also an element of rigid planning in the circulation pattern, perhaps going back to Middle Minoan IIB and IIIA, which allowed participants in a ceremony to split up at the bottom of the Grand Staircase and take part in different rites before meeting again in the great Hall of the Double Axes, probably for the culmination of the ritual.

The rest of the East Slope was given over to attractive courts and reception rooms (e.g., the Great East Hall, perhaps with relief frescoes and storage beneath in the Magazine of the Medallion Pithoi). To the north, an attractive North East Entrance was lined with fine ashlar masonry. From Middle Minoan III, a series of architectural modifications led to the creation of the North Entrance Passage, with its bastions and with the relief wall painting of a raging bull, one of the great animal icons of Knossos (figure 40.2). The wall painting has been dated anywhere between Middle Minoan IIIA and Late Minoan IB (late 18th to early 16th centuries B.C.); whatever its true date, wall paintings were of great importance at Knossos and eventually throughout Crete from Middle Minoan III to Late Minoan I and later. Some of the Knossian frescoes may have immortalized real ceremonies (e.g., the Miniature Frescoes, probably of Late Minoan I date and found just southwest of the Northern Entrance).

We know little of how the Second or New Palace was run since there are few deposits that contained documents of any kind. The palace had not yet reached the bureaucratic frenzy of Late Minoan IIIA, but goods stored and moved were recorded and sealed, and 'letters' were sent between Minoan centers (see Weingarten this volume). The nature of activities inside the palace may not have differed greatly in the Protopalatial and Neopalatial periods. There was, however, a marked change in the perceived quality of life, which was achieved through architectural and artistic developments that spread throughout the island and beyond and ultimately put flesh on 'Helladic' mainland material culture to allow the creation of 'Mycenaean.'

The town of Knossos was made up of a combination of modest houses and fine mansions, the largest of which was the Little Palace, about 300 meters west of the palace along the Royal Road. These town houses adopted many of the palatial architectural formulas, so much so that the closest parallel for the Little Palace is the Domestic Quarter of the palace. The general size of houses had increased greatly, and terracing on the slopes around the palace had been consolidated to create larger building platforms (e.g., area of the Southwest Houses). As in the Palace itself, the houses exude an impression of increased affluence; it may be important that most

Figure 40.2. The North Entrance Bastion and the reconstructed Throne Room area floors are visible from the Northeast Entrance (photograph by Colin Macdonald).

were built after the first phase of the expansion of Knossian interest abroad, perhaps as the benefits of this bold movement were reaped.

THE FINAL PALACE PERIOD (1450–1300 BC)

There may be some signs that the palace suffered destruction around 1450 BC (Late Minoan IB); some of the buildings in the town of Knossos were certainly burnt and never rebuilt. This was also the time of destructions throughout the island. Certainly, after 1450 BC Knossos looked different. Although many aspects of the following periods (Late Minoan II to IIIA) can be used to demonstrate a *floruit* in the arts and crafts, notably metalworking (see, e.g., Popham, Catling, and Catling 1974, 195–257), other aspects (e.g., architecture) give the impression of a period of decline. Astonishingly, no more limestone ashlar masonry was cut after the Late Minoan IB destructions that afflicted most of Crete, including Knossos. Gypsum was used extensively in Late Minoan II, as demonstrated, for example, by one of the unpublished Southwest Houses (S.VII), which reuses broken limestone ashlar in its walls, frames windows with gypsum, and also uses it for traditional pier-and-door partition jambs, unless these are reused from an earlier structure.

So too, in the palace, many rough walls were inserted to change circulatory patterns or to control access, although many of these were removed with little more than a nod by Sir Arthur Evans. Evans had stripped most of the palace down to its Middle Minoan III to Late Minoan I skeleton, so that its later plan is now difficult to reconstruct. In addition, there may well have been a great difference between the way the palace looked in Late Minoan II–IIIA1, when the great Palace-Style Jars were so prominently used, and the way it appeared in the last days of the Linear B administration in Late Minoan IIIA2, so well evoked by Mervyn Popham (1987, 297–99), with scribes working in both palatial halls in the west wing and on cramped landings in the domestic quarter.

The period following the Late Minoan IB destructions has been variously described as 'Mycenaean,' 'Monopalatial,' and 'Final Palatial'; the only one that is acceptable for Knossos is the last, yet it should be used only as a term of convenience rather than defining a 'Third' and Final palace. The controversy concerning the date of the final destruction of the Knossos palace (LM II, LM IIIA, or IIIB: e.g., Palmer and Boardman 1963; Popham 1970; Driessen 1990) has not been adequately resolved. A date toward the end of the 14th century (LM IIIA2) seems most likely, if certain deposits can be placed in an earlier phase, LM IIIA1, when palace-style jars were still in use. The date of the destruction of the Knossos palace is important since we need to know at what point this major economic center leaves the Mediterranean stage and lapses into a ceremonial twilight—destroyed but remembered. My own view is that a date for the final destruction of the Linear B palace around 1325–1300 BC would seem appropriate, just before the inception of Late Minoan IIIB pottery styles.

The most obvious change between Late Minoan I and Late Minoan II–III is that from 'Minoan' Linear A to the 'Mycenaean' Linear B script; the latter was not widely used in Crete, in contrast to Linear A, which is written on pots, metalwork, and ritual objects, as well as on tablets. The script is not so changed as is the language used for the economic records of the palace. The British architect Michael Ventris identified the language as Greek in 1952, thereby transforming Aegean Late Bronze Age studies (Chadwick 1976; also see J. Rutter [http://projectsx.dartmouth.edu/classics/history/bronze_age/lessons/bib/25bib.html#21] for a carefully devised bibliography of Linear B studies). However, there are also many aspects of continuity, so much so that we might even be tempted to put the 'Mycenaean Greek' language into the mouths of 'Minoans.' This particular aspect of cultural change needs more careful examination. The presence of mainlanders can be considered highly likely, but in what capacity we do not know.

The end of the palace, when it came, was accompanied by a fire that baked tablets and clay sealings, as most crashed to the ground from upper stories. The tablets document a rather frenetic final economic year but give no hint of the disaster to come. If earthquake was the cause, why did the Knossians not rebuild and repair as they had done countless times before? Other factors undoubtedly caused the abandonment of the palace as an institution that had lasted more than half a millennium.

POSTPALATIAL KNOSSOS (1300–1000 BC)

The 13th century at Knossos probably saw a reduction in occupation until around 1200, when a new settlement may have been founded. The inhabitants' activities were now so different from before that the archaeological layers are defined by a gray, ashy earth, as compared to the red-brown decayed mud brick of earlier centuries. The town flourished and had contacts outside Crete as far afield as Italy and Cyprus.

Inside the former palace area (Popham 1964), there is little evidence of activity in LM IIIB, a notable exception being the Shrine of the Double Axes (Evans 1928, 335–44), perhaps a shrine to serve any informal (i.e., nonpalatial) ceremonies that could still take place in the area of the old Central Court. However, we must admit that a notable amount of evidence from the palace area was lost or removed during the original excavations. Nearby, in the area of the southwest houses, the first activity after a major LM IIIB destruction is represented by an Early Protogeometric pit that dates to about 1000 BC, which was sunk to extract masonry from one of the houses (Coldstream and Macdonald 1997, 197, 203–204). The pit was backfilled with the debris removed from the destruction levels of the Late Minoan II house, including most of a magnificent palace-style jar, the significance of which these robbers will not have understood.

BIBLIOGRAPHY

Brown, Ann. 1994. *Arthur Evans and the Palace of Minos*. Oxford: Ashmolean Museum.

Cadogan, Gerald. 1987. "What Happened at the Old Palace of Knossos?" In *Function of the Minoan Palaces*, 71–73.

———, Eleni Hatzaki, and A. Vasilakis. 2004. *Knossos*.

Chadwick, J. 1967. *The Decipherment of Linear B*. 2nd ed. Cambridge: Cambridge University Press.

Coldstream, J. Nicolas, and Colin F. Macdonald. 1997. "Knossos: Area of South-west Houses, Early Hellenic Occupation." *BSA* 92: 191–245.

Driessen, Jan. 1990. *An Early Destruction in the Mycenaean Palace at Knossos: A New Interpretation of the Excavation Field-notes of the South-east Area of the West Wing*. Acta Archaeologica Lovaniensia, Monographiae 2. Leuven: Katholieke Universiteit Leuven.

———, and Colin F. Macdonald. 1997. *The Troubled Island: Crete before and after the Santorini Eruption*. Aegaeum 17. Liège: Université de Liège.

Driessen, Jan, Ilse Schoep, and Robert Laffineur. 2002. *Monuments of Minos*.

Evans, Arthur J. 1921–1936. *PM* I–IV and index.

Evely, Doniert G., Helen Hughes-Brock, and Nicoletta Momigliano, eds. 1994. *Knossos: A Labyrinth of History*.

Evely, Doniert G., Irene S. Lemos, and E. Susan Sherratt, eds. 1996. *Minotaur and Centaur: Studies in the Archaeology of Crete and Euboea Presented to Mervyn Popham*. BAR-IS 638. Oxford: Tempus Reparatum.

Graham, James W. 1969. *The Palaces of Minoan Crete*. Princeton: Princeton University Press.

Hägg, Robin, and Nanno Marinatos, eds. 1987. *Function of the Minoan Palaces*.

Hatzaki, Eleni. 2005. *Knossos: The Little Palace*. BSA Supplementary vol. 38. London: British School of Athens.

Hood, M. Sinclair F., and William Taylor. 1987. *The Bronze Age Palace at Knossos*. BSA Supplementary vol. 13. London: British School of Athens.

Macdonald, Colin F. 2002. "The Neopalatial Palaces of Knossos." In *Monuments of Minos*, 35–54.

———. 2005. *Knossos*. London: Folio Society.

———. 2007. "Knossos." In *Great Moments in Greek Archaeology* (in Greek and English). Athens: Capon.

———, and Jan Driessen. 1988. "The Drainage System of the Domestic Quarter in the Palace at Knossos." *BSA* 83: 235–58.

Macdonald, Colin F., and Carl J. Knappett. 2007. *Knossos: Protopalatial Deposits in Early Magazine A and the South-west Houses*. BSA Suppl. 41. London: British School at Athens.

MacGillivray, J. Alexander. 1998. *Knossos: Pottery Groups of the Old Palace Period*. BSA Studies 5. London: British School of Athens.

Momigliano, Nicoletta. 2007. *Knossos Pottery Handbook*.

Palmer, Leonard R., and John Boardman. 1963. *On the Knossos Tablets*. Oxford: Clarendon.

Panagiotaki, Marina. 1999. *The Central Palace Sanctuary at Knossos*. BSA Suppl. 31. London: British School at Athens.

Pendlebury, John D. S. 1954. *A Handbook to the Palace of Minos*. London: Parrish.

Popham, Mervyn R. 1964. *The Last Days of the Palace of Knossos*. SIMA 5. Lund: Åström.

———. 1970. *The Destruction of the Palace of Knossos*. SIMA 12. Gothenberg: Åström.

———, Elizabeth A. Catling, and Hector W. Catling. 1974. "Sellopoulo Tombs 3 and 4: Two Late Minoan Graves near Knossos." *BSA* 68: 195–258.

Raison, Jacques. 1969. *Le grand palais de Knossos: Répertoire photographique et bibliographique*. Incunabula Graeca 34. Rome: Ist. di Studi Micenei e Egeo Anatolici.

———. 1988. *Le palais du second millénnaire à Knossos*. Vol. 1, *Le Quartier nord*. Paris: L'École française d'Athène.

Shaw, Joseph W., and Arron Lowe. 2002. "The 'Lost' Portico at Knossos: The Central Court Revisited." *AJA* 106(4): 513–23.

Warren, Peter M. 1987. "The Genesis of the Minoan Palace." In *Function of the Minoan Palaces*, 47–56.

———. 1994. "The Minoan Roads of Knossos." In *Knossos: A Labyrinth of History*. Evely, Doniert G., Helen Hughes-Brock, and Nicoletta Momigliano, eds. 187–210.

Weingarten, Judith, and Colin F. Macdonald. 2005. "The Earliest Administrative Sealed Documents from Knossos (MM IB): Three Noduli in the So-called Early Magazine A." In *Studi in onore di Enrica Fiandra* ed. Massimo Perna, 393–404. Paris: De Boccard.

Wiener, Malcolm H. 2007. "Neopalatial Knossos: Rule and Role." In *Krinoi Kai Limenai*, 231–42.

CHAPTER 41

KOMMOS

JOSEPH SHAW

MARIA SHAW

LOCATION

The Minoan and Greek site of Kommos (figure 41.1) lies next to the Libyan Sea in south central Crete, along the western edge of the great Mesara Plain. It is almost due south of the inland Hagia Triadha site and is southwest of palatial Phaistos, which it apparently served as epineion during the Minoan period (Shaw and Shaw 1985, 2006). Kommos is due west of the modern town of Pitsidia and a few kilometers north of Matala, a port town of Greek and Roman Phaistos.

BRIEF HISTORY OF SETTLEMENT AND USE

Kommos was lightly settled as early as the Late Neolithic/Early Minoan period, especially on the sloping side of the small southernmost hills known as Tou Spanou Ta Kephalia ("the heads of the hairless one," a reference to its relatively bare profile during recent times). Like most Minoan sites, Kommos was mainly an agricultural community, with its inhabitants sustained by farming and herding but also by the sea. The settlement expanded during the prosperous Middle Minoan period, perhaps to 1.5 hectares. Resettlement and expansion followed, possibly after an earthquake, in MM III/LM I, perhaps to 3.5 hectares, followed by sporadic and somewhat casual use until the end of LM IIIB, ca. 1200 BC, when the site was deserted (J. Shaw 1996, 1–14, 379–400; 2002, 2006a–c). In about 1020 BC, locals established a small temple upon the Minoan ruins.

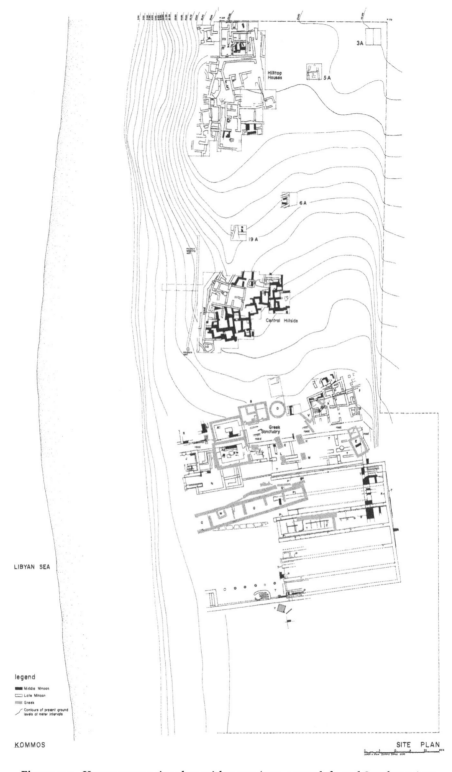

Figure 41.1. Kommos area site plan, with town (top, center left, and Southern Area (below) (by Giuliana Bianco).

THE MINOAN TOWN

A major topographical landmark at the site of Kommos is a slab-paved road that leads to the sea (figure 41.1, lower center, left ["road"]). It also divides the Minoan settlement into two parts: a town that sprawls north, up the slope of a hill, and the relatively flat area to its south, where a number of monumental buildings rose in succession over time, largely one atop the other.

As exposed in excavation, the maximum settled area of the town was perhaps 3.5 hectares. The pottery found shows it to have been settled as early as MM IB and to have continued into LM III, falling into decline by the later part of the latter period, especially in LM IIIB. This long history of occupation splits in two main parts, before and after MM III when, we believe, a destruction occurred, likely the result of an earthquake, necessitating major rebuilding.

Naturally, the period after the destruction is the one about which we are the best informed, at least architecturally, as the earlier buildings were generally overlain by the new ones. There is also the difference that, in the period preceding the seismic event, houses were not usually built with open spaces around them, as they were later. This makes it more difficult to speak of individual "houses," and, since it is a widespread phenomenon at other sites, it has led, in more recent literature, to the use of the term "household," shifting the emphasis to the inhabitants themselves—extended families occupied the same building over long periods of time (Wright 2007). The term is equally useful with reference to the Late Minoan houses, where the longevity of use by members of the same family still applies.

Volume 1, part 2 of the Kommos series (Shaw and Shaw 1996) concentrates on the area of the town, its roads, public spaces, and the houses. Contributing to the publication of the houses were often the very people who excavated them: Lucia F. Nixon, James C. Wright, John McEnroe, and Maria C. Shaw. Other members of the team contributed to the study of the finds (Shaw and Shaw 1996, chapter 4, 243–345), and there are chapters with general discussions by Maria C. Shaw, on the "Town Arrangement and Domestic Architecture" (345–77), and another by Joseph W. Shaw, on "Domestic Economy and Site Development" (379–400).

The pottery was published in separate volumes, split chronologically between Philip P. Betancourt (*Kommos*, vol. 2, 1990: down to and including the MM III period) and L. Vance Watrous (*Kommos*, vol. 3, 1992: on the Late Bronze Age). Foreign pottery was found throughout the site, including the town, though the higher concentrations were in the southern area of the site, both in the Civic Buildings and in what we labeled House X, which was built next to them. The location marks it as elite, though there may have been other houses that were eventually covered over by the buildings associated with the later Greek Sanctuary.

Of additional interest is that House X, compared to the other houses, yielded the most imports, including a Cypriot pithos. Yet, surprisingly, a kind of foreign pottery was found on the Hilltop and Hillside areas of the town that was not found there, the simple reason being that this kind of pottery, identified as coming from Sardinia (Watrous 1992, 163–68) came from LM IIIB levels, which were not always preserved in the more eroded southern area where House X was—a fact commented upon by Jeremy B. Rutter (*Kommos*, vol. 5, 2006, 674) in his recent publication of the pottery from the monumental buildings there.

With this broad review in mind, we can turn to specific aspects relating to the town: its topography, the architectural character of the houses, and the activities as implied both by architectural features and finds. With regard to town planning, we are aware of one main road that ran north to south, which we nicknamed the Rampa dal Mare. On the south, this road stopped nearly across from a major entrance into palatial Building T, and, in a parallel arrangement, another north-south road that ran alongside the east side of House X stopped right at an entrance located in T's northeast corner.

The majority of the houses in the town of Kommos belong to a category defined by McEnroe (1982) as Minoan *Type 3* Houses—a study that has now been widely accepted as a dependable model for gauging house status architecturally. Two houses, positioned along the Rampa dal Mare and nicknamed by us the "North House" and the "House with the Snake Tube," were of this type. They are among neither the humblest of Minoan houses nor the most sophisticated when compared with houses at some other sites, those at Knossos, Malia, Zakros, and Palaikastro, for instance.

House X at Kommos approximates a McEnroe *Type 2* house, the criteria for which include the numerous rooms, which vary in size, and a pillared portico (the range suggests a degree of specialization in space use). Like the North House, which is also among the better built of *Type 3* houses, House X was provided with two staircases, the smaller built in the innermost part of the house, allowing perhaps for privacy for some of its residents. Finally, and exceptionally in terms of the areas exposed at the site, House X was decorated with frescoes. The favored theme was landscape, including one of excellent quality depicting lilies.

There is evidence for household activities of a more ordinary type and evidence that goes somewhat beyond such a category. An example of the former is the food processing indicated by the many stone querns and mortars and the hand tools that were used to crush substances. Such tools and implements became the subject of a now classic study on the subject, written by Blitzer (1995, 403–535). Included in this category are stone presses (spouted slabs with a circular central depression). These were found set on built platforms and were evidently used to press grapes to produce wine or olives to produce oil. Another activity for which there is evidence at Kommos is weaving—loomweights and spindle whorls, which are the subject of a systematic study by Dabney (1996, 244–62).

More appealing to the needs of the mind and the spirit are objects like seals, one with a beautiful composition of two antithetical fish, another with a hybrid creature of a known type: half bird/half woman. The latter was found in what archaeologists usually refer to as a Household Shrine, in House X. Another cultic object, the so-called Snake Tube, was found in a house named after this find. These "shrines" occur at other Minoan sites during LM III and are often associated with times of decline.

This impression is reinforced at Kommos, for in both houses in which such "shrines" were found, there is evidence for a lack of initiative, at least as far as the

maintenance of the house is concerned. This is the time when houses were subdivided and when use shrank to fewer rooms. Oddly, at Kommos, this is also the time
of a flourishing international trade, contrasting with the decline on the domestic
front. One can only hypothesize that whoever ruled Kommos at that time did not
have the wellbeing of the local population in mind.

THE CIVIC OR SOUTHERN AREA

From as early as MM IIB, long after the settlement was founded, the lower, southern
part of the southernmost hillside and flatter shoreline adjoining it were chosen as
the site for special monumental construction, a tradition that was to last for hundreds of years.

The first phase may have begun with a building in the lower, flat area east of
the shoreline. Because of later successive construction, nothing of that building
remains, but a broad, paved walkway similar to those in the west courts of Minoan
palaces led up from the shore to where the building may have stood (figure 41.1, in
the central court at lower left, center).

The second phase, in MM IIB, began with excavation for a broad east-west
road cut into the hillside, beginning at the shoreline and extending at least sixty-
six meters to the east. At some further point, it probably became a track branching
off in different directions to inland settlements, especially those to the east and the
north. South of this road was then laid out a huge rectangular platform, for Building
AA, which was supported by walls retaining fill brought in from somewhere nearby.
Its eastern and southern walls were cleared during excavation; the northern was
obscured by later construction, while the western one has been washed away by the
sea. Although details of the overall plan of AA remain unknown, it probably featured a central court with a stoa bordering it along the south side and perhaps the
north (see J. Shaw 2006b for details).

In MM III, the beginning of the New Palaces Period in Crete, AA was replaced
by a new building, T. Like AA, T had the plan of a palace (built wings around a rectangular court), and its court measured 28.64 m. wide (east-west) by 39.10 m. long
(north-south). Six columns fronting stoas bordered it on the north and the south.
Both stoas and court were used for gatherings. There were two large wings on east
and west. The former featured long, corridor-like rooms that served for storage.
The western wing, now unfortunately partly destroyed by the sea, had two stories.
A large area of first-floor rooms no doubt served mariners and others arriving or
leaving by ship in the harbor area. The exterior walls of Building T are good examples of monumental ashlar masonry containing some of the largest blocks known in
Aegean Bronze Age architecture (J. Shaw 1983a). The impressive size of the building
and the few entrances found leading into it combine to suggest that security was
constantly in the builders' minds (Shaw and Shaw 2006, 845–78).

Figure 41.2. Restored LM III Building P, the ship sheds (by Joseph Shaw, Maria C. Shaw, and Giuliana Bianco).

Building T was to fall into ruin not long after it was built, perhaps because of a combination of destruction caused by nature (earthquake) and neglect resulting from shifting priorities in the governing power structure in the western Mesara. Parts of it were reused (e.g., J. Shaw et al. 2001). Then, during the Postpalatial period, in LM IIIA2, another large building, "P" (figure 41.2), was constructed above T's eastern wing, with a new plan but from materials reused from T. Building P was composed of six large galleries, each about six meters wide and forty meters long, with their open ends facing the shore. Earlier, much of T's western wing had already been destroyed by wave action brought about by a change in relative sea level (J. Shaw 2006b, 60n203; Gifford 1995, 78–79).

What was P's function? The excavators have proposed that its huge galleries functioned to store commercial and/or military ships of the local fleet during the winter, nonsailing months (M. Shaw 1985; Shaw and Shaw 1997, 1999, 2006, 845–78). Their argument is based on the positioning of the open galleries facing the sea and set back from the highest line of wave reach. Also, the very size of the galleries, without parallels on inland Minoan palatial sites, suggests that extremely large objects could have been stored safely within them—their side-by side plans also suggest storage. Especially pertinent is that in plan they parallel groups of Classical Greek ship sheds, which were about the same size and were also open toward the sea. In the latter case, they were set right next to the sea and built so that triremes and other warships could be winched up sloping ramps for storage and repair.

Recent events have increased the likelihood of the "ship shed" explanation. The first is the discovery in a harbor town of Knossos, at Katsamba, of a similar building of the same date with parallel galleries also set facing the sea (Whitley 2007, 109). The second is that quantities of hematite, found on the earthen floors of galleries in Kommos's Building P (Shaw and Shaw 2006, 78, 82, pl. 38d), can now be reasonably associated with the painting of the exteriors of the hulls of ancient (Roman) ships as a way to discourage marine organisms from attaching themselves to the hulls (Colombini et al. 2003, 661–62, 673). It is possible that this tradition, now also traceable back into the Classical Greek period (Blackman and Lentini 2006, 196), originated during the Bronze Age or perhaps even earlier.

A HARBOR TOWN: BRONZE AGE
KOMMOS AND THE SEA

During the Classical Greek era, "enclosed" harbors, formed by projecting head-lands, between which could be stretched ropes or chains, were preferred (J. Shaw 1990). Such harbors, often well sheltered from wave action, protected commercial and military ships from enemy attack by sea. During the Bronze Age in the Aegean, however, two harbor types were most frequented. The first was a peninsular site, with open harbors on either side offering a variety of approaches to sailing ships during windy weather, such as at Aghia Irene on Kea, or Knidos, or, probably, Akrotiri on Santorini (Shaw and Luton 2000; see also Doumas 2007). The second harbor type was on an open shoreline, sometimes partially sheltered by an offshore islet or island, as was Amnisos on Crete (Schäfer et al. 1992). Such was also the case with Kommos, on a north-south shoreline, with an islet (the "Priest's Slab" or Papadoplaka) a few hundred meters offshore. The town was set with its back to the prevailing northwest wind.

Because it was situated on the coast, Kommos may have had the disadvantage of being exposed to piratical raids. Its inhabitants had the advantage, however, of being able to harvest the wealth of the sea by fishing either from the shore or from numerous small oared or sailing boats that they could anchor off shore in good weather or pull up on shore when strong winds were blowing. Evidence for fishing activity lies in the numerous bronze fishhooks, barbed and unbarbed, often with flattened shank ends for line attachment, found in MM and LM houses (Blitzer 1995, pl. 8:85; J. Shaw 2006c).

In addition, the same terracotta loomweights used in the process of weaving functioned as weights to keep down the lower edges of nets suspended from floats (J. Shaw 2006c, 841n13; Dabney 1996, 2000). Water sieving of promising floor accumu-lations has provided the bones of fish consumed, from the commonest small shore-line fish (wrasse, bream, parrot fish) to the larger ones, such as groupers, which find shelter under projecting slabs and boulders, to large, deepwater schooling fish such as tuna, which frequent, then as now, the deeper waters out beyond the Paximadia islands, which can be seen some kilometers offshore (Rose 1995, 204–40).

Kommos was also situated so as to play a role in local and international trade. We can be confident that cargos such as metals bound for inland Cretan centers were unloaded there to be transshipped inland. In addition, agricultural and locally manufactured products were most likely sent abroad in exchange.

Our best evidence for networks of interchange (e.g., from Gavdos Island and from Knossos, both local Cretan) is the pottery discovered in the town houses and civic buildings, especially in Late Minoan contexts, where fragmentary vessels (but sometimes also complete pots) can be traced, because of their fabric, shape, or dec-oration, to Anatolia, Cyprus, Syria, Palestine, and Egypt and, for the LM IIIB period, to Sardinia to the west (Rutter 1999; Rutter and Van de Moortel 2006, esp. 630–88; Watrous 1985, 1989, 1992; Watrous, Day, and Jones 1998). While the pottery on most

Minoan sites is almost invariably local, that at Kommos represents numerous sites on Crete and elsewhere and constitute an ongoing study. The collection of international pottery from the Kommos site is greater than that recovered from any other Aegean site, mute witness to the frequency of commerce passing through during its long period of use. That many of the ships arriving there were of substantial size is suggested by the large anchors recovered (J. Shaw 1983b, 1995) and the size of the galleries (figure 41.2) in which at least some of the ships were most likely sheltered (mentioned earlier).

SOME SIGNIFICANT FEATURES OF THE KOMMOS EXCAVATION

When considered along with other Minoan settlements, Kommos becomes an informative example of a Minoan harbor town built next to a broad exposed shoreline, like Amnisos, Kato Zakros, and Palaikastro. Uniquely at this point, extensive evidence for Aegean maritime trade with Cyprus, Egypt, Syria, Asia Minor, Sardinia, and elsewhere reflects its historic role. During Old and New Palace Periods, Kommos featured a civic building with a huge central court, an architectural feature recognized in a number of major Minoan settlements. During the Postpalatial period, even though Kommian economic activity had slowed, a large building, P, with six galleries facing the coast, was built. It probably housed military and/or commercial ships during the winter, nonsailing months.

THE KOMMOS PUBLICATIONS

The extensive publication program for the site (mentioned earlier) ranges from preliminary reports that summarize progress to date, to articles that deal with some special aspect of discovery, to the final series of interrelated volumes, now completed. The last cover a broad spectrum of consideration, including area survey and site history, geomorphology and land use (Gifford 1995; Parsons 1995), modern and ancient fauna and flora (Reese 1995; Ruscillo 2006; Shay and Shay 1995, 2000), and Minoan domestic economy, as well as typological studies of artifactual remains (e.g., Blitzer 1995), especially pottery recovered during excavation of houses and civic buildings (e.g., Betancourt 1990; Watrous 1992; Rutter and Van de Moortel 2006). Volume IV in the series of volumes published by Princeton University Press focuses on the archaeological and epigraphical studies of the three superposed temples and associated buildings within the Greek Sanctuary, as well as the role they may have played in local cultural history. A separate monograph (J. Shaw 2006a) recounts some of the events and problems of the excavation.

Accompanying the material published in printed form is a digital archive presently available at https://tspace.library.utoronto.ca/handle/1807/3004. This contains many of the separate studies referred to here, as well as the volumes in the Kommos Princeton University Press series. In the same digital archive are many of the basic excavation records, in particular the excavation notebooks and trench reports from 1976 through 1995, as well as specialists' reports and interviews with Pitsidia elders about the recent history of the area. All of these can be used to learn more about the process of excavation and examination of the evidence as experienced by the excavators themselves. They have been made available through the University of Toronto's "T Space" program, designed to permanently preserve selected research project records.

BIBLIOGRAPHY

Betancourt, Philip. 1990. *Kommos II: The Final Neolithic through the Middle Minoan III Pottery*. Princeton: Princeton University Press.

———, Michael C. Nelson, and E. Hector Williams, eds. 2007. *Krinoi Kai Limenai*.

Bikai, Patricia. M. 2000. "The Phoenician Ceramics from the Greek Sanctuary." In *Kommos IV*, 302–21.

Blackman, David, and Maria Costanza Lentini. 2006. "An Ancient Greek Dockyard in Sicily." In *IKUWA2* (Second International Congress on Underwater Archaeology), 193–97.

Blitzer, Harriet. B. 1995. "Minoan Implements and Industries." In *Kommos I:1*, 403–535.

Callaghan, Peter J., Alan Johnston, John W. Hayes, and Richard Jones. 2000. "The Iron Age Pottery from Kommos." In *Kommos IV*, 210–335.

Colombini, M. P., G. Giachi, F. Modugno, Paola Pallecci, and E. Ribechini. 2003. "The Characterization of Paints and Waterproofing Materials from the Shipwrecks Found at the Archaeological Site of the Etruscan and Roman Harbor of Pisa (Italy)." *Archaeometry* 45: 659–74.

Csapo, Eric. 1991. "An International Community of Traders in Late 8th–7th c. B.C. Kommos in Southern Crete." *ZPE* 88: 211–16.

———. 1993. "A Postscript to 'An International Community of Traders in Late 8th–7th c. B.C. Kommos in Southern Crete.'" *ZPE* 96: 235–36.

———, Alan W. Johnston, and Daniel Geagan. 2000. "The Iron Age Inscriptions." In *Kommos IV*, 101–34.

Dabney, Mary K. 1996. "Catalogue of Miscellaneous Finds: Ceramic Loomweights and Spindle Whorls," "Jewellery and Seals," and "Lead Objects." In *Kommos I:2*, 244–70.

———. 2000. "Jewellery" and "Ceramic Loomweights and Spindle Whorls." In *Kommos IV*, 341–50 and 352–57, respectively.

Doumas, Christos. 2007. "Akrotiri, Thera: Some Additional Notes on Its Plan and Architecture." In *Krinoi kai Limenai*, 85–92.

Gifford, John. 1995. "The Physical Geology of the Western Mesara and Kommos." In *Kommos I:1*, 30–90.

Hayes, John W. 2000. "Roman Pottery from the Sanctuary," "Roman Lamps from the Sanctuary," and "Glass." In *Kommos IV*, 312–20, 320–30, and 336–40, respectively.

Johnston, Alan W. 1992. "Anfore laconiche a Kommos." In *Lakonikà: Ricerche e nuovi materiali di ceramica laconica*, ed. Paola Pelagatti, 115–16. Suppl. to *BdA* 64. Rome.

———. 1993. "Pottery from Archaic Building Q at Kommos." *Hesperia* 62: 339–82.

———. 2000. "Building Z at Kommos: An Eighth-century B.C. Pottery Sequence." *Hesperia* 69: 189–226.

———. 2005. "Kommos: Further Iron Age Pottery." *Hesperia* 74: 309–93.

———, and T. de Domingo. 1997. "Trade between Kommos, Crete, and East Greece: A Petrographic Study of Archaic Transport Amphorae." In *Archaeological Sciences 1995 (Proceedings of a Conference on the Application of Scientific Techniques to the Study of Archaeology, Liverpool, July 1995)*, ed. Anthony Sinclair et al., 62–68. Oxford: Oxbow.

McEnroe, John C. 1982. "A Typology of Minoan Neopalatial Houses," *AJA* 86: 3–19.

———. 1996. "The Central Hillside at Kommos: The Late Minoan Period." In *Kommos I:2*, 199–235.

Nixon, Lucia F. 1996. "The Oblique House and the Southeast Rooms." In *Kommos I:2*, 59–92.

Parsons, Michael. 1995. "Soil and Land Use Studies at Kommos." In *Kommos I:1*, 292–324.

Payne, Sebastian. 1995. "Appendix 5.1, The Small Mammals." In *Kommos I:1*, 278–91.

Prent, Mieke. 2005. *Cretan Sanctuaries and Cults: Continuity and Change from Late Minoan IIIC to the Archaic Period*. Leiden: Brill.

Reese, David. 1995. "The Minoan Fauna." In *Kommos I:1*, 163–291.

———, Mark J. Rose, and Deborah Ruscillo. 2000. "The Iron Age Fauna." In *Kommos IV*, 415–646.

Rose, Mark J. 1995. "The Fish Remains." In *Kommos I:1*, 204–40.

———. 2000. "The Fish Remains." In *Kommos IV*, 495–560.

Ruscillo, Deborah. 2006. "Faunal Remains and Murex Dye Production." In *Kommos V*, 776–840.

Rutter, Jeremy B. 1999. "Cretan External Relations during LM IIIA2–B (ca. 1370–1200 B.C.): A View from the Mesara," in *Point Iria Wreck*, 139–86.

———. 2000. "The Short-necked Amphora of the Post-palatial Mesara." In *Eighth International Cretological Congress, Herakleion 9–14 September 1996*, 177–88. Athens: University of Crete.

———. 2004. "Ceramic Sets in Context: One Dimension of Food Preparation and Consumption in a Minoan Palatial Setting." In *Food, Cuisine, and Society in Prehistoric Greece*, ed. Paul Halstead and John C. Barrett, 63–89. Sheffield Studies in Aegean Archaeology 5. Oxford: Oxbow.

———. 2006. "Southwestern Anatolian Pottery from Late Minoan Crete: Evidence for Direct Contacts between Arzawa and Keftiu?" In *Pottery and Society: The Impact of Recent Studies in Minoan Pottery: Gold Medal Colloquium in Honor of Philip P. Betancourt, 104th Annual Meeting of the Archaeological Institute of America, New Orleans, Louisiana, 5 January 2003*, ed. Malcolm H. Wiener et al., 138–53. Boston: Archaeological Institute of America.

———, and Aleydis Van de Moortel. 2006. "Minoan Pottery from the Southern Area." In *Kommos V*, 261–715.

Schäfer, Jörg S., Stylianos Alexiou, Philip Brize, Angelos Chaniotis, Wolfgang Helck, Stefan Hiller, Paul Knoblauch, Wolf-Dietrich Niemeier, Ekaterini Stefanakis, and Veit

Stürmer. 1992. *Amnisos nach den archäologischen, historischen, und epigraphischen Zeugnissen des Altertums und der Neuzeit.* Berlin: Mann.

Shaw, Joseph W. 1983a. "The Development of Minoan Orthostates." *AJA* 87: 213–16.

———. 1983b. "Stone Weight Anchors from Kommos, Crete." *IJNA* 12: 91–100.

———. 1987. "A 'Palatial' Stoa at Kommos." In *Function of the Minoan Palaces*, 101–109.

———. 1989. "Phoenicians in Southern Crete." *AJA* 93: 165–83.

———. 1990. "Bronze Age Aegean Harborsides." In *TAW III*, 420–36.

———. 1991. "North American Archaeological Work in Crete (1880-1990)." *Expedition* 32: 5–14.

———. 1995. "Two Three-holed Stone Anchors from Kommos, Crete: Their Context, Type, and Origin." *IJNA* 24: 279–91.

———. 1996. "Introduction to the Kommos Site" and "Domestic Economy and Site Development." In *Kommos I:2*, 1–14 and 379–400, respectively.

———. 1998. "Kommos in Southern Crete: An Aegean Barometer for East-west Interconnections." In *Cyprus-Dodecanese-Crete*, 13–27.

———. 1999. "A Tale of Three Bases: New Criteria for Dating Minoan Architectural Features." In *Meletemata*, 761–67.

———. 2000. "The Architecture of the Temples and Other Buildings," "Sanctuary Furnishings," "Bronze and Iron Nails," "Stone Implements," and "Ritual and Development in the Greek Sanctuary." In *Kommos IV*, 1–100, 358–63, 373–86, 386–91, and 669–731, respectively.

———. 2002. "The Minoan Palatial Establishment at Kommos: An Anatomy of Its History, Function, and Interconnections." In *Monuments of Minos*, 99–110.

———. 2003. "Palatial Proportions: A Study of the Relative Proportions between Minoan Palaces and Their Settlements." In *METRON*, 239–45.

———. 2004. "Kommos: The Sea-Gate to Southern Crete." In *Crete beyond the Palaces: Proceedings of the Crete 2000 Conference*, ed. Leslie Preston Day, Margaret S. Mook, and James D. Muhly, 43–52. Prehistory Monographs 10. Philadelphia: INSTAP Academic Press.

———. 2006a. *Kommos: A Minoan Harbor Town and Greek Sanctuary in Southern Crete.* Princeton: Princeton University Press.

———. 2006b. "The Architecture and Stratigraphy of the Civic Buildings." In *Kommos V*, 1–116.

———. 2006c. "The History and Functions of the Minoan Buildings at Kommos." In *Kommos V*, 845–78.

Shaw, Joseph W., and Deborah Harlan. 2000. "Bronze and Iron Tools and Weapons." In *Kommos IV*, 363–73.

Shaw, Joseph W., and Marjatta Luton. 2000. "The Foreshore at Akrotiri." In *Wall Paintings of Thera*, 453–66.

Shaw, Joseph W., and Maria C. Shaw, eds. 1985. *A Great Minoan Triangle in Southcentral Crete: Kommos, Hagia Triadha, Phaistos.* Scripta Mediterranea VI. Toronto: Benben.

———. 1993. "Excavations at Kommos (Crete) 1991–1992." *Hesperia* 62: 129–90.

———, eds. 1995. *Kommos I, The Kommos Region and Houses of the Minoan Town, Part 1, The Kommos Region, Ecology, and the Minoan Industries.* Princeton: Princeton University Press.

———, eds. 1996. *Kommos I, The Kommos Region and Houses of the Minoan Town, Part 2, The Houses of the Minoan Town.* Princeton: Princeton University Press.

———. 1997. "Mycenaean Kommos." In *La Crète mycénienne*, 423–34.

———. 1999. "A Proposal for Bronze Age Aegean Ship-sheds in Crete." In *5th International Symposium on Ship Construction in Antiquity*, ed. Harry Tzalas, 369–82. Tropis V. Athens: Hellenic Institute for the Preservation of Nautical Tradition.

————, eds. 2000a. *Kommos IV, The Greek Sanctuary*. Princeton: Princeton University Press.

————. 2000b. "Κομμος. Ἡ Θέση του στην προιστορική και την ιστορική εποχή." In *H Μεσαρά μέσα από τα μνημεία της. First Archaeological Meeting of the Mesara, 5, 6, 7 September 1996*, ed. A. Vasilakis, 64–110. Athens.

————, eds. 2006. *Kommos V, The Monumental Minoan Buildings*. Princeton: American School of Classical Studies.

————. Forthcoming. *Kommos House X: A Minoan Mansion near the Sea*. Philadelphia.

Shaw, Joseph W., Aleydis Van de Moortel, Peter Day, and Vassilis Kilikoglou. 2001. *A [sic] LM IA Ceramic Kiln in South-central Crete: Function and Pottery Production*. Hesperia Suppl. 30. Princeton: American School of Classical Studies in Athens.

Shaw, Maria C. 1981. "Sir Arthur Evans at Kommos: A Cretan Village Remembers Its Past." *Expedition* 23: 4–12.

————. 1983. "Two Cups with Incised Decoration from Kommos, Crete." *AJA* 87: 443–52.

————. 1985. "Late Minoan I Building J/T, and Late Minoan III Buildings N and P at Kommos: Their Nature and Possible Uses as Residences, Palaces, and/or Emporia." In *A Great Minoan Triangle in Southcentral Crete: Kommos, Hagia Triadha, Phaistos*, ed. Joseph W. Shaw and Maria C. Shaw, 19–30. *Scripta Mediterranea VI*. Toronto: Benben.

————. 1987. "A Bronze Figurine of a Man from the Sanctuary at Kommos, Crete." In *Eilapine: Festschrift for Professor N. Platon*, 371–82. Herakleion, Crete.

————. 1990. "Late Minoan Hearths and Ovens at Kommos, Crete." In *L'habitat égéen préhistorique*, 231–54.

————. 1996. "The North House and Peripheral Areas," "The Southern Cliffside," and "The House with the Press." In *Kommos I:2*, 15–59, 92–105, and 105–38, respectively.

————. 1999. "A Bronze Age Enigma: The 'U-shaped' Motif in Aegean Architectural Representations." In *Meletemata*, 769–79.

————. 2000. "The Sculpture from the Sanctuary." In *Kommos IV*, 135–209.

————. 2004. "Religion at Minoan Kommos." In *Crete beyond the Palaces: Proceedings of the Crete 2000 Conference*, ed. Leslie Preston Day, Margaret S. Mook, and James D. Muhly, 137–52. Prehistory Monographs 10. Philadelphia: INSTAP Academic Press.

————. 2006. "Plasters from the Monumental Minoan Buildings: Evidence for Painted Decoration, Architectural Appearance, and Archaeological Event." In *Kommos V*, 117–260.

Shay, C. Thomas, and Jennifer M. Shay. 1995. "The Modern Flora and Plant Remains from Bronze Age Deposits at Kommos." In *Kommos I:1*, 91–162.

————. 2000. "The Charcoal and Seeds from Iron Age Kommos." In *Kommos IV*, 647–68.

Watrous, L. Vance. 1985. "Late Bronze Age Kommos: Imported Pottery as Evidence for Foreign Contact." In *A Great Minoan Triangle in Southcentral Crete: Kommos, Hagia Triadha, Phaistos*, ed. Joseph W. Shaw and Maria C. Shaw, 7–11. *Scripta Mediterranea VI*. Toronto: Benben.

————. 1989. "A Preliminary Report on Imported 'Italian' Wares from the Late Bronze Age Site of Kommos on Crete." *SMEA XXVII*: 69–79.

————. 1992. *Kommos III: The Late Bronze Age Pottery*. Princeton: Princeton University Press.

————, Peter M. Day, and Richard Jones. 1998. "The Sardinian Pottery from the Late Bronze Age Site of Kommos in Crete: Description, Chemical, and Petrographic Analyses and Historical Context." In *Sardinian and Aegean Chronology*, ed. Miriam Balmuth and Robert Tykot, 337–40. Studies in Sardinian Archaeology V. Oxford: Oxbow.

Watrous, L. Vance, Despoina Hadzi-Vallianou, and Harriet Blitzer. 2004. *The Plain of Phaistos: Cycles of Social Complexity in the Mesara Region of Crete. Monumenta*

Archaeologica 23. Los Angeles: Cotsen Institute of Archaeology, University of California at Los Angeles.

Whitley, James. 2007. "Archaeology in Greece." *AR* 2007: 1–122.

Wright, J. C. 1996. "The Central Hillside at Kommos: The Middle Minoan Period." In *Kommos I:2*, 140–99.

———. 2007. "Modelling Domesticity." In *Krinoi Kai Limenai*, 263–70.

CHAPTER 42

....

MALIA

....

JAN DRIESSEN

IT is unfortunate that, despite its size and the scale of the archaeological investigation, we still do not know the ancient name of the site of Malia. Some suggestions have included *setoija*—mentioned in the Knossian Linear B tablets—and Milatos, a place name assumed to have later moved eastward.

Located in a fertile, terra rossa coastal valley a few hours by foot from the main Minoan site of Knossos and majestically encircled by the Selena mountains, Malia (figure 42.1) is a type site for Minoan archaeology for several reasons. Not only was it abandoned at the end of the Bronze Age and hence its ruins were less affected by later occupation (as is the case at Knossos and Phaistos, for example), but it has also been more thoroughly excavated and documented than other Cretan sites. Its main contribution to Minoan archaeology concerns its Middle Bronze Age remains, which are exceptionally rich and well preserved.

The site was discovered in 1915 by S. Xanthoudides (Effenterre and Tzedakis 1977), who grasped the size of the operation and invited the French School at Athens to continue his work from 1920 onward, which it has done ever since with an impressive series of monographs published as *Études crétoises*. Several general works and guides have also been published (Poursat 1988, 1992; Effenterre 1980; Pelon, Andersen, and Schmid 1992).

In more recent years, collaboration between the dynamic local archaeological service and the French School at Athens, backed by European funding, has made Malia into a showcase for effective heritage conservation and new ways of presenting archaeological remains to the public, with the construction of a series of roofs that leave the ruins free and integrate relatively well in the landscape (Schmid 1990).

It is not impossible that the Malia area was already inhabited during the Early Neolithic period. It would have been attractive for Neolithic communities, and cores taken in the marsh to the northwest of the palace show the presence of possible

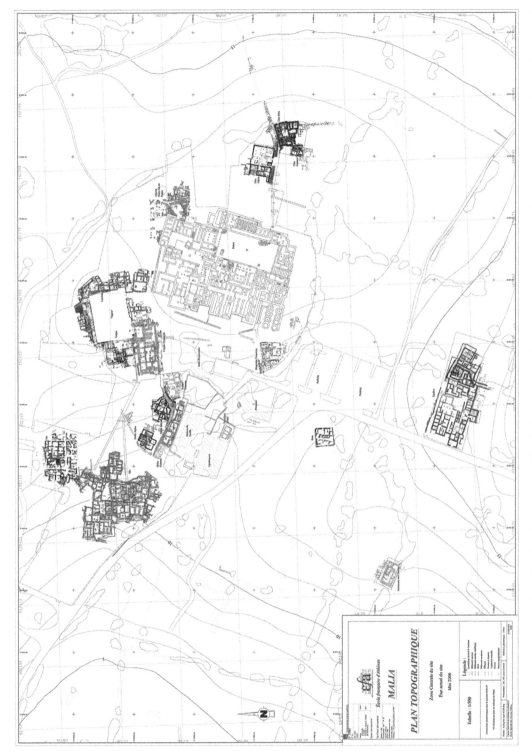

Figure 42.1. Site plan of Malia (courtesy of L'École française d'Athènes; plan no. 37863, © EfA/C. Prenez and G. Clement).

domesticated wheat from at least the 7th millennium BC onward (Dalongeville et al. 2001; Tomkins in press).

At present, Late Neolithic sherds are extremely scarce (Effenterre 1980, 83, 85, figure 107) and of uncertain provenance, but this may be more a result of intensive agricultural practices. Late Neolithic occupation has been identified by survey on the south slope of the Arkovouno hill, east of Malia (Müller 1998, 549).

So far, nothing substantial has been found on the Malia site itself before EM IIA. Sherds, usually incised, polished gray and black but sometimes painted (Agios Onouphrios, Koumasa style), and isolated walls of this period have been identified beneath the Central Court of the later palace and the area immediately north and northeast (*Abords Nord-Est*, henceforth ANE), west of the so-called Agora, around the Hypostyle Crypt and near Quartier Mu (Pelon 1986, 33; Effenterre 1980, 28, figure 38; Karantzali 1996, 56; Poursat and Darcque 1990; Farnoux 1990b). A fragmentary Koumasa figurine was also collected in the West Wing of the palace (Effenterre 1980, 87, figure 112). Note that, apart from the palace and some major buildings that have received specific names, excavated areas at Malia are usually identified by a Greek letter, as is the case with Quartier Mu.

From this evidence, one may deduce that a small village occupied what was to become the core of the palatial site, a low (14 m above sea level) hill with good views of the surrounding area, perhaps close to a series of natural waterholes situated to the northeast and south of the later palace (Müller 1990, 1991). Incidentally, sherds of this period were also collected on the Kefali hill at Sissi, 4 km east, and it is possible that a small settlement—recognized by Hood, Warren, and Cadogan during their travels in the early 1960s but now destroyed—may have existed east of the hill.

From EM IIB onward, things were rapidly changing, and surprising architectural remains have been encountered beneath the later palace. It seems very likely that some of the walls in the later West Magazines (I1) were already constructed at this time—a foundation deposit, including Vasiliki pottery, was placed within them (Driessen 2007, 84, figure 6)—and these would be incorporated within the later Middle Minoan and Late Minoan I rebuildings. Beneath the later Hypostyle Hall (IX2), north of the later Central Court, a series of rooms with more or less the same orientation as the later palace was laid out. From these rooms come a clay sealing and a gold bead (Pelon 1986, 1993; Pelon and Hue 1992). More important, one can argue that both the Central and West Courts existed even at this time (Driessen 2007, 83–86).

To the northwest of the palace, west of the court dubbed the 'Agora,' further EM IIB remains were found in connection with a small obsidian-working area. The presence of large chunks of obsidian in earlier levels in the north part of the later palace may imply that other workshops existed and that part of Malia's later success was related to its Cycladic connections, for which there is no evidence later. South of the agora, remains of a series of badly preserved Prepalatial rooms destroyed by fire were excavated. In addition, flush with the West Court of the palace, a small building with three rooms was cleared, and in them, Vasiliki sherds were found.

A complete jar in Vasiliki style was also found in an earlier level of house Db (Effenterre 1980, plate VII), and EM IIB was also identified in ANE. Soundings here and there have produced more EM IIB sherds, which suggests a settlement of about 2.58 ha. during this period. The survey has identified at least one other large EM site on the south slope of the Arkovouno close to the Malia-Sissi road, one hundred meters west of the earlier Neolithic site (Müller 1998, 549). In addition, the now destroyed settlement northeast of the Kefali hill of Sissi continued to be occupied.

Moreover, it has been argued that some of the Vasiliki ware found at Malia was imported from the Mirabello area, while some was made of clays locally exploited in the Sissi area (Pelon and Schmitt 2003). All of this clearly suggests that the site of the later palace was already significant from this early phase onward, with an open court served by several buildings especially for storage and provision for particular feasts and rituals (Driessen 2007, 90–92). The implication is that Malia by now served as a regional center for different communities in the area, including at Arkovouno and Sissi.

There seems to be a clear break between EM IIB and EM III. This is suggested not only by the presence of large quantities of EM IIB sherds in leveling layers for subsequent constructions (e.g., area V in the palace; cf. Pelon and Schmitt 2003) but also by a series of new areas that are now built upon. Pure EM III deposits are, however, still very rare (Poursat 1988, 65n8), so the EM III phase is still hard to pin down at present—although the ossuaries (charnier I) seems to have been inaugurated during this phase, as shown by a series of vases in dark on light, as well as a fine human-shaped rhyton in the same style from charnier II (Demargne 1945; Baurain 1987).

A series of soundings by Pelon (1983, 1989) suggests that the first monumentalizing activity of the building that would eventually develop into a canonical palace dates to the EM III–MM IA phase, but there is an ongoing discussion among archaeologists digging at Malia on the chronology of the different deposits (for a review see Poursat and Knappett 2005, 193–94). A foundation deposit formed by a Patrikiès-style teapot within a stone box in room IV7 (Pelon 1986) highlights the importance of this construction. Pelon (1980, 1983) has found remains of the EM III–MM IA building in many rooms, allowing a reconstruction of the general outline of its plan (cf. Schoep 2002, figure 5).

This building would remain unscathed until a violent destruction at the end of MM II (Pelon 2005, 190). Schoep (2002, 2007) has argued for a relatively modest architectural embellishment of this building but disregards the cut sideropetra blocks that characterize the earliest remains in the northwest quarter of the palace (Area V) and the reuse of such blocks within the later structure (Driessen 2007, 76n8). Sideropetra, a hard gray limestone, was much harder to cut than the sandstone used in the somewhat later Quartier Mu and Hypostyle Crypt or the Neopalatial palace.

The same limestone occurs reused in the Chrysolakkos building, the so-called royal burial building north of the site (Shaw 1973). Excavations have shown that an earlier monumental construction existed on the spot, and it has been only partly recovered beneath the eastern portico. The quality of the plan and architectural details of this earlier building contrast with what is known from elsewhere on the site, and, in general, its organization resembles that of the MM II hypostyle crypt with large, plastered rooms accessible via steps. There is nothing in this building that suggests a funerary function. The reused limestone orthostates in the later, Protopalatial Chrysolakkos building may come from this earlier building, if not from another construction. The first phase of the palace would be a good candidate because of the similar stones that still exist within the building and the uncertainty as to the original appearance of the first façade walls.

It is, furthermore, a possibility that at least part of this settlement was protected by an enclosure wall, identified to the east of Quartier Zeta and in isolated spots to the northeast and northwest, but its line cannot be followed everywhere, so it may never have been completely finished. Charniers I, II, and III were especially used during this period (EM III/M IA), but inverted pithoi with skeletons were also used as a burial method and were found in many other areas north of the site (Treuil 2005, 216). Mirabello imports continue during this phase. At Sissi, a small house tomb cemetery and a settlement with a large building on top of the Kefali hill seem to have been used from this period onward, also suggestive of a break between this period and the previous. It has been suggested that the success of the Malia settlement during EM III–MM IA was in fact the result of a voluntary *synoikismos* between the local inhabitants and those coming from the Arkovouno site (Müller 1997; Driessen 2001).

The houses south of the palace, accepted to date to MM IA/B, contrast with the regularity of the palace building and later Protopalatial constructions (Chapouthier and Demargne 1962, 13–17, and for the area to the west see Chevallier, Detournay, and Dupré 1975). The excavators distinguished between at least three houses (A, B, C) partly on the basis of fixed hearths of a type that is rather common during the Middle and early Late Bronze Age on the site, but the agglutinative plan is surprising. The remains ran beneath the later Neopalatial palace and are no longer visible. Further remains of this phase were found in Block Gamma and perhaps in the House on the Beach. It is likely that, when the town rapidly expanded during the following MM II phase, some earlier constructions were simply leveled since there seems not to have been a destruction before the end of MM II.

Despite claims that the Chrysolakkos building survived into MM II (Stürmer 1993), it may have been abandoned earlier—in MM IB (Poursat 1993, 607), implying that its reconstruction would date to the same phase or to the end of the previous one, MM IA. With its size (1156 m²), it would be one of the largest Protopalatial buildings. Although located close to the funerary zones, the nature of the Chrysolakkos building is under discussion. Human remains were few—one long bone and two skulls—and may belong to later interments made when the building was already in ruins (Treuil 2005, 214). Remains of objects of personal adornment— and half a dozen small gold pieces, including a pendant with two wasps (as well as the Aegina treasure, according to some) (Effenterre 1980, plates III, XV–XVI) were found here—and these are rare in nonfunerary contexts, but the architectural plan and elaboration, a more or less square platform building with portico, does not find ready comparison with contemporary funerary architecture.

At present MM IIA remains elusive, and, as Poursat and Knappett (2005) have shown, there is little means at present for subdividing MM II at Malia. Poursat (1988; Poursat and Knappett 2005, 194) has identified an MM IB layer—distinct from EM III–MM IA on the one hand and MM II, as represented by the Mu destruction layer, on the other—beneath Quartier Mu. Most of the palace walls, however, stayed in use during this MM IB–II phase, when the settlement expanded enormously, up to 40 or 60 hectares as has been suggested, perhaps at this stage forming the largest Middle Bronze Age settlement on the island of Crete (Whitelaw 1983, 339; Müller 1996, 1236; 1997, 52; 1998, 548, 552). It is unlikely that the occupied area was as continuously and densely occupied as its center.

The clearest sign for urbanization, apart from the buildings and courts, is the presence of a series of raised walks in sandstone slabs that crisscross the paved courts and follow some of the streets at specific locations (Driessen 2009). Indeed, taking into account the score, scale, and quality of public or semiofficial buildings on the site, a case can be made that Malia had approached statelike status with a fully integrated settlement hierarchy of several levels. Moreover, the Malia survey, which covered about 40 km², located about eighty Protopalatial sites, often situated in three almost concentric circles around the palatial settlement (Müller 1990, 1991, 1992, 1996, 1997, 1998).

Imports—whether Cretan or foreign—are more common in this period than in any other phase of the settlement's history, and Malia products, especially seal stones, are widely distributed over central Crete (Poursat and Papatsarouha 2000). Knappett (1997, 1999) has shown to what extent the tableware found at Myrtos Pyrgos (III) on the south coast resembles that found in Quartier Mu, thereby indicating that the elites of both sites may have been in close contact and perhaps even part of the same social group.

Affinities also exist with sites on the highland plateau of Lassithi, as well as with the Mirabello area, and some have recognized a Malia state during this phase (Cadogan 1990; Betancourt 2007). Several authors (Schoep 2002, 2004) have stressed the dynamic creativity of the elites at Malia, but very little progress has been made with regard to the political and social structure of the settlement during this early period.

The precise nature of the Protopalatial palace is not altogether clear because of the shallowness of stratification and the scale of the Neopalatial rebuilding. The East Magazines already existed, and large areas of the Protopalatial building, not rebuilt on afterward, have been cleared in the northwest part of the palace. These seem especially to consist of magazines and workrooms with plaster floors and connect well with those found close to the Neopalatial polythyron of the palace proper (area III), where two fine swords—one decorated with an acrobat on its gold pommel—were discovered on the plaster floor (Chapouthier 1938; Pelon 1982, 1983, 2005, 186). A polychrome fruit stand, an ivory figurine, a stone vase, and Chamaizi juglets, one of which carried a Cretan-Hieroglyphic inscription, were also found here. Some other administrative documents of this phase were found elsewhere in the palace. In the east part of the West Wing (area VI), more weapons were found, including a sword with an originally gold-plated, rock crystal pommel (Charbonneaux 1925; Pelon 2005, 189–90). Some of the West Magazines also existed during this phase, and the north side of the Central Court was already occupied by a Hypostyle Hall (IX2) (Pelon and Hue 1992; Pelon 1993). It has been suggested that the east façade of the West Wing was preceded, at least in part, by a portico.

Apart from the palace, a series of other important buildings belong to this phase, and pride of place should be given to Quartier Mu. Established in either late MM IB or early MM II, often on top of an EM III–MM I fill (Poursat and Darcque 1990, 908), Quartier Mu is remarkable for its degree of conservation, its architectural elaboration, the quantity of its finds, and the quality of its publications. The excavations of Mu have provided an extraordinary freeze-frame of the life within a sector of the Minoan town at the close of the MM II period. Among other finds, the excavations have yielded a surprising number of fine and coarse wares, stone vases, Cretan-Hieroglyphic clay administrative documents, seal stones (illustrating a real *chaîne opératoire* of seal stone production), bronze objects, stone tools, and so on (Detournay, Poursat, and Vandenabeele 1980; Godart and Olivier 1978; Poursat 1996). Among the 1,500 restorable vases and 10,000 catalogued pottery sherds, different local fabrics and many imports from the south coast, the Mesara, and the Mirabello area have been identified (Poursat and Knappett 2005), with tableware usually in local fabrics and transport and larger vases (pithoi, amphorae) often imported.

Building A of Quartier Mu was built first, and the other main building, B, was added later, when a number of workshops/houses were also constructed around the original complex, at which point the entrance was modified. Administration in Cretan-Hieroglyphic and textile production clearly took place on the upper floor. The two large buildings exhibit differences in architectural embellishment and functional organization, but the excavator, Jean-Claude Poursat, prefers to see all of the buildings that constitute Quartier Mu as interdependent, with Building A as its main center and the other buildings as dependent storage areas and workshops. Both buildings would have been under the control of a single individual (Poursat and Knappett 2005). Among the workshops/houses, at least one potter's workshop, a seal cutter's workshop, and a metal founder's workshop have been identified. It is not clear whether the extensive remains of the same period found to the north, beneath Quartier Nu, belong to the same or another similar complex (Schoep and Knappett 2003).

Of the other Protopalatial complexes, the Agora, the Hypostyle Crypt, the Dessenne Storage Area, and the Sanctuary of the Horns may be discussed briefly. The Agora is a court of ca. 30 by 40 m., partly lined with *aspropetra* orthostates, constructed in MM IB or MM II; it may have stayed in use until LM III (Effenterre and Effenterre 1969; Effenterre 1980, 191). No later construction was ever built on top of it. It was, from the beginning onward, surrounded by a series of public and domestic buildings. Some of these continued to be used in LM I and even later (Lambda quarter), whereas others were destroyed in MM II and replaced by later constructions. Some have interpreted the Agora as a meeting place, while others view it as an arena for bull games (Effenterre 1974; Graham 1974).

To the south of this court is located the Hypostyle Crypt (Amouretti 1970), an enigmatic, semiunderground building with ashlar walls, accessible via a series of steps, and perhaps used for some kind of (ritual) gathering because of the presence of benches. During MM II, it also comprised a series of spacious magazines, as well as a hall and a lightwell. It was partly reused in the Neopalatial period, at which time evidence for its earlier function was removed.

The so-called Dessenne Storage Building, southwest of the palace and located alongside one of its paved walks, consists of a series of large storage areas in which many pithoi were found. It has been suggested that, instead of a large storage complex, the complex would be formed by two individual houses (Treuil 1999). Another possible MM II construction is the Horn Sanctuary (*sanctuaire aux cornes*), which surprises observers because of its two orthostate walls with plastered horns on top. A fragment of a fresco that shows a red bucranium on a white and blue background may represent one of the earliest figurative frescos on the island. However, no other finds have been made that could confirm the cult function, in contrast with another building, now no longer visible, which contained ritual vases and has been identified as an independent sanctuary of the same period (Poursat 1966).

Within Block Epsilon, an MM II domestic structure (Epsilon beta) includes an exceptional example of a painted plaster floor (Daux 1965, 1000; 1966, 1015).

The fire that destroyed Quartier Mu was probably the same one that affected, at least partly, the Agora area, the Hypostyle Crypt, the Dessenne Storage Building, and some independent shrines, as well as other less well-preserved house remains that were often later incorporated into Neopalatial constructions. Pelon (2005, 189) argues for an earthquake destruction in the palace. The subsequent Neopalatial settlement seems smaller and more confined to the area around the palace.

The first, MM III, phase of the Neopalatial period remains elusive since few secure deposits can be attributed to this phase, apart perhaps from a pure MM III fill found in sounding 32, west of Building B of Quartier Mu (Poursat and Darcque 1990, 911). Some of the vases first dated to LM IA may now perhaps better be assigned to MM IIIB, such as those published by Hazzidakis (*PraktArchEt* 1915: 124–25, pl. 9) and the earlier destruction layer found in the Hypostyle Hall (Pelon and Hue 1992, 23; Pelon 2005, 191).

Apart from certain parts of the earlier building that may have been patched up, remains of this phase are rare, and it is not impossible that the palace building was never completed, thereby explaining the scarcity of deposits. Substantial walls, said to be MM III, were found in the northwest part of the palace and immediately north of the silos in the south wing, perhaps indicating the north and south façades of this chimerical building (Pelon in Poursat et al. 1983, 701–703, figure 22; Pelon in Poursat et al. 1984, 884–87; Poursat 1988, 75). An entrance may have led into the MM III palace from the west, where a raised walk abuts, but this was later blocked by the

LM IA rebuilding. Also, in ANE and close to the tourist pavilion, some MM III pottery was identified, but no associated architecture.

One of the most surprising buildings of the Neopalatial phase on the site is Block Epsilon, whose size (3000 m²) and architectural embellishment (ashlar, frescoes, lightwells, lustral basin) contrast with the other buildings of the same phase, even with the palace (Bradfer-Burdet 2005). Initially constructed in MM III, it was modified on several occasions, suffered minor destructions, and was eventually abandoned in LM IIIB. Did it replace the palace for a period while the latter was being reconstructed?

That the new palace was constructed late in MM IIIB or early in LM IA seems clear from a series of tests (Daux 1965, 1004; Pelon 1989, 1980, 64–65) and a foundation deposit in room IV:3 (Pelon 1986, 19; Poursat 1988, 75). This new building uses much ammouda or sandstone ashlar in its western façades and other areas but not in its eastern façade, although it was also looking out over a large court. Most of the architectural remains visible in the palace would date to this phase (Chapouthier and Demargne 1942, 1962; Chapouthier and Joly 1936).

It is also obvious that the LM I palace underwent several modifications (Driessen and Macdonald 1997, 182–86, for a detailed account), including the reduction in size of the Central Court, the blocking of the Long Corridor, and so on. These modifications may have been made following minor earthquake tremors (Pelon 1980, 55; Effenterre 1980, 377–78), perhaps connected with the Santorini eruption (Driessen and Macdonald 1997, 186).

In general, the final destruction level of the palace is somewhat surprising partly because of the scarcity of finds, the paucity of frescoes (although some examples have been noted; cf. Pelon 1980, 18), and the almost entire absence of administrative documents, despite the destruction by fire, of which many traces have been found. The early excavators suggested that, since many rooms were found empty, pillaging had preceded this fiery destruction (cited in Pelon 2005, 191n58). A finely carved leopard mace and a stone rhyton in the shape of a triton with a decoration of genii (Pelon 2005, 194; Baurain and Darcque 1983) likely come from the destruction level of the palace. Both objects may have been hidden and hence escaped pillaging. Objects that can stylistically be dated to LM IB (or early LM II) from the palace are rare: a flat, globular stirrup jar with marine decoration from room XIV2 and some vases from Magazine XXVII4, as well as an Ephyraean goblet fragment and some sherds from around the north court (Pelon 2005, 195) (i.e., close to the area where, after the destruction of the palace, the so-called Oblique Building would be constructed). It is hence perhaps more likely that the palace was destroyed earlier, late in LM IA or early in LM IB.

The main entrance to the palace at this time was probably from the north side, but several other entrances exist, perhaps each implying a specific category of visitors or users of the complex. In contrast with the palaces of Knossos, Phaistos, and Zakros, where the Minoan hall is located in the east wing, at Malia it is situated to the northwest, perhaps looking out over gardens on top of the Protopalatial remains. A north court—where, after the LM I destruction, the Oblique Building would be constructed—forms a buffer zone before the Central Court. North of the latter is the hypostyle hall with a staircase next to it, probably leading to an official reception room with columns on the upper floor.

It has been noted that the Central Courts of the Neopalatial palaces at Knossos and Malia were of almost identical original dimensions, surely indicating the fixed and ritualized nature underlying their use. The court at Malia was relaid half a dozen times, and it is the LM IA level made of Sissi earth that still shows today. The regular patches of paving at some discrete places within the court have not yet received satisfactory explanation. There is a very hard spherical stone in the northwest corner, usually identified as a baetyl, as shown in Minoan iconography, and in the center of the court are the remains of a small pillared structure, interpreted as a sacrificial hearth (Pelon 2002).

Both the east and the west wing have batteries of parallel storage rooms. The west wing comprises a series of spaces that are surprising because of their elaboration: the so-called Loggia, interpreted as a special, elevated area for admiring the various events taking place in the central court, a pillar crypt with two square pillars carrying a series of mason's marks, and a large, columnar hall, similar to that at Zakros and obviously meant to entertain larger groups. Southwest of the court is located the famous *pierre à cupules* (XVI:1), an object likely used for specific ritual or cult activities.

In the southwest wing was one of the few rooms—strangely enough accessible only from outside the palace—which still yielded objects during excavation (XVIII:1), including a small altar with incised signs, two terracotta feet, and other cult paraphernalia (Pelon 1980, 213–18; Effenterre 1980, 337). A nearby room held a deposit of stone vases, some unfinished (XVII:2). The south wing probably also contained a series of workshops and service areas.

Outside the palace, to the southwest, a series of circular structures was excavated, usually interpreted as grain silos, perhaps having a capacity of as much as 4,000 hectoliters (Pelon 1980, 222). A number of paved courts surround the palace, and many paved roads serve the town. Although the system was Protopalatial, it may have largely been maintained during the Neopalatial period, although it was encroached upon in different places (Blocks Epsilon, Zeta, Delta). Most of the excavated areas have shown traces of occupation during the Neopalatial period (Villa A, Block Nu), but there are also some good examples that illustrate the standard of living of the period.

In Block Delta, House Da, for example, preserved a Minoan Hall, as well as a lustral basin and one of the best-preserved Minoan stone toilets, which was connected to a waste system outside. Destroyed by fire probably late in LM IA, it included a few seal stones, figurines, a lead ring, and a bronze double ax among its finds. House Db, originally a Protopalatial construction, was reused and modified in LM IA, only to be destroyed by fire during this same period. In it were found a fine stone lamp and a lid depicting a bird, pithoi, a large bronze basin, and a fair number of bronze tools.

East of the palace, three houses in the Zêta Quarter were excavated (Za, Zb, Zγ), and all three seem to have been destroyed in LM IB. House Za consists of two wings that seem to show a more public part (with a Minoan Hall and a lustral basin) to the west and storerooms and living areas to the east. Much pottery comes from these last rooms, including a Marine Style alabastron. House Zb also contains a Minoan Hall, a slightly sunken lustral basin, and a hearth in its central room. The building preserved many finds, including pottery (two Marine Style vases), seal stones, loomweights, bronze tools, a large collection of obsidian, and a stone sphinx. House Zγ also yielded a large collection of bronze tools and weapons.

As mentioned, Block Epsilon, built in MM III, was considerably modified during LM I to include a series of spacious halls, lightwells, and a lustral basin and was embellished with ashlar and frescoes. The reoccupation of the building makes it difficult to determine which parts of the complex were destroyed in LM IA, LM IB, or later. The building also yielded much pottery, many stone vases, seal stones, and a series of bronze daggers. House Ea is a simpler construction and seems to have gone out of use as early as LM IA. To the northeast of the site, close to the Agia Varvara bay, a modest LM I building was excavated, perhaps a simple farm (Pelon 1966).

Funerary evidence for this period is scanty, although Charniers II and III were also used in MM III–LM IA on a limited scale (Treuil 2005). The survey around Malia has shown that the number of sites dropped considerably from the Protopalatial to the Neopalatial period, even if some of the sites grew larger. There is an obvious loss of integration where settlement hierarchy is concerned, and it has been suggested that the Malia (and Phaistos) polity was henceforth demoted to a secondary settlement, with Knossos remaining the single primary settlement in the center of the island (Driessen 2001).

Precisely what happened during LM II–IIIA1 at Malia is not yet clear, nor do we know for certain whether the traces of occupation that have been identified represent continuity or reoccupation by other groups (Farnoux 1997). Traces of mixed LM IB–LM II deposits exist in blocks Epsilon and Nu, and some isolated material comes from elsewhere, including the north court of the palace, where the Oblique Building, which is usually interpreted as an independent shrine, was constructed with recovered blocks amid the cleared ruins (Pelon 1997). Poursat has come upon what may be a pure LM II deposit west of Quartier Mu in sounding 28 (Poursat and Darcque 1990, 910). Politically, Malia (with Sissi, where LM II pottery has also been identified) may have remained within Knossian control since most of its pottery seems imported.

The next phase, LM IIIA1–early2, is attested only by sherds and isolated vases, especially from blocks Nu and Epsilon (Farnoux 1997). It is likely that the site suffered yet another destruction, since Quartier nu was built entirely on top of redeposited destruction material of this phase before an entirely new complex was laid out. The nature of the destruction is not clear, but it is obvious that, when Quartier nu was reconstructed in the following LM IIIA2–B, phase, Knossian influences diminished and local customs reemerged.

This is, at least at first sight, a relatively prosperous phase for the settlement, with several isolated nodes of habitation within and around the ruined landscape of the Neopalatial town. Malia is no longer an urbanized site but seems simply a collection of individual farmsteads. The survey has identified such farmsteads at different places, and, within the previous urban zone, reoccupation occurred in Quartier lambda, east of the Agora, and in the east part of Quartier epsilon (Pelon 1967, 508–11; 1970, 115–17). It has been suggested that these were occupied by clans composed of different families (Driessen and Fiasse in press). A seal impression comes from this area.

Quartier nu is formed by a large complex (750 m²) made up of four or five habitation units around a small central court, perhaps an attempt to recreate a Neopalatial past. Beneath the southern portico of this court was found a pebble mosaic showing lozenges, spirals, and diagonal lines, the earliest example of this kind of floor treatment known (Driessen and Farnoux 1990, 1994). On top of the mosaic was found a large (1 m high) terracotta house model with three or four windows and two cylindrical chimneys.

East of the complex was a kitchen with a skeleton, perhaps an earthquake victim. The different units each have a main columnar room with a hearth. In most of the rooms large pottery deposits were preserved, especially amphorae, kylikes, pyxides, and stirrup jars, of which several were inscribed with short Linear B texts (Farnoux and Driessen 1991). A clay sealing and a large terracotta female figurine, as well as many stone and bronze objects, were recovered (Farnoux 1990a, 1991; Driessen and Farnoux 1994). One of the pits found to the southwest of the complex may have been used to deposit the remains of ritual feasts. Whereas the west wing was obviously destroyed by earthquake, the east wing burned down.

Tombs of this LM IIIA2/B phase—especially cist graves, it appears (Treuil 2005, 218)—have been identified at several places to the north of the site, as well as near Malia, where a finely painted clay sarcophagus decorated with a double ax was found near the Agios Dimitrios church.

After the destruction around the middle of LM IIIB, the Malia site seems to have been abandoned, although the Kefali hill at Sissi seems to continue to be occupied until the end of the LM IIIB period. The LM IIIC occupation is limited to upland sites. The survey has identified Late Geometric sherds north of the palace site and Archaic sites elsewhere in the plain. During the Roman period, occupation seems again to have increased. The site itself seems also to have been occupied on a limited scale in the 14th century AD.

BIBLIOGRAPHY

Amouretti, Marie-Claire. 1970. *Fouilles exécutées à Mallia: Le centre politique.* Vol. 2, *Études crétoises* 18. Paris/Limoges: École française d'Athènes-Bontemps.
Baurain, Claude. 1987. "Les nécropoles de Malia." In *Thanatos*, 61–72.
———, and Pascal Darcque. 1983. "Un triton en pierre à Malia." *BCH* 107: 3–73.
Betancourt, Philip P. 2007. "Lasithi and the Malia-Lasithi State." In *Krinoi kai Limenes: Studies in Honor of Joseph and Maria Shaw*, ed. Philip P. Betancourt, Michael C. Nelson, and Hector Williams, 209–19. Philadelphia: INSTAP Academic Press.

Bradfer-Burdet, Isabelle. 2005. "Une kouloura dans le 'petit palais' de Malia." In *KRHS TEXNITHS*, 39–49.

Cadogan, Gerald. 1990. "The Lasithi Area in the Old Palace Period." *BICS* 37: 172–74.

Chapouthier, Fernand. 1938. *Mallia: Deux épées d'apparat découvertes en 1936 au palais de Mallia*. Études crétoises V. Paris: Geuthner.

———, and Pierre Demargne. 1942. *Fouilles exécutées à Mallia III: Exploration du palais, bordures orientale et septentrionale (1927, 1928, 1931, 1932)*. Études crétoises IV. Paris: Geuthner.

———. 1962. *Fouilles exécutées à Mallia IV: Exploration du palais, bordures méridionale et recherches complémentaires (1929–1935 et 1946–1960)*. Études crétoises XII. Paris: Geuthner.

Chapouthier, Fernand, and René Joly. 1936. *Fouilles exécutées à Mallia II: Exploration du palais (1925–1926)*. Études crétoises IV. Paris: Geuthner.

Charbonneaux, Jean. 1925–1926. "Trois armes d'apparat du palais de Mallia (Crète)." *Monuments et Memoires de la Fondation Piot* 28: 1–18.

Chevallier, Henry, Béatrice Detournay, and Sylvestre Dupré. 1975. *Fouilles exécutées à Mallia. Sondages au sud-ouest du Palais (1968)*. Études crétoises XX. Paris/Limoges: Ecole française d'Athènes-Bontemps.

Dalongeville, Remi et al. 2001. "Malia: Un marais parle." *BCH* 125: 67–88.

Daux, Georges. 1965. "Chronique des fouilles, 1964." *BCH* 89: 683–1007.

———. 1966. "Chronique des fouilles, 1965." *BCH* 90: 715–1019.

Demargne, Pierre. 1945. *Fouilles exécutées à Mallia : Exploration des nécropoles (1921–1933)* I. Études crétoises VII. Paris: Geuthner.

Detournay, Beatrice, Jean-Claude Poursat, and Frieda Vandenabeele. 1980. *Fouilles exécutées à Mallia: Le quartier Mu. II: Vases de pierre et de métal, vannerie, figurines et reliefs d'applique, éléments de parure et de décoration, armes, sceaux et empreintes*. Études crétoises XX. Paris/Limoges: Ecole française d'Athènes-Bontemps.

Driessen, Jan. 2001. "History and Hierarchy: Preliminary Observations on the Settlement Pattern of Minoan Crete." In *Urbanism*, 51–71.

———. 2007. "IIB or Not IIB? On the Beginnings of Minoan Monument Building." In *Power and Architecture: Monumental Public Architecture in the Bronze Age Near East and Aegean*, ed. Joachim Bretschneider, Jan Driessen, and Karel Van Lerberghe, 73–92. Orientalia Lovaniensia Analecta 156. Leuven: Peeters.

———. 2009. "Daidalos' Designs and Ariadne's Threads: Minoan Towns as Places of Interaction." In *Inside the City in the Greek World: Studies of Urbanism from the Bronze Age to the Hellenistic Period*, ed Sara Owen. and Laura Preston, 41–54. Oxford: Oxbow.

———, and Alexandre Farnoux. 1990. "Fouilles à Malia: Le Quartier Nu 1990." *BCH* 115: 735–41.

———. 1994. "Mycenaeans at Malia?" *Aegean Archaeology* 1: 54–64.

Driessen Jan, and Hubert Fiasse. In press. "Burning Down the House: Quartier Nu at Malia. An Arcview Analysis." In *STEGA: The Archaeology of Houses and Households in Crete from the Neolithic to Roman Period*, ed. Natalia Vogeikoff-Brogan and Kevin Glowacki. Hesperia Suppl. Princeton: American School of Classical Studies.

Driessen Jan, and Colin F. Macdonald. 1997. *The Troubled Island: Crete before and after the Santorini Eruption*. Aegaeum 17. Liège: Université de Liège.

Effenterre, Henri van. 1974. "Arène ou Agora?" In *Antichità Cretesi: Studi in onore di Doro Levi*, vol. 1, ed. Giovanni Pugliese Carratelli and Giovanni Rizza, 74–78. Catania: Università di Catania–Istituto di Archeologia.

———. 1980. *Le palais de Mallia et la cité minoenne: Étude de synthèse*, vols. 1–2. *Incunabula graeca* LXXVI. Rome: Edizioni dell'ateneo.

———, and Yannis Tzedakis. 1977. "Matériel inédit des premières fouilles au palais de Mallia." *Archaeological Deltion* 32: 156–81.

Effenterre, Henri van, and Micheline van Effenterre. 1969. *Fouilles exécutées à Mallia: Le centre politique I. L'Agora (1960–66).* Études crétoises XVII. Paris/Limoges: École française d'Athènes-Bontemps.

Farnoux, Alexandre. 1990a. "Malia à la fin du Bronze Récent." *Acta Archaeologica Lovaniensia* 28–29: 25–38.

———. 1990b. "Sondages autour de la Crypte Hypostyle." *BCH* 114: 921.

———. 1991. "Malia et la Crète à l'époque mycénienne." *Revue Archéologique:* 206–16.

———. 1997. "Malia au Minoen Récent II–IIIA1." In *La Crète mycénienne,* 135–47.

Farnoux, Alexandre, and Jan Driessen. 1991. "Inscriptions peintes en Linéaire B à Malia." *BCH* 115: 71–97.

Godart, Louis, and Jean-Pierre Olivier. 1978. "Écriture hiéroglyphique crétoise." In *Fouilles exécutées à Mallia: Le Quartier Mu,* vol. 1, ed. Jean-Claude Poursat, Louis Godart, and Jean-Pierre Olivier, 31–217. Études crétoises XXIII. Paris/Limoges: École française d'Athènes-Bontemps.

Graham, James W. 1974. "A New Arena at Mallia." In *Antichità Cretesi: Studi in onore di Doro Levi,* vol. 1, ed. Giovanni Pugliese Carratelli and Giovanni Rizza, 65–73. Catania: Università di Catania–Istituto di Archeologia.

Karantzali, Efi. 1996. *Le Bronze ancien dans les Cyclades et en Crète. BAR-IS* 631. Oxford: Tempus Reparatum.

Knappett, Carl. 1997. "Ceramic Production in the Protopalatial Mallia 'State': Evidence from Quartier Mu and Myrtos Pyrgos." In *TEXNH,* 305–11.

———. 1999. "Assessing a Polity in Protopalatial Crete: The Malia-Lasithi State." *AJA* 103: 615–39.

Müller, Sylvie. 1990. "Prospection de la plaine de Malia." *BCH* 114: 921–30.

———. 1991. "Prospection de la plaine de Malia." *BCH* 115: 741–49.

———. 1992. "Prospection de la plaine de Malia." *BCH* 116: 742–53.

———. 1996. "Prospection archéologique de la plaine de Malia." *BCH* 120: 921–28.

———. 1997. "L'organisation d'un territoire minoen." *Dossiers d'Archéologie* 222: 52.

———. 1998. "Malia: Prospection archéologique de la plaine." *BCH* 122: 548–52.

Pelon, Olivier. 1966. "Maison d'Hagia Varvara et architecture domestique à Mallia." *BCH* 90: 552–85.

———. 1967. "La maison E de Malia reconsidérée." *BCH* 91(2): 494–512.

———. 1970. *Fouilles exécutées à Mallia: Exploration des maisons et quartiers d'habitation (1963–1966). III. Le quartier E: Études crétoises* 16. Paris: Geuthner.

———. 1980. *Le palais de Malia V.* Études crétoises XXV. Paris/Limoges: École française d'Athènes-Bontemps.

———. 1982. "L'épée à l'acrobate et la chronologie maliote I." *BCH* 106: 165–90.

———. 1983. "L'épée à l'acrobate et la chronologie maliote II." *BCH* 107: 679–703.

———. 1986. "Un dépôt de fondation au palais de Malia." *BCH* 110: 9–16.

———. 1989. "Le palais." *BCH* 113: 771–86.

———. 1993. "La Salle à piliers du Palais de Malia et ses antécédents: Recherches complémentaires." *BCH* 117: 523–46.

———. 1997. "Le palais post-palatial à Malia." In *La Crète mycénienne,* 341–55.

———. 2002. "Contribution du palais de Malia à l'étude et à l'interprétation des 'palais' minoens." In *Monuments of Minos,* 111–21.

———. 2005. "Les deux destructions du palais de Malia." In *KRHS TEXNITHS,* 185–97.

————, Elga Andersen, and Martin Schmid. 1992. *Guide de Malia: Le palais et la nécropole de Chrysolakkos*. Sites et Monuments IX. Athens: École française d'Athènes.

Pelon, Olivier, and Michel Hue. 1992. "La Salle à piliers du palais de Malia et ses antécédents (I)." *BCH* 116: 1–36.

Pelon, Olivier, and Anne Schmitt. 2003. "Étude en laboratoire des céramiques dites de Vasiliki (Crète orientale)." *BCH* 127: 431–42.

Poursat, Jean-Claude. 1966. "Un sanctuaire du minoen moyen II à Mallia." *BCH* 90: 514–51.

————. 1988. "La ville minoenne de Malia: Recherches et publications récentes." *Revue Archéologique* 1: 61–82.

————. 1992. *Guide de Malia au temps des premiers palais: Le quartier Mu*. Sites et Monuments VIII. Athens: École française d'Athènes.

————. 1993. "Notes de céramique maliote à propos de 'La céramique de Chrysolakkos.' " *BCH* 117: 603–607.

————. 1996. *Fouilles exécutées à Malia: Le quartier Mu*. III: *Artisans minoens: Les maisons-ateliers du quartier Mu*. Études crétoises XXXII. Athens: École française d'Athènes.

————, and Pascal Darcque. 1990. "Sondages autour du Quartier Mu." *BCH* 114: 908–12.

Poursat, Jean-Claude, and Carl Knappett. 2005. *Fouilles exécutées à Malia: Le Quartier Mu IV. La poterie du Minoen Moyen II: Production et utilisation*. Études Crétoises XXXIII. Athens: École française d'Athènes.

Poursat, Jean-Claude, and Eva Papatsarouha. 2000. "Les sceaux de l'Atelier de Malia: Questions de style." In *Minoisch-mykenische Glyptik*, 257–68.

Poursat, Jean-Claude, Olivier Pelon, Claude Baurain, Pascal Darcque, and Colette Verlinden. 1984. "Rapports sur les travaux de l'École française en Grèce en 1983: Malia." *BCH* 108(2): 880–91.

Schmid, Martin. 1990. "Aménagement, sauvegarde, et protection des monuments minoens." *BCH* 114: 930–39.

Schoep, Ilse. 2002. "Social and Political Organization on Crete in the Proto-palatial Period: The Case of Middle Minoan II Malia." *JMA* 15: 101–32.

————. 2004. "Assessing the Role of Architecture in Conspicuous Consumption in the Middle Minoan I–II Periods." *OJA* 23: 243–69.

————. 2007. "Architecture and Power: The Origins of Minoan 'Palatial Architecture.' " In *Power and Architecture: Monumental Public Architecture in the Bronze Age Near East and Aegean*, ed. Joachim Bretschneider, Jan Driessen, and Karel Van Lerberghe, 213–36. Orientalia Lovaniensia Analecta 156. Leuven: Peeters.

————, and Carl Knappett. 2003. "Le Quartier Nu (Malia, Crète): L'occupation du Minoen Moyen II." *BCH* 127: 49–86.

Shaw, Joseph. 1973. "The Chrysolakkos Façades." In *Pepragmena tou C' Diethnous Kretologikou Synedriou*, vol. 1, 319–31. Athens: University of Crete.

Stürmer, Veit. 1993. "La céramique de Chrysolakkos: Catalogue et réexamen," *BCH* 117: 123–87.

Tomkins, Peter. 2008. "Time, Space, and the Reinvention of the Cretan Neolithic." In *Escaping the Labyrinth*, 21–48.

Treuil, René. 1999. "Les 'Maisons Dessenne' à Malia." In *Meletemata*, 841–45.

————. 2005. "Entre morts et vivants à Malia: La 'zone des nécropoles' et les quartiers d'habitation." In *KRHS TEXNITHS*, 209–20.

Whitelaw, Todd M. 1983. "The Settlement at Fournou Koriphi Myrtos and Aspects of Early Minoan Social Organization." In *Minoan Society*, 333–63.

CHAPTER 43

PALAIKASTRO

J. ALEXANDER MACGILLIVRAY
L. HUGH SACKETT

PALAIKASTRO (35° 12'N 26° 15'E) is fifteen kilometers south of Cape Sidero at Crete's northeastern tip. The region comprises a five-kilometer-long coastal plain with sandy beaches on either side of an isolated, limestone-capped conical hill. The hill, rising 84 meters above sea level, is called Kastri, meaning "fort." It dominates the plain's center and provides the "kastro" element in the region's modern name, which derives from the local pronunciation of *palaio* ("old") and *kastro* ("fort") in Greek. The steep Kastri promontory was a refuge acropolis at the end of the Bronze Age (ca. 1200–1100 BC).

Northwest of Kastri is the flat Kouremenos (meaning the 'shaved one,' perhaps a reference to ancient head-shaving rituals) plain, much of which until recently was marshland—the delta for the Kalogero river, which could mean either the "good" (*kalo*) and "strong" (*gero*) or the "Monk's" (*kalogero*) river. In the center of this alluvial plain is a low gravely rise called Rizoviglo, meaning "Rizo's lookout."

South of Kastri is the tiny sheltered harbor called Chiona, from the Ottoman word for "Customs House." Overlooking this harbor is the rugged blue limestone peak rising 254 meters above the sea, called Mount Petsophas—"skin eater" in Greek. The remains of east Crete's most important Bronze Age peak sanctuary, the source of many terracotta figurines and stone vases inscribed with Linear A, are situated on the top of Mount Petsophas. Nestled at the foot of Petsophas's northern flank is a little vale called Roussolakkos, meaning "red pit," named for its fine, impermeable building clay, which has a deep ruddy hue.

The quarries at Ta Skaria, meaning "the grids," east of Roussolakkos along the coast near Cape Plako, provided the aeolianite sandstone used in the town's finest ashlar masonry. A network of roads established early in the Old Palace period, approximately 1900 BC, connected Roussolakkos with Minoan sites to the north (Vai), south (Zakros), and west (Petras).

The Bronze Age cemeteries at Hellenika, Sarandari, and Patema are on the routes to the northwest and east of the ancient town and on the slopes of Petsophas and Kastri.

Excavations

The British School at Athens has carried out three excavation campaigns at Palaikastro. Robert Carr Bosanquet and Richard MacGillivray Dawkins directed the first campaign, which began in 1902 and lasted until 1906 (Bosanquet and Dawkins 1923). They revealed the main street and large urban blocks in the northwest quarter of the coastal Minoan city and the Archaic, Classical, and Roman sanctuary of Diktaian Zeus at Roussolakkos—Strabo's Diktaion. They also found outlying Bronze Age cemeteries and dwellings, as well as the Bronze Age peak sanctuary on Mount Petsophas (Myres 1903; Rutkowski 1991).

The second campaign, which began in 1962 and ran until 1963, was led by L. Hugh Sackett and Mervyn R. Popham, who concentrated on LM IB Block N at Roussolakkos and the Minoan occupation on Kastri (Sackett et al. 1965, 1970). Subsequently, Sackett and J. Alexander MacGillivray began the third campaign with a topographical and magnetic survey in 1983. Their excavations from 1986 to the present have uncovered seven Minoan buildings in the city's north sector (MacGillivray et al. 1984, 1987, 1988, 1989, 1991, 1992, 1998, 2000, 2007). In 2001 Michael Boyd and Ian K. Whitbread directed a geophysical survey that showed that the city occupied thirty-six hectares, making it the second largest Minoan urban center after Knossos. They also found indications of large structures in the Roussolakkos valley east of the present excavations (Boyd, Whitbread, and MacGillivray 2006). Rescue excavations by the Greek Archaeological Service have revealed a kiln, two houses to the east of the town, Mycenaean tombs, and more material from Petsophas.

History

Neolithic levels have not been encountered in the excavations, perhaps because trenches have not been dug in the Roussolakkos vale, where Final Neolithic (ca. 3100 BC) stone ax heads occur on the surface (figure 43.1).

The evidence for continuous occupation throughout the Bronze Age begins with the Early Minoan period (MacGillivray and Driessen 1989). Two small, possibly familial, holdings were built in EM IIA (ca. 2600 BC). These were succeeded by an imposing structure in EM IIB (ca. 2500 BC), partially excavated beneath the later Block X.

Figure 43.1. Palaikastro town plan (by Jan Driessen).

By the MM IB–IIA periods (ca. 1930–1800 BC), a well-planned town with foreign contacts emerged at roughly the same time as the first palaces in central Crete. This may imply that such a building also existed at Palaikastro, perhaps located in the Roussolakkos vale, as yet unexplored. There was widespread destruction at the end of the Old Palace period, approximately 1760 BC, followed by the reconstruction of the town with an improved paved street system with drainage channels. There is evidence of earthquake damage at the end of the MM IIIB period in approximately 1570 BC (Knappett and Cunningham 2003).

The region was covered in a blanket of ash, ca. 0.07 m thick, from the Thera eruption in Mature LM IA (ca. 1500 BC), and then immediately inundated by one or more tsunamis at least nine meters high, which reduced buildings to their foundations (Bruins et al. 2008).

Fine ashlar structures (Buildings 1, 3, 4, 5) were built in parts of the North sector in LM IB (ca. 1490–1460/40 BC), while other areas (Buildings 2 and 6) were left in ruins. The LM IB town provides the clearest example of Minoan urban planning, with wide streets defining large town blocks, impressive ashlar façades, and spacious main rooms with sunken central basins surrounded by four columns, dubbed the "Palaikastro Hall." The finds suggest that these were the dwellings of rich traders who filled their storage rooms with finely decorated pottery and stone vases and kept track of their transactions on tablets written in Linear A.

There was a sequence of fire destructions (ca. 1460–1440 BC), most likely due to human aggression, during the LM IB period, ending with widespread damage. From the latest of these destruction levels comes a wealth of fine objects, including the Palaikastro Kouros—the gold and ivory sculpture of a vibrant youth stepping forward, which is a masterpiece of Minoan craftsmanship—found scattered in a square and adjacent shrine in Building 5 (figure 43.2).

In contrast to other east Cretan towns, much of the city, including the main street, was rebuilt in the LM II and LM IIIA1 periods (ca. 1440–1400 BC), often on the same lines as before. However, it suffered a further destruction by fire early in the LM IIIA2 period (ca. 1400–1320 BC), perhaps contemporary with the final destruction of the palace at Knossos. A period of extensive rebuilding in LM IIIA2 and LM IIIB ended with an earthquake in the middle of the LM IIIB period, around 1250 BC. The city was abandoned at this point, and occupation was limited to a small refuge settlement on the top of the Kastri hill during LM IIIC (ca. 1200–1100 BC).

A sanctuary dedicated to Diktaian Zeus occupied the area of Block X from the Geometric to the Roman periods (eighth century BC–fourth century AD). This sanctuary's location is shown by the discovery of fragments of an inscription recording the "Hymn to Diktaian Zeus" in a pit near Block X (Bosanquet 1909). In this hymn, probably composed in the fourth or third centuries BC, the young god is summoned to return to Dikte, where his sacred altar stood. This leaves no doubt that the temple site at Roussolakkos was Dikte, famed in antiquity as the birthplace of Zeus. Here, so Greek myth relates, the young god was hidden from his jealous father, Kronos. Grown up, he overthrew his father and eventually returned to his birthplace to found the city, which the historian Diodorus of Sicily saw abandoned in the first century BC.

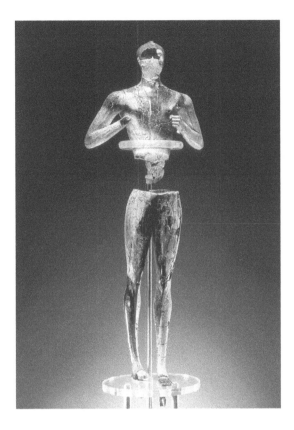

Figure 43.2. Palaikastro Kouros (photograph by Ioannis Papadakis, reproduced with the permission of the British School at Athens).

During the early centuries of cult at Roussolakkos, Diktaian Zeus was honored with bronze votive offerings of tripods, elaborately decorated shields, and other precious armor. Later, in the sixth century BC, a temple was erected and rebuilt several times, as shown by a sequence of fragmentary roof tiles. Inscriptions indicate that the sanctuary continued to function as an important place of worship for the inhabitants of the cities in eastern Crete into the Hellenistic and Roman periods. A terracotta sima with scenes of charioteers and warriors in relief, a series of antefixes with gorgon heads, and a frieze of lotus flowers and palmettes are the only decorative elements so far found from the temples that stood on this site (Thorne and Prent 2000).

MINOAN SOCIETY AT PALAIKASTRO

This town site differs from others in Minoan Crete in some significant ways. First, the town did not grow haphazardly in an agglutinative manner like the average modern Greek village or other Minoan towns or villages such as Gournia. Its main street shows evidence of organized, centrally directed, and long-lived civic planning, with new surfaces laid down in at least five phases over some four centuries

(MM III to LM IIIA), drains kept in repair, and private encroachment from adjacent buildings ruled out (Cunningham 2007).

The settlement is arranged in extensive town blocks, several of which contain one central, four-columned hall with impluvium (known as the Palaikastro Hall and found at Blocks B, Γ, Δ, and Σ), three with an adjacent lustral basin. Several also have particular rooms with public access, which may be interpreted as shops.

A reasonable inference, in terms of social organization, would be that the occupants of these house blocks consisted of extended families or clans, including people of some standing and means whose interests were coherent rather than competitive (not factions). Evidence for agricultural and trade activity comes from the storage capacity (for oil, wine, and grain) and from the presence of luxury objects, including fine ceramic wares, stone vases, ivory, some items of precious metal, and the occurrence (albeit rare) of Linear A documents.

The presence of central cult rooms (lustral basins) and of cult objects (especially rhytons, but also figurines, double ax stands, and fine Marine Style vases) also implies the participation of the occupants in common, even islandwide, cult activities.

The absence (to date) of a central administrative (or 'palatial') building might also seem a distinguishing feature, but the latest geophysical survey (Boyd, Whitbread, and MacGillivray 2006) suggests that such a building may well lie unexcavated to the south of the current excavations, so in this respect Palaikastro may well follow the normal Minoan pattern. What seems special is the widespread participation of the town's inhabitants in social activities that might elsewhere have been the sole function of the highest (Palatial) class, whether political or priestly or both.

CRAFTS AND TRADE

A wide range of crafts both supported and stemmed from the two major branches of the Palaikastro economy—agriculture and trade. In addition to the work of builders, masons, and carpenters, these crafts included ceramics (with ceramic design and the production of terracotta figures), weaving, wall painting, metalworking, stone carving, and ivory working.

Periods of extraordinary creativity in ceramic production and design burgeoned both in the Protopalatial period—especially the finest thin-walled cups with imaginative designs in the Kamares ware style—and in the Neopalatial period (the finely finished wares of the LM IA and LM IIIA1 periods and the special palatial styles of the LM IB period).

One kiln was excavated in the Roussolakkos valley, but there must have been many workshops; several potters' wheels have been found. More than a thousand locally made figurines were found dedicated at the MM I peak sanctuary on Petsofas:

many have bent arms with clenched fists on the chest, Osiris style, and foreshadow the LM IB masterwork shown in figure 43.2; others are painted and show fashionable clothing styles. An LM IIIA dancing group from a cult context in Block Δ would be quite at home in a local village festival today. Also found were unusual MM I–II ceramic bowls, some containing complex scenes of shepherd and flocks, one with a group meeting of elders, as well as interesting documents of daily life and social activities.

Weaving was a normal activity in a Palaikastro house, as shown by the presence everywhere of loomweights of varying types. Although the products of the looms are lost, it is reasonable to assume that the export of attractively designed cloth or garments was one element in the town's trade exchange. Again, it is certain that the interior walls of houses were decorated with brightly colored fresco work, though only fragments have survived, including fine floral designs—the latter found also on a fine plastered and brilliantly painted offering table. It has recently become clear that the high-quality and idiosyncratic compositions of Minoan painters (at least of those who worked at the great palatial centers) was valued overseas, both in Egypt and the Levant.

On the other hand, the crafts of metal- and ivory working were entirely dependent on imports for their raw materials, as to a lesser extent were the stone carvers. The import of bronze ingots and ivory tusks is graphically illustrated by the excavations at neighboring Zakro, and while it remains to be seen whether similar imports may also have come to a central administrative center at Palaikastro, finished objects in bronze and ivory have been found in many of the elite houses at Palaikastro, including bronze vessels, axes and knives, small ivory figurines of young boys, and relief plaques with herons and a nautilus design (from boxes?).

The existence of bronze working at the site during the late, Postpalatial, period is confirmed by the discovery of workshop debris, which included terracotta tuyères, crucibles, and molds for double axes and for a fine tripod stand (Hemingway 1996). The existence of a local ivory workshop is perhaps implied by the occurrence of a bag of bone and ivory strips found in the same context as the Palaikastro Kouros.

For their building, masons used a colorful variety of local stone and a little imported gypsum. Stone objects are very common at Palaikastro, from the greenstone axes of the earliest periods (Neo/EM) and obsidian blades of all periods to the finely shaped cups, bowls, and lamps of the Neopalatial periods. In stone carving, both the techniques and some of the materials used probably derived from Egypt, but most of the standard Minoan forms would have been made in Crete, many probably by local manufacturers.

Other materials have perished, but the craftsmen who made them were essential to the community: carpenters who built ships, houses, and furniture, leatherworkers for bags, cloth, and shields. These, along with ropes and baskets, would all have been present in people's homes.

CULT

The widespread dispersal in the settlement at Palaikastro of special objects usually associated with cult activity underscores this particular aspect of the site (Cunningham and Sackett 2009).

From the earliest times, religion was practiced in natural settings like caves, mountain peaks (cf. Petsofas, discussed earlier), and sacred groves, often represented on Minoan rings and seals. However, with the growth of towns and cities in the Neopalatial periods, worship was brought into the settlements, and the presence of house and town shrines at Palaikastro well illustrates the "urbanization" of cult. Ritual objects familiar from scenes of open-air worship, including fetishes like stalactites, triton shells, and large stone baetyls, are now found inside the settlement.

Other artifacts of cult include thymiateria (incense burners), numerous rhyta (some of the highest quality), horns of consecration, pyramidal ax stands, and the double ax (for whose manufacture in metal, stone molds have been found). The objects themselves and graphic representations of them on ceramics and frescoes (the latter especially at Knossos and Thera) show that the essence of Minoan cult was communal and ecstatic and included rituals of dancing and feasting, as well as processions and sacred offerings.

The most extraordinary cult figure from Palaikastro is a masterpiece of ivory carving, the chryselephantine Kouros, found deliberately vandalized ca. 1460/40 BC at the town shrine of Building 5 (MacGillivray and Sackett 2000). The excavators believe it to be a Minoan predecessor to Diktaian Zeus, also known as Zagreus and Cretan-born Zeus and equivalent to Greek Dionysos and Egyptian Osiris.

The earliest representations of this figure, which are shown, like Osiris, with clenched fists at the chest, are the MM terracotta effigies from the peak sanctuary on Petsofas. The prominence of this youthful male cult figure followed soon after, and may well have been validated by, the trauma and disillusionment that must have followed, the destruction of the site by the Thera eruption, with its ash fallout and tsunamis. When the time came for its own violent vandalization little more than a generation later, those responsible may have been involved in a new phase of reaction and a reversion to old beliefs or simply part of the contemporary invasion by Mycenaean marauders.

The traditional beliefs were back in style at a later town shrine, just across the street in Building 1, where, in approximately 1200 BC, we again find the female divinity, now crowned with horns of consecration and placed in a niche at the inner portal.

It is notable that the cult of Diktaean Zeus was centered on his temple at Roussolakkos, in the area of Minoan Block X, little more than 100 m. from the find place of the Palaikastro Kouros. Although the temple itself remains unexcavated, architectural elements have been found: Most important are part of an Archaic frieze and tile fragments spanning at least five successive temple roofs, as well as rich offerings, some probably from a earlier open-air altar, including a decorated bronze shield. This takes the cult back into the Geometric period. Most remarkable is the fragmentary inscribed text of a hymn to Zeus, composed in the Classical period but copied by a hand using letter forms of the 2nd century AD, thus extending the evidence for continuity of this local cult over at least a millennium.

Diet

The careful collection of bones during excavation and of other food samples through water flotation shows that there has been considerable continuity in eating habits in Crete over the ages. The Minoan diet was based on cultivated and wild plants, grains and pulses, supplemented by red meat, game, fish, and other seafood.

Evidence has been found for the consumption of emmer and einkorn wheat, barley, peas, lentils, bitter vetch, dwarf chickling, and horsebean; olives, grapes, and figs are certain, and pears, pomegranates, plums, and melons probable; wild herbs, edible weeds, bulbs, and mushrooms would have been used for both medicinal purposes and food; saffron and honey served as condiments.

Animal bones of goat and sheep are the most common, but cattle bones and snail shells also occur; duck and partridge are represented in Minoan art and are likely to have been part of the diet. Fish bones of comber, sea bream, picarel, damsel fish, horse mackerel, sand smelt, biennies, red mullet, and stingrays show that shoreline fishing was commonly done by hook and line or by nets; some deep sea fishing also took place from boats. Interest in the octopus is shown by its frequency as a motif in Minoan art.

Very common are the smallest fish (anchovies or sprat) netted close to shore; their occurrence in small ceramic jars suggests the production of *allec* or salted fish sauce, so well known in later periods (MacGillivray, Sackett, and Driessen 2007).

Many grills and cooking pots but no ovens have been found, which suggests that meat and fish were probably grilled, roasted on an open fire, or stewed with vegetables; preservation by smoking, drying, or pickling would have used olive oil and vinegar, as well as salt.

Burials

During the first phase of excavation (1902–1906), cemeteries were found outside the limits of the settlement at Roussolakkos in almost every direction: along the coast at Aspa, Patema, and Tou Galeti Kephala; on the lower slopes of Kastri at Ta Hellenika; and inland at Kephalaki, Koutsoulospilo, Sarandari, and near Angathia.

In the early phases of the Bronze Age, the tradition of secondary burial was practiced. Communal tombs, which reflected the power of the clan in society, were used. By contrast, the Late Bronze Age witnessed a significant change: bodies were now placed in individual coffins (or larnakes). This reflects a social change after the arrival of the Mycenaean Greeks, when greater emphasis was placed on the individual and the family.

The house tombs of the early periods (Prepalatial–Protopalatial or EM–MM) consisted of enclosures, probably unroofed, and covered ossuaries or narrow bone compartments. The bodies were probably prepared for burial in the open enclosures, where they may have been exposed in the rite of excarnation, and only later, when clean, removed and placed with the grave offerings inside the ossuaries. This type of burial was found at Ta Hellenika, where vases, the clay model of a boat, and a triton shell were found, and at Patema and Sarantari. The ossuaries at Tou Galeta Kephala were particularly rich: one held the remains of at least seventy-eight individuals, along with clay and stone vases, obsidian blades, and a bronze ax (average man's height 1.62 m). The disturbed burials in another were accompanied by 140 clay vessels, stone vases, a triton shell, ivory, and stone seals.

The Ellenika cemetery continued in use into the Protopalatial (or MM) periods. Reuse of Tou Galeta Kephala in the Postpalatial (Mycenaean) period was shown by the disturbed remains of a warrior with gold leaf and a bronze-studded sword.

Mycenaean larnax burials were found at Kephalaki, where one clay larnax was exquisitely painted with religious symbols and scenes of nature or paradise. Others at Koutsoulospilo contained pottery, bronze mirrors, and an ivory bead, and at Aspa a child burial was found in a larnax with an oriental-style cylinder seal. At Angathia, a unique chamber tomb with dromos held a warrior burial.

BIBLIOGRAPHY

Bosanquet, Robert C. 1909. "The Palaikastro Hymn of the Kouretes." *BSA* 15: 339–56.
———, and Richard MacGillivray Dawkins, eds. 1923. *The Unpublished Objects from Palaikastro Excavations, 1902–1906*. BSA Supplementary Paper 1. London: British School at Athens.
Boyd, Michael J., Ian K. Whitbread, and J. Alexander MacGillivray. 2006. "Geophysical Investigations at Palaikastro." *BSA* 101: 89–135.
Bruins, Hendrik J., J. Alexander MacGillivray, Costas E. Synolakis, Chaim Benjamini, Jörg Keller, Hanan J. Kisch, Andreas Klügel, and Johannes van der Plicht. 2008. "Geoarchaeological Tsunami Deposits at Palaikastro (Crete) and the Late Minoan IA Eruption of Santorini." *JAS* 35(1): 191–212.
Cunningham, Tim. 2007. "In the Shadows of Kastri: An Examination of Domestic and Civic Space at Palaikastro (Crete)." In *Building Communities: House, Settlement and Society in the Aegean and Beyond*, ed. Ruth Westgate, Nick Fisher, and James Whitley, 99–109. BSA Studies 15. London: British School at Athens.

————, and L. Hugh Sackett. 2009. "Does the Widespread Cult Activity at Palaikastro Call for a special explanation?" In *Archaeologies of Cult: Essays on Ritual and Cult in Crete*, ed. Anna Lucia D'Agata and Aleydis Van de Moortel. Hesperia Suppl. 42. Princeton: American School of Classical Studies: 79–97.

Hemingway, Sean A. 1996. "Minoan Metalworking in the Postpalatial Period: A Deposit of Metallurgical Debris from Palaikastro." *BSA* 91: 213–52.

Knappett, Carl, and Tim Cunningham. 2003. "Three Neopalatial Deposits from Palaikastro, East Crete" *BSA* 98: 107–87.

MacGillivray, J. Alexander, and Jan M. Driessen. 1989. "Minoan Settlement at Palaikastro." In *L'habitat égéen préhistorique*, 395–412.

————, and L. Hugh Sackett, eds. 2000. *The Palaikastro Kouros: A Minoan Chryselephantine Statuette and Its Aegean Bronze Age Context*. BSA Studies 6. London: British School at Athens.

MacGillivray, J. Alexander, L. Hugh Sackett, and Jan M. Driessen. 1984. "An Archaeological Survey of the Roussolakkos Area at Palaikastro." *BSA* 79: 129–59.

————, eds. 2007. *Palaikastro: Two Late Minoan Wells*. BSA Supplementary vol. 43. London: British School at Athens.

————, Robert Bridges, and David Smyth. 1989. "Excavations at Palaikastro, 1988." *BSA* 84: 417–45.

MacGillivray, J. Alexander, L. Hugh Sackett, Jan M. Driessen, Alexandre Farnoux, and David Smyth. 1991. "Excavations at Palaikastro, 1990." *BSA* 86: 121–47.

MacGillivray, J. Alexander, L. Hugh Sackett, Jan M. Driessen, and Eleni Hatzaki. 1998. "Excavations at Palaikastro, 1994 and 1996." *BSA* 93: 221–68.

MacGillivray, J. Alexander, L. Hugh Sackett, Jan M. Driessen, and Sean A. Hemingway. 1992. "Excavations at Palaikastro, 1991." *BSA* 87: 121–52.

MacGillivray, J. Alexander, L. Hugh Sackett, Jan M. Driessen, Colin F. Macdonald, and David Smyth. 1988. "Excavations at Palaikastro, 1987." *BSA* 83: 259–82.

MacGillivray, J. Alexander, L. Hugh Sackett, Jan M. Driessen, and David Smyth. 1987. "Excavations at Palaikastro, 1986." *BSA* 82: 135–54.

Myres, John L. 1903. "The Sanctuary Site of Petsophas." *BSA* 9: 356–87.

Rutkowski, Bogdan. 1991. *Petsophas: A Cretan Peak Sanctuary*. Studies and Monographs in Mediterranean Archaeology and Civilization, series 1, vol. 1. Warsaw: Polish Academy of Sciences.

Sackett, L. Hugh, and Mervyn R. Popham. 1970. "Excavations at Palaikastro. VII." *BSA* 65: 203–42.

————, and Peter M. Warren. 1965. "Excavations at Palaikastro. VI." *BSA* 60: 248–315.

Thorne, Stuart M., and Mieke Prent. 2000. "The Sanctuary of Diktaian Zeus at Palaikastro: A Re-examination of the Excavations by the British School in 1902–1906." In *Proceedings of the Eighth Cretological Congress*, ed. Alexandra Karetsou, vol. A2, 169–78. Herakleion: Etaireia Kritikon Istorikon Meleton.

CHAPTER 44

···

PHAISTOS

···

VINCENZO LA ROSA

PHAISTOS, identified by Captain Spratt in 1851–1853 (on the basis of Strabo's description) and known then as Kastri, was systematically investigated by an Italian mission from June 1900 to 1909. Investigations were resumed from 1928 to 1932, during which time small soundings were conducted in order to verify the stratigraphy encountered, and a number of restoration and consolidation works were conducted that were concluded in 1936 (Pernier 1935; Pernier and Banti 1951). Systematic excavation was resumed by the Italian archaeological school from 1950 to 1967 (Levi 1976; Levi and Carinci 1988) and again from 2000 onward (La Rosa 1998–2000, 2000, 2002a, 2004, 2005, 2007).

The name *pa-i-to* attested in the Linear B tablet archive at Knossos coincides with the Greek Φαιστος attested in Homer (*Il.* II, 648: "well inhabited"; *Od.* III, 293–96, mentioned in relation to the *lissé petre*). The site is located in a readily visible position in the Mesara plain, which is crossed by the Ieropatomos River and bordered by Mount Ida to the north and the Asterousia mountain chain to the south. The geographical characteristics make the area, even today, particularly good for primary activities (such as agriculture and husbandry) and also well delimited from a geographic point of view.

The ancient settlement of Phaistos was set out on three hills (composed of limestone and marlstone), the westernmost of which (standing at a height of 154.85 m.) is named Christòs Effendi. The middle hill (with a height of 115.15 m. and indicated as Acropoli mediana by the first excavators) is today occupied by the excavation house and magazines. The easternmost hill (with a height of 97.10 m) hosted the palace.

The river, which also lapped against the site of Ayia Triada, runs to the north of the system of hills. The hill to the north of the river (Kalivia) was occupied by the Postpalatial necropolis (end of the 15th–13th centuries BC). Habitation quarters were organized on the hill slopes (at Chalara and Ayia Photini and in the area of the small village of Haghios Ioannis).

The earliest sign of frequentation dates back to the Final Neolithic period (ca. 3600–3000 BC) and is contemporary with the most recent of the ten levels identified in the test pits opened beneath the palace at Knossos.

The occupation of the easternmost hill of Phaistos (and of its southeastern slope, Chalara) was likely subsequent to the abandonment of a small cluster of habitations (as yet unidentified), which might have been located in the area of the plain, closer to the course of the river. The move seemingly took place as a consequence of a river flood caused by intense rain (Vagnetti 1972–1973). The eastern hill was then, and continued to be, the most important part of the settlement, although it is the lowest and therefore the least defensible of the three.

A series of communal activities, with the consumption of meat, some working areas, and a particular type of ceramic production (with specialized shapes and red ochre decoration), gives some idea of the vitality of the settlement, which developed within two distinct phases of the Final Neolithic period. These activities, also documented elsewhere, served to reinforce the links between local households and also to establish relations with the households of nearby communities (Todaro and Di Tonto 2008; Di Tonto 2008, 2009).

The reexamination of old contexts, together with the information recovered during the new excavations, has allowed two moments to be stratigraphically distinguished within the Phaistian Neolithic, which can be compared respectively to the FN III and FN IV of Knossos and Sitia (Todaro and Di Tonto 2008; Todaro forthcoming b). The earlier, identified directly on the bedrock, has provided remains of rectangular huts with rounded corners and of a single circular hut; the latter, with an internal diameter of ca. 2.50 m, is built on the border of the area that was later occupied by the central court of the palace and was reoccupied with a higher floor in the EM I period. In the second phase, the dwellings moved toward the southern and western slopes of the palace hill, the top of which remained in use as a communal area for the ceremonial consumption of food and drink (Todaro forthcoming b).

The EM I period marks the third phase in the life of the settlement and is characterized by monumental architecture, with two-story rectangular buildings that have windows and painted plaster on the walls (Phaistos III: Todaro forthcoming b). The fourth phase corresponds to a mature phase of EM I and is characterized by the monumentalization of the two ceremonial areas that had been used since the Neolithic period, which coincide with the areas later used as the western and central courts of the palace (Phaistos IV: Todaro forthcoming b). It is at this time that the nearby site of Ayia Triada was first occupied.

The subsequent phases of the Prepalatial history of the site (phases V–X: Todaro 2009; forthcoming b), which correspond to the periods between EM IIA and MM IA, are marked by three large building projects that considerably changed the appearance of the hill and led to the progressive formation of the terraces above which the palace was later built. The first, at the beginning of phase V (EM IIA), brought about the terracing of the areas that were later used as the western and central courts of the palace; the second, at the beginning of phase VI (EM IIA late), led to the establishment of a habitation quarter in the area of the future *Cortile* LXX, which was connected with the top of the hill via a ramp, identified beneath the later ramp LII, and of an artisans' quarter (certainly potters), organized on terraces along the western slope of the hill (Todaro forthcoming b). The third, at the beginning of phase VIII (EM III), notably modified the morphology of the hill and led to the construction of a few buildings characterized by red clay floors (sometimes remade up to twelve times), identified beneath the western wing of the palace, beneath cortile LXX, and along the western slope. External cobbled areas and a paved ramp leading up from the area of *Cortile* LXX ensured communications between the various clusters of structures (Todaro forthcoming a).

In phase IX, which corresponds to the beginning of MM IA, the cobbled area on the top of the hill continued to be used; one of them led from the area of *Piazzale* I to the area of the central court. The artisan quarter also seems to have continued in use, although only periodically and in relation to particular events that seemingly alternate between periods of intense activity, which also brought about the gathering of several potters from the surrounding area, and periods of abandonment of some of the structures. This cyclical activity has been put in relation with the periodicity of the ceremonial activities that also took place in the area of *Piazzale* I in phase X, which coincides with the end of the MM IA period (Todaro forthcoming a, b). It is therefore possible that the settlement, rather than being unitary, was articulated in several clusters that were spread throughout the territory but which periodically gathered to celebrate their belonging to the same community (Todaro 2009; forthcoming b).

An interesting late Prepalatial site has been identified at Paterikiès, on a hill that is located halfway between Phaistos and Ayia Triada. The hundreds of teapots retrieved from a large dump (which were perhaps functional to prepare infusions of particular herbs) could represent the remains of votive offerings in the area of a sanctuary rather than the waste of a pottery workshop. The serial production of teapots (certainly not limited to local consumption) and the control of the sanctuary could be tied to the economic and political elites, who, in the following period, gave life to the palace at Phaistos.

The choice of the Phaistos hill as the location for the construction of a palace is definitely the expression of a new territorial equilibrium that assumed, perhaps for the first time, a pyramidal and hierarchical connotation. The real causes that led to this choice are not, however, very clear. Both the geographical position and the fact that the Phaistian hill offered a better projection toward the plain and therefore had better visibility could have been determinant factors in the location of the building of power.

The stimulus for the aggregation was perhaps of economic type; the means of such aggregation was perhaps religious. The basis of the Phaistian reign in the Protopalatial period has been hypothetically related to a surplus of primary activities such as agriculture and husbandry and of specialized production such as pottery (Levi and Carinci 1988) or stone vases (Palio 2008).

The palace, constructed on three different terraces, with an equal number of paved courts, was founded at the beginning of the MM IB period with an original extension of about 8,000 m² (figures 44.1, 44.2). The central court (51.50 by 22.30 m) reached about 1,100 m², in contrast to the ca. 1,250 m² of Knossos and the 1,050 m² of Malia. A paved ramp linked the lower west court (*Cortile LXX*) with the west court of the theatrical staircase (*Piazzale I*); the ramp followed the path of an earlier ramp constructed in the EM III period and reused in the MM IA period.

The thousands of sealings and associated Linear A tablets that were found in the MM IIB destruction level of the first palace demonstrate the importance of administrative activity in the life of the building (Militello 2002). They suggest the existence of oligarchies of bureaucrats who, curiously, do not seem to be suggested by the nature of the other data and finds.

The western façade (with orthostatic masonry) was, from the foundation, constructed on both the lower and the middle terraces. It has been possible to ascertain that the line of the original façade on the middle terrace coincided with that of the second palace. In the course of the MM II period, therefore, the front with the orthostats on the middle terrace was seemingly pushed forward (toward the west), thus allowing the construction of a new wing of the building (La Rosa 2007).

The southwest wing, excavated in its entirety by Levi, comprised a single three-story building rather than three superimposed palaces, as the excavator had supposed. Levi had actually based his heretical classification of the Protopalatial period on this particular reading of the stratigraphy of the area and distinguished three Protopalatial phases (the first of which was further distinguished into A and B), thus totally repudiating Evans's classification (Levi 1976).

The existence of a sacerdotal class is proved, in the case of the palace at Phaistos, not only by the rooms used as shrines or by various assemblages clearly referable to the ceremonial sphere but mainly by the large court with the theatrical staircase and raised walkways that, rather than ensuring a comfortable walk during rainfall, as previously hypothesized, were seemingly intended to be used as obligatory routes for processions and for important people or people with a particular function. The area was approximately trapezoidal and measured about 36 by 40 m, with a surface of about 1300/1400 m².

A recent revision of the stratigraphies and materials from the area of the court with the theatrical staircase (*Piazzale* I) has led to the recognition of three key elements that spanned the period between MM IB and MM IIB, which allows the western court to be considered, more than the central court, as the place for ceremonial activity par excellence. A phase of the baetyls (at least two) was identified—baetyls that had escaped the attention of the old excavators and were situated near the southern limit of the court during the MM IB period.

The second phase (MM II) seemingly had *Vasca XXX* as a ceremonial structure of reference, lined with stucco and situated immediately to the west of the paved area. The so-called *Bastione* was built in relation to this rectangular structure, but was wrongly interpreted as the location of the army entrusted with the defense of

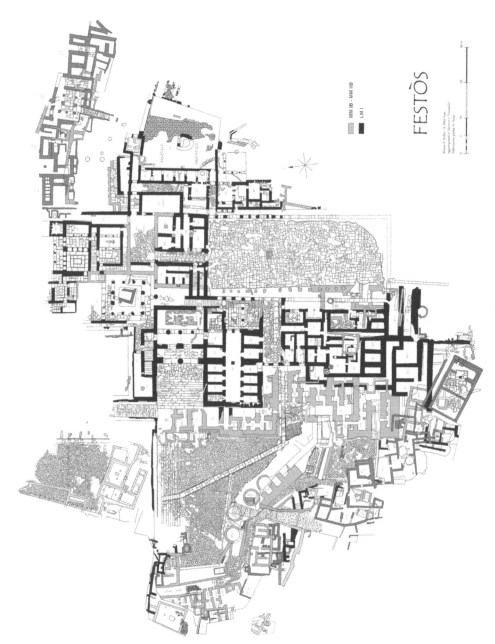

Figure 44.1. Plan of the Phaistos palace and its surroundings in the LM I period (drawing by E. Stefani, with additions by R. Oliva and B. Salmeri; elaboration by M. Tanasi).

Figure 44.2. View of the Phaistos palace from the northwest (photograph by the author).

the palace. The building, with two architectural phases, was connected to the *Vasca* via a stuccoed ramp.

The third phase within the ceremonial area is represented by the construction of the so-called *kouloures*: large circular subterranean structures (ca. 4 m in diameter, with a depth of up to 2.50–3.00 m) that have been interpreted as enclosures for sacred trees (Carinci 2001). It is possible that the paving of *Piazzale* I, with its nine-step theatrical staircase (each step of which is 24 m long, 0.60 m wide, and 0.25 m high), which had a capacity of 400–430 persons (probably standing, due to the limited height of the steps), was the ceremonial space in which the inhabitants of the palace met those who lived outside (Carinci and La Rosa 2007, 2009). The large containers on the border of the paved area, which some scholars believe to have been used as granaries, have led to the supposition that one of these ceremonies could have been related to harvesting.

The already mentioned potential of the surrounding territory (mainly agriculture and husbandry) and the richness of the ceramic production illustrate a moment of great splendor during the life of the First Palace, the mythical founder of which, according to one tradition, was Radhamanthys, the brother of Minos. This richness continued until the end of the MM IIB period. In contrast to the other palaces, such as Knossos and Malia, it is possible to hypothesize a condition of autarchy or self-sufficiency at Phaistos, which was probably outside the Mediterranean maritime trade network.

Most of the materials found in the palace, in the houses built close by, and in the quarters of Chalara and H. Photini, consist of Kamares-style pottery, which is the most beautiful type in the entire Aegean. Imported vases and local imitations of Phaistian vases (but also administrative documents such as sealings and seals) have been found in places very distant from Phaistos, such as Monastiraki and Apodolou, in the Amari valley, and are testimony to the extent of the economic interests, if not political control, of the Phaistos palace.

A recent study (Militello forthcoming) has allowed the overall nature of Protopalatial Phaistos to be sketched, with particular regard to the much-debated issue of whether the palace represented an effective building of power (with a clear distinction between residents and common people) or was simply the social arena of competing factions (Schoep 2006). The available documentation (architecture, pottery, administration, seals, etc.), analyzed from the point of view of use and consumption, has led to the conclusion that the MM II palace was not only a place for ceremonies or the gathering of people. In fact, the complex functional articulation, the independent economic activity, and the tangible degree of closeness toward the outside all suggest that the building was also the center of an established authority of theocratic nature and was restricted to a limited number of persons.

The inhabitants of the palace interacted actively with the outside world and shared the same material culture (different in terms of quantity but not in terms of quality). The palace can be assumed to have also had a double aspect from an economic point of view: as a center of production of luxury items and also as a simple consumer of agricultural and husbandry products. It therefore lived off tribute and not though the control of production, as was also the case for the Mycenaean palace.

The emerging group of the Phaistian palace needs to be placed within a social egalitarian context. This group not only controlled production but also shared in it. In this perspective, the Protopalatial period cannot be considered in a unitary way, as was characterized by qualitative changes over time.

The architectural complexity of the southwest quarter suggests the existence of a social group that was able to plan for large-scale, long-term activity at the beginning of MM IB. The building seems, from a planimetric perspective, to be open toward the outside in this first phase and therefore functionally and socially permeable.

In a second phase, during the first part of MM II, the palatial building seems to have achieved its definitive form. The emerging group, after having consolidated its power, showed a greater capability for economic and workforce management, as proved by the administrative documents. At the same time, a trend toward the manipulation of the religious sphere began, and the architectural transformations reveal a closure toward the outside. Power is, at this point, solidly in the hands of a dominant group, although some traditional forms of communal festivity localized in the paved area of the so-called theatrical staircase are also maintained, perhaps for symbolic reasons but also to uphold a certain degree of social cohesion.

In the final phase of MM II, the palatial elite apparently elaborated a foreign iconography through the adoption of royal Egyptian and Near Eastern ideologies in order to emphasize a certain distance from the mortals—a sign of a movement toward royalty that was never fully accomplished (Militello forthcoming).

A strong earthquake, probably just before 1700 BC (at the end of MM IIB) (Monaco and Tortorici 2004), destroyed the palace and the houses of the settlement, which were never rebuilt. The two lower floors of the southwest quarter of the palace were abandoned, and only the upper floor was reconstructed (La Rosa, in AA.VV. 2001).

Recent test pits have shown that the reconstruction was particularly difficult in proximity to the western façade (La Rosa 2004, 2007). The remains of five courses of foundations have been brought to light just beneath the limit of the façade of the later palace; the lower course could be referred to the construction of the original palace at the beginning of MM IB; the fourth seems to document a first attempt at reconstructing the building destroyed by the 1700 BC earthquake, with a recession of the line of the façade. The idea of the recession was eventually abandoned for unknown reasons, and it was instead decided to resume the façade that had just been destroyed, to which three small rooms functioning as shrines (probably to ward off other earthquakes) were added near the theatrical staircase, which have led some to dub this phase the "*Fase* dei sacelli" (La Rosa 2002a; Carinci and La Rosa 2007).

A large house was built to the south of the ramp for an elite group that was also involved in the religious sphere (Carinci, in AA. VV. 2001). A pottery kiln was instead built above a destroyed house near the Piazzale of the theatrical staircase and the bending of the ramp.

A second earthquake in MM IIB (only a few years after the earlier one) caused the definitive destruction of the First Palace and had heavy repercussions for the economic and political structures. In a hectic transitional period, the ruins were leveled off in a massive operation and covered with a thick layer of *calcestruzzo* (known locally as *astraki*: Altavilla et. al. 2006), when an attempt was made to construct a new palatial building during MM IIIA.

The approximate estimate of the quantity of this *calcestruzzo* (including that which remained in situ, that which was removed during the excavation, and that which degraded and was already removed in antiquity) is between 3,000 and 3,400 m³, which provides an idea of the extent of the works and of the grandeur of the reconstruction project, which, however, was never brought to completion. Only the palace was rendered partially inhabitable in MM IIIA (with an administrative activity that, judging from the few surviving documents, was reduced to a minimum).

The column bases identified on the western side of the central court have been recently attributed to this period (suggesting that the central court was certainly in use), together with staircase 6, the original shoulder of which probably marked the line of the façade that was exactly resumed in the Second Palace (Carinci and La Rosa forthcoming). A new walking level in beaten earth was prepared above the paving of the *piazzale* of the theatrical staircase (*Piazzale I*). The *Kouloures* were probably filled in, and the orthostats of the previous façade represent the limit of the space in which the theatrical staircase remained entirely in sight. Ceramic deposits along the western area of the building and a lustral basin (the first in a palatial architectural context) also document the recovery that occurred during MM IIIA (Carinci and La Rosa forthcoming).

The so-called Disk building should also be dated to the MM IIIA period palace. It was constructed near the northern limit of the hill and provided the famous and mysterious clay disk with a text written on both faces (containing 241 symbols made by forty-five stamps or puncheons), which could perhaps be interpreted as a religious formulary.

The Casa a Sud della Rampa was entirely rebuilt in MM IIIA; the houses were certainly located at Chalara and on the Acropoli mediana but not at Ayia Photini. New decorative motifs document the increased importance of the wall decoration of rooms (Militello 2001).

A new earthquake destroyed Phaistos toward the middle of the 17th century BC (end of MM IIIA), with an extraordinary consequence: the total abandonment of the palace, which was thereafter left in ruins (with the central court free and seemingly in view) for more than a century and a half. The site continued to be inhabited in the MM IIIB period (second half of the 17th century BC), as revealed by ceramic deposits in the southwest area of the palace and on the Acropoli mediana, and by an elite mansion on the northeast limit of the palace hill (buildings 103 and 104); no frequentation traces were identified in the Chalara quarter (La Rosa 2002b; Girella 2007).

It is therefore probable that the autarchic economic model typical of Protopalatial Phaistos had gone into crisis at this point, in contrast to the more dynamic model typical of the centers of the northern coast (such as Knossos and Malia), which were largely interested in maritime trade. Knossos, therefore, seemingly absorbed the effects of the last earthquake much more quickly and gradually extended its political control over central Crete. The outcome of this control was perhaps the construction of the so-called Royal Villa at Ayia Triada toward the end of the 17th century BC (end of MM IIIB–beginning of LM IA), in which a sort of vassal of the Lords of the Labyrinth seems to have been established in order to control the economy of the surrounding territory (La Rosa 1997; Puglisi 2003). Ayia Triada had at this point seemingly become the administrative capital of the ex-Phaistian kingdom in the Mesara, and Kommos had strengthened its function as a large maritime establishment and was probably less involved in the affairs of territorial control.

The palace at Phaistos remained abandoned throughout the LM IA period. Another seismic destruction at the end of that period (and probably connected to the catastrophe that occurred at Thera) apparently heavily damaged the palace at Knossos and undermined the system of territorial control that it had exercised until this point (with heavy repercussions for the Mesara plain).

The second palace at Phaistos was not reconstructed until the beginning of the LM IB. At this time it was deprived of any bureaucratic-administrative function and underwent both an integral reuse of the central court and a considerable reduction in plan through the difficult removal of entire sectors of *calcestruzzo* that had remained unused for a long time (La Rosa 2002b). On its western side, the new building had an extension of 830–850 m^2 less than the first one; the first one was, however, probably about 280 m^2 narrower. The level of the paving of the piazzale with the theatrical staircase (only three or four steps of which were still visible, proving that the group involved had also been notably restricted from a numerical point of view) was also raised with the debris from the removal.

The reconstruction project was provided with a large monumental entrance. A fourth court was created on the eastern side of the building where the traces of a further, limited subphase are visible, which, perhaps when the palace had been partially abandoned, led to the construction of a pottery kiln (Tomasello 1996). The new building was not provided with frescoes of human figures or with administrative documents (contrary to the nearby Royal Villa at Ayia Triada).

At the same time, a rich mansion was built at Chalara (Palio 2001), as well as a house at Ayia Photini (Palio in AA.VV. 2001) on the northern slope of the hill and a large structure, partially visible, on the saddle at the base of the eastern slopes of Christòs Effendi.

The construction of the Second Palace at Phaistos, an event rich in ideological connotations, presupposes economic availability and a change in power relations with a weakening Knossian leadership that was so well documented in the previous phase, although this does not necessarily imply a decline or lack of political enterprise). The floor assemblages of the new palace were not, however, particularly abundant, in striking contrast to the richness of the destruction levels of the mansion at Chalara or of the house at Ayia Photini.

It might not be a coincidence that the only three relevant deposits retrieved from the Second Palace (complex of rooms 8–11; lustral basin 63d; and staircase 51) contained ceramic shapes that relate, totally or in part, to the cultic sphere, and that the skoutelia, the plain, handleless cups (certainly used in communal libation ceremonies), were the most common shape. It is similarly meaningful that only ten pithoi, whole or fragmentary, were found within the destruction level, half of which were concentrated in room 11. The mansion at Chalara contained nine pithoi, while the villa at Ayia Triada contained about fifty.

This new palace had a brief life (perhaps less than fifty years). It was most probably destroyed by an earthquake followed by fires (as evident in the nearby villa at Ayia Triada). From an ideological point of view, it cannot be considered causal that the so-called megaron was constructed above the ruins of the villa at Ayia Triada rather than above the palace. The Second Palace at Phaistos, with its numerous courts and public areas, its monumental entrance, the elegant *peristilio 74*, and the pottery kiln set within the eastern wing continued to preserve the mysteries of an unusual Dimidiata Domus Regia (La Rosa 2002b).

Numerous questions remain about the local picture of the Mesara of this period, as exemplified by the profound qualitative and quantitative differences between the destruction levels at Phaistos and Ayia Triada, which cannot be fully explained through subsequent architectural events. It seems that the process of political restoration at Phaistos was not completed because the administrative capital of the surrounding territory remained at Ayia Triada.

The situation seems to depend on a local logic rather than a Cretan one in a period in which the area might have reached a larger autonomy, but this hypothesis would require that the various scholars reach agreement about the consistency and role of Knossos in this period, without forgetting the high quality of the pottery. The available data do not, however, allow the hypothesis that the diverse consistency of buildings such as the Second Palace at Phaistos and the villa at Ayia Triada reflect a process of differentiation of the local elites, in which the Phaistian might have had a more accentuated religious or ritual connotation.

The picture is enriched by Kommos (from MM IIB), a site to which the excavators have attributed a palatial character. It cannot be ruled out that this center was kept out of the territorial dynamics of the Mesara by its specific function and position, which inserted it into a Mediterranean network of routes and exchanges. The only noncontroversial information is, so far, the absence from Phaistos and Ayia Triada of the imports that are so well documented at Kommos.

This political trend apparently also continued in the Postpalatial period (second half of the 15th to the end of the 13th centuries BC), when a mainland dynasty controlled the palace at Knossos. Ayia Triada (with its numerous public buildings) remained the center of Mycenaean power in the Mesara, and Phaistos reacquired a dominant position in the territory only at the end of the Minoan period, toward the end of the 13th century BC.

An elite building constructed at Chalara above the ruins of the mansion of the previous period is the only construction attributable to LM IIIA1–A2. The area of the palace, which was accessed through a ramp near the southwest corner, was certainly reoccupied. A sort of stepped altar is arranged in the southeast corner of the central court. Houses and floor levels were only identified in the area immediately to the west and south of the lower western court of the first palace, while a pottery kiln was established at Chalara (Tomasello 1996).

The surviving testimonies, in other words, suggest a settlement of a certain consistency (perhaps articulated in nuclei) that was probably deprived of public or monumental buildings. Moreover, some of the rock-cut chamber tombs of the necropolis at Kalivia (datable to the end of the 15th and the beginning of the 14th centuries BC) belonged to members of the Mycenaean warrior elite who reigned at Knossos—as demonstrated by the swords, golden rings, jewelry, seals, and other precious objects of the funerary assemblages, which, unfortunately, cannot be precisely reconstructed due to the nature of their excavation (Cucuzza 2002). It is also useful to recall that two-wheeled decorated war chariots, which were privileged symbols of power and proclaimed the authority of the Knossos palace, are associated with the name *pa-i-to* (which most probably refers to a large territory rather than just to the site) in the Mycenaean archives of Knossos.

The southern Mesara area (in which it is also necessary to locate the site of *da-wo)* appears to be linked to both intense animal exploitation, especially sheep, and weaving and to be perfectly integrated into the complex system of Mycenaean textile production. In fact, 21,666 units of sheep are listed in the Mesara; tablet KN Dn 1094+1311 mentions 1,509 at *pa-i-to* and 2,440 at *da-wo;* working women who came from these two sites or settled in them are indicated as *pa-i-ti-ja* and *da-wi-ja*. In tablet KN Lc 52, the women of *da-wo* are expected to provide 207 units of wool, which is among the largest quantity ever recorded for a single group. The

Mesara, from the Knossos archive, also appears to have been a formidable wheat producer: 10,000 units of wheat (which represent the largest quantity ever recorded in Linear B, corresponding to 96,000 liters, which would require something like 1,700 pithoi to be stored) are concentrated at *da-wo* (Cucuzza 2003).

The most recent (13th century BC) and poorest nucleus of the necropolis that has been conventionally attributed to Phaistos, but might also be connected to some minor site, has been identified at Liliana. The first excavators defined the two groups of tombs of Kalivia and Liliana as "elite" and "plebeian" respectively. A sporadic resumption of the deposition is attested in the large tholos at Kamilari, and traces of frequentation have been noticed at Paterikies (Levi 1976).

The abandonment of the nearby site of Ayia Triada at the end of LM IIIB led immediately to a notable resurgence of Phaistos, for which an act of synoecism has been hypothesized. A very rich LM IIIC ceramic deposit (12th century BC) connected with communal and ritual practices was uncovered in 1955 near the Stratigraphical Museum (Borgna 2004b). A large house with several constructive phases has been excavated immediately to the west of the so-called theatrical staircase: it was probably a self-sufficient structure (also from the point of view of artisan production), for which a comparison with the *oikos* of the Homeric world has been proposed (Borgna in AA.VV. 2001; Borgna 2004b).

The data related to the sub-Minoan period (12th–11th century BC) are not very perspicuous but give the impression of more inhabited nuclei spread throughout the territory rather than a large unitary center as in the previous period (Palermo in AA.VV. 2001).

A vigorous resurgence of the center in the last quarter of the 7th century BC sees the construction of a large temple, probably a Letoon. The destruction by Gortyn in the middle of the 2nd century BC ends the long history of Phaistos.

BIBLIOGRAPHY

AA. VV. 2001. *I cento anni dello scavo di Festòs* (Atti dei Convegni Lincei, 173).Rome: Accademica Nazionale dei Lincei.

Altavilla, Claudia, E. Ciliberto, V. La Rosa, P. Militello, and S. Parlato. 2006. "Minoan 'Astraki' at Phaistos: Relationship between Technology and Archaeology." In *Proc. 2° Intern. Conf. "Ancient Greek Technology"* (Athens, 17–11.10.2005), 145–50. Athens: Technikò epimelitirio Elladas.

Borgna, Elisabetta. 2004a. "Aegean Feasting: A Minoan Perspective." In *The Mycenaean Feast*, ed. James C. Wright, 127–59. *Hesperia* 73(2). Princeton: American School of Classical Studies at Athens.

———. 2004b. *Il complesso di ceramiche TM III dall'Acropoli mediana di Festòs*. Studi di Archeologia Cretese 3. Padua: Ausilio editore.

Carinci, Filippo. 2001. "Per una diversa interpretazione delle *kulure* nei cortili occidentali dei palazzi minoici." *Creta Antica* 2: 43–60.

————, and Vincenzo La Rosa. 2007. "Revisioni festie." *Creta Antica* 8: 11–113.

————. 2009. "Revisioni festie II." *Creta Antica* 10: 147–294.

————. Forthcoming. "A New Ceremonial Building in MM IIIA Phaistos." In *Intermezzo: Intermediacy and Regeneration in Middle Minoan III Crete*. International workshop held at Knossos (Villa Ariadne, July 3–5, 2008), ed. Carl Knappett, Eleni Banou, and Colin Macdonald. *BSA* Studies.

Cucuzza, Nicola. 2002. "Osservazioni sui costumi funerari dell'area di Festòs ed Haghia Triada nel TM IIIA1–A2." *Creta Antica* 3: 133–66.

————. 2003. "Il volo del grifo: Osservazioni: Sulla Haghia Triada 'micenea.'" *Creta Antica* 4: 199–271.

Di Tonto, Serena. 2008. Il neolitico finale a Creta: L'insediamento di Festòs. PhD diss., Università di Udine.

————. 2009. "Il neolitico finale a Festòs: Per una riconsiderazione funzionale dei dati dagli scavi Levi." *Creta Antica* 9: 57–94.

Girella, Luca. 2007. "Towards a Definition of the Middle Minoan III Ceramic Sequence in South-central Crete: Returning to the Traditional MM IIIA and B Division?" In *Middle Helladic Pottery*, 233–55.

La Rosa, Vincenzo. 1997. "La 'Villa Royale' de Haghia Triada." In *The Function of the "Minoan Villa" (Athens, 6–8 June 1992)*, ed. Robin Hägg, 79–89. Acta Instituti Atheniensis Regni Sueciae, ser. in 4°, no. XLVI. Stockholm: Svenska Institutet i Athen.

————. 1998–2000. "Festòs 1994: Saggi di scavo e nuove acquisizioni." *ASAtene* LXXVI–LXXVIII: 27–134.

————. 2000. "Per i cento anni dello scavo di Festòs." *Creta Antica* I: 3–40.

————. 2002a. "Le campagne di scavo 2000–2002 a Festòs." *ASAtene* LXXX(2): 635–869.

————. 2002b. "Pour une révision préliminaire du Second Palais de Phaistos." In *Monuments of Minos*, 71–96.

————. 2004. "I saggi della campagna 2004 a Festòs." *ASAtene* LXXXII(2): 611–70.

————. 2005. "Nuovi dati sulla via di ascesa alla collina del Palazzo festio dall'età minoica alla geometrica." *Creta Antica* 6: 227–84.

————. 2007. "New Data on the Western Façade of the Phaistian Palace." In *Krinoi Kai Limenes*, 23–30.

Levi, Doro. 1976. *Festòs e la civiltà minoica*, vol. 1. Rome: Edizioni dell'Ateneo.

————, and Filippo Carinci. 1988. *Festòs e la civiltà minoica*. Vol. 2, part 2, *L'arte festia in età protopalaziale*. Rome: Edizioni dell'Ateneo.

Militello, Pietro. 2001. *Gli affreschi minoici di Festòs*. Studi di Archeologia Cretese 2, 19–216. Padua: Ausilio editore.

————. 2002. "Amministrazione e contabilità a Festòs. II: Il contesto archeologico dei documenti palatini." *Creta Antica* 3: 51–91.

————. Forthcoming. "Emerging Authority: A Functional Analysis of the MM II Settlement of Festòs." In *Back to the Beginning*.

Monaco, Carmelo, and Luigi Tortorici. 2004. "Faulting Effects of Earthquakes on Minoan Archaeological Sites in Crete (Greece)." *Tectonophysics* 382: 103–16.

Palio, Orazio. 2001. *La casa Tardo Minoico I di Chalara a Festòs*. Studi di Archeologia Cretese 2, 247–422. Padua: Ausilio editore.

————. 2008. *I vasi in pietra minoici da Festòs*. Studi di archeologia cretese 5. Padua: Ausilio editore.

Pernier, Luigi. 1935. *Il palazzo minoico di Festòs*, vol. 1. Rome: La Libreria dello Stato.

————, and Luisa Banti. 1951. *Il palazzo minoico di Festòs*, vol. 2. Rome: La Libreria dello Stato.

Puglisi, Dario. 2003. "Haghia Triada nel periodo Tardo Minoico I. " *Creta Antica* 4: 145–97.

Schoep, Ilse. 2006. "Looking beyond the First Palaces: Elites and the Agency of Power in EM III–MM II Crete." *AJA* 110: 37–64.

Todaro, Simona. 2009. "The Latest Prepalatial Period and the Foundation of the First Palace at Phaistos: A Stratigraphic and Chronological Re-assessment." *Creta Antica* 10: 105–45.

———. Forthcoming a. "Craft Production and Social Practice at Prepalatial Phaistos: The Background to the First Palace." In *Back to the Beginning.*

———. Forthcoming b. "Pottery Production in Prepalatial Mesara: The Artisans' Quarter to the West of the Palace at Phaistos." In *Back to the Starting Line: New Theoretical and Methodological Approaches to Early Bronze Age Crete* (Athens, December 21, 2007), ed. Despina Catapoti and Borjia Legarra.

———, and Serena Di Tonto. 2008. "The Neolithic Settlement of Phaistos Revisited: Evidence for Ceremonial Activity on the Eve of the Bronze Age." In *Escaping the Labyrinth*, 177–90.

Tomasello, Francesco. 1996. "Fornaci a Festòs ed Haghia Triada dall'età mediominoica alla geometrica." In *Keramika Ergastiria stin Kriti apo tin archaeotita os simera (Actes du 1er Colloque international 1995 de Margaritès, Crète)*, ed. Irini Gavrilaki, 27–37. Réthymno: Istoriki Laografiki Etaireia Rethymnis.

Vagnetti, Lucia. 1972–1973. "L'insediamento neolitico di Festòs." *ASAtene* L–LI: 7–134.

Mainland Greece

CHAPTER 45

ARGOLID

SOFIA VOUTSAKI

THE Argolid is one of the most intensively investigated and best-documented regions of the Aegean. Due to its fertile soils and its geographic position at the crossroads of communication routes, the area played an important role in social and cultural development throughout the Bronze Age.

The Argolid, as we define it on the basis of modern administrative divisions, is divided into natural subregions that witnessed different types of development throughout the Bronze Age (Wright 2004a, 115–16). The fertile Argos plain and the mountainous periphery that drains into it was—all through the Bronze Age—the heart of the Argolid, where the most important settlements were located. The valleys to the southeast, around Asine and Kandia, are reasonably fertile and had good anchorages. The Epidauria, the Methana peninsula with Troizenia, and the southern Argolid are less productive; these areas were separated from the Argos plain by mountains and were oriented more toward the Saronic Gulf.

CHRONOLOGICAL FRAMEWORK

The chronological divisions in Aegean prehistory are agreed upon in broad terms, though its subdivisions, especially the transition to the LBA, are debated (see the debate between the proponents of the 'Low Chronology,' e.g., Warren and Hankey 1989, and those favoring a 'High Chronology,' most recently Manning et al. 2006). Table 1 (at the beginning of this book) presents a simplified version of the chronological framework (full discussion, with references, can be found in Rutter 2001, 106; Shelmerdine 2001, 332).

THE EARLY HELLADIC I PERIOD

The beginning of the EBA in the Argolid is not very well documented, as EH I settlement layers are often obscured by later occupation, and only a few graves have been found in the Argolid (three graves in the settlement at Apollo Maleatas: Theodorou-Mavrommatidi 2004). Alram-Stern (2004, 587, 602, based on Weisshaar 1990) mentions thirty-three EH I sites (mostly small ones; see Dousougli-Zachou 1998, 29), but the settlement pattern is not well understood. The material culture is undistinguished, and metal is rare (Rutter 1997, lesson 3). The local pottery differs from the classic EH I assemblage of central Greece (concerning the 'Talioti assemblage,' see Dousougli 1987; Weisshaar 1990). In terms of cultural development, the phase should be seen as a terminal phase of the LN (Rutter 1997, lesson 3) rather than an embryonic stage of the EBA.

THE EARLY HELLADIC II PERIOD

The EH II period witnesses population increase, economic growth, clearer differentiation within and between communities, and the production of more elaborate and diverse material culture (see Pullen 1985; Wiencke 1989; Alram-Stern 2004; Weiberg 2007). The Argolid plays a significant role in these developments. Several excavations (Asine: Frödin and Persson 1938; Lerna: Wiencke 2000; Tiryns: Kilian 1978, 1979, 1981, 1983; Kilian, Hiesel, and Weisshaar 1982; Berbati: Säflund 1965) and intensive surface surveys (references in Rutter 2001, 97–105; see also Wright 2004a) allow us to sketch a reasonably complete picture for this period.

Demographic growth is indicated by an increase in the number of settlements occupied in this period: Cosmopoulos (1998, 43) reports fifty-three sites in use in EH II (see also Wright 2004a, 119–23). An increase in the size of settlements is also evident: Tiryns, apparently the largest settlement, may have reached 6 ha, Asine 3 ha, and Lerna 2.25 ha, but many smaller sites existed as well (Cosmopoulos 1998, 42). A site hierarchy has been reconstructed consisting of regional centers (Tiryns, Lerna, perhaps Phournoi in the southern Argolid), smaller (satellite?) sites, and hamlets/farmsteads. However, the number of tiers, as well as the criteria for placing the settlements therein are debated (Rutter 2001, 124, with full references).

The reasons underlying this demographic and economic growth are difficult to comprehend. Renfrew, in his seminal *Emergence of Civilisation* (1972), has attributed the emergence of differentiation to economic changes and the intensification of production. He has argued that the introduction of Mediterranean polyculture (the cultivation of cereals, olives, and the vine) led to agricultural specialization and the emergence of a redistributive elite. The elite used surplus to support craft specialists in order to produce valuable items for local consumption and for exchange and thereby consolidated its position within the community.

Renfrew's model has been criticized on theoretical grounds (see most recently Barrett and Halstead 2004, with full references). However, for the study of the EH period, the main problem with Renfrew's model is the weak support for the initial change: The evidence for the cultivation of the olive and the grape in the EBA Aegean is very uncertain (Hansen 1988; Hamilakis 1996). Another explanation for the expansion into more marginal land may be the 'secondary products revolution' (i.e., the use of cattle for traction and the production of dairy products and wool) (Sherratt 1983; Manning 1994). Although the archaeozoological evidence does not fully support this hypothesis (Halstead 1996, 32), a fragmentary figurine of a yoked (?) pair of oxen, found in Tsoungiza (Pullen 1992), is the first indication of the use of the plow in the prehistoric Aegean.

To return to the archaeological evidence, settlements in this period not only become larger but also acquire certain 'protourban' features: collective works (e.g., fortifications, streets), monumental buildings, and sometimes a more regular layout (Hägg and Konsola 1986).

EH II Lerna (Wiencke 2000) is the best-documented example. The fortification wall was erected in stages, and the towers and outer wall were added later. The wall was more or less contemporary to Building BG, the earlier central building that was razed to ground for the construction of the House of the Tiles. The House of the Tiles (so-called because of the terracotta tiles used for its roof), was a large (25 by 12 m) freestanding house with two floors and an open paved area around it. The ground floor had a regular axial design, with two large halls and two smaller rooms flanked by corridors (hence the type is called 'Corridor House'—Shaw 1987). It was found largely empty (perhaps it was undergoing repair at the time of destruction?) with the exception of some pottery and a mass of sealings in a small room.

Renfrew (1972) interpreted the sealings as an indication of a redistributive system and hence the House of the Tiles as the residence of the redistributive elite (see also Wiencke 1989, 504). However, new discoveries (e.g., the sealings found in the site of Petri—Kostoula 2004) have weakened the connection between sealings and central buildings. Recent studies (Nilsson 2004, 144ff., 208–14; Peperaki 2004, 226–27; Weiberg 2007, 53) prefer a more open or communal function for the House of the Tiles, but the question cannot easily be settled. It has been proposed that another monumental structure, the 'Rundbau' in Tiryns, a circular construction consisting of concentric corridors, is a granary (Kilian 1986b, 68–69; see also Haider 1980), though we have little information about its function.

As only a few EH II burials have been found in the Argolid (Cavanagh and Mee 1998, 22; Pullen 1994; Weiberg 2007, 188ff.), analysis of them does not really elucidate social relations. Strangely, most appear to be intramural, a practice usually attributed to the EH III period.

While the EH II period is characterized by intensification of exchanges across the southern Aegean (Alram-Stern 2004, 485ff.), the position of the Argolid is not very well understood as only objects from Lerna have been analyzed in detail. The list of imported raw materials includes obsidian and flint (Runnels 1985a, 143–48) and andesite from Aegina (Runnels 1985b). Carter (1999, 53–69) has argued that some coastal sites, including Lerna, acted as centers for the importation, manufacture, and further distribution of obsidian. Metal seems to have reached Lerna from Laurion, the Cyclades, and northern Greece and also possibly from sources outside the Aegean (Kayafa, Stos-Gale, and Gale 2000). Pottery in the EH Argolid (and the mainland as a whole) seems to be produced and distributed locally (Alram-Stern 2004, 477), though imports have been found in Lerna (Wiencke 2000, 634). The Argolid as a whole, in contrast to coastal sites in Attica or Euboea, received very few Cycladic imports and produced no local imitations of Cycladic types (Sampson 1988, 8; Alram-Stern 2004, 486).

THE EH III–MH I–MH II PERIOD

The transition from the EH to the MH period in the Argolid is marked by a severe discontinuity involving destructions, population decline, and social regression (Maran 1998; Rutter 2001, 113). Monumental structures such as the House of the Tiles and the Rundbau, as well as also entire settlements, are destroyed and/or abandoned. Both the number and the size of sites decrease markedly (Wright 2004a, 119–21; Zavadil in press). However, the decline is less dramatic than in other regions of the southern mainland; in fact, certain (poorly documented) sites such as Argos (Touchais 1998) or Mycenae (Shelton in press) may have remained fairly large during the earlier MH period.

The changes in settlement pattern are accompanied by pervasive changes in material culture (new pottery types, apsidal rather than rectangular houses, etc). Forsén's (1992) study has demonstrated that these changes, hitherto attributed to waves of invaders (Howell 1973; Hood 1986), do not all appear at the same time, nor are they consistently associated with destruction (or postdestruction) layers. Recent studies place more emphasis on environmental factors such as land degradation and erosion (Zangger 1993) due to overexploitation, but the dates of these phenomena and their causes (climatic or anthropogenic?) are still debated (Whitelaw 2000; for climate change, see Manning 1997). However, migration, or at least infiltrations of ethnic groups, remain part of the explanatory framework (Maran 2007).

Whatever the causes of this discontinuity were, its social consequences were profound. During the early phases of the MH period, differentiation within communities appears minimal. Settlements now consist of freestanding, randomly placed houses, and there is no evidence of collective works. House construction and contents vary little before the MH III period, though exceptions exist.

Mortuary practices confirm the absence of overt differentiation, though subtle variation between age and burial (kinship?) groups can be observed (Ingvarsson-Sundström 2003; Voutsaki 2004; Milka in Voutsaki, Triantaphyllou, and Milka 2005, 37; Triantaphyllou in press). Simple intramural graves contain as a rule single, contracted inhumations, rarely accompanied by offerings, though exceptions are found. Material culture is in general austere and rather conservative despite some technological advances (Kayafa in press; Spencer in press). The dearth of metal finds, and of precious metal in particular, further emphasizes the absence of social asymmetries. Therefore, in the Argolid at least, there is little evidence for elites or aggrandizing leaders (*contra* Kilian-Dirlmeier 1997 and Wright 2004b). It has been suggested, therefore, that social organization in early MH times was based on kin divisions (Voutsaki 2005) and that status differences emerged only toward the end of the period. This may explain the overall uniformity of material culture and the austerity of social practices in the early MH period.

However, differences between communities existed, both in size and population and also in the diversity of their economic activities. Undoubtedly, economic life must have been based on agriculture and animal husbandry (Nordquist 1987; see Hielte-Stavropoulou for pastoralism in the MBA). Craft specialization may not have exceeded the level of household industries (Nordquist 1995; Hartenberger and Runnels 2001), but activities such as metalworking are attested in only a few sites (e.g., Lerna). The disrupted contacts between the Argolid, the Aegean islands, and Crete are already reinitiated in MH I (Rutter 2001, 122–24; for the situation in EH III see Runnels 1985b; Alram-Stern 2004, 486). While the distribution of imported ceramics (Rutter and Zerner 1984, 77–78; Nordquist 1987, 62–67; Zerner 1993, 50–51) allows us to reconstruct several small-scale networks overlapping and intersecting in the Argolid, different sites received different amounts of imports. The Argolid's central position in (ceramic) exchange networks, as well as the uneven participation of various communities in these networks, may have been factors underlying the later developments.

MH III–LH I–LH II

The process of recovery from the crisis that affected the Argolid and the entire southern mainland starts in MH III and becomes consolidated during LH I–LH II (see Dietz 1991 on the transitional period). During these phases, population growth is attested by an increase in the number of sites (Zavadil in press) and in the size of some of the settlements (e.g., Mycenae, Argos). Certain areas that lay abandoned during early MH are now resettled, and survey data suggest a more intensive land use (Wright 2004a, 122). A three-tiered site hierarchy can once more be reconstructed (Rutter 2001, 130–31), although, in the absence of information on settlement size, the criterion is often the presence of rich tombs.

Indeed, the main changes take place in the funerary realm: in MH III–LH I–LH II, mortuary practices undergo a profound transformation. Extramural, formal cemeteries are used more widely, and the practice of intramural burial gradually dies out; the practice of reuse of the tomb and the secondary treatment of the body spreads; new tomb types—the shaft grave, the chamber tomb, the tholos, especially designed for reuse—are adopted; there is a general increase in the quantity, quality, and diversity of funerary offerings. These changes are manifested in the most dramatic fashion in the Grave Circles of Mycenae (Karo 1930; Mylonas 1973; Graziadio 1991). The two burial precincts must have contained the members of the emerging elites in Mycenae, a site rising suddenly to power. They were made conspicuous by the enclosures and the sculpted *stelai* and contained large and impressive shaft graves. The deceased were buried with complex rites involving sacrifices and funerary meals and were accompanied by an amazing array of elaborate and exotic funerary offerings. The conspicuous consumption of coveted goods and their acquisition via gift exchange networks become the main strategies for the creation of power and prestige in this period (Voutsaki 1997). However, while status becomes an important criterion of social classification, kinship and descent remain important, as is apparent in the introduction of multiple tombs: The chamber tomb is adopted in LH I, and the tholos tomb in LH II.

Changes are less noticeable in the domestic realm: For instance, on the Aspis the haphazardly positioned MH IIIA houses are replaced in MH IIIB by a series of houses that adjoin each other and encircle the top of the hill (i.e., following the site's possible outer enclosure) (Touchais 1998, 76). More differentiation between domestic units is evident: For example, some MH III houses in Asine are much larger and complex and built with a more regular layout than earlier MH houses (Nordquist 1987, 87–90). Evidence for the existence of some kind of central buildings is, however, scanty, as early Mycenaean layers are obliterated by later occupation. Nevertheless, the LH II fresco fragments and feasting debris found in Mycenae (French and Shelton 2005, 175–77; French 2002, 44–47) imply that some kind of mansion stood here in this early period (the situation in Tiryns is less clear—Kilian 1988; Maran 2001).

These social changes bring about changes in material culture. The local production of valuable items and the adoption of figurative elements in the hitherto uniconic MH culture (Rutter 2001, 141–42) signal a new receptivity to external stimuli. These changes need to be explained against important historical developments: the peak of the Minoan palatial power and the growth of maritime polities in the Aegean; increased mobility and interaction in the MB III–LBI Aegean; the disappearance of the important harbor town of Akrotiri because of the volcanic eruption at some point in LB I; the demise of the Minoan palaces in LM IB. The social changes on the mainland and the rise of mainland centers, especially Mycenae, cannot be understood without reference to the integration of the mainland in expanding networks of exchange (Sherratt and Sherratt 1991; Voutsaki 1997). Recent studies have suggested that the manipulation of external contacts and alliances (Voutsaki 1997, 2005; Wright 2004b) must be closely related to competition between emerging elites that was eventually resolved—as much as it was ever resolved—with the emergence of the palatial system in LH IIIA. The process of Mycenaean expansion, which starts at the end of LH II, should also be understood in this light.

LH IIIA–LH IIIB

This period represents the peak of palatial power and centralization, as well as the climax of cultural expansion across the southern Aegean—two processes that are clearly interlinked. During LH IIIA, impressive palaces and the first fortifications were built in Mycenae and Tiryns (Maran 2001; French and Shelton 2005, 177; French 2002, 57–58; Wright 2006), while the wall in Midea was built later, in LH IIIB (Demakopoulou and Divari-Valakou 1999). Circuit walls may also have existed in Argos, but their presence is debated (Touchais 1998, 11). The Argolid, with three citadels, at least two impressive palaces, elaborate royal tholoi, and several hill forts, becomes perhaps the most powerful region in the southern mainland—only Boeotia may have been a serious rival.

The LH III period is a period of population growth, extension of settlement, and more intensive land use (Cherry and Davis 2001, 153; Wright 2004a, 121ff.). Palatial sites occupy the top of a complex, four-tiered site hierarchy (Cherry and Davis 2001, 150; Wright 2004a, 125). A complex road system connects Mycenae with both secondary centers and neighboring regions.

Unfortunately, a limited number of administrative tablets have been found in Mycenae and Tiryns, but they nonetheless fully confirm the picture of a centralized and hierarchical system reconstructed on the basis of the richer Linear B evidence at Pylos. The archaeological evidence corroborates this picture of a highly stratified society. Excavations in and around Mycenae (Iakovidis 1996; French 2002; French et al. 2003) have revealed different categories of building. The palace *megaron* with its complex design, central hearth, throne, and elaborate fresco decoration must have been the reception hall of the *wanax*. The so-called Ivory Houses, large buildings with special economic functions (storage, redistribution, production of valuable items?) may represent residences of palatial officials and are closely connected to the palatial system (Tournavitou 1995; French 2002, 67–68). Finally, the Panayia houses (Mylonas-Shear 1987; French 2002, 68) must have belonged to ordinary town residents, while outside the town the farmhouse at Khania (French 2002, 69) represents one of the few Mycenaean farmsteads ever excavated.

Hierarchy is clearly expressed in the funerary realm (Mee and Cavanagh 1984; Wright 1987; French 1989): While the majority, or at least a large segment of the population is now buried in chamber tombs, the use of tholoi in the Argolid becomes restricted to palatial centers (Voutsaki 1995). Since the palatial tholoi built in LH III, those of Atreus and Clytemnestra, are the most spectacular, large, and ornate examples, and chamber tombs in this period are generally poorer, the gap between the palatial elite and the rest of the population widens. The mortuary evidence therefore attests the establishment of a hierarchical, centralized, and exploitative system. However, the emphasis on display, both in the mortuary and the domestic realm (French 1989; Wright 2006), imply that power remained contested. This is confirmed in the most tangible fashion by the 'arms race,' the expansion and

strengthening of citadels in Mycenae and Tiryns, and the construction of the fortification in Midea during LH IIIB.

Mycenaean expansion across the southern Aegean also reached its peak during this period (Mee 1988; Schallin 1993; Voutsaki 2001). As suggested earlier, the
'Mycenaeanization' of the southern Aegean should be seen as an integral part of the
process of internal competition, of the constant quest for resources, and the need to
establish political alliances with powerful neighbors. In this period, there is evidence
of Mycenaean cultural influence across the entire Aegean extending to the coast of
Asia Minor and northern Greece, while evidence for economic contacts extends to
Cyprus, the Near East, the central Mediterranean, and the Balkans (Kilian 1986a).
The mechanisms of exchange, and specifically the role of the palaces in this process
of expansion, are heavily debated (Voutsaki 2001; Sherratt 2001). The palatial records
give sufficient (albeit at times enigmatic) information on highly specialized production for export and in general about complex and sophisticated control over at least
some sectors of the economy (general discussions: Voutsaki and Killen 2001; Galaty
and Parkinson 2007; Shelmerdine 2006; for the Argolid in particular, see Burns 1999;
Sjöberg 2001; Voutsaki in press). However, we should not oversimplify the picture:
Exchanges in this period must have operated in different, though perhaps interconnected, levels and circuits: the gift exchange and diplomatic alliances between royal
elites, as well as the more ordinary trade of raw materials and resources.

While establishing the role of specific regions and centers in the process of expansion is not easy, most of the decorated pottery found in the Near East comes from
the Argolid and possibly from Berbati (Schallin 2002), a site clearly controlled by
Mycenae (Schallin 1996, 124). In addition, Mycenae has by far the highest concentration of valuable imports in the Argolid (Cline 1994, 16; Burns 1999, 87, 105; Voutsaki
in press). Therefore, in the Argolid at least, Mycenae seems to be quite successful in
restricting the flow of resources (see Burns 1999, 176–94; Sjöberg 2001, 188–96, for a
different view). The implications of this for the political organization of the Argolid
are difficult to understand. There are diverse views as to whether we are dealing with
autonomous kingdoms centered on the three citadels or one unified kingdom, with
Mycenae at its center (see discussion in Darcque 1998, 110–11; Sjöberg 2001, 13–19),
although possibilities between these two extremes should also be considered.

Whatever the causes underlying the emergence and consolidation of the mainland centers, their power was short lived: The destructions in LH IIIB and the ensuing
'arms race' imply that conditions remained (or again became) unstable during the peak
of palatial power. Finally, by the end of LH IIIB, all of the palaces were destroyed in
a series of violent conflagrations. The causes of the destructions are debated (Deger-
Jalkotzy 1991, with full references), though most recently the possibility of earthquakes
is favored most (Kilian 1980; Åström and Demakopoulou 1996). However, the collapse
of the palatial system of control should not be attributed only to a natural disaster but
also to the conflicts and tensions arising in an overcentralized and exploitative system.
Warfare, local uprisings, and movements of population may have further weakened the
Mycenaean political system, though we need not necessarily think in terms of grand
invasions or large-scale migration (an idea revived in connection with the 'Hand-made

Burnished' or 'Barbarian' ware; see Eder 1998, 20–22). External factors may also have played a role: The crisis engulfing the entire eastern Mediterranean certainly contributed to the demise of the mainland centers, which had come to depend on the supply of raw materials and symbolic capital from outside the Aegean.

LH IIIC

The last century of the Mycenaean period witnesses not only a process of decline but also localized and temporary recuperation. The destruction of the palatial centers is accompanied by the abandonment of small settlements (Foxhall 1995, 245, 247; Eder 1998, 29, 53) and a process of nucleation toward the larger sites.

While the complex palatial system collapsed after the destructions, recent studies have emphasized elements of continuity as well: The fortifications were repaired, some of the buildings within the citadels were restored, megara were built over the destroyed palaces in Tiryns and perhaps in Mycenae (French 2002, 136–38; Maran 2006), and religious activity continued above the Cult Center in Mycenae and the shrines in the Tiryns Unterburg (Maran 2006, 12). The frescoes in Mycenae and the Tiryns Treasure imply a certain affluence (Maran 2006, 127, 129ff.). Tiryns town seems to grow in size (Kilian 1985, 75ff.), and its layout is restructured (Maran 2006, 125–26). However, other important settlements or cemeteries (Mycenae, Argos, Asine, Nauplion) decrease in size. New mortuary practices are introduced (e.g., the use of the tumulus and cremation in Khania near Mycenae) (French 2002, 140).

External relations receive a serious blow by the destructions but seem to revive, if only temporarily and in certain sites (Mountjoy 1993, 174–76), despite the crisis that sweeps the entire eastern Mediterranean. However, by the end of the period, a general regression sets in: Settlements shrink or are abandoned; cemeteries fall out of use; imports cease; and the material culture is poor and carelessly made. The Mycenaean world has reached its end.

BIBLIOGRAPHY

Alram-Stern, Eva, ed. 2004. *Die ägäische Frühzeit 2. Serie: Forschungsbericht 1975–2002.* Vol. 2, part 2, *Die Frühbronzezeit in Griechenland mit Ausnahme von Kreta.* Vienna: Verlag der Österreichischen Akademie der Wissenschaften.

Åström, Paul, and Katie Demakopoulou. 1996. "Signs of an Earthquake at Midea?" In *Archaeoseismology*, eds. Stathis Stiros and Richard E. Jones, 37–40. Fitch Laboratory Occasional Paper 7. Athens: British School at Athens.

Barrett, John C., and Paul Halstead, eds. 2004. *The Emergence of Civilisation Revisited.*

Burns, Bryan E. 1999. Import Consumption in the Bronze Age Argolid (Greece): Effects of Mediterranean Trade on Mycenaean Society. PhD diss., University of Michigan.

Carter, Tristan. 1999. Through a Glass Darkly: Obsidian and Society in the Southern Aegean Early Bronze Age. PhD diss., University of London.

Cavanagh, William, and Christopher Mee. 1998. *A Private Place: Death in Prehistoric Greece.* SIMA 125. Jonsered, Sweden: Åström.

Cherry, John F., and Jack L. Davis. 2001. "'Under the Sceptre of Agamemnon': The View from the Hinterlands of Mycenae." In *Urbanism*, 141–59.

Cline, Eric H. 1994. *SWDS*.

Cosmopoulos, Michael B. 1998. "Le Bronze ancien 2 en Argolide: Habitat, urbanisation, population." In *Argos et l'Argolide: Topographie et urbanisme*, ed. Anne Pariente and Gilles Touchais, 41–50. Paris: Diffusion de Boccard.

Darcque, Paul. 1998. "Argos et la plaine argienne à l'époque mycénienne." In *Argos et l'Argolide: Topographie et urbanisme*, ed. Anne Pariente and Gilles Touchais, 103–15. Paris: Diffusion de Boccard.

Deger-Jalkotzy, Sigrid. 1991. "Die Erforschung des Zusammenbruchs der sogenannten mykenischer Kultur und der sogenannten dunkler Jahrhunderte." In *Zweihundert Jahre Homer-Forschung*, ed. Joachim Latacz, 127–54. Colloquium Rauricum Bd. 2. Stuttgart: Teubner.

Demakopoulou, Katie, and Nicoletta Divari-Valakou. 1999. "The Fortifications of the Mycenaean Acropolis of Midea." In *Polemos*, 205–15.

Dietz, Søren. 1991. *The Argolid at the Transition to the Mycenaean Age: Studies in the Chronology and Cultural Development in the Shaft Grave Period.* Copenhagen: National Museum of Denmark.

Dousougli, Angelika. 1987. "Makrovouni-Kefalari Magoula-Talioti/Bemerkungen zu den Stufen FH I und II in der Argolis." *PZ* 62(2): 164–220.

Dousougli-Zachou, Angelika. 1998. "I Argoliki pediada stin Ysteri Neolithiki kai Protohalki Epohi: Synopsi tis provlimatikis apo mia diepistimoniki proseggisi." In *Argos et l'Argolide: Topographie et urbanisme*, ed. Anne Pariente and Gilles Touchais, 24–34. Paris: Diffusion de Boccard.

Eder, Birgitta. 1998. *Argolis, Lakonien, Messenien vom ende der mykenischen Palastzeit bis zur Einwanderung der Dorier.* Mykenische Studien 17. Vienna: Verlag der Österreichischen Akademie der Wissenschaften.

Forsén, Jeannette. 1992. *The Twilight of the Early Helladics: A Study of the Disturbances in East-central and Southern Greece towards the End of the Early Bronze Age.* Jonsered, Sweden: Astrom.

Foxhall, Lin. 1995. "Bronze to Iron: Agricultural Systems and Political Structures in Late Bronze Age and Early Iron Age Greece." *BSA* 90: 239–50.

French, Elizabeth. 1989. " 'Dynamis' in the Archaeological Record at Mycenae." In *Images of Authority: Papers Presented to Joyce Reynolds on the Occasion of her 70th Birthday*, ed. Mary M. Mackenzie and Charlotte Roueché, 122–30. Cambridge Philological Society Supplementary vol. 16. Cambridge: Cambridge Philological Society.

———. 2002. *Mycenae: Agamemnon's Capital. The Site In Its Setting.* Gloucestershire: Tempus.

———, Spyros E. Iakovidis, Charalambos Ioannides, Anton Jansen, John Lavery, and Kim Shelton. 2003. *Archaeological Atlas of Mycenae.* Archaeological Society at Athens Library 229. Athens: Archaeological Society.

French, Elizabeth, and Kim Shelton. 2005. "Early Palatial Mycenae." In *Autochthon*, 175–84.

Frödin, Otto, and Axel W. Persson. 1938. *Asine: Results of the Swedish Excavations 1922–1930*. Stockholm: Generalstabens Litografiska Anstalts.

Galaty, Michael L., and William A. Parkinson. 2007. *Rethinking Mycenaean Palaces II*. Rev. and exp. 2nd ed. Los Angeles: Cotsen Institute of Archaeology, University of California at Los Angeles.

Graziadio, Gianpaolo. 1991. "The Process of Social Stratification at Mycenae in the Shaft Grave Period: A Comparative Examination of the Evidence." *AJA* 95: 403–40.

Hägg, Robin, and Dora Konsola, eds. 1986. *Early Helladic Architecture*.

Haider, Peter. 1980. "Zum frühhelladischen Rundbau in Tiryns." In *Forschungen und Funde: Festschrift Bernhard Neutsch*, ed. Fritz Krinzinger, 157–72. Innsbrucker Beiträge zur Kulturwissenschaft 21. Innsbruck: Institut für Sprachwissenschaft der Universität Innsbruck.

Halstead, Paul. 1996. "Pastoralism or Household Herding? Problems of Scale and Specialization in Early Greek Animal Husbandry." *WorldArch* 28: 20–42.

Hamilakis, Yannis. 1996. "Wine, Oil, and the Dialectics of Power in Bronze Age Crete: A Review of the Evidence." *OJA* 15: 1–32.

Hansen, Julie M. 1988. "Agriculture in the Prehistoric Aegean: Data versus Speculation." *AJA* 92: 39–52.

Hartenberger, Britt, and Curtis Runnels. 2001. "The Organization of Flaked Stone Production at Bronze Age Lerna." *Hesperia* 70(3): 255–83.

Hielte-Stavropoulou, Maria. 2004. "Sedentary versus Nomadic Life-styles: The 'Middle Helladic People' in Southern Balkan (Late 3rd and First Half of the 2nd Millennium BC)." *ActaArch* 75(2): 27–94.

Hood, Sinclair. 1986. "Evidence for Invasions at the End of the Early Bronze Age." In *The End of the Early Bronze Age in the Aegean*, ed. G. Cadogan, 31–68. Leiden: Brill.

Howell, Roger J. 1973. "The origins of the Middle Helladic Culture." In *Bronze Age Migrations in the Aegean*, ed. R. A. Crossland and Ann Birchall, 73–106. Park Ridge, N.J.: Noyes.

Iakovidis, Spyridon E. 1996. "Mycenae in the Light of Recent Discoveries." In *Atti e memorie del secondo congresso internazionale di micenologia* III, ed. Ernesto de Miro, Louis Godart, and Anna Sacconi, 1039–49. Incunabula Graeca 98. Rome: Gruppo editorial e internazionale.

Ingvarsson-Sundström, Anne. 2003. Children Lost and Found: A Bioarchaeological Study of Middle Helladic Children in Asine with a Comparison to Lerna. PhD diss., University of Uppsala.

Karo, Georg. 1930. *Die Schachtgräber von Mykenai*. Munich: Bruckmann.

Kayafa, Maria. In press. "Middle Helladic Metallurgy and Metalworking: Review of the Archaeological and Archaeometric Evidence from the Peloponnese." In *Mesohelladika*.

———, Sophie Stos-Gale, and Noel Gale. 2000. "The Circulation of Copper in the Early Bronze Age in Mainland Greece: The Lead Isotope Evidence from Lerna, Lithares, and Tsoungiza." In *Metals Make the World Go Round: The Supply and Circulation of Metals in Bronze Age Europe*, ed. Chris F. E. Pare, 39–55. Oxford: Oxbow.

Kilian, Klaus. 1978. "Ausgrabungen in Tiryns 1976: Bericht zu den Grabungen." *AA*: 449–70.

———. 1979. "Ausgrabungen in Tiryns 1977: Bericht zu den Grabungen." *AA*: 379–411.

———. 1980. "Zum Ende der mykenischen Epoche in der Argolis." *Jahrbuch des Römisch-Germanischen Zentralmuseums* 27: 166–93.

———. 1981. "Ausgrabungen in Tiryns 1978, 1979: Bericht zu den Grabungen." *AA*: 149–94.

———. 1983. "Ausgrabungen in Tiryns 1981: Bericht zu den Grabungen." *AA*: 277–328.

———. 1985. "La caduta dei palazzi micenei continentali: Aspetti archeologici." In *Le origini dei greci*, ed. Domenico Musti, 73–115. Rome: Laterza.

———. 1986a. "The Circular Building at Tiryns." In *Early Helladic Architecture*, 65–71.

———. 1986b. "Il confine settentrionale della civiltà micenea nella tarda età del bronzo." In *Traffici micenei nel mediterraneo: Problemi storici e documentazione archeologica*, ed. Massimiliano Marazzi, Sebastiano Tusa, and Lucia Vagnetti, 283–301. Magna Graecia 3. Taranto: Istituto per la storia e l'archeologia della Magna Grecia, Taranto.

———. 1988. "The Emergence of *Wanax* Ideology in the Mycenaean Palaces." *OJA* 7: 291–302.

———, Georg Hiesel, and Hans-Joachim Weisshaar. 1982. "Ausgrabungen in Tiryns 1980: Bericht zu den Grabungen." *AA*: 393–430.

Kilian-Dirlmeier, Imma. 1997. *Das mittelbronzezeitliche Schachtgrab von Ägina*. Mainz: von Zabern.

Kostoula, Maria. 2004. "Die Ausgrabungen in der frühhelladischen Siedlung von Petri bei Nemea." In *Die ägäische Frühzeit 2. Serie: Forschungsbericht 1975–2002*. Vol. 2, part 2, *Die Frühbronzezeit in Griechenland mit Ausnahme von Kreta*, ed. Eva Alram-Stern, 1135–57. Vienna: Verlag der Österreichischen Akademie der Wissenschaften.

Manning, Sturt W. 1994. "The Emergence of Divergence: Development and Decline on Bronze Age Crete and the Cyclades." In *Development and Decline in the Mediterranean Bronze Age*, ed. Clay Mathers and Simon Stoddart, 221–70. Sheffield Archaeological Monographs 8. Sheffield: Sheffield University Press.

———. 1997. "Cultural Change in the Aegean c. 2200 BC." In *Third Millennium BC Climate Change and Old World Collapse*, ed. Hasan N. Dalfes, George Kukla, and Harvey Weiss, 149–71. NATO ASI Series I, vol. 49. Berlin: Springer.

———, Christopher Bronk Ramsey, Walter Kutschera, Thomas Higham, Bernd Kromer, Peter Steier, and Eva M. Wild. 2006. "Chronology for the Aegean Late Bronze Age 1700–1400 BC." *Science* 312 (5573): 565–69.

Maran, Joseph. 1998. *Kulturwandel auf dem griechischen Festland und den Kykladen im späten 3. Jahrtausend v.Chr*. Bonn: Habelt.

———. 2001. "Zur Frage des Vorgängers des ersten Doppelpalastes von Tiryns." In *ITHAKE. Festschrift für Jörg Schäfer zum 75. Geburtstag*, ed. Stephanie Böhm und Klaus-Valtin von Eickstedt, 23–29. Würzburg: Ergon.

———. 2006. "Coming to Terms with the Past: Ideology and Power in Late Helladic IIIC." In *Ancient Greece: From the Mycenaean Palaces to the Age of Homer*, ed. Sigrid Deger-Jalkotzy and Irene S. Lemos, 123–50. Edinburgh Leventis Studies 3. Edinburgh: Edinburgh University Press.

———. 2007. "Seaborne Contacts between the Aegean, the Balkans, and the Central Mediterranean in the 3rd Millennium BC: The Unfolding of the Mediterranean World." In *BABS*, 3–23.

Mee, Christopher B. 1988. "A Mycenaean Thalassocracy in the Eastern Aegean ?" In *Problems in Greek Prehistory*, 301–305.

———, and William G. Cavanagh. 1984. "Mycenaean Tombs as Evidence for Social and Political Organization." *OJA* 3: 45–64.

Mountjoy, Penelope. 1993. *Mycenaean Pottery: An Introduction*. OUCA Monograph 36. Oxford: Oxbow.

Mylonas, Georgios. 1973. *O taphikos kyklos B ton Mykenon*. Archaeological Society at Athens Library 73. Athens: Archaeological Society.

Mylonas-Shear, Ione. 1987. *The Panagia Houses at Mycenae*. Philadelphia: University Museum, University of Pennsylvania.

Nilsson, Monika. 2004. A Civilization in the Making: A Contextual Study of Early Bronze Age Corridor Buildings in the Aegean. PhD diss., University of Gothenburg.

Nordquist, Gullög C. 1987. *A Middle Helladic Village: Asine in the Argolid*. Boreas, Uppsala Studies in Ancient Mediterranean and Near Eastern Civilization 16. Uppsala: Academia Ubsaliensis.

———. 1995. "Who Made the Pots? Production in the Middle Helladic Society." In *Politeia*, 201–207.

Peperaki, Olympia. 2004. "The House of the Tiles at Lerna: Dimensions of 'Social Complexity.'" In *Emergence of Civilisation Revisited*, 214–31.

Pullen, Daniel J. 1985. Social Organization in Early Bronze Age Greece: A Multidimensional Approach. PhD diss., Indiana University.

———. 1992. "Ox and Plow in the Early Bronze Age Aegean." *AJA* 96: 45–54.

———. 1994. "Modeling Mortuary Behavior on a Regional Scale: A Case Study from Mainland Greece in the Early Bronze Age." In *Beyond the Site: Regional Studies in the Aegean Area*, ed. P. Nick Kardulias, 113–36. Lanham, Md.: University Press of America.

Renfrew, A. Colin. 1972. *The Emergence of Civilisation: The Cyclades and the Aegean in the Third Millennium B.C.* London: Methuen.

Runnels, Curtis N. 1985a. "The Bronze Age Flaked Stone Industries from Lerna: A Preliminary Report." *Hesperia* 54(4): 357–91.

———. 1985b. "Trade and the Demand for Millstones in Southern Greece in the Neolithic and the Early Bronze Age." In *Prehistoric Production and Exchange: The Aegean and Eastern Mediterranean*, ed. A. Bernard Knapp and Tamara Stech, 30–43. UCLA Monograph 25. Los Angeles: Institute of Archaeology, University of California at Los Angeles.

Rutter, Jeremy B. 1997. *The Prehistoric Archaeology of the Aegean*. http://projectsx.dartmouth.edu/history/bronze_age/.

———. 2001. "The Pre-palatial Bronze Age of the Southern and Central Greek Mainland." In *Aegean Prehistory*, 95–156.

———, and Carol W. Zerner. 1984. "Early Hellado-Minoan Contacts." In *Minoan Thalassocracy*, 75–83.

Säflund, Gösta. 1965. *Excavations at Berbati 1936–1937*. Stockholm Studies in Classical Archaeology 4. Stockholm: Almqvist and Wiksell.

Sampson, Adamantios. 1988. "Early Helladic Contacts with the Cyclades during the EBA 2." *Aegaeum* 2: 5–10. Liège: Université de Liège.

Schallin, Anne-Louise. 1993. *Islands under Influence: The Cyclades in the Late Bronze Age and the Nature of Mycenaean Presence*. SIMA 111. Jonsered, Sweden: Åström.

———. 1996. "The Late Helladic Period." In *The Berbati-Limnes Archaeological Survey 1988–1990*, ed. Berit Wells and Curtis Runnels, 123–77. Skrifter utgivna av Svenska Institutet i Athen 4°, 44. Stockholm: Åström.

———. 2002. "Pots for Sale: The Late Helladic IIIA and IIIB Ceramic Production at Berbati." In *New Research on Old Material from Asine and Berbati in Celebration of the Fiftieth Anniversary of the Swedish Institute at Athens*, ed. Berit Wells, 141–55. Skrifter utgivna av Svenska Institutet i Athen 80, 17. Jonsered, Sweden: Åström.

Shaw, Joseph W. 1987. "The Early Helladic II Corridor House: Development and Form." *AJA* 91(1): 59–79.

Shelmerdine, Cynthia W. 2001. "Review of Aegean Prehistory VI: The Palatial Bronze Age of the Southern and Central Greek Mainland." In *Aegean Prehistory*, 329–81.

———. 2006. "Mycenaean Palatial Administration." In *Ancient Greece: From the Mycenaean Palaces to the Age of Homer*, ed. Sigrid Deger-Jalkotzy and Irene S. Lemos, 73–86. Edinburgh Leventis Studies 3. Edinburgh: Edinburgh University Press.

Shelton, Kim. In press. "Living and Dying in and around Middle Helladic Mycenae." In *Mesohelladika*.

Sherratt, Andrew. 1983. "The Secondary Exploitation of Animals in the Old World." *WorldArch* 15(1): 90–104.

———, and Susan Sherratt. 1991. "From Luxuries to Commodities: The Nature of Mediterranean Bronze Age Trading Systems." In *Bronze Age Trade*, 351–86.

Sherratt, Susan. 2001. "Potemkin Palaces and Route-based Economies." In *Economy and Politics in the Mycenaean Palace States*, ed. Sofia Voutsaki and John Killen, 214–38. Cambridge Philological Society Supplementary vol. 27. Cambridge: Cambridge Philological Society.

Sjöberg, Birgitte L. 2001. Asine and the Argolid in the Late Helladic III Period: A Socio-economic Study. PhD diss., University of Uppsala.

Spencer, Lindsay. In press. "The Regional Specialisation of Ceramic Production in the EH III through MH II Period." In *Mesohelladika*.

Theodorou-Mavrommatidi, Anthi. 2004. "An Early Helladic Settlement in the Apollon Maleatas Site at Epidauros." In *Die ägäische Frühzeit 2. Serie: Forschungsbericht 1975–2002*. Vol. 2, part 2, *Die Frühbronzezeit in Griechenland mit Ausnahme von Kreta*, ed. Eva Alram-Stern, 1167–88. Vienna: Verlag der Österreichischen Akademie der Wissenschaften.

Touchais, Gilles. 1998. "Argos à l'époque mésohelladique: Un habitat ou des habitats?" In *Argos et l'Argolide: Topographie et urbanisme*, ed. Anne Pariente and Gilles Touchais, 71–78. Paris: Diffusion de Boccard.

Tournavitou, Iphiyenia. 1995. *The "Ivory Houses" at Mycenae*. BSA Suppl. 24. London: British School at Athens.

Triantaphyllou, Sevasti. In press. "Prospects for Reconstructing the Lives of Middle Helladic Populations in the Argolid: Past and Present of Human Bone Studies." In *Mesohelladika*.

Voutsaki, Sofia. 1995. "Social and Political Processes in the Mycenaean Argolid: The Evidence from the Mortuary Practices." In *Politeia*, 55–66.

———. 1997. "The Creation of Value and Prestige in the Late Bronze Age Aegean." *Journal of European Archaeology* X: 34–52.

———. 2001. "Economic Control, Power, and Prestige in the Mycenaean World: The Archaeological Evidence." In *Economy and Politics in the Mycenaean Palace States*, ed. Sofia Voutsaki and John Killen, 195–213. Cambridge Philological Society Supplementary vol. 27. Cambridge: Cambridge Philological Society.

———. 2004. "Age and Gender in the Southern Greek Mainland, 2000–1500 BC." *Ethnographisch-archäologische Zeitschrift* 46(2–3): 339–63.

———. 2005. "Social and Cultural Change in the Middle Helladic Period: Presentation of a New Project." In *Autochthon*, 134–43.

———. In press. "From the Kinship Economy to the Palatial Economy: The Argolid in the 2nd Millennium BC." In *Political Economies in the Aegean Bronze Age*, ed. Daniel Pullen. Oxford: Oxbow.

———, and John Killen, eds. 2001. *Economy and Politics in the Mycenaean Palace States*. Cambridge Philological Society Supplementary vol. 27. Cambridge: Cambridge Philological Society.

Voutsaki, Sofia, Sevasti Triantaphyllou, and Eleni Milka. 2005. "Project on the Middle Helladic Argolid: A Report on the 2004 Season." *Pharos* 12 (2004): 31–40.

Warren, Peter, and Vronwy Hankey. 1989. *The Absolute Chronology of the Aegean Bronze Age*. Bristol: Bristol Classical Press.

Weiberg, Erika. 2007. *Thinking the Bronze Age: Life and Death in Early Helladic Greece*. Boreas, Uppsala Studies in Ancient Mediterranean and Near Eastern Civilization 29. Uppsala: Uppsala University Press.

Weisshaar, Hans-Joachim. 1990. "Die Keramik von Talioti: Ein Beitrag zum Beginn der frühen Bronzezeit in der Argolis." Tiryns XI, 1–34. Mainz: von Zabern.

Whitelaw, Todd. 2000. "Settlement Instability and Landscape Degradation in the Southern Aegean in the Third Millennium BC." In *Landscape and Land Use in Postglacial Greece*, ed. Paul Halstead and Charles Frederick, 135–61. Sheffield Studies in Aegean Archaeology 3. Sheffield: Sheffield Academic Press.

Wiencke, Martha H. 1989. "Change in Early Helladic II." *AJA* 93: 495–509.

———. 2000. *Lerna: A Preclassical Site in the Argolid*. Vol. 4.1–2, *The Architecture, Stratification, and Pottery of Lerna III*. Princeton: American School of Classical Studies at Athens.

Wright, James C. 1987. "Death and Power at Mycenae: Changing Symbols in Mortuary Practice." In *Thanatos*, 171–84.

———. 2004a. "Comparative Settlement Patterns during the Bronze Age in the Northeastern Peloponnesos, Greece." In *Side-by-side Survey: Comparative Regional Studies in the Mediterranean World*, ed. Susan E. Alcock and John F. Cherry, 114–31. Oxford: Oxbow Books.

———. 2004b. "The Emergence of Leadership and the Rise of Civilization in the Aegean." In *Emergence of Civilisation Revisited*, 64–89.

———. 2006. "The Social Production of Space and the Architectural Reproduction of Society in the Bronze Age Aegean during the 2nd Millennium B.C.E." In *Constructing Power: Architecture, Ideology, and Social Practice*, ed. Joseph Maran, Carsten Juwig, Hermann Schwengel, and Ulrich Thaler, 49–69. Geschichte Forschung und Wissenschaft 19. Hamburg: Lit Verlag.

Zangger, Eberhard. 1993. *The Geoarchaeology of the Argolid*. Argolis 2. Berlin: Mann.

Zavadil, Michaela. In press. "The Peloponnese in the Middle Bronze Age: An Overview." In *Mesohelladika*.

Zerner, Carol. 1993. "New Perspectives on Trade in the Middle and Early Late Helladic Periods on the Mainland." In *Wace and Blegen*, 39–56.

CHAPTER 46

....

BOEOTIA

....

ANASTASIA DAKOURI-HILD

BOEOTIA, a geographic area of approximately 2,580 km² in central mainland Greece, is delineated by the massifs of Elikon to the southwest, Kithairon and Pastra to the south and southeast, and Mounts Khlomon, Ptoon, and Messapion to the northwest and northeast. The Yliki and Paralimni lakes and the Euboean and Corinthian gulfs further demarcate the region from the north, east, and south, respectively. In between these ranges and coastlines extend chains of fertile alluvial plains traversed by perennial and seasonal rivers. The region is crossed by key overland routes (Buck 1979, 4–5; Fossey 1988, vol. 1, 200), while its coastal areas and harbors connect it to important maritime routes of antiquity (Heurtley 1923; Schläger, Blackman, and Schaefer 1968; Gauvin and Fossey 1985).

A number of surveys have taken place in Boeotia to date. The Cambridge-Bradford/Durham Boeotian Expedition (Bintliff 1985; 1996; Bintliff and Snodgrass 1985; Bintliff, Howard, and Snodgrass 2007) and its ongoing successor, the Leiden-Ljubljana Ancient Cities of Boeotia Project (Bintliff 2006; Bintliff and Slapšak 2007; Bintliff et al. 2001, 2002, 2004, 2004–2005), have focused on Aliartos, Thespies, Thisbe, Tanagra, and Koroneia and have employed intensive surface investigation, architectural and GIS mapping, geophysical prospection, and aerial reconnaissance. Other surveys have taken place as part of the Ohio Boeotia Thisbe Expedition (Gregory 1983, 1992), the Stanford Skourta Plain Project (Munn 1990), the Grimadha-Tanagra Project (Roller 1987), the Plataies Survey (Aravantinos, Konecny, and Marchese 2003; Konecny et al. 2008), and the Eastern Boeotia Archaeological Project (Burke, Burns, and Lupack 2007).

More specialized surface investigations have clarified Boeotian topography (e.g., Bakhuizen 1970; Hope Simpson and Dickinson 1979; Hope Simpson 1981; Fossey 1988) or have focused on the design of the Kopais water works (Munich Kopais Expedition: Knauss 1991, 2001; Knauss, Heinrich, and Kalcyk 1984). Most of the excavations have been undertaken by the Greek Archaeological Service. Archaeological fieldwork and research relating to prehistoric sites has also been conducted by early explorers (e.g., Schliemann 1881; de Ridder 1894, 1895; Noack 1894) or were carried out under the auspices of the Archaeological Society at Athens (Iakovidis 1989, 1998; cf. Iakovidis 2001; Tzavella-Evjen in prep.), the Canadian Archaeological Institute (e.g., Munn 1996; Fossey 1986; cf. Morin 2004), the American School of Classical Studies at Athens (Goldman 1931; Caskey and Caskey 1960), the Bavarian Academy and the German Archaeological Institute (e.g., Bulle 1907; Kunze 1934; Lauffer 1973–1974), and the British School at Athens (e.g., Austin 1931–1932).

The Early Bronze Age (EBA)

At least fifty-six EBA sites are known in Boeotia (figure 46.1), though few have been excavated systematically (Buck 1979, 35n18; Konsola 1981, 52; 1984, 61–68; Alram-Stern 2004, vol. 2, 691–701). Most of the known sites (ca. thirty) established in this era are located along the eastern coastline or roads to major ports (e.g., Anthedon), which suggests the importance of maritime resources (Konsola 1981, 52). Evidence of cave habitation (Spyropoulos 1972b) may be connected to transhumant pastoralism.

The transition from the Neolithic to the EH I period seems to have been relatively smooth. Buildings and Red Burnished pottery have been identified at Eutresis, Lithares, and other sites, possibly also Orchomenos (Konsola 1981, 56n48), though curiously not at Thebes, which could be due to lack of comprehensive study. The EH II and transitional EH II–III periods, characterized by Urfirnis sauceboats (cf. Theban ceramic group A), Keros-Syros imports, and Cycladic- and Anatolian-inspired pottery (cf. Theban ceramic group B/Lefkandi I) are attested at 43% of known EBA sites. The later EH III period, typified by the presence of Ayia Marina ware (cf. Theban ceramic group Γ) is known from Eutresis, Orchomenos, Lithares, Thebes, and elsewhere (Konsola 1981, 36–46; cf. Kunze 1934). The end of the transitional EH II–III period is marked by destructive fires at several sites on the Theban citadel, but such evidence has not been reported elsewhere to date. A number of regional sites were abandoned in later EH III, although apparently this was not an era of marked decline. Fire horizons dated to the end of this phase are reported from Orchomenos, Eutresis, Drosia (Konsola 1981, 43, 57) and, more recently, Thebes (Andrikou 1998).

Architecture is attested at Thebes, Orchomenos, Lithares, Eutresis, and other sites, including coastal ones (e.g., Spyropoulos 1970b; Hope Simpson and Dickinson 1979, F67, F64). Unexcavated buildings have been reported at Megali Katavothra (Konsola 1981, 38) and the west and east shorelines of Paralimni (Faraklas 1968, 1969a; Spyropoulos 1971a). Houses have stone foundations, mud-brick elevations, roofs made of logs, reeds, and clay plaster, stone thresholds with pivots, cobbled enclosed courts, and occasionally mud-brick or wooden pillars (Goldman 1931, 15–16, 25; Spyropoulos 1970b; Tzavella-Evjen and Rohner 1990). Herring-bone

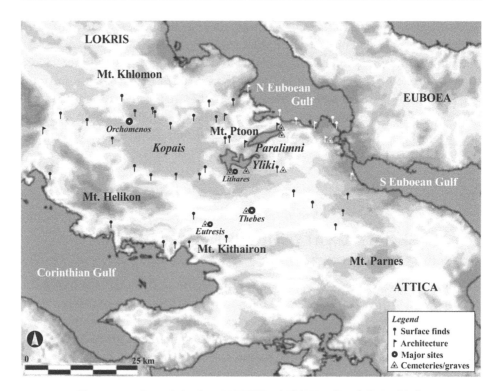

Figure 46.1. Boeotia in the EH I–III period (courtesy of the author).

masonry is presently known only from Eutresis. Domestic facilities include hearths, benches, bothroi that sometimes contain wheat (Goldman 1931, 31), built-in pithoi (Spyropoulos 1970b), stone benches, and platforms (Tzavella-Evjen and Rohner 1990). In terms of production and the economy, flour making, weaving, production of stone implements (Tzavella-Evjen 1984, 173, 175), and ornamental work using boar tusk, mother of pearl, and bone are attested (Goldman 1931, 199–220; Spyropoulos and Tzavella-Evjen 1973). Cycladic-inspired pottery has been found in domestic contexts (e.g., Tzavella-Evjen 1973–1974; 1984, 156–57, 165–68), while vessels with potter's marks are known from few sites, namely Eutresis, Lithares, and Orchomenos (see Konsola 1984, 132–33). Sealings are unattested to date, and seals are rare (Goldman 1931, 199; Aravantinos 2002).

The Lithares settlement, 0.31 ha of which has been excavated, shows a fairly regular plan with a large street (54 m long, 2.5 m wide) and smaller alleys (Tzavella-Evjen 1984, 91; cf. Tzavella-Evjen 1985). At Orchomenos and Eutresis, the houses are spaced apart and do not form a coherent town plan. House sizes and plans vary from straight-sided megara, to apsidal and round buildings, to a possible but-and-ben house (Tzavella-Evjen 1973–1974; 1984, 47). Some large EH II buildings, for instance Eutresis House L, are comparable in size to the larger Theban longhouses but the Fortified Building at Thebes (see this volume) remains exceptional. The Orchomenos round buildings (6 m average diameter; Bulle 1907, 19–25) are possibly special function buildings, possibly granaries (see Alram-Stern 2004, vol. 1, 243–46 for other inter-pretations). The Eutresis Round Building (6.40 m diameter) is associated with a debris-filled chasm (Caskey and Caskey 1960, 129, figure 6) and could be of cultic nature. Other possibly cultic spaces are Room III of Eutresis House L, which yielded a bull rhyton and a terracotta altar (Goldman 1931, 19–20), and the so-called Shrine of the Bulls at Lithares, which produced more than sixteen terracotta (mostly bull) figurines near a pile of charred debris. The excavator interpreted it as a shrine ini-tially (Tzavella-Evjen 1972; contra Tzavella-Evjen 1989); some scholars have argued for the original interpretation (e.g., Fossey 1997).

Numerous graves are known in eastern Boeotia, at Thebes and Eutresis, and at unexcavated or briefly explored sites (Papadimitriou 1931; Faraklas 1969a; Spyropoulos 1969a, 1970a). With a few exceptions (Goldman 1931, 221, 226), they belong to extramural/non-domestic cemeteries in the vicinity of settlements (Faraklas 1969a, enumerating more than one hundred tombs; Spyropoulos 1970a). The graves, which tend to accommodate single, contracted burials, are rock-cut pits of various shapes. They have small dromoi that lead to side entrances blocked with slabs or rubble, features usually interpreted as Cycladic (but see Konsola 1981, 54–56). Funerary furnishings include EH pottery and Cycladic-style artifacts, such as pyxides, frying pans, and stone vessels (Papadimitriou 1931; Faraklas 1969a; Spyropoulos and Tzavella-Evjen 1973). Marble figurines have not been found in mortuary assemblages, although a stone figurine with folded arms purchased by Bulle (1907, 121) may originate from a burial site near Orchomenos (Hope Simpson and Dickinson 1979, 238).

THE MIDDLE BRONZE AGE (MBA) AND THE SHAFT GRAVE PERIOD

Despite a relative decrease in attested settlements (at least forty-one), most sites continue to be occupied in the MBA. The region was densely inhabited, with a preference for hilly locations near fertile plains, river valleys, and coastal sites (figure 46.2). The period witnesses the rapid development of Orchomenos and Thebes as the two foci of west and east Boeotia, respectively (cf. Misiewicz 1988, 125). The latter is by far the most extensive and dense excavated settlement in the region and may well have exerted influence over, or controlled, other Boeotian settlements at this time, if not earlier.

Although the Orchomenos ceramic material has been studied (Bulle 1907; Sarri in prep.) and pottery from Thebes (Konsola 1981, 152–54) and other sites (French 1972) has been preliminarily assessed, synthetic studies are lacking. As a result, the over-all chronological framework requires refinement. The study of imported material, such as Aeginetan ware (Sarri 2007), provides a basis for interregional comparison

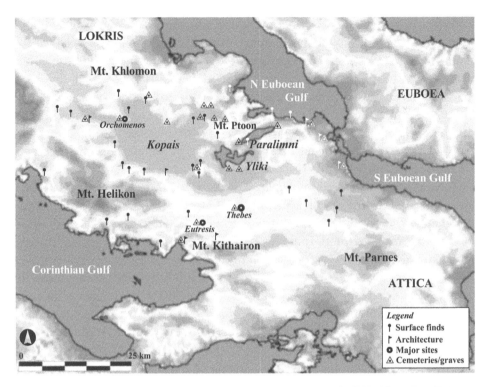

Figure 46.2. Boeotia in the MH I–III and the Shaft Grave periods (courtesy of the author).

and is helpful in this direction. Three main habitation phases can be distinguished: MH I, associated with the prevailing Gray Minyan pottery; MH II–IIIA, with Gray Minyan and simple Matt-Painted pottery; and MH IIIB–LH I (Shaft Grave period), during which Gray Minyan, fine Matt-Painted, and Polychrome pottery are in use concurrently. Red and Yellow Minyan are also attested, but Black Minyan is rare. Early Mycenaean (LH I) lustrous pottery is rarely reported, presumably due to the ongoing use of Gray Minyan and Matt Painted (Mountjoy 1999, vol. 2, 640).

Architectural remains are attested mostly at excavated sites such as Thebes, Orchomenos, Eutresis, Chaironeia, and a few other inland and coastal settlements (Konsola 1981, 35–46). Houses are straight sided and apsidal (cf. Sapouna-Sakellaraki 1993), though usually the former; both types can be in the form of a megaron. Construction techniques and materials, as well as domestic features (i.e., hearths, ovens, bothroi, clay-plastered benches), are similar to those excavated at EBA sites. The Eutresis houses are flimsier than their EBA predecessors but are well appointed with paved forecourts, water pithoi, hearths, ashpits, bothroi, baking ovens, built benches, and shelves, as well as large mortars, querns, and stone implements (Goldman 1931, 42–64). Roof materials include charred logs, reeds, and clay (Goldman 1931, 62–63). Finds at Orchomenos and Eutresis reveal a large variety of intensive crop species, indicating agricultural diversification (Bulle 1907, 60–61; Goldman 1931, 42, 64). Several clay bins in the Eutresis 'House of the

Merchant' (building F) seemingly constituted a (food?) storage facility (Goldman 1931, 41–43). Boar tusk inlays, roughouts of bone, mother of pearl, and a possible mud-brick workshop show that a range of crafts, in addition to food, lithic, and textile production, were practiced at that site (Goldman 1931, 54, 60).

At Eutresis and Orchomenos, houses are spaced wide apart, forming clusters or 'islands' (cf. Goldman 1931, 50–51). At the former site, spacious paved streets are attested. There is no evidence of large-scale communal works other than a series of earth dykes along the west and northeast shorelines of the Kopais tentatively dated to the MH period (Knauss 1995; cf. Konsola 1981, 39). An enceinte is reported at Chaironeia (Tzavella-Evjen 1991; though not in Tzavella-Evjen 1990). The final word on the MH finds (Tzavella-Evjen in prep.) from this important prehistoric site is awaited.

Graves have come to light mostly at Thebes, Eutresis, Orchomenos, Chaironeia, near Yliki and Paralimni, the Euboean coast, and the north side of Kopais. They are cists, pits, or pithoi, the former two types being common. Cists are stone built or made of stone slabs; a larger version appears from the later MBA (e.g., Spyropoulos 1971b). Some of the graves, usually transitional, are set within stone periboloi (Spyropoulos 1971a, 1973a; cf. Aravantinos 1996). Pit graves are occasionally lined with mud brick (e.g. Spyropoulos 1971b, 1972a). Stone tumuli have also been reported (Aravantinos 1996). Tombs occur in domestic/intramural locations (Bulle 1907, 61; cf. Tzavella-Evjen 1990), although the Eutresis adult burials apparently were not associated with the houses (Goldman 1931, 224; cf. Sarri 2000). They also compose separate cemeteries near settlements (Konsola 1981, 59). Burials are contracted and furnished with a few pots or are unfurnished. Interestingly, carbonized peas and traces of a coarse shroud or matting have been found in mortuary contexts at Eutresis (Goldman 1931, 223, 225). Carnelian, glass/faience, quartz, amber, gold artifacts, and bronze weapons are included in funerary assemblages in the late MBA and transitional period (e.g., Blegen 1949; Spyropoulos 1971b). A cylindrical bead with linear decoration (Aravantinos 1996) may be an import dating to this era.

THE LATE BRONZE AGE

A documented 63% increase in the number of settlements (more than sixty-seven) during the LBA suggests a population boom probably correlated with the intensification of agriculture under the auspices of the two palatial centers, Thebes and Orchomenos. Thebes, the seat of the east Boeotian palatial administration, is surrounded by satellite settlements within a 20 km radius (figure 46.3). Linear B documents have been found at Thebes, though (imported?) inscribed stirrup jars or fragments thereof are known from Orchomenos and Kreusis (Raison 1968, 118–20; Spyropoulos 1969d). The documents from Thebes (*te-qa-i*) illuminate the economic and political geography of east Boeotia (Aravantinos 1987). Other recognizable place names in these documents, such as Kreusis (*ke-re-u-so*), Eutresis (*e-u-te-re-u*), Eleon (*e-re-o*), and

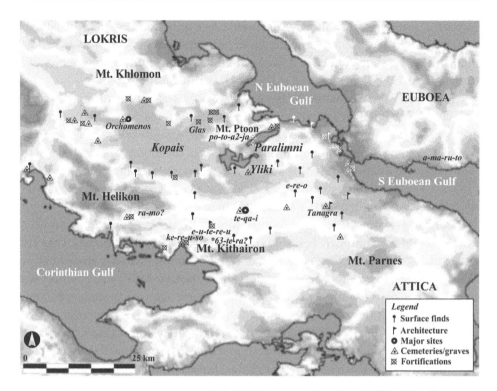

Figure 46.3. Boeotia in the LH II–LH IIIB period (courtesy of the author).

Ptoia (*po-to-a₂-ja*), confirm Theban control over the various provinces of east
Boeotia. Other place names, namely Amarynthos (*a-ma-ru-to*) and Karystos
(*ka-ru-to*), suggest that certain facilities in Euboea operated within the sphere of
Theban economic and political influence (Dakouri-Hild 2005), but whether this
points to the existence of a 'great Boeotia' encompassing south Euboea (Sergent
1994) is unclear at the moment.

The settlement pattern, in combination with archaeological evidence from Gla
and Orchomenos, suggests the existence of a separate, large polity to the west, which
controlled the fertile Kopais basin and the Larymna port and conceivably other areas
to the north (Eder 2007). The seeming absence of fortifications along the hypothesized east-west Boeotian frontier (e.g., Onchestos, Davlosis) is peculiar, given the
lack of a clear natural boundary, although this frontier (if it existed as such) could
have been defended by fortified Aliartos (Buck 1979, 38). There is no evidence on the
interrelationship and legendary discord between Orchomenos and Thebes to date.
However, the investment in major construction at Gla and other forts, which protected the enviable expanse of agricultural land afforded by the Kopais water works,
hint at potential threat (cf. Buck 1979, 39). The economic base of the west and east
polities need not have been profoundly different (see Misiewicz 1988, 124–126), but
a stronger focus on trade seems likely for Thebes within the framework of a mixed
economy (cf. Aravantinos 2003a).

The Theban Linear B documents afford glimpses of the religious landscape of east Boeotia. Industrial units of divine establishments, namely those of Hera (*e-ra*), Hermes (*e-ma-a₂*), and Potnia (*po-ti-ni-ja*), received wool allocations by the palace (Killen 1988). Possible sanctuaries of Hera (at a place called **63-te-ra*, also referred to as *di-wi-ja-me-ro*) and Haphaia (*a₂-pa-a₂*) were among the recipients of food and wine for consumption during major state feasts (cf. Killen 1992, 1994, 1999). It is likely that the shrine of Potnia was situated at present-day Potniai to the south of Thebes, also the location of the later extramural sanctuary of Demeter and Kore (cf. Schachter 1981, 167; 1994, 1–4). Notably, the Plataies Heraion at the foothills of Mount Kithairon, where Mycenaean habitation is attested, was a major religious landmark of historical Boeotia (Schachter 1981, 242–50), whereas an important shrine of Hermes dating back to the Archaic period was located at Tanagra (Schachter 1986, 44). The sanctuary of Haphaia, a nurturing deity, may have been located at Aigina at the homonymous shrine (Aravantinos 1987; Piteros, Olivier, and Melena 1990) or possibly Boeotian Akraiphia (Schachter 1994, 16–17). Possible cultic sites in the Kopais include a cave (Spyropoulos 1972b) and a hill near Gla on top of which was carved a kernos-like installation, of uncertain date (Faraklas 1969b).

Comparatively little ceramic material has been studied comprehensively (Symeonoglou 1973; Spyropoulos and Chadwick 1975; Andrikou et al. 2006; cf. Dakouri-Hild in prep.), but general stylistic studies (Mountjoy 1983, 1999, vol. 2) enable a good grasp of regional chronology. The LH II–LH IIIA2 and transitional LH IIIA2–B1 phases are represented mostly at Thebes, Orchomenos, Eutresis, and Tanagra; palace-style and Ephyraean pottery is included in the relevant assemblages (Mountjoy 1999, vol. 2, 648–71). Later material has been identified at a host of sites, but is best known from Thebes, where fire horizons have been dated to the transitional LH IIIA2–B1, LH IIIB1, and transitional LH IIIB2–C phases (cf. Dakouri-Hild 2001, 106–107). Gla shows evidence of repeated refurbishment since its establishment in LH IIIA2–B1; it burned down before LH IIIB and then again at the end of LH IIIB2 (Iakovidis 1992). At least one coastal site was devastated by fire at that time (Spyropoulos 1970b; Sapouna-Sakellaraki 1993). Parts of the Orchomenos palatial complex were abandoned in LH IIIA2 and at the end of LH IIIB, but there is no evidence of fire there (Spyropoulos 1973b). Likewise, the Eutresis settlement was abandoned without evidence of destruction (Goldman 1931, 236).

Except at Thebes, few architectural remains belong to houses (Goldman 1931, 64–68; Spyropoulos 1973c, 1974b; Hope Simpson and Dickinson 1979, G16). Traditional building techniques, materials, and domestic features were utilized (Demakopoulou 1977; Sapouna-Sakellaraki 1993). Circuit walls and segments of Cyclopean fortifications, sometimes with inner and outer rings (Hope Simpson and Dickinson 1979, G4, G6) or partial enceintes (Hope Simpson and Dickinson 1979, G11–G12) are most frequent in the north Kopais (see earlier examples and Hope Simpson and Dickinson 1979, G2, G10, G17) and protected the water-management system there. Other forts existed to the south and west of Kopais, in the east and south coastal zones, and at inland sites such as Eutresis, where some 21 ha, mostly unbuilt, are fortified (Goldman 1931, 68–75).

Palatial complexes have been brought to light at Thebes and Orchomenos. The 1903–1905 German excavations at the latter site (on and near the acropolis) revealed eroded LH architectural remains and few finds, including colored plastered fragments. Trials east of the acropolis produced fresco fragments of a possible bull-leaping scene (Bulle 1907, 81, pls. XXVIII–XXIX; cf. Immerwahr 1990, 195–96), although Boulotis (2000) prefers a siege theme, to which chariots, warriors, falling or swimming figures, and an architectural façade belong. The later excavations (1968–1973) below the acropolis brought to light three buildings, including a megaron with a hearth, as well as earlier architecture (Spyropoulos 1972a, 1973b). These structures were interpreted as palace 'wings,' but their location on the acropolis foothill and their layout, which appears to be axial, bring to mind the Mycenae House of the Oil Merchant (Iakovidis 1995; Boulotis 2000). An unpublished fresco deposit associated with the northern building included fragments of a miniature boar hunt scene (boar, spotted dogs, hunters with spears and boar tusk helmets, horse hoofs, and chariots), fragments of two youthful men, and male (possibly also female) figures engaged in an athletic contest. A fourth building in a nearby trench contained a number of bronze weapons and seals and was abandoned in LH IIIA2 (Spyropoulos 1974a).

The citadel of Gla in the northeast Kopais (23.5 ha) is encircled by massive Cyclopean fortifications (5.40–5.80 m thick, 2.8 km long), with offsets every 6–12 m and four gates. The 'melathron' to the north is an L-shaped building (1,871 m²) consisting of two semi-independent megara without throne placements or hearths. The melathron has been interpreted as the seat of two Orchomenian officials in charge of canal maintenance and cereal storage. The building is separately walled off and features monolithic stone thresholds with pivots, half-timbered wall elevations, tiled pitched roofs, an upper story in certain areas, frescoes, and horns of consecration (Iakovidis 1989). The 'agora' to the south (2,500 m²) consists of two parallel long buildings equipped with drains and ramped doorsills. This complex was apparently used for food storage in part, as suggested by burnt wheat, pithoid, and transport stirrup jars (Iakovidis 1998). The material from the agora fresco dumps is being prepared for publication (Boulotis in prep.). It includes unburnt decorative (rosettes, spirals, dadoes) and pictorial fresco fragments (micrographic architectural facades with consecration horns and double axes, windows of appearance with human figures, dolphins, octopi, nautili, seascape vegetation, and possibly a female procession) (Iakovidis 2000; 2001, pls. V-X; Boulotis 2000). Three smaller buildings, one of which is apsidal, are situated northwest, southwest, and east of the central compound.

The Kopais water-management system is a technical achievement of unprecedented scale and labor intensiveness in the Aegean. The project, which entailed the walling up of an estimated 400,000,000 m³ of stone and the transportation of some 200,000,000 m³ of earth, was apparently successful in transforming Greece's largest polje lake into the most expansive agricultural resource of the Mycenaean world (Knauss, Heinrich, and Kalcyk 1984; Knauss 1991, 1995; cf. Knauss 2001, 26–41; Hope

Simpson and Hagel 2006, 185–211). The system regulated the Kephissos and Melas rivers and drained the basin during the flood season (winter–spring); its discharge capacity has been estimated to be 150,000,000 m³ per second (Heinrich 1988). Its key components were several renovated (MH?) polder dykes, mostly along the north side of the lake; a permanent reservoir in its northwest bay; a great canal (25 km long, 40 m wide, 2.5 m deep) formed by stone-lined dams (25–30 m wide each), themselves perpendicularly reinforced with separate walls (Aravantinos, Kountouri, and Fappas 2006); a smaller canal east of Glas (Lauffer 1973–1974); and a series of natural subterranean holes or 'katavothres' to the northeast and east, through which water was funneled to the underground water table. The system created 90 km² of year-round arable land and furnished an abundant supply of water during the dry months. Moreover, the main canal was in principle navigable, whereas its wide embankments could have functioned as a road (Heinrich 1988).

Graves, mainly rock-hewn chamber tombs clustered in cemeteries, are common, though most are looted or destroyed. Aside from Thebes, significant chamber-tomb cemeteries have come to light at Aulis and Kallithea (Touloupa 1964; Spyropoulos 1971c, 1971e; Aravantinos 1983) and Tanagra. At the latter site, two cemeteries (Dendron and Ledeza, the former of which is earlier) consist of more than 250 tombs combined. The Ledeza graves are arranged in dense rows, the larger ones higher up on the hill, apparently reflecting the quality of associated furnishings and social stratification (Spyropoulos 1969c). In general, remains of funerary meals, ceramics, and other mortuary goods are plentiful (e.g., Spyropoulos 1969b, 1969c, 1970c). The so-called 'Thisbe treasure' (Evans 1925) has been discredited largely as a collection of forgeries, though some items appear to be genuine and could originate from looted chamber tombs at Thisbe (Hope Simpson and Dickinson 1979, 250). Occasionally, orientalia are among funerary furnishings (Spyropoulos 1971e, 1971g, 1977; cf. Cline 1994, 151).

The larnakes excavated at Tanagra (ca. fifty, sixteen of which are from a single grave) date to the LH IIIB–C period (cf. Phialon and Farrugio 2005, table 1; Aravantinos 2003b). Other examples of Tanagran provenance surfaced in the European art market in the 1950s (e.g., Vermeule 1965; Iakovidis 1966, esp. 46–50). The four-legged, rectangular terracotta coffins (0.43–1.07 m long, 0.23–0.38 m wide, 0.34–0.69 m high) were made in molds and have perforated sides or bases. Their (usually flat) lids are ornamented with bird-like finials, sometimes detachable, that may have been used during funerary rites and probably held an apotropaic role thereafter. The larnakes were used as collective ossuaries and sarcophagi for single burials (Spyropoulos 1969c, 1970c). Many are decorated with black, gray, and red paint in geometric, floral, and marine designs (e.g., checkered pattern, spirals, ivy, octopus). The iconography represented by the larnakes is rich and illuminating, consisting of hunting, bull leaping, and prothesis scenes, mourning processions, (mythical?) encounters with sphinxes, sacred pillars, consecration horns signifying holy precincts (Rutkowski 1979), winged 'souls' and birds, and a possible boat journey in the realm of 'shades' (cf. Spyropoulos 1973c, 1974b, 1976). The painted larnakes represent a derivative and 'stringy' style (Spyropoulos 1969c; Immerwahr 1990, 154–58; 1995) that is nevertheless expressive and powerful, encapsulating the experience of mortuary performance (cf. Merousis 2000). The form of the Tanagra larnakes relate to Cretan funerary customs and may articulate a new kind of mortuary identity in LH IIIB Boeotia (cf. Spyropoulos 1971d). Thematically and stylistically, they belong to the mainland pictorial tradition, albeit a direct line of inspiration cannot be determined (Vermeule 1965).

Other grave types include Cretan-style shafts with burial niches and benches (Spyropoulos 1977); built chambers (Hope Simpson and Dickinson 1979, G51); and traditional pits and cists, usually dating to the early Mycenaean period, though not always (e.g., Hope Simpson and Dickinson 1979, G48, G51). The so-called Treasury of Minyas at Orchomenos is the only certain tholos tomb in the region (for possible others, see Blegen 1949; Hope Simpson and Dickinson 1979, F64, G29, G51; Spyropoulos 1971f). Although its top has long collapsed and its contents have been looted (cf. Schliemann 1881), its elaborate construction and monumental size (14 m dm) is closely paralleled by the (somewhat larger) Treasury of Atreus at Mycenae. The Orchomenos tholos features ashlar masonry, for which an estimated 1,000 m³ of local limestone were quarried (Knauss 1995), a gigantic door lintel, and a side chamber with an elaborately carved ceiling (Schliemann 1881, pls. XII–XIII; cf. Aravantinos 2003a, figure 3).

In sum, Boeotia has emerged as a significant province of prehistoric Greece throughout prehistory through excavation work. The archaeological record brought about by ongoing systematic and rescue excavations continues to illuminate society, economy, and artistic production in the region during the Bronze Age.

BIBLIOGRAPHY

Alram-Stern, Eva. 2004. *Die ägäische Frühzeit. 2. Serie Forschungsbericht 1975–2002. 2. Band, Teil 1, 2, Die Frühbronzezeit in Griechenland mit Ausnahme von Kreta.* Vienna: Verlag der Österreichischen Akademie der Wissenschaften.

Andrikou, Eleni. 1998. "Οικόπεδο Δημ. Λάμπρου." *Αρχαιολογικό Δελτίο* 48 B: 173–76.

———, Vassilis Aravantinos, Louis Godart, Anna Sacconi, and Joanita Vroom. 2006. *Thèbes fouilles de la Cadmée II.2. Les tablettes en Linéaire B de la Odos Pelopidou. Le contexte archéologique. La céramique de la Odos Pelopidou et la chronologie du Linéaire B.* Rome: Istituti Editoriali e Poligrafici Internazionali.

Aravantinos, Vassilis. 1983. "Καλλιθέα Θηβών." *Αρχαιολογικό Δελτίο* 38 B: 134.

———. 1987. "Mycenaean Place-names from Thebes: The New Evidence." *Minos* 20–22: 33–40.

———. 1996. "Δαύλωση-Μεδεών." *Αρχαιολογικό Δελτίο* 51 B: 270–72.

———. 2002. "Οικόπεδο Αρχαιολογικού Μουσείου Θηβών." *Αρχαιολογικό Δελτίο* 52 B: 353–59.

———. 2003a. "La Béotie mycénienne." In *Tanagra: Mythe et archéologie,* ed. Violaine Jeammet and John M. Fossey, 18–21. Paris: Réunion des Musées Nationaux.

———. 2003b. "Les nécropoles mycéniennes de Tanagra." In *Tanagra: Mythe et archéologie,* ed. Violaine Jeammet and John M. Fossey, 68–80. Paris: Réunion des Musées Nationaux.

————, Andreas Konecny, and Ronald T. Marchese. 2003. "Plataiai in Boeotia: A Preliminary Report of the 1996–2001 Campaigns." *Hesperia* 73(3): 281–320.

Aravantinos, Vassilis, Elena Kountouri, and Yiannis Fappas. 2006. "Το μυκηναϊκό αποστραγγιστικό σύστημα της Κωπαΐδας: νέα δεδομένα και πρώτες εκτιμήσεις." In *Αρχαία Ελληνική Τεχνολογία. 2° Διεθνές Συνέδριο*, ed. Yota Kazazi, 557–64. Athens: Greek Technical Directorate.

Austin, Reginald P. 1931–1932. "Excavations at Haliartus." *BSA* 32: 180–212.

Bakhuizen, Simon C. 1970. *Salganeus and the Fortifications on Its Mountains*. Chalcidian Studies II. Groningen: Wolters-Noordhoff.

Bintliff, John L. 1985. "The Boeotia Survey." In *Archaeological Field Survey in Britain and Abroad*, ed. Sarah Macready and F. H. Thompson, 96–216. Society of Antiquaries Occasional Paper 6, London: Society of Antiquaries.

————. 1996. "The Archaeological Survey of the Valley of the Muses and Its Significance for Boeotian History." *Recherches et Rencontres* 7: 193–210.

————. 2006. "The Leiden University Ancient Cities of Boeotia Project: 2005 Season at Tanagra." *Pharos* 13: 29–38.

————, Niki Evelpidou, Emeri Farinetti, Branko Mušič, Igor Riznar, Kostas Sbonias, Lefteris Sigalos, Božidar Slapšak, Vladimir Stissi, and Andreas Vassilopoulos. 2002. "The Tanagra Survey: Report on the 2001 Season." *Pharos* 9: 33–74.

Bintliff, John L., Emeri Farinetti, Jeroen Poblome, Kalliope Sarri, Kostas Sbonias, Božidar Slapšak, Vladimir Stissi, and Athanasios Vionis. 2004. "The Leiden-Ljubljana Tanagra Project: The 2003 Season." *Pharos* 11: 35–43.

Bintliff, John L., Emeri Farinetti, Kostas Sbonias, Kalliopi Sarri, Vladimir Stissi, Jeroen Poblome, Ariane Ceulemans, Karlien De Craen, Athanasios Vionis, Branko Mušič, Dušan Kramberger, and Božidar Slapšak. 2004–2005. "The Tanagra Project: Investigations at an Ancient Boeotian City and in Its Countryside (2000–2002)." *BCH* 128–29: 541–606.

Bintliff, John L., Emeri Farinetti, Kostas Sbonias, Lefteris Sigalos, and Božidar Slapšak. 2001. "The Tanagra Survey: Report on the 2000 Season." *Pharos* 8: 93–127.

Bintliff, John L., Phil Howard, and Anthony M. Snodgrass. 2007. *Testing the Hinterland: The Work of the Boeotia Survey (1989–1991) in the Southern Approaches to the City of Thespiai*. Cambridge: MacDonald Institute for Archaeological Research.

Bintliff, John L., and Božidar Slapšak. 2007. "The Leiden-Ljubljana Ancient Cities of Boeotia Project: 2006 Season." *Pharos* 14: 15–27.

Bintliff, John L., and Anthony M. Snodgrass. 1985. "The Cambridge-Bradford Boeotian Expedition: The First Four Years." *JFA* 12(2): 123–61.

Blegen, Carl. W. 1949. "Hyria." *Hesperia Suppl.* 8 (Commemorative Studies in Honor of Theodore Leslie Shear): 39–42.

Boulotis, Christos. 2000. "Η τέχνη των τοιχογραφιών στην μυκηναϊκή Βοιωτία." In *Γ' Διεθνές Συνέδριο Βοιωτικών Μελετών (Θήβα, 4–8 Σεπτεμβρίου 1996)*, ed. Vassilis Aravantinos, 1095–1149. Vol. Γ:α. Athens: Society of Boeotian Studies.

————. In prep. *Γλας III*. Βιβλιοθήκη της εν Αθήναις Αρχαιολογικής Εταιρείας. Athens: Archaeological Society of Athens.

Buck, Robert J. 1979. *A History of Boeotia*. Edmonton: University of Alberta Press.

Bulle, Heinrich. 1907. *Orchomenos I: Die älteren Ansiedlungsschichten*. Munich: Verlag der Bayerischen Akademie der Wissenschaften.

Burke, Brendan, Bryan Burns, and Susan Lupack. 2007. "The Eastern Boeotia Archaeological Project (EBAP)." *Teiresias* 37(2): 07.0.04.

Caskey, John L., and Elizabeth G. Caskey. 1960. "The Earliest Settlements at Eutresis: Supplementary Excavations, 1958." *Hesperia* 29(2): 126–67.

Cline, Eric H. 1994. *SWDS.*

Dakouri-Hild, Anastasia. 2001. "The House of Kadmos in Mycenaean Thebes Reconsidered: Architecture, Chronology, and Context." *BSA* 96: 81–122.

———. 2005. "Breaking the Mould? Production and Economy in the Theban State." In *Autochthon,* 207–24.

———. In prep. *The House of Kadmos at Thebes, Greece: The Excavations of Antonios D. Keramopoullos (1906–1929).* Vol. 1, *Architecture, Stratigraphy, and Finds.* Biblioteca di Pasiphae, Collana di Filologia e Antichità Egea 8. Rome: Istituti Editoriali e Poligrafici Internazionali.

Demakopoulou, Katie. 1977. "Λόφος Γλύφα ή Βλίχα." *Αρχαιολογικό Δελτίο* 32 Β: 98–100.

de Ridder, A. 1894. "Fouilles de Gha." *BCH* 18: 271–310.

———. 1895. "Fouilles d'Orchomène." *BCH* 19: 137–224.

Eder, Birgitta. 2007. "The Power of Seals: Palaces, Peripheries, and Territorial Control in the Mycenaean World." In *BABS,* 35–45.

Evans, Arthur. 1925. *The "Ring of Nestor" and Gold Signet-rings and Bead-seals from Thisbe.* London: Macmillan.

Faraklas, Nikolaos. 1968. "Ἴσος." *Ἀρχαιολογικά Ἀνάλεκτα ἐξ Ἀθηνῶν* 1(2): 139–40.

———. 1969a. "Περί της κατοικήσεως τῶν Λελέγων ἐν Βοιωτίᾳ." *Ἀρχαιολογικά Ἀνάλεκτα ἐξ Ἀθηνῶν* 2(1): 96–97.

———. 1969b. "Περιοδείαι-παρατηρήσεις." *Ἀρχαιολογικά Ἀνάλεκτα ἐξ Ἀθηνῶν* 2(1): 179.

Fossey, John M. 1986. *Khóstia: Résultats des explorations et fouilles canadiennes à Khóstia en Béotie, Grèce centrale.* Amsterdam: Gieben.

———. 1988. *Topography and Population of Ancient Boeotia.* Vols. 1–2. Chicago: Ares.

———. 1997. "Boeotia in Later Prehistory: An Overview." In *Recent Developments in the History and Archaeology of Central Greece,* ed. John L. Bintliff, 3–12. *BAR-IS* 666. Oxford: Archaeopress.

French, David H. 1972. "Notes on the Prehistoric Pottery Groups from Central Greece." Unpublished typescript, British School at Athens.

Gauvin, Ginette, and John M. Fossey 1985. "Livadhostra: Un relève topographique des fortifications de l'ancienne Kreusis." In *La Béotie antique: Actes du Colloque international (Lyon, Saint-Étienne, 16–20 mai 1983),* ed. Paul Roesch and Gilbert Argoud, 77–86. Paris: CNRS.

Goldman, Hetty. 1931. *Excavations at Eutresis in Boeotia.* Cambridge, Mass.: Harvard University Press.

Gregory, Timothy. 1983. "The Ohio Boeotia Expedition Exploration of the Thisbe Basin." In *Archaeological Survey in the Mediterranean Area,* ed. Donald R. Keller and David W. Rupp, 245–47. *BAR-IS* 155. Oxford: Archaeopress.

———. 1992. "Archaeological Explorations in the Thisbe Basin." *Boeotia Antiqua* 2: 17–34.

Heinrich, Bert. 1988. "Prehistoric Hydraulic Constructions in the Copais." In *A' Διεθνές Συνέδριο Βοιωτικών Μελετών (Θήβα, 10–14 Σεπτεμβρίου 1986),* ed. Alexandros Bekiaris, 43–52. Vol. A:α. Athens: Society of Boeotian Studies.

Heurtley, William A. 1923. "Notes on the Harbours of S. Boeotia and Sea Trade between Boeotia and Corinth in Prehistoric Times." *BSA* 26: 38–45.

Hope Simpson, Richard. 1981. *Mycenaean Greece.* Park Ridge, N.J.: Noyes.

———, and Oliver T. P. K. Dickinson. 1979. *A Gazetteer of Aegean Civilization in the Bronze Age.* Vol. 1, *The Mainland and the Islands.* SIMA 52. Gothenburg: Åström.

Hope Simpson, Richard, and D. K. Hagel. 2006. *Mycenaean Fortifications, Highways, Dams, and Canals.* SIMA 133. Savedalen: Åström.

Iakovidis, Spyridon. 1966. "A Mycenaean Mourning Custom." *AJA* 70(1): 43–50 (esp. 46ff).

———. 1989. *Γλας I. Η Ανασκαφή 1955–1961.* Βιβλιοθήκη της εν Αθήναις Αρχαιολογικής Εταιρείας 107. Athens: Archaeological Society of Athens.

———. 1992. "The Mycenaean Fortress of Gla." In *Mykenaïka: Actes du IXe Colloque International sur les textes mycéniens et égéens organisé par le Centre de l'antiquite grecque et romaine de la Fondation Hellénique des recherches scientifiques et l'École française d'Athènes (Athènes, 2–6 Octobre 1990)*, ed. Jean-Pierre Olivier, 607–15. Supplément au BCH 25. Athens: L'École française d'Athènes.

———. 1995. "Γλας και Ορχομενός." In *B' Διεθνές Συνέδριο Βοιωτικών Μελετών (Λειβαδιά, 6–10 Σεπτεμβρίου 1992)*, ed. Alexandra Christopoulou, 69–81. Vol. B:α. Athens: Society of Boeotian Studies.

———. 1998. *Γλας II. Η Ανασκαφή 1981–1991*. Βιβλιοθήκη της εν Αθήναις Αρχαιολογικής Εταιρείας 173. Athens: Archaeological Society of Athens.

———. 2000. "Οι τοιχογραφίες στο Γλα και στα άλλα μυκηναϊκά κέντρα." In *Γ' Διεθνές Συνέδριο Βοιωτικών Μελετών (Θήβα, 4–8 Σεπτεμβρίου 1996)*, ed. Vassilis Aravantinos, 14–25. Vol. Γ:α. Athens: Society of Boeotian Studies.

———. 2001. *Gla and the Kopais in the 13th Century B.C.* Βιβλιοθήκη της εν Αθήναις Αρχαιολογικής Εταιρείας 221. Athens: Archaeological Society of Athens.

Immerwahr, Sara A. 1990. *Aegean Painting in the Bronze Age*. University Park: Penn State University Press.

———. 1995. "Death and the Tanagra Larnakes." In *The Ages of Homer: A Tribute to Emily Townsend Vermeule*, ed. Jane Carter and Sarah Morris, 109–21. Austin: University of Texas Press.

Killen, John T. 1988. "The Linear B Tablets and the Mycenaean Economy." In *Linear B: A 1984 Survey*, ed. Anna Morpurgo Davies and Yves Duhoux, 241–305. Louvain-la-Neuve: Peeters.

———. 1992. "Observations on the Thebes Sealings." In *Mykenaïka: Actes du IXe Colloque International sur les textes mycéniens et égéens organisé par le Centre de l'Antiquité Grecque et Romaine de la Fondation Hellénique des recherches scientifiques et l'École française d'Athènes (Athènes, 2–6 Octobre 1990)*, ed. Jean-Pierre Olivier, 365–80. Supplément au BCH 25. Athens: École française d'Athènes.

———. 1994. "Thebes Sealings, Knossos Tablets, and Mycenaean State Banquets." *BICS* 39: 67–84.

———. 1999. "Some Observations on the New Thebes Tablets." *BICS* 43: 217–19.

Knauss, Jost. 1991. "Arcadian and Boeotian Orchomenos, Centres of Mycenaean Hydraulic Engineering." *Irrigation and Drainage Systems* 5(4): 363–81.

———. 1995. "Technical and Historical Aspects of the Unfinished Ancient Drainage Tunnel at the Outmost Northeast Corner of the Kopais Basin." In *B' Διεθνές Συνέδριο Βοιωτικών Μελετών (Λειβαδιά, 6–10 Σεπτεμβρίου 1992)*, ed. Alexandra Christopoulou, 83–95. Vol. B:α. Athens: Society of Boeotian Studies.

———. 2001. *Späthelladische Wasserbauten: Erkundungen zu Wasserwirtschaftlichen Infrastrukturen der mykenischen Welt*. Bericht Nr. 90. Munich: Institut für Wasserbau und Wassermengenwirtschaft und Versuchsanstalt für Wasserbau Oskar v. Miller-Institut in Obernach Technische Universität München.

Knauss, Jost, Bert Heinrich, and Hansjörg Kalcyk. 1984. *Die Wasserbauten der Minyer in der Kopais: Die älteste Flussregulierung Europas*. Bericht Nr. 50. Munich: Institut für Wasserbau und Wassermengenwirtschaft und Versuchsanstalt für Wasserbau Oskar v. Miller-Institut in Obernach Technische Universität München.

Konecny, Andreas, Ronald T. Marchese, Michael J. Boyd, and Vassilis Aravantinos. 2008. "Plataiai in Boeotia: A Preliminary Report on Geophysical and Field Surveys Conducted in 2002–2005." *Hesperia* 77: 43–71.

Konsola, Dora. 1981. *Προμυκηναϊκή Θήβα. Χωροταξική και Οικιστική Διάρθρωση*. Athens: privately published.

———. 1984. *Η Πρώιμη Αστικοποίηση στους Πρωτοελλαδικούς Οικισμούς.* Athens: privately published.

Kunze, Emil. 1934. *Orchomenos III: Die Keramik der frühen Bronzezeit.* Munich: Verlag der Bayerischen Akademie der Wissenschaften.

Lauffer, Siegfried. 1973–1974. "Topographische Untersuchungen im Kopaisgebiet 1971 und 1973." *Ἀρχαιολογικόν Δελτίον* 29 B: 449–54.

Merousis, Nikos. 2000. "Η εικονογραφία στα πλαίσια των ταφικών πρακτικών: οι ενδείξεις από τις διακοσμημένες λάρνακες της ΥΜ III Κρήτης και της μυκηναϊκής Τανάγρας." In *Γ' Διεθνές Συνέδριο Βοιωτικών Μελετών (Θήβα, 4–8 Σεπτεμβρίου 1996),* ed. Vassilis Aravantinos, 264–85. Vol. Γ:α. Athens: Society of Boeotian Studies.

Misiewicz, Krzysztof. 1988. *Teby I Orchomenos W Epoce Brązu.* Warsaw: WUW (English summary, 124–26).

Morin, Jacques. 2004. *Khostia II: The Bronze Age: Results of Canadian Explorations and Excavations at Khostia, Boeotia, Central Greece.* Chicago: Ares.

Mountjoy, Penelope A. 1983. *Orchomenos V: Mycenaean Pottery from Orchomenos, Eutresis, and Other Boeotian Sites.* Munich: Verlag der Bayerischen Akademie der Wissenschaften.

———. 1999. *Regional Mycenaean Decorated Pottery.* Vols. 1–2. Rahden: Leidorf/Deutsches Archäologisches Institut.

Munn, Mark. 1990. "On the Frontiers of Attica and Boeotia: The Results of the Stanford Skourta Plain Project." In *Essays in the Topography, History, and Culture of Boeotia,* ed. Albert Schachter, 32–40. Teiresias Suppl. 3. Montreal: privately published.

———. 1996. "The First Excavations at Panakton on the Attic-Boeotian Frontier." *Boeotia Antiqua* 6: 47–58.

Noack, F. 1894. "Arne." *Mitteilungen der deutschen archäologischen Instituts, athenische Abteilung* 19: 405–85.

Papadimitriou, Ioannis. 1931. "Προϊστορικός συνοικισμός παρά τήν λίμνην Λικέρι τῆς Βοιωτίας." *Πρακτικά τῆς Ἀκαδημίας Ἀθηνῶν* 6: 274–76.

Phialon, Laetitia, and Sandrine Farrugio 2005. "Réflexions sur l'usage des larnakès et cercueils en Grèce mycénienne." *Revue Archéologique* 40(2): 227–54.

Piteros, Christos, Jean-Pierre Olivier, and Jose L. Melena. 1990. "Les inscriptions en Linéaire B des nodules de Thèbes (1982): La fouille, les documents, les possibilités d' interprétation." *BCH* 114: 103–84.

Raison, Jacques. 1968. *Les vases à inscriptions peintes de l'âge mycénien et leur contexte archéologique.* Incunabula Graeca 19. Rome: Istituto per gli Studi Micenei ed Egeo-Anatolici.

Roller, Duane W. 1987. "Tanagra Survey Project 1985: The Site of Grimadha." *BSA* 82: 213–32.

Rutkowski, Bogdan. 1979. "Mycenaean Pillar Cult in Boeotia." In *2nd International Boeotian Conference,* ed. John M. Fossey, 35–36. Teiresias Suppl. 2. Montreal: privately published.

Sapouna-Sakellaraki, Effie. 1993. "Ο προϊστορικός τύμβος 'του Σαλγανέα' (Λιθοσωρός) στις ακτές της Βοιωτίας." *Αρχαιολογικά Ανάλεκτα εξ Αθηνών* 21: 77–90.

Sarri, Kalliopi. 2000. "Μεδεών. Ανασκαφική έρευνα στο λόφο Μεγάλο Καστράκι." In *Γ' Διεθνές Συνέδριο Βοιωτικών Μελετών (Θήβα, 4–8 Σεπτεμβρίου 1996),* ed. Vassilis Aravantinos, 1095–1149. Vol. Γ:α. Athens: Society of Boeotian Studies.

———. 2007. "Aeginetan Matt-painted pottery in Boeotia." In *Middle Helladic Pottery,* 151–66.

———. In prep. *Orchomenos IV. Die Keramik der Mittelbronzezeit.* Munich: Verlag der Bayerischen Akademie der Wissenschaften.

Schachter, Albert. 1981. *Cults of Boeotia 1: Acheloos to Hera.* BICS University of London Suppl. 38(1). London: Institute of Classical Studies.

———. 1986. *Cults of Boeotia 2: Heracles to Poseidon.* BICS University of London Suppl. 38(2). London: Institute of Classical Studies.

———. 1994. *Cults of Boeotia 3: Potnia to Zeus, Cults of Deities Unspecified by Name.* BICS University of London Suppl. 38(3). London: Institute of Classical Studies.

Schläger, Helmut, David Blackman, and Jörg Schaefer. 1968. "Der Hafen von Anthedon mit Beiträgen zur Topographie und Geschichte der Stadt." *AA* 83: 21–102.

Schliemann, Heinrich. 1881. "Exploration of the Boeotian Orchomenus." *JHS* 2: 122–63.

Sergent, Bernard. 1994. "Les petits nodules et la grande Béotie (première partie)." *Revue des Études Anciennes* 96(3–4): 365–84.

Spyropoulos, Theodoros. 1969a. "Παραλίμνη." *Ἀρχαιολογικόν Δελτίον* 24 B: 174–75.

———. 1969b. "Τό μυκηναϊκόν νεκροταφεῖον τῆς Τανάγρας." *Ἀρχαιολογικά Ἀνάλεκτα ἐξ Ἀθηνῶν* 2(1): 20–25.

———. 1969c. "Ἀνασκαφή μυκηναϊκοῦ νεκροταφείου Τανάγρας." *Πρακτικά τῆς Ἀρχαιολογικῆς Ἑταιρείας*: 5–15.

———. 1969d. "Περιοδεῖαι." *Ἀρχαιολογικόν Δελτίον* 24 B: 185–86.

———. 1970a. "Ὕπατον Θηβῶν." *Ἀρχαιολογικόν Δελτίον* 25 B: 224–26.

———. 1970b. "Ἀνασκαφή εἰς τόν τύμβον τοῦ Σαλγανέως." *Ἀρχαιολογικόν Δελτίον* 25 B: 222–24.

———. 1970c. "Ἀνασκαφή εἰς τό μυκηναϊκόν νεκροταφεῖον Τανάγρας." *Ἀρχαιολογικά Ἀνάλεκτα ἐξ Ἀθηνῶν* 3(2): 185–97.

———. 1971a. "Ἀρχαῖαι βοιωτικαί πόλεις ἔρχονται εἰς φῶς." *Ἀρχαιολογικά Ἀνάλεκτα ἐξ Ἀθηνῶν* 4(3): 319–31.

———. 1971b. "Ὀρχομενός." *Ἀρχαιολογικόν Δελτίον* 26 B: 218–19.

———. 1971c. "Καλλιθέα." *Ἀρχαιολογικόν Δελτίον* 26 B: 213–14.

———. 1971d. "Ἀνασκαφή μυκηναϊκοῦ νεκροταφείου Τανάγρας." *Πρακτικά τῆς Ἀρχαιολογικῆς Ἑταιρείας*: 7–14.

———. 1971e. "Φάρος Αὐλίδος." *Ἀρχαιολογικόν Δελτίον* 26 B: 217–18.

———. 1971f. "Κέρησις Λεβαδείας." *Ἀρχαιολογικόν Δελτίον* 26 B: 220.

———. 1971g. "Τανάγρα." *Ἀρχαιολογικόν Δελτίον* 26 B: 214–15.

———. 1972a. "Ὀρχομενός." *Ἀρχαιολογικόν Δελτίον* 27 B: 312–14.

———. 1972b. "Κωπαΐς." *Ἀρχαιολογικόν Δελτίον* 27 B: 314–15.

———. 1973a. "Παραλίμνη." *Ἀρχαιολογικόν Δελτίον* 28 B: 265–66.

———. 1973b. "Ὀρχομενός." *Ἀρχαιολογικόν Δελτίον* 28 B: 258–63.

———. 1973c. "Ἀνασκαφή μυκηναϊκῆς Τανάγρας." *Πρακτικά τῆς Ἀρχαιολογικῆς Ἑταιρείας*: 11–21.

———. 1974a. "Τό ἀνάκτορον τοῦ Μινύου εἰς τόν Βοιωτικόν Ὀρχομενόν." *Ἀρχαιολογικά Ἀνάλεκτα ἐξ Ἀθηνῶν* 7(3): 313–25.

———. 1974b. "Ἀνασκαφή μυκηναϊκῆς Τανάγρας." *Πρακτικά τῆς Ἀρχαιολογικῆς Ἑταιρείας*: 9–33.

———. 1976. "Ἀνασκαφή μυκηναϊκῆς Τανάγρας." *Πρακτικά τῆς Ἀρχαιολογικῆς Ἑταιρείας*: 61–68.

———. 1977. "Ἀνασκαφή μυκηναϊκῆς Τανάγρας." *Πρακτικά τῆς Ἀρχαιολογικῆς Ἑταιρείας*: 25–31.

———, and John Chadwick. 1975. *Thebes Tablets II.* Minos Suppl. 4. Salamanca: Ediciones Universidad de Salamanca.

Spyropoulos, Theodoros, and Hara Tzavella-Evjen. 1973. "Lithares: An Early Helladic Settlement near Thebes." *Ἀρχαιολογικά Ἀνάλεκτα ἐξ Ἀθηνῶν* 6(3): 271–75.

Symeonoglou, Sarantis. 1973. *Kadmeia I: Mycenaean Finds from Thebes, Greece: Excavation at 14 Oedipus St.* SIMA 35. Gothenburg: Åström.

Touloupa, Evi. 1964. "Καλλιθέα." Ἀρχαιολογικόν Δελτίον 19 Β: 199.

Tzavella-Evjen, Hara. 1972. "The Lithares Idols." Ἀρχαιολογικά Ἀνάλεκτα ἐξ Ἀθηνῶν 5(3): 467–69.

———. 1973–1974. "Λιθαρές Θηβῶν." Ἀρχαιολογικόν Δελτίον 29 Β: 443–44.

———. 1984. *Λιθαρές.* Δημοσιεύματα του Αρχαιολογικού Δελτίου 32. Athens: T.A.P.A.

———. 1985. *Lithares: An Early Bronze Age Settlement in Boeotia.* Los Angeles: Cotsen Institute of Archaeology, University of California at Los Angeles.

———. 1989. "Lithares Revisited." In *Boeotia Antiqua I: Papers on Recent Work in Boeotian Archaeology and History,* ed. John M. Fossey, 5–12. Amsterdam: Gieben.

———. 1990. "Χαιρώνεια." *Το Έργον της Αρχαιολογικής Εταιρείας 1989:* 49–52.

———. 1991. "Chaeroneia Excavations, 1989: Middle Helladic Burial Practices." *AJA* 95: 306.

———. In prep. *Χαιρώνεια.* Βιβλιοθήκη της εν Αθήναις Αρχαιολογικής Εταιρείας. Athens: Archaeological Society of Athens.

———, and Dorothy R. Rohner. 1990. "Building Materials and Techniques at EH II Lithares." In *L'habitat égéen préhistorique,* 115–21.

Vermeule, Emily. 1965. "Painted Mycenaean Larnakes." *JHS* 85: 123–48.

CHAPTER 47

....

CENTRAL AND SOUTHERN PELOPONNESE

....

WILLIAM G. CAVANAGH

THE LAND AND ITS RESOURCES

....

The Peloponnese, the heartland of Mycenaean civilization, covers about 19,000 km². Of this, the Argolid, so prominent in accounts of the Bronze Age Aegean, forms only 11%, while the region considered here—roughly the modern prefectures of Messenia, Laconia (plus parts of Arkadia), and the island of Kythera—is four times larger than the Argolid and only slightly smaller than the whole of the island of Crete.

Our area's seeming obscurity is due more to accidents in its history of exploration than to real poverty. Indeed, in a later period its agricultural wealth underwrote Sparta, the dominant Classical power: it occupies the wetter, western part of Greece, making it less subject to drought and unpredictable harvests, though it still contains a mosaic of environments, including coastal lagoons, perennial rivers, a great variety of arable soils, large extents of macchia, oak woodlands, pine and fir woods, alpine meadows, and extreme landscapes such as the arid European desert of southeast Arkadia. In addition to the farming base, there are mineral resources, notably metals in the area of Neapolis, and decorative stones, *lapis Lacedaemonius* from Krokeai and *antico rosso* from Kyprianon, which were prized in Bronze Age Greece.

Physically, the landscape is dominated by the massifs of Mount Parnon (1950 m above sea level) and Taÿgetos (2450 m above sea level), which define the mountain basins of Tripolis and Megalopolis, the central plain of Laconia, and sink into the sea to form the fingers of the Malea and Tainaron peninsulas. The relief of the southwest sector is much gentler, though still marked by mountains such as Aigaleon, which divided the two provinces ruled by the palace at Pylos, and Mount Ithome.

The region enjoys a long and varied coastline with a scatter of good harbors: the trinity of Kastri (on Kythera) and then Pavlopetri and Epidauros Limera on either side of the Malea peninsula formed an important node on the trans-Aegean trade routes (Janko 2008, 558), while a sophisticated hydraulic system was developed to serve the port for the palace at Pylos (Zangger et al. 1997). It also contains large inland basins, such as those of Sparta and Arkadia; located some distance from the sea, their prosperity, greater in the former and modest in the latter, belies the notion that maritime trade was the key to success for a Bronze Age site. It must be stressed that at no time in prehistory was this a unified territory, and the generalizations imposed by a short chapter here mask important regional differences.

THE EARLY BRONZE AGE

Although not as densely settled as Thessaly during the Neolithic, the southern Peloponnese supported large villages with a rich material culture and widespread trading connections. The end of that immensely long period culminates, in the Final Neolithic, in a radical change in material culture—for example, painted pottery almost disappears, while large storage and food-processing vessels become prominent.

Silver jewelry and copper tools from Alepotrypa confirm that the region participated in a wide-ranging exchange in prestige objects reaching up into the Balkans (Phelps 2004, 12, 168–69; Zachos 1996). New parts of the landscape were settled, and the occupation of cave sites became much more common; while caves like Diros in Laconia or Spilaio ton Limnon Kalavryton in Akhaia probably also served as regional cult centers, the smaller, less prominent caves, such as Alepochori in Laconia (Karkanas 2006; Koumouzeli 1989) were used by small groups of farmers, perhaps with an emphasis on herding (Cavanagh 1999; Efstathiou-Manolakou 2008).

All the same, given the immense length of FN–EH I over which we must distribute many small, short-lived habitations, population density was not great. However, by EH II, the southern Peloponnese saw a dramatic increase in the number of sites in that climax phase, which is common to the mainland, the islands, and Crete. Archaeological surveys have revealed a range of settlement sites that vary from small farmsteads to 'towns' of 3–5 ha, which may have housed as many as a thousand inhabitants. Different areas show different patterns: the Asea valley in Arkadia (Forsén and Forsén 2003, 192–96), central Laconia (Cavanagh, Crouwel et al. 2004, 128–35), and Kythera (Broodbank and Kyriatzi 2007) all have central settlements surrounded by farmsteads/hamlets, though their histories of development vary. The Asea valley, for example, sees no clear dispersion of sites during EH I or II, whereas the area east of Sparta and Kythera both see a rise in settlement in

Figure 47.1. Drawing of EH II seal impression from Geraki, Laconia (after Crouwel 2008, figure 7).

EH II. Messenia, on the other hand, "is not richly endowed with Early Helladic...sites" (Davis et al. 1997, 417).

The region participated fully in those developments seen elsewhere in the Aegean. Excavations at Geraki (Crouwel 2009), for example, have yielded clay seal-ings (figure 47.1) (Weingarten et al. 1999) like those from Lerna and Petri, as well as fortifications of the 'kastenmauer' technique, found from Limantepe in Turkey to Lerna in the Argolid. Sophisticated architecture is also attested in this area, notably with the Corridor Houses of Akovitika but probably also at Asea and no doubt at other sites yet to be excavated.

Altogether on a different scale is the Minoan connection between Kythera and Crete, which has long been interpreted as a case of colonization, an argument now reinforced and extended by the evidence from the Kythera Island Project. Here, Minoan intervention has been attributed to a long-term process that culminated in Minoan settlement 'whose aim was to establish independent access to the Cycladic mineral resources' (Broodbank and Kyriatzi 2007, 267). Once established, Kythera's Cretan connection made itself felt through much of the region for many centuries.

The long-running controversy over the transition at the end of the Early Bronze Age in mainland Greece takes on a special emphasis in the southern Peloponnese because the critical EH III pottery has proved so elusive. In fact, EH III pottery has been found only at sites in the Asea valley (Forsén and Forsén 2003, 195), Pylos (Late EH III: Davis et al. 1997, 419; Stocker 2003), and allegedly at the Amyklaion (Forsén 1992), and one or two sherds have been reported at other sites in Laconia (Banou 1999; Efstathiou-Manolakou 2008), including a few late EH III sherds from Ayios Stephanos.

Indeed, the very rarity of EH III pottery in the southern Peloponnese has inspired the suggestion that a 'sub-EH II' style may have prevailed here, contemporary with EH III of the northern Peloponnese but continuing the earlier shapes and fabrics of the local EH II styles (Boyd 2002, 2; Broodbank and Kyriatzi 2007, 263–64; Rutter 2001, 125). Recent excavations at relevant sites have failed signally to provide any stratified context with such pottery: Geraki (Crouwel 2009) and Kouphovouno (Cavanagh, Mee, and Renard 2007; Renard 1989) have classic EH II and MH deposits but nothing resembling a local EH III; on the other hand, the very few closed EH III contexts have produced fabrics and shapes that find their closest parallels in the Lerna IV and V repertoires, not those of the preceding period (Rutter 2001, 123, on the very late EH III at Nichoria; Stocker 2003). The process of change from EBA to MBA was a gradual one (Forsén 1992), but it involved severe depopulation in many parts of the region (though not all; Kythera in particular escapes depopulation, thanks—no doubt—to its association with Crete).

THE MIDDLE BRONZE AGE

After the obscurity of the later stages of the EBA, a very different Greece emerges in the 2nd millennium BC. Some EBA sites continued into or were resettled in the MBA—natural acropolis sites (such as Geraki) and sites on the sea (such as Ayios Stephanos and Pavlopetri) commended themselves to both EBA and MBA settlers. Overall, however, most regions show a different configuration.

In particular, intensive surveys in Laconia and Messenia (though not the Asea valley survey) have identified sites founded in EH III/MH, with new settlements located on low hilltops, plateaus, or ridges (Boyd 2002, 7; Cavanagh, Crouwel et al. 2004). At Pylos, four small farmsteads of EH III date with simple, apsidal-ended houses (Stocker 2003) gave way over the course of the MBA to a nucleated settlement that covered much of the Englianos ridge (some 5.5 ha) (Bennet 1999). It appears that the Menelaion, near Sparta, underwent a similar expansion, though it started a little later. Likewise, by the end of the MH period, Nichoria was "the most substantial known settlement of the Five Rivers district" (McDonald and Wilkie 1992, 762).

Secondary MH centers in both Laconia and Messenia were smaller, and this hierarchical settlement pattern of centers dominating small territories implies a new political partition of south Greece, whose units were later to form the building blocks of the Mycenaean states. Some failures occurred (Geraki, for example, hardly survives the MBA), and for many sites we lack information on their development and that of their hinterlands (such as Palaiopyrgi, near the Vapheio tholos tomb, which may well have rivaled its neighbors at the Menelaion and Ayios Stephanos).

Settlements give the appearance of open villages with freestanding, apsidal ended or rectangular houses, perhaps of two rooms or more, simple graves in and around the houses, and perhaps large gaps between the houses. At Ayios Vasilios, a more open village plan with apsidal-ended houses is said to give way in MH II to a more densely packed settlement in which rectangular houses of several rooms were huddled into blocks separated by paved passages (Janko 2008).

Unluckily, many of the more extensively excavated sites (Pylos, Nichoria, the Menelaion, Peristeria, Kouphovouno) have yielded no coherent picture, and the dating of the various phases at Malthi is unclear. However, the impression of relative simplicity in the region's material culture can be overstated. Both Nichoria and Ayios Stephanos bear witness to the rich ceramic repertoire, including large storage pithoi (some of the burials used massive ones), underlining the importance of the storage of agricultural commodities.

The range of painted jars and serving vessels (jugs, bowls) emphasize display and consumption, and the highly burnished tablewares, such as 'Minyan,' indicate the importance of dining and commensality in MBA society. As the period advanced, these types became ever more elaborate, with a greater variety of shapes and decoration (Howell 1992; Rutter and Rutter 1976).

Metal finds are not common, but crucibles and the remains of furnaces have been reported from Nichoria (McDonald and Wilkie 1992, 23, 26–28) and Ayios Stephanos. The latter has imports of Protopalatial pottery from Crete and perhaps also Nichoria (Howell 1992, 60; certainly imitations of Minoan are reported), indicating that this region was not isolated from developments elsewhere in the Aegean.

The remains that most clearly signal a degree of complexity in the MBA society of the different regions of the southern Peloponnese are the tombs (Bennet and Galanakis 2005 emphasize the regional differences). In Messenia, in particular, even in the earlier MH period, networks of burial mounds articulated the landscape, in part placed to act as visible markers for those who lived and buried their dead there and in part embedded in earlier settlements, evidently as a symbolic claim on the past (Boyd 2002, esp. 33–39). Grave offerings were not common, at most a vase such as a kantharos, but more notable finds belonging to 'high-status' people have recently been reported from the MH I tumuli at Kastroulia (Rambach in press). As the MH period advanced, so, too, did the variety, complexity, and display in tombs increase. A snapshot of these developments follows in the next section.

THE LATE BRONZE AGE

Early Mycenaean

By the beginning of the Early Mycenaean period, a great variety of tomb types had developed: single graves of various types, tumuli covering a number of single graves or enclosing collective tombs, single built graves, rock-cut chamber tombs, and tholos tombs (Boyd 2002; Lolos 1987). The last two types were to predominate in later Mycenaean Greece and were probably invented in the southern Peloponnese. Important early (LH I) chamber tomb cemeteries are found at Epidauros Limera in Laconia and Volimidia near Pylos.

The most spectacular finds come from the tholos tombs such as Routsi tomb 2, which held inlaid daggers, long swords, arrowheads, a spear, seal stones, amber, gold, ivory pyxides, mirrors, glass, palace-style jars, and imported Minoan pottery. Many others were robbed, but a few, such as Pylos Tholos Tomb V, the tholoi at Peristeria, Epia Anthia, Kakovatos, and Vapheio, hint at a wealth of offerings comparable with those of the shaft graves at Mycenae. Two or three such prominent tombs could dominate a single site, underlining the agonistic tensions within early Mycenaean society.

If we can rely on the archaeological evidence, other sites indicate a quieter register of ostentation—the small town at Analipsis, in Arkadia, has a larger tholos, with indications of wealthier but evidently not spectacularly rich finds, to serve the leading family, accompanied by more modest, smaller tholos tombs serving others in the community (Kalogeropoulos 1998). Although robbed, the main tomb had fragments of a boar's tusk helmet, gold, ivory, silver, amber, bronze and flint arrowheads, and palace-style vases. The site of Pellana contains one very large, dominant tomb (this time a chamber tomb, again robbed, and with traces of similar finds) and a cemetery of smaller ones, though we are not sure of their dates (Spyropoulos 1998).

Nonfunerary architecture of the early Mycenaean period is harder to come by, but at Peristeria, the East House was a large, multiroomed structure that has been described as 'sprawling' (Vermeule 1964, 117) and seems to have served those buried in the wealthy tombs (surely it is no coincidence that one of the tholos tombs destroyed the house). The so-called Big House at Malthi, if MH or early LH, might fit the same picture, as could the heavily built structure at Katarrachaki (Lolos 1987, 28–41). Ayios Stephanos shrank in size, but the style of housing seems to have stayed much as before.

A new study of the remains at Pylos (Nelson 2001, referred to in Rutter 2005), indicates a sequence of buildings starting in LH I and developing into LH IIIA. These are more monumental in appearance and used carefully dressed, ashlar styles of masonry similar to those found in some of the more impressive tholos tombs of the time.

By LH II, we can point to another structure whose overall plan is more sophisticated: the first mansion at the Menelaion (figure 47.2) has a central megaron suite that measures roughly 17 by 6.5 m and a basement of organized storage magazines. The footprint of the whole building has been estimated at more than 500 m²; that is to say, it is comparable in size to the later House of Shields at Mycenae (Darcque 2005, 325).

The confrontation of the Menelaion, on one bank of the River Eurotas, with Palaiopyrgi/Vapheio some 5 km away and on the other bank, symbolizes the transformation that mainland Greece was undergoing during, roughly, the fifteenth century BC. The country was a patchwork of petty realms whose leaders, however, had at their disposal products of the most refined craftsmanship, such as the gold cups

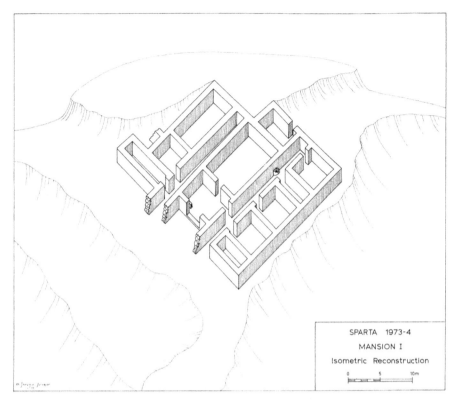

SPARTA 1973-4

MANSION I

Isometric Reconstruction

0   5   10m

Figure 47.2. Axonometric reconstruction of Mansion 1 at the Menelaion
(after Catling 1977, 28, figure 5).

and the seal stones from Vapheio. As time went on, these were amalgamated into
larger kingdoms and subjected to the discipline of a centralized economy mediated
through a literate bureaucracy when the Minoan system was adapted to Greece.

High Mycenaean

If the Menelaion marks an important next step toward the development of the
mature Mycenaean state, the process of transformation from small fiefdom to
major power has been traced most clearly for the kingdom of Pylos, where we have
the advantage of the Linear B tablets and the insight they give us into its growth and
culmination.

By its end, Pylos governed a territory of some 2000 km². Bennet (1995) has
sketched the development whereby early Mycenaean centers were either subor-
dinated to Pylos or eclipsed; thus, the important early Mycenaean princedom at
Peristeria was evidently displaced in a later period by the new, fortified, regional
center at Mouriatada; at the same time the center at Beylerbey was overtaken by
Pylos, while the site at Ordines grew in prominence under the palace's patronage
(Bennet 1999). Other, more isolated sites set relatively high in the mountains (such

as Metaxada [Gaz. D22], Romiri [D31], Misorachi [D117], Chalvatsou [D118], and Kephalovrysi [D240] in Messenia and Arkines [C9] in Laconia) might hint at the use of uplands for pasturing sheep, as wool production for textiles was an important palace industry.

Through the overthrow of its rivals by means of the exercise of favor and patronage, as well as by economic reform, the palace of Pylos reworked the inhabited landscape of Messenia. In pursuing this policy it was not unique; thus, in our region, while we cannot be certain, it appears that the Further Province may have evolved into a united principality under Leuktron before it was annexed by Pylos. Likewise, the rise of major sites such as the Menelaion (Catling 2009) and Ayios Vasilios in Laconia saw some minor centers fade while their rivals flourished (Cavanagh 1995). The important new discovery of Linear B tablets at Ayios Vasilios (announced by Vasilogamvrou and Aravantinos in April 2009) underlines that a similar political and economic revolution took place in Laconia with the rise of a palace similar to those in Pylos and central Greece.

Recent work on Kythera tells another, but related, story. In the preceding Early Mycenaean period, the island was densely covered with small farmsteads, the Minoan town of Kastri was at its most prosperous, and the richest offerings were dedicated at the peak sanctuary of Agios Georgios. During the High Mycenaean period, in contrast, many farms were abandoned, the town shrank, and the tokens of prosperity grew fewer. This decline was no doubt partly related to political changes in Crete, notably the rise and fall of Knossos, but it can be no coincidence that the tablets at Pylos recorded slave women from Kythera (Broodbank, Kiriatzi, and Rutter 2005). Undoubtedly, the rise of the various Mycenaean states brought about both losers and winners.

Nichoria gives us a good idea of the vernacular architecture of a secondary Mycenaean center. The largest structure was the LH IIIA1 'megaron,' unit IV-4A, whose main room, with an earthen floor and a central hearth lying between two single columns, measured 6.8 by 4.7 m (a little more than half the area of its equivalent in Mansion 1 at the Menelaion) (McDonald and Wilkie 1992, 433–39). Overall, the complex covered 133 m².

The majority of the houses, however, were smaller (less than 80 m²) and were scattered across the ridge in a rather open formation following the lie of the land. The majority were also multiroomed and rectangular in form, and some probably had a second story; structure III-3, however, was a simple apsidal house. Such relatively simple structures can be found in the villages of the preceding and ensuing periods; sophisticated architecture seems to have been restricted to a powerful minority.

Many more sites are known from their cemeteries, which can vary from hundreds of tombs to just a few, according to the size of the settlement. The little site of Melathria in Laconia, a hamlet of about 0.7 ha in extent, was served by a small cemetery of chamber tombs, six of which have been cleared. The settlement was newly founded in LH IIIA1 and continued in use for some two hundred years (Cavanagh and Crouwel 1992).

Final Mycenaean

The southern Peloponnese was hit hard by the destructions that more generally mark the beginning of the end of Mycenaean civilization. The palace at Pylos burned down at the transition to LH IIIC, and towns such as Nichoria were abandoned at much the same time.

Indeed, relatively few sites have produced finds of the ensuing period. In Laconia, the cult site at Amyklai continued in use, and the area was to become a significant center in the Dark Age (as indeed was Nichoria after a gap). At the Menelaion, a major disruption is witnessed with the destruction of Mansion 3, but there are signs of continued occupation into LH IIIC early (Cating 2009), and recent discoveries point to a cult site below the later Archaic sanctuary—all the same, the site was abandoned at the end of the Bronze Age. Another major center in the 12th century BC was Epidauros Limera, whose harbor served to link it into the Aegean network, which connected other coastal sites such as Asine, Perati, and Lefkandi with sites in the Cyclades, Dodecanese, and Crete. Ayios Stephanos received a fresh influx during these unsettled times.

In all, as many as sixteen sites in Laconia have LH IIIC pottery (Demakopoulou 1982), and most of these fade from view by the end of the period. Messenia, densely populated in LH IIIB (the most recent estimate suggests a population of fifty thousand people), seems to have declined even more rapidly: it has just half a dozen sites with LH IIIC pottery (e.g., Eder 1998, compare 143, figure 18, with 146, figure 19). The Early Dark Age period saw a distinctly new beginning following the devastation of the southern Peloponnese in the 12th century BC, as Greece and the Peloponnese moved from the Age of Bronze into a new epoch.

BIBLIOGRAPHY

Banou, Eleni. 1999. "New Evidence on Early Helladic Laconia." *BSA* 94: 63–79.

Bennet, John. 1995. "Space through Time: Diachronic Perspectives of the Spatial Organisation of the Pylian State." In *Politeia*, 587–601.

———. 1999. "Pylos: The Expansion of a Mycenaean Center." In *RMP*, 9–18.

———, and Ioannis Galanakis. 2005. "Parallels and Contrasts: Early Mycenaean Mortuary Traditions in Messenia and Laconia." In *Autochthon*, 144–55.

Boyd, Michael J. 2002. *Middle Helladic and Early Mycenaean Mortuary Practices in the Southern and Western Peloponnese. BAR* 1009. Oxford: British Archaeological Reports.

Broodbank, Cyprian, and Evangelia Kyriatzi. 2007. "The First Minoans of Kythera Revisited: Technology, Demography, and Landscape in the Prepalatial Aegean." *AJA* 111(2): 241–74.

———, and Jeremy Rutter. 2005. "From Pharaoh's Feet to the Slave-women of Pylos? The History and Cultural Dynamics of Kythera in the Third Palace Period." In *Autochthon*, 70–96.

Catling, Hector W. 1977. "Excavations at the Menelaion, Sparta, 1973–76." *Archaeological Reports* 23: 24–42.

———. 2009. *Sparta: Menelaion I. The Bronze Age*. BSA Supplementary vol. 45. London: British School at Athens.

Cavanagh, William. 1995. "Development of the Mycenaean State in Laconia." In *Politeia*, 81–88.

———. 1999. "Revenons à nos moutons: Surface Survey and the Peloponnese in the Late and Final Neolithic." In *Le Péloponnèse: Archéologie et histoire*, ed. Josette Renard, 31–65. Rennes: Presses Universitaires de Rennes.

———, and Joost Crouwel. 1992. "Melathria: A Small Mycenaean Rural Settlement." In *Philolakon: Lakonian Studies in Honour of Hector Catling*, ed. Jan M. Sanders, 77–86. London: British School at Athens.

———, Richard W. V. Catling, and Graham Shipley. 2004. *Continuity and Change in a Greek Rural Landscape: The Laconia Survey*, vol. 1. London: British School at Athens.

Cavanagh, William, Christopher Mee, and Peter James. 2004. *The Laconia Rural Sites Project*. BSA Supplementary vol. 36. London: British School at Athens.

Cavanagh, William, Christopher Mee, and Josette Renard. 2007. "Excavations at Kouphovouno, Laconia: Results from the 2001 and 2002 Seasons." *BSA* 102: 11–101.

Crouwel, Joost. 2009. "Prehistoric Geraki: Work in Progress." In *Sparta and Lakonia from Prehistory to Premodern: Proceedings of the Conference in Sparta Organised by the British School at Athens, the University of Nottingham, the E' Ephoreia of Prehistoric and Classical Antiquities, and the 5th Ephoreia of Byzantine Antiquities, 17–20 March 2005*, ed. William Cavanagh, Chrysanthi Gallou, and Mercouris Georgiadis, 67–76. London: British School at Athens.

Darcque, Pascal. 2005. *L'habitat mycénien: Formes et fonctions de l'espace bâti en Grèce continentale à la fin du IIe millénaire avant J.-C.* Athens: L'École française d'Athènes.

Davis, Jack, Susan Alcock, John Bennet, Yannis Lolos, and Cynthia Shelmerdine. 1997. "The Pylos Regional Archaeological Project, Part 1: Overview and the Archaeological Survey." *Hesperia* 66(3): 391–494.

Demakopoulou, Katie. 1982. *Το Μυκηναϊκό Ιερό στο Αμυκλαίο και η ΥΕ ΙΙΙΓ Περίοδος στη Λακωνία*. Athens: Athens University.

———. 1988. *The Mycenaean World: Five Centuries of Early Greek Culture 1600–1100 BC*. Athens: Greek Ministry of Culture.

Eder, Birgitta. 1998. *Argolis, Lakonien, Messenien, vom Ende der mykenischen Palastzeit bis zur Einwanderung der Dorier*. Vienna: Verlag der Österreichischen Akademie der Wissenschaften.

Efstathiou-Manolakou, Ioanna. 2008. "Archaeological Investigations in the Caves of Laconia." In *Sparta and Lakonia from Prehistory to Premodern: Proceedings of the Conference in Sparta Organised by the British School at Athens, the University of Nottingham, the E' Ephoreia of Prehistoric and Classical Antiquities, and the 5th Ephoreia of Byzantine Antiquities, 17–20 March 2005*, ed. William Cavanagh, Chrysanthi Gallou and Mercouris Georgiadis, 5–20. London: British School at Athens.

Forsén, Jeanette. 1992. *The Twilight of the Early Helladic: A Study of the Disturbances in East-central and Southern Greece towards the End of the Early Bronze Age*. SIMA-PB 116. Gothenburg: Åström.

———, and Björn Forsén. 2003. *The Asea Valley Survey: An Arcadian Mountain Valley from the Palaeolithic Period until Modern Times*. Acta Instituti Atheniensis Regni Sueciae 4°, 51. Sävedalen, Sweden: Åström.

Holmberg, Erik J. 1944. *The Swedish Excavations at Asea in Arcadia*. Gothenburg: Swedish Institute.

Howell, Roger J. 1992. "The Middle Helladic Settlement: Pottery." In *Excavations at Nichoria in Southwest Greece*. Vol. 2, *The Bronze Age Occupation*, ed. William A. MacDonald and Nancy C. Wilkie, 43–204. Minneapolis: University of Minnesota Press.

Janko, Richard. 2008. "Summary and Historical Conclusions." In *Ayios Stephanos: Excavations at a Bronze Age and Medieval Settlement in Laconia, 1973–7*, ed. William D. Taylour and Richard Janko. London: British School at Athens.

Kalogeropoulos, Konstantinos. 1998. *Die frühmykenischen Grabfunde von Analipsis (südöstliches Arkadien)*. Athens: I en Athenais Archaiologiki Etaireia.

Karkanas, Panagiotis. 2006. "Late Neolithic Household Activities in Marginal Areas: The Micromorphological Evidence from the Kouveleiki Caves, Peloponnese, Greece." *Journal of Archaeological Science* 33: 1628–41.

Koumouzeli, Maria. 1989. "Η κεραμική από την Α Κουβελέϊκη σπηλιά Αλεποχωρίου Λακωνίας." *Athens Annals of Archaeology* 22: 143–60.

Lolos, Yannis. 1987. *The Late Helladic I Pottery of the Southwestern Peloponnese and Its Local Characteristics*. Gothenburg: Åström.

McDonald, William A., and Nancy C. Wilkie. 1992. *Excavations at Nichoria in Southwestern Greece*. Vol. 2, *The Bronze Age Occupation*. Minneapolis: University of Minnesota Press.

Mee, Christopher. 2008. "Interconnectivity in Early Helladic Laconia." In *Sparta and Lakonia from Prehistory to Premodern: Proceedings of the Conference in Sparta Organised by the British School at Athens, the University of Nottingham, the E' Ephoreia of Prehistoric and Classical Antiquities, and the 5th Ephoreia of Byzantine Antiquities, 17–20 March 2005*, ed. William Cavanagh Chrysanthi Gallou, and Mercouris Georgiadis, 43–54. London: British School at Athens.

Nelson, Michael C. 2001. The Architecture of Epano Englianos, Greece. PhD diss., University of Toronto.

Phelps, William W. 2004. *The Neolithic Pottery Sequence in Southern Greece. BAR-IS* 1259. Oxford: Hadrian.

Rambach, Jörg. In press. "Recent Research in Middle Helladic Sites of the Western Peloponnese." In *Mesohelladika*.

Renard, Josette. 1989. *Le site néolithique et hélladique ancien de Kouphovounmo, Laconie: fouilles de O.-W. von Vacano (1941)*. Aegaeum 4. Liège: Université de Liège.

Rutter, Jeremy B. 2001. "The Prepalatial Bronze Age of the Southern and Central Greek Mainland." In *Aegean Prehistory*, 95–155.

———. 2005. "Southern Triangles Revisited: Lakonia, Messenia, and Crete in the 14th–12th Centuries B.C." In *Ariadne's Threads*, 17–50.

———, and Sarah Rutter. 1976. *The Transition to Mycenaean: A Stratified MH II to LH IIA Pottery Sequence from Ayios Stephanos in Laconia*. Los Angeles: University of California Institute of Archaeology.

Spyropoulos, Theodoros. 1998. "Pellana: The Administrative Centre of Prehistoric Laconia." In *Sparta in Laconia: Proceedings of the 19th British Museum Classical Colloquium, London 6–8 December 1995*, ed. William G. Cavanaghand Susan Walker, 28–38. London: British School at Athens.

Stocker, Sharon. 2003. "The Pylos Regional Archaeological Project, Part V: Deriziotis Aloni. A Small Prehistoric Site in Messenia." *Hesperia* 72(4): 341–404.

Vermeule, Emily. 1964. *Greece in the Bronze Age*. Chicago: University of Chicago Press.

Weingarten, Judith, Joost H. Crouwel, Mieke Prent, and Gillian Vogelsang-Eastwood. 1999. "Early Helladic Sealings from Geraki, Laconia." *OJA* 18: 357–76.

Zachos, Konstantinos. 1996. "Μεταλλουργεία." In *Ο Νεολιθικός Πολιτισμός στην Ελλάδα*, ed. Giorgos Papathanassopouolos, 140–43. Athens: Goulandris Foundation.

Zangger, Eberhard, Michael Timpson, Sergei Yazvenko, Falko Kuhnke, and Joost Knauss. 1997. "The Pylos Regional Archaeological Project Part II: Landscape Evolution and Site Preservation." *Hesperia* 66(4): 549–641.

Zavvou, Elena. 2008. "Archaeological Finds from the Area of Anthochori." In *Sparta and Lakonia from Prehistory to Premodern: Proceedings of the Conference in Sparta Organised by the British School at Athens, the University of Nottingham, the E' Ephoreia of Prehistoric and Classical Antiquities, and the 5th Ephoreia of Byzantine Antiquities, 17–20 March 2005*, ed. William Cavanagh, Chrysanthi Gallou, and Mercouris Georgiadis, 29–42. London: British School at Athens.

CHAPTER 48

NORTHERN AEGEAN

STELIOS ANDREOU

UNTIL the end of the 5th millennium, the northern Aegean communities were dynamic partakers of the cultural processes that transformed southeast Europe and the Aegean during the Neolithic. During the 3rd millennium, however, the dramatic developments in settlement organization, elaboration of material culture, technological advancement, and exchange caused the focus of changes to shift to the south and east. As a result, the northern Aegean found itself on the borders of this dynamic new world for the rest of the Bronze Age. This shift does not mean, however, that northern communities froze in their existing ways of life, which mainly harkened back to Neolithic times. Instead, during the following millennia, the people in the different regions of Macedonia, Thrace, and the neighboring islands were active in developing varied ways of living through the manipulation of local traditions and the selective adoption of cultural forms and technological novelties from the surrounding regions.

The survey that follows concentrates on the regions of the north, which present the strongest evidence for contacts with the cultural developments in the Aegean during the Bronze Age. These include the islands of Thasos and Samothrace, coastal Thrace, the coastal plains of central and southern Macedonia, and the peninsula of Chalkidiki. The discussion also focuses on parts of the inland basins of eastern, central, and western Macedonia and leaves out northern Macedonia, which remained outside the reach of significant Aegean influences (cf. Mitrevski 2003). Groups living in these regions took advantage of inland passes to establish and maintain at some points of their early history strong contacts with the areas farther to the south. It cannot be overemphasized, though, that throughout their early history, communities in this part of the Aegean also developed and maintained strong contacts with their neighbors to the north by taking advantage of the major river routes and the numerous mountain paths.

With the exception of two pioneering archaeological expeditions in the first half of the 20th century, the archaeological record of the Bronze Age in the north has been collected primarily during the last forty years. Consequently, information is limited, compared to many other Aegean regions, and data are largely incompletely published and unequally distributed, both temporally and geographically (Andreou, Fotiadis, and Kotsakis 2001).

THE THIRD MILLENNIUM

New ways of living become evident in the north Aegean at the end of the 4th millennium. The new manners incorporated some of the features of LN life, which were, however, reinterpreted and placed in a new frame of values and beliefs.

The evidence for a disruption of life between the late 5th millennium and the end of the 4th is as strong as in most other regions of the Aegean and the Balkans. Habitation was interrupted for a period of several centuries in Servia, Mandalo, Sitagroi, Dikili Tash, and several other tell sites (Manning 1995; Andreou, Fotiadis, and Kotsakis 2001; Ozdogan 2003b). The discontinuity may be related to a radical change in settlement numbers, size, organization, endurance, and setting during the earlier part of the 4th millennium. The extent to which the phenomenon of settlement dislocation had to do with a breakdown of traditional social structures in communities and the disintegration of the widespread regional networks of the 5th millennium or were induced by an episode of climatic disruption remains to be investigated (Manning 1995; Mayewski et al. 2004). Former explanations, however, that attribute the changes to widespread population displacements caused by an invasion of Proto-Indo-European-language speakers, have gradually lost their theoretical and archaeological support (Whittle 1996).

More than half of the EBA (ca. 3100–2000 BC) sites in the Serres basin in eastern Macedonia were new foundations of very small settlements. New settings were often chosen on higher elevations with less or no access to the richer soils of traditional LN habitation (Fotiadis 1985). The same pattern was observed in other regions as well (Andreou, Fotiadis, and Kotsakis 2001). The expansion of settlement was probably facilitated by a more diversified subsistence strategy, while the growth of maritime traffic and the resurgence of overland communications was eased by, among other factors, the novel use of donkeys (Becker 1986; Becker and Kroll 2008; Valamoti 2007). Several new EBA settlements were either short lived, leaving elusive traces, or occasionally signified by small cemeteries (Kotsakis and Andreou 1992 [1995]; Asouhidou Mantazi, and Tsolakis 1998 [2000]; Mavroidi, Andreou, and Pappa 2006 [2008]).

The reoccupation of Neolithic mounds such as Servia, Mandalo, Sitagroi, and Dikili Tash, however, indicates that during the same period other groups were marking their presence in the landscape more visibly. A rise in settlement numbers during the second half of the 3rd millennium was observed in coastal Thrace and in the almost insular peninsulas of Chalkidiki. Recent research has shown a significant increase in small EBA sites, which were often located on tiny islands, coastal hills, and promontories with access to secure ports. Some were surrounded by fortifications reminiscent of 3rd-millennium sites in the rest of the Aegean (Grammenos, Besios, and Kotsos 1997; Papadopoulos et al. 1999; Ozdogan 2003a; Smagas 2007).

Skala Sotiros on Thasos is an excavated example of such a small settlement. The near coastal site was surrounded by a fortification wall, with a façade adorned with armed anthropomorphic grave stelae in second use and stones arranged in herringbone pattern. The material culture displays several eastern Aegean features, including the characteristic "depas" cups (Davis 2001; Papadopoulos 2001 [2003]), and shows that the effects of the rising, mid-3rd-millennium, maritime network were also felt in the northern Aegean. Signs of these effects are evident up to the northern tip of the Thermaikos Gulf, which in the Bronze Age stretched beyond ancient Pella (Aslanis 1985; Schulz 1989; Mavroidi, Andreou, and Pappa 2006 [2008]; Vouvalidis et al. 2003; Akamatis in press).

Defensive walls are not evident in continental northern Aegean settlements. A typical feature of EBA habitations, however, which was shared with adjacent regions, was the elongated house with or without an apsidal end. Most were framed with posts, but mud-brick structures are also attested. Working areas, food storage and processing installations, and food consumption were consistently placed or carried out inside such houses in Sitagroi, Agios Athanasios, and Arhontiko (Elster 1997; Mavroidi, Andreou, and Pappa 2006 [2008]; Pilali and Papanthimou 2002). The variety of cultivated and wild plants and fruits, including grapes and acorns, and the remains of domesticated and wild animals, including large quantities of fishbones and shell found in the dwellings of tell sites, demonstrate the pursuit of self-sufficiency (Bökönyi 1986; Renfrew 2003; Valamoti, Papanthimou, and Pilali 2005; Theodoropoulou 2007).

The architecture and persistent inclusion of maintenance activities in houses stressed the households' autonomy and social identity, which were further underlined by infant burials underneath floors and by the reconstruction of houses on top of their predecessors. The plans of Arhontiko and Ayios Mamas during the later part of the period, with narrow paths separating insulae of long buildings with shared walls, and identical facilities for storage and food preparation, suggest the existence of an intermediary level of grouping between the household and the community and reveal distant affinities in terms of space organization with EBA settlements in the eastern and central Aegean (Pilali and Papanthimou 2002; Aslanis 2006 [2008]; Becker and Kroll 2008). Compact settlement plans, uniform house plans and orientations, clear settlement boundaries, and minimal dislocation of structures over time suggest planning in advance and the existence of well-defined social rules and practices that regulated life and prevented the expression of strong inequalities in communities.

The emphasis on the autonomous households in settlements was counterbalanced by the symbolic stress on collective identities in the idealized world of cemeteries. Small groups of compactly arranged stone circles containing individual cremations or inhumations and few, identical offerings under a common stone tumulus signaled small, short-lived communities that were colonizing the peninsulas of Chalkidiki in the middle of the 3rd millennium.

The commemoration of the collective past through tumuli was probably significant for the coherence of the fragile groups for both the display of their identity in the regional landscape and comparison with other groups. Occasionally it was amplified by the use of large anthropomorphic stelae depicting the mythical ancestors in the form of gigantic, idealized, male warriors (Asouhidou 2001; Tsigarida and Mantazi 2003 [2005]; Smagas 2007). Similar stelae have been found in second use in Thasos and several locations in Macedonia. Along with tumuli and cremation burials, they formed widespread third-millennium phenomena that demonstrate the extensive contacts of the region (cf. Whittle 1996; Bailey 2000).

In the slightly later single burial cemetery of Koilada in western Macedonia, the collective identity and cohesion of the community, despite some variability in grave types and practices, were stressed by the allocation of a special area for postfunerary rituals, the consistent orientation of graves and burials, and the lack of differentiations in burial offerings. In this case, the community was identified in the landscape through stone piles heaped primarily over single inhumation burials of males. They indicate the significance and possibly hierarchical relationship of gendered identities, which were also displayed during funerals through the consistently opposite placement of male and female bodies in the grave (Ziota 2007). Interpersonal antagonisms are, however, slightly more evident in the display of wealth and access to distant contacts in the cemeteries of large coastal communities such as Pella and Ayios Mamas (Pappa in press; Akamatis in press).

The novelties in life and death during the 3rd millennium are also evident in the new forms, techniques, and contexts in which material culture was produced and used. By the beginning of the 3rd millennium, the elaborate wares of the Neolithic had been completely replaced by coarser, dark, burnished vessels rarely decorated with channelling or incisions (figure 48.1). The most common types suggest a particular emphasis on the consumption of liquids—among which wine, known in the area from the 5th millennium on, must have held a vital position—and on the storage of grains (Sherratt 1986; Valamoti et al. 2007).

The novel forms may be partly attributed to dietary changes, but the decrease in elaboration signifies major readjustments in the symbolic significance of vessels and in the contexts of their use. The emphasis on the autonomy of households increased the importance of the display of stored agricultural wealth and the significance of serving food and drink during social occasions in the secluded space of houses. While the ceremonial aspect of these occasions was highlighted by the specialized use and the standardization of the employed vessels, the new context of display transferred the focus of symbolic expression from the vessels to the acts of storage or commensality, which had significant consequences for the appearance and technology of the pottery (Sherratt 1986).

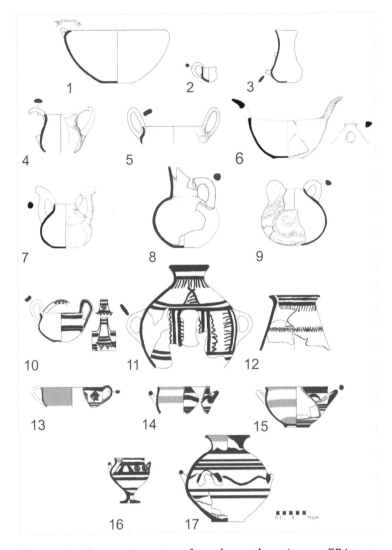

Figure 48.1. Bronze Age pottery from the northern Aegean. EBA: 1–3; EBA/MBA: 4–5; LBA brown burnished: 6–8; LBA incised and encrusted: 9; LBA matt painted: 10–12; Mycenaean: 13–17; Ayios Athanasios: 1–3; Thessaloniki Toumba: 4–17 (drawings 1–3 by Ioanna Mavroidi; 4–17 by Rania Exarhou).

Analytical evidence suggests that some northern Aegean silver and copper deposits may have been exploited during the 3rd millennium (Stos-Gale and Macdonald 1991; Renfrew and Slater 2003). Depositional preferences and the low intensity of research, however, may have been responsible for the paucity of metallic finds. Despite this, there is some evidence that the significance of metalworking for the lives of people increased and that technological innovations, such as arsenical copper and the use of two-piece molds, were adopted during the period.

The hoard of about forty chisels and four sleeve-shaft axes found in a jar near the village of Petralona offers a glimpse into the invisible part of northern Aegean metalworking (Grammenos Tzahili, and Magou 1994). Molds and several axes found in different sites suggest that the production and circulation of large tools was not unusual in communities during the mid-3rd millennium, while copper and gold slugs in settlements indicate local metalworking related to the production of jewelry and other small metal finds (Heurtley 1939; Malamidou 1997; Renfrew and Slater 2003; Ziota 2007). The fact that all of the axes belong to a circum-Pontic type, which was rare in the rest of the Aegean, demonstrates the resurgence of access to far-flung continental exchange networks after the 4th millennium disruption.

The tin bronze awl, however, in mid-3rd-millennium Sitagroi, dates from a period of westward maritime movement of Anatolian prestige objects in the form, among other things, of finished tin bronzes (cf. Nakou 1997). Objects such as the latter or the faience jewelry from the cemetery and the settlement of Ayios Mamas (among the earliest instances in the Aegean), the marble bowls from Pella and Pieria, the zoomorphic ax from Sitagroi, the EH III patterned ware tankard from Kritsana, and the eastern "depas" cups from Pella and Thasos derived their value from the biographical implications of their circulation in long-distance networks and could have played a significant role as objects of display in the muffled antagonisms for prestige between household heads during the second half of the millennium (Heurtley 1939; Renfrew, Gimbutas, and Elster 1986; Besios 1993 (1997); Akamatis in press; Pappa in press).

THE SECOND MILLENNIUM

The incomplete archaeological record for the first centuries of the 2nd millennium BC does not allow the understanding of phenomena such as the abandonment of settlements in the western part of the Thermaikos Gulf during the MBA (Hänsel 1989; Pilali and Papanthimou 2002). Important tell settlements, however, such as Assiros Toumba were founded in the same period, during which the upland migration of sites in western Macedonia was also initiated (Wardle 1980; Stefani and Merousis 2003).

At Ayios Mamas, the late EBA insulae of single-space buildings were replaced at the start of the MBA by complex, post-framed structures. Communities in Chalkidiki and Pieria, as opposed to the rest of Macedonia, continued their involvement in maritime networks, which were now focusing on the elaborate wheel-made Minyan bowls that likely originated in coastal central Greece (Hänsel 2002; Aslanis 2005 [2007]; Becker and Kroll 2008; Psaraki and Andreou in press). A novel and isolated phenomenon was the Minoan involvement in Samothrace at the end of the MBA, which was probably triggered by the interest in northern Aegean metal sources (Matsas 1995; Davis 2001).

Figure 48.2. Thessaloniki Toumba (courtesy Toumba excavation archives).

The Late Bronze Age (LBA) (ca. 1650–1050 BC) is the period with the highest number of known settlements. Sites in most regions exhibit a strong tendency to move from coastal plains, basins, and valleys to hills and spurs on higher elevations, which feature less hospitable or rugged terrain (Stefani and Merousis 2003; Lespez 2008). The example of the Langadas basin shows, however, that habitation of lowland sites was not interrupted in central Macedonia, and the LBA expansion of settlements to new ground led to a substantial increase in the number and density of sites (Andreou 2001). Fortified settlements have been confirmed only in western Thrace, but new habitation sites on elevated points and defensible heights in other regions offered protection and good control of the surrounding terrain (Fotiadis 1985; Andreou, Fotiadis, and Kotsakis 2001). Expansion to marginal lands was also triggered by the occasional extension of marshlands, further diversification of farming, a greater emphasis on animal resources, and a renewed emphasis on hunting, particularly during the end of the period (Bottema 1982; Becker 1986; Lespez 2008).

The increased mobility probably contributed to the disintegration of tell settlements in all other regions except central Macedonia. In the latter, tells not only persisted but also became the sole type of habitation site during the LBA (figure 48.2). Stone and mud-brick walls and clay banks were constructed at various levels along the periphery of several tells. It is not clear whether the early LBA, casemated, perimeter wall on the slope of the Thessaloniki Toumba and the clay bank that surrounded the Assiros Toumba were defensive, retentive, or both. They created, however, steep-sided mounds that mark clearly the places of the LBA communities in the central Macedonian landscape. Moreover, while sizes of mounds rarely exceeded 1 ha, their constructed prominence may have served as a basis for comparison among local communities. The transfer of habitation to the higher terraces in Thessaloniki and Assiros during the early LBA may have also served practical, as well as symbolic, considerations (Andreou 2001; Wardle and Wardle 2007; cf. Stefani and Merousis 2003).

Reliable information regarding planning and intrasettlement organization derives from a few systematically investigated tell sites in central Macedonia. There are evident inequalities between communities, but at the same time fluctuations in the spatial organization of individual settlements indicate the volatility and the restricted scope of the economic and political structures, which influenced life in the region during the second half of the 2nd millennium.

Communal planning and rules regulating life in settlements are manifest at Assiros, Thessaloniki, and Ayios Mamas in the definition of community boundaries and the regular network of parallel streets, which separated large, rectangular blocks of more than 150 m^2 and up to fifteen spaces each in the first two sites. Post-framed, mud-brick walls on stone foundations were evident at Ayios Mamas and Thessaloniki Toumba by the end of the MBA, and in several settlements they became the rule for the rest of the period. Other building techniques, however, well established in the area since the Neolithic, also remained in use and occasionally alternated with mud bricks in the same settlement (Andreou and Kotsakis 1996 [1997]; Hänsel 2002; Videski 2005; Chrysostomou and Georgiadou 2007).

The replication of the same house and settlement plans, with some alterations, in Assiros and Thessaloniki between the 14th and the 11th centuries BC and between the 13th and the 10th centuries BC, respectively, confirm the underpinning of the established order by ancestral values. The entrenchment of all of the maintenance activities in the houses emphasizes the autonomy of each block, but the strong similarities among buildings suggest the existence of rules that prevented the overt expression of inequalities between groups and stresses the community's collective identity. The dispersal of facilities and spaces related to storage, food preparation, and living in the 12th-century-BC blocks of Assiros and the 11th-century complexes of Thessaloniki Toumba provides some clues regarding the organizational structures of the groups that were inhabiting them (Wardle and Wardle 2007). The blocks may have been shared by small, semiautonomous descent groups. The fact that a similar pattern may be seen in a 15th-century-BC building in Ayios Mamas could indicate the long history of such a model of habitation in central Macedonia, one that may go back to the late EBA insulae of Arhontiko and Ayios Mamas (Hänsel 2002).

On the other hand, the quantity and variety of stored charred crops in the blocks of Assiros in the late 14th century BC suggest that the community of the time had the ability to store foodstuffs that may have exceeded its members' needs (Jones et al. 1986). The concentration of pithoi and bins in 12th-century-BC buildings in Thessaloniki Toumba may point to a similar situation there in a later period (Margomenou 2008). So far, there is no evidence to suggest the operation of institutional, centralized political and administrative structures in central Macedonia from the 14th to the 12th century BC that would be able to secure the mobilization of labor and the pulling of agricultural produce to local centers and administer the redistribution of regional production to smaller tell settlements.

Instead, the occurrence of luxurious drinking sets, the evidence of vinification in Thessaloniki and Assiros, and the extensive cooking facilities and large cooking pots may suggest that hospitality and feasting could have been the mechanisms that strengthened bonds among communities and facilitated the recruitment of labor and the transporting and redistribution of food by successful communities. Such processes probably resulted in asymmetrical economic and social relations among settlements at the regional level (Andreou 2001). The untidy plan, the simple houses, the limited storage space, and the periodic setbacks in the spatial organization and building techniques of Kastanas Toumba, which was located on an island in an estuary of Thermaikos Gulf, indicate a community that must have often depended for its survival on the contiguous large tell of Axiohori (Hänsel 2002). Similar local networks of sites connected by loose, hierarchical bonds are evident in several regions of central Macedonia and Chalkidiki during the later part of the LBA.

Hardly any information exists regarding the LBA treatment of the dead in central Macedonia. Although it cannot be ruled out that the invisibility of funerary remains may be accidental, there are strong indications for a real lack of interest in formal places and practices for the dead at LBA tell sites.

On the contrary, burials became the main context for the definition of social identities in most northern Aegean areas outside central Macedonia after the late 14th century BC. A new emphasis on descent is suggested by the rows of graves in Aiani in western Macedonia, the cist graves with multiple burials at Spathes on Mount Olympus, the tumuli cemeteries in western and southern Macedonia, and the multiple burial enclosures in Faia Petra and Kastri in eastern Macedonia and Thasos (Koukouli-Chrysanthaki 1992; Poulaki-Pantermali 1988 [1991]; Besios and Krahtopoulou 1994 [1998]; Karamitrou-Mentesidi 2000 [2002]; Triantafyllou 2001; Valla 2007). A greater standardization of burial practices—primarily crouched inhumations and few cremations—is contrasted by the growing variability of burial offerings. Precious local artifacts and imports or imitations of foreign products, such as gold, silver, amber, or glass jewelry, Mycenaean-type swords and seals, Mycenaean- and Danubian-style aromatic containers, and luxurious matt-painted ceramic drinking sets occurred often as prestige items in tombs.

The wall surrounding a group of burials in Aiani and the placement of the burial enclosures on a prominent hilltop in Faia Petra suggest that spatial segregation of the burial grounds may have also been used to emphasize status differences. While many details are still missing, some cemeteries seem to signify the rise of elites at the end of the 14th century BC in certain inland sites located on prominent positions or along vital passes in western and eastern Macedonia. The control of the circulation and the funerary display of prestige valuables, which often showed affinities to the Mycenaean world or the Balkans, must have been significant elements in this process (Poulaki-Pantermali 1988 [1991]; Karamitrou-Mentesidi 2000 [2002]; Valla 2007).

Significant changes are also evident in the material culture of the LBA, despite the strength of traditional values and structures in northern Aegean societies. Bronze tools, weapons, and smaller implements were widely used and manufactured at least in the later part of the LBA. Traces of metalworking have been found in all of the excavated settlements, suggesting a pattern of small-scale local production dispersed in communities irrespective of their size or significance in the regional networks (Hochstetter 1987; Koukouli-Chrysanthaki 1992; Wardle and Wardle 1999; Mavroidi Andreou, and Vavelidis 2004 [2006]).

Positive evidence also exists for gold working, and analytical results suggest the exploitation of various local gold deposits. Besides, the weak analytical indications for the origin of silver artifacts found in Grave Circle A at Mycenae from the lead mines of Chalkidiki may gain some support by the incidence of early Mycenaean pottery imports in Toroni (Papadopoulos 2005; Vavelidis and Andreou 2008). Gold and silver jewelry, however, which occurs mainly in selected graves, were quite simple in form, while personal objects made of copper, bronze, or bone and found in settlements and tombs, display a variety of types known also in the Balkans and in the southern Aegean (Hochstetter 1987; Mavroidi, Andreou, and Vavelidis 2004 [2006]).

Small-scale production of purple dye from murex shells, a new expressive technology, was first attested in the late MBA levels at Ayios Mamas and Thessaloniki Toumba. It continued to be produced and used in the various buildings of the latter site until the beginning of the Early Iron Age (EIA) (Becker 2001; Veropoulidou, Andreou, and Kotsakis 2005 [2007]; Becker and Kroll 2008).

Throughout the period, a reduction in the variety of shapes of the handmade, undecorated tablewares and a growing standardization in terms of technology are evident, reflecting greater consistency in production practices (figure 48.1). Observations on the pottery of Thessaloniki Toumba, however, suggest a pattern of small-scale ceramic production by several potters (Kiriatzi 2000). The very limited employment of two handmade decorated items at the beginning of the LBA, one incised and encrusted and the other matt painted, with distinct geographical distributions, signals the introduction of important morphological and technological innovations to the local ceramic traditions (Psaraki 2004). The incised ware has strong Balkan affinities, and analytical evidence tentatively suggests that one of its main shapes may have been used for aromatic substances (Roumbou et al. 2008). The matt-painted ware, on the other hand, displays stylistic affinities with the transitional MBA–LBA painted ceramics of Thessaly and central Greece (Horejs 2007). Its repertory of shapes suggests luxurious drinking sets, probably for the consumption of wine.

The new decorated wares, then, were intended for display at social events of feasting and body cleansing, which could have provided opportunities for distinction to those who were in a position to fund the occasions (Andreou and Psaraki 2007). It is noteworthy that this innovation coincided with the reorganization of certain major settlements, with further indications of elaboration of the material culture and with the appearance of southern and central Aegean imports and influences in coastal sites beyond Chalkidiki (Hänsel 1989; Psaraki and Andreou in press).

The adoption of wheel-made, Mycenaean-style, decorated vessels after the 14th century BC in central, western, and southern Macedonia and later in Thasos marks a major innovation in the material culture of the northern Aegean, which also sheds some light on the interactions of the local communities with the Mycenaean world (Wardle 1993; Andreou Fotiadis, and Kotsakis 2001; Jung 2002). Soon after their first appearance as imports, Mycenaean decorated vessels were imitated locally. Nevertheless, despite the intensification of local production in the 12th century, the ware always occupied only a small part of the tablewares in the area communities. The repertory of shapes was confined to a few decorated tableware forms, primarily those that were being used in the Mycenaean world for the consumption of wine and to a lesser extent as containers of aromatics. Furthermore, the wheel-made ware was clearly demarcated in terms of technology, production, and function from the traditional handmade, undecorated wares. Production of Mycenaean pottery, however, remained equally dispersed regionally and of small scale.

It is likely that the decorated Mycenaean vessels were introduced in the area in the same ceremonial contexts of feasting and body cleansing as the slightly older, handmade, matt-painted and incised wares. Their biography, however, which connected them with luxurious symposia and funerals in their esteemed places of origin and perhaps their technological qualities, provided the Mycenaean vessels with a higher prestige than their handmade equivalents, which they soon started to replace in the ceremonial contexts of use (Andreou 2003).

In inland western Macedonia, the employment of Mycenaean vessels seems to have been restricted to the highest levels of the elite, while the rest continued to use the matt-painted ware (Karamitrou-Mentesidi 1999, 2003). Uncontrolled access to the coast, however, and to incoming ships and the collective rules that regulated life in tell sites probably impeded a similar control over the circulation of the wheel-made pottery—and other incoming imports—in central Macedonia and Thasos, and this likely facilitated the wider adoption of Mycenaean vessels in these regions and the consequently faster retreat of the handmade decorated wares (Koukouli-Chrysanthaki 1992; Kiriatzi et al. 1997; Andreou 2003).

Dramatic developments, such as those seen during the LBA in the southern Aegean are missing in the north. Nevertheless, it is evident that several significant changes occurred in most aspects of social and material life. They involved a constant interplay between long-established structures, new social demands, and the selective implementation of external stimuli from a widening zone of communications and exchange. The outcome was the emergence of a variety of social formations with distinct features that not only differentiated northern Aegean societies from their outside neighbors but also distinguished developments in the various northern Aegean regions from each other. Another outcome was the employment of a series of new, complex technologies in a less rapidly changing organizational setting and the production of a richer-than-before material culture to be used in the new social contexts of consumption.

The absence of dramatic developments in the north is evident in the lack of a significant break in settlement and material culture at the end of the period and the transition to the Early Iron Age. Changes did occur, however, and they included the expansion of cemeteries to all regions of the northern Aegean, the reorganization of tell sites in central Macedonia, some of which grew considerably in size after the middle of the 9th century BC, and the further geographical expansion and increase in the number of settlements in all regions. At the same time, there are indications for the growth of clearer and more stable hierarchical social and political structures on the regional and the community level. These developments may not be unrelated to the reorganization of craft production and the considerable enrichment of most aspects of the material culture after the 10th century BC.

BIBLIOGRAPHY

Akamatis, Ioannis. In press. "Προϊστορική Πέλλα: νεκροταφείο εποχής χαλκού." In Κερμάτια.Φιλίας. Αφιερωματικός τόμος στο Γιάννη Τουράτσογλου Αθήνα: Νομισματικό.Μουσείο.

Andreou, Stelios. 2001. "Exploring the Patterns of Power in the Bronze Age Settlements of Northern Greece." In *Urbanism*, 160–73.

———. 2003. "Η μυκηναϊκή κεραμική και οι μακεδονικές κοινωνίες κατά την ύστερη εποχή του χαλκού." In *Periphery of the Mycenaean World*, 191–210.

———, Michael Fotiadis, and Kostas Kotsakis. 2001. "The Neolithic and Bronze Age of Northern Greece." In *Aegean Prehistory*, 259–328.

Andreou, Stelios, and Kostas Kotsakis. 1996 (1997). Η προϊστορική τούμπα της Θεσσαλονίκης. Παλιά και νέα ερωτήματα *Το Αρχαιολογικό Έργο στη Μακεδονία και Θράκη* 10Α: 369–87.

Andreou, Stelios, and Kiriaki Psaraki. 2007. "Tradition and Innovation in the Bronze Age Pottery of the Thessaloniki Toumba." In *The Struma/Strymon River Valley in Prehistory: Proceedings of the International Symposium Strymon Praehistoricus, Kjustendil–Blagoevgrad (Bulgaria), Serres–Amphipolis (Greece) 27.09–01.10.2004. In the Steps of James Harvey Gaul*, vol. 2, ed. Henrieta Todorova, Mark Stefanovich, and Georgi Ivanov, 397–420. Sofia: Gaul Foundation.

Aslanis, Ioannis. 1985. *Kastanas: Ausgrabungen in einem Siedlungshügel der Bronze- und Eisenzeit Makedoniens 1975–1979. Die Frühbronzezeitlichen Funde und Befunde.* Prähistorische Archäologie in Südosteuropa 4. Berlin: Wissenschaftsverlag Volker Spiess.

———. 2005 (2007). "Άγιος Μάμας Νέας Ολύνθου: η αρχιτεκτονική του μεσοελλαδικού οικισμού." *Το Αρχαιολογικό Έργο στη Μακεδονία και Θράκη* 19: 333–38.

Asouhidou, Sofia. 2001. "Καύσεις της εποχής του χαλκού στη Μακεδονία." In *Καύσεις στην εποχή του χαλκού και την πρώιμη εποχή του σιδήρου: πρακτικά του συμποσίου, Ρόδος 29 Απριλίου–2 Μαΐου 1999*, ed. Nikolaos Chr. Stampolidis, 31–45. Αθήνα: Πανεπιστήμιο Κρήτης.

———, Dimitra Mantazi, and Stefanos Tsolakis. 1998 (2000). "Ταφικός τύμβος ΠΕΧ το Κριαρίτσι Συκιάς Ν. Χαλκιδικής." *Το Αρχαιολογικό Έργο στη Μακεδονία και Θράκη* 12: 269–82.

Bailey, Douglas. 2000. *Balkan Prehistory: Exclusion, Incorporation, and Identity.* New York: Routledge.

Becker, Cornelia. 1986. *Kastanas: Ausgrabungen in einem Siedlugshügel der Bronze- und Eisenzeit Makedoniens 1975–1979. Die Tierknochenfunde.* Prähistorische Archäologie in Südosteuropa 5. Berlin: Wissenschaftsverlag Volker Spiess.

———. 2001. "Did the People in Agios Mamas Produce Purple-Dye during the Middle Bronze Age? Considerations on the Prehistoric Production of Purple-Dye in the Mediterranean." In *Animals and Man in the Past: Essays in Honor of Dr. A. T. Clason, Emeritus Professor of Archaeozoology, Rijksununiversiteit Groningen, the Netherlands.*, ed. Hilke Buitenhus and Wietske Prummel, 121–33. ARC-Publicatie 41. Groningen: Archaeological Research and Consultancy.

———, and Helmut Kroll. 2008. *Das prähistorische Olynth: Ausgrabungen in der Toumba Agios Mamas 1994–1996. Ernährung und Rohstoffnutzung im Wandel.* Prähistorische Archäologie in Südosteuropa 22. Rahden: Leidorf.

Besios, Manthos. 1993 (1997). "Ανασκαφές στη βόρεια Πιερία 1993." *Το Αρχαιολογικό Έργο στη Μακεδονία και Θράκη* 7: 215–24.

———, and Athanasia Krahtopoulou. 1994 (1998). "Ανασκαφή στο βόρειο νεκροταφείο της Πύδνας 1994." *Το Αρχαιολογικό Έργο στη Μακεδονία και Θράκη* 8: 147–50.

Bökönyi, Sandor. 1986. "Faunal Remains." In *Excavations at Sitagroi: A Prehistoric Village in Northeast Greece*, ed. Colin Renfrew, Maria Gimbutas, and Ernestine Elster, 63–96. Monumenta Archaeologica 13, vol. 1. Los Angeles: Institute of Archaeology, University of California at Los Angeles.

Bottema, Sytze. 1982. "Palynological Investigations in Greece with Special Reference to Pollen as an Indicator of Human Activity." *Palaeohistoria* 24: 257–89.

Chrysostomou, Anastasia, and Anastasia Georgiadou. 2007. "Siedlungen und Necropolen der Späten Bronze- und Frühen Eisenzeit in Almopia und äußere Einflusse." In *BABS*, 167–72.

Davis, Jack L. 2001. "The Islands of the Aegean." In *Aegean Prehistory*, 19–94.

Elster, Ernestine S. 1997. "Construction and Use of the Early Bronze Age Burnt House at Sitagroi: Craft and Technology." In *TEXNH*, 19–35.

Fotiadis, Michael. 1985. *Economy, Ecology, and Settlement among Subsistence Farmers in the Serres Basin, North-eastern Greece, 5000–1000 B.C.* PhD diss., Indiana University.

Grammenos, Dimitrios, Manthos Besios, and Stavros Kotsos. 1997. *Από τους προϊστορικούς οικισμούς της κεντρικής Μακεδονίας.* Μακεδονική Βιβλιοθήκη, τομ. 88. Θεσσαλονίκη.

Grammenos, Dimitrios, Iris Tzahili, and Eleni Magou. 1994. "Ο θησαυρός των Πετραλώνων της Χαλκιδικής και άλλα χάλκινα εργαλεία της ΠΕΧ από την ευρύτερη περιοχή." *Αρχαιολογική Εφημερίς*: 75–116.

Hänsel, Bernhard. 1989. *Kastanas: Ausgrabungen in einem Siedlugshügel der Bronze- und Eisenzeit Makedoniens 1975–1979. Die Grabung und der Baubefund.* Prähistorische Archäologie in Südosteuropa 7. Berlin: Wissenschaftsverlag Volker Spiess.

———. 2002. "Stationen der Bronzezeit zwischen Griechenland und Mitteleuropa." *Bericht der Römisch-Germanishen Kommission*, 83: 70–97.

Heurtley, William A. 1939. *Prehistoric Macedonia: An Archaeological Reconnaissance of Greek Macedonia (West of the Struma) in the Neolithic, Bronze, and Early Iron Ages.* Cambridge: University Press.

Hochstetter, A. 1987. *Kastanas: Ausgrabungen in einem Siedlugshügel der Bronze- und Eisenzeit Makedoniens 1975–1979. Die Kleinfunde.* Prähistorische Archäologie in Südosteuropa 6. Berlin: Wissenschaftsverlag Volker Spiess.

Horejs, Barbara. 2007. *Das prähistorische Olynth: Ausgrabungen in der Toumba Agios Mamas 1994–1996. Die spätbronzezeitliche handgemachte Keramik der Schichten 13 bis 1.* Prähistorische Archäologie in Südosteuropa 21. Rahden: Leidorf.

Jones, Glynis, Paul Halstead, Ken Wardle, and Diana Wardle. 1986. "Crop Storage at Assiros." *Scientific American* 254(3): 86–103.

Jung, Reinhard. 2002. *Kastanas: Ausgrabungen in einem Siedlungshügel der Bronze- und Eisenzeit Makedoniens 1975–1979. Die Drehscheibenkeramik der Schichten 19 bis 11. Teil 1 and 2.* Prähistorische Archäologie in Südosteuropa 18. Kiel: Ötker/Voges.

Karamitrou-Mentesidi, Georgia. 1999. *Βόϊον-Νότια.Ορεστίς. Αρχαιολογική έρευνα και ιστορική τοπογραφία* Θεσσαλονίκη: Θ. Αλτιντζής

———. 2000 (2002). "Αιανή 2000. Ανασκαφή νεκροταφείου ύστερης εποχής χαλκού." *Το Αρχαιολογικό Έργο στη Μακεδονία και Θράκη* 14: 591–606.

———. 2003. "Μυκηναϊκά Αιανής-Ελιμιωτίδας και Άνω Μακεδονίας." In *Periphery of the Mycenaean World*, 167–90.

Kiriatzi, Evangelia. 2000. *Κεραμική τεχνολογία και. Παραγωγή. Η κεραμική της ύστερης εποχής χαλκού από την τούμπα Θεσσαλονίκης.* PhD diss., Αριστοτέλειο Πανεπιστήμιο Θεσσαλονίκης.

———, Stelios Andreou, Sarantis Dimitriadis, and Kostas Kotsakis. 1997. "Co-existing Traditions: Handmade and Wheel Made Pottery in Late Bronze Age Central Macedonia." In *TEXNH*, 361–67.

Kotsakis, Kostas, and Stelios Andreou. 1992 (1995). "Επιφανειακή έρευνα Λαγκαδά: περίοδος 1992." *Το Αρχαιολογικό Έργο στη Μακεδονία και Θράκη* 6: 349–56.

Koukouli-Chrysanthaki, Chaido. 1992. *Πρωτοϊστορική Θάσος. Τα νεκροταφεία του οικισμού Καστρί.* Δημοσιεύματα του Αρχαιολογικού Δελτίου τομ. 45. Αθήνα: Ταμείο Αρχαιολογικών Πόρων και Απαλλοτριώσεων

Lespez, Laurent. 2008. "L'évolution des paysages du Néolithique a la periode ottoman dans la plaine de Philippes-Drama." In *Dikili Tash, village prehistorique de Macédoine Orientale. Recherche franco-helleniques dirigees par la Société archeologique d'Athènes et l'École française d'Athènes*, 21–394. Bibliothèque de la Société archeologique d'Athènes 254. Athènes: La Société archeologique d'Athènes-L'École française d'Athènes.

Malamidou, Dimitra. 1997. "Eastern Macedonia during the Early Bronze Age." In *Poliochni*, 329–44.

Manning, Sturt W. 1995. *The Absolute Chronology of the Aegean Early Bronze Age: Archaeology, History, and Radiocarbon.* Monographs in Mediterranean Archaeology 1. Sheffield: Sheffield Academic Press.

Margomenou, Despina. 2008. "Food Storage in Prehistoric Northern Greece: Interrogating Complexity at the Margins of the 'Mycenaean World.'" *JMA* 21: 191–212.

Matsas, Dimitrios. 1995. "Minoan Long-distance Trade: A View from the Northern Aegean." In *Politeia*, 235–47.

Mavroidi, Ioanna, Stelios Andreou, and Maria Pappa. 2006 (2008). "Οικισμός της πρώιμης εποχής χαλκού στον Άγιο Αθανάσιο Θεσσαλονίκης." *Το Αρχαιολογικό Έργο στη Μακεδονία και Θράκη* 20: 479–90.

Mavroidi, Ioanna, Stelios Andreou, and Michael Vavelidis. 2004 (2006). "Μεταλλικά αντικείμενα και μεταλλοτεχνικές δραστηριότητες κατά την εποχή του χαλκού στην τούμπα Θεσσαλονίκης." *Το Αρχαιολογικό Έργο στη Μακεδονία και Θράκη* 18: 315–28.

Mayewski, Paul A., Eelco E. Rohling, J. Curt Stager, Wibjfrn Karlen, Kirk A. Maasch, L. David Meeker, Eric A. Meyerson, et al. 2004. "Holocene Climate Variability." *Quaternary Research* 62: 243–55.

Mitrevski, Dragi. 2003. "Prehistory in Republic of Macedonia F.Y.R.O.M." In *Recent Research in the Prehistory of the Balkans*, ed. Dimitrios Grammenos, 13–72. Publications of the Archaeological Institute of Northern Greece 3. Thessaloniki: Archaeological Institute of Northern Greece and Archaeological Research Fund.

Nakou, Georgia. 1997. "The Role of the Northern Aegean in the Development of Aegean Metallurgy." In *Poliochni*, 634–48.

Ozdogan, Mehmet. 2003a. "The Black Sea, the Sea of Marmara, and Bronze Age Archaeology: An Archaeological Predicament." In *Troia and the Troad: Scientific Approaches*, ed. Guenter A. Wagner, Ernst Pernicka, and Hans-Peter Ürpmann, 105–15. Berlin: Springer.

———. 2003b. "The Prehistory of North-western Turkey." In *Recent Research in the Prehistory of the Balkans*, ed. Dimitrios Grammenos, 329–68. Publications of the Archaeological Institute of Northern Greece 3. Thessaloniki: Archaeological Institute of Northern Greece and Archaeological Research Fund.

Papadopoulos, John K. 2005. *The Early Iron Age Cemetery at Torone*. Monumenta Archaeologica, vol. 24. Los Angeles: Cotsen Institute of Archaeology, University of California at Los Angeles.

———, Guy M. Cross, Richard E. Jones, and Lorna Sharpe. 1999. "The Prehistoric Fortifications of Toroni." In *Polemos*, 163–70.

Papadopoulos, Stratis. 2001 (2003). "Η τελική νεολιθική και η πρώιμη εποχή του χαλκού στη Θάσο: η ανασκαφική έρευνα στις θέσεις Άγιος Ιωάννης και Σκάλα Σωτήρος." *Το Αρχαιολογικό Έργο στη Μακεδονία και Θράκη* 15: 54–65.

Pappa, Maria. In press. "Die Nekropole die frühen Bronzezeit beim prähistorische Olynth (Toumba Agios Mamas)." In *Das prähistorische Olynth: Ausgrabungen in der Toumba Agios Mamas 1994–1996*, ed. Cornelia Becker and Helmut Kroll. Rahden: Leidorf.

Pilali, Aggeliki, and Aikaterini Papanthimou. 2002. "Die Ausgrabungen auf der Toumba von Archontiko." *PZ* 77(2): 137–47.

Poulaki-Pantermali, Eftyhia. 1988 (1991). "Οι ανασκαφές του Ολύμπου." *Το Αρχαιολογικό Έργο στη Μακεδονία και Θράκη* 2: 173–80.

Psaraki, Kiriaki, 2004. Υλική και κοινωνική διάσταση του στιλ της κεραμικής: Η χειροποίητη κεραμική της εποχής του χαλκού από την τούμπα της.Θεσσαλονίκης. PhD diss., Πανεπιστήμιο Θεσσαλονίκης.

———, and Stelios Andreou. In press. "Regional Processes and Interregional Interactions in Northern Greece." In *Mesohelladika*.

Renfrew, Colin, Maria Gimbutas, and Ernestine Elster, eds. 1986. *Excavations at Sitagroi: A Prehistoric Village in Northeast Greece*. Monumenta Archaeologica 13(1). Los Angeles: Institute of Archaeology, University of California at Los Angeles.

Renfrew, Colin, and Elizabeth A. Slater. 2003. "Metal Artefacts and Metallurgy." In *Prehistoric Sitagroi: Excavations in Northern Greece, 1968–1970*. Vol. 2, *The Final Report*, ed. Ernestine Elster and Colin Renfrew, 301–24. Los Angeles: Cotsen Institute of Archaeology, University of California at Los Angeles.

Renfrew, Jane M. 2003. "Grains, Seeds, and Fruits from Prehistoric Sitagroi." In *Prehistoric Sitagroi: Excavations in Northern Greece, 1968–1970*. Vol. 2, *The Final Report*, ed. Ernestine Elster and Colin Renfrew, 3–28. Los Angeles: Cotsen Institute of Archaeology, University of California at Los Angeles.

Roumbou, Maria, Carl Heron, Glynis Jones, Evangelia Kiriatzi, Soultana M. Valamoti, and Stelios Andreou. 2008. "Detection and Identification of Organic Residues in Ceramic Vessels from Late Bronze Age Northern Greece: A Preliminary Investigation of

Consumption and Exchange of Plant Oils." Poster presented at the 37th International Symposium on Archaeometry, May 12–16, 2008, Siena, Italy.

Schulz, Horst D. 1989. "Die geologische Entwicklung der Bucht von Kastanas im Holozan." In *Kastanas: Ausgrabungen in einem Siedlugshügel der Bronze- und Eisenzeit Makedoniens 1975–1979. Die Grabung und der Baubefund*, ed. Bernhard Hänsel, 375–93. Prähistorische Archäologie in Südosteuropa 7. Berlin: Wissenschaftsverlag Volker Spiess.

Sherratt, Andrew. 1986. "The Pottery of Phases IV and V: The Early Bronze Age." In *Excavations at Sitagroi: A Prehistoric Village in Northeast Greece*, ed. Colin Renfrew, Maria Gimbutas, and Ernestine Elster, 429–76. Monumenta Archaeologica 13(1). Los Angeles: Institute of Archaeology, University of California at Los Angeles.

Smagas, Angelos D. 2007. Ανθρώπινη παρουσία και κατοίκηση στην προϊστορική Σιθωνία. PhD diss., Αριστοτέλειο Πανεπιστήμιο Θεσσαλονίκης

Stefani, Liana, and Nikos Merousis. 2003. "Τοπίο στην ομίχλη. Η 2η χιλιετία στην κεντρική Μακεδονία." In *Periphery of the Mycenaean World*, 228–42.

Stos-Gale, Zofia A., and Colin Macdonald. 1991. "Sources of Metals and Trade in the Bronze Age Aegean." In *Bronze Age Trade*, 249–88.

Theodoropoulou, Tatiana. 2007. L'exploitation de ressources aquatique en Grèce septentrionale du Néolithique a l'Age du Bronze. PhD diss., Université de Paris I.

Triantafyllou, Sevasti. 2001. *A Bioarchaeological Approach to Prehistoric Cemetery Population from Central and Western Greek Macedonia*. Oxford: Archaeopress.

Tsigarida, E. Betina, and Dimitra Mantazi. 2003 (2005). "Ανασκαφική έρευνα στην περιοχή της Νέας Σκιώνης Χαλκιδικής 2003." *Το Αρχαιολογικό Έργο στη Μακεδονία και Θράκη* 17: 369–78.

Valamoti, Soultana M. 2007. "Food across Borders: A Consideration of the Neolithic and Bronze Age Archaeobotanical Evidence from Northern Greece." In *BABS*, 281–92.

———, Maria Mangafa, Chaido Koukouli-Chrysanthaki, and Dimitra Malamidou. 2007. "Grape Pressings from Northern Greece: The Earliest Wine in the Aegean?" *Antiquity* 81: 54–61.

Valamoti, Soultana M., Aikaterini Papanthimou, and Angeliki Pilali. 2005. "Προϊστορικά μαγειρέματα στο Αρχοντικό Γιαννιτσών: Τα αρχαιοβοτανικά δεδομένα." Το *Αρχαιολογικό Έργο στη Μακεδονία και Θράκη* 17: 497–503.

Valla, Magda. 2007. "A Late Bronze Age Cemetery in Faia Petra." In *The Struma/Strymon River Valley in Prehistory: Proceedings of the International Symposium Strymon Praehistoricus, Kjustendil–Blagoevgrad (Bulgaria), Serres-Amphipolis (Greece) 27.09–01.10.2004. In the Steps of James Harvey Gaul*, vol. 2, ed. Henrieta Todorova, Mark Stefanovich, and Georgi Ivanov, 359–72. Sofia: Gaul Foundation.

Vavelidis, Michael, and Stelios Andreou. 2008. "Gold and Gold Working in Late Bronze Age Northern Greece." *Naturwissenschaften* 95: 361–66.

Veropoulidou, Rena, Stelios Andreou, and Kostas Kotsakis. 2005 (2007). "Τούμπα Θεσσαλονίκης: Η παραγωγή πορφυρής βαφής κατά την εποχή του χαλκού." *Το Αρχαιολογικό Έργο στη Μακεδονία και Θράκη* 19: 173–85.

Videski, Zlatko. 2005. "The Bronze Age at Vardarski Rid." In *Vardarski Rid*, ed. Dragi Mitrevski, 91–114. Skopje: Foundation Vardarski Rid-Skopje Institute for History of Art and Archaeology, Faculty of Philosophy, Skopje.

Vouvalidis, Kostantinos, Georgios Syridis, Theodoros Parashos, Dimitrios Psomiadis, and Michael Albanakis. 2003. "Γεωμορφολογικές μεταβολές στον κόλπο της Θεσσαλονίκης εξαιτίας της ανύψωσης της στάθμης της θάλασσας τα τελευταία 10.000 χρόνια." *Το Αρχαιολογικό Έργο στη Μακεδονία και Θράκη* 17: 313–22.

Wardle, Ken. 1980. "Excavations at Assiros Toumba 1975–79: A Preliminary Report." *BSA* 75: 229–67.

———. 1993. "Mycenaean Trade and Influence in Northern Greece." In *Wace and Blegen*, 117–41.

———, and Diana Wardle. 1999. "Metal Working in Late Bronze Age Central Macedonia." *Το Αρχαιολογικό Έργο στη Μακεδονία και Θράκη* 13: 46–55.

———. 2007. "Assiros Toumba: A Brief History of the Settlement." In *The Struma/ Strymon River Valley in Prehistory: Proceedings of the International Symposium Strymon Praehistoricus, Kjustendil-Blagoevgrad (Bulgaria), Serres-Amphipolis (Greece) 27.09–01.10.2004. In the Steps of James Harvey Gaul*, vol. 2, ed. Henrieta Todorova, Mark Stefanovich, and Georgi Ivanov, 451–80. Sofia: Gaul Foundation.

Whittle, Alasdair. 1996. *Europe in the Neolithic: The Creation of New Worlds*. New York: Cambridge University Press.

Ziota, Christina. 2007. Ταφικές πρακτικές και κοινωνίες της εποχής του χαλκού στη Δυτική.Μακεδονία. Τα νεκροταφεία στην Κοιλάδα και στις Γούλες Κοζάνης. PhD diss., Αριστοτέλειο Πανεπιστήμιο Θεσσαλονίκης.

CHAPTER 49

LERNA

MARTHA HEATH WIENCKE

ANCIENT Lerna forms a low mound of some 12,000 sq. m. on the west shore of the Bay of Argos, beside an abundant spring. The inhabitants had easy access to good farmland, timber, and main routes north to Argos (10 km.) and south into Arcadia.

Excavation at the site was carried out in the 1950s by the American School of Classical Studies under the direction of John L. Caskey (Caskey 1954–1960), when some 20% of the mound was excavated. Most of the deposits belong to the Neolithic and Early and Middle Bronze Ages; the preserved finds are kept in the Archaeological Museum of Argos.

LERNA I AND II (NEOLITHIC)

The Neolithic occupation at Lerna left three-meter-deep deposits, of which only little could be excavated. Some 10% of the Neolithic ceramic material, most frequently the painted Urfirnis (Urf), was preserved for study by Karen D. Vitelli.

By comparison with the pottery from Franchthi, which Vitelli had classified earlier (Vitelli 1993–1999), it was clear that the major Neolithic occupation at Lerna belonged to the earlier part of the Middle Neolithic (MN) period, with very little later Neolithic. It is unclear whether the first Lerna settlers used only Early Neolithic pottery. The very earliest deposits at Lerna correspond to Franchthi "F Interph 1/2," "the earliest transition to the MN" (Vitelli 2007, 128).

LERNA III (EARLY HELLADIC I–II)

After the Neolithic occupation, Lerna may have been abandoned for a time. A vigorous Early Helladic (EH) II people occupied Lerna for four or five hundred years; the evidence dates chiefly to the latter half of that period. Little more than 10% of the Lerna III deposits could be excavated (Wiencke 2000, 3). The material retained represents only a fraction of that recovered (Wiencke 2000, 315–16), but major deposits were preserved with little discard.

Although EH I inhabitants may have been resident in the first centuries after the end of the Neolithic, they left only a scattering of sherds, identified by comparison with the pottery of neighboring Tsoungiza and Talioti. Two important ceramic deposits in the earliest EH II (Early Phase A) level contained nearly all totally dark-painted fine pottery ("Urfirnis"), red or black, often well polished. No recognizable sauceboat sherds were present, but basins, early saucers, and ladles were recovered.

No constructions of Phase A could be identified. Deep areas of stony fill were found without habitational remains but containing both Neolithic and EH sherds in various percentages (Wiencke 2000, 29–33, Vitelli 2007, 135–37). These fills lie beneath the earliest walls and floors of EH II Phase B. The EH sherds recovered from the lowest "mixed fills" are clearly of an early type; many resemble the Early Phase A pottery, and some are of newer types.

The contents of these fills point to the original existence of a second, early habitation level (Late Phase A); it is here that sherds of the most characteristic EH II shape, the sauceboat, first occur, with the first light-painted pottery.

The first Phase B house walls and floors were found in widely scattered spots. The observable sequence of strata allowed for an arbitrary division of the material into three levels. No overall plan for the Phase B early and mid-occupation could be recovered, only the existence of small, usually rectangular houses, and largely dark-painted pottery, which underwent gradual changes.

In Late Phase B, an extensive, pebble-paved area with two built gutters for drainage lay beneath and south of the later Building BG. The direction of wall fragments beneath that building hint at its later orientation. Significant household deposits included early, dark-painted sauceboats (Wiencke 2000, P371–73) and other early vessels.

Many small bronze objects came from Late A through B contexts (Banks 1967, 15–80), though there was no evidence of actual bronze working. Obsidian cores, at this time and later, testify to knapping on the site, and unused blades suggest the manufacture and exchange of the imported obsidian (Hartenberger and Runnels 2001). Beans, peas, lentils, figs, and barley were available, as was wheat (emmer and einkorn; Hopf 1961, 1962) by Late B at least. Olive wood is attested in Middle B but not the pits (Hopf 1961, n70V; Wiencke 2000, 49). The increased variety of ceramic shapes, especially for storing and pouring of liquids, is notable and indicates some change in diet and social behavior. Sheep, goats, cattle, and pigs were all present; the donkey is identified in Early B (Gejvall 1969, 35–36). Animals may have been used for transport and plowing (Pullen 1992).

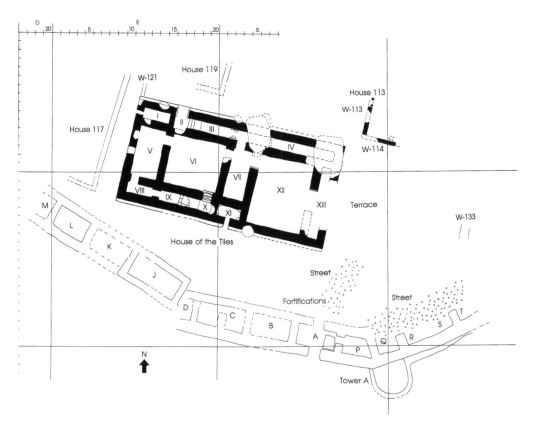

Figure 49.1. Site plan of Lerna (after *Lerna IV,* plan 8, courtesy of the
Lerna Excavations Archive, ASCSA).

There is no sign of general destruction or abandonment between Phases III B
and III C at Lerna. The pebbled area south of later Building BG remained partly
open until the end of Lerna III, and vestiges of house walls indicate a sequence of
construction throughout Phase C. The triple division of Phase III C is based on
changes in the fortifications (enclosure walls).

In Early Phase C, the eastern end of the impressive, thick, double fortification
wall and the round Tower B were constructed with an exterior broad flight of low
stairs leading up to a lost gate. In Middle C, the double wall was extended westward, and a new Tower A, perhaps a second (West), were added; the stairway was
abandoned, and a new gateway (Room A) was built (figure 49.1). This gate served
as an approach to the large corridor house, Building BG, built at some early stage of
Phase C. Building BG, which was poorly preserved, lay partly beneath the House of
the Tiles and could be only partly excavated. It had many features of the later house:
similar dimensions, heavy stone foundations, corridors along both long sides, and a
series of large rooms down the center. The front vestibule was open and very deep.
No evidence for doors could be found. A brick paving in one corridor may have

supported a stairway to the second floor. The roof had been covered with both terracotta tiles and masses of schist slabs (shale: Shriner 2007).

A westward extension of the fortification rooms (J–M) narrowed the habitation space of the site late in Phase C (Fig. 49.1). It was not connected to the earlier
wall and seems never to have been properly finished.

The Phase C household pottery was abundant and markedly different from
that of Phase B: a greater variety of shapes, many vessels only partly painted, much
unpolished light paint, some extremely fine vessels, but many more unpainted pots.
Technical researches (Shriner and Dorais 1999; Shriner and Murray 2001) identify a
change in clay source for the pottery at about this time.

The House of the Tiles

Building BG underwent some changes (a terracotta baked hearth in one corridor was certainly not in situ) and stood for some time, but the house was finally
demolished to make room for the House of the Tiles. This new House (figures
49.1, 49.2) was oriented to face east instead of south. It measured 25 meters in
length and existed only for a brief time; its burnt ruins were partly preserved by
the earth tumulus built over it. The mud brick walls still stood to over a meter
high in places, and were often plastered in clay, even with fine lime plaster in
important rooms.

The bottom clay and brick steps of two burnt stairways to the second floor
remained, as did also marks of the wooden facings along certain doorways. The
low pitched roof was covered with hundreds of fired clay tiles, coarser than earlier ones, and the eaves bore a border of schist (shale) slabs. Finds were few; the
plastering appeared incomplete. It seems likely that the House had not been long
occupied before it burned. Only one small storage room, XI, opening to the exterior, contained notable finds: many plain saucers, a few sauceboats, and many fragments of broken clay sealings, stamped when damp by some seventy different seals
with mostly geometric designs. The clay had been fired hard in the destruction. The
actual seals were of course no longer present.

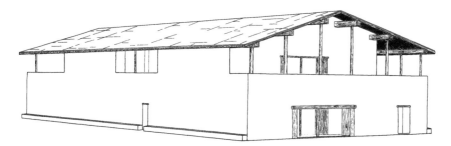

Figure 49.2. House of the Tiles (after *Lerna IV,* figure I.107a, courtesy of the Lerna
Excavations Archive, ASCSA).

The use of seals in Early Bronze Age mainland Greece had hardly been recognized in the 1950s, although numerous ivory and bone seals were known from the Early Minoan (EM) tombs of Crete. A few seal impressions were discovered in Lerna Phase C household contexts (Wiencke 1975). More recently, discoveries of clay sealings in Geraki (Laconia) and in Petri near Nemea have reinforced the importance of seal use in the EH II (Korakou) culture (Weingarten 2000; Weingarten et al. 1999; Kostoula 2000; Renfrew 1972).

The purpose of these corridor houses and of other similar ones since identified in the Peloponnesus, Aegina, and Boeotia (Karagiorga 1971; Walter and Felten 1981; Felten 1986; Aravantinos 1986; Pullen 1986) has been much discussed, but it is clear that they were not private houses. The House of the Tiles is still the best preserved and one of the latest in date (Shaw 2008). The contemporary but circular Rundbau at Tiryns exhibits the same massive walls and tiled roof and almost certainly served as a massive granary (Kilian 1986; Nilsson 2004, 146–49), but no large storage vessels were found in the House of the Tiles.

The Lerna sealings had been applied, often to wooden peg closures, on boxes or doors, and a few were used on bags or baskets (Heath 1958; Wiencke 1975, 29). The many Type B fragments bore the impressions of only three individual pegs, which had been repeatedly sealed, according to E. Fiandra (Fiandra 1968, 392). The sealings indicate the presence of marked stores, provided by or dispensed to many individuals, and the saucers suggest entertainment for guests (Peperaki 2004, 222–26), who were perhaps seated on the clay benches along the sides of the House. The plan of the House allows highly controlled access to its various rooms at both levels and provided some spaces perhaps for large public groups, while others were more private.

There were other smaller structures surrounding the House of the Tiles, and part of the fortification walls, which were awaiting repair, may have been still standing at the time of the fire. The pots in Room XI (Phase D) are somewhat different from the latest Phase C ones. The sauceboats in particular bear some resemblance to sauceboats from the Weisses Haus at Kolonna, the corridor house most closely resembling that at Lerna (Berger 2003; Felten 1986).

After the House of the Tiles had burned, a low mound (18.75 m. in diameter) was constructed out of the clay and brick debris, directly over the remains of the walls. A circle of round stones was placed at the circumference of this tumulus, and the surface within the circle was covered with small stones (Wiencke 2000, 310). It is not clear who was responsible for this monument. Scholarly consensus favors the Lerna III inhabitants, who may have been marking the spot before their departure (Banks in press). The next settlers did not at first construct any houses within the circle; possibly the space was seen as sacred.

Tumuli in later times served as burial mounds, but the contemporary EH Pelopion tumulus at Olympia, like the one at Lerna, does not lie above a grave (Forsén 1992, 232–34). A newly discovered tumulus near the new museum at Thebes was built of mud brick over both a multiple grave and late EH II apsidal houses, and its surface was not disturbed by construction for many centuries (Aravantinos and Psaraki 2007).

Final Years of EH II Period

The last years of the EH II period present many puzzles. There is no clear evidence that Lerna was abandoned after the fire. Caskey in 1960 pointed to destruction at other sites besides Lerna as evidence for invasion from abroad (Caskey 1960, 1968). Forsén has demonstrated that these destructions were not all simultaneous or universal (Forsén 1992, 248–60).

There does seem to have been a widespread collapse of the common continuum of EH II culture across the Peloponnesus and beyond, however, and a shift to more localized patterns. Architecturally, the large corridor houses were no longer built, seals were no longer in use, and the forms of sauceboat and saucer were replaced by new shapes (Rutter 2001, 113; Maran 1998, 463). The shift, however, did not take place everywhere in the same way. At nearby Tiryns, in the Übergangs transitional period, much EH II pottery was still in use, together with some early EH III. Only in the next level, Apsidenhorizont, did some of the characteristic patterned dark-on-light pottery appear (Weisshaar 1981, 1982, 1983; Rutter 1995, 645–47).

Beyond the Peloponnesus, new ceramic shapes (Lefkandi I or Kastri) derived from Anatolia appeared at Thebes, in the late EH II Thebes B (Konsola 1981, 120), at Askitario and Raphina in Attica (Theochares 1952, figures 110, 12), and in Kolonna III on Aegina (Berger 2003). At Lerna and elsewhere in the Peloponnesus, however, the Lefkandi pottery was lacking during EH II.

Lerna IV (Early Helladic III)

The Lerna IV settlers brought in great changes. Three main phases of occupation have been recognized, the first (IV.1) a small settlement beginning with a large wattle-and-daub apsidal "Chieftain's House" just outside the stone circle (Banks in press). A two-handled, marble drinking cup (rhyton?) was found nearby (Caskey 1956, 162–64, pl. 47 i, s). Other, more permanent apsidal houses (and some trapezoidal) of mud brick with stone foundations soon followed in a pattern that suggests a community directed by a headman. The settlement increased in size over the years. A reorganization and expansion of the village in IV.3, with exclusively apsidal houses in the tumulus area, coincided with a change in pottery. The older drinking vessels (Depas, ouzo cup) were replaced with new shapes (and customs), and there was an increase in both coarser pots and the use of the wheel (or tournette) for the gray ware, a forerunner of the MH Minyan (Rutter 1995, 23, 475). Potters continued to prefer the coarser clay source (metamorphic window: Shriner and Dorais 1999; Shriner and Murray 2001), which had been adopted in later Lerna III.

Bothroi, always common, increased in number in IV.3. Evidence for on-site casting of bronze and various tools showed the availability of arsenical copper, probably from Kythnos. Pottery was quite frequently imported, probably from the Corinthia, perhaps also from Aegina, the Megarid, and Boeotia (Rutter 1995, 736–49; Attas 1982; Attas, Fossey, and Yaffe 1987).

The population in Lerna IV was evidently a mixed one that likely included survivors of Lerna III. The pottery betrays some Anatolian influences; it has in fact a "highly heterogeneous" ancestry, perhaps the result of a stylistic fusion within central Greece (Rutter 1995, 649). The characteristic dark-on-light patterned ware is quite unlike that of Lerna III. The geographical extent of this culture cannot be traced precisely as yet, but it appears to have been lacking in Attica, Laconia, and Messenia (Rutter 2001, 122–23).

At Lerna, the settlement continued from EH III into Middle Helladic (Lerna V) without destruction or major changes.

Lerna V (Middle Helladic) and Lerna VI, VII (Late Helladic)

Apsidal and rectangular houses continued to be built. Habitation was continuous throughout MH, and in some areas up to nine levels of rebuilding are seen. Metalworking took place on the site. Burials, often in stone cists by the middle of the period, became common and were sometimes grouped together as a cemetery within the settlement (Zerner in preparation; Angel 1971; Voutsaki et al. 2006). Tomb gifts, which were not always present, were simple and few.

The most telling discovery from MH Lerna, however, has been Carol Zerner's analysis of the ceramic wares, which is based on the sequence of deposits from early MH I to the latest MH III and into LH I (Lerna V.1–V.3 and VI; Zerner 1988; Zerner, Betancourt, and Myer 1986). Zerner has identified some 40% of the total ceramic assemblage as imported wares. The other, local, Argive wares included the local Gray Minyan, a later yellow version (YM); the new Matt-Painted (MP) and Bichrome Matt-Painted; noncalcareous Dark Burnished wares; and coarse wares.

Of the imported wares, the commonest examples by far were of a volcanic (gold mica) fabric from Aegina of various finishes (MP, Dark Burnished, Red Slipped and Burnished, Plain, and Cooking ware) and produced in a wide range of shapes (Zerner 1993). This pottery has been found all over much of southeast Greece and seems to have reached Corinthia and Laconia by the end of the period. The distribution indicates a widely successful commercial enterprise based on Aegina, where Brophy and Shriner and team have identified the important clay source near Kolonna (Brophy, Shriner, et al. in preparation). Michael Lindblom sees the prefiring potter's marks, found on much Aegina pottery, as reflecting the economic needs of several family potting groups working together (Lindblom 2001, 41).

Other wares also reached Lerna from Kythera and the southern Peloponnesus (Lustrous Decorated), central Greece (the true wheel-made Gray Minyan), and the Cyclades and Crete. Middle Minoan pottery was now common in early MH Lerna, whether imported or made by resident Minoans. Little MH pottery reached Crete at first, although the wheel was introduced early in MM I (Rutter and Zerner 1984, 80n26).

This astonishing picture of human expansion greatly contrasts with the narrower contacts of Lerna IV and the wide, unified continuum of Lerna III (Rutter and Zerner 1984, 76).

The small MH site of Lerna, serving as a trading port for a wide area, grew prosperous. By the start of the LH period, it had acquired enough importance for persons of status to be buried there in two Shaft Graves dug into the site of the old House of the Tiles. These resemble the Shaft Graves of Mycenae in their stone grave chambers, but only a few adult bones and a pair of LH I cups remained of the original contents. The deep shafts, however, were filled with masses of shattered LH I pottery, more than half of it Aeginetan, as well as much early Mycenaean. From the presence of two LH III vessels in one shaft, it seems that the bodies were deliberately removed at that later date, and that the remains of the nearly one thousand pots, other objects, and animal bones were redeposited in the shafts with the earthen fill. Lindblom (2007) has concluded that the bulk of the pottery and the animal bones constitutes evidence for the feasting of a large company on the occasion of the original burials, commemorating among much else the importance of the Aeginetan presence at Lerna.

Early Mycenaean material at Lerna is otherwise confined to a few graves (LH I and II), two bothroi, and some mixed surface deposits. Later evidence at Lerna is largely lost. A few house remains and graves of LH III survived above MH deposits. Population had expanded by LH IIIA2, when Lerna had become part of the Mycenaean sphere (Wiencke 1998). There was a horse burial in LH IIIB (Wiencke 1998, 184–87; Reese 2008), but the site was probably abandoned by LH IIIC. Geometric graves found on the slopes of nearby Mount Pontinus, ancient wells, and other scattered finds (Erickson in preparation) indicate a modest classical occupation.

BIBLIOGRAPHY

Angel, J. Lawrence. 1971. *Lerna II: The People*. Washington, D.C.: American School of Classical Studies at Athens and Smithsonian Institution Press.

Aravantinos, Vassilios L. 1986. "The EH II Fortified Building at Thebes: Some Notes on Its Architecture." In *Early Helladic Architecture*, 57–63.

———, and Kyriaki Psaraki. 2007. "The Early Helladic Burial Mounds of Thebes." Abstract in *Helike IV: The Fourth International Conference on Ancient Helike and Aigialeia: The Early Helladic Peloponnesos; Aigion, September 1–3, 2007*, 13. Aigion: Helike Society.

Attas, Michael. 1982. Regional Ceramic Trade in Early Bronze Age Greece: Evidence from Neutron Activation Analysis of Early Helladic Pottery from Argolis and Korinthia. PhD diss., McGill University.

————, John M. Fossey, and Leo Yaffe. 1987. "An Archaeometric Study of Early Bronze Age Pottery Production and Exchange in Argolis and Korinthia (Corinthia), Greece." *Journal of Field Archaeology* 14, 77–90.

Banks, Elizabeth C. 1967. The Early and Middle Helladic Small Objects from Lerna. PhD diss., University of Cincinnati.

————. In press. *The Architecture and Stratigraphy of Lerna IV.*

Berger, Lydia M. 2003. Die frühhelladische II Keramik von Agina Kolonna und ihre Stellung im ägäischen Raum. PhD diss., University of Salzburg.

————. 2007. "The Late Early Helladic II Pottery of Aigina Kolonna." Abstract in *Helike IV: The Fourth International Conference on Ancient Helike and Aigialeia: The Early Helladic Peloponnesos; Aigion, September 1–3, 2007,* 24. Aigion: Helike Society.

Brophy, J., Christine Shriner, et al. In preparation. "A Method of Explanation for the Process of Cultural Change I: A Definition for Aeginetan Ware Based on Its Physical Properties."

Caskey, John L. 1954. "Excavations at Lerna, 1952–1953." *Hesperia* 23: 3–30.

————. 1955. "Excavations at Lerna, 1954." *Hesperia* 24: 25–49.

————. 1956. "Excavations at Lerna, 1955." *Hesperia* 25: 147–73.

————. 1957. "Excavations at Lerna, 1956." *Hesperia* 26: 142–162.

————. 1958. "Excavations at Lerna, 1957." *Hesperia* 27: 125–44.

————. 1959. "Activities at Lerna, 1958–1959." *Hesperia* 28: 202–207.

————. 1960. "The Early Helladic Period in the Argolid." *Hesperia* 29: 285–303.

————. 1968. "Lerna in the Early Bronze Age." *AJA* 72: 313–16.

Erickson, Brice. In preparation. "Post-Bronze Age Lerna."

Felten, Florens. 1986. "Early Urban History and Architecture of Ancient Aegina." In *Early Helladic Architecture,* 21–28.

Fiandra, Enrica. 1968. "A che cosa servivano le cretule di Festos?" In *Proceedings of the 2nd International Cretological Congress,* 383–97. Athens: University of Crete.

Forsén, Jeannette. 1992. *The Twilight of the Early Helladics: A Study of the Disturbances in East-central and Southern Greece towards the End of the Early Bronze Age.* Jonsered, Sweden: Aström.

Gejvall, Nils-Gustav. 1969. *Lerna I: The Fauna.* Princeton: American School of Classical Studies.

Hägg, Robin, and Dora Konsola, eds. 1986. *Early Helladic Architecture.*

Hartenberger, Britt, and Curtis Runnels. 2001. "The Organization of Flaked Stone Production at Bronze Age Lerna." *Hesperia* 70: 255–83.

Heath, Martha C. 1958. "Early Helladic Clay Sealings from the House of the Tiles at Lerna." *Hesperia* 27: 81–121.

Hopf, Maria. 1961. "Pflanzenfunde aus Lerna/Argolis." *Der Züchter* 31: 239–47.

————. 1962. "Nutzpflanzen vom lernäischen Golf." *JRGZM* 9: 1–19.

Karagiorga, Theodora G. 1971. "Akovitika Kalamatas." *ArchDelt* 26:B: 126–29.

Kilian, Klaus. 1986. "The Circular Building at Tiryns." In *Early Helladic Architecture,* 65–71.

Konsola, Dora N. 1981. *Promykenaike Theba.* Ph.D.diss., University of Athens.

Kostoula, Maria. 2000. "Die frühhelladischen Tonplomben mit Siegelabdrücken aus Petri bei Nemea." In *Minoisch-mykenische Glyptik,* 135–48.

Lindblom, Michael. 2001. *Marks and Makers: Appearance, Distribution, and Function of Middle and Late Helladic Manufacturers' Marks on Aeginetan Pottery.* SIMA M128. Jonsered, Sweden: Aström.

————. 2007. "Early Mycenaean Mortuary Meals at Lerna VI with Special Emphasis on Their Aeginetan Components." In *MH Pottery,* 115–35.

Maran, Joseph. 1998. *Kulturwandel auf dem griechischen Festland und den Kykladen im späten 3. Jahrtausend v. Chr.: Studien zu den kulturellen Verhältnissen in Südosteuropa und dem zentralen sowie östlichen Mittelmeerraum in der späten Kupfer- und frühen Bronzezeit.* Universitätsforschungen zur prähistorischen Archäologie 53. Bonn: Habelt.

Nilsson, Monica. 2004. A Civilization in the Making: A Contextual study of Early Bronze Age Corridor Buildings in the Aegean. PhD diss., Gothenburg University.

Peperaki, Olga. 2004. "The House of the Tiles at Lerna: Dimensions of 'Social Complexity.'" In *The Emergence of Civilization Revisited*, 214–31.

Pullen, Daniel J. 1986. "A 'House of the Tiles' at Zygouries? The Function of Monumental Early Helladic Architecture." In *Early Helladic Architecture*, 79–84.

———. 1992. "Ox and Plow in the Early Bronze Age Aegean." *AJA* 96: 45–54.

Reese, David. 2008. "Faunal Remains from Late Helladic Lerna (Argolid, Greece)." *Mediterranean Archaeology and Archaeometry* 8(1): 5–25.

Renfrew, Colin. 1972. *The Emergence of Civilisation: The Cyclades and the Aegean in the Third Millennium B.C.* London: Methuen.

Rutter, Jeremy B. 1995. *Lerna III: The Pottery of Lerna IV.* Princeton: American School of Classical Studies.

———. 2001. "The Prepalatial Bronze Age of the Southern and Central Greek Mainland." In *Aegean Prehistory*, 95–155.

———, and Carol Zerner. 1984. "Early Hellado-Minoan Contacts." In *Minoan Thalassocracy*, 75–83.

Shaw, Joseph W. 2008. "Sequencing the EH II 'Corridor Houses.'" *BSA* 102: 137–51.

Shriner, Christine M., and Michael J. Dorais. 1999. "A Comparative Electron Microprobe Study of Lerna III and IV Ceramics and Local Clay-rich Sediments." *Archaeometry* 41: 25–49.

Shriner, Christine M., and Haydn H. Murray. 2001. "Explaining Sudden Ceramic Change at Early Helladic Lerna: A Technological Paradigm." In *Archaeology and Clays*, ed. Isabelle C. Druc, 1–16. *BAR-IS* 942. Oxford: Hedges.

Shriner, Christine M., and Erika R. Elswick, Hannah L. Timm, Haydn H. Murray. 2007. "Clay Mineralogical Studies for Greek Bronze Age Roofing Technology." Paper for Conference of the Clay Minerals Society, June 5, 2007.

Theochares, Dimitris R. 1952. "Anaskaphe en Arapheni." *Prakt* (1955): 129–51.

Vitelli, Karen D. 1993–1999. *Franchthi Neolithic Pottery.* Bloomington: Indiana University Press.

———. 2007. *Lerna V: The Neolithic Pottery from Lerna.* Princeton: American School of Classical Studies.

Voutsaki, Sofia, Sevi Triantaphyllou, Anne Ingvarsson-Sundstrom, Kalliope Sarri, Michael Richards, Albert Nijboer, Sophia Kouidou-Andreou, Leda Kovatsi, Dimitra Nikou and Eleni Milka. 2006. "Project on the Middle Helladic Argolid: A Report on the 2006 Season, Section 1 Lerna." *Pharos* 14: 60–68.

Walter, Hans, and Florens Felten. 1981. *Alt-Aigina III.1, Die vorgeschichtliche Stadt: Befestigungen, Häuser, Funde.* Mainz am Rhein: von Zabern.

Weingarten, Judith. 2000. "EH II Sealings from Geraki in Lakonia: Evidence for Property, Textile Manufacturing, and Trade." In *Minoisch-mykenische Glyptik*, 317–28.

———, Joust H. Crowel, Mieke Prent, and Gillian Vogelsang-Eastwood. 1999. "Early Helladic Sealings from Geraki in Lakonia, Greece." *OJA* 18: 357–76.

Weisshaar, Hans-Joachim. 1981. "Ausgrabungen in Tiryns 1978, 1979: Bericht zur frühhelladischen Keramik." *AA* 1981: 250–56.

———. 1982. "Ausgrabungen in Tiryns 1980: Bericht zur frühhelladischen Keramik." *AA* 1982: 440–66.

———. 1983. "Bericht zur frühhelladischen Keramik: Ausgrabungen in Tiryns 1981." *AA* 1983: 329–58.

Wiencke, Martha H. 1975. "Lerna." In *CMS,* vol. 1, *Kleinere griechische Sammlungen, I,* ed. Ingo Pini, 23–32, 36–114. Berlin: Mann.

———. 1998. "Mycenaean Lerna." *Hesperia* 67: 125–214.

———. 2000. *Lerna IV: The Architecture, Stratification, and Pottery of Lerna III.* Princeton: American School of Classical Studies.

Zerner, Carol. 1988. "Middle Helladic and Late Helladic I Pottery from Lerna: Part II, Shapes." *Hydra* 4: 1–10.

———. 1993. "New Perspectives on Trade in the Middle and Early Late Helladic Periods on the Mainland." In *Wace and Blegen,* 39–56.

———. In preparation. *Middle Helladic Pottery from Lerna.* Princeton: American School of Classical Studies.

———, Philip P. Betancourt, and George Myer. 1986. "Middle Helladic and Late Helladic I Pottery from Lerna." *Hydra* 2: 58–74.

CHAPTER 50

....

MYCENAE

....

ELIZABETH FRENCH

MYCENAE was inhabited for several millennia before the start of the Bronze Age and remained occupied, if not prosperous, for at least a millennium after its end. The evidence for the early occupation is sporadic and tantalizing but probably often unidentified.

The site lies on a rocky knoll between two hills in the northeast corner of the Argive plain some eight miles from the sea. The location allowed exploitation of both the pasture and grazing lands of the hills, the arable lands of the adjacent uplands, and the plain below. A convenient node of routes in all directions, it also became a network of built roads in the LBA. It is probable that the environment of the Bronze Age was similar to that of the earlier part of the 20th century AD, as it seems that the north and east sections of the Argolid suffered less than other areas from poor land management in the EBA, which caused major changes in the landscape.

Mycenae was identified through both legend and Homer at least until Roman times, with the walls and Lion Gate remaining visible. It had always been assumed that the Lion Gate was never lost, but a surprising lack of mention in travelers' accounts, even of the correct placement of the site on early maps, has led to the suggestion that it was only in 1700 that the Lion Gate was rediscovered during a search for stone by the Venetians (Lavery in French and Iakovidis 2003).

The Archaeological Society of Athens began work on the site in 1841 and has continued ever since. Following the death of George E. Mylonas in 1989, Spyros E. Iakovidis has been in charge. In 1876 Heinrich Schliemann excavated test trenches widely on the acropolis and discovered Grave Circle A. Christos Tsountas (Archaeological Society) worked from 1884 to 1902 and cleared almost the whole area of the citadel, as well as more than one hundred chamber tombs.

Alan J.B. Wace (on a concession granted to the British School at Athens by the Archaeological Society) worked at intervals from 1920 to 1955, variously on the tholos and chamber tombs, the citadel, and structures outside the walls. His work on what we now know as the Cult Center was completed after his death. Its particular importance lies in the fact that this was the one area within the acropolis not touched by Schliemann or Tsountas, and it has thus given an opportunity to reassess the stratigraphic history of the site.

All recent interpretive work is based on these excavations. The extensive archival material concerning Mycenae, its discovery, and its remains can be utilized most effectively in conjunction with close study of the site itself; notable recent studies are Shelton (1993) on the chamber tombs and Tournavitou (2006) on the West House.

The first period of the Bronze Age, the Early Helladic, is attested by sherd evidence from the acropolis and several of the adjacent hills. This material appears to be largely from occupation, though occasional whole or restorable pots from near Grave Circle A may indicate that the lower West slope had already begun to be used for burials. The presence of a considerable amount of EH pottery in the fills on the very top of the citadel suggests that it might have been the site of a notable and noticeable building (Palace I), such as those known from Lerna and Tiryns.

How the various sites of the Argolid interact at this period is not clear and has not been investigated in depth. There are several small to medium-sized sites nearby, but the organizational structure cannot be determined on present evidence. The Middle Helladic period is widely documented over almost all of the site but, as previously, the evidence is largely from sherds, though now also from burials. Both types of evidence are currently under detailed study. The pottery is easily identified as it exhibits a complete change from that of the EBA, and gray burnished and matt-painted wares are particularly conspicuous. At present, pottery of the types of the transition from EH to MH, well known from Lerna, have not been identified, but this might be because the intrusive new styles were slow to penetrate to a site obviously flourishing in the EH III period.

Several walls from the deeper levels in later terraces are assigned to this period, and one structure has been excavated: a kitchen and storage area beside the later ascent to the summit from the Cult Center. It awaits full publication.

The most striking feature of the MH period is the clear growth of wealth apparent in the burial evidence of Grave Circle B. Here the series of pit graves, which gradually transform into full shaft graves and with an accompanying increase in both the number of interments and the number and quality of grave goods, documents this transformation. Manufacturing techniques in both metal and pottery develop to a high standard that will be retained throughout the LBA.

By the end of the period, pottery is being imported widely, mainly from the Cyclades, but there are also examples from northern Greece and types that are clearly imitations of Cretan wares, though actual Cretan pottery is very rare at Mycenae itself. This is in direct contrast to a site such as Lerna by the coast. It seems clear that during the later part of the period, Mycenae becomes one of the most important sites of the Argolid and that its leaders enjoy a clear degree of preeminence.

The Late Helladic period is divided into the usual canonical three divisions, which are copiously subdivided in terms of pottery development. These divisions are not on the whole helpful in defining the architectural phases, though recently it has been decided that the time of the major destructions at the end of the Palace period in the Argolid should be termed in a manner coincident with the pottery terminology (French and Stockhammer 2009).

To overcome the terminological difficulties, it is becoming customary to use the terms coined for Crete (Early Palatial, Palatial, and Postpalatial) to designate the major developments. It is particularly important to understand both that the structures visible on the site today are not necessarily contemporary, that each area within and without the citadel has an independent structural history, and that, on the whole, they can be compared one with another only hypothetically.

By chance, or perhaps because of intensity of study, we can understand the site's structural history best from one of its least well-preserved areas: the so-called Palace. The history of the site is thus discussed in relation to the phases identified there.

The Early Palatial period is particularly interesting but has been covered in some depth in a very recent account (French and Shelton 2004). For this period we have evidence (pottery, wall paintings, and domestic debris) of an élite presence on the summit of the citadel (Palace II, plan: French 2002, figure 14), possibly demarcated by a surround wall, and widespread settlement in the surrounding area. It is also marked by the climax of the shaft grave era and the transition to tholos and chamber tomb cemeteries, most of which begin to be used at this time. The prosperity of this period is apparent in the number of tholos tombs built (six of the unique total of nine).

The Palatial period as a whole covered most of the 14th and 13th centuries BC. From Palace III, as well as a pottery deposit, there are now some residual walls that show a change of alignment of the major structure on the hilltop. Traces of settlement of this period have been widely found both on the acropolis (notably below the Ramp House) and outside (on the Atreus Ridge and in the Pezoulia area).

A single, perhaps corvée, workforce was likely employed, and when work on this "maison de chef" had been completed, the workers may then have been assigned to the construction of the Treasury of Atreus, which is by far the largest and most elaborate of the tholos tombs. The period is well represented among the chamber tombs, with many richly endowed examples, and both the quantity and the quality of imported material are particularly notable. This well accords with the strong evidence of overseas expansion of Mycenaean culture in this period.

Related to this expansion is one of the structures on the Pezoulia slope known as Petsas House. Though known from preliminary work in the 1950s, it is only since 2000 that further excavation has taken place. It appears to be a workshop complex for the storage and distribution of pottery. The earliest Linear B tablets not only from Mycenae but also from mainland Greece as a whole have been found here.

The pottery can be linked closely in style to that found at Tell el-Amarna in Egypt and on the Uluburun wreck. Wood samples have been recovered, and key dating evidence, which may give important cross-cultural links, should become available. Interestingly, one vessel found in the original excavation, a handsome pictorial krater with birds, is considered to be by the same hand as one exported to Enkomi on Cyprus.

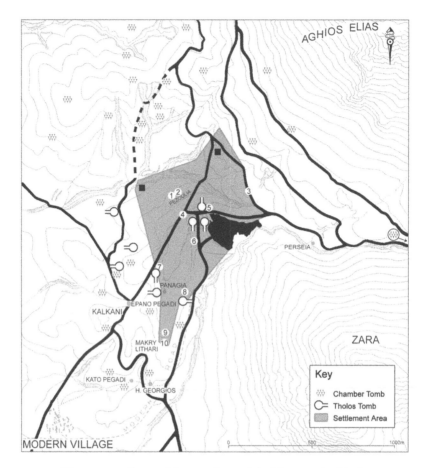

Figure 50.1. Greater Mycenae (copyright Mycenae Archive).

The first stage of the circuit wall of the acropolis was built at this time. The north wall remains today, but both the east and the west walls were altered later.

Then, using the south section as a terrace, the large and elaborate Palace IV was constructed at the very edge overlooking the gorge to the south. This was architecturally sophisticated, with decorative stone work and fresco-painted walls. The plan now shows clearly the division between public and private apartments, as well as workshops and storage areas. When this work was completed, the same workforce turned to the Tomb of Clytemnestra and then to widespread building outside the acropolis and some within.

Outside there was construction in the Pezoulia area, with occupation again in the Petsas House area (figure 50.1:2) and a new structure, possibly not completed, the Cyclopean Terrace Building (figure 50.1:1). To this period can be assigned the workshop complex, found during the construction of the new museum, known as the House of the Tripod Tomb (figure 50.1:5). It is probable that the Plakes House (figure 50.1:3) on the west slope of Aghios Elias also dates to this period.

Definitely built now are the large "houses" south of the Tomb of Clytemnestra, known as the Ivory Houses (figure 50.1:6). Farther south other less imposing houses, the Panagia Houses (figure 50.1:8), were built beside the Treasury of Atreus, and another was built at the far end of the Panagia ridge, the House of Lead (figure 50.1:9). These buildings, all well constructed, exhibit the two levels of elaboration devised to describe the nonpalatial structures of the Late Bronze Age and all varieties of plans, including hybrids among them. No evidence exists for the construction date of the other excavated areas outside the citadel (figure 50.1:4 small houses west of the modern parking lot; 1:7 Lisa's House; and 1:10 the Makri Lithari structure). The part of the lower town lying beneath the outer Hellenistic settlement is currently under investigation.

At this time there was a well-organized road network that radiated from the citadel (French 2002, figure 3), as well as other public works such as flood control (French and Iakovidis 2003, 22).

On the acropolis itself, the large and imposing South House (figure 50.2:8) was built on the west slope outside the west wall, which at that time seems to have followed the contour higher up the slope (French 2002, figure 16). The first building of the Cult Center, Shrine Gamma (figure 50.2:11) is somewhat earlier, probably the first structure in the immediate area.

It is less clear exactly when the other main component structures of the Cult Center (figure 50.2:10, 14, 15) were built, but all antedate the west extension of the Citadel Wall. Indeed, it is likely that the alterations to the Room with the Fresco (figure 50.2:15), changing its entrance from east to northwest and adding the fresco from which it takes its name, also belong to the later part of this period. The Cult Center would at this time have been approached mainly from the west and would have been situated beside the approach to the citadel entrance.

The extension of the citadel to the west to enclose the Grave Circle and the Cult Center was a very considerable enterprise and must have commanded the city's full resources. The plan included changing the approach, constructing a monumental gate (the Lion Gate, figure 50.2:1), and completely altering and refurbishing the Grave Circle (figure 50.2:3) at a higher level to make a singularly impressive sight to one entering the walled acropolis. At this point, the line of sight between the gate and the entrance to the Grave Circle was unimpeded as the Granary had not yet been built.

The old west wall of the citadel was demolished as part of this enterprise, and the whole area within the walls was covered with buildings. We know that the Northwest Quarter was built soon after the Citadel wall and probably the Southwest Quarter also. Note that this latter area is separated from the Cult Center by a built street and flight of stairs and did not form part of that complex. It seems likely that the old approach from the west was retained with a west gate at the end of that street, now hidden by Hellenistic Tower (figure 50.2:16). We await the full publication of the other building complexes within the citadel, but it is likely that they, too, in the form preserved today, were constructed sometime within this period.

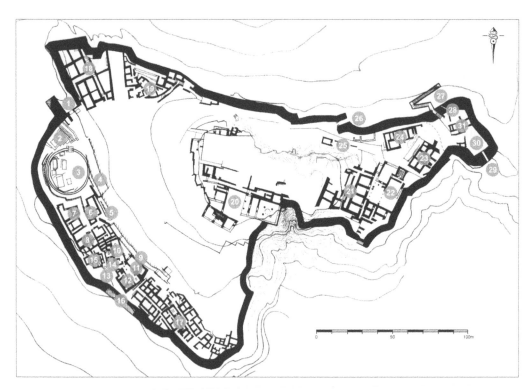

Figure 50.2. Plan of the Citadel at Mycenae: (1) Lion Gate; (2) Granary; (3) Grave Circle A; (4) Great Ramp; (5) Little Ramp; (6) Ramp House; (7) House of the Warrior Vase; (8) South House; (9) Processional Way; (10) Megaron; (11) Shrine Gamma; (12) Tsountas's House; (13) Central Court; (14) Temple; (15) Room with the Fresco; (16) Hellenistic Tower (possibly overlying the West Gate); (17) Southwest Quarter; (18) Northwest Quarter; (19) House M; (20) Palace; (21) Artisans' Quarter; (22) House of Columns; (23) House Delta; (24) House Gamma; (25) North Storerooms; (26) North or Postern Gate; (27) Underground Cistern; (28) North Sally Port; (29) South Sally Port; (30) House Alpha; (31) House Beta (copyright Mycenae Archive).

It is at this time that palatial authority becomes very apparent in the burial evidence (French 2009). There seems to have been some kind of building control that delimited the areas where chamber tombs could be cut and sumptuary rules on grave goods. There are no longer any contemporary imported objects in the tombs except for rather ill-made scarabs, and the Mycenaean pottery offerings are much less ostentatious.

This period is clearly the acme of Mycenae itself. The end was brought about by a catastrophe of some kind, evidence for which has also been found at various other sites in the northeast Peloponnese. Occupation at some did not resume. This catastrophe is attributed to a major earthquake for several reasons.

There are no traces of fire at this point, but large deposits of pottery are found on the floors. In the Cult Center, a group of cult figures with pottery and a variety of small offerings are carefully placed both in a small room that was then walled up and sealed and also in an adjacent alcove. The cult fresco is covered with a layer of whitewash before the room in which it stood was carefully filled.

The start of the next period sees widespread repairs, but they are largely of poor quality. Notable are walls with gaps infilled in pisé and the quickly laid plaster flooring of the Palace Court instead of the cement. To this phase belongs Palace V, which is visible today. It is almost identical in plan with the previous one; there were new wall paintings, but overall the repairs were shoddy.

Though this period was very considerably shorter than the one before, it saw the final alterations to the west slope and to the citadel wall. The so-called Grand Staircase of the Palace and the elaborate ramp system to the east of the Cult Center belong to this phase and seem to be connected, making a processional way between the two areas.

Alteration was also undertaken on the citadel wall. In order to construct an eastern extension, the short cross wall at the east end of the circuit was almost totally demolished, and a new Postern or North gate (figure 50.2:26) was built. This allowed two measures that seem to have been occasioned by the need for security: a lookout post at the southeast corner (figure 50.2:29) and a covered approach (figure 50.2:27) from within the circuit to the water reservoir, to which water was brought from the Perseia spring to the west. The other Argive palace sites, as well as Athens, also took precautions at this time with the apparent aim of safeguarding a water supply, but it is not clear whether these measures are the result of an actual threat or merely fashion.

This period ends with a major destruction accompanied by widespread (but not universal) burning. It may once again have been occasioned by earthquake, but the circumstances differ considerably. On this occasion almost nothing is left on the floors—a factor that has made determining the exact pottery types in use at this historic point in time extremely difficult.

There is also some evidence that conditions following the destructions were made worse by heavy rains falling on the burnt debris of the limestone walls, turning them into a concreted mass that necessitated rebuilding at a higher level.

This destruction is assumed to be the end of the Palatial period, ending the bureaucratic centralized government with its elaborate records in the Linear B script. Some form of governance, however, remained, and in a period of extreme austerity, rebuilding was organized.

The standing walls, particularly the west citadel wall, were used as extremely heavy foundations, filled with the debris of the burnt destruction, for a series of new buildings. The Granary (figure 50.2:2) is one, but there is also a pair of elaborate complexes over the west area of the Cult Center and an apparently lesser building over the House of Columns (figure 50.2:22). There may be evidence for other reoccupation of this first Postpalatial phase in the buildings of the east slope, but it is not yet published.

It has been suggested that a rectangular structure built closely over the floor of the court of the Palace may have formed some kind of central focus. This idea is based on the recent identification of a rebuilt megaron at Tiryns. At Mycenae, the artificial terrace that supported the southeast corner of the megaron of the Palace probably fell into the ravine at the time of the great destruction, thus precluding the reuse of the megaron itself. Unfortunately, this structure over the court was removed in 1920 without being sufficiently recorded. If there was such reoccupation in the Palace area, this would form Palace VI.

The later phases of the Postpalatial period see very striking prosperity, at least in terms of pottery, but the architectural evidence is extremely meagre. The Granary, following some alteration, was fully in use in this period. From it and another building over the South House Annex, we know that the period ended again with heavy burning.

There is some scanty evidence for one further phase of the Bronze Age and for some occupation throughout the first millennium, before an artificial revival as a Hellenistic *kome*.

Mycenae's prime position in the hierarchy of the Late Bronze Age is shown in the levels of craftsmanship displayed in the many finds now housed in the National Museum in Athens and the Mycenae Museum on the site itself. The grave offerings from the shaft graves are unique, not least in quantity. Other items, preserved mainly from the earlier burials in the chamber tombs, are of high quality and diverse origin. An important development is the growing use of glass ornament.

Despite the apparent sumptuary regulation of the Palatial period itself, we may note an intriguing group of artifacts from the House of Shields, consisting of locally made stone bowls, faience vessels that show the influences of a mixture of Near Eastern cultures, and the small-scale carved ivories that have become a hallmark. Several show the same stylistic features as the large-scale lion relief from the Lion Gate itself, one of the earliest examples of such monumental sculpture.

Trade can be assessed only by the materials that are preserved; imports seem to have been mainly raw materials that were often then reexported as value-added products or the invisibles. Exports, probably mainly high-value invisibles, can be traced by the distinctive pottery that served as containers or merely space-filling accompaniments. By the Palatial period, this pottery was very much a mass production of high quality. Through scientific analysis (largely Neutron Activation Analysis), we can test the provenance of this export pottery. Most interestingly, the Argolid area divides into a northern section centered on Mycenae and a southern one centered on Tiryns.

The palace archives of Mycenae have not been found, but tablets inscribed in the Linear B script have been discovered in several of the so-called Houses (French 2002, figure 61), probably indicating their commercial and administrative activities. The tablets are preserved in buildings destroyed in both the late 14th-century-BC destruction and that of the mid-13th century. Only one inscribed stirrup jar comes from a context at present known definitely to be later than this.

BIBLIOGRAPHY

French, Elizabeth B. 2002. *Mycenae, Agamemnon's Capital: The Site in its Setting.* Stroud: Tempus Publishing.
———. 2009. "Town Planning in Palatial Mycenae." In *Inside the City in the Greek World: Studies of Urbanism from the Bronze Age to the Hellenistic Period*, ed. Sara S. Owen and Laura J. Preston. Oxford: Oxbow, 55–61.

————, and Spyros E. Iakovidis, (with contributions by Anton Jansen, John Lavery and Kim S. Shelton). 2003. *Archaeological Atlas of Mycenae*. Athens: Archaeological Society of Athens.

French, Elizabeth B., and Kim S. Shelton. 2004. "Early Palatial Mycenae." In *Autochthon*, 175–84.

French, Elizabeth B., and Philipp Stockhammer. 2009. "Mycenae and Tiryns: The Pottery of the Second Half of the 13th Century BC: Contexts and Definitions." *BSA* 104: 173–230.

Shelton, Kim S. 1993. "Tsountas' Chamber Tombs at Mycenae." Αρχαιολογικη Εφημέρις 1993: 187–210.

Tournavitou, Iphiyenia. 2006. "A Mycenaean Building Reconsidered: The Case of the West House at Mycenae." *BSA* 101: 217–67.

CHAPTER 51

......

PYLOS

......

JACK L. DAVIS

THE discovery of Bronze Age Pylos followed many frustrating efforts to locate the home of Homer's hero, Nestor. The quest had occupied scholars and travelers since antiquity (McDonald and Thomas 1990).

Pausanias, the Roman author of a travel guide to Greece, identified a cave on the slopes of the medieval acropolis of Navarino as the place where Nestor and his father penned their cattle. A millennium and a half later, in 1829, soon after Greece won its independence from the Ottoman Turks, members of the great French cultural mission, the Expédition scientifique de Morée, sought Nestor's palace not far away, near a village called Pyla. In the 1880s Heinrich Schliemann dug in the medieval fortress at Navarino, looking for prehistoric remains comparable to those that he had already investigated at Mycenae, home of King Agamemnon. Others searched much farther afield, even many kilometers farther north, in Elis, in vain attempts to discover the elusive Palace of Nestor. Both in ancient and modern times, the location to which the place name Pylos was attached shifted.

Then, at the beginning of the 20th century, a Greek schoolteacher found squared limestone blocks associated with Mycenaean pottery of the 13th century BC in an olive grove on a knoll on the spine of a ridge called Englianos, overlooking the Bay of Navarino (figure 51.1; Davis 2008). Following the ridge east leads a traveler ultimately to the valley of the Pamisos River near the modern city of Kalamata. The finds were reported to the Greek Ministry of Education and came to the attention of Konstantinos Kourouniotis, director of the National Museum of Greece. Kourouniotis, in turn, discussed them with his friend Carl W. Blegen of the University of Cincinnati. In 1929 a joint excavation was proposed, but Blegen would soon become preoccupied with directing an expedition to Troy, and the collaboration did not materialize until 1939.

On the very first day of excavation at Ano Englianos, Blegen and his colleagues, including William A. McDonald (who would, in the 1960s, direct the Minnesota

Figure 51.1. Englianos Ridge and the Palace of Nestor from the Bay of Navarino
(courtesy of the Department of Classics, University of Cincinnati).

Messenian Expedition), exposed part of the archives of a Mycenaean palace of
ca. 1180 BC and uncovered the first substantial cache of clay tablets with texts written in the Linear B script ever found on the Greek mainland. The script was, of
course, already known, principally from Sir Arthur Evans's excavations at the Palace
of Minos at Knossos in central Crete.

Transcriptions of about a thousand texts were circulated among researchers
and, by 1952, had made possible the decipherment of Linear B by Michael Ventris,
an English architect (Bendall 2003a). The complex social and economic system
reflected in these documents was headed by a wanax (king), who organized some
aspects of agricultural and industrial production within an area of about two thousand square kilometers in the southwestern Peloponnese. Certain resources were
allocated for the benefit of designated elite, "collectors," and other resources were
taxed directly for the benefit of the palatial administration. Feasts that involved sacrifices are recorded, as are offerings to the gods, many of them the same as those
worshipped in historical Greece (e.g., Zeus, Poseidon, Hera, Ares, and Dionysos).

The king supported a workforce that comprised various kinds of dependent
labor, among them slaves; he appointed officials, organized feasts, and in general
played a major role in religious affairs (Bennet 2007a; Shelmerdine 2007, 2008).
The kingdom was divided into Hither and Further Provinces—the latter probably
in the valley of Kalamata, the former around the palace in the west. Within the two
provinces were a total of sixteen or seventeen districts, each headed by a governor
and a vice governor who reported to the center at Pylos.

All of the clay documents date to the final year of the palace, and none were baked on purpose. These were not intended to be part of a permanent archive. There are no legal, literary, or diplomatic texts among the surviving documents; even letters are lacking. Any such documents that would have retained significance beyond the current year may have been written on a perishable material (e.g., parchment or papyrus), which would have been long ago destroyed by the fires that ironically preserved their clay counterparts. In any case, only a few dozen scribal hands have been identified, and it is clear that literacy was restricted to a small segment of the population.

The palatial buildings and archives discovered by Blegen on that first day of excavation were finally and definitively destroyed soon after the start of the 12th century, probably ca. 1180 BC, in a fearsome conflagration. This, of course, is the traditional date of the Trojan War.

After WW II, Blegen vigorously pursued his investigations in partnership with Marion Rawson, a Cincinnati architect. Blegen and Rawson's excavations between 1952 and 1971, complemented by surface investigations in 1992–1994, also conducted under the auspices of the University of Cincinnati, documented a long history of settlement—one reaching back a millennium or more before the palace was built in a definitive and final form.

Their authoritative three-volume publication of the results of their excavations focuses on the palace of the 13th century BC and its contents and on associated cemeteries (Blegen and Rawson 1966; Lang 1969; Blegen et al. 1971). Recent reexamination of the unpublished finds from their excavations now allows much more to be said about the development of settlement on the Englianos Ridge, as well as the contacts between those who lived there and the larger Aegean world, while a definitive publication of the Linear B documents will soon appear (Bennett et al. in preparation).

The earliest finds are as yet unassociated with architecture. Fragments of pottery of the Early Helladic II period (ca. 2600 BC), including bases of small vases pierced and reused as spindle whorls have been found mixed in deposits of later date.

The first extensive remains of settlement seem to date to the time of the transition between the Early and Middle Bronze Age, not long after 2000 BC. These have been most thoroughly documented in a small excavation undertaken by Lord William Taylour (well known as the investigator of the Cult Center at Mycenae). Taylour uncovered parts of two superimposed apsidal buildings (Stocker 2003). It is now clear that houses of this same phase existed elsewhere on the Englianos Ridge, even under the later palace buildings, and it seems most probable that several separate but related hamlets coexisted.

Remains of the developed Middle Helladic period have been preserved in almost every place where excavations reached deeply. These, together with surface investigations, make it clear that even by the start of the Late Bronze Age the settlement at Englianos was quite large (Stocker and Davis in press).

Like those at sites in the Argolid such as Lerna, ceramics of Minoan Crete reached the Englianos Ridge—actual imports and imitations, at least by the time that the first palaces were established at Knossos. By the beginning of the Late Bronze Age, Cretan influence was extensive. One of the most substantial Minoan contributions was to the architecture of the settlement, where so-called ashlar masonry was used for the first time: Squared blocks of carved limestone were laid in courses, probably to adorn façades of the most significant structures of the community. Ashlar masonry was also employed about the same time in the façade of a tholos (beehive-shaped) tomb at the site of Peristeria, an hour's drive to the north of the Palace of Nestor, where two blocks are incised with mason's marks of a type appearing at the Palace of Minos at Knossos. The style of stonework has a very old history in Crete.

From ca. 1600 BC, there is evidence of intense and continuous building (Nelson 2001). Plaster floors, cut-stone column bases, and walls of orthostate construction appear, and, by 1500 BC, two or three monumental buildings had been erected on the acropolis—all with ashlar façades. The largest, Building A, on the southwestern brow of the acropolis had a massive stone façade. Building B and Building C were situated to the northeast, in the position of the later Main Building of the Palace of Nestor; it is unclear whether they were independent structures or wings of the same complex. Space between the three buildings may have formed one large open court, in a manner reminiscent of the Minoan palaces.

This older "palace" is poorly preserved, and it is not possible to say much about the activities that were conducted in it. If, as seems virtually certain, these anticipated the administrative functions of the later Palace of Nestor, there are no signs yet of a literate bureaucracy. Indeed, the earliest conclusive evidence for documents written in the Linear B script consists of the clay tablets retrieved from the debris of the Archives room, from the palace's final destruction. The Linear B script is itself, however, a legacy of contact between Crete and the Greek mainland and was in use at Mycenae as early as the 14th century BC and at Knossos in Crete before that.

In the period of the Shaft Graves at Mycenae (17th to 15th century BC), western Messenia witnessed a remarkable explosion in the construction of tholos tombs. During the Middle Helladic period, low circular mounds of earth (tumuli) had frequently been employed for tombs. A central grave, whether pit, stone cist, or box, was set in such a mound, and earth and stones were then heaped over it, with additional burials later inserted around its circumference. In at least one instance, a body was deposited in a large storage jar or pithos, positioned in the tumulus so that the mouth of the jar faced outside. Its rim was framed by three stone slabs, arranged as if to form a post-and-lintel doorway leading into the tomb. It has been suggested that mounds with burials of this sort inspired the genesis of the tholos tomb.

The first true tholos tomb that survives intact in Messenia is unprepossessing and dates to the final phase of the Middle Helladic period (Lolos 2008). It lies only a few kilometers from the Palace of Nestor, near the village of Koryphasion (formerly Osmanaga), and was dug not into the side of a hill but into dead-flat ground. The walls of the tomb are built of small, roughly coursed stones rather than the more impressive ashlar employed in some tholos tombs of the Early Mycenaean period. By the end of the 15th century in western Messenia, only those tombs associated with the Palace of Nestor were regularly in use. It is likely that their neglect elsewhere in the region reflects the rise to political ascendancy of the Palace of Nestor and a general acceptance that the right to be buried in such a tomb was the prerogative of its elite (Bennet 2007b).

In the 16th and 15th century, three tholos tombs were built on the Englianos Ridge: one, called Tholos IV by Blegen and Rawson, was excavated into the side of a low hill immediately northeast of the visitors' parking lot. The dromos (passageway) leading into it appears to have been deliberately aligned on a monumental gateway through the fortification wall that surrounded the acropolis in the Early Mycenaean period. One can easily imagine that it was placed here to serve as a visible reminder, when opened to receive a new burial, of the continuity of the power of the dynasty that held sway at Pylos. Equidistant (ca. 200 m.) to the southwest, Lord William Taylour excavated a "Grave Circle," also of the Early Mycenaean period but slightly earlier, most probably the eroded remains of another tholos tomb. Two kilometers farther toward the sea Tholos III was found, the so-called Kato Englianos tomb. These graves continued to be used throughout much of the Late Bronze Age.

Around 1400 BC, the buildings on the Englianos Ridge burned, occasioning the construction of a new complex. This final Palace of Nestor consisted of a Main Building, Southwestern Building, Northeastern Building, and Wine Magazine—structures that stood until the destruction of the site, ca. 1180 BC. The walls of the Main Building and the Southwestern Building were extensively decorated with wall paintings applied in tempera rather than true fresco technique (Brecoulaki et al. 2008).

The Main Building, as its name implies, was central to this final complex, the best-preserved and most fully excavated palace of 13th century BC Greece. From the existence of staircases, it can be deduced that the palace had an upper floor, although little of it is preserved other than fallen plaster. The Main Building was rectangular in plan, unlike the structures that preceded it. Its central rooms were the most elaborately decorated parts of the entire palatial complex and consisted of a series of axially arranged spaces oriented northwest-southeast: a Propylon with access to the Archives; a Court; and three rooms of a Megaron, culminating in a Throne Room for the wanax (figure 51.2).

It is likely that those traveling to the palace from the coast followed the floor of the valley bordering the Englianos Ridge on the north, then ascended as they approached the palace. Access to the Main Building was secure. Someone entering for the first time would have been impressed by the decorative program: first, in the Propylon, a life-sized procession of tribute bearers, then smaller figures of men, women, and animals, and architectural façades. Smaller than life-size men carrying objects decorated the walls of the Vestibule of the Megaron.

The decorative program of the Throne Room itself is only partly restored, but it certainly emphasized the role of the wanax and his significance. In the center of the room, surrounded by four fluted columns, was a large plastered hearth, its rim painted with a "flame" pattern. The columns seem to have supported a clerestory, through which smoke from the hearth vented to the sky. The floor of the room was plastered and divided into a rough checkerboard, all squares of which, except one, were decorated with geometric motifs. The exception, painted with an octopus, was

Figure 51.2. Throne Room of the Palace of Nestor. Watercolor reconstruction
by Piet de Jong, digitally restored by Craig Mauzy (courtesy of the
Department of Classics, University of Cincinnati).

set in front of a low, plastered platform that almost certainly supported a wooden
throne. To the left, one shallow basin in the floor was connected to a second by a
shallow channel; liquid offerings or libations were likely poured into it. As at the
Palace of Minos at Knossos, the king (whether in a secular capacity or that of a high
religious official), when seated on his throne was flanked by lions and griffins, symbols of his majesty and power. Elsewhere in the room were scenes of men drinking,
presumably at feasts, and of a lyre-playing bard seated on multicolored rocks, sing-
ing epic tales to diners (Bennet 2007c).

Other rooms of the palace served storage, production, or administrative functions. To the left of the entrance porch, a two-room Archives complex held ca. 80%
of all of the Linear B documents found by Blegen and Rawson's team. These had
been stored in baskets and other containers in the innermost of the two rooms;
scribes wrote the documents in the other.

Much of the remainder of the palatial complex was devoted to storage or craft
production. Pantries in the Main Building were full of pottery for consumption of
food and drink, most of it unused at the time the palace was destroyed. Large storage

jars, built into plastered benches in magazines behind the Throne Room, were filled with oil. In a freestanding structure immediately north of the Main Building was the Wine Magazine, with several dozen large storage jars. Lumps of clay, stamped with seal impressions, lay on the floor, several of them inscribed with the Linear B sign for wine. East of the Main Building, the Northeastern Building housed a shrine, perhaps dedicated to a Mistress of Horses, which Blegen and Rawson believed to be associated with a workshop partly devoted to chariot repairs. It may, however, have been a "clearing house for goods entering the palatial complex as a whole" (Bendall 2003b).

When the Main Building was newly erected, one secondary entrance led through a shallow porch in its northeast ashlar façade to a small room where a bathtub had been set into a plastered bench. Nearby, a second entrance from the outside led to a majestic complex with a megaron and central hearth similar to that of the Throne Room. Griffins and lions or lionesses adorned its walls, and a small adjacent room had a plastered floor with painted dolphins and octopuses. It is clear that these parts of the Main Building had once been of significance, but that, in the palace's final years, the secondary entrances were blocked by the construction of two courtyards—one perhaps an industrial area for the production of perfumed oils (Shelmerdine 1985).

Although the Palace of Nestor is the most fully documented of the Mycenaean palaces, much about its operation remains poorly understood. Southwest of the Main Building and parallel to it is another extensive complex of rooms. Why does this Southwestern Building contain a megaron hall (Bennet and Davis 1999)? Some scholars have imagined that it was the seat of the *lawagetas* ("leader/assembler of the people"), an official whose title suggests he may have led the kingdom in war. The wall paintings found in Hall 64, adjacent to the Megaron, do project a martial aspect. On its northeast wall, warriors clad in boars' tusk helmets and armor struggle with barbarians clothed in animal skins. A frieze of three warships in procession adorned the northwest wall.

The scenes in Hall 64 would have impressed those gathered in the broad courtyard before it to the southeast. Here it is likely that the wanax's subjects gathered to feast at his expense; they would have been supplied with drinking cups and bowls from the pantries of the palace complex. Documents suggest, in fact, that the provision of food and drink for feasts was a significant concern of the palace authorities (Wright 2004). Cattle, sheep, and pigs were inventoried for such purposes. A large heap of thigh bones and lower jawbones from at least ten head of cattle were, in fact, found gathered on the floor in the Archives, together with twice as many miniature drinking cups (Isaakidou et al. 2002; Stocker and Davis 2004). The bones, parts of the carcass typically offered to the gods, were all burned to a high temperature, probably as an offering. The meat from the sacrifice was presumably distributed to those in attendance at the feast.

The palace was well equipped to support feasting, and it is likely that both diners and drinkers would have partaken of nourishment in various parts of it, too, grouped according to their position in the palatial social hierarchy. Those of the highest status, including the king, would on some occasions have dined in the Throne Room itself (Bendall 2004).

The economic and political domination of the Palace of Nestor is reflected in the fortunes of the regions around it. Near the seacoast, the course of the river bordering the Englianos Ridge on the northwest appears to have been diverted, and an artificial basin constructed near its mouth—likely a port or harbor contemporary with the final stages of the palace (Zangger 2008). Analysis of prehistoric pollen that settled into a large lagoon north of the Bay of Navarino points to a virtual explosion in the cultivation of olives at this time, one perhaps related to the perfume oil industry supported by the palace.

There was also a proliferation in the number and size range of settlements in the area: Many of the old settlements expanded in area and presumably also in population; some, like Iklaina, displayed palatial features such as ashlar masonry and wall paintings (Cosmopoulos 2006). These are likely to be examples of the district capitals mentioned in the palatial archives. In addition, for the first time, settlements of a smaller, third-order size appear, thus packing the landscape more densely with people than would ever again be the case prior to the time of Alexander the Great.

The destruction to the Palace of Nestor ca. 1180 BC was so devastating that neither the palace nor the community subsequently recovered. Some have suggested that the agents of this calamity were invaders from outside the kingdom, Dorian Greeks or the "Peoples of the Sea" mentioned in Egyptian texts; others that the people of Pylos themselves revolted against their king. The precise causes remain undetermined, but, whatever the case, certain facts are indisputable; for instance, the Main Building burned with such intensity that the Linear B tablets in its Archive Room were fired, and jars in some of the storerooms even melted.

Before the destruction, the town around the palace extended up and down the Englianos Ridge over an area one kilometer in length, and perhaps as many as three thousand individuals were resident there. It, like the Palace of Nestor, was all but abandoned. Tombs used repeatedly for generations were neglected. The area of the Mycenaean kingdom of Pylos remained, as a whole in fact, severely depopulated for nearly a millennium. Unlike the great palaces of the Argolid, such as Mycenae and Tiryns, the ruins of the Palace of Nestor did not become a focus of worship by Greeks of historical times (Davis and Lynch in press). Still-standing walls provided some shelter to a few squatters after the Bronze Age, and small amounts of pottery, some of it as late in date as the 3rd century BC, have been found. But by then, the names Nestor and Pylos were no longer associated with the site.

BIBLIOGRAPHY

Bendall, Lisa M. 2003a. *The Decipherment of Linear B and the Ventris-Chadwick Correspondence: An Exhibition to Celebrate the 50th Anniversary of the Publication of the Decipherment.* Cambridge: Fitzwilliam Museum.
———. 2003b. "A Reconsideration of the Northeastern Building at Pylos: Evidence for a Mycenaean Redistributive Center." *AJA* 107: 181–232.

———. 2004. "Fit for a King? Hierarchy, Exclusion, Aspiration, and Desire in the Social Structure of Mycenaean Banqueting." In *Food, Cuisine, and Society in Prehistoric Greece*, ed. Paul Halstead and John C. Barrett, 105–35. Oxford: Oxbow.

Bennet, John. 2007a. "The Aegean Bronze Age." In *Cambridge Economic History of the Greco-Roman World*, ed. Walter Schiedel, Ian Morris, and Richard P. Saller, 175–210. New York: Cambridge University Press.

———. 2007b. "Pylos: The Expansion of a Mycenaean Center." In *RMP II*, 29–39.

———. 2007c. "Representations of Power in Mycenaean Pylos." In *ΣΤΕΦΑΝΟΣ ΑΡΙΣΤΕΙΟΣ: Archäologische Forschungen zwischen Nil und Istros: Festschrift für Stefan Hiller zum 65. Geburtstag*, ed. Felix Lang, Klaus Reinholdt, and Jörg Weilhartner, 11–22. Vienna: Phoibos.

———. 2008. "The Linear B Archives and the Kingdom of Nestor." In *Sandy Pylos* 2008, 111–38.

———, and Jack L. Davis. 1999. "Making Mycenaeans: Warfare, Territorial Expansion, and Representations of the Other in the Pylian Kingdom." In *Polemos*, 105–20.

Bennett, Emmett L., Jr., José L. Melena, Jean-Pierre Olivier, Thomas G. Palaima, and Cynthia W. Shelmerdine. In prep. *The Palace of Nestor in Western Messenia*. Vol. 4, *The Inscribed Documents*. Austin: University of Texas Press.

Blegen, Carl W., and Marion Rawson. 1966. *The Palace of Nestor at Pylos in Western Messenia*. Vol. 1, *The Buildings and Their Contents*. Princeton: Princeton University Press.

———, Marian Rawson, William D. Taylour, and William P. Donovan. 1971. *The Palace of Nestor at Pylos in Western Messenia*. Vol. 3, *Acropolis and Lower Town, Tholoi, Grave Circle, and Chamber Tombs: Discoveries outside the Citadel*. Princeton: Princeton University Press.

Brecoulaki, Hariklia, Caroline Zaitoun, Sharon R. Stocker, and Jack L. Davis. 2008. "An Archer from the Palace of Nestor in Pylos: A New Wall-Painting Fragment in the Chora Museum." *Hesperia* 77: 363–97.

Cosmopoulos, Michael B. 2006. "The Political Landscape of Mycenaean States: *A-pu2* and the Hither Province of Pylos." *AJA* 110: 205–28.

Davis, Jack L. 2008. "The Discovery of the Palace of Nestor." In *Sandy Pylos* 2008, 42–46.

———, and Kathleen M. Lynch. In press. "Remembering and Forgetting Nestor: Pylian Pasts Pluperfect?" In *Archaeology and Homer*, ed. Susan Sherratt and John Bennet. Sheffield: Sheffield Studies in Aegean Archaeology.

Isaakidou, Valasia, Paul Halstead, Sharon R. Stocker, and Jack L. Davis. 2002. "Burnt Animal Sacrifice at the Mycenaean 'Palace of Nestor' at Pylos." *Antiquity* 76: 86–92.

Lang, Mabel. 1969. *The Palace of Nestor in Western Messenia*. Vol. 2, *The Frescoes*. Princeton: Princeton University Press.

Lolos, Yiannos G. 2008. "Mycenaean Burial at Pylos." In *Sandy Pylos* 2008, 75–78.

McDonald, William A., and Carol G. Thomas. 1990. *Progress into the Past: The Rediscovery of Mycenaean Civilization*, 2d ed. Bloomington: University of Indiana Press.

Nelson, Michael C. 2001. The Architecture of Epano Englianos. PhD diss., University of Toronto.

Shelmerdine, Cynthia W. 1985. *The Perfume Industry of Mycenaean Pylos*. Gothenburg: Åström.

———. 2007. "Administration in the Mycenaean Palaces: Where's the Chief?" In *RMP II*, 40–46.

———. 2008. "The Palace and Its Operations." In *Sandy Pylos* 2008, 81–96.

Stocker, Sharon R. 2003. "The Pylos Regional Archaeological Project, Part IV: Deriziotis Aloni: A Small Bronze Age Site in Messenia." *Hesperia* 72(4): 341–404.

————, and Jack L. Davis. 2004. "Animal Sacrifice, Archives, and Feasting at the Palace of Nestor," Hesperia 73: 179–95.

————, and Jack L. Davis. In press. "Early Helladic and Middle Helladic Pylos: The Petropoulos Trench and Stratified Remains on the Englianos Ridge." In *Mesohelladika*.

Wright, James C., ed. 2004. *The Mycenaean Feast. Hesperia* 73(2). Princeton: American School of Classical Studies at Athens.

Zangger, Eberhard. 2008. "The Port of Nestor." In *Sandy Pylos* 2008, 69–74.

CHAPTER 52

THEBES

ANASTASIA DAKOURI-HILD

THEBES commands several alluvial plains of east Boeotia (Christodoulou 1969) extending from Kopais to the Tanagriki and from Paralimni to Parasopia. The Theban plain itself is traversed by the Thespios, Kalamitis, and Isminos riverbeds. The Dirki and Strophia torrents run along the west and east foothills of Thebes, respectively (Symeonoglou 1985, 8–11). Thebes occupies a strategic position along important overland (Buck 1979, 4–5; Fossey 1988, vol. 1, 200) and maritime routes of antiquity (Heurtley 1923; Schläger, Blackman, and Schaefer 1968; Gauvin and Fossey 1985).

The citadel of Thebes, also known as the Kadmeia, is a pear-shaped, large (800 m long, 500 m wide) and relatively low (max. 224 m) plateau, which is in part the outcome of ancient and modern earthworks. It appears to have been narrower and northwest-southeast oriented in prehistory (Konsola 1981, 68–69, map 6). Access from the west and to some extent the north slope remains arduous to this day and bespeaks the naturally defensive quality of the Theban landscape. The central east, southeast, and south slopes provide easier access to the citadel and connect it to the main routes leading to east and south Boeotia and beyond (Symeonoglou 1985, 12). The Ampheion, Kastellia, Ismenion, and Kolonaki hills, situated within a short distance (100–300 m) from the north, east, and south slopes respectively, were used as burial grounds in prehistory.

The Kadmeia had been explored by early travelers since the Renaissance, though mostly in the 19th century (Paton 1951, 38; Roller 1988). From the later 19th century, Theban topography and ancient art became the object of scholarly study (Decharme 1869; Böhlau 1888; Fabricius 1890; cf. Soteriadis 1900). Excavations were initiated at that time by Eustratios Kalopais and Dimitrios Filios and were later pursued mostly by Antonios Keramopoullos and Nikolaos Pappadakis. In the 1960–1970s Thebes underwent a dramatic urban transformation and witnessed the intensification of rescue archaeology. The contemporary city dissects the Theban landscape into hundreds of plots, which presents challenges and dilemmas (Aravantinos 1996a; Dakouri-Hild et al. 2003). Nevertheless, the Archaeological Service has brought together an impressive body of evidence substantiating the significance of Thebes throughout its occupational history of five millennia.

THE EARLY BRONZE AGE

The settlement on the Kadmeia seems to have been established in the EBA, whereas earlier habitation is attested in the plains nearby (Faraklas 1969, 176; Tsota in press). Early Helladic remains are reported from at least fifty-two plots to date (for site lists, see Konsola 1981, 81–100; Alram-Stern 2004, vol. 2, 681–90) (figure 52.1). The settlement spread as far north as the Museum hill and Gourna and covered a minimum of 14 ha but seems to have been more concentrated at Ayios Andreas and the southeast slopes. House orientation depended on local terrain and possibly other factors (Konsola 1981, 163; cf. Andrikou 2000a, 183).

Three habitation phases are distinguishable based on a preliminary study of ceramic material (Konsola 1981, 117–26): EH II with group A pottery, including Urfirnis; EH II/III (Lefkandi I) with group B pottery, including Cycladic- and Anatolian-inspired and hybridic types (Psaraki 2004); and EH III with group Γ pottery, including Ayia Marina ware. The end of the Lefkandi I phase is marked by destructive fires (e.g., Demakopoulou and Konsola 1975, 46; Demakopoulou 1976a; Aravantinos 1982a, 1983a). However, the Museum site was unaffected (Aravantinos 2002, 2004b), while one site was conflagrated in later EH III (Andrikou 1998a).

There is no evidence of a settlement enceinte (cf. Symeonoglou 1985, figure 2.1), but two large buildings, the EH II Fortified Building at the Metropolis site and the Lefkandi I apsidal building at the Museum site (figure 52.1; Aravantinos 1986, 2002), are demarcated by sizeable, tapering walls (1.65–1.80 m and 1.50–2.00 m in width, respectively) which had a retaining and probably also a protective function. Both walls have a stone socle with mud-brick elevation (1.50–2 m high) and are associated with stone-paved calderims or courtyards. The Museum wall, which forms an angle around the apsidal building, is also equipped with drains. A massive EBA mud-brick terrace covered the Lefkandi I structures at that site. Such architectural features betray planning and architectural sophistication and represent a substantial investment of labor.

Wattle-and-daub houses constructed by means of wooden posts, clay-plastered branches, and/or reeds are identifiable through rock-cut foundation pits or trenches that occasionally form elliptical plans (Konsola 1981, 104; cf. Aravantinos 2005d). While wattle-and-daub houses are not attested in EH III, stone-built houses (whether apsidal or straight-sided) are attested both in the Lefkandi I and the EH III phases. Stone-built houses are founded on stereo or brought fills and have mud-brick elevations, occasionally clay-plastered inside (Aravantinos 2002). Floors

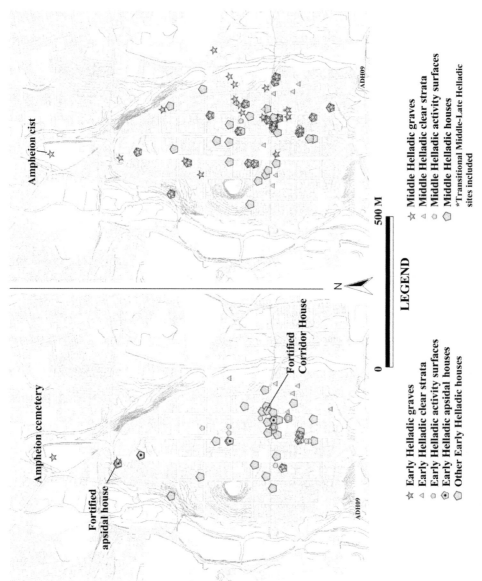

Figure 52.1. Thebes in the EH–MH period, including transitional late MH–earliest LH period (courtesy of the author).

are made of trodden earth or clay or paved with mud-brick slabs (Demakopoulou and Konsola 1975). Door openings have stone thresholds (Touloupa 1964a).

Some apsidal houses have impressive longhouse plans (12–14+ m long, 7–10 m wide). The best surviving example (Aravantinos 2002, 2004a, 2004b) was entered from the north and had three rooms and perhaps a fourth semi-apsidal room or open-air space to the west. The middle room, the main living space, is occasionally furnished with a hearth. Ancillary rooms were used for storage and cooking (Demakopoulou and Konsola 1975; Aravantinos 2002). Apsidal ones sometimes have a central column or pillar (Demakopoulou and Konsola 1975). Domestic features include exterior calderims (Demakopoulou 1978), bothroi, raised platforms (Andrikou 2000a, 2000b), and vessel placements (Aravantinos 2002; Peperaki 2000). The EH II Fortified Building stands out by virtue of its large (18 m long, 7.2 m wide) Corridor House plan. It consists of four axially arranged rooms with off-center doors and a possible upper story and is entered from a long side through a corridor (Aravantinos 1986). In general, tiles are not reported, though are illustrated in one case (Symeonoglou 1966a, figure 13).

In situ grinding stones, charred grain, and organic residues point to food production and storage (Symeonoglou 1966a; Demakopoulou 1976a; Peperaki 2000; Roumpou et al. 2007), whereas terracotta spindle whorls, loomweights, and spools (Symeonoglou 1966a; Aravantinos 1983a; Peperaki 2000) testify to domestic cloth production. Obsidian implements were produced from nuclei (Demakopoulou 1975a, 1976a; Christopoulou 2000; Peperaki 2000). A steatite mold for impressing patterns (animals, ships, insects) on soft metal, found in secondary use in a Late Helladic context (Demakopoulou 1973–1974e), has Troy IV parallels and possibly hints at the local production of sheet metal ornaments. A hoard of carpentry bronze tools (Konsola 1981, 139, figure 9; cf. Aravantinos 2004b) suggests craft specialization, as well as the valuable nature of such tools.

Gold, silver, ivory (Demakopoulou and Konsola 1975; Spyropoulos 1970b; Peperaki 2000; Aravantinos 1982b), and Cycladic-style artifacts (e.g., incised pyxides, marble vessels; cf. Demakopoulou 1976a, 1979a; Aravantinos 1982b) relate to long-distance trade. However, frying pans and a miniature folded-arms figurine of bone (Andrikou 1998b) are probably local imitations that hint at cultural ties with the Cyclades. No marble figurines have been found at Thebes to date. The interpretation of terracotta 'anchors' (Demakopoulou 1976a) is uncertain, as these objects could be either cultic (votives, figurines) or utilitarian (weights, hangers).

Early Helladic graves are rarely found (Touloupa 1964b, 1964c; Demakopoulou and Konsola 1975; Aravantinos 2004a), as elsewhere on the mainland. The known examples are cists or pits between or under houses and contained contracted burials with few or no furnishings. A mass grave at the Museum site dating to the end of EH II contained fifteen burials (cf. Vika and Richards in press), some furnished with pottery; the bodies were laid in various overlapping positions within the confines of the apsidal house atop its elevation debris. An EBA mud-brick terrace or tumulus (32 m long, 14 m wide) was built over the apsidal house and the mass burial and was later cut into by MBA cists (Aravantinos 2004a, 2004b; Aravantinos and Psaraki in press a, b).

A similar arrangement may be attested at the Ampheion hill, where remains of rock-cut EBA pits and an EBA superimposing mud-brick platform or tumulus have been found (figure 52.1; Faraklas 1967a; Spyropoulos 1981, 47). A large cist tomb at the site, the so-called tomb of Amphion and Zethos (cf. Loucas and Loucas 1987), seems to have been dug into the mud-brick structure and possibly dates to the MBA. The Ampheion tumulous has been implausibly interpreted as an Egyptianizing step pyramid (Spyropoulos 1981, 52; 2008; cf. Bernal 1988, 18; 2001, 73).

Differences in the quality of architecture, the rarity of special features and boundary walls, the limited distribution of imported commodities or artifacts made of exotic materials, and the hoarding of bronze tools indicate social complexity and differentiation, though not necessarily full-fledged stratification. The Fortified Building demonstrates a level of sophistication that is consistent with the advanced urbanistic features and 'international' outlook of EBA Thebes. Its potential significance as an elite residence and/or redistributive center is hinted at by its architectural parallels (see contributions in Hägg and Konsola 1986), but its function is not elucidated by the finds. In general, sealings have not been found in EBA Thebes, although a stone seal with linear decoration has been reported from the Museum apsidal site (Aravantinos 2002).

The Middle Bronze Age and the Shaft Grave Period

Middle Bronze Age finds are reported from eighty plots on the Kadmeia (figure 52.1), which demonstrates the expansion of the settlement to the east and west, reaching 19–20 ha in this era (Dakouri-Hild 2001a). Usage of precipitous areas (e.g., to the south and northwest of Pouros and at the east and west foothills) (e.g., Symeonoglou 1966b; Demakopoulou 1973–1974a, 1978) could suggest that space available for new construction was becoming scarce at the central, south, and southeastern parts of the citadel, where habitation was evidently dense.

Konsola (1981, 152–54) distinguishes three habitation phases based on ceramic material: MH I, associated with Gray Minyan rounded cups and kantharoi with ribbed handles, as well as Black Minyan/Argive and Adriatic incised wares; MH II–IIIA, characterized by Gray Minyan carinated kantharoi and ring-stemmed goblets and simple Matt-painted pottery; and MH IIIB–LH I (Shaft Grave period), typified by Gray Minyan cups and kantharoi with tall handles and 'beak's hawk' rims, fine Matt-painted and Polychrome pottery, and Vapheio cups in various wares. Conflagration strata are reported but are not always datable to a specific phase (Spyropoulos 1969a; Demakopoulou 1973–1974d; Andrikou 1999a). A house at the south Kadmeia was destroyed by fire, possibly preceded by an earthquake, in the advanced Shaft Grave period (Aravantinos 1981b). A megaron-like house burned down in MH IIIB–LH I; an earlier MBA destruction horizon is attested at the same site (Touloupa 1965b).

Both apsidal and straight-sided houses have come to light, sometimes side by side (Demakopoulou and Konsola 1975). The former are less frequent, but both have been dated to the MH II–IIIA and MH IIIB–LH I phases (Konsola 1981, 154). A house at the center of the citadel (Touloupa 1965b; Faraklas 1966) stands out due to its megaroid plan (9.30 m long, 5.5 m wide). It probably dates to the MH IIIB–LH I phase and consists of two axially arranged rooms (cf. Dakouri-Hild 2001a, figure 9). Its orientation and layout appear to have been determined by an earlier MBA building at the site.

In general, houses have deep stone foundations (Symeonoglou 1973, 13), mudbrick elevations, clay-plastered interior walls (Aravantinos 1983b), and troddenearth or clay floors. Roofing materials such as timber logs are occasionally reported (Faraklas 1968a). Domestic features include bothroi (e.g., Sampson 1980; Spyropoulos 1971a), benches (Symeonoglou 1973, 13), hearths and ovens (Demakopoulou and Konsola 1975), and vessel placements (Aravantinos 2005c). The distribution of domestic/intramural versus burial/extramural assemblages has been regarded as evidence for the existence of a mud-brick enceinte (Symeonoglou 1985, 19–23). However, excavation data contradict a clear-cut distinction between domestic and burial space (Dakouri-Hild 2001a). There is no evidence of an enceinte or other large-scale work, although the expansion of the settlement over the northwest and northeast slopes implies some localized terracing.

Obsidian and chert flakes and nuclei testify to the ongoing production of stone implements within individual households (Demakopoulou and Konsola 1975; Demakopoulou 1978; Aravantinos 1981a). Bone ornaments such as inlays, pendants, and pommels may be local products (Demakopoulou and Konsola 1975; Demakopoulou 1978), though a diamond-shaped decorated inlay, reportedly of ivory (Demakopoulou and Konsola 1975), is a possible import. Plant remains, including grain and vetch, and stone tools such as grindstones and pounders (Demakopoulou and Konsola 1975; Demakopoulou 1976b; Aravantinos 1981b, 2005c) are associated with food preparation and storage. Cylindrical loomweights connected to cloth production are occasionally reported (e.g., Spyropoulos 1971a).

Domestic burials are common and not reserved for infants. Stone-built cists and mud-brick- or clay-lined pits were used for burials of both children and adults. Pithos burials usually contain children, but there are exceptions (Piteros 1983). All three types are found under floors or between houses (e.g., Demakopoulou 1975a) and occasionally form crowded domestic graveyards (Demakopoulou 1978), which could relate to kin land tenure (Dakouri-Hild 2001a). Graves typically contain single interments and were evidently reused (Touloupa 1965a; Demakopoulou and Konsola 1975). Burials are in the contracted position and furnished only with pottery, if at all. Dense and extensive cist clusters along the eastern (Touloupa 1965a; Demakopoulou 1973–1974b; Aravantinos 1999) and northwestern slopes (Aravantinos 2002, 2004a; Aravantinos and Psaraki in press b) highlight a trend toward the segregation of funerary space from the MH III period onward.

A larger cist type is introduced at the end of the MBA (Touloupa 1965a; Faraklas 1968b; Demakopoulou 1973–1974b, c). Such graves are sizeable (1.60–2.5 m long,

1–1.50 m wide) but not very deep (0.90–1.10 m) and are built of large slabs. The Ampheion cist (2.20 m long, 1.15 m wide) is comparable and probably reflects the monumentalizing trends of this era (Demakopoulou and Konsola 1981, 23; Faraklas 1998, 203; cf. Rutter 1993, note 64). Three tombs of the late Shaft Grave period (Kassimi-Soutou 1980; Christopoulou 1988) resemble shaft graves proper. They are unusually large (2.15–6.15 m long, 1.50–2.50 m wide) and deep (1.20–1.90 m), of rectangular or trapezoidal shape, and stone-built or rock-hewn. A small rubble mound (Christopoulou 1988) and a belly-handled amphora (Kassimi-Soutou 1980) reportedly functioned as *semata*, though the latter seems unlikely.

The mortuary deposition of exotic artifacts and, arguably, the expression or construction of social status at death by means of such goods culminates in the MH IIIB–LH I phase. Funerary consumption of imported goods was limited. When present, such commodities sharply contrast with the average mortuary assemblage, suggesting pronounced social inequality and stratification. Infants and children were on occasion furnished with exotica (e.g., Touloupa 1965a; Demakopoulou and Konsola 1975; Demakopoulou 1979b), implying inheritance of social status. Elaborate furnishings include jewelry of gold, silver, glass/faience, amethyst, and carnelian (Touloupa 1965a; Spyropoulos 1969a; Demakopoulou and Konsola 1975; Demakopoulou 1979b; Aravantinos 1982a; Christopoulou 1988). A silver cup is also reported (Christopoulou 1988). Gold jewelry found near and inside the Ampheion cist (Faraklas 1967a; Spyropoulos 1981) find parallels in the Mycenae shaft graves (Dickinson 1977, 97–98; but see Konsola 1981, 140) and further hint at the tomb's MBA date. Bronze weapons, including Type II and Type V/Sesklo spearheads (Kassimi-Soutou 1980; Christopoulou 1988; Aravantinos 2001a, pl. 75a) and a Type A sword (Kassimi-Soutou 1980), horse remains, and boar tusk attachments (Christopoulou 1988; Kassimi-Soutou 1980) are also attested in elite funerary assemblages.

THE LATE BRONZE AGE

Late Bronze Age finds are reported from 127 plots to date, representing a 58% increase in attested sites compared to the MBA. Judging from their distribution, the settlement was dense, especially at the center and along the eastern slopes toward the Strophia riverbank. It was also remarkably extensive, covering at least 32.4 ha (i.e., most of the contemporary plateau except parts of the northwest slope and the citadel's southwest corner) (figure 52.2). Late Helladic habitation on the Kadmeia is also evidenced in hitherto uninhabited areas, some of which are precipitous (e.g., the edges of the west [Aravantinos 2001b] and south [Symeonoglou 1966c] slopes).

Theban chronology is inherently problematic because ceramic assemblages remain unpublished, with a few exceptions (Symeonoglou 1973; Spyropoulos and Chadwick 1975; Andrikou et al. 2006), and evidence from hundreds of plots can be

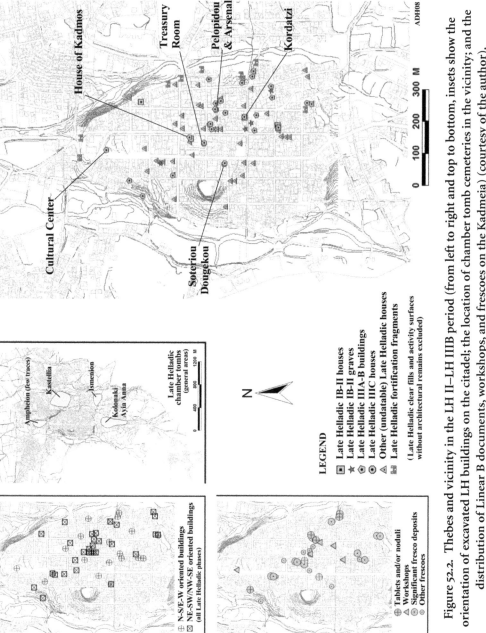

Figure 52.2. Thebes and vicinity in the LH II–LH IIIB period (from left to right and top to bottom, insets show the orientation of excavated LH buildings on the citadel; the location of chamber tomb cemeteries in the vicinity; and the distribution of Linear B documents, workshops, and frescoes on the Kadmeia) (courtesy of the author).

calibrated with difficulty due to the different methodologies and standards employed. Nevertheless, architectural remains that date to LH II (e.g., Demakopoulou 1975b, 1978), LH IIIA2–B1 (e.g., Demakopoulou 1979c; Aravantinos 1982a; Dakouri-Hild 2001b), LH IIIB1 (e.g., Symeonoglou 1973; Piteros 1983; Sampson 1985), late LH IIIB2 possibly on the transition to LH IIIC (e.g., Spyropoulos and Chadwick 1975; Piteros 1983; Aravantinos et al. in preparation; see Vitale 2006 on the late LH IIIB2–early LH IIIC transition), and later LH IIIC (e.g., Spyropoulos 1970c; Spyropoulos and Chadwick 1975, 20) hint at the chronological complexity of LBA habitation on the Kadmeia.

Accordingly, fire horizons in twenty-one plots vary in date (LH IIIA2–B1, LH IIIB1, late LH IIIB2). Destruction by earthquake is reported in at least two datable contexts, in LH IIIB1 (Sampson 1985) and late LH IIIB2 (Spyropoulos 1972b). It is likely that the citadel was fortified after a destruction in late LH IIIA2 or transitional LH IIIA2–B1 (Aravantinos 1988).

The thorny issue of palatial topography (cf. Demakopoulou 1988) is in reality a chronological problem. In the absence of published stratigraphies and pottery, architectural criteria (e.g., alignment) have been utilized to determine the relative date of buildings (Symeonoglou 1973, 1985; Spyropoulos and Chadwick 1975), especially the so-called House of Kadmos/Old Palace and the Treasury Room/New Palace (together referred to as 'the Kadmeion') (figure 52.2).

The distinction between an old and a new palace, ultimately deriving from the legends of Kadmos and the Epigonoi and bequeathed to later scholarship by Antonios Keramopoullos (1909, 1930), has proven to be influential in later excavations and research (for discussion, Dakouri-Hild 2001b; Aravantinos 2006). This notion was first challenged when a study of the House of Kadmos stirrup-jars placed the destruction of that building in LH IIIB1 (Raison 1968, 50–59), that is, close to the purported destruction of the Treasury Room (Touloupa 1964a, 1965b; Platon and Touloupa 1964a).

Comprehensive study of the bulk of pottery from the former site (Dakouri-Hild 2001b, in press b, in preparation) supports the notion that it burned during the transitional LH IIIA2–B1 period (Mylonas 1936; Catling et al. 1980). On the other hand, the buildings at the Soteriou-Dougekou plot and Pelopidou street (figure 52.2) were destroyed in late LH IIIB2 possibly on the transition to LH IIIC (Spyropoulos and Chadwick 1975; Andrikou et al. 2006). Buildings that accommodated palatial functions and finds (documents, workshop material) were affected by fire in LH IIIA2–B1, LH IIIB1, and late LH IIIB2 (see earlier).

Determining which building is part of 'the palace' and which is not becomes problematic, at least on the basis of architecture. Except for the House of Kadmos, which features half-timbered ashlar masonry, and the Treasury Room, which seemingly belongs to a massive building, architectural remains, even those associated with Linear B documents, weapon hoards, and fine workshop material, are not obviously palatial. Layouts range from tripartite buildings (Touloupa 1965a; Spyropoulos and Chadwick 1975; Sampson 1985) to corridor magazines (Aravantinos 1983b; Piteros 1983) to room clusters (Aravantinos, Godart, and Sacconi 2001). Orientation is not a chronological or palatial criterion but possibly relates to local geomorphology: east-west/north-south oriented buildings are dispersed throughout the Kadmeia, including its north and south edges, but northeast-southwest/northwest-southeast buildings are concentrated toward the center (figure 52.2, inset). The combined distribution of Linear B deposits (cf. Aravantinos 2007, in press), workshops, treasuries, and pictorial wall-paintings on the Kadmeia reveals a wide network of palatial activities and elite residences dispersed in the settlement (figure 52.2, inset). However, an architecturally integral palace of Peloponnesian type has yet to be found.

Given the spread and density of architectural remains on the Kadmeia, the rarity of houses beyond it (Spyropoulos 1972c), and the funerary nature of the areas immediately to the east, southeast, and south, it seems likely that the main settlement was intramural. Stone-built and rock-cut aqueducts, sometimes containing terracotta pipes (e.g., Keramopoullos 1917, 327–28; Symeonoglou 1966d; Faraklas 1967g) probably transported water to the citadel from the north, but their precise course (cf. Symeonoglou 1985, 50; Knauss 1995, figure 6) is unclear.

In a similar vein, the evidence on the fortification is too patchy to allow a complete reconstruction (cf. Symeonoglou 1985, 14–38), although fortification segments have come to light along the north and east slopes (figure 52.2). The best evidence comes from the southeast slope, where a thick (4.20–5 m) wall founded in a trench has been excavated (Aravantinos 1988). The wall is constructed of roughly dressed limestone blocks set in roughly horizontal courses, with a rubble and soil fill, and showed corners and traces of a square bastion along the 13.50 m of its excavated course. The fortification and a possible second bastion have been traced elsewhere on the east slope (Keramopoullos 1917, 207, 306–307; Symeonoglou 1965; Sampson 1981a; Aravantinos 1988, note 36). Reports of Cyclopean masonry in the Museum area (cf. Keramopoullos 1917, 272; Spyropoulos 1970d; Sampson 1981b) are corroborated by the discovery of a large segment west of the Museum (Aravantinos 2005b), which has offsets and was built in LH IIIA2–B1.

The construction of LH buildings upon or into earlier strata, on brought fills and terraces, leveled stereo, or a combination thereof, seem to have modified the natural landscape of Thebes considerably. Buildings have roughly dressed limestone socles reaching 1.10–1.70 m in width, mud-brick elevations, which are frequently half-timbered, and either flat or pitched/tiled roofs (cf. Demakopoulou 1990). The Kadmeion buildings almost certainly had an upper storey, as—most likely—did numerous other buildings. Floors are usually of trodden earth or clay plaster, though sometimes flagstones (Piteros 1983), lime plaster (Dakouri-Hild 2001b), or mud-brick slabs arranged in a geometric pattern (Aravantinos 1982a, pl. 101b; pers. comm.) are employed. Installations and facilities include shelves and benches (e.g., Spyropoulos and Chadwick 1975, 22), drains and a possible tank (e.g., Faraklas 1966; Symeonoglou 1973, 14), hearths and ovens (Demakopoulou 1975c; Aravantinos et al. in preparation), worktops (Demakopoulou 1973–1974e, 1980), placements for storage vessels (Faraklas 1966, 1968d), and asaminthoi (Platon and Touloupa 1964a; Spyropoulos and Chadwick 1975, 37; Piteros 1983; Andrikou 2000b).

Domestic assemblages include, other than pottery, spindle whorls and loomweights (e.g., Spyropoulos and Chadwick 1975, 38; Demakopoulou 1980), whetstones, grindstones, knives and chisels (Aravantinos 1981a; Aravantinos et al. in preparation), and traces of food remains (e.g., grain, figs, and olives) (Faraklas 1966; Spyropoulos 1970c; Piteros 1983; cf. Aravantinos et al. in preparation). Mollusks and animal bones are plentiful but are rarely included in publications (contributions in Aravantinos et al. in preparation; Dakouri-Hild in preparation).

Possible evidence of cultic activity is scant and not well understood (cf. Aravantinos 1988, note 48). Notably, cultic paraphernalia (fragments of a large idol and an anthropomorphic vessel) were brought to light in the vicinity of workshops (Demakopoulou 1974; Andrikou 2000b), but their precise context is unclear at present.

Wall-painting fragments have been found in twenty-four plots (figure 52.2, inset), mostly in the north central and southeast Kadmeia (cf. Spyropoulos 1971b; Boulotis 2000). Nine of these, in the Kadmeion area (Reusch 1948, 1953, 1956; Touloupa 1964a, 1965b; Aravantinos 1996b), the east and southeast Kadmeia (Spyropoulos 1969b, 1970e, 1972b; Aravantinos 1982a, 2005e), and the northwest slope (Symeonoglou 1966e; Spyropoulos 1969c) have yielded significant deposits. The northwest slope deposit appears to be a wall-painting dump consisting of burnt and unburnt pieces, which might well originate from the Kadmeion area a short 110–130 m (direct distance) to the southeast. In general, there are fragments with patterns (quirks, curved bands, wavy lines, dots, concentric circles, metopes, spirals and spiral waves, rosettes, tricurved arches, dadoes, possibly figure-eight shields), floral motifs (papyrus, palm tree), possible Nilotic scenes (ducks and other birds), seascapes with dolphins, hunting scenes, animals (dog/goat and feline feet), female processions (life-size at least in two cases), garments, including a man's chiton, and a miniature scene depicting a helmeted, bearded warrior in a window.

The Theban documents (352) are clay noduli and tablets—both the leaf and page type, though usually the former (Aravantinos, Godart, and Sacconi 2001, 2002; Aravantinos et al. 2005). The 56 inscribed noduli, which play a special role in Theban administration (Palaima 2000; cf. Eder 2007), carry seal and signet ring impressions and record mostly livestock collected and redistributed for a major state feast (Killen 1992, 1994; Palaima 2004; cf. Bendall 2007, 56; for a different interpretation, see Aravantinos 1987). They reportedly date to LH IIIB1 (Piteros, Olivier, and Melena 1990), but a late LH IIIB2 bowl from the same context (Piteros 1983; cf. Spyropoulos and Chadwick 1975, ph. 61; Andrikou 1999b, 93) and epigraphic connections with LH IIIB2 documents from the Treasury Room (Aravantinos, Godart, and Sacconi 2007) raise questions. Three inscribed noduli and two tablets were excavated in the Treasury Room in a late LH IIIB2 context; they deal with leather good collections, livestock, possibly timber, and allocations of an unknown commodity (Aravantinos 1996b, 2001c).

The 16 Soteriou-Dougekou tablets record wool allocations to various entities, including industrial facilities of sanctuaries (Spyropoulos and Chadwick 1975; Nosch 2001–2002, in press; Shelmerdine 1997). Furthermore, 24 tablets recording an overdue commodity (possibly an olive product [Palaima in press] rather than cuirasses as originally proposed) originate from the west side of the so-called Arsenal (Chadwick 1970; Olivier 1971). Additional fragments were found later, in a late LH IIIB2 context (Aravantinos, Godart, and Sacconi 2002, 13). Two more tablets, one recording textiles, the other registering large quantities of grain and olives—or assessing land (Killen 1999)—at Thebes, Eutresis, Eleon, and other places, were found to the northeast of the Arsenal (Aravantinos 1994), adding up to a total of 38 tablets from the site.

The bulk of the Theban corpus (236 tablets) derives from the Pelopidou street excavation, west of the Arsenal. These documents deal mostly with festive allocations of food, as well as wool allocations, livestock, food and leather acquisitions, and inventories. The interpretation of these documents, especially the divine nature of certain recipients, has been the subject of intense debate. They appear to be connected with religious banqueting and related activities, but do not seem to record cultic activities per se (e.g., offerings) (see contributions in Deger-Jalkotzy and Panagl 2006; cf. Bendall 2007, 63). The context is late LH IIIB2, which places some doubt on the dating of the main Arsenal deposit in LH IIIA2 or LH IIIB1 (Touloupa 1965a). An isolated tablet fragment from a clear LH IIIB2, context at the northwest slope of the citadel (Aravantinos 2001b; 2002, 15) suggests a wide spread of administrative activity (figure 52.2, inset).

In contrast to these documents, the painted inscriptions (seventy) on the House of Kadmos transport stirrup-jars are the product of Cretan palatial administration. They illuminate the economic geography and administrative practices of (mostly west) Crete in LH IIIB, as well as maritime trade between Crete and the mainland. The provenance of these vessels has been ardently disputed, mostly on the basis of scientific methodology (Catling and Millett 1965, 1969; Catling and Jones 1977; contra McArthur and McArthur 1974; Wilson 1976; McArthur 1978). It now seems clear that the majority were imported from west and, in part, central Crete (Catling et al. 1980; Day and Haskell 1995; Mommsen et al. 2002). Although most stirrup-jars were not made in Thebes, a group of Boeotian pseudo-transport stirrup-jars (Day and Haskell 1995) and other pottery from the House of Kadmos may well have been made at the pottery workshop of that site. Chemical analyses of a large sample of transport and pseudo-transport stirrup-jars, drinking vessels, and waste material from the kiln are expected to clarify ceramic production and consumption in the palatial ambit (Dakouri-Hild et al. in preparation).

At least five workshops operated on the LH IIIA–B Kadmeia (cf. Dakouri-Hild 2005) (figure 52.2, inset). The Kordatzi workshop (LH IIIB1) produced elaborate artifacts of various stones (lapis lazuli, steatite, quartz, agate), mother of pearl, and gold and included a small furnace. A nearby deposit of exquisite but burnt and shattered ivory artifacts (Symeonoglou 1973, 44–62) is not directly linked to the workshop. The Loukou (LH IIIB1?; Sampson 1980, 1985) and Tzortzi workshops (LH IIIA2–B1; Demakopoulou 1979c, 1988) seemingly specialized in ivory and possibly gold working. A group of stone weights was found in the former workshop (Aravantinos 1995; Aravantinos and Alberti 2006). The Koropouli workshop (LH IIIB1; Demakopoulou 1973–1974e, 1974) produced stone (quartz, agate) and metal jewelry, possibly also ivory and bone ornaments. The Cultural Center site on the northwest slope has yielded evidence of ivory-artifact production and boar-tusk harvesting (LH IIIB2; Andrikou 2000b; Snyder and Andrikou 2001). Chemical analyses indirectly illuminate the Theban production of glass (Nikita and Henderson 2006, in press); a mold for making glass jewelry has been reported (Piteros 1983), and glass artifacts have been found in several workshops, (as well as domestic spaces), but at the moment it is unclear where the production of such ornaments took place.

Mistaken or worn artifacts, roughouts, by-products, and raw material, evidently deriving from workshops elsewhere on the Kadmeia, have been found in a hoarding/ storage context (Dakouri-Hild 2006, in press a). Among other artifacts in storage at palatial sites are fine ivory throne legs, furniture parts and equestrian ornaments/ equipment (Platon and Touloupa 1964b; Aravantinos 1999, 2000; Papadaki in preparation), bronze weapons, and corslet parts (Touloupa 1964d, 1965a; Andrikou 2007), jewelry in various precious and semi-precious materials (Touloupa 1964a, 1965b), and orientalia (Aravantinos 2001c, 2005a, 2006), including the famous cache of lapis lazuli cylinder seals (Old Babylonian, Syrian-Mitannian, Kassitic; cf. Platon and Touloupa 1964a; Porada 1981). Several of the latter show traces of alteration, which probably took place in Cyprus before Theban artisans had a chance to rework them (Cline 1994, 154–60). Lapis lazuli cylinder seals were evidently reworked at Thebes to make inlays (Symeonoglou 1973, 67) and beads (Porada 1981, 4).

The latest attested prehistoric burial on the Kadmeia (LH IIIA1) is that of a child (Aravantinos 2005b). The main LBA cemeteries, which consist of chamber tombs, are situated in hills near the citadel (figure 52.2, inset). The shift from intramural to extramural graves occurred in LH IIA, if not earlier (cf. Keramopoullos 1910, 231); citadel and chamber tomb cemeteries must have coexisted for some time. Mikro and Megalo Kastelli to the east accommodated at least forty-two tombs used in LH IIB–LH IIIB (Keramopoullos 1917, 108–11; and numerous reports, Deltion 1967–1973). Ten graves (LH II–LH IIIB) have been brought to light at the Ismenion hill to the south (Keramopoullos 1917, 80–97; Faraklas 1967c, d), whereas thirty-nine graves spanning LH IIA–LH IIIC have been excavated at Kolonaki/Ayia Anna to the south (Keramopoullos 1917, 126–205, with references to earlier excavations; Faraklas 1967d, 1968c). Damaged chamber tombs have also been identified at Ampheion (Faraklas 1967b). Graves of other types are reported at Myloi, Moschopodi, and Agioi Theodoroi to the east and northeast (Keramopoullos 1910; 1917, 100; Symeonoglou 1985, 260, 263), possibly west of the Kadmeia (Keramopoullos 1910), and at Potniai (Papadaki 2000). An ongoing mapping project aims at clarifying the topography of the cemeteries, especially the location of tombs excavated in the late 19th and early 20th centuries (Aravantinos and Fappas in press); some additional study of excavated assemblages has taken place (Tzavella-Evjen and Stultz 1997).

The chamber tombs show various plans and roof types (e.g., vaulted, flat, or pitched) and have benches, drains, and floor pits. They vary significantly in size (1.32–23 m², with 3–18 m long dromoi). Two tombs stand out for their unusually large dimensions (40–80 m², dromoi 18–25 m in length; Faraklas 1967f; Spyropoulos 1972a). One of these tombs had wall-paintings (funerary procession, rocky landscape, and decorative designs), suggesting the high status of the owner(s), though traces of simpler wall-paintings have been found in other Theban graves as well (cf. Keramopoullos 1917, 159; Faraklas 1967e; Spyropoulos 1973). Although many tombs were looted in antiquity, surviving furnishings are plentiful and opulent (e.g., fine pottery, stone jewelry and vases, amber and ivory artifacts, bronze weapons, vessels and tools, gold jewelry, glass and faience artifacts, aegyptiaca [cf. Cline 1994, 172, 189, 206–207] and fragments of terracotta asaminthoi or larnakes [Keramopoullos 1917, 92; Faraklas 1967e; Spyropoulos 1972a]).

In sum, archaeological research at Thebes over the last century has been very fruitful despite the limitations posed by the configuration of excavations. Comprehensive study of Theban material has taken off in the last twenty years and continues to address publication needs. Anthropological, zooarchaeological, and archaeometric studies, which represent some of the innovative approaches in current research, are especially welcome as they reintroduce the human and environmental dimensions of assemblages into archaeological interpretation.

BIBLIOGRAPHY

Alram-Stern, Eva. 2004. *Die Ägäische Frühzeit. 2. Serie Forschungsbericht 1975–2002. 2. Band, Teil 1, 2 Die Frühbronzezeit in Griechenland mit Ausnahme von Kreta.* Vienna: Verlag der Österreichischen Akademie der Wissenschaften.

Andrikou, Eleni. 1998a. "Οικόπεδο Δημ. Λάμπρου." *Αρχαιολογικό Δελτίο* 48 B: 173–76.

———. 1998b. "An EH figurine from Thebes, Boeotia." *BSA* 93: 103–106.

———. 1999a. "Οικόπεδο Πουλιοπούλου." *Αρχαιολογικό Δελτίο* 49 B: 276–77.

———. 1999b. "The Pottery from the Destruction Layer of the Linear B Archive in Pelopidou Street, Thebes," appendix in Vassilis Aravantinos, "Mycenaean Texts and Contexts at Thebes: The Discovery of New Linear B Archives on the Kadmeia." In *Floreant Studia Mycenaea: Akten des X Internationalen Mykenologischen Colloquiums in Salzburg (vom 1–5 Mai 1995),* ed. Sigrid Deger-Jalkotzy, Stefan Hiller, and Oswald Panagl, 45–102. Vienna: Verlag der Österreichischen Akademie der Wissenschaften.

———. 2000a. "Νέα στοιχεία για την κατοίκηση στη Θήβα την Πρώιμη Εποχή του Χαλκού: αψιδωτό κτήριο στο οικόπεδο του δημοτικού συνεδριακού κέντρου Θηβαίων." In *Γ' Διεθνές Συνέδριο Βοιωτικών Μελετών (Θήβα, 4–8 Σεπτεμβρίου 1996),* ed. Vassilis Aravantinos, 173–91. Vol. Γ:α. Athens: Society of Boeotian Studies.

———. 2000b. "Συμβολή οδών Λ. Μπέλλου και Ι. Θρεψιάδου." *Αρχαιολογικό Δελτίο* 50 B: 290–94.

———. 2007. "New Evidence on Mycenaean Bronze Corselets from Thebes in Boeotia and the Bronze Age Sequence of Corselets in Greece and Europe." In *BABS,* 401–409.

———, Vassilis Aravantinos, Louis Godart, Anna Sacconi, and Joanita Vroom. 2006. *Thèbes fouilles de la Cadmée II.2. Les tablettes en Linéaire B de la Odos Pelopidou. Le contexte archéologique. La céramique de la Odos Pelopidou et la chronologie du Linéaire B.* Rome: Istituti Editoriali e Poligrafici Internazionali.

Aravantinos, Vassilis. 1981a. "Οδός Αμφίονος 25 και Οιδίποδος (οικόπεδο Δημ. Μπλάνα)." *Αρχαιολογικό Δελτίο* 36 B: 189.

———. 1981b. "Οδός Δίρκης 23 (οικόπεδο Κων. Γκέλη)." *Αρχαιολογικό Δελτίο* 36 B: 188–89.

———. 1982a. "Οδός Δίρκης και Ευριδίκης (οικόπεδο αφών Στάικου)." *Αρχαιολογικό Δελτίο* 37 B: 165.

———. 1982b. "Οδός Πελοπίδου 26 και Οιδίποδος (οικόπεδο Μητρόπολης Θηβών, πρώην Αφών Ξύδη)." *Αρχαιολογικό Δελτίο* 37 B: 165–67.

———. 1983a. "Οδός Πελοπίδου 27 (οικόπεδο Σταμ. Παυλογιαννόπουλου και Ι. Γκοβεδάρου)." *Αρχαιολογικό Δελτίο* 38 B: 131.

———. 1983b. "Οδός Οιδίποδος και πάροδος Π. Οικονόμου (οικόπεδο Ε. και Μ. Χριστοδούλου)." *Αρχαιολογικό Δελτίο* 38 B: 129–30.

———. 1986. "The Fortified Building at Thebes." In *Early Helladic Architecture*, 57–63.

———. 1987. "The Mycenaean Inscribed Sealings from Thebes: Preliminary Notes." In *Tractata Mycenaea: Proceedings of the Eighth International Colloquium on Mycenaean Studies (Held in Ohrid, 15–20 September 1985)*, ed. Petar Hr. Ilievski and Ljiljana Crepajac, 13–27. Skopje: Macedonian Academy of Sciences and Arts.

———. 1988. "Η μυκηναϊκή οχύρωση της Καδμείας: προκαταρκτική ανακοίνωση." In *Α' Διεθνές Συνέδριο Βοιωτικών Μελετών (Θήβα, 10–14 Σεπτεμβρίου 1986)*, ed. Alexandros Bekiaris, 113–36. Vol. Α:α. Athens: Society of Boeotian Studies.

———. 1994. " 'Οπλοθήκη' (οικόπεδο Δ. Παυλογιαννόπουλου, οδός Πελοπίδου 28)." *Αρχαιολογικό Δελτίο* 49 B: 274–76.

———. 1995. "Μυκηναϊκά σταθμά από την Θήβα: συμβολή στη μελέτη του μυκηναϊκού μετρικού συστήματος." In *Β' Διεθνές Συνέδριο Βοιωτικών Μελετών (Λειβαδιά, 6–10 Σεπτεμβρίου 1992)*, ed. Alexandra Christopoulou, 7–137. Vol. Β:α. Athens: Society of Boeotian Studies.

———. 1996a. "Problemi di conservazione e valorizzazione dei siti archeologici della Beozia." In *I siti archeologici: Un problema di musealizzazione all'aperto,* ed. Bruna Amendolea, Rosanna Cazzella and Laura Indrio, 397–98. Rome: Multigrafica.

———. 1996b. "Καδμείο-'Δωμάτιο του Θησαυρού.'" *Αρχαιολογικό Δελτίο* 51 B: 262–64.

———. 1999. "Οπλοθήκη (οικόπεδο Δ. Παυλογιαννόπουλου, οδός Πελοπίδου 28)." *Αρχαιολογικό Δελτίο* 49 B: 274–76.

———. 2000. "Νέα μυκηναϊκά ελεφαντουργήματα από την Καδμεία (Θήβα)." In *Γ' Διεθνές Συνέδριο Βοιωτικών Μελετών (Θήβα, 4–8 Σεπτεμβρίου 1996)*, ed. Vassilis Aravantinos, 31–120. Vol. Γ:α. Athens: Society of Boeotian Studies.

———. 2001a. "Οικόπεδο Αρχαιολογικού Μουσείου Θηβών." *Αρχαιολογικό Δελτίο* 51 B: 259–61.

———. 2001b. "Οδός Αγίων Αποστόλων και Κάδμου-έργα ΔΕΥΑΘ." *Αρχαιολογικό Δελτίο* 51 B: 266–67.

———. 2001c. "Contenu, contexte et fonction du 'trésor' du palais mycénien de Thèbes (Béotie): une approche économique et administrative." *Ktema* 26: 87–99.

———. 2002. "Οικόπεδο Αρχαιολογικού Μουσείου Θηβών." *Αρχαιολογικό Δελτίο* 52 B: 353–59.

———. 2004a. "Οικόπεδο Αρχαιολογικού Μουσείου." *Αρχαιολογικό Δελτίο* 53 B: 323–27.

———. 2004b. "New evidence about the EH II period in Thebes: a new architectural complex and a group burial within the Kadmeia." In *Die Ägäische Frühzeit. 2. Serie Forschungsbericht 1975–2002. 2. Band Teil 2 Die Frühbronzezeit in Griechenland mit Ausnahme von Kreta*, ed. Eva Alram-Stern, 1255–67. Vienna: Verlag der Österreichischen Akademie der Wissenschaften.

———. 2005a. "To Have and to Hoard: A Gold Disc from the Palace of Thebes." In *Autochthon*, 252–58.

———. 2005b. "Οικόπεδο επέκτασης Αρχαιολογικού Μουσείου." *Αρχαιολογικό Δελτίο* 54 B: 311–13.

———. 2005c. "Οδός Ζεγγίνη 3, 'Οπλοθήκη.'" *Αρχαιολογικό Δελτίο* 54 B: 313–16.

———. 2005d. "Οδός Οιδίποδος και Πελοπίδου (οικόπεδο Κυλάφη)." *Αρχαιολογικό Δελτίο* 54 B: 316.

———. 2005e. "Οικόπεδο Ε. Σπουρλή." *Αρχαιολογικό Δελτίο* 54 Β: 317–18.

———. 2006. "Le cas de Thèbes (Béotie): Mythe, idéologie, et recherche au début du XXe siècle." In *Mythos: La préhistoire égéenne du XIXe au XXIe siècle après J.-C. Actes de la Table Ronde d'Athènes (novembre 2002)*, ed. Pascal Darcque, Michael Fotiadis, and Olga Polychronopoulou, 165–74. BCH Supplément 46. Athens: L'École française d'Athènes.

———. 2007. "Le iscrizioni in Lineare B rinvenute a Tebe in Beozia. Osservazioni storico-topographiche sulle scoperte." *Pasiphae* I: 9–21.

———. In press. "The Find Places and the Contexts of the Linear B Texts from Thebes." In *Proceedings of the XII Colloquium on Mycenaean Studies, Austin, May 7th–13th, 2000.*

———, and Maria E. Alberti. 2006. "The Balance Weights from the Kadmeia, Thebes." In *Weights in Context: Bronze Age Weighing Systems of the Eastern Mediterranean. Chronology, Typology, Material, and Archaeological Contexts*, ed. Maria E. Alberti, Enrico Ascalone, and Luca Peyronel, 293–313. Rome: Istituto Italiano di Numismatica.

Aravantinos, Vassilis, Maurizio del Freo, Louis Godart, and Anna Sacconi. 2005. *Thèbes fouilles de la Cadmée IV. Les textes de Thèbes (1–433). Translitération et tableaux des scribes.* Rome: Istituti Editoriali e Poligrafici Internazionali.

Aravantinos, Vassilis, and Yiannis Fappas. In press. "Τα μυκηναϊκά νεκροταφεία της Θήβας: σχέδιο προκαταρκτικής μελέτης." *Ρέθυμνα 27 (Επιστημονική Επετηρίδα του Τμήματος Ιστορίας και Αρχαιολογίας του Πανεπιστημίου Κρήτης, Τιμητικός τόμος στον Καθηγητή Νικόλα Φαράκλα).*

Aravantinos, Vassilis, Louis Godart, and Anna Sacconi. 2001. *Thèbes fouilles de la Cadmée I. Les tablettes en Linéaire B de la Odos Pelopidou. Édition et commentaire.* Rome: Istituti Editoriali e Poligrafici Internazionali.

———. 2002. *Thèbes fouilles de la Cadmée III. Corpus des documents d'archives en Linéaire B de Thèbes (1–433).* Rome: Istituti Editoriali e Poligrafici Internazionali.

———. 2007. "La tavoletta TH Uq 434." *Pasiphae* 1: 23–33.

———, Lilian Karali, Anaya Sarpaki, and Athina Papadaki. In preparation. *Thèbes fouilles de la Cadmée II.1. Les tablettes en Linéaire B de la Odos Pelopidou. Le contexte archéologique.* Rome: Istituti Editoriali e Poligrafici Internazionali.

Aravantinos, Vassilis, and Kiki Psaraki. In press a. "Tumuli over Dwellings: The Transformation of Domestic Space to Community Monument at EH II Thebes." In *Ancestral Landscapes: Burial Mounds in the Copper and Bronze Ages (Udine, May 15–18, 2008)*, ed. Sylvie Müller Celka and Elisabetta Borgna. Travaux de la Maison de l'Orient. Lyon: Maison de l'Orient et de la Méditerranée/CNRS.

———. In press b. "Μεσοελλαδικά νεκροταφεία των Θηβών: γενική επισκόπηση και παρατηρήσεις στο φως των νέων ερευνών και ευρημάτων." In *Mesohelladika.*

Bendall, Lisa M. 2007. *Economics of Religion in the Mycenaean World: Resources Dedicated to Religion in the Mycenaean Palace Economy.* Oxford University School of Archaeology Monographs 67. Oxford: Oxford University School of Archaeology.

Bernal, Martin. 1988. *Black Athena: The Afroasiatic Roots of Classical Civilization.* Vol. 1, *The Fabrication of Ancient Greece, 1785–1985.* New Brunswick: Rutgers University Press.

———. 2001. *Black Athena Writes Back: Martin Bernal Responds to His Critics.* Durham: Duke University Press.

Böhlau, Johannes. 1888. "Boötischen Vasen." *JdI* 3: 325–64.

Boulotis, Christos. 2000. "Η τέχνη των τοιχογραφιών στην μυκηναϊκή Βοιωτία." In *Γ' Διεθνές Συνέδριο Βοιωτικών Μελετών (Θήβα, 4–8 Σεπτεμβρίου 1996)*, ed. Vassilis Aravantinos, 1095–1149. Vol. Γ:α. Athens: Society of Boeotian Studies.

Buck, Robert J. 1979. *A History of Boeotia.* Edmonton: University of Alberta Press.

Catling, Hector W., John F. Cherry, Richard E. Jones, and John T. Killen. 1980. "The Linear B–Inscribed Stirrup-jars and West Crete." *BSA* 75: 51–113.

Catling, Hector W., and Richard E. Jones. 1977. "A Re-investigation of the Provenance of the Inscribed Stirrup-jars Found at Thebes." *Archaeometry* 19(2): 137–46.

Catling, Hector W., and Anne Millett. 1965. "A Study of the Inscribed Stirrup-jars from Thebes." *Archaeometry* 8: 3–51.

———. 1969. "Theban Stirrup-jars: Questions and Answers." *Archaeometry* 11: 3–20.

Chadwick, John. 1970. "Linear B Tablets from Thebes." *Minos* 10: 115–37.

Christodoulou, Georgios. 1969. *Ἡ Γεωλογική Δομή τῆς Περιοχῆς Θηβῶν-Παραλίμνης*. Athens: Institute of Geology and Mineral Exploration.

Christopoulou, Alexandra. 1988. "Δύο πρώιμοι μυκηναϊκοί τάφοι στη Θήβα." In *Β' Διεθνές Συνέδριο Βοιωτικών Μελετών (Λειβαδιά, 6–10 Σεπτεμβρίου 1992)*, ed. Alexandra Christopoulou. Vol. Β:α. Athens: Society of Boeotian Studies (abstract).

———. 2000. "Ένα πρωτοελλαδικό σπίτι στην Καδμεία." In *Γ' Διεθνές Συνέδριο Βοιωτικών Μελετών (Θήβα, 4–8 Σεπτεμβρίου 1996)*, ed. Vassilis Aravantinos, 192–202. Vol. Γ:α. Athens: Society of Boeotian Studies.

Cline, Eric H. 1994. *SWDS*.

Dakouri-Hild, Anastasia. 2001a. "Plotting Fragments: A Preliminary Assessment of the Middle Helladic Settlement in Boeotian Thebes." In *Urbanism*, 103–118.

———. 2001b. "The House of Kadmos in Mycenaean Thebes reconsidered: architecture, chronology and context." *BSA* 96: 81–122.

———. 2005. "Breaking the Mould? Production and Economy in the Theban State." In *Autochthon*, 207–24.

———. 2006. "Something Old, Something New: Current Research on the 'Old 'Kadmeion" of Thebes." *BICS* 48: 173–86.

———. In press a. "Εργαστηριακό υλικό από την Οικία του Κάδμου: μια νέα ματιά." In *A Century of Archaeological Work at Thebes (1900–2000): Pioneers and Ongoing Research (Centenary Conference, Thebes, 16–17 November 2002)*, ed. Vassilis Aravantinos and Elena Kountouri. Athens: Ταμείο Αρχαιολογικών Πόρων και Απαλλοτριώσεων.

———. In press b. "Η 'Οικία του Κάδμου': η μέχρι τώρα (2003) έρευνα πάνω στην αρχιτεκτονική και την χρονολόγηση." In *Δ' Διεθνές Συνέδριο Βοιωτικών Μελετών (Λιβαδειά 9–13 Σεπτεμβρίου 2000)*, ed. Vassilis Aravantinos. Athens: Society of Boeotian Studies.

———. In preparation. *The House of Kadmos at Thebes, Greece: The Excavations of Antonios D. Keramopoullos (1906–1929)*. Vol. 1, *Architecture, Stratigraphy, and Finds*. Biblioteca di Pasiphae, Collana di Filologia e Antichità Egea 8. Rome: Istituti Editoriali e Poligrafici Internazionali.

———, Eleni Andrikou, Vassilis Aravantinos, and Elena Kountouri. 2003. "A GIS in Boeotian Thebes: Taking Measures for Heritage Management, Archaeological Research, and Public Outreach." In *METRON*, 49–56.

Dakouri-Hild, Anastasia, Maury Morgenstein, Malia Johnson, and Vassilis Aravantinos. In preparation. "Portable-XRF Analyses of Late Bronze Age Pottery from the House of Kadmos, Thebes."

Day, Peter M., and Halford W. Haskell. 1995. "Transport Stirrup-jars from Thebes as Evidence of Trade in Late Bronze Age Greece." In *Trade and Production in Premonetary Greece: Acquisition and Distribution of Raw Materials and Finished Products. Proceedings of the 6th International Workshop, Athens 1996*, ed. Carole Gillis, Christina Risberg, and Birgitta Sjöberg, 87–107. *SIMA-PB* 154. Jonsered, Sweden: Åström.

Decharme, Paul. 1869. *De Thebanis Artificibus*. Paris: privately published.

Deger-Jalkotzy, Sigrid, and Oswald Panagl, eds. 2006. *Die neuen Linear B-Texte aus Theben: Ihr Aufschlusswert für die mykenische Sprache und Kultur. Akten des internationalen Forschungskolloquiums an der Österreichischen Akademie der Wissenschaften (5.–6. Dezember 2002)*. Vienna: Verlag der Österreichischen Akademie der Wissenschaften.

Demakopoulou, Katie. 1973–1974a. "Ὁδός Δαγλαρίδου 14." *Ἀρχαιολογικόν Δελτίον* 29 B: 439.

———. 1973–1974b. "Ὁδός Πελοπίδου 28." *Ἀρχαιολογικόν Δελτίον* 29 B: 441.

———. 1973–1974c. "Ὁδός Κάδμου 58." *Ἀρχαιολογικόν Δελτίον* 29 B: 439–40.

———. 1973–1974d. "Ὁδός Τσεβᾶ καί Βουρδουμπᾶ." *Ἀρχαιολογικόν Δελτίον* 29 B: 437–38.

———. 1973–1974e. "Ὁδός Πινδάρου 29." *Ἀρχαιολογικόν Δελτίον* 29 B: 430–33.

———. 1974. "Μυκηναϊκόν ἀνακτορικόν ἐργαστήριον εἰς Θήβας." *Ἀρχαιολογικά Ἀνάλεκτα ἐξ Ἀθηνῶν* 7: 162–73.

———. 1975a. "Ὁδός Ἐπαμεινώνδα 58 (οἰκόπεδο Π. Μελετίου)." *Ἀρχαιολογικόν Δελτίον* 30 B: 128–31.

———. 1975b. "Ὁδός Τσεβᾶ 24 (οἰκόπεδο Σπουρλῆ)." *Ἀρχαιολογικόν Δελτίον* 30 B: 128–31.

———. 1975c. "Ὁδός Πελοπίδου 25 (οἰκόπεδο Δημ. Στέφα)." *Ἀρχαιολογικόν Δελτίον* 30 B: 131–33.

———. 1976a. "Οἰκόπεδο Στ. καί Ν. Μανίσαλη." *Ἀρχαιολογικόν Δελτίον* 31 B: 121–25.

———. 1976b. "Οἰκόπεδο Π. Ζουλάμογλου." *Ἀρχαιολογικόν Δελτίον* 31 B: 125–26.

———. 1978. "Οἰκόπεδο Σωτ. Κοροπούλη." *Ἀρχαιολογικό Δελτίο* 33 B: 108–12.

———. 1979a. "Ὁδός Ἀντιγόνης 14 (οἰκόπεδο Α. Λούκου)." *Ἀρχαιολογικό Δελτίο* 34 B: 163–65.

———. 1979b. "Ὁδός Πελοπίδου 5 (οἰκόπεδο Λ. Παυλογιαννόπουλου)." *Ἀρχαιολογικόν Δελτίο* 34 B: 165.

———. 1979c. "Ὁδός Πινδάρου 60 (οἰκόπεδο ἀδελφῶν Τζώρτζη)." *Ἀρχαιολογικό Δελτίο* 34 B: 168.

———. 1980. "Ὁδός Ζεγγίνη 3." *Ἀρχαιολογικό Δελτίο* 35 B: 215–17.

———. 1988. "Τὸ μυκηναϊκό ἀνάκτορο τῆς Θήβας: προβλήματα χρονολόγησης καὶ ταύτισης." In *Α' Διεθνές Συνέδριο Βοιωτικῶν Μελετῶν (Θήβα, 10–14 Σεπτεμβρίου 1986)*, ed. Alexandros Bekiaris, 75–85. Vol. A:α. Athens: Society of Boeotian Studies.

———. 1990. "Palatial and Domestic Architecture in Mycenaean Thebes." In *L'habitat égéen préhistorique*, 308–17.

———, and Dora Konsola. 1975. "Λείψανα πρωτοελλαδικοῦ, μεσοελλαδικοῦ καὶ υστεροελλαδικοῦ οἰκισμοῦ στῆ Θήβα." *Ἀρχαιολογικόν Δελτίον* 30 A: 44–89.

———. 1981. *Ἀρχαιολογικό Μουσείο τῆς Θήβας*. Athens: Ταμείο Ἀρχαιολογικῶν Πόρων καὶ Ἀπαλλοτριώσεων.

Dickinson, Oliver T. P. K. 1977. *The Origins of Mycenaean Civilisation*. SIMA 49. Gothenburg: Åström.

Eder, Birgitta. 2007. "The Power of Seals: Palaces, Peripheries, and Territorial Control in the Mycenaean World." In *BABS*, 35–45.

Fabricius, Ernst. 1890. *Theben: Eine Untersuchung über die Topographie und Geschichte der Hauptstadt Boeotiens*. Freiburg: Akademie Antrittsprogramm.

Faraklas, Nikolaos. 1966. "Καδμεῖον. Οἰκόπεδον Ἀ. καί Σ. Τζώρτζη (Πινδάρου καί Ἀντιγόνης)." *Ἀρχαιολογικόν Δελτίον* 21 B: 177–80.

———. 1967a. "Ἔρευνα τοῦ τύμβου τοῦ Ἀμφείου." *Ἀρχαιολογικόν Δελτίον* 22 B: 229–30.

———. 1967b. "Μυκηναϊκοί τάφοι κατά τόν λόφον τοῦ Ἀμφείου." *Ἀρχαιολογικόν Δελτίον* 22 B: 229.

———. 1967c. "Μυκηναϊκός τάφος λόφου Ἰσμηνίου." *Ἀρχαιολογικόν Δελτίον* 22 B: 227.

———. 1967d. "Ναός Ἰσμηνίου." *Ἀρχαιολογικόν Δελτίον* 22 B: 232–33.

———. 1967e. "Ναός Ταξιαρχῶν." *Ἀρχαιολογικόν Δελτίον* 22 B: 227.

———. 1967f. "Μυκηναϊκοί τάφοι εἰς λόφον Μεγάλο Καστέλλι." Ἀρχαιολογικόν Δελτίον 22 B: 227–28.

———. 1967g. "Οἰκόπεδον ἀδελφῶν Νικολιδάκη." Ἀρχαιολογικόν Δελτίον 22 B: 239.

———. 1968a. "Οἰκόπεδον Π. Λεοντάρη." Ἀρχαιολογικόν Δελτίον 23 B: 208–10.

———. 1968b. "Ἀνασκαφή οἰκοπέδου Ἰ. Παναγιωτοπούλου." Ἀρχαιολογικόν Δελτίον 23 B: 211.

———. 1968c. "Οἰκόπεδον Ἀλεξ. Μαρλάση." Ἀρχαιολογικόν Δελτίον 23 B: 219–20.

———. 1968d. "Θῆβαι: ἀνασκαφή οἰκοπέδου Λιακοπούλου-Κύρτση." Ἀρχαιολογικά Ἀνάλεκτα ἐξ Ἀθηνῶν 1 (3): 241–43.

———. 1969. "Πυρί Θηβῶν." Ἀρχαιολογικόν Δελτίον 24 B: 175–77.

———. 1998. Θηβαϊκά. Ἀρχαιολογική Ἐφημερίς 135. Athens: Archaeological Society of Athens.

Fossey, John M. 1988. Topography and Population of Ancient Boeotia. Vols. 1–2. Chicago: Ares.

Gauvin, Ginette, and John M. Fossey 1985. "Livadhostra: Un relève topographique des fortifications de l'ancienne Kreusis." In La Beotie antique: Actes du Colloque international (Lyon, Saint-Etienne, 16–20 mai 1983), ed. Paul Roesch and Gilbert Argoud, 77–86. Paris: CNRS.

Hägg, Robin, and Dora Konsola, eds. 1986. Early Helladic Architecture.

Heurtley, William A. 1923. "Notes on the Harbours of S. Boeotia and Sea Trade between Boeotia and Corinth in Prehistoric Times." BSA 26: 38–45.

Kassimi-Soutou, Maria. 1980. "Μεσοελλαδικός τάφος πολεμιστή από τη Θήβα." Ἀρχαιολογικό Δελτίο 35 A: 88–101.

Keramopoullos, Antonios. 1909. "Ἡ Οἰκία τοῦ Κάδμου." Ἀρχαιολογική Ἐφημερίς: 57–122.

———. 1910. "Μυκηναϊκοί τάφοι ἐν Αἰγίνῃ καί ἐν Θήβαις." Ἀρχαιολογική Ἐφημερίς: 209–43.

———. 1917. Θηβαϊκά. Ἀρχαιολογικόν Δελτίον 3. Athens: Estia.

———. 1930. "Αἱ βιομηχανίαι καί τό ἐμπόριον τοῦ Κάδμου." Ἀρχαιολογική Ἐφημερίς: 29–58.

Killen, John T. 1992. "Observations on the Thebes Sealings." In Mykenaïka: Actes du IXe Colloque International sur les textes myceniens et egeens organisé par le Centre de l'Antiquité grecque et romaine de la Fondation hellenique des recherches scientifiques et l'École française d'Athènes (Athènes, 2–6 Octobre 1990), ed. Jean-Pierre Olivier, 365–80. BCH Suppl. 25. Athens: L'École française d'Athènes.

———. 1994. "Thebes Sealings, Knossos Tablets, and Mycenaean State Banquets." BICS 39: 67–84.

———. 1999. "Some Observations on the New Thebes Tablets." BICS 43: 217–19.

Knauss, Jost. 1995. "Technical and Historical Aspects of the Unfinished Ancient Drainage Tunnel at the Outmost Northeast Corner of the Kopais Basin." In B' Διεθνές Συνέδριο Βοιωτικῶν Μελετῶν (Λειβαδιά, 6–10 Σεπτεμβρίου 1992), ed. Alexandra Christopoulou, 83–95. Vol. B:α. Athens: Society of Boeotian Studies.

Konsola, Dora. 1981. Προμυκηναϊκή Θήβα. Χωροταξική καὶ Οἰκιστική Διάρθρωση. Athens: privately published.

———. 1986. "Stages of Urban Transformation." In Early Helladic Architecture, 9–19.

Loucas, Ioannis, and Eveline Loucas. 1987. "La tombe des jumeaux divins Amphion et Zethos et la fertilité de la terre béotienne." In Thanatos, 95–106.

McArthur, Jennifer K., and John T. McArthur. 1974. "The Theban Stirrup-jars and East Crete: Further Considerations." Minos 15: 68–80.

McArthur, John T. 1978. "Inconsistencies in the Composition and Provenance Studies of the Inscribed Stirrup-jars Found at Thebes." Archaeometry 20(2): 177–82.

Mommsen, Hans, Eleni Andrikou, Vassilis Aravantinos, and Joseph Maran. 2002. "Neutron Activation Analysis of Bronze Age Pottery from Boeotia including Ten Linear B Inscribed Stirrup-jars of Thebes." In Archaeometry 98: Proceedings of the 31st

Symposium (Budapest, April 26–May 3, 1998), ed. Erzsebet Jerem and Katalin T. Biró, 607–12. *BAR-IS* 1043. Oxford: Archaeopress.

Mylonas, Georgios. 1936. "Ὁ ἐνεπίγραφος ἀμφορεύς τῆς Ἐλευσῖνος καί ἡ ἑλλαδική γραφή." *Ἀρχαιολογική Ἐφημερίς:* 61–100.

Nikita, Kalliopi, and Julian Henderson. 2006. "Glass Analyses from Mycenaean Thebes and Elateia: Compositional Evidence for a Mycenaean Glass Industry." *Journal of Glass Studies* 48: 71–120.

———. In press. "Τεχνολογία και παραγωγή υαλωδών υλικών στη μυκηναϊκή Θήβα." In *Ε' Διεθνές Συνέδριο Βοιωτικών Μελετών (Θήβα, 16–19 Σεπτεμβρίου 2005)*, ed. Vassilis Aravantinos. Athens: Society of Boeotian Studies.

Nosch, Marie-Louise. 2001–2002. "The Textile Industry at Thebes in the Light of the Textile Industries at Pylos and Knossos." *Studia Minora Facultatis Philosophicae Universitatis Brunensis* 6–7: 179–91.

———. In press. "The Textile Industry at Thebes, according to the Linear B Tablets." In *Δ' Διεθνές Συνέδριο Βοιωτικών Μελετών (Λιβαδειά 9–13 Σεπτεμβρίου 2000)*, ed. Vassilis Aravantinos. Athens: Society of Boeotian Studies.

Olivier, Jean-Pierre. 1971. "Notes épigraphiques sur les tablettes en Linéaire B de la série Ug de Thèbes." *Ἀρχαιολογικά Ἀνάλεκτα ἐξ Ἀθηνῶν* 4(2): 269–72.

Palaima, Thomas G. 2000. "The Palaeography of Mycenaean Inscribed Sealings from Thebes and Pylos and Their Place within the Mycenaean Administrative System and Their Links with the Extra-palatial Sphere." In *Minoisch-mykenische Glyptik*, 219–37.

———. 2004. "Sacrificial Feasting in the Linear B Documents." In *The Mycenaean Feast*, ed. James C. Wright, 97–126. Hesperia 73(2). Princeton: American School of Classical Studies at Athens.

———. In press. "The Significance of the Discovery of Linear B Tablets at Thebes: The Pioneering Years." In *A Century of Archaeological Work at Thebes (1900–2000): Pioneers and Ongoing Research (Centenary Conference, Thebes, 16–17 November 2002)*, ed. Vassilis Aravantinos and Elena Kountouri, Athens: Ταμείο Αρχαιολογικών Πόρων και Απαλλοτριώσεων.

Papadaki, Athina. 2000. "Τοπογραφικά και αρχαιολογικά Αρχαίων Ποτνιών (Τάχι, Θηβών)." In *Γ' Διεθνές Συνέδριο Βοιωτικών Μελετών (Θήβα, 4–8 Σεπτεμβρίου 1996)*, ed. Vassilis Aravantinos, 357–69. Vol. Γ:α. Athens: Society of Boeotian Studies.

———. In preparation. Das Elfenbein in mykenischen Theben. PhD diss., University of Heidelberg.

Paton, James M. 1951. *Mediaeval and Renaissance Visitors to Greek Lands*. Princeton: American School of Classical Studies at Athens.

Peperaki, Olia. 2000. "Καθημερινές δραστηριότητες στην πρωτοελλαδική Θήβα. Νέα στοιχεία από την ανασκαφή του οικοπέδου κληρονόμων Απ. Νερούτσου." In *Γ' Διεθνές Συνέδριο Βοιωτικών Μελετών (Θήβα, 4–8 Σεπτεμβρίου 1996)*, ed. Vassilis Aravantinos, 203–18. Vol. Γ:α. Athens: Society of Boeotian Studies.

Piteros, Christos. 1983. "Οδός Οιδίποδος 1 (οικόπεδο Δ. Λιάγκα)." *Αρχαιολογικό Δελτίο* 38 Β: 131–34.

———, Jean-Pierre Olivier, and Jose L. Melena. 1990. "Les inscriptions en Linéaire B des nodules de Thèbes (1982): La fouille, les documents, les possibilités d'interprétation." *BCH* 114: 103–84.

Platon, Nikolaos, and Evi Touloupa. 1964a. "Oriental Seals from the Palace of Cadmus: Unique Discoveries in Boeotian Thebes." *Illustrated London News* (November 28): 859–61.

———. 1964b. "Ivories and Linear-B from Thebes." *Illustrated London News* (December 5): 896–97.

Porada, Edith. 1981. "The Cylinder Seals Found at Thebes in Boeotia, with Contributions on the Inscriptions from Hans G. Güterbock and John A. Brinkman." *Archiv für Orientforschung* 28(1): 1–78.

Psaraki, Kiki. 2004. "A New EH Pottery Assemblage from Thebes." In *Die Ägäische Frühzeit. 2. Serie Forschungsbericht 1975–2002. 2. Band Teil 2, Die Frühbronzezeit in Griechenland mit Ausnahme von Kreta,* ed. Eva Alram-Stern, 1259–66. Vienna: Verlag der Österreichischen Akademie der Wissenschaften.

Raison, Jacques. 1968. *Les vases à inscriptions peintes de l'âge mycénien et leur contexte archéologique.* Incunabula Graeca 19. Rome: Istituto per gli Studi Micenei ed Egeo-Anatolici.

Reusch, Helga. 1948. "Der Frauenfries von Theben." *AA* 63–64: 240–53.

———. 1953. "Ein Schildfresco aus Theben." *AA* 69: 16–25.

———. 1956. *Die zeichnerische Rekonstruktion des Frauenfrieses im boötischen Theben.* Berlin: Akademie Verlag.

Roller, Duane W. 1988. *Early Travellers in Eastern Boeotia.* Amsterdam: Gieben.

Roumpou, Maria, Kiki Psaraki, Vassilis Aravantinos, and Carl Heron. 2007. "Early Bronze Age Cooking Vessels from Thebes: Organic Residue Analysis and Archaeological Implications." In *Cooking Up the Past: Food and Culinary Practices in the Neolithic and Bronze Age Aegean,* ed. Christopher Mee and Josette Renard, 158–73. Oxford: Oxbow.

Rutter, Jeremy B. 1993. "Review of Aegean Prehistory II: The Prepalatial Bronze Age of the Southern and Central Greek Mainland." *AJA* 97(4): 745–97.

Sampson, Adamantios. 1980. "Ὁδός Πελοπίδου (οἰκόπεδο Μ. Λούκου)." *Ἀρχαιολογικό Δελτίο* 35 Β: 218–20.

———. 1981a. "Πάροδος οδού Ιοκάστης (Ο.Τ. 156) (οικόπεδο αδελφών Αντ. και Δημοσθ. Ματάλα)." *Ἀρχαιολογικό Δελτίο* 36 Β: 190–91.

———. 1981b. "Πλατεία Αγίου Ιωάννη (οικόπεδο Βουδικλάρη-Κυριακού)." *Ἀρχαιολογικό Δελτίο* 36 Β: 192–93.

———. 1985. "La destruction d'un atelier palatial mycénien à Thèbes." *BCH* 109: 21–29.

Schläger, Helmut, David Blackman, and Jörg Schaefer. 1968. "Der Hafen von Anthedon mit Beiträgen zur Topographie und Geschichte der Stadt." *AA* 83: 21–102.

Shelmerdine, Cynthia W. 1997. "Workshops and Record Keeping in the Mycenaean World." In *TEXNH,* 387–98.

Snyder, Lynn M., and Eleni Andrikou. 2001. "Raw Material for a Helmet? Evidence for Boar's Tusk Harvesting in a Late Helladic Context, Thebes." *AJA* 105(2): 304 (abstract).

Soteriadis, Georgios. 1900. "Περί τῆς τοπογραφίας τῶν ἀρχαίων Θηβῶν." *Φιλολογικός Σύλλογος Παρνασσός, Ἐπετηρίς* 4: 140–70.

Spyropoulos, Theodoros. 1969a. "Οἰκόπεδον Π. Λεοντάρη." *Ἀρχαιολογικόν Δελτίον* 24 Β: 183.

———. 1969b. "Οἰκόπεδον Κωνστ. Δούρου." *Ἀρχαιολογικόν Δελτίον* 24 Β: 180.

———. 1969c. "Οἰκόπεδον ἀδελφῶν Δαγδελένη." *Ἀρχαιολογικόν Δελτίον* 24 Β: 180–82.

———. 1970a. "Οἰκόπεδον Στάικου." *Ἀρχαιολογικόν Δελτίον* 25 Β: 213–14.

———. 1970b. "Οἰκόπεδον Βρυζάκη." *Ἀρχαιολογικόν Δελτίον* 25 Β: 216–17.

———. 1970c. "Οἰκόπεδον ἀδελφῶν Σταυρῆ." *Ἀρχαιολογικόν Δελτίον* 25 Β: 214–15.

———. 1970d. "Οἰκόπεδον Νικ. Θαλασσινοῦ." *Ἀρχαιολογικόν Δελτίον* 25 Β: 217–18.

———. 1970e. "Οἰκόπεδον Ε. Φίλου." *Ἀρχαιολογικόν Δελτίον* 25 Β: 220.

———. 1971a. "Οἰκόπεδον Χαραλάμπους Βρυζάκη." *Ἀρχαιολογικόν Δελτίον* 26 Β: 202.

———. 1971b. "Μυκηναϊκά τοιχογραφήματα ἐκ Θηβῶν." *Ἀρχαιολογικόν Δελτίον* 26 Α: 104–19.

———. 1972a. "Μεγάλο Καστέλλι." *Ἀρχαιολογικόν Δελτίον* 27 Β: 309–12.

———. 1972b. "Οἰκόπεδον Κωνστ. Γκίκα." *Ἀρχαιολογικόν Δελτίον* 27 Β: 307.

————. 1972c. "Ὁδός 19, Νέαι Θῆβαι (οἰκόπεδον Τριπερίνα)." Ἀρχαιολογικόν Δελτίον 27 Β: 319–21.

————. 1973. "Μεγάλο Καστέλλι." Ἀρχαιολογικόν Δελτίον 28 Β: 252–58.

————. 1981. Ἀμφεῖον. Ἔρευνα καί Μελέτη τοῦ Μνημείου τοῦ Ἀμφείου Θηβῶν. Sparta: privately published.

————. 2008. "Ampheion at Boeotian Thebes: Burial Practices and Ritual Performances in Early Helladic Greece." In Ancestral Landscapes: Burial Mounds in the Copper and Bronze Ages (Udine, May 15–18, 2008) (abstract).

————, and John Chadwick. 1975. Thebes Tablets II. Minos Suppl. 4. Salamanca: Ediciones Universidad de Salamanca.

Symeonoglou, Sarantis. 1965. "Οἰκόπεδον Μαλαθούνη." Ἀρχαιολογικόν Δελτίον 20 Β: 237.

————. 1966a. "Οἰκόπεδον Σταμ. Σταμάτη." Ἀρχαιολογικόν Δελτίον 21 Β: 189–91.

————. 1966b. "Οἰκόπεδον Σταυροπούλου." Ἀρχαιολογικόν Δελτίον 21 Β: 192–93.

————. 1966c. "Οἰκόπεδον Κτιστάκη." Ἀρχαιολογικόν Δελτίον 21 Β: 187–88.

————. 1966d. "Οἰκόπεδον Ἀναστ. Θεοδώρου." Ἀρχαιολογικόν Δελτίον 21 Β: 188–89.

————. 1966e. "Οἰκόπεδον Γιαννοπούλου-Δημητρακοπούλου." Ἀρχαιολογικόν Δελτίον 21 Β: 183–87.

————. 1973. Kadmeia I: Mycenaean Finds from Thebes, Greece. Excavation at 14 Oedipus St. SIMA 35. Gothenburg: Åström.

————. 1985. The Topography of Thebes from the Bronze Age to Modern Times. Princeton: Princeton University Press.

Touloupa, Evi. 1964a. "Οἰκόπεδον Ἀ. καί Σ. Τζώρτζη." Ἀρχαιολογικόν Δελτίον 19 Β: 194–95.

————. 1964b. "Οἰκόπεδον Π. Θεοδώρου." Ἀρχαιολογικόν Δελτίον 19 Β: 192.

————. 1964c. "Οἰκόπεδον Ἰ. καί Κ. Τζώρτζη." Ἀρχαιολογικόν Δελτίον 19 Β: 192–94.

————. 1964d. "Ἀνασκαφή οἰκοπέδου Δημ. Παυλογιαννόπουλου." Ἀρχαιολογικόν Δελτίον 19 Β: 197.

————. 1965a. "Καδμεῖον. Οἰκόπεδον Δημ. Παυλογιαννόπουλου (Πελοπίδου 28)." Ἀρχαιολογικόν Δελτίον 20 Β: 233–35.

————. 1965b. "Καδμεῖον. Οἰκόπεδον Ἀ. καί Σ. Τζώρτζη." Ἀρχαιολογικόν Δελτίον 20 Β: 230–32.

Tsota, Evi. In press. "Ἡ απεικόνιση της ανθρώπινης μορφής στη Νεολιθική Βοιωτία. Νέα στοιχεία από την ανασκαφή της Ανισόπεδης Διάβασης Ο.Σ.Ε." In Ε' Διεθνές Συνέδριο Βοιωτικών Μελετών (Θήβα, 16–19 Σεπτεμβρίου 2005), ed. Vassilis Aravantinos. Athens: Society of Boeotian Studies.

Tzavella-Evjen, Hara, and Janet Stultz. 1997. "Reexamination of the Mycenaean Cemeteries in Thebes: Taphonomic Observations and Pottery Classification." AJA 101(2): 348–49.

Vika, Ephrosini, and Mike Richards. In press. "Θηβαίων γεύσεις: η διατροφή στην Αρχαία Θήβα από την προϊστορική στην κλασική εποχή μέσα από την ανάλυση σταθερών ισοτόπων 13C και 15N στο σκελετικό υλικό Όπισθεν Μουσείου και ΟΣΕ." In Ε' Διεθνές Συνέδριο Βοιωτικών Μελετών (Θήβα, 16–19 Σεπτεμβρίου 2005), ed. Vassilis Aravantinos. Athens: Society of Boeotian Studies.

Vitale, S. 2006. "The LH IIIB–LH IIIC Transition on the Mycenaean Mainland: Ceramic Phases and Terminology." AJA 75(2): 177–204.

Wilson, Andrew L. 1976. "The Provenance of the Inscribed Stirrup-jars Found at Thebes." Archaeometry 18(1): 51–58.

CHAPTER 53

....

THORIKOS

....

ROBERT LAFFINEUR

THORIKOS is located in the southeastern part of Attica, some three kilometers north of the modern town of Lavrio, to the east of the Laurion ridge with its metalliferous resources, and facing the island of Makronisos. The site is known in historical times as the place where Demeter landed while searching for her daughter, a sacred place that has probably been recalled by the construction of a doric temple in the nearby Adami plain.

Excavations were conducted in Thorikos in the late 1880s and early 1890s by the Ephor Valerios Staïs and have been carried out since 1963 by a Belgian mission (now the Belgian Archaeological School in Greece, which is currently working on the site). The most significant remains are the late classical theater, with the unique oblong shape of its *cavea*, and the 4th-century industrial quarter with ore washeries in the lower parts of the city, as well as cemeteries of the Geometric period and important ruins of Mycenaean date on the acropolis—the Velatouri hill. Human occupation and activity are directly connected with the availability of argentiferous lead ore, which turned into an economic and strategic richness especially at the beginning of the Mycenaean period.

The exploitation of Laurion argentiferous lead ore is attested as early as the Early Helladic period in Mine no. 3 in the Theater sector, in which late Early Helladic II pottery has been discovered (Spitaels 1984, 166–70). Traces of stone hammers from the same period have been recognized (Waelkens 1990), but no evidence of transformation of the ore has been recorded at the site at such an early date. The real beginnings of an elaborate metallurgy are documented in the Early Helladic period only in neighboring sites of Attica: cupellation, the method for separating lead and silver from the local argentiferous lead ore, has been practiced as early as the 3rd millennium, as indicated by finds of litharge, the residue of the process of cupellation, at Koropi, close to the new Athens airport, in an Early Helladic II context and in an Early Helladic house at Provatsa on the western coast of Makronisos, just opposite Thorikos (Spitaels 1984, 171). This has to be related to the results of analyses of Cycladic lead and silver, which emphasize that the two materials frequently originate from the Laurion (Gale, Stos-Gale, and Davis 1984).

At Thorikos, the earliest find of litharge so far has been made in sector I 53 (squares c5–e5 and d6) on the Velatouri, where a long sequence could be revealed between the Final Neolithic and the Archaic period. Fragments of litharge were found on a soil that the excavator has dated to the end of the 16th century (Servais 1967, 22–24; Gale and Stos-Gale 1982, 99–100). Though a relatively late testimony in comparison with the earlier-mentioned evidence from other parts of Attica, this find has great importance since it is very close in time to the period of the first main monumental development at Thorikos in the early Mycenaean phase (the construction of the oblong tomb and the tholos), if not strictly contemporary with it. It suggests that metallurgical activities, implying specific technological processes and providing specific materials, could have given an impetus to local development and that those prerequisite conditions of development were indeed present at the very beginning of the Late Bronze Age.

The architectural remains of the Mycenaean period that have been uncovered at Thorikos so far belong chiefly to funerary architecture. They are presented in chronological order here, and I stress their constructional features and define their connections with other parts of the Mycenaean mainland.

The earliest assemblage is tomb V, located immediately to the south of the oblong tomb, on the saddle between the two hills of the Velatouri (Servais and Servais-Soyez 1984, 61–66). This is a cist grave encircled by a rectangular construction of 7.80 by 5.80 m, a sort of *megaron* with partition wall and protruding *antae*, which has been covered by a tumulus supported by a circular retaining wall with a diameter of about 17.50 m. A low rectangular platform, probably connected with some kind of funerary cult, leans against the external face of the retaining wall in its northern section. The precise date of the monument is not easy to establish. The architectural structure and features, however, point to parallels such as the two earliest tumuli in Vrana-Marathon, tumuli I and II, dated respectively to the Middle Helladic and (early) Late Helladic I periods and showing a similarly built rectangular chamber in the center. The early date seems to be confirmed by the few original offerings that escaped the looters of Tomb V: in addition to Gray Minyan, Mattpainted, and bichrome matt-painted sherds, two fragments of marble jugs and the upper part of an *askos* found in a layer between the *antae* of the *megaron*, the former with parallels in Middle Minoan III and Late Minoan IA, the latter with a good parallel in grave Ypsilon in Grave circle B at Mycenae. Tomb V is in any case earlier than Tomb IV, the earth from the tumulus of which has slipped above the low rectangular platform.

Tomb IV is next in the chronological sequence. It was discovered by A. Milchhöfer in 1887 and excavated by V. Staïs in 1888 and 1893. This is the famous "oblong" tomb—not the oval or ellipsoidal tomb as it has often been called and not a tholos either since the term implies a circular shape (Servais and Servais-Soyez 1984, 16–46). The unique plan of the chamber, a rectangle with two semicircular extensions at the short sides, and the unique structure of its vault, similar to a tent with two half-conical extensions, are intriguing and without any parallels in the

Aegean—the only comparable structures are the megalithic *navetas* of the Balearic Islands, but they are geographically quite separate, their chronology is not definitely established, and though similar in general shape, they show differences as well, usually only one apsidal short side and a two-storied structure.

The tomb at Thorikos should be seen instead as an experiment by an individual architect in a period when tholos architecture had not yet achieved its canonical form and structure; this makes the importance of the monument at Thorikos even greater. The experimental character is further emphasized by the apparent correction that has been made to the original symmetrical plan of the dromos, especially the narrowing of its western face and the deviation of its axis to the east of the tomb's general axis. Another unique feature is the presence on the floor of the chamber of five long limestone blocks of rectangular section that were apparently used to form the crest line of the vault on a length of about 6 m, answering that surprising characteristic of the oblong tomb, namely the linear apex of its roof as opposed to the usual pointed apex of true tholos tombs. But the main features of the somewhat later circular tholos (Tomb III) are already present, namely the circular peribolos wall, which functions both as a retaining wall of the tumulus and as a symbolic enclosure of the tomb and is the only partially effective relieving triangle that does not drive through the whole masonry and was consequently not visible from either the dromos or the chamber. The latter adds to the tomb's experimental character.

Though the tomb had been looted in antiquity (through a hole cut in one of the lintel slabs), a sufficient number of offerings were recovered during excavation to allow a rather precise date for its construction (Servais and Servais-Soyez 1984, 46–57). These offerings include a gold sheet ornament in the shape of a butterfly, similar to examples from shaft grave III at Mycenae, two papyrus-shaped gold beads that have counterparts in shaft grave III at Mycenae, two circular gold sheets with a griffin in repoussé, a gold sheet with three rows of repoussé spirals of a variety known from Mycenae, a small gold spoon that has counterparts in the early Mycenaean period in Messenia and Laconia, and a gold rod of octagonal section, whose narrow central part is very similar to specimens from shaft grave IV at Mycenae. The ceramic material consists of sherds from the end of Late Helladic I that are probably, like the gold ornaments mentioned earlier, contemporary with the tomb's construction (just before 1500). However, quantities of Minyan and matt-painted sherds have also been found in different parts of the tomb and represent a late persistence of Middle Helladic types known from several Peloponnesian sites in Late Helladic I. The fragments of a palace-style jar of Late Helladic IIA date with zigzags and small double-ax designs are likely related to a later burial, together with fragments of four other jars of similar type with motifs of crocuses, sacral ivies, nautiloi, and foliate bands.

Tomb III, the circular tomb, the only true tholos, is next (figure 53.1). Though not one of the largest in the series, with 9.25 m for the diameter of the chamber, it offers several interesting characteristics (Gasche and Servais 1971, 17–76). The most obvious is the fact that the axis of its dromos is not perpendicular to the contour lines as usual but parallel to them. The reason for this is not clear, but it likely is related to the specific topographic conditions, especially the rather small space available and its steep lie (on the eastern slope of the acropolis).

Figure 53.1. Dromos and stomion of tholos tomb III from the north (photograph by Robert Laffineur).

An additional feature is the presence of an incomplete relieving triangle that is not entirely functional since it does not go right through the masonry above the lintels—so that Staïs was unable to reveal it. The original interpretation of the late Jean Servais is that this feature, which has been observed in Tomb IV as well, is a sign of ancient date. His suggestion that the tholos tomb of Aegisthus at Mycenae could have had the same feature has proved to be correct, thanks to a recent investigation in the masonry above the lintel of the Mycenae tomb. Significant also is the presence of a circular peribolos wall encircling the tomb and closing the dromos at its entrance—another similarity with tomb IV.

A final feature should be stressed: From a certain height in the elevation, the courses of the masonry of the chamber begin to slope inward, and this movement increases in the upper parts in such a proportion that it shows a rather high value for the last preserved course. Though the cover of the chamber is incompletely preserved, it is tempting to consider this feature as an indication that the cover was possibly approaching the structure of a true vault. This would confirm the experimental character of funerary architecture at Thorikos, which was mentioned earlier for the oblong tomb, as well as, on a more general level, the experimental character of Mycenaean funerary architecture.

This can be further emphasized, for instance, by the original relieving system of superposed horizontal slabs in the tholos tomb at Menidi in Attica and in the tholos tomb at Kopanaki in Messenia. The side faces of the stomion of the latter show an oblique profile that could be restored, if completed above the level of the last preserved courses, as an example of a corbel vault of triangular section, making the use of lintels and of a relieving triangle unnecessary. A similar feature occurs in the tholos tomb at Tourliditsa in Messenia (on this aspect of tholos tombs see Pelon 1976, 312–19).

Whatever the degree of certainty we have for the possible existence of a true vault, it remains that the sloping courses of masonry have parallels in Tholos tombs A and B at Kakovatos in Triphylia, as well as in the tholos tomb in the necropolis of the Argive Heraeum. Such relations with the Argolid and Messenia are worth remembering when it comes to an appreciation of the position of Thorikos within Mycenaean Greece. The sloping courses were able to be observed because Tholos tomb III at Thorikos is the monument for which we have the best and most certain knowledge of the structure of the masonry of the chamber, thanks to precise sections that the Belgian team was able to record, the only such precise sections to date (figure 53.2).

These have made it possible to recently apply finite element analysis to the masonry of the chamber. Modelizing different possible sections for the vault has resulted in an important observation: The presence of reinforcements of the chamber wall by thickening the masonry at the level of the lintels considerably reduces the traction stresses and consequently the risks of "opening" of the vault and thereby contributes to better stability (Cremasco and Laffineur 1999). That those reinforcements have been built exactly at the level where the stresses concentrate gives clear evidence of the empirical approach to stability problems by Mycenaean engineers. This is, of course, an obvious additional sign of the experimental character of Mycenaean funerary architecture and of funerary architecture at Thorikos in particular.

The similarities with the Tomb of Aegisthus at Mycenae mentioned earlier provide significant evidence for the date of tomb III, as proposed by Servais: "between the Aegisthus tomb as a *terminus post quem* and the second group of Wace as a *terminus ante quem*" (i.e. shortly after 1500) (Gasche and Servais 1971, 74). This date is confirmed by the few grave goods that were able to be preserved, some of them rather precisely datable to Late Helladic IIA: a palace-style jar, a small belly jar, and a squat alabastron, as well as a gold ornament in the shape of a figure-eight shield, very similar to a specimen excavated in the tholos tomb close to the Palace of Nestor at Ano Englianos in Messenia in a Late Helladic IIA context.

A similar date should be given to a fragment of ivory pyxis with running spirals and shell, which has a good parallel in tholos tomb 2 at Routsi in Messenia, about 1500 BC. All of these offerings are attributable to different burials deposited in the three shafts cut into the floor and in the two built sarcophagi leaning against the chamber wall. Though these burials were probably deposited during a rather short period of time, as indicated by a second alabastron of Late Helladic IIB date, it is impossible to individualize them because the original assemblages in the tomb had been disturbed by looters and because only a part of the original offerings were found. The later material should be attributed to a later burial of Late Helladic IIIA2/IIIB date that could not be located but contained a deep conical bowl and four terracotta Psi figurines.

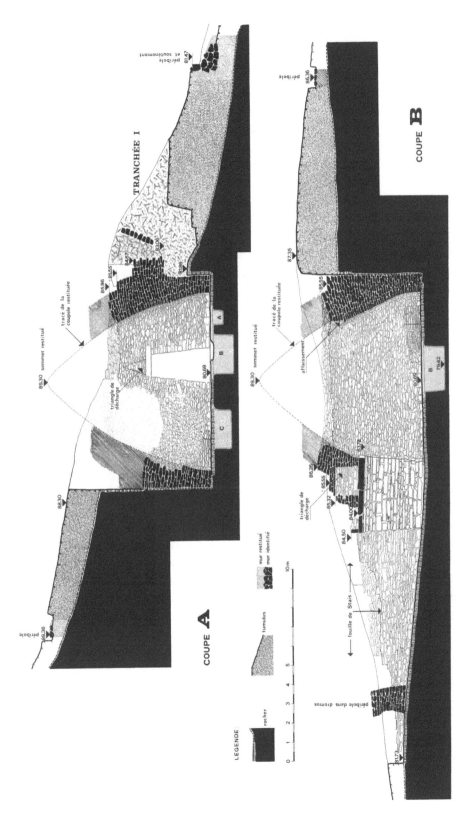

Figure 53.2. Sections of tholos tomb III (after *Thorikos V 1968, 1971*, 17–102. Drawing by H. Gasche. Copyright Belgian Archaeological School at Athens).

The last two tombs to mention, numbers I and II, belong to the class of "built chamber tombs," which are relatively rare. They are located to the east and to the west of Tomb IV, respectively.

Tomb I is of oblong shape and has a short dromos that gives access to the western part (Servais 1968, 29–41). In addition to clear evidence of a heroic cult of rather long duration in historical times, between the 7th century and the first half of the 4th (Devillers 1988), it has yielded a squat alabastron of Late Helladic IIA date, as well as stone beads and gold jewelry, including a small double ax and three rings, offerings that most probably belong to one of the original burials in the tomb.

Tomb II is L-shaped, like the "gamma tombs" at Eleusis, with a short dromos at its southern end and a partition wall closing the rectangular chamber itself (Servais 1968, 41–46). On the floor, human bones were found, together with a kylix, a find that "can be considered as the latest from the acropolis," according to Paule Spitaels (Spitaels 1982, 90), who dates it to Late Helladic IIIB/IIIC1, but which Mountjoy has placed more recently in Late Helladic IIIA2/IIIB (Mountjoy 1999, 489). This single find, in addition, might belong to a later burial, and the construction of the tomb, according to the comparable evidence from Eleusis, could well be dated to an earlier phase, possibly to Late Helladic IIIA.

A last discovery should be mentioned here, the so-called bothros of uncertain date, found close to the southwestern part of the circular retaining wall of the tumulus of tomb V. It was excavated by Staïs, who considered it as a cult place, but it could well be a tomb instead since its oblong plan is reminiscent of tomb I. It is therefore often designated as the third oval tomb on the acropolis (Hope Simpson and Dickinson 1979, 209; Mountjoy 1999, 489). In addition to the original find of black glaze sherds and Archaic terracotta figurines that could testify to a later cult similar to the heroic cult attested in tomb I, the Belgian mission has revealed Middle Helladic sherds in the lower levels, which might indicate an early construction.

With the exception of tomb II, the architectural remains of Mycenaean date at Thorikos concentrate on the Prepalatial period. Isolated finds, however, indicate that the acropolis was occupied during the palatial phases as well. The excavation of square I 53 j5 has yielded a sequence rather similar to the one in the neighboring sector, I 53 c5–e5 and d6, mentioned earlier, with a Middle Helladic child burial, a fragmentary stemmed goblet of Late Helladic IIIA date, and sub-Geometric walls, as well as some proto-Attic and proto-Corinthian sherds.

The Palatial period is also illustrated by nine vases in the Musées d'art et d'histoire in Geneva, which were purchased in Athens in 1906 by G. Nicole as coming from Thorikos (Servais 1969). The vases are of Late Helladic IIIA2 and Late Helladic IIIB1 date and show close similarities with ceramic material excavated from Attic sites. The only exception is a shallow cup that belongs most probably to Late Helladic IIB, has parallels in Prosymna, and could be an import from the Argolid.

Occupation in Late Helladic IIIA and IIIB is confirmed by Hope Simpson, who "noted fine LH IIIA and LH IIIB pottery on the surface of the acropolis hill on a visit in 1956" (Hope Simpson 1965, 104).

Occupation is finally attested at the very end of the palatial period and during Postpalatial times by finds from mine no. 3 in the theater sector. This unstratified material, which Mountjoy has published, belongs to two distinct groups that are respectively attributable to the transitional phase Late Helladic IIIB2/Late Helladic IIIC Early and to advanced Late Helladic IIIC Middle (Mountjoy 1995). The first group exhibits affinities with Attica and the eastern Peloponnese, including Corinthia, the Argolid, and Laconia. The second group duplicates shapes and decoration already known from Athens and Perati.

The provenance is not insignificant since it indicates that the exploitation of the local metal ore continued in Postapalatial times. As Mountjoy notes:

> An enormous number of tripod cooking pots [67 fragments] suggests water may have been heated, the unusually large number of dippers [48 fragments], normally not common in settlement deposits, may have been used to ladle the water into the equally large number of pouring vessels present. The boiling water may have been poured onto the surface of the rock followed by cold water in order to crack it, so the ores could be extracted. (Mountjoy 1995, 224)

Exploitation at such a late date is worth stressing in connection with the lead and silver objects from the necropolis at Perati, which have proved to be made of Laurion ore. Moreover, the similarities between pottery from mine no. 3 and ceramic material from Perati give evidence of the probable origin of the people who were engaged in this late exploitation at Thorikos.

The chronological sequence on the Velatouri hill finally appears rather complete, though with significant differences in the quantity and quality of material recovered. An additional difference concerns architectural remains. These are limited to the early Mycenaean period, which is, in the state of our present knowledge, obviously the richest phase at Thorikos. All of the remains that have been mentioned for that phase belong to the funerary sphere and to the monumental class, but Staïs has excavated remains of settlement on top of the Velatouri hill, with two succeeding phases and material that belongs to the end of Middle Helladic and to the beginning of Late Helladic.

The importance of the top of the acropolis was confirmed in 1976 by the chance discovery, in square H 53, just below the geodesic post, of sherds of a bichrome, matt-painted jar (similar to the finds by Staïs) of a fragment of a Late Minoan I cup in "rippling ware" and of sherds of a stirrup jar of Late Minoan IB date with a double ax on the bottom surface. These finds are especially interesting since they provide the first indications to date of relations between Thorikos and Minoan Crete. This appears extremely significant when it comes to defining the site's place and role in the general framework of mainland Greece in the Late Bronze Age and its evolution within the second half of the second millennium.

Whereas the external relations at the end of Mycenaean palatial times and during the Postpalatial period seem to be limited mainly to the neighboring site of Perati, as has just been pointed out, affinities and connections prove far more numerous, varied, and remote in early Mycenaean times. Most of these connections are with the Argolid, especially Mycenae, and the southwestern Peloponnese, Messenia and Triphylia and concern both the offerings—the *askos* from the *megaron* of tomb V, the jewelry from tomb IV, the gold ornament in the shape of a figure-eight shield, and the ivory pyxis with running spirals from tomb III—and some significant architectural features, including the partially efficient relieving triangle of tombs IV and III and the sloping courses of the masonry of the chamber in tomb III.

Such a difference in the range and extent of external relations is certainly due to a degree to the basically different general conditions prevailing all over mainland Greece in the two periods (i.e. claim to power, competition, and expansion in a period of formation on the one hand, and isolation and withdrawal after the destruction of palatial centers on the other). However, more specific factors must have played a decisive additional role in particular areas, and Thorikos seems to be one in which such specific conditions played an important role due to its strategic metal resources.

BIBLIOGRAPHY

Cremasco, Veronica, and Laffineur, Robert. 1999. "The Engineering of Mycenaean Tholoi: The Circular Tomb at Thorikos Revisited." In *Meletemata*, 139–48.

Devillers, Michèle. 1988. *An Archaic and Classical Votive Deposit from a Mycenaean Tomb at Thorikos. Miscellanea Graeca* 8. Ghent: Belgian Archaeological School in Greece.

Gale, Noël H., and Stos-Gale, Zofia A. 1982. "Thorikos, Perati, and Bronze Age Silver Production in the Laurion-Attica." *Studies in South Attica I, Miscellanea Graeca* 5: 97–103. Ghent: Belgian Archaeological School in Greece.

———, and Davis, Jack L. 1984. "The Provenance of Lead Used at Ayia Irini, Keos." *Hesperia* 53: 389–406.

Gasche, Hermann, and Servais, Jean. 1971. "Les fouilles sur le haut du Vélatouri." *Thorikos V 1968*: 17–102. Brussels: Belgian Archaeological School in Greece.

Hope Simpson, Richard. 1965. *A Gazetteer and Atlas of Mycenaean Sites*. London: Institute of Classical Studies.

———, and Oliver T. P. K. Dickinson. 1979. *A Gazetteer of Aegean Civilisation in the Bronze Age*. Vol. 1, *The Mainland and Islands*. Gothenburg: Åström.

Mountjoy, Penelope A. 1995. "Thorikos Mine no. 3: The Mycenaean Pottery." *BSA* 90: 195–228.

———. 1999. *Regional Mycenaean Decorated Pottery*. Rahden: Leidorf.

Pelon, Olivier. 1976. *Tholoi, tumuli, et cercles funéraires: Recherches sur les monuments funéraires de plan circulaire dans l'Egée de l'Âge du Bronze (IIIe et IIe millénaires av. J.-C.)*. Athens: L'École française d'Athènes.

Servais, Jean. 1967. "Les fouilles sur le haut du Vélatouri." *Thorikos III 1965*: 9–30. Brussels: Belgian Archaeological School in Greece.

———. 1968. "Le secteur mycénien sur le haut du Vélatouri." *Thorikos I 1963*: 27–46. Brussels: Belgian Archaeological School in Greece.

———. 1969. "Vases mycéniens de Thorikos au Musée de Genève." *Thorikos IV 1966/1967*: 53–69. Brussels: Belgian Archaeological School in Greece.

————, and Servais-Soyez, Brigitte. 1984. "La tholos 'oblongue' (Tombe IV) et le tumulus (Tombe V) sur le Vélatouri." *Thorikos VIII 1972/1976:* 15–71. Brussels: Belgian Archaeological School in Greece.

Spitaels, Paule. 1982. "An Unstratified Late Mycenaean Deposit from Thorikos (Mine Gallery no. 3) Attica." *Studies in South Attica I, Miscellanea Graeca* 5: 83–96. Ghent: Belgian Archaeological School in Greece.

————. 1984. "The Early Helladic Period in Mine no. 3 (Theatre Sector)." *Thorikos VIII 1972/1976:* 151–74. Brussels: Belgian Archaeological School in Greece.

Waelkens, Marc. 1990. "Tool Marks and Mining Techniques in Mine no. 3." *Thorikos IX 1977/1982:* 115–43. Brussels: Belgian Archaeological School in Greece.

CHAPTER 54

TIRYNS

JOSEPH MARan

The strongly fortified acropolis of Mycenaean Tiryns lies about 1.8 km from the present coast of the Bay of Nauplion, where it perches on a narrow, rocky outcrop that reaches a height of up to 28 m above sea level. The hill slopes from south to north, a topographic feature used during the Mycenaean period to create a division into an Upper Citadel, a Middle Citadel, and a Lower Citadel by demarcating the limits of the different parts of the hill with strong, supporting walls. The acropolis of Tiryns was surrounded by an extensive settlement, the Lower Town, whose size during the different phases of occupation is still difficult to determine.

Of all of the Mycenaean palatial centers, Tiryns is the one closest to the sea. This fact, together with the strong archaeological indications for its participation in long-distance exchange (Cline 1994, 54; 2007, 191–95; Maran 2004b; 2008, 50–60), underlines the site's importance as a major Mediterranean harbor during the Bronze Age. Geoarchaeological research by Eberhard Zangger (1993, 77–82; 1994) points to significant changes of the distance from the site to the coast during the Holocene. While in the third millennium BC the coastline was only a few hundred meters from the foot of the acropolis hill, in Mycenaean times the shoreline had moved outward due to massive sedimentation as a consequence of soil erosion, reaching a position approximately half as far as the current modern coast.

History of Excavations

Nowadays, the appearance of Tiryns is characterized by the Mycenaean fortification wall, which reaches a width of up to seven meters and consists of Cyclopean masonry that has remained visible since antiquity. Because of its impressive appearance, the identification of the site as ancient Tiryns was never disputed, which is why the site very early on attracted the attention of travelers and archaeologists. Tiryns was visited in antiquity by the traveler Pausanias, who admiringly compared its walls to the pyramids of Egypt, and in 1831 the Greek scholar and diplomat Alexandros Rizos-Rangavis and the German philologist Friedrich Thiersch undertook a one-day excavation on the Upper Citadel and claimed to have discovered the palace (Papadimitriou 2001, 6–13).

Heinrich Schliemann conducted a short campaign of soundings at the site in 1876 and then began a systematic excavation of Tiryns in 1884 and 1885 together with Wilhelm Dörpfeld, during which time the remains of the last Mycenaean palace on the Upper Citadel were largely uncovered. Their work was continued between 1905 and 1929 under the direction of Dörpfeld and later Georg Karo and Kurt Müller, who extended the focus of excavations to the area of the Lower Town.

In the late 1950s, restoration works under the direction of Nikolaos Verdelis revealed the underground cisterns in the Lower Citadel and thereby initiated the resumption of fieldwork by the German Archaeological Institute. These excavations extended the focus to areas that had been neglected until then, namely the Lower Citadel and the Lower Town. Of particular importance were the large-scale excavations between 1976 and 1983, directed by Klaus Kilian in the Lower Citadel, which contributed to the clarification of the long-term usage and structuvre of this part of the site. In addition, in 1984 and 1985 Kilian investigated the area of the Megara on the Upper Citadel and provided new insights into the architectural history of the central part of the Mycenaean palace. Since 1997, ongoing excavations by the German Archaeological Institute under the direction of Joseph Maran and in close cooperation with Alkestis Papadimitriou from the Greek Archaeological Service have focused on different areas of the Citadel, as well as the Lower Town.

EARLY HELLADIC PERIOD

Over the millennia, the hill of Tiryns and its immediate surroundings were repeatedly chosen as locations for settlements. The earliest signs of occupation dating to the Middle Neolithic (ca. 5900–5400 BC) have been mostly obliterated by later building activities (Kilian 1983, 323–26, 331; Alram-Stern 1996, 238). On the other end of the chronological scale, very little is also known about Byzantine Tiryns, but this is mostly due to the dismantling of post-Mycenaean structures on the Citadel by the early excavators. In the long record of human occupation, there are three periods in particular during which Tiryns seems to have had an outstanding significance: during the later part of the Early Helladic II phase (ca. 2500–2200 BC) and during the Mycenaean Palatial (ca. 1400–1200 BC) and Postpalatial periods (ca. 1200–1050 BC).

During the later part of Early Helladic II, the so-called Period of the Corridor Houses, Tiryns must have already been of considerable size since not only on the Upper and Lower Citadel but also in most excavations in the Lower Town that were deep enough to reach such levels, substantial architectural remains dating to that time have been uncovered. The most important structure of the later Early Helladic II in Tiryns is the monumental circular building on the Upper Citadel, which had a diameter of approximately 28 m and a façade that featured jutting, bastion-like projections (Müller 1930, 80–88; Kilian 1986; Maran 1998, 197–99; Marzolff 2004, 79–86).

In the third millennium BC Aegean, no other buildings even remotely resembling the Circular Building of Tiryns are known, and widely differing proposals on its function have been made, including interpretations as a residence, sanctuary, or even a granary (Maran 1998, 197–98 with earlier literature). Strikingly, in certain respects the Circular Building resembles the much later central buildings of the Mycenaean palace. Not only did its construction constitute a radical break with the former patterns of Early Helladic architectural use of the Upper Citadel, but it was also built on exactly the same plot where roughly a thousand years later the Great and the Little Megaron were built. Moreover, like Mycenaean Tiryns, the monumental structure on the Upper Citadel was contrasted by a densely organized Early Helladic settlement in the Lower Citadel (Kilian 1981a, 186–89; 1983, 327).

In positioning the main building of the settlement exactly on the highest topographical point of the hill, the builders of the Early Helladic Circular Building ensured its visibility from both sea and land (Marzolff 2004, 84). It is likely to have functioned as an imposing and fortified structure that served in times of peace as a landmark and symbol of political power and in times of war as a refuge, functions reminiscent of strong towers of medieval castles (Maran 1998, 198). However, toward the end of the Early Helladic II phase, the Circular Building and the contemporary settlement in the Lower Citadel were destroyed in an intense conflagration. This destruction marks a setback so severe that it took until the Mycenaean period for monumental architecture to reappear in the Argolid (Maran 1998, 299–301).

LATE HELLADIC PERIOD: PALATIAL ORIGINS

How Tiryns became one of the most important palatial centers of the Mycenaean period is still difficult to determine. While in the Lower Town architectural structures dating to the Middle Helladic period (2000–1700/1600 BC) are attested, there are surprisingly few signs of a contemporary occupation on the Citadel. The architectural sequence in the area of the Great Megaron on the Upper Citadel is of potential relevance here. Claims of the existence of a Middle Helladic "maison de chef" with associated fragments of painted plaster beneath the Throne Room of the Great Megaron (Kilian 1987a, 121; 1988b, 134) have been cast into doubt by a reexamination of the evidence pointing to a date of the building perhaps as late as Late Helladic I (Stülpnagel 1999, 17–25, 233; Maran 2001b, 23–25) and suggesting that the painted plaster derived from later disturbances and that no extraordinary finds were associated with the walls of this building.

While it seems that the tradition of imposing buildings on the plot of the Great Megaron cannot be traced back to Late Helladic I, let alone the Middle Helladic, the first Mycenaean architecture with features exceeding the quality of normal settlement architecture in the area of the Upper Citadel dates to Late Helladic II or IIIA1 at the latest. Excavations in the porch of the Great Megaron have uncovered remains of a building complex that did not bear any resemblance to the later palatial megara and seems to have extended over two shallow terraces linked by a flight of stairs (Maran 2001b, 25–29; figure 1; pl. 3). Connected to this building complex is probably a thick layer with a great deal of LH II pottery, as well as fresco fragments found in excavations in the adjacent eastern wing of the palace (Müller 1930, 78; Touchais 1985, 777–79; figure 32; Maran 2001b, 24, 28).

At some date during the 14th century BC (Late Helladic IIIA), the decision must have been made to impose a totally different palatial concept centering on megaron buildings. In order to create the unified space needed to construct the first Great Megaron, the entire upper terrace of the Late Helladic II/IIIA1 building complex had to be razed and leveled (Maran 2001b, 28), a fact that emphasizes the radicality of the architectural change (Kilian 1987c, 33–36; Maran 2001b, 28–29). The first Great Megaron anticipated in its measurements and ground plan the basic features of its successor but was situated a few meters to the south in comparison to the latter (Kilian 1987b, 204–207, figure 1; 1988c, 1–9, Beilage 1; Maran 2001b, 25). The LH IIIA Great Megaron was subdivided into a porch, a vestibule, and a main room that had a central hearth surrounded by columns and perhaps also a place for a throne on the inner side of the east wall. The plastered walls of the building were painted, but very little is preserved of this decoration. Under the Little Megaron, walls of an LH IIIA predecessor building came to light, so the concept of juxtaposing two megara of different size, so typical for Late Palatial Tiryns, seems to have existed since the Early Palatial period. It is unknown whether these Early Palatial megara already had courts in front of them.

At about the same time of the construction of the first megara, the Upper Citadel was encircled with a Cyclopean wall that did not yet include the Lower Citadel (Müller 1930, 55–57, pl. 4; Kilian 1988b, 134–35). How the latter was fortified during LH IIIA remains uncertain, but slightly later, in LH IIIB1, a strong fortification wall consisting of rubble stones is present in the Lower Citadel (Kilian 1988a, 139, figure 28). Besides the megara on the Upper Citadel and several houses in the Lower Citadel, little is known about how the citadel was used in LH IIIA because buildings of that date are usually concealed by superimposed later architecture. In the southern and western parts of the Lower Town, on the other hand, large building complexes dating to that time have been excavated, one of them furnished with a mosaic of dark and light pebbles (Podzuweit and Salzmann 1977; Gercke and Hiesel 1971, 3–7, Beilage 2–3).

LATE HELLADIC PERIOD: FINAL PALATIAL ACME—LH IIIB2

In the last fifty years of the Mycenaean Palatial period, during the LH IIIB2 phase, a building program of unprecedented scale was carried out in and around Tiryns (Kilian 1985, 74; 1988b, 134; Maran 2004a, 261–63). During that time, the palace discovered by Schliemann and Dörpfeld was built with the Great Megaron at its center (figure 54.1), characterized by the previously mentioned tripartite subdivision and furnished with a place for a throne, as well as a huge, central round hearth surrounded by four columns in its main room (Dörpfeld in Schliemann 1886, 230–60; Müller 1930, 139–46). The Porch of the building opened into a Great Court with a colonnade and a round hypaethral altar placed along the extension of the central axis of the Great Megaron. The Little Megaron in the neighboring eastern wing of the palace consisted of a porch and a main room and resembles a miniature version of the Great Megaron, insofar as it is roughly half of the latter's size and had not only a court but also a central hearth, as well as a place for a throne (Dörpfeld in Schliemann 1886, 268–75; Müller 1930, 157–66). The political meaning of this specific architectural layout with two megaron buildings of different size, which in this clarity is noted only in Tiryns, is disputed (Dörpfeld in Schliemann 1886, 214–18; Müller 1930, 171, 198; Kilian 1987c, 32; Maran 2006b, 84–85).

The walls and stucco floors of the megara and other palatial buildings were adorned by frescos, but the original position of the wall paintings is difficult to specify since almost all of them were found in secondary deposition in debris layers along the western slope of the Upper Citadel, where they had been dumped during clearing works after the palace's final destruction (Rodenwaldt 1912, 66–165 [frescoes of the "late palace"]; Maran 2001a, 115–16). The centrality of the Great Megaron of Tiryns manifests itself not only in its size and position but also in the fact that the most important ascent of the citadel, starting at the main entrance, was designed in such a way as to exemplify an attempt to prescribe—by architectural and esthetic means—the movement of visitors and to draw them into the depth of the citadel until they reached the Great Megaron (Müller 1930, 193–96; Wright 1994, 51–60; Küpper 1996, 111–18; Maran 2006b, 81–83; pls. 12–13).

In this last magnificent palatial building program, most of the architectural highlights that still distinguish Tiryns today were created. These include the Cyclopean fortification of the Lower Citadel, the strongly fortified West Staircase, and all of the passages and chambers within the Cyclopean wall showing the characteristic corbel vault, e.g., the North Gate and the North Passage (a newly discovered postern gate in the north of the Lower Citadel), the two stairs leading to underground cisterns in the Lower Citadel, and the East and South galleries in the Upper Citadel (Müller 1930, 57–61, 65–66, Kilian 1988b, 134; Maran 2004a, 261–275). The settlement in the Lower Citadel was redesigned by creating new terraces that run parallel to the inner side of the fortification and by constructing large building complexes on top of

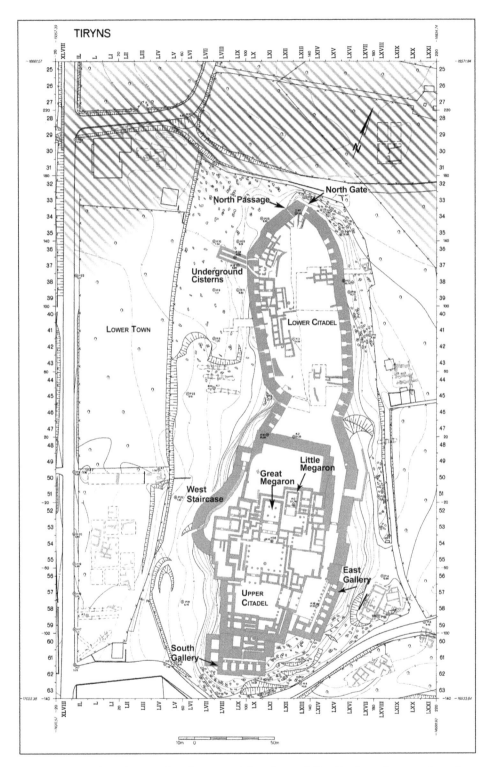

Figure 54.1. Plan of Late Palatial Tiryns with estimated distribution of stream deposits (hatched) to the north of the Acropolis (graphics by Dipl.-Arch. M. Kostoula).

them, which served for administrative activities, storage, and skilled crafting closely linked to the palace (Kilian 1988b, 134).

Of all of the measures in architecture and engineering realized in these final decades of the palace, the construction of the dam of Kofini and the redirection of a stream that had previously passed through the Lower Town of Tiryns are undoubtedly the most spectacular (Balcer 1974; Slenczka 1975; Zangger 1994, 204–207; Knauss 1995). Zangger has argued that these drastic steps may have been taken as a reaction to a catastrophic flash flood, perhaps triggered by the earthquake at the very end of the Palatial period (Zangger 1992, 82–85; 1993, 80, 82; 1994, 198–212).

However, it can be shown that the construction of the dam and the redirection of the stream must antedate the final destruction of the palace and that periodic flooding events that extended over a longer span of the 13th century BC and affected only a relatively narrow zone to the north of the acropolis are much more likely to account for the alluvial deposits in that area than a single catastrophic flash flood (Maran 2004a, 277–83, forthcoming; Maran and Papadimitriou 2006, 102–104, 127–29). Therefore, the rarity of LH IIIB2 buildings in the Lower Town in comparison to such of earlier phases of the Palatial period cannot be attributed to an extensive covering by alluvial deposits (*pace* Zangger 1994) and in all likelihood reflects a pattern of abandonment of at least certain quarters of the Lower Town.

Moreover, recent excavation results in the Lower Citadel allow the differentiation of two major phases of construction within the LH IIIB2 building program and suggest that the decision to carry out the costly measure of constructing the dam and redirecting the stream may not have been a spontaneous reaction to a natural disaster but part of a well-considered structural decision initiated by political actors of the Final Palatial period (Maran 2008, 84–90, forthcoming). To the earlier phase of the building program belong measures that point to defensive planning in politically instable times and comprise features like the Cyclopean wall, with its chambers furnished with embrasures for archers, the underground cisterns, and the newly discovered narrow postern gate (North Passage) at the northern tip of the Lower Citadel (Maran 2004a, 265–67, figures 1, 5–6; 2008, 41–49, 84–91; forthcoming; P. Marzolff in Maran 2008, 97–109).

However, shortly after the defensive architectural measures had been taken, some of them were undone and replaced by new concepts, which suggests instead a consolidation of the political situation. During this later phase of the building program, most of the chambers within the Cyclopean wall were probably walled up, while the postern gate was closed and replaced by the newly constructed and much wider North Gate, thus also suggesting a deviation from the former defensive logic. The creation of the North Gate indicates an upgrading of an approach to the citadel from the north, and in this context the building of the dam and the redirection of the stream may be seen as measures that created the precondition for developing the northern Lower Town and for allowing an unhindered access to the citadel (Maran 2008, 89, forthcoming).

If these large public works were indeed part of a visionary, Final Palatial master plan to reorganize the relation between Citadel and Lower Town, then this plan remained uncompleted. While the construction of the dam and the redirection of the stream were finished, the implementation of the idea to develop the northern Lower Town was probably thwarted by the catastrophe that struck Tiryns at the end of LH IIIB2 and destroyed the palace and the settlement in the Lower Citadel. Observations of undulating walls of Final Palatial buildings led Kilian (1996) to assume a strong earthquake as the most likely cause of the widespread destruction, and recent excavations in neighboring Midea have supported this interpretation (Demakopoulou et al. 2000–2001).

Late Helladic Period: Postpalatial Revival—LH IIIC

Arguably, the development in the years after this destruction represents the most extraordinary aspect of Mycenaean Tiryns. While the LH IIIC phase in most of the former palatial centers is accompanied by processes of shrinkage and depopulation, in 12th-century-BC Tiryns we find astonishing signs of an expansion of settlement activities and even the reestablishment of centralized political structures. Particularly intriguing is the evidence that some of the most important architectural symbols of palatial political and religious power in the heart of the destroyed palace experienced a revival. After the debris of the catastrophe had been partially cleared and leveled, the altar in the Great Court was transformed from a round to a square, platform-like structure, while in the eastern half of the ruin of the Great Megaron a narrow megaron, called Building T, was constructed (figure 54.2; Maran 2000, 2001a). The latter consisted of two rooms, an approximately square porch, and an elongated room divided into two aisles by a central row of columns that had no central hearth but integrated the location of its predecessor's throne. All traces of palatial wall paintings were carefully removed from the central area of the palace, but there was no attempt to decorate the walls of Building T with new frescos (Maran 2006a, 142–44). Apart from the Great Megaron–Great Court complex (i.e., the area with the highest political significance), the main part of the former palace, including the Little Megaron, evidently was not rebuilt. This means that Building T must have stood quite isolated on the Upper Citadel, which makes an interpretation as the residence of a specific group less likely than an identification as a communal hall in which on certain occasions gatherings took place under the direction of a ruler (Mühlenbruch 2002, 2007, 247).

In contrast to the situation in the central part of the former palace, in the Lower Citadel during LH IIIC, neither the structuring principles of palatial occupation nor any architectural forms of that time were revived. Instead, after a short phase of squatting in the immediate aftermath of the catastrophe, the Final Palatial buildings were replaced by a villagelike settlement that consisted of houses arranged around courtyards, whose basic plan remained intact until the end of the Postpalatial

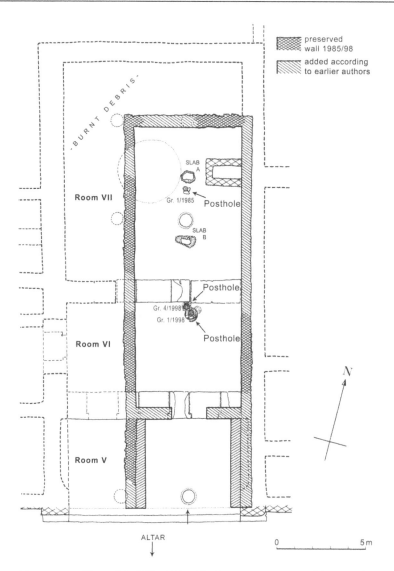

Figure 54.2. Plan of Building T inside the Great Megaron (drawing by
Dr. Peter Marzolff).

period (Kilian 1980, 185–87; 1985, 76–81; Mühlenbruch 2007). The long-term continuity of LH IIIC occupation is also exemplified by a sequence of superimposed cult
buildings with a rich inventory of cult paraphernalia that had been built over and
over again on the same plot bordering on one of the courtyards (Kilian 1981b, 1992;
Albers 1994, 104–11).

Signs of a pronounced dynamic of growth during LH IIIC are apparent in the
Lower Town, which may have reached a size of up to 25 hectares (Kilian 1980, 171;
1985, 75; 1988b, 135). While such estimations have to be treated with caution in light
of the still unsatisfactory state of research in the Lower Town, at least for the zone

to the north of the acropolis a concerted and systematic development can be demonstrated on the basis of a simultaneous start of building activities in spatially separated areas and of a similar orientation and structure of Postpalatial architecture in these areas (Kilian 1978, 449–55; Maran 2006a, 126; Maran and Papadimitriou 2006). The early start of extensive construction works within the 12th century BC in this specific area formerly affected by the stream points to the possibility that the inhabitants of Postpalatial Tiryns were aware of the aforementioned Final Palatial master plan and followed some of its objectives (Maran 2008, 89–90, forthcoming). The special significance of the Lower Town in Postpalatial times is reflected not only by its large size but also by the quality of some of the architecture. Thus, with a large building with a central row of columns (Megaron W) and a building subdivided by multiple rows of columns in the Southeastern and Northeastern Lower Town, respectively, we already know two structures outside the walls of the acropolis that stand out in size and ground plan from the rest of the contemporary architecture (Gercke and Hiesel 1971, 11–15; Gercke, Gercke, and Hiesel 1975, 8–10; Maran 2006a, 126; Maran and Papadimitriou 2006, 105–109, figures 5–6).

The driving force behind the remarkable development in 12th-century-BC Tiryns may have been the families of a new elite, who, after being freed from the constraints of palatial rule, claimed areas in the surroundings of the citadel for themselves and articulated their self-confidence by the construction of new and in some cases impressive living quarters. These families were decisive for the revival of architectural symbols of imperial power, as well as for the attempts to legitimize the claim by the possession and conspicuous use of old and new symbols of authority (Maran 2006a).

At the end of the LH IIIC phase, a process of shrinkage of the settlement in the Lower Citadel sets in, which leads within a few decades to a nearly total abandonment of the citadel (Mühlenbruch 2007, 247). For the Early Iron Age, a much more dispersed settlement structure can be inferred on the basis of groups of cist graves that have been found in many areas of the Lower Town, but very little is known about the accompanying houses (Papadimitriou 1998). The inhumation of the dead close to the houses constitutes in itself a marked break with long-standing practices since during Mycenaean times burial in chamber tombs in the nearby hill of Prophet Ilias formed the prevalent funerary practice (Rudolph 1973). The abandonment of the worlds of the living and the dead is a stark reminder that the history of Mycenaean Tiryns had come to an end.

BIBLIOGRAPHY

Albers, Gabriele. 1994. *Spätmykenische Stadtheiligtümer: Systematische Analyse und vergleichende Auswertung der archäologischen Befunde. BAR-IS* 596. Oxford: Tempus Reparatum.

Alram-Stern, Eva. 1996. *Die ägäische Frühzeit*. Vol. 1, *Das Neolithikum in Griechenland mit Ausnahme von Kreta und Zypern*. Vienna: Verlag der Österreichischen Akademie der Wissenschaften.

Balcer, Jack M. 1974. "The Mycenaean Dam at Tiryns." *AJA* 78: 141–49.

Cline, Eric H. 1994. *SWDS*.

———. 2007. "Rethinking Mycenaean International Trade with Egypt and the Near East." In *RMP II*, 190–200.

Demakopoulou, Katie, Nikoletta Divari-Valakou, Paul Åström, and Gisela Walberg. 2000–2001. "Work in Midea 1997–1999: Excavation, Conservation, Restoration." *Opuscula Atheneinsia* 25–26: 35–52.

Gercke, Peter, Wendula Gercke, and Gerhard Hiesel. 1975. "Tiryns-Stadt 1971: Graben H." In *Tiryns VIII*, 7–36. Mainz: von Zabern.

Gercke, Peter, and Gerhard Hiesel. 1971. "Grabungen in der Unterstadt von Tiryns." In *Tiryns V*, 1–19. Mainz: von Zabern.

Kilian, Klaus. 1978. "Ausgrabungen in Tiryns 1976." *Archäologischer Anzeiger*: 449–98.

———. 1980. "Zum Ende der mykenischen Epoche in der Argolis." *Jahrbuch des Römisch-Germanischen Zentralmuseum Mainz* 27: 166–95.

———. 1981a. "Ausgrabungen in Tiryns 1978, 1979." *Archäologischer Anzeiger*: 149–258.

———. 1981b. "Zeugnisse mykenischer Kultausübung in Tiryns." In *Sanctuaries and Cults*, 49–58.

———. 1983. "Ausgrabungen in Tiryns 1981. Bericht zu den Grabungen." *AA 1983*: 277–328.

———. 1985. "La caduta dei palazzi Micenei continentali: Aspetti archeologici." In *Le origini dei Greci: Dori e mondo Egeo*, ed. Domenico Musti, 73–95. Rome-Bari: Editori Laterza.

———. 1986. "The Circular Building at Tiryns." In *Early Helladic Architecture*, 65–71.

———. 1987a. "Ältere mykenische Residenzen." In *Kolloquium zur ägäischen Vorgeschichte, Mannheim 20.–22.2.1986*, 120–24. Schriften des Deutschen Archäologen-Verbandes 9. Mannheim: Deutscher Archäologen-Verband und Archäologisches Seminar Universität Mannheim.

———. 1987b. "L'architecture des résidences mycéniennes: Origine et extension d'une structure du pouvoir politique pendant l'âge du bronze récent." In *Le système palatial en Orient, en Grèce et à Rome: Actes du Colloque de Strasbourg 1985*, ed. Edmond Lévy, 203–17. Strasbourg: Centre de recherche sur le Proche-Orient et la Grèce antiques.

———. 1987c. "Zur Funktion der mykenischen Residenzen auf dem griechischen Festland." In *Function of the Minoan Palaces*, 21–38.

———. 1988a. "Ausgrabungen in Tiryns 1982/83. Bericht zu den Grabungen." *AA* 1988: 105–51.

———. 1988b. "Mycenaeans Up to Date: Trends and Changes in Recent Research." In *Problems in Greek Prehistory*, 115–52.

———. 1988c. "Die 'Thronfolge' in Tiryns." *Athenische Mitteilungen* 103: 1–9.

———. 1992. "Mykenische Heiligtümer der Peloponnes." In *Kotinos: Festschrift für Erika Simon*, ed. Heide Froning, Tonio Hölscher, and Harald Mielsch, 10–25. Mainz: von Zabern.

———. 1996. "Earthquakes and Archaeological Context at 13th Century BC Tiryns." In *Archaeoseismology*, ed. Stathis Stiros and Richard E. Jones, 63–68. Fitch Laboratory Occasional Papers 7. Athens: British School at Athens.

Knauss, Jost. 1995. "Die Flußumleitung von Tiryns." *Athenische Mitteilungen* 11: 43–81.

Küpper, Michael. 1996. *Mykenische Architektur: Material, Bearbeitungstechnik, Konstruktion, und Erscheinungsbild*. Internationale Archäologie 25. Espelkamp: Leidorf.

Maran, Joseph. 1998. *Kulturwandel auf dem griechischen Festland und den Kykladen im späten 3. Jahrtausend v. Chr. Studien zu den kulturellen Verhältnissen in Südosteuropa und dem zentralen sowie östlichen Mittelmeerraum in der späten Kupfer- und frühen Bronzezeit.* Universitätsforschungen zur prähistorischen Archäologie, vol. 53. Bonn: Habelt.

———. 2000. "Das Megaron im Megaron: Zur Datierung und Funktion des Antenbaus im mykenischen Palast von Tiryns." *Archäologischer Anzeiger:* 1–16.

———. 2001a. "Political and Religious Aspects of Architectural Change on the Upper Citadel of Tiryns: The Case of Building T." In *Potnia,* 113–22.

———. 2001b. "Zur Frage des Vorgängers des ersten Doppelpalastes von Tiryns." In *IΘAKH: Festschrift für Jörg Schäfer zum 75. Geburtstag am 25. April 2001,* ed. Stephanie Böhm and Klaus-Valtin von Eickstedt, 23–29. Würzburg: Ergon.

———. 2004a. "Architektonische Innovation im spätmykenischen Tiryns: Lokale Bauprogramme und fremde Kultureinflüsse." In *Althellenische Technologie und Technik. Tagung Ohlstadt 21.–23.3.2003,* ed. Apostolos Kyriatsoulis, 261–86. Weilheim: Verein zur Förderung der Aufarbeitung der hellenischen Geschichte.

———. 2004b. "The Spreading of Objects and Ideas in the Late Bronze Age Eastern Mediterranean: Two Case Examples from the Argolid of the 13th and 12th Centuries B.C." *BASOR* 336: 11–30.

———. 2006a. "Coming to Terms with the Past: Ideology and Power in Late Helladic IIIC." In *Ancient Greece: From the Mycenaean Palaces to the Age of Homer,* ed. Sigrid Deger-Jalkotzy and Irene S. Lemos, 123–50. Edinburgh Leventis Studies 3. Edinburgh: Edinburgh University Press.

———. 2006b. "Mycenaean Citadels as Performative Space." In *Constructing Power: Architecture, Ideology, and Social Practice,* ed. Joseph Maran, Carsten Juwig, Hermann Schwengel, and Ulrich Thaler, 75–91. Hamburg: LIT.

———. 2008. "Forschungen in der Unterburg von Tiryns 2000–2003." *Archäologischer Anzeiger:* 35–111.

———. Forthcoming. "The Crisis Years? Reflections on Signs of Instability in the Last Decades of the Mycenaean Palaces." In *Reasons for Change: Birth, Decline and Collapse of Societies between the End of the Fourth and the Beginning of the First Millennium B.C.,* ed. Andrea Cardarelli, Alberto Cazzella, Marcella Frangipane, and Renato Peroni. Scienze dell'antichità 15.

———, and Alkestis Papadimitriou. 2006. "Forschungen im Stadtgebiet von Tiryns 1999–2002." *Archäologischer Anzeiger:* 97–169.

Marzolff, Peter. 2004. "Das zweifache Rätsel Tiryns." In *Macht der Architektur: Architektur der Macht,* ed. Ernst-Ludwig Schwandner and Klaus Rheidt, 79–91. Diskussionen zur archäologischen Bauforschung, no. 8. Mainz: von Zabern.

Mühlenbruch, Tobias. 2002. Mykenische Architektur: Studien zur Siedlungsentwicklung nach dem Untergang der Paläste in der Argolis und Korinthia. MA thesis, University of Heidelberg.

———. 2007. "The Post-palatial Settlement in the Lower Citadel of Tiryns." In *LH IIIC Middle,* 243–51.

Müller, Kurt. 1930. *Tiryns III: Die Architektur der Burg und des Palastes.* Augsburg: Filser.

Papadimitriou, Alkestis. 1998. "L'évolution de l'habitat post-mycenien à Tirynthe: Les données archéologiques et leur interpretation historique (in Greek)." In *Argos et l'Argolide: Topographie et Urbanisme. Actes de la Table Ronde internationale, Athènes-Argos 28/4–1/5/1990,* ed. Anne Pariente and Gilles Touchais, 117–30. Paris: Boccard.

———. 2001. *Tiryns: A Guide to Its History and Archaeology.* Athens: Hesperos.

Podzuweit, Christian, and Dieter Salzmann. 1977. "Ein mykenischer Kieselmosaikfußboden aus Tiryns." *Archäologischer Azeiger:* 123–37.

Rodenwaldt, Gerhart. 1912. *Tiryns II: Die Fresken des Palastes.* Athens: Eleutheroudakis and
    Barth.

Rudolph, Wolf. 1973. "Die Nekropole am Prophitis Elias bei Tiryns." In *Tiryns VI*, 23–126.
    Mainz: von Zabern.

Schliemann, Heinrich. 1886. *Tiryns: Der prähistorische Palast der Könige von Tiryns.* Leipzig:
    Brockhaus.

Slenczka, Eberhard. 1975. "Damm und Kanal bei Kofini." In *Führer durch Tiryns*, ed. Ulf
    Jantzen, 70–71. Athens: German Archaeological Institute.

Stülpnagel, Hendrikje. 1999. Mykenische Keramik der Oberburg von Tiryns: Material der
    Ausgrabungen 1984, 1985 im Bereich des großen und kleinen Megarons. PhD diss.,
    University of Freiburg.

Touchais, Gilles. 1985. "Chronique des fouilles en 1984." *BCH* 109: 759–862.

Wright, James C. 1994. "The Spatial Configuration of Belief: The Archaeology of
    Mycenaean Religion." In *Placing the Gods: Sanctuaries and Sacred Space in Ancient
    Greece*, ed. Susan E. Alcock and Robin Osborne, 37–78. Oxford: Clarendon.

Zangger, Eberhard. 1992. *The Flood from Heaven: Deciphering the Atlantis Legend.* London:
    Sidgwick and Jackson.

———. 1993. *The Geoarchaeology of the Argolid.* Argolis 2. Berlin: Mann.

———. 1994. "Landscape Changes around Tiryns during the Bronze Age." *AJA* 98: 189–212.

Cyclades, Dodecanese, and Saronic Islands

CHAPTER 55

AEGINA KOLONNA

WALTER GAUSS

GENERAL INFORMATION

Aegina was one of the major centers of the Aegean Bronze Age. This chapter summarizes the most important information about the site of Kolonna, the main settlement known on the island (see figure 55.1). Excavation and research work were begun in the late 19th century and continue even today (Welter 1938; Gauss 1999; Felten 2007). Since 2002 a new series of excavations has focused on the MBA stratigraphic and ceramic sequence (Felten et al. 2003, 2004, 2005, 2006, 2007, 2008).

The importance of both the site and the entire island is mainly the result of its location in the center of the Saronic Gulf, at the maritime crossroads between central mainland Greece, the northeast Peloponnese, the Cyclades, and Crete. The material culture of Kolonna is generally associated with the Greek mainland, but foreign influences from the Cycladic islands and Crete also played a significant role, particularly in the MBA. Kolonna flourished for almost a millennium, from the late EBA II to at least the Shaft Grave period, as its impressive fortifications and wealth of material remains show.

Kolonna seems to be the earliest example of a ranked society in the Aegean, outside Crete, and a large commercial and perhaps political center in the Saronic Gulf. Jeremy Rutter has argued that "Kolonna has emerged as a Middle Helladic site without peer on the Greek mainland" (1993, 776, 780), while Wolf-Dietrich Niemeier goes even further and suggests the emergence of a state on Aegina comparable to contemporary political entities on Crete (1995).

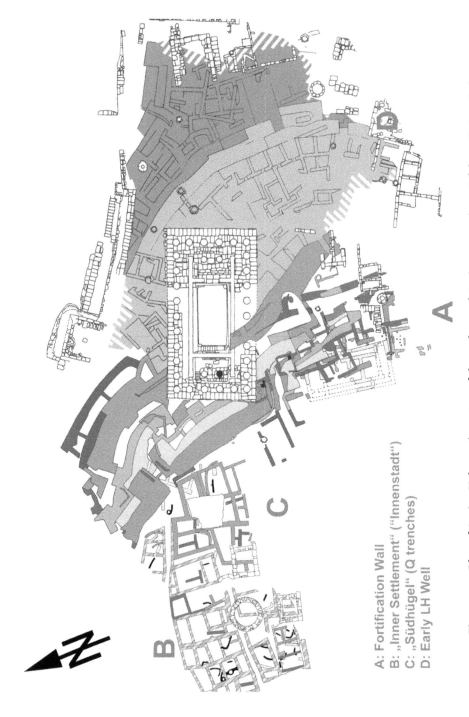

A: Fortification Wall
B: „Inner Settlement" ("Innenstadt")
C: „Südhügel" (Q trenches)
D: Early LH Well

Figure 55.1. Plan of Aegina Kolonna (courtesy of the author and Aegina excavations, Salzburg University).

LATE AND FINAL NEOLITHIC

The oldest remains at Kolonna can be dated to the Late and Final Neolithic periods (table 55.1). The pre–World War II excavations first reached Final Neolithic remains, published by Welter (1937) and restudied by Weisshaar (1994). The pottery, most of which was presumably produced locally, is characterized by pattern-burnished bowls of the Attica-Kephala culture, plastic and incised decoration, some of which have crusted decoration. Other finds of interest are a completely preserved, oval-shaped flask and the fragments of a small table. The latter, as well as the fragments with crusted decoration, indicate connections to Thessaly (Alram-Stern 1996, 220; Maran 1998, 30–31).

Above bedrock, the excavations of the 1970s and 1990s often reached a thick and hard fill layer of densely packed stones and earth, together with Final Neolithic to Early Helladic (EH) I pottery. This fill layer leveled the settlement area for the EBA II settlement and buried all earlier remains.

A number of postholes carved into bedrock and flimsy, single-rowed, straight-sided, and curved stone walls erected directly on bedrock are the only preserved architectural remains of the Kolonna I settlement phase that covers Late Neolithic to EH I. Two of the architectural remains were reconstructed: a number of postholes from an oval-shaped building ("Flechtwerkhaus") and the remains of a stone wall from a rectangular structure ("Haus mit Stützen") (Walter and Felten 1981, 10–11; Alram-Stern 1996, 220).

Recently found carinated and matt-painted sherds of the earlier stages of the Late Neolithic indicate that the nucleus of the settlement was even older than originally thought. Other important new finds are the fragments of a marble bowl, and most interesting small human clay figurines, some of them clearly male, were found in layers also containing pattern-burnished pottery (Felten and Hiller 1996, 2004). While the more recently excavated remains are not fully published, it is likely that the Final Neolithic settlement covered the entire area of the EBA settlement.

Elsewhere on Aegina there might have been other important Neolithic communities, as indicated by surface finds of two Late Neolithic female figurines of marble and seashell in the Eastern part of the island (Buchholz and Karagheorgis 1971, 98 cat. 1181–82; Papathanassopoulos 1996, 156, 318 cat. 239). Meanwhile, in the Peloponnese at Franchthi Cave, Aeginetan andesite was identified in the pottery of phase 4 (Vitelli 1993, 209), and andesite millstones originating from the Saronic Gulf region were found in Middle and Late Neolithic layers at the Athenian Agora, Franchthi, Kitsos, and Lerna, indicating early networks of exchange (Vitelli 1993, 111; Rutter 1993, 769–70).

Table 55.1. Phases of Aegina Kolonna

	Settlement Phase	Ceramic Phase	Research Areas 1 2 3 4	Imports First Appearance	Historical Chronology[c]
Neol to EH I	I	Phase A[a]		No information yet available	
EH II	II	Phase B[b]		Peloponnese (phase B or C)	
	III	Phase C[b]		Cycladic (phase B or C)	
	III (Rebuild.)	Phase C		Lefkandi I features (phase C)	EM III/MM IA transition
EH III	IV	Phase D		Peloponnese (phase D)	
	V (Destr.)	Phase E		Central Greece (phase E)	2160 to 2025 BC
	V (Reconstr.)	Phase E		Cycladic (phase F)	MM IA · 2160/2025 to 1979/1900 BC
	VI	Phase F		Local Cycladic Imitations (phase F)	MM IB · 1979/1900 to before 1800 BC
MH I	VI	Phase G		Lustrous Decorated (phase G)	MM IIA · before 1800 to 1750 BC
	VII	Phase G		Minoan (phase H)	
	VIII	Phase H		Cycladic (phase G)	
	VIIIA	Phase H			

			Local Minoan Imitations (phase I)		
MH II	IX	Phase I		MM IIB	1750 to 1700 BC
MH III	X	Phase J		MM IIIA	1700 to 1640/30 BC
LH I	X	Phase K	SE-Aegean	MM IIIB	1640/30 to 1600 BC
				LM IA	1600/1580 to 1510/1485 BC
LH II		Phase L		LM IB	1510/1485 to 1435 BC
Hiatus				LM II	1435 to 1400/1390 BC
LH IIIA		Phase M	Cypriote	LH IIIA1	1400/1390 to 1365/55 BC

[a] with subphases (A1, A2, etc.)

[b] according to L. Berger 2004

[c] after Warren-Hankey 1989, Warren 2006, 2007 and Bietak-Höfelmayer 2007

Research Areas: (1) Fortification Wall, (2) "Inner Settlement" (Innenstadt), (3) South Slope, Q-trenches (Südhügel), (4) Well Deposit ——— Vertical Stratigraphic Sequence

······· Existing Deposits, but not in Vertical Stratigraphic Sequence

Source: Based on information until September 2008 by W. Gauss, E. Kiriatzi, M. Lindblom, K. Pruckner, R. Smetana, P. Steier, F. Weninger, E.M. Wild. Table courtesy of the author.

EARLY HELLADIC I AND II

Clear statements on the site's development in EH I and during the early parts of the EH II are difficult, as the recently excavated material has not yet been published in full detail (table 55.1). Early Helladic I deposits are few and include the "Eckhaus," attributed to settlement phase Kolonna I. The pottery of this context is characterized by red, highly burnished open shapes with thickened rims (Felten and Hiller 1996, 54, pl. 12:1; Alram-Stern 1996, 219–20; 2004, 559; Maran 1998, 31). The leveling of the settlement area in advanced EH II is most likely responsible for the absence of substantial earlier architectural remains at the site (Felten and Hiller 2004, 1090).

The two following phases of occupation, Kolonna II and III, are attributed to the advanced and late EH II period. Significant amounts of pottery belonging to the first parts of EH II have not yet been isolated (Berger 2004, 1097).

The Kolonna II settlement is characterized by a corridor house, the "Haus am Felsrand," and by a large, freestanding structure, the "Herdhaus." The Haus am Felsrand was presumably two-storied and roofed with tiles (Walter and Felten 1981, 12–13; Maran 1998, 31–33; Alram-Stern 2004, 559). The excavations of the 1990s reached rich EH II layers, but only a few architectural remains were discovered, and a sequence of subsequent EH II layers was not achieved (Berger 2004, 1093).

The pottery of the Kolonna II settlement phase (ceramic phase B) is of high quality and characterized by the absence of clearly late EH II features. The repertoire of shapes and patterns is very similar to other EH II sites from the Greek mainland. Most characteristic are sauceboats in various types and bowls/saucers (flat or ring based). The overall amount of light painted (or yellow mottled, respectively, white slipped) pottery in ceramic phase B is high in comparison to phase C, and of excellent quality (Berger 2004, 1095–97). The Kolonna II settlement and its pottery of ceramic phase B are to be synchronized with Lerna phases III B late and III C (Maran 1998, 35; Berger 2004, in press)

The most important building of the Kolonna III settlement is a large corridor house ("Weißes Haus," ca. 9 by 18 m), replacing the older Haus am Felsrand. The architectural remains attributed to the Kolonna III settlement indicate that a number of large, freestanding buildings existed at the same time and at a relatively close distance to each other. One of them, the "Färberhaus," had most likely even larger dimensions (ca. 10 by 20 m) than the corridor house (Felten and Hiller 2004).

The walls of the corridor house are ca. 0.8 m thick and consist of a stone wall with mud-brick superstructure. A staircase leads to the upper story, and the building was roofed with tiles. Remains of the hearth, a round clay basin with an incised rim ("Stempelroller"), was found in one of the rooms (but not in situ) together with one pithos. Unlike the "House of the Tiles" at Lerna, no seals or seal impressions were found in the corridor house at Kolonna (for EH II seals and impression found unstratified or in later contexts: *CMS* V Suppl. 1A cat. 33; *CMS* V Suppl. 3, 1 cat. 1–2). The Kolonna III settlement was also presumably not protected by a fortification wall. The "Weißes Haus" and other buildings of that phase underwent slight modifications in their plan, perhaps indicating that the settlement lasted for some time.

The pottery of the Kolonna III settlement phase (ceramic phase C) is characterized by technological innovations and new shapes and decorations. Most important is the influence, first via appearance and then adoption, of East Aegean and Anatolian elements characteristic of the Lefkandi I-Kastri Group, such as one-handled tankards, bell-shaped cups, large shallow plates, scribble burnishing, and incised and impressed decorations (Berger 2004, 1101; in press). Flat-based bowls and saucers, some decorated with a red cross on the interior, are quite common. A new type of hybrid sauceboat that combines elements of the sauceboat and the askos makes its first appearance, as does a class of pottery with a gray core and a black slip. Light painted pottery is very rare in ceramic phase C, and dark painted pottery (already present in ceramic phase B) is now dominant (Berger 2004, 1098). Settlement phase Kolonna III and its pottery of ceramic phase C can be synchronized with Lerna phase III D (Maran 1998, 35; Berger 2004, 1097).

Small standardized weights of imported stone (e.g., marble) found in some quantities at the site are known in the central Mediterranean and indicate early standardization and trading networks at that time (Rahmstorf 2006b [for Aegina, cf. 73–79]; 2006a [for Aegina, cf. 24–28]). Recent excavations unearthed an important metal hoard of semiprecious, silver and gold jewelry in a late EH III or even an early MH context. The jewelry itself can be dated on stylistic arguments to EH II and shows connections to the Cyclades and the Near East (Reinholdt 2003, 2004, 2008).

EARLY HELLADIC III

Three phases of occupation, Kolonna IV to VI, have been distinguished for the EH III period, perhaps allowing Kolonna VI to last until the very beginning of the Middle Bronze Age (Walter and Felten 1981, 23–50, 105–122; Maran 1992, 323–25; 1998, 35–36; Gauss and Smetana 2002, 2003, 2004, 2007a, 2007b, in press a) (table 55.1).

New excavation work in the center of the prehistoric settlement has provided important stratigraphic information on the EH III to LH I sequence for not only the relative but also the absolute chronology (for recent C^{14} data see Wild et al., in press). No transitional phase EH II/III, as defined in Tiryns, was isolated at Kolonna.

The remains of the Kolonna IV settlement are few and situated on top of the ruins of the Kolonna III settlement, thus indicating a continuous habitation. The time span of the Kolonna IV settlement covers the first part of EH III, contemporary with the first phase of Lerna IV. The layout and size of the Kolonna IV settlement is unknown, and perhaps only a few houses existed at the site for some time.

The most important installation is the metal furnace that was erected in the ruins of the corridor house (the "Weißes Haus"), providing evidence for an early metal industry at the site (Walter and Felten 1981, 23–28). A number of crucibles were found in later EH III contexts, and lead ingots were reported by the pre–World War II excavators.

The pottery of the Kolonna IV settlement (ceramic phase D) is not well known. It is basically locally produced with occasional imports from the Peloponnese but no imports from the Cyclades. The range of shapes and patterns is totally different from that of the preceding ceramic phase C and characterized by the total absence of sauceboats, saucers, or any other characteristic EH II and Lefkandi I–Kastri group features. New shapes such as so-called bass bowls make their first appearance.

The Kolonna V settlement is thus far the only known fortified EH III site (Walter and Felten 1981, 28–42). Its layout and fortifications show signs of communal planning—approximately sixty to seventy houses were protected by the fortifications in the uppermost settlement area. The settlement lasted for some time—until it was destroyed in a massive fire. The time span of the Kolonna V settlement covers the middle and advanced part of the EH III period and is contemporary with the second and third phases of Lerna IV (Gauss and Smetana 2003, 2007b).

Due to the fiery destruction, rich deposits of pottery were found, characterizing ceramic phase E. The most common open and closed shapes are the bass bowls mentioned earlier (one handled cups and tankards), as well as medium-sized, belly-handled jars. The pottery is mainly locally produced and predominantly unpainted, with closest similarities to the pottery found at Lerna (Gauss and Kiriatzi in press). Imports from the Peloponnese and the mainland are attested, but none from the Cyclades are known. At Lerna, a presumable Aeginetan import was found in EH III layers (Dorias and Shriner 2002).

The massive fortifications of the Kolonna VI settlement use the ruins of the Kolonna V houses; therefore, less space is available for houses in the uppermost settlement area. The original fortification wall was rebuilt and served as an outwork until the late MH. The layout of the Kolonna VI settlement is uncertain, and Felten and Hiller (2004) note the appearance of curvilinear structures. One may assume that approximately 45 to 55 houses were protected by the fortifications. The time span of the Kolonna VI settlement covers the last and final part of the EH III period, which is contemporary with the third phase of Lerna IV. There are indications of partial destruction by fire at the end of ceramic phase F. The pottery found in these destruction deposits shows both traditional and new features and is partly inspired by the Cyclades. Imports from the mainland are known, and Cycladic imports make their first appearance since EH II (Gauss and Smetana 2007a, 2007b, 2008).

MIDDLE HELLADIC

The transition to Middle Helladic (MH) is continuous and indicates no sharp break in the material culture (table 55.1). Four subsequent settlement phases, Kolonna VII to X, have been differentiated for the MH (Walter and Felten 1981, 50–85; Maran 1992, 325–28; 1998, 36–37; Rutter 1993, 775–81). The time span of the Kolonna VII and VIII settlements covers the beginning of MH (ceramic phases G to H), while the

Kolonna IX settlement covers the middle part of MH (ceramic phases I), and the Kolonna X settlement phase covers the late MH and the beginning of LH (ceramic phases J and K [Gauss and Smetana 2007b]).

The most impressive and—for the MH period—unique architectural monument is the continuously remodeled and strengthened fortification wall, which consists of an outwork and a main wall, both built of undressed stones. The entrance system of the two main gates was continuously improved and protected by bastion-like towers.

Minoan imports and technology reach Kolonna in early MH (ceramic phase H), and we note major changes in the pottery production, as demonstrated by the first appearance of Aeginetan matt-painted pottery, a type widely distributed in the Aegean (Rutter 1993, 777, figure 12; Lindblom 2001). It is handmade, most often pot marked (Lindblom 2001), and decorated mostly in geometric motifs applied with a characteristic matt, manganese-based paint (Wünsche 1977a, 1977b; Siedentopf 1991). Recent scientific analysis programs have focused on the large-scale characterization of prehistoric Aeginetan pottery (Mommsen et al. 2001; Gauss and Kiriatzi in press).

In early MH (ceramic phase H), the nucleus of the so-called Large Building Complex was founded, the mansion of Kolonna. Situated in the center of the innermost city, it is built of massive walls and very large stone blocks. The excavations are not yet finished, and, thus, a reconstruction of its plan is still difficult. The building covered an area between 230 and 680 m², four to ten times larger than the average MH house at Kolonna, and underwent a series of architectural changes, including an extension in the time span of the Kolonna IX settlement. High-quality, locally produced and imported pottery from Crete and the Cyclades was found inside the building and emphasizes, together with new evidence, the site's extraordinary subsistence and diet (Forstenpointner et al. in press a, b), as well as its importance and wealth.

During the time of the Kolonna IX settlement (ceramic phase I), an interesting phenomenon, namely the Aeginetan local production of Minoan-type pottery, makes its first appearance. This production is remarkably different from the other, more traditionally produced, local pottery, as it is wheel made, and no potter's marks have been identified so far. The local reproduction of Cretan technological practices may indicate that Cretan craftspeople have settled on Aegina. So far mainly drinking and cooking vessels are represented (Hiller 1993; Gauss 2006; Gauss and Smetana 2007b).

This evidence, together with other interesting finds such as so-called Minoan ritual stone hammers (Reinholdt 1992) and a double-ax mason's mark on an ashlar block (Niemeier 1995), indicate a highly "Minoanized" social elite or even Minoans living at Kolonna (Gauss 2006; Gauss-Smetana 2007b, in press b). A pit inside the Large Building Complex has yielded important new finds: two cylindrical clay objects, a seal, and an object with a positive relief made of local clay and decorated with humans, animals, and spirals. Both objects are unique finds not only at Kolonna but also on the Greek mainland and may point toward administration and bureaucracy, by that time known only from Minoan Crete or even more distant areas (Gauss and Smetana in press b).

During the time of the Kolonna IX settlement, the site extended toward the east ("mittelhelladische Vorstadt") and was again protected by a massive fortification wall. Within the extension, a series of rooms was built against the wall. The function of these rooms is unclear, but some may have served as a workshop area since in one of the rooms a well-preserved MH potter's kiln was found in situ.

Another important monument of the Kolonna IX settlement, a shaft grave that at present is the earliest known on the island, is situated immediately in front of the fortification wall of the settlement extension, close to one of the gates. The grave goods consist of weapons, gold jewelry, and locally made and imported Cycladic and Cretan vessels (Kilian-Dirlmeier 1997).

LATE HELLADIC

The transition to the Late Bronze Age (LH) happened without a sharp break at Kolonna (table 55.1). At the beginning of the LH period, the settlement extended eastward and was fortified with a massive wall of large, cyclopean-like undressed stone blocks. Building activity went on there at least until LH IIA (Wohlmayr 1989, 2000, 2007; Gauss 2007; Deger-Jalkotzy 2009). Recent excavations also indicate an extension toward the south, built in Mycenaean times (Felten 2007, 19).

The mansion of Kolonna, the Large Building Complex, was in use until LH I and presumably even until LH II. Later, in LH IIIA, a large potter's kiln was erected inside its remains (Gauss 2007). Most other Mycenaean ruins of the Palatial and Postpalatial period were destroyed by later building activity at the Greek sanctuary in the first millennium BC, so the organization of the LH settlement is mostly unknown.

At present, it is difficult to be certain about the importance of the Kolonna site in the Mycenaean period. After a long period of extraordinary wealth and importance, it seems as if the growth of the major Mycenaean centers in the Argolid, Attica, the Korinthia, and Troizenia involved a slight decline in importance at Kolonna. Although the site certainly continued to be important, as is demonstrated by its fortifications and the rich finds in the nearby chamber tomb cemetery on Windmill Hill, it was not a palatial center.

Mycenaean figural pottery (Hiller 2006; Felten 2007, 20, figure 13), Cypriote white slip II, and southeast Aegean imports, as well as the remains of an undecorated clay sealing (Felten 2007, 18–19, figure 14; Gauss 2007), indicate that Kolonna was still connected to the main trade network until the LH IIIA2 and LH IIIB periods. A decrease in Kolonna's importance is particularly mirrored in the development of the local pottery production.

In the MH and the Shaft Grave periods, exported Aeginetan pottery reached its widest geographical distribution, as illustrated by the large numbers of Aeginetan drinking vessels found in the fill of the LH I shaft grave at Lerna (Lindblom 2007) and the vessels uncovered in the volcanic destruction layer at Akrotiri on Thera and at many other sites in the central Aegean (Rutter 1993, 777, figure 12; Lindblom 2001). Later, Mycenaean lustrous decorated pottery was more appreciated than the matt painted and often still handmade Aeginetan types. Only medium to large matt-painted vessels and cooking pots continued to be produced and exported (Gauss 2007, 164–65 with further references). Scientific analysis of Marine-style pottery from the site suggests that some might have been locally produced (Mountjoy, Jones, and Cherry 1978, 163, 168; Jones 1986, 447), but more detailed analysis is necessary to confirm this interpretation (Gauss and Kiriatzi in press).

A number of graves at the nearby Windmill Hill were excavated in the early 20th century and contained rich pottery finds that range in date from LH I to LH IIIB, most published by Hiller (1975). At Kolonna, LH IIIB2 and LH IIIC pottery is rare, and no contemporary graves were reported from the Windmill Hill cemetery (Hiller 1975, 55; Felten 2007, 19–20). Moreover, LH IIIC Late and sub-Mycenaean pottery is very rare, and the absence of finds may indicate that the site was gradually abandoned. A number of Protogeometric and Early Geometric cist graves of children and at least one adult provide evidence that habitation, maybe after a short break, continued in the early first millennium BC (Hiller 2003; Gauss 2005; Felten 2007, 20; Felten et al. 2003, 2004, 2006; Deger-Jalkotzy 2009; Jarosch-Reinholdt 2009).

BIBLIOGRAPHY

Alram-Stern, Eva. 1996. *Die ägäische Frühzeit, 2. Serie, Forschungsbericht 1975–2002. 1. Band, Das Neolithikum in Griechenland.* Vienna: Verlag der Österreichischen Akademie der Wissenschaften.

———. 2004. *Die ägäische Frühzeit, 2. Serie, Forschungsbericht 1975–2002. 2. Band, Teil 1 und 2, Die Frühbronzezeit in Griechenland.* Vienna: Verlag der Österreichischen Akademie der Wissenschaften.

Berger, Lydia. 2004. "Neue Ergebnisse zur FH II–Keramik aus der prähistorischen Innenstadt." In Eva Alram Stern, *Die ägäische Frühzeit, 2. Serie Forschungsbericht 1975–2002. 2. Band, Teil 2, Die Frühbronzezeit in Griechenland*, 1093–1103. Vienna: Verlag der Österreichischen Akademie der Wissenschaften.

———. In press. "Eastern Influences on the Early Helladic II Pottery of Aegina Kolonna." In *The Aegean Early Bronze Age: New Evidence*, ed. Christos Doumas, Colin Renfrew, and Ourania Koukou. Athens, April 11–14, 2008.

Buchholz, Hans-Günter, and Vassos Karageorghis. 1971. *Altägäis und Altkypros.* Tübingen: Wasmuth.

Deger-Jalkotzy, Sigrid. 2009. "Was geschah in Äigina während und nach der mykenischen Palastzeit?" In *Aiakeion. Beiträge zur Klassischen Altertumswissenschaft zu Ehren von Florens Felten*, ed. Claus Reinholdt, Peter Scherrer, and Wolfgang Wohlmayr. Vienna: Phoibos-Verl., S. 49–58.

Dorias, Michael J., and Christina M. Shriner. 2002. "An Electron Microprobe Study of P645/T390: Evidence for an EH III Lerna-Aegina Connection." *Geoarchaeology* 17: 755–78.

Felten, Florens. 2007. "The History of a Greek Acropolis." In *Middle Helladic Pottery and Synchronisms: Proceedings of the International Workshop Held at Salzburg, October 31st–November 2nd, 2004,* ed. Florens Felten, Walter Gauss, and Rudolfine Smetana, 11–34. Vienna: Verlag der Österreichischen Akademie der Wissenschaften.

———, and Stefan Hiller. 1996. "Ausgrabungen in der vorgeschichtlichen Innenstadt von Ägina-Kolonna (Alt-Ägina)." *ÖJhBeibl* 65: 29–112.

———. 2004. "Forschungen zur Frühbronzezeit auf Ägina-Kolonna 1993–2002." In *Die ägäische Frühzeit, 2. Serie Forschungsbericht 1975–2002. 2. Band, Teil 2, Die Frühbronzezeit in Griechenland,* ed. Eva Alram Stern, 1089–92. Vienna: Verlag der Österreichischen Akademie der Wissenschaften.

———, Claus Reinholdt, Walter Gauss, and Rudolfine Smetana. 2003. "Ägina-Kolonna 2002. Vorbericht über die Grabungen des Instituts für Klassische Archäologie der Universität Salzburg." *ÖJh* 72: 41–65.

———. 2004. "Ägina-Kolonna 2003: Vorbericht über die Grabungen des Instituts für Klassische Archäologie der Universität Salzburg." *ÖJh* 73: 97–128.

Felten, Florens, Claus Reinholdt, Eduard Pollhammer, Walter Gauss, and Rudolfine Smetana. 2005. "Ägina-Kolonna 2004: Vorbericht über die Grabungen des Fachbereichs für Altertumswissenschaften/Klassische und Frühägäische Archäologie der Universität Salzburg." *ÖJh* 74: 7–37.

———. 2006. "Ägina-Kolonna 2005: Vorbericht über die Grabungen des Fachbereichs für Altertumswissenschaften/Klassische und Frühägäische Archäologie der Universität Salzburg." *ÖJh* 75: 9–38.

———. 2007. "Ägina-Kolonna 2006: Vorbericht über die Grabungen des Fachbereichs für Altertumswissenschaften/Klassische und Frühägäische Archäologie der Universität Salzburg." *ÖJh* 76: 89–119.

———. 2008. "Ägina-Kolonna 2007: Vorbericht über die Grabungen des Fachbereichs für Altertumswissenschaften / Klassische und Frühägäische Archäologie der Universität Salzburg." *ÖJh* 77: 47–76.

Forstenpointner, Gerhard, Alfred Galik, Walter Gauss, Gerald Weißengruber, Ursula Thanheiser, and Stefan Zohmann. In press a. "Subsistence and More in Middle Bronze Age Aegina-Kolonna: Exploitation of Marine Resources." In *Mesohelladika.*

———. In press b. "Subsistence and More in Middle Bronze Age Aegina-Kolonna: Patterns of Husbandry, Hunting, and Agriculture." In *Mesohelladika.*

Gauss, Walter. 1999. "Aigina." In *Der neue Pauly: Enzyklopädie der Antike. Rezeptions- und Wissenschaftsgeschichte* 13, 27–32. Stuttgart: Metzler.

———. 2005. "Beobachtungen zum Apsidenbau von Ägina-Kolonna." In *Synergia: Festschrift für Friedrich Krinzinger,* ed. Barbara Brandt, Verena Gassner, and Sabine Ladstätter, 221–28. Vienna: Phoibos.

———. 2006. "Minos auf Ägina: Beobachtungen zu den Beziehungen Äginas zu Kreta." In *Timelines,* vol. 2, 435–46.

———. 2007. "Ägina Kolonna in frühmykenischer Zeit." In *Keimelion: Elitenbildung und elitärer Konsum von der mykenischen Palastzeit bis zur homerischen Epoche. Akten des internationalen Kongresses vom 3. bis 5. Februar 2005 in Salzburg,* ed. Eva Alram-Stern and Georg Nightingale, 163–72. Vienna: Verlag der Österreichischen Akademie der Wissenschaften.

———, and Evangelia Kiriatzi. In press. *Pottery Production and Supply at Bronze Age Kolonna, Aegina: an integrated archaeological and scientic study of a ceramic landscape. Ägina-Kolonna. Forschungen und Ergebnisse 5.* Vienna: Verlag der Österreichischen Akademie der Wissenschaften.

Gauss, Walter, and Rudolfine Smetana. 2002. "Untersuchung zur früh- und mittelhelladischen Keramik von Ägina Kolonna." In *Temenos: Festgabe für Florens Felten und Stefan Hiller*, ed. Beatrix Asamer, Peter Höglinger, Claus Reinholdt, Rudolfine Smetana, and Wolfang Wohlmayr, 11–19. Vienna: Phoibos.

———. 2003. "The Early Helladic III Pottery from Aigina Kolonna." In *SCIEM* II, 471–86.

———. 2004. "Bericht zur Keramik und Stratigraphie der Frühbronzezeit III aus Ägina Kolonna." In *Die ägäische Frühzeit, 2. Serie Forschungsbericht 1975–2002. 2. Band, Teil 2, Die Frühbronzezeit in Griechenland*, ed. Eva Alram-Stern, 1104–13. Vienna: Verlag der Österreichischen Akademie der Wissenschaften.

———. 2007a. "Early and Middle Bronze Age Stratigraphy and Pottery from Aegina Kolonna." In *SCIEM* III, 451–72.

———. 2007b. "The Stratigraphic Sequence of the SCIEM 2000 Project." In *MH Pottery*, 57–80.

———. 2008. "Aegina and the Cyclades in the Bronze Age." In *Horizon*, 325–38.

———. In press a. "Aegina Kolonna in Early Helladic III." In *The Aegean Early Bronze Age: New Evidence*, ed. Christos Doumas, Colin Renfrew, and Ourania Koukou. Athens, April 11–14, 2008.

———. In press b. "Middle Bronze Age Aegina Kolonna." In *Mesohelladika*.

Hiller, Stefan. 1975. *Mykenische Keramik: Alt-Ägina IV.1*. Mainz: von Zabern.

———. 1993. "Minoan and Minoanizing Pottery on Aegina." In *Wace and Blegen*, 197–99.

———. 2003. "Some Preliminary Thoughts about Aegina in the Dark Ages." In *Argosaronikos: Praktika 1. Diethnus Synedriu Historias kai Archaiologias tu Argosaroniku, Poros 26–29 Iuniu 1998*, ed. Eleni Konsolaki-Giannopoulou, 11–20. Athens: Demos Porou.

———. 2006. "Keramik mit Pictorial Style Dekor aus Ägina Kolonna." In *Figurative Painting on Mycenaean and Geometric Pottery: Pictorial Pursuits. Papers from Two Seminars at the Swedish Institute at Athens in 1999 and 2001*, ed. Eva Rystedt, and Berit Wells, 73–82. Stockholm: Aström.

Jarosch-Reinholdt, Veronika. 2009. *Die geometrische Keramik von Kap Kolonna*. Vienna: Verlag der Österreichischen Akademie der Wissenschaften (Ägina-Kolonna. Forschungen und Ergebnisse, 4).

Jones, Richard E. 1986. *Greek and Cypriot Pottery: A Review of Scientific Studies*. Fitch Laboratory Occasional Papers 1. Athens.

Kilian-Dirlmeier, Imma. 1997. *Das mittelbronzezeitliche Schachtgrab von Ägina. Alt-Ägina IV.3*. Mainz: von Zabern.

Lindblom, Michael. 2001. *Marks and Makers: Appearance, Distribution, and Function of Middle and Late Helladic Manufacturers' Marks on Aeginetan Pottery*. SIMA 128. Jonsered, Sweden: Åström.

———. 2007. "Early Mycenaean Mortuary Meals at Lerna VI with Special Emphasis on Their Aeginetan Components." In *Middle Helladic Pottery and Synchronisms: Proceedings of the International Workshop Held at Salzburg, October 31st–November 2nd, 2004*, ed. Florens Felten, Walter Gauss, and Rudolfine Smetana, 115–35. Vienna: Verlag der Österreichischen Akademie der Wissenschaften.

Maran, Joseph. 1992. *Die mittlere Bronzezeit: Die deutschen Ausgrabungen auf der Pevkakia-Magula in Thessalien III*. Bonn: Habelt.

———. 1998. *Kulturwandel auf dem griechischen Festland und den Kykladen im spätern 3. Jahrtausend v. Chr.* Universitätsforschungen zur prähistorischen Archäologie, no. 53. Bonn: Habelt.

Mommsen, Hans, Walter Gauss, Stefan Hiller, Doris Ittameier, and Joseph
    Maran. 2001. "Charakterisierung bronzezeitlicher Keramik von Ägina durch
    Neutronenaktivierungsanalyse." In *Archäologisches Zellwerk: Beiträge zur
    Kulturgeschichte in Europa und Asien. Festschrift für Helmut Roth zum 60. Geburtstag*,
    ed. Ernst Pohl, Udo Recker, and Claudia Theune, 80–96. Rahden/Westf.: Leidorf.
Mountjoy, Penelope A., Richard E. Jones, and John F. Cherry. 1978. "Provenance Studies of
    the LM IB/LH IIA Marine Style." *BSA* 73: 143–71.
Niemeier, Wolf-Dietrich. 1995. "Aegina, First Aegean State outside Crete?" In *Politeia*, 73–80.
Papathanassopoulos, George A. 1996. *Neolithic Culture in Greece*. Athens: Goulandris
    Foundation, Museum of Cycladic Art.
Rahmstorf, Lorenz. 2006a. "In Search of the Earliest Balance Weights, Scales, and Weighing
    Systems from the East Mediterranean, the Near and Middle East." In *Weights in
    Context: Bronze Age Weighing Systems of the Eastern Mediterranean. Chronology,
    Typology, Material and Archaeological Context. Proceedings of the International
    Colloquium, Rome, 22–24 November 2004*, ed. Maria E. Alberti, Enrico Ascalone, and
    Luca Peyronel, 9–45. Studi e Materiali no. 13. Rome: Istituto Italiano di Numismatica.
———. 2006b. "Zur Ausbreitung vorderasiatischer Innovation in die frühbronzezeitliche
    Ägäis." *PZ* 81: 49–96.
Reinholdt, Claus. 1992. "Ein minoischer Steinhammer in Ägina." *Archäologisches
    Korrespondenzblatt* 22: 57–62.
———. 2003. "The Early Bronze Age Jewelry Hoard from Kolonna, Aigina." In *Art of the
    First Cities: The Third Millennium b.c. from the Mediterranean to the Indus*, ed. Joan
    Aruz and Ronald Wallenfels, 260–61. New York: Metropolitan Museum of Art.
———. 2004. "Der frühbronzezeitliche Schmuck-Hortfund von Kap Kolonna/Ägina."
    In *Die ägäische Frühzeit, 2. Serie Forschungsbericht 1975–2002. 2. Band, Teil 2, Die
    Frühbronzezeit in Griechenland*, ed. Eva Alram-Stern, 1113–19. Vienna: Verlag der
    Österreichischen Akademie der Wissenschaften.
———. 2008. *Der frühbronzezeitliche Schmuckhortfund von Kap Kolonna: Ägina und die
    Ägais im Goldzeitalter des 3. Jahrtausends v.Chr. Ägina-Kolonna. Forschungen und
    Ergebnisse 2*. Vienna: Verlag der Österreichischen Akademie der Wissenschaften.
Rutter, Jeremy B. 1993. "Review of Aegean Prehistory II. The Prepalatial Bronze Age of the
    Southern and Central Greek Mainland." *AJA* 97: 745–97.
Siedentopf, Heinrich, B. 1991. *Mattbemalte Keramik der Mittleren Bronzezeit: Alt-Ägina IV.2*.
    Mainz: von Zabern.
Vitelli, Karen D. 1993. *Franchthi Neolithic Pottery*. Vol. 1, *Classification and Ceramic Phases 1
    and 2*. Excavations at Franchthi Cave, Greece, no. 8. Bloomington: Indiana University
    Press.
Walter, Hans, and Florens Felten. 1981. *Die vorgeschichtliche Stadt: Befestigungen. Häuser.
    Funde. Alt-Ägina III.1*. Mainz: von Zabern.
Weisshaar, Hans-Joachim. 1994. "Keramik des südwest-ägäischen Chalkolithikums von
    Ägina." In *Festschrift für Otto-Hermann Frey zum 65. Geburtstag*, ed. Claus Dobiat,
    675–89. Marburg: Hitzeroth.
Welter, Gabriel. 1937. "Aiginetische Keramik." *AA* 1937: 19–26.
———. 1938. *Aigina*. Berlin: Mann.
Wild, Eva-Maria, Walter Gauß, Gerhard Forstenpointner, Michael Lindblom, Rudolfine
    Smetana, Peter Steier, Ursula Thanheiser, Franz. Weninger. In press. "¹⁴C Dating of
    the Early to Late Bronze Age Stratigraphic Sequence of Aegina Kolonna, Greece." In
    Proceedings of the Eleventh International Conference on Accelerator Mass Spectometry,
    Rome, September 14–19, 2008.

Wohlmayr, Wolfgang. 1989. "Ägina Kolonna: Die schachtgräberzeitliche Siedlung." In *Transition*, 151–53.

———. 2000. "Schachtgräberzeitliche Keramik aus Ägina." In *Österreichische Forschungen zur ägäischen Bronzezeit 1998: Akten der Tagung am Institut für Klassische Archäologie der Universtität Wien, 2.–3. Mai 1998*, ed. Fritz Blakolmer, 127–36. Vienna: Phoibos.

———. 2007. "Aegina Kolonna MH III–LH I: Ceramic Phases of an Aegean Trade-domain." In *Middle Helladic Pottery and Synchronisms: Proceedings of the International Workshop Held at Salzburg, October 31st–November 2nd, 2004*, ed. Florens Felten, Walter Gauss, and Rudolfine Smetana, 44–55. Vienna: Verlag der Österreichischen Akademie der Wissenschaften.

Wünsche, Raimund. 1977a. "Die Entwicklung der mittelhelladischen mattbemalten Keramik." *Münchner Jahrbücher* 28: 7–27.

———. 1977b. *Studien zur äginetischen Keramik der frühen und mittleren Bronzezeit*. Munich: Deutscher Kunstverlag.

CHAPTER 56

....

AKROTIRI

....

CHRISTOS DOUMAS

FORTY years of continuous and systematic geological and archaeological investigations at Akrotiri on the island of Santorini (Thera) have yielded ample evidence for reconstructing the history of the site and filling gaps in the history of the wider Aegean region.

Deep soundings made throughout the excavated area have shown that the settlement was founded in the mid-fifth millennium BC and originally occupied the tip of a low promontory, following the general rule in the Cycladic islands (Doumas 2007, 85–88). This small, Late Neolithic coastal village, whose economy was based mainly on farming and fishing activities, was related culturally to other contemporary settlements in the Cyclades (Sotirakopoulou 1999), namely Saliagos near Antiparos (Evans and Renfrew 1968), Grotta on Naxos (Hadjianastasiou 1988), and Ftelia on Mykonos (Sampson 2002).

During the Early Bronze Age (3rd millennium BC), this village seems to have grown considerably, as one can infer from the extensive cemetery of rock-cut chambers on the gentle slopes of the promontory. Although architectural remains are still scarce, the moveable finds, such as pottery, marble vases, and figurines, place this EBA settlement in the orbit of the Early Cycladic culture (Sotirakopoulou 1998, 1999). Given that there is no source of good-quality marble on Thera, the Early Cycladic marble artifacts found so far must have either been made locally from imported raw material or, more likely, been imported ready made from other Cycladic islands, such as Paros and Naxos, where they are well attested. On the other hand, indirect evidence suggests that Theran pumice was used as an abrasive agent for polishing the surface of marble figurines and vessels made on other islands. It is safe to assume that commodities of a perishable nature, such as foodstuffs and timber, were also exchanged between Thera and other parts of the Aegean, the Greek mainland, and Crete.

The cemetery of rock-cut chambers is particularly interesting. In the Early Bronze Age Cyclades, inhumation in cist graves is the norm (Doumas 1977, 37–47), whereas rock-cut chambers are exceptions, previously known only from Melos (Edgar 1904, 234–37) and Epano Kouphonisi (Zapheiropoulou 2008). Outside the Cyclades but closely connected with EC burial practices, they have been found at Manika in Euboea (Papavasileiou 1910, 2–20) and at Hagia Photia in Crete (Davaras and Betancourt 2004). These are all places where stone slabs for the construction of cist graves are not easily available and where the geological substrate favors the opening of chambers: soft lava deposits in Melos and Thera, soft sedimentary deposits at Manika and Hagia Photia.

Investigation of the rock-cut chambers at Akrotiri has revealed that by the end of the third millennium BC, they had been abandoned and filled with debris almost up to their ceiling. Pithos burials of children were found in some, either beneath the debris or within it. Of particular importance is the discovery of a special construction in association with the cemetery, which corroborates sporadic evidence from various Aegean sites (Branigan 1993, 129–33; Day, Wilson, and Evangelia Kyriatzi 1998, 135; Doumas 1977, 75, 103; Murphy 1998, 36; Mylonas 1959, 106 ff.; Pantelidou-Gofa 2008). Fascinating, too, is the evidence of the use of seawater as a purifying agent from the pollution of death, a belief well documented in historical antiquity (Doumas 2008a, 174–75).

The Middle Bronze Age (Middle Cycladic) city expanded over the area of the defunct cemetery. Indeed, the filling in of the chambers may well have been an intentional measure to rehabilitate and consolidate the ground in order to facilitate this expansion. The material culture suggests that the society at Akrotiri during the transition from the Early to the Middle Bronze Age was enjoying a period of considerable prosperity. The pottery from the fill of the chambers includes large quantities of transport amphorae from different parts of the Aegean, indicating that Akrotiri was already an Aegean trading center (Wilson, Day, and Dimopoulou-Rethemiotaki 2008, 269).

The abolition of the cemetery took place after the introduction to Thera of a class of pottery that, both typologically and technically, is at home in the northeast Aegean islands, where important proto-urban settlements, such as Poliochni on Lemnos, Thermi on Lesbos, Emporio on Chios, and Heraion on Samos, had developed (Doumas 2004a, 85–93). Such vases, typical of the black and brown burnished pottery from these islands, had not previously been found as far south as Thera. Known from other Cycladic islands and mainland sites, they have been classed as the Kastri or Lefkandi group and are also characteristic of the short-lived fortified Cycladic settlements, such as Kastri on Syros and Panormos on Naxos (Doumas 2004a, 94–95).

At about this time, perhaps one or two centuries before the end of the 3rd millennium BC, the aforementioned proto-urban settlements in the north Aegean were abandoned, among them Poliochni, which has been recognized as the most important center of Early Bronze Age metallurgy in the region. It is perhaps not without significance that, along with the introduction of Kastri-style pottery, an intensification of metallurgical activities is observed in the south Aegean (Doonan, Day, and Dimopoulou-Rethemiotaki 2007, 111).

There are many reasons to believe that the development of Poliochni into the first city in Europe, as well as the earliest and most important center for the trade of metals and the practice of metallurgical technology, was due to its contacts with the Caucasus region and the Euxine Pontus (Doumas 1991). The causes of its abandonment are not known, but the loss of the possibility of transactions with the East may well have been a factor. It appears that Poliochni lost its strategic role in the trade of metals just when the demand for metals was increasing in the Aegean, particularly in Crete, where a palatial system was emerging.

Moreover, by the end of the 3rd millennium BC, Cyprus had been recognized as an inexhaustible source of copper. The strategic location of Thera on this new metal route between Crete and Cyprus is undisputable. It is, therefore, possible that the systematic practice of metallurgy at Akrotiri, documented by the presence of scoriae, crucibles, moulds, and so on, at the time of introduction of the Kastri-group pottery, was due to the arrival of displaced northeast Aegean smiths who settled and plied their skills in Thera (Doumas 1997).

Around the turn from the 3rd to the 2nd millennium BC, developments at Akrotiri gathered momentum. In the course of the Middle Bronze Age (ca. 2000–1650 BC), the settlement evolved into an urban center, features of which are communal works such as town planning, paved streets, a drainage-sewerage system, and so on (Doumas 1999a, 157). There was also clear division of labor. Although the primary sector of the economy—agriculture, animal husbandry, and fishing—was the firm basis, there is both direct and indirect evidence of increasing involvement in the secondary sector. Standardization of vase shapes and the mass production of pottery point to the existence of large workshops that covered both the local demand and the export trade. Potters, therefore, constituted a large category of specialized artisans. Metal objects found in the Middle Cycladic context might have been imported. However, the evidence mentioned earlier implies local metallurgical activities that required specialized skills. There is indirect evidence of the existence of other specialist craftspersons, such as dyers, shipwrights, masons, carpenters, and stone carvers, who were involved either seasonally or exclusively in the secondary sector.

The fact that only parts of the Middle Cycladic buildings are exposed in the trenches opened for the pillars of the new shelter does not permit any attempt at their interpretation. However, from the strong foundations and the size of their walls, one can deduce that they were large and had at least two stories. In fact, some of the impressive Late Cycladic I buildings seem to have been founded during the Middle Cycladic period.

Study of the stratigraphy has shown that the site was susceptible to earthquakes and has shed light on the inhabitants' behavior after a seismic destruction, such as removal of victims from the ruins, rescue of still usable commodities, and separating building materials for reuse (Doumas 2000, 171; Palyvou 2005, 177–78).

The Middle Cycladic (Middle Bronze Age) finds from Akrotiri are revolutionizing our knowledge about this period not only in the Cycladic islands but also in the entire Aegean. Among them are many pottery vessels decorated in bichrome technique with lustrous paint, linear motifs, and isolated plant—including the pomegranate—and animal motifs. Griffins seem to have been very popular among the Middle Cycladic exotica, where they turn up mainly on large pithoi, while narrative scenes also appear, as on the bathtub with a landscape in which birds and quadrupeds flee to the right, away from a male figure (hunter?) on the left (cf. Doumas 2008b, 30–36). It is possible that such representations were associated with Middle Cycladic mythology, but this remains in the realm of speculation. What they surely reveal is that the society at Akrotiri in the Middle Bronze Age was ready to adopt large-scale wall painting as soon as the technique and materials became available.

It is an irony of fate that our picture of the Late Bronze Age city is vivid due to its burial under pumice and volcanic ash. Although its limits still remain unknown, it appears that its plan was dictated mainly by the terrain on which it was founded and the modifications due to the accommodation of debris after earthquake destructions (figure 56.1a–b). Main streets with a general north-south direction—toward the sea—and intersected by cross streets were designed not only to facilitate communication but also to accommodate the sewage system and to prevent the rainwater from undermining the buildings. The entrance to the buildings always faces either a wide street or an open space or square (Doumas 1983, 50–51; 2007, 85–89; Palyvou 2005, 25–43).

Rectangular juxtaposed units seem to have been the pattern for the layout of both private and public buildings. Built of local volcanic stones and clay, they usually consisted of two or occasionally three stories. Their roofs were flat and were often supported by central wooden columns standing on stone bases (Doumas 1983, 50–55; 2007, 89–91; Palyvou 2005, 25–43). As a rule, storerooms and facilities for domestic tasks, such as platforms for milling grains or hearths for cooking, were located on the ground floor. The residential quarters were in the upper stories, and their furniture, examples of which have been recovered through casts made from their negatives left in the volcanic ash, evidently included looms (Doumas 1983, 116–17). The absence of household facilities of this kind from two major buildings, the so-called Xeste 3 and Xeste 4, in conjunction with their size, ashlar masonry, internal arrangement, and the iconography of their wall paintings, led to their qualification as public buildings. Indeed, Xeste 3 seems to have been used for rites of passage, while Xeste 4—not yet fully explored—gives the impression that it served an administrative function.

In each house excavated so far, at least one room was decorated with wall paintings—perhaps depending on the residents' affluence—while in the public buildings the mural decoration covered larger areas (Doumas 1992). The topographical distribution of wall paintings in the buildings is perhaps related to their meaning: In private houses upper-story rooms mainly in the north part were decorated with wall paintings that were visible from outside through large windows, whereas in public buildings the decorated walls were not restricted to any specific part of the building and were not visible from outside (Doumas 2005).

Figure 56.1. Plan of Akrotiri (courtesy of the Archaeological Society of Athens).

Study of the commodities stored in the houses, such as clay vases, stone and metal vessels, baskets, pieces of furniture, fishing nets, stone and bronze tools, and even foodstuffs enables us to reconstruct a rather clear picture of the Akrotiri community. These finds are evidence of farming, fishing, stone- and woodcarving, weaving, dyeing, metalworking, and so on. But the activity that seems to have created the city's wealth, as reflected in the architecture and the monumental art of wall painting, was maritime trade and shipping, which, as we have seen, was already established by the end of the 3rd millennium BC. The Miniature Frieze from Room 5 of the West House (figure 56.2) gives some idea of the kind of ships used by the LBA Therans in their overseas transactions and of the exotic lands they visited (Doumas 1992, 47–85).

However, it is the actual imports that provide insight into the commodities they traded. Imports and influences from Crete, at first sporadic, intensified gradually, and by the time of the volcanic eruption that buried the city, these were so ubiquitous that in the early years of the excavation many scholars were under the false impression that Akrotiri was a Cretan colony. Crete was by no means the only source of imports, however. Objects from various parts of the Aegean, as well as from East Mediterranean lands, are frequently encountered. Canaanite jars, Egyptian stone vases, ivory objects, and ostrich eggshells are among the exotica found at Akrotiri (Bichta 2003). Although evidence indicates that faience was manufactured locally, the technique was imported from the East. Three miniature wooden clappers in the form of human hands, perhaps musical instruments, discovered recently in Xeste 4, also bespeak Eastern/Egyptian influence (Mikrakis 2007). The gold figurine of an ibex, cast in the lost-wax technique, has no parallels in Aegean art, and it, too, may be of oriental provenance.

Beyond the actual materials or artifacts from the East Mediterranean at Akrotiri, the world illustrated in the wall paintings is a further source of information about the island's relations with lands in this region. The depiction of exotic landscapes with real and imaginary creatures, such as the monkey, the leopard, the antelope, and the griffin, bears witness to these contacts. The same applies to the use of pictorial and iconographic conventions common in both Aegean and East Mediterranean art (Doumas 1985; 1992, 27–29). It is also borne out by certain signs inscribed on pottery or other imported objects, particularly those employed diachronically in both the East Mediterranean and the Aegean. For example, the sign of a circle with crossbars occurs in the Aegean Linear A and Linear B scripts, in the Old Canaanite and the Phoenician alphabets for the letter *tet*, as well as in the earliest Greek alphabet as the letter *theta*. Similarly, another sign in the form of a trident is common to both Linear A and B and corresponds also to the Old Canaanite letter *kap* (Doumas 2004b, 498–501). Such finds reveal that the relations between the Aegean and the East Mediterranean were not restricted to the exchange of material goods but extended into the ideological sphere.

The merchants-entrepreneurs at Akrotiri used the same numerical, metrical, and ponderal systems as the palatial bureaucracy in Crete (Michailidou 2006), as well as Linear A script (Boulotis 1998). Their leading role in maritime trade is

Figure 56.2. Miniature Frieze (courtesy of the Archaeological Society of Athens).

attested by the archaeological finds. For example, the earliest type of the stirrup jar, undoubtedly a Cretan invention for the transportation of olive oil and wine, is represented at Akrotiri by at least 50% of the total number known from the entire Aegean region, including Crete (Haskel 1985, 225). Similarly, the lead disc–shaped balance weights at Akrotiri, which range in weight from a few grams to 15 kilograms, represent two-thirds of the total number from the entire Aegean region (Petruso 1978; Michailidou 1990).

Another compelling indication of transactions between Akrotiri and Crete is the cache of clay seal impressions found in a storeroom of Building Complex Delta. Their clay is not Theran, and their iconographic subjects are all common in Crete, which perhaps points to different producers-dispatchers or different places of origin of the goods they once sealed (Doumas 1999b). The obvious mass production and standardization of pottery shapes and sizes at Akrotiri is another clue to the operation of a bureaucracy. The capacity of vases of the same shape in different sizes and with the same decoration seems to correspond to fractions or multiples of a unit of volume (Katsa-Tomara 1990).

The end of the thriving society at Akrotiri was sudden, when the city—indeed the entire island—was buried under a thick mantle of pumice and volcanic ash. A severe earthquake, of estimated magnitude 7 on the Richter scale, preceded the eruption and caused widespread destruction in the city. However, despite the damage to buildings, no victims have been uncovered in the ruins. The evidence that, after the eruption, systematic efforts to clear the ruins and to rescue various household effects were in progress indicates that, even if there were victims, these would have been removed not only for hygienic reasons but also for appropriate burial.

Combined geological, vulcanological, and oceanographic research conducted recently in Santorini has produced a lot of new information about the Bronze Age eruption confirms that a water-filled caldera with a small islet inside already existed at that time, giving the island its crescent shape. From the absence of any horizon of atmospheric erosion between the various phases of the eruption, we can deduce that the entire event, from the first eruptions to the formation of the caldera, lasted no more than a few, perhaps two to three, days. According to the excavation data, the eruption was followed by torrential rain. The waters, seeking an exit to the sea, rapidly eroded the volcanic material and opened small ravines that went as deep as the pre-eruption soil surface. It was in one of these ravines that Marinatos started the excavation.

The most recent underwater research in the wider area around Santorini has enabled a more precise estimate of the volume of volcanic magma ejected: 60 cubic kilometers (approximately 15 billion tons), considerably more than the older estimate of 39 kilometers. This means that, in terms of magnitude, the Bronze Age eruption of the Thera volcano was the greatest in the world in the last ten thousand years (Vougioukalakis 2006).

The date of the eruption is still a matter of debate. Calibrated radiocarbon dates overwhelmingly converge toward the end of the 17th century BC, whereas scholars who invoke the so-called historical chronology of Egypt in order to accommodate the synchronisms with the Aegean place the date about one hundred years later. The problem seems to be methodological since it is illogical to compare the historical chronology of Egypt, about which even Egyptologists express skepticism, with radiocarbon dating, and for the present this vexed question, so crucial to the chronology of Aegean prehistory, remains unanswered.

BIBLIOGRAPHY

Bichta, Katerina. 2003. "Luxuria ex Oriente: Ένα προϊστορικό ταξίδι από τη Θήρα στην Ανατολή." In ΑΡΓΟΝΑΥΤΗΣ: Τιμητικός Τόμος για τον Καθηγητή Χρίστο Γ. Ντούμα από τους μαθητές του στο Πανεπιστήμιο Αθηνών (1980–2000), ed. Andreas Vlachopoulos and Kiki Birtacha, 542–53. Athens: Kathimerini.

Boulotis, Christos. 1998. "Les nouveaux documents en linéaire A d'Akrotiri: Remarques préliminaires." BCH 122: 407–11.

Branigan, Keith. 1993. Dancing with Death: Life and Death in Southern Crete c. 3000–2000 B.C. Amsterdam: Hakkert.

———, ed. 1998. Cemetery and Society in the Aegean Bronze Age. Sheffield Studies in Aegean Archaeology 1. Sheffield: Sheffield Academic Press.

Davaras, Costis, and Philip P. Betancourt. 2004. The Hagia Photia Cemetery I: The Tomb Groups and Architecture. Philadelphia: INSTAP Academic Press.

Day, Peter M., David E. Wilson, and Evangelia Kyriatzi. 1998. "Pots, Labels, and People: Burying Ethnicity in the Cemetery at Ayia Photia Siteias." In Cemetery and Society in the Aegean Bronze Age, ed. Keith Branigan, 133–49. Sheffield Studies in Aegean Archaeology 1. Sheffield: Sheffield Academic Press.

Doonan, Roger C. P., Peter M. Day, and Nota Dimopoulou-Rethemiotaki. 2007. "Lame Excuses for Emerging Complexity in Early Bronze Age Crete: The Metallurgical Finds from Poros Katsambas and Their Context." In *Metallurgy in the Early Bronze Age Aegean*, ed. Peter M. Day and Roger C. P. Doonan, 98–122. Sheffield Studies in Aegean Archaeology 7. Oxford: Oxbow.

Doumas, Christos. 1977. *Early Bronze Age Burial Habits in the Cyclades. SIMA* XLVIII. Gothenburg: Åström.

———. 1983. *Thera, Pompeii of the Ancient Aegean*. London: Thames and Hudson.

———. 1985. "Conventions artistiques à Théra et à la Méditerranée orientale à l'époque préhistorique." In *L'iconographie minoenne: Actes de la Table Ronde d'Athènes (21–22 avril 1983)*, ed. Pascal Darcque and Jean-Claude Poursat, 29–40. BCH Suppl. XI. Athens: L'École française d'Athènes.

———. 1991. "What Did the Argonauts Seek in Colchis?" *Hermathena* CL: 31–41.

———. 1992. *The Wall-Paintings of Thera*. Athens: Thera Foundation–Nomikos.

———. 1997. "Τελχίνες." In *Η Κύπρος και το Αιγαίο στην Αρχαιότητα, Διεθνές Αρχαιολογικό Συνέδριο, Λευκωσία 8–10 Δεκεμβρίου 1995*, ed. G. Hatjisavvas, 79–94. Nicosia: Department of Antiquities.

———. 1999a. "Ανασκαφή Ακρωτηρίου Θήρας." *Πρακτικά της εν Αθήναις Αρχαιολογικής Εταιρείας 1999*: 155–202.

———. 1999b. "Seal Impressions from Akrotiri, Thera: A Preliminary Report." *CMS* Beiheft 6: 57–65.

———. 2000. "Ανασκαφή Ακρωτηρίου Θήρας." *Πρακτικά της εν Αθήναις Αρχαιολογικής Εταιρείας 2000*: 171–72.

———. 2004a. "Ο Πρώιμος εξαστισμός στα νησιά του Αιγαίου." In *Η ιστορία της Ελληνικής Πόλης*, Ερμής-Αρχαιολογία και Τέχνες, ed. Alexandros Ph. Lagopoulos, 83–101. Athens: Ερμής.

———. 2004b. "Από τα σημεία κεραμέως στην αλφαβητική γραφή: Μύθος και αρχαιολογική μαρτυρία." In *Το Αιγαίο στην Πρώιμη Εποχή του Σιδήρου*, ed. Nicholas Chr. Stampolidis and Angeliki Yannikouri, 495–503. Athens: University of Crete.

———. 2005. "La repartition topographique des fresques dans les bâtiments d'Akrotiri à Théra." In *ΚΡΗΣ ΤΕΧΝΙΤΗΣ*, eds. Isabelle Bradfer-Burdet, Béatrice Detournay, and Robert Laffineur, AEGAEUM 26: 73–81.

———. 2007. "Akrotiri, Thera: Some Additional Notes on Its Plan and Architecture." In *Krinoi Kai Limenes: Studies in Honor of Joseph and Maria Shaw*, ed. Philip P. Betancourt, Michael C. Nelson, and E. Hector Williams, 85–92. Philadelphia: INSTAP Academic Press.

———. 2008a. "Chambers of Mystery." In *Horizon: A colloquium on the prehistory of the Cyclades*, eds. Neil Brodie, Jenny Doole, Giorgos Gavalas, and Colin Renfrew. Cambridge: McDonald Institute for Archaeological Research, 165–75.

———. 2008b. *The Early History of the Aegean in the Light of the Recent Finds from Akrotiri, Thera*. Athens: Association for the Study and Dissemination of Greek History.

Edgar, Campbell C. 1904. "Notes on the Tombs." In *Excavations at Phylakopi in Melos*, Thomas D. Atkinson, R. C. Bosanquet, C. C. Edgar, A. J. Evans, D. G. Hogarth, D. Mackenzie, C. Harcourt-Smith, and F. B. Welch, 234–37. Society for the Promotion of Hellenic Studies Supplementary Paper 4. London: Macmillan.

Evans, John, D., and Renfrew, Colin. 1968. *Excavations at Saliagos near Antiparos*. London: Thames and Hudson.

Hadjianastasiou, Olga. 1988. "A Late Neolithic Settlement at Grotta, Naxos." In *Problems in Greek Prehistory: Papers Presented at the Centenary Conference of the British School of Archaeology at Athens, Manchester, April 1986*, ed. Elizabeth B. French and Ken A. Wardle, 11–20. Bristol: Bristol Classical Press.

Haskel, Halford W. 1985. "The Origin of the Aegean Stirrup Jar and Its Earlier Evolution and Distribution (MB III–LB I)." *AJA* 89: 221–29.

Katsa-Tomara, Litsa. 1990. "The Pottery-Producing System at Akrotiri: An Index of Exchange and Social Activity." In *Thera and the Aegean World III*, eds. D. A. Hardy with C. G. Doumas, J. A. Sakellarakis, and P. M. Warren. London: The Thera Foundation, 31–40.

Michailidou, Anna. 1990. "The Lead Weights from Akrotiri: The Archaeological Record." In *Thera and the Aegean World III*, eds. D. A. Hardy with C. G. Doumas, J. A. Sakellarakis, and P. M. Warren. London: The Thera Foundation, 407–19.

———. 2006. "Stone Balance Weights? The Evidence from Akrotiri, Thera." *Studi e Materiali* 13: 233–63.

Mikrakis, Manolis. 2007. "Ξύλινα χειρόμορφα κρόταλα από το Ακρωτήρι», ΑΛΣ 5: 89–96.

Murphy, Joanne M. 1998. "Ideologies, Rites, and Rituals: A View of Prepalatial Minoan Tholoi." In *Cemetery and Society in the Aegean Bronze Age*, ed. Keith Branigan, 27–40. Sheffield Studies in Aegean Archaeology 1. Sheffield: Sheffield Academic Press.

Mylonas, George. 1959. *Aghios Kosmas: An Early Bronze Age Settlement and Cemetery in Attica*. Princeton: Princeton University Press.

Palyvou, Claire. 2005. *Akrotiri Thera: An Architecture of Affluence 3500 Years Old*. Philadelphia: INSTAP Academic Press.

Pantelidou-Gofa, Maria. 2008. "The EH I Deposit Pit at Tsepi, Marathon: Features, Formation, and the Breakage of the Finds." In *Horizon: A colloquium on the prehistory of the Cyclades*, eds. Neil Brodie, Jenny Doole, Giorgos Gavalas, and Colin Renfrew. Cambridge: McDonald Institute for Archaeological Research, 281–89.

Papavasileiou, George A. 1910. *Περί των εν Ευβοία αρχαίων τάφων*. Athens: Archaeological Society.

Petruso, Karl M. 1978. "Lead Weights from Akrotiri: Preliminary Observations." In *TAW* I, 547–53.

Sampson, Adamantios. 2002. *Ftelia on Mykonos: A Late Neolithic Settlement in the Cyclades*. Rhodes: University of the Aegean, Rhodes.

Sotirakopoulou, Peggy. 1998. "The Early Bronze Age Stone Figurines from Akrotiri on Thera and Their Significance for the Early Cycladic Settlement." *BSA* 93: 107–65, pls. 5–31.

———. 1999. *Ακρωτήρι Θήρας: Η Νεολιθική και η Πρώιμη Εποχή του Χαλκού επί τη βάσει της κεραμεικής*. Athens: Archaeological Society at Athens.

Vougioukalakis, Georges E. 2006. "The Minoan Eruption and the Aegean World." ΑΛΣ 4: 20–55.

Wilson, David E., Peter M. Day, and Nota Dimopoulou-Rethemiotaki. 2008. "The Gateway Port of Poros-Katsambas: Trade and Exchange between North-central Crete and the Cyclades in EBI–II." In *Horizon*, 261–70.

Zapheiropoulou, Photeini. 2008. "Early Bronze Age Cemeteries of the Kampos Group on Epano Kouphonisi." In *Horizon: A colloquium on the prehistory of the Cyclades*, eds. Neil Brodie, Jenny Doole, Giorgos Gavalas, and Colin Renfrew. Cambridge: McDonald Institute for Archaeological Research, 183–94.

CHAPTER 57

DODECANESE

TOULA MARKETOU

Kos in the Bronze Age

The elongated island of Kos, located in the narrow sea lane between the Dodecanese and Asia Minor, is one of the more fertile and better-watered islands of the Aegean. These factors determined its cultural development in prehistoric and historic times.

The earliest occupation of the island is assigned to the Final Neolithic (FN), according to some diagnostic cheese-pot fragments found in the wider area of Asklepieion, at Asklupi and Tsilimbiri, and farther west/southwest on Vouno, at Mastichari (Hope Simpson and Lazenby 1970, 57–58, 60–61, figure 7 nos. 6, 8, 9). Similar Neolithic, along with EBA III, pottery was found in the cave of Aspre Petra, near the southwest tip of the island (Levi 1925–1926, 235–312). There is evidence that during the FN and the early stages of the EBA, habitation was dispersed in the northeastern part of the island on the spur of Troulli and on the promontory of Ayios Fokas (Hope Simpson and Lazenby 1970, 55; Sampson 1987, 109, pl. 61), and farther west on the steep spur of Misonisi in the mountain village of Ziá, at Amaniú on the Kastro of Palaiopylí, and on the hill of Linopotis-Piyi (Hope Simpson and Lazenby 1970, 58–60).

The EBA II period in the Dodecanese is known mostly from Kos. Jar burials and a rounded built tomb were excavated in the wider area of Asklepieion, at Asklupi (Morricone 1972–1973, 261–71), as well as in the nearby territory of the present-day Hippokrateion Foundation (Marketou 2004, 22, figure 4). Farther west/southwest on the flat hill of Tavla, in Antimacheia (Marketou 2004, 22–23, figure 5), a repertory of jugs, amphorae, and cups assigned to EBA II was found. The most prominent burial was discovered at Mesaria (Hope Simpson and Lazenby 1970, 38; Marketou 2004). Within this jar burial, apart from the pottery, was a hoard of metal objects with daggers, chisels, an axe, a silver incised sauceboat, and an Early Cycladic II marble bowl (Marketou 2004, 20–22, figures 2–3).

This evidence strongly suggests a dispersed settlement pattern on low hills, where the settlements controlled substantial pieces of arable land bordered by streams in the middle of the island. It is remarkable, however, that during this period, which saw the rapid development of metallurgy (Renfrew 1972, 308–38), precious metal objects—mainly daggers—accumulated in burials, a fact that definitely points to the presence of an affluent society. Mortuary behavior, on the other hand, shows close interrelations with Asia Minor, not only with coastal sites like Iasos (Pecorella 1984) but also with sites in the hinterland, such as Yortan and Karataş Semayük (Özgüç 1948; Wheeler 1974).

The rapid and outstanding changes of the third millennium led to a shift toward the establishment of a nucleated proto-urban center in the territory of the major LBA settlement at Serayia (Marketou 1990b, 101–104; Morricone 1972–1973, 136–252, 280–396). (Note that the toponym of the site is actually Serayia instead of the Italian variant, Serraglio, which has so far been used in the literature.) Deep and narrow soundings below the successive LBA levels brought to light remnants of a fortification wall and elongated buildings (Marketou 1990a, 40–41; 1997, 407; 2004, 25–27, figure 7a–b). The settlement occupies a low hill (Marketou 2004, figure 6) in the southwestern part of Serayia to the north of the supposed location of the ancient acropolis (Morricone 1950, 316) and near the island's sheltered north coast. Fragmentary slipped and burnished shallow and carinated bowls, round or trefoil-mouthed jugs, dark-faced and incised duck vases, patterned and burnished pots (Marketou 2004, 26, figure 8), and tankards (Marketou 1990a, 41, figure 2) demonstrate close similarities with the neighboring EBA III settlement at Asomatos.

The occupation of the site seems to have been continuous since the Early Bronze Age, favored mainly by the fine harbor at its north end. In the succeeding Middle Bronze period, the settlement became larger and occupied almost the whole territory of the subsequent major LBA town. Carinated cups, high-necked jugs, and several types of incurving bowls define the MBA culture of Kos in the wider cultural assemblage of Rhodes, Kalymnos, Miletus, Iasos, and Samos (Marketou 1990b, 102).

In the light of this evidence, the emergence of the major LBA town—estimated around 7.5 hectares and larger than previously considered by Morricone (1972–1973, 389)—should be seen in a new context. The settlement was revealed by means of large-scale and systematic excavations undertaken by Morricone (1950, 219–46; 1972–1973, 139–396) during the period of the Italian Mission on the island. The flourishing and uninterrupted LBA occupation at Serayia is divided into four 'towns' that match the successive periods from LBA IA to LH IIIC Middle (Vitale 2005, 87–89). The stratigraphy up to the LH IIIA2/B1 periods seem broadly similar to that of Trianda.

The LBA IA town, beneath Morricone's first city, is divided into an early and a mature phase, both severely damaged by earthquakes. The ruins of the mature phase were covered by the distinctive tephra layer (Marketou 1990b, 103–104, figures 4–5). The

Figure 57.1. Serayia on Kos. Polythyron in the lower levels of the settlement. View from the west (photograph courtesy of the author).

presence of a *polythyron* with four doors (figure 57.1) and a north-south paved street that most probably leads from the harbor to the hill of the acropolis of Morricone point to a well-organized town under the usual Minoan influence (Marketou 1987b; 1990b, 103, figure 8; 1990c, figure 5; Marthari, Marketou, and Jones 1990, 178).

The Late Bronze I A pottery, however, follows the earlier local tradition. During this period, some LM IA imports arrived on Kos, but the bulk appears with light-on-dark and dark-on-light decoration. This kind of rather coarse pottery was previously described as Middle Minoan of a provincial Kamares style (Davis 1982; Marketou 1990b, 113; Momigliano 2005, 221–24; 2007; Papagiannopoulou 1985). However, according to chemical analysis by atomic absorption spectrometry, it proved to be local (Marthari, Marketou, and Jones 1990, 178–82) and is now safely dated to LBA IA/IB (Marthari, Marketou, and Jones 1990, 176–78). Close vessels of this broad Koan category were exported mainly as containers to Trianda, Akrotiri on Thera, and other sites such as Ayia Irini on Keos (Marthari, Marketou, and Jones 1990).

According to the excavator and the most recent reassessment of the stratigraphy (Marketou 1990b; Morricone 1973–1974, figure 158; Vitale 2005, 2006), Morricone's 'first city' is assigned to the end of LM IA and most probably to LBA IB/LH IIA (cf. table 58.1, this volume), which corresponds to Furumark's Trianda IIA (Furumark 1950, 179). During this period, Marine style pottery was imported at Serayia (Marketou 1987a; Morricone 1972–1973, 328–30), while the massive production of light-on-dark and dark-on-light pottery continued.

The subsequent 'second city' correlates with Furumark's Trianda IIB (cf. table 58.1, this volume); a *terminus ante quem* for this city is provided by a piriform jar (Morricone 1972–1973, 171, figure 49) assigned to LH IIB/IIIA1 (Mountjoy 1999, 1075; Vitale 2005, 83, figure 12). The period coincides with the appearance of the chamber tombs in the cemeteries of Eleona and Langada, to the southwest of Serayia (Morricone 1965–1966; Mountjoy 1999, 1077, 1084–85).

The well-organized 'third city' of Serayia is divided into two subphases; the earliest coincides with the last occupation of Trianda (LH IIIA2/IIIB1), according to pottery found on the floor of the House of the Figs (Morricone 1972–1973, 227–32, figures 155–58; Vitale 2005, 83–87; 2006, 43–44). However, the wealth of this period is displayed mainly in seventeen tombs in the cemeteries of Eleona and Langada (Mee 1982, 87; Mountjoy 1999, 1085–92). Along with imports from the Argolid (Morricone 1965–1966, 68, figures 40–41), there is an Anatolian jug—although basket vases and other products of the Rhodo-Mycenaean style are nearly unknown.

However, the apparent Mycenaean IIIB1 presence is shown in the second phase of the 'third city.' By this time, a fortification wall similarly to that at Miletus (Voigtländer 1975) has already been erected at Serayia, most recently found at the west area of the prehistoric settlement (*ArchDelt* Chronica 2000 forthcoming), while the graves in the cemeteries of Eleona and Langada represent an obvious increase in population.

The earliest European-type bronzes in the Dodecanese, a northern spearhead, a Naue II sword, and a northern spearhead (Morricone 1965–1966, 137, figures 122–25; Macdonald 1986, 145) found in warrior tomb 21 at Langada are assigned to this phase. Of great importance is also a violin-bow bronze fibula from tomb 10 (Morricone 1965–1966, 102–103, figure 84), as well as an Italian knife of the Scoglio del Tonno type from Serayia (Morricone 1972–1973, figure 239, left).

However, the Mycenaean expansion on the island has become more obvious with the discovery of architectural remains in the lower levels of the Geometric/Archaic sanctuary at the site of Heracles, near Psalidi (Skerlou 1996, 690), to the east of Serayia. Two LH IIIA2–IIIB1 chamber tombs indicate Mycenaean presence in the area (Papachristodoulou 1979; Papazoglou 1981; Skerlou 1993). Another LH IIIB1 chamber tomb was found at Mesaria (Papachristodoulou 1979; Hope Simpson 2003, 227n170). The presence of another LH IIIA2–IIIB chamber tomb found near the chapel of Ayia Paraskevi at Pyli (Benzi 2006) reinforces the argument for a considerable Mycenaean expansion on the island.

In the following LH IIIC period, Kos participated in the Aegean *koine* with close affinities with Perati and Attica. Representative of the period are several stirrup jars, kalathoi, kraters, and pottery decorated in Pictorial style, as well as the distinctive octopus pictorial stirrup jars of the Kalymnos-Pitane-Kos group (Macdonald 1986, 143–45; Mountjoy 1999, 1079–81). In the middle phase of LH IIIC, pictorial amphoroid craters decorated with bearded goats and various water birds (Macdonald 1986, 144; Morricone 1972–1973, 188, figure 73), as well as some characteristic fragments with warrior scenes (Morricone 1972–1973, 356–60, figures 356–58; Karantzali 2005, 521, figure 21), appear in the settlement at Serayia.

Nevertheless, the unpredicted discovery of two tholos tombs reinforces the assumption of the island's distinctive role in LH III. The first tomb, found at a distance of ca. 3 km west/southwest of Serayia, is dated to LH IIIA2 and was reused in LH IIIC Middle (Gregoriadou 1996). Of great importance is also the second LH IIIB tholos tomb, which was found in the western part of the modern town of Kos and is most probably associated with the settlement of Serayia (Skerlou 1997, 1110–11). The occurrence of another Mycenaean tholos at Kolophon in Asia Minor (Bridges 1974) provides important evidence of the nature of the interrelations of the eastern peripheries of the Mycenaean world.

Mycenaean Kos played an important role in the process of the Mycenaean expansion in the Dodecanese and Asia Minor, from Knidos and Ephesos to Kolophon and Klazomenai-LimanTepe. Its location in the narrow sea lane of Asia Minor leading to Iasos and Miletus and farther north to the area of the Troad shows that it might have been one of the most significant islands, perhaps one of those mentioned in the Hittite texts as being an active trade center for the operations of Ahhiyawa in Anatolia (Hope Simpson 2003, 217–24, 227–28, 237; Mountjoy 1998).

The Small Islands of the Dodecanese and the Case of the South Dodecanese: Karpathos and Kasos in the Bronze Age

The Neolithic Background and the EBA

In the 4th and early 3rd millennium BC, several—mainly coastal—sites were occupied on the north and south islands of the Dodecanese beyond Rhodes and Kos. Final Neolithic sites appear at Panormitis on Syme and on the nearby islet of Seskli, as well as in the cave of Charkadio and at the open-air site of Lakkes, near Megalo Chorio on Telos (Sampson 1987, 115). However, rather nucleated EBA sites appear on several hills, such as at Kastro on Syme and at Kastello, above the coastal plain of Livadhia on Telos (Hope Simpson and Lazenby 1970, 67–68). The same settlement pattern is also observed on the bare island of Astypalaia, the Dodecanese island closest to the Cyclades. However, the most coherent picture of the nature of the LN/FN culture and its continuity with the Bronze Age is given by the Italian excavations in the caves of Ayia Varvara, Choiromandres, and Daskalio on Kalymnos (Benzi 1993, 1997, 2008; Furness 1956; Maiuri 1928).

Excavations at Partheni and other surface finds on the island of Leros (Hope Simpson 1970, 52–53; Sampson 1987, 87–95, 109–13) have revealed an expanded FN occupation pattern indicative of the role of the prosperous island, which was in articulation with the neighboring islands of Kalymnos, Patmos, and Leipsoi. The group of islands north of Kalymnos, together with Samos, Ikaria, and the opposite mainland, make up a single cultural assemblage that provides a habitation pattern of some coastal LN/FN and EBA I sites. However, the island of Karpathos shows a dispersed pattern of LN and FN sites on promontories and mostly on hills (Melas 1985, 155–56; Zervaki 2006, 14–15), mainly in the southern part of the island, such as Leftoporos and Paliokastro in the area of Arkasa (Melas 1985, 36–38, 155–59), as well as Skopi (Sampson 1987, 108) and Lothico at Pigadhia (Melas 1985, 27), along with some evidence at Poli and other sites in the central part of Kasos (Melas 1985, 48–50, 170).

The emergence and spread of FN/EBA occupation on the islands of the Dodecanese may be the result of complex transformations and dangerous voyages to procure prestige objects and obsidian from the neighboring island of Yiali (Torrence and Cherry 1976; Buchholz and Althaus 1982, 21–30), as well as from Melos and Anatolia. The widespread circulation of cheese pots, which appear on the islets of Alimnia and Yiali (Sampson 1987, 30–31, 81, figure 102.24–32; 1988, 96–102), in the Daskalio and Choiromandres caves on Kalymnos (Benzi 2008, 96, figures 37–38), and on Astypalaia (Hope Simpson and Lazenby 1970, 164–65, figure 44.b1; 1973, 163, figure 9.5, pl. 44a.3; Zervoudaki 1971, 552) and Kasos (Hope Simpson and Lazenby 1970, 69), points to a Final Neolithic Dodecanesian *koine*.

On the other hand, the Final Neolithic curvilinear buildings revealed at Kastro on Alimnia (Sampson 1987, 79–80, pl. 37b, figure 97; 1988, 45–54, figures 33–37, plan 16a), on Yiali (Sampson 1988, 45–54, figures 33–37, plan 16a), and at Leftoporos in the area of Arkasa (Melas 1985, 37, figure 14) show close similarities with the northeast Aegean, such as Emporio VIII on Chios (Hood 1981, 100–104, figure 53, pl. 17). Moreover, the presence of crucibles for melting bronze on the island of Yiali (Sampson 1988, 108, figure 38) and the bronze needles in the Koumelo and Aghios Georghios caves on Rhodes indicate the appearance of metallurgy during the final stages of the Neolithic and the smooth transition to the EBA.

Scanty EB II evidence from Nisyros, Kalymnos, and Karpathos shows close similarities with the relevant culture of Kos, which correlates with the Keros-Syros culture in the Cyclades (Renfrew 1972, 170–85). To this culture is assigned a Cycladic idol of the Dokathismata variety in the Berlin Museum, said to have come from Nisyros (Bean and Cook 1957, 119; Hope Simpson and Lazenby 1962, 169; Kekule 1891, 220n575; Herbst 1936, 770). The marble idol is associated with three Early Bronze Age II vases typical of the area, which were found as well on Nisyros (Konstantinopoulos 1965, 602, pl. 768 b–c).

To the same category is also assigned a group of pottery from Chorio on Kalymnos, as well as a small amphora from Lefkos in central Karpathos (Melas 1985, 41, 75, no. 1047, pl. 104), which, according to the relevant typology of EBA II Kos, could be assigned to EB II rather than to Final Neolithic. Quite strange, however, is another, most probably cult limestone statuette, which was found at Pegadia on Karpathos (Bent 1885, 235; Melas 1985, 27, 147–48, figure 62A–B; Zervaki 2006, 15–16) and is dated to the earlier stages of EBA.

In comparison to the relatively rich EBA III evidence from Rhodes and Kos, this period is weakly represented on the other islands of the Dodecanese. The most coherent evidence for the period, however, is provided by the Daskalio cave on Kalymnos, where there is a rich repertory of dark-faced and incised duck vases, as well as red-burnished and pattern-painted EB III pottery of the known categories from Asomatos and Serayia (Benzi 1997, 384–92; Marketou 1990a, 1997), which confirms the continuous occupation of the cave from LN to LH IIIC. A distinguishing 'Trojan' IV/V amphora is indicative of the affinities with the northeast Aegean (Benzi 1997, 386–88, figure 2c).

Astypalaia, the remote island of the Dodecanese (Broodbank 2000, 131–33, figure 36), located between Kos and Ios, demonstrates close affinities with the Cyclades mainly during the EBA (Doumas 2005, 23–26; Hope Simpson and Lazenby 1973, 159–69, 171; Hope Simpson and Dickinson 1979, 374). The Cycladic character of the island is most prominent in the case of the EB II fortified site at Vathy (Hope Simpson and Lazenby 1973, 166), where a marble EC idol was found, and primitive drawings were identified on a rock (Doumas 2005, 23, figures 3–6). Several other sites on the island provided FN and undiagnostic EBA pottery and obsidian (Doumas 2005, 23–26; Hope Simpson and Lazenby 1973, 159–69; Hope Simpson and Dickinson 1979, 374).

The Middle Bronze Age

Middle and Late Bronze Age Kalymnos shows close cultural affinities with Serayia on Kos and the wider area of Ialysos on Rhodes. A carinated cup, an imported MM IB/II lamp, and a Middle Cycladic fragmentary vase found in the Daskalio cave on Kalymnos (Benzi 1993, 279, 281, pls 36c1, 37a–b) are indicative of the framework within which Rhodes and the northern islands were interrelated before the great Minoan expansion in the Aegean. The appearance of a broad category of MBA/ early LM IA pottery with a heavy black slip at Kastelli, Aspre, Kallikatsou, Aetofolia, Kampos, and Lefkes on Patmos has shown an expanded occupation pattern on the island. Similar pottery is also found on the neighboring islands of Leipsoi and Arkioi: a large carinated bowl from Leipsoi (Hope Simpson and Lazenby 1970, 52) and a hole-mouthed jar from Arkioi.

The LBA I/IB and the Mycenaean Periods

Imported LM IA conical rhyta (Benzi 1993, 277–79, pl. 34a–b) and the bronze statuette of a Minoan adorant (Marketou 1998b, 63–64, figure 21) provide strong evidence of the use of the Daskalio cave on Kalymnos as a cult place. During this period, visitors to the cave used the typical conical cups, light-on-dark and dark-on-light vases imported from Kos, and four large storage jars (Benzi 1993, 277–79, figure 1f, pls 35, 36a). The use of the cave as a cult place seems continuous until LH IIIC. In the meantime, Mycenaeans were also expanding on other parts of the island, as indicated by LH IIIB–C pottery found in Ayia Varvara cave near Pothia (Benzi 1993, 281–86, pls. 37 3d, figures 3e–f, 4, pls. 37–38, figure 5; Hope Simpson and Dickinson

1979, 366) and at the main Mycenaean center, most probably an acropolis or a settlement located on the fortified medieval hill of Perakastro or Chrysocheria, some 400 meters to the southwest of the Ayia Varvara cave (Hope Simpson and Lazenby 1962, 172). This site is closely associated with the nearby chamber tombs, which yielded around thirty vases that were sent to the British Museum (Paton 1887, 456, pl. 83; Walters 1897, 75–77; Walters and Forsdyke 1930, 9–10, pl. 8.22–28, pl. 9).

Similarly to Kos, Kalymnos yielded typical examples of LH IIIC pictorial pottery (Benzi 1993, 286, pl. 38d; Walters and Forsdyke 1930, 9, no. 27, pl. 8: 27). One of the best-known LH IIIC Middle octopus stirrup jars of the Kalymnos-Pitane-Kos group, decorated with goats, birds, scorpions, hedgehogs, crabs, and other decorative elements, which are illustrated crowded in among the octopus tentacles, was found in the early British excavations on behalf of the British Museum at Perakastro (Furumark 1972, 304, figure 49:28, 613 note 176:1; Macdonald 1986, 143; Mountjoy 1999, 1134, no. 19, fig. 464: 19, 465: 19; Paton 1887, 76, figure 13; Walters and Forsdyke 1930, 9 nos 7a-7b, pl. 9:7a–b). Similar stirrup jars from Kalymnos are also kept in the Amsterdam and Oxford museums (Crouwel 1972, 16–24, figures 3–11; 1984).

Evidence for conical cups from the site of Garipa on Telos (Sampson 1980) indicates the LBA I occupation on this island, which is located between Kos and Rhodes. Scanty LBA surface evidence has also appeared at Ayioi Anarghiroi, in the bay of Pontamos on Chalki (Melas 1988, 307, figure 14). Moreover, a Mycenaean stirrup jar is reported from the area between Dali and Ayia Triadha, above Mandraki on Nisyros (Doumas 1972–1974). A group of locally made Minoanizing LBA I pottery has been found quite unexpectedly on an undiagnostic ellipsoid mound of stones at Drakounda on Syme (Farmakidou 2003, 294–96). Further scanty evidence for Mycenaean occupation on Syme is indicated by an LH IIIA or IIIB fragmentary stemmed bowl rim from Kastro (Hope Simpson and Lazenby 1970, 63, figure 18d3).

However, Astypalaia has provided stronger evidence for a Mycenaean occupation of the island. Late Helladic IIIA2–B pottery indicates later human activities, long after the previous EBA occupation, on the steep cliffs of Kastro at Ayios Ioannes on Astypalaia, above the homonymous bay (Zervoudaki 1971, 551; Hope Simpson and Lazenby 1973, 162). A double chamber tomb with two dromoi was also investigated at Armenochori (Zervoudaki 1971, 550–51; Konstantinopoulos 1973, 120, 124; Hope Simpson and Lazenby 1973, 161). The tomb yielded 116 pots dated to LH IIIA2 and LH IIIC, along with a group of glass ornaments (Triantafyllidis 2002–2005).

Moreover, a pair of chamber tombs was excavated at Synkairos (Doumas 1975, 272), on the north coast of the island. Among the LH IIIA2 Mycenaean pottery and the other offerings, a substantial number of lead weights for nets and a fishhook were also found within one of the tombs, along with Rhodo-Mycenaean pottery, some Minoan imports, and an Anatolian stemmed krater (Doumas 1975, 272, pl. 252, top right). Similar to one example from Troy and another from Beycesultan, the shape recalls the stemmed crater from Trianda (Monaco 1941, 131n27, figure 83, illustrated upside down). Anatolian elements also appear on another painted, stemmed crater from Armenochori on Astypalaia (Konstantinopoulos 1973, 14, figure 14) and similarly on a crater from Apollakia on Rhodes (Mountjoy 1999, 1009n70, figure 412).

Karpathos and Kasos, the Dodecanese islands closest to Crete, were under strong Minoan influence not only in MMIII/LM IA but also during the Late Helladic III (Melas 1979, 1981, 1985, 159–62; Zervaki 2006, 18–31). Many sites were occupied in the southern and most fertile area of Afiartis in south Karpathos. The excavation of an LM I farmhouse at Kontokefalo in the area of Afiartis (Melas and Karantzali 2000; Platon and Karantzali 2003, 80) has yielded—among the locally produced Minoanizing pottery—a talismanic Minoan seal (Pini 2004; Zervaki 2006, 19–20). The Minoan expansion during the LBA I is also indicated by a settlement in the natural harbor at Pegadia (Hope Simpson and Lazenby 1962, 160–61; Melas 1985, 27–30; Zervaki 2006, 20–21). Farther north, in the area of the safe Vrontis Bay (Platon and Karantzali 2003, 201–202), the discovery of LM IB Palatial pottery associated with a settlement will elucidate the earlier stages of the Mycenaean presence in the south Aegean.

However, the Minoan character remained pronounced on Karpathos from the late 15th to the early 13th century BC. The Late Bronze Age III period is represented by the important settlement in the area of Xenonas at Pegadia (Hope Simpson and Lazenby 1970, 68; Melas 1985, 28; Platon and Karantzali 2003, 200–201; Zervaki 2003) and by the well-known chamber tombs in the neighboring cemetery at Makeli/Anemolyloi (Charitonides 1961–1962; Hope Simpson and Lazenby 1962, 159–63, 173), which are likely associated with the acropolis to the southwest of Pegadia (Hope Simpson and Lazenby 1962, 160; Melas 1985, 30), as well as the tombs at Sisamos in the same area (Hope Simpson and Lazenby 1962, 159; Melas 1985, 30).

The rich LH IIIA2–IIIB1 Mycenaean tomb found at Vonies in the area of Arkasa (Melas 1985, 37-40; Zachariadou 1978) has provided evidence for the Minoan mortuary tradition of placing the deceased in larnakes, as well as early cremation practices. To Mycenaean times is also assigned the area of the fortified acropolis of Arkasa (Hope Simpson and Lazenby 1962, 162–163), associated as well with the cemetery at Vonies.

A few Mycenaean cemeteries have been located in the northern part of the island—at Avlona (Platon and Karantzali 2003) and in the safe anchorage area of Diafani and the fertile land of Kambi (Hope Simpson and Lazenby 1962, 161; Melas 1979, 168–72; 1981, 119–20; 1983, 53; Walters and Forsdyke 1930, pl. 10: 8–14).

The small Dodecanesian island of Kasos is the first steppingstone from the eastern part of Crete to the Aegean islands. Kasos developed a dense MM/LM IA settlement pattern around the safe bay of Chelatros (Melas 1983, 55; 1985, 46–47), while in the Mycenaean period occupation is concentrated at Polin and Ellinokamara, both in the central part of the island (Hope Simpson and Lazenby 1962, 168; 1970, 69–71; Melas 1985, 48–50).

Overall, both the small and the large islands in the Dodecanese and the Aegean participated in the development and decline that took place in the area from the 4th to the end of the 2nd millennium, when their inhabitants interrelated with the neighboring sites and adopted Cretan, Anatolian, Greek mainland, and Eastern Mediterranean traits in different degrees. Each one maintained its individual rate of development and decline and its own cultural identity.

BIBLIOGRAPHY

Bean, G. E., and J. M. Cook. 1957. "The Carian Coast III." *BSA* 52: 58–146.

Bent, Theodore. 1885. "The Islands of Telos and Karpathos." *JHS* 6: 233–42.

Benzi, Mario. 1993. "The Late Bronze Age Pottery from Vathy Cave, Kalymnos." In *Wace and Blegen*, 275–88.

———. 1997. "The Late Early Bronze Age Finds from Vathy Cave (Kalymnos) and Their Links with the Northeast Aegean." In *Poliochni*, 383–94.

———. 2006. "A Group of Mycenaean Vases and Bronzes from Pyli, Kos." In *Aeimnestos: Miscellanea di Studi per Mauro. Christofani*, vol. 1, ed. Benedetta Adembri, 15–24. Florence: Centro Di della Edifirmi.

———. 2008. "A Forgotten Island: Kalymnos in the Late Neolithic Period." In *ANCEBA*, 85–108.

Bridges, Robert. 1974. "The Mycenaean Tholos Tomb at Kolophon." *Hesperia* 43: 264–66.

Broodbank, Cyprian. 2000. *An Island Archaeology of the Early Cyclades*. New York: Cambridge University Press.

Buchholz, Hans G., and Ergon Althaus. 1982. *Nisyros: Giali Kos. Ein Vorbericht über archäologisch-mineralogische Forschungen auf griechischen Inseln*. Archäologische Obsidian-Forschungen. Band I. Mainz am Rhein: von Zabern.

Charitonides, Seraphim. 1961–1962. "Θαλαμοειδής τάφος Καρπάθου." *ArchDelt* 17A (1963): 32–76.

Crouwel, Joost H. 1972. "Mycenaean Pictorial Pottery in Holland." *BABesch* 47: 14–30.

———. 1984. "Fragments of Another Octopus Stirrup Jar from Kalymnos in Amsterdam." *BABesch* 59: 63–68.

Davis, Jack. 1982. "The Earliest Minoans in the South-east Aegean: A Reconsideration of the Evidence." *AnatSt* 32: 33–41.

Doumas, Christos. 1972–1974. "Αρχαιότητες και μνημεία Δωδεκανήσων περιοδείαι και επισήμανσις αρχαίων. Σύμη-Νίσυρος, Περιοδείαι. "*ArchDelt* 29 (Chronica): 964–65, 981.

———. 1975. "Αρχαιότητες και μνημεία Δωδεκανήσων. Τήλος-Αστυπάλαια." *ArchDelt* 30 (Chronica): 369–372.

———. 2005. "Η Αστυπάλαια στην Πρώιμη ιστορία του Αιγαίου." *Δωδεκανησιακά Χρονικά ΙΘ'*: 17–27. Ρόδος: Στέγη Γραμμάτων και Τεχνών Δωδεκανήσου.

Farmakidou, Eleni. 2003. "Η προϊστορική περίοδος στη Σύμη." In *ΑΡΓΟΝΑΥΤΗΣ: Τιμητικός Τόμος για τον Καθηγητή Χρίστο Γ. Ντούμα από τους μαθητές του στο Πανεπιστήμιο Αθηνών (1980–2000)*, ed. Andreas Vlachopoulos and Kiki Birtacha, 292–99. Athens: Kathimerini.

Furness, Audrey. 1956. "Some Early Pottery of Samos, Kalimnos, and Chios." *PPS* 22: 173–212.

Furumark, Arne. 1950. "The Settlement at Ialysos and Aegean History c. 1550–1400 B.C." *OpArch* VI: 150–271.

———. 1972. *Mycenaean Pottery I: Analysis and Classification*. Skrifter Utgicna av Swenska Intstitut i Athen. Stockholm: Acta Instititi Atheniensis regni Sueciae 4°, XX:1.

Gregoriadou, Dora. 1996. "3° χλμ. Επαρχιακής οδού Κω-υπαίθρου, ΚΜ 49 γαιών Κω Εξοχής (οικόπεδο Δ. Γεωργαρά." *ArchDelt* 51 (Chronica): 690–92.

Herbst, Rudolf. 1936. "Nisyros." In *Paulys Real-Encyclopädie der classischen Altertumswissenschaft* XVII. 1, ed. Georg Wissowa and Wilhelm Kroll, 761–67. Stuttgart: Metzlerche.

Hood, Sinclair. 1981. *Excavations in Chios 1938–1955: Prehistoric Emporio and Ayio Gala*.
Vol. 1, BSA Supplementary vol. 15. London: British School of Archaeology at Athens.

Hope Simpson, Richard. 2003. "The Dodecanese and the Ahhiyawa Question." *BSA*
98: 203–37.

———, and Oliver T. P. K. Dickinson. 1979. *A Gazetteer of Aegean Civilisation in the Bronze
Age*. Vol. 1, *The Mainland and the Islands*. SIMA 52. Gothenburg: Åström.

Hope Simpson, Richard, and John F. Lazenby. 1962. "Notes from the Dodecanese." *BSA*
57: 154–75.

———. 1970. "Notes from the Dodecanese II." *BSA* 65: 47–76.

———. 1973. "Notes from the Dodecanese III." *BSA* 68: 127–79.

Karantzali, Efi. 2005. "The Mycenaeans at Ialysos: Trading Station or Colony?" In *Emporia*,
141–51.

Kekule, Reinhard. 1891. *Königliche Museen zu Berlin*. Beschreibung der Antiken Skulpturen.
Berlin.

Konstantinopoulos, Gregorios. 1965. "Δωδεκάνησα." *ArchDelt* 20: 602.

———. 1973. "Νέα ευρήματα εκ Ρόδου και Αστυπαλαίας." *AAA* 1973: 114–24.

Levi, Doro. 1925–1926. "La grotta di Aspri Petra a Coo." *ASAtene* 8–9: 235–310.

Macdonald, Colin. 1986. "Problems of the Twelfth Century B.C. in the Dodecanese." *BSA* 81:
125–51.

Maiuri, Amedeo. 1928. "Esplorazione di grotte con avanzi preistorici nell' isola di Calimno."
Clara Rhodos I: 104–17. Rhodes: Istituto Storico-Archeologico.

Marketou, Toula. 1987a. "Marine-style Pottery from the Seraglio in Kos." *BSA* 82: 165–69.

———. 1987b. "Συμβολή οδών Ιωάννου Θεολόγου και Απ. Παύλου (οικόπεδο Αφών
Κούκουνα)." *ArchDelt* 42 (Chronika): 625.

———. 1990a. "Asomatos and Seraglio: EBA Production and Interconnections." *Hydra* 7:
40–48.

———. 1990b. "Santorini Tephra from Rhodes and Kos: Some Chronological Remarks
Based on the Stratigraphy." In *TAW III*, 100–19.

———. 1990c. "Πόλη Κω. Σεράγια. Οδός Πασανικολάκη (οικόπεδο Κουτσουράδη).
Μινωικό πολύθυρο." *ArchDelt* 45 (Chronica): 496.

———. 1997. "Ασώματος Ρόδου. Τα μεγαρόσχημα κτήρια και οι σχέσεις τους με το
Βορειοανατολικό Αιγαίο." In *Poliochni*, 395–413.

———. 1998. "LB I Statuettes from Rhodes. " In *Cyprus-Dodecanese-Crete*, 55–72.

———. 2004. "Η Πρώιμη Εποχή του Χαλκού στην Κω." In *Χάρις Χαίρε. Μελέτες
στη μνήμη της Χάρης Κάντζια*. Τόμος Α., 17–30. Αθήνα: Υπουργείο Πολιτισμού.
Αρχαιολογικό Ινστιτούτο Αιγαιακών Σπουδών.

Marthari, Mariza, Toula Marketou, and Richard E. Jones. 1990. "LB I Ceramic Connections
between Thera and Kos." In *TAW III*, 171–84.

Mee, Christopher. 1982. *Rhodes in the Bronze Age: An Archaeological Survey*. Warminster:
Art and Phillips.

Melas, Manolis. 1979. "Νέα στοιχεία για τη μινωική αποίκηση της Καρπάθου."
Καρπαθιακαί Μελέται 1: 131–92.

———. 1981. "Νέα στοιχεία για τη μινωική αποίκηση της Καρπάθου." Καρπαθιακαί
Μελέται 2: 91–161.

———. 1983. "Minoan and Mycenaean Settlement in Kasos and Karpathos." *BICS* 30: 3–61.

———. 1985. *The Islands of Karpathos, Saros, and Kasos in the Neolithic and Bronze Age*.
SIMA 68. Gothenburg: Åström.

———. 1988. "Exploration in the Dodecanese: New Prehistoric and Mycenaean Finds."
BSA 83: 283–311.

————, and Efi Karantzali. 2000. "Ανασκαφή Μινωικής 'βίλλας' στην Κάρπαθο 1992–1994." In *Πεπραγμένα Η' Κρητολογικού Συνεδρίου. Ηράκλειο, 9–14 Σεπτεμβρίου 1996.* Vol. 2, Προϊστορική και Αρχαία Ελληνική Περίοδος, 281–98. Ηράκλειο.

Momigliano, Nicoletta. 2005. "Iasos and the Aegean Islands before the Santorini Eruption." In *Emporia*, 217–25.

————. 2007. "Kamares or Not Kamares? This Is [Not] the Question. Southeast Aegean Light-on-Dark (LOD) and Dark-on-Light (DOL) Pottery: Synchronisms, Production Centres, and Distribution." In *Middle Helladic Pottery*, 257–72.

Monaco, Giorgio. 1941. "Scavi nella zona Micenea di Jaliso (1935–36)." *Clara Rhodos* X: 41–183. Rhodes: Istituto Storico-Archeologico.

Morricone, Luigi. 1950. "Scavi e ricerche a Coo (1935–43), relazione preliminare." *BdA* 35: 219–46.

————. 1965–1966. "Eleona e Langada: Sepolcreti della tarda età del Bronzo a Coo." *ASAtene* 43–44: 5–311.

————. 1972–1973. "Scavi e scoperte nel 'Seraglio' e localita Minori (1935–43)." *ASAtene* 50–51: 139–396.

Mountjoy, Penelope A. 1998. "The East Aegean–West Anatolian Interface in the Late Bronze Age: Mycenaeans and the Kingdom of Ahhiyawa." *AnatSt* 48: 33–67.

————. 1999. *Regional Mycenaean Decorated Pottery*, vol. 2. Deutsches Archaeologisches Institut. Rahden/Westf.: Leidorf.

Özgüç, Tahsin. 1948. *Die Bestattungsgebräuche im vorgeschichtlichen Anatolien.* Ankara: Universitaet von Ankara.

Papachristodoulou, Ioannes. 1979. "Κως (Ύπαιθρος) Μεσαριά-Καστέλλες." *ArchDelt* 34 (Chronika): 457–59.

Papagiannopoulou, Angelia G. 1985. "Were the S.E. Aegean Islands Deserted in the MBA?" *AnatSt* 35: 85–92.

Papazoglou, Lena. 1981. "Μυκηναϊκός θαλαμωτός τάφος στο Κάστελλο Κω." *AAA* 14: 62–75.

Paton, W. R. 1887. "Vases from Calymnos and Carpathos." *JHS* 8: 446–60.

Pecorella, Paolo E. 1984. *La cultura preistorica di Iasos in Caria.* Missione Archeologica Italiana di Iasos I. Rome: Bretschneider.

Pini, Ingo. 2004. *Corpus der minoischen und mykenischen Siegel.* Band V, *Kleinere griechische Sammlungen.* Suppl. 3, *Neufunde aus Griechenland und der westlichen Türkei.* Vol. 2 *Nafplion-Volos und westliche Türkei.* 495, no. 333/inv. no. MA 190. Akademie der Wissenschaften und der Literatur. Mainz am Rhein: von Zabern.

Platon, Lefteris, and Efi Karantzali. 2003. "New Evidence for the History of the Minoan Presence on Karpathos." *BSA* 98: 189–202.

Renfrew, Colin. 1972. *The Emergence of Civilisation: The Cyclades and the Aegean in the Third Millennium BC.* London: Methuen.

Sampson, Adamantios. 1980. "Μινωικά από την Τήλο." *AAA* 13: 68–72.

————. 1987. *Η νεολιθική κατοίκηση στα Δωδεκάνησα.* Athens: Tameion Archaeologikon Poron kai Apallotrioseon.

————. 1988. *Η νεολιθική κατοίκηση στο Γυαλί της Νισύρου.* Athens: Euoïke Archaeophilos Etaireia.

Skerlou, Elpida. 1993. "Ηρακλής. Αγροτικός δρόμος (σε επαφή με τη δυτική πλευρά του οικοπέδου Γ. Ζορντού, ΚΜ 836)." *ArchDelt* 48 (Chronica): 553.

————. 1996. "Περιοχή Ηρακλής (οικόπεδο Μπακάλογλου)." *ArchDelt* 51 (Chronica): 689–90.

————. 1997. "Οδός Αργυροκάστρου και Κορυτσάς (οικόπεδο Π. και Φ. Θαλασσινού)." *ArchDelt* 52 (Chronica): 1110–11.

Torrence, Robin, and John F. Cherry. 1976. *Archaeological Survey of the Obsidian Source on Giali in the Dodecanese*. Unpublished manuscript in the British School at Athens.

Triantafyllidis, Paulos. 2002–2005. "Γυάλινα και φαγεντιανά κοσμήματα Αρμενοχωρίου Αστυπάλαιας." *AAA* 35–38: 165–83.

Vitale, Salvatore. 2005. "L'insediamento di 'Serraglio' durante il tardo Bronzo. Riesame dei principali contesti portati alla luce da Luigi Morricone tra il 1935 ed ol 1946." *ASAtene* 83: 72–94.

———. 2006. "The Early Late Bronze Age Pottery from Italian Excavations at 'Serraglio' on Kos: A Reassessment of the Complete or Almost Complete Local Vases with No Preserved Context." *Αγωγή* III: 43–54.

Voigtländer, Walter. 1975. "Die mykenische Stadtmauer von Milet und einzelne Wehranlagen der späten Bronzezeit." *IstMitt* 25: 17–34.

Walters, Henry B. 1897. "On Some Antiquities of the Mycenaean Age Recently Acquired by the British Museum." *JHS* 17: 63–77.

———, and Edgar J. Forsdyke. 1930. *Corpus Vasorum Antiquorum. Great Britain Fascicle 7, British Museum Fascicle 5: Attic Red-figured Vases, Mycenaean Pottery from Aegean Islands and Mainland Greece*. London: British Museum.

Wheeler, Tamara S. 1974. "Early Bronze Burial Customs in Western Anatolia." *AJA* 78: 415–25.

Zachariadou, Olga. 1978. "Θαλαμοειδής τάφος στην Αρκάσα Καρπάθου." *ArchDelt* 33 (Meletes): 249–94.

Zervaki, Foteini. 2003. "Η εγκατάσταση στα Πηγάδια Καρπάθου κατά την Ύστερη Εποχή του Χαλκού: Μια πρώτη προσέγγιση." *Καρπαθιακά* Α: 55–69. Rhodes.

———. 2006. "Η Κάρπαθος κατά τη Νεολιθική περίοδο και την Εποχή του Χαλκού, μέσα από τα εκθέματα του Μουσείου Καρπάθου." Rhodes.

Zervoudaki, Eos. 1971. "Αρχαιότητες και Μνημεία Δωδεκανήσου. Αστυπάλαια." *ArchDelt* 26 Β2 (Chronika): 549–52.

CHAPTER 58

RHODES

TOULA MARKETOU

THE cultural development of the elongated and fertile island of Rhodes is favored by its geographical diversity, its size (1,400 sq km), and its location at the crossroads of the Eastern Mediterranean, the Aegean, and Asia Minor. The spread of settlement on Rhodes was a long process that lasted from the beginning of the Late Neolithic (LN) to the synoecism of the city of Rhodes in 408/407 BC.

EARLY BRONZE AGE (EBA)

The first scanty evidence for the EBA period in Rhodes came to light during the Danish archaeological expedition on the island, which took place between 1902 and 1914. Apart from a group of Late/Final Neolithic stone tools, a jug and an incised lid dated to EB II/III were found in the process of the wider excavations at the acropolis of Lindos (Blinkenberg 1931, 23–26, 61–68, pl. 3.24 and 26).

Three EBA pots of nearly uncertain provenance were also purchased by dealers during this period. This pottery, kept in the National Museum of Copenhagen, consists of two EBA III duck vases, one said to be from Vati, in south Rhodes, and the second from Lakki, between Kretenia and Monolithos, while a burnished, white-painted jug assigned to EBA II was most probably found at Kalathos (Blinkenberg and Johansen 1926, 30, pl. 36. 1, 2; Dietz 1974). However, due to the uncertain provenance of these finds, the settlement pattern on the island during the EBA is still obscure. Our knowledge of the period has been enlightened only by the systematic excavation at Asomatos (Marketou 1990a, 1997) in the wider area of Ialysos.

The EBA at Ialysos

The settlement at Asomatos is located closest to the side of the island facing Asia Minor. About one hectare in size, it lies west of the modern village of Kremasti. The very existence of large buildings, almost unsuspected a few years ago, has filled the gap in our knowledge of the EBA in Rhodes and the southeastern Aegean. The last phase of occupation, dated to the mature phase of the EBA (EBA IIIB), is represented by oblong, freestanding buildings that are delimited by streets and alleys made of beaten earth and pebbles.

Only one of the oblong buildings revealed so far has been uncovered in its entirety. The building is subdivided along its length into two uneven sectors that give the impression of a double megaron. The three long side walls are projected beyond the narrow sides of the structure so that they form three antae, which are longer on the east side, similar to the megara of the second city of Troy. The wider, south part of the building is occupied by a single, spacious room. Nearly in the middle of this room is a hearth, and two ovens are built in the corners of its south wall. The rather narrow north part of the building is arranged into two small rooms for storage. In the later phase of the building, the long porches of the east side seem to have functioned as sheltered outdoor spaces.

Narrow-necked jars and several jugs for liquids were stocked in the adjacent small room to the west. It is obvious that everyday activities seem to have taken place around the hearth in the spacious main hall. This picture is perfectly represented by a broken cooking pot that was found next to the hearth and the fine tableware, such as large or smaller red-burnished and red-crossed painted bowls. Among the rest of the material culture found on the floor were also cattle bones, in some cases still in articulation (Marketou 1997, 402 figure 3; Trantalidou 1996–98), which complete the picture of the building's last living moments before the sudden abandonment of the settlement.

The use of the building's internal space, quite conceivable from its design and the orientation, has become more obvious from the distribution of the material culture, including the elegant handmade pottery, left in situ. Dark-faced, incised pyxides and duck vases, painted jugs, large teapots, and an elaborate, wide-necked jar (Efe 1997, 601, pl. I, nos. 15–17) of Anatolian influence bearing facial features in relief (Marketou 1997, 401, figure 5) were kept in the northwestern room.

The distribution of smashed objects and animal bones found indoors, as well as the presence of scattered material culture in the open-air areas, streets, and alleys between the houses, clearly shows a serious natural destruction, most probably a flood. On the other hand, the bulk of material culture consisting of narrow-necked amphorae, in some cases bearing potter's marks, large and smaller storage jars with refined decoration, dark-faced spindle whorls, numerous seashells, the broken cooking pot, and the deep bowls next to the hearth in the large room bespeak the settlement's self-sufficiency before its abrupt end.

According to this evidence, Asomatos was the earliest proto-urban center on Rhodes. The material culture is similar to that of the settlement at Serayia on Kos, Daskalio cave on Kalymnos (Benzi 1997), Heraion III–IV on Samos (Milojčić 1961, 65–67; Renfrew 1972, 127), the Yellow period of Poliochni on Lemnos (Bernabò-Brea 1976, 249–314), and other settlements in the hinterland of Asia Minor, such as Beycesultan X-IX and VII-VI (Lloyd 1962, 207–63) and EBA 3–4 Aphrodisias (Joukowsky 1986a, 387–407; 1986b, 582–610). The site of Asomatos demonstrates that, as early as the mid-3rd millennium BC, Rhodes was in communication not only with the east Aegean and Asia Minor but also with the Cyclades, Euboea, and Lerna in the Argolid, preparing for the remarkable development in the ensuing centuries.

However, the site was not built on virgin land. Immediately below the walls and the floors of the last phase of occupation lies a rectangular structure made of *pisé* on strong stone foundations assigned to EBA II (Marketou 1997, 396, figures 1–2). Moreover, between these phases, a middle phase—seriously damaged and leveled by the building activities of the last phase—has been revealed and assigned to EBA IIIA (Marketou 1997, 396).

THE AREA OF IALYSOS AND THE SETTLEMENT OF TRIANDA IN THE MBA

After the final abandonment of the EBA III settlement at Asomatos, habitation shifted farther east toward Phileremos and spread in the northern part of the island. The first evidence for the MBA period was uncovered during the Italian excavations in the deeper levels of the sanctuary of Athena on Phileremos (Benzi 1984; Coldstream 1969, 1n6; Marketou 2009, 73–76). Another location has been identified on the north slope of the mountain, near the chapel of Prophetes Elias (Marketou 1988, 28, figures 2–3; 1998a, 42, figure 2a). In parallel, a few plain MBA pots have been found at the settlement at Trianda as well (Monaco 1941, 84, figure 5.1–2; Papazoglou-Manioudaki 1982, 149–50, figure 5b, pl. 62a–63a).

Whereas the MBA in the Dodecanese used to be considered a "dark age" (Davis 1982; Papagiannopoulou 1985; Raymond 2007, 221), its existence and importance are now being ascertained continuously in excavations. A habitation level dated to the Middle Bronze Age, with pottery and loomweights, was revealed in the north end of the island, near the harbor of Akandia (Dreliosi-Herakleidou 1999, 24–25, pl. 1b, 2a–b). Architectural remains of houses are also located in the deepest levels of the prehistoric settlement at Trianda, while building complexes have been found farther south, outside the limits of the LBA city. Dispersed MBA installations also extend to the east, where an isolated jar burial was discovered (Marketou 1998a, 45, pl. Ib).

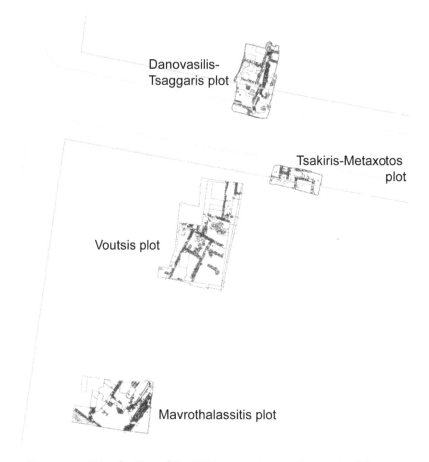

Figure 58.1. Trianda. Plan of the MBA excavations to the south of the LBA
settlement (courtesy of the author).

The recently recovered architectural remains belong to large oblong buildings with a spacious room similar to Asomatos and a number of smaller spaces.
The town layout is crowded and rather complex (figure 58.1). It comprises houses
separated by streets and alleys made of beaten earth and pebbles. The buildings
are mainly built of layers of mud, rubble and mud bricks reinforced with wooden
beams on low stone foundations, according to the earlier tradition of Asomatos.
However, there is evidence of fine white and red plaster that covered the interior
face of the walls and in some cases the floors of the houses (Marketou 1998a, 42, 43,
pl. 1a; 2009, 78–81).

In the southernmost part of the MBA occupation, located to the south of the
main LBA settlement (figure 58.1, Mavrothalassitis plot), a large room with red polished plaster on the interior face of the *pisé* walls and the floor has been uncovered (Marketou 1999, 946–947, figure 20; 2009, 79–80, figure 8). A pinkish plastered
bench is built on the west side of the room, in front of which are the remnants of a
large plastered feature set in the floor. The west side of this room is attached to the

foundation of a wide structure (1.20 m), most probably an enclosure or a fortification wall made of large pebbles aligned along two parallel rows.

The local pottery found on floor deposits in most cases is made according to the local EBA tradition. It is, however, wheel made and decorated with less careful ornamentation. Particularly popular among the numerous vase shapes are high-necked jugs and carinated cups (Marketou 1998a, 43–44, figures 1–2, pls. 4a–c; Raymond 2007, 223–25). However, the presence of some Minoan imports among the local material has so far suggested a correlation with the Cretan Middle Minoan IB-II phases (Coldstream 1969, 1n6; Benzi 1984, 98). Thus, it seems that the culture of this period developed in continuity with the EBA III, a fact that has been so far demonstrated by the stratigraphy of Serayia on Kos (Marketou 1990b, 101–102, figures 4, 6).

The LBA Settlement at Ialysos (Trianda)

Trianda, the major prehistoric settlement of the Dodecanese, is situated in the wider area of Ialysos and approximately 4.5 km to the east of Asomatos. The settlement is located at a depth of around 3–4 m, underneath a typical flood plain made of alluvial deposits. The site was originally near the coastline but has now shifted up, at a distance of around 500 m on the inland side, bordered by streams, to the north of Mount Phileremos (267 m). The branch of the main modern stream of Trianda descends from the mountain to the sea, forming a delta in the area of ancient Schedia (Inglieri 1936, 24–25n10; Papachristodoulou 1989, 87n404). It seems, however, that in the Bronze Age, ships sailing across Asia Minor from the Eastern Mediterranean and Crete would have found a similar delta formation to be navigable.

The main scope of the first excavations, conducted by the Italian Mission in 1935 and 1936, was to discover the settlement associated with the rich Mycenaean cemeteries revealed on the nearby hills of Moschou and Makria Vounara. The careful Italian excavator Giorgio Monaco (1941) investigated an area of 1,300 sq m and revealed three successive layers of the prehistoric settlement. The settlement was represented by two houses on either side of a north-south road, while part of another house was uncovered at the northeast area of the excavation (Monaco 1941, 49, pl. I, plan I).

Although the proposed chronology of the site was beyond the real synchronisms with other known Aegean sites, the detailed publication and the accurate data provided by the excavator have been of great value for further study of the site. The successive phases of the settlement were particularly discussed in the fundamental article by Arne Furumark (1950). According to his dating, based on the chronology accepted at that time, the three strata of the Italian excavation span the LM IA to the LH IIIA1 period, ca. 1550–1410 BC (Furumark 1950, 179).

Rescue excavations carried out by the Greek Archaeological Service on the site (Driessen and Macdonald 1997, 248–51; Marketou 1988, 1998a, 1998b, 1999, 2004b,

2007, 2009; Marketou et al. 2006; Papazoglou-Manioudaki 1982) have revealed small pieces of the large settlement in different locations. The excavated parts, which cover in total 5,280 sq m, have gradually defined the limits of the LBA IA town, which occupies a territory of around 18 hectares, and revealed the succeeding phases from the MBA until the last phase of the occupation, assigned to LBA IIIA2/IIIB1 (table 58.1).

It has been demonstrated that the prehistoric town suffered two severe earthquakes (Marketou 1990b, 104–11), the first in the early phase of Late Bronze IA and

Table 58.1. The Different Phases of Occupation at Trianda according to Previous and Recent Evidence

Monaco 1941	Furumark 1950	Papazoglou-Manioudaki 1982	Recent Excavations in Years BC
			MBA 2000/1900–1700
		Trianda I MM III	MBA/MM III B–LBA IA early 1700–1650
			Earthquake A/seismic destruction of Akrotiri ± 1650
		Trianda II LM IA (tephra)	LBA IA mature 1650–1630/1610
	Trianda I LM IA		Earthquake B ±1630/1610
	1550–1500 BC		Repairing phase ±1630/1610
			Tephra fall ±1630/1610
		Trianda IIIA–B	
	Trianda IIA	LM I–II–	New smaller settlement
	LM IA end– LM IB 1500–1450 BC	LH IIB/LH IIIA1	LBA/LM IB/LH IIA 1630/1610–1550
Strato inferiore	Trianda IIB		
Strato medio	LM IB end– LM II–LM IIIA1 early		LM II–LH IIB 1550–1490/1450
	1450–1410 BC		LH IIIA:1 1490/1450–1430
Strato superiore			LH IIIA: 2/ LH III B:1 1430–1410/1365

Source: Courtesy of the author.

the second in the mature phase of the same period, shortly before the eruption of the Thera volcano (Doumas 1978; Marthari 1984, 1990; Palyvou 1984) in 1630/1610 BC, according to the high chronology (Manning 1999, 7–45, table 2; Manning et al. 2002; Marketou 1990b, 104, table 1; Marketou, Fakorellis, and Maniatis 2001).

The large town was built on the MBA remains in the beginning of the LBA IA, a phase that also correlates with the Middle Minoan IIIB/early Late Minoan IA period. With the immense growth of the Cretan palaces and the Minoan expansion in the Aegean and particularly in Asia Minor, the prosperous town of Trianda adopted many elements of the Minoan style. However, the extremely complex process of 'minoanization,' also apparent in Miletus and other Aegean sites and regarded as either the 'Versailles effect' (Wiener 1990, 140) or a result of Minoan thalassocracy, deserves further consideration (Marketou 1998a, 63–65; 2009). At Trianda, as at Serayia on Kos and at Akrotiri on Thera, the Cretan style is rather noticeable during the mature LBA IA (Marketou 1988, 29–32). The Minoan influence, apparent in the presence of large quantities of conical cups, fireboxes, and clay and stone lamps, is obvious even in architecture. However, the adoption of the Minoan style seems in some cases rather eclectic.

Although the fragmentary rescue excavations give an incomplete picture, it seems that Trianda in the LBA IA was one of the great urban centers in the Aegean. The layout of the town shows at least four wide, stone-paved streets across large ashlar buildings (Marketou 1998a, 47–49; 1998b, 56–57; Marketou et al. 2006, 7–8). Three rooms with pier-and-door partitions have been recovered. A fragment of a medium-size pair of horns of consecration was found near one of the corners of the northwestern *polythyron* (Marketou 1988, 30; 1998b, 48). In the southwest sector of the settlement, two buildings situated on either side of a paved street have been excavated. Each building has at least one *polythyron* with the pier and door partitions opened to the east.

The wide distribution of fresco fragments in nearly all of the excavated areas—unfortunately not found in situ due to the clearing of the ruins after the earthquake—strongly suggests that the interiors of almost all of the houses were decorated with wall paintings. They depict floral designs, such as red on white or white on red lilies (Marketou 1998a, 60, 67; 1998b, 58; Monaco 1941, 68–72, figure 18, pl. 7), reeds and other plants, elaborate rosettes, and fragments depicting clothing of female figures. The zones flanking the upper part of each synthesis are decorated with elegant red on white or black on blue stripes or fine running spirals on a polished white background, and the lower zones of the dadoes are embellished with fine representations of veined stone or wood.

It has been shown that the wall paintings of Trianda were made by skillful painters—comparable to those at Akrotiri—who were likely traveling across the Aegean. In some cases, there are also stucco floors, either monochrome or decorated with polychrome spots that imitate pebbles. The fragmentary wall painting depicting an emblematic double axe with a sacral knot or a pendant vegetal motif (Marketou 1998a, 60; Boulotis 2005, 33) points to the cultic character of the *polythyron* at the northwest sector of Trianda (figure 58.2a).

Figure 58.2. Trianda. LBA IA. Northwest sector, area of polythyron.
The curved side of a tripod table of offerings with two acrobats
exercising on either side of a three-branched papyrus (courtesy of the
author).

The votive bronze statuettes of worshippers (Marketou 1998b) and the clay rhyta, often in the form of a bull, revealed in several houses, as well as the skulls of sacrificed animals found near the cemetery to the north of the settlement (Marketou 1998a, 60–69), hint at some aspects of domestic cult under Minoan influence. Also associated with domestic cult were several tripod offering tables of lime plaster, either monochrome or with pictorial decoration, such as the exceptional tripod table of offerings made of plaster and with the representation of two male acrobats in a performance of a reverse-vertical exercise on either side of a three-branched papyrus (figure 58.2).

The athletic exercise alludes to Egyptian iconography, as well as to Minoan images of bull leapers. Similarly, two tumblers are symmetrically designed in a flowery field on a flat cylinder from Knossos and on a lentoid gem on either side of a three-branched papyrus from Mycenae (Evans 1964, 501–508, figures 443, 444; Sakellariou 1966, 65, pl. 4e). A single tumbler is engraved on the gold-covered pommel of a sword from Malia (Chapouthier 1938, 19–62). The sophisticated use of colors and the cautiously drawn details combine to make this a masterpiece of the Aegean art of miniature painting. Tables of offerings with pictorial compositions are known from Phylakopi (Morgan 2007, 389–95), Akrotiri (Televantou 2007), Tiryns (Televantou 2007, 62n19), Miletus (Niemeier 2005, 6, color pl. 12), and Palaikastro (MacGillivray et al. 1991, 137, figure 15, pl. 14c–d).

Within the rich repertory of pottery are several fireboxes and fire stands, amphorae, jars, clay lamps, jugs and juglets, Vapheio cups, and quantities of conical cups, as well as bridge-spouted jars and conical or ovoid rhyta (Marketou

1990b, figure 18; 1998a, 49–58). Either locally made or imported from Crete, mainly from the Mesara area (Marketou et al. 2006, 8–9, 20–28), the vases are decorated with ripple patterns, running spirals, festoons, scrolls, foliate bands, reeds and trickle patterns, according to the Minoan style. Among them is also an elaborate, bronze, one-handled bowl (Matthäus 1980, 208, no. 316, pl. 38: 316; Monaco 1941, 73, figure 19).

The corpus of bronze tools, the crucibles, a bronze bun ingot, and the molds for melting tools and decorative ornaments, some of which continued to appear in the next phases of the settlement, strongly suggests the presence of workshops in the northwest area of the settlement, recalling the tradition of the mythological *Telchines* on Rhodes (Marketou 1998b, 62).

The eruption of the Thera volcano marked the end of the Late Bronze IA period. The earthquake that destroyed the buildings at Akrotiri destroyed Trianda as well. During the short interval between the earthquake and the eruption, the inhabitants cleared the ruins and began intensive reconstruction works. This picture is revealed in the excavations at Trianda, under the layer of volcanic ash that covered the ruined buildings and streets of the prehistoric city (Marketou 1990b; 1998a, 47–49). The airborne volcanic ash was dispersed to the Dodecanese, Asia Minor, Crete, and the Eastern Mediterranean. Apart from the ruined city at Trianda, tephra also covered the countryside, as ascertained in the area of Kremasti (Driessen and Macdonald 1997, 251), at the airport at Paradeisi (Doumas 1988), and Kolymbia (Marketou 1998a, 63). In addition, sporadic evidence of Late Minoan IA pottery below the tephra layers and the most recent discovery of incomplete walls at Kremasti (Marketou 2000; 2009, 90, figure 22) point to periodic habitation in the surrounding areas. Volcanic ash was also found in the interior of the Koumelo cave at Archangelos (Sampson 1987, 69–70) and farther south at Apolakkia.

The devastating preeruption earthquake, which was followed by the ash fall, had adverse effects on life on the island, especially on agriculture and stock raising, and furthermore caused a large change in the environmental conditions of the island, such as overwhelming floods. Evidence for a serious flooding in the prehistoric town at Trianda is attested by the remnants of flood-prevention works that were constructed on top of the volcanic ash layer in the posteruption phase at Trianda (Marketou 2007).

The LBA IA Cemetery

Excavations at the northernmost end of the LB settlement at Trianda, in a sandy strip of land about 500 meters from the present coastline, have revealed a rather poor cemetery (Marketou 1998a, 60–61). The deceased were buried in a crouched pose, either directly in sand or in jars, while there were also two instances of built cist graves (Marketou 1998a, pl. IV).

Almost unexpected was the presence of a horse skeleton amid a cluster of direct human burials (Marketou 1998a, pl. IIIc). The animal was found in a contracted pose and in direct association with one of the humans. This horse burial at Trianda is possibly the earliest of the known examples from the Aegean islands. The animal's small size verifies the view that the transportation of this particular kind of horse by sea was easier than horses of normal size. Indicative in this respect is the iconography of transporting a horse on a ship, found on a seal impression from the Little Palace at Knossos (Evans 1964, 827, figure 805).

The absence of grave goods and the general picture of the cemetery, along with the stratigraphical evidence, indicate that the burials were made hurriedly and simultaneously in the mature phase of LBA IA. Concurrently, the jar burials continued earlier traditions in the region, in both the Dodecanese and the hinterlands of Asia Minor, and go back to the EBA II period in Kos (Marketou 2004a, 20–23), as well as to the MBA (cf. the burial from Ialysos mentioned earlier).

The Settlement at Trianda before and after the Eruption of the Thera Volcano: Continuity of Life in the LBA IB Period

During the LBA IA, the maritime settlements of the Aegean and mainly Crete evidently participated, each to a different degree, in the network of exchanges and contacts between the Eastern Mediterranean, the Aegean, and Crete. However, Cretan products were predominant, and the strong influence of Minoan culture radiated to the Aegean settlements, as well as to Rhodes and Kos. The development of metallurgy, the empirical knowledge of astronomy, the spread of the Linear A script, and the use of a common ponderal system for weighing products, represented in Rhodes by marble and lead balance weights, facilitated voyages by sea and exchanges.

Ships traveled to the west and central Aegean for supplies of silver and copper from the sources at Laurion in Attica and on the island of Siphnos. They also journeyed to the eastern Aegean to obtain obsidian from Yiali, as well as for supplies of metals, timber, and even livestock, from Asia Minor. By the end of this period, the distinguishing light-on-dark and dark–on-light Koan vases had reached Rhodes (Marthari, Marketou, and Jones 1990).

In this active period, the eruption of the Thera volcano took place, which caused the dramatic end of Akrotiri. Nevertheless, the vigorous exchange pattern of the Aegean does not seem to have come to an end. In the succeeding LBA IB period, the new settlement of Trianda was limited to a smaller area at the northern part of the previous larger LBA I town. In the southern part of this area, strong flood-control systems were erected on the tephra layer (Marketou 1998a, 61, pl. II), as mentioned. This fact indicates that flooding was one of the serious problems caused by the earthquake and generally the eruption of the volcano. However, the architectural remains are not preserved in their entirety, as they were badly damaged by the following LH IIIA1-LH IIIA2/IIIB1 building activities (Marketou 2007).

Among these ruins, fragmentary pottery of the elegant marine, floral, or alternative styles has been found, imported from Crete or the Argolid, along with white slip I and base ring I pots and spindle bottles in red lustrous wheel-made ware that came mainly from Cyprus. In parallel, the production of local pottery and active metalworking continued at the new settlement of Trianda. A particular local category of pottery that imitates Cypriot milk bowls and spindle bottles also appears in this period (Karageorghis and Marketou 2006).

The Mycenaean Settlement at Trianda

Built on the LBA IB ruins, the new settlement in the southern part of the previous large town (Benzi 1988a; Hope Simpson and Lazenby 1973, 155–57; Karantzali 2005, 142–48; Marketou 1998a, 61–63; 2004a; 2007; Papazoglou-Manioudaki 1982, 145–49, 184–85) was once again at the epicenter of the new developments. Rhodes was the perfect station for the Mycenaeans, who wanted to enlarge their regime in the east Aegean and Asia Minor.

Mycenaean infiltration at Trianda expanded first at Ialysos in LH IIB, as attested mainly by the dissemination of pottery, imported or in local variations, as well as by the presence of rock-cut chamber tombs. The earliest tombs appeared at Ialysos in the cemeteries on the hills of Moschou and Makria Vounara, located to the southwest of the settlement (Benzi 1988b, 59–62; 1992, 209–12; Hope Simpson and Lazenby 1973, figure 2; Karantzali 2005; Mee 1982, 8–11; Mountjoy 1999, 983).

Outstanding among the architectural remains uncovered are the flood-prevention works, which remain in more or less the same position as those of the preceding period (Marketou 1998a, 62–63; 2007). However, it seems that these were unable to avert the final abandonment of the city. The results of this unavoidable destruction is evident today in the picture of the deserted city presented by recent excavations that reveal various objects of daily life that were buried beneath the alluvial deposits (Marketou 2004b, 2007). The pottery kiln found on the southeast outskirts of the Mycenaean settlement, where it was discovered in direct association with the remains of a vertical loom, provides a good example of the community's last living moments. The kiln, of the well-known horseshoe-shape type and with almost all of its main parts exceptionally well preserved, was found with fired pottery still in situ, forever covered by a layer of river pebbles and sandy earth (Marketou 2004b, figure 6). Similarly, the loomweights from the loom installation, in proximity to the kiln, are found fallen from the warp threads (Marketou 1999, 945; Marketou 2004b, figure 8).

Another catastrophe layer has been found in the southwest sector of the settlement, with a substantial group of LH IIIA2/LH IIIB1 pottery that shows the last dramatic moments of the Mycenaean settlement at Trianda before the great flood and the final desertion of the site. There is not yet evidence for the location of the Mycenaean settlement after the flooding, but a probable site might be at the southwest slope of Phileremos, below the Doric fountain of the 4th century BC.

THE MYCENAEAN CEMETERIES

The Mycenaean period in Rhodes is better known from the extended cemeteries on the island. Between 1868 and 1871 excavations undertaken by Sir Alfred Biliotti (then HBM vice consul in Rhodes) on behalf of the British Museum on Moschou Vounara at Ialysos (Forsdyke 1925, 139–77; Furtwängler and Löschke 1886, 5–7, pls. 1–11; Stubbings 1951, 5–6, 8–20) yielded the first known Mycenaean collection in the world before the outstanding discoveries of Schliemann at Mycenae in 1876 (Schliemann 1878). The following Italian excavations at Ialysos revealed a total of 170 tombs on the hills of Moschou and Makria Vounara (Maiuri 1923–1924, 83–341; Jacopi 1930–1931, 253–45) and presented the largest cemeteries of the island.

The typical cemeteries consist of clusters of chamber tombs with long and steep dromoi deeply cut into the soft rock and arranged in rows. In some cases, platforms or benches are also cut into almost rectangular or trapezoidal chambers (Benzi 1992, 227–30). In a few other cases, they include pit graves. Some pits of a late Mycenaean date also appear in Soroni (Laurenzi 1938, 51). A particular feature of the cemetery is the presence of incised, porous stone blocks *(cippi)* found in six tombs at Makria Vounara (Benzi 1992, 229, pl. 123a–b; Maiuri 1923–1924, 201, 207, 221, 228, figure 131; Mee 1982, 11), interpreted as tombs markers by Andronikos (1961–1962, 168, pls. 85 b–e; 1968, 117–18; Vermeule 1972, 302, figure 47b). In the 12th century BC, some cremations took place among the standard inhumations at Ialysos (Benzi 1992, 230–31; Mee 1982, 27–29; 1998, 139). The phenomenon appears at the same time at Müskebi in Halicarnassus (Mee 1998, 139), on Kos (Morricone 1965–1966, 30, 202–203), Karpathos (Melas 1985, 39), Astypalaia (Doumas 1975, 372), and farther northwest on Naxos and at Perati (Mee 1982, 28).

The earliest use of the cemetery at Ialysos is associated with the historical appearance of the first Mycenaeans in the settlement at Trianda in LH IIB (Benzi 1988a, 1988b, 59; Furumark 1950, 181). At the same time, Mycenaean tombs appear as well at other sites on the northwestern part of the island, namely in the area of Paradeisi (Laurenzi 1938, 49, pl. 40) and at Tholos (Jacopi 1932–1933, 44, figure 46). Stippled cups, small piriform jars, and other pots corresponding to the LH IIIA1 material from Trianda (Monaco 1941, 89–90, figure 79–80, 136, figure 86, 155, figure 117) were also found in the cemeteries (Benzi 1992, 268, pl. 31e–g; 269, pl. 32.f; 318–19, pl. 67a–1). Among the bulk of Mycenaean pottery, mostly imported from the Argolid, the percentages of Minoan imports are low, such as a piriform jar with birds and lilies, similar to one found at Makelli on Karpathos (Benzi 1992, pl. 32a; Charitonides 1961–1962, pl. 26a–b).

Other miscellaneous objects include fine pieces of jewelry and items from Cyprus and the Eastern Mediterranean, including Cypro-Syrian cylinder seals, Sandars-type Ci and Cii horned swords, a cruciform Dii sword, an Eii-type dagger (Benzi 1988b, 61, figure 4; 1992, 171–72, pl. 177; Sandars 1963, 116, 144–46), and a Cypriot-type dagger with rat tail and blade of four wing bayonet type (Benzi 1988b, 61; Catling 1964, 118), as well as a number of exotica from the Levant. Indicative of the connections with Egypt is the faience scarab of Amenhotep III from Tomb 9 of Billiotti's excavations, found along with two more scarabs of the 18th Dynasty (Cline 1994, 147–48, nos. 130–32; Forsdyke 1911, 114–15). The two Cypriot tombs, 76 and 86, at Ialysos seem to belong to this period (Benzi 1992, 384–85, 395–95; Jacopi 1930–1931, 304, 326–29; Mee 1982, 22).

During the LH IIIA2 period, the number of tombs at Ialysos increases significantly (Benzi 1988b, 63). On the other hand, the Mycenaean expansion is obvious all over the island (Benzi 1988b, 62–64, table 1; 1992, 212–14, table I; Mee 1982, 83–97). The large corpus of miscellaneous offerings derived from the tombs reflects the intensive Mycenaean trade in the Aegean during the 14th century BC, the most eloquent picture of which is given by the late 14th-century-BC shipwreck off Uluburun (Bass 1984; Bass et al. 1989; Kilian 1990; Pulak 2005).

A range of complex vases and, more often, the typical tripod basket vases, beaked jugs, and piriform jars belong to the local Rhodo-Mycenaean pottery (Mountjoy 1999, 984, figure 412). Apparent Anatolian elements that are also obvious in some products recall Trojan and mainly Beycesultan prototypes, which are more evident in an Anatolian stemmed krater found at the settlement of Trianda (Monaco 1941, 131n27, figure 83, illustrated upside down). Stirrup jars, jugs, piriform jars, and kylikes appear most frequently. Exceptional among the recent finds from the cemetery of Aspropelia at Pylona is the pictorial conical rhyton with modeled bucranium attached on the rim (Karantzali 1998; 2001, 35, color pl. 1), found in the central chamber of the triple tomb 2.

The general level of prosperity is demonstrated by the presence of gold finger rings and leaf rosettes, several beads of glass or semiprecious stones, ornaments of silver, amber, and glass, scarabs, and bronze objects, including Sandars-type B swords, razors, and cleavers, as well as a Cypriot dagger from Tholos (Benzi 1988b, 62–64; 1992, 212–14; Cline 1994, 226n831; Mee 1982, 11–22), Sandars-type IA knives, and cleavers (Benzi 1998b, 64).

The majority of the Mycenaean weapons appearing in a wide range during both the LH IIIA1 and the IIIA2 period show the Mycenaean 'militaris aura,' according to Benzi (1989b, 61–62). This is shown by swords of Dii and Ci types, Ei daggers (Sandars 1963, 131, 141), the Siana spear and knives (Sandars 1963, 140–41, pls. 27, 53–55), early spearheads of Cypriot type (Catling 1964, 118), knives, and razors. Other items include bronze vases, Syro-Palestinian mortars, and a duck-headed ivory pyxis (Furtwängler and Löschke 1886, 14, figure 3; Sakellarakis 1971, 222–23, pls. 48–49), a small ostrich rhyton, and objects made of faience.

The collapse of the Mycenaean palace system, compared with the most recent clear evidence for the overwhelming flooding that caused the final abandonment of the settlement at Trianda, provides a rather plausible explanation for the decrease in the number of tombs at Ialysos in LH IIIB. However, the scarcity of relevant material in the northwestern part of the island, apart from a few sherds at Maritsa (Hope Simpson and Lazenby 1973, 139–40; Mee 1982, 88), does not indicate a definitive abandonment of the area (Benzi 1988b, 65). Occupation appears denser in the rest of the island, mainly in the southeast, as witnessed by the abundant evidence from Vati, Lachania, Apsaktiras, and Passia (Dietz 1984), as well as at Apollakia and Ambelia at Pylona (Hope Simpson 1973, 147, 151; Mee 1982, 63–64, 73, 88).

Although many minor sites were abandoned at the beginning of the 12th century, the obvious increase in the number of burials at Ialysos cemetery demonstrates a period of prosperity in the area (Benzi 1988c). However, Rhodes is an important member of the Aegean *koine* (Desborough 1964, 115, 150, 155; Mee 1982, 90–91), correlating with the subphases of the LH IIIC known from the most recent stratigraphy at Tiryns, Mycenae, and Lefkandi. The octopus stirrup jar, represented by about forty examples, is the hallmark of the period.

Influences from the mainland are shown by the increase in the number of Mycenaean figurines (French 1971, 134). By this time, Naue II-type swords appear in Rhodes, along with other metal objects, such as five Cypriot bronze tanged mirrors (Catling 1964, 227), an Italian ring-handled knife from Tomb 15 at Ialysos (Benzi 1992, 180, 254, pl. 179h; Cline 1994, 227n844; Macdonald 1986, 141), and a large, bronze, arched fibula from tomb 4 at Pylona (Karantzali 2001, 70–71, figure 42, pl. 47a). Indicative of the connections with Egypt are also the glass vases (Benzi 1992, 201; Cline 1994, 197n558, 204n627).

However, the increase in the number of LH IIIC burials at Ialysos could also be seen as part of a process of synoecism (Macdonald 1986, 149–50) and as 'an internal migration from the peripheral areas to the main center...[rather] than an influx of settlers from the mainland and/or elsewhere in the Aegean' (Benzi 1988b, 70), as previously maintained by Mee (1982, 89–90). After this new period of affluence and trade contacts with Cyprus and the Near East, a new crisis affected the eastern Aegean and Rhodes in the early phase of the 11th century BC. By the middle of the century, the Mycenaean civilization on the island seems to have essentially come to an end.

BIBLIOGRAPHY

Andronikos, Manolis. 1961–1962. "Ελληνικά επιτάφια μνημεία." *ArchDelt* 17 (Meletes): 152–210.
———. 1968. *Totenkult: Archaeologia Homerica*. Göttingen: Vandenhoeck and Ruprecht.
Bass, George F. 1984. "A Bronze Age Shipwreck at Ulu Burun (Kas): 1984 Campaign." *AJA* 90: 269–96.

————, Cemal Pulak, Dominique Collon, and James Weinstein. 1989. "The Bronze Age Shipwreck at Ulu Burun: 1986 Campaign." *AJA* 93: 1–29.

Benzi, Mario. 1984. "Evidence for a Middle Minoan Settlement on the Acropolis at Ialysos (Mt. Philerimos)." In *Minoan Thalassocracy*, 93–105.

————. 1988a. "Mycenaean Pottery Later than LH IIIA:1 From the Italian Excavations at Trianda on Rhodes." In *Dodecanese*, 39–55.

————. 1988b. "Mycenaean Rhodes: A Summary." In *Dodecanese*, 59–72.

————. 1988c. "Rhodes in the LH IIIC Period." In *Problems in Greek Prehistory*, 253–62.

————. 1992. *Rodi e la civiltà Micenea.* Rome: Incunabula Graeca 94.

————. 1997. "The Late Early Bronze Age Finds from Vathy Cave (Kalymnos) and Their Links with the Northeast Aegean." In *Poliochni*, 383–94.

Bernabò-Brea, Luigi. 1976. *Poliochni: Città preistorica nell' isola di Lemnos*, vol. 2. Rome: Bretschneider.

Blinkenberg, Christian. 1931. *Lindos I: Fouilles de l'acropole 1902–1914. Les petit objects.* Berlin: de Gruyter and Cie. Libraires-Éditeurs.

————, and K. Frijs Johansen. 1926. *Corpus Vasorum Antiquorum.* Danemark, fasc. 2. Copenhagen: Musée National. Fasc. 2. Paris: Librairie ancienne Éduard Champion.

Boulotis, Christos. 2005. "Πτυχές θρησκευτικής έκφρασης στο Ακρωτήρι." *Άλς* 3. Περιοδική Έκδοση της Εταιρείας Στήριξης Σπουδών Προϊστορικής Θήρας: 20–75.

Catling, Hector, W. 1964. *Cypriot Bronzework in the Mycenaean World.* Oxford: Clarendon.

Chapouthier, Fernand. 1938. *Deux épées d'apparat découvertes en 1956 au palais de Mallia.* Études Crétoises V. Paris: L'École française d'Athènes.

Charitonides, Seraphim. 1961–1962. "Θαλαμοειδής τάφος Καρπάθου." *ArchDelt* 17A (1963): 32–76.

Cline, Eric H. 1994. *SWDS.*

Coldstream, Nicolas, J. 1969. "The Phoenicians at Ialysos." *BICS* 16: 1–8.

Davis, Jack. 1982. "The Earliest Minoans in the South-east Aegean: A Reconsideration of the Evidence." *AnatSt* 32: 33–41.

Desborough, Vincent R. d'A. 1964. *The Last Mycenaeans and Their Successors.* New York: Oxford University Press.

Dietz , Søren. 1974. "Two Painted Duck-vases from Rhodes." *ActaA* 45: 133–43.

————. 1984. *Excavations and Surveys in Southern Rhodes: The Mycenaean Period: Lindos IV, 1, Results of the Carlsberg Foundation Excavations in Rhodes 1902–1914.* Odense: National Museum of Denmark.

Doumas, Christos. 1975. "Αρχαιότητες και μνημεία Δωδεκανήσων. Τήλος-Αστυπάλαια." *ArchDelt* 30 (Chronica): 369–72.

————. 1978. "The Stratigraphy of Akrotiri." In *TAW* I, 778–82.

————. 1988. "The Prehistoric Eruption of Thera and Its Effects: The Evidence from Rhodes." In *Dodecanese*, 34–38.

Dreliosi-Herakleidou, Anastasia. 1999. "Παλαιά και νέα ευρήματα προ του συνοικισμού από την πόλη της Ρόδου." In *Ρόδος 2.400 Χρόνια. Η πόλη της Ρόδου από την Ίδρυσή της μέχρι την κατάληψή της από τους Τούρκους* (1523). Ρόδος, 24–29 Οκτωβρίου 1993, Τόμος Α, 21–28. Αθήνα: Ταμείο Αρχαιολογικών Πόρων και Απαλλοτριώσεων.

Driessen Jan, and Colin F. Macdonald. 1997. *The Troubled Island: Crete before and after the Santorini Eruption.* Aegaeum 17. Liège: Université de Liège.

Efe, Turan. 1997. "Pottery Links between Troad and Northwestern Anatolia." In *Poliochni*, 596–609.

Evans, Arthur, 1964. *PM* IV, ii.

Forsdyke, Edgar J. 1911. "Minoan Pottery from Cyprus and the Origin of the Mycenaean Style." *JHS* 31: 110–18.

———. 1925. *Catalogue of the Greek and Etruscan Vases in the British Museum.* Vol. 1, part 1, *Prehistoric Aegean Pottery.* London.

French, Elizabeth. 1971. "The Development of Mycenaean Terracotta Figurines." *BSA* 66: 101–87.

Furtwängler, Arne, and Löschke, Georg. 1886. *Mykenische Vasen: Vorgehellenische Thongefässe aus dem Gebiet des Mittelmeeres.* Berlin.

Furumark, Arne. 1950. "The Settlement at Ialysos and Aegean History c. 1550–1400 B.C." *OpArch* VI: 150–271.

Hope Simpson, Richard, and John F. Lazenby. 1973. "Notes from the Dodecanese III." *BSA* 68: 127–79.

Inglieri, Raffaele U. 1936. *Carta Archeologica dell' Isola di Rodi.* Florence: Istituto Storico–Archeologico FERT.

Jacopi, Giulio. 1930–1931. "Nuovi scavi nella necropoli micenea di Jalisso." *ASAtene* 13–14: 253–345.

———. 1932–1933. "Esploratione Archeologica di Camiro. II." *Clara Rhodos* VI–VII. Part 1. Rhodes: Istituto Storico Archeologico.

Joukowsky, Martha Sharp. 1986a. *Prehistoric Aphrodisias: An Account of the Excavations and Artifact Studies.* Vol. 1, *Excavations and Studies.* Archeologia Transantlantica III. Providence: Brown University Center for Old World Archaeology and Art.

———. 1986b. *Prehistoric Aphrodisias: An Account of the Excavations and Artifact Studies.* Vol. 2, *Bibliography, Catalogue, Appendix, Index.* Archeologia Transantlantica III. Providence: Brown University Center for Old World Archaeology and Art.

Karageorghis, Vassos, and Toula Marketou. 2006. "Late Bronze Age Ia/Ib Rhodian Imitations of Cypriote Ceramics: The Evidence from Trianda." In *Timelines*, vol. 2, 455–62.

Karantzali, Efi. 1998. "A New Mycenaean Pictorial Rhyton from Rhodes." In *Cyprus-Dodecanese-Crete*, 87–104.

———. 2001. *The Mycenaean Cemetery at Pylona on Rhodes.* BAR-IS 988. Oxford: Archaeopress.

———. 2005. "The Mycenaeans at Ialysos: Trading Station or Colony?" In *Emporia*, 141–51.

Kilian, Imma. 1990. "Überlegungen zum spätbronzezeitlichen Schiffswrack von Ulu Burun (Kas)." *JRGZM* 40: 333–52.

Laurenzi, Luciano. 1938. "Nuove scoperte di vasi micenei (note sulla civiltà micenea in Rodi)." *Memorie dell'Istituto F.E.R.T. di Rodi* 2: 47–54.

Lloyd, Seton, with James Mellaart. 1962. *Beycesultan.* Vol. 1, *The Chalcolithic and Early Bronze Age Levels.* Occasional Publications of the British Institute of Archaeology at Ankara 6. London: British Institute of Archaeology at Ankara.

Macdonald, Colin. 1986. "Problems of the Twelfth Century B.C. in the Dodecanese." *BSA* 81: 125–51.

MacGillivray, J. Alexander, L. Hugh Sackett, Jan Driessen, Alexandre Farnoux, and David Smyth. 1991. "Excavations at Palaikastro, 1990." *BSA* 86: 121–47.

Maiuri, Amedeo. 1923–1924. "Ialisos-Scavi della missione archeologica italiana a Rodi (parte II). *ASAtene* 6–7: 83–341.

Manning, Sturt. W. 1999. *A Test of Time: The Volcano of Thera and the Chronology and History of the Aegean and East Mediterranean in the Mid-second Millennium BC.* Oxford: Oxbow.

————, Christopher Bronk Ramsey, Christos Doumas, Toula Marketou, Gerald Cadogan, and Charlotte L. Pearson. 2002. "New Evidence for an Early Date for the Aegean Late Bronze Age and Thera Eruption." *Antiquity* 76: 733–44.

Marketou, Toula. 1988. "New Evidence on the Topography and Site History of Prehistoric Ialysos." In *Dodecanese*, 27–33.

————. 1990a. "Asomatos and Seraglio: EBA Production and Interconnections." *Hydra* 7: 40–48.

————. 1990b. "Santorini Tephra from Rhodes and Kos: Some Chronological Remarks Based on the Stratigraphy." In *TAW III*, 100–19.

————. 1997. "Ασώματος Ρόδου. Τα μεγαρόσχημα κτήρια και οι σχέσεις τους με το Βορειοανατολικό Αιγαίο." In *Poliochni*, 395–413.

————. 1998a. "Excavations at Trianda (Ialysos) on Rhodes: New Evidence for the Late Bronze Age I Period." *Rend. Mor. Acc. Lincei* s. 9, v. 9: 39–82.

————. 1998b. "LB I Statuettes from Rhodes." In *Cyprus-Dodecanese-Crete*, 55–72.

————. 1999. "Ιαλυσία-Τριάντα." *ArchDelt* 54 (Chronica): 942–47.

———— forthcoming. "Ιαλυσός." *ArchDelt* 55 (Chronica 2000).

————. 2004a. "Η Πρώιμη Εποχή του Χαλκού στην Κω." In *Χάρις Χαίρε. Μελέτες στη μνήμη της Χάρης Κάντζια*. Τόμος Α, 17–30. Αθήνα: Υπουργείο Πολιτισμού. Αρχαιολογικό Ινστιτούτο Αιγαιακών Σπουδών.

2004b. "Μυκηναϊκός κεραμικός κλίβανος στον Προϊστορικό οικισμό της Ιαλυσού (Τριάντα, Ρόδος)." In *Althellenische Technologie und Technik von der prähisto-rischen bis zur helllenistichen Zeit mit Schwerpunk auf der prähistorischen Epoche*, 133–44. Proceedings of the International Symposium in Ohlstadt, March 21–23, 2003. Weilheim/Obb.: Verein zur Förderung der Aufarbeitung der Hellenischen Geschichte.

————. 2007. "Ηφαιστειακή τέφρα και πλήμμυρες στον οικισμό της Ύστερης Χαλκοκρατίας της Ιαλυσού." In *Αρχαιολογικές έρευνες και ευρήματα στα Δωδεκάνησα. Ρόδος, Ιαλυσός, Κως, Νίσυρος και Γυαλί. Archäoligische Forschungen und Funde in der Dodekanes: Rhodos, Ialyssos, Kos, Nisyros, und Giali*, 157–80. Weilheim/Obb.: Verein zur Förderung der Aufarbeitung der Hellenischen Geschichte.

————. 2009. "Ialysos and Its Neighbouring Areas in the MBA and LB I Periods: A Chance for Peace." In *The Minoans in the Central, Eastern, and Northern Aegean: New Evidence. Acts of a Minoan Seminar 22–23 January 2005 in Collaboration with the Danish Institute at Athens and the German Archaeological Institute at Athens*, eds. Eric Hallager, Colin F. Macdonald, and Wolf-Dietrich Niemeier, 73–96. Monographs of the Danish Institute at Athens, vol. 8. Athens.

————, Giorghos Fakorellis, and Yiannis Maniatis. 2001. "New Late Bronze Age Chronology from the Ialysos Region, Rhodes." *Mediterranean Archaeology and Archaeometry* 1: 19–29.

Marketou, Toula, Efi Karantzali, Hans Mommsen, Nikos Zacharias, Vasilis Kilikoglou, and Alexander Schwedt. 2006. "Pottery Wares from the Prehistoric Settlement at Ialysos (Trianda), Rhodes." *BSA* 101: 1–55.

Marthari, Mariza. 1984. "The Destruction of the Town at Akrotiri, Thera, at the Beginning of the LC: Definition and Chronology." In *Prehistoric Cyclades*, 119–33.

————. 1990. "The Chronology of the Last Phases of Occupation at Akrotiri in the Light of the Evidence from the West House Pottery Groups." In *TAW III*, 55–70.

————, Toula Marketou, and Richard E. Jones. 1990. "LB I Ceramic Connections between Thera and Kos." In *TAW III*, 171–84.

Matthäus, Hartmut. 1980. *Die Bronzegefässe der kretisch-mykenischen Kultur.* Prähistorische Bronzefunde. Abteilung II, Band 1. Munich: Beck'sche.

Mee, Christopher. 1982. *Rhodes in the Bronze Age: An Archaeological Survey.* Warminster: Aris and Phillips.

———. 1998. "Anatolia and the Aegean in the Late Bronze Age." In *Aegean and the Orient,* 137–48.

Melas, Manolis. 1985. *The Islands of Karpathos, Saros, and Kasos in the Neolithic and Bronze Age. SIMA* 68. Gothenburg: Åström.

Milojčić, Vladimir. 1961. *Samos I: Die prähistorische Siedlung unter dem Heraion. Grabung 1953 und 1955.* Bonn: Habelt.

Monaco, Giorgio. 1941. "Scavi nella zona Micenea di Jaliso (1935–36)." *Clara Rhodos* X: 41–183. Rhodes: Istituto Storico Archeologico.

Morgan, Lyvia. 2007. "The Painted Plasters and Their Relation to the Wall Painting of the Pillar Crypt." In *Excavations at Phylakopi in Melos 1974–77,* ed. Colin Renfrew, 371–99. BSA Supplementary vol. 42. London: British School at Athens.

Morricone, Luigi. 1965–1966. "Eleona e Langada: Sepolcreti della tarda età del Bronzo a Coo." *ASAtene* 43–44: 5–311.

Mountjoy, Penelope A. 1999. *Regional Mycenaean Decorated Pottery.* Vol. 2. Deutsches Archäologisches Institut. Rahden/Westf.: Leidorf.

Niemeier, Wolf-Dietrich. 2005. "Minoans, Mycenaeans, Hittites, and Ionians in Western Asia Minor: New Excavations in Bronze Age Miletus-Millawanda." In *The Greeks in the East,* ed. Alexandra Villing, 1–36. British Museum Research Publications 157. London: British Museum.

Palyvou, Clairy. 1984. "The Destruction of the Town at Akrotiri, Thera, at the Beginning of LC I Rebuilding Activities." In *Prehistoric Cyclades,* 134–47.

Papachristodoulou, Ioannes. 1989. *Οι αρχαίοι ροδιακοί δήμοι. Ιστορική επισκόπηση. Η Ιαλυσία.* Athens: Η εν Αθήναις Αρχαιολογική Εταιρεία.

Papagiannopoulou, Angelia G. 1985. "Were the S.E. Aegean Islands Deserted in the MBA?" *AnatSt* 35: 85–92.

Papazoglou-Manioudaki, Lena. 1982. "Ανασκαφή του Μινωικού οικισμού στα Τριάντα της Ρόδου." *ArchDelt* 37 (Μελέτες): 139–87.

Pulak, Cemal. 2005. "Who Were the Mycenaeans aboard the Uluburun Ship?" In *Emporia,* 295–310.

Raymond, Amy. 2007. "Minoanization at Miletus: The Middle Bronze Age Ceramics." In *Krinoi Kai Limenai,* 221–29.

Renfrew, Colin. 1972. *The Emergence of Civilisation: The Cyclades and the Aegean in the Third Millennium BC.* London: Methuen.

Sakellarakis, Ioannis. 1971. "Ελεφάντινον πλοίον εκ Μυκηνών." *ArchEph.* 188–233.

Sakellariou, Agne. 1966. *Μυκηναϊκή Σφραγιδογλυφία.* Athens: Demosieumata Archaeologikou Deltiou no. 8.

Sampson, Adamantios. 1987. *Η νεολιθική κατοίκηση στα Δωδεκάνησα.* Athens: Tameion Archaeologikon Poron kai Apallotrioseon.

Sandars, Nancy K. 1963. "The First Aegean Swords and Their Ancestry." *AJA* 67: 117–53.

Schliemann, Heinrich. 1878. *Mycenae.* London: Murray.

Stubbings, Frank H. 1951. *Mycenaean Pottery from the Levant.* Cambridge: Cambridge University Press.

Televantou, Christina. 2007. "Επίχριστες τράπεζες προσφορών." In *Ακρωτήρι Θήρας. Δυτική οικία. Τράπεζες-λίθινα-μετάλλινα-ποικίλα,* ed. Christos Doumas, 49–70. Athens: Η εν Αθήναις Αρχαιολογική Εταιρεία no. 246.

Trantalidou, Katerina. 1996–1998. "Ασώματος Ρόδου, μια θέση της Πρώιμης Εποχής του Χαλκού στην περιοχή της αρχαίας Ιαλυσίας. Τα ζωοαρχαιολογικά κατάλοιπα (ανασκαφικές περίοδοι 1986, 1989, 1991)." *AAA* 29–31: 113–24.

Vermeule, Emily, T. 1972. *Greece in the Bronze Age.* Chicago: University of Chicago Press.

Wiener, Malcolm, H. 1990. "The Isles of Crete? The Minoan Thalassocracy Revisited." In *TAW* III, 128–61.

Wider Mediterranean

CHAPTER 59

CAPE GELIDONYA SHIPWRECK

GEORGE F. BASS

Cape Gelidonya, the Chelidonian Promontory of Pliny (*Natural History* 5.27.97), also known as Taşlıkburun, Kırlangıçburun, Kilidonya Burnu, and Anadolu Burun, lies at the western side of the mouth of the Bay of Antalya in southern Turkey. Five small islands, today called Beşadalar but known in antiquity as the Chelidoniae, extend the line of the cape southward.

The current between these islands, especially when a calm allows water backed up in the Eastern Mediterranean by the summer's prevailing northwest wind (*meltem*) to flow back westward, is as strong as any in the Mediterranean. Whether this current caused its sinking is unknown, but around 1200 BC a vessel of unknown size seems to have ripped open its bottom on a pinnacle of rock on the northeast side of the third island from land (Devecitaşı Adası).

As it sank, artifacts were strewn from the opening in its hull until it settled around 50 meters away. Its stern first rested on a large boulder. Later, perhaps as its hull disintegrated, it slipped down into a gully formed by the boulder and the base of the island. The main concentration of cargo lay at a depth of 26 to 28 meters (figure 59.1).

Over the years, the ship's wood was almost entirely devoured by marine borers, and its cargo was covered by a thick, hard layer of calcium carbonate, commonly called concretion. Almost invisible, its metal cargo was nevertheless seen by Bodrum sponge diver Kemal Aras in 1954. In 1958 he described it to American photojournalist Peter Throckmorton, who was living on Captain Kemal's sponge-diving boat while both writing about the sponge divers of Turkey and cataloging ancient shipwrecks they showed him.

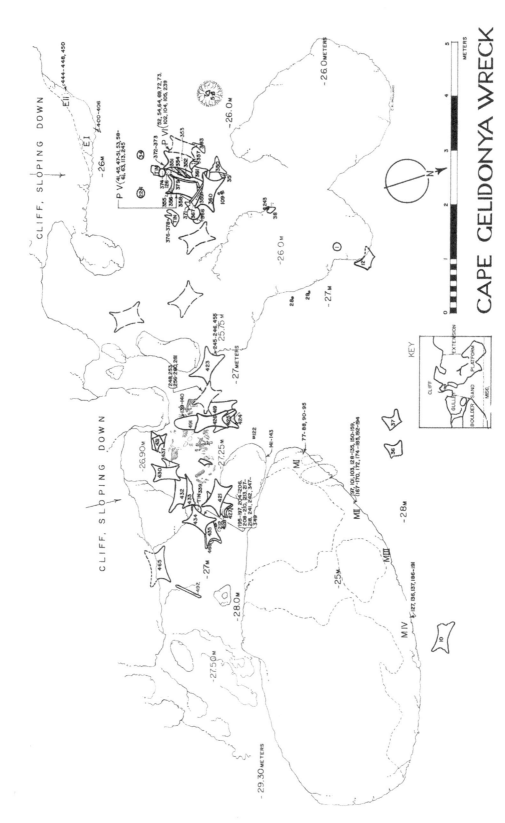

Figure 59.1. The Cape Gelidonya site (courtesy of Charles K. Williams and George F. Bass, University of Pennsylvania Museum).

Figure 59.2. Mapping the Cape Gelidonya site. Brushwood lies in the gully below the upper diver, with the boulder behind him (by Peter Throckmorton, courtesy of the INA archives).

Throckmorton had no means of going to the cape that year but noted in his log that the site seemed to be the most interesting of all those described to him. The following year he was able to reach the site and date the cargo to the Late Bronze Age on the basis of the four-handled copper ingots he saw (Throckmorton 1960). Knowing of the University of Pennsylvania Museum's involvement in archaeology in Turkey, at Gordion, he wrote to the museum and asked whether it would sponsor an expedition to demonstrate that it was possible to excavate as carefully and accurately under water as on land. I was asked by the museum to learn to dive and serve as the archaeological director (Throckmorton 1964, 176–81).

The expedition, conducted between the middle of June and the middle of September 1960 was the first to excavate an ancient shipwreck in its entirety on the seabed (figure 59.2; Throckmorton 1964, 182–253; Bass 1967, 21–43; 1975, 11–47). Results of the excavation were published in Bass (1967), and later articles responded to some of the early criticisms of that publication (Bass 1973, 1991).

In those early days of nautical archaeology, we did not recognize the small fragments of the ship's hull as being the remnants of pegged mortise-and-tenon joints

(Bass 1999) like those that held the planking of ships together from at least a century earlier (Pulak 2002) until the Late Roman period. Lying directly on the hull was a layer of brushwood dunnage, which explained for the first time the brushwood ('ὕλη) Odysseus spread out in the hull of the vessel he built to leave Calypso's island (*Odyssey* 5.257). Radiocarbon dating of the brushwood points to 1200 BC ± 50 years, a date that planned new dating with advanced techniques should be able to refine.

Preserved cargo included approximately a ton of metal, mostly in the form of thirty-four flat, four-handled ingots of nearly pure copper, averaging 25 kilograms in weight, and fragments of more. These ingots have been shown by lead-isotope analyses to have come from the Solea region of Cyprus (Stos 2001). When found at other sites, such ingots had erroneously been called "oxhide" ingots in the mistaken belief that they were cast to imitate dried ox skins, each ingot equal in value to a cow in a kind of premonetary currency.

In addition to the four-handled ingots were about twenty smaller discoid "bun ingots," weighing about three kilograms apiece, also from Cyprus and again with additional fragments. On the other hand, seventeen of eighteen smaller, flat slabs with rounded ends, all intact, whose weights were multiples of 500 grams, were made of copper from Lavrion in Greece.

With the copper ingots was a white material that was the consistency of toothpaste when discovered. Laboratory analysis subsequently showed it to be tin oxide. Concretion suggests that the tin had originally been cast as rectangular bars, similar to white bars in Egyptian tomb paintings.

The remainder of the metal cargo consisted of broken bronze tools from Cyprus, scrap that was clearly intended to be melted down and recast. Included were plowshares (incorrectly identified as picks and hoes in Bass 1967), axes, adzes, an ax-adze, chisels, pruning hooks, a spade, knives, and casting waste. Some and perhaps all of the scrap was carried in wicker baskets; the bottom of one basket was perfectly preserved between two copper ingots.

Although there is no proof for it, it is possible that a tinker accompanied this scrap bronze and the two ingredients, copper and tin, needed for making new bronze. Two stone hammerheads are similar to metalworking hammers; a bronze swage was found; a large, close-grained stone reminds us of anvils used before the introduction of iron; and there were many stone polishers and a whetstone.

At the time of the site's excavation, it was generally believed that Mycenaeans held a monopoly on maritime commerce in the Eastern Mediterranean. Thus, it was a surprise that the weights of sixty-odd stone pan-balance weights were based on Near Eastern standards such as the *qedet, nesef,* and *shekel.* Anthropologists have shown that merchants typically travel with their own sets of weights, with which they are familiar, and later convert into the weight system of the land in which they deal. This led to a closer examination of the personal items, found mostly at the end of the site that was considered to mark a living area of the ship. Without exception they, too, proved to be Near Eastern in origin: two stone mortars, a terracotta oil lamp, a razor, the stone hammers, several Syro-Palestinian imitations of Egyptian scarabs, and a merchant's cylinder seal, probably an heirloom, carved centuries earlier in north Syria.

These discoveries led to the conclusion that the ship was Near Eastern in origin (Bass 1967, 164–67), probably Syrian or Canaanite or Syro-Canaanite or proto-Phoenician (although the exact term is not important) (Bass 1973, 34n42), or perhaps Cypriot (Bass 1973, 36–37; 1991, 69). That conclusion led to a reevaluation of published evidence from both Egyptian tomb paintings and the well-known Amarna tablets found in Egypt that depict and describe shipments of tribute from Near Eastern rulers to the pharaoh in Egypt. The tomb paintings show that, with a single exception, contemporary Egyptians associated copper and tin ingots with Syrians and in no case with Mycenaeans; further, the only contemporary paintings of foreign ships arriving in Egypt, one showing four-handled copper ingots as cargo, depict Syrian ships. More recently, the only mold for casting four-handled copper ingots was found in a palace at Ras ibn Hani, the port of Ras Shamra/Ugarit on the Syrian coast.

In other words, the single ship that sank at Cape Gelidonya did not revolutionize our picture of Bronze Age maritime commerce in the Eastern Mediterranean, but its excavation was the catalyst that led to the reevaluation of existing evidence (Bass 1998). The occurrence of Near Eastern mariners in the Late Bronze Age bears on Homeric studies: The major reason for the typical dating of the *Odyssey* to the eighth century BC has been Homer's frequent mention of Phoenician mariners and metalworkers, for it was believed that these famed Semitic seafarers did not become active until the later Iron Age (Bass 1997a).

The belief in a Mycenaean monopoly on sea trade was based on the wide spread of Mycenaean pottery throughout the Near East, including Cyprus. The Cape Gelidonya shipwreck, however, suggested the existence of a large return trade in raw materials such as copper and tin, which left few traces in the archaeological record unless lost at sea, for if they reached port, they were quickly manufactured into goods typical of the importing culture. The excavation between 1984 and 1994 of the ship that sank a century earlier at the cape to the west of Cape Gelidonya, at Uluburun, provided proof of the extensive trade in raw materials from the East to the Aegean (Bass 1987, 1997b; Pulak 1998, 2008).

The excavation of terrestrial sites often lasts decades, sometimes more than a century, whereas one might think that the excavation of a shipwreck is more like the excavation of a tomb, a project undertaken and finished in a relatively brief period of time. Nearly half a century after the excavation at Cape Gelidonya, however, research continues at the site.

As excavators of the Uluburun shipwreck, we made brief visits to nearby Cape Gelidonya in the 1980s and 1990s with more advanced equipment than that available in 1960. A metal detector found not only the trail of artifacts leading to the rock that almost certainly sank the ship, as well as metal artifacts invisible under concretion, but also a large pithos in the gully we thought had been thoroughly excavated in 1960.

Battery-operated scooters allowed divers to search far and wide, leading to the discovery on this trail of the best-preserved ceramic vessels from the ship, two coarse-ware stirrup jars of Late Bronze IIIB type, about 55 meters from the gully. At nearly twice that distance, divers using the scooters found a stone anchor typical of the many examples found on the eastern littoral of the Mediterranean and on Cyprus (Bass 1999, 2005). In addition, by simply reexamining the original excavation site with care, more stone pan-balance weights were found, as was the ship's first large weapon, a bronze sword.

In addition, laboratory analyses are leading to new conclusions. Lead-isotope analyses, besides showing the Cypriot origin of the four-handled and discoid copper ingots, demonstrate that other artifacts were made of metals that came from Lavrion in Greece, the Taurus Mountains of Anatolia, the copper mines of Timna in Israel, and even Sardinia.

Similarly, petrographic analysis indicates that the ship's lamp is Cypriot, as is a pithos. The stone of the anchor suggests that it, too, is from Cyprus. Although Cyprus at this time in history was part of the Near Eastern cultural realm, a conclusion that the ship was Cypriot would still be of interest.

The new discoveries have led to the decision to undertake both a new excavation at Cape Gelidonya and a new publication that will take into account much new information.

Bibliography

Bass, George F. 1967. *Cape Gelidonya: A Bronze Age Shipwreck*. Transactions of the American Philosophical Society 57 (8). Philadelphia: American Philosophical Society.
———. 1973. "Cape Gelidonya and Bronze Age Maritime Trade." In *Orient and Occident*, ed. Harry A. Hoffner, 29–38. Kevelaer, Germany: Butzon and Bercker.
———. 1975. *Archaeology beneath the Sea*. New York: Walker.
———. 1987. "Bronze Age Shipwreck Reveals Splendors of the Bronze Age." *National Geographic Magazine* 172(6) (December): 693–733.
———. 1991. "Evidence of Trade from Bronze Age Shipwrecks." In *Bronze Age Trade*, 69–82.
———. 1997a. "Beneath the Wine Dark Sea: Nautical Archaeology and the Phoenicians of the *Odyssey*." In *Greeks and Barbarians: Essays on the Interactions between Greeks and Non-Greeks in Antiquity and the Consequences for Eurocentrism*, ed. John Coleman and Clark Walz, 71–101. Occasional Publications of the Department of Near Eastern Studies and Jewish Studies, Cornell University, no. 4. Bethesda: CDL.
———. 1997b. "Prolegomena to a Study of Maritime Traffic in Raw Materials to the Aegean during the Fourteenth and Thirteenth Centuries B.C." In *TEXNH*, 153–70.
———. 1998. "Sailing between the Aegean and the Orient in the Second Millennium BC." In *Aegean and the Orient*, 183–91.
———. 1999. "The Hull and Anchor of the Cape Gelidonya Ship." In *Meletemata*, 21–24.
———. 2005. "Cargo from the Age of Bronze: Cape Gelidonya, Turkey." In *Beneath the Seven Seas: Adventures with the Institute of Nautical Archaeology*, ed. George F. Bass, 48–55. London and New York: Thames and Hudson.

Pulak, Cemal. 1998. "The Uluburun Shipwreck: An Overview." *IJNA* 27: 188–224.

———. 2002. "The Uluburun Hull Remains." In *Tropis VII: Proceedings of the 7th International Symposium on Ship Construction in Antiquity (27–31 August, Pylos)*, ed. Harry E. Tzalas, 615–36. Piraeus: Hellenic Institute for the Preservation of Nautical Tradition.

———. 2008. "The Uluburun Shipwreck and Late Bronze Age Trade." In *Beyond Babylon: Art, Trade, and Diplomacy in the Second Millennium B.C.*, ed. Joan Aruz, Kim Benzel, and Jean M. Evans, 288–385. New York: Metropolitan Museum of Art; New Haven: Yale University Press.

Stos, Zofia Anna. 2001. "Metal Finds from the Cape Gelidonya Shipwreck: Lead Isotope and Alloy Analyses." Chapter drafted for the planned republication of the site.

Throckmorton, Peter. 1960. "Thirty-three Centuries under the Sea." *National Geographic Magazine* 117(5) (May): 682–703.

———. 1964. *The Lost Ships.* New York: Little, Brown.

CHAPTER 60

CYPRUS

LOUISE STEEL

GEOGRAPHICAL CONTEXT

Cyprus occupies a strategic position between the western Asiatic and European landmasses in the East Mediterranean. The geographical location and physical landscape had a distinct influence on the development of the island's Bronze Age societies and ensured that it played an increasingly important role in international maritime trade of the later second millennium.

Physically the island is dominated by the Troodos Mountains, which occupy much of the southwestern part of the island (figure 60.1). Largely unexploited during the Bronze Age, this vast mountainous terrain formed a massive barrier to inland communication between the communities of the west and southwest and those of the rest of the island. The lower slopes of the Troodos are ringed by pillow lavas, which contain the rich copper resources that give the island its name (Constantinou 1982, 15).

In antiquity the fertile Mesaoria plain, which lies between the Troodos and the Kyrenia mountain ranges, was probably covered by open cypress woodland (Burnet 1997, 61). Despite the undoubted importance of timber, exploitation of this resource by Bronze Age communities has not been fully explored (see, however, Burnet 1997). This might be extrapolated from later sources (Raptou 1996, 252; Given and Smith 2003, 271) that demonstrate religious and royal control of timber to sustain various industries—metallurgy, ceramic production, and shipbuilding. Timber is itemized among the tributes sent from the ruler of Alashiya (ancient Cyprus) to Thutmose III (Ockinga 1996, 42, text 67), which further illustrates the economic importance of this resource in antiquity.

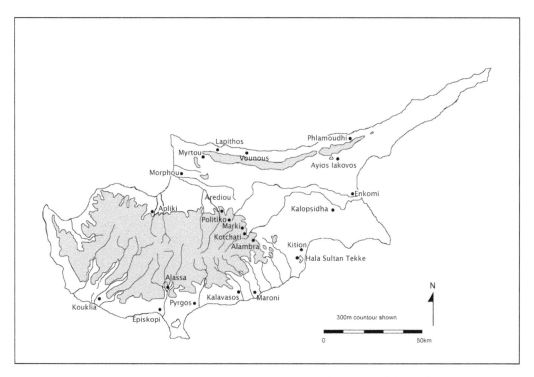

Figure 60.1. Major Bronze Age sites on Cyprus (courtesy of the author).

CHRONOLOGY

The Bronze Age of Cyprus has been organized within a tripartite chronological framework (the Early, Middle, and Late Cypriot periods), based on the typology of the local pottery styles developed by Gjerstad. The Early Cypriot (EC) period is defined by the predominant use of Red Polished pottery, which continued to be the main ware used in the Middle Cypriot (MC) period. However, this phase is distinguished from the preceding period by the appearance of White Painted ware; a significant change in the ceramic repertoire marks the transition to the Late Cypriot (LC) period, namely the disappearance of the ancient Red Polished ware and the development of the White Slip, Base Ring, and Monochrome wares.

This system is problematic (Stewart 1962a, 208, 210–11; Catling 1973, 165–66; Knapp 1990, 148–49; 1994, 274–76), and Knapp (1990, 154; 1994, 276) has proposed an alternative method that divides the Bronze Age into two major phases according to a range of cultural criteria. The EC and MC periods are grouped together as the Prehistoric Bronze Age (PreBA) on the basis that distinctions between the two periods are frequently intangible. The LC period (and the transitional MC III–LC I) is designated the Protohistoric Bronze Age (ProBA). This phase is defined according to major socioeconomic developments during the later second millennium BC. Given the greater resolution of material from this period, it has been further divided into three subphases (table 60.1).

Table 60.1. Comparison of the Traditional Relative Chronology with Knapp's (1990, 1994) Chronological Sequence, and Absolute Dates

Traditional Chronological Sequence	Knapp's Alternative Sequence	Absolute Dates
Philia	PreBA I	2500–2350 BC
EC	PreBA II	2350–2000 BC
MC	PreBA II	2000–1700
Transitional MC III–LC I	ProBA I	1700–1450
LC II (A–C)	ProBA II	1450–1200
LC III (A–B)	ProBA III	1200–1050

Source: Courtesy of the author.

PHILIA PHASE: CULTURE

The so-called Philia culture (ca. 2400–2300 BC) represents the earliest phase of the Cypriot Bronze Age and was originally identified in the cemeteries of the northwest Mesaoria. Dikaios placed the Philia material within a sequential framework at the beginning of the EC period (1962, 191–92); an alternative interpretation identified the Philia material as a regional assemblage *contemporary* with the initial phase of EC I (Stewart 1962a, 210). Excavations at Marki Alonia, however, clearly demonstrate that the Philia culture predates the EC sequence (Webb and Frankel 1999, 37–38; Frankel and Webb 2006).

The Philia phase is crucial for understanding the transition to the Bronze Age of Cyprus, in particular the evident contacts with Anatolia during this period, and for determining whether these should be viewed as evidence for a population movement, increased cultural interaction with communities beyond the island, or internal Cypriot development (Frankel, Webb, and Eslick 1996; Webb and Frankel 1999; Peltenburg 2007). The majority of Philia sites are clustered close to the island's copper resources (Webb and Frankel 1999, 8–12), suggesting that copper exploitation played a significant role in the economy (Stewart 1962a, 288–89; see discussion in Webb et al. 2006).

The Philia ceramic assemblage, in particular the introduction of the Red Polished (Philia) ware, represents a major change in the island's ceramic technology (Bolger 1991, 34; Webb and Frankel 1999, 14–23). Typical forms include flat-based jugs with an ovoid body and cutaway spout, round-based flasks or juglets, amphorae, teapots, and a variety of bowls, some with a tubular spout.

Red Polished (Philia) ware is characterized by a uniformity of fabric and a good-quality, evenly polished slip, both of which are suggestive of some degree of craft specialization—in particular control over procurement and processing of raw materials. A number of features indicate the close Anatolian connections of this ware: similar morphological and technological elements, such as the cutaway spouts, the thrust through handles, and the decorative use of incised geometric motifs (Bolger 1983, 72; Mellink 1991, 172–73). The cultural contacts suggested by the adoption of a new ceramic technology and new forms have precursors in the final stages of the Chalcolithic (ca. 2700/2800–2400/2500 BC)—exemplified by the assemblage at Kissonerga Mosphilia (Peltenburg 2007, 145–47).

Limited evidence has surfaced for copper production during the Chalcolithic period, when it was apparently restricted to small artifacts and a hammered technology. The significant innovation of the Philia phase is the introduction of a mold-made technology. The distinctive Philia metal assemblage includes heavy armbands or ring ingots, flat axes with polygonal butts, and flat-tanged knives with wide midribs (Webb and Frankel 1999, 31–32; Swiny 2003, 370–72).

Only occasional pieces of tin bronze have been identified, including four small, spiral earrings from Sotira Kaminoudhia (Webb et al. 2006, 274). Here the use of tin was purely decorative to create a gold effect (Swiny 2003, 379). Otherwise, the use of tin as an alloy is not attested on the island, except for occasional Anatolian imports, until the beginning of the Middle Cypriot period, ca. 2000 BC (Webb et al. 2006, 274).

Current research suggests that early Philia copper artifacts were not alloyed. Arsenical copper is attested from EC I, either as an intentional alloy or possibly as a by-product of smelting high-arsenic copper ores (see discussion in Webb et al. 2006, 274).

Lead-isotope analyses demonstrate Cypriot participation in a wide-ranging copper trade throughout the East Mediterranean during the mid-third millennium BC. Ores from the Cyclades (Kythnos and Seriphos) and Anatolia, as well as from Cyprus (Webb et al. 2006, 271), were used to make artifacts.

The copper was circulated in the form of ingots: ring ingots (previously identified as armbands or bracelets) (Balthazar 1990, 420; Webb et al. 2006, 275) and perforated axes (Frankel and Webb 2001, 35). A dagger-shaped object from Sotira Kaminoudhia has likewise been identified as an ingot (Giardino, Gigante, and Ridolfi 2003, 391). These ingot types were also current in the southern Aegean and western Asia and indicate both the use of a common metal 'currency' in the mid-third millennium and the movement of copper over large distances (Webb et al. 2006, 277).

EARLY–MIDDLE CYPRIOT PERIODS

The Early-Middle Cypriot period is characterized by a substantial increase in population and the number of settlements, in particular around the northwestern foothills of the Troodos massif (Swiny 1981; Knapp 1994, 277). In contrast, coastal settlements are rare, which suggests that exploitation of maritime resources played a limited part in the economy. Instead, the economic focus was the rich copper resources of the Troodos foothills. Current evidence suggests that the EC and MC settlements were primarily small villages.

Excavations at Marki Alonia, Sotira Kaminoudhia, and Alambra Mouttes have thrown light on the communities of the EC–MC periods. The introduction of rectilinear, agglutinative architecture marks a major transformation in the organization of domestic space, which is distinct from the indigenous Chalcolithic tradition of circular houses.

Although there was no uniform house plan (Swiny 1989, 20–21, figures 2.2–4.), the preferred arrangement at Marki and Alambra was of small rooms around a walled courtyard. The distribution of portable and fixed furnishings indicates spatial division of household activities (Bolger 2003, 32) and small-scale household storage. Detached, multiroomed courtyard houses have been identified at Alambra (EC III) and Kalopsidha (MC III) (Gjerstad 1926, 22–23, 27–37). The use of the courtyard space is unclear, although Gjerstad suggested it was for food preparation and cooking (Bolger 2003, 35).

Recent excavations at Pyrgos Mavroraki illustrate a different type of economic organization. Here we find clear evidence of suprahousehold production and storage activity within a large "industrial" building. Crafts identified within the building include wine and olive oil production and storage, textile production, metallurgical activity, and perfume production (Belgiorno 2004).

In addition, EC–MC burial practices reflect several important changes in social organization (Keswani 2004, 2005). Burial was separated from habitation areas and took place in large, formally organized extramural cemeteries of rock-cut chamber tombs (Keswani 2004, 39; 2005, 347–48). The complex and diverse mortuary treatments attested in the EC–MC tombs reveal elaboration of funerary ritual, in particular multistage ceremonies (Keswani 2004, 42; 2005, 352–59).

Burials were furnished with increasing quantities of grave goods: large quantities of ceramics, a limited range of metal objects (weapons, toiletry articles, and personal ornamentation), and ceramic replicas of metal artifacts, such as knives, ceramic combs, spindles, and mouthpieces. A select group of burials in the coastal cemeteries includes the combination of daggers, spearheads, and whetstones (Manning 1993, 45). Household objects were also placed in tombs: spindle whorls, figurines, and jewelry (Frankel and Webb 1996, 48).

Various scholars have suggested that the distribution of metal artifacts illustrates the emergence of social elites in Cyprus during the EC–MC periods (Swiny 1989, 27; Knapp 1990, 158; Manning 1993; Keswani 2004, 77), in particular at sites such as Lapithos Vrysi tou Barba and Vounous Bellapais. Concentrations of metal artifacts in small number of tombs might suggest some control over the dissemination of metals.

Possibly high-status grave goods include trinkets of gold, silver, and lead, faience beads, large alabaster vessels imported from Old Kingdom Egypt (Knapp 1994, 281), and, in MC III, Syrian and Old Babylonian cylinder seals (Keswani 2004, 80). Toward the end of MC III, certain Near Eastern equipment (shaft-hole axes, warrior belts) were incorporated within funerary display in wealthy tombs located near the copper-mining areas of the Troodos (Keswani 2004, 80; 2005, 380, figure 16).

Other rare grave goods are the Red Polished scenic vases, which have a limited distribution and complex imagery and were probably important emblems of identity and prestige, underpinning the new EC/MC ideological system (Keswani 2005, 250).

During the EC and MC periods, Cyprus became integrated within the maritime trade routes in the Near East, as is exemplified by the circulation of White Painted and Yahudiyeh ware juglets between Cyprus, Egypt, and the Levant. Maguire suggests that these held small quantities of a precious commodity, such as a highly coveted perfume (1995, 55, 63, figure 12). It is noteworthy that this, together with intensified exploitation of Cypriot copper, coincides with the earliest references to Alashiya during the 18th and 17th centuries BC, in texts from Mari, Babylon, and Alalakh (Sasson 1996, 17–19; Wiseman 1996, 20).

LATE CYPRIOT PERIOD

The Late Bronze Age is characterized by significant cultural transformations associated with the island's increasing contact with the civilizations of the Aegean and the Near East. Chief among these are the adoption of a completely new range of tableware (White Slip, Base Ring, and Monochrome). Nonetheless, our understanding of the political and economic organization of Cyprus is limited in contrast to our knowledge of the surrounding regions.

During this period Cyprus was the nexus of trade networks and incorporated the Aegean, Syro-Palestine, and Egypt due to the island's copper resources. The copper trade allowed the emergence of an economic and possibly political elite that controlled access to luxury imports and prestige goods. Textual evidence from Egypt and the Near East demonstrates that some individuals were involved in diplomatic exchanges with the New Kingdom pharaohs, the Hittites, and the kings of Ugarit (Beckman 1996b, 26–28; 1996a, 29; 1996c, 31–35; Knapp 1996, 8–9; Moran 1996, 21–25; Walls 1996, 36–40; Goren et al. 2003).

The MC III–LC I transition, ca. 17th–16th century BC (see Keswani 2004, 186, table 1.1) was a period of social upheaval that was characterized by regionalism, instability, and a shift in settlement toward the south and east coasts. Numerous MC villages were abandoned, and destruction horizons are evident at sites such as Kalopsidha, Episkopi Phaneromeni, and Morphou-Toumba tou Skourou, perhaps as the result of raids for livestock, agricultural produce, valuables, and human captives (Keswani 1989, 219). Mass burials are further evidence of social upheaval (Merrillees 1971, 75). Traditional interpretations attribute these to warfare or plague.

One of the more striking features of MC III–LC I is a series of forts and fortified sites located along the Karpass peninsular, the southern slopes of the Kyrenia range, and the northeastern slopes of the Troodos massif (Merrillees 1971, 75; Catling 1973, 168). In addition to their defensive role, the quantities of storage jars suggest that some forts, such as Nitovikla (figure 60.2; Hult 1992), functioned as local centers for the collection and redistribution of agricultural surplus (Peltenburg 1996, 35). The strategic position of a number of forts along the route from the copper-rich Troodos to the newly established

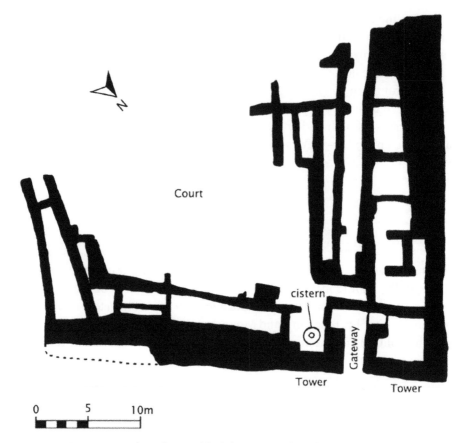

Figure 60.2. Plan of Nitovikla (after Gjerstad et al. 1934, figure 145).

coastal center of Enkomi (Crewe 2007) further indicates that many were built to protect the movement of copper (Merrillees 1982, 375; Keswani 1996, 219).

During LC II a number of towns developed along the southern coast between Enkomi in the east and Palaepaphos in the west. These were laid out on a grid system, and during the 13th century monumental construction programs, which made extensive use of ashlar (cut stone) masonry, were completed.

In addition to the coastal towns, there were also inland farming settlements and copper-mining sites around the lower reaches of the Troodos. Two mining sites have been excavated at Politiko Phorades and Apliki Karamallos. Phorades dates to around 1600 BC and appears to represent localized extraction and smelting of copper ores (Knapp, Kassianidou, and Donnelly 2002; Knapp and Kassianidou 2008). Apliki, which dates to the 13th century BC (du Plat Taylor 1952; Kling and Muhly 2007), is part of an integrated, islandwide economic system; in particular there is evidence for central suprahousehold storage within House A (Keswani 1993, 77).

The farming sites of the hinterland are less well known. However, recent excavations at Arediou Vouppes (Lithosouros) show that these were typified by well-planned architecture, control of water resources, and diverse activities (figure 60.3; Steel 2009).

Figure 60.3. Building 2, Arediou Vouppes (Lithosouros) (photograph by S. Thomas).

Funerary practices underwent several changes during the LC period, most significant of which was the move from extramural cemeteries to burial within the settlement's boundaries (Keswani 2004, 85). Tombs were placed beneath the court-yards of houses or the adjacent streets, which suggests a very private observance of death.

The typical LC tomb type is the rock-cut chamber tomb (Keswani 2004, figures 5.2–5.4), which housed collective burials. The traditional practice of secondary burial persisted (Keswani 2004, 85). More varied tomb types are attested at Enkomi and include at least five partially corbel-vaulted, ahslar-built tombs that resemble the ashlar-built tombs at Ugarit (Keswani 2004, 115). Four *tholos* tombs have also been identified (Keswani 2004, 114–15). These burial places are significantly distinct in construction and form from the Mycenaean *tholoi* of the Greek mainland, and there is no reason to suppose that these funerary monuments refer to an intrusive Aegean identity (Pelon 1973, 249–53).

The varied range of grave goods clearly demonstrates that LC burials were a visual spectacle and an important arena for competitive display (Keswani 2004, 158–60). Grave goods included small perfume containers and various ceramic vessels associated with the serving and consumption of food and drink.

Pictorial Mycenaean kraters were restricted to wealthier burials (Steel 1998, 291–92), as were vessels made from precious metals or faience (Keswani 2004, 159). Other grave goods include bronze weapons, gaming equipment, cylinder and stamp seals, toilet articles, and items of personal adornment (Webb 1992, 117; Keswani 2004, 158–59).

A number of religious sanctuaries have been identified, demonstrating a significant change in the nature and organization of communal ritual in LC II. Myrtou Pigadhes (du Plat Taylor 1957) and Athienou (Dothan and Ben-Tor 1983) were constructed in LC IIA, and in LC IIC–IIIA an explosion in religious architecture apparently occurred at the urban centers of Kition, Enkomi, and Palaepaphos (Webb 1999, 18–19, table 1).

Contemporary with the latest phase of temple construction is the increasing use of ashlar masonry. In addition, LC religious architecture is characterized by its diversity. Even so, a number of features are typical of all or most of the religious sites (Webb 1999, 157–58). Typically they are freestanding, rectangular structures with an enclosed courtyard *(temenos)*. Cult buildings are usually laid out on an east-west axis and comprise three main elements: a hall, a *cella*, and possibly a vestibule. Internal installations include benches, hearths, stone podia, horns of consecration, and stepped capitals (Webb 1999, 166–88; Knapp 2009, 51–52).

Several scholars have posited a close link between copper production and religion (Catling 1971; Knapp 1986, 1988), based on the close spatial relationship between bronze-working facilities and certain religious structures, the concentration of bronzes in sanctuaries, and representational evidence. The LC III Ingot God—of a pair of statutettes standing on what appears to be a bronze ingot (Courtois 1971, pls. XII–XIVA; Catling 1971, 15–32, figs. 3–4)—is considered to be clear evidence for religious control and divine protection of the copper industry (Catling 1971, 17; Knapp 1986, 1–2, 10–12; 1988, 144; Webb 1999, 225).

Cyprus played a pivotal role in Late Bronze Age trade in the Mediterranean, in particular the metals trade. Typically, copper was traded in the form of standardized oxhide, weighing between 25 kg and 28 kg (Stos-Gale 1997, 84). These have a wide distribution throughout the Mediterranean and in fact reach as far west as Sardinia, Sicily, and Crete (Gale 1991, 200–201, figure 2). The largest deposits are from the Gelidoniya and Uluburun shipwrecks (Bass 1986; Pulak 1988, 1997). Lead-isotope analysis indicates that much of this copper was Cypriot (Stos-Gale 1997). There is, however, intriguing evidence for a two-tier system of copper exchange and metallurgical production; while the ingots were Cypriot, lead-isotope analysis suggests the use of local copper sources to manufacture tools and weapons in Sardinia and Greece (Gale 1991, 217, 231). The implication is that the movement of copper ingots was a form of gift exchange among the palace elites, as exemplified by the Amarna archives (Moran 1996), and did not represent a convertible raw material.

Cypriot pottery was exported in large quantities to Syro-Palestine and Egypt from the beginning of the Late Bronze Age. Base Ring jugs and juglets were especially popular; the assemblage of fine Base Ring jugs and kraters from the palace of Niqme-pa at Alalakh may have been specially commissioned (Bergoffen 2005, 13, pl. 13).

Merrillees has contended that Base Ring juglets contained opium—their shape and decoration advertise the contents by referencing the seed pod of the opium poppy (Merrillees 1962, 287–92; 1968, 145–57; 1969, 167–71). This has received some support from recent chemical analyses of the residues found in Base Ring juglets (Bisset, Bruhn, and Zeuk 1996, 203–204; Koschel 1996, 159–66).

Minoan imports to Cyprus are rare; most notable is a Kamares cup from Karmi (Stewart 1962b, 202, figure 8, pl. VII), and very few Cypriot objects were exported to Crete. Manning suggests the latter were exchanged as hospitality gifts in occasional meetings between trading partners (Manning 1999, 117–18, 128, figure 34).

Mycenaean pottery is found in large quantities on Cyprus from the 14th century on (Steel 1998, 2004). The quintessential Mycenean import was the stirrup jar—a small container for a precious substance usually thought to be a perfumed oil. The pictorial krater was also popular. In contrast, Cypriot pottery is found in only small quanitities in the west, primarily at Kommos in southern Crete (Watrous 1992). Some Cypriot pottery even reached as far west as Italy and Sardinia (Lo Schiavo, MacNamara, and Vagnetti 1985, 4–9; Vagnetti and Lo Schiavo 1989, 219–20).

THE END OF THE BRONZE AGE

The beginning of the 12th century (LC IIIA) was marked by dramatic events throughout the East Mediterranean. Many sites were violently destroyed or abandoned (Karageorghis 1990). The only towns with clear evidence of occupation throughout LC IIIA are Enkomi, Kition, Kourion, and Palaepaphos, which were defended by newly constructed, Cyclopean-style fortifications. Possible defensive outposts were established at sites such as Pyla Kokkinokremos and Maa Palaeokastro (Karageorghis and Demas 1984, 1988).

These events were contemporary with a horizon of violent destructions throughout the East Mediterranean, occurrences that appear to be described on the mortuary temple of Ramses III at Medinet Habu (Ockinga 1996, 48, text 85) and in contemporary texts from Ugarit (Beckman 1996b, 27, texts 26, 27, 28).

Various changes in the archaeological record in LC IIIA have been attributed to Mycenaean settlers and have been primarily based upon large-scale, local production of Mycenaean-style pottery (Kling 1989; Sherratt 1991), which gradually ousted the indigenous tableware. A new class of coarse, handmade pottery, with parallels in the Aegean in LH IIIB and IIIC (Handmade Burnished ware or Barbarian ware), was also introduced in LC IIIA (Pilides 1994). The social changes underlying the transformation of the Cypriot pottery assemblage points toward changing modes of preparation and consumption within the household; the issue is whether this reflects a significant new ethnic component in the population or new modes of production (Sherratt 1991).

Other changes further demonstrate close cultural links with the Aegean during the 12th century BC. New metal artifacts include the violin bow fibula, socketed spears, cut-and-thrust swords, and bronze greaves (Catling 1964). The large communal hall with central hearth attests to changes in the use of domestic space, at least among the elite (Karageorghis 1998). Similar structures that are associated with Philistine settlement have been identified in the southern Levant.

The profound social changes experienced during LC III are manifest in the mortuary record. While the LC chamber tombs continued to be used, more typical was burial in shaft graves (Niklasson 1987; Keswani 2004, 159), which housed between one and three burials; moreover, the ancient practice of secondary burial was abandoned (Niklasson 1987, 222–23; Keswani 2004, 160). For the most part, the shaft graves were modestly furnished with a pottery jug and a bronze bowl. No doubt the disruption to ancient traditions reflects the unsettled conditions that affected Cypriot society during the 12th century BC and perhaps represents the burial of displaced elements of the indigenous population or even intrusive ethnic elements (Keswani 2004, 160).

TRANSITION TO THE IRON AGE

Late Cypriot IIIB (ca. 1100–1050 BC) marks the transition to the Iron Age. The phase was characterized by the introduction of a new ceramic tradition, Proto–White Painted ware (Iacovou 1988), ancestral to the Iron Age ceramic industry. There was a major shift in settlement pattern; the few remaining LBA centers were abandoned at the end of the 12th century BC, and new centers, which developed into the Iron Age city kingdoms, were gradually established (Iacovou 1994). Continuity into the 11th century is evident only at Enkomi and Kition in the area of the sanctuaries (Courtois 1971; Karageorghis and Demas 1985); however, this was short lived.

In the main, LC IIIB settlements are not archaeologically visible, and the newly established, extramural cemeteries are the main evidence for this period. Although Mediterranean maritime trade collapsed during this period, contacts persisted between Cyprus and the Levant, as indicated by the earliest imports of Phoenician pottery to the island (Bikai 1987). There is also evidence of the initial development of iron technology on the island in the form of small curved knives with ivory handles (Sherratt 1994).

Cypriot society was profoundly affected by the changes in LC IIIB—this is most evident in the transformations in the mortuary arena (Steel 1995). The reversion to extramural cemeteries reveals a fundamental shift in attitude toward the dead. While the spatial proximity typical of LC intramural tombs suggests a very close relationship between the living and their ancestors and a very private observance of death, the establishment of extramural cemeteries suggests a breakdown of ancient kinship groups and the renegotiation of new social relations.

Although material display was modest, the construction of the elaborate rock-cut chamber tombs approached by a long *dromos* within a public space indicates that funerals were important and communal occasions. This new tomb type, which is most closely paralleled by Mycenaean tombs from mainland Greece, might reflect new ethnic elements in the population.

Significant changes also occurred in religious practices, as is indicated by the deposition of large numbers of female terracotta figurines in the surviving temples

(Webb 1999, 213–15). Occasional larger wheelmade figures may be representations of deities (Webb 1999, 215). These religious changes apparently derive from the Aegean and are generally accepted as evidence of a population movement from this area. The myriad social changes documented in LC IIIB effectively laid the foundations for the development of the Cypriot Iron Age.

BIBLIOGRAPHY

Balthazar, Judith W. 1990. *Copper and Bronze Working in Early through Middle Bronze Age Cyprus. SIMA-PB* 84. Jonsered, Sweden: Åström.

Bass, George. 1986. "A Bronze Age Shipwreck at Ulu Burun (Kas): 1984 Campaign." *AJA* 90: 269–96.

Beckman, Gary. 1996a. "Akkadian Documents from Hattusa." In *Sources for the History of Cyprus*, 29.

———. 1996b. "Akkadian Documents from Ugarit." In *Sources for the History of Cyprus*, 26–28.

———. 1996c. "Hittite Documents from Hattusa." In *Sources for the History of Cyprus*, 31–35.

Belgiorno, Maria R. 2004. *Pyrgos Mavroraki: Advanced Technology in Bronze Age Cyprus*. Nicosia: Nicosia Archaeological Museum.

Bergoffen, Celia J. 2005. *The Cypriot Bronze Age Pottery from Sir Leonard Woolley's Excavations at Alalakh (Tell Atchana)*. Vienna: Verlag der Österreichischen Akademie der Wissenschaften.

Bikai, Patricia M. 1987. *The Phoenician Pottery of Cyprus*. Nicosia: Leventis Foundation.

Bisset, Norman G., Jan G. Bruhn, and Meinhart H. Zeuk. 1996. "The Presence of Opium in a 3,500-year-old Cypriote Base Ring Juglet." *Egypt and the Levant* 6: 203–204.

Bolger, Diane L. 1983. "Khrysiliou-Ammos, Nicosia–Ayia Paraskevi, and the Philia Culture of Cyprus." *RDAC*: 60–73.

———. 1991. "Early Red Polished Ware and the Origin of the Philia Culture." In *Cypriot Ceramics: Reading the Prehistoric Record*, ed. Jane A. Barlow, Diane L. Bolger, and Barbara B. Kling, 29–36. University Museum Monograph 74. Philadelphia: University of Pennsylvania.

———. 2003. *Gender in Ancient Cyprus: Narratives of Social Change on a Mediterranean Island*. Walnut Creek, Calif.: Altamira.

Burnet, Julia E. 1997. "Sowing the Four Winds: Targeting the Cypriot Forest Resource in Antiquity." In *Res Maritimae: Cyprus and the Eastern Mediterranean from Prehistory to Late Antiquity*, ed. Stuart Swiny, Robert L. Hohlfelder, and Helena W. Swiny, 59–69. CAARI Monograph 1. Atlanta: Scholars Press.

Catling, Hector W. 1964. *Cypriot Bronzework in the Mycenaean World*. Oxford: Clarendon.

———. 1971. "A Cypriot Bronze Statuette in the Bomford Collection." In *Alasia* I, ed. Claude F. A. Schaeffer, 15–32. Mission d'Archéologie d'Alasia 4. Paris: Klincksiek.

———. 1973. "Cyprus in the Middle Bronze Age." In *Cambridge Ancient History*, vol. 2, ed. I. E. S. Edwards, C. J. Gadd, and N. G. L. Hammond, 165–75. New York: Cambridge University Press.

Constantinou, Georges. 1982. "Geological Features and Ancient Exploitation of the Cupriferous Sulphide Orebodies of Cyprus." In *Early Metallurgy in Cyprus, 4000–500*

B.C.: Acta of the International Archaeological Symposium, ed. James D. Muhly, Robert Maddin, and Vassos Karageorghis, 13–24. Nicosia: Pierides Foundation in collaboration with the Department of Antiquities, Republic of Cyprus.

Courtois, Jacques-Claude. 1971. "Le sanctuaire du dieu au lingot d'Enkomi-Alasia." In *Alasia* I, ed. Claude F. A. Schaeffer, 151–362. Mission d'Archéologie d'Alasia 4. Paris: Klincksiek.

Crewe, Lindy. 2007. *Early Enkomi: Regionalism, Trade, and Society at the Beginning of the Late Bronze Age on Cyprus*. BAR-IS 1706. Oxford: Archaeopress.

Dikaios, Porphyrios. 1962. "The Stone Age." In *Swedish Cyprus Expedition*. Vol. 4.1A, *The Stone Age and Early Bronze Age*, ed. Porphyrios Dikaios and James R. Stewart, 1–203. Lund: Swedish Cyprus Expedition.

Dothan, Trude, and Amnon Ben-Tor. 1983. *Excavations at Athienou, Cyprus, 1971–1972*. Jerusalem: Hebrew University.

du Plat Taylor, Joan. 1952. "A Late Bronze Age Settlement at Apliki, Cyprus." *Antiquaries Journal* 32: 133–67.

———. 1957. *Myrtou-Pigadhes: A Late Bronze Age Sanctuary in Cyprus*. Oxford: Ashmolean Museum.

Frankel, David, and Jennifer M. Webb. 1996. *Marki Alonia: An Early and Middle Bronze Age Town in Cyprus. Excavations 1990–1994*. SIMA 123. Jonsered, Sweden: Åström.

———. 2001. "Excavations at Marki-Alonia, 2000." *RDAC*: 15–43.

———. 2006. *Marki Alonia: An Early and Middle Bronze Age Settlement in Cyprus. Excavations 1995–2000*. SIMA 123:2. Sävedalen, Sweden: Åström.

———, and Christine Eslick. 1996. "Anatolia and Cyprus in the Third Millennium B.C.E.: A Speculative Model of Interaction." In *Cultural Interaction in the Ancient Near East*, ed. Guy Bunnens, 37–50. Louvain: Peeters.

Gale, Noel H. 1991. "Copper Ingots: Their Origin and Their Place in the Bronze Age Metals Trade in the Mediterranean." In *Bronze Age Trade*, 197–239.

Giardino, Cláudio, Giovanni E. Gigante, and Stefano Ridolfi. 2003. "Archaeometallurgical Studies." In *Sotira Kaminoudhia: An Early Bronze Age Site in Cyprus*, ed. Stuart Swiny, George Rapp, and Ellen Herscher, 385–96. CAARI Monograph Series 4. Boston: American Schools of Oriental Research.

Given, Michael, and Joanna S. Smith. 2003. "Diachronic Landscape History: Geometric to Classical Landscapes." In *The Sydney Cyprus Project: Social Approaches to Regional Survey*, ed. Michael Given and A. Bernard Knapp, 270–77. Monumentum Archaeologia 21. Los Angeles: Cotsen Institute of Archaeology.

Gjerstad, Einar. 1926. *Studies in Cypriot Prehistory*. Uppsala: Uppsala Universitets Årsskrift.

Goren, Yuval, Shlomo Bunimovitz, Israel Finkelstein, and Nadav Na'aman. 2003. "The Location of Alashiya: New Evidence from Petrographic Investigation of Alashiyan Tablets." *AJA* 107: 233–55.

Hult, Gunnel. 1992. *Nitovikla Reconsidered*. Memoir 8. Stockholm: Medelhavsmuseet.

Iacovou, Maria. 1988. *The Pictorial Pottery of Eleventh-century B.C. Cyprus*. SIMA 78. Gothenburg: Åström.

———. 1994. "The Topography of Eleventh-century B.C. Cyprus." In *Cyprus in the 11th Century BC: Proceedings of the International Symposium Organized by the Archaeological Research Unit of the University of Cyprus and the A. G. Leventis Foundation, Nicosia, 30–31 October 1993*, ed. Vassos Karageorghis, 149–65. Nicosia: Leventis Foundation.

Karageorghis, Vassos 1990. *The End of the Late Bronze Age in Cyprus*. Nicosia: Pierides Foundation.

———. 1998. "Hearths and Bathtubs in Cyprus: A "Sea Peoples" Innovation?" In *Mediterranean Peoples*, 276–82.

———, and Martha Demas. 1984. *Pyla-Kokkinokremos: A Late 13th-century-B.C. Fortified Settlement in Cyprus*. Nicosia: Department of Antiquities.

———. 1985. *Excavations at Kition*. Vol. 1, *The Pre-Phoenician Levels. Areas I and II*. Nicosia: Department of Antiquities.

———. 1988. *Excavations at Maa-Palaeokastro 1979–1986*. Nicosia: Department of Antiquities.

Keswani, Priscilla S. 1989. Mortuary Ritual and Social Hierarchy in Bronze Age Cyprus. PhD diss., University of Michigan.

———. 1993. "Models of Local Exchange in Late Bronze Age Cyprus." *BASOR* 292: 73–83.

———. 1996. "Hierarchies, Heterarchies, and Urbanisation Processes: The View from Bronze Age Cyprus." *JMA* 9: 211–50.

———. 2004. *Mortuary Ritual and Society in Bronze Age Cyprus*. London: Equinox.

———. 2005. "Death, Prestige, and Copper in Bronze Age Cyprus." *AJA* 109: 341–401.

Kling, Barbara B. 1989. *Mycenaean IIIC:1b and Related Pottery in Cyprus*. SIMA 87. Gothenburg: Åström.

———, and James D. Muhly. 2007. *Joan du Plat Taylor's Excavations at the Late Bronze Age Mining Settlement at Apliki Karamallos 1*. SIMA 134:1. Sävedalen, Sweden: Åström.

Knapp, A. Bernard. 1986. *Copper Production and Divine Protection: Archaeology, Ideology, and Social Complexity on Bronze Age Cyprus*. SIMA Pocketbook 42. Gothenburg: Åström.

———. 1988. "Ideology, Archaeology, and Polity." *Man* 23: 133–63.

———. 1990. "Production, Location, and Integration in Bronze Age Cyprus." *Current Anthropology* 31: 147–76.

———. 1994. "Emergence, Development, and Decline on Bronze Age Cyprus." In *Development and Decline in the Mediterranean Bronze Age*, ed. Clay Mathers and Simon Stoddart, 271–303. Sheffield Archaeological Monographs 8. Sheffield: Sheffield University Press.

———. 1996. "Introduction." In *Sources for the History of Cyprus*, 1–13.

———. 2009. "Monumental Architecture, Identity and Memory." In *Proceedings of the Symposium: Bronze Age Architectural Traditions in the East Mediterranean: Diffusion and Diversity (Gasteig, Munich, 7–8 May, 2008)*, 47–59. Weilheim: Verein zur Förderung der Aufarbeitung der Hellenischen Geschichte e.V. 2009.

———, Vasiliki Kassianidou, and Michael Donnelly. 2002. "Excavations at Politiko-Phorades: A Bronze Age Copper Smelting Site on Cyprus." *Antiquity* 76: 319–20.

———, and Vasiliki Kassianidou. 2008. "The Archaeology of Late Bronze Age Copper Production. Politiko Phorades on Cyprus." *Anatolian Metal* 4: 135–47.

Koschel, Klaus. 1996. "Opium Alkaloids in a Cypriote Base-Ring I Vessel (Bilbil) of the Middle Bronze Age from Egypt." *Egypt and the Levant* 6: 159–66.

Lo Schiavo, Fulvia, Ellen MacNamara, and Lucia Vagnetti. 1985. "Cypriot Imports to Italy and Their Influence on Local Bronzework." *Papers of the British School at Rome* 53: 1–71.

Maguire, Louise C. 1995. "Tell el-Dab^ca: The Cypriot Connection." In *Egypt, the Aegean, and the Levant: Interconnections in the Second Millennium BC*, ed. W. Vivian Davies and Louise Schofield, 54–65. London: British Museum.

Manning, Sturt W. 1993. "Prestige, Distinction, and Competition: The Anatomy of Socio-economic Complexity in 4th–2nd Millennium BCE Cyprus." *BASOR* 292: 35–58.

———. 1999. *A Test of Time: The Volcano of Thera and the Chronology and History of the Aegean and East Mediterranean in the Mid-second Millennium BC*. Oxford: Oxbow.

Mellink, Machteld. 1991. "Anatolian Contacts with Chalcolithic Cyprus." *BASOR* 282: 165–75.

Merrillees, Robert S. 1962. "Opium Trade in the Bronze Age Levant." *Antiquity* 36: 287–92.

———. 1968. *The Cypriot Pottery Found in Egypt. SIMA* 18. Lund: Åström.

———. 1969. "Opium Again in Antiquity." *Levant* 11: 167–71.

———. 1971. "The Early History of Late Cypriote I." *Levant* 3: 56–79.

———. 1982. "Early Metallurgy in Cyprus 4000–500 B.C. Historical Summary." In *Early Metallurgy in Cyprus, 4000–500 B.C.: Acta of the International Archaeological Symposium*, ed. James D. Muhly, Robert Maddin, and Vassos Karageorghis, 371–76. Nicosia: Pierides Foundation in collaboration with the Department of Antiquities, Republic of Cyprus.

Moran, William L. 1996. "Akkadian Documents from Amarna." In *Sources for the History of Cyprus*, 21–25.

Niklasson, Karin. 1987. "Late Cypriote III Shaft Graves: Burial Customs of the Last Phase of the Bronze Age." In *Thanatos*, 219–25.

Ockinga, Boyo G. 1996. "Hieroglyphic Texts from Egypt." In *Sources for the History of Cyprus*, 42–50.

Pelon, Oliver. 1973. "Les 'tholoi' d'Enkomi." In *Acts of the International Symposium: The Mycenaeans in the Eastern Mediterranean*, ed. Vassos Karageorghis, 246–53. Nicosia: Department of Antiquities.

Peltenburg, Edgar J. 1996. "From Isolation to State Formation in Cyprus, c. 3500–1500 BC." In *The Development of the Cypriot Economy from the Prehistoric Period to the Present Day*, ed. Vassos Karageorghis and Dimitri Michaelides, 17–43. Nicosia: Leventis Foundation.

———. 2007. "East Mediterranean Interactions in the 3rd Millennium BC." In *Mediterranean Crossroads*, ed. Sophia Antoniadou and Anthony Pace, 139–59. Athens: Pierides Foundation.

Pilides, Despina. 1994. *Handmade Burnished Wares of the Late Bronze Age in Cyprus. SIMA* 105. Jonsered, Sweden: Åström.

Pulak, Cemal. 1988. "The Bronze Age Shipwreck at Ulu Burun, Turkey: 1985 Campaign." *AJA* 92: 1–37.

———. 1997. "The Ulu Burun Shipwreck." In *Res Maritimae: Cyprus and the Eastern Mediterranean from Prehistory to Late Antiquity*, ed. Stuart Swiny, Robert L. Hohlfelder, and Helena W. Swiny, 233–62. CAARI Monograph 1. Atlanta: Scholars Press.

Raptou, Eustathios. 1996. "Contribution to the Study of the Economy of Ancient Cyprus: Copper–Timber." In *The Development of the Cypriot Economy: From the Prehistoric Period to the Present Day*, ed. Vassos Karageorghis and Demetrios Michaelides, 249–60. Nicosia: University of Cyprus.

Sasson, Jack M. 1996. "Akkadian Documents from Maria and Babylonia (Old Babylonian Period)." In *Sources for the History of Cyprus*, 17–19.

Sherratt, E. Susan. 1991. "Cypriot Pottery of Aegean Type in LC II–III: Problems of Classification, Chronology, and Interpretation." In *Cypriot Ceramics: Reading the Prehistoric Record*, ed. Jane A. Barlow, Diane L. Bolger, and Barbara B. Kling, 185–98. University Museum Monograph 74. Philadelphia: University of Pennsylvania.

———. 1994. "Commerce, Iron, and Ideology: Metallurgical Innovation in 12th–11th-Century Cyprus." In *Cyprus in the 11th Century BC: Proceedings of the International Symposium Organized by the Archaeological Research Unit of the University of Cyprus and the A. G. Leventis Foundation, Nicosia, 30–31 October 1993*, ed. Vassos Karageorghis, 59–106. Nicosia: Leventis Foundation.

Steel, Louise. 1995. "Differential Burial Practices in Cyprus at the Transition from the Bronze Age to the Iron Age." In *Death in the Ancient Near East*, ed. Stuart Cambell and Anthony Green, 199–205. Oxford: Oxbow Monographs.

———. 1998. "The Social Impact of Mycenaean Imported Pottery in Cyprus." *BSA* 93: 285–96.

———. 2004. "A Reappraisal of the Distribution, Context, and Function of Mycenaean Pottery in Cyprus." In *La céramique mycénienne de l'Egée au Levant: Hommage à Vronwy Hankey*, ed. Jacqueline Balensi, Jean-Yves Monchambert, and Sylvie Müller Celka, 69–85. Lyon: Maison de l'orient et de la Méditerranée–Jean Pouilloux.

———. 2009. "Exploring Regional Settlement on Cyprus in the Late Bronze Age: The Rural Hinterland." In *The Formation of Cyprus in the 2nd Millennium BC. Studies in Regionalism During the Middle and Late Bronze Ages*, ed. I Hein, 135–45. Vienna: Austrian Academy of Sciences Press.

Stewart, James R. 1962a. "The Early Cypriote Bronze Age." In *Swedish Cyprus Expedition*. Vol. 4.1A, *The Stone Age and Early Bronze Age*, ed. Porphyrios Dikaios and James R. Stewart, 205–401. Lund: Swedish Cyprus Expedition.

———. 1962b. "The Tomb of the Seafarer at Karmi in Cyprus." *OpAth* 4: 197–204.

Stos-Gale, Zophia A. 1997. "Lead Isotope Characteristics of the Cyprus Copper Ore Deposits Applied to Provenance Studies of Copper Oxhide Ingots." *Archaeometry* 39: 83–123.

Swiny, Stuart. 1981. "Bronze Age Settlement Patterns in Southwest Cyprus." *Levant* 13: 51–87.

———. 1989. "From Round House to Duplex: A Reassessment of Prehistoric Cypriot Bronze Age Society." In *Early Society in Cyprus*, ed. Edgar J. Peltenburg, 14–31. Edinburgh: Edinburgh University Press.

———. 2003. "The Metal." In *Sotira Kaminoudhia: An Early Bronze Age Site in Cyprus*, ed. Stuart Swiny, George Rapp, and Ellen Herscher, 369–84. CAARI Monograph Series 4. Boston: American Schools of Oriental Research.

Vagnetti, Lucia, and Fulvia Lo Schiavo. 1989. "Late Bronze Age Long-distance Trade in the Mediterranean: The Role of the Cypriots." In *Early Society in Cyprus*, ed. Edgar J. Peltenburg, 217–43. Edinburgh: Edinburgh University Press.

Walls, Neal H. 1996. "Ugaritic Documents from Ugarit." In *Sources for the History of Cyprus*, 36–40.

Watrous, L. Vance. 1992. *Kommos III: The Late Bronze Age Pottery*. Princeton: Princeton University Press.

Webb, Jennifer M. 1992. "Funerary Ideology in Bronze Age Cyprus: Towards the Recognition and Analysis of Cypriote Ritual Data." In *Studies in Honour of Vassos Karageorghis*, ed. Georgios C. Ioannides, 87–99. Nicosia: Leventis Foundation.

———. 1999. *Ritual Architecture, Iconography, and Practice in the Late Cypriot Bronze Age*. SIMA-PB 75. Jonsered, Sweden: Åström.

———, and David Frankel. 1999. "Characterising the Philia Facies: Material Culture, Chronology, and the Origin of the Bronze Age in Cyprus." *AJA* 103: 3–43.

———, David Frankel, Zophia A. Stos-Gale, and Noel H. Gale. 2006. "Early Bronze Age Metal Trade in the Eastern Mediterranean: New Compositional and Lead Isotope Evidence from Cyprus." *OJA* 25: 261–88.

Wiseman, David J. 1996. "Akkadian Documents from Alalakh (Old and Middle Babylonian Periods). In *Sources for the History of Cyprus*, 20.

CHAPTER 61

···

EGYPT

···

JACKE PHILLIPS

INTRODUCTION AND CHRONOLOGY
···

Ancient Egypt essentially encompassed some 1,180 kilometers of the Nile Valley, from the First Cataract at Aswan north into the Delta, where the river fans out into multiple branches and ultimately reaches the Mediterranean Sea. The ancient Egyptians themselves viewed their homeland as the 'Two Lands,' Upper (southern, riverine) and Lower (northern, Delta) Egypt, unified by a king traditionally named Meni and over which his successors ruled for nearly three millennia.

Bronze Age Egyptian history after this unification and its succeeding Early Dynastic period is divided into the Old, Middle, and New Kingdoms, periods of centralized royal authority, separated by numbered 'Intermediate Periods,' when instability and loss of this authority divided Egypt into multiple smaller political units, some even ruled by foreigners. Despite these interruptions, the concept of Egypt as one unified 'Two Lands' remained unshakeable and all pervasive to the ancient Egyptians themselves (Shaw 2000). The chart (figure 61.1) outlines the relevant Egyptian chronological divisions, with timescales for BA Crete and mainland Greece.

Archaeology confirms a cultural dominance of Upper over Lower Egypt by about 3200/3100 BC, some two centuries before unification under the 'real' Meni, the first two Dynasty 1 kings, Nar(mer) and his successor (Hor-)Aha. The names of Egyptian kings (themselves called 'pharaoh,' from $Pr\text{-}^c3$ [Per-^{c}aa, literally 'Great House' or 'palace'], only from the reign of Akhenaten in Dynasty 18) are recorded in both contemporary and later documents and compilations. The Egyptian priest Manetho assembled our most complete list, the *Aegyptiaka*, around 280 BC. He divided his regnal list into numbered 'dynasties,' a basic outline still employed for both political and cultural histories that do not always coincide. Absolute historical

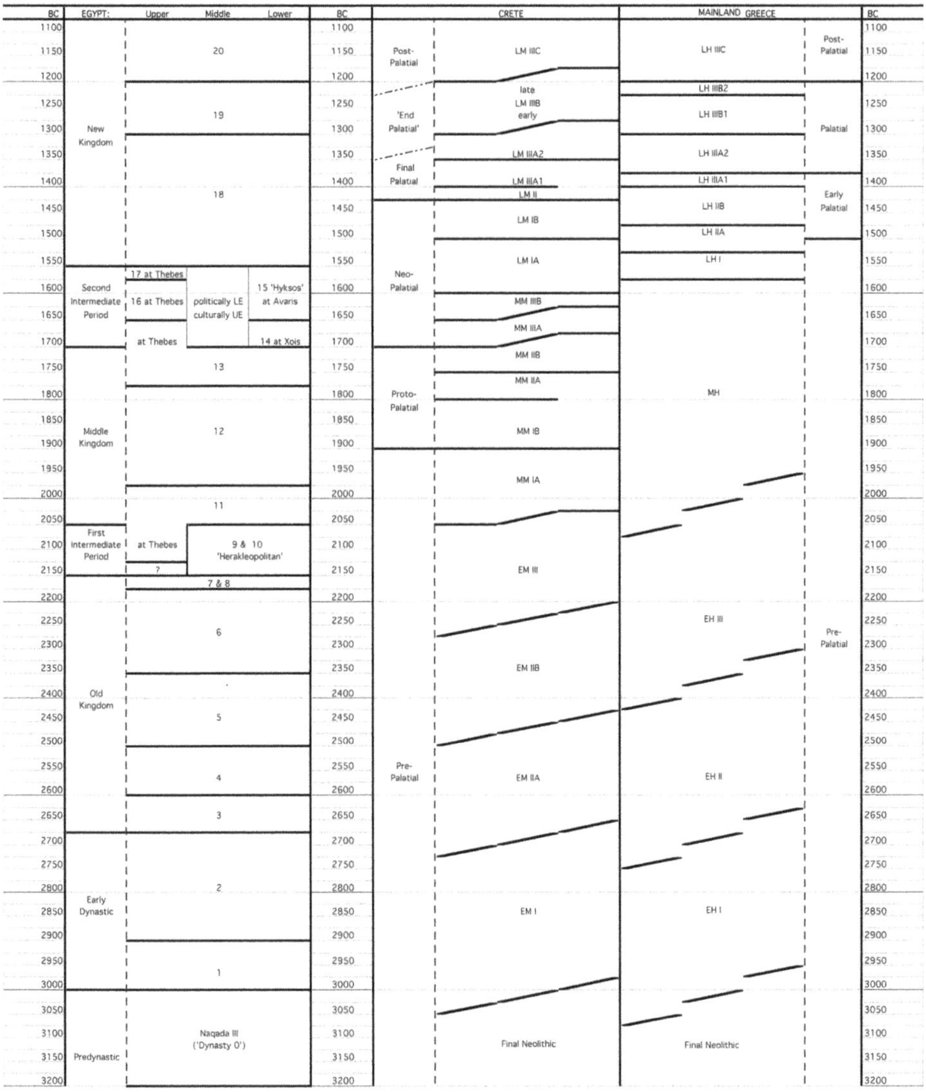

Figure 61.1. Relevant Egyptian chronological divisions with timescales for Crete and mainland Greece (courtesy of the author). Marked at 25-year divisions. For absolute Egyptian period lengths and dates, see Shaw (2000) and Hornung et al. (2006). Minoan and Mycenaean divisions are flexible, within limits.

dates in modern terms are now highly refined due to multiple, cross-referenced data sources, but slight adjustments continue as new data appear or old data are reanalyzed, most substantially by Hornung, Krauss, and Warburton (2006), where the critical definitive Sopdet dates are recalculated (see now also Van Dijk 2008; Kraus and Warburton 2009). Revisions of even a quarter century are no longer feasible from the Second Intermediate Period onward.

Flinders Petrie (1890), Arthur Evans (1899–1900), and many scholars since have employed Egyptian chronology to date Aegean material and development by correlating Aegean finds in Egypt and Egyptian finds in the Aegean, together with similarly related material found elsewhere in the Eastern Mediterranean (Phillips in press). The main rationale is Egypt's comparatively precise internal dating for its own political events and reigns, its numerous texts, and indigenous cultural material. Aegean dates also continue to be adjusted as new data appear through internal Aegean ceramic 'fine-tuning,' although not always keeping up to date with Egyptian refinements. Use of the other closely dateable historical chronology for Mesopotamia is complicated by its problematic internal chronology before the mid-LBA (although excellent afterward) and its general lack of interrelations with the Eastern Mediterranean for most of the BA, even along the coastal Levant, where all of the Eastern Mediterranean cultures interacted.

Recently, radiocarbon dating and other scientific means have been employed to independently realize a variety of 'absolute' dates for certain Aegean archaeological events (especially the Thera eruption) that have yet to be entirely reconciled with Egyptian dating. After some two decades of dedicated research, confrontation, and considerable maneuvering of individual records, adherents of both positions now acknowledge that evidence for 'the other' cannot be dismissed and have striven to reconcile theirs with it amid growing appreciation of the difficulties involved (Warburton 2009). I myself am firmly in the 'relative' camp and expect further necessary adjustments in radiocarbon dating methodologies to be recognized that will eventually allow correlation with Egyptian dating.

TEXTS AND INSCRIPTIONS

The term *Kf.tiw* (Keftiu) is now almost universally accepted for 'Crete' and 'Cretans/Minoans,' and *Ti-n3-iiw* (Tinayu) is considered to be the Greek mainland. Both names are foreign, phonetically transliterated into hieroglyphs by Egyptian scribes. The name *Kf.tiw* first appears perhaps by Dynasty 12 and certainly in the late Dynasty 15 *Papyrus Ebers*. *The Admonitions of Ipuwer* is a purely literary text of uncertain but likely similar original date. *Ti-n3-iiw* is not attested before the reign of Thutmose III (Dynasty 18).

The Egyptian term *w3ḏ wr* (Wadj-wer, 'Great Green'), attested more than three hundred times since Dynasty 5, can be variously located both in and beyond Egypt depending on textual context (Duhoux 2003; Phillips 2007). The Egyptian phrase *iww ḥriw-ib nw w3ḏ-wr* ('islands in the midst of the Great Green') is generally but not universally considered to refer to islands in the Mediterranean or perhaps the Aegean. It too is not attested before the reign of Thutmose III, although the Dynasty 12 *Tale of Sinuhe* mentions ambiguous *iww nw w3ḏ-wr* ('islands of the Great Green'), not necessarily the same thing. 'Keftiu' and the 'islands in the midst of the

Great Green' are directly associated *only* in the late Thutmose III–early Amenhotep II Theban tomb of Rekhmire (TT 100) and a (possibly copied) inscription of Rameses II (Dynasty 19) at Luxor. 'Wadj-wer' is the only term attested beyond the New Kingdom.

References chiefly are individual citations of these generic terms and are found on topographical lists and as identifications for the inhabitants of various foreign regions or the origin of their diplomatic gifts ('tribute') or rarely to identify other foreign products (Cline 1994, 108–20, 128). Longer correlations between the Egyptian and Keftiu languages are found on three mid–late Dynasty 18 texts that have phonetically transliterated Keftiu words: a 'spell' in the *London Medical Papyrus*, names stated to be Keftiu on a school writing board, and the Kom el-Heitan inscription (Kyriakides 2002). The last, on a statue base of Amenhotep III, is a unique topographical list of Aegean place names depicted as generic fettered figures, of which seven are recognizable as Amnissos (listed twice), Knossos, Kydonia, Kythera, Mycenae, Nauplion, and Phaestos. 'Keftiu' and 'Tinayu' are listed separately. The identification of another four place names is disputed, and up to four more have not survived.

Egyptian objects, chiefly scarabs, recovered in Aegean Bronze Age contexts bear the royal names Khyan (mid–Dynasty 15), Thutmose III, Amenhotep II, Amenhotep III, his wife, Tiye (all Dynasty 18), Ramesses II (Dynasty 19), and, without context, the name of the Sun Temple at Abusir of Userkaf (early Dynasty 5). All other apparent royal names are misreadings. User, whose inscribed statuette was recovered at Knossos, was a private individual.

Linear B tablets from Knossos mention two possibly Egyptian individuals (Aura Jorro 1985, 136–37, 454), a shepherd named Αιγυπτιος (*a3-ku-pi-ti-jo;* KN Db 1105.B) and a person named Μισραιος (*mi-sa-ra-jo;* KN F 841.4). Αιγυπτιος ('Aigeptios') derives from *Ḥwt-k3-Ptḥ* (Hewet-ka-Ptah, 'chapel of Ptah'), a New Kingdom name for Memphis, Egypt's administrative capital, while 'Egypt' in Semitic was *Miṣr*, and in modern Arabic is *Miṣ'r/Maṣr*. 'Egypt' in ancient Egyptian is *Kmt* (Kemet, 'Black Land').

Wall Paintings and Other Representations

Many (but not all) of the fresco fragments recovered in well-stratified but secondary palatial rubbish contexts at Avaris (Tell el-Dabᶜa) in the eastern Delta have considerable technical, stylistic, and thematic resonance in Aegean fresco painting (e.g., Bietak, Marinatos and Palivou 2007; see further in Phillips in press). Their basic production *techniques* are Aegean, but whether their artists were Minoan or Egyptian is debated. Their extensive iconographical range includes both life-size and miniature human figures, plants, wild animals, griffins, bulls, bull leapers, and abstract patterns, many of which have good visual comparanda in Aegean frescos. Their contexts ('stratum d C/3') date to the earlier half of Thutmose III's reign and thus are generally contemporary with the earliest painted 'Aegeans' at Thebes far upriver (discussed later), but stylistically most compare best with frescoes at Akrotiri at least half a century earlier. Their nearest Egyptian comparanda are 'aegaeanizing' fresco fragments from Amenhotep III's Malkata palace (Thebes, west bank), about a century later (Nikolakaki-Kentrou 2003).

Painted Aegean figures are found in ten Dynasty 18 élite Theban tombs, dating from Year 5 of Thutmose III (Useramon, TT 131) until sometime during Amenhotep III's reign (Anen, TT 120), depicted together with other foreigners (Wachsmann 1987; Martin 1989, 27; Dziobek 1994, 91–92; Pinch Brock 2000; Panagiotopoulos 2001). The earlier figures are stereotyped representatives queuing with diplomatic gifts ('tribute') for the king via his official, the tomb owner. The latest figures are symbolically fettered place names, as at Kom el-Heitan. Initially, the figures are unidentified or are labeled as from 'further Asia' or the 'islands in the midst of the Great Green.' *No* figures are labeled 'Tinayu' or, before Rekhmire, 'Keftiu.' Theban artists conflated the features of Aegean and other foreigners, but recognizable Aegean attributes include long, wavy black hair and beardless faces, the figures wearing above-ankle 'boots' and belted breechcloths with multicolored trim or elaborately patterned, multicolored pointed kilts, and carrying typically Aegean goods. Several men provisionally identified as Mycenaean warriors wear 'boar's tusk' helmets in a battle scene painted on papyrus fragments recovered at Amarna (Parkinson and Schofield 1995).

No Aegean representations of Egyptians are recognized, although generic, black-skinned 'Africans' appear on frescoes at Knossos and Akrotiri. Egyptian influence is inferred in the 'Nilotic' scenes on a dagger from Mycenae in Shaft Grave V and the West House fresco at Akrotiri, and in other iconographic details elsewhere.

Contact Routes

The earliest Egyptian references associate 'Aegeans' with regions northeast of Egypt. The most plausible contact route is a counterclockwise sailing direction from Egypt, generally hugging the coastline along the Levant, with likely stops at Cypriote and Anatolian coastal sites, then past various southern Aegean islands to Crete and the Greek mainland, with abundant, especially LBA, evidence for multinational contact throughout its entire length. Ships coming from the Aegean would travel in the reverse direction.

The Uluburun and Cape Gelidonya shipwrecks highlight the importance of this route and provide specific data for the staggering quantities and variety of raw and finished goods transported on a single LBA ship (Pulak 1998). It should be noted that the Egyptian term 'Keftiu ships' refers not to ships *of* or *from* Keftiu but rather to ships capable of reaching it. The Dynasty 19–20 model ship from Gurob (Tomb 11) has recently been identified as an Aegean-style galley (Wachsmann 2008).

Some later references instead associate 'Aegeans' with 'the West,' suggesting the counterclockwise route might have continued back to Egypt, although sea current movements argue against *direct* travel from Crete to the Delta. Moreover, a clockwise sea journey from Egypt to the Aegean, initially west along the north African coast and then north to Crete was impossible before the invention of the 'brailed sail' technology necessary to negotiate it (Wachsmann 1998, 371 n. 35). This is first illustrated, although not necessarily first employed, in Egypt during the Amarna period (Vinson 1994, 42–43).

Current research emphases on regions beyond the Nile now provide a broader picture of Egypt's relationships with interface cultures. Marsa Matruh, a coastal site 290 kilometers west of Alexandria and dating from the Amarna period into the 13th century, has LH IIIA2 (no Minoan, one sherd LH IIIA1) fine wares and open shapes, together with considerable Cypriote, Canaanite, and Egyptian vessels (White 2002; 2003). Recent excavations at the Zawiyet Umm el-Rakham fortress 20 kilometers farther west, limited to the reign of Rameses II, produced Aegean coarse ware transport stirrup jars and more Cypriote, Canaanite, and Egyptian wares (Snape 2003; Thomas 2003). Very little earlier Egyptian and no earlier Aegean or other foreign material has been recovered elsewhere along this extremely dry coast, suggesting that the brailed sail may have initiated this possible western route.

ECONOMIC AND OTHER CROSS-CULTURAL TRANSMISSIONS

Egypt to the Aegean

Although Early Dynastic stone vessels are found on Crete, the earliest physical evidence consists of a few small exotica (of obsidian, hippopotamus ivory, and faience) recovered in EM IIA contexts along northeastern coastal Crete to Knossos. Perhaps not coincidentally, evidence for Egyptian trade and diplomacy with Byblos on the Syrian coast seems to have recommenced under the last Dynasty 2 king, Khasekhem(wy), and these earliest imports likely arrived on Crete via this indirect means. The Greek mainland and its numerous islands have no archaeologically discernable contact with Egypt until the end of MH, likely via Crete initially.

Subsequent evidence for Egyptian contact with Crete is uncertain until MM IA, although Egyptian relations with Byblos continued. Evidence on Crete concentrated in its south-central Mesara plain, where imported scarabs and their locally produced versions are found in communal tombs. The earliest imports date to later Dynasty 11, precluding both their arrival *and* the manufacture of Minoan versions before MM IA. Other indigenous 'egyptianizing' types, chiefly the cylindrical stone jar with everted rim and base and the squatting baboon image (the Egyptian deity

Thoth in baboon form) excavated in these same communal tombs are less easily isolated chronologically, but these too may not have been produced until MM IA.

Middle Kingdom material found on Protopalatial Crete is limited to a very small number of scarabs, now recovered in habitation contexts, a few thin-walled stone bowls possibly employed ritually at Knossos, and the earliest ostrich eggshells and amethyst. Focus has shifted again to Knossos, judging from material concentration here. Indigenous scarab types that owe nothing more to imports are lightly scattered over the island, and two 'egyptianizing' figures with Minoan cultic associations appear: The earliest 'genius' figure was derived from the Egyptian standing hippopotamus deity, usually but (at this early date) incorrectly called Taweret (Tauert), and the MM II squatting monkey figure developed from the earlier baboon, its slimmer proportions due perhaps to importation of the animal itself. Some derivative stone vessels were produced at Knossos, perhaps also for cultic use. Egyptian amethyst is one of many hard stones used for jewelry from MM IB?/II. As some objects are undoubted Minoan types, both finished pieces *and* raw stone must have arrived from Egypt, where it was mined from late Dynasty 11 to early Dynasty 13.

Both iconographical images continue to develop their own momentum over the Neopalatial period. Early Dynastic/Old Kingdom stone jars and Middle Kingdom/Second Intermediate Period alabastra are imported initially to Knossos and in LM IB found throughout the island. Some were physically converted into Minoan vessels, a practice limited only to Neopalatial Crete, and these and unconverted imports were reexported and interred in élite tombs at Mycenae. Minoan artisans throughout the island produced variations of some Egyptian jar types. Second Intermediate Period stone alabastra were imported from MM IIIB, yet Minoan tall clay derivatives appear only in LM IB and feature details of these imports long *passé* in Egypt. Monkeys, likely imported from Egypt, appear on Cretan, Theran, and Melian frescoes.

Egyptian imports first appear on the LH I mainland, initially stone vessels via Knossos and ostrich eggshell (converted to rhyta), both found in the Mycenae shaft graves and at Akrotiri. The Minoan 'genius' was adopted by LH IIA. Buried in many early palatial tombs is a surprising quantity of jewelry elements in amethyst, long unfashionable in Egypt, and others of glass imitating amethyst.

Likely both dry and liquid goods were transported to the Minoan port of Kommos in Egyptian storage jars and amphorae of varying capacities in late LM IB through early IIIB contexts. Most are later Dynasty 18 vessels in generally contemporary LM IIIA contexts. 'Pilgrim flasks' likely contained Egyptian perfumed oils or unguents. Others, a pot stand and open bowl forms, in desert marl and Nile silt fabrics, were imported for their own sake or abandoned by ships' crews.

Imported glass vessels and an 'aegeanized' crocodile image both first appear in the Palatial mainland and Final Palatial Knossian hinterland in LH/LM IIIA1. On Crete, the ape figure disappears, and the tall clay alabastron survives only into LM IIIA1. Imported scarabs, jewelry elements, stone vessels and their conversions, and the 'genius' all continue on Crete – but not at Knossos – in LM IIIA2–B. The relative position of this period is disputed (Final or Postpalatial?) and so is here isolated as 'End Palatial.' Far more of these same types are recovered in LH IIIA2–B mainland tombs, while a few scarabs and ostrich eggshell fragments were buried in LH IIIA2–B tombs on Kos and Rhodes. Imported stone vessels recovered in all IIIB contexts are 'heirlooms,' none dating later than Dynasty 18.

Nothing is found in context on Crete during the period agreed to be Postpalatial, but many imported scarabs, other amulets, and imports have been recovered in LH IIIC (early) Perati tombs, tombs on Kos and Rhodes, and a cultic context on Melos. The LH IIIC (middle) shrine at Phylakopi is the latest dateable BA Aegean context to include an import, an ostrich eggshell converted to an Aegean rhyton. These finds suggest, at least until the dateable objects themselves are reexamined, that some Postpalatial contact was maintained.

Raw materials imported from Egypt can rarely be identified with certainty without identifiable trace element analyses, as most were also available elsewhere. Nonetheless, Egypt is the unequivocal origin of the banded 'Egyptian alabaster' (from MM III) for Aegean stone vessels, as well as amethyst (from MM IB?/II) for both jewelry and vessels. It is also the most likely source for ostrich eggshells (from EM IIB/III), both hippopotamus (from EM IIA) and elephant (from LM/LH I) ivory, and (from MM IB?/II) at least some carnelian, garnet, jasper (red, green, yellow), and possibly malachite. A strong circumstantial case may be made for at least some Aegean gold, as Egyptians mined considerable quantities of the metal throughout the BA. Wine and oil likely arrived in some of the imported vessels. Tridachna shell and 'ebony' (African blackwood) perhaps arrived via Egypt, and prepared papyrus and linen too may have been imported, although no direct evidence for the latter two survives in the Aegean.

General discussion and catalogues of Egyptian imports include Lambrou-Phillipson 1990; Cline 1994; Phillips 2008; in press. Material-specific discussion includes Warren 1969, Types 30, 43 (stone vessels); Krzyskowska 1988 (ivory); Phillips 2009 (amethyst).

The Aegean to Egypt

Aegean products imported into Egypt presumably include those not actually recovered archaeologically but mentioned in 'tribute' lists and carried by the various painted Aegeans or displayed in the Theban tombs. All but the Vapheio cups are depicted at proportionate scale, suggesting that the Theban artists had actually seen the objects they painted. A Minoan serpentine lid was recovered at Dynasty 12 Kahun (Kemp and Merrillees 1980, 78–79), and a boar's tusk helmet plaque at Dynasty 19 Qantir (Pusch 1989, 254), but the most ubiquitous archaeological finds are clay vessels, substantially complete in tombs and as sherds elsewhere.

MM IB/II (Kamares) through LM IB Minoan ceramics, both open and closed forms and many undoubtedly imported for their own sake, are recovered at a limited number of sites between the Delta and just north of the First Cataract (Kemp and Merrillees 1980). If Minoan, the Zawiyet transport stirrup jars are the only post–LM IB vessels recovered in Egypt (Snape 2003). Mycenaean open and closed forms from LH IIA through IIIB are more abundantly found in palatial, settlement, cemetery, and cultic contexts at far more Egyptian sites into Dynasty 20, all along the Nile from Tabo (just above the Third Cataract in Nubia) into the Delta, the Sinai peninsula, and along the western coast (Hassler 2008; White 2002). A key cross-cultural marker is the LH IIIA2 material at Amarna, Akhenaten's capital for less than two decades.

Egyptian artisans reproduced only two Aegean vessel forms: conical rhyta (with vertical handle not above rim level) throughout Dynasty 18 and stirrup jars from the reign of Thutmose III at least into early Dynasty 19 and possibly early Dynasty 20. Both are found in faience and clay, and stirrup jars also in calcite (Bell 1983; Ayers 2008). The rhyta retain earlier features long after their disappearance in the Aegean. The bimetallic 'funnel' Petrie (1937, 27, pl. XXXIX.25) purchased in Cairo is the only surviving possible metal conical rhyton other than the trimetallic 'Siege Rhyton.' It should represent other metal rhyta (of both cultures?) that have not survived and also recalls the four bimetallic iron/silver vessels presented in Year 42 to Thutmose III (Cline 1994, 110, 114; see Graefe 1971, 26–31 for 'iron'). Both Middle and New Kingdom vessels and frescoes also employed various 'aegeanizing' decorative elements.

Identifying imported raw materials of specifically Aegean origin is problematic, as they might equally originate elsewhere. The 'Keftiu bean' cited in *Papyrus Ebers* is not specifically identified, nor are the ingredients (likely of Keftiu origin) employed with the *London Medical Papyrus* 'spell.' The most likely imports are unguents and perfumes, perhaps mixed with a plant gum, unattested archaeologically but probably transported in stirrup jars. Evidence for the olive in Egypt is very sporadic until much later, but arguably may be an Aegean export; olive pits are first recorded at Dynasty 13 Memphis (Murray, in Nicholson and Shaw 2000, 614), and a fragmentary Amarna palace wall painting depicts a fruit-bearing olive tree (Frankfurt 1929, pl. IX.C; Weatherhead 2007, 209). Wachsmann (1987, 78–92) convincingly argues for importation of Cretan agrimi horn for New Kingdom composite bows. Barber (1991, 49 n. 6, 351) associated the (rarely found) wool recovered at Kahun and Amarna with the considerable Aegean ceramics also found there (although far earlier sites also had wool, and that at Kahun is now carbon-dated to the Roman period; Nicholson and Shaw 2000, 269). She (1991, 64–65, 351) also believed that an Aegean emigrée was buried in New Kingdom Gurob (Tomb 11) with the unique low spindle whorl of local limestone (the Aegean-style galley was also found here; Wachsmann 2008). Other materials of lesser probability are cypress wood (Nicholson and Shaw 2000, 350) and lichen (Merrillees and Winter 1972, 111–12, 113; Nicholson and Shaw 2000, 559).

Political Relationship

Opinion regarding the political relationship or relationships between Egypt and the Aegean ranges from indirect to direct and virtually nil to intense at certain periods (mainly within Dynasties 18–19), but no documentation other than Egyptian 'tribute' lists and painted figures (see earlier) survives. These suggest little or no more than an extended commercial relationship of varying intensity conducted as a royal monopoly or under royal assent, so likely including the very occasional diplomatic gift exchange at arm's length. No Egyptian king personally traveled to the Aegean, the 'Amarna Letters' include no relevant correspondence, and no military aggression is ever evident, although Aegean mercenaries may have served later pharaohs. Cross-cultural influence in both directions is minimal, restricted to certain specific materials, goods, and iconographies that reflected perceived needs at one level or another. Undoubtedly, however, both diplomatic and commercial relations were more intense than can be appreciated from the surviving evidence.

BIBLIOGRAPHY

Auro Jorro, Francisco. 1985. *Diccionario Griego-Español/Diccionario Micénico (DMic.)* 1. Madrid: Consejo Superior de Investigaciones Científicas, Instituto de Filología.

Ayers, Natasha. 2008. "Egyptian Imitations of Mycenaean Pottery." In *Tenth ICE*, 17–18.

Barber, Elizabeth J. W. 1991. *Prehistoric Textiles: The Development of Cloth in the Neolithic and Bronze Ages*. Princeton: Princeton University Press.

Bell, Martha. 1983. "'Egyptian Imitations of Aegean Vases': Some Additional Notes." *Göttinger Miszellen* 63: 13–24.

Bietak, Manfred, Nannó Marinatos, and Clairy Palivou. 2007. *Taureador Scenes in Tell el-Dabʿa (Avaris) and Knossos*. Denkschriften der Gesamtakademie 43/Untersuchungen der Zweigstelle Kairo des Österreichischen Archäologischen Institutes 27. Vienna: Verlag der Österreichischen Akademie der Wissenschaften.

Cline, Eric H. 1994. *SWDS*.

Duhoux, Yves. 2003. *Des minoens en Égypte? «Keftiou» et «des iles au milieu du Grand Vert»*. Publications de l'Institut Orientaliste de Louvain 52. London: SCM Press.

Dziobek, Eberhard. 1994. *Die Gräber des Vezirs User-Amun Theben Nr. 61 und 131*. Archaölogische Veröffentlichungen 84. Mainz: von Zabern.

Evans, Arthur J. 1899–1900. "Knossos: I. The Palace." *BSA* 6: 3–70.

Frankfort, Henri, ed. 1929. *The Mural Painting of El 'Amarnah*. London: Egypt Exploration Society.

Graefe, Erhard. 1971. *Untersuchung zur Wortfamilie* biꜣ. PhD diss., University of Cologne.

Hassler, Astrid. 2008. "Mycenaean Pottery in Egypt Reconsidered: Old Contexts and New Results." In *Tenth ICE*, 108–109.

Hornung, Erik, Rolf Krauss, and David A. Warburton, eds. 2006. *Ancient Egyptian Chronology*. Handbook of Oriental Studies 1: The Near and Middle East 83. Boston: Brill.

Kemp, Barry J., and Robert S. Merrillees. 1980. *Minoan Pottery in Second Millennium Egypt*. Mainz: von Zabern.

Krauss, Rolf, and David A. Warburton. 2009. "The Basis for the Egyptian Dates." In *Time's Up! Dating the Minoan Eruption of Santorini. Acts of the Minoan Eruption Chronology Workshop, Sandbjerg November 2007*, ed. David A. Warburton, 125–144. *Monographs of the Danish Institute at Athens* 10. Århus: Aarhus University Press.

Krzyszkowska, Olga H. 1988. "Ivory in the Aegean Bronze Age: Elephant Tusk or Hippopotamus Ivory?" *BSA* 83: 209–34.

Kyriakides, Evangelos. 2002. "Indications on the Nature of the Language of the Keftiw from Egyptian Sources." *Ägypten und Levante* 12: 211–19.

Lambrou-Phillipson, Connie. 1990. *Hellenorientalia: The Near Eastern Presence in the Bronze Age Aegean, ca. 3000–1100 B.C. plus Orientalia: A Catalogue of Egyptian, Mesopotamian, Mitannian, Syro-Palestinian, Cypriot, and Asia Minor Objects from the Bronze Age Aegean. SIMA-PB* 95. Gothenburg: Åström.

Martin, Geoffrey T. 1989. *The Memphite Tomb of Ḥoremḥeb Commander-in-Chief of Tut'ankhamūn.* Vol. 1, *The Reliefs, Inscriptions, and Commentary*. Egypt Exploration Society Memoir 55. London: Egypt Exploration Society.

Merrillees, Robert S., and J. Winter. 1972. "Bronze Age Trade between the Aegean and Egypt: Minoan and Mycenaean Pottery from Egypt in The Brooklyn Museum." In *Miscellanea Wilbouriana* 1, 101–33. Brooklyn: Brooklyn Museum.

Nicholson, Paul T., and Ian Shaw. 2000. *Ancient Egyptian Materials and Technology*. New York: Cambridge University Press.

Nikolakaki-Kentrou, Margarita. 2003. "Malkata, Site K: The Aegean-related Motifs in the Painted Decoration of a Demolished Building of Amenhotep III." In *Egyptology at the Dawn of the Twenty-first Century: Proceedings of the Eighth International Congress of Egyptologists Cairo, 2000.* Vol. 1, *Archaeology*, ed. Zahi Hawass and Lyla Pinch Brock, 352–60. New York: American University in Cairo Press.

Panagiotopoulos, Diamantis. 2001. "Keftiu in Context: Theban Tomb-paintings as a Historical Source." *OJA* 20: 263–83.

Parkinson, Richard, and Louise Schofield. 1995. "Of Helmets and Heretics: A Possible Egyptian Representation of Mycenaean Warriors on a Pictorial Papyrus from el-Amarna." *BSA* 89: 157–70.

Petrie, William M. F. 1890. "The Egyptian Bases of Greek History." *JHS* 11: 271–77.

———. 1937. *The Funeral Furniture of Ancient Egypt with Stone and Metal Vases*. Egyptian Research Account 59. London: Quaritch.

Phillips, Jacke S. 2007. Review of Duhoux 2003. *Bibliotheca Orientalis* 65: 111–14.

———. 2008. *Aegyptiaca on the Island of Crete in Their Chronological Context: A Critical Review*. Contributions to the Chronology in the Eastern Mediterranean XVIII. 2 vols. Vienna: Österreichisches Akademie der Wissenschaften. (A companion volume that reviews the Greek mainland material is in preparation.)

———. 2009. "Egyptian Amethyst in Mycenaean Greece." *Journal of Ancient Egyptian Interconnections* 1.2, 9–25 (http://jaei.library.arizona.edu).

———. In press. "The Aegean and Egypt." In *The Oxford Handbook of Egyptology*, ed. James P. Allan and Ian Shaw. New York: Oxford University Press (with many further references).

Pinch Brock, Lyla. 2000. "Art, Industry, and the Aegeans in the Tomb of Amenmose." *Ägypten und Levante* 10: 129–37.

Pulak, Çemal. 1998. "The Uluburun Shipwreck: An Overview." *IJNA* 27: 188–224.

Pusch, Edgar B. 1989. "Auslandisches Kulturgut in Qantir-Piramesse." In *Akten des Vierten Internationalen Ägyptischen Kongresses München 1985.* Vol. 2, *Archäologie Feldforschung-Prähistorie*, ed. Sylvia Schoske, 249–56. Studien zur Altägyptischn Kultur Beihefte 2. Hamburg: Buske.

Shaw, Ian, ed. 2000. *The Oxford History of Ancient Egypt*. New York: Oxford University Press (2d ed. in preparation).

Snape, Steven R. 2003. "Zawiyet Umm el-Rakham and Egyptian Foreign Trade in the 13th Century BC." In *PLOES*, 63–70.

Thomas, Susanna. 2003. "Imports at Zawiyet Umm al-Rakham." In *Egyptology at the Dawn of the Twenty-first Century: Proceedings of the Eighth International Congress of Egyptologists Cairo, 2000*. Vol. 1, *Archaeology*, ed. Zahi Hawass and Lyla Pinch Brock, 522–29. New York: American University in Cairo Press.

Van Dijk, Jacobus. 2008. "New Evidence on the Length of the Reign of Horemheb." In *Tenth ICE*, 253–54.

Vinson, Steve. 1994. *Egyptian Boats and Ships*. Shire Egyptology 24. Princes Risborough, UK: Shire.

Wachsmann, Shelley. 1987. *Aegeans in the Theban Tombs*. Orientalia Lovaniensia Analecta 20. Leuven: Peeters.

———. 1998. *Seagoing Ships and Seamanship in the Bronze Age Levant*. College Station: Texas A&M University Press (2d ed. in preparation).

———. 2008. "The Gurob Ship Model." In *Tenth ICE*, 269.

Warburton, David A., ed. 2009. *Time's Up! Dating the Minoan Eruption of Santorini. Acts of the Minoan Eruption Chronology Workshop, Sandbjerg November 2007. Monographs of the Danish Institute at Athens* 10. Århus: Aarhus University Press.

Warren, Peter M. 1969. *Minoan Stone Vases*. Cambridge: Cambridge University Press.

Weatherhead, Fran J. 2007. *Amarna Palace Paintings*. Egypt Exploration Society Memoir 78. London: Egypt Exploration Society.

White, Donald. 2002. *Marsa Matruh: The University of Pennsylvania Museum of Archaeology and Anthropology's Excavations on Bates's Island, Marsa Matruh, Egypt 1985–1989*. Prehistoric Monographs 2. Philadelphia: INSTAP Academic Press.

———. 2003. "Multum in Parvo: Bates's Island on the NW Coast of Egypt." In *PLOES*, 71–82.

CHAPTER 62

....

LEVANT

....

ASSAF YASUR-LANDAU

THE physical distance between the Aegean and the Levant is far from being an insurmountable obstacle since the Mediterranean serves as a connecting medium. Under favorable winds, a ship traveling at a speed of 2.4–3.4 knots can make the journey between Rhodes, on the southeastern border of the Aegean world, to Gaza, at the southern border of the Levant, in a mere five to seven days. In only another four days it can even make the entire trip to the Levant from Athens on mainland Greece (Casson 1971, 288).

However, the cultural distance between the regions created a formidable barrier for any type of contact. It manifested itself not only in the difference between Indo-European and Semitic languages but also in almost every aspect of behavioral patterns from cooking and weaving to the realm of religion. Moreover, the cultural and linguistic distance between the Aegean and the Levant significantly hindered any transmission of culture, especially of behavioral patterns concerning the production and/or use of artifacts because the complex processes of teaching, imitation, and other sorts of socialization needed for complete transmission are almost impossible to impart without prolonged, face-to-face contact between teacher and student (Gosselain 1998, 94–97).

This chapter deals only with the impact of the Aegean on the Levant, defined here as the coastal and nearby areas of the Eastern Mediterranean: the area from the Amuq and the Kingdom of Mukish in the north to Gaza in the south. For the topic of Near Eastern impact on the Aegean world, see Maran (2004) and Cline (1994, 2007) for further bibliography.

THE MIDDLE BRONZE I (CA. 1950–1750 BC)

It was most likely tin and copper, crucial components in any Bronze Age palatial culture, which had attracted Protopalatial Minoans to establish a presence along the land routes from Mesopotamia to the Levantine coast (Wiener 1990, 146; Betancourt 1998, 8). Ugarit, the first landfall east of Cyprus, was an important link in the trade route that connected Crete with sources of tin in the East, and the presence of Minoan merchants is attested by ARM A 1270, a tablet from Mari that records the allocation of tin to the interpreter of the Caphtorites' chief merchant in Ugarit (ARMT 23, 556, 28–31; Helzer 1989; Cline 1994, 126).

Protopalatial MM IIA–B pottery—mainly carinated cups but also bridge-spouted jars—have been found at north Levantine sites, including Ugarit, Sidon, Byblos, and Beirut (Merillees 2003). The finds in the southern Levant are even more meager, with an MM IIB cup sherd from the MB IIA "moat deposit" at Ashkelon and an MM IIB or perhaps "minoanizing" cup from an MB IIC context in Hazor (Dothan, Zuckerman, and Goren 2000; Merillees 2003, 136). The MM II pottery found in the Levant was not part of lavish diplomatic gifts, as were the Caphtorian weapons encrusted with gold and lapis lazuli recorded at Mari (e.g., ARMT 21, 231:3, 15–16; Cline 1994, 126) but were rather the residual evidence of accompanied trading items, perhaps taken by the Cretan crews of ships and intended for middle-class clients (Merrillees 2003, 139).

THE MIDDLE BRONZE II (CA. 1750–1550 BC)

The collapse of the Mari trading system, after the conquest of Mari by Hammurabi of Babylon (ca. 1750 BC, following the middle chronology, or ca. 1664 BC following the "new lower chronology"; Ben Tor 2003, 55), as well as the rise of the Hyksos in Egypt and the transition to the Neopalatial period in Crete must have created new challenges for interactions between Crete and the Levant. With the absence of any Egyptian threat and before the rise of the Hittite Empire, the Amorite kingdoms of the Levantine littoral grew unhindered and developed their own networks with Cyprus and the Aegean.

The apparent absence of MM III pottery imports (Betancourt 1998, 6) and the rather few LM IA/LH I pottery imports (Hankey and Leonard 1998, 31–32) indicate that there was no Minoan intention to broaden the commercial activity to include Aegean goods aimed for the subelites of the East. Rather, the two conspicuous examples of Aegean-style frescos found at Kabri and Alalakh—identified by the use of the *buon fresco* technique, methods of plaster preparation similar to those in the Aegean, and the use of Aegean motifs—indicate a continuation of interelite interactions (Niemeier and Niemeier 2000, 792). However, the use of the Aegean style and even symbolism does not necessarily mean the adoption of Minoan ideas but rather the deliberate use of the foreign to further entirely local causes, demonstrations of the ruler's connection with faraway lands (Niemeier and Niemeier 1998, 96) or perhaps an aspiration to belong to a more "cosmopolitan" Mediterranean narrative (Cline and Yasur-Landau 2007, 163–64; Feldman 2007).

The fresco fragments from Alalakh came from the stratum VII palace of Yarim-Lim, originating in audience hall 5, as well as from magazines 11–13, probably fallen from a large room (Woolley's grand salon) located above (Woolley 1955, 228–32; Niemeier and Niemeier 2000, 780–81). The room 5 frescoes include grasses moving in the wind, as well as a bucranium frieze, possibly with a double ax—a motif with a strong Minoan and arguably even Knossian ancestry. The grand salon fresco includes a white design on a red background, and its notched plume motif caused Niemeier and Niemeier (2000, 788–89) to interpret the scene as a large griffin crouching on a rocky terrain, painted in a distinctively Aegean style. The hypothesized *terminus post quem* for the use of the palace is the destruction of Alalakh by Hattusili I ca. 1625–1550 BC (Niemeier and Niemeier 2000, 780; Bietak 2007, 270–71), yet the frescoes themselves could have been painted anytime during the long life of stratum VII.

At Tel Kabri, excavated by Kempinski and Niemeier, a frescoed floor was found in Hall 611, within the ceremonial wing of the Canaanite palace built during the MB II period. It was decorated with a checkered design with red grid lines. Some of the squares were painted yellow; other were left white. A few squares were further decorated with marbling (stone imitation) design, while others were decorated with small dark-blue iris flowers and yellow crocuses (Niemeier and Niemeier 1998, 76).

In addition, more than two thousand tiny wall fresco fragments were found by Kempinski and Niemeier in and next to Threshold 698, located between Hall 611 and Room 740, where they had been reused as packing material (R. Oren 2002, 63; Niemeier and Niemeier 2002, 254). The fragments once belonged to an extensive miniature fresco that is similar in style, as well as in theme, to that of the West House at Akrotiri on Thera/Santorini (figure 62.1). Fragments of gray sea, crescent-shaped boats, and white and reddish-brown rocks indicate that this was a coastal scene, while fragments of architecture, reminiscent in style of the West House fresco, point to the existence of a coastal town (Niemeier and Niemeier 1998, 76–77). However, the date of the Kabri frescoes is as problematic as those at Alalakh, and they may be dated anywhere between the end of the 17th century BC and the first half of the 16th (Niemeier and Niemeier 2000, 780; Cline and Yasur-Landau 2007, 159–60).

Further indications of interactions with the Aegean are two inscriptions: a pithos sherd found in a late Middle Bronze II context in the temple courtyard at Tel Haror incised with Cretan Hieroglyphic (Day et al. 1999; Karnava 2005) and a stone basin from Lachish incised with Linear A signs (Finkelberg 1998, 267–68), the latter locally made and thus indicating the presence of a literate Aegean person at the site.

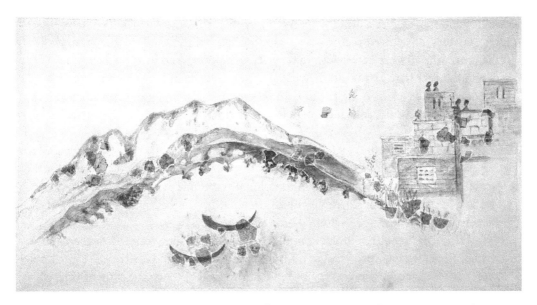

Figure 62.1. Fragments from the Kabri fresco, reconstruction by B. Niemeier and W.-D. Niemeier, conservation by R. Pelta, photograph by P. Shrago (after Cline and Yasur-Landau 2007, pl. XXXVIIIa).

A curious case is that of the importation of an Aegean legume, *Lathyrus clymenum L.* (Spanish vetchling), found at Tel Nami in a Middle Bronze Age IIA context (Artzy and Marcus 1993).

THE LATE BRONZE AGE (CA. 1550–1200 BC)

The Age of Empires and Indirect Trade Patterns

The rise of the Late Bronze Age world system, with its club of great kingdoms—Hatti, Egypt, Mitanni, Babylon, and Ahhiyawa (possibly Mycenaean Greece)—significantly changed the relations between the Levant and the Aegean. The strong Pharaohs of the early 18th dynasty led to the return of Egypt as a major player in the international trade in raw materials and elite goods, no doubt at the expense of the Levantine littoral polities. Diplomatic and high-level commercial relations with the Aegean world are evident in the commissioning of Minoan fresco art at Tel el-Dabᶜa (Bietak 2007), the Aegeans depicted in Theban tombs (Wachsmann 1987), and the Kom el-Hetan inscription (Cline 1998, 238), which may record the journey of an Egyptian ship to the Aegean.

The rise of the Egyptian and Hittite Empires left the Levantine polities as client rulers and vassals, thus diminishing their ability to conduct independent foreign policy and trade. After a hundred years of Egyptian rule, the Amarna Letters of the 14th century BC show a picture of the diminished political and military power of the Canaanite city-states. They were very likely impoverished by the accompanying demands for tribute and taxation, which led to a reduced purchasing power of elite goods, as well as a lack of ability to commission first-class Aegean art. Phenomena such as the Kabri and Alalakh frescoes never returned to the Levant during the Late Bronze Age.

At the same time, the need of these elites to strengthen their position by procuring exotic imported goods created a market for the least expensive Aegean ceramic wares. As a result, the volume of international trade in pottery increased, resulting in a related and considerable rise in the quantity of Aegean imports, mostly Mycenaean containers for perfumed oils (Dabney 2007, 191–92).

Written evidence for direct commercial interaction between the Aegean and the Levant in the Late Bronze Age is limited to the oft-quoted case of the Ugaritic merchant Sinaranu, who was exempted from several taxes by the king of Ugarit, Amistamru II, including one tax "when from Crete his ship arrives" (PRU III 16.236; Helzer 1978, 134; 1988). However, this short note pales in comparison with the rich evidence for Ugaritic interaction with Cyprus, which included diplomatic correspondence between the kings of Ugarit and Alashiya (Cyprus) dealing with both commercial and military affairs (Yon 2003, 47–48). The presence of Alashiyans in Ugarit is apparent in a census of twenty-seven Alashiyan families, possibly merchants, recorded on RS 11.857 (Schloen 2001, 323–26), as well as an Alashiyan ship mentioned in KTU 3.390 (Hoftijzer and van Soldt 1998, 339) and documents in Cypro-Minoan script found at Ugarit itself (e.g., J. Smith 2003, 284).

The lack of written records for direct contact between the Aegean and the Levant is seen also on the Aegean side, where Linear B references to the personal and ethnic names of foreigners are found (Shelmerdine 1998, 292; Cline 1994, 50; Palaima 1991, 278–79; Yasur-Landau 2003, pl. 2.1). While the Linear B tablets reflect at least a superficial knowledge of commodities and people arriving from Egypt, Cyprus, and western Anatolia, there are few references to the Levant. Most conspicuously, Ugarit, the most important gateway for Mycenaean pottery in the Levant, is not mentioned at all in the Aegean record.

In contrast to the scanty evidence of direct trade between the Aegean and the Levant at this time, we find strong indications of the important role of Cypriots rather than Mycenaeans or local merchants in the import of Mycenaean pottery to the Levant. Hankey's (1967, 146) views on the important place of Cypriots in the Mycenaean pottery trade may be strengthened by the discovery of Cypro-Minoan signs on Mycenaean and other pottery found in the Levant, either painted or incised after firing, such as the fifteen Mycenaean vessels with Cypro-Minoan signs found at Tell Abu Hawam (Hirschfeld 2004, 106). Hirschfeld (1993, 2004) sees this as a clear indication that such Mycenaean vessels traveled through Cyprus or were handled by someone accustomed to Cypriot ways, further pointing to the deep involvement of Cypriots in the trade in Mycenaean pottery.

Indeed, the volume of the trade in Mycenaean pottery exported to Canaan and the northern Levant is—in quantity—in a distant second place compared to the huge volume of pottery imports from Cyprus exported to the same area. Thus, for example, in Tyre, Cypriot imports outnumber Mycenaean imports at a ratio of 10 to 1 (Bell 2006, 56), and at Tell Abu Hawam, which yielded a number of Mycenaean imports second only to Ugarit, Cypriot pottery imports may outnumber Mycenaean vessels by a ratio of 40 to 1 (Åström 1993, 312).

Use of Mycenaean Pottery in the Levant

Mycenaean pottery is imported to the Levant in increasing numbers as early as the LH II period (Hankey and Leonard 1998, 32–33) and reach their peak in LH IIIA2; by LH IIIB they are found in at least seventy-five sites in the Levant (Wijngaarden 2002, 16–22). Provenance studies have demonstrated that in this phase most such pottery was produced in the Argolid and surrounding areas (e.g., Killebrew 1998, 160; Perlman, Asaro, and Frierman 1971; Gunneweg et al. 1992; French 2004). Clear LH IIIB2 forms are somewhat less common, although they have been found at Tell Abu Hawam (e.g., Warren and Hankey 1989, 160) and Ugarit (e.g., Hirschfeld 2000a, 149nn430, 431, 434). Transitional LH IIIB–C pottery exists at very few sites, such as Lachish and perhaps Ugarit. Pottery decorated in the LH IIIC style exists in the Levant, but it is no longer acquired from the Aegean; instead, it is either imported from Cyprus or locally made (see later discussion).

Even at the richest sites in the Levant, Mycenaean pottery constituted but a small fraction of the entire pottery assemblage; its use may have had only a limited impact on Canaanite society. In Ugarit, Cypriot and Mycenaean imports together form only about 1% of the entire ceramic finds (Bell 2006, 37). Steel, analyzing the distribution of imported Mycenaean pottery at Tel el 'Ajjul, argues—given the very small number of Mycenaean pottery imports found in habitation contexts—that "Mycenaean imports represent an exotic rarity that had a limited appeal or use within the LBA occupation of the site" (2002, 36).

Mycenaean pottery arrived at the Levantine markets through a number of coastal gateways, the most important of which was Ugarit, followed by Tell Abu Hawam, located on the coast of the Carmel (Balensi 2004; Artzy 2005). Both sites overshadow all others in both quantity—more than 1,000 Mycenaean imports at Ugarit and circa 700 at Tell Abu Hawam (Leonard 1994, 201–202, 208–209; Hirschfeld 2000a, 91; Wijngaarden 2002, 109; Balensi 2004, 145; Bell 2006, 37)—and the variety of forms (Balensi 1985, 66; 2007, figure 7a–c). Other coastal sites, such as Sarepta, Akko, Tel Nami, and Ashdod (Artzy 2005; Bell 2006, 41–44, 47–48) may have also served as entry points for both Cypriot and Mycenaean imports.

Functionally, most of the imported Mycenaean vessels were small containers, and the small stirrup jar was the most frequent Mycenaean import to the Levant in the LH IIIA–B period (Leonard 1994, 50–66; Hirschfeld 2000b, 71). Other closed forms include stirrup jars, pithoid/piriform jars, pyxides, and lentoid flasks (Leonard 1994, 13–22, 35–39, 50–83). These were probably used as containers for perfumed oils and ointments (Leonard 1981, 91–100). Luxurious dinnerware was a relatively less frequent import (Killebrew 1998, 160) and included amphoroid kraters (most of which are decorated with chariot scenes), semiglobular cups, and shallow angular bowls (Leonard 1994, 22–33, 96–102, 123–26). There was no importation of either cookware or coarse kitchen ware, which may indicate that Canaanites did not have any interest in Mycenaean cuisine or foodways.

The dominant role of small containers, usually more then 80% of the Mycenaean assemblage (Guzowska and Yasur-Landau 2007), suggests that most Mycenaean pottery was purchased for its contents. As for imported dinnerware, its patterns of use do not indicate the adoption of Mycenaean behavioral patterns relating to feasting but rather the adaptation of the imported pottery to local practices. Such is probably the case for explaining the rarity of the kylix in the Levant, even though it was the most common type of Mycenaean drinking vessel in the Aegean. Their almost complete absence may be the result of the profound difference between Canaanite and Aegean drinking practices and the way the vessels are physically held (Yasur-Landau 2005).

Aegean toasting is characterized by the use of stemmed cups, always firmly held by their stems using all five fingers. In contrast, depictions on the Megiddo and Tel el-Far'ah ivories show that Canaanite rulers and nobles drank from round-based drinking bowls, with the bowl resting on the open palm of the hand. This is a Syrian tradition that began in the early second millennium BC (Yasur-Landau 2005; Beck 1989, 338–40; Ziffer 1999, 195–96). It is therefore easy to understand why semiglobular cups and shallow angular bowls (Leonard 1994, 96–102, 123–26; Hirschfeld 2000b, 71) are the most commonly imported personal serving vessel, as they conform to the Canaanite practice of resting the vessel on the palm of the hand rather than holding its stem. The amphoroid krater, a favorite import during the 14th century, reflects the opposite phenomenon—it resembled in shape the common Canaanite krater and therefore could have been easily used during Canaanite feasts, as can be seen in the co-occurrence of Canaanite kraters and a Mycenaean "Chariot krater" in the elite Tomb 387 at Tel Dan.

Further evidence that a passion for Aegean tableware and drinking habits was not shared by many people in the Late Bronze Age southern Levant comes from the so-called derivative forms, sometimes referred to as "imitations of Mycenaean pottery" or "local" (Amiran 1970, 186; Killebrew 1998, 161). These were intended to answer the market demand of people with an acquired taste for Aegean pottery or for commodities inside such pottery. These derivative forms were mostly closed containers such as stirrup jars, pithoid/piriform jars, and straight-sided alabastra (e.g., Leonard 1994, 22nn157–61, 39nn474–76, 78–79nn1171, 1177–78, 1192–98; Amiran 1970, pl. 57: 2–7, 9, 11).

The fact that most imports and imitations are containers and not tableware indicates that the changes in behavioral patterns caused by Aegean imports leaned toward the consumption of exotic commodities transported in exotic containers. Imported tableware was in less demand and less frequently imitated, indicating little if any change in food preparation and food consumption habits.

Similarly, Mycenaean ceramic cultic objects such as figurines and rhyta had a limited impact on Levantine cults. Though they could be found in cultic contexts, such as the Temple rhyta in Ugarit (Wijngaarden 2002, 115), their sporadic use did not spark any significant wave of local imitation, as would be expected if their use introduced new Aegean ritual practices.

THE "INTERNATIONAL STYLE"

Luxury objects, mostly ivories, carved in the "international style" of the Late Bronze Age and combining Aegean, Syro-Canaanite, and Egyptian motifs, were a medium through which people in the Levant were exposed, albeit indirectly, to Aegean art (Crowley 1989; Rehak and Younger 1998). To Feldman, these objects, which possess "visual ambiguity" by not belonging to a specific artistic tradition, enabled a "hybridity of an imagined community" in situations of close encounters between kings, such as royal diplomatic marriages (Feldman 2006, 71, 190–91). The varied artistic influences of the international style is apparent in the mixed origin of Kothar, the Ugaritic god of crafts, who is described in the Baal cycle as both Cretan and Egyptian: Crete is "the throne where he sits," and Memphis is "the land of his heritage" (CAT 1.3 VI 14–16; M. Smith 1997, 119).

It is impossible to know the origin of these "koine" pieces and whether they had one manufacturing point or several (Kantor 1956, 167; Liebowitz 1980; Barnett 1982, 26; Feldman 2006, 96). Thus, for example, the famous pyxis lid from Minet el-Beida, which depicts a goddess flanked by two goats, has been identified by different scholars as either a Levantine, Cypriot, or an Aegean item made for the Levantine market (Feldman 2006, 63–64). It is likely that many workshops were active at the same time, as there is a wide continuum in ivory carving (Feldman 2006, 97).

Despite the fact that Levantine elites used objects made in the International style but include Aegean components, it appears that Aegean clothing did not influence their *habitus*—core of identity—and the way the rulers wished to see themselves on the inlaid furniture they used. Thus, at both Megiddo and Ugarit, sites that yielded many pieces in the International style, ivory pieces with scenes of elite life depict rulers and other male and female members of the elite in distinctively Canaanite dress and hairstyles (Loud 1939, nos. 2, 161, 162; Liebowitz 1980, 169; Sweeney and Yasur-Landau 1999, 131–32; Feldman 2006, 54–55, 97). If there were any foreign influence on the appearance of the local dignitaries, it is Egyptian, as is also evident in the Egyptian garments and hairstyles on a court scene from a Tel el-Far'a (S) ivory (Liebowitz 1980, 168).

THE 12TH CENTURY: LH IIIC–STYLE IMPORTS AND PHILISTINE MIGRANTS

During the early–middle 12th century in the Levant, imports of Mycenaean pottery essentially stopped, as did the imports of Cypriot base ring and white slip wares. Contemporary with the collapse of the Hittite empire, a wave of destruction crashed through the Levant and eliminated the kingdoms of Ugarit and Amurru. The sites on the Phoenician coast, from Byblos to the Carmel ridge, seem to have been spared, yet most urban sites in the southern Levant ceased to exist by the last third of the 12th century BC, many of them violently destroyed. The destruction of Ugarit, Amurru, and the sites on the southern coast of the Levant is usually attributed to the activities of the Sea Peoples, among whom are the Philistines, whose exploits were recorded in Ramses III's year 8 inscription at Medinet Habu:

> The foreign countries made conspiracy in their islands...No land could stand before their arms, from Hatti [central Anatolia], Qode [Cilicia, southeastern Anatolia], Carchemish, Arzawa [western Anatolia] and Alashiya [Cyprus] on, being cut off at one time....Their confederation was the Peleset [Philistines], Tjeker, Shekelesh, Denyen, and Weshesh, lands united. (Peden 1994, 29)

The utter destruction of the Late Bronze Age world system resulted in a deep change in the nature of the interaction between the Aegean and the Levant. Ugarit itself is thought to have been destroyed between 1195 and 1185 (Yon 1992, 119–20; Singer 1999, 729); the latest imported Aegean wares at Ugarit include a pictorial krater belonging to the Kos/Kalymnos group (Courtois 1978, 318–19, 346–50, figure 41:1, 2; Yon 2000, 8). These have been ascribed by Warren and Hankey to the LH IIIC Early period and by Mountjoy to the "Transitional LH IIIB–LH IIIC" phase (Mountjoy 2004). Note that there is a possible presence of LH IIIC Early pottery *within* the destruction deposits of Ugarit (Monchambert 1996; Karageorghis 2000, 64–65; Yon 2000, 15), but this may well postdate the destruction.

A similar picture of a small amount of Transitional LH IIIB–LH IIIC and LH IIIC–style pottery that predates the destruction at the end of the Late Bronze Age can be seen at Tel Kazel, where it is found in the transitional LB–Iron Age I phase, before the destruction of the site (attributed to the Sea People), as well as in the subsequent Iron Age I phase (Badre 2006; Jung 2007).

In areas that survived (at least temporarily) the wave of destructions at the beginning of the 12th century BC, a new type of imports appears, albeit in very small quantities: Aegean-type pottery, which, according to NAA analysis of samples from Israel (D'Agata et al. 2005; Mazar 2007), was produced mostly in Cyprus. This pottery appears in the southern Levant only at sites north of the Carmel Ridge: Tel Keisan, Acco, Beth Shean, and perhaps Dan. The most common type imported was the small stirrup jar, similarly to the earlier pattern of LH IIIB imports.

The Cypriot origin of the vessels from Tel Keisan, Beth Shean, and Acco suggests that Cypriot products from diverse pottery workshops—from the areas of

Palaepaphos in the west and Enkomi in the east (D'Agata et al. 2005)—replaced the Argolid-made Aegean wares after those became unavailable. These vessels were also locally imitated, as is seen in two examples of LH IIIC–style stirrup jars from Megiddo and Tel Keisan, produced in the vicinity of Acco, which clearly imitate Cypriot "Mycenaean IIIC" prototypes (Yasur-Landau 2006).

A similar picture also occurs at Phoenician sites such as Byblos, Sarepta, and Tyre. Unlike Ugarit and Amurru, these show no evidence of destruction during the transition between the Late Bronze Age and the Early Iron Age. These sites mainly yielded imported pieces of LH IIIC pottery, primarily stirrup jars, deep bowls, and kraters, reflecting a small-scale survival of trade with Cyprus in the mid- and late 12th century (Byblos: Salles 1980, 30–35, 66; Sarepta: Koehl 1985, 118–22; Anderson 1988, 612–13, pl. 28:19; Leonard 1994, 118n1757; Tyre: Bikai 1978, pl. XXXIX: 20; Leonard 1994, 120n1778).

In the southern Levant, the collapse of the Canaanite city-state system, which began in the 13th century BC, had ended with the demise of every Canaanite city by the middle of the 12th century BC (Finkelstein 1996). Although Cypriot-made LH IIIC pottery was not imported to sites south of the Carmel ridge, new Aegean-inspired material culture traits that stemmed from the LH IIIC Postpalatial world appeared at the sites of Ashdod, Ashkelon, Ekron, and Gath, which area later became known in the biblical literature as the Land of the Philistines.

The 12th-century-BC strata in these sites includes a significant percentage of locally made LH IIIC–style pottery, named in different publications "Mycenaean IIIC," "monochrome," or "Philistine monochrome" pottery (Dothan and Zuckerman 2004). The fineware repertoire is dominated by open forms, especially deep bowls, bell-shaped kraters, and shallow angular bowls. Other, more rare, open forms include cups and small kylikes. Closed forms, the most common imports during the earlier LH IIIA–B periods, appear in the "monochrome" assemblages in considerably smaller numbers than the open forms, and include stirrup jars, spouted jugs, strainer jugs, and pyxides (Dothan and Zukerman 2004). The decoration is mostly linear, although the geometric, floral, and even figural motifs appear mostly on deep bowls, kraters, strainer jugs, and stirrup jars.

Cooking practices and foodways in Philistia show a deep Aegean influence through the introduction of Aegean-type cooking vessels: cooking jugs (Yasur-Landau 2003, 174; 2003–2004; Dothan and Zukerman 2004, 28, 30) (figure 62.2). At the same time, the rectangular hearth, almost a universal feature of LH IIIC domestic architecture, appears in the Philistine sites and reflects concepts of cooking, as well as an arrangement of space foreign to the local Canaanites (Dothan 1998; Stager 1995, 347; Mazar 1986; 1988, 257–60; Karageorghis 1998; Yasur-Landau 2003, 172–74).

Another domestic activity that shows an Aegean influence is weaving, including the introduction of unperforated loomweights or spools, many dozens of which have been found at Ashkelon and Ekron (Master 2005, 342; Mazow 2005, 167). These are unbaked or poorly fired clay spools, either cylindrical or hourglass shaped, a common feature of LH IIIC/LM IIIC material culture assemblages. They are found

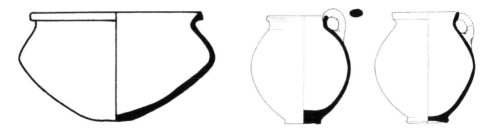

Figure 62.2. Canaanite cooking pot from Megiddo (left) and Aegean-style cooking
jugs from Tel Miqne/Ekron (after Yasur-Landau 2005, figure 3: 1, 4).

in great numbers at sites from Lefkandi in Euboea, Tiryns, and Asine in the Argolid
to Halasmenos and Chania in Crete (Rahmstorf 2003). The proof of their use as
loomweights comes from Ashkelon (Stager 1991, 14–15), where in several instances
these objects were found in a row along walls, together with linen fibers. Finally, new
types of locally made figurines, "mourning figurines," inspired by the Mycenaean
"tau" and "psi" figurines, and "Ashdoda" seated figurines, show an Aegean (and perhaps Aegean and Cypriot) impact on domestic cults (Yasur-Landau 2001).

These changes in material culture are commonly explained as the arrival of a new
population, the Philistines, from the Aegean to the southern Levant (e.g., Dothan
1982; Mazar 1985; Bietak 1993; Stager 1995; Bunimovitz and Faust 2001; Finkelstein
1995, 1998; Barako 2000; Yasur-Landau 2005; Killebrew 2006, 197–245; *contra* Sherratt
[1992, 1998], who posed a nonmigrationist explanation for the Aegean cultural traits
found on Cyprus and in Philistia, preferring a process of cultural diffusion and elite
emulation connected with the early post-Bronze Age trade). According to these views,
the profound change in domestic behavioral patterns seen at Ashdod, Ekron, and
Ashkelon could not have occurred simply through the influence of traded Aegean
items but must rather have taken place as a result of the arrival of migrants from the
Aegean and their close interaction with local populations, which facilitated a long-
term process of cultural transmission.

While most scholars seem to accept the general concept of an Aegean migration to the Levant, there are serious disagreements regarding almost all aspects of
such a migration. These include the number of migrants, their ethnic makeup (were
they mostly Aegean or a mixture of Canaanites, Syrians, and Aegeans?), the routes
they took, and the process of settlement and its chronology (Stager 1995; Finkelstein
1996, 1998, 2007; Sweeney and Yasur-Landau 1999; Bunimovitz and Faust 2001;
Yasur-Landau 2007; Killebrew 2006).

With the assimilation of the Aegean migrants into the local population, as well
as the demise of Aegean material culture traits in Philistia during the 10th century
BC, little was left of the Aegean Bronze Age impact on the Levant. However, some
names and terms persisted into the Iron Age. The Philistines, whose name may
have derived from the pre-Greek *Pelasgoi* (Singer 1988; W.-D. Niemeier 1998, 17–18,
46–47), gave their name to the southern coast of the Levant and, even in the 7th

century BC, the Philistine ruler of Ekron still carried an Aegean name, Achish, perhaps meaning "the Achaean" (Naveh 1998). Finally, the name "Caphtor" for Crete remained in constant use in the Levant from the Middle Bronze Age until the 7th century BC, when the alternative term "Cherethites" (Cretans) entered the biblical narrative (Finkelstein 2002, 148).

BIBLIOGRAPHY

Amiran, Ruth. 1970. *Ancient Pottery of the Holy Land from Its Beginnings in the Neolithic Period to the End of the Iron Age.* New Brunswick: Rutgers University Press.

Anderson, William Paul. 1988. *Sarepta I: The Late Bronze and Iron Age Strata of Area II, Y: The University Museum of the University of Pennsylvania Excavations at Sarafand, Lebanon.* Beirut: Université Libanaise.

Artzy, Michal. 2005. "Emporia on the Carmel Coast? Tel Akko, Tell Abu Hawam, and Tel Nami of the Late Bronze Age." In *Emporia*, 355–61.

Åström, Paul. 1993. "Late Cypriot Bronze Age Pottery in Palestine." In *Biblical Archaeology Today, 1990: Proceedings of the Second International Congress on Biblical Archaeology. Jerusalem, June–July 1990*, ed. Avraham Biran and Joseph Aviram, 307–13. Jerusalem: Israel Exploration Society.

Badre, Leila. 2006. "Tell Kazel-Simyra: A Contribution to a Relative Chronological History in the Eastern Mediterranean during the Late Bronze Age." *BASOR* 343: 65–95.

Balensi, Jacqueline. 1985. "Revising Tell Abu Hawam." *BASOR* 257: 65–74.

———. 2004. "Relativité du phénomène mycénien à Tell Abou Hawam: Un 'proto-marketing'?" In *La céramique mycénienne de l'Egée au Levant: Hommage à Vronwy Hankey,* ed. Jacqueline Balensi, Jean-Yves Monchambert, and Sylvie Müller Celka, 141–81. Lyon: Maison de l'orient et de la Méditerranée-Jean Pouilloux.

Barako, Tristan. J. 2000. "The Philistine Settlement as Mercantile Phenomenon?" *AJA* 104: 513–30.

Barnett, Richard David. 1982. *The Ancient Ivories of the Middle East: Qedem 14.* Jerusalem: Institute of Archaeology, Hebrew University of Jerusalem.

Beck, Pirhiya. 1989. "Stone Ritual Artifacts and Statues from Area A and H at Hazor." In *Hazor III–IV: An Account of the Third and Fourth Seasons of Excavations, 1957–1958: Text,* ed. Yigael Yadin et al., 322–38. Jerusalem: Israel Exploration Society.

Bell, Carol. 2006. *The Evolution of Long-distance Trading Relationships across the LBA/Iron Age Transition on the Northern Levantine Coast: Crisis, Continuity, and Change. BAR-IS 1574.* Oxford: Archaeopress.

Ben-Tor, Amnon. 2003. "Hazor and Chronology." *Egypt and the Levant* 14: 45–67.

Betancourt, Philip. 1998. "Middle Minoan Objects in the Near East." In *Aegean and the Orient,* 5–11.

Bietak, Manfred. 1993. "The Sea Peoples and the End of the Egyptian Administration in Canaan." In *Biblical Archaeology Today, 1990: Proceedings of the Second International Congress on Biblical Archaeology. Jerusalem, June–July 1990,* ed. Avraham Biran and Joseph Aviram, 292–306. Jerusalem: Israel Exploration Society.

———. 2007. "Bronze Age Paintings in the Levant: Chronological and Cultural Considerations." In *SCIEM* III, 269–300.

Bikai, Patricia Maynor. 1978. *The Pottery of Tyre*. Warminster: Aris and Phillips.

Bunimovitz, Shlomo, and Avraham Faust. 2001. "Chronological Separation, Geographical Segregation, or Ethnic Demarcation? Ethnography and the Iron Age Low Chronology." *BASOR* 322: 1–10.

Casson, Lionel. 1971. *Ships and Seamanship in the Ancient World*. Princeton: Princeton University Press.

Cline, Eric H. 1994. *SWDS*.

———. 1998. "Amenhotep III, the Aegean, and Anatolia." In *Amenhotep III: Perspectives on His Reign*, ed. David B. O'Connor and Eric H. Cline, 236–50. Ann Arbor: University of Michigan Press.

———. 2007. "Rethinking Mycenaean International Trade." In *RMP II*, 190–200.

———, and Assaf Yasur-Landau. 2007. "Poetry in Motion: Canaanite Rulership and Minoan Narrative Poetry at Tel Kabri." In *EPOS*, 157–66.

Courtois, Jacques-Claude. 1978. "Corpus céramique de Ras Shamra-Ugarit, niveaux historique: Bronze Moyen et Bronze Récent." In *Ugaritica* VII, ed. Claude Frédéric-Armand Schaeffer, 131–370. Paris: Librairie orientaliste P. Geuthner.

Crowley, Janice L. 1989. *The Aegean and the East: An Investigation into the Transference of Artistic Motifs between the Aegean, Egypt, and the Near East in the Bronze Age*. Jonsered, Sweden: Åström.

Dabney, M. 2007. "Marketing Mycenaean Pottery in the Levant." In *Krinoi Kai Limenai*, 191–97. Philadelphia: INSTAP Academic Press.

D'Agata, Anna Lucia, Yuval Goren, Hans Mommsen, Alexander Schwadt, and Assaf Yasur-Landau. 2005. "Imported Pottery of LH IIIC Style from Israel: Style, Provenance, and Chronology." In *Emporia*, 371–79.

Day, Peter M., Eliezer D. Oren, Louise Joyner, and Patrick S. Quinn. 1999. "Petrographic Analysis of the Tel Haror Inscribed Sherd: Seeking Provenance from Crete." In *Meletemata*, 191–96.

Dietler, Michael, and Ingrid Herbich. 1998. "*Habitus*, Techniques, Style: An Integrated Approach to the Social Understanding of Material Culture and Boundaries." In *The Archaeology of Social Boundaries*, ed. Miriam T. Stark, 232–63. Washington, D.C.: Smithsonian Institution Press.

Dothan, Trude. 1982. *The Philistines and Their Material Culture*. New Haven: Yale University Press.

———, and Alexander Zukerman. 2004. "A Preliminary Study of the Mycenaean IIIC: 1 Pottery Assemblages from Tel Miqne-Ekron and Ashdod." *BASOR* 333: 1–54.

Dothan, Trude, Sharon Zuckerman, and Yuval Goren. 2000. "Kamares Ware from Hazor." *IEJ* 50: 1–15.

Feldman, Marian H. 2006. *Diplomacy by Design: Luxury Arts and an "International Style" in the Ancient Near East, 1400–1200 BCE*. Chicago: University of Chicago Press.

———. 2007. "Knowing the Foreign: Power, Exotica, and Frescoes in the Middle Bronze Age Levant." In *Proceedings of the 51st Recontre Assyriologique Internationale*, ed. Robert D. Biggs, Jennie Myers, and Martha T. Roth, 281–86. Chicago: Oriental Institute of the University of Chicago.

Finkelberg, Margalit. 1998. "Bronze Age Writing: Contacts between East and West." In *Aegean and the Orient*, 265–71.

———, Alexander Uchitel, and David Ussishkin. 1996. "A Linear A Inscription from Tel Lachish (Lach ZA 1)." *Tel Aviv* 23: 195–207.

Finkelstein, Israel. 1996. "The Philistine Countryside." *IEJ* 46: 225–42.

———. 1998. "Philistine Chronology: High, Middle, or Low?" In *Mediterranean Peoples,* 140–47.

———. 2002. "The Philistines in the Bible: A Late-Monarchic Perspective." *JSOT* 27: 131–67.

———. 2007. "Is the Philistine Paradigm Still Viable?" In *SCIEM* III, 517–23.

French, Elizabeth B. 2004. "The Contribution of Chemical Analysis to Provenance Studies." In *La céramique mycénienne de l'Egée au Levant: Hommage à Vronwy Hankey,* ed. Jacqueline Balensi, Jean-Yves Monchambert, and Sylvie Müller Celka, 15–25. Lyon: Maison de l'orient et de la Méditerranée-Jean Pouilloux.

Gosselain, Olivier P. 1998. "Social and Technical Identity in Clay Crystal Ball." In *The Archaeology of Social Boundaries,* ed. Miriam T. Stark, 78–106. Washington, D.C.: Smithsonian Institution Press.

Gunneweg, Jan, Frank Asaro, Helen V. Michel, and Isadore Perlman. 1992. "On the Origin of a Mycenaean IIIA Chariot Krater and Other Related Mycenaean Pottery from Tomb 387 at Laish/Dan." *Eretz Israel* 23: 54*–63*.

Guzowska, Marta, and Assaf Yasur-Landau. 2007. "The Mycenaean Pottery from Tel Aphek: Chronology and Patterns of Trade." In *SCIEM* III, 537–45.

Hankey, Vronwy. 1967. "Mycenaean Pottery in the Middle East: Notes on Finds since 1951." *BSA* 62: 107–147.

———, and Albert Leonard Jr. 1998. "Aegean LB I and II Pottery in the East: 'Who Is the Potter, Pray, and Who the Pot?'" In *Aegean and the Orient,* 29–36.

Helzer, Michael. 1978. *Goods, Prices, and the Organization of Trade in Ugarit.* Wiesbaden: Reichert.

———. 1988. "Sinaranu, Son of Siginu, and the Trade Relations between Ugarit and Crete." *Minos* 23: 7–13.

———. 1989. "The Trade of Crete and Cyprus with Syria and Mesopotamia and the Eastern Tin-Sources in the XVIII–XVII Centuries B.C." *Minos* 24: 7–28.

Hirschfeld, Nicolle. 1993. "Incised Marks (Post-firing) on Aegean Wares." In *Wace and Blegen,* 311–18.

———. 2000a. "The Catalogue." In *Céramique mycénienne d'Ougarit,* ed. Marguerite Yon, Vassos Karageorghis, and Nicolle Hirschfeld, 75–161. Ras Shamra Ougarit 13. Paris: Editions recherche sur les civilisations.

———. 2000b. "Introduction to the Catalogue." In *Céramique mycénienne d'Ougarit,* ed. Marguerite Yon, Vassos Karageorghis, and Nicolle Hirschfeld, 67–73. Ras Shamra Ougarit 13. Paris: Editions recherche sur les civilisations.

———. 2004. "Eastwards via Cyprus? The Marked Mycenaean Pottery of Enkomi, Ugarit, and Tell Abu Hawam." In *La céramique mycénienne de l'Egée au Levant: Hommage à Vronwy Hankey,* ed. Jacqueline Balensi, Jean-Yves Monchambert, and Sylvie Müller Celka, 97–104. Lyon: Maison de l'orient et de la Méditerranée-Jean Pouilloux.

Hoftijzer, Jacob, and Wilfred H. van Soldt. 1998. "Appendix: Text from Ugarit Pertaining to Seafaring." In *Seagoing Ships and Seamanship in the Bronze Age Levant,* ed. Shelley Wachsmann, 333–44. College Station: Texas A&M University Press.

Jung, Reinhard. 2007. "Tell Kazel and the Mycenaean Contacts with Amurru (Syria)." In *SCIEM* III, 551–70.

Kantor, Helene J. 1956. "Syro-Palestinian Ivories." *JNES* 15: 153–74.

Karageorghis, Vassos. 1998. "Hearths and Bathtubs in Cyprus: A 'Sea Peoples' Innovation?" In *Mediterranean Peoples,* 276–82.

———. 2000. "Mycenaean and Other Sherds in the Louvre." In *Céramique mycénienne d'Ougarit,* ed. Marguerite Yon, Vassos Karageorghis, and Nicolle Hirschfeld, 37–65. Ras Shamra-Ougarit 13. Paris: Editions recherche sur les civilisations.

Karnava, Artemis. 2005. "The Tel Haror Inscription and Crete: A Further Link." In *Emporia*, 837–43.

Killebrew, Ann. 1998. "Mycenaean and Aegean-style Pottery in Canaan during the 14th–12th Centuries BC." In *Aegean and the Orient*, 158–66.

———. 2006. *Biblical People and Ethnicity: An Archaeological Study of Egyptians, Canaanites, Philistines, and Early Israel 1300–1100 B.C.E.* Leiden: Brill.

Kislev, Mordechai E., Michal Artzy, and Ezra Marcus. 1993. "Import of an Aegean Food Plant to a Middle Bronze IIA Coastal Site in Israel." *Levant* 25: 145–54.

Koehl, Robert B. 1985. *Sarepta III: The Imported Bronze and Iron Age Wares from Area II, X.* Beirut: Université Libanaise.

Leonard, Albert, Jr. 1981. "Consideration of Morphological Variations in the Mycenaean Pottery from the Southeastern Mediterranean." *BASOR* 241: 87–101.

———. 1994. *An Index to the Late Bronze Age Aegean Pottery from Syria Palestine.* Jonsered, Sweden: Åström.

Liebowitz, Harold. 1980. "Military and Feast Scenes on Late Bronze Palestinian Ivories." *IEJ* 30: 162–69.

Loud, Gordon. 1939. *The Megiddo Ivories: Oriental Institute Publications* 52. Chicago: University of Chicago Press.

Maran, Joseph. 2004. "The Spreading of Objects and Ideas in the Late Bronze Age Eastern Mediterranean: Two Case Examples from the Argolid of the 13th and 12th Centuries B.C." *BASOR* 336: 11–30.

Master, Daniel. M. 2005. "Iron I Chronology at Ashkelon: Preliminary Results of the Leon Levy Expedition." In *The Bible and Radiocarbon Dating*, ed. Thomas E. Levy and Thomas Higham, 337–48. London: Equinox.

Mazar, Amihai. 1985. "The Emergence of the Philistine Material Culture." *IEJ* 35: 95–107.

———. 1986. "Excavations at Tell Qasile 1982–1984." *IEJ* 36: 1–15.

———. 1988. "Some Aspects of the 'Sea Peoples' Settlement." In *Society and Economy in the Eastern Mediterranean (c. 1500–1000 B.C.)*, ed. Michael Heltzer and Edward Lipinski, 251–60. Louvain: Peeters.

———. 2007. "Myc IIIC in the Land of Israel: Its Distribution, Date, and Significance." In *SCIEM* III, 571–82.

Mazow, Laura B. 2005. Competing Material Culture: Philistine Settlement at Tel Miqne-Ekron in the Early Iron Age. PhD diss., University of Arizona.

Merrillees, Robert S. 2003. "The First Appearance of Kamares Ware in the Levant." *Egypt and the Levant* 13: 127–42.

Monchambert, Jean-Yves. 1996. "Du Mycénien III C à Ougarit." *Orient Express* 2 (1996): 45–46.

Mountjoy, Penelope A. 2004. "Miletos: A Note." *BSA* 99: 190–200.

Naveh, Joseph. 1998. "Achish-Ikausu in the Light of the Ekron Dedication." *BASOR* 310: 35–37.

Niemeier, Barbara, and Wolf-Dietrich Niemeier. 2000. "Aegean Frescoes in Syria-Palestine: Alalakh and Tel Kabri." In *Wall Paintings of Thera*, 763–800.

———. 2002. "The Frescoes in the Middle Bronze Age Palace." In *Tel Kabri: The 1986–1993 Excavation Seasons*, ed. Aharon Kempinski, Na'ama Scheftelowitz, and Ronit Oren, 254–85. Tel Aviv: Emery and Claire Yass Publications in Archaeology.

Niemeier, Wolf-Dietrich. 1998. "The Mycenaeans in Western Anatolia and the Problem of the Origin of the Sea Peoples." In *Mediterranean Peoples*, 17–65.

———, and Barbara Niemeier. 1998. "Minoan Frescoes in the Eastern Mediterranean." In *Aegean and the Orient*, 69–98.

Oren, Eliezer D. 1997. "The 'Kingdom of Sharuhen' and the Hyksos Kingdom." In *The Hyksos: New Historical and Archaeological Perspectives,* ed. Eliezer D. Oren, 253–83. Philadelphia: University Museum, University of Pennsylvania.

Oren, Ronit. 2002. "Area D." In *Tel Kabri: The 1986–1993 Excavation Seasons,* ed. Aharon Kempinski, Na'ama Scheftelowitz, and Ronit Oren, 55–72. Tel Aviv: Emery and Claire Yass Publications in Archaeology.

Palaima, Thomas G. 1991. "Maritime Matters in the Linear B Tablets." In *Thalassa,* 273–310.

Peden, Alexander J. 1994. *Egyptian Historical Inscriptions of the Twentieth Dynasty. Documenta Mundi Aegyptiaca* 3. Jonsered, Sweden: Åström.

Perlman, Isadore, Frank Asaro, and Jay D. Frierman. 1971. "Provenience Studies of Tel Ashdod Pottery Employing Neutron Activation Analysis." In *Ashdod II–III: The Second and Third Seasons of Excavations 1963, 1965, Sounding in 1967. Text and Plates,* ed. Moshe Dothan, 216–19. Atiqot English Series 9–10. Jerusalem: Israel Exploration Society.

Rahmstorf, Lorenz. 2003. "Clay Spools from Tiryns and Other Contemporary Sites: An Indication of Foreign Influence in LH IIIC?" In *Periphery of the Mycenaean World,* 397–410.

Rehak, Paul, and John G. Younger. 1998. "International Styles in Ivory Carving in the Bronze Age." In *Aegean and the Orient,* 229–54.

Salles, Jean-François. 1980. *La Nécropole "K" de Byblos. Recherche sur les grandes civilisations,* Mémoir no. 2. Paris: Éditions ADPF.

Schloen, J. David. 2001. *The House of the Father as Fact and Symbol: Patrimonialism in Ugarit and the Ancient Near East.* Winona Lake, Ind.: Eisenbrauns.

Shelmerdine, Cynthia W. 1998. "Where Do We Go from Here? And How Can the Linear B Tablets Help Us Get There?" In *Aegean and the Orient,* 292–98.

Sherratt, E. Susan. 1992. "Immigration and Archaeology: Some Indirect Reflections." In *Acta Cypria: Acts of an International Congress on Cypriote Archaeology Held in Göteborg on 22–24 August 1991,* Part 2, ed. Paul Åström, 316–47. *SIMA-PB* 117. Jonsered, Sweden: Åström.

———. 1998. " 'Sea Peoples' and the Economic Structure of the Late Second Millennium in the Eastern Mediterranean." In *Mediterranean Peoples,* 292–313.

———. 2006. "The Chronology of the Philistine Monochrome Pottery: An Outsider's View." In *"I Will Speak the Riddles of Ancient Times": Archaeological and Historical Studies in Honor of Amihai Mazar on the Occasion of His Sixtieth Birthday,* ed. Aren M. Maeir and de Pierre de Miroschedji, 361–74. Winona Lake, Ind.: Eisenbrauns.

Singer, Itamar. 1988. "The Origin of the Sea People and Their Settlement on the Coast of Canaan." In *Society and Economy in the Eastern Mediterranean (c. 1550–1000 B.C.),* ed. Michael Heltzer and Edward Lipinski, 239–50. Louvain: Peeters.

———. 1999. "A Political History of Ugarit." In *Handbook of Ugaritic Studies,* ed. Wilfred G. E. Watson and Nicolas Wyatt, 603–733. Boston: Brill.

Smith, Joanna. 2003. "Writing Styles in Clay of the Eastern Mediterranean Late Bronze Age." In *PLOES,* 277–89.

Smith, Mark S. 1997. "The Baal Cycle." In *Ugaritic Narrative Poetry,* ed. Simon B. Parker, 81–180. Atlanta: Scholars Press.

Stager, Lawrence E. 1991. *Ashkelon Discovered: From Canaanites and Philistines to Romans and Moslems.* Washington, D.C.: Biblical Archaeological Society.

———. 1995. "The Impact of the Sea Peoples in Canaan (1185–1050 BCE)." In *The Archaeology of Society in the Holy Land,* ed. Thomas E. Levy, 332–48. New York: Facts on File.

Steel, Louise. 2002. "Consuming Passions: A Contextual Study of the Local Consumption of Mycenaean Pottery at Tell el-Ajjul." *JMA* 15(1): 25–51.

Sweeney, Deborah, and Assaf Yasur-Landau. 1999. "Following the Path of the Sea Persons: The Women in the Medinet Habu Reliefs." *Tel Aviv* 26: 116–45.

Tzedakis, Yannis, and Holly Martlew. 1999. *Minoans and Mycenaeans: Flavours of Their Time: National Archaeological Museum, 12 July–27 November 1999.* Athens: Greek Ministry of Culture, General Directorate of Antiquities.

Wachsmann, Shelley. 1987. *Aegeans in the Theban Tombs: Orientalia Lovaniensia Analecta* 20. Louvain: Peeters.

Wiener, Malcolm. 1990. "The Isles of Crete?: The Minoan Thalassocracy Revisited." In *TAW III,* 128–61.

Wijngaarden, Gert Jan van. 2002. *Use and Appreciation of Mycenaean Pottery in the Levant, Cyprus, and Italy (ca. 1600–1200).* Amsterdam: Amsterdam University Press.

Woolley, Leonard. 1955. *Alalakh: An Account of the Excavations at Tell Atchana in the Hatay, 1937–1949.* London: Society of Antiquaries.

Yasur-Landau, Assaf. 2001. "The Mother(s) of All Philistines: Aegean Enthroned Deities of the 12th–11th Century Philistia." In *Potnia,* 329–43.

———. 2003. Social Aspects of the Aegean Migration to the Levant in the End of the 2nd Millennium BCE. PhD diss., Tel Aviv University.

———. 2003–2004. "The Last *Glendi* in Halasmenos: Social Aspects of Cooking in a Dark Age Cretan Village." *Aegean Archaeology* 7: 49–66.

———. 2005. "Old Wine in New Vessels: Intercultural Contact, Innovation, and Aegean, Canaanite, and Philistine Foodways." In *Between East and West: Eretz Israel and the Ancient Near East—Intercultural Ties and Innovations in the Second Millennium BCE: The Sonia and Marco Nadler Institute of Archaeology Annual Symposium, April 29, 2004,* ed. Yoram Cohen and Assaf Yasur-Landau, 168–91. *Tel Aviv* 32(2).

———. 2006. "A LH IIIC Stirrup Jar from Area K." In *Megiddo IV: The 1998–2002 Seasons,* ed. Israel Finkelstein, David Ussishkin, and Baruch Halpern, 299–302. Tel Aviv: Emery and Claire Yass Publications in Archaeology.

———. 2007. "Let's Do the Time Warp Again: Migration Processes and the Absolute Chronology of the Philistine Settlement." In *SCIEM* III, 609–20.

Yon, Marguerite. 1992. "The End of the Kingdom of Ugarit." In *The Crisis Years: The 12th Century B.C. from beyond the Danube to the Tigris,* ed. William A. Ward and Martha Sharp Joukowski, 111–22. Dubuque: Kendall/Hunt.

———. 2000. "Répartition et contextes." In *Céramique mycénienne d'Ougarit,* ed. Marguerite Yon, Vassos Karageorghis, and Nicolle Hirschfeld, 1–27. Ras Shamra-Ougarit 13. Paris: Editions recherche sur les civilisations.

———. 2003. "The Foreign Relations of Ugarit." In *PLOES,* 41–51.

Ziffer, Irit. 1999. Metamorphosis of Ancient Near Eastern Metaphors of Rulership: The Towel, the Flower, and the Cup. PhD diss., Tel Aviv University (Hebrew).

CHAPTER 63

···

TROY

···

PETER JABLONKA

THE site today known as Troy (Turkish Hisarlık, Homer's Ilios, Greek and Roman Ilion/Ilium) is situated in northwestern Asia Minor, five kilometers from the present coastline at the Dardanelles (ancient Hellespont), at 26°14′E and 39°52′N. Its sequence of occupation spans several millennia from the beginning of the Bronze Age (3000 BC) to the Byzantine period (12th century AD).

Troy's high profile is obviously due to the fact that it has been regarded as the scene of the Trojan War, a story told in Homer's *Iliad* and still part of popular culture. Since this story also lies at the heart of Greek ethnic identity both ancient and modern, Troy has been considered "Aegean" although it is actually part of "Anatolia." Whether these terms are meaningful at all, apart from reflecting a division of scholarship along modern political boundaries, remains to be shown.

HISTORY OF EXCAVATIONS

The attempt to determine whether this place can really be identified with the setting of the *Iliad* has been the incentive for large-scale archaeological research that has continued at the site for the past 140 years. Based on coins and inscriptions that were found at Hisarlık, Edward Daniel Clarke identified the site with ancient Ilion in 1801. Charles Maclaren concluded in 1822 that, according to ancient tradition, Ilion must also be Homer's Troy. Nevertheless, the quest for Troy was continued at other sites in the vicinity, probably influenced by Strabo, who believed that the Troy of the *Iliad* was not the city Ilion of his own time. Until the second half of the 19th century, many scholars, following Marie-Gabriel A. F. Choiseul-Gouffier and

Jean-Baptiste Lechevalier, claimed that Homer's Troy was on the nearby hilltop of the Ballı Dağ.

In 1863 Frank Calvert—a British expatriate and an amateur scholar living in the region—started excavations at Hisarlık/Ilion. When Heinrich Schliemann, a retired German merchant and self-made millionaire looking for a second career, arrived in the Dardanelles in 1868, Calvert pointed the site out to him (Heuck Allen 1999; Robinson 2007).

Seizing the opportunity, Schliemann continued excavations from 1870 until his death in 1890 (Traill 1995; Easton 2002). When he found treasures, including jewelry and vessels made from gold and silver, in what looked like the remains of a burnt citadel, he mistakenly took this for evidence that the Trojan War had actually taken place at Hisarlık. Later it became clear that these finds were from the Early Bronze Age, at least thousand years older than any possible date for the events related by Homer.

After Schliemann's death, Wilhelm Dörpfeld continued the excavations in 1893 and 1894 and published the results of his own, as well as Schliemann's, excavations (Dörpfeld 1902). From 1932 to 1938, a team from the University of Cincinnati under the directorship of Carl W. Blegen undertook a reassessment of earlier results (Blegen 1963; Blegen et al. 1950, 1951, 1953, 1958). In 1988, excavations were resumed by an international team directed by Manfred Korfmann of the University of Tübingen, Germany, with the collaboration of the University of Cincinnati (Korfmann 2006; *Studia Troica* 1991–2007). Since Manfred Korfmann's death in 2005, work at Troy has continued to the present day (2010) under the direction of Ernst Pernicka.

In the course of this long history of research, Troy—its mythological or literary associations notwithstanding—has become an important archaeological site in its own right. This is only partly due to the attention and research that have gone into the investigation of the site. With its unique, continuous sequence of important settlements spanning the entire Bronze Age, Troy is certainly one of the most prominent archaeological sites in Anatolia and the Aegean.

THE ARCHAEOLOGY OF TROY

The archaeological site of Troy (cf. Korfmann and Mannsperger 2005) occupies the northwestern corner of a low plateau that overlooks what is today an alluvial plain at the mouth of the river Karamenderes Çayı (ancient Scamander). Early Bronze Age Troy, however, was a coastal settlement on the shores of a wide but shallow bay at the mouth of the region's largest river (Kayan et al. 2003; Kraft et al. 2003). During the past six thousand years, the Scamander and Simoeis (Dümrek) rivers have prograded more than 6 km into this bay, accompanied by accelerated erosion in their catchments. The bay and its shores have been buried under several meters of sediment, rivers have frequently changed their courses, and the coastline has slowly moved to its present position, thus making archaeological investigation of the floodplain nearly impossible.

Excavations have always focused on a settlement mound ("citadel") 300 by 200 m wide on the edge of the plateau. Its 15 m of deposits contain the remains of superimposed and increasingly larger Bronze Age settlements with their ramparts, the sanctuary of Athena Ilias, and other public buildings from the Hellenistic and Roman periods. Schliemann and Dörpfeld have subdivided the sequence into nine major periods of occupation: the "cities" Troy I–IX. This chronology is still being used today. It has been revised and refined by Blegen and radiocarbon-dated by recent excavations (Korfmann and Kromer 1993; Kromer, Korfmann, and Jablonka 2003).

Ruins of classical Ilion and Bronze Age settlements outside the citadel are located on the slopes and plateau to the south and east of the mound ("lower city").

TROY I (CA. 3000–2550 BC)

Several Late Neolithic/Chalcolithic sites have been discovered in the Troad and on the island of Imbros (Kumtepe A and B, ca. 5000–3000 BC). The earliest settlement at Troy itself, Troy I, was a small village. Houses with stone and mud-brick walls were attached to each other, and some of these were "megaron" buildings consisting of a large room with a porchlike anteroom. The settlement was surrounded by stone ramparts that were repeatedly reinforced. Pottery is dark, handmade, and decorated with white incrustation. Although the majority of metal artifacts were still made from copper, bronze artifacts have been found in Troy I–levels at nearby Beşiktepe (Begemann 2003). Architecture and finds at contemporaneous sites on the shores and islands of the northern Aegean (e.g., Poliochni on Lemnos or Thermi on Lesbos) resemble what has been found at Troy (Séfériadès 1985; Kouka 2002). On the other hand, similar house plans have been discovered at Demircihüyük near Eskişehir (Korfmann 1983) or Bademağacı Höyük north of Antalya. Rather than being either Aegean or Anatolian, Troy I appears to belong to a distinctively Aegean–West Anatolian cultural sphere.

TROY II (CA. 2550–2300 BC)

At the center of the citadel, freestanding megaron buildings up to 40 m long were erected inside a courtyard and were very likely used for assemblies, audiences, or religious ceremonies. The fortifications of the citadel now consisted of mud-brick walls that crowned stone ramparts and included several monumental gates. Some but not all of the pottery shapes at Troy II were wheel made, notably large quantities of plates. The famous treasures found by Schliemann in levels most likely belonging to Troy II (Easton 1994; Tolstikow and Treijster 1996; Korfmann 2001a; Sazcı and Treister 2006) included thousands of objects made from gold, silver, electrum, bronze, carnelian, and lapis lazuli. Raw materials came from regions as far away as Afghanistan and central Asia. Comparanda for vessels like the two-handled cup ("depas amphikypellon"), jewelry, and other objects have been found in Bulgaria, Greece, Anatolia, Syria, and Mesopotamia.

An area of 9 ha. to the south of the citadel was protected by a palisade uncovered during recent excavations (Jablonka 2001). Houses have been discovered immediately outside the citadel. For the first time, the citadel of Troy II was surrounded by a larger settlement.

Troy II was twice destroyed by fire. After the first destruction, monumental buildings were replaced by densely clustered blocks of smaller houses in a development similar to what once again can be observed in Late Bronze Age Troy VIIa. After the second destruction, possible survivors were not able to reclaim the treasures. The following settlements Troy III–V were markedly less prosperous.

This course of events is typical of the second half of the third millennium BC. In Egypt, Mesopotamia, and Syria, states, urban centers, and writing had already been established. At the periphery, from Anatolia to Greece, secondary centers acted as nodes in a network of exchange and contact with these more developed areas (Sherratt 1997; Maran 1998; Korfmann 2001b). However, growth was not sustainable. At the end of the millennium, Troy was only one among many places struck by a crisis that affected the larger region from Greece and Anatolia to Egypt and the Middle East.

Troy III (ca. 2300–2200 BC), IV (ca. 2200–2000 BC), and V (ca. 2000–1750 BC)

In his attempt to expose the center of Troy II, Schliemann removed large parts of these levels without sufficient documentation. Blegen ascribed much of what Dörpfeld had called Troy III to a late phase of Troy II. The chronology of the period is still somewhat ambiguous. The impression that Troy III–V were rather modest villages may partly be due to the current state of research (cf. Sazcı 2001; Blum 2006).

The area of the citadel was covered by densely packed houses with stone and mud-brick walls. In Troy IV, domed ovens were introduced. Like the "red-cross bowls" of Troy V, this seems to be an influence from Anatolia. At the end of Troy V, however, Minoan imports appear.

During Troy III, the ramparts of Troy II might still have been in use. Houses from Troy V have been excavated to the west of the citadel, a clear sign that the settlement was growing once again.

TROY VI (CA. 1750–1300 BC)

The citadel of Troy VI by far surpassed its predecessors in size and workmanship (figures 63.1, 63.2). Regrettably, its center was removed when the mound was leveled in the Hellenistic period to make room for the temple of Athena, and more has been dug away by Schliemann.

At the end of the period, the fortification walls (cf. Klinkott 2004) enclosed an area of two hectares. The walls, built of large limestone blocks, are five meters wide and still preserved to a height of eight meters. Several towers were built against the walls. From the south gate, a paved and drained street led into the citadel. Inside the walls, large, two-storied, freestanding buildings with stone walls that resemble the fortification were built on terraces rising toward the center, almost each with a different layout. Megaron houses still occur, but there are also halls with pillars or columns or irregular floor plans. The massive house walls without ground-floor windows may have served defensive purposes, possibly indicating conflicts among the leading families.

The citadel was surrounded by a larger settlement that has been called the "lower city" (Korfmann 1995, 1997; Jablonka and Rose 2004; Becks 2006; Jablonka 2006). Its ill-preserved remains are covered by Hellenistic and Roman Ilion and can therefore be excavated only with difficulty and in small patches. This larger settlement was surrounded by a rock-cut defensive ditch comprising an area of ca. 30 hectares. The area inside was rather densely built up close to the citadel, but houses have also been found farther away. A systematic surface-find collection demonstrates that Late Bronze Age pottery is scattered across the whole area encompassed by the ditch. A small cemetery excavated by Blegen 450 meters south of the citadel is situated outside this area near a gate bridging the ditch.

No effort was spared to secure the settlement's water supply. A "cave" and spring 200 m southwest of the citadel previously known to Schliemann but only recently excavated is in fact a system of artificial tunnels and shafts that tap two aquifers (Frank, Mangini, and Korfmann 2002; Korfmann, Frank, and Mangini 2006). The citadel's northeast bastion was built around a large rectangular well accessible through a gate from the "lower city" outside.

Details of Late Bronze Age Troy resemble Mycenaean (megaron buildings, sawtooth vertical offsets that divide walls into sections) and Hittite (citadel-city, rectangular towers) architecture. Taken as a whole, however, the layout of the site is unparalleled.

The beginning of Troy VI is marked by important innovations. For the first time, horses were kept at Troy. Also making an appearance is a new, gray, wheelmade type of burnished pottery that is virtually identical with the Middle Helladic Minyan Gray ware of Greece (Pavúk 2005). With changing shapes, production of this West Anatolian Gray Ware continues until Troy VIIb. Beginning in mid-Troy VI, Tan Ware was produced from the same clays by using different firing techniques. Mycenaean shapes were imitated in both wares. Although only a small fraction of

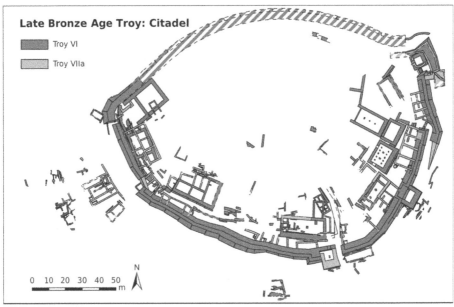

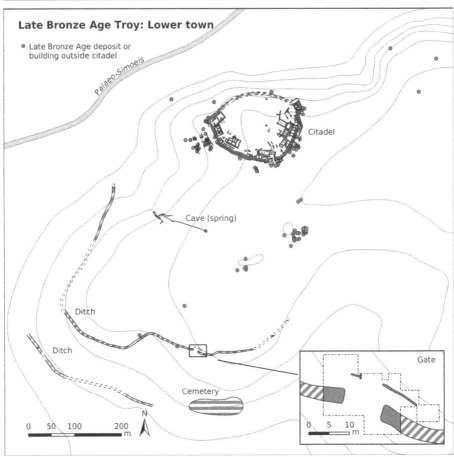

Figure 63.1. Plan of Late Bronze Age Troy. Citadel, Lower town with contemporary topography, rock-cut ditch, and gate (Troy VI) (copyright Peter Jablonka and Troia-Projekt, University of Tübingen).

Figure 63.2. Late Bronze Age Troy, partial view of the ruins. Citadel walls, tower, and East gate (foreground), Houses VI E and VI F (Troy VI), walls of smaller houses (Troy VII) just behind citadel wall (background) (copyright Troia-Projekt, University of Tübingen).

the pottery was imported, Minoan, Mycenaean, Cypriot, and Levantine imported pottery occurred throughout Troy VI and VII. West Anatolian Gray Ware has been found on Cyprus and along the Levantine coast. However, pottery or other finds from Hittite Anatolia are missing.

It is not clear whether an earthquake, a war, or an internal uprising caused a partial destruction of the city at the end of Troy VI.

TROY VIIA (CA. 1300–1180 BC)

The city was soon rebuilt (figures 63.1, 63.2). Some of the buildings inside the citadel were reused. Empty spaces were filled with smaller houses. In many rooms, storage vessels were sunk into the ground. This replacement of the almost palacelike buildings from Troy VI most likely reflects changes in society. Towers and mud-brick breastworks were added to the citadel walls, but at the same time new houses were also built outside (Becks, Rigter, and Hnila 2006). A stretch of yet another rock-cut ditch has been discovered to the south of the first one. The area of the settlement might therefore have been even larger than during Troy VI. Troy VIIa once again suffered destruction by fire.

TROY VIIB (CA. 1180–950 BC)

The first phase of Troy VIIb looks very much like a continuation of Troy VIIa. Houses were rebuilt inside and outside the citadel, the citadel walls reused, pottery—including some Mycenaean imports from Greece—remains almost the same, even if some handmade wares ("barbarian ware") begin to appear. Inside a house from Troy VIIb1 a biconvex bronze seal has been found, the only evidence of writing at Bronze Age Troy so far (Hawkins and Easton 1996). The Luwian hieroglyphic inscription gives the names of a woman and a man whose profession is specified as scribe.

In later phases of Troy VIIb, a new building technique—walls using upright stones ("orthostates")—and a handmade, knobbed ceramic ware ("Buckelkeramik") are introduced, both similar to finds from southeastern Europe and along the shores of the Black Sea. This has been thought to reflect the arrival of immigrant population groups.

Troy VIIb continued into the Iron Age, when Protogeometric amphoras were imported from Greece (Catling 1998; Becks 2003). Two phases of Troy VIIb ended in destruction by fire.

TROY VIII AND IX (BEGINNING CA. 950 BC)

South of the citadel wall, a complete sequence of layers from Troy VI into the Roman period has recently been excavated (Chabot Aslan 2002). This shows that, contrary to what Blegen believed, even during the "dark ages" that followed the end of the second millennium BC, Troy was never completely abandoned. The oldest houses of Greek Ilion are from the end of the 8th century BC. At the same time, ritual activities commenced at a sanctuary to the west of the Bronze Age citadel, whose magnificent walls were still visible. The city of Ilion prospered during the Hellenistic and Roman periods, not least by exploiting its ties with a mythical past politically and as a source of income from travelers. After all, even Roman emperors believed their ancestors descended from Troy's royal family.

HISARLIK, HITTITES, AND HOMER

Any discussion of the significance of archaeological remains uncovered at the site of Hisarlık-Troy inevitably leads back to the questions that Heinrich Schliemann naïvely asked: Is this the Troy of the *Iliad?* Did the Trojan War really happen?

If Schliemann had found nothing beneath the ruins of Greek and Roman Ilion, which could well have happened, the question would have been decided. But what he found is probably the most important Bronze Age site of western Anatolia and the northern Aegean. It has an exceptionally long, uninterrupted sequence of occupation. It always was a well-fortified stronghold, and its walls were renewed and enlarged after each of several destructions. Twice in the course of its long history— during Troy II and Troy VI–VII—it showed several characteristics of a central place that was urbanized at least in comparison to its regional setting: monumental and symbolic architecture, a citadel surrounded by a large settlement, finds that reflect craft specialization and foreign contacts. Late Bronze Age Troy was as large as medium-sized Hittite cities. On the other hand, several characteristics of Bronze Age civilizations seem to be absent: sculpture or wall paintings, and, with the exception of one seal, writing or other administrative practices.

Manfred Korfmann's reconstruction of Late Bronze Age Troy VI and VIIa with a densely built-up lower city surrounded not only by a ditch but also by fortifications modeled on the casemate walls known from Hittite cities has been subject to considerable criticism (Hertel and Kolb 2003; Kolb 2004; cf. Bryce 2006, 62–64). Even if Korfmann's interpretation of his findings was overly enthusiastic, much of this criticism is certainly going too far and can be refuted (Easton et al. 2002; Jablonka and Rose 2004). There is solid evidence for several phases of Late Bronze Age buildings outside, even far away, from the citadel. It has been shown that the ditches that encompass the lower city served a defensive purpose, and next to them bedrock-cuttings for a wooden construction supporting a rampart or wall have been found.

It has been said that Troy owed its prosperity at least in part to its geographic position between two continents and seas, at the crossing point of land routes from Anatolia to the Balkans and sea routes from the Aegean to the Black Sea (Korfmann 1986; Wright 1997; Höckmann 2003). Because of prevailing northerly winds and strong currents flowing into the Aegean, entry into the Dardanelles is difficult. Ships had to wait for favorable conditions, using anchorages in the Beşik Bay on the Aegean shore near Troy or in the bay at the mouth of the Scamander. This could have put Troy in a position to control and profit from traffic. There is indeed archaeological evidence for Late Bronze Age contacts between the Aegean and the Black Sea: Oxhide ingots and stone anchors of Aegean type have been found along the coast of Bulgaria, Aegean weapon types are common in the hinterland of the Black Sea, and a stone scepter from Romania has been found on the Uluburun shipwreck (Höckmann 2003). Minoan and Mycenaean pottery has been found at Troy and on the northeast Aegean islands but not along the shores of the Sea of Marmara or the Black Sea. This could mean that goods reached Troy from both directions but had to be exchanged there.

Late Bronze Age Troy may therefore be termed the capital of a city-state that controlled the surrounding landscape, the Troad. But are there written sources relating to its history? As early as 1923–1924, Emil Forrer and Paul Kretschmer noted that certain names of persons and countries on cuneiform tablets from the Hittite capital, Hattusa, were similar to names in the *Iliad*: Wilusa = (W)ilios; Alaksandu = Alexandros (the

Trojan prince Paris's other name); Ahhiyawa = Achaioi (Greeks). Based on other documents found since then, most scholars agree that Ahhiyawa was Mycenaean Greece or a part of it, that Wilusa was a country in northwest Anatolia, and that Troy most likely was its capital (Starke 1997; cf. Beckman 1999 for an English translation of relevant Hittite sources; Latacz 2004).

Very little is known of Wilusa's history. Around 1400 BC, Wilusa—at that time part of the land of Assuwa—first made contact with the Hittites. In the second half of the 14th century BC, Kukunni was king of Wilusa. Around 1300 BC, the Arzawan prince Pijamaradu attacked Alaksandu of Wilusa. Seeking protection, Alaksandu signed a treaty with the Hittite king Muwattalli II. Wilusa became a vassal state of the Hittite empire. At the end of the 13th century BC King Walmu of Wilusa was overthrown and reinstalled with help from the Hittites.

Conflicts between this kingdom of Wilusa and Mycenaean groups during the period of unrest at the end of the second millennium are not unlikely (Niemeier 1999). A faint remembrance of such conflicts may have survived the fall of Troy, the Hittite empire, and the Mycenaean palaces and could have become the core of the story of the Trojan War (Latacz 2004; cf. also Cline 1996, 1997).

Archaeological evidence for Hittite-Mycenaean contacts is scarce. Virtually no Hittite objects have been found west of Eskişehir, and Mycenaean finds from within the Hittite empire are rare. However, artifact distributions do not necessarily correspond to politics. In addition, a Mycenaean sword, booty from the war against Assuwa and dedicated to the storm god by King Tudhalya II, has been found in the Hittite capital, Hattusa (Ertekin and Ediz 1993; Cline 1996).

This scenario, which is based on circumstantial evidence, may be speculative, but it brings all of the available sources—Bronze Age archaeology, Hittite texts, Greek epic tradition—into one consistent narrative. Given the fragmentary nature of archaeological and textual sources, no more than that can probably be achieved.

BIBLIOGRAPHY

Beckman, Gary. 1999. *Hittite Diplomatic Texts*, 2d ed. Society of Biblical Literature Writings from the Ancient World, no. 7. Atlanta: Society of Biblical Literature Writings.

Becks, Ralf. 2003. "Troia VII: The Transition from the Late Bronze Age to the Early Iron Age." In *Identifying Changes: The Transition from Bronze to Iron Ages in Anatolia and Its Neighbouring Regions. Proceedings of the International Workshop, Istanbul, November 8–9, 2002*, ed. Bettina Fischer, Hermann Genz, Éric Jean, and Kemalettin Köroğlu, 41–53. Istanbul: Ege Yayınları.

———. 2006. "Troia in der späten Bronzezeit: Troia VI und Troia VIIa." In *Troia: Archäologie eines Siedlungshügels und seiner Landschaft*, ed. Manfred O. Korfmann, 155–66. Mainz: von Zabern.

———, Wendy Rigter, and Pavol Hnila. 2006. "Das Terrassenhaus im westlichen Unterstadtviertel von Troia." *Studia Troica* 16: 87–88.

Begemann, Friedrich. 2003. "On the Composition and Provenance of Metal Finds from Beşiktepe (Troia)." In *Troia and the Troad: Scientific Approaches. Natural Science in Archaeology*, ed. Günther A. Wagner, Ernst Pernicka, and Hans-Peter Uerpmann, 173–201. Berlin: Springer.

Blegen, Carl W. 1963. *Troy and the Trojans*. Ancient Peoples and Places. London: Thames and Hudson.

———, Cedric G. Boulter, John L. Caskey, and Marion Rawson. 1958. *Troy 4: The Settlements VIIa, VIIb, and VIII*. Princeton: Princeton University Press.

Blegen, Carl W., John L. Caskey, and Marion Rawson. 1951. *Troy 2: The Third, Fourth, and Fifth Settlements*. Princeton: Princeton University Press.

———. 1953. *Troy 3: The Sixth Settlement*. Princeton: Princeton University Press.

———, and Jerome W. Sperling. 1950. *Troy 1: The First and Second Settlements*. Princeton: Princeton University Press.

Blum, Stephan W. E. 2006. "Troia an der Wende von der frühen zur mittleren Bronzezeit: Troia IV und Troia V." In *Troia: Archäologie eines Siedlungshügels und seiner Landschaft*, ed. Manfred O. Korfmann, 145–54. Mainz: von Zabern.

Bryce, Trevor R. 2006. *The Trojans and Their Neighbours*. London: Routledge.

Catling, Richard. 1998. "The Typology of the Protogeometric and Subprotogeometric Pottery from Troia and Its Aegean Context." *Studia Troica* 8: 151–88.

Chabot Aslan, Carolyn. 2002. "Ilion before Alexander: Protogeometric, Geometric, and Archaic Pottery from D9." *Studia Troica* 12: 81–129.

Cline, Eric H. 1996. "Aššuwa and the Achaeans: The 'Mycenaean' Sword at Hattušas and Its Possible Implications." *BSA* 91: 137–51.

———. 1997. "Achilles in Anatolia: Myth, History, and the Aššuwa Rebellion." In *Crossing Boundaries and Linking Horizons: Studies in Honor of Michael Astour on His 80th Birthday*, ed. Gordon D. Young, Mark W. Chavalas, and Richard E. Averbeck, 189–210. Bethesda: CDL.

Dörpfeld, Wilhelm. 1902. *Troia und Ilion: Ergebnisse der Ausgrabungen in den vorhistorischen und historischen Schichten von Ilion 1870–1894*. Athens: Beck and Barth. Reprint, Osnabrück: Zeller, 1968.

Easton, Donald F. 1994. "Priam's Gold: The Full Story." *AnatSt* 44: 221–43.

———. 2002. *Schliemann's Excavations at Troia 1870–1873*. Studia Troica Monographien no. 2. Mainz: von Zabern.

———, J. David Hawkins, Andrew G. Sherratt, and E. Susan Sherratt. 2002. "Troy in Recent Perspective." *AnatSt* 52: 75–109.

Ertekin, Ahmet, and İsmet Ediz. 1993. "The Unique Sword from Boğazköy/Hattuša." In *Aspects of Art and Iconography: Anatolia and Its Neighbors. Studies in Honor of Nimet Özgüç*, ed. Machteld J. Mellink, Edith Porada, and Tahsin Özgüç, 719–26. Ankara: Türk Tarih Kurumu Basımevi.

Frank, Norbert, Augusto Mangini, and Manfred Korfmann. 2002. "230TH/U Dating of the Trojan 'Water Quarries.' " *Archaeometry* 44: 305–14.

Hawkins, J., David and Donald F. Easton. 1996. "A Hieroglyphic Seal from Troia." *Studia Troica* 6: 111–19.

Hertel, Dieter, and Frank Kolb. 2003. "Troy in Clearer Perspective." *AnatSt* 53: 71–88.

Heuck Allen, Susan. 1999. *Finding the Walls of Troy: Frank Calvert and Heinrich Schliemann at Hisarlık*. Berkeley: University of California Press.

Höckmann, Olaf. 2003. "Zu früher Seefahrt in den Meerengen." *Studia Troica* 13: 133–60.

Jablonka, Peter. 2001. "Eine Stadtmauer aus Holz: Das Bollwerk der Unterstadt von Troia II." In *Troia: Traum und Wirklichkeit. Begleitband zur Ausstellung*, ed. Archäologisches Landesmuseum Baden-Württemberg et al., 391–94. Stuttgart: Theiss.

———. 2006. "Leben außerhalb der Burg: Die Unterstadt von Troia." In *Troia: Archäologie eines Siedlungshügels und seiner Landschaft*, ed. Manfred O. Korfmann, 167–80. Mainz: von Zabern.

———, and Charles Brian Rose. 2004. "Late Bronze Age Troy: A Response to Frank Kolb." *AJA* 108: 615–30.

Kayan, İlhan, Ertuğ Öner, Levent Uncu, Beycan Hocaoğlu, and Serdar Vardar. 2003. "Geoarchaeological Interpretations of the Troian Bay." In *Troia and the Troad: Scientific Approaches*, ed. Günther A. Wagner, Ernst Pernicka, and Hans-Peter Uerpmann, 379–401. Berlin: Springer.

Klinkott, Manfred. 2004. "Die Wehrmauern von Troia VI: Bauaufnahme und Auswertung." *Studia Troica* 14: 33–85.

Kolb, Frank. 2004 "Troy VI: A Trading Center and Commercial City?" *AJA* 108: 577–613.

Korfmann, Manfred. 1983. *Architektur, Stratigraphie, und Befunde: Demircihüyük. Die Ergebnisse der Ausgrabungen 1975–1978, no. 1.* Mainz: von Zabern.

———. 1986. "Troy: Topography and Navigation." In *Troy and the Trojan War: A Symposium Held at Bryn Mawr College, October 1984*, ed. Machteld J. Mellink, 1–16. Bryn Mawr, Penn.: Bryn Mawr College.

———. 1995. "Troia: A Residential and Trading City at the Dardanelles." In *Politeia*, 173–83.

———. 1997. "Troia, an Ancient Anatolian Palatial and Trading Center: Archaeological Evidence for the Period of Troia VI/VII." In *The World of Troy: Homer, Schliemann, and the Treasures of Priam*, ed. Deborah Boedeker, 51–73. Washington, D.C.: Society for the Preservation of the Greek Heritage.

———. 2001a. "Der 'Schatz A' und seine Fundsituation: Bemerkungen zum historischen und chronologischen Umfeld des 'Schatzfundhorizontes' in Troia." In *Beiträge zur vorderasiatischen Archäologie, Winfried Orthmann gewidmet*, ed. Jan-Waalke Meyer, Mirko Novák, and Alexander Pruß, 212–35. Frankfurt: Archäologisches Institut der Universität.

———. 2001b. "Troia als Drehscheibe des Handels im 2. und 3. vorchristlichen Jahrtausends: Erkenntnisse zur Troianischen Hochkultur und zur Maritimen Troiakultur." In *Troia: Traum und Wirklichkeit. Begleitband zur Ausstellung*, ed. Archäologisches Landesmuseum Baden-Württemberg et al., 355–68. Stuttgart: Theiss.

———, ed. 2006. *Troia: Archäologie eines Siedlungshügels und seiner Landschaft*. Mainz: von Zabern.

———, Norbert Frank, and Augusto Mangini. 2006. "Eingang in die Unterwelt: Die Höhle von Troia und ihre Datierung." In *Troia: Archäologie eines Siedlungshügels und seiner Landschaft*, ed. Manfred O. Korfmann, 337–42. Mainz: von Zabern.

Korfmann, Manfred, and Bernd Kromer. 1993. "Demircihüyük, Beşik-Tepe, Troia: Eine Zwischenbilanz zur Chronologie dreier Orte in Westanatolien." *Studia Troica* 3: 135–72.

Korfmann, Manfred O., and Dietrich Mannsperger. 2005. *Troia/Wilusa: General Background and a Guided Tour*. Istanbul: Çanakkale-Tübingen Troia Vakfı/Ege Yayınları.

Kouka, Ourania. 2002. *Siedlungsorganisation in der Nord- und Ostägäis während der Frühbronzezeit*. Internationale Archäologie, no. 58. Rahden (Westfalen): Leidorf.

Kraft, John C., İlhan Kayan, Helmut Brückner, and George Rapp. 2003. "Sedimentary Facies Patterns and the Interpretation of Paleogeographies of Ancient Troia." In *Troia and the Troad: Scientific Approaches*, ed. Günther A. Wagner, Ernst Pernicka, and Hans-Peter Uerpmann, 361–77. Berlin: Springer.

Kromer, Bernd, Manfred Korfmann, and Peter Jablonka. 2003. "Heidelberg Radiocarbon Dates for Troia I to VIII and Kumtepe." In *Troia and the Troad: Scientific Approaches*, ed. Günther A. Wagner, Ernst Pernicka, and Hans-Peter Uerpmann, 43–54. Berlin: Springer.

Latacz, Joachim. 2004. *Troy and Homer: Towards a Solution of an Old Mystery*. New York: Oxford University Press.

Maran, Josef. 1998. *Kulturwandel auf dem griechischen Festland und den Kykladen im späten 3. Jahrtausend v. Chr. Studien zu den kulturellen Verhältnissen in Südosteuropa und dem zentralen Mittelmeerraum in der späten Kupfer- und frühen Bronzezeit*. Universitätsforschungen zur Prähistorischen Archäologie, no. 53. Bonn.

Niemeier, Wolf-Dietrich. 1999. "Mycenaeans and Hittites in War in Western Asia Minor." In *Polemos*, 141–55.

Pavúk, Peter. 2005. "Aegeans and Anatolians: A Trojan Perspective." In *Emporia*, 269–79.

Robinson, Marcelle. 2007. *Schliemann's Silent Partner: Frank Calvert (1828–1908). Pioneer, Scholar, and Survivor*. Philadelphia: Xlibris.

Sazcı, Göksel. 2001. "Gebäude mit vermutlich kultischer Funktion: Das Megaron in Quadrat G6." In *Troia: Traum und Wirklichkeit. Begleitband zur Ausstellung*, ed. Archäologisches Landesmuseum Baden-Württemberg et al., 384–90. Stuttgart: Theiss.

———, and Mikhail Treister. 2006. "Troias Gold: Die Schätze des dritten Jahrtausends vor Christus." In *Troia: Archäologie eines Siedlungshügels und seiner Landschaft*, ed. Manfred O. Korfmann, 209–18. Mainz: von Zabern.

Séfériadès, Michel. 1985. *Troie I: Matériaux pour l'étude des sociétés du Nord-Est égéen au début du bronze ancien*. Cahiers (Éditions Recherche sur les civilisations), no. 15. Paris: Éditions Recherche sur les civilisations.

Sherratt, Andrew G. 1997. "Troy, Maikop, Altyn Depe: Bronze Age Urbanism and Its Periphery." In *Economy and Society in Prehistoric Europe: Changing Perspectives*, ed. Andrew G. Sherratt, 457–70. Edinburgh: Edinburgh University Press.

Starke, Frank. 1997. "Troia im Kontext des historisch-politischen Umfeldes Kleinasiens im 2. Jahrtausend." *Studia Troica* 7: 447–88.

Studia Troica. 1991–2007. Vols. 1–17. Mainz: von Zabern. Vols. 1–15 ed. Manfred Korfmann; vols. 16–17 ed. Peter Jablonka, Ernst Pernicka, and Brian Rose.

Tolstikow, Wladimir P., and Michail J. Trejster. 1996. *Der Schatz aus Troja: Schliemann und der Mythos des Priamos-Goldes: Katalogbuch Ausstellung Puschkin-Museum Moskau 1996/97*. Stuttgart: Belser.

Traill, David A. 1995. *Schliemann of Troy: Treasure and Deceit*. New York: St. Martin's.

Wright, James C. 1997. The Place of Troy among the Civilizations of the Bronze Age. In *The World of Troy: Homer, Schliemann, and the Treasures of Priam*, ed. Deborah Boedeker, 33–43. Washington, D.C.: Society for the Preservation of the Greek Heritage.

CHAPTER 64

ULUBURUN SHIPWRECK

CEMAL PULAK

EXCAVATION of the Uluburun shipwreck near Kaş in southern Turkey has yielded one of the largest and richest assemblages of Bronze Age trade goods and raw materials ever found (figure 64.1). The finds provide significant insight into, and our clearest glimpse of, Late Bronze Age maritime and terrestrial trade in the Mediterranean.

The 1984–1994 excavation of the shipwreck, under the auspices of the Institute of Nautical Archaeology (INA) at Texas A&M University (Bass 1986; Bass, Pulak, Collon, and Weinstein 1989; Pulak 1988, 1997, 1998, 2001, 2005a, 2005b, 2008, 288–305), revealed an immense cargo of raw materials, manufactured goods, a collection of premium, exotic items, personal effects, items for shipboard use, ship's equipment, and a small portion of the hull. The conservation and analysis of nearly seventeen tons of artifacts recovered from the site demonstrate the diversity and complexity of the assemblage.

THE SITE

The site was briefly visited by archaeologists for the first time in the fall of 1982, and an extended survey of the site in 1983 revealed several dozen copper ingots arranged in four rows. The ingots, along with several types of pottery vessels from the wreck, suggested that the ship sank sometime during the late 14th century BC. Full-scale excavations began in 1984 (Bass, Frey, and Pulak 1984).

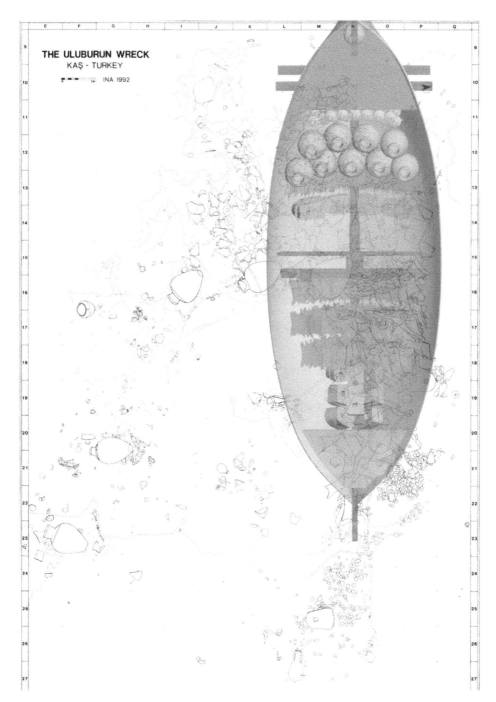

Figure 64.1. Plan and reconstructed ship shown in final resting position on the seabed before disintegrating and spilling cargo and other artifacts down the steep slope (plan by author; ship graphics by Shih-Han Lin).

Due to the depth of the site (44–61 m), the cargo had been spared from both salvage and pillaging. Unfortunately, the depth limited divers to short periods on the sea bottom, making excavation difficult. Over the eleven seasons of excavation, more than 22,400 dives were logged, totaling more than 6,600 hours spent excavating an area of approximately 250 square meters.

The majority of artifacts were scattered over the steep, rocky bottom on which the ancient ship had come to rest at an angle of about 30 degrees, with the bow facing downslope, and at a 15 degree list to starboard. As the ship settled under the weight of its cargo, the wooden hull gradually collapsed and deteriorated. Some of the artifacts settled into level spots, while others tumbled down the slope. Despite provenience problems involving the displaced cargo, detailed documentation and computer modeling have permitted a reasonably accurate reconstruction of the ship and the original placement of the cargo within the hold.

THE SHIP'S CARGO

The Uluburun ship had a carrying capacity of at least twenty tons burden. This was calculated by tallying the recovered objects, including about ten tons of copper and one ton of tin ingots, pottery storage jars, and other objects, as well as twenty-four stone anchors and approximately one ton of cobble ballast. The overall estimate is based on the assumption that all of the ceramic storage jars were filled with materials that approximated the density of water. It is impossible to determine exactly how much of the original perishable cargo disappeared due to the marine environment, but some fragments of delicate organic items did survive. Most of the ship's cargo is of Syro-Canaanite and Cypriot origin; along with other factors, this suggests that the vessel was heading for a destination in the Aegean.

The ship's cargo, perhaps of an elite or royal nature, consisted mostly of raw materials, although finished goods were also present. The primary freight consisted of about ten tons of copper ingots and about one ton of tin ingots. Also on board were discoid glass ingots, terebinth resin (*Pistacia* sp.) and oil in Canaanite jars, hippopotamus and elephant teeth, African blackwood (Egyptian ebony: *Dalbergia melanoxylon)* logs, spices and condiments, murex shell opercula (probably for use as an incense ingredient), and orpiment.

Manufactured articles include Cypriot pottery packed in large storage jars (pithoi), copper-alloy vessels, glass and faience beads, inlaid seashell rings, ostrich eggshell vases, duck-shaped ivory containers and containers made of boxwood, and probably garments or textiles, among other items. Galley wares, tools, fishing implements, and foodstuffs were for shipboard use, while beam balances and balance weights, assorted beads, cylinder seals (Collon 2005, 2008), writing boards, weapons, and a hoard of gold and silver jewelry and

Figure 64.2. Excavation of one of four rows of copper oxhide ingots carried on the ship. The oxhide ingots were laden from one side of the ship to the other in an overlapping, herringbone configuration in order to prevent slippage of ingots during transit (courtesy of the author and the Institute of Nautical Archaeology).

scrap precious metals represent some of the personal effects of those on board. Several of the artifacts are unique, and the number of finds has vastly enhanced our understanding of Late Bronze Age trade as it is known from the terrestrial archaeological record.

Some of the objects found during the excavation are of a perishable nature and survived only because they were quickly covered by sediment or became trapped between or beneath copper ingots, which later generated corrosion products that preserved them. Study of the Uluburun ship's artifacts has shown that the ship transported, at least in part, a shipment of high-end goods both in the form of raw materials and manufactured items likely en route from the elite of one polity to another.

The Uluburun shipwreck has yielded the single largest assemblage of Bronze Age metal ingots (figure 64.2). The primary freight excavated from the wreck consists of about ten tons of Cypriot copper in the form of 348 large rectangular slab ingots, each with an average weight of about twenty-four kilograms but originally heavier before corrosion (Pulak 2000b, 140–46; 2001, 18–22).

Of these, 317 are of the typical oxhide shape with a protrusion at each of the four corners. In addition, 31 unique ingots, while of similar form, have only two protrusions, both of which are on one side of the longitudinal axis. There are also six small rectangular slab ingots with less-pronounced corner protrusions than the oxhide ingots, which weigh about 10 kilograms each. Also found were about 120 plano-convex discoid or bun-shaped copper ingots.

The ingots are made of pure copper (Hauptmann, Maddin, and Prange 2002, 13). Lead-isotope analysis of the oxhide and bun ingots indicate an origin consistent with Cypriot copper ores and suggest that the great majority were cast with copper from the same source, likely obtained from the Apliki and other mines located in the Solea axis ores of northwestern Cyprus (Pulak 2000b, 147–50; Gale 2005). The Uluburun copper ingots, therefore, were obtained from Cyprus, as is true of nearly all contemporary and later oxhide ingots discovered in the Mediterranean.

The Uluburun ingots were stored in four distinct rows, overlapping one another like roof shingles. Potential slippage between ingots during transit was minimized by careful stowage and orientation. The bottom layers were placed on cushioning beds of brushwood and branches, also known as dunnage, to distribute the weight of the load and to protect the hull timbers.

In addition to the carefully stowed copper ingots, about one ton of tin ingots was carried on board in several shapes, but mostly in the oxhide form. Many of the tin ingots had been cut into sections (mostly quadrants) before being placed on board, indicating that they were not pristine ingots obtained directly from the original source but mostly gathered after having been cut up and distributed (Pulak 2000b, 150–53; 2001, 22–23).

Much of the tin on the wreck had been transformed into a nonmetallic phase of tin with the consistency of toothpaste, which disintegrated when disturbed. Chemical analysis revealed the tin to be surprisingly pure (Hauptmann, Maddin, and Prange 2002, 16). It is impossible to determine the exact amount of tin originally on the ship since some of it was lost due to corrosion, but one ton of tin was recovered in the excavation. This amount, when alloyed with the copper, would have produced eleven tons of bronze in the commonly used alloy ratio of 1 to 10.

Generally assumed to be lacking in the Bronze Age Mediterranean, tin was likely obtained through trade and shipped from the Levantine coast. Although sources of Bronze Age tin remain unknown, ancient texts indicate that it was obtained from regions east of Mesopotamia, probably in the Middle East or central Asia (Dossin 1970, 101–106; Muhly 1985, 282–83). Lead-isotope analysis, however, suggests that the Uluburun tin ingots originated from two separate sources: the Taurus Mountains in south-central Turkey and a source outside the Mediterranean, probably located to the east—near or in Afghanistan (Pulak 2000b, 153–55; Weeks 1999, 60–61). It is likely that both the copper and the tin ingots were transshipped and stored at an entrepôt on the Syro-Palestinian coast before being loaded on the Uluburun ship.

Glass ingots, each generally in the shape of a roughly truncated cone or disk, were also part of the cargo. Due to the partial or complete deterioration of some of the glass ingots, it is not possible to calculate the exact number carried on board;

a minimum estimate, which takes into account completely deteriorated fragments, is about 175 pieces. With an average weight of about 2 kilograms per ingot, the ship was carrying an estimated 350 kilograms of glass in at least four colors: dark blue (imitating lapis lazuli), light blue (imitating turquoise), purple (imitating amethyst), and dark yellow (probably imitating amber), with the last two colors represented by only three ingots. The ingots represent glass that was being transported as a raw material to be melted down and formed into beads and other objects. These glass ingots are likely the *mekku* and *ehlipakku* of the Amarna letters, also mentioned in an Ugaritic text as having been exported from cities along the Syro-Palestinian coast (Pulak 2001, 25–30).

More than two-thirds of the approximately 150 Canaanite jars aboard the Uluburun ship together contained more than half a ton of a yellowish substance chemically identified as a *Pistacia* sp. resin or terebinth resin, likely from the *Pistacia atlantica* tree, making it the second largest consignment on the ship after the copper and tin ingots (Pulak 2001, 33–36). The resin on the Uluburun ship provided the first opportunity for chemical identification of this material by modern analytical methods (Mills and White 1989; Hairfield and Hairfield 1990); it represents the largest ancient deposit of this material ever found.

Analysis of the pollen extracted from the resin (Jacobsen, Bryant, and Jones 1998), combined with malacological evidence of endemic terrestrial snails found in the jars (Welter-Schultes 2008), suggests that the resin was gathered from trees growing in the western and northern regions of the Dead Sea in Israel. The discovery of such a large quantity of resin in a commercial context means that terebinth resin may now be added to the list of important raw materials exported from the Levant.

The Uluburun ship carried a cut section of a large elephant tusk and fourteen hippopotamus teeth, consisting of eight incisors and six canines (Pulak 2001, 37–39). Bronze Age ivory was routinely carved into various objects, including combs, plaques, furniture inlays, containers, and pins. Elephant tusk was the material of choice since it yielded large sizes and quantities of solid ivory, but hippopotamus teeth were more commonly used due to their availability. As differentiation between the two types of ivory requires specialist diagnosis, the full extent of the trade in hippopotamus ivory is only recently being assessed. A study of carved ivory objects from Ugarit in the fourteenth and thirteenth centuries BC, however, shows that the majority were made of hippopotamus rather than elephant ivory (Caubet and Poplin 1992, 92).

African blackwood (*Dalbergia melanoxylon*) was an important component of Bronze Age trade. This is the *hbny* or 'ebony' of ancient Egyptians, which originated in tropical Africa. More than two dozen small logs and fragments thereof were found on the Uluburun ship, although it cannot be known how many logs were originally aboard (Pulak 2001, 30–31). The ebony component of the cargo fits well with elite goods constituting some of the cargo, but its export in log form suggests that its destination was a palace or similarly centralized entity with a workshop capable of transforming this difficult-to-carve wood into luxury items.

Coriander, black cumin or nigella, and safflower were all carried on the Uluburun ship, together with sumac (Haldane 1993, 352; Pulak 2001, 37). Ancient oils were pretreated with astringents like coriander and then scented with rose and sage. The oil base was usually made from olives, almonds, and other seeds. Both olives and almonds were recovered from the Uluburun ship, but it is not known whether these items were intended for shipboard use or export.

Alongside raw materials, the Uluburun ship also carried manufactured goods, predominantly in the form of Cypriot pottery. Nine large pithoi and a pithoid-krater were found on the shipwreck, serving both as containers during transit and probably also as items of export. These jars are of typical Cypriot types known from various sites on and outside of Cyprus. Most contained perishable cargo, probably oils or grain, along with fruit (pomegranates) and perhaps other commodities, but at least three of them contained additional Cypriot pottery.

The approximately 155 pieces of Cypriot pottery contained in the pithoi include oil lamps, wall brackets, jugs, various bowls, and other vessels (Hirschfeld 2005; 2008). The most common vessels are white shaved juglets, white slip II milk bowls, oil lamps, and base ring II bowls (Pulak 2001, 40–42; 103–104). The sheer quantity of the Cypriot wares at Uluburun contrasts with what has been found in the Aegean to date. The ship carried more than twice the amount of Cypriot wares known from sites all around the Late Bronze Aegean. This disparity demonstrates that the archaeological record, even with respect to nonperishable goods, does not necessarily reflect the full nature and magnitude of the trade in question.

Copper-alloy and tin vessels were carried aboard the Uluburun ship (Pulak 2001, 42–43). Many of these artifacts had mostly disintegrated through corrosion, although sturdier components survived to reveal their approximate shapes and sizes. Elements such as a riveted spout hint at the variety of metal forms that were present but which may never be fully reconstructed due to the lack of sufficient preservation. Excavated tin vessels include a pilgrim flask, a plate, and a twin-handled mug. Only one example of each tin vessel was found, suggesting that these were special-purpose items, probably prestige gifts. Bronze Age tin objects are extremely rare, and those from the Uluburun shipwreck have nearly doubled the number of tin objects known.

In addition to the raw glass, glass beads were also recovered. Many have lost their original colors due to decomposition, and some were likely carried in perishable containers such as cloth or leather bags, which have since disintegrated. Smaller glass beads found packed inside a Canaanite jar were intended for export (Pulak 2005b, 590). Faience beads of red, yellow, green, black, and blue were found dispersed throughout the wreck, as well as an encrusted cluster estimated to include seventy thousand beads (Pulak 2005b, 590).

An oblong ovoid lid and a circular base from two boxwood containers were recovered from a pithoid-krater. These likely fell into the jar after the ship sank, were quickly covered with sediment, and were thus preserved. Poorly preserved fragments of other objects indicate that wooden vessels of high-quality material and artistry were carried on the ship, although nearly all of this cargo has likely perished, making it difficult to discern the exact quantity and nature of these items.

The Uluburun ship carried three ostrich eggshells, one of which was found intact (Pulak 2008, 324–25). These were exotica likely destined to be transformed by Aegean artisans into ornate vases by the addition of spouts and bases of faience, precious metals, or other materials. A blue glass disk with concave surfaces found separately, however, may have served as a base for one of the eggshells. If so, then at least one Uluburun eggshell was exported as a finished vase, probably to serve as a value-laden gift for elite tastes, representing the first documented shipment of ostrich eggshell vases from the Levant to the Aegean.

Gold and silver, mostly in the form of intact and scrap jewelry but also as a gold ring ingot, silver bar ingots, and amorphous lumps, were found (Pulak 2001, 23–25; 2005b, 594–97). The weight of a single gold chalice constitutes nearly half of the approximately 530 grams of gold found on the ship (Pulak 2008, 353–55). Much of the gold and silver, whether intact or scrap, was excavated in the same general area of the site that corresponds to the stern of the ship, suggesting that it was likely kept together and used as bullion when required. Even pristine jewelry may have been used as bullion, for a number of silver bangles and various gold pieces had sections cut off with a chisel. Most of the gold and silver jewelry is of Canaanite origin (Pulak 2008, 347–48, 350–52, 355–58), but several Egyptian pieces, including a unique gold scarab naming the Egyptian queen Nefertiti (Weinstein 1989, 17–23; 2008), were also present.

Trade

A counterclockwise route has been proposed for the Uluburun ship specifically and for Late Bronze Age, long-distance maritime trade in the Eastern Mediterranean generally. The Uluburun ship epitomizes the means by which disparate raw materials and finished goods reached the Late Bronze Age Aegean and regions beyond. The wreck is dated to the last quarter of the fourteenth century BC, one of the most active and colorful periods of the Bronze Age Eastern Mediterranean.

During this century, seafaring Canaanites traded extensively with Egypt, Cyprus, and the Aegean, and these lands served as hubs for overland trade that connected Egypt, Mesopotamia, and the Hittite Empire. While the exact nature of long-distance trade is not fully understood, ancient textual evidence suggests that much of it was conducted as directed trade at the palace level under the guise of 'royal gift exchange.' However, private enterprises that involved opportunistic, coastal trade undoubtedly existed on a smaller scale, as exemplified by the Cape Gelidonya ship (Bass 1967), which sank about a century later than the Uluburun ship.

Long-distance trade was a high-risk endeavor that necessitated extensive preparations, provisions for en-route security, and investment of substantial capital for the procurement of goods. Such demanding requirements, along with most aspects of social, economic, political, and military life, were best provided by the state (Liverani 1987; Peltenberg 1991, 161–70). While private merchants engaged in retail domestic trade and, to some extent, modest interregional commerce, much of the long-distance interregional exchange in the Late Bronze Age Near East was likely controlled or influenced by the palaces or elite centers under the guise of gift exchange. Even seemingly private mercantile enterprises appear to have been conducted by merchants who were in some manner connected to or operating around the palace.

Gift exchange is a form of directed trade. A vessel is loaded in one port for a specific destination rather than engaging in opportunistic coastal trading or cabotage between minor ports. Such is the nature of trade illustrated by many of the Amarna letters (Sherratt and Sherratt 1991). Gift exchange is high commerce, prestigious trade, probably based on the concept of reciprocity. Luxurious gifts may have served specific purposes such as dowries, commemoration of special occasions, or tribute, while the exchange of raw and finished goods, probably operating through the use of credit, would also have been accompanied by prestige gifts. Concepts of prestige and peer groups were probably prevalent in the Late Bronze Age and may have fueled some of this interregional trade.

The Likely Route of the Uluburun Ship

Assigning a specific home port for the ship and its crew is not easy, but certain artifacts point to a regional source. Stone anchors are good indicators of a ship's home port, as they were not cargo and were probably not transported very far before being loaded onto a ship. Galley wares, such as lamps and pots used by the crew, are also useful in identifying a ship's home port.

Preliminary petrographic analysis suggests that the source of the clay used for the Uluburun galley wares, including the oil lamps, and the stone used for the anchors was in the general area between the northern coast of Israel and southernmost coastal Lebanon. A coastal port site in this region, such as Tell Abu Hawam, may have been the home port of the Uluburun ship or at least the origin of its final voyage. The site's well-placed location on the coast, its prominence among coastal sites in the region, the period during which it flourished as a port city, its identification as the port associated with the major inland site of Megiddo, and the presence at the site of many objects similar to those found on the Uluburun ship render it a likely candidate as the departure point from which the Uluburun ship began its ill-fated journey westward.

Significant quantities of Cypriot pottery found at Tell Abu Hawam suggest that these were imported from Cyprus and stockpiled for export aboard ships like the one that sank at Uluburun with its large cargo of Cypriot pottery. Other goods, such as the Cypriot copper ingots, tin ingots, and ebony logs obtained from distant lands, were also likely stockpiled in warehouses at Tell Abu Hawam before they were loaded on the ship. That the Cypriot pottery aboard the Uluburun ship came from an entrepôt like Tell Abu Hawam rather than directly from a Cypriot port is suggested by the nature of the Cypriot pottery assemblage itself and the manner in which it was stacked inside larger storage jars aboard the ship. The considerable variation in the style, size, and artisanship among the individual examples of a given vessel type suggests an assemblage of leftover pieces in a warehouse rather than direct procurement from a specific production site on Cyprus, which would have resulted in a more homogenous pottery collection. Moreover, in one of the storage jars aboard the ship, a locally made bowl was stacked together with Cypriot bowls, an arrangement that would be less likely had the Cypriot pottery been loaded at Cyprus itself.

From its point of origin, the Uluburun vessel headed north along the Syro-Palestinian coast, past Cyprus, and then sailed west along the southern coast of Turkey, where it sank. Contemporary shipwrecks along the southern coast of Turkey suggest that ships navigating this route hugged the coast during their journeys westward. After negotiating the prominent cape at Uluburun, westbound ships continued toward the southern corner of the Anatolian peninsula, whence they sailed either west, in the direction of southern Greece, or north, into the Aegean Sea.

Why the wreck occurred at Uluburun will probably never be known with certainty, but while sailing in a northwesterly direction, the ship may have come dangerously close to the promontory before tacking and failed to clear it. It is also conceivable that the vessel was dashed against the rocky promontory by an unexpected southerly wind or that it experienced some navigational difficulty while trying to negotiate the cape.

PEOPLE ON BOARD THE SHIP

It is impossible to know the fate of the crew and passengers on the Uluburun ship, but surviving artifacts offer insight into their identities. The ship was crewed by Canaanite merchants and sailors who were accompanied by two Mycenaean Greeks of elite status and a third individual who may have been from an area north of Greece.

Analysis of approximately 150 balance pan weights suggests the presence of four Canaanite merchants aboard, one of whom was the chief merchant. The majority of the weights were based on a mass standard with a unit (shekel) of ca. 9.3 grams. Each of the four merchants was equipped with two sets of weights based on this mass standard, one consisting of sphendonoid weights with small denominations for precision weighing of precious objects and metals and a second, larger set consisting of domed weights for bulk weighing of heavier, everyday goods (Pulak 2000a).

A few additional sets of precision sphendonoid weights that conformed to other Near Eastern mass standards of 8.3 and 7.4 grams were probably kept for use as reference sets (Pulak 2000a, 259, 261). A unique set of bronze animal-shaped (zoomorphic) weights was most likely the possession of the chief merchant, reflecting his high status (Pulak 2000a, 256, 262). The four Canaanite merchants proposed for the Uluburun ship compare favorably with a maritime scene in the tomb of Kenamun (T. 162) at Thebes (Davies and Faulkner 1947, 40–46), which depicts a Syrian merchant fleet arriving in Egypt.

The number of excavated weapons also appears to agree with the proposed presence of four merchants aboard. The chief merchant, who may also have been the ship's captain, was in charge of the ship and its cargo; he must have carried the only Canaanite sword found on the ship. Almost fully preserved, it is a solid-cast bronze weapon with its hilt embellished with ebony and ivory inlays, indicative of the owner's elite status (Pulak 1988, 20–23; 1997, 246–48). Among the daggers recovered, two are similar to the Canaanite sword in design and embellishment (Pulak 2008, 366–67). These daggers were visible symbols of status roughly equivalent to the sword. A Canaanite tanged dagger may have belonged to the fourth merchant.

Little can be determined about the rest of the crew since their personal effects would not have included distinctive and valuable items. Among the objects recovered are several relatively plain daggers, knives, simple pendants, and other basic personal effects. The exact number of the crew is unknown, but it is certain that they used Canaanite lamps and galley wares.

Mycenaean objects such as fine tableware, swords, spears, glass relief beads, faience and amber beads, knives, razors, broad chisels, and lentoid seals were also aboard the ship (Pulak 2005c). Since the lentoid seals, broad chisels, and double axes are of the variants found on the Greek mainland rather than on Crete, the Mycenaeans aboard were more likely associated with the mainland than with Crete, which also implies that the ship's ultimate destination lay somewhere on the Greek mainland (Pulak 2005c, 296). Some of the items of the assemblage, such as the swords, the glass relief beads, and the seals, occur in pairs and were probably the personal effects of two elite Mycenaeans. These individuals were probably emissaries or the 'messengers' of ancient texts, who served as representatives of the recipients, overseeing the safe delivery of the precious goods carried on the Uluburun ship.

A final individual may be attested by the presence of a sword—for which parallels are found in southern Italy and Sicily (Vagnetti and Lo Schiavo 1989, 223–24; Pulak 2001, 45–47; Lo Schiavo 2005, 399–400), and Albania—a bronze pin, spearheads, and a scepter-mace with parallels in Romania and Bulgaria (Pulak 1997, 253–54; Buchholz 1999; Buchholz and Weisgerber 2005, 149). This shadowy figure, who probably hailed from a region to the north of Greece, may have been another messenger or a temporary mercenary seeking to elevate his local status through service to the Mycenaeans (Pulak 2001, 45–48). The presence of swords and spears on board the vessel may hint at the dangers of piracy in the Late Bronze Age Mediterranean.

THE HULL

Since most of the hull and some of the cargo perished long before the excavation commenced, estimates of the ship's size and shape are partly speculative. Even so, the distribution of the recovered remains and surviving portions of the hull suggest that the ship had a length of ca. 15 m and a beam of ca. 5 m, with a cargo capacity of at least twenty tons burden. The hull was built of Lebanese cedar (*Cedrus libani*), and the hull planks were fastened to each other with pegs and tenons of Kermes oak (*Quercus coccifera*) (Pulak 1999). Archaeological examples such as the Egyptian funerary ships of Khufu (ca. 2589–2566 BC) and Senusret III (ca. 1874–1855 BC) at Dashur, as well as the Cape Gelidonya wreck on Turkey's southern coast, dated to ca. 1200 BC, were also built of Lebanese cedar.

The cedar hull planking was joined edge-to-edge with mortise-and-tenon joints. In this type of construction, a mortise, or socket, was cut into the faces of the two planks to be joined. A rectangular piece of wood, called a tenon, was inserted into each mortise, and the two pieces of planking were joined together. An oak peg driven through the joint on either side of the plank seam locked the assembly; the closely spaced tenons added considerable strength to the planking. Although the earliest documented nonmaritime use of this type of joint in the Near East dates from the Middle Bronze IIB period—much later than in Egypt—the use of pegged mortises and tenons in shipbuilding most likely developed on the Levantine littoral and spread westward.

Perhaps the most unusual feature of the Uluburun hull is its keel, the primary longitudinal member that forms the ship's spine; this is the earliest archaeologically documented example of its use. The Uluburun keel, which is slightly wider than it is high and extends upward into the hull, may best be described as a 'proto-keel' (Pulak 2002). It demonstrates an understanding that a hull needed to be reinforced by the addition of a strong longitudinal member. Unlike true keels that project well beyond the exterior of the hull in later sailing ships, however, such a keel would have contributed little in helping the ship hold course when sailing against unfavorable winds.

SUMMARY

Excavation of the Uluburun ship has revealed one of the largest and most impressive assemblages of Bronze Age goods ever found. The ship's cargo consisted mostly of raw materials, although finished goods were also present. Galley wares, tools, and some foodstuffs were for shipboard use, while cylinder seals, weapons, jewelry, and balance scales and weights represent some of the personal effects of the Canaanite merchants and crew on board.

Petrographic analysis of the ship's galley wares and stone anchors suggests that an area somewhere between the northern coast of Israel and the southern coast of southern Lebanon was the ship's most likely home port. The origins of the ship's cargo indicate that the vessel was westward bound, and the Mycenaean personal effects on board indicate the presence of two Mycenaean 'messengers' and a third 'foreigner,' who was most likely from northern Greece or a region to the north of Greece. This evidence suggests that the ship's destination lay in the Aegean, likely on the Greek mainland.

The Uluburun ship, therefore, captures in transit tangible evidence of the flow of goods and raw materials from the Levant toward the Aegean during the Late Bronze Age. At the same time, it provides a rare and precious glimpse of those people involved in long-distance trade and the ships on which they traveled.

BIBLIOGRAPHY

Bass, George F. 1967. *Cape Gelidonya: A Bronze Age Shipwreck. Transactions of the American Philosophical Society* 57(8). Philadelphia: American Philosophical Society.

———. 1986. "A Bronze Age Shipwreck at Ulu Burun (Kaş): 1984 Campaign." *AJA* 90: 269–96.

———, Donald A. Frey, and Cemal Pulak. 1984. "A Late Bronze Age Shipwreck at Kaş, Turkey." *IJNA* 13: 271–79.

Bass, George F., Cemal Pulak, Dominique Collon, and James Weinstein. 1989. "The Bronze Age Shipwreck at Ulu Burun: 1986 Campaign." *AJA* 93: 1–29.

Buchholz, Hans-Günther. 1999. "Ein aussergewöhnliches Steinzepter im östlichen Mittelmeer." *PZ* 74: 68–78.

———, and Gerd Weisgerber. 2005. "Prominenz mit Steingerät." In *Das Schiff von Uluburun: Welthandel vor 3000 Jahren, Katalog der Ausstellung des deutschen Bergbau-Museums Bochum vom 15. Juli 2005 bis 16. Juli 2006*, ed. Ünsal Yalçın, Cemal Pulak, and Rainer Slotta, 149–53. Bochum: Deutsches Bergbau-Museum Bochum.

Caubet, Annie, and François Poplin. 1992. "La place des ivoires d'Ougarit dans la production du Proche Orient ancien." In *Ivory in Greece and the Eastern Mediterranean from the Bronze Age to the Hellenistic Period*, ed. J. Lesley Fitton, 91–100. British Museum Occasional Papers 85. London: British Museum Press.

Collon, Dominique. 2005. "Rollsiegel aus dem Schiffswrack von Uluburun." In *Das Schiff von Uluburun: Welthandel vor 3000 Jahren, Katalog der Ausstellung des deutschen Bergbau-Museums Bochum vom 15. Juli 2005 bis 16. Juli 2006*, ed. Ünsal Yalçın, Cemal Pulak, and Rainer Slotta, 109–14. Bochum: Deutsches Bergbau-Museum Bochum.

———. 2008. "Cylinder Seals." In *Beyond Babylon: Art, Trade, and Diplomacy in the Second Millennium B.C.*, ed. Joan Aruz, Kim Benzel, and Jean M. Evans, 362–65. The Metropolitan Museum of Art, New York: Yale University Press.

Davies, Norman de Garis, and Raymond O. Faulkner. 1947. "A Syrian Trading Venture to Egypt." *JEA* 33: 40–46.

Dossin, G. 1970. "La route de l'étain en Mésopotamie au temps de Zimri-Lim." *Revue d'Assyriologie* 64: 97–106.

Gale, Noel. 2005. "Die Kupferbarren von Uluburun." In *Das Schiff von Uluburun: Welthandel vor 3000 Jahren, Katalog der Ausstellung des deutschen Bergbau-Museums Bochum vom 15. Juli 2005 bis 16. Juli 2006*, ed. Ünsal Yalçın, Cemal Pulak, and Rainer Slotta, 141–47. Bochum: Deutsches Bergbau-Museum Bochum.

Hairfield, Hampton H., and Elizabeth M. Hairfield. 1990. "Identification of a Late Bronze Age Resin." *Analytical Chemistry* 62(1): 41A–45A.

Haldane, Cheryl. 1993. "Direct Evidence for Organic Cargoes in the Late Bronze Age." *World Archaeology* 2: 348–60.

Hauptmann, Andreas, Robert Maddin, and Michael Prange. 2002. "On the Structure and Composition of Copper and Tin Ingots Excavated from the Shipwreck of Uluburun." *BASOR* 328: 1–30.

Hirschfeld, Nicolle. 2005. "Die Zyprische Keramik aus dem Schiffswrack von Uluburun." In *Das Schiff von Uluburun: Welthandel vor 3000 Jahren, Katalog der Ausstellung des deutschen Bergbau-Museums Bochum vom 15. Juli 2005 bis 16. Juli 2006*, ed. Ünsal Yalçın, Cemal Pulak, and Rainer Slotta, 103–108. Bochum: Deutsches Bergbau-Museum Bochum.

———. 2008. "Cypriot Pottery." In *Beyond Babylon: Art, Trade, and Diplomacy in the Second Millennium B.C.*, ed. Joan Aruz, Kim Benzel, and Jean M. Evans, 321–23. The Metropolitan Museum of Art, New York: Yale University Press.

Jacobsen, Maria, Vaughn M. Bryant, Jr., and John G. Jones. 1998. "Preliminary Pollen Analysis of Terebinth Resin from a Bronze Age Mediterranean Shipwreck." In *New Developments in Palynomorph Sampling, Extraction, and Analysis*, ed. Vaughn M. Bryant and John H. Wrenn, 75–82. AASP Contributions Series no. 33. Houston: American Association of Stratigraphic Palynologists Foundation.

Liverani, Marco. 1987. "The Collapse of the Near Eastern Regional System at the End of the Bronze Age: The Case of Syria." In *Centre and Periphery in the Ancient World*, ed. Michael Rowlands, Mogens Larsen, and Kristian Kristiansen, 66–73. New Directions in Archaeology. New York: Cambridge University Press.

Lo Schiavo, Fulvia. 2005. "Metallhandel im zentralen Mittelmeer." In *Das Schiff von Uluburun: Welthandel vor 3000 Jahren, Katalog der Ausstellung des deutschen Bergbau-Museums Bochum vom 15. Juli 2005 bis 16. Juli 2006*, ed. Ünsal Yalçın, Cemal Pulak, and Rainer Slotta, 399–414. Bochum: Deutsches Bergbau-Museum Bochum.

Mills, John S., and Raymond White. 1989. "The Identity of the Resins from the Late Bronze Age Shipwreck at Ulu Burun (Kaş)." *Archaeometry* 31: 37–44.

Muhly, James D. 1985. "Sources of Tin and the Beginnings of Bronze Metallurgy." *AJA* 89: 275–91.

Peltenberg, Edgar. 1991. "Greeting Gifts and Luxury Faience: A Context for Orientalising Trends in Late Mycenaean Greece." In *Bronze Age Trade*, 162–79.

Pulak, Cemal. 1988. "The Bronze Age Shipwreck at Ulu Burun, Turkey: 1985 Campaign." *AJA* 92: 1–37.

———. 1997. "The Uluburun Shipwreck." In *Res Maritimae: Cyprus and the Eastern Mediterranean from Prehistory to Late Antiquity, Proceedings of the Second International Symposium "Cities on the Sea," Nicosia, Cyprus, October 18–22, 1994*, ed. Stuart Swiny, Robert L. Hohlfelder, and Helena W. Swiny, 233–62. Cyprus American Archaeological Research Institute Monograph Series 1. Atlanta: Scholars Press.

———. 1998. "The Uluburun Shipwreck: An Overview." *IJNA* 27: 188–224.

———. 1999. "The Late Bronze Age Shipwreck at Uluburun: Aspects of Hull Construction." In *Point Iria Wreck*, 209–38.

———. 2000a. "The Balance Weights from the Late Bronze Age Shipwreck at Uluburun." In *Metals Make the World Go Round: The Supply and Circulation of Metals in Bronze*

Age Europe. Proceedings of a Conference Held at the University of Birmingham in June 1997, ed. Christopher F. E. Pare, 247–66. Oxford: Oxbow.

———. 2000b. "The Cargo of Copper and Tin Ingots from the Late Bronze Age Shipwreck at Uluburun." In *Anatolian Metal*, vol. 1, ed. Ünsal Yalçın, 137–57. Der Anschnitt, Beiheft 13. Bochum: Deutsches Bergbau-Museum Bochum.

———. 2001. "The Cargo of the Uluburun Ship and Evidence for Trade with the Aegean and Beyond." In *Italy and Cyprus in Antiquity, 1500–450 BC: Proceedings of an International Symposium Held at the Italian Academy for Advanced Studies in America at Columbia University, November 16–18, 2000*, ed. Larissa Bonfante and Vassos Karageorghis, 13–60. Nicosia: Severis Foundation.

———. 2002. "The Uluburun Hull Remains." In *Tropis VII: 7th International Symposium on Ship Construction in Antiquity: Pylos 1999 Proceedings*, ed. Harry E. Tzalas, 615–34. Athens: Hellenic Institute for the Preservation of Nautical Tradition.

———. 2005a. "Discovering a Royal Ship from the Age of King Tut: Uluburun, Turkey." In *Beneath the Seven Seas: Adventures with the Institute of Nautical Archaeology*, ed. George F. Bass, 34–47. London: Thames and Hudson.

———. 2005b. "Das Schiffswrack von Uluburun." In *Das Schiff von Uluburun: Welthandel vor 3000 Jahren, Katalog der Ausstellung des deutschen Bergbau-Museums Bochum vom 15. Juli 2005 bis 16. Juli 2006*, ed. Ünsal Yalçın, Cemal Pulak, and Rainer Slotta, 55–102, with accompanying catalog, 559–633. Bochum: Deutsches Bergbau-Museum Bochum.

———. 2005c. "Who Were the Mycenaeans aboard the Uluburun Ship?" In *Emporia*, 295–310.

———. 2008. "The Uluburun Shipwreck and Late Bronze Age Trade." In *Beyond Babylon: Art, Trade, and Diplomacy in the Second Millennium B.C.*, ed. Joan Aruz, Kim Benzel, and Jean M. Evans, 288–305, 306–10, 313–21, 324–33, 336–42, 345–48, 350–58, 366–78. The Metropolitan Museum of Art, New York: Yale University Press.

Sherratt, Susan, and Andrew Sherratt. 1991. "From Luxuries to Commodities: The Nature of Mediterranean Bronze Age Trading Systems." In *Bronze Age Trade*, 351–86.

Vagnetti, Lucia, and Fulvia Lo Schiavo. 1989. "Late Bronze Age Long-distance Trade in the Mediterranean: The Role of the Cypriots." In *Early Society in Cyprus*, ed. Edgar Peltenburg, 217–43. Edinburgh: Edinburgh University Press.

Weeks, Lloyd. 1999. "Lead Isotope Analyses from Tell Abraq, United Arab Emirates: New Data Regarding the 'Tin Problem' in Western Asia." *Antiquity* 73: 49–64.

Weinstein, James. 1989. "The Bronze Age Shipwreck at Ulu Burun: 1968 Campaign, Part 3: The Gold Scarab of Nefertiti from Ulu Burun: Its Implications for Egyptian History and Egyptian-Aegean Relations." *AJA* 93: 17–29.

———. 2008. "Nefertiti Scarab." In *Beyond Babylon: Art, Trade, and Diplomacy in the Second Millennium B.C.*, ed. Joan Aruz, Kim Benzel, and Jean M. Evans, 358. The Metropolitan Museum of Art, New York: Yale University Press.

Welter-Schultes, Francisco W. 2008. "Bronze Age Shipwreck Snails from Turkey: First Direct Evidence for Oversea Carriage of Land Snails in Antiquity." *Journal of Molluscan Studies* 74: 79–87.

CHAPTER 65

WESTERN ANATOLIA

ALAN M. GREAVES

DESPITE its physical proximity to the region, western Anatolia is often overlooked in discussions of the Bronze Age Aegean (Renfrew 2005, 153–54). This is partly due to a lack of identified sites (compare sites in Greece with those in Turkey in Hope Simpson 1965) and perhaps also to a tendency among scholars to retroject the modern Greek-Turkish political border onto past societies (Greaves 2007, 3). Factors that have resulted in this lack of identified Bronze Age sites include the sheer size of the Anatolian region, the dynamic character of its coastline (Brükner et al. 2006), and the relatively late adoption of extensive survey as a method of site prospection (Greaves 2007, 7). The excavation of some key coastal, multiperiod sites is also hampered by the overburden of later deposits (Greaves 2007, 7–9). Nevertheless, new findspots of Aegean material appear annually, and important new excavations have been initiated, especially at Bademgediği Tepe and Çine-Tepecik.

Although there is as yet no single synthetic survey volume, a number of useful publications do exist (e.g., Mee 1978; Niemeier 2007b; Erkanal et al. 2008). The purpose of this chapter is to highlight and critique those core themes that scholars most frequently revisit. These include the date and nature of the earliest contact between the cultures of the Aegean and those of western Anatolia, the Minoan 'colonization' of Miletus, Mycenaean pottery and materials in the region, and questions of the historical-archaeological interface (see figure 65.1).

EARLIEST AEGEAN-ANATOLIAN CONTACTS

The Troad dominated discussions of the interaction between the prehistoric Aegean and Anatolia for much of the twentieth century (Şahoğlu 2004, 97). In particular, much has been made of the significance (or otherwise) of Troy-Hisarlık I/II, the

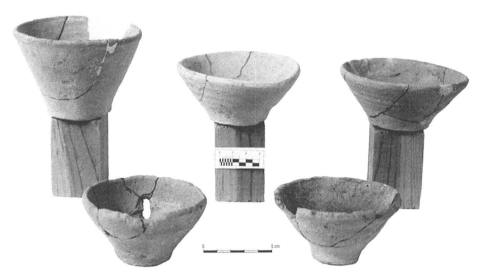

Figure 65.1. Conical cups from Iasos, including imports from Miletus (Momigliano 2008, figure 18) (courtesy of Nicoletta Momigliano).

level of the great treasure and the so-called Troia Maritime Culture. Until relatively recently, therefore, the central and southern areas of western Anatolia were under-represented in both data and discussion, and it was even possible to consider that the region may have been only thinly populated (Yakar 1991).

The state of our information improved considerably with the discovery and excavation of a number of sites around the Bay of İzmir as a consequence of the initiation of the Izmir Region Excavations and Research Project (IRERP), which has provided us with a wealth of data about the bay, a key area of the west coast of Anatolia (Tuncel 2008). Here, two excavated sites have revealed important early strata—Bakla Tepe and Liman Tepe. The inland site of Bakla Tepe is positioned within easy reach of the sea and has a burial area that included grave goods from central and western Anatolia and the west Aegean (Şahoğlu 2005, 346–49).

Liman Tepe is a coastal, multiperiod *höyük* (or settlement mound), the lower part of which, including a built harbor, is now under water. Here, connections to the Aegean cultures can be securely detected from the EBI fortified settlement. In the EBII period, the site featured a massive tower, a fortification wall, and a central 'corridor building' of a type known in Greece. The site was a regional center, and this building may represent its 'central authority,' although religious paraphernalia suggest a cult dimension to its function. Through its status as a harbor, Liman Tepe had contacts that extended beyond the Aegean to the Eastern Mediterranean, the Balkans, and the Caucasus.

Farther south, extensive regional surveys have now identified a number of inland *höyüks* (Günel 2003, 2005), but investigation of the major coastal sites of Ephesos, Miletus, and Iasos is hampered by their classical period remains, which make the exposure of extensive horizontal strata difficult (Şahoğlu 2005, 346n8; Greaves 2007, 7).

Settlements across western Anatolia appear to be strategically located to take advantage of landscape features that are advantageous to trade (Günel 2005; Şahoğlu 2005). Major sites are often typified by having an upper citadel and a lower town (Şahoğlu 2005). Most of the identified sites take the form of *höyüks,* but Miletus and Iasos appear to have been flat, which suggests different depositional or postdepositional histories.

Even from the Anatolian LNI period, similarities exist in assemblages from the Troad to the east Aegean islands, the Cyclades, and the Balkans (Takaoğlu 2006). Western Anatolia was evidently already part of an extensive sphere of cultural interaction that encompassed the Aegean, which was to be the backdrop of extensive EB interaction. Questions about the nature of earliest Aegean-Anatolian interaction have therefore shifted from 'when' and 'if' the two regions were in contact to 'how' and 'why.'

Procurement of raw materials was a key factor in early Aegean-Anatolian interactions. Aegean obsidian from Melos and Yali is found in western Anatolia (Joukowsky 1986, 279–85; Georgiadis 2008). Anatolian copper and tin found their way into the Aegean (Gale 2008), and trade in these most precious Bronze Age commodities is likely to have been of central importance (Greaves 2002, 32–37; Şahoğlu 2005, 341).

Exchange was not only in raw materials but also in behaviors. Cycladic figurines are reported from Cnidus (Bent 1888, 82) and from Miletus, a site that has also yielded six Anatolian-type figurines (W.-D. Niemeier 2005, 2–3, pl. 3). These may represent direct east-west trade, prestige goods radiating out from the islands, or ritual activity (Broodbank 2000, 308; Niemeier 2005, 2). There is also evidence of the adoption of Anatolian drinking behaviors at EH III Lerna, Kastri, and Lefkandi I (Rutter 2008).

Two models for understanding EBA trade networks have been proposed: Vasif Şahoğlu's maritime 'Anatolian Trade Network' (2005), spanning Anatolia and with 'colonies' in the Aegean; and Turan Efe's terrestrial 'Great Caravan Route' (2007), crossing Anatolia from Cilicia to the Troad but essentially bypassing southwest Anatolia and the Aegean altogether. These models provide a useful basis for future discussion and impetus for further survey, excavation, and scientific analysis.

'Minoans' in Western Anatolia

In the Middle Bronze Age, the issue of western Anatolia's interaction with the Aegean becomes one of understanding 'Minoan' involvement in the region. In this context, Miletus appears to have been an exceptional site by whatever criteria one judges it. Then situated on an island, it was well positioned to access both the Aegean, by means of its harbor, and central Anatolia via the adjacent Büyük Menderes (ancient Maeander) Valley. The site has provided rich evidence of sustained Minoan involvement. Although other sites on the west coast of Anatolia, most notably Iasos but also Çeşme, Troy, Kömüradası, and Tavşanadası, have yielded Minoan material, none as yet have the same quantities of material as Miletus.

Excavations at Miletus have shown that the earliest settlement, founded on bedrock, dates to the Late Chalcolithic (Aegean Final Neolithic) period (Miletus I) and was followed by an EBA 'offering place' (II) (Niemeier 2005, 2). In the next level (III), finds included imported MM IB and MM II Kamares pottery, Minoan domestic forms produced in local fabric, a kiln of a type known from Crete, two seals, and a sealing. This phase of the site has been connected with Cretan expansion in the Protopalatial period, the so-called Eastern String, and trade in metals (Niemeier 1998a).

The next phase of the settlement (IVa) was destroyed at the time of the Thera eruption, which also affected Iasos and other regions of Anatolia (Huber, Bichler, and Musilek 2003), and was then leveled off and rebuilt (IVb). Miletus IV featured much imported pottery from across Crete, hundreds of conical cups, a predominance of Minoan-style domestic pottery made in local clay, a fragment of a potter's wheel, a disc-shaped weight, two seals, and the active use of Linear A inscribed on local pots before firing. In Miletus IVa, the remains so far uncovered appear to indicate a cult area featuring figurines, the remains of animal sacrifice, wall paintings, and thirteen plaster offering tables set around a series of square, mud-brick altars that the excavator describes as "a typical Minoan feature" (Niemeier 2005, 6).

At Iasos, contact with Crete began in the Protopalatial period, as evidenced by three sherds found in later contexts (Momigliano 2008, 20–21). Stronger evidence comes for contact between the site and Neopalatial Crete (MM IIIB–LM 1A) and includes the Minoan-style architecture of the "almost monumental" Building F (Momigliano 2008, 22), Linear A potters' marks incised on local clay before firing, stone objects, and abundant pottery, including about fifty imported pieces, hundreds of conical cups, and a few dozen loomweights. Local potters evidently made imitations of Minoan styles, but Minoan imports and Minoan-type pottery still constitute only 5% of an essentially Anatolian-dominated assemblage. This level of the site was sealed by a thick layer of ash from Thera, dating to LM IA. After this, contact with Crete declined and eventually ended with the destruction of the "flimsy" Building B probably in LM IB; contact with the Aegean was not renewed until LH IIIA1.

Farther north on the Anatolian coast, Minoan materials at Çeşme and Troy appear to have come from neighboring 'Minoanized' centers in the north Aegean through their engagement in local trade networks rather than through direct contacts with Crete (Momigliano 2008, 33). In LM IA–B contexts across the Dodecanese and the Carian-Ionian coast, finds of southeast Aegean light-on-dark and dark-on-light wares (previously thought to be Kamares or Kamares Imitation but probably made at Seraglio on Kos) tell a complex story of emulation of Minoan styles and of trade (Momigliano 2007).

Figure 65.2. An imported Mycenaean bowl of a type found widely in
LHIII B1–2 and C, from Çine-Tepecik (Günel 2006, figure 3)
(courtesy of Sevinç Günel).

This extensive and complex pattern of evidence demands careful attention to
the precise nature of the material, as well as its contexts and relative quantities.
For example, although Nicoletta Momigliano (2008) has demonstrated that there
is evidence for the presence of 'Minoans' at Iasos at least in the person of potters
and architects, there is no evidence for direct contact with the island of Crete itself,
as many of the Minoan or Minoan-style products found there could have been
traded through intermediary settlements such as Miletus. In fact, a number of conical cups found at the site are apparently made in Milesian fabric (see figure 65.2).
Even at Miletus itself, with its wealth of Minoan material, the evidence is complex
and requires careful consideration of its precise form and context (e.g., Kaiser 2005;
Raymond 2005).

Due to the limited extent of the horizontal exposures at Miletus, it is not possible to fully apply Keith Branigan's (1981) model of Minoan colonization, which is
based on sitewide understandings of architecture and ethnicity. Therefore, in order
to better define and understand the nature of any Minoan presence, Niemeier and
Niemeier have produced a set of diagnostic criteria (1997; 1999, 544–45). Applying
these and noting especially the 95% predominance of Minoan-style domestic
wares, they argue that there was indeed a Minoan presence at Miletus IV but rule
out Branigan's 'community colony' in favor of his 'governed' or 'settlement' models
(W.-D. Niemeier 2005, 9).

New studies of Minoan overseas settlements have furthered debate and
opened up new avenues for consideration by separating Cretans and processes

of 'Minoanization' from direct Minoan political control (Broodbank 2004), for questioning what we mean by 'Minoans' in Anatolian contexts (Momigliano 2008), and for considering Minoan materials and behaviors within local contexts (Knappett and Nikolakopoulou 2008). However, as Branigan's model might be used to portray Minoans as colonizers and Anatolian populations as the colonized, we need to consider theoretical modes of interaction between Crete and Anatolia that do not necessarily always place Minoan culture in the ascendant. For example, Momigliano (2008) has recast Iasos as a site at which the local Anatolian elite 'consumed' Minoan-style architecture, imports, and imitations executed in local materials by presumably itinerant 'Minoan' artisans.

When one looks to the interior of western Anatolia, evidence for Minoan influence is less apparent. The palace at Beycesultan is comparable in size to those of Crete, but direct evidence of Minoan materials here and at Aphrodisias is nonexistent. The intriguing bull-leaping scene on a vase from Hüseyindede (Taracha 2002) and a mud-brick platform comparable to that found at Miletus IVa from Acem Höyük (Öztan 2003, 43–44, figure 10) show that images and behaviors that one might consider typically Minoan can also appear in Anatolian contexts. The processes by which such intercultural exchanges may have occurred, under what circumstances, and even in which direction they traveled are likely to be items of much future research.

ANATOLIA AND THE MYCENAEAN AEGEAN

The refined typology of Mycenaean pottery makes it an essential dating tool in western Anatolia, where the long-running sequences of the dominant local pottery tradition, exemplified by Beycesultan, cannot be so closely defined. However, its usefulness for dating should not lead us to think that Mycenaean political influence extended into the region. New findspots of Mycenaean pottery in Anatolia are reported almost annually (e.g., Günel 2006 at Çine-Tepecik; see figure 65.3), and local imitations abound (e.g., Özgünel 1996; Meriç and Mountjoy 2001, 2002). At Miletus V, an apparently Mycenaean settlement, eight pottery kilns were found, and its products were widely distributed (Niemeier 2005, 10–16).

Once again, understanding the precise context of discovery during stratigraphic excavation calls for careful consideration of a number of issues. The relative quantities of Mycenaean/local wares will affect the interpretation of their function, but such quantification is not always an easy task. At Miletus, for example, estimates of the ratio of Mycenaean pottery at the site have varied from just 5% of the total to the majority of it (Ünal 1991, 23–25; Niemeier 2005, 12, respectively).

Different levels of intensity of Mycenaean pottery can be observed north and south of the Samsun Dağı peninsula, with higher concentrations to the south. Explanations for this observed distribution pattern have included the existence

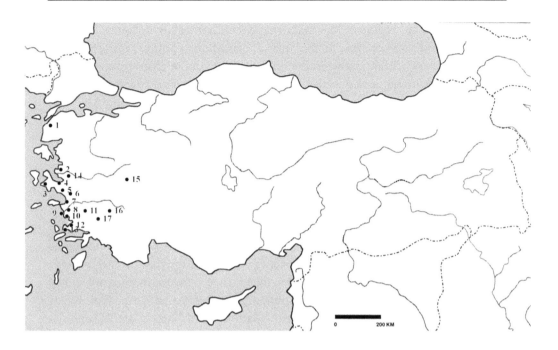

	Modern Name	Classical Name	Bronze Age Name
1	Hisarlık (Troy)	Ilion	Wilusa
2	Panaztepe	?	?
3	Çeşme	?	?
4	Liman Tepe	Klazomenai	?
5	Bakla Tepe	?	?
6	Torbali, Bademgediği Tepe	Metropolis	Puranda (?)
7	Selçuk–Ayasoluk Hill	Ephesos	Apaša
8	Balat	Miletus	Millawanda
9	Tavşanadası	?	?
10	Kömüradası	Teichioussa	?
11	Beşparmak Dağı	Mt. Latmos	?
12	Kiyikişlacik	Iasos	?
13	Müskebi (Ortakent)	?	?
14	Karabel	?	?
15	Beycesultan	?	?
16	Geyre	Aphrodisias	?
17	Çine-Tepecik	?	?

Key Bibliography

1. Blegen, Caskey, Rawson, Sperling 1950; Blegen, Caskey, Rawson 1951, 1953; Blegen, Boulter, Caskey, Rawson 1958; Mellink 1986; Easton et al. 2002; Hertel, Kolb 2004. 2. Günel 1999. 3. Şahoğlu 2007. 4. Erkanal 2008b. 5. Erkanal 2008a; Erkanal, özkan 1997, 1998. 6. Meriç 2003, 2007; Meriç, Mountjoy 2002. 7. Bammer, Muss 1996; Büyükkolanci 2007. 8. Greaves 2002; Kaiser 2005; Niemeier & Niemeier 1997, 1999; Niemeier 1997, 1998a, 2005, 2007a; Raymond 2005, 9. Joukowsky 1986, 722–24. 10. Voigtländer 2004. 11. Peschlow-Bindokat 2001. 12. Benzi 2005; Momigliano 2005, 2007, 2008. 13. Boysal 1967. 14. Hawkins 1998. 15. Lloyd, Mellaart 1962, 1965; Lloyd 1972; Mellaart, Murray 1995. 16. Joukowsky 1986. 17. Günel 2006, 2007.

Figure 65.3. Modern, Classical, and Bronze Age sites. On the accompanying table, the numbers in the left-hand column relate to the numbered sites on the map (courtesy of the author).

of some form of regional Mycenaean-type cultural entity (Mountjoy 1998). Mycenaean pottery penetrated farther inland than Minoan pottery, and the reason for its extensive circulation and imitation is evidently more than just aesthetic—for instance, its presence in burials suggests that it had a valued funerary purpose. In fact, many of the most important findspots are burials, including Müskebi, Miletus (Değirmentepe), Ephesos (Ayasoluk), and Panaztepe. At Müskebi, forty-eight chamber tombs were found of typical Mycenaean type and usage, but at Panaztepe, Mycenaean pottery, swords, jewelry, and tombs were incorporated into a distinctively local, hybrid funerary culture (Mee 1998, 140–45). There are fewer settlement sites than burials, and only at Miletus can funerary and settlement evidence be compared.

Again, the distribution of Aegean materials in Anatolia cannot be divorced from their meaning to the local populations of western Anatolia. However, understanding those populations has often been overshadowed not only by the Aegean cultures but also by the Hittites of central Anatolia. Just as Mycenaean finds are widely reported, so, too, are new Hittite findspots such as Beşparmak Dağı, Kadı Kalesi (Greaves and Helwing 2004), and Ephesos (Bammer and Muss 2007). Substantial Hittite monuments have been found in the region, including Hittite-style walls of Miletus and carved rock reliefs at Ephesos (İçten and Krinzinger 2004), Beşparmak Dağı, and Karabel.

However, questions of Hittite-Aegean interaction in western Anatolia, rather than their respective interactions with local populations, have commanded, indeed commandeered, much of the academic discussion of the region to an unhealthy degree (Ünal 1991). The local population were the agents who determined the nature and extent of the penetration of Mycenaean culture into western Anatolia, but relatively little is known about these people and their encounter with the materials and behaviors of the Aegean. This situation is now changing, but one cannot escape the fact that the start and end points of many discussions of the region have been a narrow range of historical controversies rather than the study of the region and its people in their own right and, subsequent to that, their relations with their Aegean and central Anatolian neighbors.

HISTORICAL CONTROVERSIES

Discussions of Bronze Age western Anatolia are frequently dogged by attempts to equate its archaeology with textual references, such as the Cretan origins of Miletus and the so-called Troy Question and Ahhiyawa Question.

Various classical sources cite foundation myths that somehow connect Miletus to Crete (Ephorus *ap.* Strabo 14.1.6; Apollodorus 3.2; Pausanias 7.2.1–3; Ovid *Met.* 9.450). However, these sources are chronologically distanced and likely to preserve negligible historical evidence (Greaves 2002, 67–68). In fact, they are a distraction from the proper investigation of Miletus's first settlement since they can be read to imply a single act of foundation on virgin territory, which is at odds with its complex archaeology.

More controversial is the so-called Troy Question, that is, the question of whether the site of Hisarlık can be identified with the Troy of the Homeric epics. Blegen linked Troy VIIA with the Trojan War, but even recently scholars have disagreed about the importance or otherwise of the site. This debate was an academic explosion, but one that ultimately produced more heat than light (Easton et al. 2002; Hertel and Kolb 2004).

The Ahhiyawa Question revolves around locating certain place names known from records in the Hittite capital at Boğazköy-Hattusa, with archaeological phenomena on the ground (see figure 65.1, column 3). One of these names, Ahhiyawa, has been related to a putative Mycenaean state in one form or another.

New archaeological and epigraphic discoveries make frequent additions to these topics of debate (e.g., Hawkins 1998; Meriç and Mountjoy 2002; W.-D. Niemeier 1998b, 2007b). However, although connecting sites with sources may potentially be useful, for example, by providing a context of vacillating political control at Miletus-Millawanda that can aid its interpretation, the importance of such connections is overvalued. To put it in context, of the ca. twenty-five thousand tablets in the Hittite archives, only twenty-eight refer to Ahhiyawa and then almost always in connection with the troublesome Anatolian power of Arzawa. Wherever Ahhiyawa was, its dealings with the Hittite state were peripheral to the latter party. A more appropriate objective for research might be to better understand the indigenous cultures of western Anatolia, such as Arzawa, and to locate their dealings with the Aegean and Hittite cultures within local contexts.

Summary

In all periods, it is necessary to understand the presence of Aegean materials, behaviors, and people within the context of the local cultures of western Anatolia, which are generally less well understood than those of their Aegean neighbors. Issues of a disparity in quantity and nature of the evidence between the two, particularly away from the Aegean coast, and the pursuit of historical *topoi* will continue to pose problems to the proper discussion of this region. However, our paradigms for understanding the nature of interaction between these two are shifting away from ones of Aegeo-centric 'colonization' toward more subtle discussions of interaction that seek to validate the agency of local populations. New and ongoing field projects will continue to make western Anatolia an exciting arena for archaeological research and debate.

BIBLIOGRAPHY

Bammer, Anton, and Ulrike Muss. 1996. *Das Artemision von Ephesos.*Mainz: von Zabern.

———. 2007. "Ein frühes Quellheiligtum am Ayasolukhügel in Ephesos." *Anatolia Antiqua* 15: 95–101.

Bent, J. Theodore. 1888. "Discoveries in Asia Minor." *JHS* 9: 82–87.

Benzi, Mario. 2005. "Mycenaeans at Iasos? A Reassessment of Doro Levi's Excavations." In *Emporia*, 205–16.

Blegen, Carl W., Cedric G. Boulter, John L. Caskey, and Marion Rawson. 1958. *Troy IV: Settlements VIIa, VIIb, and VIII.* Princeton: Princeton University Press.

Blegen, Carl W., John L. Caskey, and Marion Rawson. 1951. *Troy II: General Introduction: The Third, Fourth, and Fifth Settlements.* Princeton: Princeton University Press.

———. 1953. *Troy III: General Introduction: The Sixth Settlement.* Princeton: Princeton University Press.

———, and Jerome Sperling. 1950. *Troy I: General Introduction: The First and Second Settlements.* Princeton: Princeton University Press.

Boysal, Yusuf. 1967. "New Excavations in Caria." *Anadolu (Anatolia)* 11: 31–56.

Branigan, Keith. 1981. "Minoan Colonisation." *BSA* 76: 23–33.

Broodbank, Cyprian. 2000. *An Island Archaeology of the Early Cyclades.*New York: Cambridge University Press.

———. 2004. "Minoanisation." *PCPS* 50: 46–91.

Brückner, Helmut, Marc Müllenhoff, Roland Gehrels, Alexander Herda, Maria Knipping, and Andreas Vött. 2006. "From Archipelago to Floodplain: Geographical and Ecological Changes in Miletus and Its Environs during the Past Six Millennia (Western Anatolia, Turkey)." *Zeitschrift für Geomorphologie* N.F., Suppl. vol. 142: 63–83.

Büyükkolancı, Mustafa. 2007. "Apaša, das alte Ephesos und Ayasoluk." In *Frühes Ionien eine Bestandsaufnahme*, ed. Justus Cobet, Volkmar von Graeve, Wolf-Dietrich Niemeier, and Konrad Zimmermann, 21–26. Mainz am Rhein: von Zabern.

Easton, Donald, J. David Hawkins, Andrew Sherratt, and E. Susan Sherratt. 2002. "Troy in Recent Perspective." *AnatSt* 52: 75–109.

Efe, Turan. 2007. "Theories of the 'Great Caravan Route' between Cilicia and Troy: The Early Bronze Age III Period in Inland Western Anatolia." *AnatSt* 57: 47–64.

Erkanal, Hayat. 2008a. "Liman Tepe: New Light on Prehistoric Aegean Cultures." In *ANCEBA* 179–90.

———. 2008b. "Die neuen Forschungen in Bakla Tepe bei İzmir." In *ANCEBA*, 165–77.

Erkanal, Hayat, and Turan Özkan. 1997. "1995 Bakla Tepe Kazıları." *Kazı Sonuçları Toplantası* 18(1): 261–80.

———. 1998. "1996 Bakla Tepe Kazıları." *Kazı Sonuçları Toplantası* 19(1): 399–425.

Erkanal, Hayat, Harald Hauptmann, Vasıf Şahoğlu, and Rıza Tuncel (eds.). 2008. *The Aegean in the Neolithic, Chalcolithic, and the Early Bronze Age.* Ankara: Ankara Üniversitesi.

Gale, Noel. 2008. "Metal Sources for Early Bronze Age Troy and the Aegean." In *ANCEBA*, 203–22.

Georgiadis, Mercouris. 2008. "The Obsidian in the Aegean beyond Melos: An Outlook from Yali." *OJA* 27(2): 101–17.

Greaves, Alan M. 2002. *Miletos: A History.* London: Routledge.

———. 2007. "Trans-Anatolia: Examining Turkey as a Bridge between East and West." *AnatSt* 57: 1–15.

————, and Barbara Helwing. 2004. "Archaeology in Turkey: The Stone, Bronze, and Iron Ages 2002." *TÜBA-AR (Turkish Academy of Sciences Journal of Archaeology)* 7: 225–50.

Günel, Sevinç. 1999. *Panaztepe 2: M.Ö. 2 bine tarihlendirilen Panaztepe seramiğinin batı Anadolu ve Ege arkeolojisindeki yeri ve önemi.* Ankara: Türk Tarih Kurumu.

————. 2003. "Vorbericht über die Oberflächenbegenungen in den Provinzen Aydın und Muğla." *Anatolia Antiqua* 11: 75–100.

————. 2005. "The Cultural Structure of the Aydın-İkizdere Region in the Prehistoric Age and Its Contribution to the Archeology of the Aegean Region." *Anatolia Antiqua* 13: 29–40.

————. 2006. "Çine-Tepecik Höyüğü 2004 Yılı Kazıları." *Kazı Sonuçları Toplantası* 27(1): 19–28.

————. 2007. "Çine-Tepecik Höyüğü 2005 Yılı Kazıları." *Kazı Sonuçları Toplantası* 28(1): 231–46.

Hawkins, David. 1998. "Tarkasnawa King of Mira: 'Tarkondemos,' Boğazköy, Sealings and Karabel." *AnatSt* 48: 1–32.

Hertel, Dieter, and Frank Kolb. 2004. "Troy in a Clearer Perspective." *AnatSt* 53: 71–88.

Hope Simpson, Richard. 1965. *A Gazetteer and Atlas of Mycenaean Sites.* BICS Supplementary Series no. 16. London: Institute of Classical Studies.

Huber, Heinz, Max Bichler, and Andreas Musilek. 2003. "Identification of Pumice and Volcanic Ash from Archaeological Sites in the Eastern Mediterranean Using Chemical Fingerprinting." *Egypt and the Levant* 13: 83–105.

İçten, Cengiz, and Friedrich Krinzinger. 2004. "Ein wiederentdecktes Felsrelief aus Ephesos." *ÖJh* 73: 159–63.

Joukowsky, Martha S. 1986. *Prehistoric Aphrodisias.* Providence: Brown University, Center for Old World Archaeology and Art.

Kaiser, Ivonne. 2005. "Minoan Miletus: A View from the Kitchen." In *Emporia*, 193–98.

Knappett, Carl, and Nikolakopoulou, Irene. 2008. "Colonialism without Colonies? A Bronze Age Case Study from Akrotiri, Thera." *Hesperia* 77(1): 1–42.

Lloyd, Seton. 1972. *Beycesultan 3.1: Late Bronze Age Architecture.* London: British Institute of Archaeology at Ankara.

————, and James Mellaart. 1962. *Beycesultan 1: The Chalcolithic and Early Bronze Age Levels.* London: British Institute of Archaeology at Ankara.

————. 1965. *Beycesultan 2: Middle Bronze Age Architecture and Pottery.* London: British Institute of Archaeology at Ankara.

Mee, Christopher. 1978. Aegean Trade and Settlement in Anatolia in the Second Millennium BC. *AnatSt* 28: 121–56.

————. 1998. "Anatolia and the Aegean in the Late Bronze Age." In *Aegean and the Orient*, 137–48.

Mellaart, James, and Anne Murray. 1995. *Beycesultan 3.2: Late Bronze Age and Phrygian Pottery and Middle and Late Bronze Age Small Objects.* London: British Institute of Archaeology at Ankara.

Mellink, Machteld, ed. 1986. *Troy and the Trojan War: A Symposium Held at Bryn Mawr College, October 1984.* Bryn Mawr, Penn.: Bryn Mawr College.

Meriç, Recip. 2003. "Excavations at Bademgediği Tepe (Puranda) 1999–2002: A Preliminary Report." *Istanbuler Mitteilungen* 53: 79–98.

————. 2007. "Ein Vorbericht über eine spätbronzezeitliche befestige Höhensiedlung bei Metropolis in Ionien: Die Arzawa-Stadt Puranda?" In *Frühes Ionien eine Bestandsaufnahme*, ed. Justus Cobet, Volkmar von Graeve, Wolf-Dietrich Niemeier, and Konrad Zimmermann, 27–36. Mainz am Rhein: von Zabern.

————, and Penelope Mountjoy. 2001. "Three Mycenaean Vases from Ionia." *Istanbuler Mitteilungen* 51: 137–41.

————. 2002. "Mycenaean Pottery from Bademgediği Tepe (Puranda) in Ionia: A Preliminary Report." *Istanbuler Mitteilungen* 52: 79–98.

Momigliano, Nicoletta. 2005. "Iasos and the Aegean Islands before the Santorini Eruption." In *Emporia*, 217–25.

————. 2007. "Kamares or Not Kamares? This Is [Not] the Question. Southeast Aegean Light-on-Dark (LOD) and Dark-on-Light (DOL) Pottery: Synchronisms, Production Centers, and Distribution." In *Middle Helladic Pottery*, 257–72.

————. 2008. "Minoans at Iasos?" In *The Minoans in the Central, Eastern, and Northern Aegean*, ed. Erik Hallager, Colin MacDonald, and Wolf-Dietrich Niemeier, 17–36. Athens: Danish Institute at Athens.

Mountjoy, Penelope. 1998. "The East Aegean: West Anatolian Interface in the Late Bronze Age." *AnatSt* 48: 33–68.

Niemeier, Barbara, and Wolf-Dietrich Niemeier. 1997. "Milet 1994–1995, Projekt 'Minoisch-Mykenisches bis Protogeometrisches Milet': Zielsetzung und Grabungen auf dem Stadionhügel und am Athenatempel." *AA* (1997): 189–248.

————. 1999. "The Minoans of Miletus." In *Meletemata*, 543–54.

Niemeier, Wolf-Dietrich. 1997. "The Mycenaean Potter's Quarter at Miletus." In *TEXNH*, 347–52.

————.1998a. "The Minoans in the South-eastern Aegean and in Cyprus." In *Cyprus-Dodecanese-Crete*, 29–47.

————. 1998b. "The Mycenaeans in Western Anatolia and the Problem of the Origins of the Sea Peoples." In *Mediterranean Peoples*, 17–65.

————. 2005. "Minoans, Mycenaeans, Hittites, and Ionians in Western Asia Minor: New Excavations in Bronze Age Miletus-Millawanda." In *The Greeks in the East*, ed. Alexandra Villing, 1–36. London: British Museum.

————. 2007a. "Milet von den Anfängen menschlicher Besiedlung bis zur Ionischen Wanderung." In *Frühes Ionien: Eine Bestandsaufnahme*, ed. Justus Cobet, Volkmar von Graeve, Wolf-Dietrich Niemeier, and Konrad Zimmermann, 3–20. Mainz am Rhein: von Zabern.

————. 2007b. "Westkleinasien und Ägäis von den Anfängen bis zur Ionischen Wanderung: Topographie, Geschichte, und Beziehungen nach dem archäologischen Befund und den hethitischen Quellen." In *Frühes Ionien: Eine Bestandsaufnahme*, ed. Justus Cobet, Volkmar von Graeve, Wolf-Dietrich Niemeier, and Konrad Zimmermann, 37–96. Mainz am Rhein: von Zabern.

Özgünel, Coşkun. 1996. *Mykenische Keramik in Anatolien.*Bonn: Habelt.

Öztan, Aliye. 2003. "2001 Yılı Acemhöyük Kazıları." *Kazı Sonuçları Toplantısı* 24(1): 39–48.

Peschlow-Bindokat, Anneliese. 2001. "Eine hethitische Grossprinzeninschrift aus dem Latmos. Vorläufiger Bericht." *AA* 3 (2001): 363–78.

Raymond, Amy. 2005. "Importing Culture at Miletus: Minoans and Anatolians at Middle Bronze Age Miletus." In *Emporia*, 185–91.

Renfrew, Colin. 2005. "Round a Bigger Pond." In *Prehistorians Round the Pond: Reflections on Aegean Prehistory as a Discipline*, ed. John F. Cherry, Despina Margomenou, and Lauren E. Talaly, 151–59. Ann Arbor: Kelsey Museum of Archaeology, University of Michigan.

Rutter, Jeremy B. 2008. "The Anatolian Roots of Early Helladic III Drinking Behaviour." In *ANCEBA*, 461–81.

Şahoğlu, Vasif. 2004. "Interregional Contacts around the Aegean during the Early Bronze Age: New Evidence from the İzmir Region." *Anadolu/Anatolia* 27: 97–108.

———. 2005. "The Anatolian Trade Network and the İzmir Region during the Early Bronze Age." *OJA* 24(4): 339–61.

———. 2007. "Çeşme-Bağlararası: A New Excavation in Western Anatolia." In *Middle Helladic Pottery*, 309–22.

Takaoğlu, Turan. 2006. "The Late Neolithic in the Eastern Aegean: Excavations at Gülpınar in the Troad." *Hesperia* 75(3): 289–315.

Taracha, Piotr. 2002. "Bull-leaping on a Hittite Vase: New Light on Anatolia and Minoan Religion." *Archaeologica Warsawa* 53: 7–20.

Tuncel, Rıza. 2008. "The İzmir Regional Excavations and Research Project (İRERP) Survey Programme: New Prehistoric Settlements in the İzmir Region." In *ANCEBA*, 581–92.

Ünal, Ahmet. 1991. "Two Peoples on Both Sides of the Aegean Sea: Did the Achaeans and the Hittites Know Each Other?" *Bulletin of the Middle Eastern Culture Center in Japan* 4: 16–44.

Voigtländer, Walter. 2004. *Teichiussa: Näherung und Wirklichkeit*. Rahden: Leidorf.

Yakar, Jak. 1991. *Prehistoric Anatolia: The Neolithic Transformation and the Early Chalcolithic Period*. Tel Aviv: Tel Aviv University.

CHAPTER 66

WESTERN MEDITERRANEAN

LUCIA VAGNETTI

THE Aegean area, including Crete, mainland Greece, and the Cycladic islands, was part of a complex network that connected human groups who lived along the Mediterranean coasts. Interconnections vary in extension and intensity in the different periods since the Neolithic and become more and more systematic in the Bronze Age.

During the Early and Middle Bronze Age, Minoan Crete plays the most active role, looking mainly eastward (Egypt, Levant, Cyprus) and developing a local network inside the Aegean, in particular with the Cyclades and the Peloponnese. With the emergence of complex societies in mainland Greece and the formation of the Mycenaean civilization, the network begins extending westward and eventually involves the central Mediterranean (i.e., peninsular Italy, Sicily, and Sardinia, as well as minor islands such as the Aeolian and the Phlaegrean archipelago).

The evidence for the western interconnection is supported almost entirely by archaeological finds, as there is no significant reference to this part of the world in Linear B texts, and writing was not yet in use among the communities of the Central and Western Mediterranean.

The earliest discovery of Aegean Bronze Age material from the Central Mediterranean goes back to the late 19th century. The great explorations by Paolo Orsi in Sicily resulted in the discovery of several Bronze Age necropoleis in which Mycenaean pottery was fairly common. In 1899–1900, the important Bronze Age settlement of Scoglio del Tonno near Taranto, in Apulia, located at one of the most strategic harbor settings in the Mediterranean, was excavated by Q. Quagliati (Biancofiore 1967). The large quantity and variety of Mycenaean pottery from these early discoveries remain a substantial source of information today.

A milestone in the development of research has been established by systematic archaeological excavations carried out on the Aeolian Islands after World War II. There, for the first time, Mycenaean pottery was found in stratified association with the local Bronze Age material, offering the first framework for a comparative chronology (Bernabò Brea and Cavalier 1968, 1980, 1991). A summary of the evidence up to the 1950s was collected and discussed in a monograph by Lord William Taylour (1958), whose experience in Mycenaean archaeology provided an appropriate classification of the material, including chronology, distribution, and historical implications.

More than fifty years have passed since the publication of Taylour's monograph, and during that time both systematic excavations and chance finds have enormously enlarged our database. In the late 1970s, new systematic excavations started on the small island of Vivara in the Gulf of Naples (Marazzi and Tusa 1994; Merkouri 2005) and in southern Italy, at Broglio di Trebisacce (Peroni 1984; Peroni and Trucco 1994) and Torre Mordillo (Trucco and Vagnetti 2001), in the region presently known as Sibaritide (from the Greek colony of Sybaris, established in the area in the 8th century BC).

Explorations at Termitito, a Bronze Age site near Greek Metaponto, started in the same period (De Siena and Bianco 1982). Soon after, new research in Sardinia, in particular at Antigori, made it possible to include the land of the nuraghi in the general picture (Ferrarese Ceruti 1982, 1986; Ferrarese Ceruti, Vagnetti, and Lo Schiavo 1987).

The substantial increase in the available evidence, the improvement in excavation techniques that allowed a more careful contextual analysis of the finds, and the widening and refinement of methodological approaches attracted new interest in the subject and prompted the organization of international conferences, during which the new evidence from the central Mediterranean was presented and discussed in a broader Mediterranean framework, together with an evaluation of the main methodological issues involved in research (Vagnetti 1982; Marazzi, Tusa and Vagnetti 1986; Balmuth 1987; Giardino 1999).

Some of the main concerns during those years were an effort toward a thorough publication of the evidence, especially from new sites; the progressive use of information technology (IT) in building databases; and the elaboration of theoretical frameworks for the interpretation of the data (Peroni 1983; Bietti Sestieri 1988). During the same decade, archaeological science came into action, providing several hundred analyses of Mycenaean and other Aegean-derivative pottery from Italy, thereby adding a new dimension to the picture (Jones 1986; Jones and Day 1987; Jones and Vagnetti 1991; Jones, Levi, and Vagnetti 2002; Jones et al. 2002; Jones, Levi, and Bettelli 2005; Vagnetti 1999; Vagnetti and Jones 1988; Vagnetti et al. in preparation).

Field research continues, and the list of sites where finds either from the Aegean or of Aegean derivation have come to light is now well beyond one hundred (figure 66.1). Among these are sites of unprecedented importance for the quality and variety of the evidence they have thus far revealed. The extraordinary site of Rocavecchia

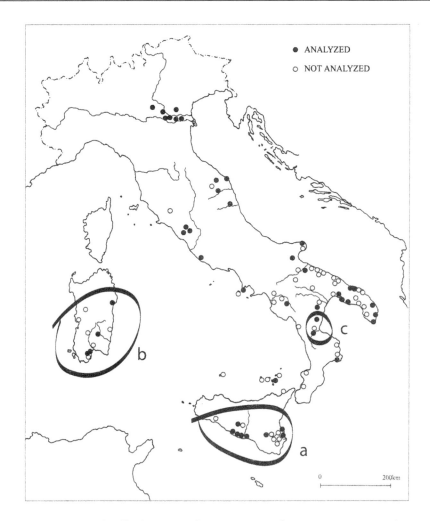

Figure 66.1. Distribution map of Mycenaean- and Aegean-type pottery in Italy. Black dots indicate sites included in the program of archaeometric analyses; white dots indicate sites not yet included in the program. The three outlined clusters correspond to three regional case studies: Sicily, Sardinia, and Sybaris plain (after Vagnetti et al. 2006, figure 1).

in Apulia (Guglielmino 2003, 2005; Pagliara 2003, 2005; Pagliara et al. 2007, 2008), the new finds from Tolentino in the Marche region (Vagnetti et al. 2006) and from Afragola in the vicinity of Naples (Laforgia et al. 2007), as well as the sparse but significant evidence from the Po valley (Jones et al. 2002; Salzani et al. 2006), represent new challenges for further research and refinements in interpretation. New sites in southern Sicily such as Monte Grande (Castellana 1998, 2000) and Cannatello (De Miro 1996) allow a wider chronological and spatial framework for the long-distance interconnections of the island.

The international interest produced by the progress of research has also been a stimulus for doctoral dissertations, in which aspects of the available evidence are collected, discussed, and interpreted (Bettelli 2002; van Wijngaarden 2002; Vianello 2005), for monographs that focus on specific problems such as comparative chronology (Jung 2006), and for conferences devoted to regional studies (La Rosa 2004) or to a specific class of evidence such as ivories (Vagnetti, Bettelli and Damiani 2005). Papers on the Western Mediterranean evidence are increasingly included in conferences devoted to the general problem of Bronze Age trade and long-distance interconnections (*Emporia*). The subject has become a chapter of the Mediterranean protohistoric studies and cannot be ignored by specialists of the Aegean Bronze Age and, in general, of the so-called archaeology of trade.

CHRONOLOGICAL FRAMEWORK

The chronological framework of the interconnections between the Aegean area and the Central and Western Mediterranean encompasses, in Aegean terms, the formative phase and the entire duration of the Mycenaean civilization up to the Postpalatial period, ca. 1650–1050 BC (Late MH, LH I–IIIC and Submycenaean). This long period corresponds, in relative chronology, to the MBA–LBA–FBA2 in the sequence in use for the Central Mediterranean. The approximate correspondence between the two series is shown in table 66.1 (after Alberti and Bettelli 2005; see also Jung 2006).

Late Helladic I–II

Toward the end of the Middle Helladic period, a remarkable social differentiation emerges in mainland Greece, one that is especially mirrored in tomb groups and burial customs in the Argolid and Messenia. During this period, a complex network of contacts is established between Greece and southern Italy, in particular with the Adriatic coast of Apulia, the Taranto Gulf, the Ionian coast of Calabria, the southern coast of Sicily, the Aeolian Islands, and the Phlaegrean Islands in the Gulf of Naples.

Table 66.1. Chronological Framework of the Aegean Area and the Central and Western Mediterranean

Aegean	Italy
LH I–II	MBA 1–2
LH IIIA	MBA3
LH IIIB–IIIC early–middle–advanced (part)	RBA
LH IIIC advanced, late, and Submycenaean	FBA1–2

Source: After Alberti and Bettelli 2005; see also Jung 2006.

This network seems to antedate the establishment of regular interconnections between mainland Greece and the Eastern Mediterranean, where Minoan interests were still very active. The most important evidence for the period, due to quantity, variety, quality of the finds, and related contextual information is concentrated on the Aeolian Islands (mainly Lipari and Filicudi). Other important finds come from the small island of Vivara in the Gulf of Naples, from Porto Perone and a few other sites in Apulia, and from Capo Piccolo and Torre Mordillo in the Sibaritide, as well as from Monte Grande in Sicily.

Late Helladic IIIA–IIIB Early

Toward the end of the 15th and in the early 14th century BC, important changes take place within the Aegean area. The palatial civilization of Crete comes to an end, and the island falls under the influence, not to say rule, of mainland Greece. During the 14th century BC, mainland influence extends toward the eastern Aegean and the Dodecanese. Cyprus, Egypt, and the Levant receive massive quantities of Mycenaean goods. The cargo found on the shipwreck at Uluburun, along the Turkish coast, presents a vivid picture of the variety, quality, and quantity of goods exchanged in the Mediterranean at the end of the 14th century BC (Yalçin, Pulak, and Slotta 2005).

This development has its counterpart in the Central Mediterranean, where a process of stabilization in regular interconnections between the two areas clearly emerges from the archaeological evidence. At Scoglio del Tonno, the high concentration of Aegean imports and evidence for regular contacts with other parts of Italy characterize the site as a pivotal point in the east-west trade network.

The Aeolian Islands, Thapsos, and other sites in eastern Sicily are very active, especially in the 14th century BC, as the significant quantity of Aegean and Cypriot imported pottery found in Bronze Age Aeolian settlements and in contemporary Sicilian necropoleis clearly shows.

Isolated finds, such as an LH IIIA alabastron from Nuraghe Arrubiu at Orroli are, at the moment, the earliest indication of Sardinia's involvement in international trade (Lo Schiavo and Vagnetti 1993).

In southern Italy, several sites located at some distance from the coast, but in view of the sea, such as Termitito in Basilicata, Torre Mordillo and Broglio di Trebisacce in Calabria, emerge.

Late Helladic IIIB Late–IIIC Advanced

The main new development of the period is a gradual change in the nature of the interconnections between the two areas. A careful examination of the archaeological evidence, which is also supported by a vast archaeometric project (Jones, Levi, and Bettelli 2005; Vagnetti et al. in preparation), shows that imported pottery is concentrated at specific spots, such as the area of Taranto in Apulia and Nuraghe Antigori in Sardinia. In other areas, imports become rarer and are gradually replaced by local production of Aegean-type wares. Trade is now integrated by a very impressive technology transfer that gives rise to several production centers located in Apulia, Basilicata, Calabria, Sardinia, and possibly areas of central Italy (Buxeda i Garrigós et al. 2003; Bettelli et al. 2006).

This change in the nature of the relationship seems to have started during the 14th century BC, judging from a very few and sometimes not entirely diagnostic sherds that are apparently of local production (from the Sibaritide) and that were found in local late MBA contexts, (Jones Levi, and Bettelli 2005).

The increase in production of locally made, Aegean-type pottery during the local RBA (corresponding to LH IIIB and LH IIIC early to developed and advanced) makes it less easy to equate typological affinities and chronology, especially in the case of highly fragmentary sherds. During this period, the distribution map of Mycenaean and Aegean-type finds shows a higher density of spots along the coasts of southern Italy, sparse evidence from Lipari and from Sicily (in particular at Cannatello, near Agrigento), and clusters of sites in Sardinia, central Italy, and the Po valley.

Other pottery fabrics derived from Aegean technology but entirely locally made are distinctive productions of southern Italy, with a high concentration in the Sibaritide. These are the Grey Wheelmade ware, also known as "Pseudominyan ware," and a class of large storage jars, manufactured with levigated and tempered clay, locally called "dolia," derived from Aegean pithos ware. They are the best example of the role played by both technology transfer and trade between the two areas (Bettelli 2002; Bettelli and Levi 2003; Levi and Schiappelli 2004; Belardelli and Bettelli 2007).

Late Helladic IIIC Advanced to Late

Interconnections between the Aegean and Italy continue in the 12th century BC and later, although on a more limited scale. Imports are rare but not unknown; the local production of pottery reflects a good knowledge of the parallel developments in the Aegean and indicates a continuity in contacts that is especially well represented in the extreme south of Apulia, in particular at Rocavecchia (Guglielmino 2003, 2005) and Santa Maria di Leuca (Benzi and Graziadio 1996).

Nature of the Evidence

Concerning the nature of the evidence, clearly pottery plays the main role, at least with regard to the quantity of finds and the chronological span. In fact, among the archaeological indications of trade and exchange between the Aegean and the central Mediterranean in the Bronze Age, Mycenaean and related pottery is a common and easily recognizable item. It is "common" because it is known over several centuries and encompasses the entire duration of the Mycenaean civilization and

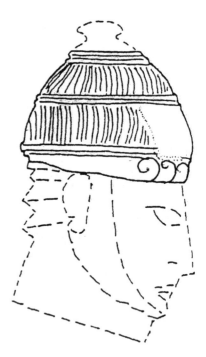

Figure 66.2. Reconstructive drawing of a Mycenaean ivory plaque representing a warrior with a boar-tusk helmet from Mitza Purdia–Decimoputzu (Sardinia) (after Vagnetti and Poplin 2005, figure 1b).

also because its distribution covers a large part of southern Italy, Sicily, Sardinia, and the minor Italian islands. It is easily recognizable because it appears in local contexts that have a completely different pottery tradition, that is, wheel-made vessels of levigated clay with painted decoration, fired in high-temperature kilns (Mycenaean), vs. handmade vessels of heavily tempered clay with burnished surface, plain or decorated with incised patterns and fired at a lower temperature (local *impasto*).

Among the imports and close imitations, the other classes of evidence are clay figurines (Taylour 1958, pls. 8:3, 13:24–25), ivory objects, including a Mycenaean warrior's head from Sardinia (figure 66.2) made of hippo tusk (Vagnetti and Poplin 2005), a few seal stones (Pacciarelli 2000; Cucuzza 2006), and objects of vitreous material related to Aegean types (Rahmstorf 2005; Bellintani et al. 2006, with ample bibliography). Each of these categories deserves a detailed treatment at some point in the future.

The study of the exchange system related to metalwork is complex and includes the circulation of metal as raw material, the possible import of specific items, and imitations of other items. Oxhide ingots, complete or in fragments, are known from Sicily, the Aeolian Islands, and, above all, Sardinia. They have been the subject of a vast archaeological and archaeometric project carried out under the direction of Fulvia Lo Schiavo. Preliminary and partial results have been published in a number of papers, and a complete monograph is forthcoming (Lo Schiavo 2003; Lo Schiavo et al. 2009).

Thanks to the multidisciplinary approach, it is now clear that oxhide ingots found in the Central Mediterranean were made of Cypriot copper. This result sounds rather surprising, given the current hypothesis about the Mycenaeans' interest in metals as a primary stimulus to establish systematic exchanges with the Central Mediterranean. However, the association of Cyprus with specific types of metal objects found in the Central Mediterranean, in particular bronze vessels, tripod stands, mirrors, some types of figurines, double axes, and smithing tools, is well known and has been extensively discussed (Lo Schiavo, Macnamara, and Vagnetti 1985).

In Italy and the Aegean, especially in the 13th century BC, various metal objects such as swords, daggers, knives, tools, and fibulas follow a parallel typological development known as "metalwork koiné." Imports from the Aegean into Italy are not many, while some specific Italian types, such as the Peschiera daggers, seem particularly appreciated in the Aegean (Matthäus 1981; Bettelli 2002).

Certain architectural features offer a stimulus for reflection: powerful fortifications as in the case of Rocavecchia in Apulia (Guglielmino 2005; Pagliara 2005); complex, multiroomed buildings organized in a planned urban setting, as in Thapsos (Militello 2004; Tomasello 2004); tholos-like tombs carved in the rock as in several Sicilian necropoleis (Tomasello 1995–1996); and the introduction and use of specialized technological devices such as the potter's wheel and the high-temperature kiln (Levi et al. 1999; Buxeda i Garrigós et al. 2003). The adoption of storage facilities such as the large pithoi, typical of southern Italy (Levi et al. 1999; Guglielmino 1999; Levi and Schiappelli 2004), and of a possible system of weight (Cardarelli, Pacciarelli, and Pallante 1997) is also an important indication of the Aegean's manifold influence on local communities.

The nature of the evidence can be examined in spatial, chronological, typological, contextual, and functional terms. The spatial distribution of Mycenaean and related pottery, plus metalwork, seals, ivory, and other minor objects found in the Central Mediterranean, includes now more than hundred findspots densely distributed in southern Italy (Bettelli, Levi, and Vagnetti 2001–2002), Sicily, the Aeolian and Phlaegrean islands, and Sardinia. A minor cluster is located in central Italy, looking toward the Tyrrhenian Sea (Bettelli, Jones, and Vagnetti 2006), while a cluster in the Marche region and another in the Po valley are closely related to the Adriatic (Jones et al. 2002; Vagnetti et al. 2006, Salzani et al. 2006). Isolated finds from Malta (recently Blakolmer 2005) and Pantelleria (Marazzi and Tusa 2005) should be considered in the framework of the evidence from Sicily, while the few records from the Iberian peninsula are, at least in part, open to discussion (Martin de la Cruz 1990, 1996; Podzuweit 1990; Almagro Gorbea and Fontes 1997).

The chronological framework has already been outlined. A further important piece of information to consider is the kind of context in which Mycenaean and Aegean-type material is found. Apart from a minority of findspots of uncertain definition, the basic contexts are local settlements and cemeteries. In only four cases (that we know of)—Giovinazzo and Torre Santa Sabina in Apulia, Thapsos and Milena in Sicily—are settlement and cemetery related to the same site.

Importantly, no purely Mycenaean context is yet known in the Central Mediterranean; we always deal with settlements and cemeteries of the local type, in most cases established well before the appearance of any archeological evidence of interconnections with the Aegean. Moreover, the percentage of Mycenaean and Aegean-type pottery in the general ceramic assemblage of a specific site is rarely more than 5% and usually much lower.

One should also remember that the informative value of the findspots is highly variable, according to the circumstances of the find and the quantity of material recovered. The finds recovered at the great majority of the sites (up to 70%) have been very limited: between one and ten Mycenaean or Aegean-type sherds. In this respect, another factor to consider is the kind of research carried out at the various sites; as a matter of fact, a single sherd from an extensively excavated site has a completely different value from one found during a surface survey.

As mentioned before, the results of a vast program of pottery analysis has offered strategic information to be integrated into the archaeological interpretation of the data. The distinction between imports and local imitations and the definition of the imports' main areas of provenance represent an important element for a differentiated interpretation of the picture.

A recent study (Jones, Levi, and Bettelli 2005) offers a parallel view of three different geographic areas: Sicily, Sardinia, and the Sibaritide, each representative of a specific attitude in the distribution of imports and Italo-Mycenaean pottery. In Sicily, the majority of Mycenaean ceramics are imported; in Sardinia, in particular at Antigori, both imports and local productions are well represented; and in the Sibaritide and Basilicata, the majority of ceramic finds are locally made.

As regards the provenance, the imports in these three areas come mainly from the Peloponnese, but imports from Crete and Cyprus are known in Sicily and Sardinia. The plurality of the Aegean terminals involved in long-distance trade with the Central Mediterranean and beyond is also reflected in the typological and stylistic inspiration recognizable in Italo-Mycenean pottery.

Although the vast majority of parallels appear in the standard Peloponnesian repertoire, influence from Postpalatial Crete has a strong impact on the production of local Mycenean pottery in the Sibaritide (figure 66.3) and, to some extent, on the local Mycenaean pottery from Sardinia (Vagnetti 2003).

If we take a global approach to the archaeological evidence mentioned here, we can recognize that different patterns of interconnections are operating at the same time. On one side, we see the results of long-distance Mediterranean Bronze Age trade, with exchanges of goods in the form of raw materials and finished products. What remains are the durable materials, mainly pottery, but a variety of perishable material, today invisible, such as oils, spices, perfumes, and textiles, should have been much more important. On the other side, we see the circulation of know-how, as the introduction of the specialized manufacture of pottery in the Sibaritide and other areas of Italy or the adoption of specialized metallurgical tools of Cypriot derivation in Sardinia clearly show.

Figure 66.3. Locally
produced, two-handled jar
from Broglio di Trebisacce
(Calabria) (after Vagnetti
et al. 2006, figure 3).

At the beginning, during the formative phase of the Mycenaean civilization, Aegean traders probably opened paths to areas where they could get strategic raw materials such as metals. As a more complex social system grew in Greece and the Mycenaeans gained a strong political and economic position in the Mediterranean, the interest in the Central and Western Mediterranean became more widespread and stable. Over the course of time, especially during LH/LM IIIB and IIIC, one starts to also see some feedback, with the presence of Nuragic imported pottery at Kommos and handmade burnished ware of western inspiration at some of the main Mycenaean and Cretan sites, such as Mycenae, Tiryns, Lefkandi, and Chania (Watrous 1992; Rutter 1999; Rutter and van de Moortel 2006; Bettelli 2002; Hallager and Hallager 2003; Evely 2006; Kilian 2007; Belardelli and Bettelli 2007).

This is the time when workshops that produced Italo-Mycenaean pottery and other Aegean derivative wares were established at various locations in peninsular Italy and Sardinia, making the presence and activity of potters of Aegean provenance or training in these areas highly probable.

To sum up, on the basis of what we know today, we can state that the interconnections between the Aegean and the Central and Western Mediterranean in the Bronze Age represent a long-lasting relationship that was differentiated by space and time. The general outline of the picture seems to some extent clear, but details are changing rapidly as new data are found, processed, and interpreted against the known framework.

The pace of development in our knowledge has greatly increased in the last twenty-five years, and more data are already awaiting study, interpretation, and publication. What seems solidly acquired is that the study of the subject should be tackled with a perspective that includes both an Aegean point of view and an insight into the development of the Bronze Age societies of the Central and Western Mediterranean.

BIBLIOGRAPHY

Alberti, Lucia, and Marco Bettelli. 2005. "Contextual Problems of Mycenaean Pottery in Italy." In *Emporia*, 547–57.

Almagro Gorbea, Martin, and Fernando Fontes. 1997. "The Introduction of Wheel-made Pottery in the Iberian Peninsula: Mycenaeans or Pre-orientalizing Contacts?" *OJA* 16: 345–61.

Balmuth, Miriam S., ed. 1987. *Studies in Sardinian Archaeology III: Nuragic Sardinia and the Mycenaean World. BAR-IS* 387. Oxford: British Archaeological Reports.

Belardelli, Clarissa, and Marco Bettelli. 2007. "Different Technological Levels of Pottery Production: Barbarian and Grey Ware between the Aegean and Europe in the Late Bronze Age." In *BABS*, 481–86.

Bellintani, Paolo, Ivana Angelini, Gilberto Artioli, and Angela Polla. 2006. "Origini dei materiali vetrosi italiani: Esotismi e localismi." In *Materie prime e scambi nella preistoria italiana: Atti della XXXIX Riunione Scientifica dell'Istituto Italiano di Preistoria e Protostoria (Firenze, novembre 2004)*, 1495–1531. Florence: Istituto Italiano di Preistoria e Protostoria.

Benzi, Mario, and Giampaolo Graziadio. 1996. "The Last Mycenaeans in Italy?" *SMEA* XXXVIII (1996): 95–138.

Bernabò Brea, Luigi, and Madeleine Cavalier. 1968. *Meligunìs Lipàra, III. Stazioni preistoriche delle isole Panarea, Salina, e Stromboli.* Palermo: Flaccovio.

———. 1980. *Meligunìs Lipàra IV. L'Acropoli di Lipari nella preistoria.* Palermo: Flaccovio.

———. 1991. *Meligunìs Lipàra, VI. Filicudi: Insediamenti dell'età del bronzo.* Palermo: Accademia di Scienze, Lettere, ed Arti.

Bettelli, Marco. 2002. *Italia meridionale e mondo miceneo: Ricerche su dinamiche di acculturazione e aspetti archeologici, con particolare riferimento ai versanti adriatico e ionico della penisola italiana.* Florence: All'insegna del giglio.

———, and Sara T. Levi. 2003. "Lo sviluppo delle produzioni ceramiche specializzate in Italia meridionale nell'età del Bronzo in rapporto ai modelli egei e alla ceramica d'impasto indigena." In *Le comunità della preistoria italiana: Studi e ricerche sul neolitico e l'età dei metalli. Atti della XXXV Riunione Scientifica dell'Istituto Italiano di Preistoria e Protostoria (Lipari, giugno 2000)*, 435–54. Florence: Istituto Italiano di Preistoria e Protostoria.

———, Richard E. Jones, and Lucia Vagnetti. 2006. "Le ceramiche micenee in area medio tirrenica: Nuove prospettive." In *Studi di Protostoria in onore di Renato Peroni*, 399–406. Florence: All'insegna del Giglio.

Bettelli, Marco, Sara T. Levi, and Lucia Vagnetti. 2001–2002. "Cronologia, topografia, e funzione dei siti con testimonianze micenee in Italia meridionale." *Geographia Antiqua* X–XI: 65–95.

Biancofiore, Franco. 1967. *Civiltà micenea nell'Italia meridionale.* Incunabula Graeca XXII. Rome: Edizioni dell'Ateneo.

Bietti Sestieri, Anna Maria. 1988. "The 'Mycenaean Connection' and Its Impact on Central Mediterranean Societies." *Dialoghi di Archeologia* 6(1): 23–51.

Blakolmer, Fritz. 2005. "Relations between Prehistoric Malta and the Aegean: Myth and Reality." In *Emporia*, 653–62.

Buxeda i Garrigós, Jaume, Richard E. Jones, Vassili Kilikoglou, Sara T. Levi, Yannis Maniatis, John Mitchel, Lucia Vagnetti, Ken Wardle, and Stelios Andreou. 2003. "Technology Transfer at the Periphery of the Mycenaean World: The Cases of Mycenaean Pottery Found in Central Macedonia (Greece) and the Plain of Sybaris (Italy)." *Archaeometry* 45: 263–84.

Cardarelli, Andrea, Marco Pacciarelli, and Paolo Pallante. 1997. "Pesi da bilancia dell'età del bronzo?" In *Le Terramare: La più antica civiltà padana*, ed. Maria Bernabò Brea, Andrea Cardarelli, and Mauro Cremaschi, 628–42. Milan: Electa.

Castellana, Giuseppe. 1998. *Il santuario castellucciano di Monte Grande e l'approvvigionamento dello zolfo nel Mediterraneo nell'età del Bronzo.* Agrigento: Regione Siciliana.

———. 2000. *La cultura del Medio Bronzo nell'Agrigentino ed i rapporti con il mondo miceneo.* Agrigento: Regione Siciliana.

Cucuzza, Nicola. 2006. "Un sigillo miceneo da Lipari?" *SMEA* XLVIII: 73–88.

De Miro, Ernesto. 1996. "Recenti ritrovamenti micenei nell'Agrigentino e il villaggio di Cannatello." In *Atti e Memorie del Secondo Congresso Internazionale di Micenologia (Roma-Napoli 1991)*, ed. Ernesto De Miro, Louis Godart, and Anna Sacconi, 995–1012. Rome: Gruppo Editoriale Internazionale.

De Siena, Antonio, and Salvatore Bianco. 1982. "Termitito (Montalbano Ionico, Matera)." In *Magna Grecia e mondo miceneo: Nuovi documenti*, ed. Lucia Vagnetti, 69–96. Taranto: Istituto per la Storia e l'Archeologia della Magna Grecia.

Evely, Don, ed. 2006. *Lefkandi IV: The Bronze Age. The Late Helladic IIIC Settlement at Xeropolis.* Oxford: British School at Athens.

Ferrarese Ceruti, Maria Luisa. 1982. "Il complesso nuragico di Antigori (Sarroch, Cagliari)." In *Magna Grecia e mondo miceneo: Nuovi documenti*, ed. Lucia Vagnetti, 167–76. Taranto: Istituto per la Storia e l'Archeologia della Magna Grecia.

———. 1986. "I vani c, p, q del complesso nuragico di Antigori (Sarroch, Cagliari)." In *Traffici micenei nel Mediterraneo: Problemi storici e documentazione archeologica. Atti del Convegno di Palermo (11–12 maggio e 3–6 dicembre 1984)*, ed. Massimiliano Marazzi, Sebastiano Tusa, and Lucia Vagnetti, 183–92. Taranto: Istituto per la storia e l'archeologia della Magna Grecia.

———, Lucia Vagnetti, and Fulvia Lo Schiavo. 1987. "Minoici, Micenei, e Ciprioti in Sardegna nella seconda metà del II millennio a.C." In *Studies in Sardinian Archaeology III: Nuragic Sardinia and the Mycenaean World*, ed. Miriam S. Balmuth, 7–37. *BAR-IS* 387. Oxford: British Archaeological Reports.

Giardino, Claudio, ed. 1999. *Culture marinare nel Mediterraneo centrale e occidentale fra il XVII e il XV secolo a.C.* Rome: Bagatto Libri.

Guglielmino, Riccardo. 1999. "I dolii cordonati di Roca Vecchia (LE) e il problema della loro derivazione egea." In *Epi ponton plazomenoi: Simposio italiano di studi egei dedicato a Luigi Bernabò Brea e Giovanni Pugliese Carratelli*, ed. Vincenzo La Rosa, Dario Palermo, and Lucia Vagnetti, 475–86. Rome: Scuola Archeologica Italiana di Atene.

———. 2003. "Il sito di Roca Vecchia: Testimonianze di contatti con l'Egeo." In *L'archeologia dell'Adriatico dalla Preistoria al Medioevo, Convegno Internazionale (Ravenna, 7–9 giugno 2001)*, ed. Fiamma Lenzi, 91–119. Florence: All'insegna del giglio.

———. 2005. "Rocavecchia: Nuove testimonianze di relazioni con l'Egeo e il Mediterraneo orientale nell'età del Bronzo." In *Emporia*, 637–50.

Hallager, Erik, and Birgitta P. Hallager. 2003. *The Greek-Swedish Excavations at the Agia Aikaterini Square, Kastelli, Chania, 1970–1987 and 2001, III.* Stockholm: Svenska Institutet i Athen.

Jones, Richard E. 1986. "Chemical Analysis of Aegean-type Late Bronze Age Pottery Found in Italy." In *Traffici micenei nel Mediterraneo: Problemi storici e documentazione archeologica. Atti del Convegno di Palermo (11–12 maggio, 3–6 dicembre 1984),* 205–14, ed. Massimiliano Marazzi, Sebastiano Tusa, and Lucia Vagnetti. Taranto: Istituto per la storia e l'archeologia della Magna Grecia.

———, and Peter M. Day. 1987. "Aegean-type Pottery on Sardinia: Identification of Imports and Local Imitations by Chemical Analysis." In *Studies in Sardinian Archaeology, III. Nuragic Sardinia and the Mycenaean World,* ed. Miriam S. Balmuth, 257–70. Oxford: British Archaeological Reports.

Jones, Richard E., Sara T. Levi, and Marco Bettelli. 2005. "Mycenaean Pottery in the Central Mediterranean: Imports, Imitations, and Derivatives." In *Emporia,* 539–45.

Jones, Richard E., Sara T. Levi, and Lucia Vagnetti. 2002. "Connections between the Aegean and Italy in the Later Bronze Age: The Ceramic Evidence." In *Modern Trends in Scientific Studies on Ancient Ceramics: Papers presented at the 5th European Meeting on Ancient Ceramics (Athens 1999),* ed. Vasili Kilikoglou, Anno Hein, and Yannis Maniatis, 171–84. *BAR-IS* 1011. Oxford: Archaeopress.

Jones, Richard E., and Lucia Vagnetti. 1991. "Traders and Craftsmen in the Central Mediterranean: Archaeological Evidence and Archaeometric Research." In *Bronze Age Trade,* 127–47.

Jones, Richard E., Lucia Vagnetti, Sara T. Levi, John Williams, David Jenkins, and Armando De Guio. 2002. "Mycenaean and Aegean-type Pottery from Northern Italy: Archaeological and Archaeometric Studies." *SMEA* 44: 221–61.

Jung, Reinhard. 2006. *Χρονολογία comparata: Vergleichende Chronologie von Südgriechenland und Süditalien von ca. 1700/1600 bis 1000 v.u.Z.* Vienna: Verlag der Österreichischen Akademie der Wissenschaften.

Kilian, Klaus. 2007. *Die Handgemachte geglättete Keramik mykenischer Zeitstellung: Tiryns XV.* Wiesbaden: Reichert.

Laforgia, Elena, Giovanna Boenzi, Marco Bettelli, Fulvia Lo Schiavo, and Lucia Vagnetti. 2007. "Recenti rinvenimenti dell'età del bronzo ad Afragola (Napoli)." In *Strategie di insediamento fra Lazio e Campania in età preistorica e protostorica: Atti della XL Riunione scientifica dell'Istituto Italiano di Preistoria e Protostoria (Roma, Napoli, Pompei, novembre–dicembre 2005),* 935–39. Florence: Istituto Italiano di Preistoria e Protostoria.

La Rosa, Vincenzo, ed. 2004. *Le presenze micenee nel territorio siracusano.* Padua: La Bottega di Erasmo.

Levi, Sara T., et al. 1999. *Produzione e circolazione della ceramica nella Sibaritide protostorica. I, Impasto e Dolii.* Florence: All'insegna del giglio.

Levi, Sara T., and Andrea Schiappelli. 2004. "I pithoi di ispirazione egea del tardo Bronzo nell'Italia meridionale: Tecnologia, contenuto, immagazzinamento, e circolazione." In *Metodi ed approcci archeologici: L'industria ed il commercio nell'Italia antica (Roma 18–20 aprile 2002),* ed. Eric C. de Sena and Hélène Dessalles, 96–108. *BAR-IS* 1262. Oxford: Archaeopress.

Lo Schiavo, Fulvia. 2003. "Sardinia between East and West: Interconnections in the Mediterranean." In *PLOES,* 15–34.

———, Ellen Macnamara, and Lucia Vagnetti. 1985. "Late Cypriot Imports to Italy and Their Influence on Local Bronzework." *PBSR* LIII, 1–71.

Lo Schiavo, Fulvia, James D. Muhly, Robert Maddin, and Alessandra Giumlia-Mair, eds. 2009. *Oxhide Ingots in the Central Mediterranean*. Biblioteca di Antichità Cipriote, 8. Rome: Istituto di studi sulle civiltà dell'Egeo e del Vicino Oriente.

Lo Schiavo, Fulvia, and Lucia Vagnetti. 1993. "Alabastron miceneo dal nuraghe Arrubiu di Orroli (Nuoro)." *RendLinc* s. IX, IV: 121–48.

Marazzi, Massimiliano, and Sebastiano Tusa, eds. 1994. *Vivara: Centro commerciale mediterraneo dell'età del bronzo*. Vol. 2, *Le tracce dei contatti con il mondo egeo (scavi 1976–1982)*. Rome: Bagatto Libri.

———. 2005. "Egei in Occidente: Le più antiche vie marittime alla luce dei nuovi scavi sull'isola di Pantelleria." In *Emporia*, 599–609.

———, and Lucia Vagnetti, eds. 1986. *Traffici micenei nel Mediterraneo: Problemi storici e documentazione archeologica. Atti del Convegno di Palermo (11–12 maggio, 3–6 dicembre 1984)*. Taranto: Istituto per la storia e l'archeologia della Magna Grecia.

Martin de la Cruz, José C. 1990. "Die erste mykenische Keramik von der Iberischen Halbinsel." *PZ* 65: 49–52.

———. 1996. "Nuevas ceramicas de importacion en Andalucia (Espana): Sus implicaciones culturales." In *Atti e Memorie del Secondo Congresso Internazionale di Micenologia (Roma-Napoli 1991)*, ed. Ernesto De Miro, Louis Godart, and Anna Sacconi, 1551–60. Rome: Gruppo Editoriale Internazionale.

Matthäus, Hartmut. 1981. "Italien und Griechenland in der ausgehenden Bronzezeit." *JdI* XCV: 109–39.

Merkouri, Christina. 2005. "I contatti transmarini fra occidente e mondo miceneo sulla base del materiale ceramico d'importazione rinvenuto a Vivara (Napoli-Italia)." In *Emporia*, 611–21.

Militello, Pietro. 2004. "Commercianti, architetti, ed artigiani: Riflessioni sulla presenza micenea nell'area iblea." In *Le presenze micenee nel territorio siracusano*, ed. Vincenzo La Rosa, 296–336. Padua: La Bottega di Erasmo.

Pacciarelli, Marco. 2000. *Dal villaggio alla città: La svolta protourbana del 1000 a.C. nell'Italia tirrenica*. Florence: All'insegna del giglio.

Pagliara, Cosimo. 2003. "Il sito di Roca Vecchia nell'età del Bronzo." In *L'archeologia dell'Adriatico dalla Preistoria al Medioevo, Convegno Internazionale (Ravenna, 7–9 giugno 2001)*, ed. Fiamma Lenzi, 74–90. Florence: All'insegna del giglio.

———. 2005. "Rocavecchia (Lecce): Il sito, le fortificazioni, e l'abitato dell'età del Bronzo." In *Emporia*, 629–34.

———, Giovanna Maggiulli, Teodoro Scarano, Corrado Pino, Riccardo Guglielmino, Jacopo De Grossi Mazzorin, Michela Rugge, Girolamo Fiorentino, Milena Primavera, Lucio Calcagnile, Marisa D'Elia, Gianluca Quarta, "La sequenza cronostratigrafica delle fasi di occupazione dell'insediamento protostorico di Roca (Melendugno, Lecce). Relazione preliminare della campagna di scavo 2005—Saggio X." *Rivista di Scienze Preistoriche* 57: 311–62.

———, Riccardo Guglielmino, Luigi Coluccia, Ilaria Malorgio, Marco Merico, Daria Palmisano, Michela Rugge, Francesco Minonne, "Rocavecchia (Melendugno, Lecce), SAS, IX: relazione stratigrafica preliminare sui livelli di occupazione protostorici (campagne di scavo 2005–2006)" *Rivista di Scienze Preistoriche* 58: 239–80.

Peroni, Renato. 1983. "Presenze micenee e forme socio-economiche nell'Italia protostorica." In *Magna Grecia e mondo miceneo: Atti del XXII Convegno di Studi sulla Magna Grecia (Taranto, 7–11 ottobre 1982)*, 211–84. Taranto: Istituto per la Storia e l'Archeologia della Magna Grecia.

———, ed. 1984. *Nuove ricerche sulla protostoria della Sibaritide*. Rome: Paleani.

———, and Flavia Trucco, eds. 1994. *Enotri e Micenei nella Sibaritide.* Taranto: Istituto per la Storia e l'Archeologia della Magna Grecia.

Podzuweit, Christian. 1990. "Bemerkungen zur mykenische Keramik von Llanete de los Moros, Montoro, Prov. Cordoba." *PZ* 65: 53–58.

Rahmstorf, Lorenz. 2005. "Terramare and Faience: Mycenaean Influence in Northern Italy during the Late Bronze Age." In *Emporia,* 663–74.

Rutter, Jeremy B. 1999. "Cretan External Relations during Late Minoan IIIA2–B (ca. 1370–1200 BC): A View from the Mesara." In *Point Iria Wreck,* 139–86.

———, and Aleydis van de Moortel. 2006. "Minoan Pottery from the Southern Area." In *Kommos V,* 261–715.

Salzani, Luciano, Lucia Vagnetti, Richard E. Jones, and Sara T. Levi. 2006. "Nuovi ritrovamenti di ceramiche di tipo egeo dall'area veronese: Lovara, Bovolone, e Terranegra." In *Materie prime e scambi nella preistoria italiana: Atti della XXXIX Riunione Scientifica dell'Istituto Italiano di Preistoria e Protostoria (Firenze, novembre 2004),* 1145–57. Florence: Istituto Italiano di Preistoria e Protostoria.

Taylour, Lord William. 1958. *Mycenean Pottery in Italy and Adjacent Areas.* Cambridge: Cambridge University Press.

Tomasello, Francesco. 1995–1996. "Le tombe a tholos della Sicilia centro-meridionale." *Cronache di Archeologia* 34–35: 149–215. Catania: Centro di studio sull'archeologia greca.

———. 2004. "L'architettura micenea nel siracusano: *TO-KO-DO-MO A-PE-O* o *DE-ME-O-TE?*" In *Le presenze micenee nel territorio siracusano,* ed. Vincenzo La Rosa, 187–215. Padua: La Bottega di Erasmo.

Trucco, Flavia, and Lucia Vagnetti, eds. 2001. *Torre Mordillo 1987–1990: Le relazioni egee di una comunità protostorica della Sibaritide.* Incunabula Graeca, vol. CI. Rome: Istituto per gli studi micenei ed egeo-anatolici.

Vagnetti, Lucia, ed. 1982. *Magna Grecia e mondo miceneo.* Nuovi Documenti. XXII Convegno di Studi sulla Magna Grecia (Taranto, 7–11 ottobre 1982). Taranto: Istituto per la Storia e l'Archeologia della Magna Grecia.

———. 1999. "Mycenaean Pottery in the Central Mediterranean: Imports and Local Productions in Their Context." In *The Complex Past of Pottery: Production, Circulation, and Consumption of Mycenaean and Greek Pottery (Sixteenth to Early Fifth Centuries BC). Proceedings of the ARCHON International Conference (Amsterdam, November 1996),* ed. Jan P. Crielaard, Vladimir Stissi, and Gert J. van Wijngaarden. Amsterdam: Gieben.

———. 2003. "The Role of Crete in the Exchanges between the Aegean and the Central\ Mediterranean in the Second Millennium BC." In *PLOES,* 53–61.

———, Marco Bettelli, and Isabella Damiani, eds. 2005. *L'avorio in Italia nell'età del bronzo.* Incunabula Graeca, CII. Rome: Istituto di studi sulle civiltà dell'Egeo e del Vicino Oriente.

Vagnetti, Lucia, and Richard E. Jones. 1988. "Towards the Identification of Local Mycenaean Pottery in Italy." In *Problems in Greek Prehistory,* 335–48.

———, Sara T. Levi, and Marco Bettelli. 2006. "Circolazione a vasto raggio di ceramiche protostoriche: Il caso della ceramica micenea." In *La ceramica in Italia quando l'Italia non c'era: Atti della 8° Giornata di Archeometria della Ceramica (Vietri sul Mare, 27–28 aprile 2004),* ed. Bruno Fabbri, Sabrina Gualtieri, and Matilde Romito, 11–21. Bari: Edipuglia.

———. In preparation. *The Mycenaeans and Italy: The Archaeological and Archaeometric Ceramic Evidence.*

Vagnetti, Lucia, Edvige Percossi, Mara Silvestrini, Tommaso Sabbatini, Richard E. Jones, and Sara T. Levi. 2006. "Ceramiche egeo-micenee dalle Marche: Analisi archeometriche e inquadramento preliminare dei risultati." In *Materie prime e scambi nella preistoria italiana: Atti della XXXIX Riunione Scientifica dell'Istituto Italiano di Preistoria e Protostoria (Firenze, novembre 2004)*, 1159–72. Florence: Istituto Italiano di Preistoria e Protostoria.

Vagnetti, Lucia, and François Poplin. 2005. "Frammento di applique raffigurante un elmo a denti di cinghiale da Mitza Purdia-Decimoputzu (Cagliari)." In *L'avorio in Italia nell'età del bronzo*, ed. Lucia Vagnetti, Marco Bettelli, and Isabella Damiani, 111–14. Incunabula Graeca, CII. Rome: Istituto di studi sulle civiltà dell'Egeo e del Vicino Oriente.

van Wijngaarden, Gert J. 2002. *Use and Appreciation of Mycenaean Pottery in the Levant, Cyprus, and Italy (ca. 1600–1200 BC)*. Amsterdam: Amsterdam University Press.

Vianello, Andrea. 2005. *Late Bronze Age Mycenaean and Italic Products in the West Mediterranean: A Social and Economic Analysis*. BAR-IS 1439. Oxford: Archaeopress.

Watrous, Vance L. 1992. *Kommos III: The Late Bronze Age Pottery*. Princeton: Princeton University Press.

Yalçin, Ünsal, Çemal Pulak, and Rainer Slotta, eds. 2005. *Das Shiff von Uluburun: Welthandel vor 3000 Jahren. Katalog der Ausstellung des Deutschen Bergbau-Museums Bochum (Juli 2005–Juli 2006)*. Bochum: Deutsches Bergbau-Museum.

INDEX

Lightning Source UK Ltd.
Milton Keynes UK
UKHW032056111120
373188UK00015B/531